GLOBAL MARKETING

SEVENTH EDITION

GLOBAL MARKETING

SVEND HOLLENSEN

PEARSON

Harlow, England • London • New York • Boston • San Francisco • Toronto • Sydney • Auckland • Singapore • Hong Kong
Tokyo • Seoul • Taipei • New Delhi • Cape Town • São Paulo • Mexico City • Madrid • Amsterdam • Munich • Paris • Milan

PEARSON EDUCATION LIMITED
Edinburgh Gate
Harlow CM20 2JE
United Kingdom
Tel: +44 (0)1279 623623
Web: www.pearson.com/uk

First published 1998 by Prentice Hall (print)
Second edition published 2001 by Pearson Education Limited (print)
Third edition published 2004 (print)
Fourth edition published 2007 (print)
Fifth edition published 2011 (print)
Sixth edition published 2014 (print and electronic)
Seventh edition published 2017 (print and electronic)

© Prentice Hall Europe 1998 (print)
© Pearson Education Limited 2001, 2011 (print)
© Pearson Education Limited 2014, 2017 (print and electronic)

ISBN: 978-1-292-10011-1 (print)
       978-1-292-10014-2 (PDF)
       978-1-292-14421-4 (ePub)

British Library Cataloguing-in-Publication Data
A catalogue record for this book is available from the British Library

Library of Congress Cataloging-in-Publication Data
A catalog record for this book is available from the Library of Congress

10 9 8 7 6 5 4 3
20 19 18 17

Cover image © Thomas Vogel/Getty Images

Print edition typeset in 10/12 Basic Commercial LT Com by Spi Global
Print edition printed in Slovakia by Neografia

NOTE THAT ANY PAGE CROSS REFERENCES REFER TO THE PRINT EDITION

BRIEF CONTENTS

CONTENTS

PART II   DECIDING WHICH MARKETS TO ENTER   181

PART IV DESIGNING THE GLOBAL MARKETING PROGRAMME 491

Companion Website

For open-access **student resources** specifically written to complement this textbook and support your learning, please visit **www.pearsoned.co.uk/hollensen**

Lecturer Resources

For password-protected online resources tailored to support the use of this textbook in teaching, please visit **www.pearsoned.co.uk/hollensen**

PREFACE

Globalization is the growing interdependence of national economies – involving primarily customers, producers, suppliers and governments in different markets. Global marketing therefore reflects the trend of firms selling and distributing products and services in many countries around the world. It is associated with governments reducing trade and investment barriers, firms manufacturing in multiple countries and foreign firms increasingly competing in domestic markets.

For many years, the globalization of markets, caused by the convergence of tastes across borders, was thought to result in very large multinational enterprises that could use their advantages in scale economies to introduce world-standardized products successfully.

In his famous 1994 book, *The Global Paradox*, John Naisbitt has contradicted this myth, especially the last part:[1]

> The mindset that in a huge global economy the multinationals dominate world business couldn't have been more wrong. The bigger and more open the world economy becomes, the more small and middle sized companies will dominate. In one of the major turn-arounds in my lifetime, we have moved from 'economies of scale' to 'diseconomies of scale'; from bigger is better to bigger is inefficient, costly and wastefully bureaucratic, inflexible and, now, disastrous. And the paradox that has occurred is, as we move to the global context: The smaller and speedier players will prevail on a much expanded field.

When the largest corporations (e.g. IBM, ABB) downsize, they are seeking to emulate the entrepreneurial behaviour of successful SMEs (small and medium-sized enterprises) where the implementation phase plays a more important role than in large companies. Since the behaviours of smaller and (divisions of) larger firms (according to the above quotation) are convergent, the differences in the global marketing behaviour between SMEs and LSEs (large-scale enterprises) are slowly disappearing. What is happening is that the LSEs are downsizing and decentralizing their decision-making process. The result will be a more decision- and action-oriented approach to global marketing. This approach will also characterize this book.

In light of their smaller size, most SMEs lack the capabilities, market power and other resources of traditional multinational LSEs. Compared with the resource-rich LSEs, the complexities of operating under globalization are considerably more difficult for the SME. The success of SMEs under globalization depends in large part on the decision and implementation of the right international marketing strategy.

The primary role of marketing management, in any organization, is to design and execute effective marketing programmes that will pay off. Companies can do this in their home market or they can do it in one or more international markets. Going international is an enormously expensive exercise, in terms of both money and, especially, top management time and commitment. Due to the high cost, going international must generate added value for the company beyond extra sales. In other words, the company needs to gain a competitive advantage by going international. So, unless the company gains by going international, it should probably stay at home.

The task of global marketing management is complex enough when the company operates in one foreign national market. It is much more complex when the company starts

---

[1] Naisbitt, J. (1994) *The Global Paradox*, Nicholas Brealey Publishing, London, p. 17.

operations in several countries. Marketing programmes must, in these situations, adapt to the needs and preferences of customers that have different levels of purchasing power as well as different climates, languages and cultures. Moreover, patterns of com-petition and methods of doing business differ between nations and sometimes also within regions of the same nation. In spite of the many differences, however, it is important to hold on to simi-larities across borders. Some coordination of international activities will be required, but at the same time the company will gain some synergy across borders, in the way that experience and learning acquired in one country can be transferred to another.

Objectives

This book's value chain offers the reader an analytic decision-oriented framework for the development and implementation of global marketing programmes. Consequently, the reader should be able to analyse, select and evaluate the appropriate conceptual frame-works for approaching the five main management decisions connected with the global marketing process: (1) whether to internationalize; (2) deciding which markets to enter; (3) deciding how to enter the foreign market; (4) designing the global marketing programme; and (5) implementing and coordinating the global marketing programme.

Having studied this book, the reader should be better equipped to understand how the firm can achieve global competitiveness through the design and implementation of market-responsive programmes.

Target audience

This book is written for people who want to develop effective and decision-oriented global marketing programmes. It can be used as a textbook for undergraduate or graduate courses in global/international marketing. A second audience is the large group of people joining 'global marketing' or 'export' courses on non-university programmes. Finally, this book is of special interest to the manager who wishes to keep abreast of the most recent developments in the global marketing field.

Prerequisites

An introductory course in marketing.

Special features

This book has been written from the perspective of the firm competing in international markets, irrespective of its country of origin. It has the following key features:

- a focus on SMEs as global marketing players;
- a decision/action-oriented approach;
- a value chain approach (both the traditional product value chain and the service value chain);
- a value network approach (including different actors vertically and horizontally);
- a social media marketing approach is integrated throughout the book;

- coverage of global buyer–seller relationships;
- extensive coverage of born globals and global account management (GAM), as an extension of the traditional key account management (KAM);
- presents new interesting theories in marketing, for example, service value chain, value innovation, blue ocean strategy, social marketing, corporate social responsibility (CSR), global account management, viral branding and sensory and celebrity branding;
- aims to be a 'true' global marketing book, with cases and exhibits from all parts of the world, including Europe, the Middle East, Africa, the Far East, North and South America;
- provides a complete and concentrated overview of the total international marketing planning process;
- many new up-to-date exhibits and cases illustrate the theory by showing practical applications.

Outline

As the book has a clear decision-oriented approach, it is structured according to the five main decisions that marketing people in companies face in connection with the global marketing process. The 20 chapters are divided into five parts. The schematic outline of the book in Figure 1 shows how the different parts fit together. Global marketing research is considered to be an integral part of the decision-making process, therefore it is included in the book (Chapter 5), so as to use it as an important input to the decision about which markets to enter (the beginning of Part II). Examples of the practice of global marketing by actual companies are used throughout the book, in the form of exhibits. Furthermore, each chapter and part ends with cases, which include questions for students.

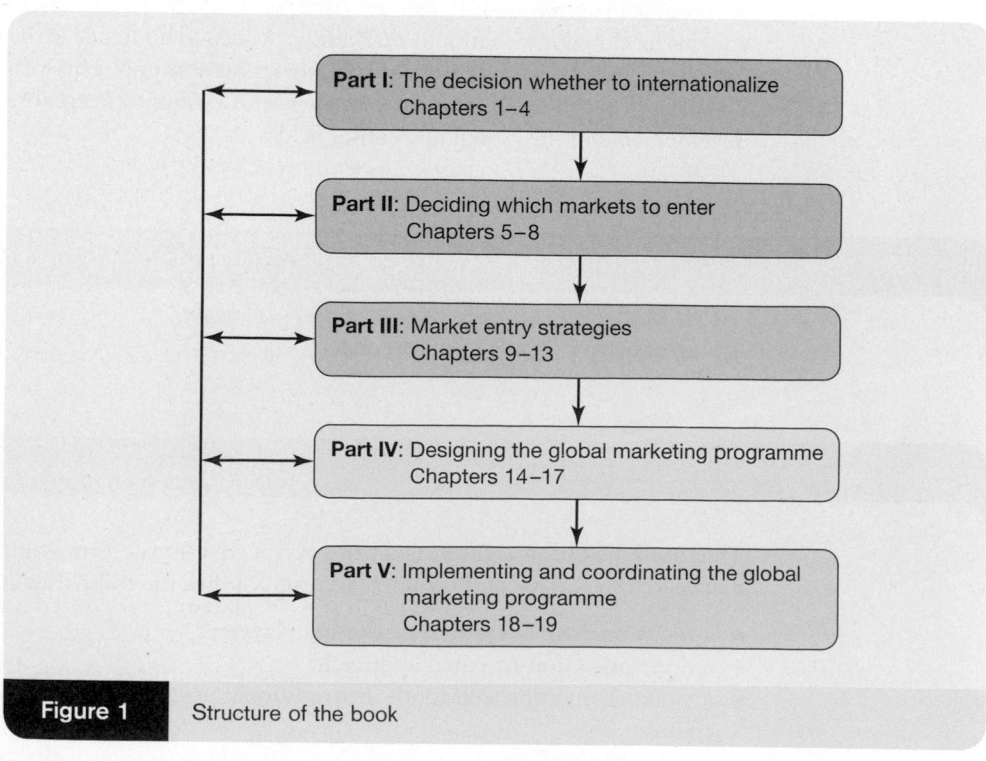

| Figure 1 | Structure of the book |

What's new in the seventh edition?

The new seventh edition is concentrated around two major themes: 'glocalization' and the 'internet of everything'. The glocalization concept which runs throughout this new edition enables international marketers to utilize the synergies arising from being both 'local' and 'global' at the same time. An important aspect of this new edition is its emphasis on the so-called 'internet of everything', which is becoming incorporated in all parts of the daily communication and buying behaviour of consumers around the world. Consequently, this increasing ubiquity of the internet is reflected in its inclusion in every chapter and in most of the cases and exhibits. The book is still structured around the well-known stages that SMEs go through when they internationalize as shown in Figure 1.

The book's chapters and cases are totally updated with newest journal articles and company information. Besides that, the following new issues are introduced in the individual chapters:

- Chapter 1 – the concept of providing customer value through the product value chain and the service value chain is now extended by adding 'customer experiences' as value generator. Augmented reality (AR) can be seen as a form of experiential marketing because it focuses not only on a single product/service, but also on an entire experience created for the customers. AR technology enhances the customer's current perception of reality.

- Chapter 2 – the 'inverted U-shaped curve' is introduced as a means of identifying, in terms of internationalization, the optimum point that results in the maximum number of countries that should be served. Internationalization incurs costs for the expanding company which explains why further internationalization can have a negative influence on profitability and why over-internationalized companies may reduce their degree of internationalization.

- Chapter 4 – introduces the concept of the 'sharing economy', where individuals are able to lease assets (products or services) owned by someone else, typically through an online marketplace. There are several ways of selling use of a product rather than ownership. Hilti is introduced as a company which provides products, systems and services to the global construction industry, but which focuses not only on selling the hand-held power tools but also on selling the use of the products. This chapter also introduces Barney's VRIO analysis in order to determine the competitive potential of a given firm's resource.

- Chapter 5 – here Amazon is used as an example of how companies can use big data and analytics in order to create competitive advantage. Amazon is now offering and selling their algorithm services to other companies, e.g. through Amazon Web Services (AWS).

- Chapter 6 – shows how a company like Google is confronted with political risks. In China, the company experienced political risks, and the chapter shows how they coped with it. Google's involvement in an EU antitrust case is also examined.

- Chapter 8 – introduces the GLOBE model, which is an updated extension of Hofstede's original work. This chapter also discusses the effects of cultural dimensions on ethical decision-making.

- Chapter 12 – presents a framework for analysing the cultural interaction between organizations in different countries, i.e. between HQ and the specific subsidiary/the host country.

- Chapter 14 – introduces e-services through 'cloud computing'. Furthermore, 3-D printing is introduced as a possible new industrial revolution in customization. In the last part, global mobile app marketing is discussed as the new global marketing tool – one which is attracting increasing attention due to the global roll out of 3G and 4G mobile services, together with the increasing penetration of smartphones and tablets. Mobile value-added services (MVAS) represent a special case where the app offers services that are not directly tied to sales but are designed to help customers solve problems or make decisions. Such an app enriches the total customer experience of a product/service offering.

- Chapter 15 – introduces the Freemium (Free + Premium = Freemium) pricing strategy, a pricing strategy by which a product or service is provided free of charge (Free), but changes are introduced afterwards for more advanced features or functionality (Premium).
- Chapter 16 – in connection with the introduction of the omnichannel retailing (or multichannel retailing) approach, a 2×2 matrix is introduced, based on two basic dimensions: information delivery and transaction fulfilment.
- Chapter 17 – now contains the transition from the traditional one-way market communication – playing 'bowling' – to playing 'pinball'. In a social media marketing world, the bowling metaphor no longer fits. In this new arena, marketing can be better described as playing 'pinball': companies serve up a 'marketing ball' (the brand) into a dynamic and chaotic market environment.
- Several new exhibits with real updated company examples are added to vaiours chapters.
- Many completely new and exciting chapter case studies are now available:
  - Case 4.2: **DJI Technology Co. Ltd** – a Chinese 'born global' is dominating the world market for drones with its Phantom
  - Video case 5.3: **BMW i3** – the electric car
  - Video case 7.3: **Allergan** – the maker of Botox and breast implants
  - Video case 8.3: **Oreo Mondelēz**
  - Video case 13.3: **Kone elevators and escalators**
  - Video case 14.3: **Burberry** branding
- Two new part introduction video case studies are now available:
  - Part I Video case study: **Uber**
  - Part II Video case study: **HondaJets**
- Furthermore, completely new part cases have been added:
  - Case II.1: **SodaStream** – managing profitable growth in an increasingly competitive global environment
  - Case II.3: **Zalando** – how can the online apparel retailer turn financial losses into positive profits?
  - Case II.4: **Ferrari** – international market selection (IMS) for the exclusive sports car brand
  - Case III.2: **Netflix Inc.** – the US internet subscription service company is dominating the television and movies and streaming world
  - Case IV.3: **Dyson** – the iconic vacuum cleaner manufacturer launches the robotic version
- In total 6 (chapter cases) + 2 (part video cases) + 5 (part cases) = **13 new cases** have been added to the book, making a total of:
- **38** chapter case studies (two per chapter) + **5** part video case studies (one per part) + **19** chapter video case studies (one per chapter) + **25** part case studies (five per part) = **87** case studies in all.
- Furthermore **16 completely new exhibits** have been added to the book. The total number of exhibits is now **72**.

Pedagogical/learning aids

One of the strengths of *Global Marketing* is its strong pedagogical features:

- Chapter objectives tell readers what they should be able to do after completing each chapter.
- Real-world examples and exhibits enliven the text and enable readers to relate to marketing models.

- End-of-chapter summaries recap the main concepts.
- Each chapter contains two case studies, which help the student relate the models presented in the chapter to a specific business situation.
- Questions for discussion allow students to probe further into important topics.
- Part cases studies – for each part there are five comprehensive case studies covering the themes met in the part. To reinforce learning, all case studies are accompanied by questions. Case studies are based on real-life companies. Further information about these companies can be found on the internet. Company cases are derived from many different countries representing all parts of the world. Tables 1 and 2 present the chapter and part case studies.
- Multiple choice questions.
- Part video case studies: each part is introduced by a video case which highlights a general decision problem from the part.

Table 1	Chapter case studies: overview (the video case studies can be viewed at www.pearsoned.co.uk/hollensen)				
Chapter	Case study title, subtitle and related websites	Country/area of company headquarters	Geographical target area	Target market	
				B2B	B2C
Chapter 1 Global marketing in the firm	Case study 1.1 **Green Toys, Inc.** A manufacturer of eco-friendly toys is going international www.greentoys.com	US	US, World	✓	✓
	Case study 1.2 **Hunter Boot Ltd** The iconic British brand is moving into exclusive fashion www.hunterboots.com	UK	World		✓
	Video case study 1.3 **Nivea** (8.56) www.nivea.com	Germany	World		✓
Chapter 2 Initiation of internationalization	Case study 2.1 **LifeStraw** Vestergaard-Frandsen transforms dirty water into clean drinking water www.vestergaard.com	Switzerland	World (developing countries)	✓	✓
	Case study 2.2 **Elvis Presley Enterprises Inc. (EPE)** Internationalization of a cult icon www.elvis.com	US	World		✓
	Video case study 2.3 **TOMS Shoes** www.toms.com	US	World (developing countries)		✓
Chapter 3 Internationalization theories	Case study 3.1 **Zumba** A dance phenomenon is going global www.zumba.com	US	World	✓	✓
	Case study 3.2 **DreamWorks Classics** Internationalization of Postman Pat http://classics.dreamworksanimation.com	UK	World		✓

Table 1	Continued				
Chapter	Case study title, subtitle and related websites	Country/area of company headquarters	Geographical target area	Target market	
				B2B	B2C
	Video case study 3.3 **Reebok** (9.09) www.reebok.com www.adidas-group.com	US	World	✓	✓
Chapter 4 Development of the firm's international competitiveness	Case study 4.1 **Nintendo Wii** Nintendo's Wii took first place in the world market – but it didn't last www.nintendo.com	Japan	World	✓	✓
	Case study 4.2 **DJI Technology Co. Ltd** A Chinese 'born global' is dominating the world market for drones with its Phantom www.dji.com	China	World	✓	✓
	Video case study 4.3 **Nike** (14.03) www.nike.com	US	World		✓
Chapter 5 Global marketing research	Case study 5.1 **Teepack Spezialmaschinen GmbH** Organizing a global survey of customer satisfaction www.teepack.com	Germany	World	✓	
	Case study 5.2 **LEGO Friends** One of the world's largest toy manufacturers moves into the girl's domain www.lego.com	Denmark	World		✓
	Video case 5.3 **BMW i3** The electric car www.bmw.com	Germany	World		✓
Chapter 6 The political and economic environment	Case study 6.1 **G-20 and the economic and financial crises** What on earth is globalization about? Protests during a meeting in Brisbane, Australia, November 2014 www.theguardian.com/world/ g20-brisbane-2014	US	World	✓	✓
	Case study 6.2 **Danfoss Power Solutions** Which political/economic factors would affect a manufacturer of hydraulic components? www.powersolutions.danfoss.com	Denmark, US, Germany	World	✓	

Table 1	Continued				
Chapter	Case study title, subtitle and related websites	Country/area of company headquarters	Geographical target area	Target market	
				B2B	B2C
	Video case study 6.3 **Debate on globalization** No website available	US	US	✓	✓
Chapter 7 The sociocultural environment	Case study 7.1 **Cirque du Soleil Inc.** The show that revolutionized the circus arts is expanding its global scope www.cirquedusoleil.com	Canada	World		✓
	Case study 7.2 **IKEA catalogue** Are there any cultural differences? www.ikea.com	Sweden, Holland	World		✓
	Video case study 7.3 **Allergan** The maker of Botox and breast implants www.allergan.com			✓	✓
Chapter 8 The international market selection process	Case study 8.1 **Tata Nano** International market selection with the world's cheapest car www.tatamotors.com	India	World (emerging countries)	✓	✓
	Case study 8.2 **Philips Lighting** Screening markets in the Middle East www.philips.com	Holland	World		✓
	Video case study 8.3 **Oreo (Mondelēz)** www.oreo.com	US	World		✓
Chapter 9 Some approaches to the choice of entry mode	Case study 9.1 **Jarlsberg** The king of Norwegian cheeses is deciding on entry modes into new markets www.jarlsberg.com	Norway	World	✓	✓
	Case study 9.2 **Ansell condoms** Is acquisition the right way to gain market shares in the European condom market? www.anselleurope.com www.lifestyles.com	Australia, Belgium	Europe, World		✓
	Video case study 9.3 **Understanding entry modes into the Chinese market** No website available	World	China	✓	

Table 1	Continued				
Chapter	**Case study title, subtitle and related websites**	**Country/area of company headquarters**	**Geographical target area**	**Target market**	
				B2B	**B2C**
Chapter 10 Export modes	Case study 10.1 **Lysholm Linie Aquavit** International marketing of the Norwegian Aquavit brand www.linie.com	Norway	Germany, the rest of the world	✓	✓
	Case study 10.2 **Parle Products** An Indian biscuit manufacturer is seeking agents and cooperation partners in new export markets www.parleproducts.com	India	World	✓	✓
	Video case study 10.3 **Honest Tea** www.honesttea.com	US	World, US		✓
Chapter 11 Intermediate entry modes	Case study 11.1 **Hello Kitty** Can the cartoon cat survive the buzz across the world? www.sanrio.com	Japan	World	✓	✓
	Case study 11.2 **Kabooki** Licensing in the LEGO brand www.legowear.dk	Denmark	World	✓	✓
	Video case study 11.3 **Marriott** (9.36) www.marriott.com	US	World	✓	✓
Chapter 12 Hierarchical modes	Case study 12.1 **Polo Ralph Lauren** Polo moves distribution for South-east Asia in-house www.ralphlauren.com	US	World, Asia	✓	✓
	Case study 12.2 **Durex Condoms** SSL will sell Durex condoms in the Japanese market through its own organization www.durex.com	UK	World	✓	✓
	Video case study 12.3 **Starbucks** www.starbucks.com	US	World	✓	✓
Chapter 13 International sourcing decisions and the role of the subsupplier	Case study 13.1 **ARM** Challenging Intel in the world market of computer chips www.arm.com	UK	World	✓	

Table 1	Continued				
Chapter	**Case study title, subtitle and related websites**	**Country/area of company headquarters**	**Geographical target area**	**Target market**	
				B2B	B2C
	Case study 13.2 **Bosch Indego** How to build B2B and B2C relationships in a new global product market – robotic lawnmowers www.bosch.com	Germany	World	✓	✓
	Video case study 13.3 **Kone elevators and escalators** www.kone.com	Finland	World	✓	
Chapter 14 Product decisions	Case study 14.1 **Danish Klassic** Launch of a cream cheese in Saudi Arabia www.arla.com (regarding the Puck brand)	Denmark	Saudi Arabia Middle East	✓	✓
	Case study 14.2 **Zippo Manufacturing Company** Has product diversification beyond the lighter gone too far? www.zippo.com	US	World	✓	✓
	Video case study 14.3 **Burburry branding** www.burberry.com	UK	World		✓
Chapter 15 Pricing decisions and terms of doing business	Case study 15.1 **Harley-Davidson** Does the image justify the price level? www.harley-davidson.com	US	US, Europe		✓
	Case study 15.2 **Gillette Co.** Is price standardization possible for razor blades? www.gillette.com	US	World	✓	✓
	Video case study 15.3 **Vaseline pricing strategy** www.vaseline.com	US	US, World		✓
Chapter 16 Distribution decisions	Case study 16.1 **De Beers** Forward integration into the diamond industry value chain www.debeers.com	South Africa, UK, Luxembourg	Europe, World	✓	✓
	Case study 16.2 **Tupperware** The global direct distribution model is still working www.tupperware.com	US	World	✓	✓
	Video case study 16.3 **DHL** www.dhl.com	Germany	World	✓	

Table 1	Continued				
Chapter	**Case study title, subtitle and related websites**	**Country/area of company headquarters**	**Geographical target area**	**Target market**	
				B2B	**B2C**
Chapter 17 Communication decisions	Case study 17.1 **Helly Hansen** Sponsoring fashion clothes in the US market www.hellyhansen.com	Norway	US	✓	✓
	Case study 17.2 **Morgan Motor Company** Can the British retro sports car brand still be successful after 100 years? www.morgan-motor.co.uk	UK	World (Europe and US)	✓	✓
	Video case study 17.3 **BMW Motorcycles** www.bmwmotorcycles.com www.bmw.com	Germany	US, World	✓	✓
Chapter 18 Cross-cultural sales negotiations	Case study 18.1 **ZamZam Cola** Marketing of a 'Muslim' cola from Iran to the European market www.zamzamrefreshment.com	Iran	Europe, Middle East	✓	✓
	Case study 18.2 **TOTO** The Japanese toilet manufacturer seeks export opportunities for its high-tech brands in the US www.toto.co.jp/en/				
	Video case study 18.3 **Dunkin' Donuts** www.DunkinDonuts.com www.dunkinbrands.com				
Chapter 19 Organization and control of the global marketing programme	Case study 19.1 **Mars Inc.** Merger of the European food, pet care and confectionery divisions www.mars.com	US	World	✓	✓
	Case study 19.2 **Henkel** Should Henkel shift to a more customer-centric organization? www.henkel.com	Germany	World	✓	✓
	Video case study 19.3 **McDonald's** www.mcdonalds.com	US	World	✓	

Table 2	Part case studies: overview				
Part	Case study title, subtitle and related websites	Country/area of company headquarters	Geographical target area	Target market	
				B2B	B2C
Part I The decision whether to internationalize	Part video case study **Uber** www.uber.com	US	World		✓
	Case study I.1 **Zara** The Spanish retailer goes to the top of world fashion www.inditex.com/en	Spain	World	✓	✓
	Case study I.2 **Manchester United** Still trying to establish a global brand www.manutd.com	UK	World, US	✓	✓
	Case study I.3 **Adidas** The No. 2 in the global sportswear market is challenging the No. 1, Nike www.adidas.com	Germany	World	✓	✓
	Case study I.4 **Cereal Partners Worldwide (CPW)** The no. 2 world player is challenging the no. 1, Kellogg www.generalmills.com/en/Company/Businesses/international/joint-ventures www.nestle.com/asset-library/documents/media/news-and-features/2011-february/cpw-brochure.pdf	Switzerland, US	World	✓	✓
Part II Deciding which markets to enter	Part video case study **HondaJets** Honda enters the small-sized business jet market http://www.hondajet.com/	Japan	World	✓	
	Case study II.1 **SodaStream** Managing profitable growth in an increasingly competitive global environment www.sodastream.com	Israel	World	✓	✓
	Case study II.2 **The female Health Company (FHC)** The Female condom is seeking a foothold in the world market for contraceptive products www.femalehealth.com	US	World (governmental organizations)	✓	✓
	Case study II.3 **Zalando** How can the online apparel retailer turn financial losses into positive profits? www.zalando.com	Spain	World		✓

Table 2	Continued				
Part	**Case study title, subtitle and related websites**	**Country/area of company headquarters**	**Geographical target area**	**Target market**	
				B2B	**B2C**
	Case study II.4 **Ferrari** International market selection (IMS) for the exclusive sports car brand	Italy	World		✓
Part III Market entry strategies	Part video case study **Müller Yogurts** www.muellergroup.com	Germany	US	✓	✓
	Case study III.1 **Raleigh Bicycles** Does the iconic bicycle brand still have a chance on the world market? www.raleigh.co.uk	UK	World	✓	✓
	Case study III.2 **Netflix Inc.** The US internet subscription service company is dominating the television and movies and streaming world www.Netflix.com	US	World		✓
	Case study III.3 **Autoliv Airbags** Transforming Autoliv into a global company www.autoliv.com	Sweden, US	World	✓	
	Case study III.4 **IMAX Corporation** Globalization of the film business www.imax.com	Canada	World	✓	✓
Part IV Designing the global marketing programme	Part video case study **Tequila Avión** www.tequilaavion.com	US	World	✓	
	Case study IV.1 **Absolut Vodka** Defending and attacking for a better position in the global vodka market www.pernod-ricard.com www.pernod-ricard.com/525/brands/see-all-brands/strategic-brands/absolut-vodka	France, Sweden	World, Eastern Europe		✓
	Case study IV.2 **Guinness** How can the iconic Irish beer brand compensate for declining sales in the home market? www.diageo.com www.guinness.com	UK, Ireland	World	✓	✓
	Case study IV.3 **Dyson** The iconic vacuum cleaner manufacturer launches the robotic version www.dyson.co.uk	UK	US, the rest of the world	✓	✓

Table 2	Continued					
Part	**Case study title, subtitle and related websites**	**Country/area of company headquarters**	**Geographical target area**	**Target market**		
				B2B	**B2C**	
	Case study IV.4 **Triumph Motorcycles Ltd** Rising from the ashes in the international motorcycle business www.triumph.co.uk	UK	World		✓	
Part V Implementing and coordinating the global marketing programme	Part video case study **Stella & Dot** www.stelladot.com	US	World	✓	✓	
	Case study V.1 **Sony Music Entertainment** New worldwide organizational structure and the marketing, planning and budgeting of Pink's new album www.sonymusic.com	US, Japan	World	✓	✓	
	Case study V.2 **Red Bull** The global market leader in energy drinks is considering further market expansion www.redbull.com	Austria	World	✓	✓	
	Case study V.3 **Tetra Pak** How to create B2B relationships with the food industry on a global level www.tetrapak.com	Holland	World	✓		
	Case study V.4 **Polaroid Eyewear** Can the iconic brand achieve a comeback in the global sunglasses industry? www.polaroideyewear.com	Switzerland, Italy	World		✓	

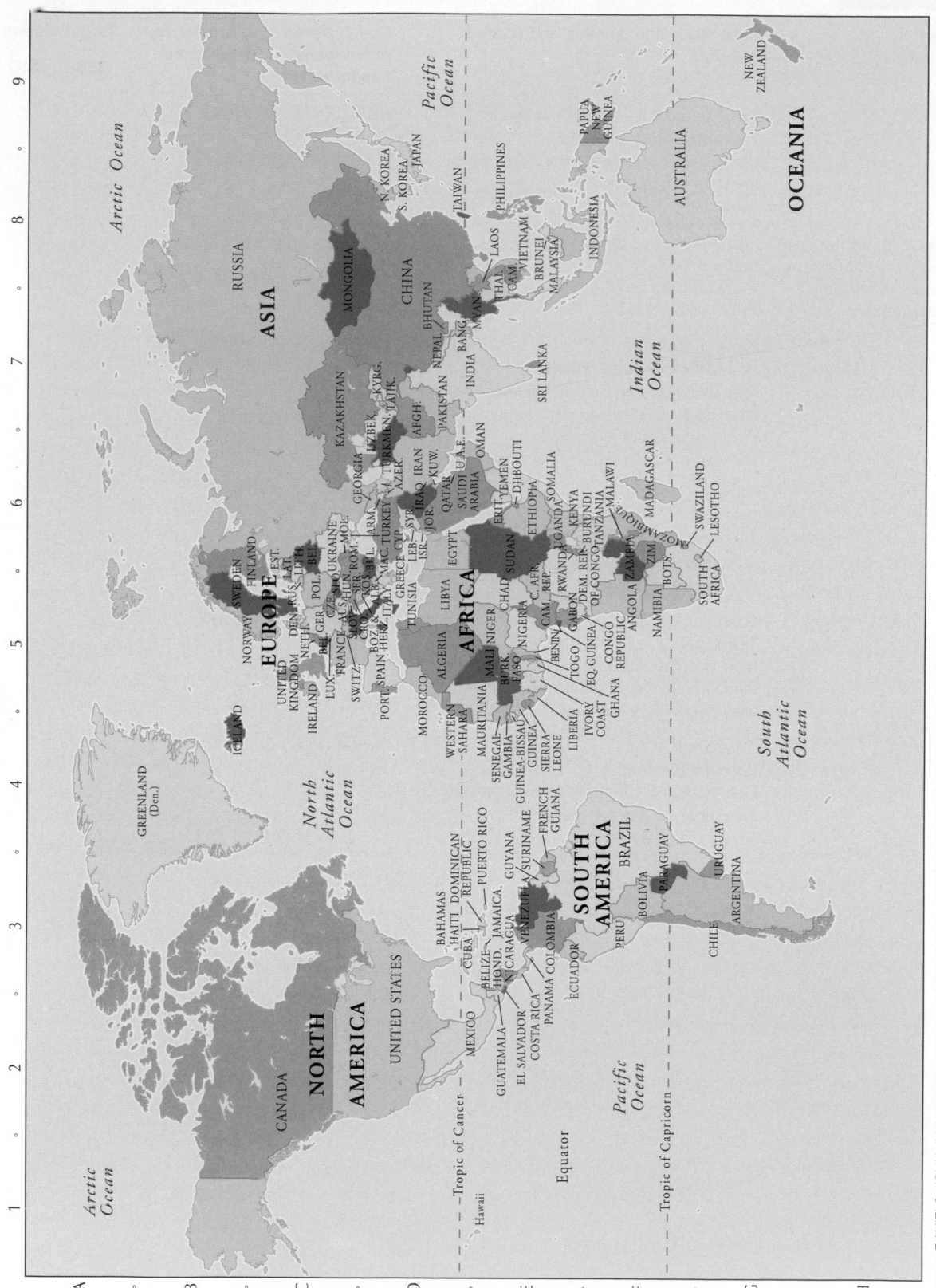

ACKNOWLEDGEMENTS

Writing any book is a long-term commitment and involves time-consuming effort. The successful completion of a book depends on the support and generosity of many people and the realization of this book is certainly no exception.

I wish to thank the many scholars whose articles, books and other materials I have cited or quoted. However, it is not possible to acknowledge everyone by name. In particular, I am deeply indebted to the following individuals and organizations. I thank you all for your help and contributions:

University of Southern Denmark

- Management at University of Southern Denmark provided the best possible environment for writing and completing this project. I would especially like to thank the Head of the Department of Border Region Studies, Elisabeth Vestergaard, for her support during the writing process.
- Colleagues provided encouragement and support during the writing process. I would especially like to thank the Secretaries, Charlotte Lund Hansen, Angela Hansen and Janne Øe Hobson, and the Project Coordinator, Simon Kleinschmidt Salling, at the University of Southern Denmark, Campus Sønderborg for their helpfulness and support during the writing process.
- The library at the University of Southern Denmark provided articles and books from different worldwide sources.

Reviewers

- Reviewers provided suggestions which were useful in improving many parts of the text.
- In the development of this text, a number of reviewers have been involved, whom I would like to thank for their important and valuable contribution.

Endorsers

I would like to thank the users of the book who have endorsed my *Global Marketing* on Amazon, on my LinkedIn profile or on other social media. I am especially grateful to the front- and backcover endorsers of this edition:

- Professor Philip Kotler, Northwestern University, USA
- Professor Michael R. Solomon, Saint Joseph's University, USA
- Dr Elisabeth Götze, Vienna University of Economics and Business, Austria
- Giovanna Battiston, Sheffield Hallam University, UK

Case contributors

- Wim Wils, Fontys Eindhoven, for Case 8.2: Philips Lighting.
- Vlad Stefan Wulff, for Case 19.2 Henkel.

I also wish to acknowledge the help from the following firms whose managers have provided valuable material that has enabled me to write the cases mentioned. I have been in direct personal contact with most of the case companies and thank the managers involved for their very useful comments. In particular, I would like to thank:

Chapter cases

- The founders of Green Toys, Inc. for Case 1.1 on Green Toys.
- Family Vestergaard-Frandsen for Case 2.1 on LifeStraw.
- Elvis Presley Enterprises, Inc. for Case 2.2 on EPE.
- Zumba Fitness, Florida, for Case 3.1 on Zumba.
- Teepack Spezialmaschinen GmbH, Düsseldorf, Germany for Case 5.1 on Teepack Spezialmaschinen.
- LEGO, Billund, Denmark on Case 5.2 on LEGO Friends.
- Danfoss Power Solutions for Case 6.2 on Danfoss Power Solutions.
- IKEA, Sweden for Case 7.2 on the IKEA Catalogue.
- Jarlsberg, Norway for Case 9.1 on Jarlsberg.
- Arcus AS, Oslo, Norway for Case 10.1 on Lysholm Linie Aquavit.
- Sanrio, Europe for Case 11.1 on Hello Kitty.
- Kabooki, Ikast, Denmark for Case 11.2 on Kabooki.
- Polo Ralph Lauren, USA for Case 12.1 on Polo Ralph Lauren.
- ARM, Cambridge, UK for Case 13.1 on ARM.
- Vaseline, UK for Case 15.3 on Vaseline pricing strategy.
- Morgan Motor Company, UK for Case 17.2 on the Morgan Motor Company.
- Henkel, Germany for Case 19.2 on Henkel.

Part cases

- Inditex, Spain for Case I.1: Zara.
- Raleigh Bicycles, UK for Case III.1: Raleigh Bicycles.
- Autoliv AB, Stockholm, Sweden for Case III.3: Autoliv airbags.
- IMAX Corporation, Toronto, Canada for Case III.4: Imax Corporation.
- The Absolut Company, a division of Pernod Ricard for Case IV.1: Absolut Vodka.
- Sony Music Entertainment, New York, USA for Case V.1: Sony Music Entertainment.
- Red Bull, Austria for Case V.2: Red Bull.

I would like to thank The Tussauds Group for their contribution to Exhibit 14.4.

I would also like to thank Husqvarna AB (Sweden), especially Vice President for Brand and Marketing, Torsten Bollweg, for his permission to show the 'Husqvarna consumer wheel' in Exhibit 17.2.

I am also grateful to the following international advertising agencies, which have provided me with examples of standardized and/or localized advertising campaigns:

- Walter Thompson (JWT Europe), London, who contributed with a European ad for LUX soap.
- Hindustan Thompson (HTA), Bombay, India, who contributed with an ad for Kellogg's Basmati Flakes in India and an ad for LUX soap in India.

I would also like to thank LEGO and Danfoss for their contributions to different examples in the book.

I am grateful to my publisher, Pearson Education. I would like to thank Donna Goddard, Rachel Gear, Rufus Curnow and Anita Atkinson for their commitment to this book project.

I also extend my greatest gratitude to my colleagues at the University of Southern Denmark for their constant help and inspiration.

Finally, I thank my family for their support through the revision process. I am pleased to dedicate this version to Jonna, Nanna and Julie.

Svend Hollensen
University of Southern Denmark, Sønderborg,
May 2016
svend@sam.sdu.dk

PUBLISHER'S ACKNOWLEDGEMENTS

We are grateful to the following for permission to reproduce copyright material:

Figures

Figure 1.2 from *Essentials of Global Marketing*, Financial Times Prentice Hall (Hollensen, S. 2008) figure 1, pp. 6–9, copyright © Pearson Education Ltd; Figure 1.3 from The strategy concept I: five Ps for strategy, *California Management Review*, 30(1), pp. 11–24 (Mintzberg, H. 1987), p. 14, © Regents of the University of California. Published by the University of California Press; Figure 1.4 from Rethinking incrementalism, *Strategic Management Journal*, 9, pp. 75–91 (Johnson, G. 1988), copyright © 1988 John Wiley & Sons Ltd, reproduced with permission; Figure 1.6 from A framework for analysis of strategy development in globalizing markets, *Journal of International Marketing*, 5(1), p. 11 (Solberg, C.A. 1997), reprinted by permission of American Marketing Association; Figure 1.10 adapted from *Competitive Advantage: Creating and Sustaining Superior Performance* (Porter, M.E. 1985) figure 2-2, p. 37, copyright © 1985, 1998 by Michael E. Porter, adapted with the permission of The Free Press of Simon & Schuster, Inc., all rights reserved; Figure 1.13 from *Essentials of Global Marketing*, Financial Times Prentice Hall (Hollensen, S. 2008) figure 1.5, p. 17, copyright © Pearson Education Ltd; Figure 2.4 from *Essentials of Global Marketing*, Financial Times Prentice Hall (Hollensen, S. 2008) p. 47, copyright © Pearson Education Ltd; Figure 2.5 from *Essentials of Global Marketing*, Financial Times Prentice Hall (Hollensen, S. 2008) p. 48, copyright © Pearson Education Ltd; Figure 3.1 adapted from *International føretagsekonomi*, Norstedts (Forsgren, M. and Johanson, J. 1975) p. 16, with permission from Mats Forsgren; Figures 3.2 and 3.3 from Internationalization: evolution of a concept, *Journal of General Management*, 14(2), pp. 36–64 (Welch, L.S. and Loustarinen, R. 1988), reproduced with permission from The Braybrooke Press Ltd; Figure 3.6 adapted from *Internationalization Handbook for the Software Business*, Centre of Expertise for Software Product Business (Âijö, T., Kuivalainen, O., Saarenketo, S., Lindqvist, J. and Hanninen, H. 2005) p. 6; Figure 4.7 adapted from Competitive advantage: merging marketing and competence-based perspective, *Journal of Business and Industrial Marketing*, 9(4), pp. 42–53 (Jüttner, U. and Wehrli, H.P. 1994), with permission from Hans P. Wehrli; Figure 4.8 from Exploiting the core competences of your organization, *Long Range Planning*, 27(4), p. 74 (Tampoe, M. 1994), with permission from Elsevier; Figure 4.11 adapted from The business case for corporate social responsibility: a company-level measurement approach for CSR, *European Management Journal*, 26(4), pp. 247–61 (Weber, M. 2008), with permission from Elsevier; Figure 4.14 adapted from Value innovation: the strategic logic of high growth, *Harvard Business Review*, 75(1), pp. 102–12 (Kim, W.C. and Mauborgne, R. 1997), Harvard Business School Publishing; Figure 5.5 adapted from *Marketing Research Essentials*, 5th ed. (McDaniel Jr, S. and Gates, R. 2005) p. 228, © 2005 John Wiley & Sons, Inc., reproduced with permission; Figure 5.8 from *Marketing Research: An International Approach*, Financial Times Prentice Hall (Schmidt, M.I. and Hollensen, S. 2006) p. 587, copyright © Pearson Education Ltd; Figure 6.3 from *Global Marketing*, South-Western (Czinkota, M.R. and Ronkainen, I.A. 1996) p. 112, reproduced with permission of Harcourt College Publishers in the format Republish in a book via Copyright Clearance Center; Figure 7.3 from *Marketing Across Cultures*, 3rd ed., Pearson Education Ltd (Usunier, J-C. and Lee, J.A. 1999), copyright © Pearson Education Ltd; Figure 8.1 from

Marketing Management: A Relationship Approach, 3rd ed., Pearson Education Ltd (Hollensen, S. 2015) p. 61, copyright © Pearson Education Ltd; Figure 8.6 adapted from *European Business: An Issue-based Approach*, Pearson Education Ltd (Welford, R. and Prescott, K. 1996), copyright © Pearson Education Ltd; Figure 8.13 from *Global Marketing Management*, 2nd ed., Pearson Education, Inc. (Keegan, W.J. and Green, M. 2000) p. 410, reprinted and electronically reproduced by permission of Pearson Education, Inc., Upper Saddle River, New Jersey; Figure 8.14 from *International Marketing Strategy*, 2nd ed., Prentice Hall (Bradley, F. 1995), copyright © Pearson Education Ltd; Figure 8.15 from Market expansion strategies in multinational marketing, *Journal of Marketing*, 43, Spring, p. 84 (Ayal, I. and Zif, J. 1979), reprinted by permission of American Marketing Association; Figure 8.16 adapted from Bajaj Auto, www.bajajauto.com; Figure 1 on page 310 from A Nano car in every driveway? How to succeed in the ultra-low-cost car market, *Executive Agenda*, XI(2), pp. 55–62 (Oxyer, D., Deans, G., Shivaraman, S., Ghosh, S. and Pleines, R. 2008), figure 1, copyright © A.T. Kearney, 2008, all rights reserved, http://www.atkearney.com/paper/-/asset_publisher/dVxv4Hz2h8bS/content/a-nano-car-in-every-driveway/10192, reprinted with permission; Figure 11.2 from *International Marketing Strategy*, 2nd ed., Prentice Hall (Bradley, F. 1995) p. 388, adapted from Lowe, J. and Crawford, N. (1984) *Technology Licensing and the Small Firm*, England: Gower, copyright © Pearson Education Ltd, with permission from Julian Lowe; Figure 11.3 from *Essentials of Global Marketing*, Financial Times Prentice Hall (Hollensen, S. 2008) p. 233, copyright © Pearson Education Ltd; Figure 11.6 adapted from *Strategiske allianser i globale strategier*, Norges Eksportråd (Lorange, P. and Roos, J. 1995) p. 16, reprinted by permission of Index Publishing/Norwegian Trade Council; Figures 11.7 and 11.8 from *Strategies for Joint Ventures*, Lexington Books (Harrigan, K.R. 1985) p. 50 and p. 52; Figure 12.2 from *Essentials of Global Marketing*, Financial Times Prentice Hall (Hollensen, S. 2008) p. 245, copyright © Pearson Education Ltd; Figure 12.4 from Toward a theory of international new ventures, *Journal of International Business Studies*, 25(1), pp. 45–64 (Oviatt, B.M. and McDougall, P.P. 1994), Palgrave Macmillan; Figure 12.5 from Organizational dimensions of global marketing, *European Journal of Marketing*, 23(5), pp. 43–57 (Raffée, H. and Kreutzer, R. 1989), reprinted by permission of Emerald Group Publishing Ltd, www.emeraldinsight.com; Figure 12.6 from Why are subsidiaries divested? A conceptual framework, *Working Paper No. 3–93*, figure 2 (Benito, G. 1996), reprinted by permission of Institute of International Economics and Management, Copenhagen Business School; Figure 13.1 adapted from Alihankintajarjestelma 1990-luvulla [Subcontracting system in the 1990s], *Publications of SITRA*, 114, p. 22 (Lehtinen, U. 1991), reprinted by permission of SITRA; Figure 13.3 from A total cost/value model for supply chain competitiveness, *Journal of Business Logistics*, 13(2), pp. 285–301 (Cavinato, J.L. 1992), Council of Logistics Management; Figure 13.4 adapted from Interactive strategies in supply chains: a double-edged portfolio approach to SME, *Subcontractors Positioning Paper presented at the 8th Nordic Conference on Small Business Research* (Blenker, P. and Christensen, P.R. 1994); Figure 13.6 from Relationship marketing from a value system perspective, *International Journal of Service Industry Management*, 5, pp. 54–73 (Jüttner, U. and Wehrli, H.P. 1994), reprinted by permission of Emerald Group Publishing Ltd, www.emeraldinsight.com; Figure on page 495 adapted from Standardization: an integrated approach in global marketing, *European Journal of Marketing*, 22(10), pp. 19–30 (Kreutzer, R. 1988), reprinted by permission of Emerald Group Publishing Ltd, www.emeraldinsight.com; Figure 14.2 from *International Marketing*, 4th ed., Dryden Press (Czinkota, M.R. and Ronkainen, I.A. 1995) p. 526, reproduced with permission of Dryden Press, in the format Republish in a book via Copyright Clearance Center; Figure 14.3 from *Marketing Management: A Relationship Approach*, 2nd ed., Pearson Education Ltd (Hollensen, S. 2010) figure 11.7, copyright © Pearson Education Ltd; Figure 14.4 from *Marketing Management: A Relationship Approach*, 2nd ed., Pearson Education Ltd (Hollensen, S. 2010) figure 7.5, copyright © Pearson Education Ltd; Figure 14.7 adapted from Competitive analysis using matrix displays, *Long Range Planning*, 17(3), pp. 98–114 (McNamee, P. 1984), copyright 1984, with permission from Elsevier; Figure 14.8 from *International Marketing: Analysis and Strategy,* 2nd ed. (Onkvisit, S. and Shaw, J.J. 1993) p. 483, reprinted by permission of Sak Onkvisit; Figures 14.11 and 14.12 from New products: cutting the time to market, *Long Range Planning,* 28(2), pp. 61–78 (Töpfer, A. 1995), copyright 1995, with permission from Elsevier; Figure 14.15 from *International Marketing: Analysis and Strategy,* 2nd ed. (Onkvisit, S. and Shaw, J.J. 1993) p. 534, reprinted by permission of Sak Onkvisit; Figure 15.3 from *Strategic Management: An Integrative Perspective* (Hax, A.C. and Majluf, N.S. 1984) p. 121, © 1984, electronically reproduced by permission of Pearson Education, Inc., Upper Saddle River, New Jersey; Figure 15.4 from *Marketing Management: Analysis, Planning, Implementation and Control,* 7th ed., Prentice Hall (Kotler, P. 1991) p. 350, © 1991, electronically reproduced by permission of Pearson Education, Inc., Upper Saddle River, New Jersey; Figure 15.5 from Pricing conditions in the European Common Market, *European Management Journal,* 12(2), p. 168 (Diller, H. and Bukhari, I. 1994), copyright 1994, with permission from Elsevier; Figure 15.6 adapted from A taxonomy of the pricing practices of exporting firms: evidence from Austria, Norway and the United States, *Journal of International Marketing,* 14(1), pp. 23–48 (Solberg, C.A., Stöttinger, B. and Yaprak, A. 2006), reprinted by permission of American Marketing Association; Figure 15.7 from The European pricing bomb – and how to cope with it, *Marketing and Research Today,* February, pp. 25–36 (Simon, H. and Kucher, E. 1993), ESOMAR; Figure 15.8 from *Dynamics of Trade Finance,* Chase Manhattan Bank (1984) p. 5; Figure 15.9 from *International Marketing Strategy: Analysis, Development and Implementation,* Routledge (Phillips, C., Doole, I. and Lowe, R. 1994) p. 454, copyright © 1994, reproduced by permission of Cengage Learning EMEA Ltd; Figures 16.2, 16.3 and 16.4 from *Marketing Management: An Overview,* The Dryden Press (Lewison, D.M. 1996) p. 271 and p. 279, with permission from Dale M. Lewison; Figure 16.10 adapted from How to win in an omnichannel world, *MIT Sloan Management Review,* 56(1), pp. 44–53 (Bell, D.R., Gallino, S. and Moreno, A. 2014), © 2014 from MIT Sloan Management Review/Massachusetts Institute of Technology. All rights reserved. Distributed by Tribune Content Agency; Figure 16.11 adapted from *Food, Inc. – Corporate Concentration from Farm to Consumer,* UK Food Group (Vorley, B. 2003) figure 7.2, p. 52, with permission from UK Food Group; Figure 16.13 from *International Marketing,* Heinemann (Paliwoda, S. 1993) p. 300, reprinted with permission from Butterworth-Heinemann Publishers, a division of Reed Educational & Professional Publishing Ltd; Figure 19.12 from *International Marketing: Planning and Practice,* Macmillan (Samli, A.C., Still, R. and Hill, J.S. 1993) p. 421, with permission from Professor Coskun Samli.

Maps

Map on page xxxii from *International Business,* 12th ed., Pearson Education, Inc. (Daniels, J., Radebaugh, L. and Sullivan, D. 2009) p. 37, M1 World View, © 2009, reprinted and electronically reproduced by permission of Pearson Education, Inc., Upper Saddle River, New Jersey; Map on page 76 from *The World's Water 1998–1999: The Biennial Report on Freshwater Resources,* Island Press (Gleick, P.H. 1998) p. 41, map 2.1, ISBN 9781559635929, copyright © 1998 Island Press, reproduced by permission of Island Press, Washington, DC.

Tables

Table 2.1 adapted from *International Marketing and Export Management,* 2nd ed., Addison Wesley (Albaum, G., Strandskov, J., Duerr, E. and Dowd, L. 1994) p. 31, reprinted by permission of Pearson Education Ltd; Table 4.1 from Composite strategy: the combination of collaboration and competition, *Journal of General Management,* 21(1), pp. 1–23

(Burton, J. 1995), reproduced with permission from The Braybrooke Press Ltd; Table 6.1 after World Bank 2015 statistics, © The World Bank; Table 7.2 adapted from *International Marketing Strategy: Analysis, Development and Implementation*, Thomson Learning (Phillips, C., Doole, I. and Lowe, R. 1994) p. 96, copyright © 1994, reproduced by permission of Cengage Learning EMEA Ltd; Table 7.4 from *Going International: How to Make Friends and Deal Effectively in the Global Marketplace*, Random House (Copeland, L. and Griggs, L. 1985), The Sagalyn Agency; Table 1 on page 330 adapted from The World Bank, © The World Bank; Tables 2, 3 and 4 on pages 330–31 adapted from Euromonitor International; Table 5 on page 332 from *Marketing Management: A Relationship Approach*, 3rd ed., Pearson Education Ltd (Hollensen, S. 2015) p. 64, © Pearson Education Ltd; Table 6 on page 333 from *Marketing Management: A Relationship Approach*, 3rd ed., Pearson Education Ltd (Hollensen, S. 2015) p. 65, copyright © Pearson Education Ltd; Table 10.1 from *Entry Strategies for International Markets*, second revised and expanded edition, Jossey Bass (Root, F.R. 1998) pp. 68–9, John Wiley and Sons; Table 11.3 adapted from *International Market Entry and Development*, Harvester Wheatsheaf/Prentice Hall (Young, S., Hamill, J., Wheeler, S. and Davies, J.R. 1989) p. 233, copyright © Pearson Education Ltd and Stephen Young; Table 13.1 from Relationship marketing from a value system perspective, *International Journal of Service Industry Management*, 5, pp. 54–73 (Jüttner, U. and Wehrli, H.P. 1994), reprinted by permission of Emerald Group Publishing Ltd, www.emeraldinsight.com; Table on page 496 from *Essentials of Global Marketing*, Financial Times Prentice Hall (Hollensen, S. 2008) table 1, p. 299, copyright © Pearson Education Ltd; Table 14.2 adapted from The international dimension of branding: strategic considerations and decisions, *International Marketing Review*, 6(3), pp. 22–34 (Onkvisit, S. and Shaw, J.J. 1989), reprinted by permission of Emerald Group Publishing Ltd, www.emeraldinsight.com; Table 16.2 adapted from *Online Retail Report 2016–17*, Centre for Retail Research, Nottingham (Bamfield, J.A.N. 2015); Table 17.3 adapted from *International Marketing Strategy: Analysis, Development and Implementation*, Routledge (Phillips, C., Poole, I. and Lowe, R. 1994) p. 362, copyright © 1994, reproduced by permission of Cengage Learning EMEA Ltd; Table 17.5 from Guidelines for managing an international sales force, *Industrial Marketing Management*, 24, p. 138 (Honeycutt, E.D. and Ford, J.B. 1995), copyright 1995, with permission from Elsevier; Table 19.1 adapted from *Principles and Practice of Marketing*, McGraw-Hill (Jobber, D. 1995), © 1995 McGraw-Hill, with the kind permission of the McGraw-Hill Publishing Company; Table 19.2 from *International Marketing: Planning and Practice*, Macmillan (Samli, A.C., Still, R. and Hill, J.S. 1993) p. 425, with permission from Professor Coskun Samli; Table 19.3 from *Marketing Management: Analysis, Planning, Implementation and Control*, 9th ed., Prentice Hall (Kotler, P. 1997) table 24-2, p. 765, © 1991, electronically reproduced by permission of Pearson Education, Inc., Upper Saddle River, New Jersey; Table 19.4 from *Marketing Management: A Relationship Approach*, 2nd ed., Pearson Education Ltd (Hollensen, S. 2010) p. 583, copyright © Pearson Education Ltd.

Text

Exhibit 2.4 from *Essentials of Global Marketing*, Financial Times Prentice Hall (Hollensen, S. 2008) pp. 47–8, copyright © Pearson Education Ltd; Exhibit 4.3 adapted from Erbitterter Kampf und die Lufthoheit, *Der Standard*, 30/06/2012 (Ruff, C.), Issue 7122, p. 14; Case Study on page 327 from *Marketing Management: A Relationship Approach*, 3rd ed., Pearson Education Ltd (Hollensen, S. 2015) pp. 59–66, copyright © Pearson Education Ltd; Case Study 11.1 from Top Cat: how 'Hello Kitty' conquered the world – Japan's new tourism ambassador, *The Independent*, 21/05/2008 (Walker, E.), http://www.independent.co.uk/news/world/asia/top-cat-how-hello-kitty-conquered-the-world-831522.html, The Independent; Exhibit 13.1 from Network sourcing: a hybrid approach, *Journal of Supply Chain Management* (formerly *The International Journal of Purchasing and Materials*

Management), 31(1), pp. 17–24 (Hines, P. 2006), John Wiley & Sons, Inc.; Exhibit 14.9 adapted from Monsanto Europe S.A.; Case Study 15.3 adapted from History of Vaseline, http://www.vaseline.co.uk, with the kind permission of Unilever; Extract on page 611 from *International Marketing Management*, 5th ed., South-Western, a division of Thomson Learning (Jain, S.C. 1996) p. 523, with permission from Professor Subhash C. Jain; Exhibit 16.3 adapted from *Food, Inc. – Corporate Concentration from Farm to Consumer*, UK Food Group (Vorley, B. 2003) p. 53, with permission from UK Food Group; Case Study 19.1 adapted from Can Mars bridge gaps in merger?, *Marketing Week*, News Analysis, 13 January (McCawley, I. 2000), with permission from Centaur Media plc.

Photographs

The publisher would like to thank the following for their kind permission to reproduce their photographs:

(Key: b–bottom; c–centre; l–left; r–right; t–top)

AB Electrolux: 255; **Adidas:** 104, 165; **Alamy Images:** Action Plus Sports Images 152, Adrian Sherratt 696t, Andrew Twort 413, AW Photography 14, Charlotte Allen 264, Convery flowers 23, David Pearson 309tl, epa european pressphoto agency b.v. 477tl, Helen Sessions 647, Ian Leonard 16, IanDagnall Computing 474, J.F.T.L Images 103, Jeffrey Blackler 50, Joerg Boethling 301, LOOK Die Bildagentur der Fotografen GmbH 488, Mark Scheuern 668, Markus Mainka 415, P. Cox 309br, Pickture 439; **Ansell:** 360; **Arcus Gruppen AS:** 382; **Arla Foods:** 549; **ARM Ltd:** 458b; **Autoliv Inc.:** 482; **Bajaj Auto:** 305; **CNH Industrial America LLC:** 41t, 41b; **Corbis:** Car Culture 676, Carlo Allegri/ Reuters 477br, Guy Corbishley/Demotix 323, Hannibal Hanschke/Reuters 703, Imagine China 624, Imaginechina 431, Jo Yong-Hak/Reuters 605, Motoo Naka/AFLO/Nippon News 544; **Dell, Inc.:** 608; **Det Danske Spirituskompagni A/S:** 658l, 658r; **DK Images:** Tony Souter 139; **Elvis Presley Enterprises:** 78; **Getty Images:** 498bl, Ari Perilstein 712, Bloomberg 4, 146, 277, 319, 356, 657t, Brian Ach 498tr, Daniel Munoz 247, David Maung/ Bloomberg 151r, David Paul Morris/Bloomberg 553, Donato Sardella 79, Ethan Miller 151l, 800, FOX 648, Hassan Ammar 551, Kevork Djansezian 145, 649t, 778, Kristian Dowling 95, MacFormat Magazine 572, Mike Coppola 321, Nicholas Ratzenboeck/AFP 121, PonyWang 271, Robyn Beck/AFP 148, Ulrich Baumgarten 329; **Godrej & Boyce Manufacturing Company Limited:** 240; **Green Toys, Inc:** 46t, 46b; **Husqvarna AB:** 636; **IKEA Ltd:** 42, 276; **Intel Corporation:** 458t; **iRobot Corporation:** 698; **KONE plc:** 465; **Lego Group:** 213, 214t/Penguin Books Ltd, 214b, 416, 643, 659tl, 659tr; **Lofthouse of Fleetwood Ltd:** 374; **Madame Tussauds:** 524l, 524r; **Marriott Hotels International Limited:** 417; **Monsanto Company:** 533; **Nivea and Beiersdorf UK Ltd:** 52b; Otsuka Pharmaceutical Co. Ltd: 267; **Reuters:** Yuya Shino 183; **Rex Shutterstock:** Buzz Foto 52t, David Pearson 698, Startraks Photo 101, Xinhua News Agency/REX Shutterstock 239; **Robert Bosch GmbH:** 463; **Sauer-Danfoss Ltd:** 249; Shutterstock.com: Adriano Castelli 705, Annette Shaff 142, Costi Iosif 784, Dutourdumonde Photography 335, Emka74 566, Frederic Legrand - COMEO 216, GoBOb 18, InsectWorld 630, Ivan Garcia 221, lzf 225, Melica 592, Nenov Brothers Images 316, Northfoto 738, Roman Samokhin 770, saknakorn 773, Sorbis 64, Thinglass 604, TonyV3112 591, urbanbuzz 347; **Société des Produits Nestlé S.A:** 173, 534, the Nestlé name and image is reproduced with kind permission; **Sunquick:** 299, 300; **Tetra Pak:** 792, 794, 795, 797; **The Absolut Company AB:** 680, 681, 685, used under permission from The Absolut Company AB. Absolut® Vodka. Absolut Country of Sweden Vodka & logo, Absolut, Absolut bottle design and Absolut calligraphy are trademarks owned by The Absolut Company AB, © The Absolut Company AB; **The Female Health Company:** 324; **Threadless:** 513; **Tine SA:** 359, 659bl, 659br, 660l, 660r; **TOTO:** 736; **Unilever PLC:** 593, reproduced with kind permission of Unilever PLC and group companies; **Vestergaard Frandsen:** 75, 77; **Vodacom:** 243; **Zalando:** 327; **Zippo:** 552bl, 552br.

ABBREVIATIONS

ACs	advanced countries
APEC	Asia-Pacific Economic Cooperation
AR	augmented reality
ASEAN	Association of South East Asian Nations
B2B	business to business
B2C	business to consumer
BATNA	best alternative to a negotiated agreement
BDA	before–during–after
BERI	Business Environment Risk Index
BMI	Business Monitor International
BOP	bottom of the pyramid
BRIC	Brazil, Russia, India and China
BT	British Telecommunications
C2C	consumer to consumer
CAGR	compound annual growth rate
CATI	computer-aided telephone interviews
CDB	China Development Bank
CEO	chief executive officer
CFR	cost and freight
CIF	cost, insurance and freight
CIP	carriage and insurance paid to
CMM-SEI	Carnegie Mellon University's Software Engineering Institute
COO	country of origin
CPM	cost per thousand
CPT	carriage paid to
CPV	customer perceived value
CRM	customer relationship management
CSR	corporate social responsibility
DAF	delivered at frontier
DAP	delivered at place
DAT	delivered at terminal
DDP	delivered duty paid
DDU	delivered duty unpaid
DEQ	delivered ex-quay
DES	delivered ex-ship
DMR	digital remastering
DSS	decision support system
EBIT	earnings before interest and taxes
ECB	European Central Bank
ECSC	European Coal and Steel Community
EEA	European Economic Area
EEC	European Economic Community
EFTA	European Free Trade Area
EMC	export management company
EMEA	Europe, Middle East and Africa
EMU	European Economic and Monetary Union

EPAC	electronically power-assisted cycles
EPRG	ethnocentric, polycentric, regiocentric, geocentric
EU	European Union: title for the former EEC used since the ratification of the Maastricht Treaty in 1992
EURATOM	European Atomic Energy Community
EXW	ex-works
FAB	flavoured alcoholic beverages
FAS	free alongside ship
FCA	free carrier
FDA	Food and Drug Administration (US)
FDI	foreign direct investment: a market entry strategy in which a company invests in a subsidiary or partnership in a foreign market (joint venture)
FHI	Family Health International
FMCG	fast-moving consumer goods
FOB	free on board: the seller quotes a price covering all expenses up to the point of shipment
FSC	Foreign Sales Corporation
G-D	goods dominant
GA	global account
GAM	global account management
GATT	General Agreement on Tariffs and Trade
GDP	gross domestic product
GEL	General Electric Lighting
GNI	gross national income
GNP	gross national product: the total 'gross value' of all goods and services produced in the economy in one year
GPC	global pricing contract
GRP	gross rating point
GSM	global system for mobile communications (wireless mobile)
GWD	guinea worm disease
HHP	household penetration
HLL	Hindustan Latex Ltd
HOG	Harley Owners Group
ICC	International Chamber of Commerce
IDR	intermediation–disintermediation–reintermediation
IMC	integrated marketing communications
IMF	International Monetary Fund
IMS	international market selection
IMUSA	Independent Manchester United Supporters Association
IP	intellectual property
IPLC	international product life cycle
ISO	International Standards Organization
ISP	internet service provider
IT	information technology
KAM	key account management
KSF	key success factor
L/C	letter of credit
LCC	low-cost car
LDCs	less developed countries
LSEs	large-scale enterprises
LTO	long-term orientation
M&A	merger and acquisition

MACS	market attractiveness/competitive strengths
MFN	most-favoured nation
MIS	marketing information system
MNCs	multinational corporations
MNE	multinational enterprise
MS	market share
MSRP	manufacturer's suggested retail price
MVAS	mobile value-added services
NAFTA	North American Free Trade Agreement: a free trade agreement to establish an open market between the US, Canada and Mexico
NASSCOM	National Association of Software and Service Companies
NGO	non-governmental organization
NICs	newly industrialized countries
NPD	new product development
NSB	National Standards Board
OE	operational effectiveness
OECD	Organization for Economic Cooperation and Development: a multinational forum that allows the major industrialized nations to discuss economic policies and events
OEM	original equipment manufacturer (outsourcer)
OLI	ownership-location-internalization
OPEC	Organization of Petroleum Exporting Countries
OTC	over the counter
OTS	opportunity to see
PEST	political/legal, economic, social/cultural, technological
PLB	private-label brand
PLC	product life cycle: a theory that characterizes the sales history of products as passing through four stages: introduction, growth, maturity, decline
PPP	purchasing-power parity
PR	public relations
QDF	quality deployment function
R&D	research and development
RM	relationship marketing
RMC	regional management centre
ROA	return on assets
ROI	return on investment
RTD	ready to drink
S-D	service-dominant
SaaS	software-as-a-service
SBU	strategic business unit: a single business or a collection of related businesses that can be planned separately from the rest of the company
SEM	search-engine marketing
SGVC	sustainable global value chain
SMEs	small and medium-sized enterprises
SMS	short message service
SRC	self-reference criterion
STD	sexually transmitted disease
STP	software technology park
SWOT	strengths, weaknesses, opportunities, threats
TC	transaction cost
TCA	transaction cost analysis

TF	trade fair
TLC	technological life cycle
TQM	total quality management
TTM	time to market
ULCC	ultra low-cost car
UNAIDS	Joint United Nations Programme on AIDS
UNFPA	United Nations Population Fund
USAID	United States Agency for International Development
USP	unique selling proposition
VAT	value added tax
VER	voluntary export restraint
VRIO	value, rarity, imitability, organization
WHO	World Health Organization
WoM	word-of-mouth
WTO	World Trade Organization (successor to GATT)

ABOUT THE AUTHOR

Svend Hollensen is an Associate Professor of International Marketing at the University of Southern Denmark. He holds an MSc (Business Administration) from Aarhus Business School. He has practical experience working as an International Marketing Coordinator in a large Danish multinational enterprise and as an International Marketing Manager in a company producing agricultural machinery.

After working in industry, Svend received his PhD in 1992 from Copenhagen Business School.

With Pearson Education he has published *Marketing Management – A Relationship Approach* (the third edition was published in 2015) as well as *Marketing Research – An International Approach* (2006), together with Marcus Schmidt. *Essentials of Global Marketing* was published in 2008 with a second edition in 2012. *Global Marketing* has been translated into Russian and Chinese. An Indian edition (co-authored with Madhumita Banerjee) was published in September 2009 and a Spanish edition (co-authored with Jesus Arteaga) was published in May 2010.

Furthermore, Svend has published in internationally well-recognized journals, like *California Management Review*, *Journal of Family Business Strategy*, *Journal of Brand Strategy* and *Marketing Intelligence & Planning*.

Svend has also worked as a business consultant for several multinational companies, as well as global organizations such as the World Bank.

The author may be contacted via:

University of Southern Denmark
Alsion 2
DK-6400 Sønderborg
Denmark
e-mail: svend@sam.sdu.dk

PART I
The decision whether to internationalize
Chs 1–4

PART II
Deciding which markets to enter
Chs 5–8

PART III
Market entry strategies
Chs 9–13

PART IV
Designing the global marketing programme
Chs 14–17

PART V
Implementing and coordinating the global marketing programme
Chs 18–19

Part I Contents

1 Global marketing in the firm
2 Initiation of internationalization
3 Internationalization theories
4 Development of the firm's international competitiveness

Part I Case studies

I.1 **Zara:** the Spanish retailer goes to the top of world fashion

I.2 **Manchester United:** still trying to establish a global brand

I.3 **Adidas:** the no. 2 in the global sportswear market is challenging the no. 1, Nike

I.4 **Cereal Partners Worldwide (CPW):** the no. 2 world player is challenging the no. 1, Kellogg

PART I
The decision whether to internationalize

Introduction to Part I

It is often the case that a firm going into an export adventure should have stayed in the home market because it did not have the necessary competences to start exporting. Chapter 1 discusses competences and global marketing strategies from the value chain perspective. Chapter 2 discusses the major motivations of the firm to internationalize. Chapter 3 concentrates on some central theories that explain firms' internationalization processes. Chapter 4 discusses the concept of international competitiveness from a macro level to a micro level.

PART I VIDEO CASE STUDY Uber

download from **www.pearsoned.co.uk/hollensen**

Uber Technologies Inc. (www.uber.com) is an American international transportation network company headquartered in San Francisco, California. The company develops, markets and operates the Uber mobile app, which allows consumers with smartphones to submit a trip request which is then routed to Uber drivers who use their own cars. Uber now operates in 311 cities in 58 countries, providing more than 1 million rides each day. On 1st August 2015, Uber's market value was around US$51 billion with expected revenues for 2015 around US$2 billion. However, since it began operation in 2012, Uber's net income has been negative.

Source: Bloomberg/Getty Images.

Consumers appreciate Uber, and rival services like Lyft in the US, Didi Kuaidi in China and GrabTaxi in South-east Asia, because they are cheaper than conventional taxis, clean and reliable. Uber's freelance drivers (who typically pay Uber around 20 per cent of their fares) enjoy flexible working hours and are spared the formalities of qualifying as a conventional cabbie.

Uber is a case study in how to construct a 'platform', a digital service on top of which other businesses can be built. As it arrives in a city, it launches a vigorous recruiting programme for drivers, offering them incentives to sign up. Its fares are 'dynamic' – they undercut conventional taxis most of the time, but go up when it rains, or when there is some other reason why demand for rides is high.

This encourages more of its drivers onto the roads when they are most needed. This in turn means that customers can always get a car quickly, even if it sometimes costs a bit more. This encourages them to keep using Uber, in turn providing lots of work for its drivers. Uber has now begun experimenting with local delivery services, with the aim of becoming as disruptive in logistics as it has been in the taxi business.

Uber's presence in cities has provoked a reaction among regulators. Taxi drivers have also taken on the company with protest and violence against Uber drivers. For example, Uber took the decision to suspend its service in France after 65 of its taxi drivers were attacked in the latter half of June 2015. French taxi drivers, who have to pay up to €240,000 for a traditional licence, held demonstrations across the country protesting against the Uber service.

Questions

1. What are the basic principles in the 'sharing economy'?

2. Explain the competitive advantage of Uber.

3. Why is it so important for Uber to get into so many countries so fast?

Source: based on different public sources.

Please look at the video links at **www.pearsoned.co.uk/hollensen**

CHAPTER 1
Global marketing in the firm

Contents

Learning objectives

After studying this chapter you should be able to:

- Characterize and compare the management style in SMEs (small and medium-sized enterprises) and LSEs (large-scale enterprises)
- Identify drivers of global integration and market responsiveness
- Explain the role of global marketing in the firm from a holistic perspective
- Describe and understand the concept of the value chain
- Identify and discuss different ways of internationalizing the value chain
- Explain the difference between the 'product value chain' and the 'service value chain'
- Understand how 'customer experience' can extend the traditional value perspective.

1.1   Introduction to globalization

After two years (2008–10) in economic crisis mode, business executives are again looking to the future. As they are re-engaging in global marketing strategy thinking, many executives are wondering if the turmoil was merely another turn of the business cycle or a restructuring of the global economic order. However, although growth in the globalization of goods and services has stalled for a period, because international trade has declined along with demand, the overall globalization trend is unlikely to reverse (Beinhocker *et al.*, 2009).

In 2005 Thomas L. Friedman published his international bestselling book *The World is Flat* (Freidman, 2005). It analyses globalization, primarily in the early twenty-first century, and the picture has changed dramatically. The title is a metaphor for viewing the world as a level playing field in terms of commerce, where all players and competitors have an equal opportunity. Companies from every part of the world will be competing with each other in every corner of the world's markets – for customers, resources, talent and intellectual capital. Products and services will flow from many locations to many destinations. Friedman mentions that many companies in, for example, the Ukraine, India and China provide human-based subsupplies for multinational companies. In this way, these companies in emerging and developing countries are becoming integral parts of complex global supply chains for large multinational companies, like Dell, SAP, IBM and Microsoft.

Pankaj Ghemawat has contradicted Friedman's view of the world being flat (Ghemawat, 2008). In his latest book, Ghemawat introduces World 3.0, a world that is neither a set of distinct nation-states (World 1.0) nor the stateless ideal (World 2.0) that seems implicit in the 'The world is flat' strategies of so many companies. In such a World 3.0 (Ghemawat, 2011a), home matters, but so do countries abroad. Ghemawat argues that when distances (geographic, cultural, administrative/political and economic) increase, cross-border trade tends to decrease (Ghemawat, 2011b). Ghemawat thinks that it is certainly possible to have a global strategy and a global organization in such a world. But the global strategy must be based not on the elimination of differences and distances among people, cultures and places, but on an understanding of them.

1.2   The process of developing the global marketing plan

As the book has a clear decision-oriented approach, it is structured according to the five main decisions that marketing people in companies face in connection with the global marketing process. The 15 chapters are divided into five parts (Figure 1.1).

In the end, the firm's global competitiveness is mainly dependent on the end-result of the global marketing stages: *the global marketing plan* (see Figure 1.2). The purpose of the marketing plan is to create sustainable competitive advantages in the global marketplace. Generally, firms go through some kind of mental process in developing global marketing plans. In small and medium-sized enterprises (SMEs) this process is normally informal; in larger organizations it is often more systematized. Figure 1.2 offers a systematized approach to developing a global marketing plan – the stages are illustrated using the most important models and concepts, which are explained and discussed throughout the chapters. Readers are advised to return to this figure throughout the book.

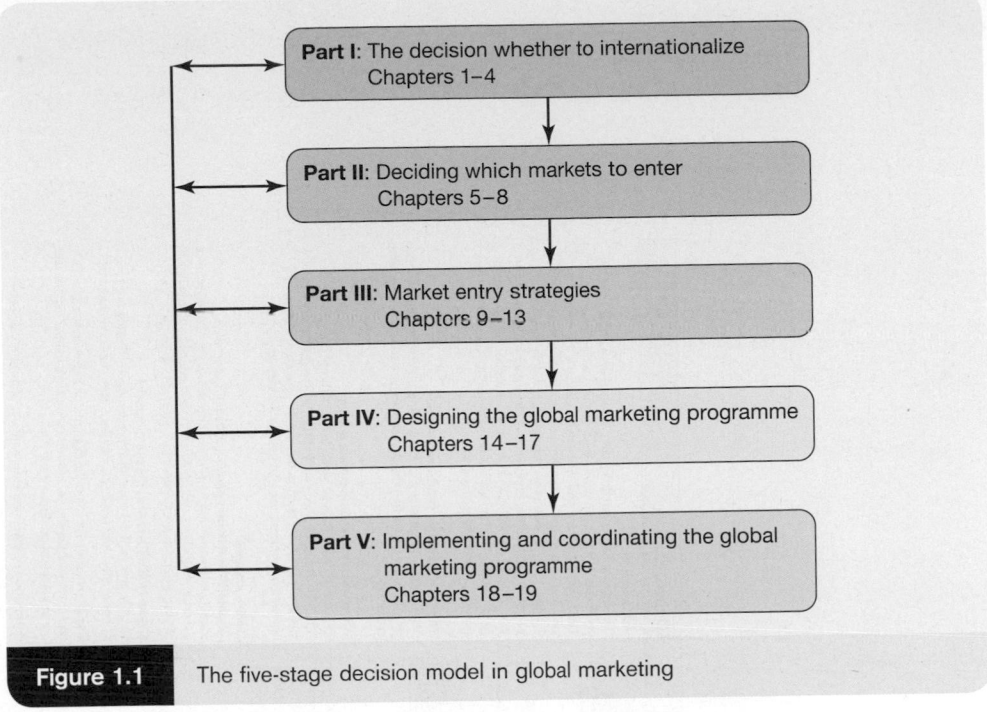

Figure 1.1   The five-stage decision model in global marketing

1.3 Comparison of the global marketing and management style of SMEs and LSEs

LSEs
According to the
EU definition, LSEs
(large-scale enterprises)
are firms with more
than 250 employees.
Although LSEs account
for less than 1 per cent
of companies, almost
one-third of all jobs in the
EU are provided by LSEs.

The reason underlying this 'convergence' is that many large multinationals (such as IBM, Philips, GM and ABB) have begun downsizing operations, so in reality many **LSEs** act like a confederation of small, autonomous, entrepreneurial and action-oriented companies. One can always question the change in orientation of **SMEs**. Some studies (e.g. Bonaccorsi, 1992) have rejected the widely accepted proposition that firm size is positively related to export intensity. Furthermore, many researchers (e.g. Julien *et al.*, 1997) have found that SMEs as exporters do not behave as a homogeneous group.

Table 1.1 gives an overview of the main qualitative differences between management and marketing styles in SMEs and LSEs. We will discuss each of the headings in turn.

Resources

SMEs
SMEs (small and
medium-sized enterprises)
occur commonly in the
EU and in international
organizations. The EU
categorizes companies
with fewer than 50
employees as 'small',
and those with fewer
than 250 as 'medium'.
In the EU, SMEs (250
employees and less)
comprise approximately
99 per cent of all firms.

- *Financial*. A well-documented characteristic of SMEs is the lack of financial resources due to a limited equity base. The owners put only a limited amount of capital into the business, which quickly becomes exhausted.
- *Business education/specialist expertise*. In contrast to LSEs, a characteristic of SME managers is their limited formal business education. Traditionally, the SME owner/manager is a technical or craft expert and is unlikely to be trained in any of the major business disciplines. Therefore specialist expertise is often a constraint because managers in small businesses tend to be generalists rather than specialists. In addition, global marketing expertise is often the last of the business disciplines to be acquired by an expanding SME; finance and production experts usually precede the acquisition of a marketing counterpart. Therefore it is not unusual to see owners of SMEs closely involved in sales, distribution, price setting and, especially, product development.

Tools used in different stages (references to the book)

Tools used in different stages (references to the book)	Process stages	Description

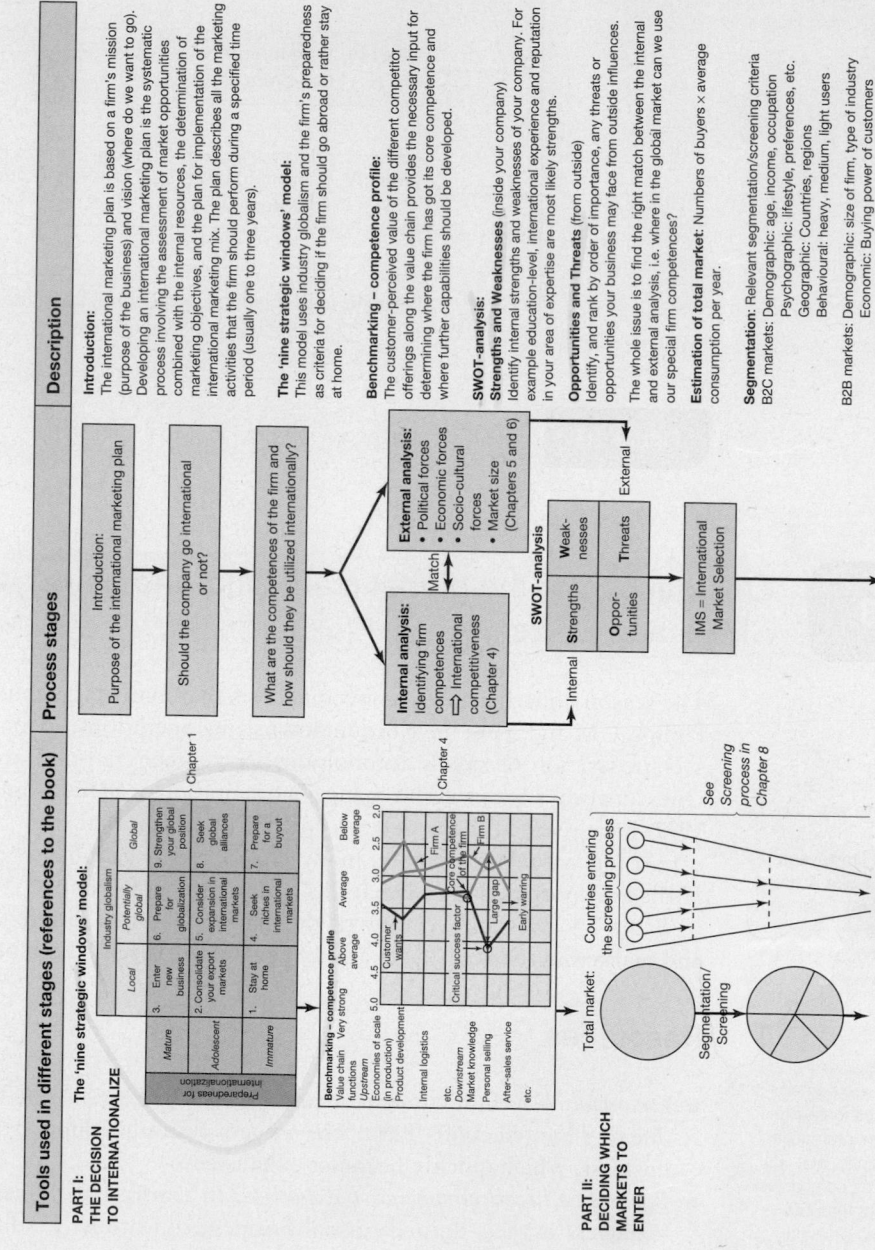

PART I: THE DECISION TO INTERNATIONALIZE

The 'nine strategic windows' model:

Preparedness for Internationalization

	Industry globalism		
	Local	Potentially global	Global
Mature	3. Enter new business	6. Prepare for globalization	9. Strengthen your global position
Adolescent	2. Consolidate your export markets	5. Consider expansion in international markets	8. Seek global alliances
Immature	1. Stay at home	4. Seek niches in international markets	7. Prepare for a buyout

Benchmarking – competence profile

Value chain functions — Upstream (In production): Economies of scale, Product development, Internal logistics, etc. Downstream: Market knowledge, Personal selling, After-sales service, etc.

Scale: Very strong 5.0 Above average 4.5 4.0 Average 3.5 3.0 Below average 2.5 2.0

Customer wants — Critical success factor — Core competence of the firm — Firm A — Firm B — Large gap — Early warning

PART II: DECIDING WHICH MARKETS TO ENTER

Total market: Countries entering the screening process

Segmentation / Screening

See Screening process in Chapter 8

Process stages

Introduction: Purpose of the international marketing plan *(Chapter 1)*

Should the company go international or not?

What are the competences of the firm and how should they be utilized internationally? *(Chapter 4)*

Internal analysis: Identifying firm competences → International competitiveness (Chapter 4)

External analysis: Political forces, Economic forces, Socio-cultural forces, Market size (Chapters 5 and 6)

Match

SWOT-analysis: Strengths, Weaknesses, Opportunities, Threats — Internal, External

IMS = International Market Selection

Description

Introduction:
The international marketing plan is based on a firm's mission (purpose of the business) and vision (where do we want to go). Developing an international marketing plan is the systematic process involving the assessment of market opportunities combined with the internal resources, the determination of marketing objectives, and the plan for implementation of the international marketing mix. The plan describes all the marketing activities that the firm should perform during a specified time period (usually one to three years).

The 'nine strategic windows' model:
This model uses industry globalism and the firm's preparedness as criteria for deciding if the firm should go abroad or rather stay at home.

Benchmarking – competence profile:
The customer-perceived value of the different competitor offerings along the value chain provides the necessary input for determining where the firm has got its core competence and where further capabilities should be developed.

SWOT-analysis:
Strengths and Weaknesses (inside your company)
Identify internal strengths and weaknesses of your company. For example education-level, international experience and reputation in your area of expertise are most likely strengths.

Opportunities and Threats (from outside)
Identify, and rank by order of importance, any threats or opportunities your business may face from outside influences.
The whole issue is to find the right match between the internal and external analysis, i.e. where in the global market can we use our special firm competences?

Estimation of total market: Numbers of buyers × average consumption per year.

Segmentation: Relevant segmentation/screening criteria
B2C markets: Demographic: age, income, occupation
Psychographic: lifestyle, preferences, etc.
Geographic: Countries, regions
Behavioural: heavy, medium, light users
B2B markets: Demographic: size of firm, type of industry
Economic: Buying power of customers

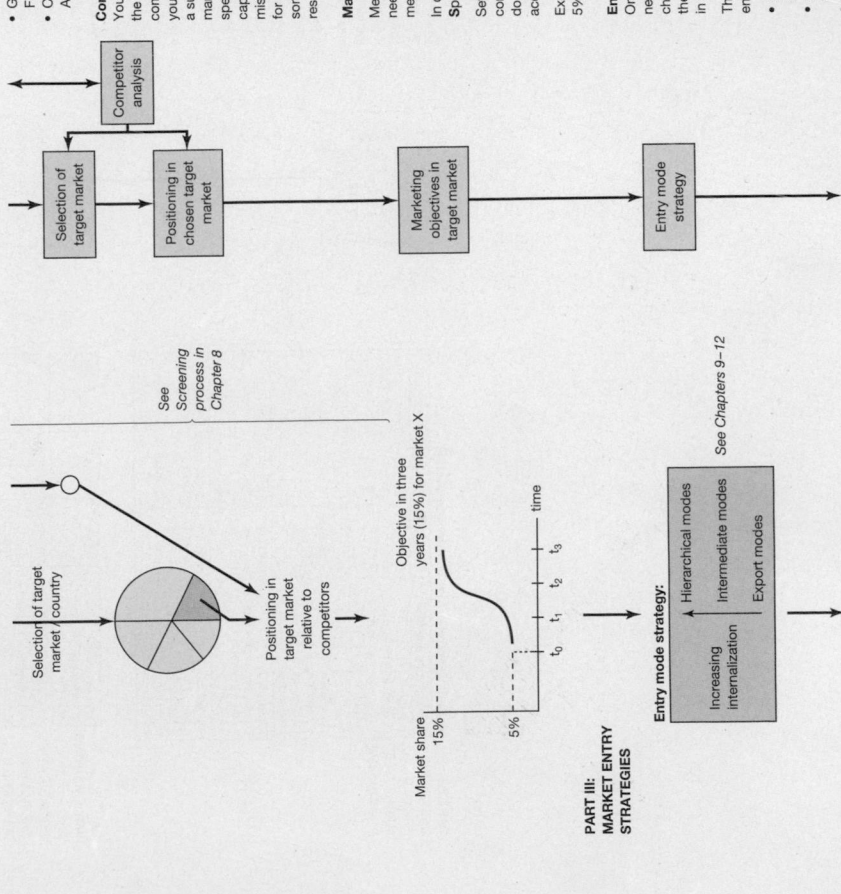

- Geographical market: region (Western Europe, Eastern Europe, Far East, North America etc.) country or area in a country
- Customer type: end-customer, middlemen, OEMs, Global Accounts (GAs)

Competitor analysis:

You'll discover your company's competitive advantage – the reason customers do business with you instead of your competition. By observing the actions of your competitors, you might learn more about your market. For example, does a successful competitor offer reduced prices in a specific market? If so, what might that tell you about the market's spending habits? If you find that your market is saturated with capable competitors ('red ocean'), you can avoid the costly mistake of selecting a target market without adequate demand for your offer. You can then redirect your efforts toward something that will generate more profit with the existing resources base in your company ('blue-ocean strategy').

Marketing objectives:

Meeting marketing objectives should lead to sales. (If not, you need to set different marketing objectives.) They should be clear, measurable, and have a stated time frame for achievement. In other words the objectives should follow the SMART-concept: **S**pecific, **M**easurable, **A**chievable, **R**ealistic, **T**imeable

Setting your marketing objectives and finalizing the remaining components of your marketing plan may serve as a reality check: do you have the resources and competences necessary to accomplish your objectives?

Example: Increase market share in target market from now (t_0) 5% to 15% in three years (t_3) – Is that realistic?

Entry mode strategy:

Once the firm has set its target objectives in target markets the next step is to choose the best way to enter the market. The chosen entry mode can be regarded as the first decision level in the vertical chain that will provide distribution to the next actors in the vertical chain at the national level.

The following characteristics are connected to the three types of entry modes (seen from the manufacturer's perspective):

- Export modes (agent, distributor); Low control, low risk, high flexibility
- Intermediate mode (joint venture, strategic alliance); shared control and risk, split ownership
- Hierarchical modes (Own subsidiary); High control, high risk, low flexibility

Figure 1.2   Development of an international marketing plan

PART IV: DESIGNING THE GLOBAL MARKETING PROGRAMME

Marketing mix plan (per country and overall)

Marketing mix (activities)	Year 1 (t_1)	Year 2 (t_2)	Year 3 (t_3)
Product Features, quality, name, guarantees, packaging, support services	New variant	New product line and services	Develop new technology/ product
Price List price, additional services prices, credit facilities, terms/conditions, allowances	Keep skimming price	Lower price	Stabilize price
Place Distributors, wholesalers, retailers, locations, transport	Selective dist.	Expand distr. with new partners	New int. markets
Promotion Advertising, direct mail, email, publicity, sales promotion, personal selling, company literature, Internet	Keep current advertising media	Development of social media campaign	Personal selling

See Chapters 14–17

Developing the international marketing mix (the 4 Ps)

Development of the marketing mix:

The international marketing mix section of your plan (the 4 Ps or alternatively the 7 Ps) outlines your game plan to achieve your marketing objectives internationally. It is, essentially, the heart of the marketing plan. The marketing mix section should include information about:

- Product – your offering; product(s) and services
- Price – what you'll charge customers for delivered products and services
- Promotion – how you will promote or create awareness and interest for your product in the marketplace
- Place (distribution) – how you will bring your product(s)/services together with your customers through different channels? How can you create extra value by developing relationships with your customer?

Implementation:

To translate the strategy into action (organizing):

- Assemble the 4P-mix for each product/service (SBU)
- Organize the marketing effort
- Who is responsible for the implementation of the activities?
- When will the activities take place?
- Internal marketing plan: Sell the the marketing plan inside the organization before going outside. Are there any internal barriers that should be considered?

Cross-border negotiation:

The most fundamental gap influencing the negotiation climate between buyer and seller is the cultural distance, represented by differences in communication and negotiation behaviour, the concepts of time, space and work patterns, and the nature of social norms. The cultural distance can be reduced by cultural training and market research.

PART V: IMPLEMENTING AND COORDINATING THE GLOBAL MARKETING PROGRAMME

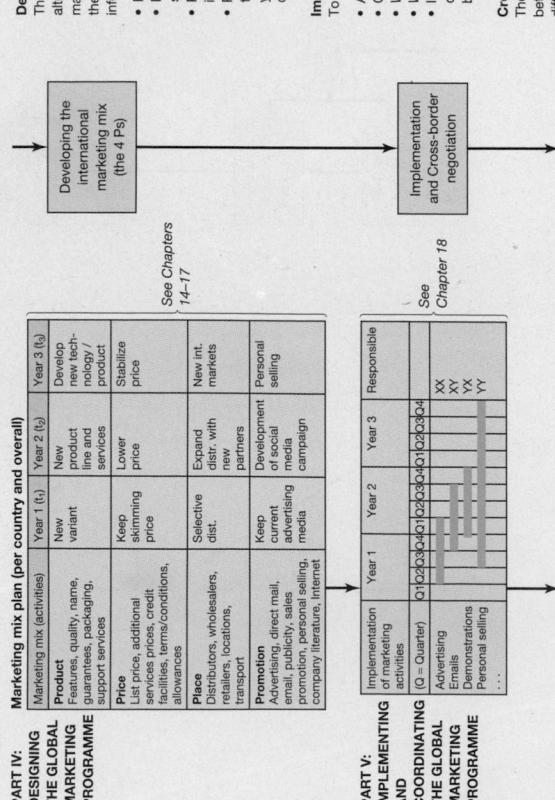

Implementation of marketing activities (Q = Quarter)	Year 1 Q1 Q2 Q3 Q4	Year 2 Q1 Q2 Q3 Q4	Year 3 Q1 Q2 Q3 Q4	Responsible
Advertising				XX
Emails				XY
Demonstrations				YX
Personal selling				YY
....				

See Chapter 18

Implementation and Cross-border negotiation

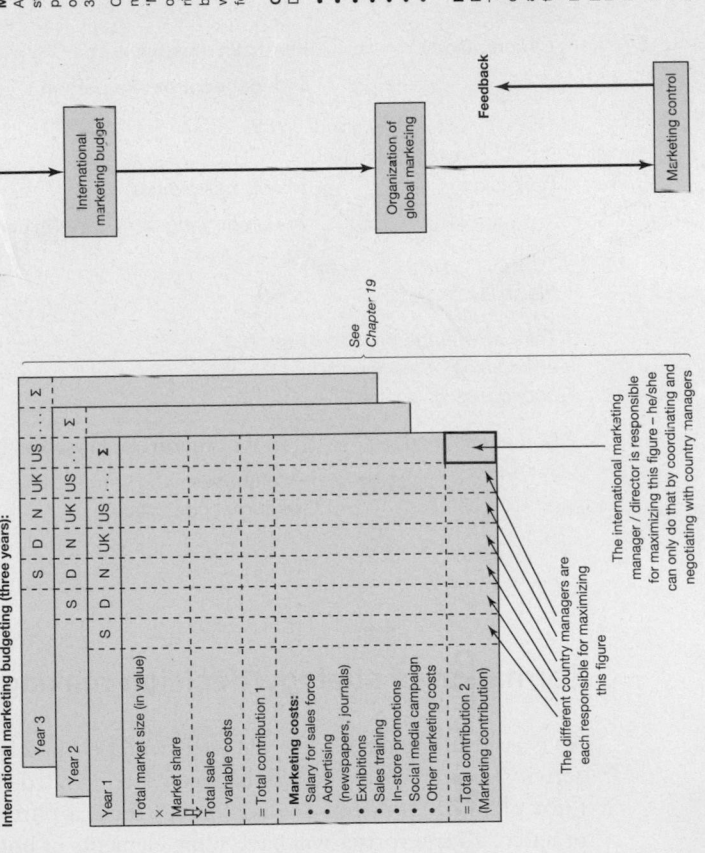

Marketing budget:
A marketing budget derived from a tactical marketing strategy must have adequate resources allocated to meet the performance objectives of the strategic market plan. An estimate of market and profit performance is made for each year of a 3 year strategic market planning horizon.

Concerning the figure at the left, the international marketing manager / director is responsible for maximizing the total 'Marketing contribution' for the whole world (Σ). In order to optimize this total marketing contribution (Σ), this person has the right to coordinate and transfer marketing resources across borders, by cooperation and negotiation with country managers, who are responsible for maximizing the 'Marketing contribution' for their single countries.

Organization of global marketing activities:
Different options for organizing these activities:

- Ad hoc exporting
- Functional structure
- International division structure
- Product structure
- Geographical (customer) structure
- Matrix structure
- Global Account Management (GAM)

Marketing control:
Planning and budgeting are the main formal control methods. The budget spells out the objectives and necessary marketing costs to achieve these objectives. Control consists of measuring actual figures against budget figures. If there is tolerable variance then no action is usually taken.

Performance is evaluated by measuring actual against planned performance. The problem is setting a performance standard. Usually it is based on historical performance with some kind of industry average.

Problems of international comparison inevitably occur, like how budgets in different countries are affected by currency fluctuations during the budget period.

International marketing budget

Organization of global marketing

Feedback

Marketing control

See Chapter 19

International marketing budgeting (three years):

Year 3
Year 2
Year 1

	S	D	N	UK	US	.....	Σ

Total market size (in value)
× Market share
= Total sales
− variable costs
= Total contribution 1

− Marketing costs:
- Salary for sales force
- Advertising (newspapers, journals)
- Exhibitions
- Sales training
- In-store promotions
- Social media campaign
- Other marketing costs

= Total contribution 2 (Marketing contribution)

The different country managers are each responsible for maximizing this figure

The international marketing manager / director is responsible for maximizing this figure – he/she can only do that by coordinating and negotiating with country managers

Figure 1.2   *Continued*

Source: Hollensen, S. (2008) *Essentials of Global Marketing*, FT/Prentice Hall, pp. 6–9. Copyright © Pearson Education Limited.

Table 1.1	The characteristics of LSEs and SMEs	
	LSEs	**SMEs**
Resources	Many resources	Limited resources
	Internalization of resources	Externalization of resources (outsourcing of resources)
	Coordination of: – personnel – financing – market knowledge, etc.	
Formation of strategy/ decision-making processes	Deliberate strategy formation (Mintzberg, 1987; Mintzberg and Waters, 1985) (see Figure 1.3)	Emergent strategy formation (Mintzberg, 1987; Mintzberg and Waters, 1985) (see Figure 1.3)
	Adaptive decision-making mode in small incremental steps (logical incrementalism) (e.g. each new product: small innovation for the LSE) (see Figure 1.4)	The entrepreneurial decision-making model (e.g. each new product: considerable innovation for the SME) (see Figure 1.5)
		The owner/manager is directly and personally involved and will dominate all decision-making throughout the enterprise
Organization	Formal/hierarchical	Informal
	Independent of one person	The owner/entrepreneur usually has the power/charisma to inspire/control a total organization
Risk-taking	Mainly risk-averse	Sometimes risk-taking/sometimes risk-averse
	Focus on long-term opportunities	Focus on short-term opportunities
Flexibility	Low	High
Take advantage of economies of scale and economies of scope	Yes	Only limited
Use of information sources	Use of advanced techniques: – databases – external consultancy – internet	Information gathering in an informal manner and an inexpensive way: – internal sources – face-to-face communication

Formation of strategy/decision-making processes

As is seen in Figure 1.3, the realized strategy (the observable output of an organization's activity) is a result of the mix between the intended ('planned') strategy and the emergent ('not planned') strategy. No companies form a purely deliberate or intended strategy. In practice, all enterprises will have some elements of both intended and emergent strategy.

In the case of the deliberate (planned) strategy (mainly LSEs), managers try to formulate their intentions as precisely as possible and then strive to implement these with a minimum of distortion.

This planning approach 'assumes a progressive series of steps of goal setting, analysis, evaluation, selection and planning of implementation to achieve an optimal long-term direction for the organization' (Johnson, 1988). Another approach for the process of strategic management is so-called *logical incrementalism* (Quinn, 1980), where continual adjustments

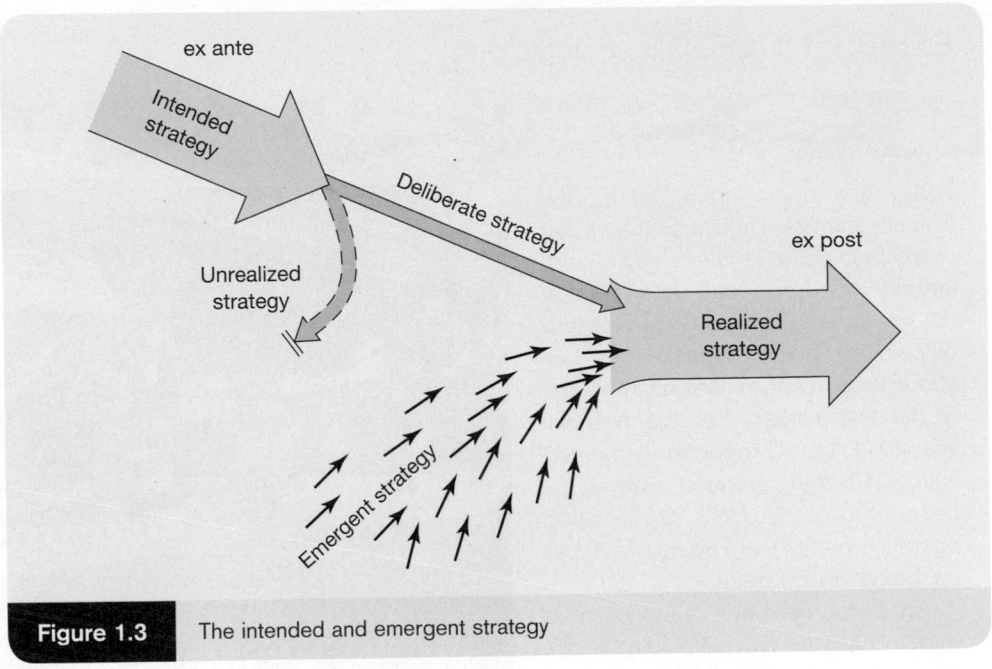

Figure 1.3   The intended and emergent strategy

Source: Mintzberg (1987, p. 14). Copyright © 1987, by The Regents of the University of California. Reprinted from the *California Management Review,* Vol. 30, No. 1.

in strategy proceed flexibly and experimentally. If such small movements in strategy prove successful then further development of the strategy can take place. According to Johnson (1988) managers may well see themselves as managing incrementally, but this does not mean that they succeed in keeping pace with environmental change. Sometimes the incrementally adjusted strategic changes and the environmental market changes move apart and a *strategic drift* arises (see Figure 1.4).

Exhibit 1.1 gives an example of strategic drift.

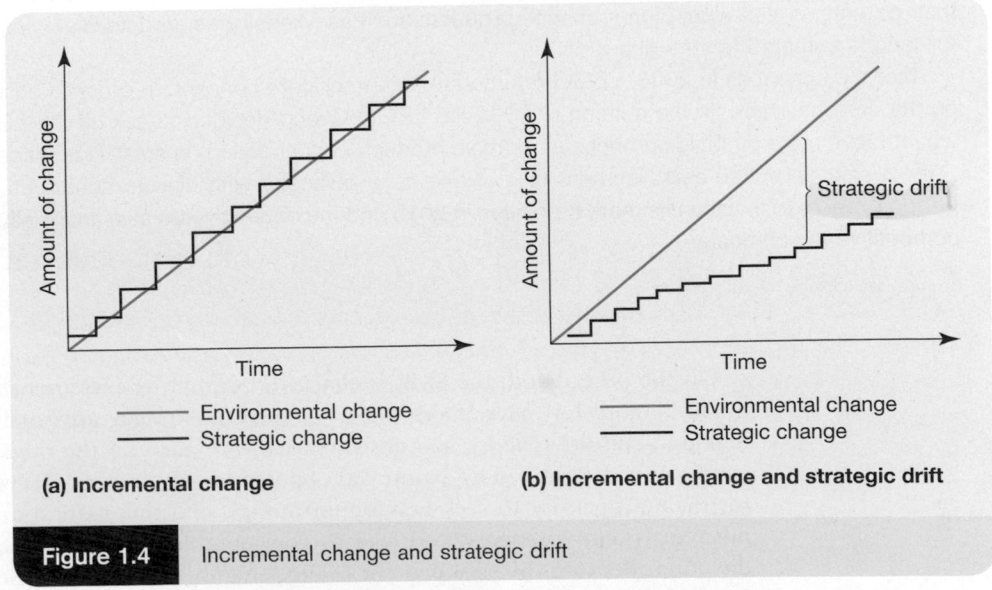

Figure 1.4   Incremental change and strategic drift

Source: Johnson, G. (1988) 'Rethinking incrementalism', *Strategic Management Journal*, 9. pp. 75–91. Copyright 1988 © of John Wiley & Sons Ltd. Reproduced with permission.

EXHIBIT 1.1 LEGO's strategic drift

Today (the beginning of 2013), the Danish family-owned LEGO group (www.lego.com) is the world's third largest toy producer after Mattel (known for the Barbie doll) and Hasbro (known for Trivial Pursuit). Lego has about 8 per cent market share of the global toy market. For the financial year 2011, LEGO reported (compared with 2010) that revenues were up 17 per cent to nearly US$3.50 billion and operating profits were up nearly 20 per cent to US$1.06 billion.

But things have not always been so rosy. In 2003, the firm suffered a net loss of approximately US$3.19 billion. LEGO strongly believed that its unique concept was superior to other products, but the company was under pressure in the

Source: A W Photography/Alamy Images.

competition for children's time. The famous LEGO bricks were under increasing competition from TV, videos, CD-ROM games and the internet. It seemed that in LEGO's case there was a 'strategic drift' around 2003 – the LEGO management's blind faith in its unique and pedagogical toys was not in harmony with the way in which the world was developing. Many working parents had less and less time to 'control' their children's play habits, and spectacular computer games were displacing the 'healthy' and pedagogical toys produced by LEGO. These fast-moving developments forced LEGO to re-evaluate its strategy regarding product programmes and marketing.

LEGO had been trying to extend its traditional concepts and values into media products for children aged 2–16 years. These new categories – including PC and console software, books, magazines, TV, film and music – aimed to replicate the feelings of confidence and trust already long established among children and their parents. It also went high-tech with products such as Mindstorms, and its Bionicles toys appeared in a full-length animated feature film.

After the huge loss in 2003, LEGO returned to its former core concept. In order to ensure increased focus on the core business, in the autumn of 2004 the LEGO Group decided to sell off the LEGOLAND Parks. It would focus more on building bricks as its main product, concentrating on small kids' eagerness to assemble.

Focusing on the re-establishment of a strong core business with classic construction toys, the LEGO Group expects to maintain its market position in 2015 and the coming years as a financially stronger and more competitive toy company.

Source: adapted from different public media.

On the other hand, the SME is characterized by the entrepreneurial decision-making model (Figure 1.5). Here more drastic changes in strategy are possible because decision-making is intuitive, loose and unstructured. In Figure 1.5 the range of possible realized strategies is determined by an interval of possible outcomes. SME entrepreneurs are noted for their propensity to seek new opportunities, and this natural propensity for change, inherent in entrepreneurs, can lead to considerable changes in the enterprise's growth direction. Because the entrepreneur changes focus, this growth is not planned or coordinated and can therefore be characterized by sporadic decisions that have an impact on the overall direction in which the enterprise is going.

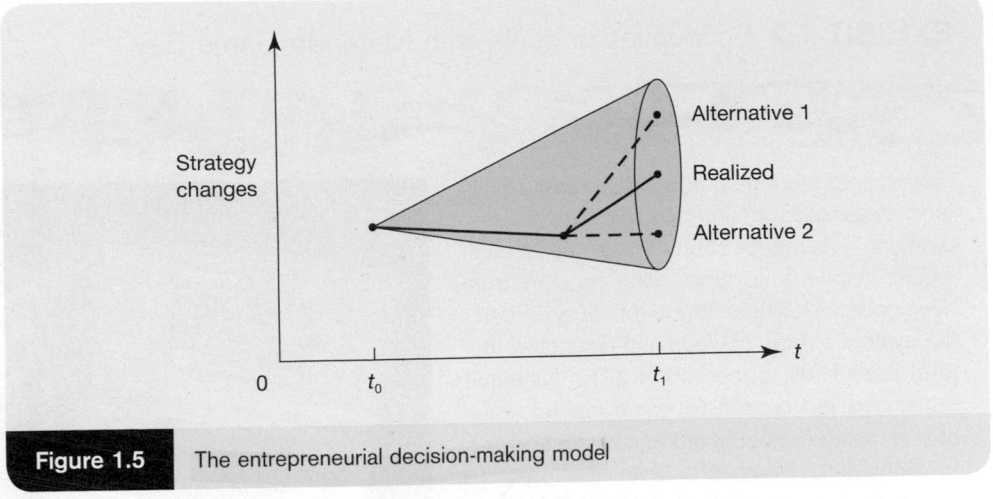

| Figure 1.5 | The entrepreneurial decision-making model |

Organization

Compared with LSEs, the employees in SMEs are usually closer to the entrepreneur and, because of the entrepreneur's influence, these employees must conform to his or her personality and style if they are to remain employees.

Risk-taking

There are, of course, different degrees of risk. Normally the LSEs will be risk-averse because of their use of a decision-making model that emphasizes small incremental steps with a focus on long-term opportunities.

In SMEs, risk-taking depends on the circumstances. It can occur in situations where the survival of the enterprise may be under threat, or where a major competitor is undermining the activities of the enterprise. Entrepreneurs may also be taking risks when they have not gathered all the relevant information, and thus may have ignored some important facts in the decision-making process.

On the other hand, there are, of course, some circumstances in which an SME will be risk-averse. This often occurs when an enterprise has been damaged by previous risk-taking and the entrepreneur is reluctant to take any kind of risk until confidence returns.

Flexibility

Because of the shorter communication lines between the enterprise and its customers, SMEs can react in a quicker and more flexible way to customer enquiries.

Economies of scale and economies of scope

Economies of scale

Economies of scale
Accumulated volume in production, resulting in lower cost price per unit.

Accumulated volume in production and sales will result in lower cost price per unit due to 'experience curve effects' and increased efficiency in production, marketing, etc. Building a global presence automatically expands a firm's scale of operations, giving it larger production capacity and a larger asset base. However, larger scale will create a competitive advantage only if the company systematically converts scale into **economies of scale**.

EXHIBIT 1.2 Economies of scale with Nintendo Game Boy

Having sold more than 300 million Game Boys (and its successor Nintendo DS: 'Developers' System' – Nintendo hoped that the system would inspire innovative game design from developers; DS also stands for 'dual screen', the system's most obvious and distinctive feature) from 1989 to the end of 2012, Nintendo dominates the hand-held game market, even as it is losing market share in console systems to Sony and Microsoft. Over the past 15 years, such companies as Sega, NEC, SNK and even cellphone manufacturer Nokia have launched several competing portable game systems without much success.

Source: Ian Leonard/Alamy Images.

The economies of scale primarily relate to the manufacturing of the hardware. In the software market, economies of scale are limited. Many different types of game have to be offered and the popularity of most of them is short-lived. This is especially so in the case of software linked to a film: the popularity of the game diminishes as the film ceases to be shown in cinemas.

Source: based on various public sources.

In principle, the benefits of economies of scale can appear in different ways (Gupta and Govindarajan, 2001):

- Reducing operating costs per unit and spreading fixed costs over a larger volume due to experience curve effects.
- Pooling global purchasing gives the opportunity to concentrate global purchasing power over suppliers. This generally leads to volume discounts and lower transaction costs.
- A larger scale gives the global player the opportunity to build centres of excellence for the development of specific technologies or products. In order to do this, a company needs to focus a critical mass of talent in one location.

Because of size (bigger market share) and accumulated experience, the LSEs will normally take advantage of these factors (see Exhibit 1.2 about Nintendo's Game Boy). SMEs tend to concentrate on lucrative, small, market segments. Such market segments are often too insignificant for LSEs to target, but can be substantial and viable in respect of the SME. However, they will only result in a very limited market share of a given industry.

Economies of scope

Synergy effects and global scope can occur when the firm is serving several international markets: global scope is not taking place if an international marketer is serving a customer that operates in just one country. The customer should purchase a bundle of identical products and services across a number of countries. This global customer could source these products and services either from a horde of local suppliers or from a single global supplier (international marketer) that is present in all of its markets. Compared with a horde of local suppliers, a single global supplier (marketer) can provide value for the global customer through greater consistency in the quality and features of products and services across countries, faster and smoother coordination across countries and lower transaction costs.

Economies of scope
Reusing a resource from one business/country in additional businesses/countries.

The challenge in capturing the **economies of scope** at a global level lies in being responsive to the tension between two conflicting needs: the need for central coordination of most marketing mix elements, and the need for local autonomy in the actual delivery of products and services (Gupta and Govindarajan, 2001).

The LSEs often serve many different markets (countries) on more continents and are thereby able to transfer experience acquired in one country to another. Typically, SMEs serve only a very limited number of international markets outside their home market. Sometimes the SME can make use of economies of scope when it enters into an alliance or a joint venture with a partner who has what the particular SME is missing in the international market in question: a complementary product programme or local market knowledge.

Another example of economies of scale and scope can be found in the world car industry. Most car companies use similar engines and gearboxes across their entire product range so that the same engines or gearboxes can be installed in different models of cars. This generates enormous potential cost savings for companies such as Ford or Volkswagen. It provides both economies of scale (decreased cost per unit of output), by producing a larger absolute volume of engines or gearboxes, and economies of scope (reusing a resource from one business/country in additional businesses/countries). It is not surprising that the car industry has experienced a wave of mergers and acquisitions aimed at creating larger global car companies of sufficient size to benefit from these factors.

Use of information sources

Typically, LSEs rely on commissioned market reports produced by reputable (and well-paid!) international consultancy firms as their source of vital global marketing information. SMEs usually gather information in an informal manner through the use of face-to-face communication. The entrepreneur is able to synthesize this information unconsciously and use it to make decisions. The acquired information is mostly incomplete and fragmented, and evaluations are based on intuition and often guesswork. The whole process is dominated by the desire to find a circumstance that is ripe for exploitation.

Furthermore, the demand for complex information grows as the SME selects a more and more explicit orientation towards the international market and as the firm evolves from a production-oriented ('upstream') to a more marketing-oriented ('downstream') firm (Cafferata and Mensi, 1995).

As a reaction to pressures from international markets, both LSEs and SMEs evolve towards a globally integrated but market-responsive strategy. However, the starting points of the two firm types are different (see Figure 1.3). The huge global companies have traditionally based their strategy on taking advantage of economies of scale by launching standardized products on a worldwide basis. These companies have realized that a higher degree of market responsiveness is necessary to maintain competitiveness in national markets. On the other hand, SMEs have traditionally regarded national markets as independent of each other. However, as international competences have evolved, they have begun to realize that there is interconnectedness between their different international markets. They now recognize the benefits of coordinating the different national marketing strategies in order to utilize economies of scale in research and development (R&D), production and marketing.

Exhibit 1.3 shows that LSEs (illustrated here by the recent Ford Focus case) still try to focus on 'economies of scale' by reducing the number of variations among cars in different countries ('One Ford').

EXHIBIT 1.3 Ford Focus Global Marketing Plan

The global marketing campaign for the 2012 Ford Focus compact car, including that for the US launch, was developed by a European team, a move that runs counter to the conventional wisdom that marketing is best developed locally. Ten years earlier ago, Ford's marketing leaders for North America, Europe and Asia did not collaborate on how many websites to use for a model launch, how to unify public relations or how best to use auto shows before a launch. Ford's marketing departments in 110 countries had the authority to create their own programmes. Ford used up to 15 advertising campaigns for individual countries when it launched the Focus globally.

The Focus 2012 global marketing plan approach was thus the latest iteration of the drive for 'One Ford' – a company free of regional barriers that can create global products sharing design, parts and engineering for a single Ford brand. The Focus is in many ways a logical car for a global marketing campaign. It was developed globally for markets around the world. The US and European versions, for example, share 80 per cent of their parts, setting a new high for transatlantic cooperation.

The task of developing a global marketing campaign for Focus was given to the European Ford headquarters because of their expertise in marketing cars of a similar size, which are the heart of the European market. In a multinational company like Ford it is also a question of realizing where the main competences are for developing the marketing plan. For trucks it might be in North America, but for this type of car it is in Europe.

Ford did not intend limiting global marketing strategy to the Focus, saying rather that all future vehicle launches would follow a similar approach. There would be one central group in a chosen region heading the marketing effort around the world for that vehicle. Marketing managers in a country or region would choose which of one or two main campaigns to use, but they could not start from scratch and make their own.

The Ford Focus global marketing theme

The Ford Focus is normally perceived as a compact-car brand. Car buyers normally look at smaller cars like the Ford Focus as a commodity, but the global Ford Focus team wanted to make customers see these cars as premium brands. The Focus TV spots therefore had to convey a premium message despite its compact-car status.

In developing the overall global marketing campaign, the global Ford Focus team was inspired by European luxury car companies, e.g. BMW's over-all campaign theme 'ultimate driving machine'. The BMW commercial on its own is premium, as is its portrayal of the product. BMW makes the engine look beautiful – when people see it, they immediately think it is very expensive. One example of Ford's premium approach is an ad developed in Europe for the 2012 Focus global campaign, which highlights the sedan's self-parking system.

Source: GoBOb/Shutterstock.com.

The global Ford Focus team worked for two years on the Focus global marketing approach. The resulting 50 Focus TV spots featured the same technology and message no matter where they were aired around the world.

A global approach saves money

The economic downturn pushed marketers to embrace any strategy that saves money, and going global should do this. In the past, a host of TV commercials, photographic sessions and motor show displays were produced locally for global launches. Now, Ford insists that global departments work together to share resources and reduce costs.

Consider photographs. Typically, each region and operating group – including design, marketing and public relations – took their own set of photographs to support a vehicle launch. For the Focus, Ford's management insisted that all picture requests be handled by a single photo shoot. Ford received 800 photo requests for the global Focus launch from different countries. A few differed, asking for a city street scene, say, rather than a country road backdrop. But the Ford Focus global marketing team realized that there was a lot of overlap between the different photo requests.

The global advertising launch budget for a car such as the Focus would typically be about US$100 million. Production costs, which cover photographs, printing and so on, make up 5–10 per cent of the usual ad budget for a vehicle launch. By eliminating the duplication and overlap, Ford cut those costs by 70 per cent, which could mean cost savings of around US$5 million.

Source: based on various public media sources, among others www.ford.com.

1.4   Should the company internationalize at all?

Globalization
Reflects the trend of firms buying, developing, producing and selling products and services in most countries and regions of the world.

Internationalization
Doing business in many countries of the world, but often limited to a certain region (e.g. Europe).

In the face of **globalization** and an increasingly interconnected world, many firms attempt to expand their sales into foreign markets. International expansion provides new and potentially more profitable markets, helps to increase the firm's competitiveness, and facilitates access to new product ideas, manufacturing innovations and the latest technology. However, **internationalization** is unlikely to be successful unless the firm prepares in advance. Advance planning has often been regarded as important to the success of new international ventures (Knight, 2000).

Solberg (1997) discusses the conditions under which the company should 'stay at home' or further 'strengthen the global position' as two extremes (see Figure 1.6). The frame-work in Figure 1.3 is based on the dimensions industry globalism and preparedness for internationalization.

Industry globalism

In principle, the firm cannot influence the degree of industry globalism, as it is mainly determined by the international marketing environment. Here the strategic behaviour of firms depends on the international competitive structure within an industry. In the case of a high degree of industry globalism there are many interdependencies between markets, customers and suppliers, and the industry is dominated by a few large, powerful players (*global*), whereas the other end (*local*) represents a multidomestic market environment, where markets exist independently of one another. Examples of very global industries are those making PCs, IT (software), CDs, films and aircraft (the two dominant players being Boeing and Airbus). Examples of more local industries are those that are more culture-bounded, such as hairdressing, foods and dairies (e.g. brown cheese in Norway).

Preparedness for internationalization

This dimension is mainly determined by the firm. The degree of preparedness is dependent on the firm's ability to carry out strategies in the international marketplace, i.e. the actual skills in international business operations. These skills or organizational capabilities may consist of personal characteristics (e.g. language, cultural sensitivity), managers' international experience or financial resources. The well-prepared company (*mature*) has a good basis for dominating the international markets and consequently it would gain higher market share.

		Industry globalism		
		Local	*Potentially global*	*Global*
Preparedness for internationalization	*Mature*	3. Enter new business	6. Prepare for globalization	9. Strengthen your global position
	Adolescent	2. Consolidate your export markets	5. Consider expansion in international markets	8. Seek global alliances
	Immature	1. Stay at home	4. Seek niches in international markets	7. Prepare for a buyout

Figure 1.6   The nine strategic windows

Source: Solberg (1997, p. 11). Reprinted with kind permission. In the original article Solberg has used the concept 'globality' rather than 'globalism'.

In the global/international marketing literature the 'staying at home' alternative is not discussed thoroughly. However, Solberg (1997) argues that with limited international experience and a weak position in the home market there is little reason for a firm to engage in international markets. Instead the firm should try to improve its performance in its home market. This alternative is window number 1 in Figure 1.6.

If the firm finds itself in a global industry as a dwarf among large multinational firms, Solberg (1997) argues that it may seek ways to increase its net worth so as to attract partners for a future buyout bid. This alternative (window number 7 in Figure 1.6) may be relevant to SMEs selling advanced high-tech components (as subsuppliers) to large industrial companies with a global network. In situations with fluctuations in the global demand, the SME (with limited financial resources) will often be financially vulnerable. If the firm has already acquired some competence in international business operations, it can overcome some of its competitive disadvantage by going into alliances with firms that have complementary competences (window number 8). The other windows in Figure 1.6 are further discussed by Solberg (1997).

1.5   Development of the 'global marketing' concept

Basically 'global marketing' consists of finding and satisfying global customer needs better than the competition, and coordinating marketing activities within the constraints of the global environment. The nature of the firm's response to global market opportunities depends greatly on the management's assumptions or beliefs, both conscious and unconscious, about doing business around the world. This world view of a firm's business activities can be described according to the EPRG framework (Perlmutter, 1969; Chakravarthy and Perlmutter, 1985), the four orientations of which are summarized as follows:

1. *Ethnocentric*: the home country is superior and the needs of the home country are most relevant. Essentially the headquarters extends its ways of doing business to its foreign

affiliates. Controls are highly centralized and the organization and technology implemented in foreign locations will be largely the same as in the home country.

2. *Polycentric* (multidomestic): each country is unique and should therefore be targeted in a different way. The polycentric enterprise recognizes that there are different conditions for production and marketing in different locations and tries to adapt to those different conditions in order to maximize profits in each location. The control is highly decentralized among affiliates, and communication between headquarters and affiliates is limited.

3. *Regiocentric*: the world consists of regions (e.g. Europe, Asia, the Middle East). The firm tries to integrate and coordinate its marketing programme within regions, but not across them.

4. *Geocentric* (global): the world is getting smaller and smaller. The firm may offer global product concepts but with local adaptation ('think global, act local').

The regio- and geocentric firm (in contrast to the ethnocentric and polycentric) seeks to organize and integrate production and marketing on a regional or global scale. Each international unit is an essential part of the overall multinational network, and communications and controls between headquarters and affiliates are less top-down than in the case of the ethnocentric firm.

Many international markets are converging, as communication and logistic networks are integrated on a global scale. At the same time, other international markets are becoming more diverse as company managers are encountering economic and cultural heterogeneity. This means that firms need to balance tensions in adapting to different demands from customers in divergent markets, which require different skills and resources while attempting to transfer knowledge and learning between the established markets and these new markets (Douglas and Craig, 2011).

This leads us to a definition of global marketing:

Global marketing is defined as the firm's commitment to coordinate its marketing activities across national boundaries in order to find and satisfy global customer needs better than the competition. This implies that the firm is able to:

- develop a global marketing strategy, based on similarities and differences between markets;
- exploit the knowledge of the headquarters (home organization) through worldwide diffusion (learning) and adaptations;
- transfer knowledge and 'best practices' from any of its markets and use them in other international markets.

There follows an explanation of some key terms:

- *Coordinate its marketing activities*: coordinating and integrating marketing strategies and implementing them across global markets, which involves centralization, delegation, standardization and local responsiveness.
- *Find global customer needs*: this involves carrying out international marketing research and analysing market segments, as well as seeking to understand similarities and differences in customer groups across countries.
- *Satisfy global customers*: adapting products, services and elements of the marketing mix to satisfy different customer needs across countries and regions.
- *Being better than the competition*: assessing, monitoring and responding to global competition by offering better value, lower prices, higher quality, superior distribution, great advertising strategies or superior brand image.

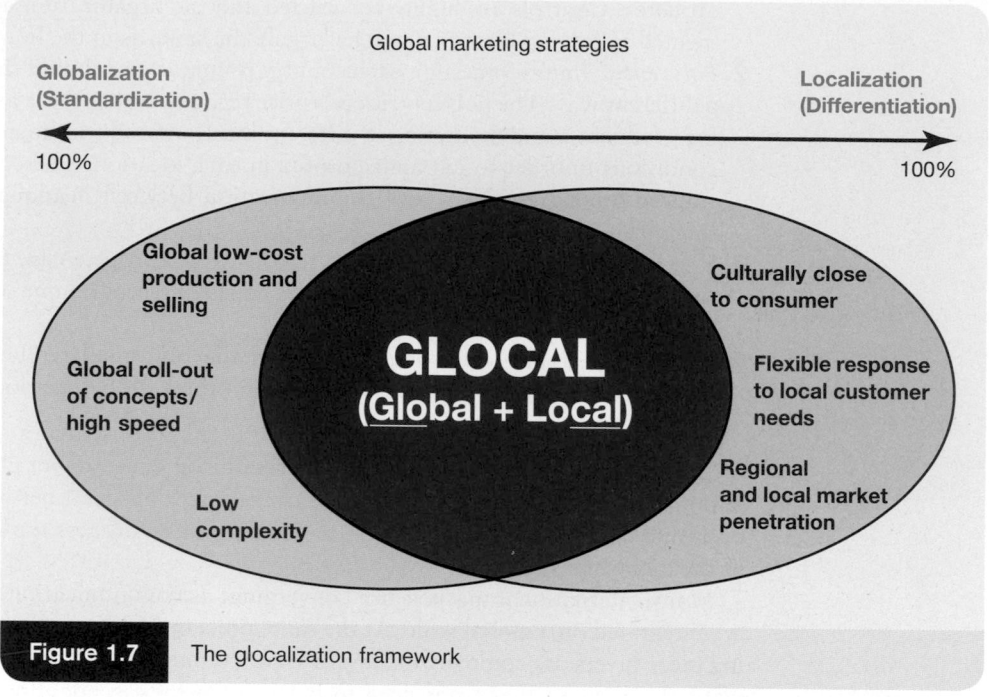

Figure 1.7   The glocalization framework

The second part of the global marketing definition is also illustrated in Figure 1.7 and further commented on in the following.

This global marketing strategy strives to achieve the slogan 'think globally but act locally' (the so-called '**glocalization**' framework) through dynamic interdependence between headquarters and subsidiaries. Organizations following such a strategy coordinate their efforts, ensuring local flexibility while exploiting the benefits of global integration and efficiencies, as well as ensuring worldwide diffusion of innovation (see Exhibit 1.5).

Principally, the value chain function should be carried out where there is the highest competence (and the greatest cost-effectiveness), and this is not necessarily at head office (Bellin and Pham, 2007).

The two extremes in global marketing, globalization and localization, can be combined into the 'glocalization' framework, as shown in Figure 1.7.

A key element in knowledge management is the continuous learning from experiences. In practical terms, the aim of knowledge management as a learning-focused activity across borders is to keep track of valuable capabilities used in one market that could be used elsewhere (in other geographic markets), so that firms can continually update their knowledge. This is also illustrated in Figure 1.8 with the transfer of knowledge and 'best practices' from market to market. However, knowledge developed and used in one cultural context is not always easily transferred to another. The lack of personal relationships, the absence of trust and 'cultural distance' all conspire to create resistance, frictions and misunderstandings in cross-cultural knowledge management.

With globalization becoming a centrepiece in the business strategy of many firms – be they engaged in product development or providing services – the ability to manage the 'global knowledge engine' to achieve a competitive edge in today's knowledge-intensive economy is one of the keys to sustainable competitiveness. However, in the context of global marketing the management of knowledge is *de facto* a cross-cultural activity, whose key task is to foster and continually upgrade collaborative cross-cultural learning (this will be further discussed in Chapter 14). Of course, the kind and/or type of knowledge that is strategic for an organization and which needs to be managed for competitiveness varies depending on the business context and the value of different types of knowledge associated with it.

Glocalization
The development and selling of products or services intended for the global market, but adapted to suit local culture and behaviour. (Think globally, act locally.)

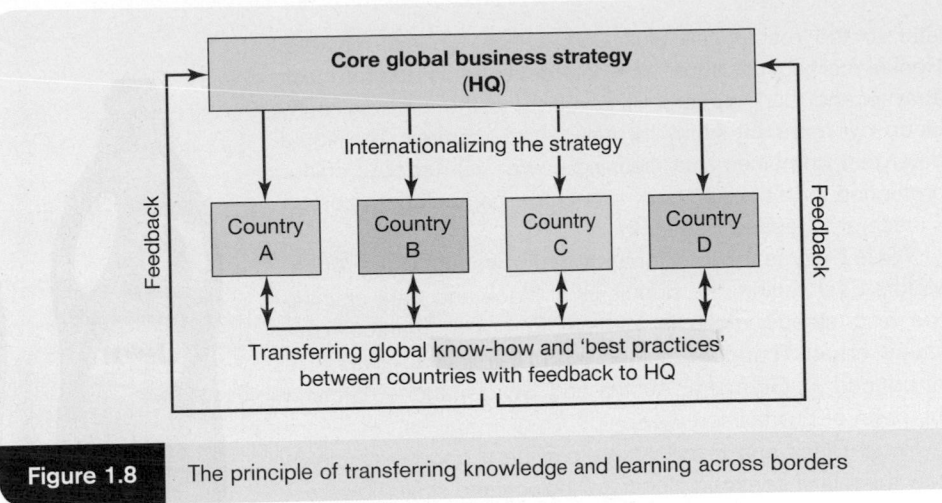

| Figure 1.8 | The principle of transferring knowledge and learning across borders |

EXHIBIT 1.4 Helly Hansen is using 'localization' through geo-targeting technology

Brands are increasingly seeking to fine-tune their localization strategies by using the newest technology. In June 2015, outdoor apparel maker Helly Hansen from Norway revealed that it had grown sales in some countries by using geo-targeting technology to locate potential customers and lead them to the right Helly Hansen website.

The company pairs local weather forecasts with specific on-site experiences. When rain was forecasted over a five-day period in Germany, for example, the brand used geotargeting to present a rainwear banner on the homepage, rather than promoting winter skiwear. This resulted in a 52 per cent uplift in conversions from awareness of the brand to actual purchase.

Source: Convery flowers/Alamy Images.

Source: based on Bacon (2015).

EXHIBIT 1.5 Persil Black & Persil Abaya = glocalization (same product, but different packaging and market communication)

Founded in 1876, Henkel holds globally leading market positions in both the consumer and industrial businesses with well-known brands such as Persil, Schwarzkopf and Loctite.

With headquarters in Düsseldorf, Germany, Henkel has some 47,000 employees worldwide. In 2011, Henkel generated revenues of €15.6 billion and net profits of €1.2 billion. In 2011, Henkel reinforced its position in the emerging markets, where 42 per cent of its sales are generated and 54 per cent of its people are employed. Persil Abaya is a liquid detergent that Henkel introduced to the Saudi Arabian market in 2007 and later to the rest of the Gulf Cooperation Council markets. Henkel markets this liquid as a detergent specialized for black abayas and dark apparel. The abaya is the predominantly black overgarment worn by most Arab women. The liquid detergent combines true cleaning power with special colour protection for black and dark garments – particularly important if these are washed frequently.

While black is the traditional shade for women in the Africa/ Middle East region, the popularity of black and dark clothing has also steadily risen in western European markets over recent years. Therefore in June 2011, Persil Black was also introduced in Germany, Austria and Switzerland – catching the crest of this fashion wave.

Persil Black and Persil Abaya provide a good example of how the mix of common global technology and scale (low-cost production) can be combined with local market. The two Persil brands have similar product formulations, but regionally tailored product marketing, in the form of different packaging and market communication.

Source: Henkel AG & Co KGaA.

Persil Abaya was launched in the Gulf States through a mix of TV commercials and a very successful viral online marketing campaign. An interactive website was set up and Henkel also sponsored a reality TV designer competition, in order to show that the abaya has transcended from traditional garment to individual fashion statement. In the western European markets, the consumer campaign for Persil Black relied mainly on classic TV advertising, complemented by social media activities such as a game on Facebook.

Sources: based on Henkel Annual Report 2011–2015 (*www.henkel.com*); Hollensen and Schimmelpfennig (2015).

1.6   Forces for global integration and market responsiveness

In Figure 1.9 it is assumed that SMEs and LSEs are learning from each other. The consequence of both movements may be an action-oriented approach, where firms use the strengths of both orientations. The following section will discuss the differences in the starting points of LSEs and SMEs in Figure 1.9. The result of the convergence movement of LSEs and SMEs into the upper-right corner can be illustrated by Figure 1.9.

An example of a LSE's movement from 'left' to 'right' is given in Exhibit 1.6, where McDonald's has adapted its menus to the local food cultures. SMEs have traditionally been strong on 'high degree of responsiveness', but their tendency to decentralization and local decision-making has made them more vulnerable to a low degree of coordination across borders (which, by contrast, is the strength of LSEs).

The terms 'glocal strategy' and 'glocalization' have been introduced to reflect and combine the two dimensions in Figure 1.9: globalization (*y*-axis) and localization (*x*-axis). The glocal strategy approach reflects the aspirations of a global integrated strategy, while recognizing the importance of local adaptations/market responsiveness. In this way, glocalization tries to optimize the balance between standardization and adaptation of the firm's international marketing activities (Svensson, 2001, 2002; Bailey *et al.*, 2015).

First let us try to explain the underlying forces for global coordination/**global integration** and **market responsiveness** in Figure 1.9.

Global integration
Recognizing the similarities between international markets and integrating them into the overall global strategy.

Market responsiveness
Responding to each market's needs and wants.

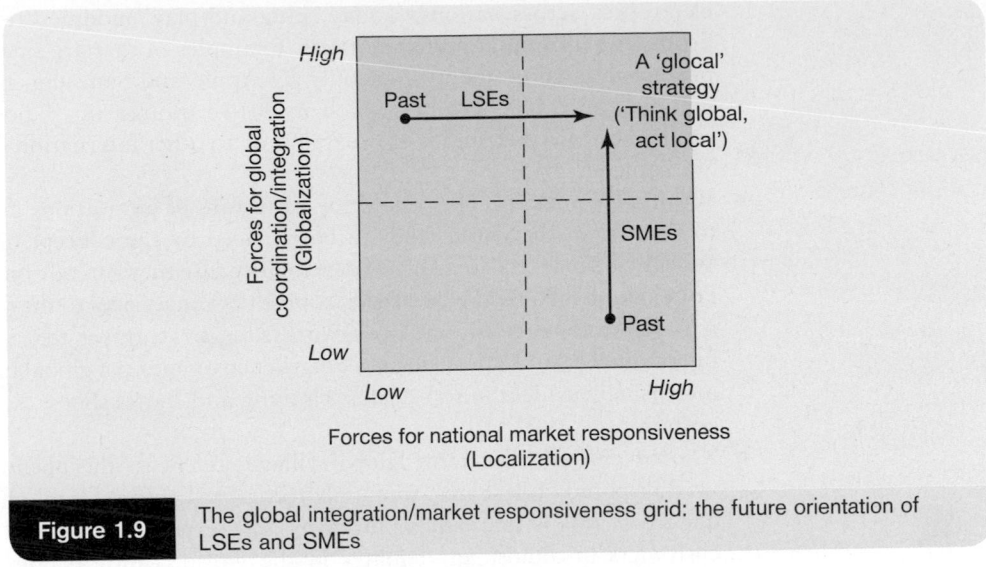

| Figure 1.9 | The global integration/market responsiveness grid: the future orientation of LSEs and SMEs |

Forces for 'global coordination/integration'

In the shift towards integrated global marketing, greater importance will be attached to transnational similarities for target markets across national borders and less on cross-national differences. The major drivers for this shift are as follows (Sheth and Parvatiyar, 2001; Segal-Horn, 2002):

● *Removal of trade barriers (deregulation).* Removal of historic barriers, both tariff (such as import taxes) and non-tariff (such as safety regulations), which have constituted barriers to trade across national boundaries. Deregulation has occurred at all levels: national, regional (within national trading blocs) and international. Thus deregulation has an impact on globalization, as it reduces the time, costs and complexity involved in trading across boundaries.

● *Global accounts/customers.* As customers become global and rationalize their procurement activities, they demand that suppliers provide them with global services to meet their unique global needs. Often this may consist of global delivery of products, assured supply and service systems, uniform characteristics and global pricing. Several LSEs, such as IBM, Boeing, IKEA, Siemens and ABB, make such 'global' demands on their smaller suppliers, typical SMEs. For these SMEs, managing such global accounts requires cross-functional customer teams, in order to deploy quality consistency across all functional units.

● *Relationship management/network organization.* As we move towards global markets it is becoming increasingly necessary to rely on a network of relationships with external organizations, for example, customer and supplier relationships to pre-empt competition. Firms may also have to work with internal units (e.g. sales subsidiaries) located in many and various parts of the world. Business alliances and network relationships help to reduce market uncertainties, particularly in the context of rapidly converging technologies and the need for higher amounts of resources to cover global markets. However, networked organizations need more coordination and communication.

● *Standardized worldwide technology.* Earlier differences in world market demand were due to the fact that advanced technological products were primarily developed for the defence and government sectors before being scaled down for consumer applications. However, today the desire for gaining scale and scope in production is so high that worldwide availability of products and services should escalate. As a consequence we may witness more homogeneity in the demand and usage of consumer electronics across nations. Today 'plug-and-play' modules are combined to create products very similar across markets. Examples of that are smartphones, that can be produced at good quality, not only by Apple and Samsung, but also by a Chinese manufacturer, like Xiaomi, which in 2014 captured no. 1 position in the Chinese smartphone market, and is now expanding to other international markets (Santos and Williamson, 2015).

- *Worldwide markets*. The concept of 'diffusions of innovations' from the home country to the rest of the world tends to be replaced by the concept of worldwide markets. Worldwide markets are likely to develop because they can rely on world demographics. For example, if a marketer targets its products or services to the teenagers of the world, it is relatively easy to develop a worldwide strategy for that segment and draw up operational plans to provide target market coverage on a global basis. This is becoming increasingly evident in soft drinks, clothing and sports shoes, especially in the internet economy.

- *'Global village'*. The term 'global village' refers to the phenomenon in which the world's population shares commonly recognized cultural symbols. The business consequence of this is that similar products and services can be sold to similar groups of customers in almost any country in the world. Cultural homogenization therefore implies the potential for the worldwide convergence of markets and the emergence of a global marketplace, in which brands such as Coke, Nike and Levi's are universally desired.

- *Worldwide communication*. New internet-based 'low-cost' communication methods (e.g. e-mailing, e-commerce) ease communication and trade across different parts of the world. As a result, customers within national markets are able to buy similar products and similar services across parts of the world.

- *Global cost drivers*. These are categorized as 'economies of scale' and 'economies of scope'. In the drive to reduce costs, many established multinationals have focused increasingly on activities with the highest returns. This means that lower-value activities are outsourced to emerging and developing countries with lower labour costs. The result is that once-closed value chains have been opened up, enabling local players to source 'plug-and-play' modular designs to big multinationals, or even to develop local brands themselves (Santos and Williamson, 2015).

Forces for 'market responsiveness'

These are as follows:

- *Cultural differences*. Despite the advent of the 'global village', cultural diversity clearly continues to exist. Cultural differences often pose major difficulties in international negotiations and marketing management. These cultural differences reflect differences in personal values and in the assumptions people make about how business is organized. Every culture has its opposing values. Markets are people, not products. There may be global products, but there are not global people.

- *Regionalism/protectionism*. Regionalism is the grouping of countries into regional clusters based on geographic proximity. These clusters (such as the European Union or the North American Free Trade Agreement) have formed regional trading blocs, which may represent a significant barrier to globalization, since regional trade is often seen as incompatible with global trade. In this case, trade barriers that are removed from individual countries are simply reproduced for a region and a set of countries. Thus all trading blocs create outsiders as well as insiders. Therefore one may argue that regionalism results in a situation where protectionism reappears around regions rather than individual countries.

Deglobalization
Moving away from the globalization trends and regarding each market as special, with its own economy, culture and religion.

● **Deglobalization** *trend.* More than 2,500 years ago the Greek historian Herodotus (based on observations) claimed that everyone believes their native customs and religion are the best. Current movements in Arab countries, the big demonstrations accompanying conferences such as the World Economic Forum in Davos or the World Trade Organization (WTO) meetings show that there could be a return to old values, promoting barriers to the further success of globalization. Rhetorical words such as 'McDonaldization' and 'Coca-Colonization' describe in a simple way fears of US cultural imperialism.

Exhibit 2.4 presents an example of British Telecommunications' experience with de-internationalization of their American and Asian strategy (Turner and Gardiner, 2007).

EXHIBIT 1.6 McDonald's is moving towards a higher degree of market responsiveness

McDonald's (www.mcdonalds.com) has now expanded to about 30,000 restaurants in over 100 countries. Executives at the headquarters of McDonald's Corp. in Oak Brook, Illinois, have learned that despite the cost savings inherent in standardization, success is often about being able to adapt to the local environment. Here are some examples.

Japan

McDonald's first restaurant in Japan opened during 1971. At that time fast food in Japan consisted of either a bowl of noodles or miso soup.

With its first-mover advantage, McDonald's kept its lead in Japan. By 1997, it had over 1,000 outlets there, selling more food in Japan than any other restaurant company, including 500 million burgers a year.

Among the offerings of McDonald's Co. (Japan) Ltd are chicken tatsuta, teriyaki chicken and the Teriyaki McBurger. Burgers are garnished with a fried egg. Beverages include iced coffee and corn soup.

McDonald's in Japan imports about 70 per cent of its food needs, including pickles from the US and beef patties from Australia. High volumes facilitate bargaining with suppliers, in order to guarantee sourcing at a low cost.

India

McDonald's, now with seven restaurants in India, was launched there in 1996. It has had to deal with a market that is 40 per cent vegetarian; meat eaters who dislike beef or pork; consumers with a hostility to frozen meat and fish; and a general Indian fondness for spice with everything.

The Big Mac was replaced by the Maharaja Mac, made from mutton, and the outlets also offer vegetarian rice-patties flavoured with vegetables and spice.

Other countries

In tropical markets, guava juice was added to the McDonald's product line. In Germany, McDonald's did well selling beer as well as McCroissants. Banana fruit pies became popular in Latin America and McSpaghetti noodles became a favourite in the Philippines. In Thailand, McDonald's introduced the Samurai Pork Burger with sweet sauce. Meanwhile, McDonald's in New Zealand launched the Kiwiburger served with beetroot sauce and optional apricot pie.

In Singapore, where fries came to be served with chilli sauce, the Kiasuburger chicken breakfast became a bestseller. Singapore was among the first markets in which McDonald's introduced a delivery service.

As indicated, McDonald's has achieved economies of scale and cost savings through standardization and in its packaging. In 2003, McDonald's announced that all its restaurants would soon be adopting the same brand packaging for menu items. According to a company press release, the new packaging would feature photographs of real people doing things they enjoy, such as listening to music, playing soccer and reading to their children. McDonald's global chief marketing officer was quoted as saying, 'It is the first time in our history that a single set of brand packaging, with a single brand message, will be used concurrently around the world.' Two years later, in 2005, the company had to pull back when it announced plans to *localize* its packages (Frost, 2006).

Sources: adapted from a variety of public media.

1.7   The value chain as a framework for identifying international competitive advantage

The concept of the value chain

Value chain
A categorization of the firm's activities providing value for the customers and profit for the company.

The **value chain** shown in Figure 1.10 provides a systematic means of displaying and categorizing activities. The activities performed by a firm in any industry can be grouped into the nine generic categories shown.

At each stage of the value chain there exists an opportunity to contribute positively to the firm's competitive strategy by performing some activity or process in a way that is

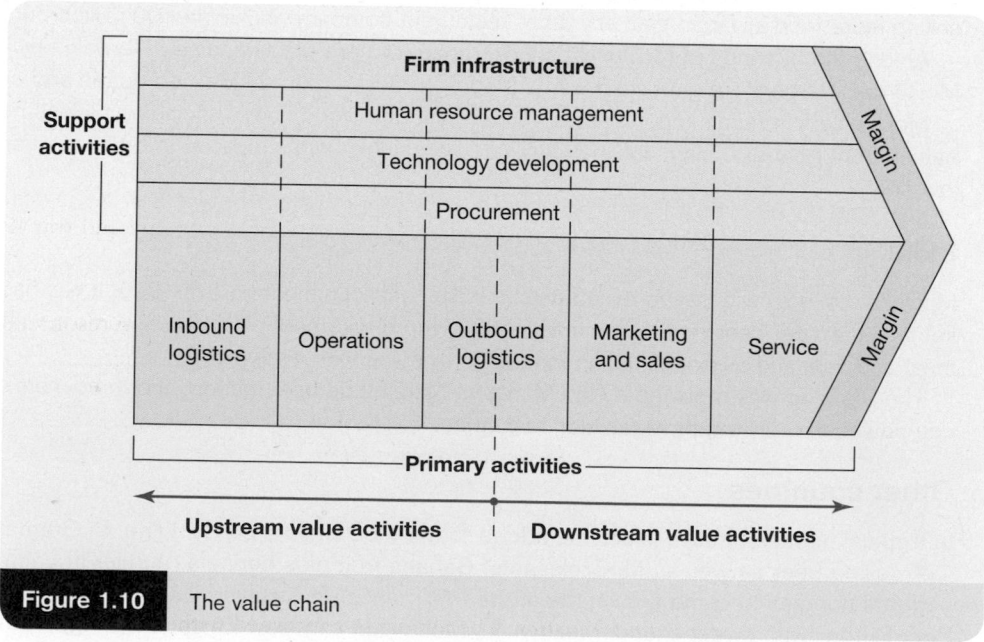

| **Figure 1.10** | The value chain |

better than and/or different from the competitors' offer, and so provide some uniqueness or advantage. If a firm attains such a competitive advantage, which is sustainable, defensible, profitable and valued by the market, then it may earn high rates of return, even though the industry structure may be unfavourable and the average profitability of the industry modest.

In competitive terms, value is the amount that buyers are willing to pay for what a firm provides them with (perceived value). The value chain includes both cost and value drivers. Drivers are the underlying structural factors that explain why the cost/value generated by a firm's activities differs from that of its rivals. Basically, a firm is profitable if the value it commands exceeds the costs involved in creating the product. Creating value for buyers that exceeds the cost of doing so is the goal of any generic strategy. Sometimes value, instead of cost, must be used in analysing competitive position, since firms often deliberately raise their costs in order to command a premium price via differentiation. The concept of buyers' perceived value will be discussed further in Section 4.4.

Before going into the details of the various value chain activities, it is important to realize that the firm's value chain is embedded in a larger stream of network activities in the total supply chain. Suppliers, the firm itself and business customers all have their *own* value chain, starting from the basic raw materials and going right through to those engaged in the delivery of the final product and service to the final customer.

The Porter concept of the value chain

Porter's (1986) original value chain displays total value and consists of value activities and margin. Value activities are the physically and technologically distinct activities that a firm performs. These are the building blocks with which a firm creates a product valuable to its buyers. Margin is the difference between total value (price) and the collective cost of performing the value activities.

Competitive advantage is a function of either providing comparable buyer value more efficiently than competitors (lower cost), or performing activities at comparable cost but in unique ways that create more customer value than the competitors are able to offer and, hence, command a premium price (differentiation). The firm might be able to identify elements of the value chain that are not worth the costs. These can then be unbundled and produced outside the firm (outsourced) at a lower price.

Value activities can be divided into two broad types, primary activities and support activities. *Primary activities*, listed along the bottom of Figure 1.10, are the activities involved in the physical creation of the product, its sale and transfer to the buyer, as well as after-sales assistance. In any firm, primary activities can be divided into the five generic categories shown in the figure. *Support activities* support the primary activities and each other by providing purchased inputs, technology, human resources and various firm-wide functions. The dotted lines reflect the fact that procurement, technology development and human resource management can be associated with specific primary activities as well as supporting the entire chain. Firm infrastructure is not associated with particular primary activities, but supports the entire chain.

Primary activities

The primary activities of the organization are grouped into five main areas, as follows:

1. *Inbound logistics.* The activities concerned with receiving, storing and distributing the inputs to the product/service. These include materials, handling, stock control and transport.

2. *Operations*. The transformation of these various inputs into the final product or service, e.g. machining, packaging, assembly, testing.

3. *Outbound logistics*. The collection, storage and distribution of the product to customers. For tangible products this would involve warehousing, material handling and transport; in the case of services it may be more concerned with arrangements for bringing customers to the service if it is in a fixed location (e.g. sports events).

4. *Marketing and sales*. These provide the means whereby consumers/users are made aware of the product/service and are able to purchase it. This would include sales administration, advertising and selling. In public services, communication networks that help users access a particular service are often important.

5. *Service*. These are all the activities that enhance or maintain the value of a product/service. Asugman *et al.* (1997) have defined after-sales service as 'those activities in which a firm engages after purchase of its product that minimize potential problems related to product use, and maximize the value of the consumption experience'. After-sales service consists of the following: the installation and start-up of the purchased product, the provision of spare parts for products, the provision of repair services, technical advice regarding the product, and the provision and support of warranties.

Each of these groups of primary activities is linked to support activities.

Support activities

These can be divided into four areas:

1. *Procurement*. This refers to the process of acquiring the various resource inputs to the primary activities (not to the resources themselves). As such, it occurs in many parts of the organization.

2. *Technology development*. All value activities have a 'technology', even if it is simply 'know-how'. The key technologies may be concerned directly with the product (e.g. R&D, product design), with processes (e.g. process development) or with a particular resource (e.g. raw material improvements).

3. *Human resource management*. This is a particularly important area that transcends all primary activities. It is concerned with the activities involved in recruiting, training, developing and rewarding people within the organization.

4. *Infrastructure*. The systems of planning, finance, quality control, etc. are crucially important to an organization's strategic capability in all primary activities. Infrastructure also consists of the structures and routines of the organization that sustain its culture.

As indicated in Figure 1.10, a distinction is also made between the production-oriented, 'upstream' activities and the more marketing-oriented, 'downstream' activities.

Figure 1.11 shows a simplified version of the value chain in Figure 1.10. This simplified version, characterized by the fact that it contains only the primary activities of the firm, will be used in most parts of this book.

Although value activities are the building blocks of competitive advantage, the value chain is not a collection of independent activities, but a system of interdependent activities. Value activity is related by horizontal linkages within the value chain. Linkages are relationships between the way in which one value activity is dependent on the performance of another.

Furthermore, the chronological order of the activities in the value chain is not always as illustrated in Figure 1.11. In companies where orders are placed before production of the final product (build-to-order), the sales and marketing function takes place before production.

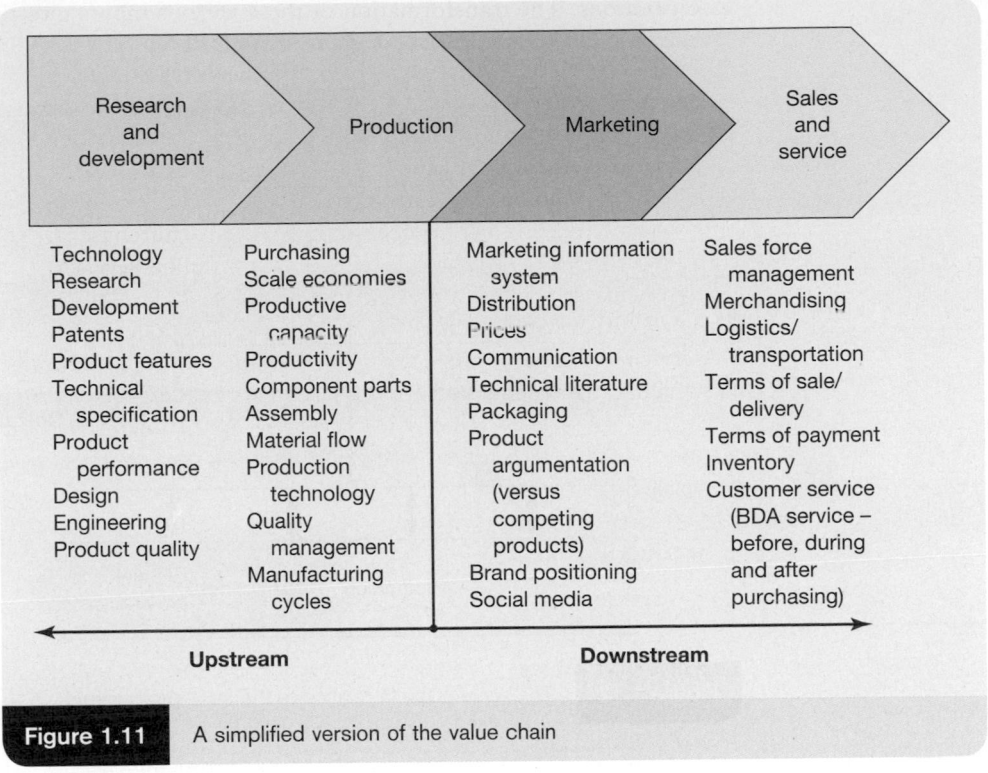

Research and development	Production	Marketing	Sales and service
Technology	Purchasing	Marketing information	Sales force
Research	Scale economies	system	management
Development	Productive	Distribution	Merchandising
Patents	capacity	Prices	Logistics/
Product features	Productivity	Communication	transportation
Technical	Component parts	Technical literature	Terms of sale/
specification	Assembly	Packaging	delivery
Product	Material flow	Product	Terms of payment
performance	Production	argumentation	Inventory
Design	technology	(versus	Customer service
Engineering	Quality	competing	(BDA service –
Product quality	management	products)	before, during
	Manufacturing	Brand positioning	and after
	cycles	Social media	purchasing)

Upstream   Downstream

Figure 1.11   A simplified version of the value chain

In understanding the competitive advantage of an organization, the strategic importance of the following types of linkage should be analysed in order to assess how they contribute to cost reduction or value added. There are two kinds of linkage:

1. *internal linkages* between activities within the same value chain, but perhaps on different planning levels within the firm;
2. *external linkages* between different value chains 'owned' by the different actors in the total value system.

Internal linkages

There may be important links between the primary activities. In particular, choices will have been made about these relationships and how they influence value creation and strategic capability. For example, a decision to hold high levels of finished stock might ease production scheduling problems and provide a faster response time to the customer. However, it will probably add to the overall cost of operations. An assessment needs to be made of whether the added value of 'stocking' is greater than the added cost. Suboptimization of the single value chain activities should be avoided. It is easy to miss this point in an analysis if, for example, the marketing activities and operations are assessed separately. The operations may look good because they are geared to high-volume, low-variety, low-unit-cost production. However, at the same time the marketing team may be selling quickness, flexibility and variety to the customers. When put together these two potential strengths are weaknesses because they are not in harmony, which is what a value chain requires. The link between a primary activity and a support activity may be the basis of competitive advantage. For example, an organization may have a unique system for procuring materials. Many international hotels and travel companies use their computer systems to provide immediate 'real time' quotations and bookings worldwide from local access points.

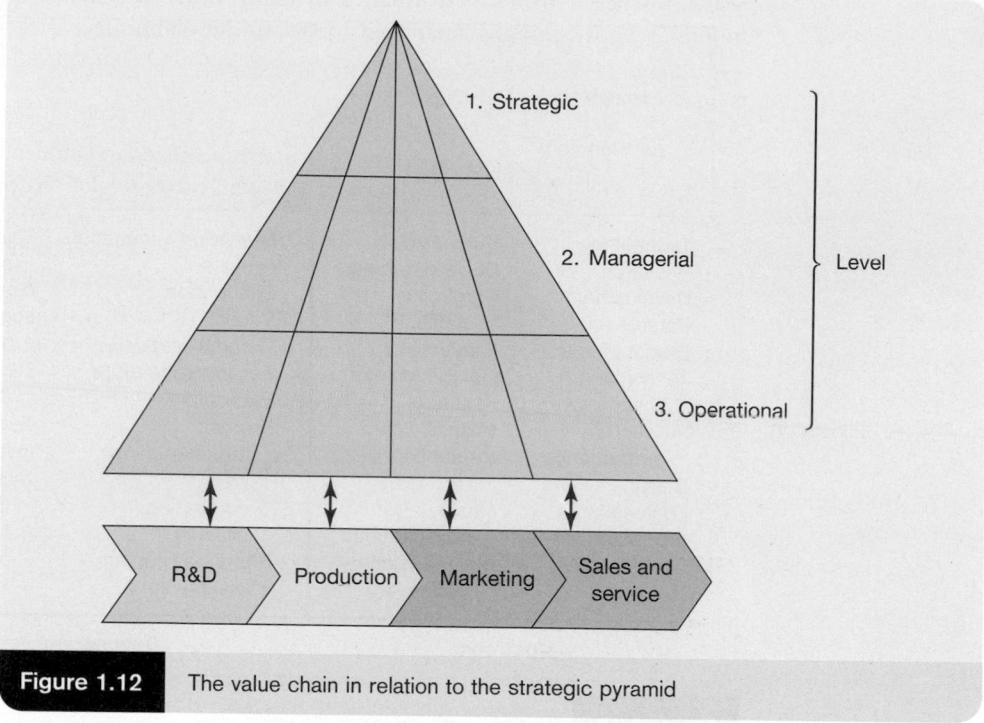

Figure 1.12   The value chain in relation to the strategic pyramid

As a supplement to comments about the linkages between the different activities, it is also relevant to regard the value chain (illustrated in Figure 1.11 in a simplified form) as a thorough-going model on all three planning levels in the organization.

In purely conceptual terms, a firm can be described as a pyramid as illustrated in Figure 1.12. It consists of an intricate conglomeration of decision and activity levels, having three distinct levels, but the main value chain activities are connected to all three strategic levels in the firm:

1. The *strategic level* is responsible for formulation of the firm's mission statement, determining objectives, identifying the resources that will be required if the firm is to attain its objectives, and selecting the most appropriate corporate strategy for the firm to pursue.
2. The *managerial level* has the task of translating corporate objectives into functional and/or unit objectives and ensuring that resources placed at its disposal (e.g. in the marketing department) are used effectively in the pursuit of those activities that will make the achievement of the firm's goals possible.
3. The *operational level* is responsible for the effective performance of the tasks that underlie the achievement of unit/functional objectives. The achievement of operational objectives is what enables the firm to achieve its managerial and strategic aims. All three levels are interdependent, and clarity of purpose from the top enables everybody in the firm to work in an integrated fashion towards a common aim.

External linkages

One of the key features of most industries is that a single organization rarely undertakes all value activities from product design to distribution to the final consumer. There is usually a specialization of roles, and any single organization usually participates in the wider value system that creates a product or service. In understanding how value is created it is not enough to look at the firm's internal value chain alone. Much of the value creation will occur in the supply and distribution chains, and this whole process needs to be analysed and understood.

Suppliers have value chains that create and deliver the purchased inputs used in a firm's chain (the upstream part of the value chain). Suppliers not only deliver a product, but can also influence a firm's performance in many other ways. For example, Benetton, the Italian fashion company, managed to sustain an elaborate network of suppliers, agents and independent retail outlets as the basis of its rapid and successful international development during the 1970s and 1980s.

In addition, products pass through the value chain channels on their way to the buyer. Channels perform additional activities that affect the buyer and influence the firm's own activities. A firm's product eventually becomes part of its buyer's value chain. The ultimate basis for differentiation is a firm and its product's role in the buyer's value chain, which is determined by buyer needs. Gaining and sustaining competitive advantage depend on understanding not only a firm's value chain, but also how the firm fits into the overall value system.

There are often circumstances where the overall cost can be reduced (or the value increased) by collaborative arrangements between different organizations in the value system. It will be seen elsewhere (Chapter 10) that this is often the rationale behind downstream collaborative arrangements, such as joint ventures, subcontracting and outsourcing between different organizations (e.g. sharing technology in the international motor manufacture and electronics industries).

Internationalizing the value chain

All internationally oriented firms must consider an eventual internationalization of the value chain's functions. The firm must decide whether the responsibility for the single value chain function is to be moved to the export markets or is best handled centrally from head office. Principally, the value chain function should be carried out where there is the highest competence (and the most cost-effectiveness), and this is not necessarily at head office.

A distinction immediately arises between the activities labelled downstream in Figure 1.11 and those labelled upstream activities. The location of downstream activities, those more related to the buyer, is usually tied to where the buyer is located. If a firm is going to sell in Australia, for example, it usually provide services in Australia, and it must have sales-people stationed there. In some industries it is possible to have a single sales force that travels to the buyer's country and back again; other specific downstream activities, such as the production of advertising copy, can sometimes also be performed centrally. More typically, however, the firm must locate the capability to perform downstream activities in each of the countries in which it operates. By contrast, upstream activities and support activities are more independent of where the buyer is located (Figure 1.13). However, if the export

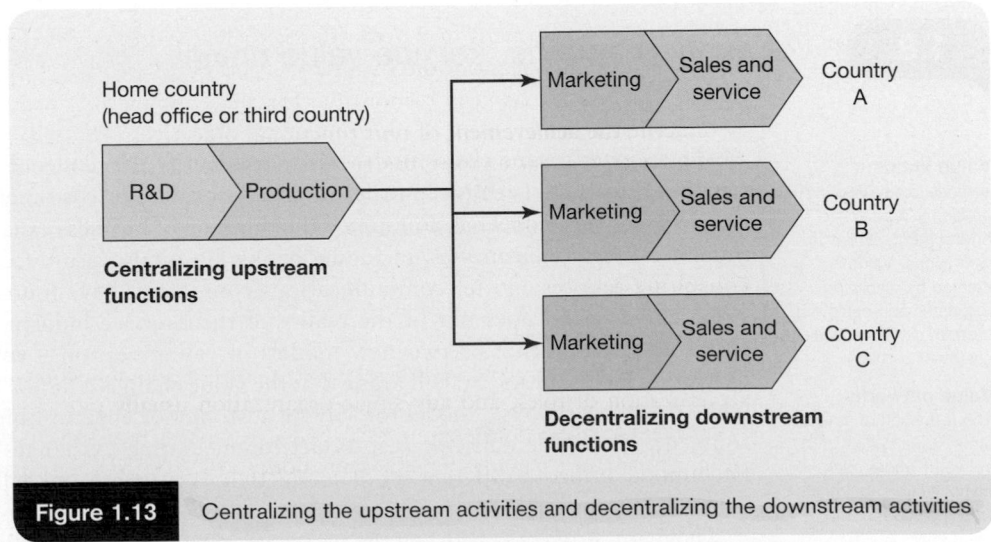

Figure 1.13   Centralizing the upstream activities and decentralizing the downstream activities

markets are culturally close to the home market, it may be relevant to control the entire value chain from head office (home market).

This distinction carries some interesting implications. First, downstream activities create competitive advantages that are largely country-specific: a firm's reputation, brand name and service network in a country grow largely out of its activities and create entry/mobility barriers largely in that country alone. Competitive advantage in upstream and support activities often grows more out of the entire system of countries in which a firm competes than from its position in any single country.

Secondly, in industries where downstream activities or other buyer-tied activities are vital to competitive advantage, there tends to be a more multidomestic pattern of international competition. In many service industries, for example, not only downstream activities but frequently upstream activities are tied to buyer location, and global strategies are comparatively less common. In industries where upstream and support activities such as technology development and operations are crucial to competitive advantage, global competition is more common. For example, there may be a large need in firms to centralize and coordinate the production function worldwide to be able to create rational production units that are able to exploit economies of scale. Today it is very popular among companies to outsource production to the Far East, e.g. China.

Furthermore, as customers increasingly join regional cooperative buying organizations, it is becoming more and more difficult to sustain a price differentiation across markets. This will put pressure on the firm to coordinate a European price policy. This will be discussed further in Chapter 11.

The distinctive issues of international strategies, in contrast to domestic, can be summarized in two key dimensions of how a firm competes internationally. The first is called the *configuration* of a firm's worldwide activities, or the location in the world where each activity in the value chain is performed, including the number of places. For example, a company can locate different parts of its value chain in different places – for instance, factories in China, call centres in India and retail shops in Europe. IBM is an example of a company that exploits wage differentials by increasing the number of employees in India from 9,000 in 2004 to 50,000 by mid-2007 and by planning for massive additional growth. Most of these employees are in IBM Global Services, the part of the company that is growing fastest but has the lowest margins – which the Indian employees are supposed to improve, by reducing (wage) costs rather than raising prices (Ghemawat, 2007).

The second dimension is called *coordination,* which refers to how identical or linked activities performed in different countries are coordinated with each other (Porter, 1986).

1.8　　Value shop and the 'service value chain'

Value shops
A model for solving problems in a service environment, similar to workshops. Value is created by mobilizing resources and deploying them to solve a specific customer problem.

Value networks
The formation of several firms' value chains into a network, where each company contributes a small part to the total value chain.

Michael Porter's value chain model claims to identify the sequence of key generic activities that businesses perform in order to generate value for customers. Since its introduction in 1985, this model has dominated the thinking of business executives. Yet a growing number of service businesses, including banks, hospitals, insurance companies, business consulting services and telecommunications companies, have found that the traditional value chain model does not fit the reality of their service industry sectors. Stabell and Fjeldstad (1998) identified two new models of value creation – **value shops** and **value networks**. Fjeldstad and Stabell argue that the value chain is a model for making products, while the value shop is a model for solving customer or client problems in a service environment. The value network is a model for mediating exchanges between customers. Each model utilizes a different set of core activities to create and deliver distinct forms of value to customers.

The main differences between the two types of value chains are illustrated in Table 1.2.

Table 1.2	The traditional value chain versus the service value chain

Traditional value chain model	Service value chain ('value shop') model
Value creation through transformation of inputs (raw material and components) to products.	Value creation through customer problem-solving. Value is created by mobilizing resources and activities to resolve a particular and unique customer problem. Customer value is not related to the solution itself but to the value of solving the problem.
Sequential process ('first we develop the product, then we produce it, and finally we sell it')	Cyclical and iterative process.
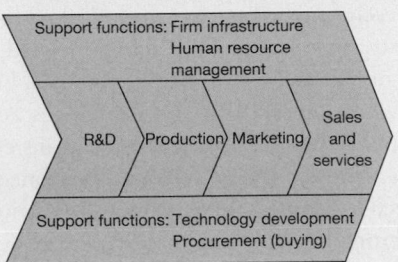	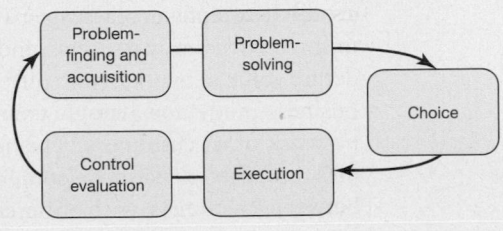
The traditional value chain consists of primary and support activities. **Primary activities** are directly involved in creating and bringing value to customers: upstream (product development and production) and downstream activities (marketing and sales and service). **Support activities** enable and improve the performance of the primary activities, e.g. procurement, technology development, human resource management and firm infrastructure.	The **primary activities** of a value shop are: 1. *Problem-finding*: activities associated with the recording, reviewing and formulating of the problem to be solved and choosing the overall approach to solving the problem. 2. *Problem-solving*: activities associated with generating and evaluating alternative solutions. 3. *Choice*: activities associated with choosing among alternative problem solutions. 4. *Execution*: activities associated with communicating, organizing and implementing the chosen solution. 5. *Control and evaluation*: activities associated with measuring and evaluating to what extent implementation has solved the initial statement.
Examples: production and sales of furniture, consumer food products, electronic products and other mass products.	*Examples*: banks, hospitals, insurance companies, business consulting services and telecommunications companies.

Source: based on Stabell and Fjeldstad (1998).

Value shops (as in workshops, not retail stores) create value by mobilizing resources (e.g. people, knowledge and skills) and deploying them to solve specific problems such as curing an illness, delivering airline services to the passengers or delivering a solution to a business problem. Shops are organized around making and executing decisions – identifying and assessing problems or opportunities, developing alternative solutions or approaches, choosing one, executing it and evaluating the results. This model applies to most service-oriented organizations such as building contractors, consultancies and legal organizations. However, it also applies to organizations that are primarily configured to identify and exploit specific market opportunities, such as developing a new drug, drilling a potential oilfield or designing a new aircraft.

Different parts of a typical business may exhibit characteristics of different configurations. For example, production and distribution may resemble a value chain; research and development a value shop.

Value shops make use of specialized knowledge-based systems to support the task of creating solutions to problems. However, the challenge is to provide an integrated set of applications that enable seamless execution across the entire problem-solving or opportunity–exploitation process. Several key technologies and applications are emerging in value shops – many focus on utilizing people and knowledge better. Groupware, intranets, desktop videoconferencing and shared electronic workspaces enhance communication and collaboration between people, essential to mobilizing people and knowledge across value shops. Integrating project planning with execution is proving crucial, for example, in pharmaceutical development, where bringing a new drug through the long, complex approval process a few months early can mean millions of dollars in revenue. Technologies such as inference engines and neural networks can help to make knowledge about problems and the process for solving them explicit and accessible.

The term 'value network' is widely used but imprecisely defined. It often refers to a group of companies, each specializing in one piece of the value chain, and linked together in some virtual way to create and deliver products and services. Stabell and Fjelstad (1998) define value networks quite differently – not as networks of affiliated companies, but as a business model for a single company that mediates interactions and exchanges across a network of its customers. This model clearly applies best to telecommunications companies, but also to insurance companies and banks, whose business, essentially, is mediating between customers with different financial needs – some saving, some borrowing, for example. Key activities include operating the customer-connecting infrastructure, promoting the network, managing contracts and relationships, and providing services.

Some of the most IT-intensive businesses in the world are value networks – banks, airlines and telecommunications companies, for instance. Most of their technology provides the basic infrastructure of the 'network' to mediate exchanges between customers. But the competitive landscape is now shifting beyond automation and efficient transaction processing to monitoring and exploiting information about customer behaviour.

The aim is to add more value to customer exchanges through better understanding of usage patterns, exchange opportunities, shared interests and so on. Data mining and visualization tools, for example, can be used to identify both positive and negative connections between customers.

Competitive success often depends on more than simply performing your primary model well. It may also require the delivery of additional kinds of complementary value. Adopting attributes of a second value configuration model can be a powerful way to differentiate your value proposition or defend it against competitors pursuing a value model different to your own. It is essential, however, to pursue another model only in ways that leverage the primary model. For example, Harley-Davidson's primary model is the chain – it makes and sells products. Forming the Harley Owners Group (HOG) – a network of customers – added value to the primary model by reinforcing the brand identity, building loyalty and providing valuable information and feedback about customers' behaviours and preferences. Amazon.com is a value chain like other book distributors, and initially used technology to make the process vastly more efficient. Now, with its book recommendations and special interest groups, it is adding the characteristics of a value network. Our research suggests that the value network, in particular, offers opportunities for many existing businesses to add more value to their customers, and for new entrants to capture market share from those who offer less value to their customers.

Combining the product value chain and the service value chain

Blomstermo *et al.* (2006) make a distinction between *hard* and *soft services*. Hard services are those where production and consumption can be decoupled. For example, software services can be transferred into a CD or some other tangible medium, which can be mass-produced, making standardization possible. With soft services, where production and consumption occur simultaneously, the customer acts as a co-producer, and decoupling is not viable. The soft-service provider must be present abroad from its first day of foreign operations.

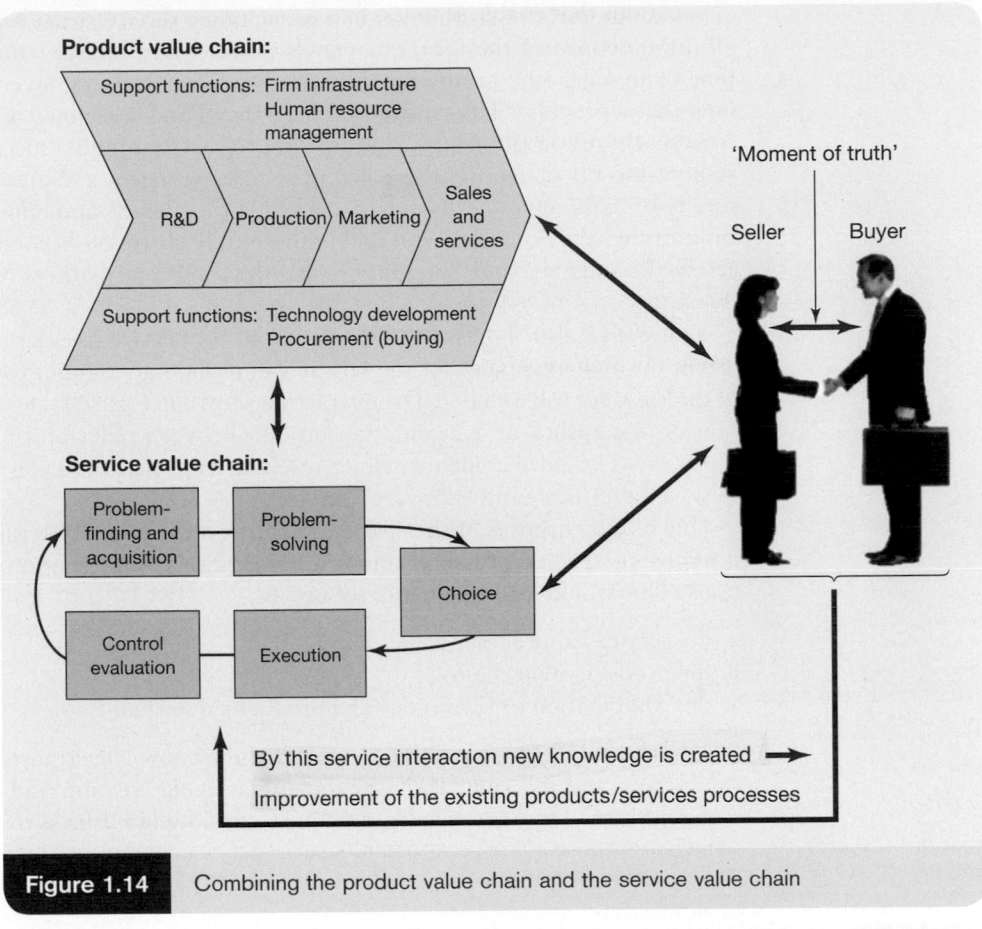

Figure 1.14   Combining the product value chain and the service value chain

Figure 1.14, showing the combination of the product and service value chains, is mainly valid for soft services, but at the same time in more and more industries we see that physical products and services are combined.

Most product companies offer services to protect or enhance the value of their product businesses. Cisco, for instance, built its installation, maintenance and network-design service business to ensure high-quality product support and to strengthen relationships with enterprise and telecom customers. A company may also find itself drawn into services when it realizes that competitors use its products to offer services of value. If it does nothing, it risks not only the commoditization of its own products – something that is occurring in most product markets, irrespective of the services on offer – but also the loss of customer relationships. To make existing service groups profitable – or to succeed in launching a new embedded service business – executives of product companies must decide whether the primary focus of service units should be to support existing product businesses or to grow as a new and independent platform.

When a company chooses a business design for delivering embedded *services* to customers, it should remember that its strategic intent affects which elements of the delivery life cycle are most important. If the aim is to protect or enhance the *value* of a product, the company should integrate the system for delivering it and the associated *services* in order to promote the development of product designs that simplify the task of *service* (e.g. by using fewer subsystems or integrating diagnostic software). This approach involves minimizing the footprint of *service* delivery and incorporating support into the product whenever possible. If the company wants the *service* business to be an independent growth platform, however, it should focus most of its delivery efforts on constantly reducing unit costs and making the *services* more productive (Auguste *et al.*, 2006).

In the 'moment of truth' (e.g. in a consultancy service situation), the seller represents all the functions of the focal company's product and service value chain – at the same time. The seller (the product and service provider) and the buyer create a service in an interaction process: 'The service is being created and consumed as it is produced.' Good representatives on the seller's side are vital to service brands' successes, being ultimately responsible for delivering the seller's promise. As such, a shared understanding of the service brand's values needs to be anchored in their hearts and minds to encourage brand-supporting behaviour. This internal brand-building process becomes more challenging as service brands expand internationally, drawing on workers from different global domains.

Figure 1.14 also shows the cyclic nature of the service interaction ('moment of truth') where the post-evaluation of the service value chain gives input for the possible redesign of the 'product value chain'. The interaction shown in Figure 1.14 could also be an illustration or a snapshot of a negotiation process between seller and buyer, where the seller represents a branded company, which is selling its projects as a combination of 'hardware' (physical products) and 'software' (services).

One of the purposes of the 'learning nature' of the overall decision cycle in Figure 1.14 is to pick up the best practices among different kinds of international buyer–seller interactions. This would lead to a better set-up of:

● the service value chain (value shop);
● the product value chain;
● the combination of the service and product value chain.

Johansson and Jonsson (2012) emphasized the knowledge transfer between the product value chain and the value shop, by looking at value creation and utilizing the synergies between them. This is especially relevant to consider in business to business (B2B) project selling.

1.9   Global experimental marketing

Customer experience
The use of products in combination with services to engage the individual customer in a way that creates a memorable event. This can be characterized into one of four groups: entertainment, educational, aesthetic or escapist.

The previous section describes and explains value creation as a result of both the product and service offerings. However, as services increasingly become commoditized – think of smartphone services sold solely on price – 'experiences' have emerged as the next step in providing 'customer value'. This process of generating customer value from a product solution, services and finally customer experiences is shown in Figure 1.15. A **customer experience** occurs when a company intentionally uses products in combination with services to engage individual customers in a way that creates a *memorable* event (Pine and Gilmore, 1998).

Experiential marketing is a growing trend worldwide, evident in most sectors of the global economy. The term essentially describes marketing initiatives that give customers in-depth, tangible experiences in order to provide them with sufficient information to make a purchasing decision. It has evolved as a response to a perceived transition from a service economy to one personified by the experiences in which consumers participate.

Unless companies want to be in a commoditized business, they will be compelled to upgrade their offerings to the next stage of customer value creation: customer experience. This applies to both B2C (business to consumer) and B2B businesses.

B2C businesses

It is increasingly the case that consumers are involved in the processes of both defining and creating value, and the co-created experience of consumers through the holistic brand value structure becomes the very basis of marketing.

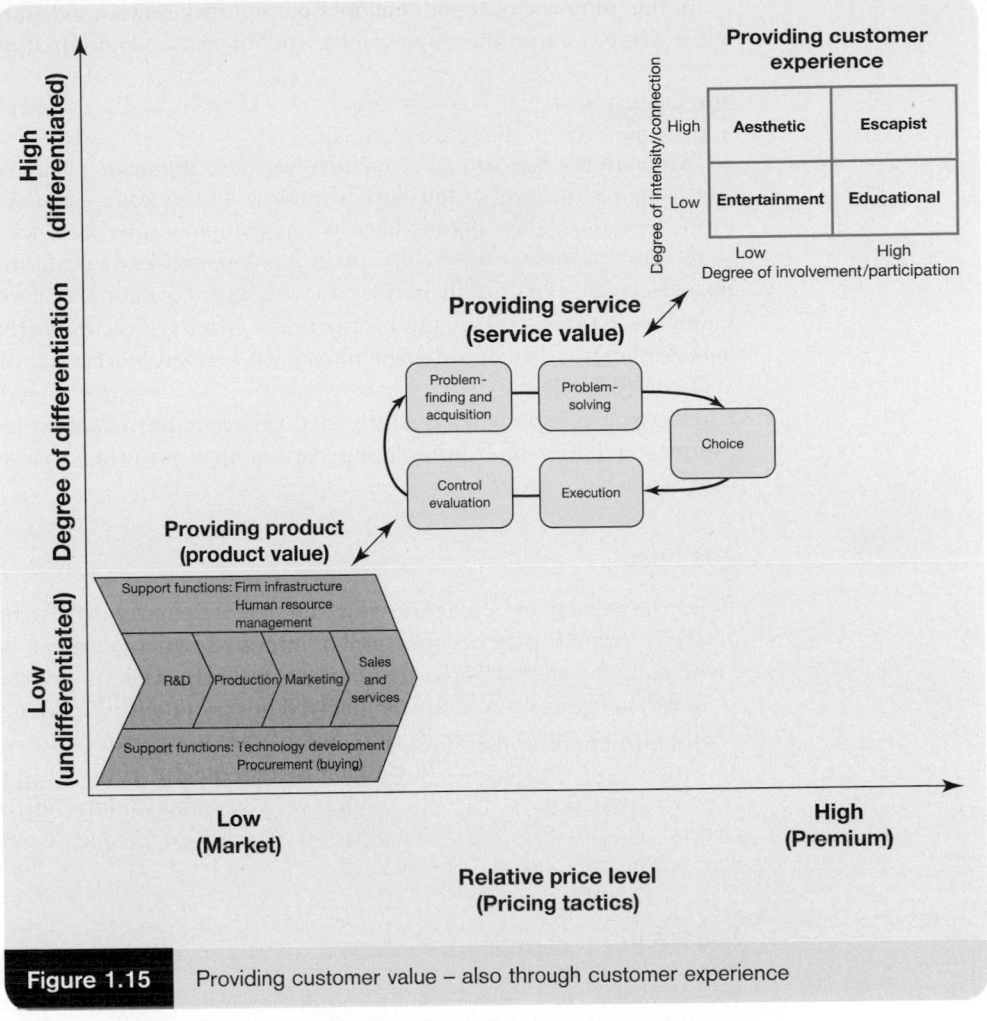

| | **Figure 1.15** | Providing customer value – also through customer experience |

Sources: based on Pine and Gilmore (1998); Atwal and Williams (2009).

Pine and Gilmore (1998) suggest that we think about experiences across two bi-polar constructs:

- *Involvement/participation.* This dimension refers to the level of interactivity between the supplier and the customer. At 'low degree' there is passive participation, where the participants experience the event as observers or listeners, e.g. classical symphony-goers. At the other end of the spectrum lies 'active participation' in which customers play key roles in creating the performance or event, e.g. going to a rock concert.
- *Intensity/connection.* This dimension refers to the strength of feeling towards the inter-action. Watching a film in the cinema (e.g. an IMAX theatre) with an audience, 3D screen and advanced sound is associated with a 'high degree' of intensity/connection compared with watching the same film at home on a DVD.

We can sort experiences into four broad categories according to where they fall along the spectra of the two dimensions:

Entertainment

Entertainment can be defined as something that amuses, pleases or diverts (especially a performance or show), or as the pleasure afforded by being entertained and amused. For example, fashion shows in designer boutiques and upmarket department stores, involving a low degree of customer involvement and intensity, would qualify as 'entertainment'.

Educational

Activities in the *educational* zone involve those in which participants are more actively involved, but the level of intensity is still low. In this zone, participants acquire new skills or increase those they already have. Many company offerings include educational dimensions. For example, cruise ships often employ well-known authorities to provide semi-formal lectures as part of their itineraries, a concept commonly referred to as 'edutainment'. Likewise, the Ferrari Driving Experience is a two-day precision driving school designed to narrow the gap between driving ability and a Ferrari's performance capability (Atwal and Williams, 2009).

This type of experience typically involves active participation by the consumer in educational activities of a stimulating nature, thus ensuring that the event provides an experience.

Aesthetic

When the element of activity is reduced to a more passive involvement, the event becomes *aesthetic*. Admiring the architectural or interior design of designer boutiques, for example, involves high degree of intensity but it has little effect on its environment.

In this category customers are involved in very intense experiences (e.g. a tourist viewing the Grand Canyon from its rim), but they are not personally involved in the event (such as climbing down the Grand Canyon as they might in the escapism category). Luxury brand activity is of an aesthetic nature, with customers immersing themselves in the experience but with little active participation. Watching a Cirque du Soleil show (see case 7.1) is a customer experience of this kind.

Escapism

Escapism can be defined as a tendency to escape from daily realities or routines by indulging in daydreams, fantasies or entertainment that provide a break from reality. *Escapist* activities are those that involve a high degree of both involvement and intensity, and are clearly a central feature of much of luxury consumption and lifestyle experiences, often connected to the fitness trend. This is clearly evident in the luxury tourism and hospitality sector, with the growth of specialized holiday offerings, in which customers are closely involved in co-creating their experiences. Joining a Zumba dance course (see case 3.1) is similar to this kind of customer experience.

B2B businesses

Like B2C companies, B2B businesses also need to continuously innovate how they attract, engage and excite customers by finding new possibilities for creating value. Leading industrial equipment suppliers, for instance, are learning that creation of customer value needs to be based on how customers experience the job they need to do now or how they prepare to transform themselves to succeed in the future.

Mass customization

One of the best ways to create customer value is to engage customers and create experience by mass customizing goods and services for them. One of the benefits of digital technology is that B2B companies can mass customize offerings, efficiently serving customers uniquely, differentiating offerings from any competition and locking customers in. This is

Mass customization
Mass customization can be viewed as collaborative efforts between customers and manufacturers to jointly search for solutions that best match customers' individual specific needs with manufacturers' customization capabilities. This combines the low unit costs of mass production processes with the flexibility of individual customization.

because mass customizing a product automatically turns it into a service. An integrated part of the **mass customization** process is the intangible service of helping customers figure out exactly what it is they want. So when B2B companies mass customize a product, they compete in the service business of helping their individual business customers define their needs, and then make and deliver customized products to meet those needs for each of their customers.

Furthermore, mass customizing a service turns it into an experience because, when businesses design a custom service that is just right for a particular customer at a particular point in time, the result is an inherently personal, and memorable, interaction.

More and more customers seek out suppliers that want to become partners in their customers' success, that help customers help their customers and that think beyond the value of the equipment they sell to the far greater value that accrues from helping customers use that equipment effectively. B2B businesses need to realize that customers don't really want just products, systems or even solutions. They want a better business. Customers that are growing and adapting to their markets do not just buy industrial equipment today because they want the equipment; it is always a means to create a better and more profitable business. The 'Case Construction' exhibit (Exhibit 1.7) illustrates this point.

EXHIBIT 1.7 Case Construction Equipment is using experiential marketing

In 1999, CNH (Case New Holland) was established as a result of a merger between Case and New Holland. CNH manufactures its products (agricultural and construction equipment and machines) in 37 facilities throughout the world and distributes its products in approximately 170 countries through approximately 11,500 full line dealers and distributors.

One of the brands under CNH is Case Construction Equipment (www.casece.com).

In North America, Case Construction Equipment operates its Tomahawk Experience Center in Northern Wisconsin so potential business customers can try out its excavators, loaders, forklifts, backhoes and other equipment in a multi-day experience. It lets construction company owners and managers who grew up in the business get back in touch with their inner operator again, provides the opportunity for Case's experts to answer whatever questions they have and enables dealers to form close relationships with these customers.

The Tomahawk Customer Center has been serving customers for more than 60 years.

The facility stands on the site of the Drott Manufacturing proving grounds, which date back to the early 1900s. After acquiring Drott in 1968, Case transformed the property into a world-class facility dedicated to serving Case customers.

Source: CNH Industrial America LLC.

Source: CNH Industrial America LLC.

Today's Tomahawk Customer Center features state-of-the-art training, a line-up of more than 60 pieces of new equipment to operate, log cabin-style lodges for comfortable accommodation and memorable hospitality. The outcome?

Case has experienced that when a normal potential customer heads to a dealer it has about a 20 per cent chance of getting the business, but when the dealer brings the customer to Tomahawk, the close rate goes up to 80 per cent.

Sources: based on www.cnh.com, www.casese.com; Pine (2015).

Augmented Reality (AR)

Argmented Reality is a live view of a physical, real-world environment whose elements are augmented (or supplemented) by computer-generated sensory input such as sound, video, graphics or GPS data. AR technology allows consumers to virtually interact with three-dimensional product visualizations displayed on users' screens.

Augmented Reality (AR)

The way in which **Augmented Reality (AR)** has been used in marketing campaigns can be seen as a form of experiential marketing because it focuses not only on a single product/service, but also on an entire experience created for the customers. The technology enhances the customer's current perception of reality. By contrast, virtual reality replaces the real world with a simulated one. With the help of advanced AR, information about the surrounding real world of the user becomes interactive and digitally manipulable.

EXHIBIT 1.8 IKEA's use of AR

In the 2014 catalogue, IKEA has produced an interactive online catalogue based on AR, in which viewers can actually see a piece of furniture in their home before buying it. Viewers can accelerate their decision-making by easily dragging an item from the catalogue and placing it anywhere in the simulated space on their smartphone or tablet screen, and then immediately taking a screenshot of that selection. Such technology allows for more personally interactive catalogues and enhances playfulness and convenience, as well as stimulating consumers buying intentions and impressions of a brand.

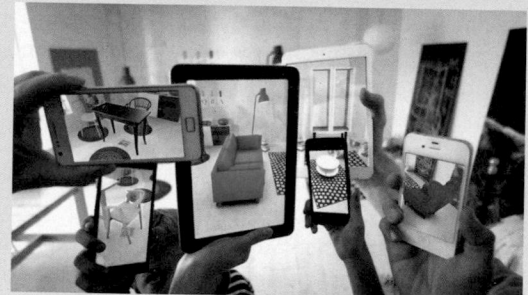

Source: used with the permission of Inter IKEA Systems B.V.

See also: http://www.youtube.com/watch?v=vDNzTasuYEw

Source: based on Lung-Huang and Liu (2014).

Experiential marketing is recognized as an important means of creating value for the end consumer, who will be motivated to make faster and more positive purchasing decisions. Consequently AR experiential marketing is considered as mainly affecting the pre-purchase stage due to the fact that AR has the most impact at the pre-purchase stage. At this stage the consumer is evaluating their choices before taking the final purchase decision and AR has the power to 'put the product in the hand of the users' giving them the opportunity to test the product as if they already own it. Furthermore, AR has the potential to provide customers with an experience they appreciate and that they will tell their friends about.

In conclusion, whereas traditional marketing frameworks view consumers as rational decision-makers focused on the functional features and benefits of products, experiential marketing views consumers as emotional beings, focused on achieving memorable experiences. In this connection the use of new technologies, such as social media, has also increased the potential for experiential marketing. This is of particular relevance given the increasing significance of the internet as a communication and distribution channel within the luxury sector.

Finally, the more a company engages all five senses in the creation of a customer experience, the more effective and memorable it can be.

1.10 Information business and the virtual value chain

Most business managers would agree that we have recently entered a new era, 'the information age', which differs markedly from the industrial age. What have been the driving forces for these changes?

The consensus has shifted over time. To begin with, it was thought to be the automation power of computers and computation; then it was the ability to collapse time and space through telecommunications. More recently it has been seen as the value-creating power of information, a resource that can be reused, shared, distributed or exchanged without any inevitable loss of value; indeed, value is sometimes multiplied. Today's fascination with competing on invisible assets means that people now see knowledge and its relationship with intellectual capital as the critical resource, because it underpins innovation and renewal.

One way of understanding the strategic opportunities and threats of information is to consider the **virtual value chain** as a supplement to the physical value chain (Figure 1.16).

By introducing the *virtual value chain,* Rayport and Sviokla (1996) have made an extension to the conventional value chain model, which treats information as a supporting element in the value-adding process. Rayport and Sviokla (1996) show how information in itself can be used to create value.

Virtual value chain
An extension of the conventional value chain, where the information processing itself can create value for customers.

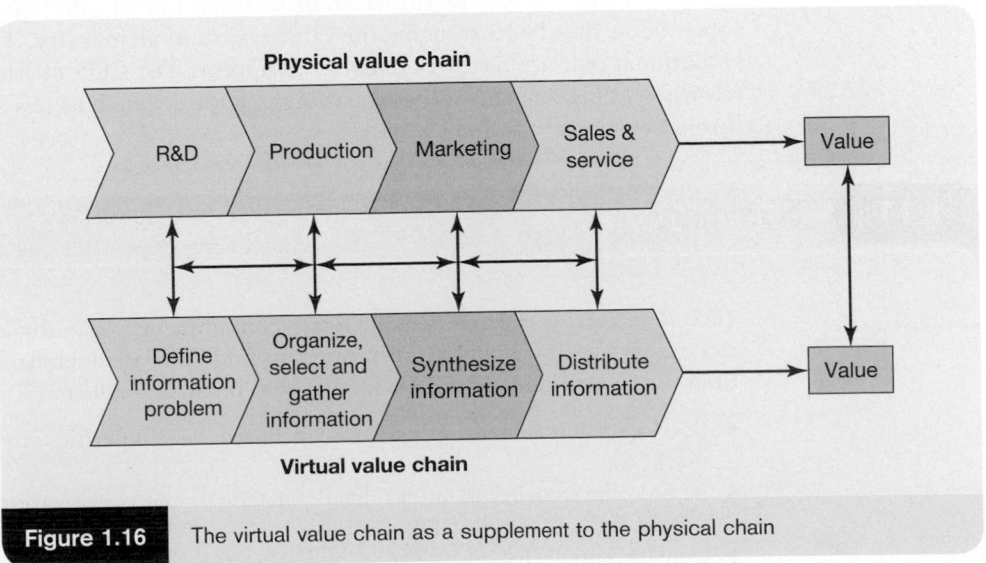

Figure 1.16   The virtual value chain as a supplement to the physical chain

Source: based on Rayport and Sviokla (1996).

Fundamentally, there are four ways of using information to create business value (Marchand, 1999):

1. *Managing risks.* In the twentieth century the evolution of risk management stimulated the growth of functions and professions such as finance, accounting, auditing and controlling. These information-intensive functions tend to be major consumers of IT resources and people's time.

2. *Reducing costs.* Here the focus is on using information as efficiently as possible to achieve the outputs required from business processes and transactions. This process view of information management is closely linked with the re-engineering and continuous improvement movements of the 1990s. The common elements are focused on eliminating unnecessary and wasteful steps and activities, especially paperwork and information movements, and then simplifying and, if possible, automating the remaining processes.

3. *Offering products and services.* Here the focus is on knowing one's customers, and sharing information with partners and suppliers to enhance customer satisfaction. Many service and manufacturing companies focus on building relationships with customers and on demand management as ways of using information. Such strategies have led companies to invest in point-of-sale systems, account management, customer profiling and service management systems.

4. *Inventing new products.* Finally, companies can use information to innovate – to invent new products, provide different services and use emerging technologies. Companies such as Intel and Microsoft are learning to operate in 'continuous discovery mode', inventing new products more quickly and using market intelligence to retain a competitive edge. Here, information management is about mobilizing people and collaborative work processes to share information and promote discovery throughout the company.

Every company pursues some combination of the above strategies.

In relation to Figure 1.16, each of the physical value chain activities might make use of one or all four information-processing stages of the virtual value chain, in order to create extra value for the customer. This is the reason for the horizontal double arrows between the different physical and virtual value chain activities in the figure. In this way information can be captured at all stages of the physical value chain. Obviously such information can be used to improve performance at each stage of the physical value chain and to coordinate elements across it. However, it can also be analysed and repackaged to build content-based products or to create new lines of businesses.

A company can use its information to reach out to other companies' customers or operations, thereby rearranging the value system of an industry. The result might be that traditional industry sector boundaries disappear. The CEO of Amazon.com, Jeff Bezos, clearly sees his company as being not in the book-selling business but in the information-broker business.

1.11   Summary

Global marketing is defined as the firm's commitment to coordinate its marketing activities across national boundaries in order to find and satisfy global customer needs better than the competition does. This implies that the firm is able to:

- develop a global marketing strategy based on similarities and differences between markets;
- exploit the knowledge of the headquarters (home organization) through worldwide diffusion (learning) and adaptations;
- transfer knowledge and 'best practices' from any of its markets and use them in other international markets.

Porter's original value chain model was introduced as a framework model for major parts of this book. In understanding how value is created, it is not enough to look at the firm's internal value chain alone. In most cases the supply and distribution value chains are interconnected, and this whole process needs to be analysed and understood before considering an eventual internationalization of value chain activities. This also involves decisions about configuration and coordination of the worldwide value chain activities.

As a supplement to the traditional (Porter) value chain, the service value chain (based on the so-called 'value shop' concept) has been introduced. Value shops create value by mobilizing resources (people, knowledge and skills) and deploying them to solve specific problems. Value shops are organized around making and executing decisions in the specific service interaction situation with a customer – identifying and assessing service problems or opportunities, developing alternative solutions or approaches, choosing one, executing it and evaluating the results. This model applies to most service-oriented organizations.

Many product companies want to succeed with embedded services: as competitive pressures increasingly commoditize product markets, services will become the main differentiator of *value* creation in coming years. However, companies will need a clearer understanding of the strategic rules of this new game – and will have to integrate the rules into their operations – to realize the promise of these fast-growing businesses.

Today, the right combination of the product value chain and the service value chain is not a sufficient competitive differentiator. Adding 'customer experiences' occurs when a company intentionally uses products in combination with services, to engage individual customers in a way that creates a memorable event that can be characterized in one of four groups: entertainment, educational, aesthetic or escapist.

At the end of the chapter the virtual value chain was introduced as a supplement to the physical value chain, thus using information to create further business value.

CASE STUDY 1.1

Green Toys, Inc.: a manufacturer of eco-friendly toys is going international

In 2006, Robert von Goeben, a venture capitalist and an electronic toy designer in San Francisco, contemplated shifting course again. Instead of making more toys that required electricity and intricate parts, he listened to his wife and created a simpler line that would appeal to parents who identified with the green movement. More and more parents are starting to look at toys like they look at food. A toy used to be a plastic thing and parents did not question what was in it. Now green has gone mainstream, and parents want to know what is in their toys.

In August 2006, Mattel Inc. recalled more than 10 million Chinese-made toys, including the popular Barbie and Polly Pocket toys, because of lead-paint hazards and tiny magnets that could be swallowed. The US government warned parents to make sure that children would not play with any of the recalled toys.

As questions about toy safety made more headlines in 2007 with recall of more than 17 million

Chinese-made toys, von Goeben partnered with former marketing executive Laurie Hyman, a business acquaintance. Green Toys Inc. was profitable from its first year on.

Together Robert von Goeben and Laurie Hyman founded Green Toys Inc. in 2006 and started right away with manufacturing of eco toys from recycled plastic milk jugs.

In November 2013 the private investment firm, The Friend Group (represented by the businessman Howard Friend), bought a majority stake in Green Toys Inc. but still Von Goeben and Hyman maintain their duties until today (February 2016).

The founders of Green Toys Inc.

The two co-founders of Green Toys – Robert von Goeben (responsible for product) and Laurie Hyman (responsible for marketing) – have different backgrounds and competences:

Robert von Goeben was the founder of Propellerhead Studios, a leading Silicon Valley design studio specializing in electronic toys and games. At Propellerhead Studios, he worked with many major toy companies, including Mattel and Wild Planet. Before that, he was the founder and managing director of Starter Fluid, a seed-stage venture capital fund backed by institutional and corporate investors, including Compaq computers and the University of Chicago. Von Goeben's career began in the entertainment industry where he started and managed the online division of Geffen Records. He has an MBA from the University of Southern California and a BA in Mathematics from the State University of New York. He holds two US patents in the field of toys and games.

Laurie Hyman used to work as a marketing executive for several online consumer-marketing companies, including, most recently, Ingenio, a pioneer in combining the power of the internet and

phone to connect buyers and sellers. Before that, she was the first member of the marketing team at Webvan, where she managed relationships with some of the world's largest consumer packaged goods companies, including P&G, Nestlé, Coca-Cola, Kraft, General Mills and Pillsbury. Hyman also served as the director of marketing at Goodcompany.com, one of the internet's first online social networks. She has an MBA from the University of Southern California and a BA in Business from Indiana University.

Green Toys Inc. today

Green Toys Inc. makes a line of classic children's toys constructed from recycled plastic and other environmentally friendly materials. This helps reduce fossil fuel use and greenhouse gas emissions, improving the overall health of the planet. In 2014, the company had a turnover of approximately US$20 million. At that time the average number of employees was 80.

Unlike its half-dozen eco-friendly competitors that manufacture or buy raw materials for their toys overseas, Green Toys contracts only with companies in California. Sourcing locally means burning less fossil fuel and creating or maintaining more US jobs. Green Toys can also track the chemical content of toys better than its counterparts.

Source: Green Toys Inc.

Green Toys' customers and marketing strategy

Green Toys' key customer segment consists of parents between the ages of 25 and 40, and they are predominantly female. The largest part of these mothers is well-educated and online. The whole world of bloggers, especially parents, who are blogging and searching online about products and trends for their children, is huge.

Green Toys' products are about 30 per cent more expensive than similar toys from major players. Green Toys should be able to narrow that price difference by at least two-thirds as the company grows and it can utilize 'economies of scale', though it is unclear how popular its market segment will become. In 2014 eco-friendly toys generated just US$40 million in sales, a fraction of the US$22 billion for the US toy industry as a whole.

Green Toys' products are sold in 5,000 US stores, including Pottery Barn, Barnes & Noble, Whole Food and Buy Buy Baby. Some of the biggest Green Toys retailers are also selling online. Consequently, the majority of the Green Toys' marketing budget is spent online.

Source: Green Toys Inc.

Green Toys' internationalization strategy

Green Toys also has distributors in 35 countries, but until now 90 per cent of Green Toys' sales have been from the US market. Until now Green Toys has had no plans to move production out of the US. However, in the future they do not exclude the possibility of manufacturing abroad with local sourcing of materials.

The following report explains current and future trends in the global toy industry.

The global toy industry

In 2014 the size of the global toy market was US$ 84 billion.

Development of Green Toys' end-customers: the world's children

The global child population has been declining due to falling family sizes: globally, birth rates were 19.6 per 1,000 people in 2010 compared with 21.8 in 2000, while fertility (the average number of children per woman) was 3.0 in 2010 compared with 3.4 in 2000. The world total of children aged 0–14 shrank in the first decade of the new millennium, dropping, on average, by 0.1 per cent per annum. This is a comparatively recent trend, as the child population grew 0.6 per cent per year between 1990 and 2000 and 0.1 per cent per year between 1980 and 1990. As of 2010, 0–14 year-olds made up 26.3 per cent of the global population compared with 35.2 per cent in 1980 (see Table 1).

This trend reflects cultural and social changes towards smaller family sizes in both developed and developing markets. Regionally, Eastern Europe has seen the largest decrease in the child population, at an annual average rate of 2 per cent between 2000 and 2010, which is partly due to large-scale migration to Western Europe and also due to the transition period from communism in the 1990s and 2000s when fertility and life expectancy fell due to economic hardship.

However, many of the world's developing countries still have sizeable and rising child populations. The child population in some developed countries is also rising.

The overall downturn in the child population globally has meant smaller household sizes and greater consumer expenditure per child, which has created more allowance for discretionary spending on non-essentials for children. This has important implications for toys and games companies targeting parents of 0–14 year-olds. The number of 65+ year-olds rose by an average of 2.5 per cent annually from 2000 and 2010 to account for 7.9 per cent of the total population globally. By 2020, this group is forecast to account for just fewer than 10 per cent of the global population.

In absolute terms, Asia-Pacific and the Middle East and Africa are the biggest regions in terms of 0–14 year-olds, followed by Latin America. In 2014, more than 128 million babies were born in the world and Asia-Pacific accounted for more than half. The Philippines, Egypt and Saudi Arabia are the top three countries in terms of birth rates, recording between 23 and 25 per 1,000 inhabitants. Over the period 2009–2014, birth rates declined in most countries, but continued to be high in young fast-growing markets, such as India and South Africa, where there were around 21 births per 1,000 inhabitants in 2014.

By contrast, in the ageing developed markets of Germany and Japan, the birth rate was extremely low, at just eight births per 1,000 inhabitants in 2014. Russia is unusual in that it is one of the very few markets where the birth rate increased substantially over the review period, from 10.0 births per 1,000 inhabitants in 2003 to 13 births per 1,000 inhabitants in 2014.

Between 2004 and 2009, Russia, Spain, Australia and the UK all recorded over 10 per cent increases in their 0–4 year-old populations. Spain was the third country globally with a 15 per cent increase in its 5–9 year-old population in the past five years.

For a number of years, birth rates have been falling around the world, as women wait longer before having children. Young adults can now afford interests and lifestyles that are not compatible with large families, not only in more affluent countries, but also in a number of developing countries. They often choose to postpone childbirth, in favour of building a career or simply enjoying their freedom.

The oldest mothers at first childbirth in the world are in western Europe, specifically the UK, Germany, Switzerland and the Netherlands. By contrast, the

Table 1	The global population by age group, 1980–2020				
Age groups (years)	1980 (%)	1990 (%)	2000 (%)	2010 (%)	2020 (%)
0–14	35.2	32.6	29.8	26.3	24.5
15–64	58.9	61.2	63.2	65.8	65.9
65+	5.9	6.2	7.0	7.9	9.6
Total	100	100	100	100	100

Source: adapted from Euromonitor.com and other public sources.

average age of women at first childbirth in the US is relatively low, at 25 years in 2014. This is partly due to the importance of the Hispanic population, which tends to have larger families from an earlier age.

Spending on Green Toys' target end-consumers: the world's 0–3 year-olds

The distribution of total spending on 0–3 year-olds (baby care, infant clothing, baby food, nappies/diapers and toys) is shown in Table 2.

There are 'two worlds' of spending: the markets of western Europe, North America and Japan where, despite low birth rates, spending is high, and the fast-growing markets of Asia-Pacific, Latin America and Middle East and Africa, where children are plentiful and spending is much lower. The top five countries (Germany, UK, France, Japan and US) all recorded over US$1,500 per-capita spending on 0–3 year-olds.

When fewer babies are born into a family, they are often more cherished, with more money spent on them by both parents and grandparents alike. One of the best examples of this is the so-called 'little emperor' syndrome in China. Children in China tend to get spoiled with toys and clothing when they are young (according to Table 2, toys for 0–3 year-olds represent 26 per cent of total spending for this age group). As they get older they are spoilt in different ways, including with mobile phones, education and leisure activities. That said, there are many, especially in rural areas, who are not spoilt at all.

Many parents in Asia believe that pre-school toys can increase a child's intelligence and improve cognitive ability, benefiting the child at school later on. Most parents in cities pay much more attention to the role of toys and games in supporting their children's education and stimulating their intellectual development, encouraging manufacturers to develop a plethora of toys for the pre-school age group.

China is the most fragmented traditional toys and games market in the world. Although overall unit prices recorded a decline in 2014, thanks to the 'little emperors', more expensive toys have been gaining ground. Almost all multinational players, including Mattel, Namco Bandai, LEGO and Hasbro, enjoyed very high growth in their sales in China.

In countries where the average number of children per household is higher than one, spending on traditional toys and games per child does not exceed US$50 in a given year.

Overall, the older the average age of a woman at childbirth, the higher the spend on traditional toys and games per child. As modern mothers continue to work, for various reasons, the limits on parental time require products that can fill this gap.

Single-parent households tend to be among the poorest, creating a need for cheaper products. Low-priced, high-volume toys tend to find success in markets where single-parent households are more common.

Distribution of toys

Supermarkets/hypermarkets have continued to expand their toy and game offerings and their private label portfolios. However, sales of toys and games through store-based retailers are being affected by the growing popularity of new distribution channels, such as the internet retailing and TV home shopping.

In North America, the strength of retail giants WalMart and Target greatly contributed to the large share held by mixed retailers in 2009. The increase in Wal-Mart's market share slowed in 2014 as supermarkets, drug stores, hardware retailers and online outlets expanded their offerings of traditional toys and games.

Store-based retailers are increasingly backing up their brick-and-mortar sales efforts by offering online shopping. They have found that online sites help them to promote niche brands and gain wider market

Table 2	Breakdown of average total spending on 0–3 year-olds, by product category, in 2014									
	France (%)	UK (%)	Germany (%)	Russia (%)	US (%)	Brazil (%)	South Africa (%)	China (%)	Japan (%)	India (%)
Baby care	5	5	5	6	4	18	3	4	5	12
Infant clothing	18	35	30	12	35	16	30	10	20	6
Baby food	35	18	20	37	22	18	22	40	18	45
Nappies/diapers	22	26	27	37	22	40	40	20	40	15
Toys	20	16	18	8	17	8	5	26	17	22
Totals	100	100	100	100	100	100	100	100	100	100

Source: adapted from Euromonitor and other public sources.

exposure. Online sites also help consumers compare prices and features of new toys and games. In Japan, the rapid growth of internet retailing has helped drive sales of the newest video game releases.

The convenience of home shopping appeals to a wide range of consumers, especially older consumers. For distributors this channel is growing in importance, as it helps build brand image.

Generally there is an increasing share of grocery retailers in the toys and games sector in many countries. Grocery retailing is slowly becoming the most popular channel in the western European retail sector.

Italians still prefer making in-store product purchases. The only significant development in the country's distribution channels over the past 10 years has been the rise of grocery retailers, who have increasingly varied their non-grocery offerings, including toys and games. In France, the fastest-growing channel has been leisure and personal goods retailers, with growth driven by the development of specialized toys and video games centres. Approximately 800 specialized toys and games stores opened between 2010 and 2014, an indication of the sector's dynamism.

The leading toy distribution channel in Germany is also leisure and personal goods retailers. Though online shopping has increased in Germany, most consumers still prefer to see and feel the products they are buying. In addition, consumers welcome the opportunity to get professional opinions and advice on product quality and features from in-store staff.

In Russia specialist retailers are developing rapidly. The most popular places to buy toys and games are retail chains, followed by shopping centres. Specialist distribution channels are more popular in the main cities of Russia where the population is generally, 1 million and more. In smaller cities, non-store distribution is still popular.

In Latin America, hypermarkets and other grocery retailers enjoyed increased toy sales, especially during the end-of-the-year holidays and Children's Day, when important advertising campaigns are conducted and discounts and special deals are increasingly offered.

In Brazil, specialist stores control an important part of the market due to the expansion of toy stores in large cities. The concentration of this format has strengthened the competitive environment, encouraged a greater variety in product offerings and lessened the impact of the seasonality on sales.

Generally, in Latin America specialist toy retailers remain the most important channel, based on their offering a greater variety of products. Also, they are easy to find as they are located in a greater number of retail venues, particularly shopping centres.

Competition in the toy industry

The world's top 10 toys and games companies accounted for nearly half of the global total value of sales from 2010 to 2015. Mattel, LEGO and Namco Bandai held the top three positions.

Summary and future trends

Infant and pre-school toys will remain recession-proof as parents continue to invest in their children's enjoyment and education.

Environmentally friendly, hazard-free features will continue to be among the main selling points of traditional toys and games.

Multinational companies will weather the storm brought about by the global financial crisis. Consolidation is expected in the sector, with mergers and acquisitions of small and independent companies likely.

Sales via internet retailers are expected to grow dramatically over the forecast period, particularly in light of the demise of small and independent toys and games retailers.

Based on this case and the toy industry trends, answer the following questions.

QUESTIONS

1. What are the key success factors in the world toy industry?

2. What are Green Toys' key competitive advantages in the international toy market?

3. Should Green Toys Inc. consider a higher degree of international expansion of their products?

4. If yes, which countries/regions should they target and how?

Source: based on www.greentoys.com and other public sources.

CASE STUDY 1.2

Hunter Boot Ltd: The iconic British brand is moving into exclusive fashion

The Hunter boot brand (www.hunter-boot.com) has become a symbol of British country life and celebrity fashion. Hunter boots, designed over 150 years ago, were originally created to deal with Britain's rugged and unpredictable weather. Today, Hunter is firmly established as a fashion brand beloved by Hollywood celebrities.

Arthur Wellesley, the first Duke of Wellington, instructed his shoemaker, Hoby of St James Street, London, to modify his eighteenth-century boot. They designed the boots in soft calfskin leather, removed the trim and made the cut closer around the leg. It was hard to wear the new boots in battle but it was said that the Duke of Wellington wore the boots at the famous Battle of Waterloo in 1815. The boots were dubbed 'Wellingtons' or 'wellies' and the name stuck.

Wellingtons quickly caught on with patriotic British gentlemen eager to emulate their war hero. The original Wellington boots were made of leather; however, in America, where there was more experimentation in shoemaking, producers were beginning to manufacture using rubber. One such entrepreneur, Mr Henry Lee Norris, moved to Scotland in search of a suitable site to produce rubber footwear. Eventually he found it on the farm of the Castle Mill in Edinburgh. Norris began his boot-making company, the North British Rubber Company (the company changed its name to the Hunter Rubber Company in 2004), in 1856. Committed to fit, comfort, durability and performance, Hunter Wellington boots bear two rare and coveted stamps of approval of the British royal family.

Production of the Wellington boot was dramatically boosted with the advent of World War I, due to the demand for a sturdy boot suitable for the conditions in flooded trenches. This made the wellies a functional necessity.

By the end of World War I, the North British Rubber Company had produced more than 1.8 million pairs of boots for soldiers. Shoe production ran 24 hours a day.

Again the Wellington made an important contribution during World War II. At the outbreak of war in September 1939, although trench warfare was not a feature, those forces assigned the task of clearing Holland of the enemy had to work in terrible flooded conditions. By the end of the war, the Wellington had become popular among men, women and children for wear in wet weather. The boot had developed to become far roomier with a thick sole and rounded toe. Also, with the rationing of shoes at that time, labourers began to use them for daily work.

The company's most famous welly, the original Green Wellington, was made over 50 years ago in the winter of 1955. It was launched alongside the Royal Hunter – another boot that remains in Hunter's range today.

From 1966 to 2005 a number of ownership changes took place and, in 2006, the Hunter Rubber Company was placed into administration as a result of cash flow problems. In spite of a reported turnover of over £5 million, accountants from KPMG said the firm suffered from high manufacturing costs, including fuel costs, and made a loss from the expansion of its business to the US. Hunter reported a loss of £600,000 from September 2003 to the end of February 2005, when it had a net debt of £2.03 million.

In 2006, a private consortium led by Lord Marland, Peter Mullen and Julian Taylor bought Hunter out of administration and Hunter Boot Ltd was born. After rapid restructuring of the company, new supply routes and distribution partners were found in the UK and the US and the Hunter portfolio was rationalized to core products exhibiting the key skills and tradition of the company.

Hunter re-established itself as a major player in the traditional country and leisure footwear market in the UK in the aftermath of the 2006 acquisition and positioned itself as a strong contender in the US – opening showrooms on Seventh Avenue in New York

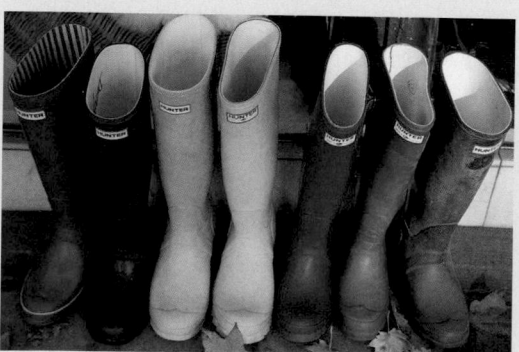

Source: Jeffrey Blackler/Alamy Images.

and Carnaby Street in London. A new management team was also put in place.

One Hunter Wellington tall boot is made from 28 individual parts. Each part is individually tailored and assembled by hand to support specific parts of the foot, calf and ankle. Hunters continue to be made and finished by hand from natural rubber. Because of this degree of 'handmade' in the production of Hunter boots, the management moved manufacturing from Scotland to China to cut production cost. Retail prices were also increased by 20 per cent, and modern ranges in a selection of colours and textures were added.

A major breakthrough for Hunter in the realm of fashion, as opposed to farms, came in 2006 when Kate Moss was seen wearing an Original pair in black at the Glastonbury music festival. Since then, the Hunter boot has become a familiar sight among celebrities, on catwalks and on high streets, as well as in the countryside.

In September 2008, following the 2008 Olympics in Beijing, China, Hunter Boot Ltd sent specially made gold Wellington boots to every member of the Great Britain Olympic team who had won a gold medal at the Games.

In 2010 the UK Prime Minister David Cameron bought pink and purple pairs of Hunter boots for his US trip, as gifts for Barack Obama's daughters.

Hunter Boot Ltd today

Since the downturn in 2006, Hunter has expanded its sales and profits rapidly, as seen in Table 1.

Hunter has since seen strong growth with international distribution in 30 countries.

Hunter is moving into alliances with exclusive fashion designers

In January 2009, Hunter announced that it would be collaborating with London-based luxury fashion designer Jimmy Choo for a limited-edition black Wellington boot, embossed with signature Jimmy Choo crocodile print and containing gold rivets and a leopard-print lining. Another boot was then launched in 2011. The boots costs £250 and were sold exclusively online at www.jimmychoo.com (the original version normally costs around £80).

Jimmy Choo and Hunter Boot Ltd received a tremendous reaction from customers; the online waiting list opened on 1 May, and by 16 May more than 4,000 fashion-conscious customers had already joined it. Today, the luxurious Wellington boots have become a classic lifestyle item at Jimmy Choo and can be purchased regardless of the season, and not only in traditional black, but in several variations.

In March 2012, J. Mendel and Hunter – two iconic brands dating back to the nineteenth century – joined forces in a special collaboration to produce the most glamorous of Wellington boots: exclusive to North America, these limited-edition boots brought together the sumptuous look and feel of J. Mendel with the timeless functionality of Hunter Boot. The boots went on sale in November 2012 and retailed at from US$585 (£366) to US$795 (£497) at Saks, Nordstrom, Gorsuch and hunter-boot.com.

Hunter Boot Ltd has always been highly dependent on the celebrity factor. It has become something of a sport to collect photographs of celebrities wearing different Hunter boots. Here are some examples of the Hunter brand preferred by some celebrities:

- Jennifer Aniston – Original Black Hunter wellies
- Drew Barrymore – Original Navy Hunter wellies
- Kate Moss – Original Black Hunter wellies
- Sandra Bullock – Original Navy Hunter wellies
- Alexandra Burke – Short Original Black Hunter boots
- Kings of Leon (Group) – WaterAid Hunter wellies

Table 1	Hunter Boot Ltd's financial performance, 2011–2013		
	Millions of £		
	2013	**2012**	**2011**
Sales (% for export)	81.6 (62%)	74.4 (57%)	77.7 (53%)
Cost of sales	39.5	37.1	39.4
Gross profit	42.1	37.3	38.3
Pre-tax profit	14.6	13.8	22.1
Profit after tax	10.4	10.4	15.9
Number of employees	125	85	73

Source: based on various data on www.hunter-boot.com.

Source: Buzz Photo/Rex Features.

- Angelina Jolie – Original Red Hunter wellies
- Madonna – Original Navy Hunter wellies

- Gwyneth Paltrow – Original Aubergine Hunter wellies
- Kelly Rowland – Original Red Hunter wellies

QUESTIONS

1. What are the main reasons for the recent international marketing success of the Hunter Boots?

2. Recently Hunter has added outerwear (leather footwear and hand-bags) to their international product range. What are the pros and cons of extending the product range in this way? Should Hunter Boots Ltd include further products like eyewear and watches?

Sources: based on www.Hunter-boot.com; bevan2bade's Blog: 'Hunter Wellington Boots and Celebrities' (http://bevan2bader.blogs. experienceproject.com/770875.html)

VIDEO CASE STUDY 1.3 Nivea

download from **www.pearsoned.co.uk/hollensen**

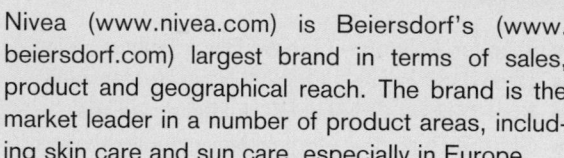

Nivea (www.nivea.com) is Beiersdorf's (www. beiersdorf.com) largest brand in terms of sales, product and geographical reach. The brand is the market leader in a number of product areas, including skin care and sun care, especially in Europe.

Questions

1. Which degree of market responsiveness and global coordination/integration does Nivea represent?

2. Do you think that the Nivea Vital commercial (shown in the video) is able to cross borders without any adaptation? If not, which elements should be adapted?

3. Which marketing problems does Nivea anticipate when penetrating the US market?

Source: Nivea and Beiersdorf UK Ltd.

For further resources, see this book's website at **www.pearsoned.co.uk/hollensen**

Questions for discussion

1. What is the reason for the 'convergence of orientation' in LSEs and SMEs?
2. How can an SME compensate for its lack of resources and expertise in global marketing when trying to enter export markets?
3. What are the main differences between global marketing and marketing in the domestic context?
4. Explain the main advantages of centralizing upstream activities and decentralizing downstream activities.
5. Explain how a combination of the product value chain and the service value chain can create further customer value.
6. How is the virtual value chain different from the conventional value chain?

References

Asugman, G., Johnson, J.L. and McCullough, J. (1997) 'The role of after-sales service in international marketing', *Journal of International Marketing*, 5(4), pp. 11–28.

Atwal, G. and Williams, A. (2009) 'Luxury brand marketing – the experience is everything', *Brand Management*, 16(5/6), pp. 338–346.

Auguste, B.G., Harmon, E.P. and Pandit, V. (2006) 'The right service strategies for product companies', *McKinsey Quarterly*, 1 March, pp. 10–15.

Bacon, J. (2015) 'How to avoid your message getting lost in translation', *Marketing Week*, 18 June, pp. 23–25.

Bailey, C.K., Knepler, B., and Vaanlombeek, P. (2015) 'Creating flexible global brnads in federated organisations: A case study from a global not-for-profit', *Journal of Brand Strategy*, 3(4), pp. 350–356.

Beinhocker, E., Davis, I. and Mendonca, L. (2009) '10 trends you have to watch', *Harvard Business Review*, July–August 2009, pp. 55–60.

Bellin, J.B. and Pham, C.T. (2007) 'Global expansion: balancing a uniform performance culture with local conditions', *Strategy & Leadership*, 35(6), pp. 44–50.

Blomstermo, A., Sharma, D.D. and Sallis, J. (2006) 'Choice of foreign market entry mode in service firms', *International Marketing Review*, 23(2), pp. 211–229.

Bonaccorsi, A. (1992) 'On the relationship between firm size and export intensity', *Journal of International Business Studies*, fourth quarter, pp. 605–635.

Cafferata, R. and Mensi, R. (1995) 'The role of information in the internationalization of SMEs: a typological approach', *International Small Business Journal*, 13(3), pp. 35–46.

Chakravarthy, B.S. and Perlmutter, H.V. (1985) 'Strategic planning for a global business', *Columbia Journal of World Business*, 20(2), pp. 3–10.

Douglas, S.P. and Craig, C.S. (2011) 'Convergence and divergence: developing a semiglobal marketing strategy', *Journal of International Marketing*, 19(1), pp. 82–101.

Friedman, T. (2005) *The World is Flat*. Farrar, Straus and Giroux, New York.

Frost, R. (2006) 'Global Packaging: What's the difference?', www.Brandchannel.com, 16 January 2006.

Ghemawat, P. (2011a) *World 3.0: Global Prosperity and How to Achieve It*. Harvard Business Review Press, Boston, MA.

Ghemawat, P. (2011b) 'The cosmopolitan corporation', *Harvard Business Review*, May, pp. 92–99.

Ghemawat, P. (2008) 'Globalization is an option not an imperative. Or, why the world is not flat', *Ivey Business Journal*, Jan–Feb, 72(1), pp. 1–11.

Ghemawat, P. (2007) 'Managing differences – the central challenge of global strategy', *Harvard Business Review*, March, pp. 59–68.

Gupta, A.K. and Govindarajan, V. (2001) 'Converting global presence into global competitive advantage', *Academy of Management Executive*, 15(2), pp. 45–56.

Hollensen, S. and Schimmelpfennig, C. (2015) 'Developing a glocalisation strategy – experiences from Henkel's product launches in Middle East and Europe, *Journal of Brand Strategy*, 4(3), pp. 201–211.

Johnson, G. (1988) 'Rethinking incrementalism', *Strategic Management Journal*, 9, pp. 75–91.

Johansson, M. and Jonsson, A. (2012) 'The package logic: a study on value creation and knowledge flows', *European Management Journal*, 30, pp. 1–17.

Julien, P.E., Joyal, A., Deshaies, L. and Ramangalahy, C. (1997) 'A typology of strategic behaviour among small and medium-sized exporting businesses: a case study', *International Small Business Journal*, 15(2), pp. 33–49.

Knight, G. (2000) 'Entrepreneurship and marketing strategy: the SME under globalization', *Journal of International Marketing*, 8(2), pp. 12–32.

Lung-Huang, T. and Liu, F.H. (2014) 'Formation of augmented reality – interactive technology's persuasive effects from the perspective of experiential value', *Internet Research*, 24(1), pp. 82–109.

Marchand, D.A. (1999) 'Hard IM choices for senior managers', Part 10 of 'Your guide to mastering information management', *Financial Times*, 5 April.

Mintzberg, H. (1987) 'The strategy concept I: five Ps for strategy', *California Management Review*, 30(1), pp. 11–24.

Mintzberg, H. and Waters, A. (1985) 'Of strategies, deliberate and emergent', *Strategic Management Journal*, 6, pp. 257–272.

Perlmutter, H.V. (1969) 'The tortuous evolution of the multinational corporation', *Columbia Journal of World Business*, 9(January–February), pp. 9–18.

Pine, B.J. (2015) 'How B2B companies create economic value by designing experiences and transformations for their customers', *Strategy & Leadership*, 43(3), pp. 2–6.

Pine, B.J. and Gilmore, J.H. (1998) 'Welcome to the experience economy', *Harvard Business Review*, July/August, pp. 97–105.

Porter, M.E. (1986) 'Competition in global industries: a conceptual framework', in Porter, M.E. (ed.), *Competition in Global Industries*, Harvard Business School Press, Boston, MA.

Quinn, J.B. (1980) 'Strategies for change: logical incrementalism', *Sloan Management Review*, 20(1), pp. 7–21.

Rayport, J.F. and Sviokla, J.J. (1996) 'Exploiting the virtual value chain', *McKinsey Quarterly*, 1, pp. 21–36.

Santos, J.F.P. and Williamson, P.J. (2015) 'The New Mission for Multinationals', *MIT Sloan Management Review*, 56(4), pp. 44–54.

Segal-Horn, S. (2002) 'Global firms: heroes or villains? How and why companies globalize', *European Business Journal*, 14(1), pp. 8–19.

Sheth, J.N. and Parvatiyar, A. (2001) 'The antecedents and consequences of integrated global marketing', *International Marketing Review*, 18(1), pp. 16–29.

Solberg, C.A. (1997) 'A framework for analysis of strategy development in globalizing markets', *Journal of International Marketing*, 5(1), pp. 9–30.

Stabell, C.B. and Fjeldstad, Ø.B. (1998) 'Configuring value for competitive advantage: on chains, shops, and networks', *Strategic Management Journal*, 19, pp. 413–437.

Svensson, G. (2001) '"Glocalization" of business activities: a "glocal strategy" approach', *Management Decision*, 39(1), pp. 6–18.

Svensson, G. (2002) 'Beyond global marketing and the globalization of marketing activities', *Management Decision*, 40(6), pp. 574–583.

Turner, C. and Gardiner, P.D. (2007) 'De-internationalization and global strategy: the case of British Telecommunications (BT)', *Journal of Business & Industrial Marketing*, 22(7), pp. 489–497.

CHAPTER 2
Initiation of internationalization

Contents

Case studies

Learning objectives

After studying this chapter you should be able to:

- Discuss the reason (motives) why firms go international
- Explain the difference between proactive and reactive motives
- Analyse the triggers of export initiation
- Explain the difference between internal and external triggers of export initiation
- Describe different factors hindering export initiation
- Discuss the critical barriers in the process of exporting.

2.1   Introduction

Internationalization occurs when a firm expands its research and development (R&D), production, selling and other business activities into international markets. In many larger firms, internationalization may occur in a relatively continuous fashion, with the firm undertaking various internationalization stages on various foreign expansion projects simultaneously, in incremental steps, over a period of time. However, for small and medium-sized enterprises (SMEs), internationalization is often a relatively discrete process; that is, one in which management regards each internationalization venture as distinct and individual.

In the pre-internationalization stages, SME managers use information to achieve enough relevant knowledge to initiate internationalization (Freeman, 2002). Figure 2.1 illustrates the different stages in pre-internationalization, and the rest of this chapter refers to the stages in this figure.

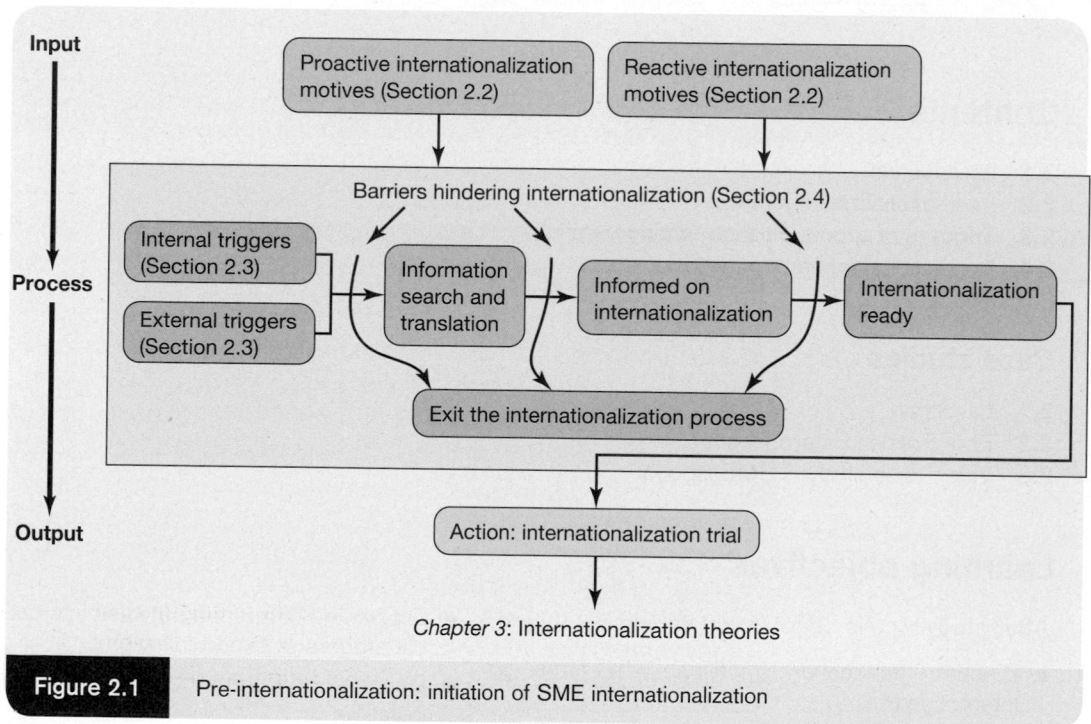

Figure 2.1   Pre-internationalization: initiation of SME internationalization

2.2   Internationalization motives

The fundamental reason for exporting, in most firms, is to make money. But, as in most business activities, one factor alone rarely accounts for any given action. Usually a mixture of factors results in firms taking steps in a given direction.

The discussion of internationalization motives can be traced back to the work of John H. Dunning, who distinguished between four main motives (Dunning, 1993; Benito, 2015):

1. Market-seeking: companies go abroad to find new customers.
2. Efficiency-seeking: companies go abroad to lower the costs associated with performing economic activities and/or with the aim of rationalizing their already existing operations in various locations.

3. Resource-seeking: companies venture abroad to access resources that are not readily available at home or that can be obtained at a lower cost abroad.

4. Strategic asset-seeking: companies go abroad to obtain strategic assets (tangible or intangible), which may be critical to their long-term strategy but that are not available at home.

Internationalization motives
The fundamental reasons – proactive and reactive – for internationalization.

Table 2.1 provides an overview of the major **internationalization motives**. They are differentiated into proactive and reactive motives. *Proactive motives* represent stimuli to attempt strategy change, based on the firm's interest in exploiting unique competences (e.g. a special technological knowledge) or market possibilities. *Reactive motives* indicate that the firm reacts to pressures or threats in its home market or in foreign markets and adjusts passively to them by changing its activities over time.

Let us take a closer look at each export motive.

Table 2.1	Major motives for starting export
Proactive motives	**Reactive motives**
• Profit and growth goals • Managerial urge • Technology competence/unique product • Foreign market opportunities/market information • Economies of scale • Tax benefits	• Competitive pressures • Domestic market: small and saturated • Overproduction/excess capacity • Unsolicited foreign orders • Extend sales of seasonal products • Proximity to international customers/psychological distance

Source: adapted from *International Marketing and Export Management,* 2nd ed., Addison Wesley (Albaum, G., Strandskov, J., Duerr, E. and Dowd, L. 1994), p. 31, reprinted by permission of Pearson Education Ltd.

Proactive motives

Profit and growth goals

The desire for short-term profit is especially important for SMEs that are at the stage of an initial interest in exporting. The desire to grow may also be of particular importance in a firm's decision to start exporting.

Increasing profits on a longer term can result from selling more or buying better and/or cheaper. If the company is expanding abroad to sell more, it exploits its existing resources and capabilities to obtain access to larger international markets and increased revenues. In the case of buying better and/or cheaper the company does so by accessing the comparative advantage of the host country and utilizing the competitive advantages of companies there. That would be the case if the company chooses to reduce operations in the home market and increase operations abroad, for example by placing production in a low-cost country.

Over time, the firm's attitude towards growth will be influenced by the type of feedback received from past efforts. For example, the profitability of exporting may determine management's attitude towards it. Of course, the perceived profitability, when planning to enter international markets, is often quite different from the profitability actually attained. Initial profitability may be quite low, particularly in international start-up operations. The gap between perception and reality may be particularly large when the firm has not previously engaged in international market activities. Despite thorough planning, sudden influences often shift the profit picture substantially. For example, a sudden shift in exchange rates may drastically alter profit forecasts, even though they were based on careful market evaluation.

The stronger the firm's motivation to grow, the greater will be the activities it generates, including search activity for new possibilities, in order to find means of fulfilling growth and profit ambitions.

EXHIBIT 2.1 Jägermeister: the famous herbal liqueur is going global as a result of 'managerial urge' in the family-owned company

The herbal liqueur Jägermeister was created by Curt Mast in Wolfenbüttel, Germany, almost 100 years ago. Taking over his father's vinegar production plant in 1918, Mast changed the direction of the company and began dealing in wine. He also began experimenting with the production of spirits. By 1934 he had hit upon a liqueur recipe made with 56 herbs, blossoms, roots and fruits.

Mast was an enthusiastic hunter. Translated literally, *Jägermeister* means 'hunting master', combining Jäger (hunter) and *Meister* (master, in the sense of an accomplished professional). The Jägermeister logo, a stag and gleaming cross, was derived from Saint Hubertus, the patron saint of hunters.

Jägermeister is a type of liqueur called Kräuterlikör (herbal liqueur). It is similar to other central European liqueurs, such as Kümmel and Ratzeputz from Germany, Gammel Dansk from Denmark, Unicum from Hungary, Becherovka from the Czech Republic, Fernet Branca from Italy, Demanovka from the Slovakia and Pelinkovac from Croatia. In contrast to those beverages, Jägermeister has a sweeter taste.

In the 1960s, the popularity of Jägermeister grew, leading to a growing export market in Scandinavia, Austria, the Benelux region and the US. Over time it has conquered markets as far away as South America, Africa, Australia and Asia.

Jägermeister expanded its global sales from 87.1 million bottles (0.7 litre) in 2011 to 89.2 million bottles in 2012. This corresponds to an increase of just under 2.5 per cent compared with 2011, making Jägermeister number 7 on the influential Impact International ranking list of the top 100 premium spirits. Jägermeister thus continued to be the world's best-selling liqueur brand and is the only German spirit in the top 70 in this ranking. In 2012, Jägermeister was marketed in over 90 countries with Mast-Jägermeister SE employing around 600 people. A family-owned company, over the years the globalization of Jägermeister has been driven by the 'managerial urge' of its senior staff, as discussed in the main text.

Source: Owen Sweeney/Rex Features.

In 2012, today about 80 per cent of the total sales of Jägermeister came from outside Germany. Jägermeister's biggest market was the US (where it is the best-selling imported liqueur), followed by the UK (where 6 million bottles were sold in 2012) and Germany (its home market).

While the product, the vivid green bottle and the logo remain the same in all markets, the brand image may be different. In much of Europe, the drink remains familiar to many as a digestif, while in the Netherlands traditional pubs serve it from a unique bottle to fit the round cooling racks behind the bar. In the US, Jägermeister is served sub-ice-cold on tap and in the UK consumers often order it as a shot mixed with Red Bull.

Jägermeister's international marketing is driven by sponsorship activities. Generally Jägermeister does only a little international mass advertising. Instead the brand relies on trade promotions (in bars, etc.), experimental marketing and sponsoring activities.

From the 1970s until 2000, the Jägermeister brand developed an association with motor racing, and they have sponsored various European racing teams, primarily those fielding BMWs and Porsches. In the 1970s, Jägermeister was associated with German football, especially the Bundesliga (the Eintracht Braunschweig team).

In the UK, Jägermeister mostly associates itself with the rock music scene, sponsoring rock concerts as well as attending rock music festivals throughout the summer months, using these marketing events to drive trials. The core target are persons socializing with their friends and having a good time. Jägermeister hopes to reach more customers within its 20–30 year-old target group but also attract new (older) drinkers, educating them about the 'perfect ice-cold shot' which it believes represents the biggest growth opportunity for the brand.

Jägermeister aims to develop its brand abroad by taking account of cultural and

Source: Leonard Zhukovsky/Shutterstock.com.

country-specific circumstances in each market, working principally with local distribution partners so that marketing concepts are tailored to the needs of the market. Jägermeister associates the brand with rock music in Europe, the US and Australia; for example, in the US, Jägermeister became popular through sponsoring the 'Jägermeister Music Tour' and through association with heavy metal bands such as Metallica, Mötley Crüe, Pantera, Megadeth and Slayer.

Jägermeister also sponsors more than 160 rock bands there. Jägermeister supplies the bands with giveaway items, such as posters, T-shirts and hats. The items are branded with the Jägermeister logo and the name of the band. Jägermeister also encourages the bands to mention the drink between the sets, enjoying a shot on the stage, hanging up a few banners or wearing a T-shirt.

Source: based on www.jagermusic.com, www.jagermeister.com; http//newsroom.jagermeister.de.

Managerial urge

Managerial urge
Managers' commitment and motivation that reflect the desire and enthusiasm to drive internationalization forward.

Managerial urge is a motivation that reflects the desire, drive and enthusiasm of management towards global marketing activities. This enthusiasm can exist simply because managers like to be part of a firm that operates internationally. Further, it can often provide a good reason for international travel. Often, however, the managerial urge to internationalize is simply a reflection of general entrepreneurial motivation – of a desire for continuous growth and market expansion.

Managerial attitudes play a critical role in determining the exporting activities of the firm. In SMEs, export decisions may be the province of a single decision-maker; in large-scale enterprises (LSEs), they might be made by a decision-making unit. Irrespective of the number of people involved in the export decision-making process, the choice of a foreign market entry strategy is still dependent on the decision-maker's perceptions of foreign markets, expectations concerning these markets and the company's capability of entering them.

The internationalization process may also be encouraged by the cultural socialization of the managers. Managers who either were born or have the experience of living or travelling abroad may be expected to be more internationally minded than other managers. Prior occupation in exporting companies, or membership in trade and professional associations, may also reinforce key decision-makers' perceptions and evaluations of foreign environments.

Technology competence/unique product

A firm may produce goods or services that are not widely available from international competitors or may have made technological advances in a specialized field. Again, real and perceived advantages should be differentiated. Many firms believe that their products or services are unique, even though this may not be the case in the international market. If products or technology are unique, however, they can certainly provide a sustainable competitive edge and result in major business success abroad. One issue to consider is how long such a technological or product advantage will continue. Historically, a firm with a competitive edge could count on being the sole supplier to foreign markets for many years after entry. In recent times, however, this type of advantage has shrunk dramatically because of competing technologies and a frequent lack of international patent protection.

However, a firm producing superior products is more likely to receive enquiries from foreign markets because of the perceived competence of its offerings. Several dimensions in the product offering affect the probability that a potential buyer will be exposed to export stimuli. Furthermore, if a company has developed unique competences in its domestic market, the possibilities of spreading unique assets to overseas markets may be very high, because the opportunity costs of exploiting these assets in other markets will be very low.

Foreign market opportunities/market information

It is evident that market opportunities act as stimuli only if the firm has, or is capable of securing, those resources necessary to respond to the opportunities. As market entry is costly and risky, decision-makers are likely to consider a rather limited number of foreign market opportunities in planning their foreign entry. Moreover, such decision-makers are likely to explore first those overseas market opportunities perceived as having some similarity with the opportunities in their home market (Benito, 2015).

From time to time, certain overseas markets grow spectacularly, providing tempting opportunities for expansion-minded firms. The attraction of the South-east Asian markets is based on their economic successes, while the attraction of the eastern European markets is rooted in their new-found political freedoms and desire to develop trade and economic relationships with countries in western Europe, North America and Japan. Other countries that are likely to increase in market attractiveness as key internal changes occur include the People's Republic of China and South Africa.

Specialized marketing knowledge or access to information can distinguish an exporting firm from its competitors. This includes knowledge about foreign customers, marketplaces or market situations that is not widely shared by other firms. Such specialized knowledge may result from particular insights based on a firm's international research, special contacts a firm may have, or simply being in the right place at the right time (e.g. recognizing a good business situation during a vacation trip). Past marketing success can be a strong motivator for future marketing behaviour. Competence in one or more of the major marketing activities will often be a sufficient catalyst for a company to begin or expand exports.

Economies of scale – learning curve

In this situation, the company exploits the resources and capabilities that form the basis for its competitive advantage at home, transferring them abroad and benefiting from economies of scale (Cuervo-Cazurra et al., 2015).

Becoming a participant in global marketing activities may enable the firm to increase its output and therefore climb more rapidly on the learning curve. Ever since the Boston Consulting Group showed that a doubling of output can reduce production costs by up to

30 per cent, this effect has been very much sought. Increased production for the international market can therefore also help in reducing the cost of production for domestic sales and make the firm more competitive domestically as well. This effect often results in seeking market share as a primary objective of firms (see Exhibits 1.2 and 2.1 as examples of this). At an initial level of internationalization this may mean an increased search for export markets; later on it can result in opening foreign subsidiaries and foreign production facilities.

EXHIBIT 2.2 Global marketing and economies of scale in Japanese firms

Japanese firms exploit foreign market opportunities by using a penetration pricing strategy – a low entry price to build up market share and establish a long-term dominant market position. They accept losses in the early years, as they view it as an investment in long-term market development. This can be achieved because much of Japanese industry (especially the *keiretsu* type of organization) is supported or owned by banks or other financial institutions with a much lower cost of capital.

Furthermore, because of the lifetime employment system, labour cost is regarded as a fixed expense, not a variable as it is in the West. Since all marginal labour cost will be at the entry salary level, raising volume is the only way to increase productivity rapidly. As a result, market share, not profitability, is the primary concept in Japanese firms, where scale of operation and experience allow economies of scale, which also help to reduce distribution costs. The international trading companies typically take care of international sales and marketing, allowing the Japanese firm to concentrate on economies of scale, resulting in lower cost per unit.

Source: Genestre *et al.* (1995).

Through exporting, fixed costs arising from administration, facilities, equipment, staff work and R&D can be spread over more units. For some companies a condition for exploiting scale effects on foreign markets to the fullest extent is the possibility of standardizing the marketing mix internationally. For others, however, standardized marketing is not necessary for scale economies.

Tax benefits

Tax benefits can also play a major motivating role. In the US, a tax mechanism called the Foreign Sales Corporation (FSC) has been instituted to assist exporters. It is in conformity with international agreements and provides firms with certain tax deferrals. Tax benefits allow the firm either to offer its products at a lower cost in foreign markets or to accumulate a higher profit. This may therefore tie in closely with the profit motivation.

However, anti-dumping laws enforced by the World Trade Organization (WTO) punish foreign producers for selling their products on local markets at very low prices, in order to protect local producers. Every country that has signed the WTO agreement (and most countries have signed) must abide by these laws.

Reactive motives

Competitive pressures

A prime form of reactive motivation is reaction to competitive pressures. A firm may fear losing domestic market share to competing firms that have benefited from economies of scale gained by global marketing activities. Further, it may fear losing foreign markets permanently to domestic competitors that decide to focus on these markets, knowing that market share is most easily retained by the firm that obtains it initially. Quick entry may result in similarly quick withdrawal once the firm recognizes that its preparations have been insufficient. In addition to this, knowing that other firms, particularly competitors, are internationalizing provides a strong incentive to internationalize. Competitors are an important external factor stimulating internationalization. Coca-Cola became international much earlier than Pepsi did, but there is no doubt whatever that Coca-Cola's move into overseas markets influenced Pepsi to move in the same direction.

Domestic market: small and saturated

A company may be pushed into exporting because of a small home market potential. For some firms, domestic markets may be unable to sustain sufficient economies of scale and scope, and these companies automatically include export markets as part of their market entry strategy. This type of behaviour is likely for industrial products that have few, easily identified customers located throughout the world, or for producers of specialized consumer goods with small national segments in many countries.

A saturated domestic market, whether measured in sales volume or market share, has a similar motivating effect. Products marketed domestically by the firm may be in the declining stage of the product life cycle. Instead of attempting a push-back of the life cycle process, or in addition to such an effort, firms may opt to prolong the product life cycle by expanding the market. In the past, such efforts were often met with success, as customers in many developing countries only gradually reached a level of need and sophistication already attained by customers in industrialized nations. Some developing nations are still often in need of products for which the demand in the industrialized world is already on the decline. In this way, firms can use the international market to prolong the life cycle of their product (see also Chapter 11 for further discussion).

Many US appliance and car manufacturers initially entered international markets because of what they viewed as near-saturated domestic markets. US producers of asbestos products found the domestic market legally closed to them but, because some overseas markets had more lenient consumer protection laws, they continued to produce for overseas markets.

Another perspective on market saturation is also relevant for understanding why firms may expand overseas. Home market saturation suggests that unused productive resources (such as production and managerial slack) exist within the firm. Production slack is a stimulus for securing new market opportunities, and managerial slack can provide those knowledge resources required for collecting, interpreting and using market information.

Overproduction/excess capacity

If a firm's domestic sales of a product are below expectations, the inventory can be above desired levels. This situation can be the trigger for starting export sales via short-term price cuts on inventory products. As soon as the domestic market demand returns to previous levels, global marketing activities are curtailed or even terminated. Firms that have used such a strategy may encounter difficulties when trying to employ it again, because many foreign customers are not interested in temporary or sporadic business relationships. This reaction from abroad may well lead to a decrease in the importance of this motivation over time.

In some situations, however, excess capacity can be a powerful motivation. If equipment for production is not fully utilized, firms may see expansion into the international market as an ideal possibility for achieving broader distribution of fixed costs. Alternatively, if all fixed costs are assigned to domestic production, the firm can penetrate international markets with a pricing scheme that focuses mainly on variable costs. Although such a strategy may be useful in the short term, it may result in the offering of products abroad at a lower cost than at home, which in turn may stimulate parallel importing. In the long run, fixed costs have to be recovered to ensure replacement of production equipment. A market penetration strategy based on variable cost alone is therefore not feasible over the long term.

Sometimes excess production capacity arises because of changing demand in the domestic market. As domestic markets switch to new and substitute products, companies making older product versions develop excess capacity and look for overseas market opportunities.

Unsolicited foreign orders

Many small companies have become aware of opportunities in export markets because their products generated enquiries from overseas. These enquiries can result from advertising in trade journals that have a worldwide circulation, through exhibitions and by other means. As a result, a large percentage of exporting firms' initial orders are unsolicited.

Extend sales of seasonal products

Seasonality in demand conditions may be different in the domestic market from other international markets. This can act as a persistent stimulus for foreign market exploration that may result in a more stable demand over the year.

For example, a producer of agricultural machinery in Europe experienced demand from its domestic market primarily in the spring months of the year. In an attempt to achieve a more stable demand over the year, it directed its market orientation towards the southern hemisphere (e.g. Australia, South Africa), where the summer months coincide with the northern hemisphere, winter in and vice versa.

Proximity to international customers/psychological distance

Physical and psychological proximity to the international market can often play a major role in the export activities of a firm. For example, German firms established near the Austrian border may not even perceive their market activities in Austria as global marketing. Rather, they are simply an extension of domestic activities, without any particular attention being paid to the fact that some of the products go abroad.

Unlike US firms, most European firms automatically become international marketers simply because their neighbours are so close. As an example, a European firm operating in Belgium needs to go only 100 kilometres to be in multiple foreign markets. Geographic proximity to foreign markets may not necessarily translate into real or perceived closeness to the foreign customer. Sometimes cultural variables, legal factors and other societal norms make a foreign market that is geographically close seem psychologically distant. For example, research has shown that US firms perceive Canada as psychologically much closer than Mexico. Even the UK, mainly because of the common language, is perceived by many US firms as much closer than Mexico or other Latin American countries, despite the geographic distances. The recent extensive expansion of many Greek firms (especially banks) into the Balkans is another example of proximity to international customers.

In a study of small UK firms' motives for going abroad, Westhead *et al.* (2002) found the following main reasons for firms starting to export their products/services:

- being contacted by foreign customers who place orders;
- one-off order (no continuous exporting);
- the availability of foreign market information;
- part of the growth objective of the firm;
- export markets are actively targeted by the key founder/owner/manager.

The results of the Westhead *et al.* (2002) study also showed that the bigger the firm, the more likely it would be to cite *proactive* stimuli/motives.

EXHIBIT 2.3 Internationalization of Haier – proactive and reactive motives

Haier Group, the Chinese manufacturer of home appliances (e.g. refrigerators), was near bankruptcy when Mr Zhang Ruimin was appointed plant director in 1984, the fourth one that year. It is under Zhang's leadership that the company has grown into the world's sixth largest home appliance manufacturer.

Proactive motives

Zhang Ruimin had an internationalization mindset that set the initial stage of Haier's development. In 1984, soon after joining the plant, he introduced technology and equipment from Liebherr, a German company, to produce several popular refrigerator brands in China. At the same time he actively expanded cooperation with Liebherr by manufacturing refrigerators based on its standards which were then sold to Liebherr, as a way of entering the German market. In 1986, the value of Haier's exports reached US$3 million for the first time. Zhang later commented on this strategy: 'Exporting to earn foreign exchange was necessary at that time.'

Source: Sorbis/Shutterstock.com.

When Haier invested in a plant in the US, Zhang thought it gained location advantage by setting up plants overseas to avoid tariffs and reduce transportation costs. Internalization advantage had been attained through controlling services and marketing/distribution, and ownership advantage had been achieved by developing design and R&D capabilities through utilizing high-quality local human resources.

In January 2016 Haier Group said it would buy General Electric Co's appliance business for $5.4 billion, the Chinese company's latest attempt to boost its presence in the lucrative United States market.

Reactive motives

The entry of global home appliance manufacturers into the Chinese market forced Haier to seek international expansion. In particular, since China joined the WTO, almost every international competitor has invested in China, establishing wholly-owned companies. The best defensive strategy for Haier would be to have a presence in its competitors' home markets.

The saturation of the Chinese home appliance market, with intensifying competition, has been a major motive. After the mid-1990s, price wars broke out one after another in various categories of the market. At the end of 2000, Haier's market shares in China of refrigerators, freezers, air conditioners and washing machines had reached 33, 42, 31 and 31 per cent, respectively. The potential for further development in the domestic market was therefore limited.

One of the important external triggers for the internationalization of Haier has been the Chinese government. Being an international player, Haier gained some special conditions that other Chinese companies could not obtain. For instance, Haier had already been approved to establish a financial company, to be the majority shareholder of a regional commercial bank, and to form a joint venture with a US insurance company. Without its active pursuit of internationalization, as well as a dominant position in the home appliance sectors, it would normally be impossible for a manufacturer to get approval to enter the financial sector.

Source: based on Liu and Li (2002) and other public sources.

The results of Suárez-Ortega and Àlamo-Vera (2005) suggest that the main driving forces motivating internationalization are found within the firm, and therefore they are based on the management's strengths and weaknesses. They conclude that it is not the external environment that mainly influences the internationalization activities, but the pool of resources and capabilities within the firm that might be appropriately combined to succeed in international markets. Consequently, the speed and intensity of internationalization can be emphasized through programmes aimed at enhancing managers' skills and capabilities. Also export promotion programmes aiming to get more non-exporters to become interested in exporting should emphasize activities that increase managers' awareness of export advantages.

2.3   Triggers of export initiation (change agents)

Internationalization triggers
Internal or external events taking place to initiate internationalization.

For internationalization to take place, someone or something within or outside the firm (so-called change agents) must initiate the process and carry it through to implementation (see Table 2.2). These are known as **internationalization triggers**. One conclusion from the research done in this area is that it is rare that an isolated factor will trigger a firm's internationalization process. In most cases it is a combination of factors that initiates the internationalization process (Rundh, 2007).

Table 2.2	Triggers of export initiation	
Internal triggers		**External triggers**
• Perceptive management		• Market demand
• Specific internal event		• Network partners
• Importing as inward internationalization		• Competing firms
		• Trade associations and other outside experts
		• Financing

Internal triggers

Perceptive management

Perceptive managers gain early awareness of developing opportunities in overseas markets. They make it their business to become knowledgeable about these markets, and maintain a sense of open-mindedness about where and when their companies should expand overseas. Perceptive managers include many cosmopolitans in their ranks.

A trigger factor is frequently foreign travel, during which new business opportunities are discovered or information is received that leads management to believe that such opportunities exist. Managers who have lived abroad, have learned foreign languages or are particularly interested in foreign cultures are likely, sooner rather than later, to investigate whether global marketing opportunities would be appropriate for their firm.

Often managers enter a firm having already had some global marketing experience in previous jobs and try to use this experience to further the business activities of their new firm. In developing their goals in the new job, managers frequently consider an entirely new set of options, one of which may be global marketing activities.

Specific internal event

A significant event can be another major change agent. A new employee who firmly believes that the firm should undertake global marketing may find ways to motivate management. Overproduction or a reduction in domestic market size can serve as such an event, as can the receipt of new information about current product uses. For instance, a company's research activity may develop a by-product suitable for sale overseas, as happened with a food-processing firm that discovered a low-cost protein ideal for helping to relieve food shortages in some parts of Africa.

Research has shown that in SMEs the initial decision to export is usually made by the chief executive, with substantial input provided by the marketing department. The carrying out of the decision – that is, the initiation of actual global marketing activities and the implementation of these activities – is then primarily the responsibility of the marketing personnel. Only in the final decision stage of evaluating global marketing activities does the major emphasis rest again with the chief executive of the firm. In order to influence a firm internally, it therefore appears that the major emphasis should be placed first on convincing the chief executive to enter the international marketplace and then on convincing the marketing department that global marketing is an important activity. Conversely, the marketing department is a good place to be if one wants to become active in international business.

In a recent study of internationalization behaviour in Finnish SMEs, Forsman *et al.* (2002) found that the three most important triggers for starting up operations internationally were as follows:

1. management's interest in internationalization;
2. foreign enquiries about the company's products/services;
3. inadequate demand in the home market.

In this study it is interesting to note that companies do not regard contacts from chambers of commerce or other support organizations as important for getting their international activities going. However, chambers of commerce are often used for obtaining further information about a foreign country after an initial trigger has led to the consideration of going international.

Inward/outward internationalization

Internationalization has traditionally been regarded as an outward flow and most internationalization models have not dealt explicitly with how earlier inward activities, and thereby gained knowledge, can influence later outward activities. A natural way of internationalizing would be first to get involved in inward activities (imports) and thereafter in outward activities (exports). Relationships and knowledge gathered from import activities could thus be used when the firm engages in export activities (Welch *et al.*, 2001).

Inward/outward internationalization
Imports (inward) as a preceding activity for the later market entries (outward) in foreign markets.

Welch and Loustarinen (1993) claim that **inward internationalization** (importing) may precede and influence **outward internationalization** (international market entry and marketing activities) – see Figure 2.2.

A direct relationship exists between inward and outward internationalization in the way that effective inward activities can determine the success of outward activities, especially in the early stages of internationalization. The inward internationalization may be initiated by one of the following:

● *the buyer*: active international search of different foreign sources (buyer initiative reverse marketing);
● *the seller*: initiation by the foreign supplier (traditional seller perspective).

During the process from inward to outward internationalization, the buyer's role (in country A) shifts to that of seller, both to domestic customers (in country A) and to foreign customers. Through interaction with the foreign supplier, the buyer (importer) obtains

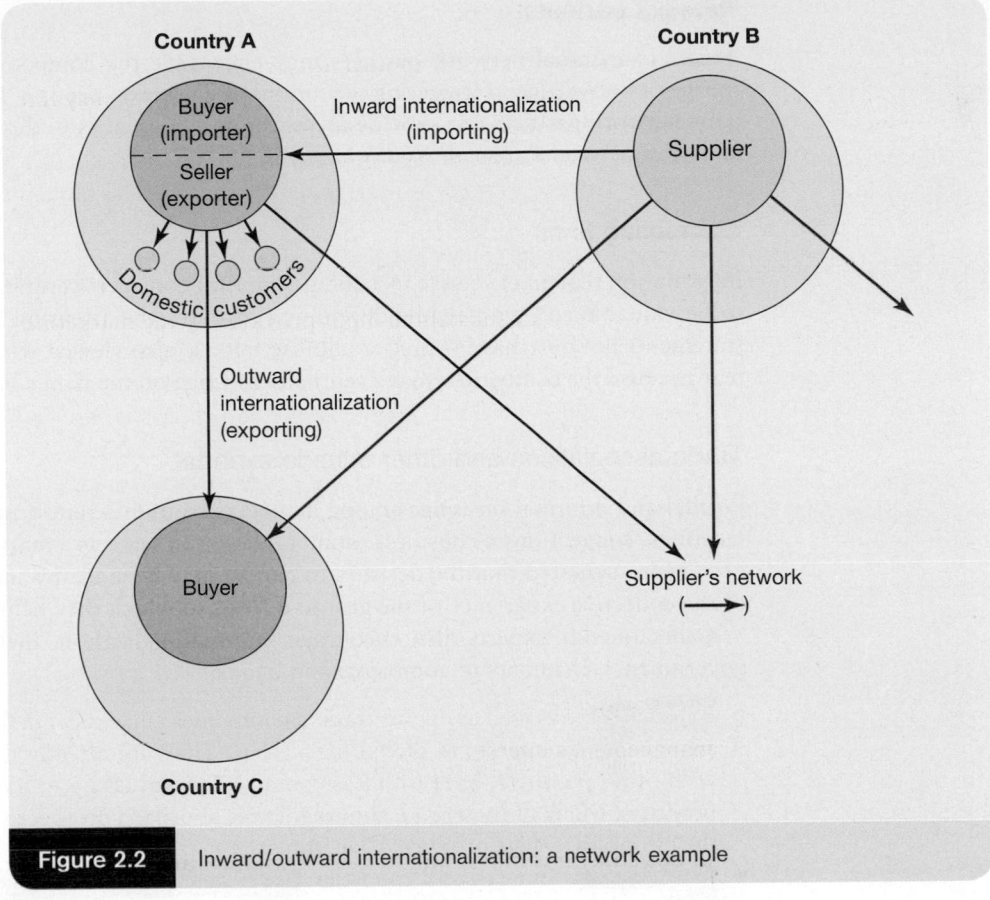

Country A

Buyer
(importer)

Inward internationalization
(importing)

Country B

Supplier

Seller
(exporter)

Domestic customers

Outward
internationalization
(exporting)

Buyer

Supplier's network
(——➤)

Country C

| Figure 2.2 | Inward/outward internationalization: a network example |

access to the network of the supplier, so that at some later time there may be an outward export to members of this network.

Inward international operations thus usually cover a variety of different forms used to strengthen a firm's resources. Of course, inward flows imply importing products needed for the production process, such as raw materials and machinery. But inward operations can also include finances and technology through different operational forms, such as franchising, direct investments and alliances (Forsman *et al.*, 2002). In some cases inward foreign licensing may be followed by outward technology sales. According to Fletcher (2001) and Freeman (2002), inward and outward activities and the links between them can develop in different ways. The links are most tangible in counter-trade arrangements (where the focal firm initiates exporting to the same market from which importing takes place), but they can also be found in the networks of relationships between subunits within a multinational enterprise and in strategic alliances.

External triggers

Market demand

Growth in international markets also causes the demand for the products of some companies to grow, pushing the makers of these products into internationalization. Many pharmaceutical companies entered international markets when growth in the international demand for their products first began. The US-based company Squibb entered the Turkish market before it was large enough to be profitable, but the market was growing rapidly, which encouraged Squibb to internationalize further.

Network partners

Access to external network partners may encourage the company to use this as a key source of knowledge in triggering the internationalization process. For example, the company network partners can provide access to international sales through their distribution and sales networks abroad (Vissak *et al.*, 2008).

Competing firms

Information that an executive in a competing firm considers certain international markets to be valuable and worthwhile developing captures the attention of management. Such statements not only have source credibility but are also viewed with a certain amount of fear because the competitor may eventually infringe on the firm's business.

Trade associations and other outside experts

Formal and informal meetings among managers from different firms at trade association meetings, conventions or business round tables often serve as a major change agent. It has even been suggested that the decision to export may be made by small firms on the basis of the collective experience of the group of firms to which they belong.

Other outside experts also encourage internationalization, including export agents, governments, chambers of commerce and banks:

- *Export agents* as well as export trading companies and export management firms generally qualify as experts in global marketing. They are already dealing internationally with other products, have overseas contacts and are set up to handle other exportable products. Many of these trade intermediaries approach prospective exporters directly if they think that their products have potential markets overseas.
- *Governments*. In nearly all countries, governments try to stimulate international business through providing global marketing expertise (export assistance programmes). For example, government stimulation measures can have a positive influence not only in terms of any direct financial effects that they may have, but also in relation to the provision of information.
- *Chambers of commerce* and similar export production organizations are interested in stimulating international business, both exports and imports. These organizations seek to motivate individual companies to get involved in global marketing and provide incentives for them to do so. These incentives include putting the prospective exporter or importer in touch with overseas business, providing overseas market information, and referring the prospective exporter or importer to financial institutions capable of financing global marketing activity.
- *Banks* and other financial institutions are often instrumental in getting companies to internationalize. They alert their domestic clients to international opportunities and help them to capitalize on these opportunities. Of course, they look forward to their services being used more extensively as domestic clients expand internationally.

Financing

Financial resources are required to fund international activities, such as exhibiting at international trade fairs, and to bring about the changes required within the firm for internationalization, such as the development of its capabilities (particularly the firm's production, managerial and marketing capabilities). The financial resources available to the company may be influenced by several factors, including the firm's willingness to borrow funds from financial institutions.

Government grants (for R&D purposes, in order to sell products and services worldwide) can be a useful source of finance (and knowledge) in the early stages of internationalization.

However, they are not sufficient to build an internationalized business. Unless a firm enjoys a dominant position in the domestic marketplace, it will need to raise the necessary funds through industry grants, debt and/or equity finance. This may mean taking greater risks (Graves and Thomas, 2008).

Information search and translation

Of all resources, information and knowledge are perhaps the most critical factor in the initiation of the internationalization process in the SME (see also Figure 2.1).

Because each international opportunity constitutes a potential innovation for the SME, its management must acquire appropriate information. This is especially important to SMEs that typically lack the resources to internationalize in the manner of LSEs. Consequently, management launches an *information search* and acquires relevant information from a number of sources relevant to the intended internationalization project, such as internal written reports, government agencies, trade associations, personal contacts or the internet. In the information translation stage, the internationalization information is transformed by managers into knowledge within the firm. It is through the information search and translation into knowledge that management becomes informed on internationalization. At this stage, the firm has entered a cycle of continuous search and translation into internationalization knowledge. This cycle continues until management is satisfied that it has sufficiently reduced the uncertainty associated with the internationalization project to ensure a relatively high probability of success. Once sufficient information has been acquired and translated into usable knowledge, the firm leaves the cycle, becoming internationalization-ready. It is here that the firm proceeds to action, that is, internationalization trial. 'Action' refers to behaviours and activities that management executes based on the knowledge that it has acquired. At this stage the firm could be said to have an embedded internationalization culture, where even the most challenging foreign markets can be overcome, leading to further internationalization and 'storage' of actual internationalization knowledge in the heads of the managers. This description represents the firm more or less in isolation. However, the network theory recognizes the importance of the firm's membership in a constellation of firms and organizations. By interacting within such a constellation, the firm derives advantages well beyond what it could obtain in isolation.

At the most basic level, knowledge is created by individuals. Individuals acquire explicit knowledge via specific means and tacit knowledge through 'hands on' experience (experiential learning).

The nature of the pre-internationalization process (illustrated in Figure 2.1) will be unique in each firm because of several factors at the organization and individual levels within the firm (Knight and Liesch, 2002). For example, for SMEs it seems that the managers' personal networks tend to speed up the pre-internationalization process. These personal networks are used for creating cross-border alliances with suppliers, distributors and other international partners (Freeman *et al.*, 2006).

Throughout the process depicted in Figure 2.1, the firm may exit from the pre-internationalization process at any time, as a result of the barriers hindering internationalization. The manager may decide to 'do nothing', an outcome that implies exiting from pre-internationalization.

2.4 Internationalization barriers/risks

A wide variety of barriers to successful export operations can be identified. Some problems mainly affect the export start; others are encountered in the process of exporting. The incremental character of internationalization (according to the Uppsala model – see

Section 3.2) is largely attributed to a lack of market information. This lack of market information will strongly influence the manager's perceived psychic distance (see Chapter 3) from the home country to the host country. Increasing the foreign market knowledge will decrease the psychic distance. However, the distortion of information transmission associated with psychic distance implies the necessity of trust development. This means that trust plays a crucial role in overcoming the challenges to successful international relationship building to the foreign partners (Khojastehpour and Johns, 2015).

Barriers hindering internationalization initiation

Critical factors hindering *internationalization initiation* include the following (mainly internal) barriers:

- insufficient finances;
- insufficient market knowledge;
- lack of foreign market connections;
- lack of export commitment;
- lack of capital to finance expansion into foreign markets;
- lack of productive capacity to dedicate to foreign markets;
- lack of foreign channels of distribution;
- management emphasis on developing domestic markets;
- cost escalation due to high export manufacturing, distribution and financing expenditures.

Inadequate information on potential foreign customers, competition and foreign business practices is a key barrier facing active and prospective exporters. Obtaining adequate representation for overseas distribution and service, ensuring payment, import tariffs and quotas, and difficulties in communicating with foreign distributors and customers are also major concerns. Serious problems can also arise from production disruptions resulting from a requirement for non-standard export products. This will increase the cost of manufacturing and distribution.

In a study of craft micro-enterprises (fewer than ten employees) in the UK and Ireland, Fillis (2002) found that having sufficient business in the domestic market was the major factor in the decision not to export. Other reasons of above-average importance were lack of export inquiries, relating to the reactive approach to business; complicated exporting procedures; poor levels of exporting assistance; and limited government incentives. Similar results were supported by a study by Westhead *et al.* (2002), who found that for small firms 'focus on local market' was the main reason for not exporting any of their products.

Barriers hindering the further process of internationalization

Critical barriers in the *process of internationalization* (sometimes resulting in more costs than benefits) may generally be divided into three groups: general market risks, commercial risks and political risks, all seen from the company perspective.

General market risks

General market risks include the following:

- *Comparative market distance:* each additional foreign market creates additional organizational costs, and differences in culture and language will increase the amount of information that managers must collect to effectively manage and coordinate across the foreign markets.

- *Adaptation to foreign markets*: the products and services that companies produce abroad are often the same as at home but, even in that case, producing and selling abroad involve higher costs than doing it at home. It requires modifications to the production process and marketing mix.
- Competition from other firms in foreign markets.
- Adapting products and services to new local conditions.
- Difficulties in finding the right distributor in the foreign market.
- Differences in product specifications in foreign markets.
- Complexity of shipping services to overseas buyers.

Commercial risks

The following fall into the commercial risks group:

- exchange rate fluctuations when contracts are made in a foreign currency;
- failure of export customers to pay due to contract dispute, bankruptcy, refusal to accept the product or fraud;
- delays and/or damage in the export shipment and distribution process;
- difficulties in obtaining export financing.

Political risks

Among the political risks resulting from intervention by home and host country governments are the following:

- foreign government restrictions (think about the Russian–Ukrainian conflict in 2014, which resulted in import restrictions, imposed by the Russian government);
- national export policy (think about the Russian–Ukrainian conflict in 2014, which resulted in EU boycott of certain products exported to Russia);
- foreign exchange controls imposed by host governments that limit the opportunities for foreign customers to make payment;
- lack of governmental assistance in overcoming export barriers;
- lack of tax incentives for companies that export;
- high value of the domestic currency relative to those in export markets;
- high foreign tariffs on imported products;
- confusing foreign import regulations and procedures;
- complexity of trade documentation;
- enforcement of national legal codes regulating exports;
- civil strife, revolution and wars disrupting foreign markets.

The importance of these risks must not be overemphasized, and various risk management strategies are open to exporters, including the following:

- Avoid exporting to high-risk markets.
- Diversify overseas markets and ensure that the firm is not overdependent on any single country.
- Insure risks when possible – government schemes are particularly attractive.
- Structure export business so that the buyer bears most of the risk. For example, price in a hard currency and demand cash in advance.

In Fillis (2002), over one-third of the exporting craft firms indicated that they encountered problems once they entered export markets. The most common problem was connected with the choice of a reliable distributor, followed by difficulties in promoting the product and matching competitors' prices.

De-internationalization

De-internationalization
A process, determined by internal and external factors, where the multinational company shifts to a strategic configuration that has a lower international presence.

The above explained barriers can sometimes be so serious that the internationalization process can go in a different direction from what was expected. The **de-internationalization** process can be defined as the process whereby the multinational company shifts to a strategic configuration that has a lower international presence (Turner, 2012). Both external and internal factors determine the adoption of a de-internationalization strategy, which is characterized by the transition of various stages that culminates in the reorientation of the company's strategy, whether through a tactical withdrawal seen as a failure, or a strategic withdrawal seen as an opportunity for growth in other markets.

For example, at one point Carrefour (the world's second largest retailer) decided to go into many new countries based on selected criteria, mainly market size, geographical proximity and compatibility of operations. Entering so many new countries meant that Carrefour was also confronted with different regulations in the retail markets on the basis of religion, culture and taste. To recover its profitability, around 2005 Carrefour decided to separate from its non-strategic and unprofitable assets, mainly outside Europe (Buigues *et al.*, 2015).

Researchers have questioned to what extent companies should continue to expand internationally if this strategy is not always profitable. Empirical studies (Turner, 2012; Buigues et al., 2015) have evidenced an optimum point in terms of internationalization that results in the 'inverted U-shaped curve' (Figure 2.3), where – at a company level – there should be a maximum of countries that should be served. Internationalization incurs costs for the expanding company which explains why further internationalization can have negative influence on profitability and why overinternationalized companies may reduce their degree of internationalization.

Figure 2.3 shows that from a certain stage in the firm's internationalization process (the 'optimal' level), the costs of further international expansion outweigh the marginal financial benefits, producing a lower profitability, in terms of return on investment (ROI). The shape of Figure 2.3 has been confirmed by a study of Buigues et al. (2015), which showed that when levels of internationalization were below the 'optimal' level, companies generally continued their international expansion. Conversely, when the level of internationalization

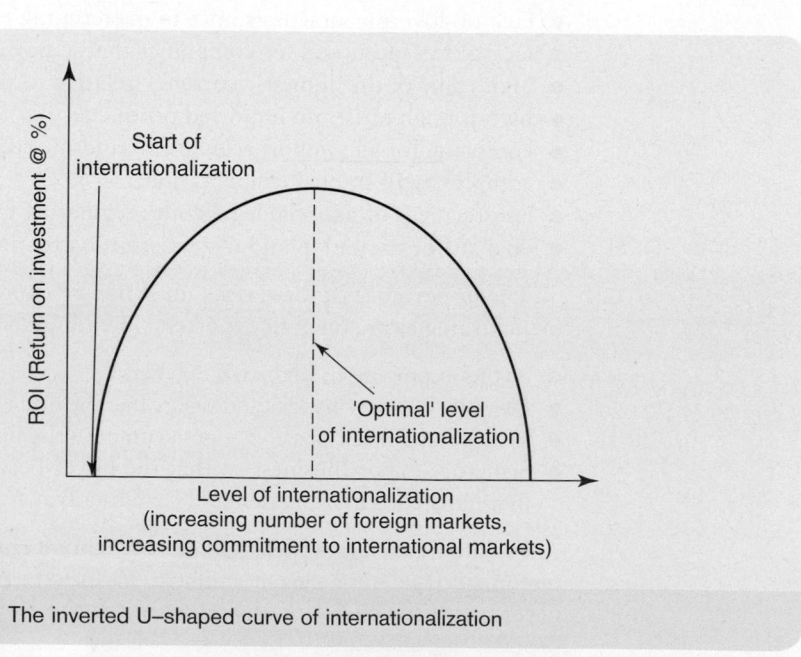

Figure 2.3   The inverted U–shaped curve of internationalization

was beyond the optimum (measured by profitability metrics, like ROI), a majority of the companies actually decreased their level of internationalization. From a managerial point of view, this implies that managers should always have a close look at the balance between the costs and benefits of internationalization. See also Exhibit 2.4 for a more in-depth view on BT's de-internationalization process.

EXHIBIT 2.4 De-internationalization at British Telecommunications (BT)

BT started its internationalization in the mid-1990s. Over the following years, BT built a global strategy, seeking to position itself as a leading supplier of telecommunication services to multinational companies in different countries. However, the percentage increase in international activities has slowed down over the years. In 1994, less than 1 per cent of total turnover came from international activities. In 2002, this had increased to 11 per cent, and by 2007 it had increased to 15 per cent of its £20 billion turnover. So, although BT overall has experienced a sharp increase in turnover from international activities, it has also experienced some setbacks in the internationalization process, especially in the beginning, as indicated in Figure 2.4.

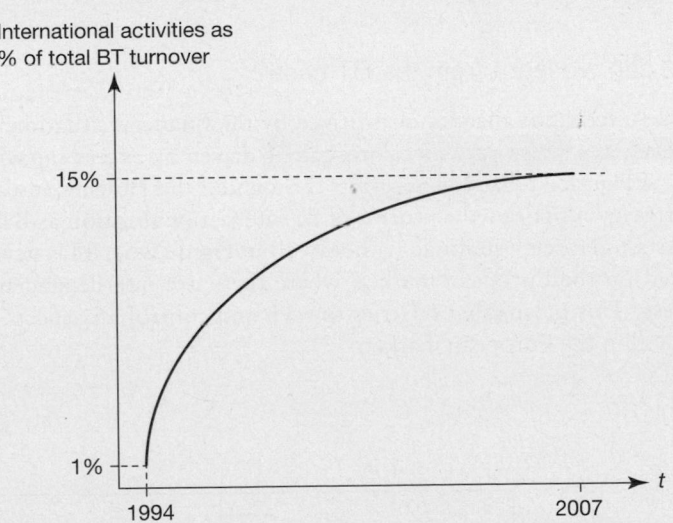

| **Figure 2.4** | Illustration of BT's internationalization 1994–2007 |

Source: Hollensen, S. (2008) *Essentials of Global Marketing*, FT/Prentice all, p. 47. Copyright © Pearson Education Limited.

At the beginning of the internationalization process, BT built its international strategy around three guiding principles:

1. Not over-committing itself by building its own infrastructure based on uncertain traffic flows.
2. Achieving quick and reliable access to targeted marketplaces by entering distribution partnerships and equity joint ventures. This strategy involved relatively low risk and allowed speedy access into marketplaces with partners who had intimate knowledge of local market conditions.
3. Ensuring that the strategy gave BT sufficient strategic flexibility to be able to adjust rapidly to changing market conditions.

At its height in 1999, BT had 25 equity joint ventures and 44 distribution partnerships. Within the equity joint ventures, BT took a minority stake, with the stated intention to gradually upgrade this stake to a controlling investment over time. BT would also often take a stake in its distribution partners as a means of giving them incentives to sell BT's products.

De-internationalization at BT

In 2002, BT launched a new corporate strategy that was considerably more defensive than its predecessor. There were mainly two problems with the series of joint ventures and partnerships:

1. BT needed different skills and competences for different partners. This made coordination of activities between partners very complex. As a consequence, BT found itself on a steep learning curve with this large number of partners.
2. The strategy of only taking a minority stake in the joint ventures rebounded on BT. Furthermore, there was little incentive for partners to fully support the roll-out of BT products, especially where these were in competition with their own offerings. When BT attempted to increase its financial stake within the partnership, it often found that the other shareholders had exactly the same intention.

Subsequently, BT made divestments, both in North America and in Asia.

Sources: adapted from Turner and Gardiner (2007); BT Financial Report (2007).

What can we learn from the BT case?

BT's de-internationalization was driven by the financial situation, where the high cost of market entry combined with falling prices (driven by excess capacity in the telecommunication sector) led to declining profits throughout the 1990s. Consequently, the new defensive strategy represented a process of de-internationalization as BT retreated from the US and Asian markets ('multiple withdrawal' in Figure 2.5). BT's new international strategy is based on the European market, where there are interdependencies with the core UK business. This means that BT tries to own and control all aspects of the delivery mechanism within the European market.

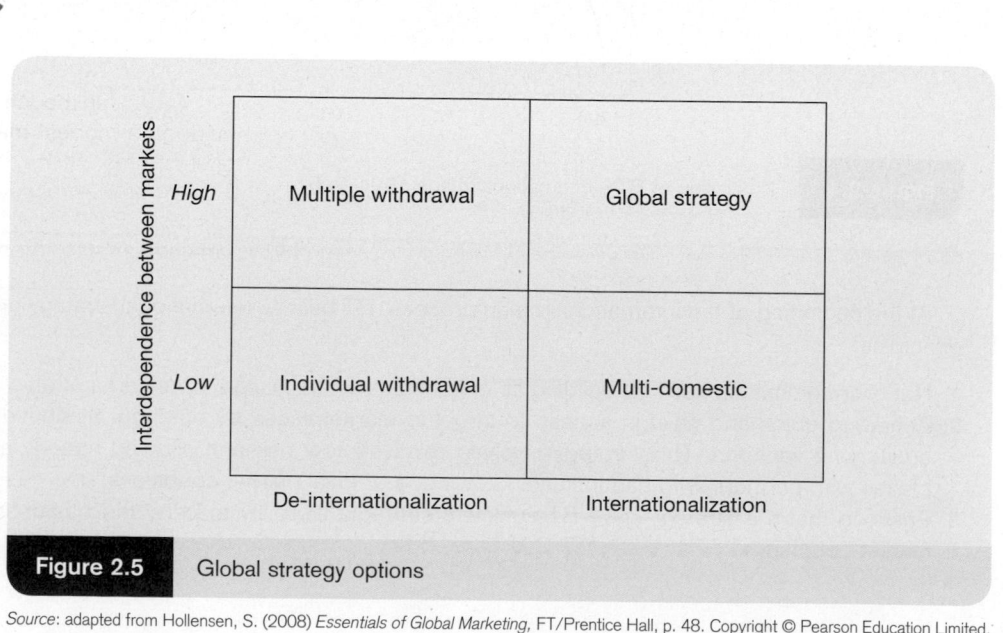

Figure 2.5   Global strategy options

Source: adapted from Hollensen, S. (2008) *Essentials of Global Marketing*, FT/Prentice Hall, p. 48. Copyright © Pearson Education Limited.

This BT case demonstrates that the future development of the global marketing strategy can work in both directions. If the globalization of markets goes well in a company, the interdependence and synergies between markets can be further utilized to strengthen the global strategy (upper-right corner in Figure 2.5). However, the case also shows that divestment in individual locations cannot occur in isolation without damaging the firm's global value proposition. Therefore, BT's de-internationalization also meant (because of the high dependence of markets) that it had to make multiple market withdrawals.

If we talk about SMEs (not the case with BT!), there is often a low interdependence between markets, and in that case one talks about a 'multidomestic' strategy if internationalization is increased (lower-right corner in Figure 2.5) and individual withdrawal if internationalization is decreased (lower-left corner in Figure 2.5).

2.5 Summary

This chapter has provided an overview of the pre-internationalization process. The chapter opened with the major motives for firms to internationalize. These were differentiated into proactive and reactive motives. Proactive motives represent internal stimuli to attempt strategy change, based on the firm's interest in exploiting unique competences or market possibilities. Reactive motives indicate that the firm reacts to pressures or threats in its home market or in foreign markets and adjusts passively to them.

For internationalization to take place, someone or something ('triggers') inside or outside the firm must initiate it and carry it through. To succeed in global marketing the firm has to overcome export barriers. Some barriers mainly affect the export initiation and others are encountered in the process of exporting.

CASE STUDY 2.1

LifeStraw: Vestergaard-Frandsen transforms dirty water into clean drinking water

Creating products to save people's lives in the developing world is the mission of a company – Vestergaard-Frandsen (VF) (www.vestergaard-frandsen.com) – based in Lausanne, Switzerland. The 'profit for a purpose' approach has turned humanitarian responsibility into VF's core business. The company is offering complex emergency response and disease-control products.

Source: Vestergaard-Frandsen.

Vestergaard Frandsen began life over 55 years ago in Denmark as a modest manufacturer of hotel and restaurant uniforms. Today, its headquarters are in Lausanne, and the sole focus of the 150 employees is on what the CEO Mikkel Vestergaard Frandsen calls 'humanitarian entrepreneurship'. Originally a textile company that began in Denmark in 1957, they now develop innovative products that prevent the transmission of water-borne and insect-borne diseases in developing countries. For water-borne diseases VF has its LifeStraw – see below for a description. For insect-borne diseases VF is one of the world's leading producers of bed nets impregnated with insecticide. The purpose is to prevent malaria, caused by the bloodsucking bites of mosquitoes. Besides mosquito intensive areas, this product is used in refugee camps and disaster areas all over the world. Vestergard Frandsen, which is family-owned, does not disclose financial data, but over the years it has sold over 250 million mosquito nets, and the company makes a profit.

The concept for the LifeStraw began with the work of the Carter Center, founded by Jimmy and Rosalynn Carter. It has been their mission since 1986 to eradicate guinea worm disease (GWD) in Africa and Asia. The most effective way to prevent this disease is to filter drinking water, so that the tiny water fleas are not ingested to begin the life cycle of GWD. The LifeStraw has played a substantial role in the prevention of this disease, and many other bacterial and viral infections caused by a lack of safe drinking water in many developing countries.

The lack of safe drinking water

Water in drinking form is becoming scarcer in certain places, and its availability is a major social and economic concern. Currently, about a billion people around the world routinely drink unhealthy water.

About 99.7 per cent of the Earth's water is contained in undrinkable forms such as oceans, underground, ice caps and glaciers. Due to increased contamination and pollution both above and below the ground, the condition of the remaining 0.3 per cent is now questionable, with many countries finding it increasingly difficult to source drinkable water that is of an acceptable quality.

Throughout history, clashes between and within countries have occurred over water and its supply. Many people believe that in the future conflicts and even wars will be waged over water supplies, particularly as uncontaminated water becomes increasingly scarce.

More than 780 million people in the world do not have access to safe drinking water. The average distance that women in Africa and Asia walk to collect water is 6 km.

The LifeStraw product

LifeStraw water filters remove disease-causing pathogens that are major causes of water-borne diseases such as cholera, typhoid and diarrhoea in the developing world, enabling people to access safe drinking water. LifeStraw technologies have been distributed to more than 64 countries where they are a vital tool for some of the 780 million people who don't have ready access to safe drinking water.

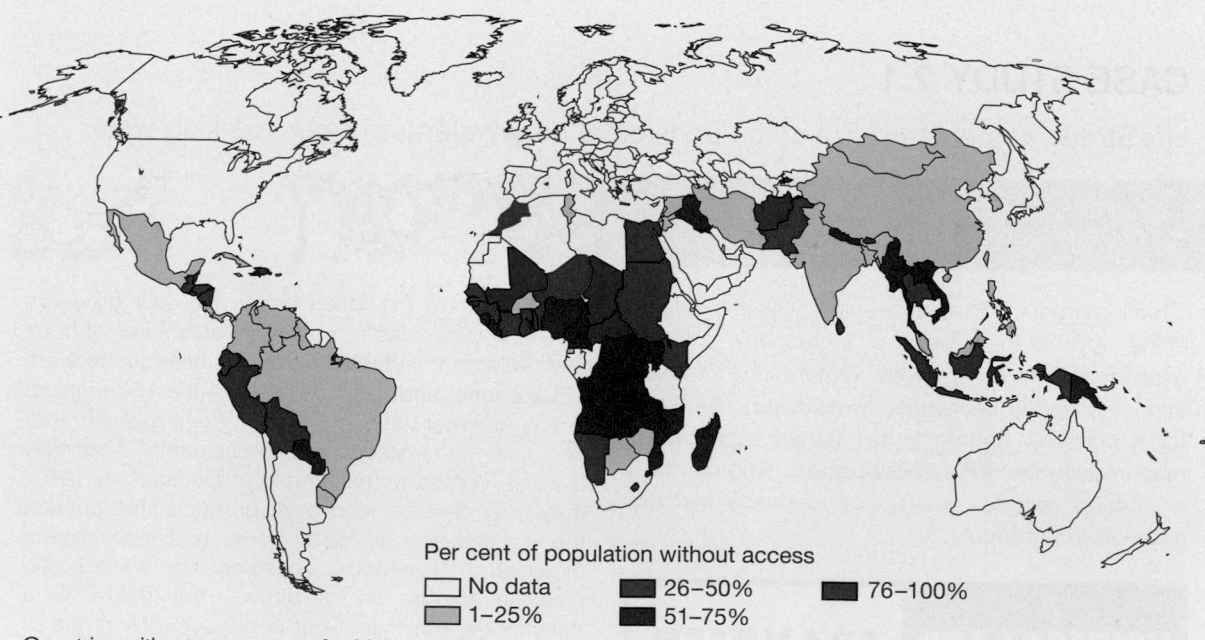

Per cent of population without access
☐ No data   ▣ 26–50%   ■ 76–100%
▣ 1–25%   ■ 51–75%

Countries without access to safe drinking water

Source: from *The World's Water 1998–1999* by Peter H. Gleick. Copyright © 1998 Island Press. Reproduced by permission of Island Press, Washington, DC.

LifeStraw filters are easy to use, and require no electricity, batteries or replacement parts. The personal version is ideal for out-of-home use by hikers, campers or people displaced by natural disasters. LifeStraw Family, used in homes, provides an average family of five with safe water for at least three years. LifeStraw Community is designed for schools, health facilities and institutions where it will deliver an estimated 70,000 to 100,000 litres of safe drinking water over its lifetime.

Five million people die each year (mainly children) from water-borne diseases. The World Health Organization (WHO) estimates that safe water could prevent 1.4 million child deaths from diarrhoea each year.

A product as simple and inexpensive as the LifeStraw could change these numbers and do it right at the point of consumption.

Children drinking water from the LifeStraw in India
Source: Vestergaard-Frandsen.

How does the LifeStraw function?

LifeStraw uses advanced hollow fibre technology. Water is forced through narrow fibres under high pressure. Clean water exits through tiny pores in the walls of the hollow fibres, but bacteria, protozoa and other contaminants are trapped inside the hollow fibres and are flushed out by backwashing. This is a highly efficient method of filtration.

For the personal version of LifeStraw, the user draws the unfiltered water through the LifeStraw, the same way they would when using a straw. For LifeStraw Family and LifeStraw Community, untreated water is poured into the top of the unit which has a pre-filter that removes coarse particles. The ultrafiltration hollow-fibre membrane cartridge then stops all turbidity particles and smaller pathogens, including all bacteria, viruses and protozoan cysts. Particles and microbes larger than 20 nanometres stay on the dirty side of the membrane and clean/purified water passes through the membrane. The blue tap releases purified water.

Customers and distribution of LifeStraw

Customers are mainly foreign governmental aid agencies, international relief and development organizations, foundations and charities.

The best way for people (end users) in these risky areas to get a LifeStraw is through a charitable organization, which funds and sometimes also buys the products. The non-governmental organizations (NGOs) then take the product to the rural households where the poorest people live.

QUESTIONS

1. In McNeil (2009), Kevin Starace states: 'Vestergaard is just different from other companies we work with. They think of end users as a consumer rather as a patient or a victim.' What do you think is the meaning behind this statement?

2. What are the most critical factors in the further internationalization process of Vestergaard Frandsen?

Sources: www.vestergaard-frandsen.com; Donald G. McNeil Jr (2009) 'A company prospers by saving poor people's lives,' *New York Times – Science Times*, 3 February.

CASE STUDY 2.2

Elvis Presley Enterprises Inc. (EPE): internationalization of a cult icon

More than 25 years after his death, Elvis Presley has one of the most lucrative entertainment franchises in the world. Despite the sorry state of his affairs in 1977, the Elvis empire has thrived, due in large part to the efforts of the people who handled his estate after his grandmother died in 1980, including his ex-wife Priscilla Beaulieu Presley, his daughter Lisa Marie and Jack Soden, the CEO of Elvis Presley Enterprises Inc. (www.elvis.com), the company that handles all the official Elvis properties.

Priscilla Presley was involved in the masterstroke decision to open Elvis's mansion, Graceland, to the public in 1982. Graceland gets more than 600,000 visitors per year, according to EPE's website. That means that Graceland is the second most visited private residence in US, behind the White House in Washington DC. Attendance ranges from a few hundred visitors on a weekday in the dead of winter to 2,000–3,500 visitors per day in the spring and early summer, to over 4,000 per day in July at the height of the travel season. Over half of Graceland's visitors are under the age of 35. While visitors come from all parts of the world, the majority still come from different parts of the US. The Graceland tour costs $25, which means that EPE makes $15 million on those tickets alone, plus what it receives from photographs, hotel guests, meals and souvenirs.

EPE's other revenue streams include a themed restaurant called Elvis Presley's Memphis; a hotel, down at the end of Lonely Street, called Heartbreak Hotel; licensing of Elvis-related products; the development of Elvis-related music, film, video, TV and stage productions, and more.

Ironically, EPE gets very little money from Elvis's actual songs, thanks to a deal Elvis's infamous former manager, Colonel Tom Parker, made with RCA in 1973, whereby Elvis traded the rights to all future royalties from the songs he had recorded up to that point for a measly US$5.4 million – half of which he had to give to Parker.

In 2002, the 25th anniversary of his death was an international spectacle. A remix of the 1968 Elvis song 'A Little Less Conversation' became a global hit single and the CD *Elvis: 30 #1 Hits* went triple platinum. In mid-2004, to commemorate the 50th anniversary of Presley's first professional recording, 'That's All Right' was re-released, and made the charts around the world, including the top three in the UK and top 40 in Australia.

In mid-October 2005, *Variety* named the top 100 entertainment icons of the twentieth century, with Presley landing in the top 10, along with the Beatles, Marilyn Monroe, Lucille Ball, Marlon Brando, Humphrey Bogart, Louis Armstrong, Charlie Chaplin, James Dean and Mickey Mouse.

Until 2005, EPE was wholly owned by the Elvis Presley Trust/Lisa Marie Presley. In February 2005, the media and entertainment company CKX Inc. acquired an 85 per cent interest in EPE, including its physical and intellectual properties. Lisa Marie Presley retained a 15 per cent ownership in the company and continued to be involved, as did her mother Priscilla. The pre-existing EPE management team remained in place, but Priscilla Presley has withdrawn from the position as chairperson and CEO of EPE. In November 2013, the 85 per cent interest in EPE was sold to Authentic Brands Group, who now owns the rights to the library of photographic imagery, video and audio assets, including television appearances and music specials. Authentic Brands Group has also acquired the rights to the management of Graceland Operations. The ownership of Graceland itself is still in the hands of Lisa Marie Presley.

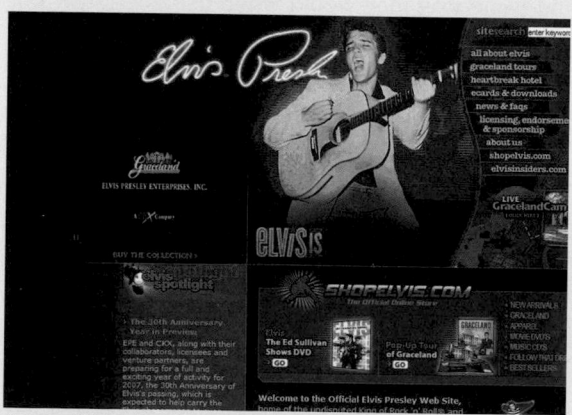

Source: © Elvis Presley Enterpises, Inc. Used by permission.

For 2014, EPE reported revenue of US$75 million compared with US$57 million for 2010. Operating income in 2014 was US$15 million compared with US$10 million in 2010.

QUESTIONS

1. What are the main motives for the internationalization of EPE?

2. What can EPE do to maintain a steady income stream from abroad?

3. What are the most obvious assets for further internationalization of EPE?

Sources: http://www.elvis.com/corporate/elvis_epe.asp; money.cnn.com/2002/08/15/news/elvis.

VIDEO CASE STUDY 2.3 TOMS Shoes

download from **www.pearsoned.co.uk/hollensen**

TOMS Shoes (www.tomsshoes.com) was founded in 2006 on a simple premise, as stated on their website 'With every pair you purchase, TOMS will give a pair of new shoes to a child in need. One for One.' Using the purchasing power of individuals to benefit the greater good is what the company is all about. The company name is derived from the words '**tom**orrow' and '**s**hoes' (evolved from the original concept, the 'shoes for Tomorrow Project').

In 2006, Blake Mycoskie, an American traveller, went to Argentina and found that many children there had no shoes to protect their feet. Wanting to help, he created TOMS Shoes, a company that would match every pair of shoes purchased with a pair of new shoes given to a child in need. Blake returned to Argentina with a group of family, friends and staff later that year with 10,000 pairs of shoes, all made possible by caring TOMS customers.

In developing countries, wearing shoes prevents feet from getting cuts and sores on unsafe roads and from contaminated soil. These injuries are not only painful, but, when wounds become infected, they are dangerous. The leading cause of disease in developing countries is soil-transmitted parasites which penetrate the skin through open sores. Wearing shoes can prevent this and ultimately the risk of amputation.

From the beginning in 2006 up to the end of 2012, TOMS gave over 10 million pairs of shoes to children in need (in 60 developing countries) through the 'One for One' model. In 2011, TOMS launched its eyewear line. When Toms sells a pair of glasses, part of the profit is used to save or restore the eyesight of people in developing countries. At the end of 2014, more than 700 retailers worldwide were carrying the brand.

TOMS' marketing activities have included fashion shows, high-profile events, university campus marketing, social media and temporary pop-up stores. TOMS' recent marketing plan also includes an advertisement with AT&T showing one of Toms' shoe drops in Uruguay.

Source: Donato Sardella/Getty Images.

TOMS is built on the loyalty of customers who choose a better tomorrow with every purchase. TOMS has one of the coolest internship programmes in the country, according to *Inc. Magazine*. Many of those passionate interns stay with TOMS and become hard-working, full-time employees.

TOMS Shoes' headquarters are in Santa Monica, California.

TOMS had estimated revenue of US$250m in 2014, with 30 per cent of sales coming from its website. All of its consumer shoes – priced between US$55 and US $85 – are made in China, as are the vast majority of its giveaway shoes. From 2016,

TOMS plans to have one-third of all shoes produced in the countries in which it operates its donation programmes.

Questions

1. What would be the key barriers in the early days of internationalization if TOMS Shoes decided to expand to Europe?

2. What have been the driving forces (motives) for the early internationalization of TOMS Shoes?

3. What are the key drivers of TOMS shoes' internationalization today?

Source: based on information from www.tomsshoes.com.

For further resources, see this book's website at **www.pearsoned.co.uk/hollensen**

Questions for discussion

1. Export motives can be classified as reactive or proactive. Give examples of each group of export motives. How would you prioritize these motives? Can you think of motives other than those mentioned in the chapter? What are they?

2. What is meant by 'change agents' in global marketing? Give examples of different types of change agent.

3. Discuss the most critical barriers to the process of exporting.

4. What were the most important change agents in the internationalization of Haier (Exhibit 2.3)?

5. What were the most important export motives in Japanese firms (Exhibit 2.2)?

References

Albaum, G., Strandskov, J., Duerr, E. and Dowd, L. (1994) *International Marketing and Export Management* (2nd edn). Addison-Wesley, Reading, MA.

Buigues, P.-A., Lacoste, D. and Lavigne, S. (2015) 'When over internationalized companies reduce their international footprint', *International Business Review*, http://dx.doi.org/10.1016/j.ibusrev.2015.04.006 (article in press, no page numbers).

Cuervo-Cazurra, A., Narula, R., C. and Un, A. (2015), 'Internationalization motives: sell more, buy better, upgrade and escape', *Multinational Business Review*, 23(1), pp. 25–35.

Dunning, J.H. (1993) *Multinational Enterprises and the Global Economy*, Addison-Wesley, Harlow.

Benito, G.R.G. (2015) 'Why and how motives (still) matter', *Multinational Business Review*, 23(1), pp. 15–24.

Fillis, I. (2002) 'Barriers to internationalization: an investigation of the craft microenterprises', *European Journal of Marketing*, 36(7–8), pp. 912–927.

Fletcher, R. (2001) 'A holistic approach to internationalization', *International Business Review*, 10, pp. 25–49.

Forsman, M., Hinttu, S. and Kock, S. (2002) 'Internationalization from an SME perspective', Paper presented at the *18th Annual IMP Conference*, September, Dijon, pp. 1–12.

Freeman, S. (2002) 'A comprehensive model of the process of small firm internationalization: a network perspective', Paper presented at the *18th Annual IMP Conference*, September, Dijon, pp. 1–22.

Freeman, S., Edwards, R. and Schroder, B. (2006) 'How smaller born-globals firms use networks and alliances to overcome constraints to rapid internationalization', *Journal of International Marketing*, 14(3), pp. 33–63.

Genestre, A., Herbig, D. and Shao, A.T. (1995) 'What does marketing really mean to the Japanese?', *Marketing Intelligence and Planning*, 13(9), pp. 16–27.

Graves, C. and Thomas, J. (2008) 'Determinants of the internationalization pathways of family firms: an examination of family influence', *Family Business Review*, XXI(2), pp. 151–165.

Khojastehpour, M. and Johns, R. (2015) 'From pre-internationalization to post-internationalization: relationship marketing perspective', *Journal of Strategic Marketing*, 23(2), pp. 157–174.

Knight, G.A. and Liesch, P.W. (2002) 'Information internalization in internationalizing the firm', *Journal of Business Research*, 55, pp. 981–995.

Liu, H. and Li, K. (2002) 'Strategic implications of emerging Chinese multinationals: the Haier case study', *European Management Journal*, 20(6), pp. 699–706.

Rundh, B. (2007) 'International marketing behaviour amongst exporting firms', *European Journal of Marketing*, 41(1/2), pp. 181–198.

Suárez-Ortega, S.M. and Àlamo-Vera, F.R. (2005) 'SMEs' internationalization: firms and managerial factors', *International Journal of Entrepreneurial Behavior & Research*, 11(4), pp. 258–279.

Turner, C. (2012) 'Deinternationalisation: towards a coevolutionary framework', *European Business Review*, 24(2), pp. 92–105.

Turner, C. and Gardiner, P.D. (2007) 'De-internationalisation and global strategy: the case of British Telecommunications (BT)', *Journal of Business & Industrial Marketing*, 22(7), pp. 489–497.

Vissak, T., Ibeh, K. and Paliwonda, S. (2008) 'Internationalising from the European periphery: triggers, processes, and trajectories', *Journal of Euromarketing*, 17(1), pp. 35–48.

Welch, L.S., Benito, G.R.G., Silseth, P.R. and Karlsen, T. (2001) 'Exploring inward–outward linkages in firms' internationalization: a knowledge and network perspective', Paper presented at the *17th Annual IMP Conference*, September, Oslo, pp. 1–26.

Welch, L.S. and Loustarinen, R.K. (1993) 'Inward–outward connections in internationalization', *Journal of International Marketing*, 1(1), pp. 44–56.

Westhead, P., Wright, M. and Ucbasaran, D. (2002) 'International market selection strategies selected by "micro" and "small" firms', *Omega – The International Journal of Management Science*, 30, pp. 51–68.

CHAPTER 3
Internationalization theories

Contents

Case studies

Learning objectives

After studying this chapter you should be able to:

- Analyse and compare the three theories explaining a firm's internationalization process:
  (i)   the Uppsala internationalization model
  (ii) the transaction cost theory
  (iii) the network model
- Explain the most important determinants for the internationalization process of small and medium-sized enterprises (SMEs)

- Discuss the different factors that influence internationalization of services
- Explain and discuss the relevance of the network model for an SME serving as a subcontractor.
- Explain the term 'born global' and its connection to internet marketing.

3.1   Introduction

Having discussed the barriers to starting internationalization in Chapter 2, we will begin this chapter by presenting the different theoretical approaches to international marketing and then choose three models for further discussion in Sections 3.2–Section 3.4.

Historical development of internationalization

Much of the early literature on internationalization was inspired by general marketing theories. Later on, internationalization dealt with the choice between exporting and foreign direct investment (FDI). During the past 10–15 years there has been much focus on internationalization in networks, where a firm has different relationships not only with customers but also with other actors in the environment.

The traditional marketing approach

The Penrosian tradition (Penrose, 1959; Prahalad and Hamel, 1990) reflects the traditional marketing focus on the firm's core competences combined with opportunities in the foreign environment.

The cost-based view of this tradition suggested that the firm must possess a 'compensating advantage' in order to overcome the 'cost of foreignness' (Kindleberger, 1969; Hymer, 1976). This led to the identification of technological and marketing skills as the key elements in successful foreign entry.

'Life cycle' concept for international trade

Sequential modes of internationalization were introduced by Vernon's (1966) 'product cycle hypothesis', in which firms go through an exporting phase before switching first to market-seeking FDI and then to cost-oriented FDI. Technology and marketing factors combine to explain standardization, which drives location decisions.

Vernon's hypothesis is that producers in advanced countries (ACs) are 'closer' to the markets than producers elsewhere; consequently the first production facilities for these products will be in the ACs. As demand expands, a certain degree of standardization usually takes place. 'Economies of scale', through mass production, become more important. Concern about production cost replaces concern about product adaptations. With standardized products the less developed countries (LDCs) may offer competitive advantages as production locations. One example of this is the movement of production locations for personal computers from ACs to LDCs.

The Uppsala internationalization model

The Scandinavian 'stages' models of entry suggest a sequential pattern of entry into successive foreign markets, coupled with a progressive deepening of commitment to each market. Increasing commitment is particularly important in the thinking of the Uppsala School (Johanson and Wiedersheim-Paul, 1975; Johanson and Vahlne, 1977). The main consequence of this **Uppsala internationalization model** is that firms tend to intensify their commitment to foreign markets as their experience grows (see also Section 3.2).

Uppsala internationalization model
Additional market commitments are made in small incremental steps: choosing additional geographic markets with small psychic distances, combined with choosing entry modes with few additional risks.

The internationalization/transaction cost approach

In the early 1970s, intermediate forms of internationalization such as licensing were not considered interesting. Buckley and Casson (1976) expanded the choice to include licensing as a means of reaching customers abroad. But in their perspective the multinational firm would usually prefer to 'internalize' transactions via direct equity investment rather than license its capability. Joint ventures were not explicitly considered to be in the spectrum of governance choices until the mid-1980s (Contractor and Lorange, 1988; Kogut, 1988).

Buckley and Casson's focus on market-based (externalization) versus firm-based (internalization) solutions highlighted the strategic significance of licensing in market entry. Internationalization involves two interdependent decisions – location and mode of control.

The internalization perspective is closely related to the transaction cost (TC) theory (Williamson, 1975). The paradigmatic question in internalization theory is that, upon deciding to enter a foreign market, should a firm do so through internalization within its own boundaries (a subsidiary) or through some form of collaboration with an external partner (externalization)? The internalization and TC perspectives are both concerned with the minimization of TC and the conditions underlying market failure. The intention is to analyse the characteristics of a transaction in order to decide on the most efficient, i.e. TC minimizing, governance mode. The internalization theory can be considered the TC theory of the multinational corporation (Rugman, 1986; Madhok, 1998).

Dunning's eclectic approach

In his eclectic ownership–location–internalization (OLI) framework, Dunning (1988) discussed the importance of locational variables in foreign investment decisions. The word 'eclectic' represents the idea that a full explanation of the transnational activities of firms needs to draw on several strands of economic theory. According to Dunning, the propensity of a firm to engage itself in international production increases if the following three conditions are being satisfied:

1. *Ownership advantages*. A firm that owns foreign production facilities has bigger ownership advantages compared with firms of other nationalities. These 'advantages' may consist of intangible assets, such as know-how.
2. *Locational advantages*. It must be profitable for the firm to continue these assets with factor endowments (labour, energy, materials, components, transport and communication channels) in the foreign markets. If not, the foreign markets would be served by exports.
3. *Internalization advantages*. It must be more profitable for the firm to use its advantages rather than selling them, or the right to use them, to a foreign firm.

The network approach

The basic assumption in the network approach is that the international firm cannot be analysed as an isolated actor but has to be viewed in relation to other actors in the international environment. Thus the individual firm is dependent on resources controlled by others. The relationships of a firm within a domestic network can be used as connections to other networks in other countries (Johanson and Mattson, 1988).

In the following three sections (Sections 3.2–3.4) we will concentrate on three of the approaches presented in this section.

The difference between cultural distance and psychic distance

Cultural distance (discussed in Chapter 7) refers to the (macro) cultural level of a country and is defined as the degree to which (factual) cultural values in one country are different from those in another country, i.e. 'distance' between countries.

Psychic distance (as used in this text, e.g. in the geographical dimension of Figure 3.1) can be defined as the individual manager's perception of the differences between the home

Psychic distance
The individual's perception of difference between two markets, in terms of differences in 'country' and 'people' characteristics, which disturbs the flow of information, goods and services between the firm and the market.

and the foreign market, and it is a highly subjective interpretation of reality. The purpose of psychic distance is to capture the individual managers' perceptions and understandings of the 'distance' between two international markets, whereas 'cultural distance' focuses on a national level analysis (Avloniti and Filippaios, 2014). Therefore, psychic distance cannot only be measured with factual indicators, such as publicly available statistics on level of education, religion, language and so forth. Sousa and Lages (2011) suggest that the definition of 'psychic distance' should consist of two dimensions of 'distance':

- *Country characteristics distance*: level of economic development, communication infrastructure, marketing structure, technical requirements, market competitiveness and legal regulations.
- *People characteristics distance*: per-capita income, purchasing power of customers, customer lifestyles and preferences, level of education, language and cultural values (beliefs, attitudes and traditions).

By assessing psychic distance at the individual level on different dimensions, it is possible to take appropriate steps to reduce the manager's psychic distance towards foreign markets (Sousa and Bradley, 2005, 2006). We would expect that the manager's perception of psychic distance toward a foreign market will have an impact on the degree of adaptation/standardization of the different elements in the international marketing mix. Specifically, we expect that the higher the psychic distance between two markets, the greater the adaptation of the international marketing mix (product, price, place and promotion) is needed.

3.2 The Uppsala internationalization model

The stage model

During the 1970s, a number of Swedish researchers at the University of Uppsala (Johanson and Wiedersheim-Paul, 1975; Johanson and Vahlne, 1977) focused their interest on the internationalization process. Studying the internationalization of Swedish manufacturing firms, they developed a model of the firm's choice of market and form of entry when going abroad. Their work was influenced by Aharoni's (1966) seminal study.

With these basic assumptions in mind, the Uppsala researchers interpreted the patterns in the internationalization process they had observed in Swedish manufacturing firms. They had noted, first of all, that companies appeared to begin their operations abroad in markets that were fairly close geographically and only gradually penetrated more far-flung markets. Second, it appeared that companies entered new markets through exports. It was very rare for companies to enter new markets with sales organizations or manufacturing subsidiaries of their own. Wholly-owned or majority-owned operations were established only after several years of exports to the same market.

Johanson and Wiedersheim-Paul (1975) distinguish between four different modes of entering an international market, where the successive stages represent higher degrees of international involvement/market commitment:

- Stage 1: no regular export activities (sporadic export)
- Stage 2: export via independent representatives (export modes)
- Stage 3: establishment of a foreign sales subsidiary
- Stage 4: foreign production/manufacturing units.

The assumption that the internationalization of a firm develops step by step was originally supported by evidence from a case study of four Swedish firms. The sequence of stages was restricted to a specific country market. This market commitment dimension is shown in Figure 3.1.

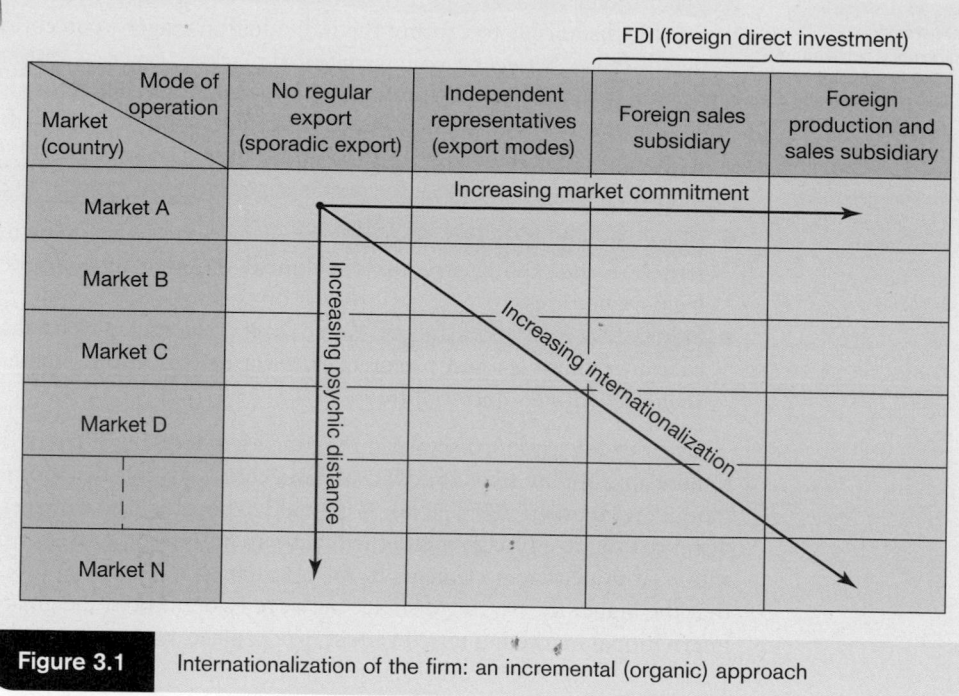

Market (country) / Mode of operation	No regular export (sporadic export)	Independent representatives (export modes)	FDI (foreign direct investment)	
			Foreign sales subsidiary	Foreign production and sales subsidiary
Market A				
Market B				
Market C				
Market D				
Market N				

Figure 3.1   Internationalization of the firm: an incremental (organic) approach

Source: adapted from Forsgren and Johanson (1975, p. 16).

The concept of market commitment is assumed to contain two factors – the amount of resources committed and the degree of commitment. The amount of resources could be operationalized to the size of investment in the market (marketing, organization, personnel, etc.), while the degree of commitment refers to the difficulty of finding an alternative use for the resources and transferring them to the alternative use.

International activities require both general knowledge and market-specific knowledge. Market-specific knowledge is assumed to be gained mainly through experience in the market, whereas knowledge of the operations can be transferred from one country to another; the latter will thus facilitate the geographic diversification in Figure 3.1. A direct relation between market knowledge and market commitment is postulated: knowledge can be considered as a dimension of human resources. Consequently, the better the knowledge about a market, the more valuable are the resources and the stronger the commitment to the market.

Figure 3.1 implies that additional market commitment as a rule will be made in small incremental steps, both in the market commitment dimension and in the geographical dimension. There are, however, three exceptions. First, firms that have large resources experience small consequences of their commitments and can take larger internationalization steps. Second, when market conditions are stable and homogeneous, relevant market knowledge can be gained in ways other than experience. Third, when the firm has considerable experience from markets with similar conditions, it may be able to generalize this experience to any specific market (Johanson and Vahlne, 1990).

The geographical dimension in Figure 3.1 shows that firms enter new markets with successively greater psychic distance. Psychic distance is defined by the individual manager's perception of the differences in terms of factors such as differences in language, culture and political systems, which disturb the flow of information between the firm and the market. Thus firms start internationalization by going to those markets they most easily understand. There they will see opportunities, and the perceived market uncertainty will be low (Brewer, 2007).

The original stage model has been extended by Welch and Loustarinen (1988), who operate with six dimensions of internationalization (see Figure 3.2):

1. *sales objects* (what?): goods, services, know-how and systems;
2. *operations methods* (how?): agents, subsidiaries, licensing, franchising management contracts;
3. *markets* (where?): political/cultural/psychic/physical distance differences between markets;
4. *organizational structure*: export department, international division;
5. *finance*: availability of international finance sources to support the international activities;
6. *personnel*: international skills, experience and training.

Of the six dimensions in Figure 3.2, three of these (4, 5 and 6) are concerned with an internal resource-based view, which is also consistent with a recent categorization of internationalization archetypes which uses the following six dimensions (Cerrati et al., 2015):

1. internationalization from the demand side (ratio of foreign sales to total sales);
2. resources located abroad (amount of resources that go overseas);
3. geographical scope (number of countries or regions in which the firm operates);
4. international orientation (percentage of managers with international work experience);
5. business networks (percentage of foreign sales that go through external agents/distributors vs own subsidiaries – FDI);
6. financial internationalization (share of foreign ownership).

The underlying assumption in the Uppsala model is that internationalization is a slow, time-consuming and iterative process. This was confirmed by a recent case study on the

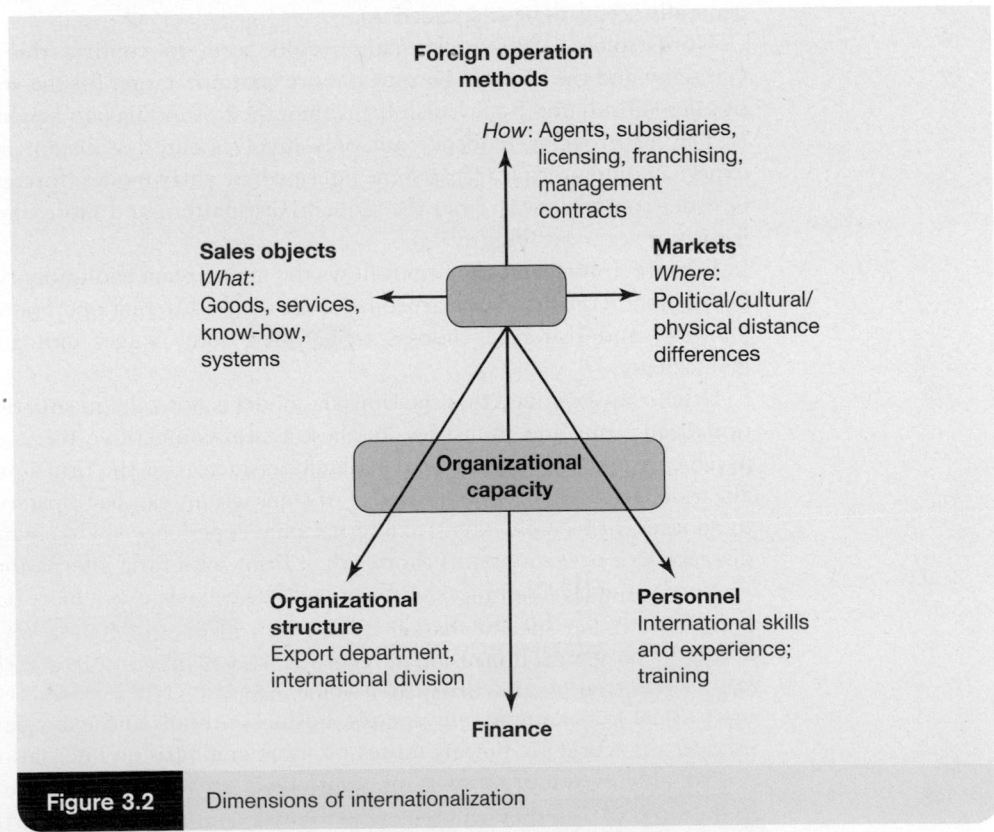

Figure 3.2   Dimensions of internationalization

Source: Welch and Loustarinen (1988). Reproduced with permission from The Braybrooke Press Ltd.

Volvo heavy truck business, in which Vahlne *et al.* (2011) concluded that, when the industry is highly complex and uncertainties involved are immense, internationalization decisions made too quickly and too boldly run a real risk of failure, with potentially large and negative consequences. The globalization process of the Volvo heavy truck business showed that learning plays an important role and that the creation of new structures, systems and relationships is required. This means that the management has to accept that the globalization of the company may proceed at a slower pace to allow for learning and adjustment to take place.

Critical views of the original Uppsala model

Various criticisms of the Uppsala model have been put forward: one is that the model is too deterministic (Reid, 1983; Turnbull, 1987).

It has also been argued that the model does not take into account interdependencies between different country markets (Johanson and Mattson, 1986). It seems reasonable to consider a firm more internationalized if it views and handles different country markets as interdependent than if it views them as completely separate entities.

Studies have shown that the internationalization process model is not valid for service industries. In research into the internationalization of Swedish technical consultants – a typical service industry – it has been demonstrated that the cumulative reinforcement of foreign commitments implied by the process model is absent (Sharma and Johanson, 1987).

The criticism has been supported by the fact that the internationalization process of new entrants in certain industries has recently become more spectacular. Firms have lately seemed prone to *leapfrog* stages in the establishment chain, entering 'distant' markets in terms of psychic distance at an early stage, and the pace of the internationalization process generally seems to have speeded up.

Nordström's (1990) preliminary results seem to confirm this argument. The UK, Germany and the US have become a more common target for the very first establishment of sales subsidiaries by Swedish firms than their Scandinavian neighbours.

The leapfrogging tendency not only involves entering distant markets. We can also expect a company to leapfrog some intermediate entry modes (foreign operation methods) in order to move away from the sequentialist pattern and more directly to some kind of foreign investment (Figure 3.3).

In market number 1 the firm follows the mainstream evolutionary pattern, but in market number 6 the firm has learned from the use of different operation methods in previous markets, and therefore chooses to leapfrog some stages and go directly to foreign investment.

Others have claimed that the Uppsala model is not valid in situations of highly internationalized firms and industries. In these cases, competitive forces and factors override psychic distance as the principal explanatory factor for the firm's process of internationalization. Furthermore, if knowledge of transactions can be transferred from one country to another, firms with extensive international experience are likely to perceive the psychic distance to a new country as shorter than firms with little international experience.

Nordström (1990) argues that the world has become much more homogeneous and that consequently psychic distance has decreased. Firms today also have quicker and easier access to knowledge about doing business abroad. It is no longer necessary to build up knowledge in-house in a slow and gradual trial-and-error process. Several factors contribute to this. For example, universities, business schools and management training centres all over the world are putting more and more emphasis on international business.

Probably even more important, continuous growth in world trade and foreign direct investment has resulted in an increase over time of the absolute number of people with experience of doing business abroad. Hence it has become easier to hire people with the experience and knowledge needed, rather than develop it in-house.

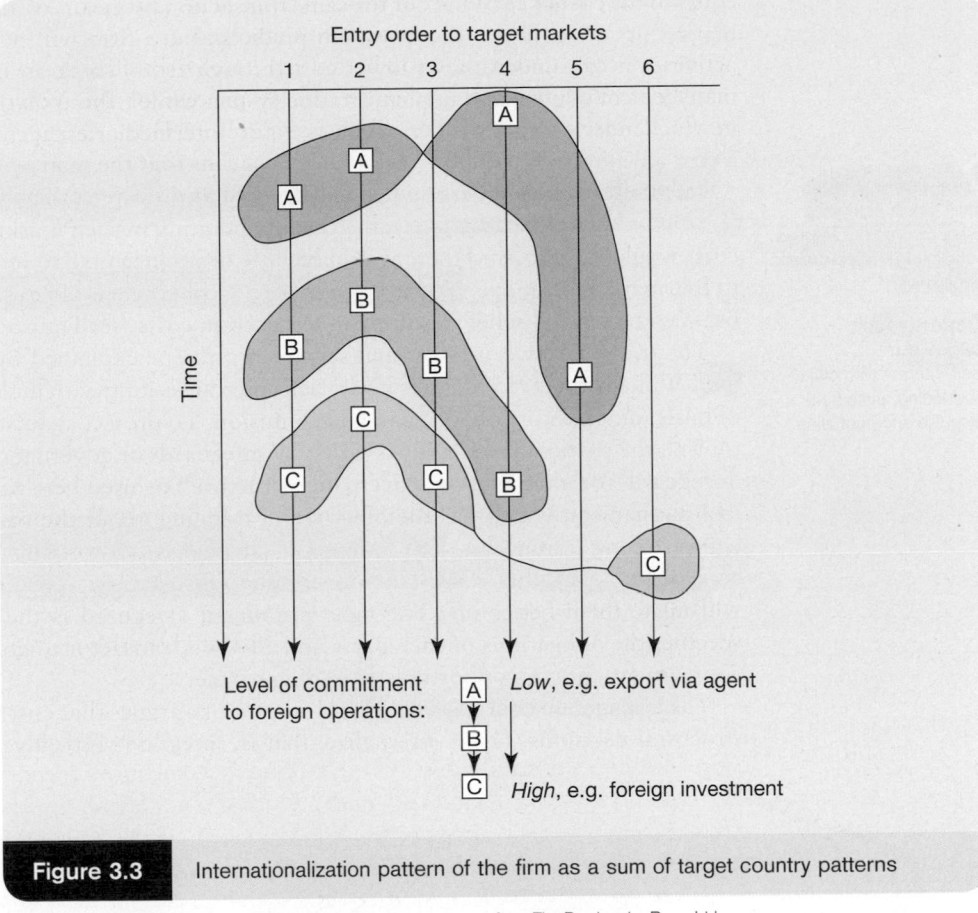

| **Figure 3.3** | Internationalization pattern of the firm as a sum of target country patterns |

Source: Welch and Loustarinen (1988). Reproduced with permission from The Braybrooke Press Ltd.

The spectacular development of information technologies, in terms of both absolute performance and diminishing price/performance ratios, has made it easier for a firm to become acquainted with foreign markets, thus making a leapfrog strategy more realistic (see also Section 3.5 on internet-based born globals).

In spite of the criticisms, the Uppsala model has gained strong support in studies of a wide spectrum of countries and situations. The empirical research confirms that commitment and experience are important factors explaining international business behaviour (Cumberland, 2006). In particular, the model receives strong support regarding export behaviour, and the relevance of cultural distance has also been confirmed.

In a more recent article, Johanson and Vahlne (2009) updated their model in parallel with the new findings on companies' internationalization. In their updated model they have put more emphasis on networks (as initiated by Johanson and Mattson, 1988) and opportunity recognition within the internationalization process. They see a firm's problems and opportunities as becoming less a matter of becoming familiar with certain export countries, and more related to relationships and networks. They recognize that new knowledge is mainly developed in relationships, and not so much in specific international markets.

3.3   The transaction cost analysis (TCA) model

The foundation for this model was made by Coase (1937). He argued that 'a firm will tend to expand until the cost of organizing an extra transaction within the firm will become equal to the cost of carrying out the same transaction by means of an exchange on the open market' (p. 395). It is a theory which predicts that a firm will perform internally those activities it can undertake at lower cost through establishing an internal ('hierarchical') management control and implementation system while relying on the market for activities in which independent outsiders (such as export intermediaries, agents or distributors) have a cost advantage.

Transaction costs emerge when markets fail to operate under the requirements of perfect competition ('friction free'); the cost of operating in such markets (i.e. the transaction cost) would be zero, and there would be little or no incentive to impose any impediments to free market exchange. However, in the real world there is always some kind of 'friction' between buyer and seller, resulting in transaction costs (see Figure 3.4).

The friction between buyer and seller can often be explained by **opportunistic behaviour**. Williamson (1985) defines it as a 'self-interest seeking with guile'. It includes methods of misleading, distortion, disguise and confusion. To protect against the hazards of opportunism, the parties may employ a variety of safeguards or governance structures. The term 'safeguard' (or alternatively 'governance structure') as used here can be defined as a control mechanism, which has the objective of bringing about the perception of fairness or equity among transactors. The purpose of safeguards is to provide, at minimum cost, the control and 'trust' that is necessary for transactors to believe that engaging in the exchange will make them better off. The most prominent safeguard is the legal contract, which specifies the obligations of each party and allows a transactor to go to a third party (i.e. a court) to sanction an opportunistic trading partner.

The **transaction cost analysis** (TCA) framework argues that cost minimization explains structural decisions. Firms internalize, that is, integrate vertically, to reduce transaction

Transaction costs
The 'friction' between buyer and seller, which is explained by opportunistic behaviour.

Opportunistic behaviour
Self-interest with guile – misleading, distortion, disguise and confusion.

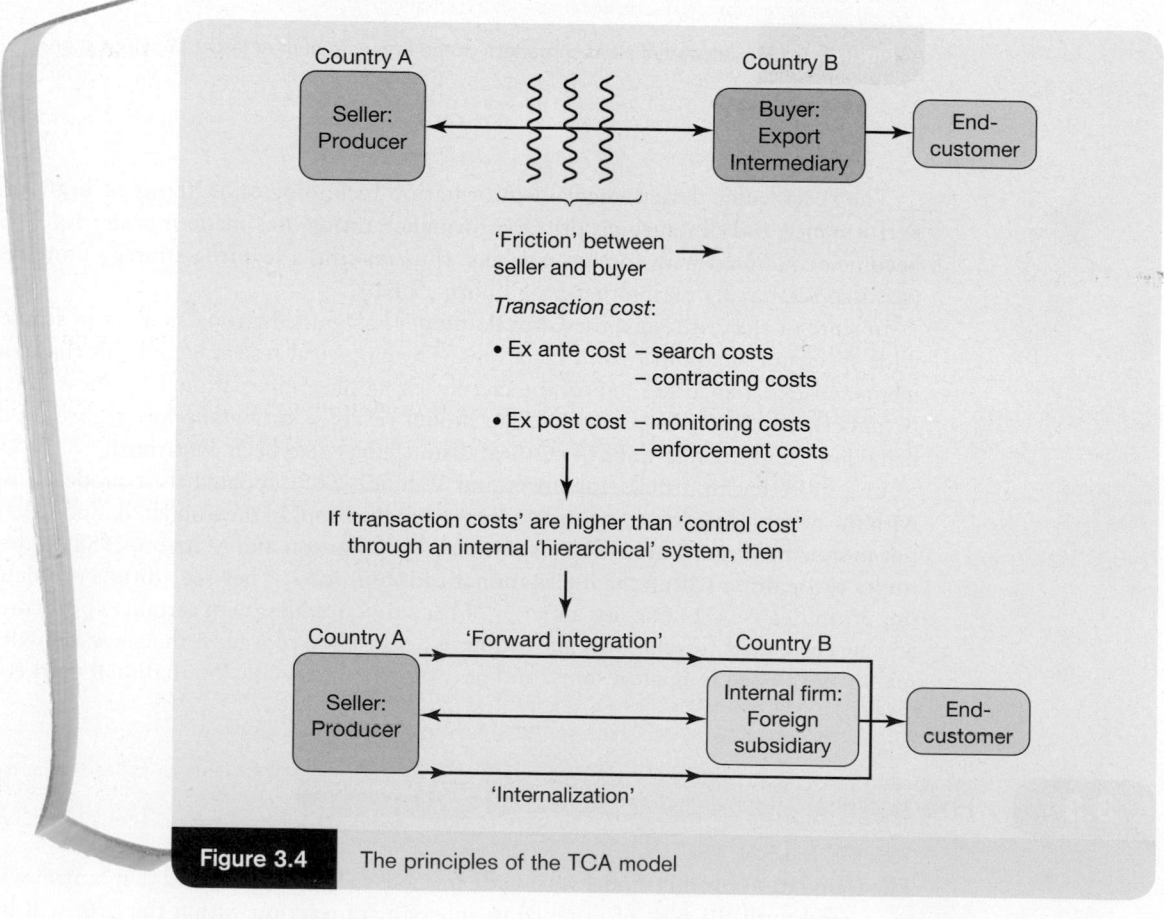

Figure 3.4   The principles of the TCA model

Transaction cost analysis
Transaction cost analysis concludes that, if the 'friction' between buyer and seller is higher than through an internal hierarchical system, then the firm should internalize.

costs. Transaction costs can be divided into *different forms of costs* related to the transactional relationship between buyer and seller. The underlying condition for the following description of the cost elements is the equation:

$$\text{Transaction cost} = ex\ ante\ \text{costs} + ex\ post\ \text{costs}$$
$$= (\text{search costs} + \text{contracting costs}) +$$
$$(\text{monitoring costs} + \text{enforcement costs})$$

Ex ante costs

- *Search costs* include the cost of gathering information to identify and evaluate potential export intermediaries. Although such costs can be prohibitive to many exporters, knowledge about foreign markets is critical to export success. The search costs for distant, unfamiliar markets, where available (published) market information is lacking and organizational forms are different, can be especially prohibitive (e.g. exports from the UK to China). In comparison, the search costs for nearby, familiar markets may be more acceptable (e.g. export from UK to Germany).
- *Contracting costs* refer to the costs associated with negotiating and writing an agreement between seller (producer) and buyer (export intermediary).

Ex post costs

- *Monitoring costs* refer to the costs associated with monitoring the agreement to ensure that both seller and buyer fulfil the predetermined set of obligations.
- *Enforcement costs* refer to the costs associated with the sanctioning of a trading partner who does not perform in accordance with the agreement.

A fundamental assumption of transaction cost theory is that firms will attempt to minimize the combination of these costs when undertaking transactions. Thus, when considering the most efficient form of organizing export functions, transaction cost theory suggests that firms will choose the solution that minimizes the sum of *ex ante* and *ex post* costs.

Williamson (1975) based his analysis on the assumption of transaction costs and the different forms of governance structure under which transactions take place. In his original work, Williamson identified two main alternatives of governance markets: externalization and internalization ('hierarchies'). In the case of **externalization**, market transactions are by definition external to the firm, and the price mechanism conveys all the necessary governance information. In the case of **internalization**, the international firm creates a kind of internal market in which the hierarchical governance is defined by a set of 'internal' contracts.

Externalization
Doing business through an external partner (importer, agent, distributor).

Internalization
Integration of an external partner into one's own organization.

Externalization and internalization of transactions are equated with intermediaries (agents, distributors) and sales subsidiaries (or other governance structures involving ownership control), respectively.

In this way, Williamson's framework provides the basis for a variety of research into the organization of international activity and the choice of international market entry mode. We will return to this issue in Part III of this book.

The conclusion of the transaction cost theory is:

If the transaction costs (defined above) through externalization (e.g. through an importer or agent) are higher than the control cost through an internal hierarchical system, then the firm should seek internalization of activities, i.e. implementing the global marketing strategy in wholly-owned subsidiaries. Or more popularly explained: if the 'friction' between buyer and seller is too high then the firm should internalize instead, in the form of its own subsidiaries.

Limitations of the TCA framework

Narrow assumptions of human nature

Ghoshal and Moran (1996) criticized the original work of Williamson as having overly narrow assumptions of human nature (opportunism and its equally narrow interpretation of economic objectives). They also wondered why the theory's mainstream development has remained immune to such important contributions as Ouchi's (1980) insight on social control. Ouchi (1980) pointed to the relevance of intermediate forms (between markets and hierarchies), such as the clan, where governance is based on a win–win situation (in contrast to a zero–sum game situation).

Sometimes firms would even build trust with their externalized agents and distributors by turning them into partners. In this way the firms would avoid large investments in subsidiaries around the world.

Excluding 'internal' transaction costs

The TCA framework also seems to ignore the 'internal' transaction cost, assuming zero friction within a multinational firm. One can imagine severe friction (resulting in transaction cost) between the head office of a firm and its sales subsidiaries when internal transfer prices have to be settled.

Relevance of 'intermediate' forms for SMEs

One can also question the relevance of the TCA framework to the internationalization process of SMEs (Christensen and Lindmark, 1993). The lack of resources and knowledge in SMEs is a major force for the externalization of activities. But since the use of markets often raises contractual problems, markets in many instances are not real alternatives to hierarchies for SMEs. Instead, the SMEs have to rely on intermediate forms of governance, such as contractual relations and relations based on clan-like systems created by a mutual orientation of investments, skills and trust-building. Therefore SMEs are often highly dependent on the cooperative environment available. Such an approach is presented and discussed in the next section on the network model.

Importance of production cost is understated

It can be argued that the importance of transaction cost is overstated and that the importance of production cost has not been taken into consideration. Production cost is the cost of performing a particular task/function in the value chain, such as R&D costs, manufacturing costs and marketing costs. According to Williamson (1985), the most efficient choice of internationalization mode is one that will help to *minimize the sum of production and transaction costs*.

3.4   The network model

Basic concept

Business networks are a mode of handling activity interdependences between several business actors. As we have seen, other modes of handling or governing interdependences in a business field are markets and hierarchies.

Business networks
Actors are autonomous and linked to each other through relationships, which are flexible and may alter accordingly to rapid changes in the environment. The 'glue' that keeps the relationships together is based on technical, economic, legal and, in particular, personal ties.

Network model
The relationships of a firm in a domestic network can be used as bridges to other networks in other countries.

The **network model** differs from the market with regard to relations between actors. In a market model, actors have no specific relationships to each other. The interdependences are regulated through the market price mechanism. By contrast, in the business network the actors are linked to each other through exchange relationships, and their needs and capabilities are mediated through the interaction taking place in the relationships.

The industrial network differs from the hierarchy in the way that the actors are autonomous and handle their interdependences bilaterally rather than via a coordinating unit on a higher level. Whereas a hierarchy is organized and controlled as one unit from the top, the business network is organized by each actor's willingness to engage in exchange relationships with some of the other actors in the network. The networks are more loosely coupled than are hierarchies; they can change shape more easily. Any actor in the network can engage in new relationships or break off old ones, thereby modifying its structure. Thus business networks can be expected to be more flexible in response to changing conditions in turbulent business fields, such as those where technical change is very rapid.

It can be concluded that business networks will emerge in fields where coordination between specific actors can give strong gains and where conditions are changing rapidly. Thus the network approach implies a move away from the firm as the unit of analysis, towards exchange between firms and between a group of firms and other groups of firms as the main object of study. However, it also implies a move away from transactions towards more lasting exchange relationships constituting a structure within which international business takes place and evolves.

Evidently, business relationships and consequently industrial networks are subtle phenomena, which cannot easily be observed by an outsider: that is, a potential entrant. The actors are tied to each other through a number of different bonds, including technical, social, cognitive, administrative, legal and economic.

A basic assumption in the network model is that the individual firm is dependent on resources controlled by other firms. The companies get access to these external resources through their network positions. Since the development of positions takes time and depends on resource accumulations, a firm must establish and develop positions in relation to counterparts in foreign networks.

To enter a network from outside requires that other actors be motivated to engage in interaction, something that is resource-demanding and that may require several firms to make adaptations in their ways of performing business. Thus foreign market or network entry of the firm may very well be the result of interaction initiatives taken by other firms that are insiders in the network in the specific country. However, the chances of being the object of such initiatives are much greater for an insider.

The networks in a country may well extend far beyond country borders. In relation to the internationalization of the firm, the network view argues that the internationalizing firm is initially engaged in a network that is primarily domestic.

The relationships of a firm in a domestic network can be used as bridges to other networks in other countries. In some cases, the customer demands that the supplier follows it abroad if the supplier wants to keep the business at home. An example of an international network is shown in Figure 3.5. It appears that one of the subsuppliers established a subsidiary in country B. Here the production subsidiary is served by the local company of the subsupplier. Countries E and F, and partly country C, are sourced from the production subsidiary in country B. Generally it can be assumed that direct or indirect bridges exist between firms and different country networks. Such bridges can be important both in the initial steps abroad and in the subsequent entry of new markets.

The character of the ties in a network is partly a matter of the firms involved. This is primarily the case with technical, economic and legal ties. To an important extent, however, the ties are formed between the people engaged in the business relationships, which is the case with social and cognitive ties. Industries as well as countries may differ with regard to the relative importance of firm and personal relationships. But it can be expected

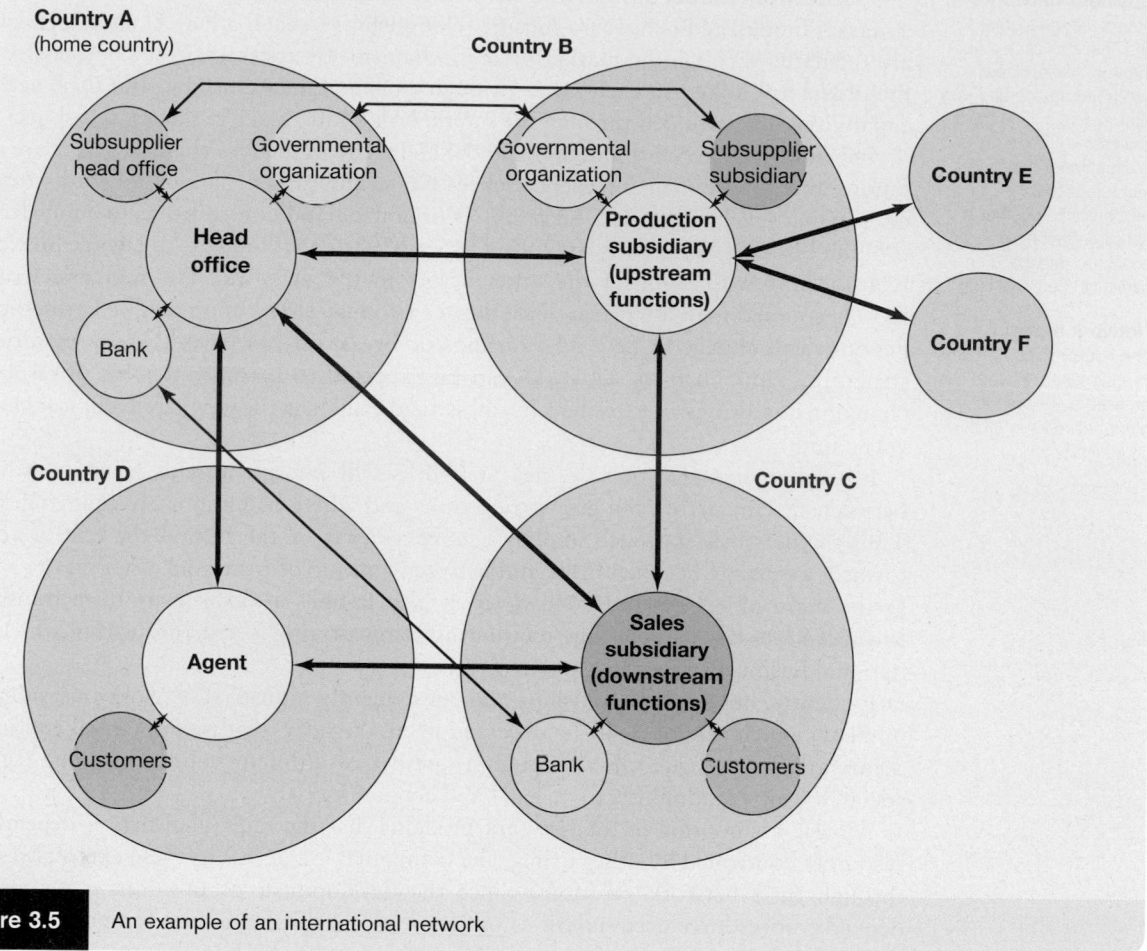

| **Figure 3.5** | An example of an international network |

that the personal influence on relationships is strongest in the early establishment of relationships. Later in the process, routines and systems will become more important.

When entering a network, the internationalization process of the firm will often proceed more quickly. In particular, SMEs in high-tech industries tend to go directly to more distant markets and to set up their own subsidiaries more rapidly. One reason seems to be that the entrepreneurs behind those companies have networks of colleagues dealing with the new technology. Internationalization, in these cases, is an exploitation of the advantage that this network constitutes.

3.5   Born globals

In recent years, research has identified an increasing number of firms that certainly do not follow the traditional stages pattern in their internationalization process. By contrast, they aim at international markets, or possibly even the global market, right from their birth.

Born global

A firm that from its 'birth' globalizes rapidly without any preceding long-term internationalization period.

A **born global** can be defined as 'a firm that from its inception pursues a vision of becoming global and globalizes rapidly without any preceding long-term domestic or internationalization period' (Oviatt and McDougall, 1994; Gabrielsson and Kirpalani, 2004).

Born globals represent an interesting case of firms operating under time and space compression conditions that have allowed them to assume a global geographic scope from the moment of their start-up. This 'time–space compression' phenomenon (Harvey, 1996) means that geographical processes can be reduced and compressed into 'here and now' trade and information exchange over the globe – if available infrastructure, communication and IT devices are put in place, together with skilled people. The global financial market is a good example of the phenomenon (Törnroos, 2002).

Oviatt and McDougall (1994) grouped born globals (or 'international new ventures' as they call them) into four different categories, dependent on the number of value chain activities performed combined with the number of countries involved. For example, they distinguish the 'export/import start-up' from the 'global start-up', where the latter – in contrast with the former – involves many activities coordinated across many countries.

EXHIBIT 3.1 K-pop – a 'born global' phenomenon has worldwide success

South Korea is emerging in the twenty-first century as a major exporter of popular culture. The wave has had considerable impact on the South Korean economy, as well as on the political and cultural influence of South Korea. Korean culture exports were predicted to reach US$4.5 billion in revenue in 2013, a 10 per cent increase on the previous year.

K-pop (Korean pop) is a musical genre consisting of dance, electro-pop, hip hop and R&B music originating in Korea. The term is commonly used for songs performed by Korean teen idols like Super Junior and Girls' Generation.

Source: Kristian Dowling/Getty Images.

Many K-pop music videos have colourful visuals and a catchy beat. Dance is an integral part of K-pop. When combining multiple singers, the singers often switch their positions while singing and dancing by making prompt movements in synchrony. K-pop is also recognized for its boy and girl groups whose members are young and attractive. Indeed, some critics suggest that Korean girl groups recruit members for their looks, and that they later undergo plastic surgery.

Most K-pop groups are owned by a handful of entertainment agencies. To guarantee the high probability of success of new talent, these agencies (such as S.M. Entertainment, which represents the boy group Super Junior and the girl group Girls' Generation) fully subsidize and oversee the professional lives and careers of the group members, often spending a lot to train and launch a new group.

South Korean entertainment companies have developed a process for training the singers and dancers in their groups. In many cases, potential group members enter the system at the age of 10 and live together in a house under tight rules. They attend school during the day and take singing and choreography classes at night.

The largest production company, SM Entertainment, alone made overseas revenues of about US$100 million in 2014, up from US$8 million in 2008. The company has produced two iterations of one of its most popular boy bands: the six members of EXO-K sing in Korean, while their counterparts in EXO-M perform the same songs in Mandarin for the huge Chinese market.

Globalization of K-pop through the internet and social media

The rise of social media networks (e.g. Facebook) since the mid-2000s has given K-pop an opportunity to reach a previously inaccessible audience, and the phenomenon has spread via the internet and through smartphone devices more rapidly than ever. The Korean wave has quickly spread K-pop to Europe, Asia and Africa.

One example of this phenomenon was the 2012 music video *Gangnam Style,* by Korean satirical rapper PSY. This music video became a worldwide viral phenomenon and was the first YouTube video to reach 1 billion hits. The single reached number 1 in both the UK and the US.

The use of K-pop (Super Junior) in LG's endorsement activities

In April–May 2012, Korea's LG Electronics selected idol Korean group, Super Junior, as the newest models to endorse their new L series of smartphones, which were introduced in Asia during that time.

To celebrate the launch of their new smartphones, LG Electronics hosted a 'LG Optimus Super Concert' Facebook event in collaboration with Super Junior.

The event was mainly for fans residing in Southeast Asia, and lasted for six weeks in countries such as Indonesia, the Philippines, Vietnam, Singapore, Malaysia and Hong Kong, among others. Each fan who clicked the 'like' button on their country's individual 'LG Mobile' Facebook page was entered as an event participant, and had an opportunity to receive virtual messages from Super Junior and to feel as though they were attending a live performance by their idols.

Source: Imaginechina/Corbis.

In addition, around 2,000 participants were selected by LG to receive footage of the members filming their *Mr Simple* music video.

Source: based on different public sources.

Born-again global
A firm that previously focused on its domestic markets but that suddenly embraces rapid and dedicated internationalization. The internationalization can be a result of critical events, such as a change in ownership and management or a takeover by another company. In this way, the acquired firm can gain access to more financial resources, managerial capability and international market knowledge.

Born globals are typically characterized as SMEs with fewer than 500 employees, with annual sales under US$100 million – and with a reliance on cutting-edge technology in the development of relatively unique product or process innovations. The most distinguishing feature of born global firms, however, is that they tend to be managed by entrepreneurial visionaries who view the world as a single, borderless marketplace from the time of the firm's founding. These small, technology-oriented companies operate in international markets from the earliest days of their establishment, and there is growing evidence of the emergence of born globals in numerous countries of the developed world.

More recently the concept of the **born-again global** firms has been proposed, i.e. long-established firms that previously focused on their domestic markets but that suddenly embrace rapid and dedicated internationalization (Bell *et al.*, 2001). The internationalization can be a result of critical events, such as a change in ownership and management, a takeover by another company or client followership, where a domestic customer internationalizes its operations by following its main customer to foreign markets. The change in ownership can bring in new decision-makers with an international focus. The acquisition can help the firm gain access to more financial resources, managerial capability, international market knowledge and the existing networks of the company taking it over (Kontinen and Ojala, 2012).

Born regional
A firm that starts international activities early and with significant international shares, but its international activities are only in its home region.

Furthermore, it seems that there can be *true-born globals* (focusing on both low- and high-distance markets) and apparently born globals, that is *born internationals,* which mainly focus on low-distance markets (Kuivalainen *et al.*, 2007). A **born regional** also starts international activities early and with significant international shares, but its international activities only take place in its home region, e.g. Europe, Asia or South America (Lopez *et al.*, 2009).

Internet-based born globals are emerging

A very important trend in favour of born globals is the recent advance in *communications technology,* which has accelerated the speed of information flows. Gone are the days of large, vertically integrated firms where information flows were expensive and took a considerable time to be shared. With the invention of the internet, e-mail and other telecommunication aids such as smartphones, iPads and other computer-supported technologies, managers of even small firms can manage operations efficiently across borders. Information is now readily and more quickly accessible to everyone. Everything is getting smaller and faster, allowing information to reach more people and places around the globe.

The internet revolution offers new opportunities for young SMEs to establish a global sales platform by developing e-commerce websites. Today many new and small firms are born globals in that they are 'start-ups' on the internet and sell to a global audience via a centralized e-commerce website. A recent study of the born globals usage of international sales channels showed that born globals are relatively quick to adopt internet-based sales channels (Gabrielsson and Gabrielsson, 2011). However, many of these firms not only rely on internet-based channels, but also use combinations of conventional channels and the internet. For example, in the case of *hybrid sales channels,* the channel functions are shared between the producer and the middleman, using the internet to integrate the activities. Customers and sales leads may be generated by internet-based promotion, but the actual product fulfilment (handling of stocks, distribution control and other reselling/retailing functions) is the responsibility of the 'physical' intermediaries.

The implementation of hybrid sales channels has to be handled with care in order to avoid channel conflicts.

Born globals are challenging traditional theories

Born globals may be similar to the 'late starter' or the 'international among others' (Johanson and Mattson, 1988). In the latter situation, both the environment and the firm are highly internationalized. Johanson and Mattson (1988) pointed out that internationalization processes of firms will be much faster in internationalized market conditions, because, among other reasons, the need for coordination and integration across borders is high. Since relevant partners/distributors will often be occupied in neighbouring markets, firms do not necessarily follow a 'rings in the water' approach to market selection. In the same vein, their 'establishment chain' need not follow the traditional picture because strategic alliances, joint ventures and the like are much more prevalent; firms seek partners with supplementary skills and resources. In other words, internationalization processes of firms will be much more individual and situation-specific in internationalized markets.

Many industries are characterized by *global sourcing activities* and also by networks across borders. The consequence is that innovative products can very quickly spread to new markets all over the world – because the needs and wants of buyers are becoming more homogeneous. Hence the internationalization process of subcontractors may be quite diverse and different from the stages models. In other words, the new market conditions pull the firms into many markets very quickly. Finally, financial markets have also become international, which means that entrepreneurs can seek financial sources all over the world.

Cavusgil and Knight (2015) conclude that the born global firms are often driven by change agents (founders and employees) who initiate the first export sales. It can be argued that the background of the decision-maker (founder) has a big influence on the internationalization path followed (Freeman and Cavusgil, 2007; Hagen and Zuchella, 2014). Market knowledge, personal networking of the entrepreneur and international contacts and experience transmitted from former occupations, relations and education are examples of such international skills obtained prior to the birth of the firm. Factors such as education, experience of living abroad, experience of other internationally oriented jobs, and so on mould the mind of the founder and decrease the psychic distances to specific product markets significantly; the previous experience and knowledge of the founder extend the network across national borders, opening up possibilities for new business ventures (Madsen and Servais, 1997).

Often born globals govern their sales and marketing activities through a specialized network in which they seek partners that complement their own competences; this is necessary because of their limited resources.

In many ways the slow organic (Uppsala model) process and the accelerated born global pathways are opposites, at the two extremes of a spectrum (see Figure 3.6). They also often represent the choice of doing it alone (the organic pathway), while the born global pathway is based on different types of cooperation and partnerships in order to facilitate rapid growth and internationalization.

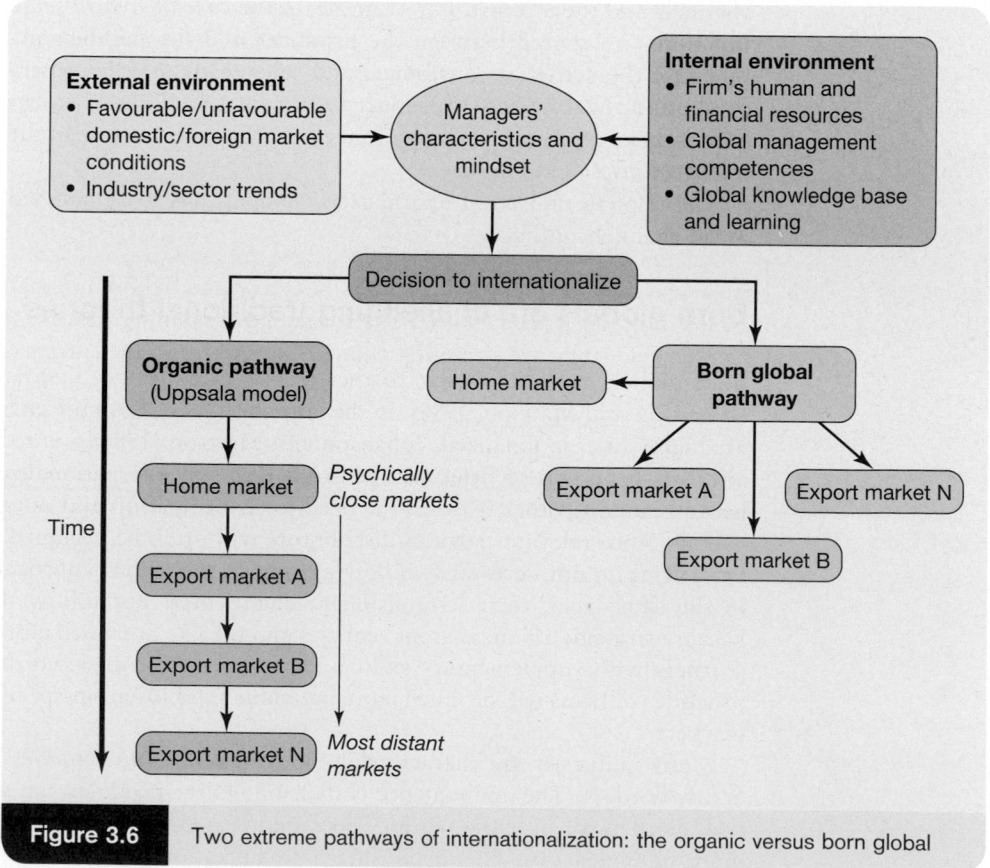

Figure 3.6   Two extreme pathways of internationalization: the organic versus born global

Source: adapted from Âijö et al. (2005, p. 6).

In spite of the different time-frames and prerequisites for the pathways, there are also some common characteristics in all models. Internationalization is seen as a process where knowledge, learning and commitment go hand in hand, even when it is rapid. Past knowledge and experience contribute to current knowledge of the company (Johanson and Martín, 2015). Firms aiming for the born global pathway do not have time to develop these skills in an organic way (inside the firm) – they need to possess them beforehand or acquire them along the way, i.e. through collaborating with other firms that already possess these supplementary competences.

Born globals must often choose a business area with homogeneous and minimal adaptation of the marketing mix. The argument is that these small firms cannot take a multi-domestic approach as can large firms, simply because they do not have sufficient scale in operations worldwide. They are vulnerable because they are dependent on a single product (niche market) that they have to commercialize in lead markets first, no matter where such markets are situated geographically. The reason is that such markets are the key to broad and rapid market access, which is important because these firms often incur relatively high fixed R&D costs, which occur 'up front', i.e. before any sales are made. Since this is the key factor influencing the choice of the initial market, the importance of psychic distance as a market selection criterion is reduced. In order to survive, firms must quickly catch the growth track to cover the initial expenses. Finally, competition for a typical born global is very intense and its products may become obsolete rather quickly (e.g. in the case of software). If a company is to take full advantage of the market potential during its 'global window of opportunity', it may be forced to penetrate all major markets simultaneously (Âijö et al., 2005).

More recent studies (e.g. Trudgen and Freeman, 2014) propose that some born globals initially select psychically proximate markets for the purpose of risk reduction, but are then able to utilize technical expertise, networks and entrepreneurial skill to move very quickly to psychically distant markets with more opportunities.

3.6   Summary

The main conclusions of this chapter are summarized in Table 3.1.

Born globals represent a relatively new research field in international marketing. They share some fundamental similarities: they possess unique assets, focus on narrow global market segments, are strongly customer-oriented, and the entrepreneur's vision and competences are of crucial importance. In the end, for these firms, being global does not seem to be an option but a necessity. They are pushed into globalization by global customers and national/regional market segments that are too small. They can sustain their immediate global reach thanks to entrepreneurial vision and competences, and a deep awareness and knowledge of their competitive advantage in foreign markets.

Table 3.1	Summary of the three models explaining the internationalization process of the firm		
	Uppsala internationalization model	Transaction cost analysis model	Network model
Unit of analysis	The firm	The transaction or set of transactions	Multiple inter-organizational relationships between firms Relationships between one group of firms and other groups of firms

Table 3.1	Continued		
	Uppsala internationalization model	**Transaction cost analysis model**	**Network model**
Basic assumptions about firms' behaviour	The model is based on behavioural theories and an incremental decision-making process with little influence from competitive market factors. A gradual learning-by-doing process from simple export to foreign direct investment (FDI)	In the real world there are 'friction'/transactional difficulties between buyer and seller. This friction is mainly caused by opportunistic behaviour: the self-conscious attention of the single manager (i.e. seeking of self-interest with guile)	The 'glue' that keeps the network (relationships) together is based on technical, economic, legal and especially personal ties. Managers' personal influence on relationships is strongest in the early phases of the establishment of relationships. Later in the process, routines and systems will become more important
Explanatory variables affecting the development process	The firm's knowledge/market commitment Psychic distance between home country and the firm's international markets	Transactional difficulties and transaction costs increase when transactions are characterized by asset specificity, uncertainty, frequency of transaction	The individual firms are autonomous. The individual firm is dependent on resources controlled by other firms Business networks will emerge in fields where there is frequent coordination between specific actors and where conditions are changing rapidly
Normative implications for international marketers	Additional market commitments should be made in small incremental steps: – Choose new geographic markets with small psychic distances from existing markets – Choose an 'entry mode' with few marginal risks	Under the above-mentioned conditions (i.e. prohibitively high transaction costs), firms should seek internalization of activities (i.e. implement the global marketing strategy in wholly-owned subsidiaries). Overall, the firm should select the entry mode for which transaction costs are minimized	The relationships of a firm in a domestic network can be used as bridges to other networks in other countries. Such direct or indirect bridges to different country networks can be important in the initial steps abroad and in the subsequent entry of new markets. Sometimes an SME can be forced to enter foreign networks, e.g. if a customer requires that the subsupplier (an SME) follows it abroad.

CASE STUDY 3.1

ZUMBA: a dance phenomenon is going global

It is the opening day at the fifth annual Zumba (www.zumba.com) conference in 2012, a five-day event in Orlando, Florida, where 8,000 Zumba instructors from across the world have gathered in shiny neon crop-tops and cargo pants. By 10am, there are clear signs of the excitement buzzing through the hall; people dressed in luminous green and pink are jiggling up and down in anticipation. Once the room is packed to capacity, the speaker takes to the stage and the crowd breaks out in excitement.

Greeting them this morning is the company's CEO and co-founder Alberto Perlman. Dressed for business in a shirt and glasses, Perlman is often referred to as the brains behind the business partner and co-founder, Alberto 'Beto' Perez.

Once the applause has settled, Perlman – who worked in IT before joining the company 11 years ago – greets the crowd in the steamy conference hall: 'We are the United Nations of Zumba!' he shouts, and once again the audience roars. 'Anyone who's here for the first time stand up,' he continues. 'Now, those standing on the right of those who are here for the first time, stand up, turn to your neighbour and give them a hug. That's a Zumba welcome!'

By 2012, Zumba Fitness had become the largest branded fitness programme in the world, with about 12 million people taking Zumba classes weekly at 110,000 locations in at least 125 countries. In the US alone, there were some 82,500 locations offering classes from Zumba-certified instructors (so-called ZINs – see later).

Source: Startraks/Rex Features.

How it all started. . .

Perez fell in love with dancing at the age of seven while watching a video of the 1978 movie *Grease,* starring John Travolta. At 16, he was teaching aerobics classes for $1 an hour. One day, he forgot his prepared music. All he had in his backpack was a cassette tape of merengue and salsa music that he had recorded off the radio.

His morning class was full of mothers who had dropped their kids off at school. 'I can't say, "Hey sorry, I forgot my music",' Perez said. 'I say to the people, "I have a new class I prepared for a long time." It was not true. I improvised for one hour.'

He soon moved to the Colombian capital of Bogotá, where he continued those classes and became a choreographer for Sony Music and Shakira.

In 1999, Perez went to the US for the first time. He pounded the pavement on South Beach, going from gym to gym. Nobody was interested in this new dance exercise class by a man who couldn't speak English.

On his fourth trip to Miami he landed a job at the swanky Williams Island Spa in a development where several Colombians lived. Some had even taken classes with him in Bogotá.

Within a year, Perez was in demand, teaching 22 classes all over south Florida. At the same time, Alberto Perlman and Alberto Aghion, both entrepreneurs in their mid-20s and natives of Colombia, were looking for a new business venture after the dot-com bubble had burst, bringing down their internet company, Spydre Labs, an incubator for internet start-ups related to Latin America.

Zumba Fitness was founded in Aventura, Florida, in 2001 by the 'three Albertos' Perez and boyhood friends Perlman and Aghion. The trio's original plan was simple: produce VHS workout tapes and DVDs of Perez's popular south Florida classes to sell around the country on infomercials.

To create a demonstration video to show to investors, the three stayed up all night laying down boards to create a dance floor on the beach outside a Sunny Isles hotel. About 200 of Perez's students paid $20 each for the class, raising an additional $4,000.

When the infomercial began running on TV, people rang the call centre in Ohio to buy the videos and a few also asked how to become Zumba instructors. Those callers were forwarded to Zumba's office – at Aghion's home. After a few 2am wake-up calls, Aghion realized this was another business opportunity.

The business model

Since 2001, when Perlman, Perez and Aghion first started trying, initially quite unsuccessfully, to sell DVDs of their euphoric, Latino-inspired dance workouts, their brand has gone global.

Today, Zumba (which is a registered trademark) is everywhere: 15 million weekly participants take to the dancefloor (and church halls and community centres and tin shacks) in more than 200,000 locations in 180 countries across the world – and after the US, Britain is Zumba's biggest market. With Zumba now the biggest branded fitness programme in the world, the possibilities for its creators have proved limitless.

Part of the Zumba programme's popularity can be explained by its adoption by celebrities all over the world. Jennifer Lopez and Kirstie Alley are known to take Zumba classes as part of their workout routines, while Jackie Chan has been caught on video performing the exercises. Other celebrity fans of Zumba include Emma Watson, Victoria Beckham and Halle Berry.

Zumba Fitness also has greatly benefited from internet advertising and social media. Many people discovered Zumba via YouTube videos. Zumba Fitness started a Facebook page about a year ago and now has more than 3 million fans. Zumba is mentioned every 11 seconds in social media platforms.

Alongside traditional Zumba classes, there is also Zumbatomic for kids, Zumba Gold for the mature student, Aqua Zumba, Zumba Toning, Zumba Gold Toning, Zumba in the Circuit and now Zumba Sentao, a new body-busting Zumba workout with chairs. Zumba may look easy but it involves loud music, gyrating with chairs and imaginary lassoes, and leaves participants after an hour's class both whooping with joy and on the verge of collapse. The physical results are fierce, with participants burning as much as 2,000 calories an hour while throwing their bodies around to very loud music.

Zumba Fitness makes its money on its instructors' academy, instructors' courses, monthly fees from instructors in its network and its brand merchandise. The company has built its own line of hip, colourful clothing and footwear, workout DVDs, two video games, original music and a lifestyle magazine, *Z-Life*.

With instructors across the world charging, on average, between US$8 and US$16 (£5–£10) per person for an hour's packed-out session, serious cash is changing hands, and yet the classes only make up a tiny fraction of this fast-expanding empire. To date, more than 10 million copies of the four different Zumba Fitness DVDs have been sold worldwide. Zumba was the first branded fitness programme to launch a video game on all three major gaming platforms: Wii, Xbox and PS3. Their best-selling video game has sold more than 6 million copies and dominated the video-game charts for nearly 40 weeks.

The clothing range is a key part of Zumba's growing business model, which seems to be not so much about diversification as about creating a brand that is entirely self-sufficient. When in 2002 they launched their DVDs, and people started seeing them and asking how they could become instructors, they launched their training programme; when, five years later, they had the idea of selling a few clothing items to publicize their brand, they put 500 T-shirts and 500 cargo pants on sale online – they sold out within a month, and they decided there was something in it. Rather than licensing their clothing range, Zumba decided to keep that in-house as well. Their market research is cheap: instead of focus groups, members of their 25-strong clothing team go out to Zumba events and see what the people are wearing and how they customise their clothes, and then repackage those ideas back to the consumers. It works. The clothing range, which launched in 2007, has fast become a phenomenon in itself. In 2012, Zumba had a revenue of US$10 million in clothes sales. The company sold 3 million units in 2012, compared with 1.8 million units in 2011.

The real cash-cow – the ZINs

Zumba has access to a captive global audience of 12 million people a week through its network of instructors, the so-called ZINs (members of the Zumba® Instructor Network), of whom there are now 30,000 around the world. In 2005, the Zumba Academy was launched to license instructors to teach Zumba classes.

ZINs are affiliated instructors who pay around US$30 a month for membership and, in return, get their literature and cards printed by one of the brand's many sponsors, as well as new choreography and CDs, and the chance to sell the clothes for a small profit. In order to become a ZIN, the potential Zumba instructors have to pay around US$480 to do a day's training, then pay for insurance and various other costs including ongoing training. Signing up to become a ZIN also provides access to a special social networking site, giving members instant links to fellow fanatics around the world.

Zumba does not charge licensing fees to gyms or fitness centres – this is all taken care of by the ZINs who act as independent business entrepreneurs.

QUESTIONS

1. Which of the internationalization models presented in this chapter best fits the internationalization of Zumba?

2. Why has Zumba's global business model been so successful?

Sources: based on www.zumba.com; Noel P. (2012), Zumba Instructor Certification, www.ehow.com/about_6304817_zumba-instructor-certification.html; Clark, C. (2012) 'Zumba's Latin rhythms on the move in the fitness world', *The Seattle Times*, February 20, 2012, http://seattletimes.com/html/businesstechnology/2017556695_zumbabiz21.html.

CASE STUDY 3.2

Dreamworks Classics: internationalization of Postman Pat

On 23 July 2012, movie studio DreamWorks Animation (the company behind box office hits such as *Shrek* and *Madagascar*) acquired Classic Media for US$155 million. The company became a division of DreamWorks Animation and was renamed DreamWorks Classics, which now controls Classic Media's portfolio of over 450 films and 6,100 episodes of TV shows, including *Lassie, The Lone Ranger, Postman Pat, Noddy* and *Rocky and Bullwinkle*.

In 2012, Classic Media had a net revenue of $82.2 million and an operating profit of $19.2 million.

By acquiring Classic Media, DreamWorks Classics obtained control of Postman Pat, one of the most popular characters among children of pre-school age.

Postman Pat

Set in the fictional Yorkshire village of Greendale, Postman Pat and his faithful companion, Jess the Cat, began delivering post on the UK's BBC1 channel in September 1981. *Postman Pat* continues to air on the BBC, with episodes licensed and the broadcast platform secured beyond 2010. The target viewer group for the show is the pre-school age (2–6 years).

Postman Pat TV shows have now been shown in more than 100 countries around the world. With sales in so many international markets, it is important that the brand awareness created by the TV platform is leveraged through the development of a strong licensing and merchandising line. For example, in the UK in 2004 Marks & Spencer acquired the rights to use the characters in 70 of its top stores. The programme included a range of nightwear, underwear, slippers, watches and puzzles for children aged 3–6. Postman Pat and Jess the Cat proved an irresistible gift buy for parents, grandparents, guardians and others.

In May 2009, Classic Media secured a partnership with one of the UK's largest theme parks – Flamingo Land in North Yorkshire – for Postman Pat and other characters from the Special Delivery service to take up residence. A say 2009, over 12 million Postman Pat books had been sold worldwide and some 20 titles were released in the UK in 2013. This growing collection includes Postman Pat storybooks, integrated learning books, colouring books and multi-character magazines.

The long-anticipated 3D movie *Postman Pat: The Movie – You Know You're The One* was released at the end of May 2013. The film finds Pat, everyone's favourite postman, coming face to face with the temptations of money, status and a shiny new suit when he enters a national TV talent show that threatens to tear him away from his hometown of Greendale and the friends he loves.

QUESTIONS

1. List the criteria that you should use for choosing new international markets.

2. If you were to advise DreamWorks Classics would you recommend them to use the 'organic' or 'born global' pathway for the internationalization of Postman Pat?

3. What values/benefits can DreamWorks Classics transfer to the license partners for consumer products apart from using the Postman Pat characters?

Source: based on different public sources.

Source: JFTL Images/Alamy Images.

VIDEO CASE STUDY 3.3 Reebok
download from **www.pearsoned.co.uk/hollensen**

Source: Reebok International Limited. The 'Reebok logo' is a registered trade mark of Reebok International Limited, used with permission.

Reebok (www.reebok.com and www.adidas-group. com) specializes in the design, marketing and distribution of sports and fitness products, including footwear, apparel and accessories, as well as footwear and apparel for non-athletic use. In August 2005, Adidas bought Reebok for US$3.8 billion, giving the company about 20 per cent of the US market and the potential to challenge market leader Nike.

Questions

1. Which of the internationalization theories best explains Adidas's acquisition of Reebok?

2. What could be the motives behind Adidas's acquisition of Reebok?

3. Which of the three internationalization theories is best for explaining whether Reebok follows the establishment of its retailers, e.g. Foot Locker, in international markets?

4. Is Reebok able to adopt its US marketing approach (connecting to the youth segment through famous rappers, like 50 Cent) in other international markets?

For further resources, see this book's website at **www.pearsoned.co.uk/hollensen**

Questions for discussion

1. Explain why internationalization is an ongoing process in constant need of evaluation.

2. Explain the main differences between the three theories of internationalization: the Uppsala model, the transaction cost theory and the network model.

3. What is meant by the concept of 'psychological' or 'psychic' distance?

References

Aharoni, Y. (1966) *The Foreign Investment Decision Process*. Harvard Business School Press, Boston, MA.

Âijö, T., Kuivalainen, O., Saarenketo, S., Lindqvist, J. and Hanninen, H. (2005) *Internationalization Handbook for the Software Business*. Centre of Expertise for Software Product Business, Espoo, Finland.

Avloniti, A. and Filippaios (2014) 'Unbundling the difference between Psychic and Cultural Distance: An empirical examination of the existing measures', *International Business Review*, 23(3), pp. 660–674.

Bell, J., McNaughton, R. and Young, S. (2001) 'Born-again global firms: an extension to the born global phenomenon', *Journal of International Management*, 7(3), pp. 173–190.

Brewer, P.A. (2007) 'Operationalizing psychic distance: a revised approach', *Journal of International Marketing*, 15(1), pp. 44–66.

Buckley, P.J. and Casson, M. (1976) *The Future of the Multinational Enterprise*. Holmes & Meier, New York.

Cavusgil, S.T. and Knight, G. (2015) 'The born global firm: An entrepreneurial and capabilities perspective on early and rapid internationalization', *Journal of International Business Studies*, 46(1), pp. 3–16.

Cerrati, D., Crosato, L. and Depperu, D. (2015) 'Archetypes of SME internationalization: A configurational approach'. *International Business Review*, http://dx.doi.org/10.1016/j.ibusrev.2015.05.010 (article in press, no page numbers)

Christensen, P.R. and Lindmark, L.L. (1993) 'Location and internationalization of small firms', in Lindquist, L. and Persson, L.O. (eds), *Visions and Strategies in European Integration*. Springer Verlag, Berlin and Heidelberg.

Coase, R.H. (1937) 'The nature of the firm', *Economica*, 4(16), pp. 386–405.

Contractor, F.J. and Lorange, P. (eds) (1998) *Cooperative Strategies in International Business*. Lexington Books, Lexington, MA.

Cumberland, F. (2006) 'Theory development within international market entry mode – an assessment', *The Marketing Review*, 6(4), pp. 349–373.

Dunning, J.H. (1988) *Explaining International Production*. Unwin, London.

Forsgren, M. and Johanson, J. (1975) *International føretagsekonomi*. Norstedts, Stockholm.

Freeman, S. and Cavusgil, S.T. (2007) 'Towards a typology of commitment states among managers of born-global firms: a study of accelerated internationalization', *Journal of International Marketing*, 15(4), pp. 1–40.

Gabrielsson, M. and Gabrielsson, P. (2011) 'Internet-based sales channel strategies of born global firms', *International Business Review*, 20, pp. 88–89.

Gabrielsson, M. and Kirpalani, M.V.H. (2004) 'Born globals; how to reach new business space rapidly', *International Business Review*, 13, pp. 555–571.

Ghoshal, S. and Moran, P. (1996) 'Bad for practice: a critique of the transaction cost theory', *Academy of Management Review*, 21(1), pp. 13–47.

Hagen, B. and Zuchella, A. (2014) 'Born global or born to run? The long-term growth of born global firms', *MIR Management International Review*, 54(4), pp. 497–525.

Harvey, D. (1996) *Justice, Nature and the Geography of Difference*. Basil Blackwell, Oxford.

Hymer, S.H. (1976) 'The international operations of national firms: a study of direct foreign investment'. Unpublished 1960 Ph.D. thesis, MIT Press, Cambridge, MA.

Johanson, M. and Martín (2015) 'The incremental expansion of Born Internationals: A comparison of new and old Internationals', *International Business Review*, 24(3), pp. 476–496.

Johanson, J. and Mattson, L.G. (1986) 'International marketing and internationalization processes: some perspectives on current and future research', in Paliwoda, S. and Turnbull, P. (eds), *Research in Developments in International Marketing*. Croom Helm, Beckenham (UK).

Johanson, J. and Mattson, L.G. (1988) 'Internationalization in industrial systems', in Hood, N. and Vahlne, J.E. (eds), *Strategies in Global Competition*. Croom Helm, Beckenham (UK).

Johanson, J. and Vahlne, J.E. (1977) 'The internationalization process of the firm: a model of knowledge development and increasing foreign market commitment', *Journal of International Business Studies*, 8(1), pp. 23–32.

Johanson, J. and Vahlne, J.E. (1990) 'The mechanism of internationalization', *International Marketing Review*, 7(4), pp. 11–24.

Johanson, J. and Vahlne, J.E. (2009) 'The Uppsala internationalization process model revisited: from liability of foreignness to liability of outsidership', *Journal of International Business Studies*, 40(9), pp. 1411–1431.

Johanson, J. and Wiedersheim-Paul, F. (1975) 'The internationalization of the firm: four Swedish cases', *Journal of Management Studies*, October, pp. 305–322.

Kindleberger, C.P. (1969) *American Business Abroad*. Yale University Press, New Haven, CT.

Kogut, B. (1988) 'Joint ventures: theoretical and empirical perspective', *Strategic Management Journal*, 9, pp. 319–332.

Kontinen, T. and Ojala, A. (2012) 'Internationalization pathways among family-owned SMEs', *International Marketing Review*, 29(5), pp. 496–518.

Kuivalainen, O., Sundqvist, S. and Servais, P. (2007) 'Firms' degree of born-globalness, international entrepreneurial orientation and export performance', *Journal of World Business,* 42, pp. 253–267.

Lopez, L.E., Kundu, S.K. and Ciravegna, L. (2009) 'Born global or born regional? Evidence from an exploratory study in the Costa Rican software industry, *Journal of International Business Studies,* 40(7), pp. 1228–1238.

Madhok, A. (1998) 'The nature of multinational firm boundaries: transaction cost, firm capabilities and foreign market entry mode', *International Business Review,* 7, pp. 259–290.

Madsen, T.K. and Servais, P. (1997) 'The internationalization of born globals: an evolutionary process?', *International Business Review,* 6(6), pp. 561–583.

Nordström, K.A. (1990) 'The internationalization process of the firm: searching for new patterns and explanations', research paper, Stockholm School of Economics.

Ouchi, W.G. (1980) 'Markets, bureaucracies and clans', *Administrative Science Quarterly,* 25, pp. 129–142.

Oviatt, B. and McDougall, P. (1994) 'Towards a theory of international new ventures', *Journal of International Business Studies,* 25(1), pp. 45–64.

Penrose, E. (1959) *The Theory of the Growth of the Firm.* Blackwell, London.

Prahalad, C.K. and Hamel, G. (1990) 'The core competence and the corporation', *Harvard Business Review,* May, pp. 71–97.

Reid, S.D. (1983) 'Firm internationalization, transaction costs and strategic choice', *International Marketing,* 1(2), p. 44.

Rugman, A.M. (1986) 'New theories of the multinational enterprise: an assessment of internationalization theory', *Bulletin of Economic Research,* 38(2), pp. 101–118.

Sharma, D.D. and Johanson, J. (1987) 'Technical consultancy in internationalization', *International Marketing Review,* Winter, pp. 20–29.

Sousa, C.M.P. and Bradley, F. (2005) 'Global markets: does psychic distance matter?' *Journal of Strategic Marketing,* 13 (March), pp. 43–59.

Sousa, C.M.P. and Bradley, F. (2006) 'Cultural distance and psychic distance: two peas in a pod?', *Journal of International Marketing,* 14(1), pp. 49–70.

Sousa, C.M.P. and Lages, L.F. (2011) 'The PD scale: a measure of psychic distance and its impact on international marketing strategy', *International Marketing Review,* 28(2), pp. 201–222.

Trudgen, R. and Freeman, S. (2014) 'Measuring the Performance of Born-Global Firms Throughout Their Development Process: The Roles of Initial Market Selection and Internationalisation Speed', *MIR Management International Review,* 54(4), pp. 551–579.

Turnbull, P.N. (1987) 'Interaction and international marketing: an investment process', *International Marketing Review,* Winter, pp. 7–19.

Törnroos, J.-Å. (2002) 'Internationalization of the firm: a theoretical review with implications for business network research', Paper presented at the 18th Annual IMP Conference, September, Lyon, pp. 1–21.

Vahlne, J.E., Ivarsson, I. and Johanson, J. (2011) 'The tortuous road to globalization for Volvo's heavy truck business: extending the scope of the Uppsala model', *International Business Review,* 20, pp. 1–14.

Vernon, R. (1966) 'International investment and international trade in the product cycle', *Quarterly Journal of Economics,* 80, pp. 190–207.

Welch, L.S. and Loustarinen, R. (1988) 'Internationalization: evolution of a concept', *Journal of General Management,* 14(2), pp. 36–64.

Williamson, O.E. (1975) *Markets and Hierarchies: Analysis and Antitrust Implications.* The Free Press, New York.

Williamson, O.E. (1985) *The Economic Institutions of Capitalization.* The Free Press, New York.

CHAPTER 4

Development of the firm's international competitiveness

Contents

Learning objectives

After studying this chapter you should be able to:

- Define the concept of international competitiveness in a broader perspective from a macro to a micro level
- Discuss the factors influencing the firm's international competitiveness
- Explain how Porter's traditional competitive-based five forces model can be extended to a collaborative (five sources) model
- Explore the idea behind the competitive triangle
- Analyse the basic sources of competitive advantage
- Explain the steps in competitive benchmarking
- Explain how a company can create customer value by the use of Blue Ocean Strategy.

4.1   Introduction

The topic of this chapter is how the firm creates and develops competitive advantages in the international market. Development of a firm's international competitiveness takes place interactively with the environment. The firm must be able to adjust to customers, competitors and public authorities. To be able to participate in the international competitive arena, the firm must have established a competitive basis consisting of resources, competences and relations to others in the international arena.

To enable an understanding of the development of a firm's international competitiveness in a broader perspective, a model in three stages (see Figure 4.1) will be presented:

1. analysis of national competitiveness (the Porter diamond) – macro level;
2. competition analysis in an industry (Porter's five forces) – meso level;
3. value chain analysis – micro level:
    (a) competitive triangle;
    (b) benchmarking.

The analysis starts at the macro level and then moves into the firm's competitive arena through Porter's five-forces framework. Based on the firm's value chain, the analysis is concluded with a discussion of which activities/functions in the value chain are the firm's core competences (and must be developed internally in the firm) and which competences must be placed with others through alliances and market relations.

The graphical system used in Figure 4.1 (which will be referred to throughout this chapter) places the models after each other in a hierarchical windows logic, where you get from stage 1 to stage 2 by clicking on the icon box: 'Firm strategy, structure and rivalry'. Here Porter's five-forces model appears. From stage 2 to 3 we click the middle box labelled 'Market competitors/Intensity of rivalry' and the model for a value chain analysis/competitive triangle appears.

Individual competitiveness

In this chapter the analysis ends at the firm level, but it is possible to go a step further by analysing individual competitiveness (Veliyath and Zahra, 2000). The factors influencing the capacity of an individual to become competitive would include intrinsic abilities, skills, motivation levels and the amount of effort involved.

4.2   Analysis of national competitiveness (the Porter diamond)

Analysis of national competitiveness represents the highest level in the entire model (Figure 4.1). Michael E. Porter called his work *The Competitive Advantage of Nations* (1990), but as a starting point it is important to say that it is firms that are competing in the international arena, not nations. Yet the characteristics of the home nation play a central role in a firm's international success. The home base shapes a company's capacity to innovate rapidly in technology and methods, and to do so in the proper directions. It is the place from which competitive advantage ultimately emanates and from which it must be sustained. Competitive advantage ultimately results from an effective combination of national circumstances and company strategy. Conditions in a nation may create an environment in which firms can attain international competitive advantage, but it is up to a company to seize the opportunity. The national diamond becomes central to choosing the industries to compete with, as well as the appropriate strategy. The home base is an important determinant of a firm's strengths and weaknesses relative to foreign rivals.

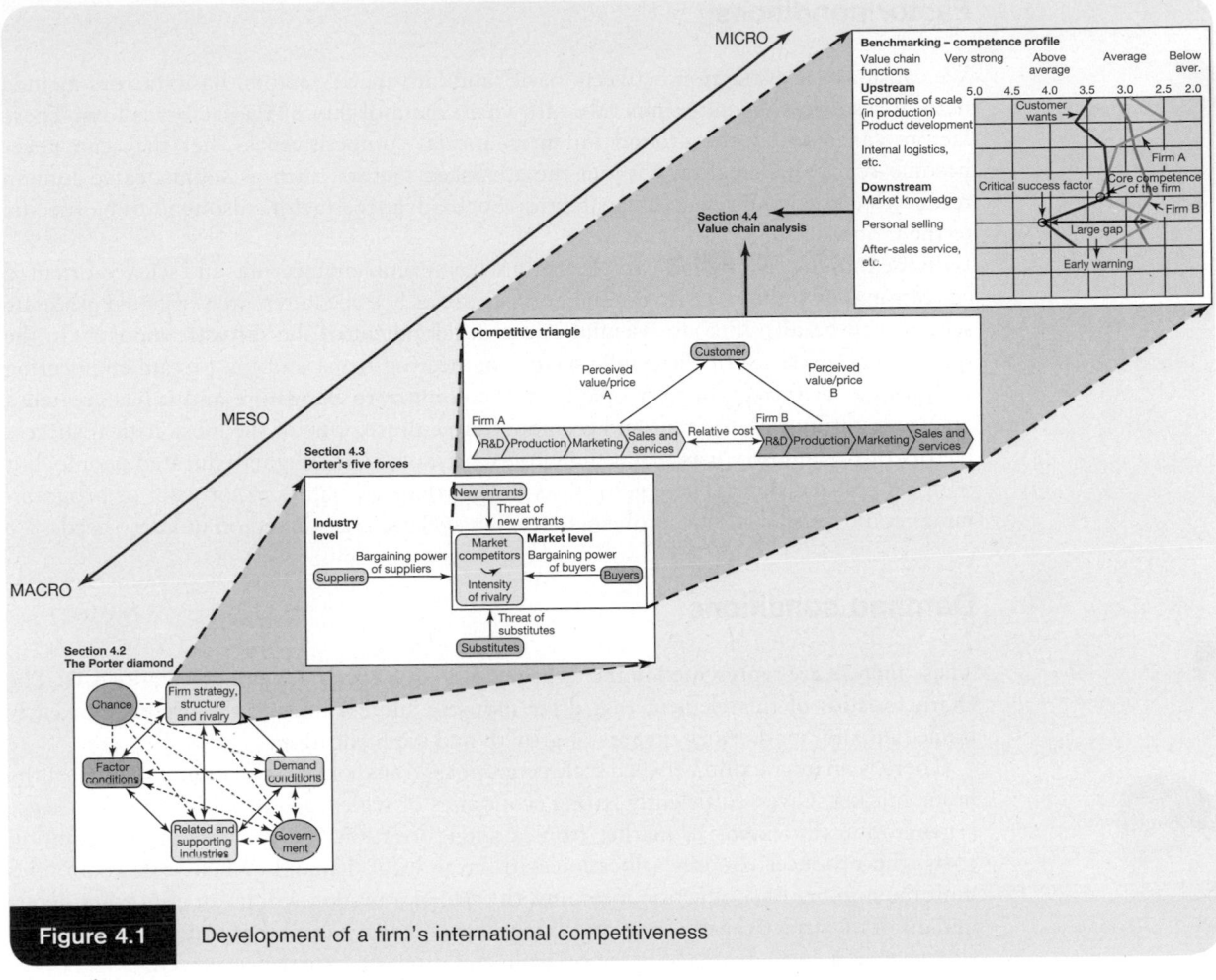

| Figure 4.1 | Development of a firm's international competitiveness |

Understanding the home base of foreign competitors is essential when analysing them. Their home nation yields them advantages and disadvantages. It also shapes their likely future strategies.

Porter (1990) describes a concentration of firms within a certain industry as industrial clusters. Within such industrial clusters, firms have a network of relations to other firms in the industry: customers (including firms that work on semi-manufactured goods), suppliers and competitors. These industrial clusters may spread worldwide, but they will usually have their starting point and location in a certain country or region of a country.

A firm gains important competitive advantages from the presence in its home nation of world-class buyers, suppliers and related industries. They provide an insight into future market needs and technological developments. They contribute to a climate for change and improvement, and become partners and allies in the innovation process. Having a strong cluster at home unblocks the flow of information and allows deeper and more open contact than is possible when dealing with foreign firms. Being part of a cluster localized in a small geographic area can be even more valuable, so the central question we can ask is: what accounts for the national location of a particular global industry? The answer begins, as does all classical trade theory, with the match between the factor endowments of the country and the needs of the industry.

Let us now take a closer look at the different elements in **Porter's diamond**. Throughout the analysis the Indian IT/software industry (especially illustrated by the Bangalore area) will be used as an example (Nair *et al.*, 2007).

Porter's diamond
The characteristics of the 'home base' play a central role in explaining the international competitiveness of the firm – the explaining elements consist of factor conditions, demand conditions, related and supporting industries, firm strategy – structure and rivalry, government and chance.

Factor conditions

We can make a distinction between 'basic' and 'advanced' factors. Basic factors include natural resources (climate, minerals, oil) where the mobility of the factors is low. These factors can also lay the ground for international competitiveness, but they can never become real value creation without the advanced factors, such as sophisticated human resources (skills) and research capabilities. Such advanced factors also tend to be specific to the industry.

In the Indian software industry, Bangalore has several engineering- and science-oriented educational institutions. Also the Indian Institute of Science (a research-oriented graduate school) can be identified as essential in the development of the software industry in the region. The presence of the public-sector engineering firms and the private engineering colleges has attracted young people from the country to Bangalore and it has created a diverse, multilingual, tolerant and cosmopolitan culture. One of the most critical success factors of the industry was the availability of advanced- and higher-educated people, but with generalized skills. These generalists (rather than specialists in software or programming) could be trained into problem-solvers in specific areas based on industry needs.

Demand conditions

These factors are represented in the right-hand box of Porter's diamond (Figure 4.1). The characteristics of this element that drive industry success include the presence of early home demand, market size, its rate of growth and sophistication.

There is an interaction between scale economies, transportation costs and the size of the home market. Given sufficiently strong economies of scale, each producer wants to serve a geographically extensive market from a single location. To minimize transportation costs, the producer chooses a location with large local demand. When scale economies limit the number of production locations, the size of a market will be an important determinant of its attractiveness. Large home markets will also ensure that firms located at that site develop a cost advantage based on scale and often on experience as well.

An interesting pattern is that an early large home market that has become saturated forces efficient firms to look abroad for new business. For example, the Japanese motorcycle industry with its large home market used its scale advantages in the global marketplace after an early start in Japan. The composition of demand also plays an important role.

A product's fundamental or core design nearly always reflects home market needs. In electrical transmission equipment, for example, Sweden dominates the world in the high-voltage distribution market. In Sweden there is a relatively large demand for transporting high voltage over long distances, as a consequence of the location of population and industry clusters. In this case, the needs of the home market shaped the industry that was later able to respond to global markets (with ABB as one of the leading producers in the world market).

The sophistication of the buyer is also important. The US government was the first buyer of computer chips and remained the only customer for many years. The price inelasticity of government encouraged firms to develop technically advanced products without worrying too much about costs. Under these conditions the technological frontier was clearly pushed much further and much faster than it would have been had the buyer been either less sophisticated or more price sensitive.

The Indian software industry was kicked off as a result of the Y2K problem (a problem caused due to a coding convention in older systems that assigned only two digits for the year count, thereby creating a potential disruption as the calendar year turned 2000) because US firms contracted with Indian software firms that had employees who were skilled in older programming languages such as Cobol and Fortran. As their experience with US firms increased and the Y2K problems were solved, Indian-based software firms began diversifying and offering more value-added products and services. Serving demanding US customers forced the Indian software firms to develop high-quality products and services. Later on this experience helped to address the needs of IT customers in Germany, Japan and other markets.

Related and supporting industries

The success of an industry is associated with the presence of suppliers and related industries within a region. In many cases competitive advantages come from being able to use labour that is attracted to an area to serve the core industry, but which is available and skilled enough to support this industry. Coordination of technology is also eased by geographic proximity. Porter argues that Italian world leadership in gold and silver jewellery has been sustained in part by the local presence of manufacturers of jewellery-making machinery. Here the advantage of clustering is not so much transportation cost reductions, but technical and marketing cooperation. In the semiconductor industry, the strength of the electronics industry in Japan (which buys the semiconductors) is a strong incentive to the location of semiconductors in the same area. It should be noted that clustering is not independent of scale economies. If there were no scale economies in the production of intermediate inputs, then the small-scale centres of production could rival the large-scale centres. It is the fact that there are scale economies in both semiconductors and electronics, coupled with the technological and marketing connections between the two, that gives rise to clustering advantages.

In the beginning, Bangalore's lack of reliable supporting industries, like telecommunications and power supplies, was a problem, but many software firms installed their own generators and satellite communication equipment. Recently, firms that provide venture capital, recruitment assistance, network, hardware maintenance and marketing/accounting support have emerged in the Bangalore area to support the software firms. Also the presence of consulting firms like KPMG, PricewaterhouseCoopers and Ernst & Young helps incoming multinational companies to enter the Indian market, by solving problems linked to currency, location and the like. Consequently, a whole system of support has now evolved around the software industry.

Firm strategy, structure and rivalry

This fairly broad element includes the way in which companies are organized and managed, their objectives and the nature of domestic rivalry.

One of the most compelling results of Porter's study of successful industries in 10 different nations is the powerful and positive effect that domestic competition has on the ability to compete in the global marketplace. In Germany, the fierce domestic rivalry among BASF, Hoechst and Bayer in the pharmaceutical industry is well known. Furthermore, the process of competition weeds out inferior technologies, products and management practices, and leaves as survivors only the most efficient firms. When domestic competition is vigorous, firms are forced to become more efficient, adopt new cost-saving technologies, reduce product development time and learn to motivate and control workers more effectively. Domestic rivalry is especially important in stimulating technological developments among global firms.

The small country of Denmark has three producers of hearing-aids (William Demant, Widex and GN Resound/Danavox), which are all among the top 10 of the world's largest producers of hearing aids. In 1996, Oticon (the earlier William Demant) and Widex fought a violent technological battle to be the first in the world to launch a 100 per cent digitalized hearing aid. Widex (the smaller of the two producers) won, but forced Oticon at the same time to keep a leading edge in technological development.

In relation to the Indian software industry, most firms in the Bangalore area experience fierce competition. The competition about future customers is not just with local firms, but also with firms outside Bangalore and multinational companies such as IBM and Accenture. Competition has resulted in a pressure on firms to deliver quality products and services, but also to be cost-effective. It has also encouraged firms to seek international certifications, with a rating in software development. Today, the Bangalore area has the world's highest concentration of companies with the so-called CMM-SEI (Carnegie Mellon University's Software Engineering Institute) Level 5 certification (the highest quality rating).

Government

According to Porter's diamond model, governments can influence and be influenced by each of the four main factors. Governments can play a powerful role in encouraging the development of industries within their own borders that will assume global positions. Governments finance and construct infrastructure, providing roads, airports, education and health care, and can support use of alternative energy (e.g. wind turbines) or other environmental systems that affect factors of production.

In relation to the Indian software industry, the federal government in Delhi had already targeted software as a growth area in the 1970s, because of its high skill requirements and labour intensity. Through the 1970s and 1980s, the industry was mainly dominated by public-sector companies like CMC. In 1984, the government started liberalizing industrial and investment policies, which gave access to IT companies from abroad (e.g. Texas Instruments). One of the new initiatives was also setting up 'technology parks', e.g. the Software Technology Park (STP) in Bangalore. The liberation policy continued throughout the 1980s and 1990s. In 1988, the National Association of Software and Service Companies (NASSCOM) was formed. NASSCOM is an association of IT firms, which acts as a catalyst for industry growth by supporting IT research and education in India. In 1999, the Ministry of Information Technology was set up to coordinate the IT initiatives at government, academic and business levels. Thus Bangalore's success in becoming a software hub was contributed to by the state government's active role in the early and later stages of the industry's evolution.

Chance

According to Porter's diamond, national/regional competitiveness may also be triggered by random events.

When we look at the history of most industries we also see the role played by chance. Perhaps the most important instance of chance involves the question of who comes up with a major new idea first. For reasons having little to do with economics, entrepreneurs will typically start their new operations in their home countries. Once the industry begins in a given country, scale and clustering effects can cement the industry's position in that country.

In relation to the development of competitiveness of the Indian software industry (especially in Bangalore) two essential events can be identified:

1. the Y2K problems (described earlier), which created an increased demand for services of Indian software firms;
2. the collapse of the dotcom boom in 2001 in the US and Europe, resulting in a search for ways to cut costs by outsourcing software functions to India.

From the firm's point of view, the last two variables, chance and government, can be regarded as exogenous variables that the firm must adjust to. Alternatively, the government may be considered susceptible through lobbying, interest organizations and mass media.

In summary, we have identified six factors that influence the location of global industries: factors of production, home demand, the location of supporting industries, the internal structure of the domestic industry, chance and government. We have also suggested that these factors are interconnected. As industries evolve, their dependence on particular locations may also change. For example, the shift in users of semiconductors from the military to the electronics industry has had a profound effect on the shape of the national diamond in that industry. To the extent that governments and firms recognize the source of any locational advantages they have, they will be better able to both exploit those differences and anticipate their shifts.

In relation to the software industry in India (Bangalore), which was used throughout the diamond model, the following conclusions may be arrived at (Nair *et al.*, 2007):

● The software industry in Bangalore started off by serving not only its domestic customers but also the demanding North American customers. Also the rivals for software firms tend not to be so much local but global.

● The support needed for software services is much less sophisticated than for manufacturing. For the manufacturing sector it is also important to have access to a well-functioning physical infrastructure (transport, logistics, etc.), which is not necessary for the software industry where most of the logistics can be done over the internet. That is one of the reasons why Bangalore's software industry created international competitiveness but the manufacturing sector did not.

● The software industry is very much dependent on advanced and well-educated human resources as the key factor input.

While the Bangalore-based firms started off at the low end of the value chain (performing coding work for the Y2K problem) they have continuously moved in the direction of delivering more value-added services in emerging areas.

The 'double diamond' and 'multiple diamond' framework

Double diamond
The international competitiveness of an industry in a country is not only dependent on its home country diamond conditions but also on those of trading partners.

A key limitation of Porter's (1990) diamond model is its main focus on solely home country conditions (Rugman *et al.*, 2012). The **double diamond** framework addresses this concern. Rugman and D'Cruz (1993) suggested that the international competitiveness of Canadian firms depended not only on their home country diamond conditions but also on those of their trading partner, the US. Consequently, the sources of a firm's international competitive advantage are not only limited to the home country advantages, according to Porter's single diamond model, but they can also be achieved by sensing and developing competitive advantages in relationship with multiple 'diamonds' in several host countries.

4.3   Competition analysis in an industry

The next step in understanding the firm's competitiveness is to look at the competitive arena in an industry, which is the top box in the diamond model (see Figure 4.1).

One of the most useful frameworks for analysing the competitive structure was developed by Porter. Porter (1980) suggested that competition in an industry is rooted in its underlying economic structure and goes beyond the behaviour of current competitors. The state of competition depends upon five basic competitive forces, as shown in Figure 4.1. Together these factors determine the ultimate profit potential in an industry, where profit is measured in terms of long-run return on invested capital. The profit potential will differ from industry to industry.

Porter's five-forces model
The state of competition and profit potential in an industry depends on five basic competitive forces: new entrants, suppliers, buyers, substitutes and market competitors.

Marketing myopia
The failure of a company to define its organisational purpose from a broad consumer orientation.

To make things clearer we need to define a number of key terms. An *industry* is a group of firms that offer a product or class of products that are close substitutes for each other. Examples are the car industry and the pharmaceutical industry (Kotler, 1997, p. 230). A *market* is a set of actual and potential buyers of a product and sellers. A distinction will be made between industry and market level, as we assume that the industry may contain several different markets. This is why the outer box in Figure 4.1 is designated 'industry level' and the inner box 'market level'.

Thus the *industry level* (**Porter's five-forces model**) consists of all types of actors (new entrants, suppliers, substitutes, buyers and market competitors) that have a potential or current interest in the industry.

The *market level* consists of actors with a current interest in the market, i.e., buyers and sellers (market competitors). In Section 4.4 (value chain analysis) this market level will be further elaborated on, as the buyers' perceived value of different competitor offerings will be discussed.

Although division into the above-mentioned two levels is appropriate for this approach, Levitt (1960) pointed out the danger of '**marketing myopia**', where the seller defines the competition field (i.e. the market) too narrowly. For example, European luxury car manufacturers showed this myopia with their focus on each other rather than on the Japanese mass manufacturers, who were new entrants into the luxury car market.

The goal of competition analysis is to find a position in industry where the company can best defend itself against the five forces, or can influence them in its favour. Knowledge of these underlying pressures highlights the critical strengths and weaknesses of the company, shows its position in the industry, and clarifies areas where strategy changes yield the greatest payoff. Structure analysis is fundamental for formulating competitive strategy.

Each of the five forces in the Porter model in turn comprises a number of elements that combine to determine the strength of each force, and its effect on the degree of competition. Dobbs (2014) provide practitioners and students with a practical and highly recommended set of templates for applying Porter's five forces framework for industry analysis. Each of the five forces is now discussed.

Market competitors

The intensity of rivalry between existing competitors in the market depends on a number of factors:

- *The concentration of the industry.* Numerous competitors of equal size will lead to more intense rivalry. There will be less rivalry when a clear leader (at least 50 per cent larger than the second) exists with a large cost advantage.
- *Rate of market growth.* Slow growth will tend towards greater rivalry.
- *Structure of costs.* High fixed costs encourage price cutting to fill capacity.
- *Degree of differentiation.* Commodity products encourage rivalry, while highly differentiated products, which are hard to copy, are associated with less intense rivalry.
- *Switching costs.* When switching costs are high because the product is specialized, the customer has invested a lot of resources in learning how to use the product or has made tailor-made investments that are worthless with other products and suppliers (high asset specificity), rivalry is reduced.
- *Exit barriers.* When barriers to leaving a market are high due to such factors as lack of opportunities elsewhere, high vertical integration, emotional barriers or the high cost of closing down plant, rivalry will be more intense than when exit barriers are low.

Firms need to be careful not to spoil a situation of competitive stability. They need to balance their own position against the well-being of the industry as a whole. For example, an intense price or promotional war may gain a few percentage points in market share, yet lead to an overall fall in long-run industry profitability as competitors respond to these moves. It is sometimes better to protect industry structure than to follow short-term self-interest.

Suppliers

The cost of raw materials and components can have a major bearing on a firm's profitability. The higher the bargaining power of suppliers, the higher the costs. The bargaining power of suppliers will be higher in the following circumstances:

● Supply is dominated by few companies and they are more concentrated than the industry they sell to.
● Their products are unique or differentiated, or they have built up switching costs.
● They are not obliged to contend with other products for sale to the industry.
● They pose a credible threat of integrating forwards into the industry's business.
● Buyers do not threaten to integrate backwards into supply.
● The market is not an important customer to the supplier group.

A firm can reduce the bargaining power of suppliers by seeking new sources of supply, threatening to integrate backwards into supply and designing standardized components so that many suppliers are capable of producing them.

Buyers

The bargaining power of buyers is higher in the following circumstances:

● Buyers are concentrated and/or purchase in large volumes.
● Buyers pose a credible threat of integrating backwards to manufacture the industry's product.
● Products they purchase are standard or undifferentiated.
● There are many suppliers (sellers) of the product.
● Buyers earn low profits, which create a great incentive to lower purchasing costs.
● The industry's product is unimportant to the quality of the buyer's products, but price is very important.

Firms in the industry can attempt to lower buyer power by increasing the number of buyers they sell to, threatening to integrate forward into the buyer's industry and producing highly valued, differentiated products. In supermarket retailing, the brand leader normally achieves the highest profitability, partly because being number one means that supermarkets need to stock the brand, thereby reducing buyer power in price negotiations.

Customers who purchase the product but are not the end user (such as original equipment manufacturers [OEMs] or distributors) can be analysed in the same way as other buyers. Non-end-customers can gain significant bargaining power when they can influence the purchasing decision of customers downstream (Porter, 2008). Over the years, ingredient supplier DuPont has created enormous clout by advertising its Teflon brand not only to the manufacturers of cooking equipment, but also to downstream end-customers (households). (See also 'ingredient branding' in Section 14.8.)

Substitutes

The presence of substitute products can reduce industry attractiveness and profitability because they put a constraint on price levels.

If the industry is successful and earning high profits, it is more likely that competitors will enter the market via substitute products in order to obtain a share of the potential profits available. The threat of substitute products depends on the following factors:

- the buyer's willingness to substitute;
- the relative price and performance of substitutes;
- the costs of switching to substitutes.

The threat of substitute products can be lowered by building up switching costs. These costs may be psychological. Examples are the creation of strong, distinctive brand personalities, and maintaining a price differential commensurate with perceived customer values.

New entrants

New entrants can serve to increase the degree of competition in an industry. In turn, the threat of new entrants is largely a function of the extent to which barriers to entry exist in the market. Some key factors affecting these entry barriers include the following:

- economies of scale;
- product differentiation and brand identity, which give existing firms customer loyalty;
- capital requirements in production;
- switching costs – the cost of switching from one supplier to another;
- access to distribution channels.

Because high barriers to entry can make even a potentially lucrative market unattractive (or even impossible) to enter for new competitors, the marketing planner should not take a passive approach but should actively pursue ways of raising barriers to new competitors.

High promotional and R&D expenditures and clearly communicated retaliatory actions to entry are some methods of raising barriers. Some managerial actions can unwittingly lower barriers. For example, new product designs that dramatically lower manufacturing costs can make entry by newcomers easier.

Strategic groups

Strategic group
A group of firms (or strategic business units, or brands) operating within an industry where the firms (or strategic business units, or brands) within the group compete for the same group of customers (segment), using similar market-related strategies.

A **strategic group** can be defined as a group of companies (or strategic business units, or brands) operating within an industry where the firms (or strategic business units, or brands) within the group compete for the same group of customers (segment), using similar market-related strategies. An industry could have only one strategic group if all the firms followed essentially the same strategy. At the other extreme, each firm could be a different strategic group.

Companies in different strategic groups compete for a different group of customers using strategies that are different from those of other strategic groups. So different strategic groups do not compete with each other, as they are pursuing different groups of customers.

Strategic group analysis is then a technique used to provide management with information about the firm's position in the market and a tool to identify their direct competitors. The five-forces industry analysis will form the first step in this process (Porter, 1980). After having identified the forces, the major competitors in the industry based on competitive variables will also be outlined. Competitors will then be divided into strategic groups based on similarities in strategies and competitive positions. For this purpose, Porter's three generic strategies (low cost, differentiation and focus) can be used (Porter, 1985).

For example, in the car industry, consumers who buy low-priced brands, such as Suzuki, Kia or Hyundai, buy them because they are inexpensive (low-cost strategy), while those who buy a Toyota Camry or Honda Accord, say (differentiation strategy), are willing to pay a higher price for a car that is bigger, has more features/options, is more reliable, and so on. Finally, people who buy a Rolls-Royce or Jaguar (focus strategy) are willing to pay a fortune for something that is unique and prestigious.

Often a two-dimensional grid is made to position firms along an industry's two most important dimensions in order to distinguish direct rivals (those with similar strategies or business models) from indirect rivals. Firms may try to shift to a more favourably situated group, and how hard such a move proves to be will depend on whether entry barriers for the target strategic group are high or low.

The collaborative five-sources model

Porter's original model is based on the hypothesis that the competitive advantage of the firm is best developed in a very competitive market with intense rivalry relations.

The five-forces framework thus provides an analysis for considering how to squeeze the maximum competitive gain out of the context in which the business is located – or how to minimize the prospect of being squeezed by it – on the five competitive dimensions that it confronts.

Over the past decade, however, an alternative school (e.g. Reve, 1990; Kanter, 1994; Burton, 1995) has emerged which emphasizes the positive role of cooperative (rather than competitive) arrangements between industry participants, and the consequent importance of what Kanter (1994) has termed 'collaborative advantage' as a foundation of superior business performance.

An all-or-nothing choice between a single-minded striving for either competitive or collaborative advantage would, however, be a false one. The real strategic choice problem that all businesses face is where (and how much) to collaborate, and where (and how intensely) to act competitively.

Put another way, the basic questions that firms must deal with in respect of these matters are as follows:

- choosing the combination of competitive and collaborative strategies that are appropriate in the various dimensions of the industry environment of the firm;
- blending the two elements together so that they interact in a mutually consistent and reinforcing (and not counterproductive) manner;
- in this way, optimizing the firm's overall position, drawing upon the foundation and utilization of both collaborative and competitive advantage.

This points to the imperative in the contemporary context of complementing the competitive strategy model with a sister framework that focuses on the assessment of collaborative advantage and strategy. Such a complementary analysis, which is called the *five-sources framework* (Burton, 1995), is outlined below.

Corresponding to the array of five competitive forces that surround a company – as elaborated in Porter's treatment – there are also five potential sources for the building of collaborative advantage in the industrial environments of the firm (the **five-sources model**). These sources are listed in Table 4.1.

In order to forge an effective and coherent business strategy, a firm must evaluate and formulate its collaborative and competitive policies side by side. It should do this for two purposes:

1. to achieve the appropriate balance between collaboration and competition in each dimension of its industry environment (e.g. relations with suppliers, policies towards customers/channels);
2. to integrate them in a way that avoids potential clashes and possibly destructive inconsistencies between them.

Five-sources model
Corresponding to Porter's five competitive forces, there are also five potential sources for building collaborative advantages together with the firm's surrounding actors.

Table 4.1	The five-sources model and the corresponding five forces in the Porter model
Porter's five-forces model	**The five-sources model**
Market competitors	Horizontal collaborations with other enterprises operating at the same stage of the production process/producing the same group of closely related products (e.g. contemporary global partnering arrangements among car manufacturers)
Suppliers	Vertical collaborations with suppliers of components or services to the firm – sometimes termed vertical quasi-integration arrangements (e.g. the *keiretsu* formations between suppliers and assemblers that typify the car, electronics and other industries in Japan)
Buyers	Selective partnering arrangements with specific channels or customers (e.g. lead users) that involve collaboration extending beyond standard, purely transactional relationships
Substitutes	Related diversification alliances with producers of both complements and substitutes. Producers of substitutes are not 'natural allies', but such alliances are not inconceivable (e.g. collaborations between fixed-wire and mobile telephone firms in order to grow their joint network size)
New entrants	Diversification alliances with firms based in previously unrelated sectors, but between which a 'blurring' of industry borders is potentially occurring, or a process (commonly due to new technological possibilities) that opens up the prospect of cross-industry fertilization of technologies/business that did not exist before (e.g. the collaborations in the emerging multimedia field)

Source: Burton, 1995. Reproduced with permission from The Braybrooke Press Ltd.

This is the terrain of composite strategy, which concerns the bringing together of competitive and collaborative endeavours.

4.4   Value chain analysis

Until now we have discussed the firm's international competitiveness from a strategic point of view. To get closer to the firm's core competences we will now look at the market-level box in Porter's five-forces model, which treats buyers and sellers (market competitors). Here we will look more closely at what creates a competitive advantage among market competitors towards customers at the same competitive level.

Customer perceived value

Perceived value
The customer's overall evaluation of the product/service offered by a firm.

Success in the marketplace is dependent not only upon identifying and responding to customer needs, but also upon our ability to ensure that our response is judged by customers to be superior to that of competitors (i.e. high **perceived value**). Several writers (e.g. Porter, 1980; Day and Wensley, 1988) have argued that causes of difference in performance within a market can be analysed at various levels. The immediate causes of differences in the performance of different firms, these writers argue, can be reduced to two basic factors (D'Aveni, 2007): the *perceived value* compared with the *customer's perceived sacrifice (costs)*.

Perceived value is the *relation* between the benefits customers realize from using the product/service (the numerator in Figure 4.2) and the costs, direct and indirect, that they incur in finding, acquiring and using it (the denominator in Figure 4.2). The higher this relation is, the better the perceived value for the customer and the better the competitiveness.

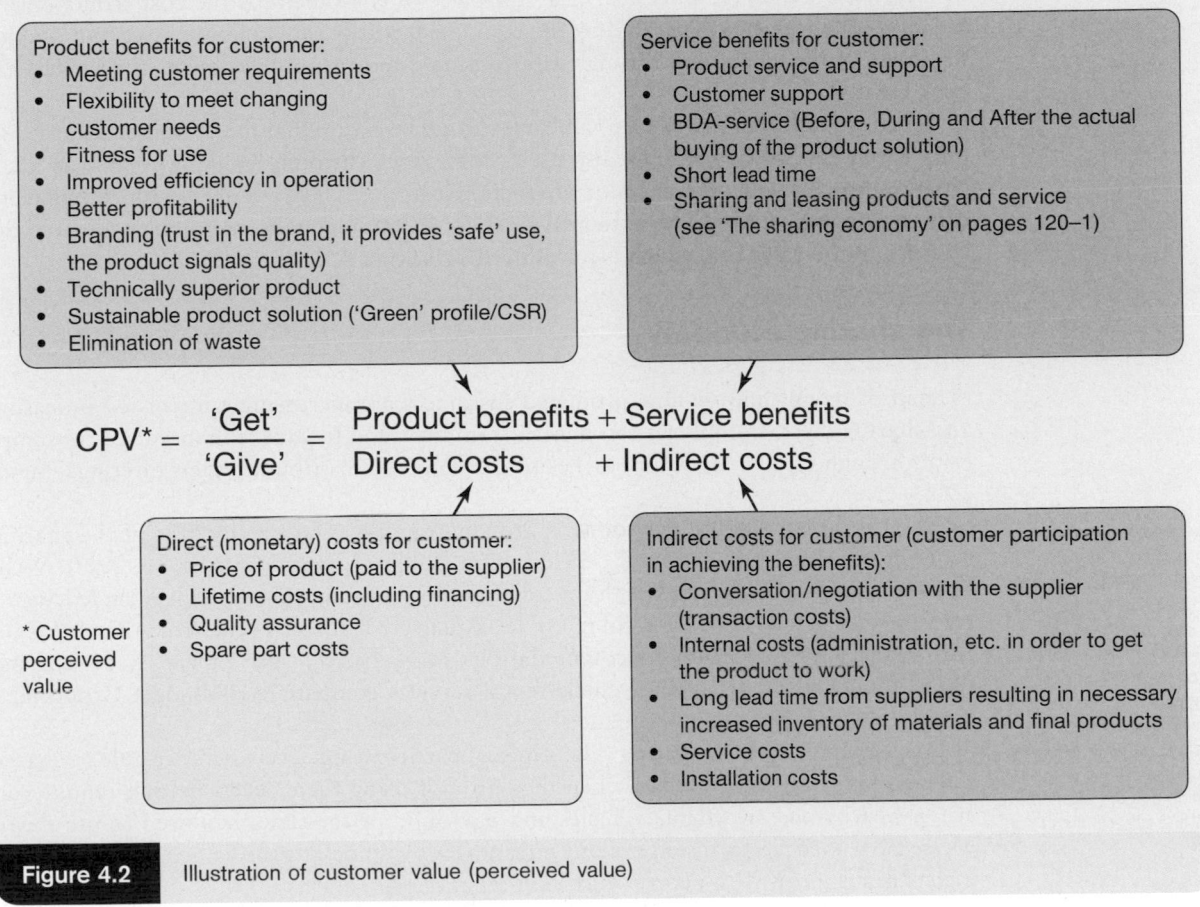

Product benefits for customer:
- Meeting customer requirements
- Flexibility to meet changing customer needs
- Fitness for use
- Improved efficiency in operation
- Better profitability
- Branding (trust in the brand, it provides 'safe' use, the product signals quality)
- Technically superior product
- Sustainable product solution ('Green' profile/CSR)
- Elimination of waste

Service benefits for customer:
- Product service and support
- Customer support
- BDA-service (Before, During and After the actual buying of the product solution)
- Short lead time
- Sharing and leasing products and service (see 'The sharing economy' on pages 120–1)

$$CPV^* = \frac{\text{'Get'}}{\text{'Give'}} = \frac{\text{Product benefits} + \text{Service benefits}}{\text{Direct costs} + \text{Indirect costs}}$$

* Customer perceived value

Direct (monetary) costs for customer:
- Price of product (paid to the supplier)
- Lifetime costs (including financing)
- Quality assurance
- Spare part costs

Indirect costs for customer (customer participation in achieving the benefits):
- Conversation/negotiation with the supplier (transaction costs)
- Internal costs (administration, etc. in order to get the product to work)
- Long lead time from suppliers resulting in necessary increased inventory of materials and final products
- Service costs
- Installation costs

Figure 4.2   Illustration of customer value (perceived value)

Sources: adapted from Anderson *et al.* (2007, 2008); McGrath and Keil (2007); Smith and Nagle (2005).

Please do not think about Figure 4.2 as a mathematical formula for calculating an exact measure of 'customer perceived value' (CPV). Instead think about what the customer 'gets' compared with what the customer 'gives' in order to be able to use or consume the product/service.

After the product/service has been purchased and is being used or consumed, the level of the customer's satisfaction can be evaluated. If the actual customer satisfaction with both purchase and quality exceeds the initial expectations, then the customer will tend to buy the product/service again and the customer may become loyal towards the company's product/service (brand loyalty).

The components driving customer benefits include product values, service values, technical values and commitment value, but always remember what Theodore Levitt wrote (he actually attributes the famous quote to Leo McGinnera):

People don't want to buy a quarter-inch drill – they want a quarter inch hole.
(Levitt, 1983, p. 128)

The components driving cost fall into two categories: those that relate to the price paid and those representing the internal costs incurred by the customer. These components can be unbundled into salient attributes. Commitment to value, for example, includes investment in personnel and customer relations. Internal cost might reflect set-up time and expense, maintenance, training and individual physical energy.

If the benefits exceed the costs, then a customer will at least consider purchasing your product. For example, the value to an industrial customer may be represented by the rate of return earned on the purchase of a new piece of equipment. If the cost reductions or revenue enhancements generated by the equipment justify the purchase price and operating costs of the equipment through an acceptable return on investment, then value has been created.

When we talk about customer value, we should be aware that the customer value is not only being created by the company itself. Sometimes customer value is created in a co-creation process with customers or suppliers (Grönroos, 2009), or even with complementors and/or competitors. This extended version of 'customer value creation' leads us to the concept of the value net, which is introduced in Section 4.7.

The sharing economy

Instead of buying and owning products, customers are increasingly interested in leasing and sharing them. Companies can benefit from the trend toward 'collaborative consumption' through creative new approaches to defining and distributing their offerings (Stein, 2015).

The sharing economy
An economic model in which individuals are able to lease assets (products or services) owned by someone else, typically through an online marketplace. The sharing economy model is most likely to be used when the price of a particular asset is high and the asset is not fully utilized all the time.

This so-called '**sharing economy**' is growing rapidly. The size in 2014 of the sharing economy is estimated at around US$30 billion (Malhotra and Van Alstyne, 2014). Well-known examples of start-ups built on collaborative consumption systems include Uber, a transportation (taxi) network company headquartered in San Francisco, Airbnb Inc., a San Francisco-based online accommodations marketplace, and Zipcar, a car-sharing brand that is now part of the vehicle rental services company Avis Budget Group Inc., based in New Jersey.

For example, with car sharing (like Zipcar), participating car owners are able to charge a fee to rent out their vehicles when they are not using them. Participating renters can access nearby and affordable vehicles and pay only for the time they need to use them. These two-sided platforms offer many advantages by unlocking the value inherent in sharing spare resources with people who want them.

In line with the service-dominant logic (Bettencourt et al., 2014), there is a move away from an approach based on selling a product to one where the company sells the use of something and so provides the customer with a service. The company in effect serves the customer by helping him or her to accomplish a job (Slimane and Chaney, 2015). There are several means by which a company can sell use of a product rather than ownership. Hilti (based in Liechtenstein), is a company which provides products, systems and services to the global construction industry, but they focus not only on selling the hand-held power tools but also on selling the use of the products (Matzler et al., 2015; Slimane and Chaney, 2015). See also Exhibit 4.1.

EXHIBIT 4.1 Hilti is selling the 'use' – not the product

In the late 1990s, Hilti experienced sales losses to competitors' inexpensive small tools. The company then sought to learn from its customers how the company could improve its offerings. In the process, the company learned that many workers sometimes saw cheap small tools as disposable and basically they could not get them to work with other higher-end and more expensive power tools. This frustrated construction site managers who saw their site overloaded with cheap incompatible hand-held power tools. Furthermore, the site managers experienced time delays and increasing project costs because of the non-working power tools.

Although the low-cost tools represented a threat to Hilti sales, it also opened up an opportunity to compete by providing customers with convenience and a service, known as *'tool fleet management'*. Now, Hilti's construction customers no longer have to purchase individual tools. Instead, they can lease them at a fixed monthly rate within a defined usage time. On top of gaining flexibility and efficiency from the leasing arrangement, customers also receive an all-inclusive repair service. In this way, Hilti managed to capitalize on what initially seemed to be a threat to its core competencies. Hilti's change in strategy and the approach which it encompasses are illustrated in Figures 4.3 and 4.4.

Source: Nicholas Ratzenboeck/AFP/Getty Images.

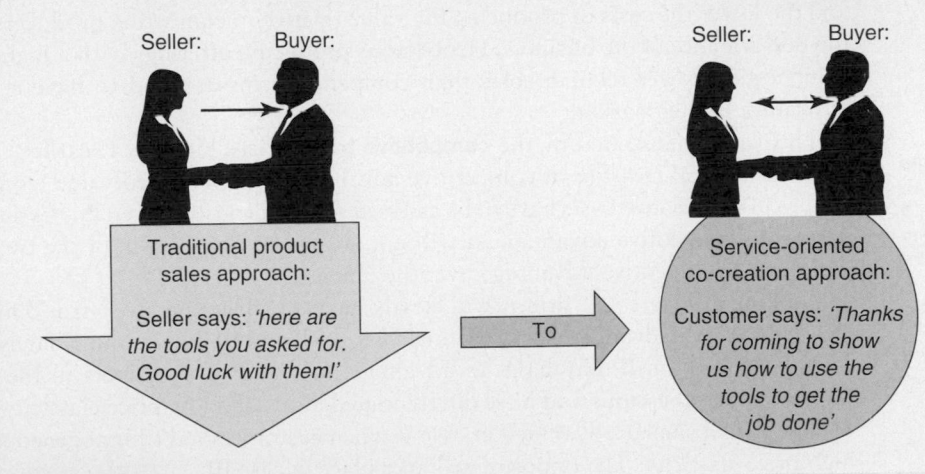

Figure 4.3   Hilti's changing strategy from traditional product sales approach to a service-oriented co-creation approach

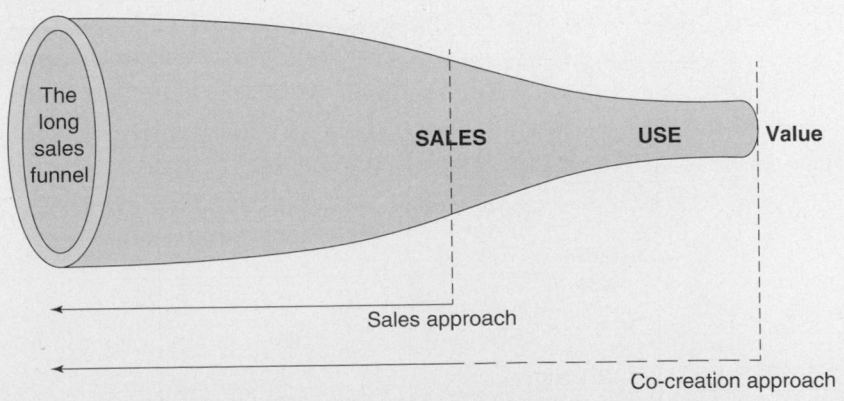

Figure 4.4   The process lasts until the customer obtains the value the salesperson promised them him or her.

Sources: based on Matzler et al. (2015); Slimane and Chaney (2015).

The competitive triangle

Success in the marketplace is dependent not only upon identifying and responding to customer needs, but also upon our ability to ensure that our response is judged by customers to be superior to that of competitors (i.e. high perceived value). Several writers (e.g. Porter, 1980; Day and Wensley, 1988) have argued that causes of difference in performance within a market can be analysed at various levels. The immediate causes of differences in the performance of different firms, these writers argue, can be reduced to two basic factors (D'Aveni, 2007):

1. The *perceived value* of the product/services offered, compared with the *perceived sacrifice*. The perceived sacrifice includes all the 'costs' the buyer faces when making a purchase, primarily the *purchase price,* but also acquisition costs, transportation, installation, handling, repairs and maintenance (Ravald and Grönroos, 1996). In the models presented, the (purchase) price will be used as a representative of the perceived sacrifice. D'Aveni (2007) presents a strategic tool for evaluating how much a customer is willing to pay for a perceived benefit of a product/service.
2. The firm-related *costs* incurred in creating this perceived value.

These two basic factors will be further discussed later in this section.

The more value customers perceive in a market offering relative to competing offerings, and the lower the costs in producing the value relative to competing producers, the higher the performance of the business. Hence firms producing offerings with a higher perceived value and/or lower relative costs than competing firms are said to have a competitive advantage in that market.

Competitive triangle
Consists of a customer, the firm and a competitor (the 'triangle'). The firm or competitor 'winning' the customer's favour depends on perceived value offered to the customer compared with the relative costs between the firm and the competitor.

This can be illustrated by the **competitive triangle** (see Figure 4.1, earlier). There is no one-dimensional measure of competitive advantage, and perceived value (compared with the price) and relative costs have to be assessed simultaneously. Given this two-dimensional nature of competitive advantage, it will not always be clear which of the two businesses will have a competitive advantage over the other.

Looking at Figure 4.5, firm A will clearly have an advantage over firm B in case I, and clearly have a disadvantage in case IV, while cases II and III do not immediately allow such a conclusion. Firm B may have an advantage in case II if customers in the market are highly quality-conscious and have differentiated needs and low price elasticity, while firm A may have a similar advantage in case II when customers have homogeneous needs and high price elasticity. The opposite will take place in case III.

		Perceived value (compared to the purchase price)	
		Higher for A	*Higher for B*
Relative costs	*Lower for A*	I	II
	Lower for B	III	IV

Figure 4.5   Perceived value, relative costs and competitive advantage

Even if firm A has a clear competitive advantage over firm B, this may not necessarily result in a higher return on investment for A, if A has a growth policy and B has a hold policy. Thus performance would have to be measured by a combination of return on investment and capacity expansion, which can be regarded as postponed return on investment.

While the relationship between perceived value and relative costs is rather intricate, we can retain the basic statement that these two variables are the cornerstone of competitive advantage. Let us take a closer look at these two fundamental sources of competitive advantage.

Perceived value advantage

We have already observed that customers do not buy products, they buy benefits. Put another way, the product is purchased not for itself but for the promise of what it will 'deliver'. These benefits may be intangible, i.e. they may relate not to specific product features but rather to such things as image or reputation. Alternatively, the delivered offering may be seen to outperform its rivals in some functional aspect.

Perceived value is the customer's overall evaluation of the product/service offered. So, establishing what value the customer is actually seeking from the firm's offering (value chain) is the starting point for being able to deliver the correct mix of value-providing activities. It may be some combination of physical attributes, service attributes and technical support available in relation to the particular use of the product. This also requires an understanding of the activities that constitute the customer's value chain.

Unless the product or service we offer can be distinguished in some way from its competitors there is a strong likelihood that the marketplace will view it as a 'commodity', and so the sale will tend to go to the cheapest supplier. Hence the importance of seeking to attach additional values to our offering to mark it out from the competition.

What are the means by which such value differentiation may be gained? If we start in the value chain perspective (see Section 1.7), we can say that each activity in the business system adds perceived value to the product or service. Value, for the customer, is the perceived stream of benefits that accrue from obtaining the product or service. Price is what the customer is willing to pay for that stream of benefits. If the price of a good or service is high, it must provide high value, otherwise it will be driven out of the market. If the value of a good or service is low, its price must be low, otherwise it will also be driven out of the market. Hence, in a competitive situation, and over a period of time, the price that customers are willing to pay for a good or service is a good proxy measure of its value.

If we look especially at the downstream functions of the value chain, a differential advantage can be created with any aspect of the traditional '4P' marketing mix: product, distribution, promotion and price are all capable of creating added customer perceived value. The key to whether improving an aspect of marketing is worthwhile is to know if the potential benefit provides value to the customer.

If we extend this model, particular emphasis must be placed upon the following (see Booms and Bitner, 1981; Magrath, 1986; Rafiq and Ahmed, 1995):

- *People*. These include both consumers, who must be educated to participate in the service, and employees (personnel), who must be motivated and well trained in order to ensure that high standards of service are maintained. Customers identify and associate the traits of service personnel with the firms they work for.
- *Physical aspects*. These include the appearance of the delivery location and the elements provided to make the service more tangible. For example, visitors experience Disneyland by what they see, but the hidden, below-ground support machinery is essential for the park's fantasy fulfilment.
- *Process*. The service is dependent on a well-designed method of delivery. Process management assures service availability and consistent quality in the face of simultaneous

consumption and production of the service offered. Without sound process management, balancing service demand with service supply is extremely difficult.

Of these three additional Ps, the firm's *personnel* occupies a key position in influencing customer perception of product quality. As a consequence, the *image* of the firm is very much influenced by the personnel. It is therefore important to pay particular attention to the quality of employees and to monitor their performance. Marketing managers need to manage not only the service provider – customer interface – but also the actions of other customers; for example, the number, type and behaviour of other people will influence a meal at a restaurant.

Relative cost advantage

Each activity in the value chain is performed at a cost. Getting the stream of benefits that accrue from the good or service to the customer is thus done at a certain 'delivered cost', which sets a lower limit to the price of the good or service if the business system is to remain profitable. Decreasing the price will thus imply that the delivered cost be first decreased by adjusting the business system. As mentioned earlier, the rules of the game may be described as *providing the highest possible perceived value to the final customer, at the lowest possible delivered cost.*

A firm's cost position depends on the configuration of the activities in its value chain versus that of competitors and its relative location on the cost drivers of each activity. A cost advantage is gained when the cumulative cost of performing all the activities is lower than competitors' costs. This evaluation of the relative cost position requires an identification of each important competitor's value chain. In practice, this step is extremely difficult because the firm does not have direct information on the costs of competitors' value activities. However, some costs can be estimated from public data or interviews with suppliers and distributors.

Relative cost advantage
A firm's cost position depends on the configuration of the activities in its value chain versus that of its competitors.

Creating a **relative cost advantage** requires an understanding of the factors that affect costs. It is often said that 'big is beautiful'. This is partly due to economies of scale, which enable fixed costs to be spread over a greater output, but more particularly it is due to the impact of the *experience curve*.

The experience curve is a phenomenon that has its roots in the earlier notion of the learning curve. The effects of learning on costs were seen in the manufacture of fighter planes during World War II. The time taken to produce each plane gradually fell as learning took place. The combined effect of economies of scale and learning on cumulative output has been termed the experience curve. The Boston Consulting Group estimated that costs reduced on average by approximately 15–20 per cent each time cumulative output doubled.

Subsequent work by Bruce Henderson, founder of the Boston Consulting Group, extended this concept by demonstrating that all costs, not just production costs, would decline at a given rate as volume increased. In fact, to be precise, the relationship that the experience curve describes is between real unit costs and cumulative volume.

This suggests that firms with greater market share will have a cost advantage through the experience curve effect, assuming that all companies are operating on the same curve. However, a move towards a new manufacturing technology can lower the experience curve for adopting companies, allowing them to leapfrog over more traditional firms and thereby gain a cost advantage even though cumulative output may be lower.

The general form of the experience curve and the leapfrogging to another curve are shown in Figure 4.6.

Leapfrogging the experience curve by investing in new technology is a special opportunity for small and medium-sized enterprises (SMEs) and newcomers to a market, as they will (as a starting point) have only a small market share and thereby a small cumulative output.

The implications of the experience curve for the pricing strategy will be discussed further in Chapter 15. According to Porter (1980) there are other cost drivers that determine the costs in value chains:

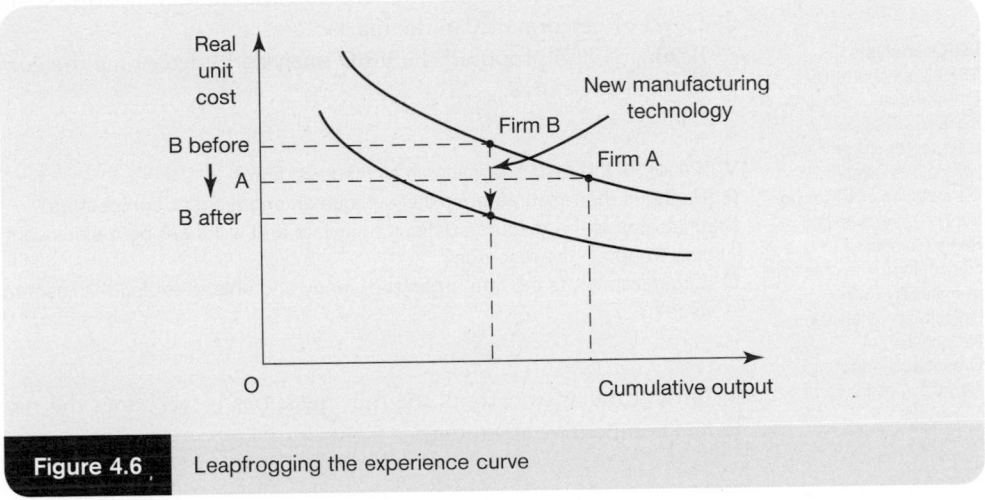

Figure 4.6   Leapfrogging the experience curve

- *Capacity utilization.* Underutilization incurs costs.
- *Linkages.* Costs of activities are affected by how other activities are performed. For example, improving quality assurance can reduce after-sales service costs.
- *Interrelationships.* For example, different strategic business units' sharing of R&D, purchasing and marketing will lower costs.
- *Integration.* For example, deintegration (outsourcing) of activities to subsuppliers can lower costs and raise flexibility.
- *Timing and time compression.* First movers in a market can gain cost advantage. Time compression represents a factor that reduces costs and improves quality, since it reduces set-up times and down-times in production, and involves human resources in the increase in productivity. Customers may be willing to pay a higher price for a new product that is delivered more quickly to the customer than a competitor's product. Shorter time-to-market is equal to improved global competitiveness (Demartini and Mella, 2011).
- *Policy decisions.* Product width, level of service and channel decisions are examples of policy decisions that affect costs.
- *Location.* Locating near suppliers reduces in-bound distribution costs. Locating near customers can lower out-bound distribution costs. Some producers locate their production activities in eastern Europe or the Far East to take advantage of low wage costs.
- *Institutional factors.* Government regulations, tariffs, local content rules and the like will affect costs.

Resources
Basic units of analysis –
financial, technological,
human and organizational
resources – found in the
firm's different
departments.

Competences
Combination of different
resources into capabilities
and later competences –
being something that the
firm is really good at.

The basic sources of competitive advantage

The perceived value created and the costs incurred will depend on the firm's **resources** and its **competences** (see Figure 4.7).

Resources

Resources are the basic units of analysis. They include all inputs into the business processes – financial, technological, human and organizational resources. Although resources provide the basis for competence building, on their own they are barely productive.

Resources are necessary in order to participate in the market. The competitors in a market will thus not usually be very different with regard to these skills and resources, and the latter will not explain differences in created perceived value, relative costs and the resulting performance. They are failure-preventers, but not success-producers. They may, however, act as barriers to entry for potential new competitors, and hence raise the average level of performance in the market.

Barney (1997) proposed the **VRIO analysis** to determine the competitive potential of a given firm's resource:

V (Value): Is the resource valuable to the focal firm?
R (Rarity) Is the resource absolutely unique among a set of competitors?
I (Imitability): Is the resource difficult to imitate and will there be a significant disadvantage to a firm trying to obtain the resource?
O (Organization): Is the firm organized, ready and able to exploit the resource in order to capture the value?

Only if the answer to all the four questions is 'yes' does the resource represent a 'sustained competitive advantage'.

VRIO analysis
VRIO is an abbreviation for the four questions that the firm asks about a resource to determine its *competitive sustainability*: the question of **V**alue (to the firm), the question of **R**arity (compared to competitors), the question of **I**mitability (ease/difficulty to imitate) and the question of **O**rganization (ability to exploit the resource or capability).

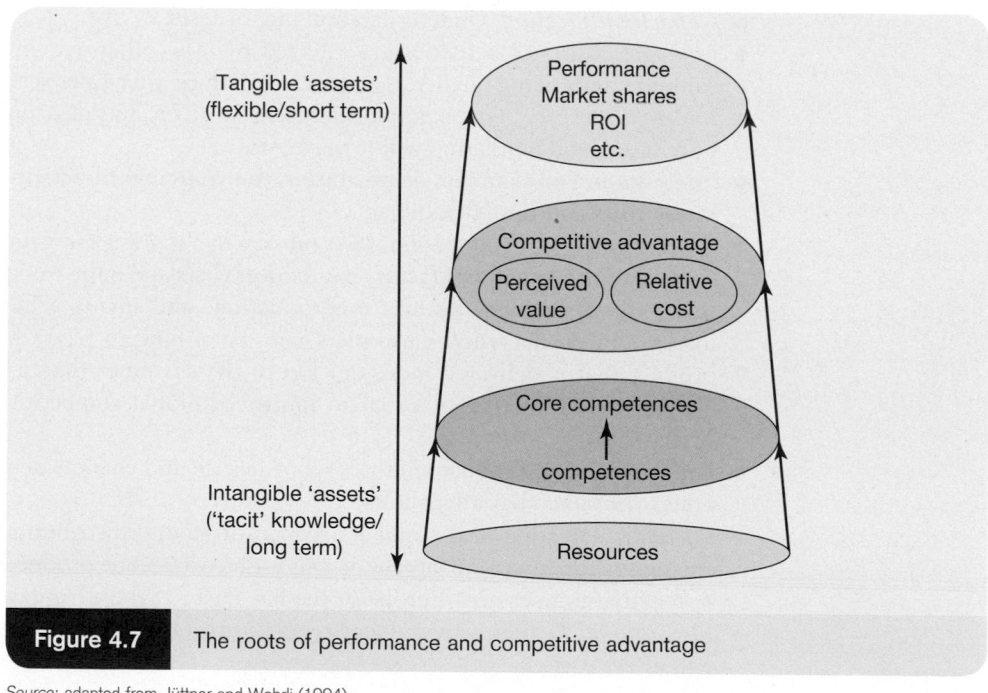

Figure 4.7   The roots of performance and competitive advantage

Source: adapted from Jüttner and Wehrli (1994).

Competences

Competences – being components of a higher level – result from a combination of the various resources. Their formation and quality depend on two factors. The first factor is the specific capabilities of the firm in integrating resources. These capabilities are developed and improved in a collective learning process. On the other hand, the basis for the quality of a competence is the resource assortment. This forms a potential for competences, which should be exploited to the maximum extent.

Cardy and Selvarajan (2006) classify competences into two broad categories: *personal* and *corporate*. Personal competences are possessed by individuals and include characteristics such as knowledge, skills, abilities, experience and personality. Corporate competences belong to the organization and are embedded processes and structures that tend to reside within the organization, even when individuals leave. These two categories are not entirely independent. The collection of personal competences can form a way of doing things or a culture that becomes embedded in the organization. In addition, corporate characteristics can determine the type of personal competences that will best work or fit in the organization.

Core competences
Value chain activities in which the firm is regarded as better than its competitors.

A firm can have a lot of competences, but only a few of them are **core competences**, i.e. a value chain activity in which the firm is regarded as a better performer than any of its competitors (see Figure 4.8).

In Figure 4.8 a core competence is represented by a strategic resource (asset) that competitors cannot easily imitate and which has the potential to earn long-term profit. The objective of the firm will be to place products and services at the top-right corner. The top-left corner also represents profit possibilities, but the competitive advantage is easier to imitate, so the high profit will only be short term. The bottom-left corner represents the position of the price-sensitive commodity supplier. Here the profits are likely to be low because the product is primarily differentiated by place (distribution) and especially price.

Competitive benchmarking

The ultimate test of the efficiency of any marketing strategy has to be in terms of profit. Those companies that strive for market share but measure market share in terms of volume sales may be deluding themselves to the extent that volume is bought at the expense of profit.

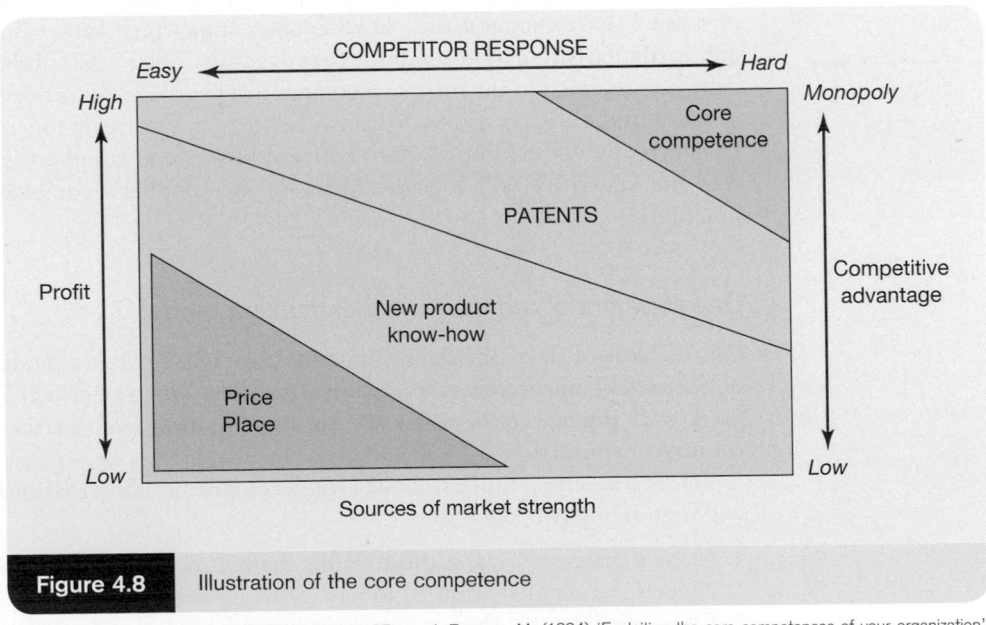

| **Figure 4.8** | Illustration of the core competence |

Source: reprinted from *Long Range Planning*, vol. 27, no. 4, Tampoe, M. (1994) 'Exploiting the core competences of your organization', p. 74, Copyright 1994, with permission from Elsevier.

Because market share is an 'after the event' measure, we need to utilize continuing indicators of competitive performance. This will highlight areas where improvements in the marketing mix can be made.

Competitive benchmarking
A technique for assessing relative marketplace performance compared with main competitors.

In recent years, a number of companies have developed a technique for assessing relative marketplace performance, which has come to be known as **competitive benchmarking**. Originally the idea of competitive benchmarking was literally to take apart a competitor's product, component by component, and compare its performance in a value engineering sense with your own product. This approach has often been attributed to the Japanese, but many western companies have also found the value of such detailed comparisons.

The concept of competitive benchmarking is similar to what Porter (1996) calls operational effectiveness (OE), meaning performing similar activities better than competitors perform them. However, Porter (1996) also thinks that OE is a necessary, but not a sufficient, condition for outperforming rivals. Firms also have to consider strategic (or market) positioning, meaning the performance of *different* activities from rivals or performing similar activities in different ways. Only a few firms have competed successfully on the basis of OE over a long period. The main reason is the rapid diffusion of best practices. Competitors can rapidly imitate management techniques and new technologies with support from consultants.

However, the idea of benchmarking is capable of extension beyond this simple comparison of technology and cost-effectiveness. Because the battle in the marketplace is for 'share of mind', it is customers' perceptions that we must measure.

The measures that can be used in this type of benchmarking programme include delivery reliability, ease of ordering, after-sales service, the quality of sales representation and the accuracy of invoices and other documentation. These measures are not chosen at random, but are selected because of their importance to the customer. Market research, often based on in-depth interviews, would typically be employed to identify what these 'key success factors' (KSF) are. The elements that customers identify as being the most important (see Figure 4.8) then form the basis for the benchmark questionnaire. This questionnaire is administered to a sample of customers on a regular basis: for example, German Telecom carries out a daily telephone survey of a random sample of its domestic and business customers to measure customers' perceptions of service. For most companies, an annual survey might suffice; in other cases, a quarterly survey might be more appropriate, particularly if market conditions are dynamic. The output of these surveys might typically be presented in the form of a competitive profile, as in the example in Figure 4.9.

Most of the criteria mentioned above relate to downstream functions in the value chain. Concurrently with closer relations between buyers and suppliers, especially in the industrial market, there will be more focus on the supplier's competences in the upstream functions.

Development of a dynamic benchmarking model

On the basis of the value chain's functions, we will suggest a model for the development of a firm's competitiveness in a defined market. The model will be based on a specific market, as the market demands are assumed to differ from market to market, and from country to country.

Before presenting the basic model for development of international competitiveness, we will first define two key terms:

1. *Critical success factors*: those value chain functions where the customer demands/ expects the supplier (firm X) to have a strong competence.
2. *Core competences*: those value chain functions where firm X has a strong competitive position.

The strategy process

The model for the strategy process is shown in Figure 4.10.

Examples of value chain functions (mainly downstream functions)	Customer Importance to customer (key success factors)					Own firm (Firm A) How do customers rate performance of our firm?					Key competitor (Firm B) How do customers rate performance of key competitor?				
	High importance				Low importance	Good				Bad	Good				Bad
	5	4	3	2	1	5	4	3	2	1	5	4	3	2	1
Uses new technology															
High technical quality and competence															
Uses proven technology															
Easy to buy from															
Understands what customers want															
Low price															
Delivery on schedule															
Accessible for enquiries															
Takes full responsibility															
Flexible and quick															
Known contact person															
Provides customer training															
Takes account of future requirements															
Courteous and helpful															
Specified invoices															
Gives guarantees															
ISO 9000 certified															
Right first time															
Can give references															
Environment conscious															

Figure 4.9 Competitive benchmarking (example with only a few criteria)

Stage 1: Analysis of situation (identification of competence gaps)

We will not go into detail here about the problems there have been in measuring the value chain functions. The measurements cannot be objective in the traditional way of thinking, but must rely on internal assessments from firm representatives (interviews with relevant managers) supplemented by external experts ('key informants') who are able to judge the market's (customers') demand now and in the future.

The competence profile for firm A in Figure 4.1 (top-right diagram) is an example of how a firm is out of kilter with the market (= customer) demand. The company has its core competences in parts of the value chain's functions where customers place little importance (market knowledge in Figure 4.1).

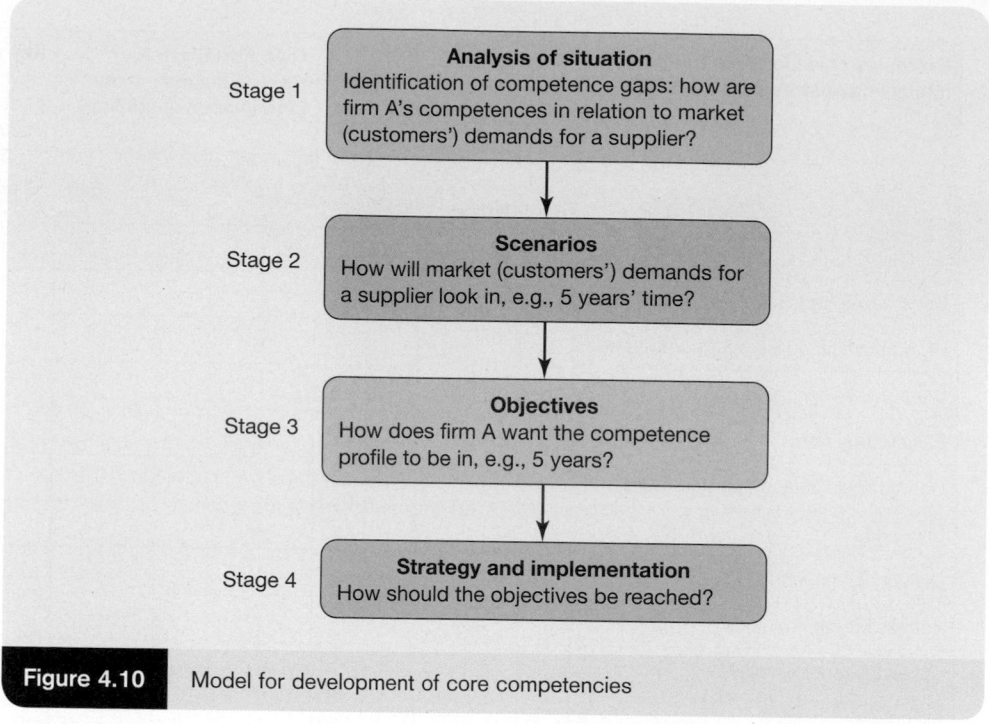

Figure 4.10 Model for development of core competencies

If there is generally a good match between the critical success factors and firm A's initial position, it is important to concentrate resources and improve this core competence to create sustainable competitive advantages.

If, on the other hand, there is a large gap between customers' demands and the firm's initial position in critical success factors in Figure 4.1 (as with the personal selling functions), it may give rise to the following alternatives:

● improve the position of the critical success factor(s);
● find business areas where firm A's competence profile better suits the market demand and expectations.

As a new business area involves risk, it is often important to identify an eventual gap in a critical success factor as early as possible. In other words, an 'early warning' system must be established that continuously monitors the critical competitive factors so that it is possible to start initiatives that limit an eventual gap as early as possible.

In Figure 4.1 the competence profile of firm B is also shown.

Stages 2 and 3: Scenarios and objectives

To be able to estimate future market demand, different scenarios are drawn of the possible future development. These trends are first described generally, and the effect of the market's future demand/expectations on a supplier's value chain function is then concretized.

In this way, the described 'gap' between market expectations and firm A's initial position becomes more clear. At the same time, the biggest gap for firm A may have moved from personal sales to, for example, product development. From knowledge of the market leader's strategy, it is possible to complete scenarios of the market leader's future competence profile.

These scenarios may be the foundation for a discussion of objectives and of which competence profile the company wants in, say, five years' time. Objectives must be set realistically and with due consideration of the organization's resources (the scenarios are not shown in Figure 4.1).

Stage 4: Strategy and implementation

Depending on which of firm A's value chain functions are to be developed, a strategy is prepared. This results in implementation plans that include the adjustment of the organization's current competence level.

4.5   The sustainable global value chain

A value chain comprises all activities necessary to 'bring a product from conception to market'. Therefore, it includes product development, different phases of production, extraction of raw materials, semi-finished materials, component production and assembly, distribution, marketing and even recycling. As these activities may be spread over several different firms and countries, the value chain can become global (see also Chapter 1).

In order that the value chain should also be strategic, Porter and Kramer (2006) wrote that corporate social responsibility (CSR) should contribute to firm value chain practices and/or improve the context of competitiveness. Building on this example, it can be advocated that company CSR programmes could be so designed that the CSR activity forms part of the firm value chain by contributing to the primary activities and/or the support activities. Such CSR initiatives help firms to secure purchased inputs, reduce operational costs, smooth logistics and/or contribute to the marketing and sales function of the value chain. Similarly, CSR activities could also be intelligently planned to contribute to the support activities such as procurement, and manpower development of the company's value chain.

Shared value
A company's strategies and operating practices that globally enhance the competitiveness of the company, while simultaneously advancing the social conditions in the international communities in which it operates.

A company's value chain inevitably affects – and is affected by – several societal issues, such as natural resources and water use, health and safety, and working conditions. In a recent article, Porter and Kramer (2011) introduced the concept of **shared value**. Shared value creation focuses on identifying and expanding the connection between societal and company added value. Shared value can be defined as the strategies and operating practices that enhance the competitiveness of a company, while at the same time advancing the social values in the communities in which it operates. Many so-called externalities actually increase the internal costs of the firm, even in the absence of regulations and resource taxes. Excess packaging of products and greenhouse gases are costly not just to the environment, but also to the company, and reducing these costs would bring 'shared value'.

Porter and Kramer (2011) use the example of Walmart's initiatives, which were able to address both issues by reducing its packaging and rescheduling its trucks to cut 100 million miles from its delivery routes in 2009, saving US$200 million even as it shipped more products. Innovation in disposal of plastic used in Walmart stores has also saved other millions in lower disposal cost to landfills.

4.6   Corporate social responsibility (CSR)

The traditional corporate paradigm has always supported a strong external customer relationship, because customers buy the firm's product and ultimately deliver profits to the stockholders. The concept of **corporate social responsibility (CSR)** has become a relatively visible phenomenon in the marketing literature, shifting the narrow notion of customer-based marketing to a broader corporate-level marketing concept.

Corporate social responsibility (CSR)
A number of corporate activities that focus on the welfare of stakeholder groups other than investors, such as charitable and community organizations, employees, suppliers, customers and future generations.

A prevailing understanding of CSR is based on the notion of stakeholders' expectations, which are of important concern to corporate marketing. This means that an organization operates within a network of different stakeholders who can influence it directly or indirectly. Therefore, the scope of CSR should focus on the organization's commitment to avoid harm and improve stakeholders' and society's well-being.

Corporate social responsibility comprises a number of corporate activities that focus on the welfare of stakeholder groups other than investors, such as charitable and community organizations, employees, suppliers, customers and future generations.

For example, in the 1990s, Nike was accused over several Asian sweatshop issues. Nike used their Nikebiz.com website to inform the audience about the company's core values by emphasizing its commitment to economically empowering individual women in under-developed countries, in this way responding indirectly to media charges that Nike routinely tolerated the violation of its Asian female workers' human rights. Nikebiz.com successfully associated Nike with those working for positive change in the lives of poor women across Asia and Africa (Waller and Conaway, 2011).

One important category of CSR activities includes 'green' production practices, such as conserving energy, reducing emissions, using recycled materials, reducing packaging materials and sourcing materials from vendors located geographically close to manufacturing facilities. For example, in 2006 Walmart announced a programme to measure suppliers on their ability to reduce packaging, with a goal of eliminating 5 per cent of total packaging between 2008 and 2013. Similarly, Hewlett-Packard provides free recycling of toner cartridges for customers (Sprinkle and Maines, 2010).

Definitions of CSR, and the very actions of CSR, vary among countries, regions, societies and communities. One very broad definition of CSR may be what a business puts back into the local or state economy in return for what it takes out. Many definitions of CSR include management practices, linking the inner circle of management with the outer circle of the community-at-large. Managers have a direct impact on companies' abilities to manage the business processes in a way that produces an overall positive impact on society.

Thus the concept of CSR refers to the belief that modern businesses have a responsibility to society that extends beyond delivering profits to the stockholders or investors in the firm. These other societal stakeholders typically include consumers, employees, the community at large, government and the natural environment. The CSR concept applies to organizations of all sizes, but discussions have tended to focus on large organizations because they tend to be more visible and have more power – and, as many have observed, with power comes responsibility.

Corporate social responsibility must be rooted deep in the company's resource base (see also Figure 4.7), which means that short-term gain must take a clear second place to long-term thinking. Exhibit 4.2 shows a company (Chiquita), which managed to integrate this long-term view into its resource base and improve its international competitiveness as a result.

In the following we will analyse some specific conditions under which a sustainable global value chain (SGVC) might gain international competitiveness. Here, we use a bottom-line definition of international competitiveness: a global value chain is competitive internationally as long as its products can be profitably sold on export markets. In addition, we define SGVC as the global value chains in which the products and the production process result from environmental, social and/or economical concerns and practices. Considering the growing number of contributions to sustainable development and CSR literature, we recognize that many different types of SGVC could be identified (related to specific social or environmental issues) with different specificities.

Value added from CSR activities can occur if revenues increase or costs decrease due to the CSR involvement of a company (Figure 4.11).

CSR benefits

CSR-induced revenue increases can come from additional sales due to increases in sales quantities, prices or margins. These can be stimulated by cause-related marketing

EXHIBIT 4.2 Chiquita – integrating CSR in the resource base

The time it can take to embed CSR successfully into a brand, and then see a return on that investment, is illustrated by US-based fruit and vegetable producer Chiquita Brands Inc., one of the world's biggest importers of bananas that oversees a maze of local labour partnerships. Anticipating that its European business was going to be threatened by lower-priced competitors, Chiquita began overhauling its entire sourcing infrastructure around ethical credentials. This process, which cost the firm US$20 million, began in 1992, and culminated with certification by the activist group Rainforest Alliance in 2000. However, it only began actively to communicate a sustainability and responsibility message to consumers in 2005.

Many strategies suffer from a failure in perhaps one of the most critical aspects of their deployment – making the resource base visible and tangible to the external stakeholders. CSR is no different. Adopting CSR is one thing but, like all business tools, in order to bring success it must be adequately monitored. As for Chiquita, this ongoing assessment process is a vital part of the chain.

In 1998, executives at Chiquita were horrified to see their company splashed all over the newspapers after an undercover investigation into 'dangerous and illegal business practices' throughout its Latin American operations. Chiquita had to make a dramatic review of its entire business.

Chiquita's CEO declared his commitment to breaking new ground in responsible management and pledged that the company would do much more than merely repair the damage brought about by the media. Ten years later, and despite changes at the corporate management level, Chiquita's CSR policy was still in full flight and its long-term international competitiveness improved as a result.

In the meantime, Chiquita also signed a global agreement with local and international food unions. Furthermore, it embraced sustainable farming techniques and allowed products to be certified for environmental and other standards.

Sources: based on Curtis (2006); *Economist* (2012).

campaigns, CSR-specific product line changes or improved possibilities of winning public tenders, e.g. due to the use of environmentally friendly technologies. CSR-induced revenue increases can also refer to CSR grants and subsidies. The sales may increase as a result of:

- better branch value;
- better customer attraction and retention (higher repurchase rates, higher market shares);
- higher employed attractiveness (more applications per vacancy, better hiring rate);
- higher employee motivation and retention (lower fluctuation rate, absenteeism).

Savings from CSR-induced cost decreases can result from internal cost savings due to efficiency improvements or can be triggered by CSR-specific collaborations with, for example, non-governmental organization (NGOs) that provide knowledge or contacts to critical stakeholders such as public authorities, reducing the costs for product or market development. Cost savings can also come from tax concessions or reductions of certain duties granted by governments to promote CSR activities, e.g. tax concessions for environmentally friendly technologies.

When evaluating CSR benefits, managers need to carefully consider the time period involved. As CSR benefits often occur after a time lag, evaluations should focus on longer time periods. As argued above, for some CSR benefits it is difficult to isolate the impact of CSR from other influencing factors. In this context, the evaluation of complementary figures as well as CSR key performance indicators can be helpful.

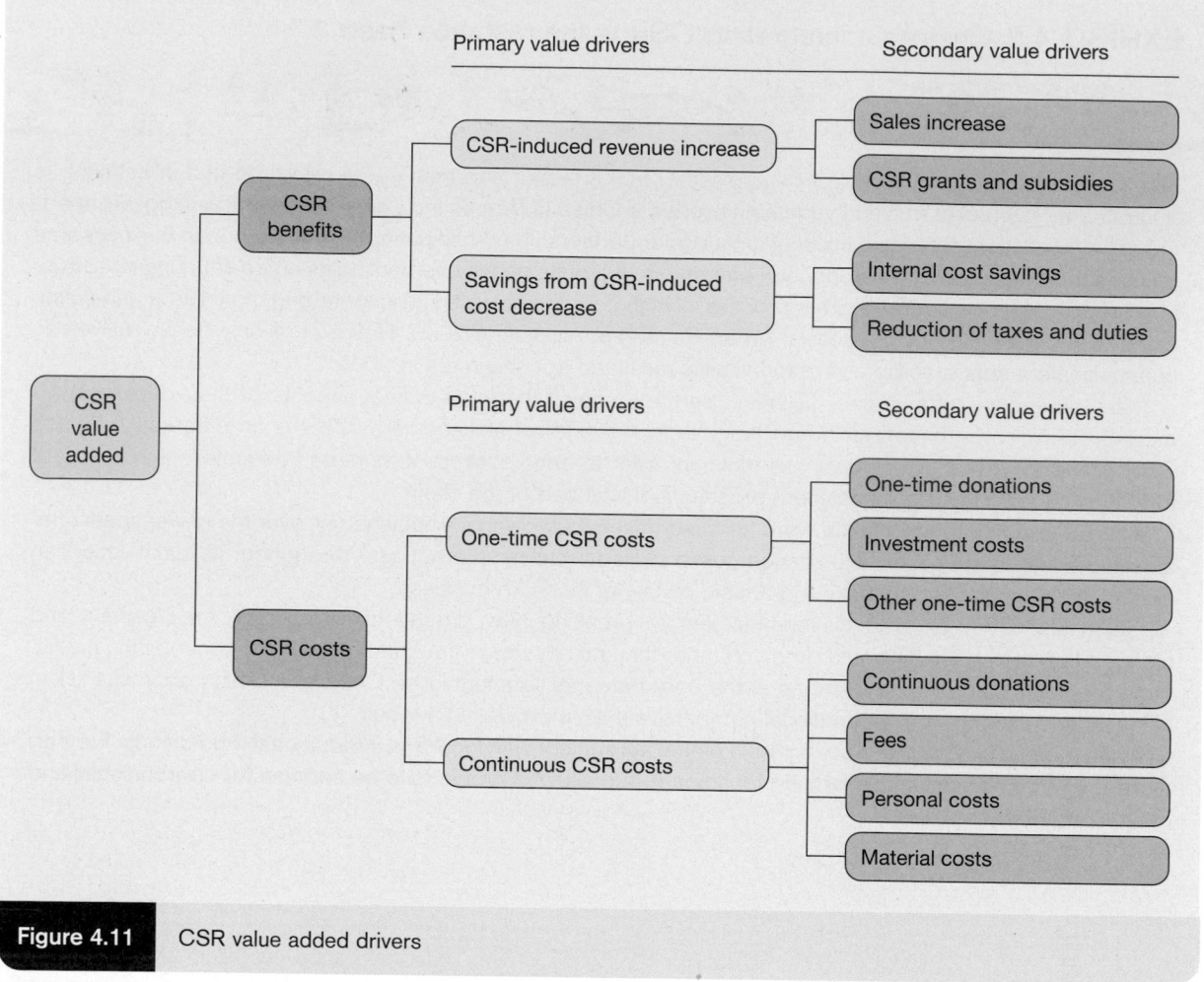

Figure 4.11   CSR value added drivers

Source: adapted from Weber, M. (2008) 'The business case for corporate social responsibility: a company-level measurement approach for CSR,' *European Management Journal*, 26, 4: 247–61. Reproduced with permission from Elsevier.

CSR costs

One-time CSR costs include one-time donations, such as those given to support the tsunami victims in 2004. One-time CSR costs also include investment costs, e.g. for the installation of smoke filters that are beyond legal requirements, and other one-time costs caused by the CSR activities in scope.

Continuous CSR costs include donations intended to continuously support a certain cause and fees such as licence fees to use certain labels or patents, which are paid on a continuous basis. They also include recurring personnel and material costs such as the costs of managers coordinating CSR projects or material costs for the production of promotion materials, e.g. in cause-related marketing campaigns.

It is often difficult to assess CSR costs using conventional cost accounting systems, as these do not distinguish between CSR and non-CSR costs. Conventional cost accounting assigns overhead costs to products based on volume indicators such as production volume.

While CSR in a company's value chain and context of competitiveness are certain actual activity descriptions, other CSR activities can also provide new business opportunities for a firm, and in the next two sections these aspects are explored further.

Society has a multitude of social and environmental problems that vary in type and magnitude. Two major problems, and consequently business market opportunities, are widespread: poverty and environmental degradation – the 'green' market. Poverty is a threat for the healthy existence of future generations. But these two issues can also create business opportunities, which are further discussed in Hollensen (2010), Chapter 6.

4.7 The value net

Value net
A company's value creation in collaboration with suppliers and customers (vertical network partners) and complementors and competitors (horizontal network partners).

Value chain analysis (Section 4.4) implies a linear process, ignoring inputs from outside the chain – many firms may have an input into the process at various stages (Neves, 2007). The reality is therefore that the value chain becomes a value network, a group of interrelated entities, which contribute to the overall creation of value through a series of complex relationships, and the result is the so-called **value net** (Brandenburger and Nalebuff, 1996; Teng, 2003; Holmberg and Cummings, 2009).

The value net reveals two fundamental symmetries. Vertically, customers and suppliers are equal partners in creating value. The other symmetry is on the horizontal for competitors and complementors. The mirror image of competitors is complementors. A complement to one product or service is any other product or service that makes the first one more attractive, e.g. computer hardware and software, hot dogs and mustard, catalogues and overnight delivery service, red wine and dry cleaners. The value net helps you understand your competitors and complementors 'outside in'. Who are the players and what are their roles and the interdependences between them? Re-examine the conventional wisdom of 'Who are your friends and who are your enemies?' The suggestion is to know your business inside out and create a value net with the other players.

With Figure 4.12 in mind, we can also think about how the different actors can add value to the total global value chain. For example, the Swedish furniture giant IKEA provides an example of customer co-creation. The retailer enables customers to pay less for furniture but also encourages them to transport and then assemble the furniture themselves. Compared with a traditional furniture store, IKEA's business model is very much dependent on the value creation on the customer side (Michel *et al.*, 2008).

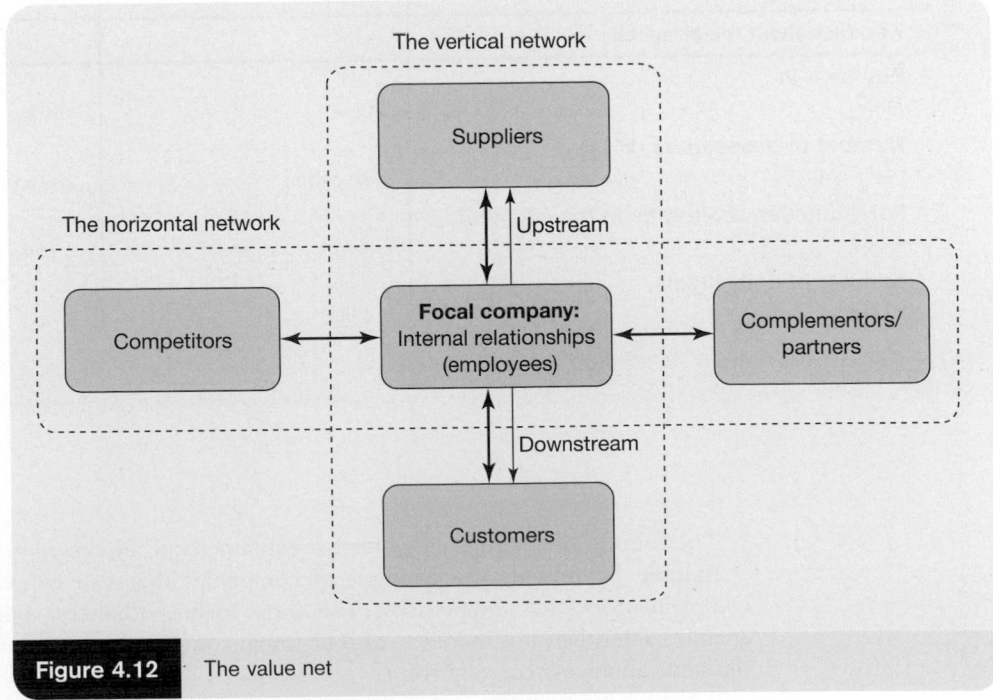

Figure 4.12   The value net

EXHIBIT 4.3 Value net – cooperation/competition between competitors within each airline alliance. The three alliances are competing against each other

Star Alliance members	Skyteam members	One World members
Adria Airways	Aeroflot	airberlin/Niki
Aegean Airlines	Aeromexico	American Airlines
Air Canada	Air Europa	British Airways
Air China	Air France	Cathay Pacific
Air New Zealand	Alitalia	Finnair
ANA	China Airlines	Iberia
Asiana Airlines	China Eastern	Japan Airlines
Austrian	China Southern	LAN
Avianca AV, TACA Airlines	Czech Airlines	Mexicana
Blue1	Delta Air Lines	Qantas
Brussels Airlines	Kenya Airways	Royal Jordanian
Copa Airlines	KLM	S7 Airlines
Croatia Airlines	Korean Air	
EGYPTAIR	Saudi Arabian Airlines	
Ethiopian Airlines	TAROM	
LOT Polish Airlines	Vietnam Airlines	
Lufthansa		
Scandinavian Airlines		
Singapore Airlines		
South African Airways		
SWISS		
TAM Airlines		
TAP Portugal		
THAI		
Turkish Airlines		
United		
US Airways		

Key data about the alliances		
Founded in: 1997	2000	1999
Number of passengers (2011) 654 million	487 million	288 million
Total number of aircrafts in the alliance: 4,386	3,542	2,194
Number of daily flights: 21,230	14,500	8,750

Source: adapted from Ruff (2012).

The concept of a 'value net' is further explained and discussed in Hollensen (2010).

Exhibit 4.2 provides an example of companies that can co-exist as both partners/complementors and competitors. The three airline alliances shown compete fiercely against each other, but there can also be tough competition between airline companies in the same alliance on certain routes.

4.8   Blue ocean strategy and value innovation

Red oceans
Tough head-to-head competition in mature industries often results in nothing but a bloody red ocean of rivals fighting over a shrinking profit pool.

Blue oceans
The unserved market, where competitors are not yet structured and the market is relatively unknown. Here it is about avoiding head-to-head competition.

Kim and Mauborgne (2005a,b,c) use the ocean as a metaphor to describe the competitive space in which an organization chooses to swim. **Red oceans** refer to the frequently accessed marketspaces where the products are well defined, competitors are known and competition is based on price, product quality and service. In other words, red oceans are an old paradigm that represents all the industries in existence today.

By contrast, **blue oceans** denote an environment where products are not yet well defined, competitors are not structured and the market is relatively unknown. Companies that sail in the blue oceans are those beating the competition by focusing on developing compelling value innovations that create uncontested marketspace. Adopters of blue ocean strategy believe that it is no longer valid for companies to engage in head-to-head competition in search of sustained, profitable growth.

In Michael Porter's work (1980, 1985) companies are fighting for competitive advantage, battling for market share and struggling for differentiation. Blue ocean strategists argue that cut-throat competition results in nothing but a bloody red ocean of rivals fighting over a shrinking profit pool. Blue ocean is a marketspace that is created by identifying an unserved set of customers, then delivering to them a compelling new value proposition. This is done by reconfiguring what is on offer to better balance customer needs with the economic costs of doing so. This is as opposed to a red ocean, where the market is well defined and heavily populated by the competition.

Blue ocean strategy should not be a static process but a dynamic one. Consider The Body Shop. In the 1980s, it was highly successful, and rather than compete head-on with large cosmetics companies, it invented a whole new marketspace for natural beauty products. During the 1990s, The Body Shop also struggled, but that does not diminish the excellence of its original strategic move. Its genius lay in creating a new marketspace in an intensely competitive industry that historically competed on glamour (Kim and Mauborgne, 2005b).

Kim and Mauborgne (2005a) is based on a study of 150 strategic moves that spanned more than 100 years (1880–2000) and 30 industries. Their first point in distinguishing this strategy from the traditional strategic frameworks is that in the traditional business literature, the company forms the basic unit of analysis, and the industry analysis is the means of positioning the company. Their hypothesis is that since markets are constantly changing in their levels of attractiveness, and companies over time vary in their level of performance, it is the particular *strategic move of the company,* and not the company itself or the industry, that is the correct criterion for evaluating the difference between red and blue ocean strategies.

Value innovation

Value innovation
A strategic approach to business growth, involving a shift away from a focus on the existing competition to one of trying to create entirely new markets. Value innovation can be achieved by implementing a focus on innovation and creation of new marketspace.

Kim and Mauborgne (2005a) argue that tomorrow's leading companies will succeed not by battling competitors, but by making strategic moves, which they call **value innovation.**

The combination of value with innovation is not just marketing and taxonomic positioning. It has consequences. Value without innovation tends to focus on value creation on an incremental scale, and innovation without value tends to be technology-driven, market-pioneering or futuristic, often overshooting what buyers are ready to accept and pay for. Conventional Porter logic (1980, 1985) leads companies only to compete at the margin for incremental share. The logic of value innovation starts with an ambition to dominate the market by offering a tremendous leap in value. Many companies seek growth by retaining and expanding their customer base. This often leads to finer segmentation and greater customization of offerings to meet specialized needs. Instead of focusing on the differences between customers, value innovators build on the powerful commonalities in the features that customers value (Kim and Mauborgne, 1997).

Value innovation is intensely customer-focused, but not exclusively so. Like value chain analysis, it balances the costs of delivering the value proposition with what the buyer values are, and then resolves the trade-off dilemma between the value delivered and the costs involved. Instead of compromising the value wanted by the customer, because of the high costs associated with delivering it, costs are eliminated or reduced if there is no or less value placed on the offering by the customer. This is a real win–win resolution that creates the compelling proposition. Customers get what they really want for less, and sellers get a higher rate of return on invested capital by reducing start-up and/or operational delivery costs. The combination of these two is the catalyst of blue ocean market creation. Exhibit 4.4 illustrates this using the case of Formule 1.

The output of the value innovation analysis is the value curves of the different marketers in the industry (also called the 'strategy canvas' in Kim and Mauborgne (2005a) – see Exhibit 4.4). These different value curves raise four basic questions for the focal firm:

1. Which factors should be reduced well below the industry standard?
2. Which of the factors that the industry takes for granted should be eliminated?
3. Which factors should be raised well above the industry standard?
4. Which factors should be created that the industry has never offered?

These four questions can be reduced to two simple strategies in order to create 'value innovation' (see Figure 4.13):

● reducing costs (1 and 2);
● increasing customer value (3 and 4).

When both strategies are being realized at the same time, the 'overlapping' area in Figure 4.13 will be higher (= increasing 'value innovation').

The resulting new value curve should then determine if the firm is on its way into the 'blue ocean'.

A decade after the 'Blue Ocean Strategy' was launched, Kim and Mauborgne (2015) evaluated their many conversations with managers about the barriers in executing market-creating strategies. They found that although the managers' mental models can help make decisions that are critical to survival, they also undermine the ability to think in new ways in order to create new markets. Consequently, the managers' mental models may create 'red ocean traps' that anchor managers in red oceans and prevent them from entering 'blue oceans' with uncontested market space including ample new potential.

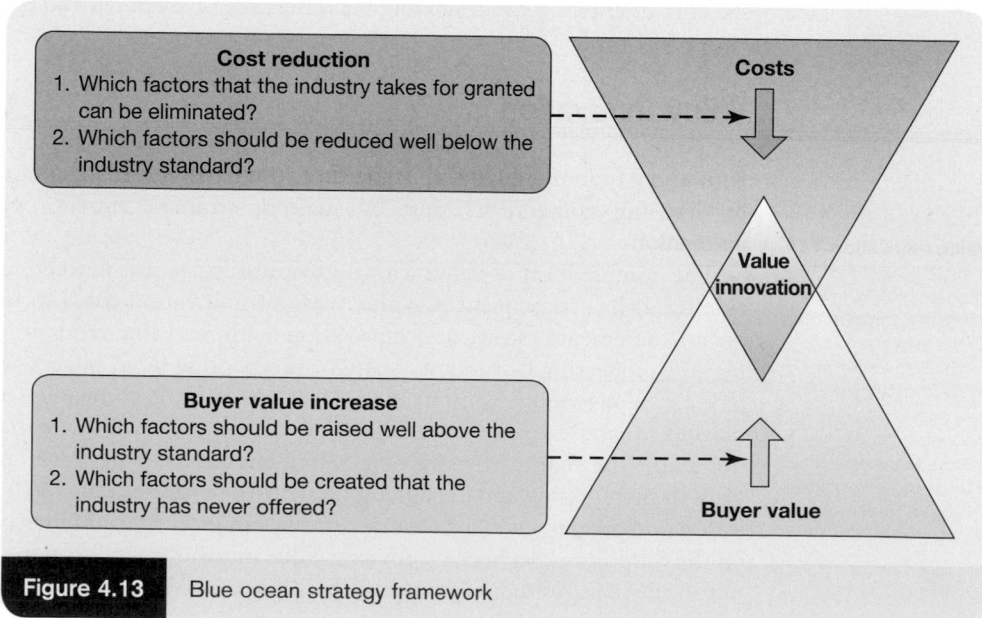

Cost reduction
1. Which factors that the industry takes for granted can be eliminated?
2. Which factors should be reduced well below the industry standard?

Costs

Value innovation

Buyer value increase
1. Which factors should be raised well above the industry standard?
2. Which factors should be created that the industry has never offered?

Buyer value

Figure 4.13   Blue ocean strategy framework

EXHIBIT 4.4 Hotel Formule 1 – value innovation in action

When Accor launched Formule 1 (a line of French budget hotels) in 1985, the budget hotel industry was suffering from stagnation and over-capacity. The top management urged the managers to forget everything they knew of the existing rules, practices and traditions of the industry. There were two distinct market segments in the industry. One segment consisted of no-star and one-star hotels (very cheap, around €20 per room per night) and the other segment was two-star hotels, with an average price of €40 per room. These more expensive two-star hotels attracted customers by offering better sleeping facilities than the cheap segment. Accor's management undertook market research and found

Source: Tony Souter/DK Images.

out what most customers of all budget hotels wanted: a good night's sleep at a low price. Then they asked themselves (and answered) the four fundamental questions:

1. Which of the factors that the budget hotel industry took for granted should be eliminated? The Accor management eliminated such standard hotel features as costly restaurants and appealing lounges. Accor reckoned that they might lose some customers, but they also knew that most customers could live without these features.
2. Which factors should be reduced well below the industry standard? Accor also believed that budget hotels were overperforming along other dimensions. For example, at Formule 1 receptionists are on hand only during peak check-in and check-out hours. At all other times, customers use an automated teller. The rooms at Formule 1 are small and equipped only with a bed and bare necessities – no desks or decorations. Instead of closets, there are a few shelves for clothing.
3. Which factors should be raised well above the industry standard? As seen in Formule 1's value curve (Figure 4.14) the following factors were raised above the relative level of the one- and two-star hotels:
   - the bed quality
   - hygiene
   - room quietness.
   The price performance was perceived as being at the same level as the average one-star hotels.
4. Which new factors (that the industry had never offered) should be developed? These covered cost-minimizing factors such as the availability of room keys via an automated teller. The rooms themselves are modular blocks manufactured in a factory, a method which may not result in the nicest architectural aesthetics but gives economies of scale in production and considerable cost advantages. Formule 1 has cut the average cost of building a room in half and its staff costs (in relation to total sales) dropped below the industry average (approximately 30 per cent) to between 20 and 23 per cent. These cost savings have allowed Accor to improve the features, that customers value most ('a good night's sleep at a low price').

Note that, in Figure 4.14, if the price is perceived as relatively low, it is regarded as a strong performance.

What has happened with Accor and Formule 1?

Accor is the owner of several hotel chains (besides Formule 1) – Etap, Mercure, Sofitel, Novotel, Ibis and Motel 6. In 2008, the sales of the Accor Group were €7.7 billion with operating profits of €875 million.

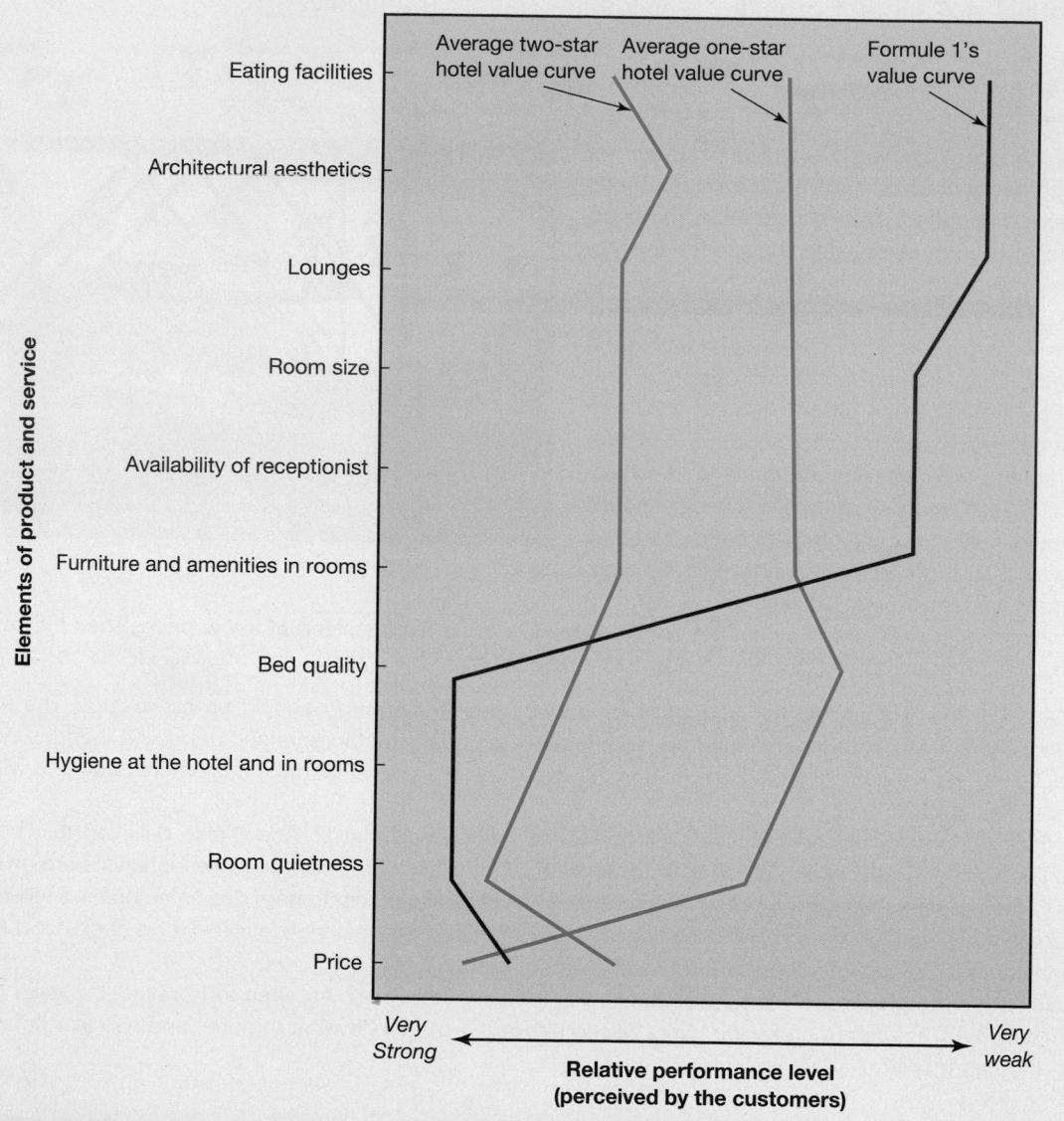

Figure 4.14   Formule 1's value curve

Source: adapted from Value innovation: the strategic logic of high growth, *Harvard Business Review*, Vol. 75(1), pp. 102–112 (W. Chan Kim and Renée Mauborgne 1997), January/February, Copyright © 1997 by Harvard Business Publishing, all rights reserved, reprinted by permission of Harvard Business Review.

In France, Formule 1 has abbreviated its name to Hotel F1. In the rest of Europe, the brand name has been incorporated into the Etap hotels. Outside Europe, 55 hotels are operated under the Formule 1 brand (in South Africa, Australia, Brazil, Indonesia, Japan and New Zealand). In 2008, Accor's market share in the European budget hotel segment was approximately 50 per cent.

Sources: www.accor.com; www.hotelformule1.com; Kim and Mauborgne (1997).

4.9 Summary

The main focus of this chapter is how the firm creates and develops competitive advantages in the international marketplace. A three-stage model allows us to understand the development of a firm's international competitiveness in a broader perspective:

1. analysis of national competitiveness (the Porter diamond);
2. competition analysis (Porter's five forces);
3. value chain analysis:

   (a) competitive triangle
   (b) benchmarking.

Analysis of national competitiveness

The analysis starts at the macro level, where the Porter diamond indicates that the characteristics of the home nation play a central role in the firm's international success.

Competition analysis

The next stage is to move to the competitive arena where the firm is the unit of analysis. Porter's five-forces model suggests that competition in an industry is rooted in its underlying economic structure and goes beyond the behaviour of current competitors. The state of competition depends upon five basic competitive forces, which determine the profit potential in an industry.

Value chain analysis

Here we look at what creates a competitive advantage at the same competitive level (among industry competitors). According to the *competitive triangle,* it can be concluded that firms have a competitive advantage in a market if they offer products with the following:

- a higher perceived value to the customers;
- lower relative costs than competing firms.

A firm can find out its competitive advantages or core competences by using *competitive benchmarking,* a technique whereby customers measure marketplace performance of the firm against that of a 'first-class' competitor. The measures in the value chain that can be used include delivery reliability, ease of ordering, after-sales service and quality of sales representation. These value chain activities are chosen on the basis of their importance to the customer. As customers' perceptions change over time, it may be relevant to try to estimate customers' future demands on a supplier of particular products.

According to the blue ocean strategy, the red oceans represent all the industries in existence today. This is *known* marketspace. Blue oceans denote all the industries not in existence today. This is *unknown* marketspace.

In the red oceans, industry boundaries are defined and accepted, and the competitive rules of the game are known. Here companies try to outperform their rivals to grab a greater share of existing demand. As the marketspace gets more and more crowded, prospects for profits and growth are reduced. Products become commodities, and cut-throat competition turns the red ocean bloody.

Blue oceans, by contrast, are defined by untapped marketspace, demand creation and the opportunity for highly profitable growth. While blue oceans are occasionally created well beyond existing industry boundaries, most are created by expanding existing industry boundaries. In blue oceans, competition is irrelevant as the rules of the game are waiting to be set.

Once a company has created a blue ocean, it should prolong its profit and growth sanctuary by swimming as far as possible in the blue ocean, making itself a moving target, distancing itself from potential imitators and discouraging them in the process. The aim here is to dominate the blue ocean over imitators for as long as possible. But, as other companies' strategies converge on your market, and the blue ocean turns red with intense competition, companies need to reach out to create a new blue ocean to break away from the competition yet again.

CASE STUDY 4.1

Nintendo Wii: Nintendo's Wii took first place on the world market – but it didn't last

When it was launched, very few analysts would have predicted that Nintendo Wii would one day be market leader in the games console market against the established PlayStation 3 (PS3) and Xbox 360 brands. But analysts can be wrong: in the week ending 23 August 2007, www.Vgchartz.com data, which is based on sample data from retailers all over the world, indicated that Nintendo's Wii (which was released in November 2006 – one year after the Xbox 360) had passed the Xbox 360's lifetime unit sales, making Nintendo the new world market leader in both the games and console businesses.

This had a big impact on third-party publishers and also influenced the decisions that the three major players (Microsoft, Sony and Nintendo) would make in the future.

One factor that no doubt helped Nintendo's Wii to grow so quickly was the console's broad appeal across all age groups, demographics and countries. However, Nintendo's first place in the world market came under massive attack from both Sony and Microsoft's new sensing devices (see below).

Nintendo Group (including subsidiaries) employs about 5,200 people.

The Nintendo Wii
Source: Annette Shaff/Shutterstock.com.

Nintendo – key facts and financial data

Nintendo Co. was founded in 1889 as the Marufuku Company to make and sell 'hanafuda', Japanese game cards. Abandoning previous ventures in favour of toys in the 1960s, Nintendo then developed into a video game company in the 1970s, ultimately becoming one of the most influential in the industry and Japan's third most valuable listed company with a market value of over US$85 billion.

Today Nintendo (www.nintendo.co.jp) is engaged in the creation of interactive entertainment products. It manufactures and markets hardware and software for its home video game systems. The company primarily operates in Japan, Europe and America. It is headquartered in Kyoto, Japan. In total the whole

In the fiscal year 2014, Nintendo's recorded revenues were US$5.6 billion. There was a loss in the company of US$0.2 billion during fiscal year 2014. Approximately 80 per cent of the company's revenue is generated from regions outside Japan.

Over the years, Nintendo has managed to achieve higher returns on its investments, assets and equity compared with the industry average. Nintendo has not raised any capital through debt in the past few years. The company's total debt to equity ratio at the beginning of 2015 was close to zero compared with industry average of 12 per cent. Debt-free status indicates the company's ability to finance its operations efficiently. Additionally, having no debt obligation provides the company with significant liquidity and financial flexibility.

The video game console industry

The interactive entertainment software market is characterized by short product life cycles and frequent introductions of new products.

The game consoles are relatively expensive at the beginning of the product life cycle. Hard-core game freaks pay dearly to have a console early, but sales really jump in years two and three, as Moore's law and economies of scale drive prices down and third-party developers release must-have games. By year four the buzz will have begun about the next generation, and the games consoles will often be found at the local grocery store at discount prices.

Nintendo has been operating in the video game console market since 1977 with colour television games, and is considered the oldest company in this market. It is one of the largest console manufacturers in the world, and a leader in the hand-held console market. The company released six generations of consoles over the past two decades, including the Nintendo Entertainment System, Super Nintendo Entertainment System, Nintendo 64, GameCube, Wii and Wii U. Nintendo has dominated the hand-held games market since its release of the original Game Boy hand-held system in 1989. Nintendo DS, the current hand-held console of Nintendo, had, by the end of December 2014, already had lifetime sales of more than 150 million.

Nintendo's launch of Wii

Nintendo launched the Wii in November 2006. Nintendo's arguments for using this brand name were:

- Wii sounds like 'we', which emphasizes this console is for everyone.
- Wii can easily be remembered by people around the world, no matter what language they speak.
- Wii has a distinctive 'ii' spelling that symbolizes both the unique controllers and the image of people gathering to play.

The genius of the Wii is that it has changed the rules and invented a type of gaming with massively enhanced interaction between player and game.

Wii's first attack – the blue ocean strategy

Nintendo was attempting to create a blue ocean by creating a unique gaming experience and keeping the cost of its system lower than Sony's and Microsoft's.

In a Forbes.com interview, Perrin Kaplan, vice president of marketing and corporate affairs for Nintendo of America, discussed its implementation of blue ocean:

Inside Nintendo, we call our strategy 'blue ocean.' This is in contrast to a 'red ocean.' Seeing a blue ocean is the notion of creating a market where there initially was none – going out where nobody has yet gone. Red ocean is what our competitors do – heated competition where sales are finite and the product is fairly predictable. We're making games that are expanding our base of

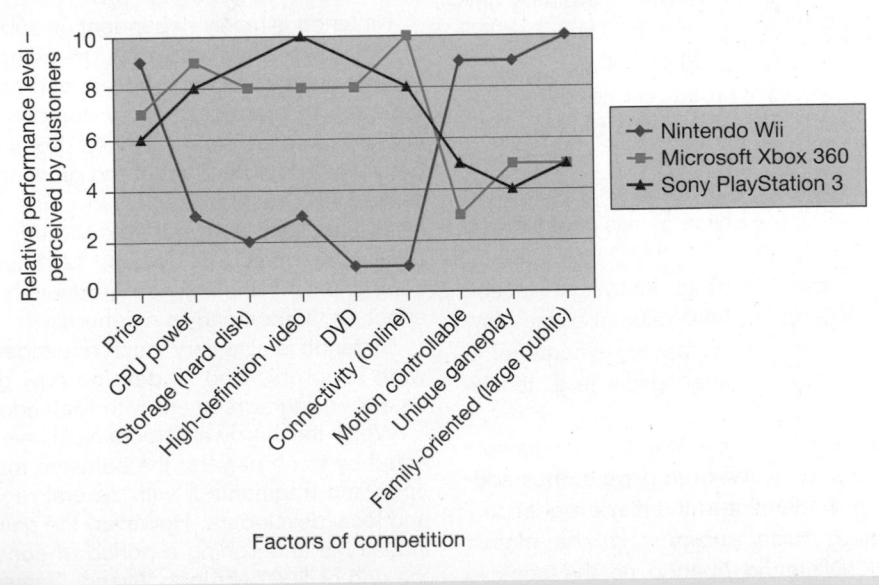

| **Figure 1** | Value curves (strategy canvas) – Wii versus Xbox and PS3 |

consumers in Japan and America. Yes, those who've always played games are still playing, but we've got people who've never played to start loving it with titles like Nintendogs, Animal Crossing and Brain Games. These games are blue ocean in action.

(Rosmarin, 2006)

Part of blue ocean strategy involves creating a strategy canvas that depicts the current market-space and relative offering level for major attributes that companies compete on. It helps visualize which offerings cost more to compete on. It also helps companies to identify which values to eliminate, reduce and/or raise and, finally, it helps to identify new values that aren't currently competed on.

Figure 1 shows a strategy canvas for the Nintendo Wii, compared with Microsoft's Xbox 360 and Sony's PlayStation 3, at the point of introduction in late 2006. The x-axis of the graph lists the primary sources of Wii's competitive advantages, at the time of introduction (end of 2006):

- *Price*: Wii was 30–40 per cent cheaper than Xbox 360 and Sony PlayStation 3.
- *CPU power*: Wii had a comparatively low processor speed and no Dolby 5.1 (sound system). Both PS3 and Xbox 360 had processors that were far more powerful than you would find in most PCs.
- *Storage (hard disk)*: in the basic model, Wii had no hard disk.
- *High-definition video*: both PS3 and Xbox 360 used high-end graphics chips that supported high-definition games and were prepared for high-definition TV. Wii's graphics were marginally better than the PS2 and the original Xbox, but Wii paled next to the PS3 and Xbox 360.
- *DVD*: both Sony and Microsoft provided the DVD opportunity. Sony even included a Blu-Ray DVD drive.
- *Connectivity (online)*: the Xbox especially had positioned itself as the online games console with multi-player functions.
- *Motion-controllable*: with its innovative motion control stick Wii added new value to game playing. The stick integrated the movements of a player directly into the video game (e.g. tennis, golf, sword fights).
- *Unique gameplay*: the new Wii gaming console sensed depth and motion from players, thus adding a whole new element to the play experience.
- *Family-oriented (large public)*: with the motion control stick, Nintendo opened up the console world to a completely new public of untapped

non-gamers from the age of around 30. Parents and even grandparents enjoyed playing the Wii.

Wii's market shares compared with Microsoft (Xbox) and Sony (SP3)

Table 1 shows the worldwide sales of games consoles from 2005 to 2014, together with the corresponding market share.

Current Wii U sales are pretty evenly split between the three major markets – 30 per cent have been sold in Japan, the American market (including Canada and South America) accounts for 40 per cent, and other markets (including Europe and Australia and a few niche markets) for 30 per cent. The sales of Sony (PS3 and PS4) and Microsoft (Xbox 360 and Xbox One) have been more unequally distributed: Microsoft sells in North America, whereas Sony's biggest markets are Japan, China and the rest of Asia.

At the retail level, games consoles are sold through a variety of electronic and audio/video retailers, supermarkets, discount stores, department stores and internet retail stores.

Nintendo's strategy

Wii managed to become a market leader by emphasizing its simplicity and lower price (than Sony and Microsoft) to break down barriers for new customers.

Nintendo has attracted non-traditional users, such as women and those over 60 years old, with easy-to-play titles such as *Brain Training* and *Wii Fit* (launched in April/May 2008).

Nintendo is highly dependent on subsuppliers, for both hardware and software. The company commissions a number of subsuppliers and contract manufacturers to produce the key components of game consoles and assemble finished products. The company was not able to meet the growing demand for its new Wii console, after its November 2006 launch, as its suppliers were not able to ramp up their production to meet the demand. A shortage of key components or the finished products had a negative effect on the company's revenues.

Nintendo is also very much dependent on its software suppliers, who all develop new games based on a licensing agreement with Nintendo.

While the hardware (consoles) market is dominated by three players, the software market is more open and fragmented, with several regional players and local developers. However, the games software industry is undergoing a period of consolidation. At the end of 2007, French Vivendi Games acquired a 52 per cent stake in Activision and created a new

Table 1   World sales of games consoles (units) and market shares

	2005		2006		2007		2008		2009		2010		2011		2012		2013		2014	
	Mill units	%	Mill units	%	Mill units	%	Mill units	%	Mill units	%	Mill units	%	Mill units	%	Mill units	%	Mill units	%	Mill units	%
Sony PS4 (+ earlier versions)	16.8	69	12.9	53	15.8	40	17.7	33	17.5	35	17.4	35	14.1	36	11.9	40	12.8	47	17.7	55
Microsoft Xbox One (+ earlier versions)	4.8	20	7.5	31	7.8	20	11.2	21	10.2	21	13.6	28	13.8	35	10.5	35	9.3	34	10.5	32
Nintendo Wii U (+ earlier version, incl. GameCube)	2.7	**11**	4.0	**16**	15.5	**40**	24.8	**46**	21.8	**44**	18.1	**37**	11.6	**29**	7.5	**25**	5.0	**19**	4.2	**13**
Total	24.3	100	24.4	100	39.1	100	53.7	100	49.5	100	49.2	100	39.5	100	30.0	100	27.1	100	32.4	100

Source: based on www.Vgchartz.com.

entity, Activision Blizzard, which in size was close to that of the market leader, Electronic Arts.

Wii's second attack – the Wii U

After the two competitors, Sony and Microsoft, had launched their new Playstation Move and Xbox Kinect in 2010, Nintendo came out with what they thought should be the new Blue Ocean Strategy.

In November 2012, Nintendo's new Wii U was released for worldwide sale. The Wii U console and controller prototypes were first revealed at the E3 2011 exhibition. The Wii U GamePad is the main controller for the Wii U. It features a built-in touchscreen, which can either supplement or replicate the game play shown on the main display. When using the 'Off TV Play' function, the controller can act as a standalone screen without the use of a TV.

Table 1 shows the worldwide sales of games consoles (in millions units) from 2005 to 2014, together with the corresponding market shares, which are illustrated in Figure 2.

The Wii U is available at two prices: basic (US$300 in the US) and deluxe (US$350). At these prices Nintendo will make a loss on selling the hardware but, from the moment the consumer buys one piece of software, that entire customer relationship becomes positive in terms of profits for Nintendo. The purpose of the business model is to

drive the installation base for the hardware, and then to drive a strong tie-in ratio with all the software (games).

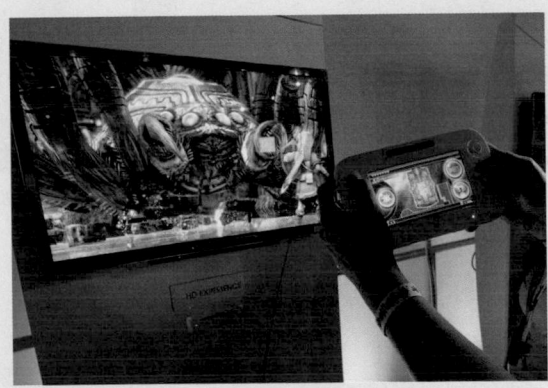

The Nintendo 'Wii U'
Source: Kevork Djansezian/Getty Images.

In 2013, the new *Super Mario Bros. U* was one of the best-selling Wii U games. Also released in 2013 was the popular *LEGO City: Undercover*. In this original LEGO game, exclusive to Wii U, players assume the role of Chase McCain, a tough police officer who is a master of disguise.

When the plans for Wii U were announced at the end of 2011, the stock market was a bit disappointed. The question now was whether Nintendo could create another 'blue ocean'. These concerns about

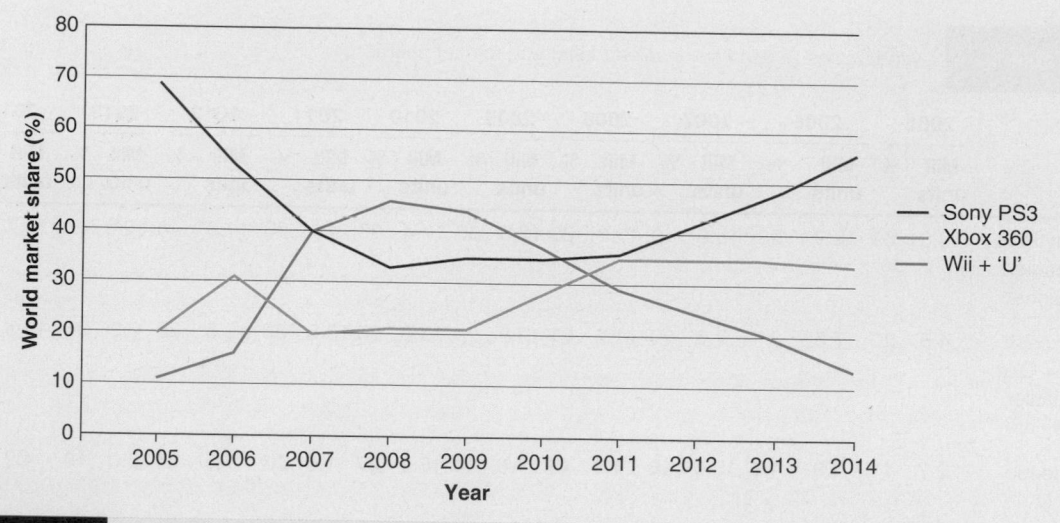

| **Figure 2** | Development of world market shares for SP3 (Move), Xbox 360 (Kinect) and Wii ('U') |

Source: based on www.Vgchartz.com.

Satoru Iwata, President of Nintendo, introduces the Wii U at the Electronic Entertainment Expo (ov E3) in Los Angeles, 7 June 2011

Source: Bloomberg/Getty Images.

Nintendo's Wii U also came at a time when smartphones and tablet PCs are taking shares away from games consoles.

The competitors' response to Nintendo's Wii U

The two main Wii competitors have both undergone some dramatic changes since the first console was introduced, as discussed in the following.

Sony PlayStation

In 2008, cumulative sales of the PlayStation 2 (PS2) reached 130 million units, making it the world's best-selling game platform. However, the 2006–07 launch of Sony's new-generation PS3 did not translate into the immediate success that the company had hoped for. It was not as successful as the Nintendo Wii. Sony suffered from a perception that it was a complex console only to be used in a darkened room by qualified young men. The core age group used to be a tight demographic group of 14–30 year-old men.

In September/October 2010, Sony launched the PlayStation Move, a motion-sensing game controller platform for the PlayStation 3 (PS3) video game console. Based on a hand-held motion controller wand, PlayStation Move uses the PlayStation Eye camera to track the wand's position and inertial sensors in the wand to detect its motion.

In November 2013, Sony launched its new Sony PlayStation 4 (SP 4), which is now the world market leader.

Microsoft Xbox

The original Xbox was introduced in 2001 – six years after the first Sony PlayStation 1 (PS 1). Microsoft continues to target the 'serious' gamer segment with the Xbox 360. The Xbox graphics, games and Xbox Live internet gaming have been popular with the core user segment, primarily young males. The US market remains the most important so far, accounting for nearly 50 per cent of the overall Xbox sales.

Xbox is the console with the highest 'game attach' rate. This is defined as the average number of games each console owner buys. For the Xbox 360, Microsoft managed a 'games per console' average of 8 to 1 in 2008, the highest in the industry.

The strength of Microsoft's software distribution network has also kept the company alive in the business, allowing Microsoft to have a presence in more worldwide markets than Nintendo. Microsoft is strongly positioned in countries like China, India, Malaysia and South Africa, all of which are growth markets, and this is promising for future sales of Xbox.

In November 2010, Kinect for Xbox 360, or simply Kinect, was introduced worldwide. It is a motion-sensing input device for the Xbox 360 video game console. Unlike its rivals, Microsoft's Kinect does not use a controller. Instead, a series of sensors allow the gamer to control the action using gestures, movement and speech. Based around a webcam-style add-on peripheral for the Xbox 360 console, it enables users to control and interact with the Xbox 360 without the need to touch a game controller, through a natural user interface using gestures and spoken commands.

The new Xbox One was launched in November 2013. Prior to its official release, the Xbox One received mixed reviews.

Overall the 'rough' comparison between the three competitors is as shown in Table 2.

Microsoft has been aggressive in price cuts since the launch. In June 2014, they cut the price from US$500 to US$400, by taking the Kinect out of the standard package. In February 2015, they further cut the price to US$350. The increase in sales volume has been quite strong since the beginning of 2015, so industry experts think it is only a question of time before Sony has to react.

Nielsen market study

In early 2015, retail monitor Nielsen (Pike, 2015) released the results of its latest gaming study, this one examining the top factors shoppers considered when buying their new-generation console. The study, called the 'Nielsen 360 Gaming Report' asked 4,400 respondents in the US what were the driving factors behind the purchase of their consoles. For gamers aged 13 and up, 'better resolution' was a top driving factor for PlayStation 4, while 'brand' was the leading quality for Xbox One. Meanwhile, people gravitated most toward the Wii U for its 'fun-factor', which may also be the reason why the Wii U is mostly popular among kids. Besides 'fun factor', the Wii U owners also bought their console because of the competitive price, and the kid-friendly game library that Nintendo is known for. Mario Kart 8 and Smash Bros. are both examples of exclusive titles aimed at kids.

Technically the Wii U is not as strong in processing power or in screen resolution as the other two consoles but, besides the 'fun factor' and competitive price, Wii U does have further selling points. Nintendo takes their time with development of new games through flagship franchises and puts a lot of time and energy into new game ventures.

In the first year of the PS4 and Xbox One lifecycle, a major talking point was resolution. Some multiplatform games were able to achieve higher resolution on PS4 than on their Xbox One counterparts.

Nielsen's gaming study also shows that the vast majority of new-generation system owners have owned a home console before. In fact, between 80 per cent and 90 per cent had earlier owned a PlayStation 3, Xbox 360 or Wii.

However, the PS4, showed that it was successful in capturing not only previous PS3 owners (66 per

Table 2	Comparison of Wii U, PS 4 and Xbox One		
Brand	**Wii U**	**PlayStation 4 (PS4)**	**Xbox One**
Manufacturer	Nintendo	Sony	Microsoft
Launch dates	November 2012	November 2013	November 2013
Launch prices	US$ 300	US$ 400	US$ 500 (including Kinect)
Lifetime sales (as at 1st January 2015)	10.2 million	18.7 million	11.0 million

Source: based on different public sources.

cent), but also Xbox 360 (59 per cent) and Wii (72 per cent). This might explain why the PS4 started so well in sales, leading the early sales race against the Xbox One and Wii U.

QUESTIONS

1. What were Microsoft's motives in entering the games console market with Xbox back in 2001?

2. What are the competitive advantages of Microsoft's Xbox One and Sony's PlayStation 4?

3. What are the competitive advantages of the original Wii and the new Wii U?

4. Do you have any ideas of how Nintendo can create a new 'Blue Ocean' with a successor of Wii U?

Sources: based on different public media; Pike N. (2015).

CASE STUDY 4.2

DJI Technology Co. Ltd: a Chinese 'born global' is dominating the world market for drones with its Phantom

Chinese drone maker DJI Technology Co Ltd has established a strong early lead in the world commercial market as companies turn to its inexpensive, light-weight flying devices for a host of uses from shooting films to mapping and site inspections.

Founded in 2006 by Chinese entrepreneur Frank Wang, DJI generated nearly US$500 million in revenue in 2014, up from US$130 million in 2013. A revenue of US$1 billion is expected in 2015. DJI netted about US$120 million in profit in 2014. In 2014, around 30 per cent of its revenue was achieved in North America, 30 per cent in Europe and 30 per cent in Asia. The remaining 10 per cent goes to South America and Africa. The percentage for the North American market is estimated to be reduced in the coming years. The subsidiary DJI North America was opened in July 2012.

Back in 2006, Frank Wang was a student at the Hong Kong University of Science and Technology. Originally DJI was centred on building flight control systems for model helicopters, which Wang had loved since childhood. But as multi-rotor drones began to gain popularity, Wang deftly turned the company toward that market. Before the Phantom, most highly capable consumer drones were sold to serious hobbyists and required a lot of assembly and know-how. The French company, Parrot, had a simple, popular unit with its A.R. Drone, but that was not a very powerful craft. The Phantom represented the first relatively cheap drone that came ready to fly out of the box, but boasted top-of-the-line flight control systems. Phantom debuted in January 2013. In April 2015, its latest Phantom 3 was introduced.

With over 2,800 employees, DJI now has offices in Shenzhen, Hong Kong, Los Angeles, Rotterdam, Tokyo and Kobe. It sells several different variations of its Phantom drone, as well as its higher-end 'prosumer' unit, the Inspire One, and its much larger S-class units. It also has a popular line of gimbals used for stabilizing cameras during flight, and has translated that technology into a hand-held camera stabilizer, the Ronin, used by film and TV professionals.

Source: Robyn Beck/AFP/Getty Images.

DJI is also currently raising a new round of funding at a US$10 billion valuation and Wang, who owns about 45 per cent, will be worth about US$4.5 billion.

Shenzhen-based DJI, whose best-selling Phantom 2 Vision drone retails for around US$1,200 in the US, estimates that it already has about 70 per cent of the drone market worldwide (a larger portion of the consumer market, than for the commercial market).

The Phantom is simple enough for beginners, but powerful enough to interest serious hobbyists, professional photographers and film-makers.

Federal records also suggest that DJI is quickly expanding its US market share, thanks in part to a new process speeding federal exemptions for companies that intend to use drones previously vetted by regulators. DJI accounted for about a half of the roughly 100 exemptions for the commercial market granted by the Federal Aviation Administration (FAA) from September 2014 to September 2015. The FAA has granted nearly twice as many commercial drones exemptions for photo and video drone use than any other market, with inspection and monitoring trailing as the second largest use of drones. A drone costing just a few thousand dollars can deliver high wow-factor shots that were impossible to get before, or could only be captured using expensive cranes, stabilizing equipment, and a manned helicopter.

Footage from a drone has been used in movies like *The Hunger Games, Skyfall* and *The Dark Knight Rises.*

Industry experts say basic drones such as DJI's are likely to drive the US commercial market for the foreseeable future, meeting business demand for uses such as aerial photography for site inspections, real estate promotions and video production.

The US market for more sophisticated unmanned aerial vehicles (UAVs) is being limited by FAA policy that restricts commercial drone flights to line-of-sight operations at altitudes of 500 feet (152 metres) or less. Those rules are complicating efforts by e-commerce giants Amazon.com and Google Inc. to develop high-tech drones capable of delivering packages over long distances. Those limitations effectively rule out larger UAVs, which are not going to be cost-effective with that sort of restriction. This is really going to drive products towards the lower end of the market.

The world market for drones (only civilian use)

Consumer drones are typically defined as those marketed at individual consumers for personal use at a price point low enough that one doesn't need a corporate budget to buy and operate. Commercial drones make up a more sophisticated, more expensive category of aircraft aimed at businesses that want to use drones as part of a for-profit enterprise. The fiscal boundary separating consumer and commercial drones is itself somewhat unclear. Some industry analysts place drones costing US$10,000 or less in the consumer category (unless they are being used specifically for a commercial purpose), while others draw the line at US$5,000. In Table 1 the line between consumer and commercial drones is set at US$5,000.

Table 1	World drone market (defence market is excluded – the market estimate is only for the civilian use of drones)	
	2015	**2020 (estimate)**
Total world market for drones (only civilian use)	$1.5 billion **% split** Commercial (professional): 70% Consumer (retail): 30% Total 100%	$5.0 billion **% split** Commercial (professional): 50% Consumer (retail): 50% Total 100%
% market share of manufacturers:	**% market share**	**% market share**
DJI (China)	70%	50%
Parrot (France)	15%	20%
3-D Robotics	5%	10%
Others	10%	20%
Total	100%	100%

Source: own estimates based on different public sources.

The US market accounts for approximately 50 per cent of the total drone market in 2015. This percentage is expected to be reduced in the coming years.

Creating competitive advantages

How does a company come to dominate fast-growing markets like this one so quickly? In the case of DJI, it comes down to four key 'innovation capabilities' that separate it from its competitors:

1. *Rapid prototyping.* The company excels at rapid prototyping and new product development (NPD). It has developed a keen sense of where the market is headed and is rolling out a new product every five months. For example, when DJI noticed that customers were attaching GoPro cameras to their Flame Wheel drones, they quickly released the camera-wielding Phantom. This rapid response to customer behaviour, in part driven by a healthy fear that competitors will beat them to the punch, is key to the company's success.

2. *Agile manufacturing.* An agile manufacturing operation has enabled DJI to pivot quickly to adjust production for new products. Consider that the popular Phantom drone sells for about US$1,000, while most of its competitors are US$5,000 or more. This lower price is key for civilian buyers. One amateur photographer in New Hampshire reported that he got on DJI's waiting list as soon as he read about the low-priced Phantom.

3. *Horizontal marketing.* DJI has leveraged existing products to pursue horizontal markets that have vast potential. The company launched its Spreading Wings product line that features advanced steering and image stabilization systems. The product sells for more than US$10,000 and is used in industries from film production to construction and agriculture. Using their existing know-how and infrastructure lowers the cost of market entry into these related markets.

4. *Ancillary products.* In addition to related markets, DJI is pursuing the accessory and ancillary side of the drone market as well. The company sells drone components and parts (providing recurring revenue), cameras, imaging, control, and stabilization systems. It also designed a hand-held camera mount for professional film-makers, called Ronin, which is based on its experience and knowledge with image stabilization.

In many ways, DJI is a typical start-up in a highly attractive industry. There is no inherent competitive advantage in its technologies, location or intellectual property. Yet, the company has carved out a dominant position and is poised to continue its rapid growth into the foreseeable future.

So, what can entrepreneurs learn from the DJI example? The first lesson comes from the founder who has had a life-long interest in radio-controlled aircraft. Entrepreneurs frequently find their greatest success in industries for which they have a seemingly innate or inborn passion.

Second, it's important to be agile. DJI has a lean operation with just 2,800 employees. That equals sales in excess of US $46,000 per employee which enables the company to invest substantial resources in research and development in its core product areas.

Finally, priorities are a must. Any start-up will need to make trade-offs with its scarce resources. In the case of DJI, that trade-off means lower investment in customer service while it focuses on growth and innovation. Over the longer term, the company will need to address its customer service to retain customers but, for now, its focus is on its most immediate goals: developing dominant market share and brand identity.

DJI is facing increasing competition

In the coming years, DJI is estimated to face increasing market share and they will find it hard to defend their current world market share of 70 per cent.

Parrot (France)

Parrot is expected to triple its drone revenue in 2015. The drone business has benefited from the dynamic performance in terms of launches for the MiniDrones and Parrot Bebop, released at the end of 2014. During the first half of 2015, Parrot presented 13 new MiniDrones (public retail price of €99–189 including tax). Parrot's powerful quadcopter, the Bebop, is taking direct aim at getting market shares from DJI's Phantom line.

3D Robotics (USA)

In the world of consumer drones, DJI is industry leader, but Chris Anderson, CEO of Berkeley-based 3D Robotics, thinks his company can change all that. In June 2015, 3D Robotics (or 3DR) released its latest consumer drone offering, called Solo, in Best

Source: Ethan Miller/Getty Images.

Source: David Maung/Bloomberg/Getty Images.

Buy across North America (it is also available online). The somewhat blurred distinction between 'consumer drones' and 'commercial drones' is exactly what 3DR has taken aim at with Solo. What differentiates 3DR's new drone from competitors – including DJI's new Phantom 3 (launched in April 2015), which packs its own suite of similar features – is a higher degree of onboard computer intelligence and an open software architecture.[1] Both individual consumers and commercial enterprises can develop or buy different cameras and sensors for their aircraft, design task-specific software interfaces or custom apps for the platform, and otherwise bend Solo to their needs. All the interesting stuff is going to happen on the software side: more apps, more features, more cloud services. 3DR likes to analogize Solo with the smartphone, which didn't really take off until third parties were able to develop an ecosystem of apps around the hardware. So 3D Robotics hopes to take market share from DJI on this competitive platform.

GoPro (USA)

GoPro Inc. (the main action-camara supplier for the drone manufacturers) is set to launch a quadcopter drone in the first half of 2016, and the action-camera company could be a behemoth that challenges current drone makers for market dominance. DJI initially

relied on the GoPro in its original 'Phantom' line, supplying customers with a mount for their GoPro on the drone. However, DJI recently transitioned to making its own drone cameras. 3D Robotics continues to partner with GoPro as a supplier of cameras for its drones.

You are hired by Peter Wang as a specialist in international marketing, and you are tasked with answering the following questions:

QUESTIONS

1. What are the main differences in the customers' needs and values in the consumer (retail) and commercial (professional) drone market?

2. What are the main reasons for DJI's competitiveness in the drone market?

3. How can DJI defend its world market share in a market with increasing competition?

Source: based on different public sources.

[1] As a supplement, you are welcome to read the interesting article: Stuart, T. and Anderson, C. (2015) '3D Robotics: disrupting the drone market', *California Management Review*, 57(2), pp. 91–112.

VIDEO CASE STUDY 4.3 Nike

download from **www.pearsoned.co.uk/hollensen**

Nike (www.nike.com) is the largest seller of athletic footwear and athletic apparel in the world. Nike's strategy for growth around the globe is to develop greater reach into diverse market segments. The three main segments are: (1) performance athletes, (2) participant athletes and (3) those who influence the world and the culture of sport. Partnerships are formed with athletes not just because of their status, but also because they are integral to the product development process. For example, to increase market share in Europe, Nike needed to produce a strong soccer product, which it did with the help of star soccer players.

Questions

1. Discuss how Nike's growth can be attributed to its targeting of diverse market global segments.

2. Why and how did Nike penetrate the European soccer footwear market?

3. What are the key driving forces behind Nike's international competitiveness (versus Adidas) in soccer footwear?

Source: Action Plus Sports Images/Alamy Images.

For further resources, see this book's website at **www.pearsoned.co.uk/hollensen**

Questions for discussion

1. How can analysis of national competitiveness explain the competitive advantage of the single firm?

2. Identify the major dimensions used to analyse a competitor's strengths and weaknesses profile. Do local, regional and global competitors need to be analysed separately?

3. How can a country with high labour costs improve its national competitiveness?

4. As the global marketing manager for Coca-Cola, how would you monitor reactions around the world to a major competitor such as Pepsi?

References

Anderson, J.C., Kumar, N. and Narus, J.A. (2007) 'Value merchants', *Marketing Management*, March/April, pp. 31–35.

Anderson, J.C., Kumar, N. and Narus, J.A. (2008) 'Certified value sellers', *Business Strategy Review*, Spring, pp. 48–53.

Barney, J. (1997) *Gaining and Sustaining Competitive Advantage*. Addison Wesley Longman, Reading, MA.

Bettencourt, L.A., Lusch, R.F. and Vargo, S.L. (2014) 'A Service Lens on Value Creation: Marketing's Role in Achieving Strategic Advantage', *California Management Review*, 57(1), pp. 44–66.

Booms, B.H. and Bitner, M.J. (1981) 'Marketing strategies and organization structures for service firms', in Donnelly, J.H. and George, W.R. (eds), *Marketing of Services*, American Marketing Association, Chicago, IL.

Brandenburger, A.M. and Nalebuff, B.J. (1996) *Co-operation and Co-ompetition*. Doubleday, New York.

Burton, J. (1995) 'Composite strategy: the combination of collaboration and competition', *Journal of General Management*, 21(1), pp. 1–23.

Cardy, R.L. and Selvarajan, T.T. (2006) 'Competencies: alternative frameworks for competitive advantage', *Business Horizons*, 49, pp. 235–245.

Curtis, J. (2006) 'Why don't they trust you with CSR?', *Marketing*, 13 September, pp. 30–31.

Day, G.S. and Wensley, R. (1988) 'Assessing advantage: a framework for diagnosing competitive superiority', *Journal of Marketing*, 52(2), pp. 1–20.

D'Aveni, R.A. (2007) 'Mapping your competitive position', *Harvard Business Review*, November, pp. 111–120.

Demartini, C. and Mella, P. (2011) 'Time competition. The new strategic frontier', *iBusiness*, 3, June, pp. 136–146.

Dobbs, M.F. (2014) 'Guidelines for applying Porter's five forces framework: a set of industry analysis templates', *Competitiveness Review*, 24(1), pp. 32–45.

Economist (2012) 'Going Bananas – Chiquita has tried hard to be good and got no credit for it', *Economist*, 31st March, p. 32.

Grönroos, C. (2009) 'Marketing as promise management: regaining customer management for marketing', *Journal of Business & Industrial Marketing*, 24(5/6), pp. 351–359.

Hollensen, S. (2010) *Marketing Management – A Relationship Approach*, 2nd edn. Pearson Education, Harlow.

Holmberg, S.R. and Cummings, J.L. (2009) 'Building successful strategic alliances', *Long Range Planning*, 42, pp. 164–193.

Jüttner, U. and Wehrli, H.P. (1994) 'Competitive advantage: merging marketing and competence-based perspective', *Journal of Business and Industrial Marketing*, 9(4), pp. 42–53.

Kanter, R.M. (1994) 'Collaborative advantage: the art of alliances', *Harvard Business Review*, July–August, pp. 96–108.

Kim, W.C. and Mauborgne, R. (1997) 'Value innovation: the strategic logic of high growth', *Harvard Business Review*, 75(1), pp. 102–112.

Kim, W.C. and Mauborgne, R. (2005a) *Blue Ocean Strategy: How to Create Market Space and Make the Competition Irrelevant*. Harvard Business School Publishing Corporation, Boston, MA.

Kim, W.C. and Mauborgne, R. (2005b) 'Value innovation: a leap into the blue ocean', *Journal of Business Strategy*, 26(4), pp. 22–28.

Kim, W.C. and Mauborgne, R. (2005c) 'Blue ocean strategy – from theory to practice', *California Review*, 47(3), pp. 105–121.

Kim, W.C. and Mauborgne, R. (2015) 'Red Ocean Traps – The mental models that undermine market-creating strategies', *Harvard Business Review*, March, pp. 68–73.

Kotler, P. (1997) *Marketing Management: Analysis, Planning, Implementation, and Control* (9th edn). Prentice-Hall, Englewood Cliffs, NJ.

Levitt, T. (1960) 'Marketing myopia', *Harvard Business Review*, July–August, pp. 45–56.

Levitt, T. (1983) *The Marketing Imagination*, The Free Press, New York/London

Magrath, A.J. (1986) 'When marketing service's 4 Ps are not enough', *Business Horizons*, May–June, pp. 44–50.

Malhotra, A. and Van Alstyne, M. (2014) 'Economic and business dimensions – the dark side of the sharing economy and how to lighten it', *Communications of the ACM*, 57(11), pp. 24–27.

Matzler, K., Veider, V. and Kathan, W. (2015) 'Adapting to the sharing economy', *MIT Sloan Management Review*, 56(2), pp. 71–77.

McGrath, R.G. and Keil, T. (2007) 'The value captor's process – getting the most out of your new business ventures', *Harvard Business Review*, May, pp. 128–136.

Michel, S., Brown, S.W. and Gallan, A.S. (2008) 'Service-logic innovations: how to innovate customers, not products', *California Management Review*, 50(3), pp. 49–65.

Nair, A., Ahlstrom, D. and Filer, L. (2007) 'Localized advantage in a global economy: the case of Bangalore', *Thunderbird International Business Review*, 49(5), pp. 591–618.

Neves, M.F. (2007) 'Strategic marketing places and collaborative networks', *Marketing Intelligence & Planning*, 25(2), pp. 175–192.

Pike, N. (2015) 'No stranger to the (video) game: most eight gen gamers have previously owned consoles', Nielsen Games, New York, http://www.nielsen.com/us/en/insights/news/2015/no-stranger-to-the-video-game-most-eighth-generation-gamers-have-previously-owned-consoles.html.

Porter, M.E. (1980) *Competitive Strategy*. The Free Press, New York.

Porter, M. (1985), *Competitive Advantage: Creating and Sustaining Superior Performance*. The Free Press, New York.

Porter, M.E. (1990) *The Competitive Advantage of Nations*. The Free Press, New York.

Porter, M.E. (1996) 'What is strategy?', *Harvard Business Review*, November–December, pp. 61–78.

Porter, M.E. (2008) 'The competitive forces that shape strategy', *Harvard Business Review*, January, pp. 78–93.

Porter, M.E. and Kramer, M.R. (2006) 'Strategy and society: the link between competitive advantage and corporate social responsibility', *Harvard Business Review*, 84(12), pp. 56–68.

Porter, M.E. and Kramer, R.M. (2011), 'Creating shared value', *Harvard Business Review*, January–February, pp. 62–77.

Rafiq, M. and Ahmed, P.K. (1995) 'Using the 7Ps as a generic marketing mix', *Marketing Intelligence and Planning*, 13(9), pp. 4–15.

Ravald, A. and Grönroos, C. (1996) 'The value concept and relationship marketing', *European Journal of Marketing*, 30(2), pp. 19–30.

Reve, T. (1990) 'The firm as a nexus of internal and external contracts', in Aoki, M., Gustafsson, M. and Williamson, O.E. (eds), *The Firm as a Nexus of Treaties*, Sage, London.

Rosmarin, R. (2006) 'Nintendo's New Look', 02.07.2006, Forbes.com.

Ruff, C. (2012) Erbitterter Kampf und die Lufthoheit, 30.06.2012, *Der Standard*, Issue number 7122, p. 14.

Rugman, A.M., Hoon Oh, C. and Lim, D.S.K. (2012) 'The regional and global competitiveness of multinational firms', *Academy of Marketing Science*, 40, pp. 218–235.

Rugman, A.M. and D'Cruz, J.R. (1993) 'The "double diamond" model of international competitiveness: the Canadian experience', *Management International Review*, 33(2), pp. 17–39.

Slimane, K.B. and Chaney, D. (2015) 'Towards marketing of functionality: insight from Michelin and Hilti, *Journal of Strategic Marketing*, 23(3), pp. 224–237.

Smith, G.E. and Nagle, T.T. (2005) 'A question of value', *Marketing Management*, July/August, pp. 38–43.

Sprinkle, G.B. and Maines, L.A. (2010) 'The benefits and costs of corporate social responsibility', *Business Horizons*, Vol. 53, pp. 445–453.

Stein, J. (2015) 'Baby, you can drive my car', *Time*, 9 February, pp. 32–40.

Teng, B.-S. (2003) 'Collaborative advantage of strategic alliances: value creation in the value net', *Journal of General Management*, 29(2), pp. 1–22.

Veliyath, R. and Zahra, S.A. (2000) 'Competitiveness in the 21st century: reflections on the growing debate about globalization', *ACR*, 8(1), pp. 14–33.

Waller, R.L. and Conaway, R.N. (2011) 'Framing and counterframing the issue of corporate social responsibility: the communication strategies of Nikebiz.com', *Journal of Business Communication*, 48(1), pp. 83–116.

CASE STUDY I.1

Zara: the Spanish retailer goes to the top of world fashion

Zara (www.inditex.com) is a fashion retail chain of Inditex Group owned by the Spanish businessman, Amancio Ortega, who also owns brands such as Massimo Dutti, Pull & Bear, Oysho, Uterqüe, Stradivarius and Bershka. The Inditex group (of which Zara is a part) is headquartered in La Coruña, north-west Spain, where the first Zara store opened in 1975. It is claimed that Zara needs just two weeks to develop a new product and get it to stores, compared with a two-month industry average. Zara has resisted the industry-wide trend towards outsourcing fast fashion production to low-cost countries. Its most unusual strategy is its policy of zero advertising; the company prefers to invest a percentage of revenues in opening new stores instead.

Main shareholder of Inditex, Amancio Ortega
Source: Copyright © Inditex.

Zara's business model

Zara is a vertically integrated retailer. Unlike similar apparel retailers, Zara controls most of the steps on the supply chain: it designs, produces and distributes itself.

Zara is a fashion imitator and focuses its attention on understanding the current fashion trend, which is what customers want, and then delivering it, ratherthan promoting predicted season's trends via fashion shows and similar channels of influence, as traditionally done by the fashion industry.

Of the products Zara sells, 50 per cent are manufactured in Spain, 26 per cent in the rest of Europe and 24 per cent in Asian and African countries and the rest of the world. So while some competitors (e.g. Gap) outsource all production to Asia, Zara makes its most fashionable items – half of all its merchandise – at a dozen company-owned factories in Spain and Portugal, particularly in Galicia and northern Portugal where labour is cheaper than most of Western Europe. Clothes with a longer shelf life, such as basic T-shirts, are outsourced to low-cost suppliers, mainly in Asia and Turkey.

The store acts as a point of sale and also influences the design and speed of production. It is the end and starting point of the business system. Zara's business cycle starts with customers' judgments on the new designs, as well as information collected by staff members who travel to fashion cities, observing people on the streets, browsing publications and visiting venues frequented by their potential customers.

What distinguishes Zara from its competitors is the feedback that Zara's managers get from the customers at the point of sale in the stores about new clothing lines they are interested in. Store managers report customer demands and sales trends to the headquarters on a daily basis. Members of the design group (over 300 designers for Inditex – 200 for Zara alone) use the feedback to create new articles or to modify existing goods and then deliver the items to the stores. All stores receive goods twice a week and each shipment contains new products (Figure 1). These frequent shipments also avoid the need for large inventories. In the stores, around 60 per cent of Zara products are permanent and the remaining 40 per cent vary continually.

Zara can offer considerably more products than similar companies. It launches about 30,000 model items annually compared with 10,000 items for its key competitors. The company has been able to shorten the product life cycle which means greater success in meeting consumer preferences. If a design doesn't sell well within a week, it is withdrawn from shops, further orders are cancelled and a new design is pursued. No design stays on the shop floor for more than four weeks, which encourages Zara fans to make repeat visits. An average high-street store in Spain expects

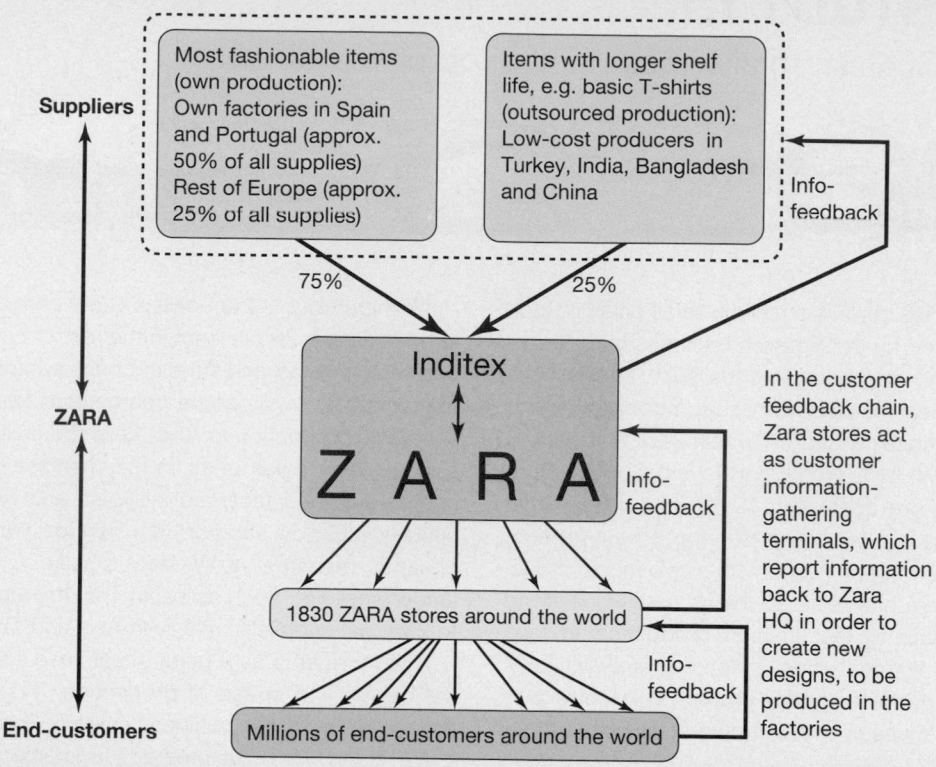

Figure 1   Zara's business model

Zara store in Moscow, Russia
Source: Copyright © Inditex.

customers to visit three times a year, but that figure will be up to 17 times for Zara.

Zara's core competence lies in the ability to recognize and assimilate the continuous changes in fashion, rapidly designing new models that respond to customer needs and wants. Zara uses its flexible business model to adapt to changes occurring during a season, reacting to them by bringing new products to the stores in a short time. For Zara the keys to global competitiveness are the time factor and the ability to adapt the offer precisely and quickly to the customer desires. The logistics system, based on software designed by the company's own teams, means that the time between receiving an order at the distribution centres (in Spain only) to the delivery of the goods in the store is on average 24 hours for European stores and a maximum of 48 hours for American or Asian stores.

Zara's (Inditex's) store brand portfolio

Between 1975 and 2008 Inditex built a portfolio of brands (see Table 1b for details) through brand acquisition – Massimo Dutti in 1991 and Stradivarius in 1999 – and brand development by using a multi-brand strategy and an extension strategy. In line with the multi-brand development strategy, Zara was created in 1975, Pull & Bear in 1991, Bershka in 1998, Oysho in 2001 and Uterqüe in 2008. The extension strategy was applied to Zara Home. Inditex used the name of the existing Zara brand to take advantage of the transfer of associations between the parent brand and the extended one, Zara Home.

Table 1	Inditex's brand store portfolio							
	Zara (including Zara Kids)	**Pull & Bear**	**Massimo Dutti**	**Bershka**	**Stradivarius**	**Oysho**	**Zara Home**	**Uterqüe**
Year of foundation	1975	1991	1991	1998	1999	2001	2003	2008
Number of stores (2011)	1830	750	600	800	700	450	300	80
Product	Fast fashion clothing	Casual clothes	Quality and conventional fashion	Avant-garde clothing	Trendy clothing	Lingerie	Household clothing (textiles for bed, bath and table)	Accessories (handbags, footwear, leather goods and costume jewellery)
Target end-customer	Women, men and children, ages 0–45	Women, and men, ages 13–23	Women, and men, ages 25–45	Women, and men, ages 13–23	Women, ages 15–25	Youths (Women)	–	Mainly women, ages 15–45
Price/quality	Medium-low/medium	Medium-low/medium	Medium-high	Medium-low/medium	Medium-low/medium	Medium-low/medium	Medium-low/medium	Medium-high/high

Source: based on Lopez and Fan (2009).

- Zara is the flagship chain (66 per cent of total Inditex turnover). It encompasses many different styles, from daily clothes, more informal, to the more serious or formal, through dresses and suits for festival events. Fashion for women, men and children.
- Pull & Bear focuses on youth fashion, with a very urban style. Aimed primarily at teens and pre-teens, for both girls and boys.
- Massimo Dutti highlights are designs that are more elegant, classic and studied, for daily and formal clothes. It is more expensive than the other stores of the group. Fashion for women, men and, recently, children.
- Bershka began distributing fashion for girls and, more recently, for boys too. It also has a youthful style, although not as urban as Pull & Bear.
- Stradivarius is aimed at the young woman. A mix between Pull & Bear and Bershka, but more similar to the latter.
- Oysho lingerie and women's underwear (but also includes pyjamas, accessories, bathing suits in the summer and more); also includes collections for little girls and babies.

- Zara Home interiors, utensils for household furnishings, accessories, kitchenware, Zara Home Kids (for children).
- Uterqüe is the latest addition to Inditex, selling accessories including shoes, handbags, jewellery and sunglasses. Intends to present a sober image, inspired by the English clubs, but at the same time is clear and modern. More costly than the group's other brands, except for Massimo Dutti, it still aims to be price-competitive with the big brands in the market.

All these brands were built within the domestic market and then launched for international markets. This multi-brand portfolio has allowed Inditex to target different segments more effectively. However, the cost of maintaining several brands and the risk of cannibalization are the major drawbacks of this strategy. Inditex tries to tackle cannibalization by differentiating the brands mainly through the product, target markets (customer groups and countries), store presentation and retail image.

Zara has attractive pricing with an average selling price €15–20. The company's market share is below 1 per cent of the general clothing market in most countries.

Human resource policy and training

The stores continue to be the main motor of employment in the company, representing 89 per cent of the total number of employees in the Group. The fact that Inditex's particular business model is designed to constantly adapt to customers' needs means that management considers training and internal promotion of its professionals as key elements of its activity.

Training of the staff is also a huge investment each year. The internal training plans are adapted to the needs of the group professionals according to their activity and are of a diverse nature:

- entry training for new employees
- management and administration of teams
- languages
- information systems
- new technologies
- individual training plans
- store management systems
- presentation of collections

- training in products, raw materials and corporate social responsibility (CSR).

In the linguistic sphere, the Spanish and English language are priorities. The materials taught on each course vary according to the nature of the activity of each professional and the specific vocabulary required.

Competition

Zara's major global competitors in terms of market share are Gap Inc. and H&M. The following presents some information about the two companies (see also Table 2 for a direct comparison of the three global competitors).

Gap Inc.

Gap, Inc. is an American clothing and accessories retailer based in San Francisco, California, and founded in 1969 by Donald Fisher and Doris F. Fisher. The company has five primary brands: the namesake Gap banner, Banana Republic, Old Navy, Piperlime and Athleta. Despite its publicly traded status, the founding

Table 2	The three main global competitors in fashion retailing (end of 2011)		
2011 figures	Inditex-Zara (Spain)	Gap, Inc. (US)	H&M (Sweden)
Net sales (million €)	13,793	11,280	14,842
Net profits (million €)	1,946	641	1,823
Growth in sales (%) compared with 2007	+10%	−1%	+1.5%
% international sales (outside home country)	Inditex: 66% Zara: 70%	19%	93%
Number of employees	109,000	132,000	67,000
Number of stores and global reach	Inditex: 5,500 stores in 85 countries Zara: 1,830 stores in 82 countries	3,100 stores in 45 countries	2,206 stores in 53 countries
Business model and production	High degree of vertical integration – mainly own production facilities	Partial vertical integration – control over design, distribution and sales; production is outsourced	Partial vertical integration – control over design, distribution and sales; production is outsourced
Promotion and advertising	Only 0.3% of turnover. The store is the main promotional tool	3–3.5% of turnover spent on advertising	4% of turnover spent on advertising
Brand portfolio	Eight brand stores: Zara, Pull & Bear, Massimo Dutti, Bershka, Stradivarius, Oysho, Zara Home and Uterqüe	Five brand stores: Gap, Banana Republic, Old Navy, Piperlime and Athleta	One brand store: single format

Source: based on various public sources.

Fisher family remains deeply involved in Gap Inc.'s business. Donald Fisher served as chairman of the board until 2004; when he stepped down, he was succeeded by his son, Robert J. Fisher. Today Glenn K. Murphy serves both as chairman and CEO, but the Fisher family still has family members on the board.

H&M

The company was established in 1947 in Västerås, Sweden, by Erling Persson, though at the time it only sold women's clothing and was called Hennes, Swedish for 'hers'. In 1968, Persson acquired the premises and inventory of a Stockholm hunting equipment store named Mauritz Widforss. Included in the inventory was a supply of men's clothing, prompting Persson to expand into menswear. Accordingly, he renamed the store Hennes & Mauritz, later abbreviated to H&M. The Persson family is still in control. In 2009 Karl-Johan Persson took over as president and chief executive.

Today the majority of H&M's clothing is outsourced and manufactured in Turkey and Bangladesh.

H&M describes its mission as 'fashion and quality at the best price'. H&M's goals for 2008 were to intensify sales in the existing stores, as well as to increase the number of new stores by 10–15 per cent per year.

H&M has an extensive network throughout much of Europe, but its main markets are in northern Europe. The biggest markets are Germany, the UK and Sweden. H&M opened its first US store in New York (Manhattan) in March 2000. By January 2012, it had at least 235 individual stores in that country. The first store in mainland China was opened in 2007; there are now 100 of them in operation.

Internationalization strategy

Zara opened its first store in 1975 in La Coruña, northwest Spain. During the 1980s, Zara focused on and expanded within the domestic market, opening stores in all Spanish cities with a population of greater than 100,000 inhabitants. The maturity of the Spanish market led Zara to search for international opportunities in 1988. Portugal was an attractive and familiar market due to its geographical and cultural proximity to Spain, and international expansion of Zara started with the opening of a store in Oporto. Through establishment in Portugal, Zara acquired international market experience and knowledge and realized that it would have to adjust its business model to suit the new international markets.

During the next stages of internationalization, Zara expanded into international markets with a minimum level of psychic (cultural) distance from Spain, adding one or two countries per year to its market portfolio. In 1990, Zara started operating in France (Paris), a geographically contiguous country, a fashion capital and a starting point for the later expansion in northern Europe.

Mexico was added in 1992. This market, though geographically distant, is culturally (language, etc.) close to the home country, Spain, and provided reference for the later expansion to the South American market. The experience gained in the international environment made Zara more determined and intent on a rapid global expansion, regardless of cultural or geographical proximity. They began this stage by opening a store in Israel in 1997. One year later, Zara entered eight countries, consolidating its presence in the Middle East with Kuwait, Lebanon and the United Arab Emirates. Between 2000 and 2003, Zara consolidated its position in the European market as opposed to gaining a foothold in new countries (the enlargement of the European Union in 2004 justifies the considerable number of European countries that were incorporated that year). Between 2003 and 2009, a lot of new store openings were made in new countries, and Zara (Inditex) now has over 5,500 in 82 countries (October 2012).

On April 20, 2011 the first Zara flagship store opened in Australia. Today, Inditex is the biggest fashion group in the world.

During the early stages of internationalization, the management at Zara followed an ethnocentric orientation, whereby the stores in foreign countries were a replication of the Spanish stores. However, this approach encountered unexpected difficulties in some countries due to cultural differences. Therefore, Zara decided to move towards a geocentric orientation, allowing some stores abroad to adopt local solutions rather than merely replicate the home market. The company sells a largely homogeneous product for a global market, but some adjustments have to be made to its product offerings, for example as a consequence of customers' size differences in Asian and European countries.

Once the entry decision is made for a particular country, Zara follows a pattern of expansion strategy known as 'oil stain' (dominate strongly in one place, then spread across the surface of the country, like an oil stain on water). Zara opens its first store, the so-called flagship store, in a strategic area with the purpose of getting information about the market and acquiring expertise. The experience guides Zara in the later phases of expansion in that country.

Entry mode strategy

Over time Zara has mainly used the hierarchical and intermediate modes.

Hierarchical modes

Zara has adopted the hierarchical modes (direct investment) in most European and southern European countries, resulting in full ownership of the stores. Those markets where the hierarchical model is used are characterized by high growth potential and relatively low sociocultural distance (low country risk) between Spain and the target market.

The intermediate modes (joint venture and franchising) are mainly used in countries where the sociocultural distance is high.

Joint ventures

This is a cooperative strategy in which facilities and know-how of the local company are combined with the international fashion expertise of Zara. This mode is especially used in large, competitive markets where it is difficult to acquire property to set up retail outlets or where there are other kinds of obstacles that require cooperation with a local company. For example, in 1999, Zara entered into a 50–50 joint venture with the German firm Otto Versand, which had experience in the distribution sector and market knowledge in one of Europe's largest markets, Germany. Zara has also entered a joint venture in Japan.

In 2009, Inditex and the Tata Group signed an agreement to form a joint venture to develop Zara stores in India. This deal gave Zara control of 51 per cent of the venture with the remaining 49 percent in the hands of Trent Limited, a Tata Group company. The partnership opened its first stores in 2010 in New Delhi, Mumbai and other major cities of India.

Tata is one of the largest conglomerates in India, with a corporate history dating back more than 140 years and operations spanning seven industries: information systems and communications, engineering, materials, services, energy, consumer products and chemicals. In many of these industries, Tata Group companies are among the largest conglomerates in the world.

Zara viewed their entry into the Indian market as one of significant strategic importance. India is one of the most important countries in the world by GDP, growing by around 6 per cent per annum in recent years and is also the second most populated country, with a population of more than 1.1 billion. Ten areas have a population of more than 3 million, including Mumbai, Delhi, Bangalore and Kolkata.

Franchising

Zara chooses this mode for high-risk countries which are socioculturally distant or have small markets with low sales forecasts, such as Kuwait, Andorra, Puerto Rico, Panama or the Philippines. At the beginning of 2009, there were 500 franchised stores.

Zara's franchisees follow the same business model as its own stores regarding the product, store location, interior design, logistics and human resources strategy. However, franchisees are responsible for investing in fixed assets and recruiting the staff. Zara gives franchisees the opportunity of exclusivity in their geographic area, although Zara has the right to open its own stores in the same location after a fixed number of years.

QUESTIONS

1. Which theory is the best representative of Zara's (Inditex's) internationalization?

2. Please evaluate the competitive strategy of the three world market leaders. Which of the three will be the future winner with regard to global retailing in the fashion world?

3. What are the advantages and disadvantages of Zara's (Inditex's) multi-brand store strategy?

4. How successful do you think Zara has been in meeting the 'risk of cannibalization' as a consequence of the multi-brand strategy?

5. What are the advantages and disadvantages of going into a joint venture with Tata in India?

Sources: Lopez, C. and Fan, Y. (2009) 'Case study: Internationalisation of the Spanish fashion brand Zara', *Journal of Fashion Marketing and Management*, 13(2), pp. 279–296; www.inditex.com; Zara press release: Inditex and Trent of the Tata Group agree to open stores in India beginning 2010, 5 February 2009, http://www.inditex.com/en/press/press_releases/extend/00000689; Datamonitor: www.datamonitor.com.

CASE STUDY I.2

Manchester United: still trying to establish a global brand

Manchester United (abbreviated as Man Utd, www.manutd.com) has developed into one of the most famous and financially successful football clubs in the world, being recognized in virtually every country, even those with little interest in the sport. In Deloitte's football money league the top five by revenue in 2014 were: 1, Real Madrid (€549.5 million); 2, Manchester United (€518 million); 3, Bayern Munich (€487.5 million); 4, FC Barcelona (€484.6 million); and 5, Paris Saint-Germain (€474.2 million) (Deloitte; 2015).

According to Forbes' valuation estimates (Forbes, 2015), at US$3.10 billion Man Utd is the 4th highest-valued professional sports club in the world. The top five in 2015 were: 1, Real Madrid (US$3.26 billion); 2, Dallas Cowboys (US$3.20); 3, New York Yankees (US$3.20); 4, Manchester United (US$3.10 billion); and 5, Los Angeles Lakers (US$2.60 billion).

The intangible assets of Man Utd

Where does Man Utd's wealth stem from?

- great histories of success, and with historical success comes an ability to create superior brand identity;
- league-generated wealth;
- team-specific wealth stemming from local media deals or new sports facilities;
- loyal fan base;
- advantageous geographic marketplace;
- revenue-aggressive ownerships keep the team on top of the national league;
- providing international fans with a taste of the excitement at a game, through TV and internet coverage, is the key to maintaining and building the brand.

American football certainly doesn't have the same type of worldwide appeal. Baseball is popular in Central America, Japan, Korea and Taiwan, but has nothing like the global reach of soccer.

Furthermore, consider these facts about Man Utd:

- It has an estimated 360 million supporters worldwide, including 200 million in Asia and 15 million Facebook fans.

- Commercial revenue of $122 million is growing at a double-digit annual rate thanks to deals with Turkish Airlines, Adidas and several telecommunications companies.
- Man Utd's share of broadcast revenues from playing in the Premier League has increased considerably because of good performance and results over the years.

Since the mass commercialization of football in 1992, Man Utd has unquestionably been the team to beat. In the past 20 seasons, it has collected 14 Premier League titles, four FA Cups and two Champions League trophies. Old Trafford regularly attracts more than 75,000 fans paying above and beyond £45 a ticket, 30 or so times a season.

Source: Manchester United Ltd.

Brand assets

ManUtd's brand assets include the *physical aspects* of logos, colours, names and facilities, and the *intangible aspects* of reputation, image and perception. The official mascot of the team is the Red Devil. Although centrally featured in Man Utd's logo, the mascot doesn't play a prominent role in promotions. The team's nickname is the Reds, which seems logical enough, given the dominant colour of its home jerseys but, unfortunately, Liverpool, another top team in the Premier League, is also referred to as the Reds.

International brand evolution

For British fans of Man Utd, passions run deep. Although the brand is solidly entrenched in British soccer fans' psyches, it is in transition. Man Utd is no longer simply a British brand; it is a world brand. It boasts an incredible number of fans in China. A survey of China's 12 largest markets showed that 42 per cent of fans are between 15 and 24, and that 26 per cent are between 25 and 34. The team is positioned to take advantage of China's growing middle class, with members who are anxious to enjoy the good life and associate themselves with successful western brands. As an early entrant, Man Utd has the chance to establish itself as one of Asia's dominant brands (Olson *et al.*, 2006).

Although the absolute numbers are much smaller, the US also represents fertile ground. Of course, international football must compete with established groups such as Major League Baseball, the National Football League, the National Basketball Association and the National Hockey League, but soccer has become a staple at schools across the country. A recent, unprompted awareness study of European soccer teams revealed that among North American fans, the most frequently mentioned team was Man Utd, at 10 per cent; Liverpool, Real Madrid and Barcelona each generated 3 per cent, and Arsenal generated 2 per cent. The study also showed that awareness of Man Utd is strongest in the north-eastern and western parts of the US.

In order to be successful in foreign markets, Man Utd must generate memberships, sell kits and other merchandise, have access to media markets (including TV, internet, mobile phones and publishing), set up soccer schools, form licensing agreements with strong local sponsors and embark on tours to create halo effects.

The challenge Man Utd faces is accomplishing this transition without destroying what made it distinctly British and highly successful. Today's team is composed of players from around the globe. (Although Man Utd still has British players, the Premier League is no longer dominated by them.) This raises another concern: strong teams employ strong players who become brands themselves. Most notable for Man Utd was the rise of David Beckham to the ranks of superstar, on the pitch and in the media, through his marriage to Victoria, a former Spice Girl. Man Utd considered that Beckham's market value was greater than they could afford, so they sold him to Real Madrid one year before his contract expired. Now the brand building of Man Utd depends on other stars such as Wayne Rooney. At the same time as these stars are Man Utd brand-builders, they are also able to build their own personal brand.

Brand challenges

Man Utd is in the enviable position of market leader during a time of dramatic media growth in the world's most popular game. However, leaders can stumble and the team is not immune to the sensitive nature of sports fans. To address this concern, Man Utd has developed a customer relationship management (CRM) database of more than three million fans. Many of these database members are game-day customers.

A substantial group of US Man Utd fans are not loyal. They climb on the bandwagon of the team when it has success, only to climb off the instant it stumbles.

Chinese fans don't possess the same level of experience with professional teams as UK fans. Nevertheless, cultural and physical barriers exist between British and Chinese fans. To develop deeper loyalties in Chinese markets, Man Utd established a Mandarin website, started a soccer school in Hong Kong, and is constantly planning Asian tours while looking to add Asian players to the roster. Although these are sound moves to build brand loyalty, well-funded competitors such as Chelsea or Liverpool can copy Man Utd.

Even in England, Man Utd faces significant challenges. Especially after the Glazer invasion (see below) it generates a love-them-or-hate-them mentality. Fans of opposing teams have been thrilled to see Chelsea, Arsenal and Liverpool also secure championships.

Then Glazer came . . .

In the late 1990s and the early part of the 2000s, an increasing source of concern for many Man Utd supporters was the possibility of the club being taken over. The supporters' group IMUSA (Independent Manchester United Supporters' Association) were extremely active in opposing a proposed takeover by Rupert Murdoch in 1998. However, they could do nothing in May 2005 when the US sports tycoon Malcolm Glazer (who also owns the American Football team Tampa Bay Buccaneers) paid US$1.4 billion for a 98 per cent stake in Man Utd, following a nearly year-long takeover battle. So is the Man Utd brand worth US$1.5 billion? Glazer seemed to think so, as he paid roughly US$200 million more than the team's open-market stock valuation.

It was a hostile takeover which plunged the club into massive debt, as his bid was heavily funded by borrowing on the assets owned already by Man Utd, and the takeover was fiercely opposed by many fans of the club. Many supporters were outraged and some formed a new club called F.C. United of Manchester.

After the takeover, the Glazer family (Malcolm Glazer and his three sons) took big steps to shore up the club's finances. They cut more than 20 staff members, including some executives. They also raised ticket prices and lent 23 players to other clubs, saving Man Utd more than US$20 million in fees and salaries. In general, they have been cutting expenses wherever they can.

Malcolm Glazer, the patriarch of the Glazer family that owns the club, died on 28 May 2014.

Man Utd in recent seasons

In 2009–10, in the battle for the national Premier League title Man Utd was ultimately beaten by Chelsea by a single point. They also had the chance to be the first team to reach three consecutive Champions League finals since Juventus in 1998, but they were knocked out in the quarter-finals by Bayern Munich.

In the 2010–11 season, United won their 19th title, surpassing Liverpool's record of 18 titles, which they equalled in the 2008–09 season. This is the first time in the club's history that it has held the outright record.

The 2011–12 season was not as good for Man Utd. They ended the season second in the Premier League (behind Manchester City), and third in the Champions League group stage.

Man Utd secured their 20th Premier League league title in 2012–13. In the Champions League they lost against Bayern Munich in the quarter final in Spring 2014.

On 8 May 2013, Alex Ferguson announced that he was to retire as manager at the end of the football season. The club announced the next day that Everton manager David Moyes would replace him from 1 July 2013, having signed a six-year contract. Ryan Giggs took over as interim player–manager 10 months later, on 22 April 2014, when Moyes was sacked after a poor 2013–14 season in which the club failed to defend their Premier League title. A seventh place in the league was Man Utd's lowest finish since 1990 and meant that they had missed out on European qualification. On 19 May 2014, it was confirmed that Louis van Gaal would replace Moyes as Man Utd manager on a three-year deal, with Giggs as his assistant.

Man Utd ended the 2014–15 season in fourth place – three places, and six points higher than the previous season, ensuring that the Red Devils would compete in the Champions League in the 2015–16 season, following a one-year absence.

Sponsorships

In August 2014, Man Utd announced a 10-year contract with the German manufacturer Adidas to be the club's new kit sponsor for a record-breaking minimum £750 million. The agreement started at the beginning of the 2015–16 season and it ends Nike's 13-year relationship with Man Utd.

Adidas also sponsors other of the world's top football clubs including Real Madrid, FC Bayern Munich, AC Milan and Chelsea.

The club's current official sponsorship partners also include world-leading brands such as AON (principal sponsor), Chevrolet (official automotive partner) and DHL (official logistics partner), as well as local brands such as Kagome (official partner of Man Utd for Japan), Thomas Cook (official travel partner) and Turk Telekom (official integrated telecommunications partner for Turkey).

The club typically enters into official partnership agreements for a period of 2–5 years and is currently pursuing a two-fold strategy to increase revenue from sponsorship:

1. Firstly, Man Utd continues to pursue expansion of its portfolio of global and regional sponsors and there is evidence that, in recent years, it has been successful in identifying and securing new sponsors. Since the beginning of 2011, a number of high-profile partner agreements have been signed, most notably with companies in the Asia-Pacific region. New agreements have not, however, been limited to the Far East with bwin, Chevrolet and Hublot all committing to deals since 2011.

2. In addition to developing its global sponsorship portfolio, the club is focused on expanding a regional sponsorship model, segmenting new opportunities by product category and territory. As part of this strategy, the club has opened an office in Asia and is in the process of establishing a permanent presence in the potentially lucrative North American market.

This two-fold strategy and the new local offices will augment the club's current geographic presence which has, to this point, been mainly in its home market of the UK.

Financial situation

Man Utd Ltd's last three years look like this:

	2013/14	2012/13	2011/12
Revenues (£m)	433	286	278
Net profits after tax (£m)	+24	−80	+48

The biggest cost element is the players' wages: in 2013/14 they accounted for around £150 million, or around 40 per cent of the operating expenses. On the surface the financial figures look very good, but Man Utd's revenue is expected to drop around £50 million in 2014/15 just from missing out on the Champions League in 2013/14. At the same time, expenses have risen after the club signed multiple players. This means that the net profits after tax are expected to be negative in 2014/2015. Man Utd's debt has also risen to £380.5 million.

So there are some mixed clouds on the horizon for Man Utd . . .

QUESTIONS

1. How do you evaluate the international competitiveness of Man Utd after the takeover by Malcolm Glazer?

2. Discuss and explain how the different alliances can increase the international competitiveness of Man Utd.

3. What are the main threats to retaining 'Manchester United' as a global brand?

Sources: Deloitte (2015) *Football Money League,* Sports Business Group, January; Forbes (2015) *The World's 50 Most Valuable Sports Teams 2015,* Forbes/Business, July, 15 (online version).

CASE STUDY I.3

Adidas: the No. 2 in the global sportswear market is challenging the No. 1, Nike

Besides Nike, Adidas AG (www.adidas.com) is one of the largest companies in the sporting goods industry. The company offers its products through three main brands: Adidas, Reebok and TaylorMade-Adidas Golf. Adidas operates through more than 170 subsidiaries in Europe, the US and Asia, each focusing on a particular market or part of the manufacturing process.

Adidas is currently based in Herzogenaurach, Germany, along with Puma, which is a competitor. The company operates through three business segments, wholesale, retail and other businesses:

- The wholesale segment comprises all business activities relating to the distribution of Adidas and Reebok products to retail customers.
- The retail segment comprises all business activities relating to the sale of Adidas and Reebok products directly to end-consumers through own retail. Adidas and Reebok branded products include footwear, apparel and other goods, such as bags and balls.
- The other businesses include TaylorMade-Adidas Golf, Rockport and Reebok-CCM Hockey, as well as other centrally managed brands. Among others, this part contains Adidas Golf branded products including golf footwear, apparel and accessories.

To minimize production costs, Adidas outsources a major part of its production to external suppliers in the Far East (as does its main competitor, Nike). Adidas outsources over 95 per cent of production to independent third-party suppliers, primarily located in Asia. Furthermore, 32 per cent of all suppliers are located in China. Since the company procures its merchandise from foreign manufacturers, it has little control over the product quality.

History

Adidas AG was founded by Adolf Dassler in 1949 following a split between Adolf and his older brother Rudolf in 1947. The company name is actually a formed from 'Adi' (a nickname for Adolf) and 'Das' (from Dassler). It launched its first pair of football boots with removable studs in 1954. By the 1960s, the company was manufacturing equipment across various sports, including equipment for fringe sports. In 1975, the company launched one of the world's most popular football boots: the Copa Mundial.

After the split, Rudolf formed a new firm that he called Ruda – from **Ru**dolf **Da**ssler, later rebranded as Puma. Puma and Adidas entered into a fierce and bitter rivalry after the split.

In August 2005, Adidas decided to buy British rival Reebok for US$3.8 billion. This takeover was completed in January 2006 and meant that the company would have business sales closer to those of Nike in North America. The acquisition of Reebok also allowed Adidas to compete head-to-head with Nike worldwide as the number two athletic shoemaker in the world.

Source: Adidas.

Key data comparison between the world's two main sportswear competitors

Over recent decades, worldwide sports suppliers Nike and Adidas have become synonymous with the sportswear industry. The rivalry between the two key players is tougher than ever.

Table 1	Global sportswear (shoes + clothing) market shares – Top 5 – 2013–14	
Company	**% value 2013**	**% value 2014**
Nike Inc	15.0	15.9
Adidas Group	10.7	10.5
VF Corp	3.3	3.5
Kering SA	2.0	2.0
Asics Corp	1.7	1.7

Source: based on various public sources.

Table 2	Key economic data for Adidas and Nike (€1 = US$1.20)	
	Adidas (2014, million €)	**Nike (2014, million €)**
Revenue	14,292	23,166
Net profit (% of revenue)	961 (6.6%)	2,244 (9.7%)
Employees (end of year)	53,700	56,000
Revenue split (%)		
Product type		
Apparel	43	31
Footwear	46	62
Other	11	7
Total	100	100
Region		
North America	20	47
Western Europe	28	18
Asia-Pacific	25	21
Eastern Europe	10	4
Latin America	11	6
Middle East and Africa	5	3
Australasia	1	1
World total	100	100

Source: based on various data from www.euromonitor.com.

Table 1 shows that Nike Inc and Adidas Group lead the global sportswear market, with a combined share of 26 per cent in 2014, up marginally from 2009. Second placed Adidas was the only leading player to suffer a market share decline in 2014 due to recent problems in Russia and unfavourable currency exchanges.

The positions between the two key world player have changed over recent years:

- *2010–2011*: Adidas copes with the global economic crisis better than Nike, thanks to less exposure to North America, the world's largest sportswear market.
- *2012–2013:* Ongoing weakness in western Europe, Adidas's key market, and problems retooling the Reebok brand mean the company struggles to maintain pace with Nike.

- *2013–2014*: Depressed consumer sentiment in Russia, weakness in the global golf market and currency headwinds further impact Adidas's performance in 2014. But Adidas also made gains on Nike in a number of key markets in 2014, notably China, helped by a more developed retail network than Nike.

Table 2 details the key economic data of the two world players.

Adidas's sales channel strategy

Wholesale – sales via third party retail channels – remained the largest part of the company's business in 2014, generating 68 per cent of total revenue. Wholesale was among the more problematic areas of the company's business over the review period, in part because third-party retailers in many countries responded to the economic crisis by price-cutting; this, in turn, undercut brand equity for Adidas and Reebok.

Historically, the company has distributed its products through third-party retail accounts, principally footwear, sporting goods and department stores. Other sports brands, including Nike and Puma, have followed this strategy.

However, like its peers, Adidas is seeking to take greater charge of its brands, pursuing a strategy it describes as 'controlled space'. This includes not only rolling out more company-owned and -operated stores (it intends to open at least 550 Adidas and Reebok stores by 2018) but also extending its mono-brand franchise operations, especially in China.

It is also seeking to develop more shop-within-a-shop operations with its principal wholesaling partners. Adidas aims to generate 50 per cent of total sales from these controlled space operations by 2020, compared with 40 per cent in 2014.

At the same time, it is also looking to improve its internet business, which it seeks to grow to €500 million by 2015. In 2014, Adidas operated online stores in the US, Asia and Europe, and opened its first online outlet in Latin America in 2012 as part of its strategy to add 10 new online markets over that year.

Adidas's social media strategy

Adidas has been able to develop exceptionally high levels of brand awareness for the Adidas and Reebok brands among the consumer base. Sports and non-sports buyers make repeat purchases of these brands and have characteristically shown a lack of price sensitivity if the perceived aesthetic or function of a new apparel product is high enough.

However, because for many users there is a great deal of interchangeability between sports brands, Adidas is looking to strengthen its relationship with consumers by increasing its use of social media. This is an increasingly important strategy among apparel companies, especially those targeting the 18–35 year-old demographic.

Adidas primarily uses existing networks; its Adidas Originals Facebook page, for example, added 5 million followers in 2014 to reach 15 million. It has also developed mobile phone apps including miCoach Football and miCoach Running that allow users to upload statistics to an interactive training site. The company uses these tools to build product awareness and engage directly with consumers, for example offering the opportunity to participate in brand design.

Adidas slightly lags behind its principal rival Nike in this strategy, largely because Nike dominates the North American market where consumer use of these media is at its most developed. These are extremely effective platforms to disseminate new product information, build brand loyalty and heighten product awareness, especially among young consumers; at the same time, it supports the brand position for Adidas and Reebok in particular as tech-led, early adopting and youthful.

Adidas versus Nike in the global apparel market

The global market for apparel is comparatively

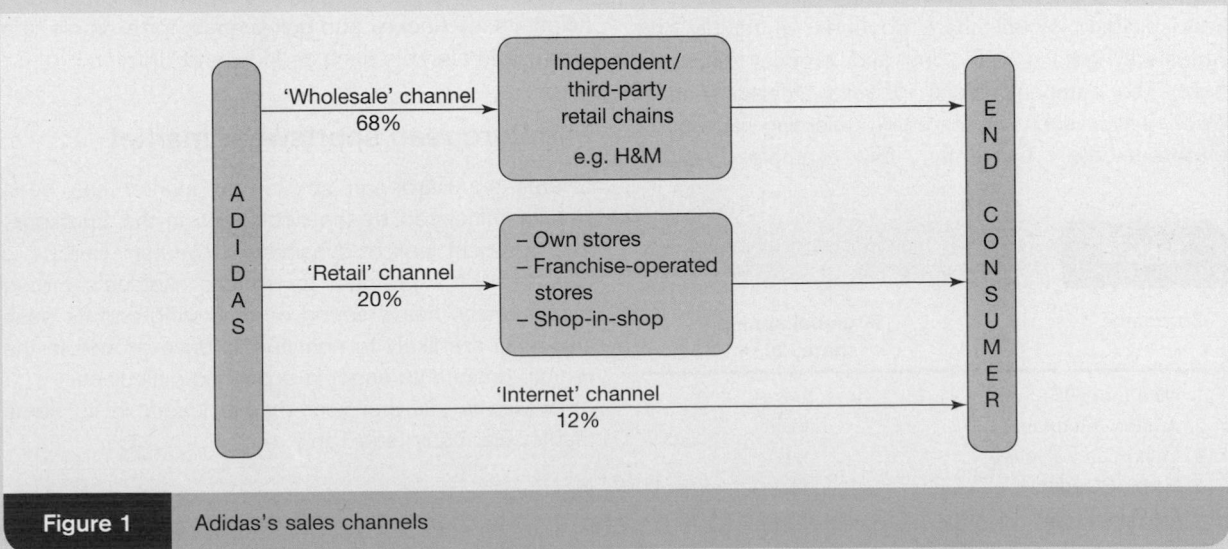

Figure 1   Adidas's sales channels

Sources: based on www.adidas.com and other public media.

fragmented, reflecting, in part, strong localized fashion preferences (Table 3). The fact that the two leading brands, Nike and Adidas, are sports brands may reflect this; the theoretical function of the products should cut across regional tastes. However, global share for these brands is mostly underpinned by massive marketing expenditure, and consumers of the two brands do not always buy them for exercise.

Leading manufacturers' push into emerging markets such as China has underpinned growth in global share for five of the 10 leading producers. However, a significant brand is yet to emerge from these markets, although much of the manufacture is outsourced to them.

Producers that have lost share have typically failed to adapt to new market conditions; Gap, for example, has failed to follow the new, flexible fashion model of a rapid turnover of design and extensive clothing ranges, and as a result has lost ground to peer brands such as Inditex's Zara.

Nike is the largest apparel single brand in the world, with a 2.4 per cent share of sales in 2014. Adidas's principal two brands, with which Nike competes on almost every front, held a combined 2014 global share of 1.6 per cent, up from 1.3 per cent in 2006, and ranked second and 12th.

The competitive environment in sports apparel is extremely intense. There is a high risk of substitution for consumers using these products for exercise, as these brands offer basically the same products. Developing differentiation is difficult, although sports brands have begun to develop greater consumer loyalty through massive marketing expenditure, brand control via retail and social media initiatives.

The environment is also one in which competitors aggressively pursue market share. Adidas's ability to keep building global share depends on rapidly and repeatedly getting marketing and product decisions right. The company seeks to build differentiation in other ways, such as carefully selecting its sports endorsements. Currently, for example, Adidas

produces the strip for football giants Real Madrid, while Nike produces that of chief Spanish rivals FC Barcelona. AC Milan and Inter Milan are also equipped by the two different brands.

Adidas – geographical dimensions

Adidas's largest regional market remains domestic western Europe, which generated 28 per cent of global revenues in 2014. However, Asia-Pacific is set to overtake this going forward, generating 26 per cent of value in 2014 compared with 19 per cent in 2006. Although the company lags behind Nike in the key Chinese market, it is the number one brand in India. Like Nike, Adidas is seeking to extend its retail operations, allowing for improved brand control.

Adidas has identified two 'attack markets', geographical regions it is focusing on: North America (where Reebok is the company's key brand following acquisition in 2006), greater China and Russia/CIS – these markets are anticipated by Adidas to produce 50 per cent of future growth to 2018. The focus is therefore on emerging markets, and leverage of the Adidas brand itself is used to grow global sales. The brand generated 75 per cent of revenue in 2014, compared with 67 per cent in 2006.

Adidas has supported this brand in particular with some of its highest-profile sports sponsorships, supplying uniforms to football teams including Real Madrid, AC Milan and the World Cup-winning Spanish national team. At the same time, it has used fashion designers, including Stella McCartney and Yohji Yamamoto, to develop a fashion position for the brand. These strategies have underpinned global awareness, and made the Adidas brand the principal tool for expansion. The fact that it is less characterized by specialization also helps; its ice hockey and golf brands, for example, are less use in markets such as India and Brazil.

The European sportswear market

Overall the European sportswear market has been heavily influenced by the debt crisis in the Eurozone. The apparent lack of dynamism in western Europe is now less of a problem for Adidas. Adidas's strong brand equity, heavy spend on marketing and its push into retail are likely to continue to drive growth in the region, despite its ongoing economic difficulties.

Adidas is still the clear market leader in its home market Germany (see Table 4).

UK

Surprisingly, Adidas regards the UK as a market with considerable opportunity; this is despite the fact that

Table 3	Top five in the global apparel market by value share
Company	**% global apparel share, 2014**
1. Nike Inc. (US)	2.4
2. Adidas (Germany)	1.6
3. Inditex/Zara (Spain)	1.1
4. H&M (Sweden)	1.0
5. GAP Inc. (US)	0.9

Source: based on various data from www.euromonitor.com.

consumer confidence in 2012 fell to new lows and the country is faced with a double-dip recession. Adidas was a principal sponsor at the London 2012 Olympics, for example choosing British designer Stella McCartney to design the uniforms for the British team, designs that were well received in the fashion press.

Premiership football in the UK also continues to be a vital marketing tool for the company. English football is among the most in-demand and watched in the global market, and Adidas uses the league to showcase product development in both the Adidas and Reebok brands as well as repeatedly underlining brand awareness. Again the company is seeking to expand its retail operations in what it regards as a crucial market; its importance appears to be as much about its global visibility as actual sales.

Russia

Russia (and Ukraine) have consistently generated the company's strongest sales over the last five years. Part of the company's success has been its ability to develop a strong retail division in eastern Europe. In what it reports as European Emerging Markets, wholesale sales of the Reebok and Adidas brands generated 5 per cent of global values, and retail generated 38 per cent.

Again, rising wage levels and relatively low unemployment have underpinned demand for sporting goods, and the newness of these markets means that the company has been able to control its offer more effectively.

Russia, in particular, is a core market for the company, and in 2011 was its third largest national market after the US and China. However, although Russia is a key focus market for Adidas, growth was threatened by the recession in 2015, as a result of the political and economic boycott of Russia. The group's heavy investment in retail puts it at more risk than Nike.

Markets outside Europe

Countries outside Europe, including Brazil, Russia,

Table 4	Market share of sportswear brands in the biggest European countries (2014)							
Market share of sportswear brands	Germany	UK	France	Spain	Italy	Russia	Poland	Turkey
Total market for sportswear (shoes + clothing) – retail value (million €)	3,219	3,048	2,692	1,720	2,318	2,000	1,225	1,400
	%	%	%	%	%	%	%	%
Nike	6.5	17.9	8.1	9.7	6.9	11.2	6.6	2.9
Adidas	10.8	14.6	4.7	8.5	1.7	17.4	3.8	2.0
Reebok (Adidas)	1.2	6.8	3.2	0.9	–	4.6	3.7	–
Puma	3.8	3.0	3.6	–	1.0	–	2.6	1.3
Asics	2.5	1.5	–	–	0.5	–	1.1	–
Other brands (the mentioned brands are the most important after the main brands, singled out above)	75.2 (Esprit, Schöffel, The North Face, H&M, Jack Wolfskin, etc.)	56.2 (Umbro/ Nike, The North Face, Timberland, Berghaus, etc.)	80.4 (H&M, Aigle, Quechua/ Tribord, Latuma, Geox, etc.)	80.9 (H&M, Forum Sport, Foot Locker, Zara, Timberland, Converse/ Nike, Geox, etc.)	89.9 (Original Marines, Geox, Lotto, Sportmax, etc.)	66.8 (Demix, Columbia, Centrobuv, Decathlon, Ecco, Sala, Finn Flare, etc.)	82.2 (H&M, Timberland, Zara, Wolverine, etc.)	93.8 (Koton, LCW, Mavi, Zara, DeFacto, Colin's, H&M, etc.)
Total	100	100	100	100	100	100	100	100

Source: based on various data from www.euromonitor.com.

Table 5	Market shares in markets outside Europe: Adidas vs Nike		
Seven markets (outside Europe) with expected strongest market growth, 2014–19	Market size: Million US$ absolute market growth, 2014–19	Market share, 2014: Adidas	Market share 2014: Nike
1. USA	10,400	5	21
2. China	6,200	14	15
3. India	2,400	16	5
4. Mexico	1,800	10	9
5. Canada	1,600	7	15
6. Japan	1,200	17	13
7. Brazil	700	6	13

Source: based on various public sources.

India and China (the so-called BRIC countries) still represent good potential for sales growth going forward in the global apparel market. However, the scale of the market in China (where Nike is the leading apparel brand) makes it the number one target for Adidas and other manufacturers of international branded apparel.

Table 5 shows the Adidas vs Nike market share in the key markets outside Europe. Please note that the market sizes here represent the expected absolute market growth in million US$ from 2014 to 2019.

China

The economic crisis in the Eurozone (one of Adidas's largest export markets) and growing demands from trading partners for China to raise the value of its currency, making Chinese exports more expensive, may cool demand for consumer goods there. However, it is the scale of the consumer base and its long-term potential that make it particularly key to Adidas' strategy.

Adidas's Asia-Pacific operations has been improved; it ranked fifth in China in 2007 compared with second in 2014, very close to Nike. Adidas is well set up in India, and the boom in middle-class consumers in both markets offers plenty of marketing opportunities for the company. Other emerging markets, notably Latin America, where Adidas is the no. 2 apparel company (after Nike), offer similar trends and opportunities.

Adidas believes that despite the growth in share of domestic manufacturers, international brand producers are the key drivers of growth in the Chinese sportswear market.

Adidas has also sought to develop a stronger relationship with recreational athletes in China, an increasingly important area of the consumer base. It sponsors the Beijing marathon, and is seeking to develop more running sponsorships in smaller cities. The company has also sought to increase visibility via fitness chains, giving clothing to fitness instructors and buying advertising space in locker rooms and over treadmills. The emphasis is very much on urban consumers, with smaller cities, whose middle-class consumer bases are less developed, a particular priority.

However, its key China development strategy appears to be to increase its retail presence. Adidas has invested heavily in its retail operations, and is extending the number of its mono-branded franchise stores. For example, in China's central city of Wuhan, five Adidas stores that were identical outlets five years ago have now been split up to focus on different sporting interests, for example basketball. Adidas is also making a push in the direction of fashion, hiring talent from retailers H&M and Zara.

India

Adidas is the leading sportswear company in India with a 16 per cent share of value sales based on its Reebok and Adidas brands. The Indian apparel market is anticipated to see a compound announced growth note (CAGR) of 5 per cent over 2015–20, and will show the fourth largest growth of all global markets in absolute terms. Growth over the review period has been exponential, with the company generally hitting high double figures.

Reebok is the stronger of the two brands, based on its dominance of the cricket market; it supplies clothing to the Indian Premier League, one of the most dynamic sports franchises in the world, as well as equipment, apparel and footwear. Cricket is a national obsession, and the marketing opportunities are enormous.

Most importantly, the company had the market

largely to itself in 2014, as Nike has yet to develop a visible presence, despite manufacturing in the country (and also supplying the uniform for India's 2014 Cricket World Cup-winning team).

However, Adidas may be on the point of jeopardizing its success in India. At a time when the Indian government has indicated it may greatly liberalize foreign direct investment in the retail market, Adidas announced plans in May 2012 to close a third of its 1,000 Reebok stores in India.

United States

In 2011, the total apparel market in the US represented a value of €525 billion with Nike was the clear market leader. Despite recent efforts following the acquisition of Reebok, Adidas has so far failed to build share in this lucrative region.

In 2014, the Adidas brand lost its number two position in the US to 'Under Armour'. Nike still leads, with a 21 per cent share, compared to Under Armour's 3 per cent. Under Armour is well regarded as a women's brand in the US. It is best known as an apparel business, but is seeking to expand its footwear sales.

Between 2009 and 2014 Adidas was able to increase its market share in the US market, though not enough, by focusing on the most dynamic parts of its market there, including running and training, and increasingly basketball. Historically, the Adidas and Reebok brands have lagged behind Nike in the NBA; however, Adidas has increased its spending on basketball sponsorship, providing uniforms for the teams, as well as tying up stars such as Derrick Rose to sponsorship deals.

Distribution strategy has also been crucial to brand growth for the Adidas portfolio; as in other geographies, it seeks to control its portfolio via a tightened grip on retail. Where possible, it has sought to expand retail operations into high-quality malls and sporting goods stores; e-commerce is also a key part of its regional sales. As such, North America has been designated one of its key attack markets for the future, despite a CAGR of only 1 per cent forecast for the region between 2015 and 2020.

QUESTIONS

1. Please compare and evaluate Adidas's and Nike's global competitiveness and global strategies.

2. Which region would you recommend Adidas to focus on during the next five years?

3. What should Adidas do to become No. 1 in the global sportswear industry?

Sources: based on data from www.adidas.com; www.nike.com; www.euromonitor.com; other public data.

CASE STUDY I.4

Cereal Partners Worldwide (CPW): the No. 2 world player is challenging the No. 1, Kellogg

On a lovely spring morning in 2011, while giving her kids some Cheerios, the CEO of Cereal Partners Worldwide S.A. (CPW), Carol Smith, thinks about how CPW might expand international sales and/or capture further market shares in the saturated breakfast cereals market. Right now, CPW is the No. 2 in the world market for breakfast cereals, but it is a tough competition, primarily with the Kellogg Company, which is the world market leader.

Perhaps there are other ways of gaining new sales in this competitive market? Carol has just read the business best-seller *Blue Ocean Strategy* and she is fascinated by the thought of moving competition in the cereals breakfast market from the red to the blue ocean. The question is: how?

Maybe it would be better just to take the head-on battle with Kellogg Company. After all, CPW has managed to beat Kellogg in several minor international markets (e.g. in the Middle and Far East).

The children have finished their Cheerios and it is time to drive them to the kindergarten in Lausanne, Switzerland, where CPW has its headquarters. Later that day, Carol has to present the long-term global strategy for CPW, so she hurries to her office, and starts preparing the presentation. One of her marketing managers has prepared a background report about CPW and its position in the world breakfast cereals market. The following shows some important parts of the report.

History of breakfast cereals

Ready-to-eat cereals first appeared during the late 1800s. According to one account, John Kellogg, a doctor who belonged to a vegetarian group, developed wheat and corn flakes to extend the group's dietary choices. John's brother, Will Kellogg, saw potential in the innovative grain products and initiated commercial production and marketing. Patients at a Battle Creek, Michigan, sanitarium were among Kellogg's first customers.

Another cereal producer with roots in the nineteenth century is the Quaker Oats Company. In 1873, the North Star Oatmeal Mill built an oatmeal plant in Cedar Rapids, Iowa. North Star reorganized with other enterprises and together they formed Quaker Oats in 1901.

The Washburn Crosby Company, a predecessor to General Mills, entered the market during the 1920s. The company's first ready-to-eat cereal, Wheaties, was introduced to the American public in 1924. According to General Mills, Wheaties was developed when a Minneapolis clinician spilled a mixture of gruel that he was making for his patients on a hot stove.

Cereal Partners Worldwide

Cereal Partners Worldwide was formed in 1990 as a 50:50 joint venture between Nestlé and General Mills (see Figure 1), in order to produce and sell ready-to-eat breakfast cereals worldwide outside the US and Canada. CPW has a portfolio of over 50 brands, including Cheerios, Nesquik and Shredded Wheat.

General Mills

General Mills, a leading global manufacturer of consumer food products, operates in more than 30 global markets and exports to over 100 countries. It has 66 production facilities: 34 are located in the US; 15 in the

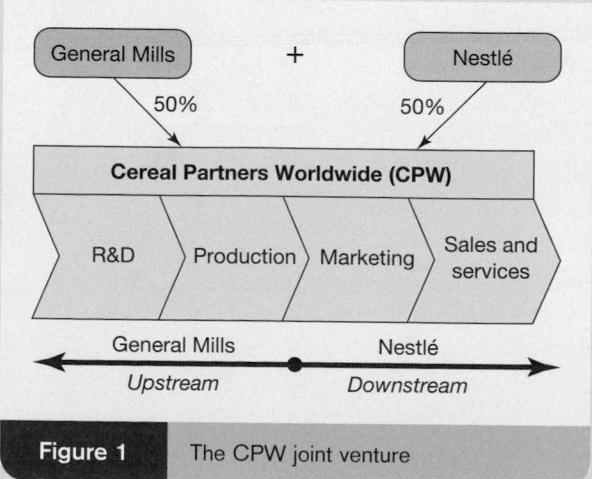

| Figure 1 | The CPW joint venture |

Source: Société des Produits Nestlé SA. The Nestlé name and image are reproduced with kind permission of Société des Produits Nestlé SA.

Asia-Pacific region; six in Canada; five in Europe; five in Latin America and Mexico; and one in South Africa. The company is headquartered in Minneapolis, Minnesota. In financial year 2009, the total net sales were US$15.9 billion of which 15 per cent came from outside the US. The company has 30,000 employees.

In October 2001, General Mills completed the largest acquisition in its history when it purchased the Pillsbury Company from Diageo. The US$10.4 billion deal almost doubled the size of the company, and consequently boosted General Mills' worldwide ranking, making it one of the world's largest food companies.

Source: The Nestlé name and image is reproduced with kind permission of Société des Produits Nestlé S.A.

However, the company was heavily debt-laden following its Pillsbury acquisition, which would continue to eat into operating and net profits for the next few years.

The company now has more than 100 US consumer brands, including Betty Crocker, Cheerios, Yoplait, Pillsbury Doughboy, Green Giant and Old El Paso. Integral to the successes of General Mills has been its ability to build and sustain huge brand names and maintain continued net growth. Betty Crocker, originally a pen name invented in 1921 by an employee in the consumer response department, has become an umbrella brand for products as diverse as cookie mixes to ready meals. The Cheerios cereal brand, which grew rapidly in the US post-war generation, remains one of the top cereal brands worldwide.

However, heavy domestic dependence leaves the company vulnerable to variations in that market, such as supermarket price-cutting or sluggish sales in prominent product types such as breakfast cereals.

Internationally, General Mills uses its 50 per cent stake in CPW to sell its breakfast cereals outside North America. Cereal sales have faced tough competition recently, leading to significant drops in sales, particularly tough competition from private labels.

Nestlé

Founded in 1866, Nestlé is the world's largest food and beverage company in terms of sales. The company began in the field of dairy-based products and diversified to food and beverages in the 1930s. Nestlé is headquartered in Vevey, Switzerland, and has 500 factories in 83 countries. It has about 406 subsidiaries located across the world. The company employs 247,000 people around the world, of which 131,000 employees work in factories, with the remainder working in administration and sales.

Nestlé's businesses are classified into six divisions based on product groups, which include beverages; milk products, nutrition and ice cream; prepared dishes and cooking aids; chocolate, confectionery and biscuits; pet care; and pharmaceutical products. Nestlé's global brands include Nescafé, Taster's Choice, Nestlé Pure Life, Perrier, Nestea, Nesquik, Milo, Carnation, Nido, Nestlé, Milkmaid, Sveltesse, Yoco, Mövenpick, Lactogen, Beba, Nestogen, Cerelac, Nestum, PowerBar, Pria, Nutren, Maggi, Buitoni, Toll House, Crunch, Kit-Kat, Polo, Chef, Purina, Alcon and L'Oréal (in which it has an equity stake).

Nestlé reported net sales of US$120 billion for the fiscal year 2010.

CPW

CPW markets cereals in more than 130 countries, except for the US and Canada, where the two companies market themselves separately. The joint venture was established in 1990 and the agreement also extends to the production of private-label cereals in the UK. Average yearly volume growth for CPW was 4 per cent for the period 2005–10. The company's cereals are sold under the Nestlé brand, although many originated from General Mills. Brand names manufactured (primarily by General Mills) under the Nestlé name under this agreement include Corn Flakes, Crunch, Fitness, Cheerios and Nesquik. Shredded Wheat and Shreddies were once made by Nabisco (before their acquisition by General Mills), but are now manufactured by General Mills and marketed by CPW.

The CPW turnover in 2014 was a little less than US$3 billion. CPW has 14 factories in 11 countries: UK, two factories; France, two factories; Poland, two factories; one factory in each of Portugal, Russia, China, the Philippines, Australia, Mexico, Chile and Brazil.

There are four research and development centres: US, UK, Switzerland and Australia. The research centres focus on breakfast cereal solutions that deliver consumer benefits, such as improved nutritional content, freshness, taste and texture. CPW employs nearly 4,000 people all over the world.

When CPW was established in 1990, each partner brought distinctive competences into the joint venture.

- General Mills
  - Proven cereal marketing expertise
  - Technical excellence in products and production processes (upstream competences)
  - Broad portfolio of successful brand.
- Nestlé
  - World's largest food company
  - Strong worldwide organization
  - Deep marketing and distribution knowledge (downstream competences).

CPW is number two in most international markets, but it is also market leader in some of the smaller breakfast cereal markets like China (60 per cent), Poland (50 per cent), Turkey (50 per cent), East/Central Europe (40 per cent) and South-east Asia (40 per cent).

The world market for breakfast cereals

In the early 2000s, breakfast cereal makers were facing stagnant, if not declining, sales. Gone are the days of the family breakfast, of which a bowl of cereal was standard fare. The fast-paced American lifestyle has more and more consumers eating breakfast on the go. Fast-food restaurants like McDonald's, ready-to-eat breakfast bars, bagels and muffins offer consumers less labour-intensive alternatives to cereal. Although the value of product shipped by cereal manufacturers

Table 1	Breakfast cereal consumption per capita per year – 2014

Region	Per-capita consumption per year (kg)
Sweden	9.0
Canada	7.0
UK	6.0
Australia	6.0
US	5.0
South-west Europe (France, Spain)	1.5
South-east Asia	0.1
Russia	0.1
China	0.1

Source: based on different public sources.

Table 2	World market for breakfast cereals by region – 2014	
Region	Billion US$	%
North America	12	38
Europe (west + east)	10	31
Rest of the world	10	31
Total	**32**	**100**

Source: based on different public sources.

has grown in absolute figures, increased revenues came primarily from price hikes rather than market growth.

English-speaking nations represented the largest cereal markets. Consumption in non-English markets was estimated at only one-quarter the amount consumed by English speakers (see Table 1), where the breakfast cereal consumption per capita is 6 kg in the UK, but only 1.5 kg in south-west Europe (France, Spain and Portugal). On the European continent, consumption per capita averaged 1.5 kg per year.

Growth in the cereal industry has been slow to non-existent in this century. The question at hand for the industry is how to remake cereal's image in light of the new culture. Tinkering with flavourings and offerings, such as the recent trend toward the addition of dried fresh fruit, provides some relief, but with over 150 different choices on store shelves and 20 new offerings added annually, variety has done more to overwhelm than to excite consumers. In addition, cereal companies are committing fewer dollars to their marketing budgets.

Development in geographical regions

As seen in Table 2, the US is by far the largest breakfast cereals market in the world. In total North America accounted for 42 per cent of the global sales of US$28 billion in 2014. The US accounted for about 90 per cent of the North American market.

The European region accounted for 31 per cent of global sales, at US$10 billion in 2014. By far the largest market is the UK, contributing nearly 40 per cent of the regional total, with France and Germany as the key countries in breakfast cereals. Eastern Europe is a minor breakfast cereal market, reflecting the product's generally new status in the region. However, the market is vibrant, as new lifestyles born from growing urbanization and westernization – key themes in emerging market development – have fuelled steady sales growth. Despite its low level of per-capita spending, Russia is the largest market in Eastern Europe, accounting for over 35 per cent of regional sales in 2014. The continued growth of this has lately been threatened by the boycott policy in Europe and in Russia. However, cereals remain a niche market in Russia, as they do across the region, with the product benefiting from a perception of novelty. A key target for manufacturers has been children and young women, at whom advertising has been aimed.

The Australasian breakfast cereals sector, like western Europe and North America, is dominated by a single nation, Australia, and is becoming increasingly polarized. In common with the key US and UK markets, breakfast cereals in Australia are suffering from a high degree of maturity, with annual growth at a low single-digit level.

The Latin American breakfast cereals sector is the third largest in the world, but at US$2 billion in 2014, it is notably overshadowed by the vastly larger North American and western European markets. However, in common with these developed regions, one country plays a dominant role in the regional make-up: Mexico, accounting for nearly 60 per cent of the overall breakfast cereal markets in Latin America.

In common with Eastern Europe, breakfast cereal sales, whilst small in Africa and the Middle East, have displayed marked growth in recent years as a direct result of greater urbanization and a growing trend (in some areas) towards westernization. Given the overriding influence of this factor on market development, sales are largely concentrated in the more developed regional markets, such as Israel and South Africa, where the investment by multinationals has been at its highest.

In Asia, the concept of breakfast cereals is relatively new, with the growing influence of western culture fostering a notable increase in consumption in major urban cities. Market development has been rapid in China, reflecting the overall rate of industry expansion in the country, with breakfast cereals sales rising by 10–15 per cent in 2014, although the per capita consumption is still very low (see Table 1). In the region's developed markets, in particular Japan, market performance is broadly similar, although the key growth driver is different, in that it is health. Overall, in both developed and developing markets, breakfast cereals are in their infancy. Per-capita consumption rates (Table 1) are still very low, leaving considerable scope for future growth.

CPW penetrates emerging markets, like Russia and China

Cereal Partners Worldwide has performed best in developing markets such as Russia and China, where market leader Kellogg has not yet established a strong presence. Although in 2014 the Russian and Chinese markets were still relatively small in global terms, they are growing rapidly. Moreover, per-capita consumption rates are still very low (particularly in China), leaving considerable scope for future growth.

The Nestlé brand has had a presence in the Chinese packaged food market since 1990, providing an excellent springboard for the launch of CPW in the country. CPW itself entered the Chinese breakfast cereals market in 2004, when it opened a manufacturing facility in the city of Tianjin, and it has relied on a combination of strong branding and intensive marketing to gain market share, particularly in children's cereals, where its market share stood at 60 per cent in 2008.

All of CPW's breakfast cereals are marketed under the name 'Que Cao', which means bird's nest in Mandarin. This name, together with a universal visual identity/logo and the tagline 'Choose quality, choose Nestlé', is the cornerstone of its Chinese marketing strategy, appearing on packaging, point-of-sale materials and media advertising. In-store promotions and sampling are also utilized. Moreover, unlike many of its indigenous rivals, CPW can afford to spend heavily on television advertising.

Thus the marketing of these breakfast cereals is integrated into a wider portfolio of products. However, this approach is not without its dangers, as demonstrated in 2005 when Nestlé's reputation in China took a hit after its baby formula was found to be contaminated with iodine. In this case, the fallout from the scandal does not seem to have had a serious impact on the Chinese operations of CPW.

In addition, CPW's marketing strategy in China is predicated on segmenting the market into two groups: urban and rural customers. It targets its latest and most innovative products at the wealthier urban population, which became the majority in 2011, emphasizing issues relating to health and wellness. In terms of China's diminishing rural population, who have significantly less disposable income than their urban counterparts, it takes a lower-cost approach, adapting existing product lines and highlighting such issues as basic nutrition and affordability, as well as quality and safety.

In China there are two contradictory forces at play. Although the country's birth rate fell significantly, mainly due to the government's one-child policy, disposable income is rising rapidly, so families now have much more money to spend on each child. As a result, the current generation, dubbed China's 'little emperors' by some marketers, would appear to be a ripe market for premium and value-added products, which CPW will have to exploit if its leadership of this category is not to be overtaken. None of CPW's three children's breakfast cereals brands in China, Trix, Star and Koko Krunch, are particularly healthy, which may make the company vulnerable to competitors with stronger health and wellness plays, as issues such as childhood obesity come more to the fore in China.

Another risk for CPW is that it is relatively weak in hot cereals, which accounted for more than 50 per cent of the total Chinese breakfast cereals sales in 2010.

Health trend

With regard to health, breakfast cereals have been hurt by the rise of fad diets such as the Atkins and South Beach diets, which have heaped much scorn on carbohydrate-based products. The influence of these diets is on the wane, but their footprint remains highly visible on national eating trends. In addition, the high sugar content of children's cereals has come under intense scrutiny, which caused a downturn in this sector, although the industry is now coming back with a range of 'better for you' variants.

Regarding convenience, this trend, once a growth driver for breakfast cereals, has now become a threat, with an increasing number of consumers opting to skip breakfast. Portability has become a key facet of convenience, a development that has fed the emergence and expansion of breakfast bars at the expense of traditional foods, such as breakfast cereals. In an increasingly cash-rich, time-poor society, consumers are opting to abandon a formal breakfast meal and instead are relying on an 'on-the-go' solution, such as breakfast bars or pastries. These latter products, in particular breakfast bars, are taking a share from cereals, a trend that looks set to gather pace in the short term.

Trends in product development

The market for breakfast products will continue to be influenced by factors such as the speeding up of society, the entry of more women into the workforce and the further growth of single- and two-person households as people delay marriage and have fewer children. These trends will fuel demand for products that are portable and/or easy to prepare as an increasing number of consumers grab breakfast on the way to work or school.

Consumer awareness of health and nutrition has also played a major part in shaping the industry in recent years. Cereal manufacturers began to tout the benefits of eating breakfast cereal right on the package – vitamin-fortified, low in fat and a good source of fibre. Another trend, begun in the 1990s and picking up steam in the 2000s, is adding dehydrated whole fruits to cereal, which provides colour, flavour and nutritional value. Yet touting health benefits to adults and marketing film characters to children have not been sufficient to reinvigorate this mature industry.

Under the difficult market conditions, cereal packaging is receiving new attention. Packaging was a secondary consideration, other than throwing in special offers to tempt kids. These days, with meal occasions boiled down to their bare essentials, packaging and delivery have emerged as key weapons in the cereal marketer's arsenal. New ideas circulating in the industry usually include doing away with the traditional cereal box, which has undergone little change in its lifetime. Alternatives range from clear plastic containers to a return of the small variety six-packs.

Trends in distribution

The ways in which breakfast products are brought to market in the developed world are not expected to change a great deal. The distribution of breakfast foods is already characterized by a high percentage of sales through supermarkets/hypermarkets, for reasons of convenience and economy. However, supermarkets/hypermarkets will face more intense competition from hard discounters such as Aldi and Lidl, which have been increasing their penetration, notably in Europe. Hard discounters appeal to price-conscious consumers, and continued economic uncertainty in key markets such as France and Germany has fuelled growth in this segment.

Discounters are also widening their reach in emerging market regions, such as eastern Europe, where price sensitivity is high, and are stepping up their private-label development with premium breakfast products that compete effectively with established brands. As a result of the fierce competition between supermarkets/hypermarkets and hard discounters, independent food stores are likely to lose out further in the future, as they will find it increasingly difficult to compete in times of tighter margins and heavy promotion.

In an increasingly time-poor, cash-rich culture, consumers are also proving ever more willing to frequent convenience or impulse stores for the purchase of 'on-the-go' breakfast solutions such as cereals in pots complete with milk, in-cup porridge, cereal bars and artisanal rolls and pastries. Successful formats include outlets such as service station forecourts and urban supermarket formats, which are well placed to allow consumers to pop in on their way to work, college or school. This trend is expected to become more pronounced in the future, as people have less time to eat at home.

While e-commerce is not generally suited to breakfast products, due to their fresh and perishable nature, manufacturers will likely make greater use of their websites to inform consumers about nutritional issues and new products, as well as to suggest recipes or generally increase brand visibility. In developing markets, the growing use of the internet will serve to make consumers increasingly aware of western brands.

Independent food stores (where breakfast cereals are traditionally sold) have suffered a decline during the past years. They have been at a competitive disadvantage compared with their larger and better resourced chained competitors.

Trends in advertising

Advertising expenditures of most cereal companies were down in recent years due to decreases in consumer spending. However, there are still a lot of marketing activities going on.

Celebrity endorsements continue to play a critical part of, for example, General Mills's marketing strategies, in particular its association with sporting personalities dating back to the 1930s with baseball sponsorship. One of the main lines of celebrity endorsement involves Wheaties boxes, which have featured a long line of sports people since the 1930s. In 2001, Tiger Woods, spokesman for the Wheaties brand, appeared on special-edition packaging for Wheaties to commemorate his victory of four Grand Slam golf titles.

Private-label competition intensifies

Across many categories, rising costs have led to price increases in branded products which have not been matched by any pricing actions taken by private labels. As a result, the price gaps between branded and private-label products have increased dramatically and, in some cases, can be as much as 30 per cent.

This creates intense competitive environments for branded products, particularly in categories such as cereals, e.g. for Kellogg's and CPW, as consumers have started to focus more on price than on brand identity. This shift in focus is partly the result of private labels' increased quality as they compete for consumer loyalty and confidence in their label products.

The following Table 3 shows a ranking of the 10 countries where CPW has the highest market shares.

Competitors

The competitive situation in three main markets (Germany, UK and US) is shown in Table 4.

Kellogg's

The company that makes breakfast foods and snacks for millions began with only 25 employees in Battle Creek in 1906. In 2014, Kellogg Company employed more than 25,000 people, manufactures in 17 countries and sold its products in more than 180 countries.

Kellogg was the first American company to enter the foreign market for ready-to-eat breakfast cereals. Company founder Will Keith (W.K.) Kellogg was an early believer in the potential of international growth and began establishing Kellogg's as a global brand with the introduction of Kellogg's Corn Flakes in Canada in 1914. As success followed and demand grew, Kellogg Company continued to build manufacturing facilities around the world, including Sydney, Australia (1924), Manchester, England (1938), Queretaro, Mexico (1951), Takasaki, Japan (1963), Mumbai, India (1994) and Toluca, Mexico (2004).

Kellogg Company is the leader among global breakfast cereal manufacturers, with sales revenue in 2011 of US$13.2 billion (operating profit was $2 billion). Walmart Stores, Inc. and its affiliates accounted for approximately 18 per cent of consolidated net sales during 2011.

Kellogg Company was the world's market leader in ready-to-eat cereals throughout most of the twentieth century. In 2014, Kellogg had 30 per cent of the world market share for breakfast cereals (see Table 4). Canada, the UK and Australia represented Kellogg's three largest overseas markets.

The most well-known Kellogg products are Corn Flakes, Kellogg's Special K, Frosted Mini-Wheats, Corn Pops and Fruit Loops.

PepsiCo (Quaker)

In August 2001, PepsiCo merged with Quaker Foods, thereby expanding its existing portfolio. Quaker's family of brands includes Quaker Oatmeal, Cap'n Crunch and Life cereals, Rice-A-Roni and Near East side dishes, and Aunt Jemima pancake mixes and syrups.

Table 3	CPW 'top ten' market shares
Country	**CPW market shares in breakfast cereals in 2014 (%)**
1. Indonesia	80
2. Malaysia	73
3. Turkey	53
4. Thailand	51
5. Chile	50
6. Russia	48
7. Saudi Arabia	48
8. Ukraine	38
9. Brazil	35
10. Singapore	34

Source: based on a General Mills (public available) PP presentation.

Table 4	The world market for breakfast cereals, by company – 2014. Figures are percentage market share			
Manufacturer	**Germany**	**UK**	**US**	**World**
Kellogg Company	27	30	30	30
CPW (General Mills + Nestlé)	12	15	30	20
PepsiCo (Quaker)	–	6	14	10
Weetabix	–	10	–	5
Private label	35	15	10	15
Others	26	24	16	20
Total	**100**	**100**	**100**	**100**

In the US, General Mills and Nestlé market each of their breakfast cereal products independently, because CPW only covers international markets outside the US. The CPW global market share (30 per cent) includes General Mills' global market share, which alone is around 10 per cent, because of its strong position in the US.

Source: based on various public sources.

Quaker Foods' first puffed product, Puffed Rice, was introduced in 1905. In 1992, Quaker Oats held an 8.9 per cent share of the ready-to-eat cereal market, and its principal product was Cap'n Crunch. Within the smaller hot cereal segment, however, the company held approximately 60 per cent of the market. In addition to cereal products, Quaker Oats produced Aunt Jemima Pancake mix and Gatorade sports drinks.

The PepsiCo brands in the breakfast cereal sector include Cap'n Crunch, Puffed Wheat, Crunchy Bran, Frosted Mini Wheats and Quaker. Despite recent moves to extend its presence into new markets, PepsiCo tends to focus on its North American operations.

Weetabix

Weetabix is a British manufacturer, with a relatively high market share (10 per cent) in the UK. It sells its cereals in over 80 countries and has a product line that includes Weetabix, Weetos and Alpen. Weetabix is headquartered in Northamptonshire, UK. In 2011 Weetabix had an estimated turnover of around US$1 billion.

In May 2012, China's state-owned 'Bright Food' took over Weetabix. Bright Food has extensive experience across all aspects of the food industry, including the primary (agriculture/farming), secondary (manufacturing of food products) and tertiary (retail and distribution) industries. In addition, it owns several well-known trademarks and branded products in Asia's food processing industry.

Bright Food will also offer a good 'route-to-market' through its broad retail platform. In 2014, Bright Food generated revenues of US$19 billion and had a net profit of US$500 million. Bright Food now sees a big opportunity for Weetabix in China, where breakfast is a very important meal and there is a trend towards healthy eating.

QUESTIONS

Carol has heard that you are the new global marketing specialist, so you are called in as a last-minute consultant before the presentation to the board of directors. You are confronted with the following questions, which you are supposed to answer as best you can:

1. How can General Mills and Nestlé create international competitiveness by joining forces in CPW?

2. Evaluate the international competitiveness of CPW compared with the Kellogg Company.

3. Suggest how CPW can create a blue ocean strategy.

4. Where and how can CPW create further international sales growth?

Sources: www.cerealpartners.co.uk; www.generalmills.com; www.nestle. com; www.euromonitor.com; www.datamonitor.com; www.marketwatch. com; Bowery, J. (2006) 'Kellogg broadens healthy cereals portfolio', *Marketing,* 8 February, p. 5; Sanders, T. (2006) 'Cereals spark debate', *Food Manufacture,* August, 81(8), p. 4; Reyes, S. (2006) 'Saving private label', *Brandweek,* 5 August, 47(19), pp. 30–34; Hanson, P. (2005) 'Market focus breakfast cereals', *Brand Strategy,* March, 190, p. 50; Pehanich, M. (2003) 'Cereals run sweet and healthy', *Prepared Foods,* March, pp. 75–76; Vignali, C. (2001) 'Kellogg's – internationalisation versus globalisation of the marketing mix', *British Food Journal,* 103(2), pp. 112–130.

PART I
The decision whether
to internationalize
Chs 1–4

PART II
Deciding which
markets to enter
Chs 5–8

PART III
Market entry strategies
Chs 9–13

PART IV
Designing the global
marketing programme
Chs 14–17

PART V
Implementing and
coordinating the global
marketing programme
Chs 18–19

Part II Contents

5 Global marketing research

6 The political and economic environment

7 The sociocultural environment

8 The international market selection process

Part II Case studies

II.1 **SodaStream**: managing profitable growth in an increasingly competitive global market

II.2 **The Female Health Company (FHC):** the female condom is seeking a foothold in the world market for contraceptive products

II.3 **Zalando:** how can the online approval retailer turn financial losses into positive profits?

II.4 **Ferrari:** international market selection (IMS) for the exclusive sports car brand

PART II
Deciding which markets to enter

Introduction to Part II

After considering the initial phase in Part I, the decision whether to internationalize, the structure of this part follows the process of selecting the 'right' international market. First, Chapter 5 presents the most important international marketing research tools for analysing the internal and external environments. The political and economic environment (Chapter 6) and the sociocultural environment (Chapter 7) are then used as inputs to the process from which the output is the target market(s) that the firm should select as a basis for development of the international marketing mix (see Part IV). The structure of Part II is shown in Figure II.1.

As Figure II.1 shows, the research tools presented in Chapter 5, and the forces in Chapters 6 and 7, provide the environmental framework that is necessary for:

- the selection of the right market(s) (Chapter 8)
- the subsequent development of the global marketing mix.

The discussion following Chapters 6 and 7 will be limited to the major macroenvironmental dimensions affecting market and buyer behaviour and thus the global marketing mix of the firm.

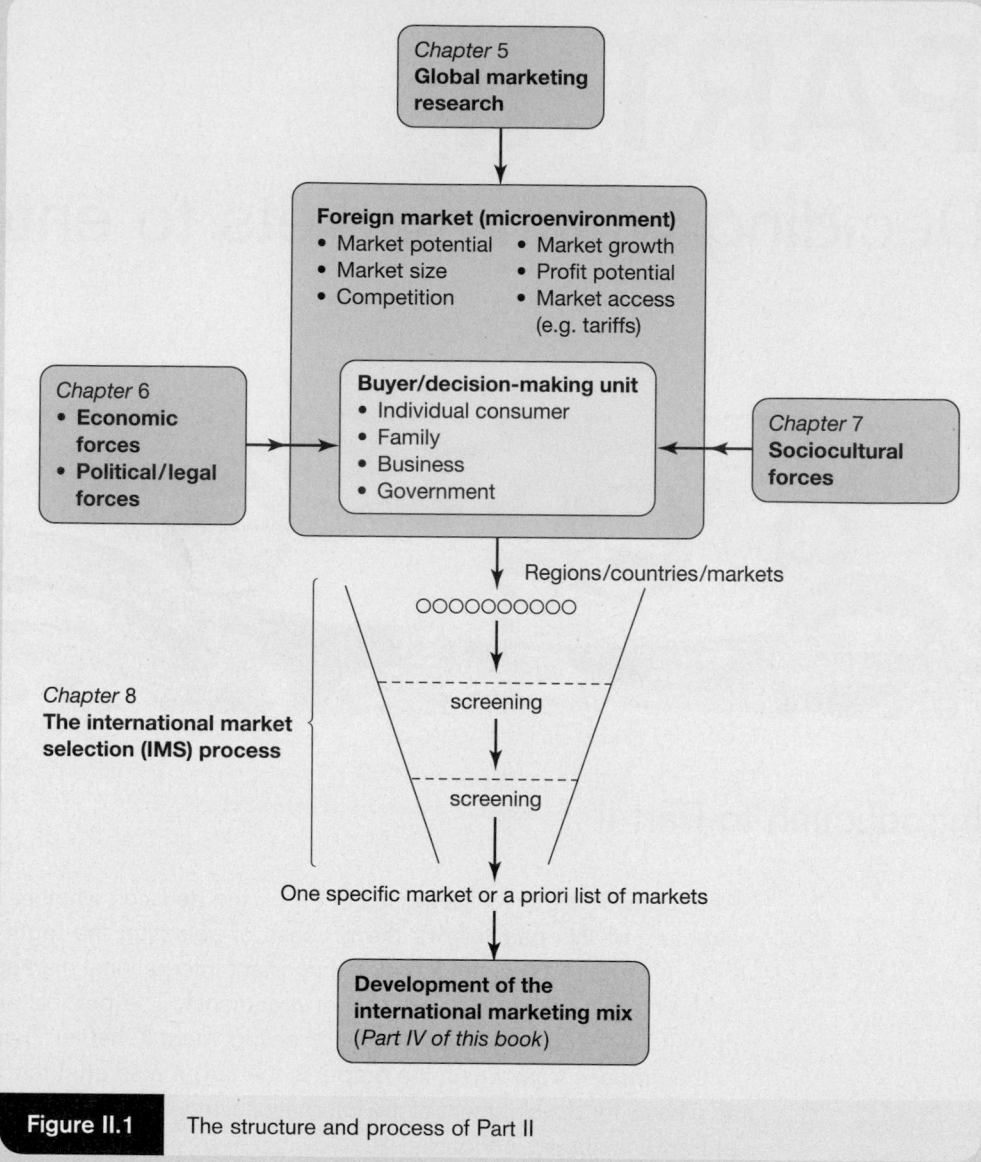

Figure II.1 The structure and process of Part II

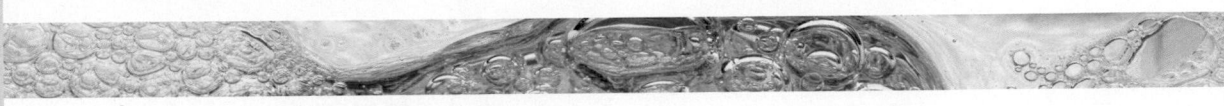

PART II VIDEO CASE STUDY HondaJets – Honda enters the small-sized business jet market

download from **www.pearsoned.co.uk/hollensen**

Honda Motor Co. is a Japanese multinational corporation primarily known as a manufacturer of cars and motorcycles. At the same time, they are world famous for their core competency in small engines, which are used in a variety of products requiring such engines (motorcycles, jet skis, lawn mowers, etc.). Now Honda has also pioneered new technology in its HondaJet, manufactured by its subsidiary Honda Aircraft Company, which allows increased aerodynamics and fuel efficiency thus reducing operating costs.

The Honda Aircraft was formed as a separate entity in August 2006 under the leadership of president and CEO Michimasa Fujino. The corporate headquarters are located at the Piedmont Triad International Airport in Greensboro, North Carolina, where the prototype HondaJet was also developed and flight tested. The company received more than 100 orders for the seven-seater jet in three days when it began taking orders in 2006, promising a quieter engine, 20 per cent better fuel economy over competing models and operational costs of two-thirds or less. The jet is powered by a pair of fuel-efficient turbofan jet engines, which were developed under a joint venture between Honda and General Electric. The 13-meter-long HondaJet is priced at US$4.5 million.

The only problem for Honda Aircraft Company has been to get final approval to sell and fly the aircraft officially. It was April 2015 when Honda got US approval to go ahead with the final tests of its Honda-Jet, before generating real revenues. Now the people behind the HondaJet are quite optimistic and hope to gain one-third of the market for these small-sized business jets (up to 10 seats). That is equal to between 100 and 200 HondaJets per year.

Source: Yuya Shino/Reuters.

Questions

1. Which demand factors would influence future sales of business jets in general?

2. How could Honda Aircraft Company estimate the future total market for these small-sized business jets (total number of small business jets sold per year)?

3. Which screening criteria would you recommend Honda Aircraft Company to use in order to find the most attractive markets (countries) for their small business jets in the International Market Selection (IMS) process?

4. What kind of market research (primary and/or secondary) would you recommend Honda Aircraft Company to do, in order to use this input for their decision about IMS?

Please look at the video clips at **www.pearsoned.co.uk/hollensen**

CHAPTER 5
Global marketing research

Contents

Learning objectives

After studying this chapter you should be able to:

- Explain the importance of having a carefully designed international information system

- Link global marketing research to the decision-making process

- Discuss the key problems in gathering and using international market data

- Distinguish between different research approaches, data sources and data types

- Discuss opportunities and problems with qualitative market research methods

- Understand how online surveys are carried out

- Understand the relevance of the internet as an important data source in global marketing research

- Understand the growing role of social networks and other online communities (Web 2.0 as sources of information).

5.1   Introduction

Information is a key ingredient in the development of successful international marketing strategies. Lack of familiarity with customers, competitors and the market environment in other countries, coupled with the growing complexity and diversity of international markets, makes it increasingly critical to collect information in relation to these markets.

In contrast to a researcher concerned with only one country, an international market researcher has to deal with a number of countries that may differ considerably in a number of important ways. Therefore many international marketing decisions are concerned with priorities and allocation of resources between countries.

The prime function of global marketing is to make and sell what international buyers want, rather than simply selling whatever can be most easily made. Therefore what customers require must be assessed through marketing research and/or through establishing a decision support system, so that the firm can direct its marketing activities more effectively by fulfilling the requirements of the customers.

The term 'marketing research' refers to gathering, analysing and presenting information related to a well-defined problem. Hence the focus of marketing research is a specific problem or project with a beginning and an end.

Marketing research differs from a decision support system (DSS) or marketing information system (MIS), which is information gathered and analysed on a continual basis. In practice, marketing research and DSS/MIS are often hard to differentiate, so they will be used interchangeably in this context.

At the end of this chapter a proposal for setting up an international MIS will be presented.

5.2   The changing role of the international researcher

The role of international market research is primarily to act as an aid to the decision-maker. It is a tool that can help to reduce the risk in decision-making caused by the environmental uncertainties and lack of knowledge in international markets. It ensures that the manager bases a decision on the solid foundation of knowledge and focuses strategic thinking on the needs of the marketplace rather than on the product.

Earlier marketing research was regarded as a staff function and not a line function. Marketing researchers had little interaction with marketing managers and did not participate in marketing decision-making. Likewise, external providers of marketing research had little interaction with marketing managers. However, as we have moved into the new millennium, this line of demarcation between marketing research and marketing, and thus the distinction between marketing researchers and marketing managers, has become thinner and thinner.

As the line and staff boundary blurs, marketing managers are becoming increasingly involved in marketing research. This trend towards making marketing research more of a line function, rather than a staff function, is likely to continue and even accelerate in the near future where 'sense and respond' will increasingly characterize firms' approach to business. Thus the traditional marketing researcher in a commercial firm narrowly focused on the production of presentations and reports for management will become a rare breed. The transition of marketing researchers to researchers-cum-decision-makers has already begun. Indeed, some of the most effective researchers of customer satisfaction are not only participating in decision-making but are also deployed as part of the team to implement organizational changes in response to customer satisfaction surveys.

The availability of better decision tools and decision support systems is facilitating the transition of research managers to decision-makers. Senior managers can now directly access internal and external secondary data from computers and internet sites around the world.

In this millennium good marketing researchers will be good marketing managers, and vice versa.

5.3   Linking global marketing research to the decision-making process

Global marketing research should be linked to the decision-making process within the firm. The recognition that a situation requires action is the initiating factor in the decision-making process.

Even though most firms recognize the need for domestic marketing research, this need is not fully understood for global marketing activities. Most small and medium-sized enterprises (SMEs) conduct no international market research before they enter a foreign market. Often decisions concerning entry into and expansion in overseas markets and the selection and appointment of distributors are made after a subjective assessment of the situation. The research done is usually less rigorous, less formal and less quantitative than in large-scale enterprises (LSEs). Furthermore, once an SME has entered a foreign market, it is likely to discontinue any research of that market. Many business executives therefore appear to view foreign market research as relatively unimportant.

A major reason that firms are reluctant to engage in global marketing research is a lack of sensitivity to cross-cultural customer tastes and preferences. What information should the global marketing research/DSS provide?

Table 5.1 summarizes the principal tasks of global marketing research, according to the major decision phases of the global marketing process. As can be seen, both internal (firm-specific) and external (market) data are needed. The role of a firm's internal information system in providing data for marketing decisions is often forgotten.

Table 5.1	Information for the major global marketing decisions
Global marketing decision phase	**Information needed**
1. Deciding whether to internationalize	Assessment of global market opportunities (global demand) for the firm's products Commitment of the management to internationalize Competitiveness of the firm compared with local and international competitors Domestic versus international market opportunities
2. Deciding which markets to enter	Ranking of world markets according to market potential of countries/regions Local competition Political risks Trade barriers Cultural/psychic distance to potential market
3. Deciding how to enter foreign markets	Nature of the product (standard versus complex product) Size of markets/segments Behaviour of potential intermediaries Behaviour of local competition Transport costs Government requirements
4. Designing the global marketing programme	Buyer behaviour Competitive practice Available distribution channels Media and promotional channels
5. Implementing and controlling the global marketing programme	Negotiation styles in different cultures Sales by product line, sales force customer type and country/region Contribution margins Marketing expenses per market

Primary data
Information that is collected first-hand, generated by original research tailor-made to answer specific research questions.

Secondary data
Information that has already been collected for other purposes and is thus readily available.

How the different types of information affect the major decisions is thoroughly discussed in the different parts and chapters of this book. Besides the split between internal and external data, the two major sources of information are **primary data** and **secondary data**:

1. *Primary data.* This can be defined as information that is collected first-hand, generated by original research tailor-made to answer specific current research questions. The major advantage of primary data is that the information is specific (fine-grained), relevant and up to date. The disadvantages of primary data, however, are the high costs and amount of time associated with its collection.
2. *Secondary data.* This can be defined as information that has already been collected for other purposes and is thus readily available. The major disadvantage is that the data is often more general and coarse-grained in nature. The advantages of secondary data are the low costs and amount of time associated with its collection. For those who are unclear on the terminology, secondary research is frequently referred to as desk research.

The two basic forms of research (primary and secondary) will be discussed in further detail later in this chapter.

If we combine the split of internal/external data with primary/secondary data, it is possible to place data in four categories. In Figure 5.1, this approach is used to categorize indicator variables for answering the following marketing questions. Is there a market for the firm's product A in country B? If yes, how large is it and what is the possible market share for the firm? Note that in Figure 5.1 only a limited number of indicator variables are

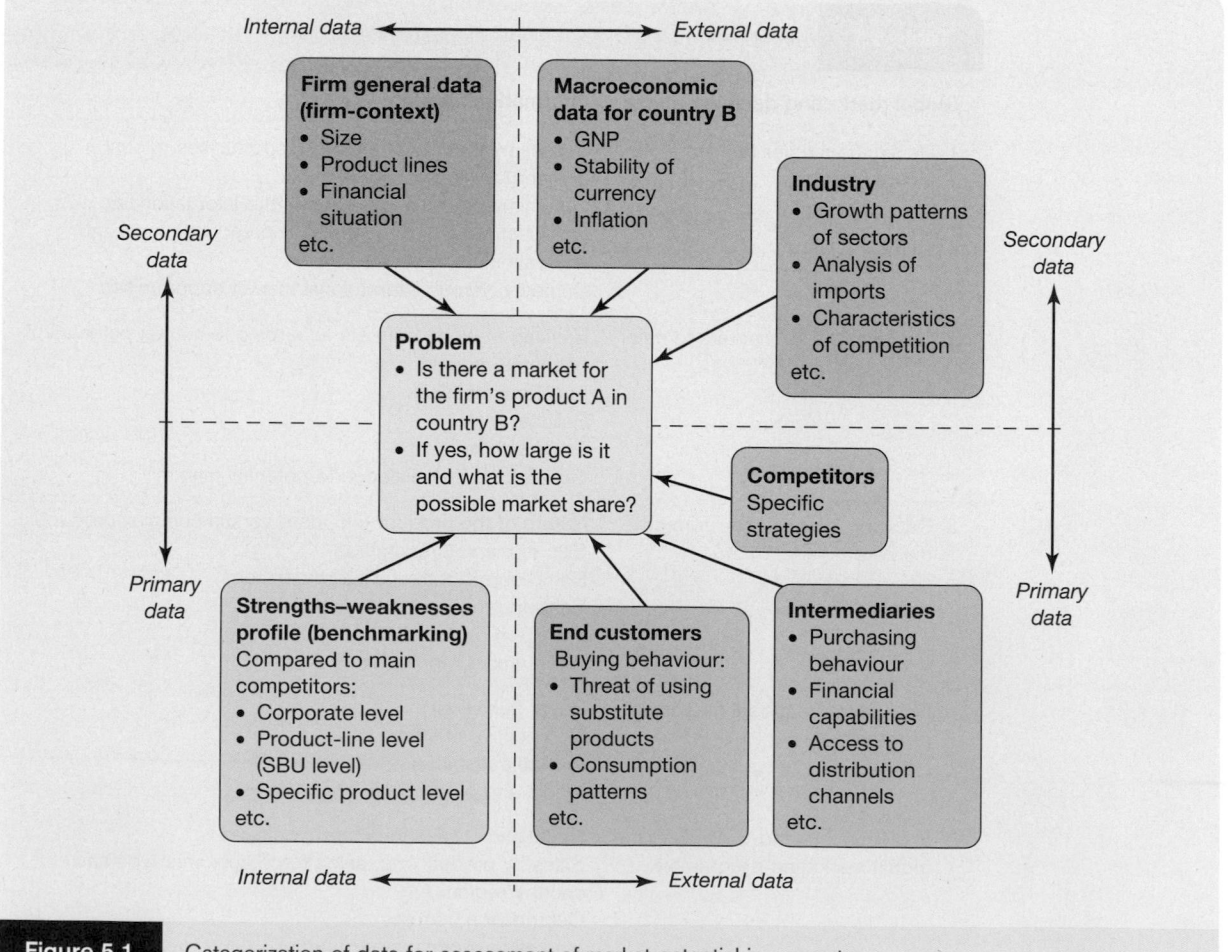

Figure 5.1 Categorization of data for assessment of market potential in a country

shown. Of course, the one-market perspective in Figure 5.1 could be expanded, to cover not only country B (as in Figure 5.1) but a range of countries, e.g. the EU.

As a rule, no primary research should be done without first searching for relevant secondary information, and secondary data should be used whenever available and appropriate. Secondary data often helps to define problems and research objectives. In most cases, however, secondary sources cannot provide all the information needed and the company must collect primary data.

In Figure 5.1 the most difficult and costly kind of data to obtain is probably the strengths–weaknesses profile of the firm (internal and primary data). However, because it compares the profile of the firm with those of its main competitors, this quadrant is a very important indicator of the firm's international competitiveness. The next two sections discuss different forms of secondary and primary research.

With many international markets to consider, it is essential that firms begin their market research by seeking and utilizing secondary data.

5.4 Secondary research

Advantages of secondary research in foreign markets

Secondary research conducted from the home base is less expensive and less time-consuming than research conducted abroad. No contacts have to be made outside the home country, thus keeping commitment to possible future projects at a low level. Research undertaken in the home country about the foreign environment also has the benefit of objectivity. The researcher is not constrained by overseas customs. As a preliminary stage of a market-screening process, secondary research can quickly generate background information to eliminate many countries from the scope of enquiries.

Disadvantages of secondary research in foreign markets

Problems with secondary research in foreign countries are:

- *Non-availability of data.* In many developing countries, secondary data is very scarce. These weak economies have poor statistical services – many do not even carry out a population census. Information on retail and wholesale trade is especially difficult to obtain. In such cases, primary data collection becomes vital.
- *Reliability of data.* Sometimes political considerations may affect the reliability of data. In some developing countries, governments may enhance the information to paint a rosy picture of the economic life in the country. In addition, due to the data collection procedures used, or the personnel who gathered the data, much data lacks statistical accuracy. As a practical matter, the following questions should be asked to judge effectively the reliability of data sources (Cateora, 1993, p. 346):
    - Who collected the data? Would there be any reason for purposely misrepresenting the facts?
    - For what purpose was the data collected?
    - How was the data collected (methodology)?
    - Are the data internally consistent and logical in the light of known data sources or market factors?
- *Data classification.* In many countries the data reported is too broadly classified for use at the micro level.
- *Comparability of data.* International marketers often like to compare data from different countries. Unfortunately the secondary data obtainable from different countries is not readily comparable because national definitions of statistical phenomena differ from one country to another. The term 'supermarket', for example, has a variety of

meanings around the world. In Japan, a supermarket is quite different from its UK counterpart. Japanese 'supermarkets' usually occupy two- or three-storey structures; they sell daily necessities such as foodstuffs, but also clothing, furniture, electrical home appliances and sporting goods, and they have a restaurant.

In general, the availability and accuracy of recorded secondary data increase as the level of economic development increases. However, there are many exceptions: India is at a lower level of economic development than other countries but has accurate and complete development of government-collected data.

Although the possibility of obtaining secondary data has increased dramatically, the international community has grown increasingly sensitive to the issue of data privacy. Readily accessible large-scale databases contain information valuable to marketers but that is considered privileged by the individuals who have provided the data. The international marketer must therefore also pay careful attention to the privacy laws in different nations and to the possible consumer response to using such data. Neglecting these concerns may result in research backfiring and the corporate position being weakened.

In doing secondary research or building a decision support system, there are many information sources available. Generally these secondary data sources can be divided into internal and external sources (Figure 5.1). The latter can be classified as either international/global or regional/country-based sources.

Internal data sources

Internal company data can be a most fruitful source of information. However, it is often not utilized as fully as it should be.

The global marketing and sales departments are the main points of commercial interaction between an organization and its foreign customers. Consequently a great deal of information should be available, including:

- *Total sales*. Every company keeps a record of its total sales over a defined time period, e.g. weekly records, monthly records and so on.
- *Sales by country*. Sales statistics should be split up by countries. This is partly to measure the progress and competence of the export manager or the salesperson (sometimes to influence earnings because commission may be paid on sales) and partly to measure the degree of market penetration in a particular country.
- *Sales by products*. Very few companies sell only one product. Most companies sell a range of products and keep records for each kind of product or, if the range is large, each product group.
- *Sales volume by market segment*. Such segmentation may be geographical or by type of industry. This will give an indication of segment trends in terms of whether they are static, declining or expanding.
- *Sales volume by type of channel distribution*. Where a company uses several different distribution channels, it is possible to calculate the effectiveness and profitability of each type of channel. Such information allows marketing management to identify and develop promising channel opportunities, and results in more effective channel marketing.
- *Pricing information*. Historical information relating to price adjustments by product allows the organization to establish the effect of price changes on demand.
- *Communication mix information*. This includes historical data on the effects of advertising campaigns, sponsorship and direct mail on sales. Such information can act as a guide to the likely effectiveness of future communication expenditure plans.
- *Sales representatives' records and reports*. Sales representatives should keep a visit card or file on every 'live' customer. In addition, sales representatives often send reports to the sales office on such matters as orders lost to competitors and possible reasons why, as well as on firms that are planning future purchasing decisions. Such information can help to bring improvements in marketing strategy.

External data sources

One very basic method of finding international business information is to begin with a public library or a university library. The internet can also help in the search for data sources. The internet has made thousands of databases for intelligence research available (i.e. research on competitors). In addition, electronic databases carry marketing information ranging from the latest news on product development to new thoughts in the academic and trade press and updates on international trade statistics. However, the internet will not totally replace other sources of secondary data. Cost compared with data quality will still be a factor influencing a company's choice of secondary data sources.

Secondary data used for estimation of foreign market potential

Secondary data are often used to estimate the size of potential foreign markets. In assessing current product demand and forecasting future demand, reliable historical data is required. As previously mentioned, the quality and availability of secondary data are frequently inadequate. Nevertheless, estimates of market size must be attempted in order to plan effectively. Despite limitations, there are approaches to forecasting future demand in a market with a minimum of information. A number of techniques are available (see Craig and Douglas, 2000). Here four are examined in some detail: proxy indicators, the chain ratio method, lead–lag analysis and estimation by analogy.

Proxy indicators

Proxy indicators
Used when direct measures are hard to obtain. Indirect variables serve as surrogate or proxy.

Proxy indicators are useful in situations where a direct measure is difficult to obtain. Indirect variables serve as surrogate or proxy.

Ownership of durables by households has also been suggested as a proxy for a country's economic development. For example, consumption of refrigerators or any other household appliance can be a good proxy for washing machines. Even television consumption can be used as a proxy. Another proxy could be the total number of households connected with resident telephone lines. In developing countries, relatively privileged people have a telephone in their homes. The assumption is that the households with resident telephones have the potential to buy a washing machine.

The method can provide robust estimation and is relatively inexpensive and convenient to implement, but the use of proxy variables can also cause validity problems. The degree of precision depends on the choice of proxy variable (Waheeduzzaman, 2008). For example, the Big Mac Index (the relative Big Mac prices in different countries) is used as a proxy variable for the likely future currency development against the US$.

Chain ratio method

Chain ratio method
A method of calculating total market demand for a product by using several percentages in order to reduce a base population to the relevant target group and the final realistic demand.

The **chain ratio method** is a simple arithmetic technique where ratios are used to reduce a base population. The purpose of the reduction technique is to derive a realistic demand. It can provide reasonably precise estimates if the ratios are logical and make practical sense. For example, the market potential for household air conditioners in a country is dependent on the rate of urbanization (percentage of people living in cities), total number of households, percentage of population having access to electricity and percentage of population who can afford the product. Multiplying these metrics provides a rough estimate for the potential air conditioner market in a country. If the market researcher wanted to estimate the total market potential for washing machines in Thailand, he would do it like this: Thailand has 17.6 million households, 82 per cent of these households have electricity and 50 per cent have a running water supply. Multiplying these variables $17.6 \times 0.82 \times 0.50$, the total market potential comes out at 7.2 million.

Though robust, the method can offer estimates that are close to real data. It is relatively inexpensive and convenient to implement (Waheeduzzaman, 2008).

Lead–lag analysis

This technique is based on the use of time-series data from one country to project sales in other countries. It assumes that the determinants of demand in the two countries are the same, and that only time separates them. This requires that the diffusion process, and specifically the rate of diffusion, is the same in all countries. Of course, this is not always the case, and it seems that products introduced more recently diffuse more quickly (Craig and Douglas, 2000).

Lead–lag analysis
Determinants of demand and the rate of diffusion are the same in two countries, but time separates the two.

Figure 5.2 shows the principle behind the **lead–lag analysis** with an illustrative example in the Video-On-Demand (VOD) market, where one of the major players is Netflix with their subscription service. By the end of 2013, it was assumed that 55 per cent of the 120 million US TV households would have access to VOD, whereas it was assumed that 'only' 20 per cent of Italian households would have access to VOD. In Figure 5.2 we define the time-lag between the American and the Italian VOD market as two years. So if we were to estimate the future penetration of VOD in Italian households (and as a consequence also demand), we could make a parallel displacement of the S-formed US penetration curve by two years, as illustrated in Figure 5.2. However, there is a tendency that such online products, like VOD, would have shorter time-lags from the original market (US) to subsequent markets. This also shows how rapidly new products (especially IT products) today are diffused from market to market. The difficulty in using the lead–lag analysis includes the problem of identifying the relevant time-lag and the range of factors that have an impact on future demand. However, the technique has considerable intuitive appeal to managers and is likely to guide some of their thinking.

When data are not available for a regular lead–lag analysis, estimation by analogy can be used.

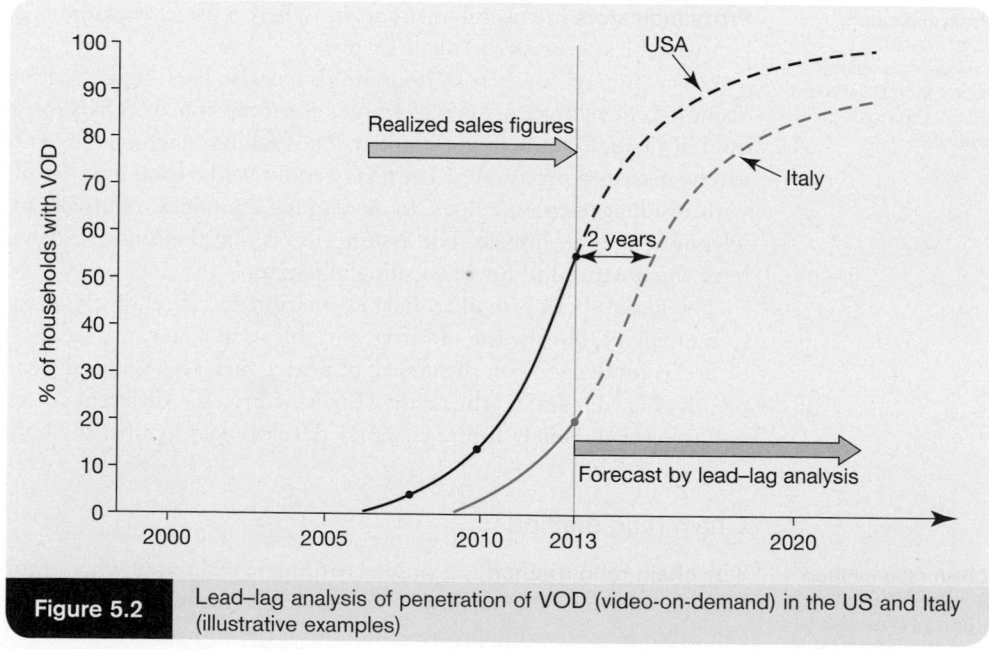

| **Figure 5.2** | Lead–lag analysis of penetration of VOD (video-on-demand) in the US and Italy (illustrative examples) |

Estimation by analogy

Estimation by analogy
A correlation value (between a factor and the demand for the product) for one market is used in another international market.

Estimation by analogy is essentially a single-factor index with a correlation value (between a factor and demand for a product) obtained in one country applied to a target international market. First a relationship (correlation) must be established between the demand to be estimated and the factor which is to serve as the basis for the analogy. Once the known relationship is established, the correlation value then attempts to draw an analogy between the known situation and the market demand in question.

Example

We want to estimate the market demand for refrigerators in Germany. We know the market size in the UK but we do not know it in Germany. As nearly all households in the two countries already have a refrigerator, a good correlation could be number of households or population size in the two countries. In this situation we choose to use population size as the basis for the analogy:

Population size in the UK = 60 million

Population size in Germany = 82 million

Furthermore we know that the number of refrigerators sold in the UK in 2002 was 1.1 million units.

By analogy we estimate the sales to be the following in Germany:

(82/60) × 1.1 million units = 1.5 million units

A note of caution

Generally caution must be used with estimation by analogy because the method assumes that factors other than the correlation factor used (in this example, population size) are similar in both countries, such as the same culture, buying power of consumers, tastes, taxes, prices, selling methods, availability of products, consumption patterns and so forth. Despite the apparent drawbacks it is still useful where international data are limited.

5.5 Primary research

Qualitative and quantitative research

Quantitative research
Data analysis based on questionnaires from a large group of respondents.

Qualitative research
Provides a holistic view of a research problem by integrating a larger number of variables, but asking only a few respondents.

If a marketer's research questions are not adequately answered by secondary research it may be necessary to search for additional information in primary data. These data can be collected by **qualitative research** and **quantitative research**. Quantitative and qualitative techniques can be distinguished by the fact that quantitative techniques involve getting data from a large, representative group of respondents.

The objective of qualitative research techniques is to give a holistic view of the research problem. Therefore these techniques must have a large number of variables and few respondents (see Figure 5.3). Choosing between quantitative and qualitative techniques is a question of trading off breadth and depth in the results of the analysis.

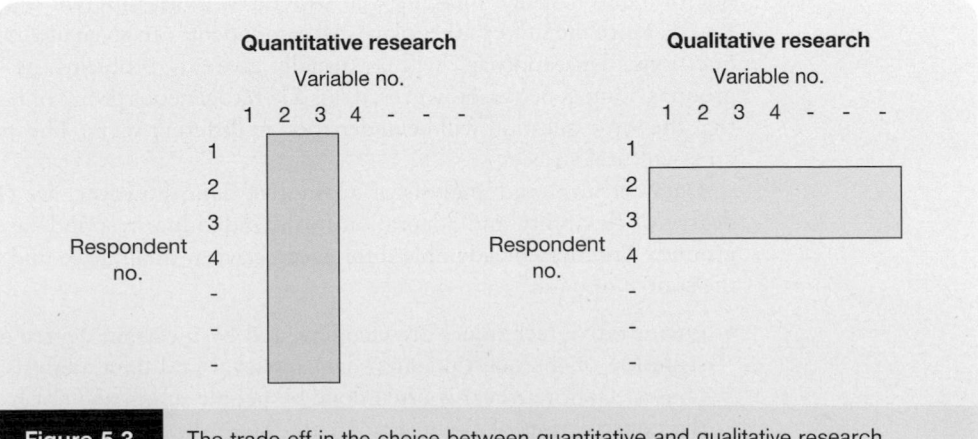

| **Figure 5.3** | The trade-off in the choice between quantitative and qualitative research |

Table 5.2	Quantitative versus qualitative research	
Comparison dimension	Quantitative research (e.g. a postal questionnaire)	Qualitative research (e.g. a focus group interview or the case method)
Objective	To quantify the data and generalize the results from the sample to the population of interest	To gain an initial and qualitative understanding of the underlying reasons and motives
Type of research	Descriptive and/or casual	Exploratory
Flexibility in research design	Low (as a result of a standardized and structured questionnaire: one-way communication)	High (as a result of the personal interview, where the interviewer can change questions during the interview: two-way communication)
Sample size	Large	Small
Choice of respondents	Representative sample of the population	People with considerable knowledge of the problem (key informants)
Information per respondent	Low	High
Data analysis	Statistical summary	Subjective, interpretative
Ability to replicate with same result	High	Low
Interviewer requirements	No special skills required	Special skills required (an understanding of the interaction between interviewer and respondent)
Time consumption during the research	*Design phase:* high (formulation of questions must be correct) *Analysis phase:* low (the answers to the questions can be coded)	*Design phase:* low (no 'exact' questions are required before the interview) *Analysis phase:* high (as a result of many 'soft' data)

Other differences between the two research methodologies are summarized in Table 5.2. Data retrieval and analysis of quantitative respondent data are based on a comparison of data between all respondents. This places heavy demands on the measuring instrument (the questionnaire), which must be well structured (with different answering categories) and tested before the survey takes place. All respondents are given identical stimuli, i.e. the same questions. This approach will not usually give any problems, as long as the respondent group is homogeneous. However, if it is a heterogeneous group of respondents, it is possible that the same question will be understood in different ways. This problem is intensified in cross-cultural surveys.

Data retrieval and analysis of qualitative data, however, are characterized by a high degree of flexibility and adaptation to the individual respondent and their special background. Another considerable difference between qualitative and quantitative surveys is the source of data:

● Quantitative techniques are characterized by a certain degree of distance, as the construction of the questionnaire, data retrieval and data analysis take place in separate phases. Data retrieval is often done by people who have not had anything to do with the construction of the questionnaire. Here the measuring instrument (the questionnaire) is the critical element in the research process.

● Qualitative techniques are characterized by proximity to the source of data, where data retrieval and analysis are done by the same person, namely, the interviewer. Data retrieval is characterized by interaction between the interviewer and the respondent, where each new question is to a certain degree dependent on the previous question. Here it is the interviewer and his or her competence (or lack thereof) which is the critical element in the research process.

Qualitative techniques imply a less sharp separation between data retrieval and analysis/interpretation, since data retrieval (e.g. the next question in a personal interview) will be dependent on the interviewer's interpretation of the previous answer. The researcher's personal experience from fieldwork (data retrieval) is generally a considerable input into the analysis phase. In the following section the two most important qualitative research methods are presented.

Triangulation: mixing qualitative and quantitative research methods

Quantitative and qualitative research methods often complement each other. Combined use of quantitative and qualitative research methods in the study of the same phenomenon is termed triangulation (Denzin, 1978; Jick, 1979). The triangulation metaphor is from navigation and military strategy, which use multiple reference points to locate an object's exact position. Similarly, market researchers can improve the accuracy and validity of their judgments by collecting both quantitative and qualitative data. Sometimes qualitative research methods explain or reinforce quantitative findings and even reveal new information.

Sometimes it is relevant to use qualitative data collected by, for example, in-depth interview of a few key informants as exploratory input to the construction of the best possible questionnaire for the collection of quantitative data. In this way, triangulation can enrich our understanding of a research question before a structured and formalized questionnaire is designed.

Research design

Figure 5.4 shows that designing research for primary data collection calls for a number of decisions regarding research approaches, contact methods, sampling plan and research instruments. The following pages will look at the various elements of Figure 5.4 in further detail.

Research problem/objectives

Companies are increasingly recognizing the need for primary international research. As the extent of a firm's international involvement increases, so does the importance and complexity of its international research. The primary research process should begin with a definition of the research problem and the establishment of specific objectives. The major difficulty here is translating the business problem into a research problem with a set of specific researchable objectives. In this initial stage, researchers often embark on the research process with only a vague grasp of the total problem. Symptoms are often mistaken for causes, and action determined by symptoms may be oriented in the wrong direction.

Research objectives may include obtaining detailed information for better penetrating the market, for designing and fine-tuning the marketing mix, or for monitoring the political climate of a country so that the firm can expand its operations successfully. The better defined the research objective is, the better the researcher will be able to determine the information requirement.

Research approaches

In Figure 5.4 three possible research approaches are indicated: observation, surveys and experiments.

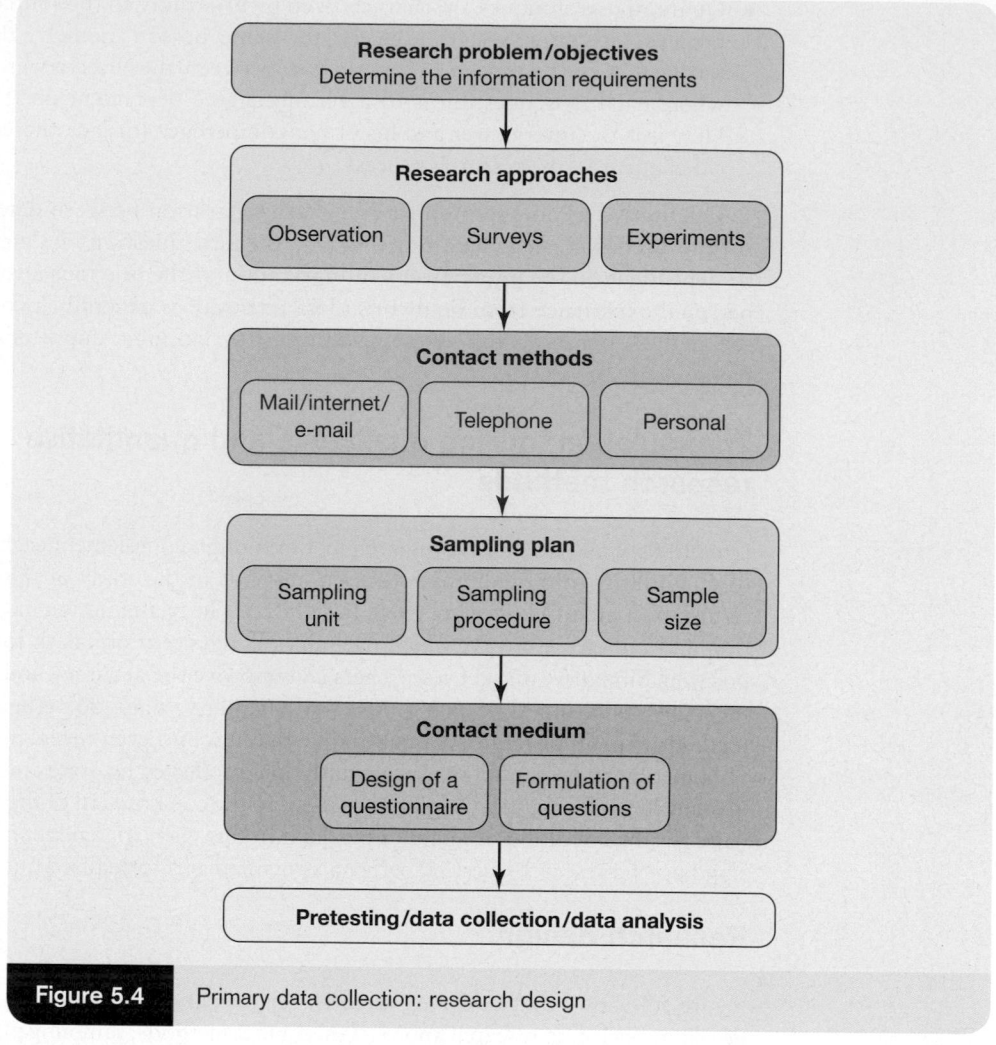

| **Figure 5.4** | Primary data collection: research design |

Observation

This approach to the generation of primary data is based on watching and sometimes recording market-related behaviour. Observational techniques are more suited to investigating what people do rather than why they do it. Here are some examples of this approach:

- Store checks: a food products manufacturer sends researchers into supermarkets to find out the prices of competing brands or how much shelf space and display support retailers give its brands. To conduct in-store research in Europe, for example, store checks, photo audits of shelves and store interviews must be scheduled well in advance and need to be preceded by a full round of introductions of the researchers to store management and personnel.
- Mechanical observations are often used to measure TV viewership.
- Cash register scanners can be used to keep track of customer purchases and inventories.

Observational research can obtain information that people are unwilling or unable to provide. In some countries, individuals may be reluctant to discuss personal habits or consumption. In such cases observation is the only way to obtain the necessary information. By contrast, some things are simply not observable, such as feelings, attitudes and motives, or private behaviour. Long-term or infrequent behaviour is also difficult to observe. Because of these limitations, researchers often use observation along with other data collection methods.

Experiments

Experiments gather casual information. They involve selecting matched groups of subjects, giving them different treatments, controlling unrelated factors and checking for differences in group responses. Thus experimental research tries to explain cause-and-effect relationships.

The most frequently used marketing research application of experiments is in test marketing. This is a research technique in which a product under study is placed on sale in one or more selected localities or areas, and its reception by consumers and the trade is observed, recorded and analysed. In order to isolate, for example, the sales effects of advertising campaigns, it is necessary to use relatively self-contained marketing areas as test markets.

Performance in these test markets gives some indication of the performance to be expected when the product goes into general distribution. However, experiments are difficult to implement in global marketing research. The researcher faces the task of designing an experiment in which most variables are held constant or are comparable across cultures. To do so represents a major challenge. For example, an experiment that intends to determine a casual effect within the distribution system of one country may be difficult to transfer to another country where the distribution system is different. As a result, experiments are used only rarely, even though their potential value to the international market researcher is recognized.

Surveys

The survey research method is based on the questioning of respondents and represents, in both volume and value terms, perhaps the most important method of collecting data. Typically the questioning is structured: a formal questionnaire is prepared and the questions are asked in a prearranged order. The questions may be asked verbally, in writing or via a computer.

Survey research is used for a variety of marketing issues, including:

- customer attitudes
- customer buying habits
- potential market size
- market trends.

Unlike experimental research, survey research is usually aimed at generating descriptive rather than casual data. Unlike observational research, survey research usually involves the respondent.

Because of the importance and diversity of survey research in global marketing, it is on this particular aspect that we now concentrate.

Contact methods

The method of contact chosen is usually a balance between speed, degree of accuracy and cost. In principle, there are four possibilities when choosing a contact method: mail surveys, internet/e-mail, telephone interviews and personal (face-to-face) interviews. Each method has its own strengths and weaknesses. Table 5.3 gives an overview of these.

Mail

Mail surveys are among the least expensive. The questionnaire can include pictures – something that is not possible over the phone. Mail surveys allow respondents to answer at their leisure, rather than at the often inconvenient moment they are contacted for a phone or personal interview. For this reason, they are not considered to be as intrusive as other kinds of interviews. However, mail surveys take longer than other kinds. You will need to wait several weeks after mailing out questionnaires before you can be sure that you have obtained most of the responses. In countries with lower educational and literacy levels, response rates to mail surveys are often too small to be useful.

Table 5.3	Strengths and weaknesses of the four contact methods			
Questions/questionnaire	Mail	Internet/e-mail	Telephone	Personal
Flexibility (ability to clarify problems)	Poor	Fair	Good	Excellent
Possibility of in-depth information (use of open-ended questions)	Fair	Poor	Fair	Excellent
Use of visual aids	Good	Excellent	Poor	Good
Possibility of a widely dispersed sample	Excellent	Excellent	Excellent	Fair
Response rates	Poor	Fair	Good	Fair
Asking sensitive questions	Good	Poor	Poor	Fair
Control of interviewer effects (no interviewer bias)	Excellent	Fair	Fair	Poor
Speed of data collection	Poor	Excellent	Excellent	Good
Costs	Good	Excellent	Excellent	Poor

Internet/e-mail surveys (online surveys)

These can collect a large amount of data that can be quantified and coded into a computer. A low research budget combined with a widely dispersed population may mean that there is no alternative to the e-mail/internet survey. E-mail surveys are both very economical and very fast. It is possible to attach pictures and sound files. However, many people dislike unsolicited e-mails even more than unsolicited regular mail.

One of the advantages of online surveys in international market research is the saving on travelling costs. Often researchers have to travel to countries in which research is conducted, especially in the case of face-to-face interviews (Adiham *et al.*, 2009). This leads to high travelling costs and increases the time needed to execute the fieldwork. In online research the respondents can be recruited and interviewed from any computer anywhere in the world. Most of the people who are connected to the internet know how to use chatrooms and speak English.

Online surveys can be conducted through e-mail or they can be posted on the web. When a wide audience is targeted, the survey can be designed as a pop-up survey, which would appear as a web-based questionnaire in a browser window while users are browsing the respective websites. Such a web-based survey is appropriate for a wide audience, where all the visitors to certain websites have an equal chance to enter the survey. However, the researcher's control over respondents entering the web-based surveys is lower than with e-mail surveys.

Telephone interviews

In some ways these are somewhere between personal and mail surveys. They generally have a response rate higher than mail questionnaires but lower than face-to-face interviews, their cost is usually less than with personal interviews, and they allow a degree of flexibility when interviewing. However, the use of visual aids is not possible and there are limits to the number of questions that can be asked before respondents either terminate the interview or give quick (invalid) answers to speed up the process. With computer-aided telephone interviewing (CATI), centrally located interviewers read questions from a computer monitor and input answers via the keyboard. Routing through the questionnaire is computer-controlled, helping the process of interviewing. Some research firms set up terminals in shopping centres, where respondents sit down at a terminal, read questions from a screen and type their answers into the computer.

Personal interviews

Personal interviews take two forms – individual and group interviewing. *Individual interviewing* involves talking with people in their homes or offices, in the street or in shopping arcades. The interviewer must gain the cooperation of the respondents. *Group interviewing* (*focus-group interviewing*) consists of inviting six to 10 people to gather for a few hours with a trained moderator to talk about a product, service or organization. The moderator needs objectivity, knowledge of the subject and industry and some understanding of group and consumer behaviour. The participants are normally paid a small sum for attending.

Personal interviewing is quite flexible and can collect large amounts of information. Trained interviewers can hold a respondent's attention for a long time and can explain difficult questions. They can guide interviews, explore issues and probe as the situation requires. Interviewers can show subjects actual products, advertisements or packages and observe reactions and behaviour.

The main drawbacks of personal interviewing are the high costs and sampling problems. Group interview studies usually employ small sample sizes to keep time and costs down, but it may be hard to generalize from the results. Because interviewers have more freedom in personal interviews, the problem of interviewer bias is greater.

Thus there is no 'best' contact method – it all depends on the situation. Sometimes it may even be appropriate to combine the methods.

Sampling plan

A scheme outlining the group (or groups) to be surveyed in a marketing research study, how many individuals are to be chosen for the survey, and on what basis this choice is made.

Sampling plan

Except in very restricted markets, it is both impractical and too expensive for a researcher to contact all the people who could have some relevance to the research problem. This total number is known statistically as the 'universe' or 'population'. In marketing terms, it comprises the total number of actual and potential users/customers of a particular product or service.

The population can also be defined in terms of elements and sampling units. Suppose that a lipstick manufacturer wants to assess consumer response to a new line of lipsticks and wants to sample females over 15 years of age. It may be possible to sample females of this age directly, in which case a sampling unit would be the same as an element. Alternatively, households might be sampled and all females over 15 in each selected household interviewed. Here the sampling unit is the household, and the element is a female over 15 years old.

What is usually done in practice is to contact a selected group of consumers/customers to be representative of the entire population. The total number of consumers who could be interviewed is known as the 'sample frame', while the number of people who are actually interviewed is known as the 'sample'.

Sampling procedure

There are several kinds of sampling procedures, with probability and non-probability sampling being the two major categories:

- *Probability sampling.* Here it is possible to specify in advance the chance that each element in the population will have of being included in a sample, although there is not necessarily an equal probability for each element. Examples are simple random sampling, systematic sampling, stratified sampling and cluster sampling (see Malhotra, 1993 for more information).
- *Non-probability sampling.* Here it is not possible to determine the above-mentioned probability or to estimate the sampling error. These procedures rely on the personal judgment of the researcher. Examples are convenience sampling, quota sampling and snowball sampling (see Malhotra, 1993 for more information).

Given the disadvantages of non-probability samples (results are not projectable to the total population, and sampling error cannot be computed) one may wonder why they are used so frequently by marketing researchers. The reasons relate to the inherent advantages of non-probability sampling:

- Non-probability samples cost less than probability samples.
- If accuracy is not critical, non-probability sampling may have considerable appeal.
- Non-probability sampling can be conducted more quickly than probability sampling.
- Non-probability sampling, if executed properly, can produce samples of the population that are reasonably representative (e.g. by use of quota sampling) (Malhotra, 1993, p. 359).

Sample size

Once we have chosen the sampling procedure, the next step is to determine the appropriate sample size. Determining the sample size is a complex decision and involves financial, statistical and managerial considerations. Other things being equal, the larger the sample, the smaller the sampling error. However, larger samples cost more money, and the resources (money and time) available for a particular research project are always limited.

In addition, the cost of larger samples tends to increase on a linear basis, whereas the level of sampling error decreases at a rate only equal to the square root of the relative increase in sample size. For example, if the sample size is quadrupled, data collection costs will be quadrupled too, but the level of sampling error will be reduced by only one-half. Among the methods for determining the sample size are:

- *Traditional statistical techniques* (assuming the standard normal distribution).
- *Budget available*. Although seemingly unscientific this is a fact of life in a business environment, based on the budgeting of financial resources. This approach forces the researcher to consider carefully the value of information in relation to its cost.
- *Rules of thumb*. The justification for a specified sample size may boil down to a 'gut feeling' that this is an appropriate sample size, or it may be a result of common practice in the particular industry.
- *Number of subgroups to be analysed*. Generally speaking the greater the number of subgroups that need to be analysed, the larger the required total sample size.

In transnational market research, sampling procedures become a rather complicated matter. Ideally a researcher wants to use the same sampling method for all countries in order to maintain consistency. Sampling desirability, however, often gives way to practicality and flexibility. Sampling procedures may have to vary across countries in order to ensure reasonable comparability of national groups. Thus the relevance of a sampling method depends on whether it will yield a sample that is representative of a target group in a certain country, and on whether comparable samples can be obtained from similar groups in different countries.

Contact medium/measurement instrument

Designing the questionnaire

A good questionnaire cannot be designed until the precise information requirements are known. It is the vehicle whereby the research objectives are translated into specific questions. The type of information sought, and the type of respondents to be researched, will have a bearing upon the contact method to be used, and this in turn will influence whether the questionnaire is relatively unstructured (with open-ended questions), aimed at depth interviewing, or relatively structured (with closed-ended questions) for 'on the street' interviews.

In cross-cultural studies, open-ended questions appear useful because they may help to identify the frame of reference of the respondents. Another issue is the choice between direct and indirect questions. Societies have different degrees of sensitivity to certain questions. Questions related to the income or age of the respondent may be accepted differently in different countries. Thus the researcher must be sure that the questions are culturally acceptable. This may mean that questions that can be asked directly in some societies will have to be asked indirectly in others.

Formulation (wording) of questions

Once the researcher has decided on specific types of questions, the next task is the actual writing of the questions. Four general guidelines are useful to bear in mind during the wording and sequencing of each question:

- *The wording must be clear*. For example, try to avoid two questions in one.
- Select words so as to avoid biasing the respondent. For example, try to avoid leading questions.
- *Consider the ability of the respondent to answer the question*. For example, asking respondents about a brand or store that they have never encountered creates a problem. Since respondents may be forgetful, time periods should be relatively short. For example: 'Did you purchase one or more cola(s) within the last week?'
- *Consider the willingness of the respondent to answer the question*. 'Embarrassing' topics that deal with things such as borrowing money, sexual activities and criminal records must be dealt with carefully. One technique is to ask the question in the third person or to state that the behaviour or attitude is not unusual prior to asking the question. For example: 'Millions of people suffer from haemorrhoids. Do you or does any member of your family suffer from this problem?' It is also a feasible solution to ask about embarrassing topics at the end of the interview.

The impact of language and culture is of particular importance when wording questions. The goal for the global marketing researcher should be to ensure that the potential for misunderstandings and misinterpretations of spoken or written words is minimized. Both language and cultural differences make this issue an extremely sensitive one in the global marketing research process.

In many countries, different languages are spoken in different areas – in Switzerland, for example, German is used in some areas and French and Italian in others – and the meaning of words often differs from country to country. For example, in the US the concept of 'family' generally refers only to the parents and children. In the southern part of Europe, the Middle East and many Latin countries it may also include grandparents, uncles, aunts and cousins.

When finally evaluating the questionnaire, the following items should be considered:

- Is a certain question necessary? The phrase 'It would be nice to know' is often heard, but each question should either serve a purpose or be omitted.
- Is the questionnaire too long?
- Will the questions achieve the survey objectives?

Pretesting

Pretesting
Conducting limited trials of a questionnaire or some other aspect of a study to determine its suitability for the planned research project. In the context of advertising, research carried out beforehand on the effectiveness of an advertisement. It begins at the earliest stages of development and continues until the advertisement is ready for use.

No matter how comfortable and experienced the researcher is in international research activities, an instrument should always be pretested. Ideally such **pretesting** is carried out with a subset of the population under study, but a pretest should at least be conducted with knowledgeable experts and/or individuals. The pretest should also be conducted in the same mode as the final interview. If the study is to be on the street or in the shopping arcade, then the pretest should be the same. Even though a pretest may mean time delays and additional cost, the risks of poor research are simply too great for this process to be omitted.

Data collection

The global marketing researcher must check that the data is gathered correctly, efficiently and at a reasonable cost. The market researcher has to establish the parameters under which the research is conducted. Without clear instructions, the interviews may be conducted in different ways by different interviewers. Therefore the interviewers have to be instructed about the nature of the study, start and completion time and sampling methodology. Sometimes a sample interview is included with detailed information on probing and quotas. Spot checks on these administration procedures are vital to ensure reasonable data quality.

Data analysis and interpretation

Once data have been collected, the final steps are the analysis and interpretation of findings in the light of the stated problem. Analysing data from cross-country studies calls for substantial creativity as well as scepticism. Not only are data often limited, but frequently results are significantly influenced by cultural differences. This suggests that there is a need for properly trained local personnel to function as supervisors and interviewers; alternatively, international market researchers require substantial advice from knowledgeable local research firms that can also take care of the actual collection of data. Although data in cross-country analyses are often of a qualitative nature, the researcher should, of course, use the best and most appropriate tools available for analysis. On the other hand, international researchers should be cautioned against using overly sophisticated tools for unsophisticated data. Even the best of tools will not improve data quality. The quality of data must be matched by the quality of the research tools.

Problems with using primary research

Most problems in collecting primary data in international marketing research stem from cultural differences among countries, and range from the inability of respondents to communicate their opinions to inadequacies in questionnaire translation (Cateora *et al.*, 2000).

Sampling in field surveys

The greatest problem of sampling stems from the lack of adequate demographic data and available lists from which to draw meaningful samples. For example, in many South American and Asian cities, street maps are unavailable, streets are not identified and houses are not numbered. In Saudi Arabia, the difficulties with probability sampling are so acute that non-probabilistic sampling becomes a necessary evil. Some of the problems in drawing a random sample include:

- no officially recognized census of population;
- incomplete and out-of-date telephone directories;
- no accurate maps of population centres, and therefore no area samples can be made.

Furthermore, door-to-door interviewing in Saudi Arabia is illegal.

Non-response

Non-response is the inability to reach selected elements in the sample frame. As a result, opinions of some sample elements are not obtained or properly represented. A good sampling method can only identify elements that should be selected; there is no guarantee that such elements will ever be included.

The two main reasons for non-response errors are:

1. *Not being at home.* In countries where males are still dominant in the labour force, it may be difficult to contact a head of household at home during working hours. Frequently only housewives or servants are at home during the day.
2. *Refusal to respond.* Cultural habits in many countries virtually prohibit communication with a stranger, particularly among women. This is the case in the Middle East, much of the Mediterranean area and throughout most of South-east Asia – in fact, wherever strong traditional societies persist. Moreover, in many societies such matters as preferences for hygienic products and food products are too personal to be shared with an outsider. For example, in many Latin American countries a woman may feel ashamed to talk with a researcher about her choice of brand of sanitary towel, or even hair shampoo or perfume. Respondents may also suspect that the interviewers are agents of the government, seeking information for the imposition of additional taxes. Finally, privacy is becoming a big issue in many countries: for example, in Japan the middle class is showing increasing concern about the protection of personal information.

Language barriers

This problem area includes the difficulty of exact translation, which creates problems in eliciting the specific information desired and in interpreting the respondents' answers.

In some developing countries with low literacy rates, written questionnaires are completely useless. Within some countries the problem of dialects and different languages can make a national questionnaire survey impractical – this is the case in India, which has 25 official languages.

The obvious solution of having questionnaires prepared or reviewed by someone fluent in the language of the country is frequently overlooked. In order to find possible translation errors, marketers can use the technique of *back translation*, where the questionnaire is translated from one language to another, and then back again into the original language. For example, if a questionnaire survey is going to be carried out in France, the English version is translated into French and then translated back to English by a different translator. The two English versions are then compared and, where there are differences, the translation is checked thoroughly.

Measurement

The best research design is useless without proper measurements. A measurement method that works satisfactorily in one culture may fail to achieve the intended purpose in another country. Special care must therefore be taken to ensure the **reliability** and **validity** of the measurement method.

In general, 'how' you measure refers to reliability, and 'what' you measure refers to validity.

If we measure the same phenomenon over and over again with the same measurement device and we get similar results then the method is reliable. There are three types of validity:

- *Construct validity* establishes correct operational measures for the concepts being studied. If a measurement method lacks construct validity it is not measuring what it is supposed to.
- *Internal validity* establishes a causal relationship, whereby certain conditions are shown to lead to other conditions.
- *External validity* is concerned with the possible generalization of research results to other populations. For example, high external validity exists if research results obtained for a marketing problem in one country will be applicable to a similar marketing problem in another country. If such a relationship exists, it may be relevant to use the analogy method for estimating market demand in different countries. Estimating by analogy assumes, for example, that the demand for a product develops in much the same way in countries that are similar.

The concepts of reliability and validity are illustrated in Figure 5.5. In the figure, the bull's eye is what the measurement device is supposed to 'hit'. *Situation 1* shows holes all over the target, which could be due to the use of a bad measurement device. If a measurement instrument is not reliable, there are no circumstances under which it can be valid. However, just because an instrument is reliable it does not mean it is automatically valid. We see this in *situation 2*, where the instrument is reliable but is not measuring what it is supposed to measure. The shooter has a steady eye, but the sights are not adjusted properly. *Situation 3* is the ideal situation for the researcher to be in. The measurement method is both reliable and valid.

An instrument proven to be reliable and valid in one country may not be so in another. The same measurement scales may have different reliabilities in different cultures because of various levels of consumers' product knowledge. Therefore it may be dangerous simply to compare results in cross-country research. One way to minimize the problem is to adapt measurement scales to local cultures by pretesting measures in each market of interest until they show similar and satisfactory levels of reliability.

Reliability

If the same phenomenon is measured repeatedly with the same measurement device and the results are similar then the method is reliable (the 'how' dimension).

Validity

If the measurement method measures what it is supposed to measure, then it has high validity (the 'what' dimension). There are three types of validity: construct, internal and external.

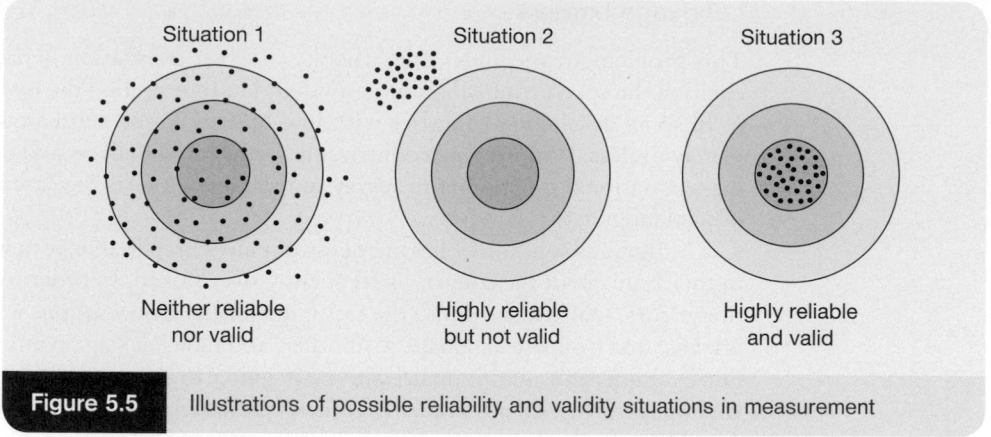

Figure 5.5   Illustrations of possible reliability and validity situations in measurement

Source: McDaniel and Gates (2007, p. 321).

However, as different methods may have varying reliabilities in different countries, it is essential that these differences can be taken into account in the design of a multicultural survey. Thus, a mail survey could be most appropriate to use in country A and personal interviews in country B. In collecting data from different countries, it is more important to use techniques with equivalent levels of reliability than to use the same techniques across countries.

5.6   Other types of marketing research

A distinction is made between ad hoc and continuous research.

Ad hoc research

An ad hoc study focuses on a specific marketing problem and collects data at one point in time from one sample of respondents. Examples of ad hoc studies are usage and attitude surveys, and product and concept tests via custom-designed or multi-client studies. More general marketing problems (e.g. total market estimates for product groups) may be examined by using Delphi studies (see below).

Custom-designed studies

These are based on the specific needs of the client. The research design is based on the research brief given to the marketing research agency or internal marketing researcher. Because they are tailor-made, such surveys can be expensive.

Multi-client studies

These are a relatively low-cost way for a company to answer specific questions without embarking on its own primary research. There are two types of multi-client study:

1. *Independent research studies.* These are carried out totally independently by research companies (e.g. Frost and Sullivan Inc.) and then offered for sale.
2. *Omnibus studies.* Here a research agency will target specified segments in a particular foreign market and companies will buy questions in the survey. Consequently interviews (usually face-to-face or by telephone) may cover many topics. Clients will then

Omnibus studies
A regular survey usually operated by a market research specialist company which asks questions of respondents.

receive an analysis of the questions purchased. For **omnibus studies** to be of use, the researcher must have clearly defined research needs and a corresponding target segment in order to obtain meaningful information.

Delphi studies

This type of research approach clearly aims at qualitative rather than quantitative measures by aggregating the information of a group of experts. It seeks to obtain answers from those who possess particular in-depth expertise instead of seeking the average responses of many with only limited knowledge.

The area of concern may be future developments in the international trading environment or long-term forecasts for market penetration of new products. Typically 10–30 key informants are selected and asked to identify the major issues in the area of concern. They are also requested to rank their statements according to importance and explain the rationale behind the ranking. Next the aggregated information is returned to all participants, who are encouraged to state clearly their agreements or disagreements with the various rank orders and comments. Statements can be challenged and then, in another round, participants can respond to the challenges. After several rounds of challenge and response, a reasonably coherent consensus is developed.

One drawback of the technique is that it requires several steps, and therefore months may elapse before the information is obtained. However, the emergence of e-mail may accelerate the process. If done properly the Delphi method can provide insightful forecast data for the international information system of the firm.

Continuous research (longitudinal designs)

A longitudinal design differs from ad hoc research in that the sample or panel remains the same over time. In this way a longitudinal study provides a series of pictures that give an in-depth view of developments taking place. The panel consists of a sample of respondents who have agreed to provide information at specified intervals over an extended period.

There are two major types of panel:

1. *Consumer panels*. These provide information on their purchases over time. For example, a grocery panel would record the brands, pack sizes, prices and stores used for a wide range of supermarket brands. By using the same households over a period of time, measures of brand loyalty and switching can be achieved, together with a demographic profile of the type of person or household who buys particular brands.
2. *Retailer panels*. By gaining the cooperation of retail outlets (e.g. supermarkets), sales of brands can be measured by laser scanning the barcodes on goods as they pass through the checkout. Although brand loyalty and switching cannot be measured in this way, retail audits can provide accurate assessments of sales achieved by store. The A.C. Nielsen Company is a major provider of retail data.

Sales forecasting

A company can forecast its sales either by forecasting the market sales (called *market forecasting*) and then determining what share of this will accrue to the company or by forecasting the company's sales directly. Techniques for doing this are dealt with later in this chapter. The point is that planners are only interested in forecasts when the forecast comes down to individual products in the company.

We will now examine the applicability and usefulness of the short-, medium- and long-term forecasts in so far as company planners are concerned, and then look at each from individual company departmental viewpoints:

- *Short-term forecasts*. These are usually for periods up to three months ahead, and as such are really of use for tactical matters such as production planning. The general trend of sales is less important here than short-term fluctuations.
- *Medium-term forecasts*. These have direct implications for planners. They are of most importance in the area of business budgeting, the starting point for which is the sales forecast. Thus if the sales forecast is incorrect, the entire budget is incorrect. If the forecast is over-optimistic then the company will have unsold stocks, which must be financed out of working capital. If the forecast is pessimistic then the firm may miss out on marketing opportunities because it is not geared up to produce the extra goods required by the market. More to the point, when forecasting is left to accountants they will tend to err on the conservative side and will produce a forecast that is lower than actual sales, the implications of which have just been described. This serves to re-emphasize the point that sales forecasting is the responsibility of the sales manager. Such medium-term forecasts are normally for one year ahead.
- *Long-term forecasts*. These are usually for periods of three years or more depending on the type of industry being considered. In industries such as computers, three years is considered long term, whereas for steel manufacture 10 years is a long-term horizon. Long-term forecasts are worked out from macroenvironmental factors such as government policy and economic trends. Such forecasts are needed mainly by financial accountants for long-term resource implications, but such matters are, of course, boards of directors' concerns. The board must decide what its policy is to be in establishing the levels of production needed to meet the forecast demand; such decisions might mean the construction of a new factory and the training of a workforce. Forecasts can be produced for different horizons, starting at an international level and then ranging down to national levels, by industry and then by company levels until we reach individual product-by-product forecasts. This is then broken down seasonally over the time span of the forecasting period, and geographically right down to individual salesperson areas. It is these latter levels that are of specific interest to sales management, or it is from this level of forecasting that the sales budgeting and remuneration system stems.

Figure 5.6 shows an example of trend forecasting. The unit sales and trend are drawn in as in the figure. The trend line is extended by sight (and it is here that the forecaster's skill and intuition must come in). The deviations from trend are then applied to the trend line, and this provides the sales forecast.

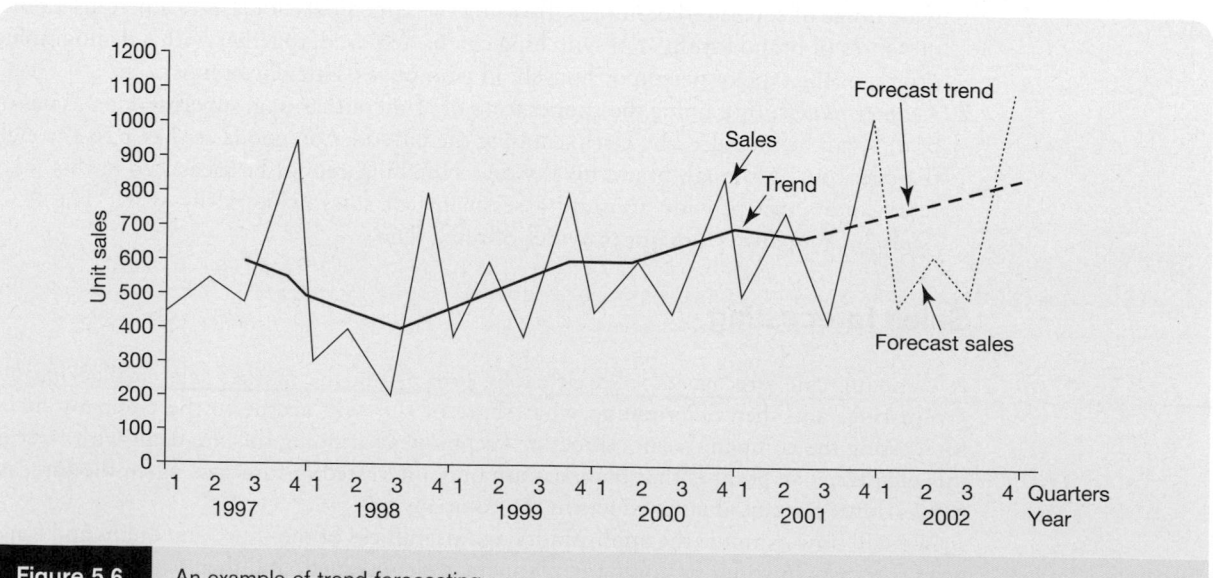

Figure 5.6   An example of trend forecasting

In this particular example, it can be seen that the trend line has been extended slowly upwards, similar to previous years. The technique, as with many similar techniques, suffers from the fact that downturns and upturns cannot be predicted, and such data must be subjectively entered by the forecaster through manipulation of the extension to the trend line.

Scenario planning

Scenarios are stories about plausible alternative futures (Wright, 2005). They differ from forecasts in that they explore possible futures rather than predict a single point future. Figure 5.7 shows two different scenarios – A and B – where the outcome – measured on two dimensions – is influenced by both **convergent** and **divergent forces**.

Figure 5.7 shows that the diverging and converging factors have to be balanced. Time flows from the left to the right and the courses of the scenarios pass through a number of time windows, each made up of the key dimensions the scenario writers want to highlight. In Figure 5.7, two 'time windows' are shown: one in two years from now and another one in five years from now. The two dimensions could be, for example, 'worldwide market share' and 'worldwide market growth' for one of the company's main products. The 'convergent forces' would mean that scenarios A and B would come nearer to each other over time. The 'divergent forces' would have the opposite effect.

Examples of *convergent* forces are:

- a high degree of macroeconomic stability in key international markets;
- increasing standardization of products across borders.

An example of a *divergent* force is cultural diversity among target markets.

Scenario planning allows us to consider a range of alternative futures, each of which is dramatically different from the other and from the current operating environment. Rather than rely on a single 'most likely' forecast, it is possible to compare and contrast alternative opinions on how your industry may evolve.

Because it is externally oriented, scenario planning is very effective at identifying growth strategies for the company as well as potential threats to its market position. Scenarios can also help to identify the specific external industry changes that are causing falling market share or margins.

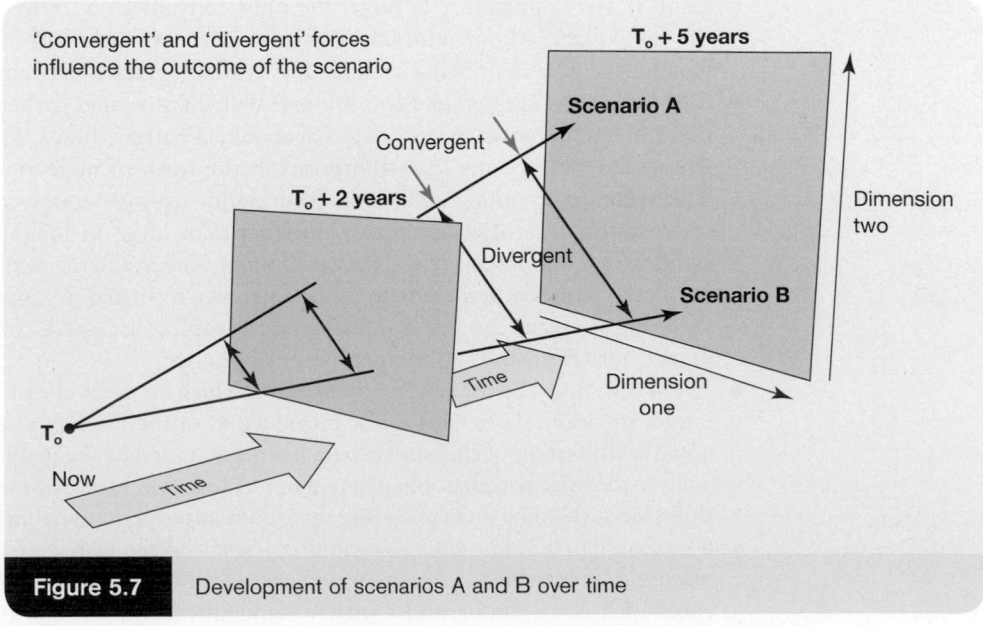

Figure 5.7   Development of scenarios A and B over time

Guidelines for scenario planning

- *Establish a core planning team.* Analysing the strategic implications of scenarios is best done in teams. The creative dynamics of an effective group are likely to provide the types of breakthrough that will make the scenario process worthwhile. What seems obvious to one person will be surprising to another. A good rule of thumb is to have five to eight people in the planning group.
- *Get a cross-section of expertise.* Include the heads of all functional areas – sales, marketing, operations, purchasing, information technology, personnel, etc. We also recommend including individuals beyond the top executives. This injects new perspectives on your company or your line of trade. This is a great time to involve the rising stars and innovative thinkers in the organization.
- *Include outside information and outside people.* Focus on injecting interesting and challenging perspectives into the discussion. In a group composed solely of insiders, it will be hard to achieve breakthrough insights. Outsiders may be customers, suppliers or consultants. If possible, involve an executive from another line of trade or even from outside wholesale distribution. However, many executives feel uncomfortable letting outsiders participate in the planning process of their companies.

5.7 Marketing research based on Web 2.0

Today, maybe 80 per cent of international marketers' needs for international marketing data are addressed by conducting a market-research project. In future the leading edge multinational enterprises (MNEs) – probably led by consumer packaged goods and technologically driven companies – will look for answers to 80 per cent of their marketing issues by 'catching' already available data.

Some of the data sources and tools available through the Web 2.0 will include the following (Micu et al., 2011):

- *Mobile data.* One of the biggest opportunities for marketers is the opportunity to collect real-time geographic information about consumers and to geo-target consumers. GPS-enabled smartphones penetrating worldwide markets at an exponential rate coupled with an ongoing increase in cellular bandwidth and data processing speed will result in the opportunity to target the right consumer not only at the right time but at the right place. Major information firms such as Google and innovative start-ups are leading the way in utilizing such readily available data sources in real time.
- *User-generated content and text mining.* Web 2.0 provides gathering places for internet users in social-network sites (e.g. Facebook, Twitter), blogs, forums and chatrooms. These assembly points leave footprints in the form of huge amounts of textual data. The difficulty in obtaining insights from online user-generated content is that consumers' postings are often extremely unstructured, large in magnitude and not easy to syndicate. Commercial (e.g. Nielsen Online) and academic text-mining tools provide marketers and researchers with an opportunity to 'listen' to consumers in the market. By doing so, firms can better understand the topics discussed, consumers' opinions, the market structure and the competitive environment.
- *Web browsing.* The use of clickstream data, which contains click-by-click web page-viewing information, dates back to the introduction of the Internet to the mass market. Until now the utilization of clickstream data has been limited by the inability to collect, store and analyse the huge data sets, often in real time. However, now firms use cross-organizational skills for developing and converting these data into international market insights.
- *Social networks and online communities.* Some of the fastest growing sources of information flow are the social-networking sites of which the most visible and powerful presences include Facebook and Twitter. Somehow consumers are turning from searching

for information at news websites and search engines back to the traditional approaches of asking their friends their advice. Of course, the networking element means that they have a much wider circle of 'friends', which can also be used for more formal but 'quick-and-dirty' questionnaire surveys. Although social-networking sites have become ubiquitous, the full international marketing utilization of these sites is still untapped. The integration of social networking sites with other sources of information such as online retailers and media sources will amplify the opportunities to derive actionable marketing insights from online word-of-mouth content. Furthermore, by observing consumers' social-networking habits and purchase behaviour, researchers can leverage the social relationship information to identify and target opinion leaders. Furthermore, with the emergence of Web 2.0, many consumer goods companies such as Nike, Harley-Davidson and Procter & Gamble have started to build their own brand communities. Brand communities open an opportunity for firms not only to enhance the interactions among consumers but to fully observe these interactions. Furthermore, brand communities open a direct of communication channel between the firm and its customer. As consumers move toward obtaining much of the information from other consumers, brand communities are likely to become a major component of the information flow.

- *Customer decision-making data.* Increasingly firms are interested not only in understanding the outcome of (or exposure to) the marketing effort but in understanding the *entire process* customers go though in arriving at a decision. This interest has been sparked by several technological advances in areas such as radio frequency identification (RFID), video-recognition tools and eye tracking. RFID technology allows researchers to track consumers in the retail environment, a capability to track items with the goal of improving the efficiency of supply-chain systems. Marketers can get the full picture of what is happening in the store and enable tracing consumers and product flow. The difficulty with converting these extremely valuable data into international marketing insights lies in the magnitude of data and the complexity of analysis.

- *Consumer usage data.* More and more products now are being embedded with sensors and wireless devices that can allow marketers to track consumers geographically and over time. For example, sensors on cars and consumer packaged goods can open new windows into their usage and consumption in addition to the purchase of products.

- *Neuromarketing.* Neuromarketing, referring to the use of neuroscience for marketing applications, potentially offers the ability to observe directly what consumers are thinking. Neuromarketing is often used to study brain activity in response to exposure to brands, product designs or advertising. Neuromarketing is a relatively new tool for marketers, mainly owing to technological barriers, difficulty in transforming the neuroscience results into actionable business insights, and the high costs of collecting the data. We expect, however, that the next decade will see improvement on all of these fronts, making neuromarketing a common component of the customer insights tool kit.

EXHIBIT 5.1 Amazon.com – sustaining a competitive advantage through market research and analytics

'Analytics' can be thought of as data (including market research data) and the algorithms that extract useful information from that data. Amazon is an example of a company that has sustained an advantage from its analytics by using analytics in its internal processes and is now offering and selling their algorithm services to other companies, e.g. through Amazon Web Services (AWS).

The fact that Amazon founder and CEO Jeff Bezos was educated as an engineer may explain why Amazon today is a leading data-driven company using a factual, experimental approach to constant innovation. Analytics at Amazon has clearly enjoyed exceptional CEO support. Moreover, Bezos invented the Amazon business model from scratch. His strategy was one of constant innovation supported through experimentation, data collection and analytics. While Amazon's storeyed warehouses and supplier list garner many headlines, Amazon's analytics algorithms and capabilities are arguably its most important strategic asset.

For example, AWS offers a collection of algorithms called Amazon Mobile Analytics, which is sold to developers of apps (typically SMEs) who can then measure app usage, app revenue, user retention, etc. The app developer can then make data-driven decisions to increase engagement and monetization for the app.

Source: based on Bell (2015).

5.8 Setting up an international marketing information system (MIS)

Once research has been conducted and the data collected and analysed, the next step is to incorporate this information into management decision-making. More and more businesses are now concerned with increasing the productivity of their marketing efforts, especially in their marketing research departments.

A massive amount of data is available from a wide variety of sources. The trick is to transform that data, ranging from statistics and facts to opinions and predictions, into information that is useful to the organization's marketing decision-makers. The importance of a timely and comprehensive information system is becoming more evident with the increased need to develop closer customer relationships, the increasing costs of making wrong marketing decisions, the greater complexity of the marketplace and the elevated level of competitor aggressiveness. The need for current and relevant knowledge may result in the development and implementation of information systems that incorporate data management procedures involving generating new data or gathering existing data, storing and retrieving data, processing data into useful information and disseminating information to those individuals who need it. The **international marketing information system** is an interacting organization of people, systems and processes devised to create a regular, continuous and orderly flow of information essential to the marketer's problem-solving and decision-making activities. As a planned, sequential flow of information tailored to the needs of a particular marketing manager, the international MIS can be conceptualized as a four-stage process consisting of locating, gathering, processing and utilizing information. Figure 5.8 illustrates the central issues to be addressed in each of the four international MIS-stages.

In this holistic international MIS model, input data flow into the system from three major sources: the microenvironment, the macroenvironment and functional areas of the firm. The output information will then be made available to management for analysis, planning, implementation and control purposes. The proposed model meets the exigencies of the ever-expanding role of the MIS professional that has to provide timely, accurate and objective information for management to be able to navigate its way through the complex and fast-changing world of business globalization. Against the backdrop of a dynamic business environment, companies are increasingly developing their MISs to provide managers with real-time market information. Likewise, they are expanding from local to national to global operations while consumers are becoming ever more selective in their product choices.

International marketing information system
An interacting organization of people, systems and processes devised to create a regular, continuous flow in information essential to the international marketer's problem-solving and decision-making activities around the world.

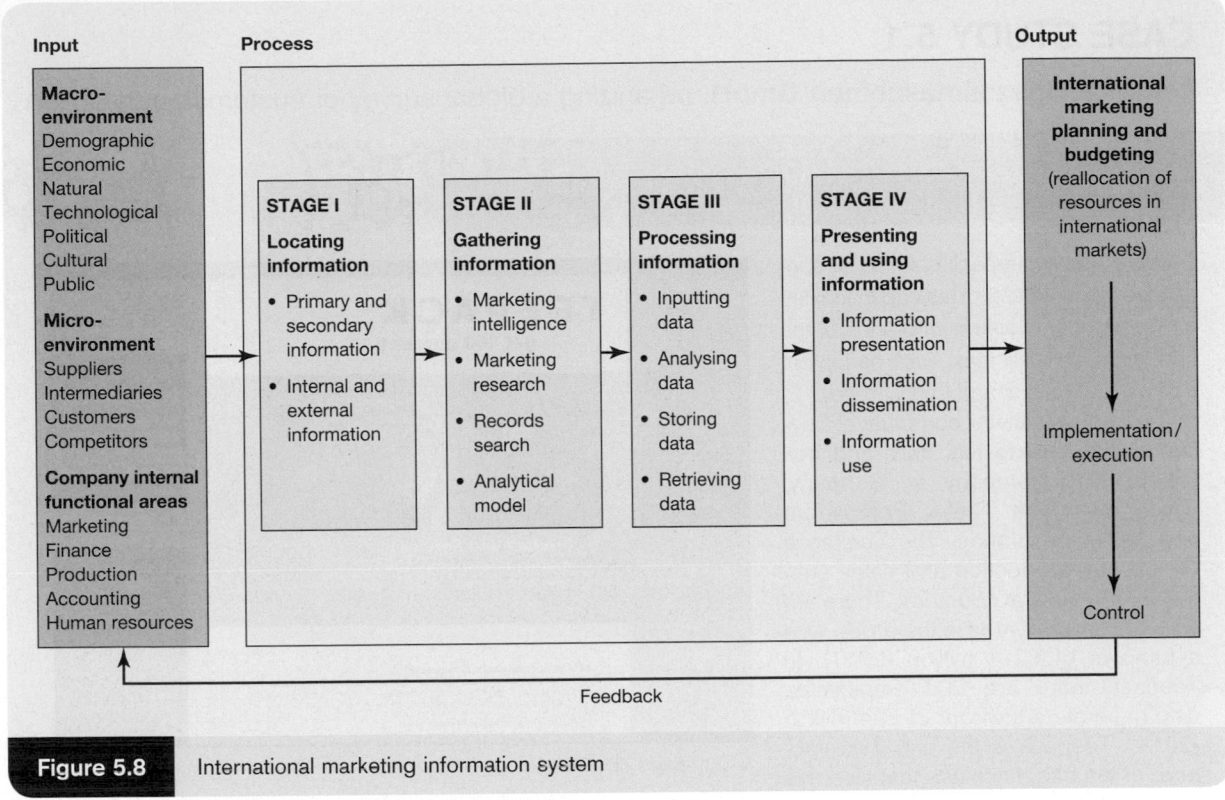

Figure 5.8 International marketing information system

Source: Marketing Research: An International Approach, FT/Prentice Hall (Schmidt, M.I. and Hollensen, S. 2006) p. 587, Copyright © Pearson Education Limited.

5.9 Summary

The basic objective of the global marketing research function is to provide management with relevant information for more accurate decision-making. The objective is the same for both domestic and global marketing. However, global marketing is more complex because of the difficulty of gathering information about multiple and different foreign environments.

In this chapter, special attention has been given to the information collection process and the use of marketing information. This coverage is far from being exhaustive, and the reader should consult marketing research textbooks for specific details related to particular research topics.

An international marketer should initiate research by searching first for any relevant secondary data. Typically a great deal of information is already available, and the researcher needs to know how to identify and locate the international sources of secondary data.

If it is necessary to gather primary data, the international marketer should be aware that it is simply not possible to replicate the methodology used in one country elsewhere. Some adaptation of the research method to different countries is usually necessary.

The firm should set up a decision support system or an international MIS to handle the gathered information efficiently. This system should integrate all information inputs, both internal and external. In addition, an international MIS can support managers in their marketing decision-making by providing interlinkage and integration between functional departments or international divisions. However, in the final analysis, every international marketer should keep in mind that an information system is no substitute for sound judgment.

The Web 2.0 age provides the international marketer with a lot of opportunities to utilize the new online technologies to obtain relevant cross-border customer information and make better international marketing decisions.

CASE STUDY 5.1

Teepack Spezialmaschinen GmbH: organizing a global survey of customer satisfaction

Teepack (www.teepack.com) is a specialized manufacturer of tea bag machines for the world's best-known brands of tea and herbs and fruit teas, such as Lipton, Pickwick, Twinings and Lyons/Tetley.

Teepack is a sister company of Teekanne, the leading tea, herb and fruit tea packing company in Germany, which owns the Teefix, Pompadour and Teekanne brands. The Teekanne Group has production and sales subsidiaries in several countries. There are about 700 employees in the group with a turnover of €211 million (2011). In Teepack there are 200 employees, who generate a turnover of €34 million (2011). Teepack is the only manufacturer of tea bag machines that also has an ownership relation to a major tea bag brand manufacturer (Teekanne).

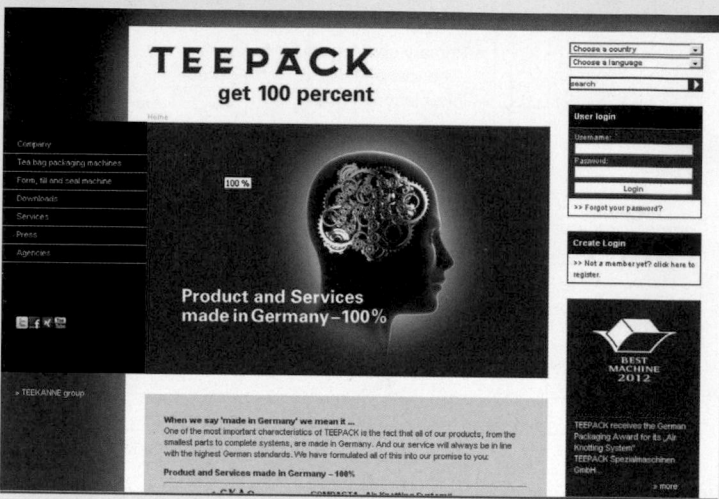

Source: Teepack Spezialmaschinen GmbH & Co. KG.

The invention of the automatic tea bag-packaging machine by Teepack in 1949 revolutionized the tea market with the double-chamber tea bag. It meant that production volumes could be increased dramatically. Today, the latest generation of these machines is capable of production speeds of almost 400 tea bags per minute, i.e. some 4 billion a year.

The tea bag produced by Teepack machines has the highest sales of any double-chamber tea bag in the world. Important benefits are that it has considerably larger space between the two bag chambers and offers maximum tea bag stability and durability without adding glue or heat-sealing.

The popularity of this practical tea bag has continued to grow. For example, in Germany, 82 per cent of tea sales are in double-chamber tea bags; in the UK, the figure is about 90 per cent and in Europe, if you omit the UK, the figure is close to 100 per cent. Even in the former UK colony, Australia, the double-chamber tea bag has almost convinced consumers. 'Down under', sales of UK tea bags and the double-chamber tea bag are more or less equal.

Since 1950, Teepack GmbH has been the number one producer of double-chamber tea bag-packaging machines in the world and has sold more than 2,000 of its 'Constanta' machine. Thanks to Teepack's packaging machines, Lipton is the leader of the international tea market. By 1957, Teepack had sold more than 100 tea bag-packaging machines in the US.

Technical innovation resulted in Teepack engineers developing a new, even more efficient machine – the 'Perfecta'. Since 1990, more than 200 Perfecta machines have been sold worldwide.

In 2011, Teepack had a market share of about 70 per cent of the global double-chamber tea bag machine market. Their product range includes more than 200 machines.

QUESTIONS

Please visit www.teepack.com before you answer the following questions:

1. How would you forecast worldwide demand for tea bag machines?

2. How can Teepack and Teekanne use their relationship to each other with regard to collecting relevant market research data for both companies?

3. Argue the case for the market analysis method you would choose if you had to evaluate the competitiveness of Teepack Spezialmaschinen on the global tea bag-packaging machine market.

4. In order to achieve better customer feedback, the top management of Teepack is interested in learning how to measure customer satisfaction. Propose a questionnaire design that contains some of the themes it would be relevant to include in the questionnaire.

Sources: based on www.teepack.com.

CASE STUDY 5.2

LEGO Friends: one of the world's largest toy manufacturers moves into the girls' domain

LEGO (www.lego.com) is the second largest toymaker globally after Mattel, with total revenues in 2014 of DKK 28.6 billion (€3.8 billion) and DKK 7.0 billion (€0.9 billion) in net profit. Its main category presence is in construction toys, where LEGO holds the leading company share in the vast majority of countries.

While the majority of LEGO products fall within the construction toy category, the company maintains a diverse product portfolio, with a mix of licensed and non-licensed properties, and different toys. LEGO continues to experiment with the brick toys concept. The product range is designed to appeal to all age groups. LEGO maintains a strong relationship with licence owners such as Disney and LucasArts, and uses many licences on its products.

In general, the majority of toy production is outsourced to China. However, LEGO has retained a large part of production capabilities in-house rather than outsourcing to the Far East, focusing on product quality and innovation rather than price. This strategy has paid off, with customers proving that they are willing to pay a price premium as long as the product quality is perceived as high.

Many traditional toy makers are having a tough time as competition intensifies from digital games. Aging populations in Europe present another big challenge, shrinking the market for toys. But LEGO, owned by Denmark's richest family, is expecting continued sales growth in the coming years. Demand for its Lego City and LEGO Star Wars product lines continues.

In 2014, LEGO's sales were lifted substantially by the success of 'The Lego Movie'. Not only did LEGO make a specific line of toys based on the movie – there was a 'halo effect' from the media attention, which helped sales.

Part of LEGO's long-term strategy is to turn east and cash in on the growth of the Asian toy market. LEGO's sales in China rose 50 per cent year-to-year, after a similar expansion in 2013. In April 2014, LEGO laid the foundations for its first Chinese factory, due to

Source: Teepack Spezialmaschinen GmbH & Co. KG.

start manufacturing in 2015 and reach full-scale production in 2017.

LEGO is entering the girls' segment with LEGO Friends (http://friends.lego.com)

The main target of LEGO products is the 5–12 year-old age group, but LEGO has a diversified range of products and licences to keep its brand appeal high across various age groups. For example, as part of its Duplo range, LEGO has The Winnie the Pooh licence from Disney that is tailored to the pre-school age range. As children grow older, other licences become more popular. LEGO has Pirates of the Caribbean, for example, which is especially popular among 5–12 year-olds. For older age groups, Lego offers the Technic range, among others, aimed more at 12–16 year-olds.

LEGO products do not have a firm gender distinction in the same way as dolls or action figures, but its main product lines appeal mostly to boys. Until the launch of LEGO Friends, 90 per cent of

Source: © The LEGO Group.

LEGO's end-customers were boys and only 10 per cent girls. This was the main trigger for the LEGO management's decision to launch LEGO Friends, which was designed to appeal primarily to girls.

Introduced in January 2012, the theme includes unique 'mini-doll' figures, which are about the same size as the traditional minifigures but are more detailed and realistic. The sets include pieces in pink and purple colour schemes and depict scenes from suburban life set in the fictional town of Heartlake City.

The Friends product range replaces LEGO's previous female-oriented theme, LEGO Belville, which had been in production since 1994. Other related LEGO product ranges for girls have included Homemaker (1971–1982), Paradisa (1991–1997) and Scala (1997–2001).

The LEGO Friends story centres on the everyday lives and personalities of five girls in a fictional hometown called Heartlake City. Each of the friends has a distinct personality and interests, such as animals, performing arts, invention and design, that are reflected in the models. Building sets reflect different parts of town where the girls' adventures take place – downtown, the suburbs, the beach, camping grounds and mountains.

The launch of LEGO Friends generated some controversy, with critics claiming that the new product line panders to gender stereotypes.

LEGO has also released accompanying products branded under the Friends name. In June 2012, a book was released based on the Friends theme: *Lego Friends: Welcome to Heartlake City*. Here, girls can meet the LEGO Friends as they hang out at all the hotspots, such as the tree house, beauty parlour, idyllic whispering woods and their favourite café.

In terms of sales, LEGO Friends has done surprisingly well since the launch. The LEGO Group sold twice as many LEGO Friends as expected in the first six months. As a result, LEGO increased production to meet the demand for LEGO Friends in the important pre-Christmas period.

The themes of LEGO Friends change over time:

● The first winter wave of sets released in 2012 followed the adventures of the girls in a suburban setting, the summer wave also focused on a more rural setting with Emma and Stephanie going to a horse-back riding camp outside of Heartlake City and Olivia taking a camping trip. The 2013 winter wave went back to the suburban setting and added two water-themed sets, which go outside Heartlake City to the beach and ocean. The summer 2013 wave added a high school and other suburban-themed sets, while expanding the characters' interests to include soccer and music; a large yacht rounded out the sets.

Source: © The LEGO Group.

- The winter 2014 wave saw several farm and agriculture-themed sets, including a farmers' market, a horse barn and a set where one of the characters nursed a newborn lamb. A beachside house was also added. The summer of 2014 saw several animal rescue and nursing sets, playing off the polybag sets featuring animals such as baby bear and tiger cubs, birds and other wildlife; each of these sets are set in a jungle. A camping caravan set and a large shopping mall – the largest Friends set yet – went on sale to round out the suburbia theme.
- Several of the winter 2014–15 sets were new versions of sets issued during the original wave, the most notable examples being a new veterinary clinic and hair salon; also, Emma's House replaced Olivia's House (the last original set still in release in late 2014). All-new sets included a hot-air balloon, a beachfront lighthouse and a pizzeria stand; the summer of 2015 brought a private jet, airport, tourist kiosk, a small grocery market, skateboard park and a hotel.
- The summer of 2015 brought a new subtheme: 'Pop Star' sets, centred on the life of Livi, a pop music recording artist who apparently lives in Heartlake City and is friends with the main 'Friends' gang. Sets in the initial wave represented a recording studio, a backstage dressing room, a performance stage and a tour bus. Planned for January 2016 was a mansion where Livi lives, along with a television studio.

QUESTIONS

1. Emerging markets like China, India and Indonesia offer long-term opportunities for organic growth. However, LEGO still has a small share in developing economies. What kind of market data would you collect in order to increase market shares in the three countries?

2. Was it a good idea to launch LEGO Friends? Why/why not?

3. LEGO Friends has been introduced as a supplement to the current product range. How would you recommend that LEGO management measure the degree of market success for LEGO Friends?

Sources: based on www.lego.com; friends.lego.com; www.euromonitor.com; other public available data.

VIDEO CASE STUDY 5.3 BMW i3 – the electric car
download from **www.pearsoned.co.uk/hollensen**

High levels of air pollution and carbon emissions, as well as a perceived energy shortage, are all cited as reasons why electric vehicles will surely become a major factor in the global auto industry going forward. The flip side of that coin is that high costs, short driving ranges, long charging times, lack of charging facilities and battery maintenance issues are major obstacles faced by all electric vehicle manufacturers.

So far, the negatives of electric vehicles appear to outweigh the positives in the minds of individual consumers. Despite the media hype, electric cars have not yet grabbed a meaningful share in any of the three major auto markets — North America, western Europe or China — which collectively account for 60 per cent of the total global auto market. Moreover, declining oil prices and the increase in energy supply caused by the development of shale gas reserves threaten to halt any momentum that may have been achieved in recent years when oil was trading above US$100 per barrel. At the current price of US$40–50 per barrel (September 2015), with no bottom yet in sight, the economics of electric vehicles to the consumer have become less attractive.

Despite these facts, the global number of electric vehicles has exploded since 2011. But the 320,000 electric cars bought worldwide in 2014 should be seen in comparison with the roughly 71 million new passenger cars that were bought worldwide in 2014.

In February 2011, BMW announced a new sub-brand, BMW i. To market the vehicles produced

Sources: Frederic Legrand, COMEO/Shutterstock.com.

under Project i BMW began selling the BMW i3 at the end of 2013, with a starting price in the UK of £30,680. In 2014 the company achieved global sales of 16,052 vehicles, making them sixth among 2014's top 10 global best selling plug-in electric cars. In 2014, the best selling electric car globally was Nissan Leaf which sold 61,027 units.

Questions

1. Which research market research method would you use to estimate the total world market for electric cars?

2. Which research market research method would you use to estimate the total world sales of BMW i3 electric cars?

For further resources, see this book's website at **www.pearsoned.co.uk/hollensen**

Questions for discussion

1. Explore the reasons for using a marketing information system in the international market. What are the main types of information you would expect to use?

2. What are some of the problems that a global marketing manager can expect to encounter when creating a centralized marketing information system? How can these problems be solved?

3. What are the dangers of translating questionnaires (which have been designed for one country) for use in a multi-country study? How would you avoid these dangers?

4. Identify and classify the major groups of factors that must be taken into account when conducting a foreign market assessment.

5. A US manufacturer of shoes is interested in estimating the potential attractiveness of China for its products. Identify and discuss the sources and the types of data that the company will need in order to obtain a preliminary estimate.

6. Identify and discuss the major considerations in deciding whether research should be centralized or decentralized.

7. Distinguish between internal and external validity. What are the implications of external validity for international marketers?

8. Would Tokyo be a good test market for a new brand planned to be marketed worldwide? Why or why not?

9. If you had a contract to conduct marketing research in Saudi Arabia, what problems would you expect in obtaining primary data?

10. Do demographic variables have universal meanings? Is there a chance that they may be interpreted differently in different cultures?

11. In forecasting sales in international markets, to what extent can the past be used to predict the future?

12. How should the firm decide whether to gather its own intelligence or to buy it from outside?

References

Adiham, P.T., Gajre, S. and Kejriwal, S. (2009) 'Cross-cultural competitive intelligence strategies', *Marketing Intelligence & Planning*, 27(5), pp. 666–680.

Bell, P.C. (2015) 'Sustaining an analytics advantage', *MIT Sloan Management Review*, Spring, pp. 20–24.

Cateora, P.R. (1993) *International Marketing*, 8th edn. Irwin, Homewood, IL.

Cateora, P.R., Graham, J.L. and Ghauri, P.N. (2000) *International Marketing*. European edition, McGraw-Hill Publishing, Maidenhead.

Craig, S.C. and Douglas, S.P. (2000) *International Marketing Research*, 2nd edn. John Wiley & Sons, Chichester.

Denzin, N.K. (1978) *The Research Act*, 2nd edn. McGraw-Hill, New York.

Jick, T.D. (1979) 'Mixing qualitative and quantitive methods: triangulation in action', *Administrative Science Quarterly*, 24, December, pp. 602–611.

Malhotra, N.K. (1993) *Marketing Research: An Applied Orientation*. Prentice-Hall, Englewood Cliffs, NJ.

Micu, A.C., Dedeker, K., Lewis, I., Moran, R., Wetzer, O., Plummer, J. and Robinson, J. (2011) 'The shape of marketing research in 2021', *Journal of Advertising Research*, March, pp. 213–221.

McDaniel, C. Jr and Gates, R. (2007) *Marketing Research*, 8th edn. John Wiley & Sons, Inc., Hoboken, NJ.

Schmidt, M. and Hollensen, S. (2006) *Marketing Research – An International Approach*. FT/Prentice Hall, Harlow (UK).

Waheeduzzaman, A.N.M. (2008) 'Market potential estimation in international markets: a comparison of methods', *Journal of Global Marketing*, 21(4), pp. 307–320.

Wright, A. (2005) 'Using scenarios to challenge and change management thinking', *Total Quality Management*, 16(1), pp. 87–103.

CHAPTER 6
The political and economic environment

Contents

Case studies

Learning objectives

After studying this chapter you should be able to:

- Discuss how the political/legal environment will affect the attractiveness of a potential foreign market
- Distinguish between political factors in the home country environment and the host country environment
- Explain the steps in a political risk analysis procedure
- Distinguish between tariff barriers and non-tariff barriers
- Describe the major trading blocs

- Explore why the structure of consumption is different from country to country
- Explain how managers can influence local politics
- Define regional economic integration and identify different levels of integration
- Discuss the benefits and drawbacks associated with regional economic integration
- Evaluate consequences of the EMU and the euro on European business
- Explain what the term BRIC stands for, and what the main differences are between the BRIC countries.

6.1   Introduction

This chapter is devoted to macroenvironmental factors that explain the many forces to which a firm is exposed. Marketers have to adapt to a more or less uncontrollable environment within which they plan to operate. In this chapter, the environmental factors in the foreign environment are limited to the political/legal forces and the economic forces.

6.2   The political/legal environment

This section will concentrate mainly on political issues. The political/legal environment comprises primarily two dimensions:

● the home country environment
● the host country environment.

Besides these two dimensions there is also a third:

● the general international environment (see Figure 6.1).

Home country environment

A firm's home country political environment can constrain its international operations as well as its domestic operations. It can limit the countries that the international firm may enter.

The best-known example of the home country political environment affecting international operations was South Africa. Home country political pressure induced some firms to leave the country altogether. After US companies left South Africa, the Germans and the Japanese remained as the major foreign presence. German firms did not face the same political pressure at home that US firms had. However, the Japanese government was embarrassed when Japan became South Africa's leading trading partner. As a result, some Japanese companies reduced their South African activity.

One challenge facing multinationals is the triple-threat political environment. Even if the home country and the host country do not present problems, they may face threats in third markets. Firms that did not have problems with their home government or the South African government, for example, could be troubled or boycotted about their South African operations in third countries, such as the US. Today European firms face problems in the US if they do business in Cuba. Nestlé's problems with its infant formula controversy were most serious, not at home in Switzerland, or in African host countries, but in a third market – the US.

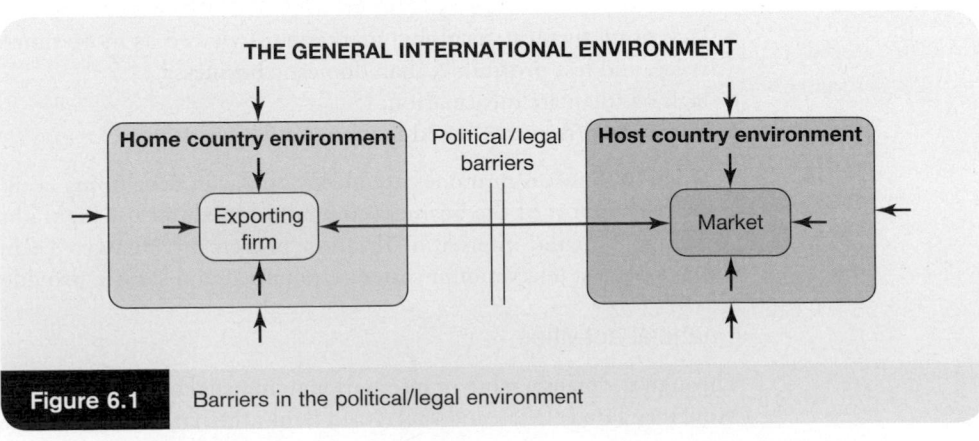

Figure 6.1   Barriers in the political/legal environment

A third area in which some governments regulate global marketing concerns bribery and corruption. In many countries, payments or favours are a way of life, and an 'oiling of the wheels' is expected in return for government services. In the past, many companies doing business internationally routinely paid bribes or did favours for foreign officials in order to gain contracts.

Many business managers argue that their home country should not apply its moral principles to other societies and cultures in which bribery and corruption are endemic. If they are to compete globally, these managers argue, they must be free to use the most common methods of competition in the host country. Particularly in industries that face limited or even shrinking markets, such stiff competition forces firms to find any edge possible to obtain a contract.

On the other hand, applying different standards to management and firms, depending on whether they do business abroad or domestically, is difficult to envisage. Also, bribes may open the way for shoddy performance and loose moral standards among managers and employees, and may result in a concentration on how best to bribe rather than on how best to produce and market products.

The global marketer must carefully distinguish between reasonable ways of doing business internationally – including compliance with foreign expectations – and outright bribery and corruption.

Promotional activities (sponsored by governmental organizations)

The programmes adopted by governmental organizations to promote exporting are an increasingly important force in the international environment. Many of the activities involve implementation and sponsorship by government alone, while others are the results of the joint efforts of government and business.

Furthermore, so-called regulatory supportive activities are direct government attempts to make its country's products more competitive in world markets. There are also attempts to encourage greater participation in exporting, particularly by smaller companies.

The granting of subsidies is of special interest: export subsidies are to the export industries what tariffs are to domestic industries. In both cases, the aim is to ensure the profitability of industries and individual firms that might well succumb if exposed to the full force of competition. For export industries, revenue is supplemented by subsidies, or costs are reduced by subsidies to certain input factors. Subsidies can be given through lower taxes on profits attributable to export sales, refunding of various indirect taxes, etc. Furthermore, a subsidy may take the form of a direct grant, which enables the recipient to compete against companies from other countries that enjoy cost advantages, or may be used for special promotion by recipient companies.

In a broader sense, government export promotion programmes, and programmes for global marketing activities in general, are designed to deal with the following internal barriers (Albaum *et al.*, 2002):

- lack of motivation, as global marketing is viewed as more time-consuming, costly and risky, and less profitable, than domestic business;
- lack of adequate information;
- operational/resource-based limitations.

Some of these programmes are quite popular in developing countries, especially if they enjoy the support of the business community. Exhibit 6.1 highlights the role of the home government in the internationalization process of Huawei Technologies Corporation, China's biggest telecommunications equipment and service provider.

Financial activities

Through the membership of international financial organizations such as the International Monetary Fund (IMF) and the World Bank, the national government can assume its role as an international banker. The granting of subsidies is another financially based promotional activity of national governments.

One of the most vital determinants of the results of a company's export marketing programme is its credit policy. The supplier that can offer better payment terms and financing conditions may make a sale, even though its price may be higher or the quality of its product inferior to that of its competitors.

If the credit terms are extended, the risks of non-payment increase, and many exporters are reluctant to assume the risks. Consequently, it may be necessary to offer exporters the opportunity of transferring some of the risk to governmental organizations through credit insurance. *Export credit insurance* and guarantees cover certain commercial and political risks that might be associated with any given export transaction.

EXHIBIT 6.1 Huawei Technologies Corporation: the role of home government in the internationalization process

By 2011, Huawei Technologies Corporation had become the largest telecom vendor in China, with reported revenues in 2014 of US$ 46.5 billion and net profits of US$ 5.5 billion. The number of employees at the end of 2014 was over 170,000. While Huawei has a strong national identity, it is seeking international expansion at a time when global telecommunication giants have already established their global brands in major trading blocs.

Government-run corporations remain the main driver for the Chinese national economy. Historically, the telecommunication sector in China has been closely controlled by the central government through the Ministry of Information Industry (MII). However, it is apparent that the Chinese telecommunication sector is in a process

Huawei is rapidly penetrating the Asian markets for smartphones

Source: Ivan Garcia/Shutterstock.com.

of transformation from a centrally controlled sector to a semi-capitalist industry. This transformation process is also as a result of China's commitment to the principles of the World Trade Organization (WTO). China will have to open up to more foreign investments. But China's central government will continue to play a central role in stimulating technical progress through alliances, mergers and acquisitions. The political and business leaders see the global telecommunication giants (such as Motorola, Nokia, Alcatel and Siemens) as catalysts for China's development and huge concessions have already been made to these companies, in cases where they have invested in China. Also Huawei receives plenty of state support, including soft loans to help with its international expansion. In 2004, the China Development Bank (CDB) extended a credit facility of US$10 billion to help overseas customers to fund the purchase of Huawei's products.

The MII also continued to encourage local Chinese operators such as China Mobile and China Telecom to purchase telecommunications equipment from Chinese manufacturers [e.g. Huawei, ZTE (Zhongxing), Datang and Great Dragon].

So the key future challenge for Huawei is competing in two market environmental structures – one local and the other global.

Sources: www.huawei.com; Low (2007).

Information services

Many large companies can collect the information they need themselves. Other firms, even if they do not possess the expertise to do their own research, can afford to hire outside research agencies to do the necessary research. However, a large number of companies are not in a position to take either of these approaches. For these firms, generally smaller companies or newcomers to global marketing, their national government is the major source of basic marketing information.

Although the information relevant for international/export marketers varies from country to country, the following kinds are typically available (Albaum *et al.*, 2002, pp. 119–120):

- economic, social and political data on individual countries, including their infrastructure;
- summary and detailed information on aggregate global marketing transactions;
- individual reports on foreign firms;
- specific export opportunities;
- lists of potential overseas buyers, distributors and agents for various products in different countries;
- information on relevant government regulations both at home and abroad;
- sources of various kinds of information not always available from the government, e.g. foreign credit information;
- information that will help the company manage its operation, e.g. information on export procedures and techniques.

Most types of information are made available to firms through published reports or through the internet. In addition, government officials often participate in seminars and workshops aimed at helping the international marketer.

Export-facilitating activities

A number of national government activities can stimulate export. These include the following (Albaum *et al.*, 2002, pp. 119–120):

- trade development offices abroad, either as a separate entity or as part of the normal operations of an embassy or consulate;
- government-sponsored trade fairs and exhibitions – a trade fair is a convenient marketplace in which buyers and sellers can meet, and in which an exporter can display products;
- sponsoring trade missions of business people who go abroad for the purpose of making sales and/or establishing agencies and other foreign representation;
- operating permanent trade centres in foreign market areas, which run trade shows often concentrating on a single industry.

From the national government's point of view, each of these activities represents a different approach to stimulating the growth of exports. From the point of view of an individual company, these activities provide relatively low-cost ways of making direct contact with potential buyers in overseas markets.

Promotion by private organizations

Various non-governmental organizations play a role in the promotion of global marketing. These include the following (Albaum *et al.*, 2002, p. 120):

- industry and trade associations, national, regional and sectoral industry associations, associations of trading houses, mixed associations of manufacturers and traders, and other bodies;

- chambers of commerce: local chambers of commerce, national chambers, national and international associations of chambers, national chambers abroad and binational chambers;
- other organizations concerned with trade promotion: organizations carrying out export research, regional export promotion organizations, world trade centres, geographically oriented trade promotion organizations, export associations and clubs, international business associations, world trade clubs and organizations concerned with commercial arbitration;
- export service organizations, banks, transport companies, freight forwarders, export merchants and trading companies.

The type of assistance available to firms includes information and publications, education and assistance in 'technical' details, and promotion in foreign countries.

State trading

Many of the former communist countries are now allowing some private trading activities, either through joint ventures or as a result of privatization of state-owned enterprises. However, there are still countries with some state trading, such as Cuba and 'to some extent' China.

Private businesses are concerned about state trading for two reasons. First, the establishment of import monopolies means that exporters have to make substantial adjustments in their export marketing programmes. Second, if state traders wish to utilize the monopolistic power they possess, private international marketers will have a difficult time.

Host country environment

Managers must continually monitor the government, its policies and its stability to determine the potential for political change that could adversely affect operations of the firm.

Political risks

There is political risk in every nation, but the range of risks varies widely from country to country. In general, political risk is lowest in countries that have a history of stability and consistency. Three major types of political risk can be encountered:

1. *ownership risk*, which exposes property and life;
2. *operating risk*, which refers to interference with the ongoing operations of a firm;
3. *transfer risk*, which is mainly encountered when companies want to transfer capital between countries.

Political risk can be the result of government action, but it can also be outside the control of government. The types of action and their effects can be classified as follows:

- *Import restrictions.* Selective restrictions on the import of raw materials, machines and spare parts are fairly common strategies to force foreign industry to purchase more supplies within the host country and thereby create markets for local industry. Although this is done in an attempt to support the development of domestic industry, the result is often to hamstring and sometimes interrupt the operations of established industries. The problem then becomes critical when there are no adequately developed sources of supply within the country.
- *Local-content laws.* In addition to restricting imports of essential supplies to force local purchase, countries often require a portion of any product sold within the country to have local content, i.e. to contain locally made parts. This requirement is often imposed on foreign companies that assemble products from foreign-made components.

Local-content requirements are not restricted to developing countries. The European Union (EU) has a 45 per cent local-content requirement for foreign-owned assemblers. This requirement has been important for Far East car producers.

- *Exchange controls.* Exchange controls stem from shortages of foreign exchange held by a country. When a nation faces shortages of foreign exchange, controls may be levied over all movements of capital or, selectively, against the most politically vulnerable companies to conserve the supply of foreign exchange for the most essential uses. A problem for the foreign investor is getting profits and investments into the currency of the home country (transfer risks).

- *Market control.* The government of a country sometimes imposes control to prevent foreign companies from competing in certain markets. Some years ago the US government threatened to boycott foreign firms trading with Cuba. The EU countries have protested against this threat.

- *Price controls.* Essential products that command considerable public interest, such as pharmaceuticals, food, petrol and cars, are often subjected to price controls. Such controls can be used by a government during inflationary periods to control the environmental behaviour of consumers or the cost of living.

- *Tax controls.* Taxes must be classified as a political risk when used as a means of controlling foreign investments. In many cases, they are raised without warning and in violation of formal agreements. In underdeveloped countries, where the economy is constantly threatened with a shortage of funds, unreasonable taxation of successful foreign investments appeals to some governments as the most convenient and quickest way of finding operating funds.

- *Labour restrictions.* In many nations labour unions are very strong and have great political influence. Using their strength, unions may be able to persuade the government to pass very restrictive laws that support labour at heavy cost to business. Traditionally labour unions in Latin America have been able to prevent lay-offs and plant shutdowns. Labour unions are gradually becoming strong in western Europe as well. For example, Germany and a number of other European nations require labour representation on boards of directors.

- *Change of government party.* A new government may not honour an agreement that the previous government has made with the company. This is especially an issue in the developing countries, where the governing party changes quite often. For example, in late December 2008, the international aluminium industry was rocked by a troubling development. The death of Guinean President Lansana Conté immediately sparked a military coup. The new leaders of Guinea – the nation that holds the world's largest reserves of bauxite, the raw material used in the production of primary aluminium – subsequently announced the suspension of all bauxite mining activity, and forced foreign mining companies to renegotiate the contracts (Jakobsen, 2010).

Nationalization
Takeover of foreign companies by the host government.

- **Nationalization** *(expropriation).* Defined as official seizure of foreign property, this is the ultimate government tool for controlling foreign firms. This most drastic action against foreign firms is fortunately occurring less often as developing countries begin to see foreign direct investment as desirable.

- *Domestication.* This can be thought of as creeping expropriation and is a process by which controls and restrictions placed on the foreign firm gradually reduce the control of the owners. The firm continues to operate in the country while the host government is able to maintain leverage on the foreign firm through imposing different controls. These controls include greater decision-making powers accorded to nationals; more products produced locally rather than imported for assembly; gradual transfer of ownership to nationals (demand for local participation in joint ventures); and promotion of a large number of nationals to higher levels of management. Domestication provides the host country with enough control to regulate the activities of the foreign firm carefully. In this way, any truly negative effects of the firm's operations in the country are discovered and prompt corrective action may be taken.

EXHIBIT 6.2 Google is experiencing political risk in China

After a long period of planning and negotiating with the Chinese government, Google created its Chinese domain Google.cn in January 2006. At first, Google was quite successful, quickly grabbing about one-third of the Chinese search engine market. However, just a few years after Google's entry, Google became unhappy with the Chinese government's censorship demands and suspected that the government might be behind hacker attacks on Google originating from China.

Source: lzf/Shutterstock.com.

Google and the Chinese government were on poor terms almost from the start. Shortly after the initial bargain was struck, Google indicated that it viewed these terms of entry as temporary terms that would be revisited, perhaps with 'guidance' from the Chinese government. This was likely not received favourably by the Chinese government, which views censorship as non-negotiable. Furthermore, Google upset the Chinese government by explicitly alerting users that their search results were being censored in accordance with Chinese law.

As the conflict escalated, Google took steps in 2010 to reduce its presence in China after threatening to pull out entirely. As a result, Google has seen its market share in China plummet. After capturing approximately 35 per cent of the market by the fourth quarter of 2009, Google dropped to under 2 per cent of search engine volume in China by the start of 2014, falling into fourth place behind Chinese competitors Baidu, Qihoo 360 and Sogou.

Sources: based on Karamchandani *et al.* (2011); other public resources.

Trade barriers from home country to host country

Free trade between nations permits international specialization. It also enables efficient firms to increase output to levels far greater than would be possible if sales were limited to their own domestic markets, thus permitting significant economies of scale. Competition increases, prices of goods in importing countries fall, while profits increase in the exporting country.

While countries have many reasons for wishing to trade with each other, it is also true to say that, all too frequently, an importing nation will take steps to inhibit the inward flow of goods and services by effecting **trade barriers**.

Trade barriers
Trade laws (often tariffs) that favour local firms and discriminate against foreign ones.

One of the reasons why international trade is different from domestic trade is that it is carried on between different political units, each one a sovereign nation exercising control over its own trade. Although all nations control their foreign trade, they vary in the degree of control. Each nation or trading bloc invariably establishes trade laws that favour its indigenous companies and discriminate against foreign ones.

There are two main reasons why countries levy tariffs:

1. *To protect domestic producers.* Because import tariffs raise the effective cost of an imported good, domestically produced goods can appear more attractive to buyers. In this way, domestic producers gain a protective barrier against imports. Although producers receiving tariff protection can gain a price advantage, protection can keep them from increasing efficiency in the long run. A protected industry can be destroyed if protection encourages complacency and inefficiency when it is later thrown into the lion's den of international competition.

Protectionism in the form of industry policy is most evident in France. On 31 August 2005, France announced that it would protect 11 domestic industries defined as strategic from buyouts by foreign companies. The protected industries include defence, biotechnology, telecommunications, casinos, encryption, IT security and antidote production. This was done primarily to frustrate Italian energy group Enel's bid for Suez, a French concern. The French prime minister described the measure as an example of economic patriotism. Paris argued that its actions would comply with EU economic laws, which allow each country to define 'strategic' sectors in accordance with national interests. (Enderwick, 2011).

2. *To generate revenue.* Using tariffs to generate government revenue is most common among relatively less-developed nations. The main reason is that these nations tend to have less formal domestic economies that presently lack the capability to record domestic transactions accurately. The lack of accurate record-keeping makes the collection of sales taxes within the country extremely difficult. Nations solve the problem by simply raising their needed revenue through import and export tariffs. Those nations obtaining a greater portion of their total revenue from taxes on international trade are mainly the poorer nations.

Trade distortion practices can be grouped into two basic categories: tariff and non-tariff barriers.

Tariff barriers

Tariffs
A tool used by governments to protect local companies from outside competition. The most common forms are specific, ad valorem and discriminatory.

Tariffs are direct taxes and charges imposed on imports. They are generally simple, straightforward and easy for the country to administer. While they are a barrier to trade, they are a visible and known quantity and so can be accounted for by companies when developing their marketing strategies.

Tariffs are used by poorer nations as the easiest means of collecting revenue and protecting certain home industries. They are a useful tool for politicians to show indigenous manufacturers that they are actively trying to protect their home markets.

The most common forms of tariffs are as follows:

- *Specific.* Charges are imposed on particular products, by either weight or volume, and usually stated in the local currency. For example, the EU charges duties on certain dairy products based on the weight of lactic matter in the product.
- *Ad valorem.* The charge is a straight percentage of the value of the goods (the import price) – for example, a 5 per cent tariff means that the import tariff is 5 per cent of the appraised value of the good in question.
- *Discriminatory.* In this case, the tariff is charged against goods coming from a particular country, either where there is a trade imbalance or for political purposes. Under the WTO agreements, countries cannot normally discriminate between their trading partners. If one country grants another country a special favour (such as a lower customs duty rate for one of their products), the first country will have to do the same for all other WTO members. This principle is known as most-favoured-nation (MFN) treatment. Some exceptions are allowed. Countries can give developing countries special access to their markets, or raise barriers against products that are considered to be traded unfairly from specific countries.

Non-tariff barriers

Non-tariff trade barriers
Non-monetary barriers to foreign products, such as biases against a foreign company's bids, or product standards that go against a foreign company's product features.

In the past 40 years, the world has seen a gradual reduction in tariff barriers in most developed nations. However, in parallel to this, **non-tariff barriers** have substantially increased. Non-tariff barriers are much more elusive and can be more easily disguised. However, in some ways the effect can be more devastating because they are an unknown quantity and are much less predictable.

Among non-tariff barriers the most important (not mentioned earlier) are as follows.

Quotas

A restriction on the amount (measured in units or weight) of a good that can enter or leave a country during a certain period of time is called a *quota*. After tariffs, a quota is the second most common type of trade barrier. Governments typically administer their quota systems by granting quota licences to the companies or governments of other nations (in the case of import quotas) and to domestic producers (in the case of export quotas). Governments normally grant such licences on a year-by-year basis.

There are two reasons why a government imposes *import quotas*:

1. It may wish to protect its domestic producers by placing a limit on the amount of goods allowed to enter the country. This helps domestic producers maintain their market shares and prices because competitive forces are restrained. In this case, domestic producers win because of the protection of their markets. Consumers lose because of higher prices and less selection due to lower competition. Other losers include domestic producers whose own production requires the import to be slapped with a quota. Companies relying on the importation of so-called 'intermediate' goods will find the final cost of their own products increases.

2. It may impose import quotas to force the companies of other nations to compete against one another for the limited amount of imports allowed. Thus those wishing to get a piece of the action will likely lower the price that they are asking for their goods. In this case, consumers win from the resulting lower prices. Domestic producers of competing goods win if external producers do not undercut their prices, but lose if they do.

Likewise, there are at least two reasons why a country imposes *export quotas* on its domestic producers:

1. It may wish to maintain adequate supplies of a product in the home market. This motive is most common among countries exporting natural resources that are essential to domestic business or the long-term survival of a nation.

2. It may restrict exports to limit supply on world markets, thereby increasing the international price of the good. This is the motive behind the formation and activities of the Organization of Petroleum Exporting Countries (OPEC). This group of nations from the Middle East and Latin America attempts to restrict the world's supply of crude oil to earn greater profits.

A unique version of the export quota is called a *voluntary export restraint* (VER) – a quota that a nation imposes on its exports usually at the request of another nation. Countries normally self-impose a voluntary export restraint in response to the threat of an import quota or total ban on the product by an importing nation. The classic example of the use of a voluntary export restraint is the automobile industry in the 1980s. Japanese car makers were making significant market share gains in the US market. The closing of US car makers' production facilities in the US was creating a volatile anti-Japan sentiment among the population and the US Congress. Fearing punitive legislation in Congress if Japan did not limit its car exports to the US, the Japanese government and its car makers imposed a voluntary export restraint on cars headed for the US.

Consumers in the country that imposes an export quota benefit from greater supply and the resulting lower prices if domestic producers do not curtail production. Producers in an importing country benefit because the goods of producers from the exporting country are restrained, which may allow them to increase prices. Export quotas hurt consumers in the importing nation because of reduced selection and perhaps higher prices. However, export quotas might allow these same consumers to retain their jobs if imports were threatening to put domestic producers out of business. Again, detailed economic studies are needed to determine the winners and losers in any particular export quota case.

Embargoes

A complete ban on trade (imports and exports) in one or more products with a particular country is called an *embargo*. An embargo may be placed on one or a few goods or may completely ban trade in all goods. It is the most restrictive non-tariff trade barrier available and is typically applied to accomplish political goals. Embargoes can be decreed by individual nations or by supranational organizations such as the United Nations. Because they can be very difficult to enforce, embargoes are used less today than in the past. One example of a total ban on trade with another country has been the US embargo on trade with Cuba.

Administrative delays

Regulatory controls or bureaucratic rules designed to impair the rapid flow of imports into a country are called *administrative delays*. This non-tariff barrier includes a wide range of government actions such as requiring international air carriers to land at inconvenient airports; requiring product inspections that damage the product itself; deliberately understaffing customs offices to cause unusual time delays; and requiring special licences that take a long time to obtain. The objective of such administrative delays for a country is to discriminate against imported products – in a word, it is protectionism.

Although Japan has removed some of its trade barriers, many subtle obstacles to imports remain. Products ranging from cold pills and vitamins to farm products and building materials find it hard to penetrate the Japanese market.

Local-content requirements

Laws stipulating that a specified amount of a good or service be supplied by producers in the domestic market are called local-content requirements. These requirements can state that a certain portion of the end product consist of domestically produced goods, or that a certain portion of the final cost of a product have domestic sources.

The purpose of local-content requirements is to force companies from other nations to employ local resources in their production processes – particularly labour. Similar to other restraints on imports, such requirements help protect domestic producers from the price advantage of companies based in other, low-wage countries. Today companies can circumvent local-content requirements by locating production facilities inside the nation stipulating such restrictions.

Historical development of barriers

Non-tariff barriers become much more prevalent in times of recession. The US and Europe have witnessed the mobilization of quite strong political lobby groups as indigenous industries, which have come under threat, lobby their governments to take measures to protect them from international competition. The last major era of protectionism was in the 1930s. During that decade, under the impact of the most disastrous trade depression in history, most countries of the world adopted high tariffs.

After World War II there was a reaction against the high tariff policy of the 1930s and significant efforts were made to move the world back to free trade. World organizations (such as GATT and its successor, the WTO) have been developed to foster international trade and provide a trade climate in which such barriers can be reduced.

The political risk analysis procedure

The goal of this procedure is to help firms make informed decisions based on the ratio of the return to risk, so that firms can enter or stay in a country when the ratio). is favourable and avoid or leave a country when the ratio for them is poor (see Figure 6.2).

Generally political risks are addressed through the building of relationships with the various stakeholders of the company (Erevelles *et al.*, 2005):

- the government
- customers
- employees
- the local community.

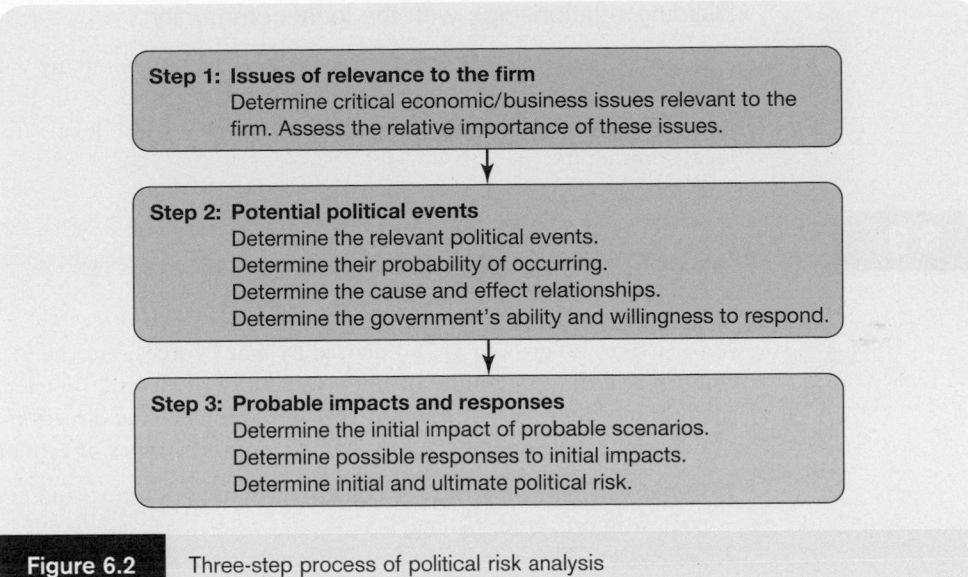

Figure 6.2 Three-step process of political risk analysis

Building relationships with government

Managers must be able to deal with the political risks, rules and regulations that apply in each national business environment. Moreover, laws in many nations are susceptible to frequent change, with new laws continually being enacted and existing ones modified. To influence local politics in their favour, managers can propose changes that positively affect their local activities:

- *Lobbying*. Influencing local politics always involves dealing with local lawmakers and politicians, either directly or through lobbyists. Lobbying is the policy of hiring people to represent a company's views on political matters. Lobbyists meet with local public officials and try to influence their position on issues relevant to the company. They describe the benefits that a company brings to the local economy, natural environment, infrastructure and workforce. Their ultimate goal is getting favourable legislation passed and unfavourable legislation rejected.
- *Corruption/bribery*. Although illegal in most countries, bribes are common for gaining political influence and building relationships with political decision-makers. This issue is further discussed in Section 18.6 on transnational bribery in cross-cultural negotiations.

Building relationships with customers

Local customers support companies that have provided them with desirable products and services. For example, in the case of expropriation, the firm that has excelled in relationship-building with its customers will have considerable support from them, as they will fear losing the benefits that the firm provides.

Building relationships with employees

Local employees can be very protective of a company, even in times of instability, especially if they perceive that their jobs could be affected by government interference. Therefore, well-treated employees will usually be interested in the company's survival, because they perceive it to be key to their own survival.

Building relationships with the local community

The local community may be concerned that a foreign company will extract materials and labour and make a profit, but fail to give something back to the local environment and the local people. Therefore the company needs to be a good 'local citizen' and reinvest in the local community.

6.3 The economic environment

Market size and growth are influenced by many forces, but the total buying power in the country and the availability or non-availability of electricity, telephone systems, modern roads and other types of infrastructure will influence the direction of that spending.

Economic development results from one of three types of economic activity:

1. *Primary*. These activities are concerned with agriculture and extractive processes (e.g. coal, iron ore, gold, fishing).
2. *Secondary*. These are manufacturing activities. There are several evolutions. Typically countries will start manufacturing through processing the output of primary products.
3. *Tertiary*. These activities are based upon *services*, e.g. tourism, insurance and health care. As the average family income in a country rises, the percentage of income spent on food declines, the percentage spent on housing and household activities remains constant, and the percentage spent on service activities (e.g. education, transport and leisure) will increase.

How exchange rates influence business activities

Times of crisis are not the only occasions during which companies are affected by exchange rates. In fact, movement in a currency's exchange rate affects the activities of both domestic and international companies. Let us now examine how exchange rate changes affect the business decisions of companies, and why stable and predictable rates are desirable.

Exchange rates affect demand for a company's products in the global marketplace. When a country's currency is *weak* (valued low relative to other currencies), the price of its exports on world markets declines and the price of imports increases. Lower prices make the country's exports more appealing on world markets. They also give companies the opportunity to take market share away from companies whose products are highly priced in comparison.

Furthermore, a company selling in a country with a *strong* currency (one that is valued high relative to other currencies) while paying workers in a country with a weak currency improves its profits.

The international lowering of the value of a currency by the nation's government is called devaluation. The reverse, the intentional raising of its value by the nation's government, is called revaluation. These concepts are not to be confused with the terms *weak* and *strong* currencies, although their effects are similar.

Devaluation lowers the price of a country's exports on world markets and increases the price of imports because the country's currency is now worth less on world markets. Thus a government might devalue its currency to give its domestic companies an edge over competition from other countries. It might also devalue to boost exports so that a trade deficit can be eliminated. However, such a policy is not wise because devaluation reduces consumers' buying power. It also allows inefficiencies to persist in domestic companies because there is now less pressure to be concerned with production costs. In such a case, increasing inflation may be the result. *Revaluation* has the opposite effect: it increases the price of exports and reduces the price of imports.

As we have seen, unfavourable movements in exchange rates can be costly for both domestic and international companies. Therefore, managers prefer that exchange rates be *stable*. Stable exchange rates improve the accuracy of financial planning, including cash flow forecasts. Although methods do exist for insuring against potentially adverse exchange rate movements, most of these are too expensive for small and medium-sized enterprises (SMES). Moreover, as the unpredictability of exchange rates increases, so too does the cost of insuring against the accompanying risk.

Law of one price

An exchange rate tells us how much of one currency we must pay to receive a certain amount of another. But it does not tell us whether a specific product will actually cost us more or less in a particular country (as measured in our own currency). When we travel to another country we discover that our own currency buys more or less than it does at home. In other words, we quickly learn that exchange rates do not guarantee or stabilize the buying power of our currency. Thus we can lose purchasing power in some countries while gaining it in others.

The law of one price stipulates that an identical product must have an identical price in all countries when price is expressed in a common-denominator currency. For this principle to apply, products must be identical in quality and content in all countries, and must be entirely produced within each particular country.

Big Mac Index/Big MacCurrencies

The usefulness of the law of one price is that it helps us determine whether a currency is overvalued or undervalued. Each year *The Economist* magazine publishes what it calls its 'Big MacCurrencies' exchange-rate index.

The index is based on the theory of purchasing-power parity (PPP), the notion that a dollar should buy the same amount in all countries. Purchasing-power parities are not only calculated for individual products; they are calculated for a 'basket' of products, and PPP is meaningful only when applied to such a 'basket'. The theory naturally relies on certain assumptions, such as negligible transportation costs, that goods and services must be 'tradeable', and that a good in one country does not differ substantially from the same good in another country. Thus, in the long run, the exchange rate between two currencies should move towards the rate that equalizes the prices of an identical basket of goods and services in each country. In this case the 'basket' is a McDonald's Big Mac, which is produced in about 120 countries. The Big Mac PPP is the exchange rate that would mean hamburgers cost the same in the US as abroad. Comparing actual exchange rates with the PPP indicates whether a currency is under- or overvalued.

This index uses the law of one price to determine the exchange rate that should exist between the US dollar and other major currencies. It employs the McDonald's Big Mac as its single product to test the law of one price. Why the Big Mac? Because each Big Mac is fairly identical in quality and content across national markets and almost entirely produced within the nation in which it is sold. The underlying assumption is that the price of a Big Mac in any world currency should, after being converted to dollars, equal the price of a Big Mac in the US. A country's currency would be overvalued if the Big Mac price (converted to dollars) is higher than the US price. Conversely, a country's currency would be undervalued if the converted Big Mac price was lower than the US price.

Such large discrepancies between a currency's exchange rate on currency markets and the rate predicted by the Big Mac Index are not surprising, for several reasons. For one thing, the selling price of food is affected by subsidies for agricultural products in most countries. Also, the Big Mac is not a 'traded' product in the sense that one can buy Big Macs in low-priced countries and sell them in high-priced countries. Prices can also be affected because Big Macs are subject to different cost prices of Big Mac and different marketing strategies in different countries. Finally, countries impose different levels of sales tax on restaurant meals.

The drawbacks of the Big Mac Index reflect the fact that applying the law of one price to a single product is too simplistic a method for estimation of exchange rates. Overall, the price of a Big Mac will be a reflection of its local production and delivery cost, the cost of advertising (considerable in some areas) and, most importantly, what the local market will bear. Until now the assumption in the Hamburger Standard has been that relative differences in prices of Big Macs (in $) may be explained by differences in exchange. However, a better prediction of future possible currency movement might be done if we also compensate and adjust the raw index with the GDP per person, because a low GDP per person would also indicate a relatively low relative price of Big Macs, because that would be what the local market can bear.

Nonetheless, a recent study finds that currency values, especially in the medium to longer term, do tend to change in the direction suggested by the Big Mac Index (Clements *et al.*, 2010). For example, when the euro was launched in 1999, the widespread prediction was that it would immediately rise against the dollar. The Big Mac index disagreed, showing that the euro was already significantly overvalued, and it fell against the US$ over the coming years.

Classification by income

GNP
Gross national product is the value of all goods and services produced by the domestic economy over a one-year period, including income generated by the country's international activities.

GNP per capita
Total GNP divided by its population.

Countries can be classified in a variety of ways. Most classifications are based on national income and the degree of industrialization. The broadcast measure of economic development is **gross national product (GNP)** – the value of all goods and services produced by a country during a one-year period. This figure includes income generated both by domestic production and by the country's international activities. *Gross domestic product* (GDP) is the value of all goods and services produced by the domestic economy over a one-year period. In other words, when we add to GDP the income generated from exports, imports and the international operations of a nation's companies, we get GNP. A country's **GNP per capita** is simply its GNP divided by its population. GDP per capita is calculated similarly.

Both GNP per capita and GDP per capita measure a nation's income per person. *In this regard GNI (gross national income) can be regarded as the same as GNP.*

Less developed countries (LDCs)

This group includes underdeveloped countries and developing countries. The main features are a low GDP per capita (less than US $3,000), limited amount of manufacturing activity and a very poor and fragmented infrastructure. Typical infrastructure weaknesses are in transport, communications, education and health care. In addition, the public sector is often slow-moving and bureaucratic.

It is common to find that LDCs are heavily reliant on one product and often on one trading partner. The typical pattern for single-product dependence is the reliance on one agricultural crop or on mining. Colombia (coffee) and Cuba (sugar) are examples of extreme dependence upon agriculture. The risks posed to the LDC by changing patterns of supply and demand are great. Falling commodity prices can result in large decreases in earnings for the whole country. The resultant economic and political adjustments may affect exporters to that country through possible changes in tariff and non-tariff barriers.

A wide range of economic circumstances influences the development of the LDCs in the world. Without real prospects for rapid economic development, private sources of capital are reluctant to invest in such countries. This is particularly the case for long-term infrastructure projects. As a result, important capital spending projects rely heavily on world aid programmes.

The quality of distribution channels varies considerably between countries. There are often great differences between the small-scale, undercapitalized distribution intermediaries in LDCs and the distributors in more advanced countries. Retailers, for example, are more likely to be market traders. The incidence of large-scale self-service outlets will be comparatively low.

Newly industrialized countries (NICs)

Newly industrialized countries are countries with an emerging industrial base, one that is capable of exporting. Examples of NICs are the 'tigers' of South-east Asia: Hong Kong, Singapore, South Korea and Taiwan. Brazil and Mexico are examples of NICs in South America. In NICs, although the infrastructure shows considerable development, high growth in the economy results in difficulties with producing what is demanded by domestic and foreign customers.

Advanced industrialized countries

These countries have considerable GDP per capita, a wide industrial base, considerable development in the services sector and substantial investment in the infrastructure of the country.

This attempt to classify the economies of the world into neat divisions is not completely successful. For example, some of the advanced industrialized countries (e.g. the US and France) have important agricultural sectors.

Regional economic integration

Economic integration has been one of the main economic developments affecting world markets since World War II. Countries have wanted to engage in economic cooperation to use their respective resources more effectively and to provide large markets for member-country producers.

Some integration efforts have had quite ambitious goals, such as political integration; some have failed as a result of perceptions of unequal benefits from the arrangement or a parting of the ways politically. Figure 6.3, a summary of the major forms of economic cooperation in regional markets, shows the varying degrees of formality with which integration can take place. These economic integration efforts are dividing the world into trading blocs.

The levels of economic integration will now be described.

Free trade area

The free trade area is the least restrictive and loosest form of economic integration among nations. In a free trade area all barriers to trade among member countries are removed. Each member country maintains its own trade barriers vis-à-vis non-members.

The European Free Trade Area (EFTA) was formed in 1960 with an agreement by eight European countries. Since that time EFTA has lost much of its original significance due to its members joining the European Union. All EFTA countries have cooperated with the European Union through bilateral free trade agreements, and since 1994 through the European Economic Area (EEA) arrangement that allows for free movement of people, products, services and capital within the combined area of the European Union and EFTA. Of the EFTA countries, Iceland and Liechtenstein have decided not to apply for membership of the European Union and Norway turned down membership after a referendum in 1994. Switzerland has also decided to stay out of the European Union.

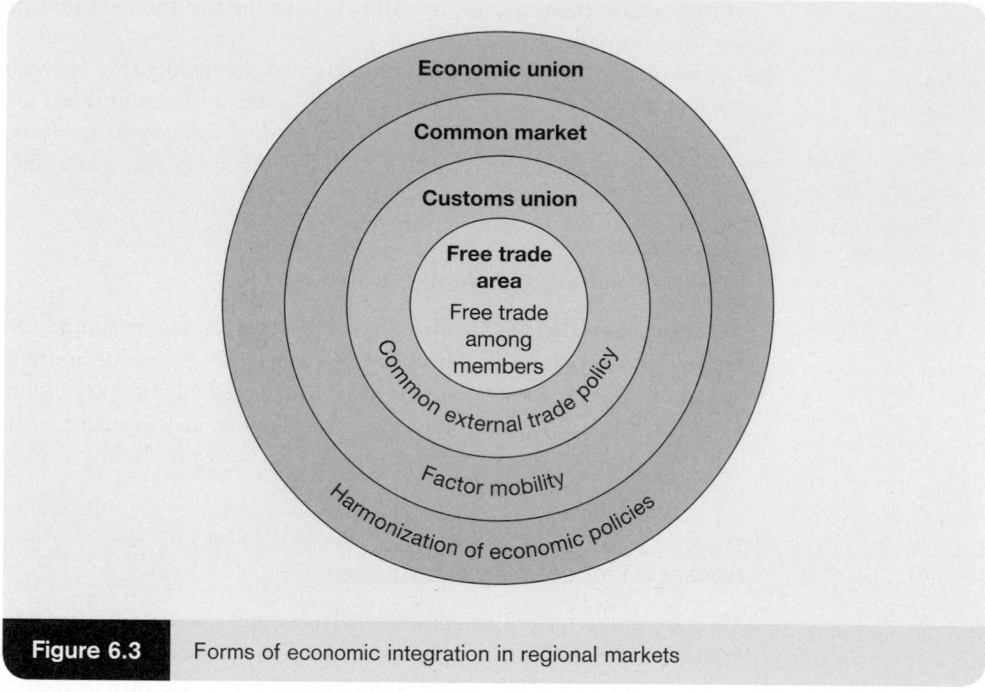

| Figure 6.3 | Forms of economic integration in regional markets |

Source: from Czinkota/Ronkainen. *Global Marketing,* 1e. © 1996 South-Western, a part of Cengage Learning, Inc. Reproduced by permission. www.cengage.com/permissions.

After three failed efforts during the last century, the US and Canada signed a free trade agreement that went into effect in 1989. North American free trade expanded in 1994 with the inclusion of Mexico in the North American Free Trade Agreement (NAFTA).

Customs union

The customs union is one step further along the spectrum of economic integration. As in the free trade area, goods and services are freely traded among members. In addition, however, the customs union establishes a common trade policy with respect to non-members. Typically this takes the form of a common external tariff, whereby imports from non-members are subject to the same tariff when sold to any member country. The Benelux countries formed a customs union in 1921 that later became part of wider European economic integration.

Common market

The common market has the same features as a customs union. In addition, factors of production (labour, capital and technology) are mobile among members. Restrictions on immigration and cross-border investment are abolished. When factors of production are mobile, capital, labour and technology may be employed in their most productive uses.

The removal of barriers to the free movement of goods, services, capital and people in Europe was ratified by the passing of the Single European Act in 1987 with the target date of 31 December 1992 to complete the internal market. In December 1991, the EEC agreed in Maastricht that the so-called 1992 process would be a step towards cooperation beyond the economic dimension. While many of the directives aimed at opening borders and markets were completed on schedule some sectors, such as cars, will take longer to open up.

Economic union

The creation of true economic union requires integration of economic policies in addition to the free movement of goods, services and factors of production across borders. Under an economic union, members harmonize monetary policies, taxation and government spending. In addition, a common currency is used by members and this could involve a system of fixed exchange rates. The ratification of the Maastricht Treaty in late 1993 resulted in the European Union (EU) being effective from 1 January 1994. Clearly the formation of a full economic union requires the surrender of a large measure of national sovereignty to a supranational body. Such a union is only a short step away from political unification, but many countries in the EU (especially in the northern part of Europe) are sceptical about this development because they fear a loss of national identity.

Enlargement of the EU

The EU can already look back on a history of successful enlargements. The Treaties of Paris (1951), establishing the European Coal and Steel Community (ECSC), and Rome (1957), establishing the European Economic Community (EEC) and EURATOM, were signed by six founding members: Belgium, France, Germany, Italy, Luxembourg and the Netherlands. The EU then underwent four successive enlargements: 1973, Denmark, Ireland and the UK; 1981, Greece; 1986, Portugal and Spain; 1995, Austria, Finland and Sweden.

After growing from six to 15 members, the EU prepared for its biggest enlargement ever in terms of scope and diversity. Thirteen countries have applied to become new members and 10 of these – Cyprus, the Czech Republic, Estonia, Hungary, Latvia, Lithuania, Malta, Poland, the Slovack Republic and Slovenia – joined on 1 May 2004. Bulgaria and Romania joined on 1 January 2007, while Turkey is not currently negotiating its membership. However, Turkey wants to be a member of the EU and the issue will be taken up again in the future.

The current 28 member states of the EU as on 1 July 2015 are: Austria, Belgium, Bulgaria, Croatia, Cyprus, Czech Republic, Denmark, Estonia, Finland, France, Germany, Greece, Hungary, Ireland, Italy, Latvia, Lithuania, Luxembourg, Malta, the Netherlands, Poland, Portugal, Romania, Slovakia, Slovenia, Spain, Sweden and the UK.

New countries wanting to join the EU need to fulfil the economic and political conditions known as the 'Copenhagen criteria', according to which a prospective member must be a stable democracy, respecting human rights, the rule of law and the protection of minorities; have a functioning market economy; and adopt the common rules, standards and policies that make up the body of EU law.

EXHIBIT 6.3 EU's antitrust regulator complains about competition practices of Google

In April 2015, the EU Competition Chief, Margrethe Vestager, officially raised an antitrust complaint against Google Inc. for their alleged practice of highlighting its own service, Google Shopping, ahead of links to similar services run by rivals.

Such 'search bias' is important because more than 90 per cent of Internet searches in Europe are conducted on Google. Given that dominance, promoting its own services while demoting others may be illegal under EU law, which intends to provide fair and open market access along with consumers' interests.

On their side, Google claims that they compete side by side with other search services, such as Apple Inc.'s Siri and Microsoft Corp's Cortana, as well as specialized services from Amazon.com Inc., eBay Inc. and others. Google argues that their rivals do exactly the same as they do. Google claims that the competitors who run other comparison-shopping sites, as well as competitors in other 'vertical' areas such as travel, maps and local services, bolster its own offerings in those areas, and directs users to its services, ahead of links to others.

Besides Google Shopping, the EU's antitrust regulator also opened a formal investigation into the Google mobile operating system (Android) to see if Google:

- required smartphone manufacturers to exclusively pre-install its own apps or services;
- prevented phone and tablet manufacturers from developing competing versions of Android;
- hindered rival apps by bundling Google apps with other Google services.

Source: based on Barr (2015).

6.4 The European Economic and Monetary Union and the euro

The Maastricht Treaty resulted in the European Economic and Monetary Union (EMU), which also included the new common European currency, the euro (introduced on 1 January 1999). The euro involves the extension of the 'law of one price' across a market comprising more than 320 million consumers, representing one-fifth of the world economy, which should promote increased trade and stimulate greater competition. Consequently, the development of this 'new' Europe has an importance beyond the relatively small group of nations currently involved in its creation.

Today, the euro is one of the world's most powerful currencies, used by more than 320 million Europeans in 23 countries. As at 1 January 2015, the 19 Eurozone countries that officially use the euro are:

- Belgium, Germany, Ireland, Spain, France, Italy, Luxembourg, the Netherlands, Austria, Portugal and Finland (joined 1999)
- Greece (joined 2001)
- Slovenia (joined 2007)
- Cyprus, Malta (joined 2008)
- Slovakia (joined 2009)
- Estonia (joined 1 January 2011)
- Latvia (joined 1 January 2014)
- Lithuania (joined 1 January 2015)

Notably, the UK, Denmark and Sweden have thus far decided not to join the euro. Other new EU member countries are working towards becoming part of the Eurozone.

On the other hand, Andorra, Kosovo, Montenegro, Monaco, San Marino and the Vatican City are not EU members but do officially use the euro as their currencies. A total of $19 + 6 = 25$ countries are using the euro as at 1 January 2015.

The consequences of European economic integration will not be restricted to so-called 'European' business. Most obviously the developments associated with the EMU will have a direct impact upon all foreign subsidiaries located within the new euro market. These companies will be forced to adapt their accounting, personnel and financial processes to accommodate the new currency.

The EMU will also affect the international competitiveness of European companies. Reductions in transaction costs, exchange rate risk, intensified domestic competition and the possibilities of gleaning additional economies of scale should all facilitate reductions in the cost structures of European firms, with inevitable consequences upon their external competitors. However, this may be negated by the impact of demands for wage equalization and restrictions imposed by regulations.

With so many important issues in the EMU, there is no single economic consensus concerning the likely development of the European economy.

Supporters of EMU claim that the greater nominal exchange rate stability, lower transaction costs (by the introduction of the euro) and price transparency (across European borders) resulting in reduction of information costs will increase the international competitiveness of European business, raising consumer welfare together with the demand for cheaper products. The establishment of an independent European Central Bank (ECB) is anticipated to ensure a low level of inflation, reduce real interest rates and thereby stimulate investment, output and employment.

Opponents of the EMU claim the following:

- The loss of national economic policy tools will have a destabilizing impact.
- The lack of 'real' convergence of participating economies is likely to increase the problem of asymmetric shocks.

● The ECB's attempts at stabilization by the use of a single instrument, a common interest rate, are likely to prove insufficient because the common monetary policy affects EU members differently due to differences in factors such as the concentration of owner-occupation and variable interest borrowing.

Major trading blocs

Gross domestic product (GDP)
Plus/minus net income from assets (e.g. subsidiaries abroad) is GNI (= GNP).

Table 6.1 shows the major trading blocs together with their population, GNI and GNI per capita. GNI (= GNP) is the current income indicator used by the World Bank. Previously the World Bank used **gross domestic product (GDP)** which is the total value of all goods and services produced by capital and workers in a country. GNI is GDP plus net income from assets abroad (e.g. subsidiaries). This means that GNI is the total value of all goods and services produced by a country's residents or corporations, regardless of their location (World Bank, 2015a).

The size and economic importance of the EU, the US and Japan stand out. The affluence of Luxembourg and Denmark – both small countries – is marked by high values of GNI per capita.

Besides the major trading blocs mentioned in Table 6.1, the most important global market will be the 'triad'.

Table 6.1		Major trading blocs as of 1 January 2015 (figures are from 2014 – World Bank)			
Organization	Type	Members	Population (million)	GNI (US $ billion)	GNI per capita (US $)
European Union	Political and economic union	Austria	8.5	427.3	50,390
		Belgium	11.2	528.0	47,030
		Bulgaria	7.2	53.6	7,420
		Croatia	4.2	55.2	13,020
		Cyprus	1.2	22.5	26,370
		Czech Republic	10.5	199.4	18,970
		Denmark	5.6	345.8	61,310
		Estonia	1.3	24.3	18,530
		Finland	5.5	266.0	48,910
		France	66.2	2,851.7	43,080
		Germany	80.9	3,853.5	47,640
		Greece	11.0	242.0	22,090
		Hungary	9.9	132.9	13,470
		Ireland	4.6	206.0	44,660
		Italy	61.3	2,102.8	34,280
		Latvia	2.0	31.2	15,660
		Lithuania	2.9	45.0	15,380
		Luxembourg	0.6	38.0	69,880
		Malta	0.4	8.9	21.000
		Netherlands	16.9	863.0	51,210
		Poland	38.0	521.8	13,730
		Portugal	10.4	221.7	21,320
		Romania	19.9	186.6	9,370
		Slovakia	5.4	96.4	17,810
		Slovenia	2.1	47.8	23,220
		Spain	46.4	1395.9	29,940
		Sweden	9.7	596.9	61,600
		UK	64.5	2754.1	42,690
		Total	**508.3**	**18,133**	**35,673**

Table 6.1	Continued				
Organization	Type	Members	Population (million)	GNI (US $ billion)	GNI per capita (US $)
Association of South East Asian Nations (ASEAN)	Limited trade and cooperation agreement	Brunei	0.4	15.1	36,710
		Cambodia	15.4	15.6	1,010
		Indonesia	252.8	923.7	3,650
		Laos	6.9	11.0	1,600
		Malaysia	30.2	321.7	10,660
		Myanmar	53.7	68.1	1,270
		Philippines	100.1	344.0	3,440
		Singapore	5.5	301.6	55,150
		Thailand	67.2	363.4	5,410
		Vietnam	90.7	171.9	1,890
		Total	**622.9**	**2,536.1**	**4,071**
Asia-Pacific Economic Cooperation (APEC, excl. ASEAN, US and Canada)	Formal institution	Australia	23.5	1,519.4	64,680
		China (incl. Taiwan)	1,364.3	10,069.2	7,380
		Japan	127.1	5,339.1	42,000
		New Zealand	4.5	174.6	39,300
		South Korea	50.4	1,365.8	27,090
		Total	**1,569.8**	**16,948.7**	**10,797**
North American Free Trade Area (NAFTA)	Free trade area	Canada	35.5	1,836.9	51,690
		Mexico	123.8	1,235.7	9,980
		US	318.9	17,601.1	55,200
		Total	**478.2**	**20,673.7**	**43,232**

Source: based on World Bank (2015a).

6.5 BRIC – the slowing growth is hitting the emerging countries

The acronym BRIC – which stands for Brazil, Russia, India and China – was coined in 2001 by Goldman Sachs. These are countries to watch, the emerging markets where we will see high future growth. The BRIC term is also used by companies who consider these countries as key to their emerging markets strategies. The term 'Chindia' (for China and India) is also often used.

Together, the four BRIC countries account for 42 per cent of the world's population and approximately 20 per cent of the world's gross domestic product (GDP; World Bank, 2015b).

However, some have questioned the BRIC categorization from the start. Fundamentally, the four countries have very little in common. Two countries are manufacturing-based economies and big importers (China and India), and two are huge exporters of natural resources (Brazil and Russia).

Academics and experts have suggested that China is in a league of its own compared with the other BRIC countries. The 'growth gap' between China and other large emerging economies such as Brazil, Russia and India can be attributed, to a large extent, to China's early focus on ambitious infrastructure projects.

In the meantime, the financial markets are already on the lookout for the next emerging countries. South Africa, South Korea, Indonesia and Mexico have sometimes been added to the list. Others advise that a close eye should be kept on Africa.

The BRICS summit in Ufa, Russia, 8–9 July 2015. Front row, left to right: President Jacob Zuma (South Africa), President Xi Jinping (China), President Vladimir Putin (Russia), Prime Minister Narendra Modi (India) and President Dilma Rousseff (Brazil)
Source: Xinhua News Agency/REX Shutterstock.

In 2009, the BRIC political leaders met for the first BRIC summit. Following a meeting in Brasilia in 2010, to which South Africa was invited as a guest, the group invited South Africa to join as a full member in 2011 and the group formerly called BRIC officially became BRICS.

In the future, BRIC economies will face challenges from:

- a slow-growing global economy;
- a reversal of investor risk appetite moving capital from the BRICs (and other emerging markets) to safe havens;
- a loss of confidence in the BRICs.

As a result, a slowdown of growth in the BRICs happened between 2012 and 2015. However, the authorities and governments in these economies have plenty of scope to loosen monetary policy and provide fiscal support, so it is expected that policy measures can provide another economic boost in coming years.

For example, the Chinese economy experienced a moderation in growth to 6.5 per cent in 2015 on account of slowing services and a slowing manufacturing sector. The 'low' growth has continued in 2016. The key risks to China's economic outlook are from its trade exposure to the slowing growth in Europe and a sharp correction in property prices, but the Chinese government has plenty of financial ammunition with which to respond if a sharper slowdown becomes evident. China's authorities are trying to engineer a controlled slowdown as they seek to transform the country's growth model to one driven by consumer spending, as opposed to heavy infrastructure investment.

Russia is officially forecasting that its economy will slide into recession in 2016. The news comes amid a raft of bad economic figures, western sanctions, a weakening ruble and falling oil prices.

In the past few years, Brazil's economy has disappointed. It grew by 2.2 per cent a year, on average, during President Dilma Rousseff's first term in office in 2011–14, a slower rate of growth than in the other BRIC countries. In 2014, GDP barely grew at all. In 2015, a negative growth is expected by as much as 2 per cent.

The Indian economy – today the eighth largest by total GDP (purchasing power) – would become the world's third largest by 2030. While China's growth has slowed, India's GDP is still growing (approximately 7 per cent in 2015) making it the fastest-growing major economy among the BRIC countries.

EXHIBIT 6.4 Chotukool – Indian Godrej is creating a disruptive innovation (a low-cost refrigerator) for the BOP market

A disruptive innovation is a technology whose performance does not currently meet the requirements of the mainstream market (point B in Figure 6.4). However, it does meet the requirements of a lower-end market (point A), with customers who have lower performance requirements and who are more sensitive to price. Often, this lower-end market did not exist previously, and was created by the advent of the disruptive technology.

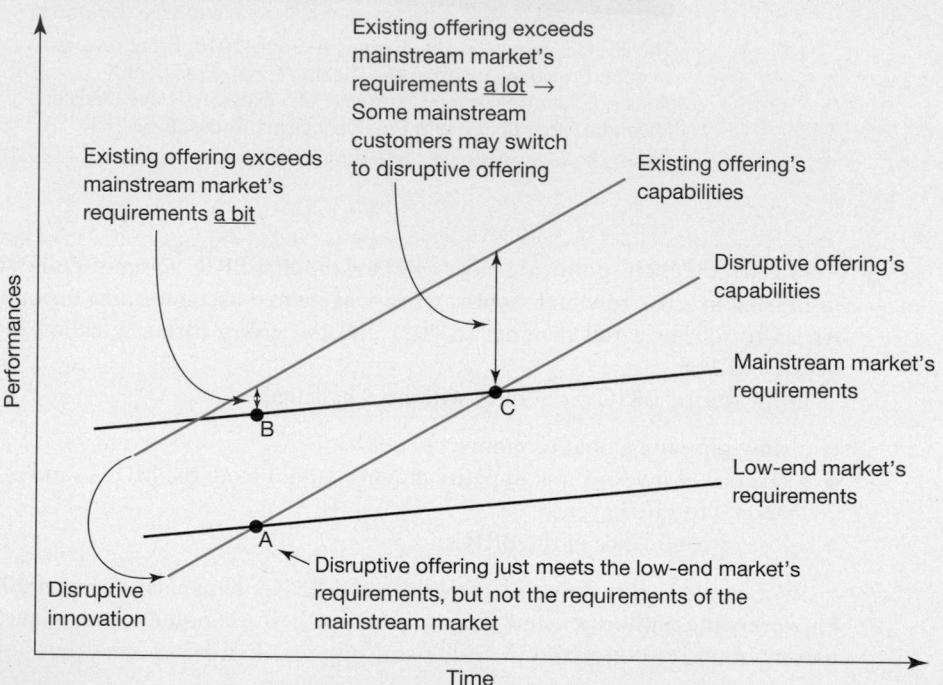

| Figure 6.4 | The principle of disruptive innovations |

Source: based on Christensen (1997).

As time progresses, the performance requirements of both the mainstream and the lower-end markets grow, as we see on the diagram. However, and this is key, the performance of the existing offering and of the disruptive offering grows more quickly. At some point (point C in the diagram), the disruptive innovation's performance meets the performance requirements of the existing market. This existing offering still has better performance, but it now offers more than what the mainstream market needs. At this point, mainstream customers begin to move, in large numbers, to the disruptive innovation, which meets their needs at a cheaper price.

Source: Godrej & Boyce Manufacturing Co. Ltd.

Companies following disruptive innovation in their initial stages have the following characteristics – lower gross margins, smaller target markets and simpler products and services that may not appear as attractive as existing solutions when compared against traditional performance metrics.

The situation in India concerning refrigerators

Currently, in urban India, about 50 per cent of all households have refrigerators. On the other hand, in rural India, only 8 per cent of households have them. Several factors are responsible for the low uptake of conventional refrigerators in rural India, such as the low purchasing power of households and the absence of a regular power supply. However, these factors have also created the opportunity for a disruptive innovation in the area of refrigeration in India.

Godrej (one of the largest manufacturers of home appliances in India, headquartered in Mumbai) decided to address this concern by developing an innovative product for the customers at the bottom of the pyramid (BOP).

The R&D team at Godrej began work on the 'ChotuKool' (meaning 'small cooler') in 2007. The team adopted a different approach to developing the product. For a better understanding of consumer needs, the Godrej team decided to involve the villagers in determining the key features of the new product, instead of using a market research agency. The prototype went through multiple iterations based on the feedback received from rural women.

In 2009, the outcome of the R&D process was a highly portable refrigerator plastic cube, 40 litres in volume and with colour options ranging from a quiet blue-grey to a striking candy-red. It opens on top to conserve cold air. The unconventional opening ensures that cold air settles down in the cabinet to minimize heat loss and power consumption. A power socket sits embedded in the lid, next to two axial fans that dispel heat. When it is empty, it weighs 7-kg. When it's plugged in, it can cool its contents to 20 degrees below the ambient temperature. The ChotuKool does not attempt to be an icebox; it aspires only to be a serviceable domestic refrigerator. Instead of traditional compressors, ChotuKool is based on a thermoelectric chip that maintains a cool temperature using a 12-volt DC current or an external battery.

Priced at about US $65, less than half of an entry-level refrigerator, ChotuKool creates a new product category, with a targeted value proposition that serves the BOP segment of customers.

Godrej plans to involve village girls in selling the products on a commission of US $3 per product sold. This plan will help to reduce distribution and marketing costs by 40 per cent. This community initiative will help drive the cause of inclusive growth.

In 2012, Godrej set out to sell 100,000 ChotuKools, mainly on the Indian market. Godrej is also looking for foreign market opportunities.

Sources: based on www.godrej.com; www.chotukool.in; Christensen (1997).

6.6   'Bottom of pyramid' (BOP) as a market opportunity

Poverty is a widespread reality in the modern world. Two-thirds of the world's population earn less than US $2,000 per year. The poor people's market has been seen as a gold mine for reaping business profits and it has been called the 'bottom of the pyramid' (BOP) market (Prahalad, 2004). According to Prahalad, focus on the BOP market should be a part of core business and not just corporate social responsibility (CSR) initiatives: catering to the BOP market (by satisfying unmet social needs and new consumer preferences), business organizations can create market opportunities of substantial value. The development of the business of microfinance is one such example.

According to Prahalad (2004), marketers who believe that the BOP is a valuable unserved market also believe that even the poor can be good customers. Despite their low level of income, they are discerning consumers who want value and are well aware of the value brands favoured by more affluent consumers. This school of thought recognizes the obstacles created by low income. It postulates that if companies take the correct steps and devote sufficient resources to satisfying the needs of the BOP market, they can overcome barriers to consumption.

Prahalad recognizes that serving the low-income sector requires a commercial strategy in response to the needs of those people; to succeed, other players have to get involved – mainly local and central government, financial institutions and non-governmental organizations (NGOs). He proposes four key elements to thrive in the low-income market:

1. creating buying power;
2. shaping aspirations through product innovation and consumer education;
3. improving access through better distribution and communication systems;
4. tailoring local solutions.

In the following we will focus on the BOP market in relation to:

● the poor as consumers;
● the poor as marketers of products and services.

The poor as consumers

Poverty is a matter of degrees and involves subjective judgments. Prahalad (2004) uses the criterion of US $2 per day at PPP rates in 1990 prices (equivalent to US $3.50 at 2008 prices). At this level of poverty, the basic needs of survival are met, but just barely.

Prahalad claims that the potential BOP market is US $13 trillion at PPP. According to Karnani (2007) this grossly overestimates the size of the BOP market. The *average* consumption of poor people is US $1.25 per day. Assuming there are 2.7 billion poor people, this implies a BOP market size off US $1.2 trillion at PPP in 2002. Karnani suggests this may also be an overestimated figure and he thinks that the global BOP might be as little as US$0.3 trillion, compared with the US$11 trillion economy in the US alone.

According to Hammond *et al.* (2007), the BOP is concentrated in four regional areas: Africa, Asia, eastern Europe and Latin America and the Caribbean: 12.3 per cent of the BOP market live in Africa, 72.2 per cent in Asia, 6.4 per cent in eastern Europe and the remaining 9.1 per cent in Latin America and the Caribbean. Rural areas dominate most BOP markets in Africa and Asia, while urban areas dominate most in eastern Europe and Latin America and the Caribbean.

In order to reach the BOP customers, Gollakota *et al.* (2010) propose a two-stage model:

1. *Deep cost management*. It is obvious that costs need to be reduced, but before this happens the core value of the product and service for BOP customers must be identified. Lifestyle and circumstances of people at the BOP are very different from those of even the poorest in western markets. The cultural norms are different and there are differences in perceptions of value experienced by BOP customers. Companies must understand the essential needs that the product/service satisfies. Once the organization has identified its core value proposition to match its BOP customers' needs and wants, the next step is to re-engineer the value chain to reduce costs. This may involve stripping out elements that only add costs and avoiding all the frills, e.g. by lowering costs using cheaper inputs or reducing package sizes (repackaging in small amounts). Other cost-saving solutions include using credit (when available) to reduce the up-front payments and accepting payment in instalments. Another possibility is to adopt pay-per-use strategies that allow the customer to pay for the use of the asset without paying the full capital cost (Karamchandani *et al.*, 2011).

2. *Deep benefit management*. Even a deep cost management strategy may still not enable a company to reach BOP customers. Instead, companies often need to recognize that BOP customers' needs and wants are very different from those of more affluent customers.

In these cases, a more fundamental redesign may be necessary. In some cases, this means adding new features that are important for BOP customers; in other cases, it might mean offering convenient locations, transport or other services that are essential for BOP customers.

EXHIBIT 6.5 Vodacom – reaching both BOP (bottom of pyramid) customers and BOP entrepreneurs in Africa

Vodacom is a pan-African mobile tele-communications company, and was the first cellular network in South Africa. It provides GSM services to over 50 million customers in South Africa, Tanzania, Lesotho, Mozambique and the Democratic Republic of the Congo.

At some point Vodacom recognized that although only few individuals in BOP areas within Africa could afford a mobile phone for his or her exclusive personal use, one could be affordable by sharing it and its cost among a number of users. This shared mobile phone would meet the basic need of communication but would not meet the needs of privacy or allow the BOP customer to be always accessible. Moving

Vodacom: a pan-African, cellular, telecommunications network

Source: Vodacom.

beyond the value of a mobile phone as a communication device, Vodacom added a new value proposition by positioning the mobile phone as an income-earning asset. With this new value proposition, a mobile phone could be sold to a local entrepreneur who would act as a franchisee for Vodacom (franchisor) by charging users in the local community for using it. In this way, Vodacom added value to the mobile phone by offering not just a mode of communication, but also a way of earning a livelihood.

Source: adapted from Gollakota *et al.* (2010)

The poor as marketers of products and services

In order for the BOP to develop successful entrepreneurs, there are three critical aspects that should be fulfilled in order to serve the BOP market (Pitta *et al.*, 2008):

- access to credit (microfinance);
- the establishment of alliances;
- adaptation of the marketing mix (not discussed here – but see Exhibits 6.2 and 6.3 for good examples of marketing mix adaptation).

Access to credit (microfinance)

The concept that a poor consumer could gain a small loan and become a producer contributing to family income and independence is tantalizing. There is evidence that micro-loans have succeeded in aiding the BOP. There is also evidence that many of the would-be entrepreneurs failed to capitalize on such credit (Karnani, 2007).

Formal commercial credit has been unavailable to this market and the cost of accessing and getting financial services in the informal financial market is enormous.

The decision to award the 2006 Nobel Peace Prize to Muhammad Yunus and the Grameen Bank in Bangladesh has underlined the potential of microfinance in developing countries. Microfinance banks have been set up in most African countries over the past decade, but the sheer scale of the Grameen operations is staggering. Providing individuals or very small businesses with access to what are often very small sums of money may seem like a marginal contribution to economic growth, but it can widen a nation's economic base and promote the kind of growth that leads to real increases in living standards.

Grameen Bank has now provided credit to over 7 million people, 97 per cent of them women. Most loans are very small and rarely exceed $100. In Bangladesh, the bank usually operates in local temples or village halls. Loans are often used to improve irrigation or to buy new tools to improve efficiency. As part of the Nobel Prize, Yunus was awarded 10 million Swedish Krona (US $1.35 million), which will be used to find new ways of helping poor people set up their own businesses.

EXHIBIT 6.6 Voltic Cool Pac – distribution of water in Ghana

In the early 2000s, Voltic, Ghana's leading producer of bottled water, was concentrated on higher-income Ghanaians servicing high-end outlets including hotels, bars and restaurants. However, for the Voltic management, the BOP water market held significant potential, but with low prices and little brand loyalty among consumers, it was viewed as a segment with high volume but very low value.

The company clearly had to rethink its business strategy in order to compete. Voltic realized that transporting water from centralized bottling facilities to the respective markets and high traffic areas was too costly. Furthermore, with smaller package sizes the transportation cost per litre would increase, as sachets (or pouches) are not really known for stowability. Poor infrastructure and transport utilization in emerging markets compounded the problem. So, Voltic took a radical step to decentralize its bottling process through more than a dozen franchisees and, in the process, brought their water product closer to the market.

Voltic made radical changes to its business model, decentralizing production through franchising, establishing a separate brand, and optimizing sales by using informal street hawkers to peddle the US $0.03 500 ml sachets. Franchisees are local entrepreneurs with the ability to invest and grow the business. This includes bottling (including quality control) and distribution. In this partnership, Voltic pays for just over half the capital cost, with the rest of the costs covered by the entrepreneur. Voltic and the franchisees split the operating margin.

Voltic introduced a new brand called Cool Pac and priced it at a slight premium above the numerous informal competitors. In the BOP segment where water functions more as a commodity, Voltic changed all of that with a strong emphasis on the brand and quality. Even though Voltic outsourced bottling and distribution, the company maintains close control over all brand-building activities.

The sachets are distributed using a network of informal street hawkers. Sachets (500-ml) are sold to consumers for US $0.03 per sachet on a cash-and-carry basis. Today, more than 10,000 street hawkers sell nearly 480,000 Cool Pac sachets daily.

Following Voltic's success, private equity firm Aureos made two successful investments in the company beginning in 2004 and, in 2009, Voltic was acquired by SABMiller.

Source: Svend Hollensen.

Source: based on Karamchandani *et al.* (2011).

The establishment of alliances

The BOP market requires the involvement of multiple players, including private companies, governments, NGOs, financial institutions and other organizations, e.g. communities.

By infusing the profit motive into value creation, the hope is that private companies will take the leading role in serving the BOP and, thus, the purpose of alleviating poverty will be more likely to succeed.

Lastly, the public sector has an important role in developing the BOP proposition. The focus is changing from traditional governmental assistance delivery to different ways of creating a sustainable environment for aiding the BOP. For example, the provision of funding and training to entrepreneurs is a way governments can support consumers and producers at the BOP.

Alliances in the health care sector are also very important. For example, the cost of a 10-day supply of a life-saving antibiotic cannot be reduced realistically using the 'smaller package size' option. The implication would be either reduced daily doses or fewer full-strength doses. Both are likely to breed drug-resistant organisms and thereby threaten the life of the patient and society. To remedy this situation, other players, such as governments and NGOs, will be important and marketers must realize that collaborating with them is important.

6.7   Summary

In this chapter, we have concentrated on analysing the political/legal and economic environments as they affect the firm in international markets. Most companies are unable to influence the environment of their markets directly, but their opportunities for successful business conduct depend largely on the structure and content of that environment. A marketer serving international markets, or planning to do so, therefore, has to assess carefully the political and legal environments of the markets served or under consideration to draw the appropriate managerial consequences.

Political environment

The international marketer's political environment is complex because of the interaction among domestic, foreign and international politics. When investing in a foreign country, firms have to be sensitive to that country's political concerns. The firm should prepare a monitoring system that allows it to evaluate the political risks – such as expropriation, nationalization and restrictions against exports and/or imports – systematically. Through skilful adaptation and control, political risks can be reduced or neutralized.

Tariffs have traditionally been used as barriers to international trade. International trade liberalization during the last decade of the twentieth century led to a significant reduction of tariff barriers. Therefore governments have been increasingly using non-tariff barriers to protect those of their countries' industries they think are unable to sustain free international competition. A government may also support or deter international business through its investment policy, that is, the general rules governing legislation concerning domestic as well as foreign participation in the equity or ownership of businesses and other organizations of the country.

There are various trade barriers that can inhibit global marketing. Although nations have used the WTO to lessen many of the restrictions, several of these barriers will undoubtedly remain.

The political risk perspective of a nation can be studied using factors such as:

- a change in government policy;
- the stability of the government;

- the quality of the host government's economic management;
- the host country's attitude towards foreign investment;
- the host country's relationship with the rest of the world;
- the host country's relationship with the parent company's home government;
- the attitude towards the assignment of foreign personnel;
- the closeness between the government and people;
- the fairness and honesty of administrative procedures.

The importance of these factors varies from country to country and from firm to firm. Nevertheless, it is desirable to consider them all to ensure a complete knowledge of the political outlook for doing business in a particular country.

International terrorism is an increasing problem for companies but, with appropriate strategic and operational thinking, the effects of terrorism can be anticipated and planned for. While new procedures intended to minimize terrorism's harm may prove costly, they must be weighed against the substantial savings afforded by corporate preparedness for both the direct and indirect effects of terrorism. In the long run, manufacturers should increasingly incorporate product value chains that facilitate rapid switching to alternative parts and components in the event of supply shocks to critical input goods.

Economic environment

The economic environment is a major determinant of market potential and opportunity. Significant variations in national markets originate in economic differences. Population characteristics, of course, represent one major dimension. The income and wealth of the nation's people are also extremely important because these key figures determine people's purchasing power. Countries and markets may be at different stages of economic development, each stage having different characteristics.

The Maastricht Treaty resulted in the European Economic and Monetary Union (EMU), which also included the new common European currency, the euro. Although the EMU is currently limited to 19 of the 28 member states, it nevertheless involves the extension of the 'law of one price' across a market comprising 300 million consumers, representing one-fifth of the world economy, which should promote increased trade and stimulate greater competition. Consequently the development of this 'new' Europe has an importance beyond the relatively small group of nations currently involved in its creation.

Formal methods for gauging economic development in other nations include: (a) national production, such measures as gross national product and gross domestic product; (b) purchasing-power parity, or the relative ability of two countries' currencies to buy the same 'basket' of goods in those two countries. This index is used to correct comparisons that are made.

BRIC stands for Brazil, Russia, India and China. The economic growth and emerging middle class in these countries will probably have enormous influence on the rest of the world.

CASE STUDY 6.1

G-20 and the economic and financial crises: what on earth is globalization about?
Protests during a meeting in Brisbane, Australia, November 2014

The Group of Twenty (G-20) finance ministers and central bank governors was established in 1999 to bring together important industrialized and developing economies to discuss key issues in the global economy on a regular basis. The G-20 was created as a response both to the financial crises of the late 1990s and to a growing recognition that key emerging-market countries (represented in the G-8) were not adequately included in the core of global economic discussion and governance. The inaugural meeting of the G-20 took place in Berlin, on 15–16 December 1999, hosted by German and Canadian finance ministers. The G-20 is made up of the finance ministers and central bank governors of 19 countries: Argentina, Australia, Brazil, Canada, China, France, Germany, India, Indonesia, Italy, Japan, Mexico, Russia, Saudi Arabia, South Africa, South Korea, Turkey, the UK, the US and the European Union (the 20th member of the G-20).

On 15–16 November 2014, the world leaders from the G-20 countries – representing 85 per cent of the world's output – met in Brisbane, Australia. They came together in the shadow of the euro crises and the pro-Russian actions in Ukraine earlier in the year. European leaders have come under pressure to show that they can stop the risk of a Greek exit from the Eurozone and the threat to the bigger economies in the single currency (euro) area, such as Spain and Italy. They have been, and continue to be, pressed to show that they can take steps to fix the fundamental problems that have dogged the euro.

As has occurred at other World Bank or G-8 meetings, there were massive protests and demonstrations planned. However, a demonstration likely to have drawn up to 120,000 people at the G20 summit in Brisbane was reduced to as few as 1,000 because of protest laws implemented by Queensland's government just a few weeks before the summit in Brisbane.

The motives for protests at G-20 meetings are multifaceted: the protesters range from anti-war campaigners and environmentalists (wanting the G-20 to consider moving away from fossil fuels)

Source: Daniel Munoz/Getty Images.

to anti-globalization activists. The arguments for and against globalization are outlined in the following.

For globalization

For consumers and avowed capitalists, globalization is largely a good thing. The fall of protectionist barriers has stimulated free movement of capital and paved the way for companies to set up several bases around the world. The rise of the internet and recent advances in telecommunications have spurred on the already surging train. Vigorous trade has made for more choice on the high street, greater spending, rising living standards and a growth in international travel. Supporters of globalization say it has promoted information exchange, led to a greater understanding of other cultures and allowed democracy to triumph in most countries.

Against globalization

As the street protests indicate, there is a growing opposition to the forces of globalization. The anti-globalization movement developed in the late twentieth century to combat the globalization of corporate economic activity and the free trade with developing nations that might result from such activity.

Critics say the West's gain has been at the expense of developing countries. Demonstrators say rich countries should forgive the debts of the poorest nations. Generally speaking, protesters believe that these global institutions and agreements (WTO, World Bank/IMF, G-8, G-20) undermine local decision-making methods. Many governments and free trade institutions are seen as acting for the good of transnational (or multinational) corporations (e.g. Microsoft, Unilever).

The already low share of the global income of the poorest people in the world has dropped even more in the past decade, but in the developed world not everyone has been a winner. The freedoms granted by globalization have led to increased insecurity in the workplace. Manual workers, in particular, are under threat as companies shift their production lines overseas to low-wage economies.

Developing countries are demanding that the EU and the US cut back their agricultural subsidy programmes and provide market access for products like Central American sugar and Brazilian orange juice. However, as agribusiness is focal in several EU countries and in the US, and with thousands of agricultural jobs at stake in these areas, it is unlikely that the US or the EU administration will negotiate seriously on these issues in the near future.

At the heart of the demonstrators' concerns is the fact that huge transnational companies are becoming more powerful and influential than democratically elected governments, putting shareholder

interests above those of communities and even customers. Ecological campaigners say corporations are disregarding the environment in the stampede for worldwide mega-profits. Human rights groups say corporate power is restricting individual freedom. Even business people behind small firms have sympathy for the movement, afraid as they are that global economies of scale will put them out of work.

The mere fact that the debate can take place simultaneously across countries and continents, however, may well show that the celebrated global village is already here.

QUESTIONS

1. What were the key arguments of the anti-globalization groups?

2. How could these protests affect the operations of multinational companies?

3. How could the G-20 do a better marketing job in communicating its views to the global audience?

Source: based on http://www.theguardian.com/world/2015/apr/18/g20-laws-cut-protest-numbers-from-likely-120000-to-1000-inquiry-told.

CASE STUDY 6.2

Danfoss Power Solutions: which political/economic factors would affect a manufacturer of hydraulic components?

Danfoss Power Solutions (www.powersolutions. danfoss.com) is a comprehensive subsupplier of mobile hydraulic solutions as either components or integrated systems to manufacturers of mobile equipment in agriculture, construction, material handling and road building, as well as speciality vehicles in forestry and on-highway.

The name of the division changed from Sauer-Danfoss to Danfoss Power Solutions on September 17, 2013, when Danfoss A/S acquired all the remaining publicly held shares of Sauer-Danfoss Inc. Today, Danfoss Power Solutions is a part of the privately held Danfoss Group, which in 2014 generated

€4.6 billion in net sales, with EBIT of €584 million. Globally Danfoss has around 24,000 employees.

Danfoss Power Solutions has around 20 factories in North America, Europe and South-east Asia and is among the largest manufacturers and suppliers of mobile hydraulics in the world today. Danfoss Power Solutions has its principal business centres in Ames, Iowa (US), Neumünster (Germany) and Nordborg (Denmark).

Danfoss Power Solutions' competitors in mobile hydraulic solution include Bosch Rexroth (Germany), Parker Hannifin Corporation (US) and Eaton Corporation (US).

QUESTIONS

1. Which political and economic factors in the global environment would have the biggest effect on the future global sales of Danfoss Power Solutions' hydraulic components/systems to:

   (a) manufacturers of construction and mining equipment (e.g. Caterpillar)?

   (b) manufacturers of agricultural machinery (e.g. John Deere)?

2. What are the biggest problems in forecasting future demand for a subsupplier such as Danfoss Power Solutions?

Sources: www.powersolutions.danfoss.com/home/; other public sources.

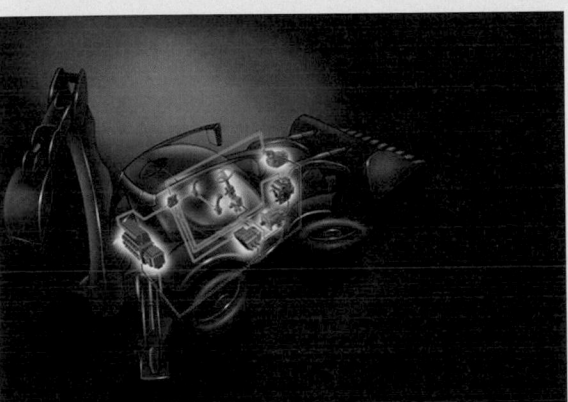
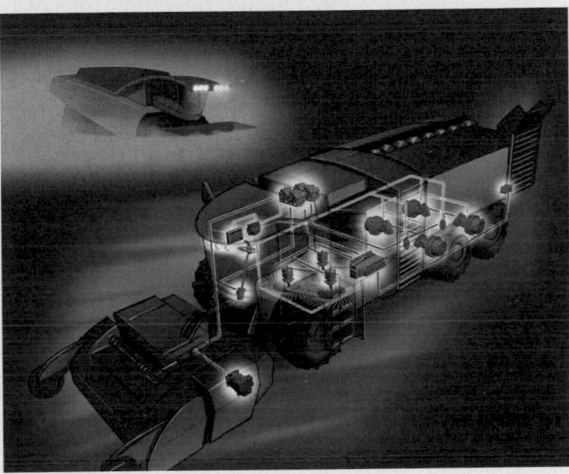

The two blue images represent the construction market (backhoe loader) and the agricultural market (beet harvester)

Source: Sauer-Danfoss Ltd.

VIDEO CASE STUDY 6.3 Debate on globalization

download from **www.pearsoned.co.uk/hollensen**

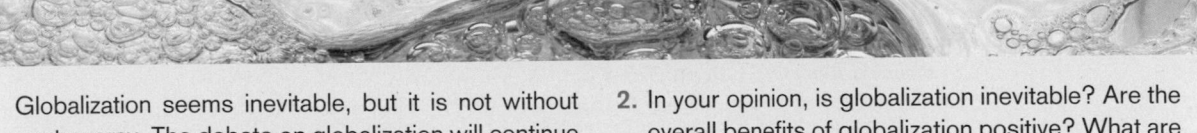

Globalization seems inevitable, but it is not without controversy. The debate on globalization will continue as people try to make sure that the benefits of global trade outweigh the costs for all countries, not just a select few. Despite the pervasive influence of globalization, it is hard to pin down one definition that will suit everybody. For our purposes, globalization refers to an interdependent world economy – in which people in one part of the world interact with people in another part as buyers, sellers or intermediaries.

Questions

1. What are the dimensions that go into the concept of 'globalization'?

2. In your opinion, is globalization inevitable? Are the overall benefits of globalization positive? What are the gains and losses from globalization?

3. What external influences does a company encounter when determining how and where to conduct business globally?

4. What are the motives behind for example Nike's globalization strategy? What are the pros and cons behind the sourcing of products from developing countries?

For further resources, see this book's website at **www.pearsoned.co.uk/hollensen**

Questions for discussion

1. Identify different types of barrier to the free movement of goods and services.

2. Explain the importance of a common European currency to firms selling goods to the European market.

3. How useful is GNP when undertaking a comparative analysis of world markets? What other approaches would you recommend?

4. Discuss the limitations of per-capita income in evaluating market potential.

5. Distinguish between: (a) free trade area, (b) customs union, (c) common market, (d) economic and monetary union and (e) political union.

6. Why are international marketers interested in the age distribution of the population in a market?

7. Describe the ways in which foreign exchange fluctuations affect: (a) trade, (b) investments, (c) tourism.

8. Why is political stability so important for international marketers? Find some recent examples from the press to underline your points.

9. How can the change of major political goals in a country have an impact on the potential for success of an international marketer?

10. A country's natural environment influences its attractiveness to an international marketer of industrial products. Discuss.

11. Explain why a country's balance of trade may be of interest to an international marketer.

References

Albaum, G., Strandskov, J. and Duerr, E. (2002) *International Marketing and Export Management*, 4th edn. Financial Times/Pearson Education, Harlow.

Barr, A. (2015) 'EU Case turns on "Search Bias"', *The Wall Street Journal*, April 17, p. 19.

Christensen, C.M. (1997) *The Innovator's Dilemma: When New Technologies Cause Great Firms to Fail*. Harvard Business School Press, Boston, MA, USA.

Clements, K.W., Lan, Y. and Seah, S.P. (2010) 'The Big Mac Index two decades on: an evaluation on Burgernomics', Discussion Paper 10.14, University of Western Australia.

Enderwick, P. (2011) 'Understanding the rise of global protectionism', *Thunderbird International Business Review*, 53(3), pp. 325–336.

Erevelles, M.S., Horton, V. and Marinova, A. (2005) 'The triadic model: a comprehensive framework for managing country risk', *The Marketing Journal*, 15(2), pp. 1–17.

Gollakota, K., Gupta, V. and Bork, J.T. (2010) 'Reaching customers at the base of the pyramid – a two-stage business strategy', *Thunderbird International Business Review*, 52(5), pp. 355–367.

Hammond, A., Kramer, W.J., Tran, J., Katz, R. and Walker, C. (2007) *The Next 4 Billion*. World Resource Institute, Washington.

Jakobsen, J. (2010) 'Old problems remain, new ones crop up: political risk in the 21st century', *Business Horizons*, 53, pp. 481–490.

Karamchandani, A., Kubzansky, M. & Lalwani, N. (2011) 'Is the bottom of the pyramid really for you?', *Harvard Business Review*, March, pp. 107–111.

Karnani, A. (2007) 'The mirage of marketing to the bottom of the pyramid: how the private sector can help alleviate poverty', *California Management Review*, 49, pp. 90–111.

Low, B. (2007) 'Huawei Technologies Corporation: from local dominance to global challenge?', *Journal of Business & Industrial Marketing*, 22(2), pp. 138–144.

Pitta, D.A., Guesalaga, R. and Marshall, P. (2008) 'The quest for the fortune and the bottom of the pyramid: potential and challenges', *Journal of Consumer Marketing*, 25(7), 393–401.

Prahalad, C.K. (2004) *Fortune at the Bottom of the Pyramid: Eradicating Poverty through Profits*. Upper Saddle River, NJ: Wharton School Publishing.

World Bank (2015a) World Development Indicators database, World Bank, 1 July 2011.

World Bank (2015b) *World Development Indicators 2012*. The World Bank – Development Data Group, Washington.

CHAPTER 7
The sociocultural environment

Contents

Case studies

Learning objectives

After studying this chapter you should be able to:

- Discuss how the sociocultural environment will affect the attractiveness of a potential market

- Define culture and name some of its elements

- Explain the '4 + 1' dimensions in Hofstede's model

- Discuss the strengths and weaknesses of Hofstede's model

- Discuss whether the world's cultures are converging or diverging.

7.1 Introduction

The importance of culture to the international marketer is profound. Culture is a pervasive influence which underlies all facets of social behaviour and interaction. It is embodied in the objects used in everyday life and in modes of communication in society. The complexity of culture is reflected in its multitude of definitions (Craig and Douglas, 2006). Every author who has dealt with culture has defined it differently. Tylor's (1881) definition is one of the most widely accepted: 'Culture is a complex whole which includes knowledge, belief, art, morals, law, custom and any other capabilities and habits acquired by man as a member of the society'.

Culture is an obvious source of differentiation between international markets. Some cultural differences are easier to manage than others. In tackling markets in which buyers speak different languages or follow other religions, for instance, the international marketer can plan in advance how to manage specific points of difference. Often a greater problem is to understand the underlying attitudes and values of buyers in different countries.

The concept of culture is broad and extremely complex. It encompasses virtually every part of a person's life. The way in which people live together in a society is influenced by religion, education, family and reference groups. It is also influenced by legal, economic, political and technological forces. There are various interactions between these influences. We can look for cultural differences in the ways different societies communicate: different spoken languages are used, and the importance of spoken and other methods of communication (e.g. the use of space between people) will vary. The importance of work, the use of leisure and the types of reward and recognition that people value vary from culture to culture. In some countries, people are highly motivated by monetary rewards, while in other countries and cultures, social position and recognition are more important.

Culture develops through recurrent social relationships which form patterns that are eventually internalized by members of the entire group. In other words, a culture does not stand still, but changes slowly over time. Finally, cultural differences are not necessarily visible but can be quite subtle, and can surface in situations where one would never notice them.

It is commonly agreed that a culture must have these three characteristics:

1. *It is learned*: that is, acquired by people over time through their membership of a group that transmits culture from generation to generation. In the case of a national culture, you learn most intensively in the early years of life. By the age of five you are already an expert in using your language. You have internalized values associated with such functions as:
   ● interacting with other members of your family;
   ● eliciting rewards and avoiding punishments;
   ● negotiating for what you wanted;
   ● causing and avoiding conflict.
2. *It is interrelated*: that is, one part of the culture is deeply connected with another part, such as religion and marriage, business and social status.
3. *It is shared*: that is, tenets of a culture extend to other members of the group. The cultural values are passed on to an individual by other members of the culture group. These include parents, other adults, family and institutions such as schools, and friends.

Culture can be thought of as having three other levels (Figure 7.1). The tangible aspects of a culture – things you can see, hear, smell, taste or touch – are artefacts or manifestations of underlying values and assumptions that a group of people share. The structure of these elements is like that of an iceberg.

The part of the iceberg that you see above the water is only a small fraction of what is there. What you cannot see are the values and assumptions that can sink your ship if you mistakenly run into them. Daily behaviour is influenced by values and social morals that work closer to the surface than the basic cultural assumptions. The values and social

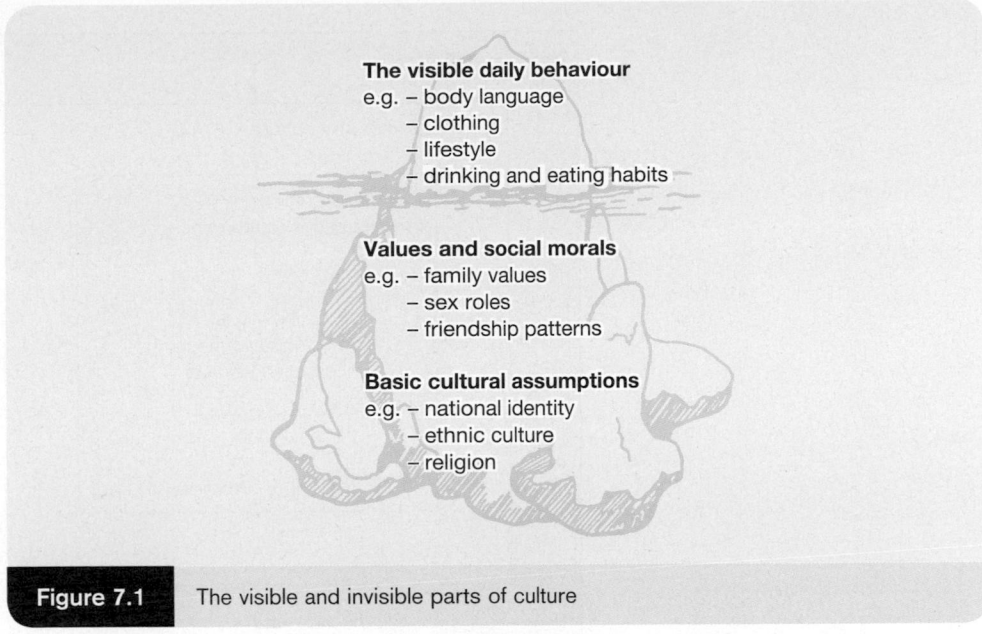

The visible daily behaviour
e.g. – body language
    – clothing
    – lifestyle
    – drinking and eating habits

Values and social morals
e.g. – family values
    – sex roles
    – friendship patterns

Basic cultural assumptions
e.g. – national identity
    – ethnic culture
    – religion

Figure 7.1	The visible and invisible parts of culture

norms help people to make adjustments to their short-term daily behaviour; these standards change over shorter periods of time (10 or 20 years), whereas the basic cultural assumptions are probably formed over centuries.

For the purposes of this book we will define **culture** as the learned ways in which a society understands, decides and communicates.

One way to approach the analysis of cultural influences is to examine cultures by means of a high-context/low-context analysis. Because languages are an important component of culture and an important means of communication, we will look at both spoken languages and silent languages.

The differences between some cultures may be large. Language and value differences between the Swiss and Chinese cultures, for instance, are considerable. There are also differences between the Spanish and Italian cultures, but these are much fewer. Both have languages based on Latin – they use the same written form of communication and they have similar, although not identical, values and norms.

The use of communication techniques varies in different cultures. In some languages, communication is based strictly on the words that are said or written; in others, the more ambiguous elements such as surroundings or the social status of the message-giver are important variables in the transmission of understanding. Hall (1960a) used this finding to make a generalized division between what he referred to as 'low-context cultures' and 'high-context cultures'.

Culture
The learned ways in which a society understands, decides and communicates.

7.2   Layers of culture

The norms of behaviour accepted by the members of the company organization become increasingly important with the company's internationalization. When people with increasingly diverse national cultural backgrounds are hired by international firms, the layers of culture can provide a common framework to understand the various individuals' behaviour and their decision-making process of how to do business.

The behaviour of the individual person is influenced by different layers of culture. The national culture determines the values that influence business/industry culture, which then determine the culture of the individual company.

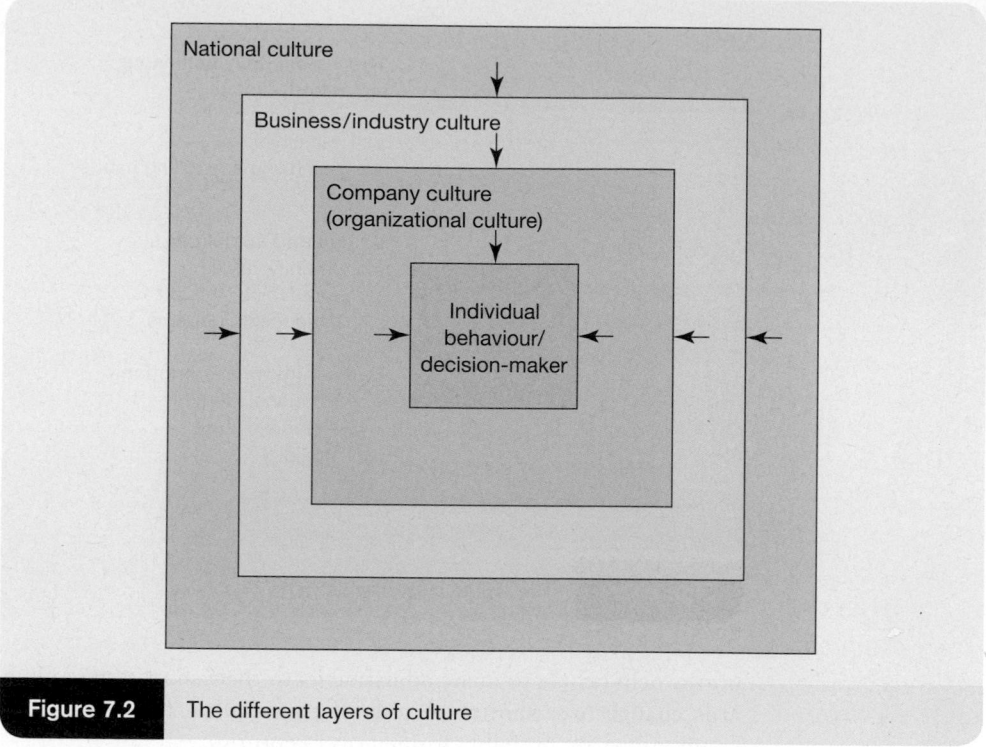

| Figure 7.2 | The different layers of culture |

Figure 7.2 illustrates a typical negotiation situation between a seller in one country and a buyer in another country. The behaviour of the individual buyer or seller is influenced by cultural aspects on different levels, which are interrelated in a complex way. Each of the different levels influences the individual's probable behaviour.

In Figure 7.2 the different levels are looked at from a 'nesting' perspective, the levels being nested into each other in order to grasp the cultural interplay between them. The total nest consists of the following levels:

- *National culture*. This gives the overall framework of cultural concepts and legislation for business activities.
- *Business/industry culture*. Every business is conducted within a certain competitive framework and within a specific industry (or service sector). Sometimes these may overlap but, in general, a firm should be able to articulate quite clearly what business it is in. This level has its own cultural roots and history, and the players within this level know the rules of the game. Industry culture is very much related to a branch of industry, and this culture of business behaviour and ethics is similar across borders. For example, shipping, the oil business, international trading and electronics have similar characteristics across national borders.
- *Company culture (organizational culture)*. The total organization often contains sub-cultures of various functions. Functional culture is expressed through the shared values, beliefs, meanings and behaviours of the members of a function within an organization (e.g. marketing, finance, shipping, purchasing, top management and blue-collar workers).
- *Individual behaviour*. The individual is affected by the other cultural levels. In the inter-action environment, the individual becomes the core person who 'interacts' with the other actors in industrial marketing settings. The individual is seen as important because there are individual differences in perceiving the world. Culture is learned; it is not innate. The learning process creates individuals due to different environments in learning and different individual characteristics.

EXHIBIT 7.1 Electrolux is adapting its vacuum cleaner for the Japanese market

Electrolux is one of the world's largest producers of vacuum cleaners. It opened its first vacuum-cleaner plant outside Sweden as early as 1926, and its vacuum cleaners are currently sold in more than 50 countries around the world.

Vacuum cleaners are suitable for 'globalization', as the shipping costs per unit are relatively low. Consequently, the vacuum cleaner industry is more globalized than those of kitchen and laundry appliances, and most vacuum cleaners are produced in low-cost countries.

Source: AB Electrolux.

However, this does not mean that a manufacturer should just sell exactly the same vacuum cleaner all over the world. The brand may also vary across regions. All Electrolux vacuum cleaners sold in Asia and Latin America are Electrolux brands. In Europe, Electrolux is the dominant manufacturer and here its brands include Volta, Tornado, Progress, AEG-Electrolux and Zanussi. In the US, most of its vacuum cleaners are sold under the Eureka brand and the more exclusive Electrolux branded models.

It has been especially challenging for Electrolux to adapt its vacuum cleaner for the Japanese market. Japanese homes are relatively small and vacuum cleaners need to be quiet in order not to disturb family members and neighbours. Japanese customers are also very careful about cleanliness in their homes and thus clean them regularly.

In order to meet all these demands, the R&D team (together with Electrolux's marketing and design team) developed an ultra-compact vacuum cleaner especially suited to the Japanese market.

The new 'Electrolux Ergothree' vacuum cleaner was introduced in Tokyo in late 2011 with more than 100 Japanese journalists attending the event.

Sources: based on Electrolux Annual Report (2011); and www.electrolux.com.

7.3   High- and low-context cultures

Low-context cultures
Rely only on spoken and written language ('get everything down in the written contract'). Low degree of complexity in communication.

High-context cultures
Use more elements surrounding the message. The cultural context in where the message is communicated has a lot to say. High degree of complexity in communication.

Edward T. Hall (1960a) introduced the concept of high and low contexts as a way of understanding different cultural orientation.

- **Low-context cultures** rely on spoken and written language for meaning. Senders of messages encode their messages, expecting that the receivers will accurately decode the words used to gain a good understanding of the intended message.
- **High-context cultures** use and interpret more of the elements surrounding the message to develop their understanding of the message. In high-context cultures the social importance and knowledge of the person and the social setting add extra information, and will be perceived by the message receiver.

Table 7.1 summarizes some of the ways in which high- and low-context cultures differ.

Figure 7.3 shows the contextual differences in the cultures around the world. At one extreme are the low-context cultures of northern Europe. At the other extreme are the

Table 7.1	General comparative characteristics of cultures	
Characteristic	**Low-context/individualistic (e.g. western Europe, US)**	**High-context/collectivistic (e.g. Japan, China, Saudi Arabia)**
Communication and language	Explicit, direct	Implicit, indirect
Sense of self and space	Informal handshakes	Formal hugs, bows and handshakes
Dress and appearance	Dress for individual success, wide variety	Indication of position in society, religious rule
Food and eating habits	Eating is a necessity, fast food	Eating is social event
Time-consciousness	Linear, exact, promptness is valued, time = money	Elastic, relative, time spent on enjoyment, time = relationships
Family and friends	Nuclear family, self-oriented, value youth	Extended family, other oriented, loyalty and responsibility, respect for old age
Values and norms	Independence, confrontation of conflict	Group conformity, harmony
Beliefs and attitudes	Egalitarian, challenge authority, individuals control destiny, gender equity	Hierarchical, respect for authority, individuals accept destiny, gender roles
Mental process and learning	Lateral, holistic, simultaneous, accepting life's difficulties	Linear, logical, sequential, problem-solving
Business/work habits	Deal-oriented ('quickly getting down to business'), rewards based on achievement, work has value	Relationship-oriented ('first you make a friend, then you make a deal'), rewards based on seniority, work is a necessity

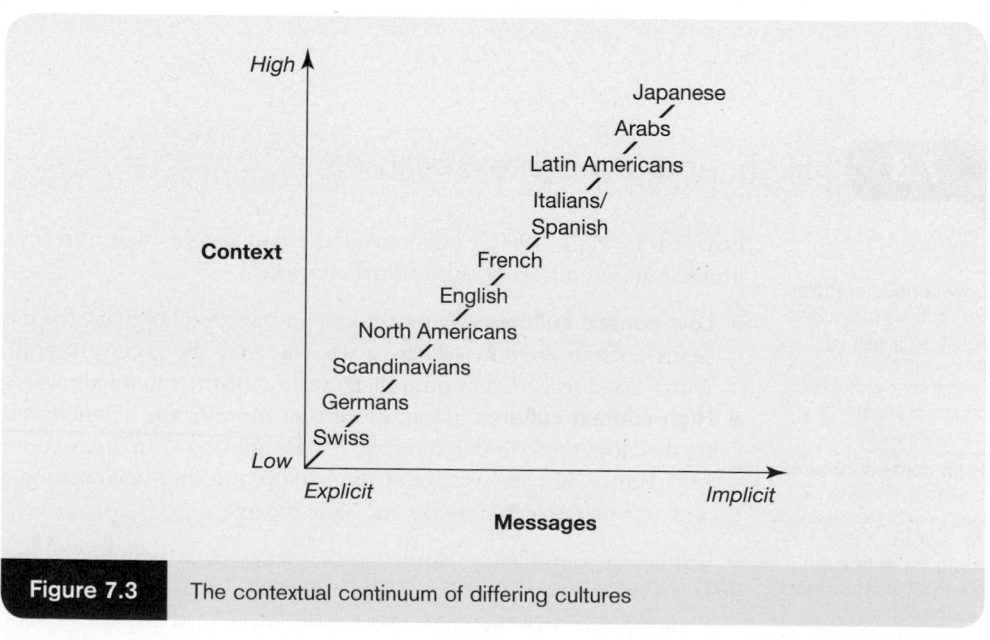

| Figure 7.3 | The contextual continuum of differing cultures |

Source: *Marketing Across Cultures*, 3rd ed., Pearson Education Ltd. (Usunier, J-C. and Lee, J.A. 1999) Copyright © Pearson Education Ltd.

high-context cultures. The Japanese and Arabs have a complex way of communicating with people according to their sociodemographic background.

In an analysis of industrial buyer behaviour in Arab countries, Solberg (2002) found that building trust with partners willing to endorse one's products takes more time in Arab countries than is customary in the west. Networking – using the power of other partners – seems to play a far greater role for Arab buyers. In Arab countries, the position of the agent and his network with prominent families may be critical for success. 'Falling in love' with the wrong agent may therefore spoil the exporter's chances of spending a long period of time in the market.

Special cultural issues in China

In China, many western executives and expatriates approach their assignment with a narrow focus on driving sales. First of all, most westerners underestimate the role of the Chinese government. In most industries, it is impossible to do well in China without the government's back-up.

Secondly, attracting and retaining people in China isn't just about pay or providing opportunities for advancement; it's also about creating a workplace that engages the whole person. For many Chinese, the company is as much a social community as a place of work, and they want their boss to be more than a taskmaster or a distant professional. To reach people on a more personal level, smart executives make themselves more responsive and their companies more caring. For instance, they increase the sponsorship of worker-organized events and expand employee involvement in community and civic-responsibility programmes.

For many western executives, time spent on soft issues like these is time lost on hard ones such as achieving performance targets and improving productivity. However, contrary to popular belief, sincere concern for employees' welfare can be a key factor in driving performance improvement in China. This is not only true at the manager–employee level, it is also the case on the government level. In China, people and the government expect multinational companies to be good corporate citizens to a greater degree than in low-context countries. Companies can demonstrate their commitment by investing in China's development. Samsung's programme to build long-term ties between its operating companies and remote farming villages that need a helping hand, Ericsson's efforts to install mobile telecommunications technology in rural China and GE's involvement in training China's senior leaders are all integral to the businesses' strategic positioning, not optional extras (Paine, 2010).

Getting too involved in the work of employees is understood in the west as micromanagement. In China, because of inexperience, employees usually want more guidance on how to reach their goals and are more likely to look to the boss for detailed instructions. That is why effective Chinese leaders closely oversee subordinates' work, taking the opportunity to lead by example or intervene when teachable moments arise.

The greater the context difference between those trying to communicate, the greater the difficulty in achieving accurate communication.

7.4 Elements of culture

There are varying definitions of the elements of culture, including one (Murdoch, 1945) that counts 73 'cultural universals'.

The following elements are usually included in the concept of culture.

EXHIBIT 7.2 In China the Citroën C4 brand name was changed to Citroën c-Quatre

The number 4 is considered an unlucky number in Chinese because in pronunciation it is very similar to the word 'death' (死 pinyin *sǐ*). As a result, many numbered product lines skip the '4', e.g. Nokia mobile phones (there is no series beginning with a 4). In South-east Asia, some buildings do not have a fourth floor (comparable with the western practice of some buildings not having a 13th floor, because 13 is considered unlucky.) In Hong Kong, some high-rise residential buildings omit all floor numbers with '4', e.g. 4, 14, 24, 34 and all 40–49 floors, in addition to not having a 13th floor.

Building on the success of the Citroën C4 in Europe, Citroën wanted to penetrate the market in China with this model, but because of the sensitive '4' Citroën decided to change the model brand name to c-Quatre when it introduced it in 2012. It is based on the first generation Citroën C4 and made in China by the Dongfeng-PSA joint venture.

Source: based on Feyter, T. (2012) Facelifted Citroen C4 hits the China car market, 19 May, CarNewsChina.com, www.carnewschina.com/2012/05/19/facelifted-citroen-c4-hits-the-china-car-market/.

Language

A country's language is the key to its culture and can be described as the mirror of the culture. Thus, if one is to work extensively with any one culture, it is imperative to learn the language. Learning a language well means learning the culture, because the words of the language are merely concepts reflecting the culture from which it derives.

Language can be divided into two major elements. The verbal language of vocal sounds in patterns that have meaning is the obvious element. Non-verbal language is less obvious, but it is a powerful communicator through body language, silences and social distance.

Verbal language

Verbal language is an important means of communication. In various forms, such as plays and poetry, the written word is regarded as part of the culture of a group of people. In the spoken form, the actual words spoken and the ways in which the words are pronounced provide clues to the receiver about the type of person who is speaking.

Language capability plays four distinct roles in global marketing:

1. Language is important in information-gathering and evaluation efforts. Rather than rely completely on the opinions of others, the manager is able to see and hear personally what is going on. People are far more comfortable speaking their own language, and this should be treated as an advantage. The best intelligence is gathered on a market by becoming part of the market rather than observing it from the outside. For example, local managers of a global corporation should be the firm's primary source of political information to assess potential risk. But take care, they may also be biased.

2. Language provides access to local society. Although English may be widely spoken, and may even be the official company language, speaking the local language could make a dramatic difference. For example, firms that translate promotional materials and information are seen as being serious about doing business in the country.

3. Language capability is increasingly important in company communications, whether within the corporate family or with channel members. Imagine the difficulties encountered by a country manager who must communicate with employees through an interpreter.

4. Language provides more than the ability to communicate; it extends beyond mechanics to the interpretation of contexts.

A very important dimension of the language that can vary by culture is the extent to which communication is explicit or implicit. In explicit-language cultures, managers are taught that to communicate effectively you should 'say what you mean, and mean what you say'. Vague directives and instructions are seen as a sign of poor communication abilities. The assumption in explicit-language cultures is that the burden of effective communication is on the speaker. By contrast, in implicit-language cultures (mostly high context), the assumption is that the speaker and listener both share the burden of effective communication. Implicit communication also helps avoid unpleasant and direct confrontations and disagreements.

Estimates of the numbers of speakers of the main languages around the world are given in Table 7.2. Chinese is spoken as the mother tongue (or first language) by three times more people than the next largest language, English. However, Chinese is overtaken by English when spoken business-language population numbers are taken into account.

It should be noted that official languages are not always spoken by the whole population of a country. For example, French is an official language in Canada, but many Canadians have little or no fluency in French.

Hence English is often, but by no means always, the common language between businesspeople of different nationalities.

Table 7.2	Official languages and spoken languages in the world
Mother tongue (first language)	**No. of speakers (million)**
Chinese	1,000
English	350
Spanish	250
Hindi	200
Arabic	150
Bengali	150
Russian	150
Portuguese	135
Japanese	120
German	100
French	70
Punjabi	70

Note: Chinese is composed of a number of dialects of which Mandarin is the largest.
Source: adapted from Phillips *et al.* (1994), p. 96.

Non-verbal language

Non-verbal language
More important in high-context cultures: time, space (conversational distance between people), material possessions, friendship patterns and business agreements.

Non-verbal language is a powerful means of communication, according to Hall (1960a). The importance of non-verbal communication is greater in high-context countries. In these cultures, people are more sensitive to a variety of different message systems, while in the low-context Anglo-Germanic cultures many of these non-verbal language messages would not be noticed.

Non-verbal language messages, according to Hall (1960b), communicate up to 90 per cent of the meaning in high-context cultures. Table 7.3 describes some of the main non-verbal languages.

Table 7.3	The main non-verbal languages in international business
Non-verbal language	**Implications for global marketing and business**
Time	The importance of being 'on time'. In high-context cultures (e.g. Middle East, Latin America), time is flexible and not seen as a limited commodity.
Space	Conversational distance between people. *Example*: Individuals vary in the amount of space they want between themselves and others. Arabs and Latin Americans like to stand close to people they are talking to. If an American, who may not be comfortable with such proximity, backs away from an Arab, this might be mistaken as a negative reaction.
Material possessions	The relevance of material possessions and interest in the latest technology. This can have a certain importance in both low-context and high-context countries.
Friendship patterns	The significance of trusted friends as a social insurance in times of stress and emergency. *Example*: In high-context countries, extended social acquaintance and the establishment of appropriate personal relations are essential to conducting business. The feeling is that one should often know one's business partner on a personal level before transactions occur.
Business agreements	Rules of negotiations based on laws, moral practices or informal customs. *Example*: Rushing straight to business will not be rewarded in high-context cultures because deals are made not only on the basis of the best product or price, but also on the entity or person deemed most trustworthy. Contracts may be bound by handshakes, not complex agreements – a fact that makes some, especially western, business people uneasy.

EXHIBIT 7.3 Sensuality and touch culture in Saudi Arabian versus European advertising

Although Saudi Arabia has a population of only about 9 million people (including 2 million immigrants) the country is the sixth biggest fragrance market in the world behind the US, Japan, Germany, France and Italy. Saudi Arabia also has the world's highest per-capita consumption of fragrance, leaving all other countries far behind.

In promoting perfumes, the big importers generally use the same advertising materials used by marketers in Europe. What is specifically Arabian in the campaigns is often dictated by Arabian morals.

Saudi Arabia is a high-touch culture, but the inappropriate use of touch in advertising messages can cause problems. The Drakkar Noir pictures show two advertisements for the men's perfume, in which Guy Laroche (via the advertising agency Mirabelle) tones down the sensuality for the Arab version. The European version (left) shows a man's hand clutching the perfume bottle and a woman's hand seizing his bare forearm. In the Saudi version (right), the man's arm is clothed in a dark jacket sleeve, and the woman is touching the man's hand only with her fingertip.

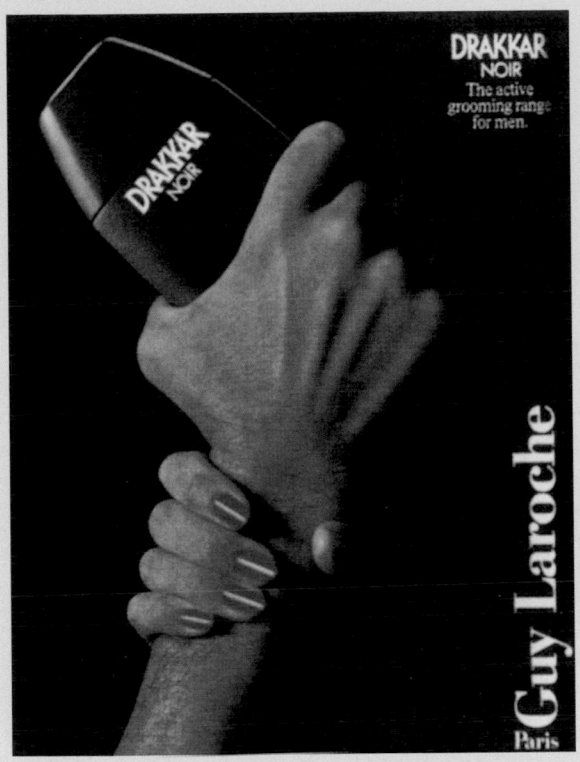

Drakkar Noir: Sensuality and touch culture in Europe and Saudi Arabia

Source: Field (1986). Photos from Guy Laroche.

Manners and customs

Changes occurring in manners and customs must be carefully monitored, especially in cases that seem to indicate a narrowing of cultural differences between peoples. Phenomena such as McDonald's and Coca-Cola have met with success around the world.

Understanding manners and customs is especially important in negotiations because interpretations based on one's own frame of reference may lead to a totally incorrect conclusion. To negotiate effectively abroad, one needs to read all types of communication correctly.

In many cultures, certain basic customs must be observed by the foreign businessperson. One of them concerns the use of the right and left hands. In so-called right-hand societies, the left hand is the 'toilet hand' and using it to eat, for example, is considered impolite.

Technology and material culture

Material culture results from technology and is directly related to how a society organizes its economic activity. It is manifested in the availability and adequacy of the basic economic, social, financial and marketing infrastructures.

With technological advancement comes cultural convergence. Black-and-white television sets extensively penetrated the US market more than a decade before they reached similar levels in Europe and Japan. With colour television, the lag was reduced to five years. With videocassette recorders, the difference was only three years, but this time the Europeans and the Japanese led the way, while Americans concentrated on cable systems. With the compact disc, penetration rates were equal after only one year. Today, with the internet or MTV available by satellite across Europe, no lag exists at all.

Social institutions

Social institutions – business, political, family or class related – influence the behaviour of people and the ways in which people relate to each other. In some countries, for example, the family is the most important social group, and family relationships sometimes influence the work environment and employment practices.

In Latin America and the Arab world, a manager who gives special treatment to a relative is considered to be fulfilling an obligation. From the Latin point of view, it makes sense only to hire someone you can trust. In the US and Europe, however, it is considered favouritism and nepotism. In India there is a fair amount of nepotism, but it is consistent with the norms of the culture. By knowing the importance of family relationships in the workplace and in business transactions, embarrassing questions about nepotism can be avoided.

An important part of the socialization process of consumers worldwide is *reference groups*. These groups provide the values and attitudes that become influential in shaping behaviour. Primary reference groups include the family, co-workers and other intimate groupings, whereas secondary groups are social organizations in which less continuous interaction takes place, such as professional associations and trade organizations.

Social organizations also determine the roles of managers and subordinates and how they relate to one another. In some cultures, managers and subordinates are separated. In other cultures managers and subordinates are on a more common level, and work together in teams.

Education

Education includes the process of transmitting skills, ideas and attitudes, as well as training in particular disciplines. Even primitive peoples have been educated in this broader sense. For example, the Bushmen of South Africa are well educated for the culture in which they live.

One function of education is the transmission of the existing culture and traditions to the new generation. However, education can also be used for cultural change. The promotion of a communist culture in the People's Republic of China is a notable example, but this, too, is an aspect of education in most nations. Educational levels will have an impact on various business functions. Training programmes for a production facility will have to take the educational backgrounds of trainees into account.

The global marketing manager may also have to be prepared to overcome obstacles in recruiting a suitable sales force or support personnel. For example, Japanese culture places a premium on loyalty, and employees consider themselves to be members of the corporate family. If a foreign firm decides to leave Japan, employees may find themselves stranded in mid-career, unable to find a place in the Japanese business system. University graduates are therefore reluctant to join all but the largest and most well-known of foreign firms.

If technology is marketed, the level of sophistication of the product will depend on the educational level of future users. Product adaptation decisions are often influenced by the extent to which targeted customers are able to use the product or service properly.

Values and attitudes

Our attitudes and values help to determine what we think is right or appropriate, what is important and what is desirable. Some relate to marketing, and these are the ones we will look at here.

The more rooted values and attitudes are in central beliefs (such as religion), the more cautiously the global marketing manager has to move. Attitude towards change is basically positive in industrialized countries, whereas in more tradition-bound societies change is viewed with great suspicion, especially when it comes from a foreign entity.

In a conservative society there is generally a greater reluctance to take such risks. There-fore the marketer must also seek to reduce the risk involved in trying a new product as perceived by customers or distributors. In part this can be accomplished through educa-tion; guarantees, consignment selling or other marketing techniques can also be used.

Aesthetics

Aesthetics
What is meant by good taste in art, music, folklore and drama may vary a lot from culture to culture.

Aesthetics refers to attitudes towards beauty and good taste in the art, music, folklore and drama of a culture. The aesthetics of a particular culture can be important in the interpre-tation of symbolic meanings of various artistic expressions. What is and what is not acceptable may vary dramatically, even in otherwise highly similar markets. Sex in adver-tising is an example.

It is important for companies to evaluate in depth such aesthetic factors as product and package design, colour, brand name and symbols. For instance, some conventional brand names that communicate positive messages in the US have a totally different meaning in another country, which may substantially damage corporate image and marketing effec-tiveness (see Table 7.4).

Table 7.4	US brand names and slogans with offensive foreign translations			
Company	**Product**	**Brand name or slogan**	**Country**	**Meaning**
ENCO	Petroleum	Former name of EXXON	Japan	'Stalled car'
American Motors	Automobile	Matador	Spain	'Killer'
Ford	Truck	Fiera	Spain	'Ugly old woman'
Pepsi	Soft drink	'Come alive with Pepsi'	Germany	'Come out of the grave'

Source: Going International: How to Make Friends and Deal Effectively in the Global Marketplace, Copyright © Lennie Copeland and Lewis Griggs (Random House, 1985); all rights reserved.

Religion

The major religions are shared by a number of national cultures:

- Christianity is the most widely practised. The majority of Christians live in Europe and the Americas, and numbers are growing rapidly in Africa.
- Islam is practised mainly in Africa, the Arab countries and around the Mediterranean, and in Indonesia. There has been a recent rise in Islamic fundamentalism in Iran, Paki-stan, Algeria and elsewhere.
- Hinduism is most common in India. Beliefs emphasize the spiritual progress of each person's soul rather than hard work and wealth creation.
- Buddhism has adherents in central and South-east Asia, China, Korea and Japan. Like Hinduism, it stresses spiritual achievement rather than wealth, although the continuing development of these regions shows that it does not necessarily impede economic activity.
- Confucianism has adherents mainly in China, Korea and Japan. The emphasis on loy-alty and obligation between superiors and subordinates has influenced the development of family companies in these regions.

Religion can provide the basis for transcultural similarities under shared beliefs in Islam, Buddhism or Christianity, for example. Religion is of the utmost importance in many countries. In the US and Europe, substantial efforts are made to keep government and church matters separate. Nevertheless there remains a healthy respect for individual religious differences. In some countries, such as Lebanon and Iran, religion may be the very foundation of the government and a dominant factor in business, political and educational decisions.

Religion may affect the global marketing strategy directly in the following ways:

- Religious holidays vary greatly among countries, not only from Christian to Muslim, but even from one Christian country to another. In general, Sundays are a religious holiday in all nations where Christianity is an important religion. In the Muslim world, however, the entire month of Ramadan is, for all practical purposes, a religious holiday.

  In Saudi Arabia, for example, during the month of Ramadan, Muslims fast from sunrise to sunset. As a consequence, worker productivity drops. Many Muslims rise earlier in the morning to eat before sunrise and may eat what they perceive to be enough to last until sunset. This affects their strength and stamina during the working day. An effort by management to maintain normal productivity levels will probably be rejected, so managers must learn to be sensitive to this and similar customs.

- Consumption patterns may be affected by religious requirements or taboos. Fish on Friday for Catholics used to be the classic example. Taboos against beef for Hindus and pork for Muslims and Jews are other examples. The pork restriction exists in Israel as well as in Islamic countries in the Middle East, such as Saudi Arabia, Iraq and Iran, and South-east Asian countries such as Indonesia and Malaysia.

- Islamic worshippers pray facing the holy city of Mecca five times each day. Visiting westerners must be aware of this religious ritual. In Saudi Arabia and Iran, it is not unusual for managers and workers to place carpets on the floor and kneel to pray several times during the day.

- The economic role of women varies from culture to culture, and religious beliefs are an important cause. In the Middle East women may be restricted in their capacity as consumers, as workers or as respondents in a marketing study. These differences can require major adjustments in the approach of a management conditioned to western markets. Women are, among other things, required to dress in such a way that their arms, legs, torso and faces are concealed. An American female would be expected to honour this dress code while in the host country.

EXHIBIT 7.4 Polaroid's success in Muslim markets

During the past 30 years Polaroid's instant photography has been largely responsible for breaking down taboos against taking pictures in the Arab world, especially those concerning women revealing their faces.

When Polaroid entered the market in the mid-1960s, it discovered that instant photography had a special appeal. Because of religious constraints there were only a few photo-processing laboratories. But with Polaroid's instant cameras, Arab men were able to photograph their wives and daughters without fear of a stranger in a film laboratory seeing the women unveiled and without the risk of someone making duplicates.

Source: Charlotte Allen/Alamy Images.

Source: Harper (1986).

Hofstede's model (the '4 + 1' dimensions model) versus the GLOBE model

While an international manager may have neither the time nor the resources to obtain a comprehensive knowledge of a particular culture, a familiarity with the most pervasive cultural 'differentiators' can provide useful guidance for corporate strategy development. One approach to identifying these pervasive fundamental differences of national cultures is provided by Hofstede (1983). Hofstede tried to find an explanation for the fact that some concepts of motivation did not work in the same way in all countries. Hofstede based his research on an extensive IBM database from which – between 1967 and 1973 – 116,000 questionnaires (from IBM employees) were used in 72 countries and in 20 languages.

According to Hofstede, the way people in different countries perceive and interpret their world varies along four dimensions: power distance, uncertainty avoidance, individualism and masculinity:

1. *Power distance* refers to the degree of inequality between people in physical and educational terms (i.e. from relatively equal to extremely unequal). In high power distance societies, power is concentrated among a few people at the top who make all the decisions. People at the other end simply carry these decisions out. They accept differences in power and wealth more readily. In low power distance societies, on the other hand, power is widely dispersed and relations among people are more egalitarian. The lower the power distance, the more individuals will expect to participate in the organizational decision-making process. A high power distance score was observed in Japan. The US and Canada record a middle-level rating on power distance, but countries such as Denmark, Austria and Israel exhibit much lower ratings.

2. *Uncertainty avoidance* concerns the degree to which people in a country prefer formal rules and fixed patterns of life, such as career structures and laws, as means of enhancing security. Another important dimension of uncertainty avoidance is risk-taking. High uncertainty avoidance is probably associated with risk aversion. Organization personnel in low uncertainty avoidance societies face the future as it takes shape without experiencing undue stress. In high uncertainty avoidance cultures, managers engage in activities such as long-range planning to establish protective barriers to minimize the anxiety associated with future events. On uncertainty avoidance, the US and Canada score quite low, indicating an ability to be more responsive in coping with future changes. But Japan, Greece, Portugal and Belgium score high, indicating their desire to meet the future in a more structured and planned fashion.

3. *Individualism* denotes the degree to which people in a country learn to act as individuals rather than as members of groups. In individualistic societies, people are self-centred and feel little need for dependency on others. They seek fulfilment of their own goals over those of the group. In collectivistic societies, members have a group mentality. They are interdependent on each other and seek mutual accommodation to maintain group harmony. Collectivistic managers have high loyalty to their organizations, and subscribe to joint decision-making. The UK, Australia, Canada and the US show very similar (high) ratings on individualism, while Japan, Brazil, Colombia, Chile and Venezuela exhibit very low ratings.

4. *Masculinity* relates to the degree to which 'masculine' values, such as achievement, performance, success, money and competition, prevail over 'feminine' values, such as quality of life, maintaining warm personal relationships, service, care for the weak, preserving the environment and solidarity. Masculine cultures exhibit different roles for men and women, and perceive anything big as important. The feminine cultures value 'small as beautiful', and stress quality of life and environment over materialistic ends. A relatively high masculinity index was observed for the US, Italy and Japan. In

low-masculinity societies such as Denmark and Sweden, people are basically motivated by a more qualitative goal set as a means to job enrichment. Differences in masculinity scores are also reflected in the types of career opportunity available in organizations and associated job mobility.

5. *Time perspective.* In a 23-country study, some years after Hofstede's original work, Hofstede and Bond (1988) identified a fifth dimension that they first termed Confucian dynamism and then renamed 'time orientation'. This time orientation is defined as the way members in an organization exhibit a pragmatic future-oriented perspective rather than a conventional history or short-term point of view. The consequences of a high score on the long-term orientation (LTO) index are persistence, ordering relationships by status and observing this order. The opposite is short-term orientation, which includes personal steadiness and stability (Minkov and Hofstede, 2011).

Most South-east Asian markets, such as China, Hong Kong, Taiwan and South Korea, score high on the LTO index. This tendency has something to do with the Confucian traditions prevalent there, with high emphasis on ordering of relationships, embracing all kinds of human relationships in society, by determining the social roles, obligations and status of each person in the social networking system (Venaik and Prewer, 2013). On the other hand, many European countries are short-term-oriented, with emphasis on quick results rather than long-term fulfillment. In countries scoring high on the LTO index, the respondents said they valued thrift, and in fact these countries have higher saving rates than countries scoring more short-term. More savings means more money for future productive investment (Hofstede, 2007).

Brief introduction to the GLOBE model

The GLOBE study was designed to replicate and expand on Hofstede's original (1980) work, and to test various hypotheses that had been developed, in particular, on leadership topics.

GLOBE is a long-term programmatic research effort designed to explore the complex effects of culture on leadership, organizational effectiveness, economic competitiveness of societies and the human condition of members of the societies studied (House *et al.*, 2004). Conducted in the mid-1990s, the major purpose of the GLOBE study was to increase knowledge and understanding of cross-cultural interactions. The GLOBE researchers measured cultural practices and values at the levels of industry (financial services, food processing, telecommunications), organization (several in each industry), and society (62 cultures). The results were presented in the form of quantitative data based on responses of about 17,000 managers from 951 organizations functioning in 62 societies throughout the world. The questionnaire reports of managers were complemented by interview findings, focus group discussions and formal content analyses of printed media.

GLOBE produced a set of nine dimensions:

uncertainty avoidance, power distance, institutional collectivism, in-group collectivism, gender egalitarianism, assertiveness, future orientation, performance orientation and humane orientation.

The Globe researchers measured Hofstede's 'collectivism' with two constructs: institutional collectivism and in-group collectivism. Similarly, Hofstede's 'masculinity' dimension was measured with the two constructs: gender egalitarianism and assertiveness. Hofstede's LTO is similar to GLOBE's future orientation. Finally, there are two additional dimensions of culture in GLOBE – performance orientation and humane orientation – that are not measured by Hofstede.

All in all, GLOBE researchers were heavily influenced by Hofstede's work in their choice of variables to assess, and some of their nine societal scales share labels with the Hofstede dimensions.

One of the key questions raised is whether the relative positions of countries on the national culture dimensions have changed over time since Hofstede's (1980) original work. Work by Beugelsdijk *et al*. (2015) indicates that the country pair differences (i.e. cultural distances) are relatively stable. There is no indication that cultural distance has decreased over time. For distances towards the US, however, Beugelsdijk *et al*. (2015) find a reduction in the average cultural distance. This decrease in distance seems driven by a process of the US shifting towards the centre of the global distribution rather than the rest of the world moving closer to the US.

EXHIBIT 7.5 Pocari Sweat – a Japanese soft drink expands sales in Asia

Pocari Sweat is a popular Japanese soft health drink, manufactured by Otsuka Pharmaceutical Co. Ltd. The brand started selling in Japan in 1980 and has secured a good foothold for international expansion. The drink is now distributed in other countries in the region, including China (Hong Kong), South Korea, Taiwan, Thailand, Indonesia, Vietnam and the United Arab Emirates. In addition, it can be obtained in the 'Chinatown' areas of many cities around the world.

Source: Otsuka Pharmaceutical Co. Ltd.

Pocari Sweat's slogan is as follows: 'Pocari Sweat – A drink with Properties of your Body's own Fluids'. The phrase '60 per cent of the human body is made up of body fluids' is also included in the advertising.

Contrary to the odd name and its translucent-white colour, Pocari Sweat does not taste like sweat; it is a mild-tasting, relatively light, sweet drink.

● What do you think about the brand name (Pocari Sweat) and its slogan?

Sources: Otsuka Pharmaceutical Co. Ltd; www.otsuka.co.jp/poc/; Pocari Sweat's official website.

7.6 Managing cultural differences

Having identified the most important factors of influence from the cultural environment on the firm's business and having analysed those factors, the international marketer is able to take decisions about how to react to the results of the analysis.

In accordance with Chapter 8, less attractive markets will not be considered further. On the other hand, in the more attractive markets, marketing management must decide to what extent adaptions to the given cultural specifics are needed.

For example, consider *punctuality*. In the most low-context cultures – the Germans, Swiss and Austrians, for example – punctuality is considered extremely important. If you have a meeting scheduled for 9.00am and you arrive at 9.07am you are considered 'late'. Punctuality is highly valued within these cultures, and to arrive late for a meeting (thus 'wasting' the time of those forced to wait for you) is not appreciated.

By contrast, in some southern European nations, and within Latin America, a somewhat 'looser' approach to time may pertain. This does not imply that one group is 'wrong' and the other is 'right'. It simply illustrates that different approaches to the concept of time have evolved for a variety of reasons, over many centuries, within different cultural groups. Culture can and does influence the business sector in different parts of the world to function in distinct ways.

Another example of how cultural differences influence the business sector concerns the presentation of business cards. In the US – which has a very 'informal' culture – business cards are typically presented in a very casual manner. Cards are often handed out quickly and are just as quickly placed into the recipient's pocket or wallet for future reference.

In Japan, however – which has a comparatively 'formal' culture – the presentation of a business card is a more carefully orchestrated event. There, business cards are presented by holding the card up with two hands while the recipient carefully scrutinizes the information it contains. This procedure ensures that one's title is clearly understood – an important factor for the Japanese, where one's official position within one's organizational 'hierarchy' is of great significance.

To simply take the card from a Japanese person and immediately place it in one's cardholder could well be viewed (from a Japanese perspective) in a negative light. However, in the US, to take several moments to carefully and deliberately scrutinize an American's business card might also be taken in a negative way, perhaps suggesting that the person's credibility is in doubt.

These examples – the sense of time/punctuality and the presentation of the business card – illustrate just two of the many ways in which cultural factors can influence business relationships.

In attempting to understand another culture we inevitably interpret our new cultural surroundings on the basis of our existing knowledge of our own culture.

In global marketing it is particularly important to understand new markets in the same terms as buyers or potential buyers in that marketplace. For the marketing concept to be truly operational, the international marketer needs to understand buyers in each marketplace and be able to use marketing research in an effective way.

Lee (1966) used the term *self-reference criterion* (SRC) to characterize our unconscious reference to our own cultural values. He suggested a four-step approach to eliminate SRC:

1. Define the problem or goal in terms of home country culture, traits, habits and norms.
2. Define the problems or goals in terms of the foreign culture, traits, habits and norms.
3. Isolate the SRC influence in the problem and examine it carefully to see how it complicates the problem.
4. Redefine the problem without the SRC influence and solve for the foreign market situation.

It is therefore of crucial importance that the culture of the country is seen in the context of that country. It is better to regard the culture as different from, rather than better or worse than, the home culture. In this way, differences and similarities can be explored and the reasons for differences can be sought and explained.

7.7   Convergence or divergence of the world's cultures

As we have seen earlier in this book, the right mix between local knowledge of different cultures and globalization/integration of national marketing strategies is the key to success in global marketing.

There seems to be a great difference in attitude towards the globalization of cultures among different age groups, youth culture being more international/global than other age groups (Smith, 2000).

Youth culture

Countries may be at different stages in the evolution of particular product and service categories, but in most cases youth is becoming more homogeneous across national markets. Youth cultures are more international than national. There are still some strong national characteristics and beliefs, but they are being eroded. The McDonald's culture is spreading into southern Europe, and at the same time we can see satellite TV taking the values of MTV, *The Simpsons* and Ricki Lake all over the world, with English language culture in their wake.

Differences between youth and adult markets are changing in several key respects, the professionals agree. Younger consumers differ from adults in emphasizing quality and being both discerning and technically literate. Younger consumers are now much more self-reliant and take responsibility far earlier. They are sensible, sophisticated and grown-up at an early age.

Generational barriers are now very blurred. The style leaders for many young people – musicians, sports stars and so on – are often in their 30s and 40s. Cultural and family influences remain very strong throughout Europe and the rest of the world. Few young people have 'role models', but they respect achievers, particularly in music and sport, and their parents, particularly if they have succeeded from humble beginnings.

The lack of clarity in age-group targeting has to be weighed against a growth in cross-border consistencies. But marketers should beware of strategies aimed too blatantly at younger consumers. Young people tend to reject marketing and promotions that are obviously targeted at 'youth'. They perceive these to be false and hypocritical (Smith, 1998).

Today's young people have greater freedom than previous generations had. They are more culturally aware and are reluctant to take anything – or anyone – at face value. Pasco (2000) argues that getting youngsters to relate to celebrities is increasingly difficult. Celebrities often fail or disappoint young people, and again they 'sell out', giving up the integrity for which they were admired in the first place.

Disillusion with celebrities has led young people to look elsewhere for inspiration. They select values from a range of individuals rather than buying wholesale into one. Despite their mistrust of corporations, the young increasingly aspire to, and engage with, brands. It appears safer to invest emotionally in brands than in celebrities.

7.8 The effects of cultural dimensions on ethical decision-making

As more and more firms operate globally, an understanding of the effects of cultural differences on ethical decision-making becomes increasingly important for avoiding potential business pitfalls and for designing effective *international marketing* management programmes.

Culture is a fundamental determinant of ethical decision-making. It directly affects how an individual perceives ethical problems, alternatives and consequences. In order to succeed in today's international markets, managers must recognize and understand how ideas, values and moral standards differ across cultures, and how these in turn influence marketing decision-making.

Some countries, such as India, are well known for 'requiring' small payments if customs officials are to allow goods to enter the country. While this may indeed be a bribe and illegal, the ethics of that country seem to allow it (at least to a certain extent). The company is then left with a problem: does it bribe the official, or does it wait for normal clearance and let its products sit in the customs warehouse for a considerably longer time?

Fees and commissions paid to a firm's foreign intermediate or to consultant firms for their services are a particular problem – when does the legal fee become a bribe? One reason for employing a foreign representative or consultants is to benefit from their contacts with decision-makers, especially in a foreign administration. If the export intermediary uses part of the fee to bribe administrators, there is little that the firm can do.

Thus every culture – national, industry, organizational or professional – establishes a set of moral standards for business behaviour, i.e. a code of business ethics. This set of standards influences all decisions and actions in a company, including, for example, what and how to manufacture (or not), what wages are appropriate to pay, how many hours personnel should work and under what conditions, how to compete, and what communication guidelines to follow. Which actions are considered right or wrong, fair or unfair, in the conduct of business and which are particularly susceptible to ethical norms are heavily influenced by the culture in which they take place (the question of bribery is further discussed in Chapter 18).

The ethical commitment of an international company is illustrated in Figure 7.4 as a continuum from unacceptable ethical behaviour to the most ethical decision-making.

The adherence only to the letter of the law reflects minimally acceptable ethical behaviour. A classification of a company as 'most ethical' requires that the firm's code of ethics should address the following six major issues:

1. *Organizational relations,* including competition, strategic alliances and local sourcing.
2. *Economic relations,* including financing, taxation, transfer prices, local reinvestment, equity participation.
3. *Employee relations,* including compensation, safety, human rights, non-discrimination, collective bargaining, training and sexual harassment.
4. *Customer relations,* including pricing, quality and advertising.
5. *Industrial relations,* including technology transfer, research and development, infrastructure development and organizational stability/longevity.
6. *Political relations,* including legal compliance, bribery and other corrupt activities, subsidies, tax incentives, environmental protection and political involvement.

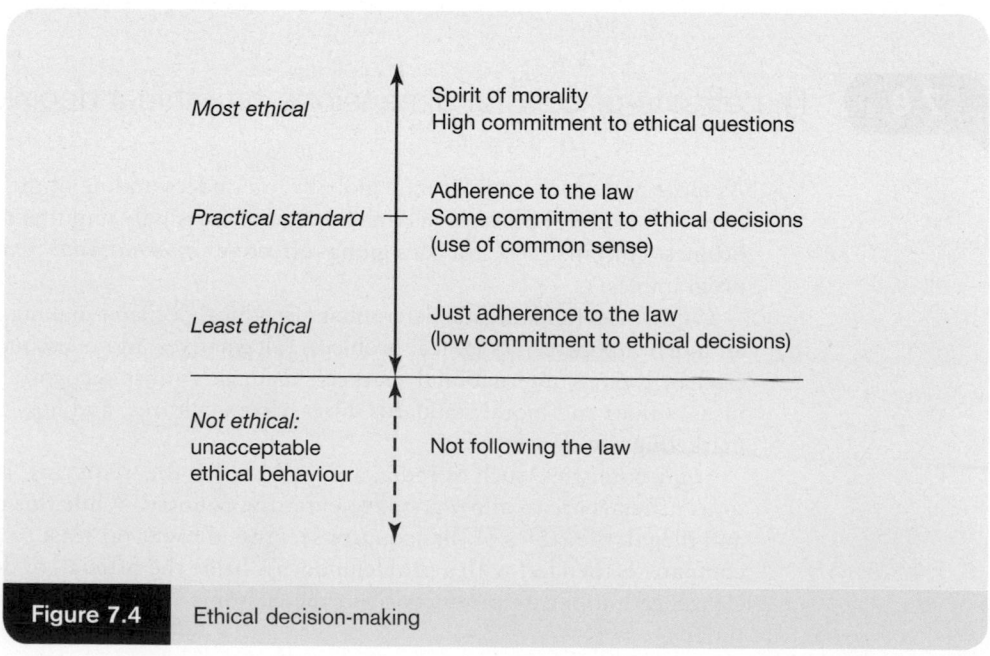

Figure 7.4   Ethical decision-making

EXHIBIT 7.6 The quest for beauty opens a huge market for whitening products in Asia

In Asia, beauty is believed to open many doors, especially for women. Young girls dream of the day when they can get their eyes and nose done, and appear more attractive. Some of them admit that a pretty face is key to clinching a good job or landing the spouse of choice. While these ideas might seem strange to outsiders, it should not come as a surprise, as many cultures around the world place a premium on external beauty.

For example, it is also common for clinics in South Korea to admit patients who are in their teens. Parents, too, are more than happy to pay the bill. Many teenagers are even offered cosmetic surgery from their parents as a reward for doing well in their exams.

Source: Pony Wang/Getty Images.

Among wealthier Asian women, in particular, there is a tremendous interest in plastic surgery that can also be traced back to the detailed definition of what constitutes beauty in Asia. Small sharp features, large eyes with a double eyelid, a high nose, pale skin and full lips are considered ideal, but this is essentially a western idea of perfection. Few Asian women are born with such features, which partly explains their willingness to attempt surgery.

One of the most important beauty features in Asia is pale skin. One reason for this is that traditionally people of noble blood in South Korea were fair-skinned. The upper class rarely went out in the heat of the day, whereas the working classes usually sported a tanned complexion from hours of toil in the sun. This led to a deep-rooted psychological belief relating pale skin to 'upper class'.

The passion for pale skin has given rise to a booming skincare sector that features the latest laser treatments, high-tech facials and over-the-counter formulas. Given the cultural ideal for pale skin, a strong demand for skin whiteners has arisen, also thanks to the rising disposable incomes in the emerging Asian countries.

This is generating interest from multinational players keen to capture a share of the market. As a result there has been an influx of new products with whitening properties from facial care brands. Many of the leading personal care players, such as Procter & Gamble and L'Oréal, heavily promoted their whitening facial skin care products in 2011.

As a result, growth in key skin whitening markets is far outperforming the 3 per cent global growth in facial care in 2011; for example, Thailand recorded 9 per cent, India 13 per cent and China 11 per cent.

In several Asian countries more than 50 per cent of the total number of facial moisturizers sold contain 'whitening' chemical components.

The key consumer base for whitening products remains young women, particularly those in urban areas who typically earn more and are willing to pay extra for premium whitening products. With workers being hit by the recession in Asia-Pacific, intensified competition in the job market means the whitening trend is very unlikely to die down as workers associate pale skin with job success. Parallels can be drawn with the effect of the recession in western markets such as the US, where the distinct rise in cosmetic surgery procedures as job insecurity increases reflects the fact that western consumers are also looking to outward appearance to stay ahead.

Source: based on various public media and informal interviews in Asia.

It is easy to generalize about the ethics of political payoffs and other types of payments; it is much more difficult to make the decision to withhold payment of money when the consequences of not making the payment may affect the company's ability to do business profitably, or at all. With the variety of ethical standards and levels of morality that exist in different cultures, the dilemma of ethics and pragmatism facing international business cannot be resolved until more countries decide to deal effectively with the issue.

7.9   Summary

For international marketers, it is important to understand customers' personal values and accepted norms of behaviour in order to market to them properly. At the same time, marketers must search for groups with shared cognitions that result in shared views of the marketer's offerings and similar product-related behaviour to simplify their task. Such groups may even exist across country borders.

How we perceive other cultures stems from our own cultural mindset and it is very difficult not to take an ethnocentric point of view when classifying other cultures. Classification of cultures is necessary to develop marketing and advertising strategies in the global marketplace. Classifying cultures on dimensions has proved to be the most constructive method. It helps in vocalizing and labelling cultural differences and similarities. Many of the cultural differences are reflected in the type of communication culture used. In this chapter, different models for classification have been discussed.

High/low-context cultures

The difference between high- and low-context communication cultures helps us understand why, for example, Asian (high-context) and western (low-context) styles are so different, and why Asians prefer indirect verbal communication and symbolism over the direct assertive communication approaches used by westerners. Other dimensions, such as different concepts of time, can also explain major differences between east and west.

Hofstede's model

In order to construct a more refined classification system, Hofstede developed a model of '4 + 1' dimensions for comparing work-related values, based on data collected in an extensive study. This model also proves useful for comparing cultures with respect to consumption-related values. As a result, it can explain the variety of values and motivations used in marketing and advertising across cultures.

It can also explain differences in actual consumption behaviour and product use and can thus assist in predicting consumer behaviour or effectiveness of marketing strategies for cultures other than one's own. This will be particularly useful for companies that want to develop global marketing and advertising strategies.

The problem of business ethics is infinitely more complex in the international marketplace because value judgments differ widely among culturally diverse groups. What is commonly accepted as right in one country may be completely unacceptable in another. Giving business gifts of high value, for example, is generally condemned in western countries, but in many countries of the world gifts are not only accepted but expected.

CASE STUDY 7.1

Cirque du Soleil Inc.: the show that revolutionized the circus arts is expanding its global scope

Cirque du Soleil Inc. ('Circus of the Sun'; www.cirquedusoleil.com) is a Canadian entertainment company, self-described as a 'dramatic mix of circus arts and street entertainment'. Based in Montreal, Quebec, the company was founded in 1984 by two former street performers, Guy Laliberté and Gilles Ste-Croix. Today Laliberté is the CEO of the company.

With numerous prizes and distinctions to its credit, Cirque du Soleil is a unique organization which has reinvented and revolutionized the circus arts. Since its beginnings in 1984, Cirque du Soleil has been entertaining the public with a novel show concept that is as original as it is non-traditional: an astonishing, theatrical blend of circus arts and street performance, wrapped up in spectacular costumes and fairyland sets and staged to spellbinding music and magical lighting. There are no animals in a Cirque du Soleil production – only sheer human energy is at work.

The internationalization of Cirque du Soleil

Cirque du Soleil was founded in 1984 to produce an event in Quebec celebrating the 450th anniversary of Canada's discovery by Jacques Cartier. It did so with a $1.3 million grant from the Canadian government.

During the first years, Cirque du Soleil was in serious financial trouble several times and in 1986 it came very close to bankruptcy.

These first two years for Cirque du Soleil consisted of touring around Quebec and neighbouring Ontario. By the end of 1986, however, the Cirque du Soleil management had become convinced of the concept's broad-based appeal, and prepared to export it on a broad scale to their southern neighbours. Thus, in 1987, Cirque du Soleil made its debut in the US.

The company's managers were forward-thinking and objective-oriented, formulating and then pursuing successive five-year plans. The shows themselves were expressions of artistic and athletic ability, but the stewardship of the company was conducted in a businesslike way. This approach

fuelled the geographic expansion of Cirque du Soleil's touring schedule, diversified the company's activities into new revenue-generating areas and, eventually, helped the Cirque du Soleil name become as well known as a popular consumer brand. Although the maturation of the Cirque du Soleil concept into an eccentric yet formidable marketing force did not gain momentum until the mid-1990s, some lucrative projects were started during the late 1980s. In 1988, the company began negotiations that would continue for the next four years for an Asian tour. In 1989, Cirque du Soleil sold its concept for European performances to Circus Knie (Switzerland), which subsequently began producing its own version in Europe.

Cirque du Soleil embarked on its first tour of Asia in 1990, financed by a $40 million investment from Fuji Televisions Network, which handled ticket sales and promotion for the tour. The production, whose budget rivalled that of a major Broadway musical, featured 72 international artists and musicians.

Cirque du Soleil also began a tour organized in partnership with Circus Knie, putting on shows in 60 towns in Switzerland. Busy on all fronts, the company also appeared in Las Vegas for the first time, bringing *Nouvelle Experience* to the Mirage Hotel for a year-long engagement in a tent behind the hotel.

Cirque du Soleil celebrated its 10th anniversary in 1994, its management having devised and fulfilled two five-year plans. For the next five years, management laid out a diversified blueprint for growth, the implementation of which would greatly increase the company's financial stature.

Cirque du Soleil ended the 1990s with seven productions, performing in 22 countries in Asia, the Pacific, North America and Europe. Looking ahead, the company intended to use its worldwide exposure to build the Cirque du Soleil name into an internationally recognized brand.

Cirque du Soleil expanded rapidly through the 2000s, going from one show to 19 shows in over 271 cities on every continent except Antarctica.

Cirque du Soleil today

Each show is a synthesis of circus styles from around the world, with its own central theme and storyline. They draw the audience into the performance through continuous live music, with performers rather than stagehands changing the props.

The multiple permanent Las Vegas shows alone play to more than 9,000 people a night, 5 per cent of the city's visitors, adding to the 90 million people who have experienced Cirque du Soleil worldwide. In 2000, Laliberté bought out Gauthier and, with 95 per cent ownership, has continued to expand the brand. In 2008, Laliberté split 20 per cent of his share equally between two investment groups, Istithmar World and Nakheel of Dubai, in order to further finance the company's goals. In partnership with these two groups, Cirque had planned to build a residency show in the United Arab Emirates by 2012. However, as a result of Dubai's financial problems in 2010, caused by the 2008 global recession, this project was put on hold. Laliberté may be looking for another financial partner to bankroll the company's future plans. Several more shows are in development around the world, along with a television deal, women's clothing line and a possible move into other mediums such as spas, restaurants and nightclubs.

Cirque du Soleil has turned the circus on its ear, blending street entertainment, eccentric costumes and cabaret. Its shows have been seen by more than 100 million spectators in nearly 300 cities on five continents. Among its 20 productions are *O* (an aquatic show at MGM Resorts' Bellagio); *LOVE,* a Las Vegas show featuring Beatles music (with support from Paul McCartney and Ringo Starr, and from the widows of George Harrison and John Lennon); and touring shows *Quidam* and *Alegría.*

The company's latest collaboration is with the estate of Michael Jackson, and consists of a series of projects based on the 'king of pop'. The project includes a touring show (*Michael Jackson: The Immortal World Tour,* launched in North America in the autumn of 2011), and a permanent production in Las Vegas opened in MGM Resorts' Mandalay Bay in 2013. The Las Vegas show employs cutting-edge technology such as holograms, 3D and motion simulation. The deal with the Jackson estate represents Cirque du Soleil's biggest investment to date, worth some US$80 million.

Cirque du Soleil has also been busy diversifying its operations beyond live entertainment. It produces special events for private parties and corporate gatherings, as well as major public events (World Exposition Shanghai, 2010).

Source: Helga Esteb/Shutterstock.com.

The company additionally creates original content for television and on DVD through Cirque du Soleil Images, which has produced Emmy award-winning documentaries and television specials (Cirque du Soleil presents *Corteo* and *Fire Within*). Through a partnership with filmmaker James Cameron (*Avatar*), the company is developing a series of Cirque-inspired 3D projects. Cameron joined with Andrew Adamson (director of *Shrek* and *Shrek 2,* and the first two *Chronicles of Narnia* movies) to film the partnership's first movie, *Cirque du Soleil: Worlds Away.* The film was released in November 2012.

In 2010, the turnover of Cirque du Soleil Inc. was US$825 million, rising to US$950 million in 2011, with around US$200 million in profits.

Among its 5,000 employees are more than 1,300 artists, including dancers, actors and acrobats, from some 50 countries.

Michael Jackson: The Immortal World Tour

Michael Jackson: The Immortal World Tour is the official theatrical production by Cirque du Soleil which has been one of Cirque du Soleil's biggest successes. *Michael Jackson: The Immortal World Tour* unfolds Michael Jackson's artistry before the eyes of the audience. The show uses the music and vision of Michael Jackson along with Cirque du Soleil's signature acrobatic performance style to create a realistic concert experience. Aimed at lifelong fans as well as those experiencing Michael's creative genius for the first time, the show captures the essence, soul and inspiration of the King of Pop, celebrating a legacy that continues to transcend generations.

The show was produced in partnership with the Estate of Michael Jackson. Thus 'The Immortal World Tour' is owned by Cirque Jackson I.P Company, which is owned 50/50 by the conglomerate The Michael Jackson Company and Cirque Du Soleil. The arena show – which is very similar to a rock concert – began its tour on October 2, 2011 in Montreal. After touring North America for about two years, it continued on to Europe and the rest of the world. When it left North America, a resident show – more theatrical in nature – opened in 2013 at the Mandalay Bay Resort and Casino located in Las Vegas, Nevada.

The Michael Jackson Company LLC has partnered with Cirque du Soleil in order to create this concert experience. As part of the US$250 million contract with Sony allowing music publishing until 2017, an album titled *Immortal* was produced. The estate initially opened 50 venues and asked the fans to make a request if they wanted the show to come to their respective cities. The high ticket demand prompted the estate to add several venues and several show dates.

By July 2013, The Immortal World Tour had sold tickets worth over 450 million dollars. More than 2 million tickets had been sold when the world tour finished in Europe in April 2013. At that point, in total 273 shows had been performed, 218 in North America and 55 in Europe.

QUESTIONS

1. Which sociocultural factors influence the sales of tickets for 'Cirque du Soleil' shows around the world?

2. What makes the business model of 'Cirque du Soleil' globally so successful?

3. What should be the criteria for selection of a theme for Cirque du Soleil's next world tour?

Sources: based on www.cirquedusoleil.com/; other public media.

CASE STUDY 7.2

The IKEA catalogue: are there any cultural differences?

IKEA was founded in Älmhult, Sweden, in 1943 by Ingvar Kamprad. The company name is a composite of the first letters in his name, in addition to the first letters of the names of the property and the village in which he grew up: **I**ngvar **K**amprad **E**lmtaryd **A**gunnaryd.

The IKEA business philosophy is: 'We shall offer a wide range of well-designed, functional home furnishing products at prices so low that as many people as possible will be able to afford them.'

In the late 1940s, the first IKEA advertisements appeared in local newspapers. Demand for IKEA products soared, and Ingvar Kamprad quickly outgrew his ability to make individual sales calls. As a result, he began operating a mail order catalogue and distributed his products via the county milk van. This resourceful solution to a difficult problem led to the annual IKEA catalogue.

First published in Swedish in 1951, the IKEA catalogue was in 2010 published in 55 editions, in 27 languages for 36 countries, and is considered to be the main marketing tool of the retail giant, consuming 70 per cent of the company's annual marketing budget. In terms of publishing quantity, the catalogue has surpassed the Bible as the world's most published work – at an estimated 160 million copies (in 2010) worldwide – triple that of its less materialistic counterpart. However, since the catalogue is free of charge, the Bible continues to be the most purchased non-fiction work.

In Europe alone, the catalogue reaches more than 250 million people annually. Containing over 300 pages and about 12,000 products, it is distributed free of charge both in stores and by mail. Furthermore, there were also over 500 million visitors to the IKEA websites during 2010. The annual catalogue is distributed in August/September of each year and is valid for a full year. Prices in the catalogue are guaranteed not to increase while the catalogue is valid. Most of the catalogue is produced by IKEA Catalogue Services AB in IKEA's home town of Älmhult, Sweden.

At the beginning of 2011, there were 276 IKEA stores in 25 countries operating under a franchise from Inter IKEA Systems Bv. Total IKEA turnover in 2010 was €23.5 billion.

IKEA accounts for just 5 to 10 per cent of the furniture market in each country in which it operates. More important is that the awareness of the IKEA brand is much bigger than the size of the company. That is because IKEA is far more than a furniture merchant. It sells a Scandinavian lifestyle that customers around the world embrace.

Cultural difference

There are about 12,000 products in the total IKEA product range. Each store carries a selection of these 12,000 products depending on store size. The core range is the same worldwide but, as shown, there are differences in how the IKEA catalogue displays its products in the different national editions. Below are two different illustrations featuring the same product. In this case the two illustrations for the same product are taken from the Danish and the Chinese catalogues.

QUESTIONS

1. Discuss the advantages and disadvantages of having the same product range shown in all IKEA catalogues around the world.

2. The catalogue is the most important element in IKEA's global marketing planning. Discuss whether there could be some cultural differences in the effectiveness of the catalogue as a marketing tool.

3. Explain some cultural differences which are illustrated by the two different illustrations of the same product (from the Danish and Chinese IKEA catalogues).

Source: www.ikea.com.

Illustration of the same product in the IKEA Catalogue in Denmark and Shanghai
Source: IKEA Ltd.

VIDEO CASE STUDY 7.3 Allergan – the maker of Botox and breast implants
download from **www.pearson.co.uk/hollensen**

Allergan, headquartered in Irvine, California, is a leading maker of eye care, skin care and aesthetic products, including best-selling pharmaceutical *Botox*. Originally used to treat muscle spasms (as well as eye spasms and misalignment), Botox has found another, more popular application in

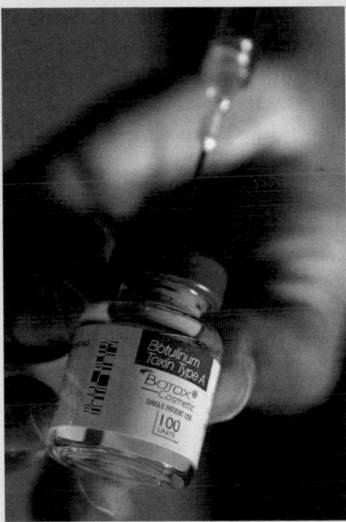

Source: Bloomberg/Getty Images.

diminishing facial wrinkles. Allergan also sells implants used in breast enlargement. Its products are sold in 100 countries via direct sales and distributors.

Total revenues in 2014 were US$7.3 billion, with US$1.5 billion in net profits.

On the 23 November 2015, US drugs giant Pfizer sealed a deal to buy Botox-maker Allergan for US$160 billion (£106 billion) in what was then the biggest pharmaceuticals deal in history. The merged business would be called Pfizer Plc. The companies expected the deal to be completed in the second half of 2016, subject to regulatory approval in the US and Europe.

Questions

1. Cultural differences need to be considered when communicating across borders. What characteristics of a country's culture need to be researched to ensure business success across borders in the case of Allergan's Botox and breast implants?

2. In which cultures and countries would there be the best and worst chances of selling Allergan's Botox and breast implants?

For further resources, see this book's website at **www.pearsoned.co.uk/hollensen**

Questions for discussion

1. As English is the world language of business, is it necessary for UK managers to learn a foreign language?

2. According to Hofstede and Hall, Asians are (a) more group-oriented, (b) more family-oriented and (c) more concerned with social status. How might such orientations affect the way you market your product to Asian consumers?

3. Do you think that cultural differences between nations are more or less important than cultural variations within nations? Under what circumstances is each important?

4. Identify some constraints in marketing to a traditional Muslim society. Use some of the examples in the chapter.

5. What layers of culture have the strongest influence on business people's behaviour?

6. The focus of this chapter has mainly been the influence of culture on international marketing strategies. Try also to discuss the potential influences of marketing on cultures.

7. What role does the self-reference criterion play in international business ethics?

8. Compare the role of women in your country with their role in other cultures. How do the different roles affect women's behaviour as consumers and as business people?

References

Beugelsdijk, S., Maseland, R. and van Hoorn, A. (2015) 'Are Scores on Hofstede's Dimensions of National Culture Stable over Time? A Cohort Analysis', *Global Strategy Journal*, 5, pp. 223–240.

Craig, C.S. and Douglas, S.P. (2006) 'Beyond national culture: implications of cultural dynamics for consumer research', *International Marketing Review*, 23(3), pp. 322–342.

Field, M. (1986) 'Fragrance marketers sniff out rich aroma', *Advertising Age* (special report on 'marketing to the Arab world'), 30 January, p. 10.

Hall, E.T. (1960a) *The Silent Language*. Doubleday, Garden City, NY.

Hall, E.T. (1960b) 'The silent language in overseas business', *Harvard Business Review*, May–June, pp. 87–97.

Harper, T. (1986) 'Polaroid clicks instantly in Moslem market', *Advertising Age* (special report on 'Marketing to the Arab world'), 30 January, p. 12.

Hofstede, G. (1980) *Cultural Consequences: International Differences in Work-related Values*, Sage, Beverly Hills, CA and London.

Hofstede, G. (1983) 'The cultural relativity of organizational practices and theories', *Journal of International Business Studies*, Fall, pp. 75–89.

Hofstede, G. (2007) 'Asian Management in the 21st century', *Asia Pacific Journal of Management*, 24, pp. 411–420.

Hofstede, G. and Bond, M.R. (1988) 'The Confucius connection: from cultural roots to economic growth', *Organizational Dynamics*, 16(4), pp. 4–21.

House, R. J., Hanges, P. J., Javidan, M., Dorfman, P. W. and Vipin. G. (2004) *Culture, Leadership, and Organizations: The GLOBE study of 62 societies Sage*, Thousand Oaks, CA.

Lee, J. (1966) 'Cultural analysis in overseas operations', *Harvard Business Review*, March–April, pp. 106–114.

Murdoch, G.P. (1945) 'The common denominator of cultures', in Linton, R. (ed.), *The Science of Man in the World Crises*. Columbia University Press, New York.

Minkov, M. and Hofstede, G. (2011) 'The evolution of Hofstede's doctrine', *Cross Cultural Management: An International Journal*, 18(1), pp. 10–20.

Paine, L.S. (2010) 'The China Rules', *Harvard Business Review*, June, pp. 103–108.

Pasco, M. (2000) 'Brands are replacing celebrities as role models for today's youth', *Kids Marketing Report*, 27 January.

Phillips, C., Doole, I. and Lowe, R. (1994) *International Marketing Strategy: Analysis, development and implementation*. Routledge, London.

Smith, D.S. (1998) 'Europe's youth is our future', *Marketing*, 22 January.

Smith, K.V. (2000) 'Why SFA is a tough sell in Latin America', *Marketing News*, 3 January.

Solberg, C.A. (2002) 'Culture and industrial buyer behaviour: the Arab experience', Paper presented at the 18th IMP Conference, pp. 1–34.

Tylor, E.B. (1881) *Anthropology: An Introduction to the study of Man and Civilization*. D. Appleton, New York.

Usunier, J-C. and Lee, J.A. (1999) *Marketing Across Cultures*, 3rd edn. Pearson Education Ltd.

Venaik, S. and Brewer, P. (2013) 'Critical issues in the Hofstede and GLOBE national culture models', *International Marketing Review*, 30(5), pp. 469–482.

CHAPTER 8
The international market selection process

Contents

Case studies

Learning objectives

After studying this chapter you should be able to:

- Define international market selection and identify the problems in achieving it

- Explore how international marketers screen potential markets/countries using secondary and primary data (criteria)

- Distinguish between preliminary and 'fine-grained' screening

- Realize the importance of segmentation in the formulation of the global marketing strategy

- Choose among alternative market expansion strategies

- Distinguish between concentration and diversification in market expansion.

8.1 Introduction

Identifying the 'right' market(s) to enter is important for a number of reasons:

- It can be a major determinant of success or failure, especially in the early stages of internationalization.
- This decision influences the nature of foreign marketing programmes in the selected countries.
- The geographic location of selected markets affects the firm's ability to coordinate foreign operations.

In this chapter a systematic approach to international market selection (IMS) is presented. A study of recently internationalized US firms showed that, on average, firms do not follow a highly systematic approach. However, those firms using a systematic sequence of steps in IMS showed a better performance (Yip *et al.,* 2000; Brouthers and Nakos, 2005).

8.2 International market selection: SMEs versus LSEs

The international market selection process is different in small and medium-sized enterprises (SMEs) and large-scale enterprises (LSEs).

In SMEs, the IMS is often simply a reaction to a stimulus provided by a change agent. This agent can appear in the form of an unsolicited order. Government agencies, chambers of commerce and other change agents may also bring foreign opportunities to the firm's attention. Such cases constitute an externally driven decision in which the exporter simply responds to an opportunity in a given market.

In other cases, the IMS of SMEs is based on the following criteria (Johanson and Vahlne, 1977):

- Low psychic distance: low uncertainty about foreign markets and low perceived difficulty of acquiring information about them. Psychic distance has been defined as differences in language, culture, political system, level of education or level of industrial development.
- Low cultural distance: low perceived differences between the home and destination cultures (cultural distance is normally regarded as part of psychic distance).
- Low geographic distance.

Using any one of these criteria often results in firms entering new markets with successively greater psychic distance. The choice is often limited to the SMEs' immediate neighbours, as geographic proximity is likely to reflect cultural similarity, more knowledge about foreign markets and greater ease in obtaining information. When using this model, the decision-maker will focus on decision-making based on incrementalism where the firm is predicted to start the internationalization by moving into those markets they can most easily understand. It is generally believed that SMEs and firms that are early in their internationalization process are more likely to use a psychic distance or other rule-of-thumb procedures than LSEs with international experience (Andersen and Buvik, 2002).

By limiting their consideration to a nearby country, SMEs effectively narrow the IMS into one decision: to go or not to go to a nearby country. The reason for this behaviour can be that SME executives, usually being short of human and financial resources, find it hard to resist the temptation of selecting target markets intuitively.

In a study of internationalization in Danish SMEs, Sylvest and Lindholm (1997) found that the IMS process in 'old' SMEs (established before 1960) was very different from that in 'young' SMEs (established in 1989 or later). The young SMEs entered more distant markets much earlier than the older SMEs, who followed the more traditional step-by-step

IMS process. The reason for the more rapid internationalization of young SMEs may be their status as subsuppliers to larger firms, where they are 'pulled out' to international markets by their large customers and their international networks.

While SMEs must make first-entry decisions by selecting targets among largely unknown markets, LSEs with existing operations in many countries have to decide which of them to introduce new products into. By drawing on existing operations, LSEs have easier access to product-specific data in the form of primary information that is more accurate than any secondary database. As a result of this, the LSEs can be more proactive. Although selecting markets based on intuition and pragmatism can be a satisfying method for SMEs, the following will be based on a more proactive IMS process, organized in a systematic way with step-by-step analysis.

However, in real life the IMS process will not always be a logical and gradual sequence of activities, but instead an iterative process involving multiple feedback loops (Andersen and Strandskov, 1998). Furthermore, in many small subcontracting firms, exporting firms do not actively select their foreign markets. The decision about IMS is made by the partner obtaining the main contract (main contractor), thus pulling the SME into international markets (Brewer, 2001; Westhead *et al.*, 2002). SMEs are often selling to global customers (so-called global accounts) who have a global scope of operation and they expect delivery of the SME's product and services at multiple country sites. SMEs with already established global distribution networks and production sites in more business hubs are often better positioned to supply these global account customers, e.g. in the automotive sector (Meyer, 2009).

8.3   Building a model for international market selection

Research from the Uppsala school on the internationalization process of firms has suggested several potential determinants of firms' choice of foreign markets. These can be classified into two groups: (i) environmental characteristics, and (ii) firm characteristics (see Figure 8.1).

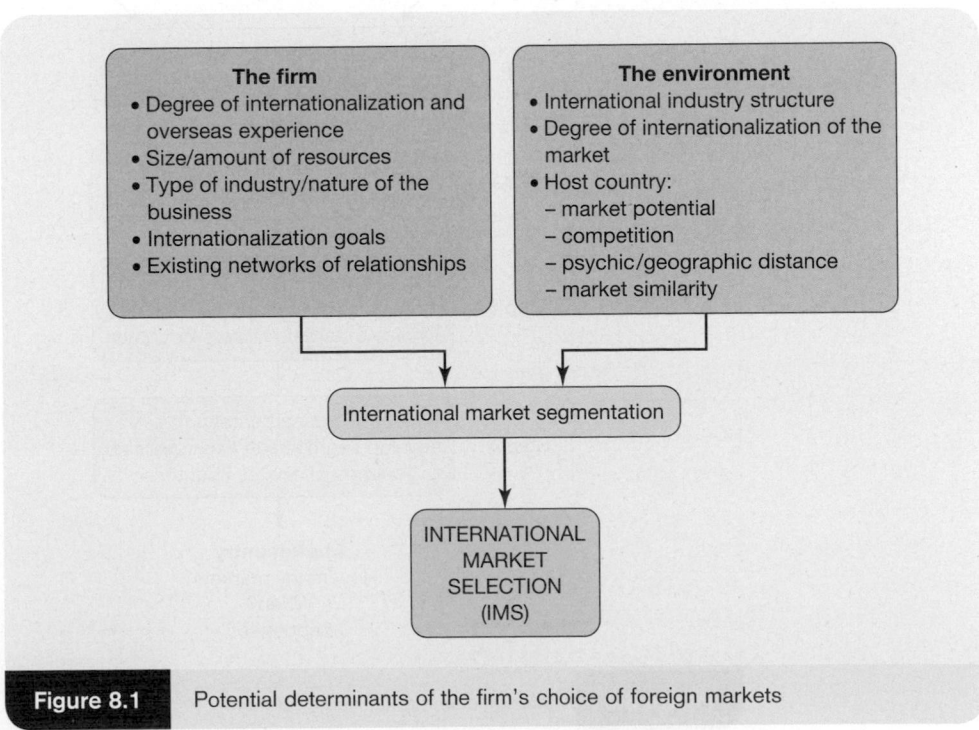

Figure 8.1   Potential determinants of the firm's choice of foreign markets

Let us look first at the environment. How do we define 'international markets'? The following approach suggests two dimensions:

1. the international market as a country or a group of countries;
2. the international market as a group of customers with nearly the same characteristics. According to this latter definition, a market can consist of customers from several countries.

Most books and studies in global marketing have attempted to segment the world market into the different countries or groups of countries. This has been done for two principal reasons:

1. International data are more easily (and sometimes exclusively) available on a nation-by-nation basis. It is very difficult to acquire accurate cross-national statistical data.
2. Distribution management and media have also been organized on a nation-by-nation basis. Most agents/distributors still represent their manufacturers only in one single country. Few agents sell their products on a cross-national basis.

However, country markets or multi-country markets are not quite adequate. In many cases, boundary lines are the result of political agreement or war and do not reflect a similar separation in buyer characteristics among people on either side of the border.

Presentation of a market-screening model

In Figure 8.1 an outline model for IMS was presented. In the following we will look in more detail at the box labelled 'international market segmentation'. The elements of IMS are shown in Figure 8.2, and the different steps are further discussed in the following sections.

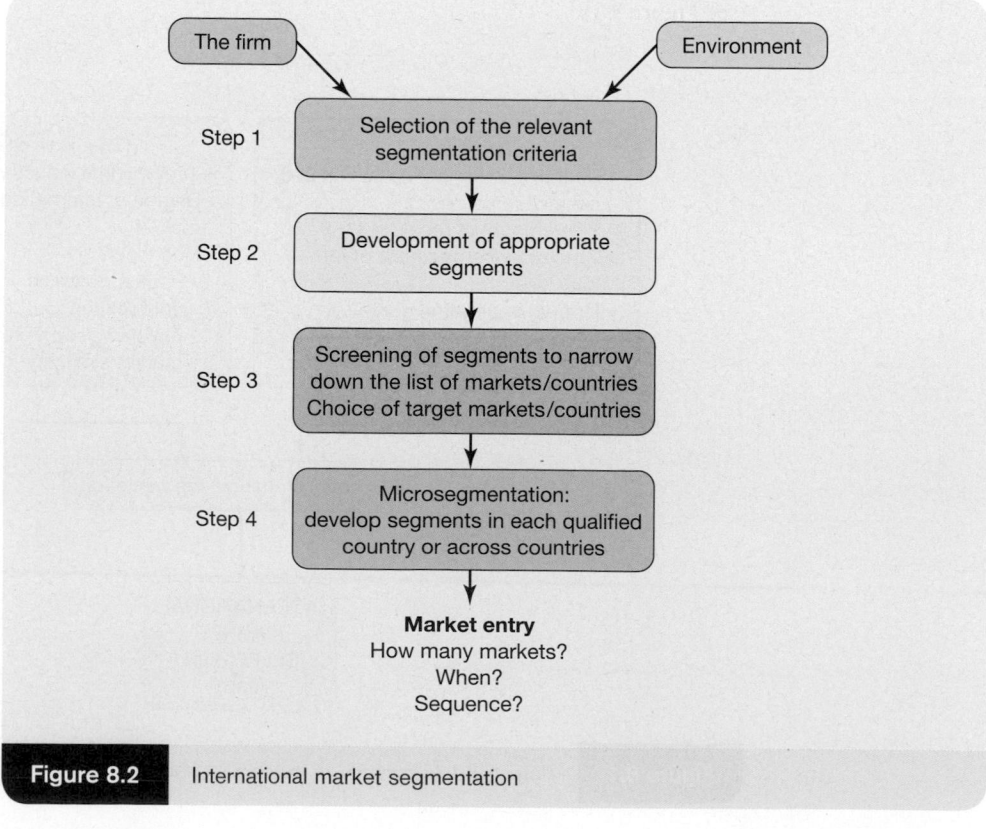

Figure 8.2   International market segmentation

Steps 1 and 2: defining criteria and developing segments

In general, the criteria for effective segmentation are as follows:

- *measurability*: the degree to which the size and purchasing power of resulting segments can be measured;
- *accessibility*: the degree to which the resulting segments can be effectively reached and served;
- *substantiality/profitability*: the degree to which segments are sufficiently large and/or profitable;
- *actionability*: the degree to which the organization has sufficient resources to formulate effective marketing programmes and 'make things happen'.

A high degree of measurability and accessibility indicates more general characteristics as criteria (at the top of Figure 8.3) and vice versa. It is important to realize that more than one measure can be used simultaneously in the segmentation process.

In Chapters 6 and 7 the different segmentation criteria in the international environment were discussed and structured according to the PEST approach:

- political/legal
- economic
- social/cultural
- technological.

We will now describe in more detail the general and specific criteria mentioned in Figure 8.3. By categorizing the criteria in this way, this approach follows the two-stage model (Gaston-Breton and Martin, 2011).

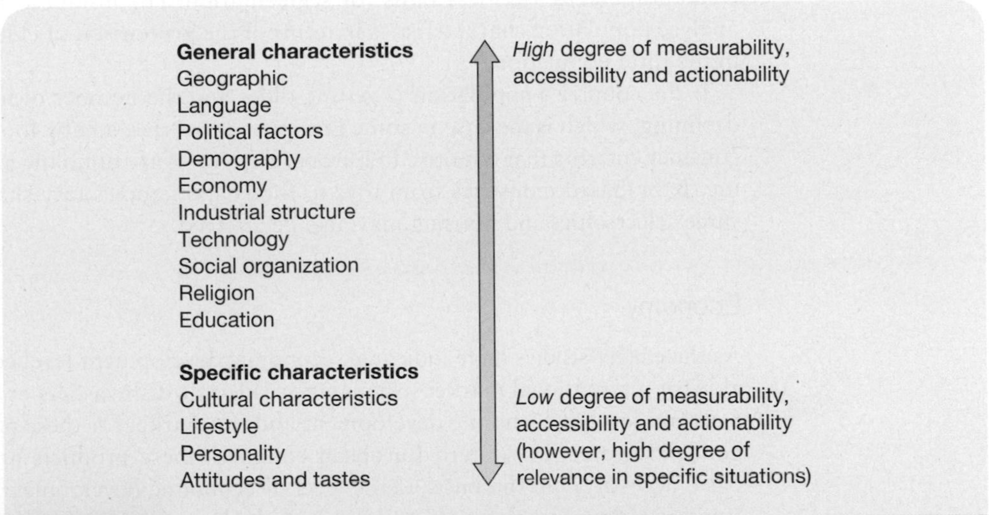

General characteristics
Geographic
Language
Political factors
Demography
Economy
Industrial structure
Technology
Social organization
Religion
Education

High degree of measurability, accessibility and actionability

Specific characteristics
Cultural characteristics
Lifestyle
Personality
Attitudes and tastes

Low degree of measurability, accessibility and actionability (however, high degree of relevance in specific situations)

Figure 8.3   The basis of international market segmentation

General characteristics

Geographic

The location of the market can be critical in terms of segmenting world markets. Scandinavian countries or Middle Eastern countries may be clustered according to their geographic proximity and other similarities. However, the geographic location alone could be a critical factor. For instance, air conditioning requirements in some of the Arab countries could make a manufacturer consider these countries as specific clusters.

Language

Language has been described as the mirror of culture. On one level, its implications for the international marketer are self-evident: advertising must be translated; brand names must be vetted for international acceptability; and business negotiations must often be conducted through expensive interpreters or through the even more expensive acquisition of a foreign translator. In the latter case, genuine fluency is essential; persuasion and contract negotiation present considerable difficulties even in a mother tongue.

Less obvious is the fact that foreign language may imply different patterns of thought and different customer motivations. In such cases, a knowledge – again, a good knowledge – of the language will do more than facilitate communication; it provides automatic insight into the relevant culture.

Political factors

Countries may be grouped and world markets segmented according to broad political characteristics. Until recently, the Iron Curtain was the basis of one such division. In general terms, the degree of power that the central government has may be the general criterion for segmentation. It is possible, for instance, that a company is producing certain chemicals, but that, due to government regulations, many of the world markets are considered too difficult to enter.

Demography

Demographics is a critical basis for segmentation. For instance, it is often necessary to analyse population characteristics in terms of the proportion of elderly people or children in the total population.

If the country's population is getting older and the number of infants per thousand is declining, which is the case in some European countries, a baby food company would not consider entering that country. In Europe, birth rates are tumbling and life spans lengthening. Baby-based industries from toys to foods and nappies face sharp competition. Consumer electronics and housing may also be affected.

Economy

As the earlier studies have indicated, economic development level could be a critical variable for international market segmentation. Electric dishwashers or washer-dryers require a certain level of economic development and the market for these products in India is not good. However, in western European countries these products are becoming almost a basic necessity. On the basis of the level of economic development, certain specific consumption patterns emerge. Societies with high personal income spend more time and money on services, education and recreation. Thus it may be possible to arrange certain income groups from different countries into clusters.

Industrial structure

A country's industrial structure is depicted by the characteristics of its business population. One country may have many small retailers, while another may rely on a large number of department stores for retail distribution. One country may be thriving on small manufacturers, whereas another may have very concentrated and large-scale manufacturing activity. The type of competition that exists at the wholesale level may be the critical specific factor for clustering international markets. The international marketer may wish to work with a series of strong wholesalers.

Technology

The degree of technological advancement or the degree of agricultural technology could easily be the basis for segmentation. A software company planning to enter international markets may wish to segment them on the basis of the number of PCs per thousand of the population, as it may not be worthwhile entering markets below a certain threshold number. On this basis, Pakistan, Iran, most Arab countries, all of Africa and the whole of eastern Europe might be less than satisfactory for entry.

Social organization

The family is an important purchasing group in any society. In Europe, marketers are accustomed to either the so-called nuclear family, with father, mother and children all living together under one roof, or, increasingly, the single-parent family. In other countries the key unit is the extended family, with three or four generations all in the same house.

In the US, for instance, socioeconomic groupings have been used extensively as segmentation tools. A six-category classification is used: upper upper class, lower upper, upper middle, lower middle, upper lower and lower lower. High-income professionals are relegated to the lower upper class, described as those 'who have earned their position rather than inherited it', the nouveaux-riches.

By contrast, it would have been hard to find useful socioeconomic groupings in Russia beyond white-collar worker, blue-collar worker and farm worker.

Religion

Religious customs are a major factor in marketing. One of the most obvious examples is the Christian tradition of present-giving at Christmas, yet even in this simple matter pitfalls await the international marketer: in some Christian countries the traditional exchange of presents takes place not on Christmas Day but on other days in December or early January.

The impact of religion on marketing is most evident in the case of Islam. Islamic laws, based on the Koran, provide guidance for a whole range of human activities, including economic activity.

Education

Educational levels are of importance to the international marketer from two main standpoints: the economic potential of the youth market and, in developing countries, the level of literacy.

Educational systems vary considerably from country to country. The compensation for on-the-job training also varies a great deal. As a result, the economic potential of the youth market is very different from country to country.

In most industrialized countries, literacy levels are close to 100 per cent and the whole range of communications media is open to the marketer. In developing countries, literacy rates can be as low as 25 per cent, and, in one or two, 15 per cent or less, although at such low levels these figures can be no more than estimates. In those same countries, television sets and even radios are economically beyond the reach of most of the population, although communal television sets are sometimes available. The consumer marketer faces a real challenge in deciding on promotional policies in these countries, and the use of visual material is more relevant.

Specific characteristics

Cultural characteristics

Cultural characteristics may play a significant role in segmenting world markets. To take advantage of global markets or global segments, firms require a thorough understanding of what drives customer behaviour in different markets. They must learn to detect the extent to which similarities exist or can be achieved through marketing activities. The cultural behaviour of the members of a given society is constantly shaped by a set of dynamic variables that can also be used as segmentation criteria, including language, religion, values and attitudes, material elements and technology, aesthetics, education and social institutions. These different elements are dealt with more extensively in Chapters 6 and 7.

Lifestyle

Typically, activity, interest and opinion research is used as a tool for analysing lifestyles. However, such a research tool has not been developed for international purposes. Consumption habits or practices could possibly be used as an indication of the lifestyle that is being studied. Type of food eaten, for example, is a general lifestyle indicator that an international food company should be ready to consider: Indian-style hot curries are not likely to be very popular in Germany, given its rather bland cooking, while very hot Arab dishes are not likely to be popular in western Europe.

Personality

Personality is reflected in certain types of behaviour. A general characteristic may be temper, so that segmentation may be based on the general temper of people. Latin Americans or Mediterranean people are known to have certain personality traits, and those traits might be a suitable basis for the segmentation of world markets. One example is the tendency to haggle. In pricing, the international firm will have to use a substantial degree of flexibility where haggling is widespread. Haggling in a country like Turkey is almost a national pastime. In the underground bazaars of Istanbul, the vendor would be almost offended if the customer accepted the first asking price.

Attitudes and tastes

These are all complex concepts, but it is reasonable to say that they can be utilized for segmentation. Status symbols can be used as indicators of what some people in a culture would consider enhances their own self-concept as well as their perception among other people.

Step 3: screening of segments (markets/countries)

The screening process can be divided into two stages (Gaston-Breton and Martin, 2011; Sinha *et al.*, 2015):

- *Preliminary screening.* This is where markets/countries are screened primarily according to external screening criteria (the state of the market). In the case of SMEs, the limited internal resources (e.g. financial resources) must also be taken into account. This would be an example of internal screening criteria.
- *Fine-grained screening.* This is where the firm's competitive power (and special competences) in the different markets can be taken into account.

Preliminary screening

The number of markets is reduced by coarse-grained, macro-oriented screening methods based on criteria such as:

- population size;
- gross national product (GNP) in total;
- gross national product (GNP) per capita;
- restrictions in the export of goods from one country to another;
- share of population with access to internet;
- smartphones owned per 1,000 of the population;
- cars owned per 1,000 of the population;
- government spending as a percentage of GNP;
- population per hospital bed.

The specific choice of preliminary screening criteria may vary, dependent on the product/service or industry. In most cases, the researcher will start with analysis of 'buying power' regarding the specific product/service. This would indicate use of some economic criteria like GNP in total or GNP per capita.

Country responsiveness
'Income elasticity' of specific product- and industry consumer-related expenditures in a country. It reflects the tendency of consumers to spend, in a specific product category, in response to a rise in their income.

Another proxy for buying power is so-called '**country responsiveness**' (Ozturk *et al.*, 2015). Country responsiveness is defined as the 'income elasticity' of specific product- and industry consumer-related expenditures. It reflects the tendency of consumers to spend, in a specific product category, in response to a rise in their income. If this tendency is high, then this country is classified as responsive. Identifying responsive and non-responsive countries can be part of the preliminary screening process and this makes country responsiveness a potent indicator for a variety of industry/product sectors. For example, in the case of the smartphone industry, if consumers in a country spend more of their income increase on smartphones than those in another country then the former country is more responsive to increasing smartphone consumption in the face of increasing income than the latter. This would support the case for expansion of a smartphone business into the former country.

'Knock-out' criteria
Screening criteria that are used to exclude countries in advance as potential future markets.

There may be a number of countries that can be excluded in advance as potential markets. The screening criteria used for this purpose are also called '**knock-out**' **criteria**. In Exhibit 8.1 Bosch Security Systems used the following 'knock-out' criteria in the first screening:

- The country must be politically stable and not be too conservative with regard to religion (Iran was 'knocked out' on this).
- The country must not already be an established market for Bosch fire detection (Egypt was 'knocked out' on this).

BERI (Business Environment Risk Index)
A tool used in the coarse-grained, macro-oriented screening of international markets.

When screening countries it is particularly important to assess the political risk of entering a country. Over recent years, marketers have developed various indices to help assess the risk factors in the evaluation of potential market opportunities, including the Business Environment Risk Index (**BERI**). Other organizations such as Business Monitor International (www.businessmonitor.com) and the Economist Intelligence Unit (www.eiu.com) also have a country risk service. Or you can follow Euromoney's country risk index: their country risk survey, published twice a year, monitors the political and economic stability of 185 sovereign countries. Results focus foremost on economics, specifically sovereign default risk and/or payment default risk for exporters. Users of these country risk analyses normally have to pay for these subscription services.

Euromoney, BMI, BERI and other services measure the general quality of a country's business climate. They assess countries several times a year on different economic, political and financial factors on a scale from 0 to 4. The overall index ranges from 0 to 100 (see Table 8.1). The BERI index has been questioned as a general management decision tool and should therefore be supplemented by in-depth country reports before final market entry decisions are made.

Table 8.1	Criteria included in the overall BERI index		
Criteria	**Weights**	**Multiplied with the score (rating) on a scale of 0–4**[a]	**Overall BERI index**[b]
Political stability	3		
Economic growth	2.5		
Currency convertibility	2.5		
Labour cost/productivity	2		
Short-term credit	2		
Long-term loans/venture capital	2		
Attitude towards the foreign investor and profits	1.5		
Nationalization	1.5		
Monetary inflation	1.5		
Balance of payments	1.5		
Enforceability of contracts	1.5		
Bureaucratic delays	1		
Communications: phone, fax, internet access	1		
Local management and partner	1		
Professional services and contractors	0.5		
Total	25	× 4 (max.)	= max. 100

[a] 0, unacceptable; 1, poor; 2, average conditions; 3, above average conditions; 4, superior conditions.
[b] Total points: > 80, favourable environment for investors, advanced economy; 70–79, not so favourable, but still an advanced economy; 55–69, an immature economy with investment potential, probably a newly industrialized country (NIC); 40–54, a high-risk country, probably a less developed country (LDC) – quality of management has to be superior to realize potential; < 40, very high risk – would only commit capital if there were some extraordinary justification.

Among other macro-oriented screening methods is the *shift-share approach* (Green and Allaway, 1985; Papadopoulos *et al.*, 2002). This approach is based upon the identification of relative changes in international import shares among various countries. The average growth rate of imports for a particular product for a 'basket' of countries is calculated and then each country's actual growth rate is compared with the average growth rate. The difference, called the 'net shift', identifies growing or declining markets. This procedure has the advantage that it takes into account both the absolute level of a country's imports and their relative growth rate. On the other hand, it examines only those criteria and does not take into account other macro-oriented criteria.

Fine-grained screening

As the BERI index focuses only on the political risk of entering new markets, a broader approach that includes the competences of the firm is often needed.

For this purpose, a powerful aid to the identification of the 'best opportunity' target countries is the application of the market attractiveness/competitive strength matrix (Figure 8.4). This market portfolio model replaces the two single dimensions in the Boston Consulting Group (BCG) growth–share matrix with two composite dimensions applied to global marketing issues. Measures on these two dimensions are built up from a large number of possible variables, as listed in Table 8.2. In the following, one of the important dimensions will be described and commented upon.

Market size

The total market volume per year for a certain country/market can be calculated as:

Production (of a product in a country)

+ import

– <u>export</u>

= theoretical market size

± <u>changes in stock size</u>

= effective market size

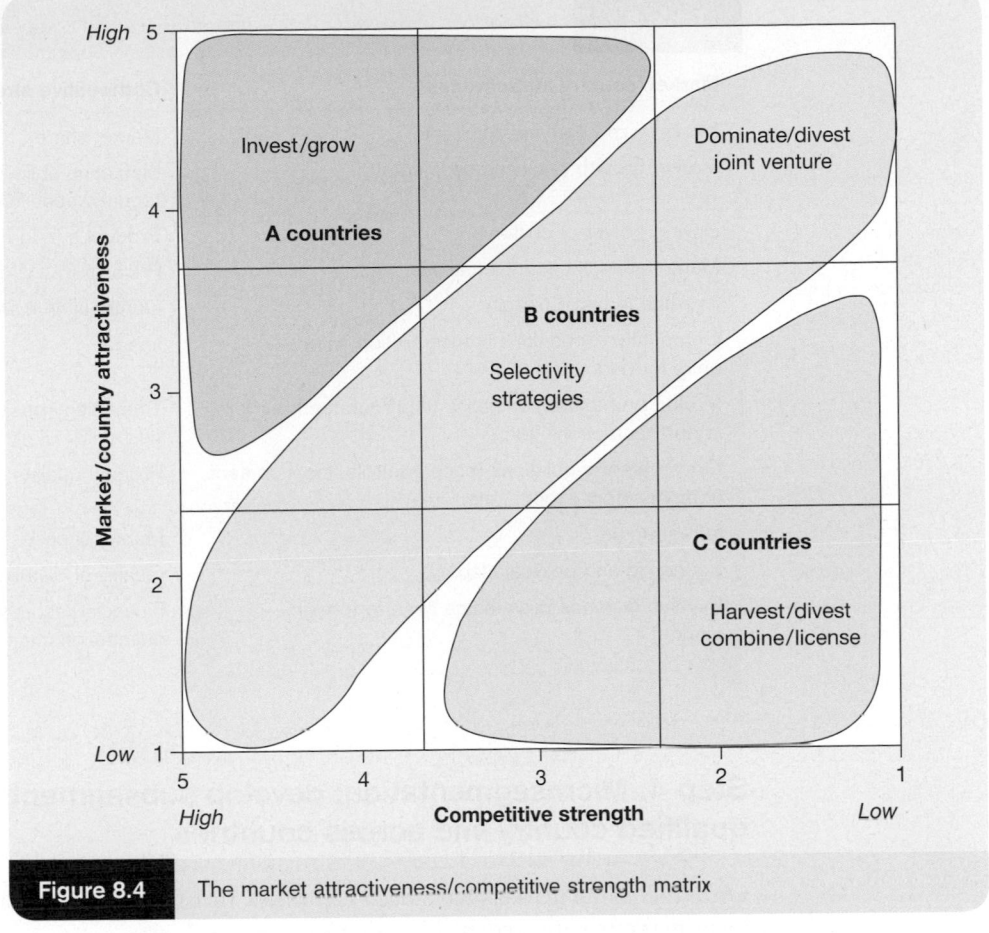

Figure 8.4   The market attractiveness/competitive strength matrix

Production, import and export figures can usually be found in the specific country's statistics, if it is a standardized product with an identifiable customs position.

A more precise location of a particular country (in Figure 8.4) may be determined by using the questionnaire in Figure 8.5.

The outcome of Figure 8.5 is a 'place/location' in Figure 8.4, representing the competitive strength (horizontal axis) and the market attractiveness (vertical axis). See also Exhibit 8.1 later in this chapter where the IMS tool is shown in practical use.

As we saw in Figure 8.4, one of the results of this process is a prioritized classification of countries/markets into distinct categories:

● *A countries*. These are the primary markets (i.e. the key markets), which offer the best opportunities for long-term strategic development. Here companies may want to establish a permanent presence and should therefore embark on a thorough research programme.
● *B countries*. These are the secondary markets, where opportunities are identified but political or economic risk is perceived as being too high to make long-term irrevocable commitments. These markets would be handled in a more pragmatic way due to the potential risks identified. A comprehensive marketing information system would be needed.
● *C countries*. These are the tertiary or 'catch what you can' markets. They will be perceived as high risk, and so the allocation of resources will be minimal. Objectives in such countries would be short-term and opportunistic; companies would give no real commitment. No significant research would be carried out.

Table 8.2	Dimensions of market/country attractiveness and competitive strength

Market/country attractiveness	Competitive strength
Market size (total and segments)	Market share
Market growth (total and segments)	Marketing ability and capacity (country-specific know-how)
Buying power of customers	Product's fit to market demands
Market seasons and fluctuations	Price
Average industry margin	Contribution margin
Competitive conditions (concentration, intensity, entry barriers, etc.)	Image
Market prohibitive conditions (tariff/non-tariff barriers, import restrictions, etc.)	Technology position
Government regulations (price controls, local content, compensatory exports, etc.)	Product quality
Infrastructure	Market support
Economic and political stability	Quality of distributors and service
Psychic distance (from home base to foreign market)	Financial resources, access to distribution channels

Step 4: Microsegmentation: develop subsegments in each qualified country and across countries

Once the prime markets have been identified, firms then use standard techniques to segment markets within countries, using variables such as:

- demographic/economic factors
- lifestyles
- consumer motivations
- geography
- buyer behaviour
- psychographics.

Thus the prime segmentation basis is geographic (by country) and the secondary is within countries. The problem here is that depending on the information basis, it may be difficult to formulate fully secondary segmentation bases. Furthermore, such an approach can run the risk of leading to a differentiated marketing approach, which may leave the company with a very fragmented international strategy.

The drawback of traditional approaches lies in the difficulty of applying them consistently across markets. If a company is to try to achieve a consistent and controlled marketing strategy across all its markets, it needs a transnational approach to its segmentation strategy.

It can be argued that companies competing internationally should segment markets on the basis of consumers, not countries. Segmentation by purely geographical factors leads to national stereotyping. It ignores the differences between customers within a nation and ignores similarities across boundaries.

Time of analysis:
Analysis of product area:
In country:

A. Market attractiveness

	1 Very poor	2 Poor	3 Medium	4 Good	5 Very good	% Weight factor	Result (grading × weight)
Market size							
Market growth							
Buying structure							
Prices							
Buying power							
Market access							
Competitive intensity							
Political/economic risks							
etc.							
Total						100	

Market attractiveness = Result : 100 = ...

B. Relative competitive strength
with regard to the strongest competitor = ...

	1 Very poor	2 Poor	3 Medium	4 Good	5 Very good	% Weight factor	Result (grading × weight)
Products fit to market demands							
Prices and conditions							
Market presence							
Marketing							
Communication							
Obtainable market share							
Financial results							
etc.							
Total						100	

Relative competitive strength = Result : 100 = ...

Figure 8.5 Underlying questionnaire for locating countries on a market attractiveness/ competitive strength matrix

Cluster analysis can be used to identify meaningful cross-national segments, each of which is expected to evoke a similar response to any marketing mix strategy. Figure 8.6 shows an attempt to segment the western European market into six clusters.

Once the firm has chosen a certain country as a target market, the next stage in the micro-segmentation process is to decide with which products or services the company wishes to become active in the individual countries. Here it is necessary to make a careful market segmentation, especially in the larger and more important foreign markets, in order to be in a position to exhaust the market potential in a differentiated manner (Figure 8.7).

In this context, it is necessary to draw attention to a specific strategic procedure, which is oriented worldwide towards similar market segments. Here it is not the country-specific market attractiveness that influences the decision on specific markets, but the recognition of the existence of similar structures of demand and similar consumer habits in segments (and perhaps only in small segments) of different markets.

An illustration of the whole international market segmentation/screening process (steps 1–4 in Figure 8.2) is seen in Figure 8.8.

The model in Figure 8.8 begins by regarding the world market as the potential market for a firm's product. However, if the firm only regards western Europe as a possible market, then it may start the screening process at this lower level. The six western

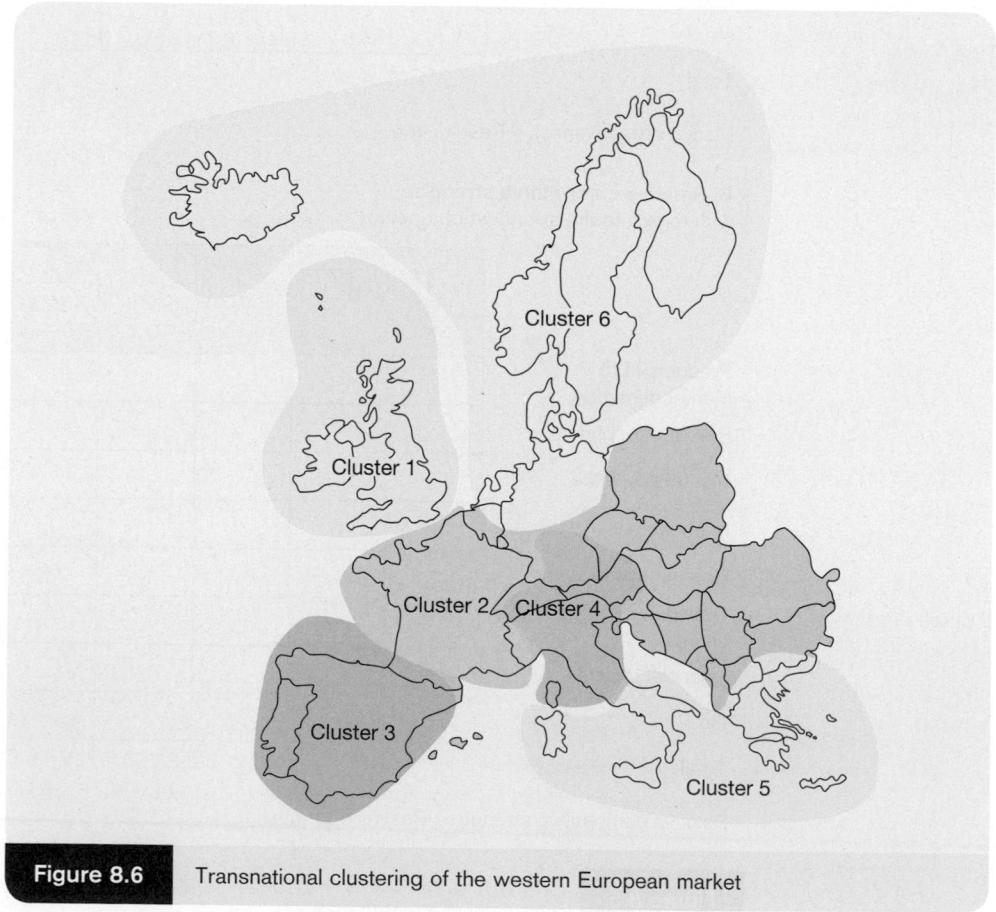

Figure 8.6   Transnational clustering of the western European market

Source: adapted from *European Business: An issue-based approach*, Pearson Education Ltd. (Welford, R. and Prescott, K. 1996) Copyright © Pearson Education Ltd.

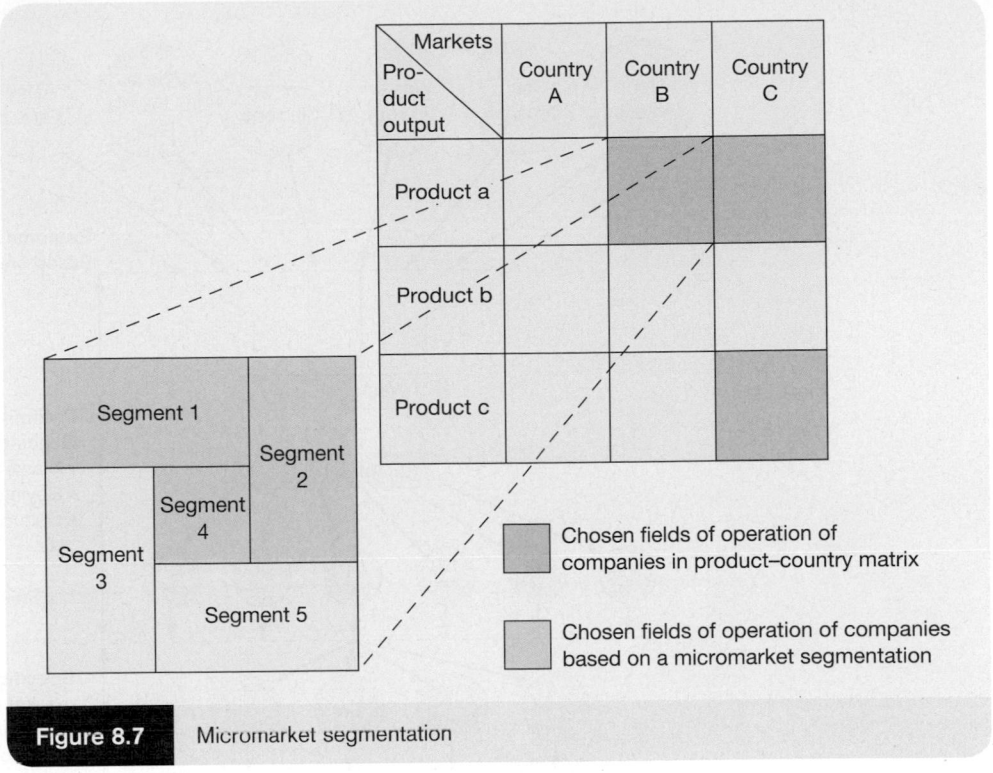

Figure 8.7   Micromarket segmentation

European clusters are based on the transnational clustering in Figure 8.6. The further down in the model, the greater the use of primary data (personal interviews, field research, etc.), as well as screening from internal criteria. Furthermore, the firm may discover a *high market potential* in some geographic segments. However, this is not the same as a *high sales potential* for the firm's product. There may be some restrictions (e.g. trade barriers) on the exporting of products to a particular country. Also the management of the company may have a policy of selecting only markets that are culturally similar to the home market. This may exclude very distant countries from being selected as target markets, although they may have a high market potential. Furthermore, to be able to transform a high market potential into a high sales potential, there must be a harmony between the firm's competences (internal criteria) and the value chain functions that customers rate as important to them. Only in this situation will a customer regard the firm as a possible supplier, equal to other possible suppliers. In other words, in making the IMS, the firm must seek synergy between the possible new target market and its own strengths, objectives and strategy. The firm's choice of new international markets is very much influenced by the existence of complementary markets and marketing skills gained in these markets.

In general, Figure 8.8 is based on proactive and systematic decision-making behaviour by the firm. This is not always a realistic condition, especially not in SMEs, where a *pragmatic approach* is required. Often firms are not able to segment from their own criteria but must expect to be evaluated and chosen (as subsuppliers) by much larger firms. The pragmatic approach to IMS can also give rise to the firm choosing customers and markets with a background similar to the managers' own personal network and cultural background. Contingencies, serendipity and 'management feel' play an important role in both early and

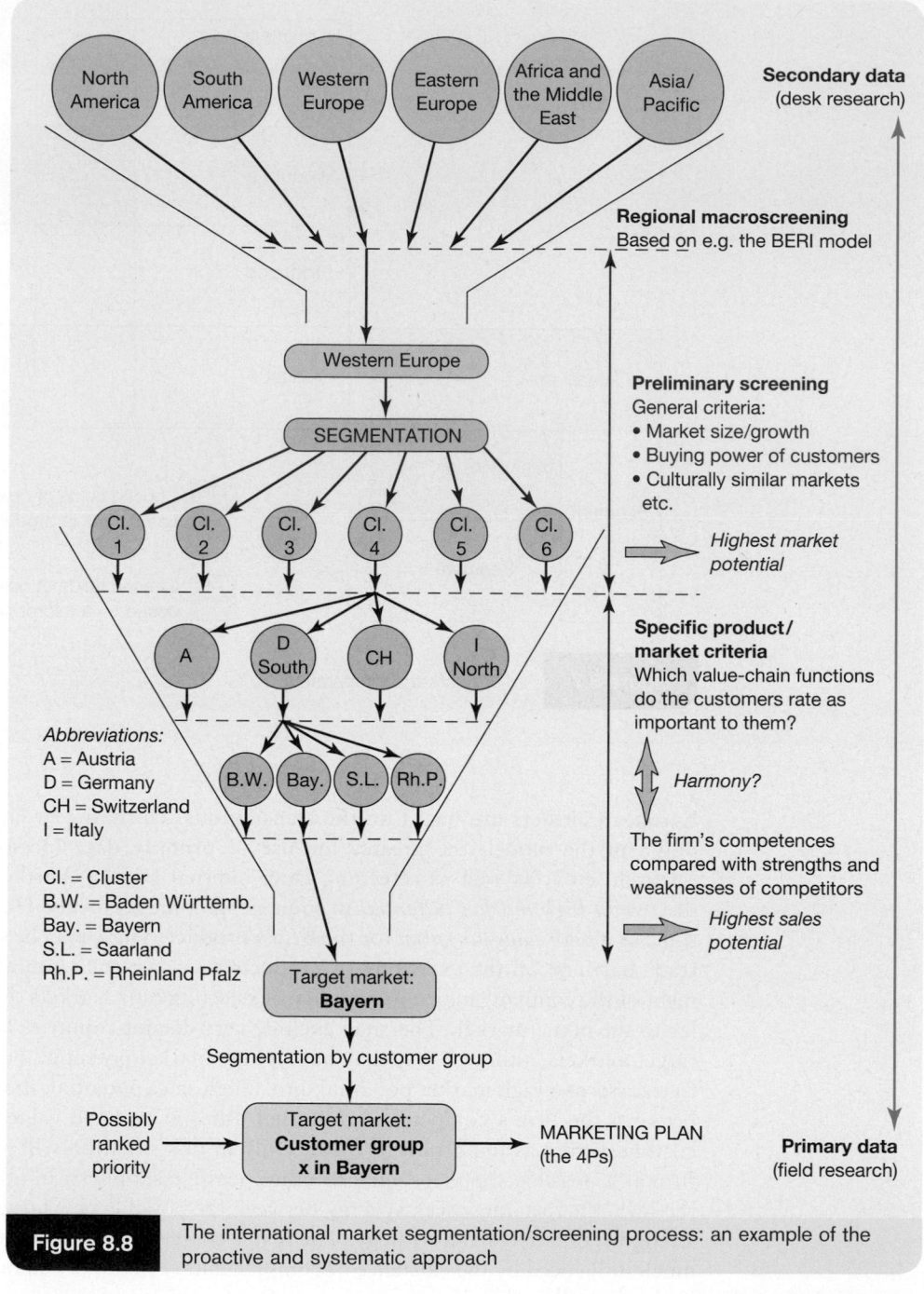

| **Figure 8.8** | The international market segmentation/screening process: an example of the proactive and systematic approach |

late phases of IMS. In a qualitative study of Australian firms, Rahman (2003) found that an important factor taken into consideration by firms at the final stage of evaluating the attractiveness of foreign markets is 'management feel'. One of the companies said (Rahman, 2003, p. 124):

> At the end of the day much of the decision depends on the management's feel about the market. There will always be some uncertainties in the market, particularly when you are deciding about the future, and international markets are no exception in this regard. So, we managers will have to make the decision within the limited information available to us, and 'gut feel' plays a big role in that.

EXHIBIT 8.1 Bosch Security Systems: IMS in the Middle East for fire detection systems

Market screening of eight leading countries in the Middle East: Egypt, Iran, Jordan, Kuwait, Oman, Qatar (QA), Saudi Arabia (SA) and the United Arab Emirates (UAE)

The following is the result of an international market selection (IMS) process that Bosch Security Systems (www.boschsecurity.com) did back in 2006.[a] Up to then, the export efforts of Bosch Security Systems in the Middle East had been rather sporadic. The firm wanted to increase its overall market share and total sales in the region. This growth strategy would require concentration of marketing resources, and consequently a systematic and proactive approach to IMS that would end up with a ranking of the most attractive market(s) for Bosch Security Systems within 'fire detection' in the Middle East.

The fire systems for buildings are generally characterized by the following:

- safety market where lives are involved;
- law driven market – most countries have very strict laws requiring fire safety systems;
- very large markets.

Typically the buildings' fire systems require the following:

- fire detection – smoke and heat detection, signalling devices, fire sound alarms, manual call points;
- alarm follow-up – dialler for external alarm; fire paging system (SMS) for alerting, for example, the hearing-impaired;
- evacuation of the building – recorded messages, LED indicators for emergency exits, etc.;
- fire-fighting – sprinkler systems, fire doors.

Bosch Security Systems is involved in all of these functions except the fire-fighting.

The overall process that the management of Bosch Security Systems went through together with the local Middle East sales managers can be illustrated as Figure 8.9 (which is similar to Figure 8.8).

The IMS process resulting in the final ranking list was quite time-consuming (several days of meetings), but these market analysis costs should be measured against the massive negative consequences of making the wrong selection. Bosch Security Systems concluded that it would be better to do their 'homework' properly. Bosch was following Chapter 8's proposed IMS process very closely.

First screening

At this stage some knock-out criteria were established and, if the countries did not meet these, they were 'kicked out' of the further screening process. In the first screening process, two major knock-out criteria were established:

- The country must be politically stable and not too 'conservative' with regard to politics and religion (Iran was 'kicked out' on this criterion).
- The country must not already be an established export market for Bosch fire detection (Egypt was 'kicked out' on this criterion).

The remaining six countries went on to the second screening process.

Second screening

Determine how you are going to 'measure' your variables! For this purpose, we use the MACS model: Market attractiveness/competitive strengths (this model is similar to Figure 8.4, p. 289, and Table 8.2, p. 290):

---

[a] Some of the original data that was used in the IMS process may have been changed in this explanation of the process. The outcome of the IMS process may not reflect the current Bosch strategy for fire detection systems in the Middle East and is solely the responsibility of the author.

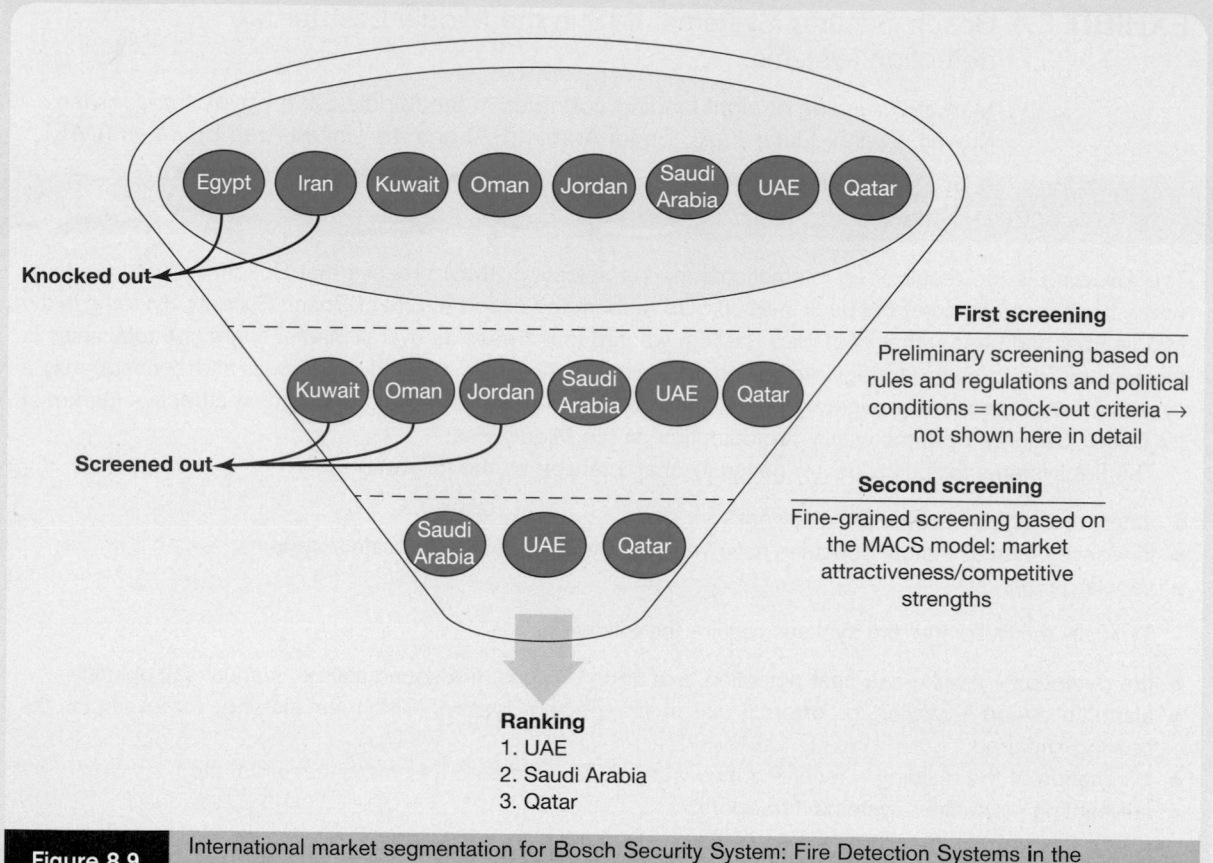

| **Figure 8.9** | International market segmentation for Bosch Security System: Fire Detection Systems in the Middle East |

- **MA screening variables – market attractiveness**
  - economic position – GDP (gross domestic product) per capita;
  - growth in construction industry – number of planned billion-dollar construction projects.

- **CS screening variables – competitive strengths**
  - strong local network – assess the quality of your local contacts;
  - sufficient local sales and technical support – number of Bosch sales advisors who are present locally.

The process then continued with:

- determining how much each screening variable affects the attractiveness of a country and the competitive strengths of your company; attach a **'weight'** per screening variable;
- researching every screening variable regarding 'performance' for each country individually and providing them with **'scores'**.

The weights of the screening variables added up to 100 per cent or to 1.0.

Before measuring the variables, it was important for Bosch Security Systems to classify the screening variables. The 'scores' were measured on a scale from 1 to 5, but was only possible to give the scores 1, 3 or 5. Table 8.3 shows the requirements that need to be fulfilled in order to assign 1, 3 or 5. Table 8.4 shows the specific scoring for the different countries.

After the classification of the different variables was made, the next stage was to evaluate each country on each screening variable. During this process, Bosch Security Systems sat down (in long meetings) with the local market specialists from the Middle East to determine a 'score' for each variable for each country.

The score given to each criterion per country is not shown in Table 8.4, only the result of weight × score. So, for example, for economic position for Saudi Arabia, a score of 3 was assigned, giving $0.05 \times 3 = 0.15$.

Table 8.3	Classification variables in the MACS model

Market attractiveness (MA)

Score	1	3	5
Economic position (GDP per capita, US$)	0–10,000	11,000–20,000	≥ 21,000
Market focus (quality or price)	Price	50/50	Quality
Construction – planned construction projects (billion-dollar projects)	0–5 projects	6–10 projects	≥ 11 projects
Market size fire business (€)	0–10 million	11–20 million	≥ 21
Market growth fire business	0–4%	5–9%	≥ 10%
Number of fire installers/dealers	0–15 dealers	16–30 dealers	≥ 31 dealers
Fire safety awareness (scale 1–10)	1, 2, 3, 4	5, 6, 7	8, 9, 10
Top verticals[a] that comply with EN standard[b]	1–2 verticals	2–3 verticals	> 3 verticals
Percentage of the market that can be served with CE[c]-certified products	0–33%	34–66%	67–100%
Exclusiveness of partnerships	1 exclusive dealer	1 premium dealer + supporting dealers	No exclusive regulations

Competitive strengths (CS)

Score	1	3	5
Local fire experience (€ sales in fire)	< 10,000	10,000–100,000	> 100,000
Local market knowledge (scale 1–10)	1, 2, 3, 4	5, 6, 7	8, 9, 10
Quality of the local business network/contact with authorities	Bad	Moderate	Good
Presence of a local Bosch fire sales representative	No	On short term < 1 year[d]	Yes
Local technical support (front office present)	No	On short term < 1 year	Yes
Contact details available of potential local fire partners	No	Partially	Yes

[a] Verticals: Industry verticals such as tourism (hotels), media, banking, fashion, health care, government.
[b] EN standards (European norms): European standards maintained by the CEN (European Committee for Standardization).
[c] CE, *conformité Européenne*, which means that the product meets the applicable European Directives.
[d] Local person available within 1 year (3) as opposed to already available (5).

Table 8.4	Measurement/evaluation of screening variables

Market attractiveness

	Weight ×	Score					
		Jordan	Kuwait	Oman	Qatar	Saudi Arabia	UAE
Economic position	0.05	0.05	0.05	0.05	0.25	0.15	0.25
Market focus (quality/price)	0.05	0.15	0.15	0.05	0.15	0.15	0.25
Construction	0.10	0.10	0.30	0.10	0.30	0.50	0.50
Market size fire business	0.15	0.15	0.45	0.15	0.45	0.75	0.75
Market growth fire business	0.15	0.75	0.45	0.45	0.75	0.75	0.75
Number of fire installers/dealers	0.10	0.10	0.30	0.10	0.30	0.50	0.50
Fire safety awareness	0.05	0.05	0.15	0.05	0.25	0.25	0.25
Top verticals that comply with EN standards	0.15	0.45	0.45	0.75	0.75	0.45	0.75
Percentage of the market for CE certified Bosch fire products	0.15	0.75	0.45	0.45	0.75	0.45	0.75
Exclusiveness of partnerships	0.05	0.15	0.25	0.05	0.15	0.25	0.25
Total	**1.00**	**2.70**	**3.00**	**2.20**	**4.10**	**4.20**	**5.00**

Table 8.4 *Continued*

Competitive strength (CS)

	Weight × Score						
		Jordan	Kuwait	Oman	Qatar	Saudi Arabia	UAE
Local experience	0.15	0.45	0.15	0.15	0.15	0.45	0.75
Market knowledge	0.15	0.15	0.15	0.15	0.15	0.45	0.45
Quality of the local business network	0.20	0.20	0.20	0.20	0.20	0.60	0.60
Presence of a local Bosch fire expert	0.20	0.20	0.20	0.20	0.60	0.60	0.60
Local technical support	0.20	0.20	0.20	0.20	0.60	0.60	1.00
Contact details potential partners	0.10	0.30	0.50	0.10	0.50	0.10	0.30
Total	**1.00**	**1.50**	**1.40**	**1.00**	**2.20**	**2.80**	**3.70**

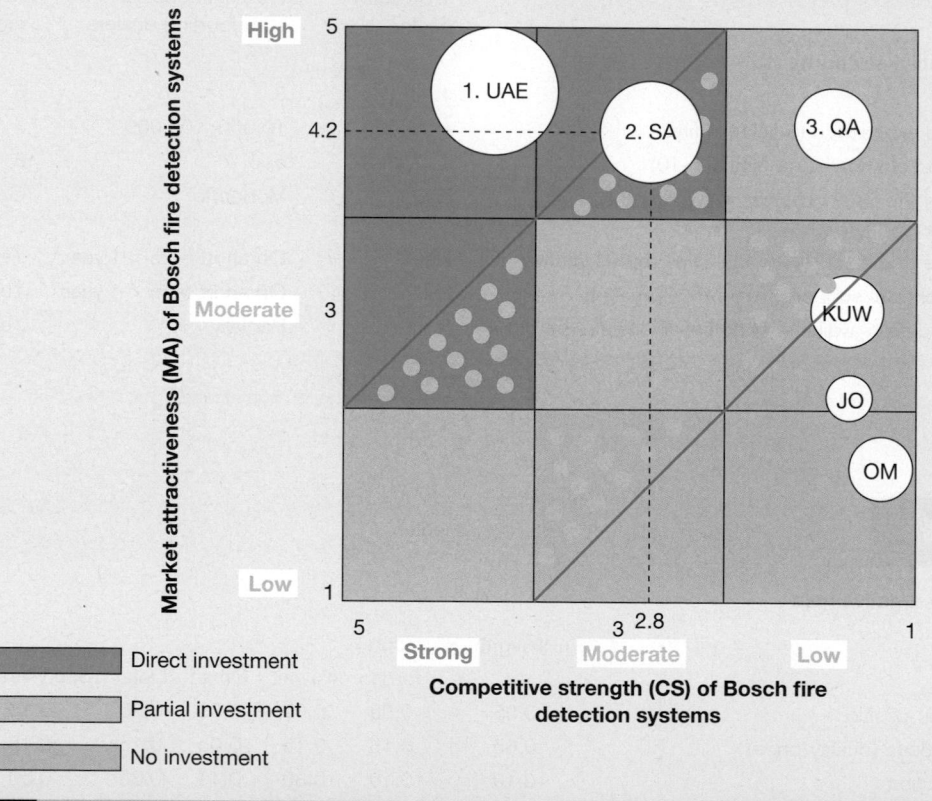

Figure 8.10 Bosch Fire Detection Systems MACS matrix

The outcomes of Table 8.4 are the centres of the 'bubbles' in Figure 8.10 (similar to the generic MACS model in Figure 8.4). Thus, Saudi Arabia (SA in the figure) gets $(x, y) = (2.8, 4.2)$. The sizes of the bubbles represent the market size of fire detection systems in different countries.

Outcome of the IMS process

The result of the project work and all the analysis was the following ranking of the most attractive countries for Bosch Security Systems (fire detection) in the Middle East:

1. United Arabic Emirates (UAE)
2. Saudi Arabia (SA)
3. Qatar (QA)

These rankings are only the start for the 'real' international marketing plan. The principal procedure is that the company chooses country number 1 in the list and decides about:

● entry mode (Part III of this book);
● marketing plan for the specific country (Part IV of this book).

After penetrating the country ranked number 1, the company can choose to do the same procedure for the countries ranked number 2, 3 and so on.

At some point, an overall cross-border coordination of all marketing activities can be initiated. This stage is discussed in Part V of this book.

The company also has to consider the competitors' current positions in the potential market. Even in situations where the potential market is very large and apparently attractive, the competitors may be so strong that it would be too resource-demanding for the company to enter the market in an attempt to gain market shares from the competitors.

8.4   Market expansion strategies

The choice of a market expansion strategy is a key decision in export marketing. First, different patterns are likely to cause development of different competitive conditions in different markets over time. For example, a fast rate of growth into new markets characterized by short product life cycles can create entry barriers towards competitors and give rise to higher profitability. On the other hand, a purposeful selection of relatively few markets for more intensive development can create higher market shares, implying stronger competitive positions.

EXHIBIT 8.2 Sunquick's waterfall approach

CO-RO, the manufacturer of Sunquick, is one of Denmark's leading companies in the development of fruit and juice-based super-concentrates. The company is focusing on developing close relationships with its licensing bottling partners, as shown in Figure 8.11.

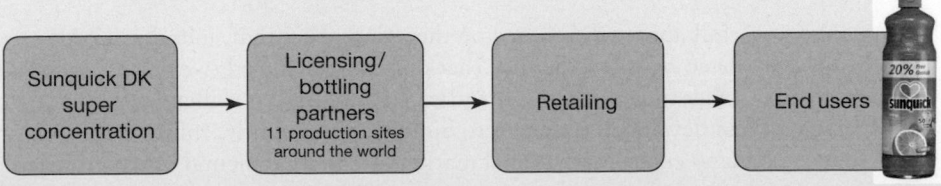

| **Figure 8.11** | Sunquick's worldwide value chain |

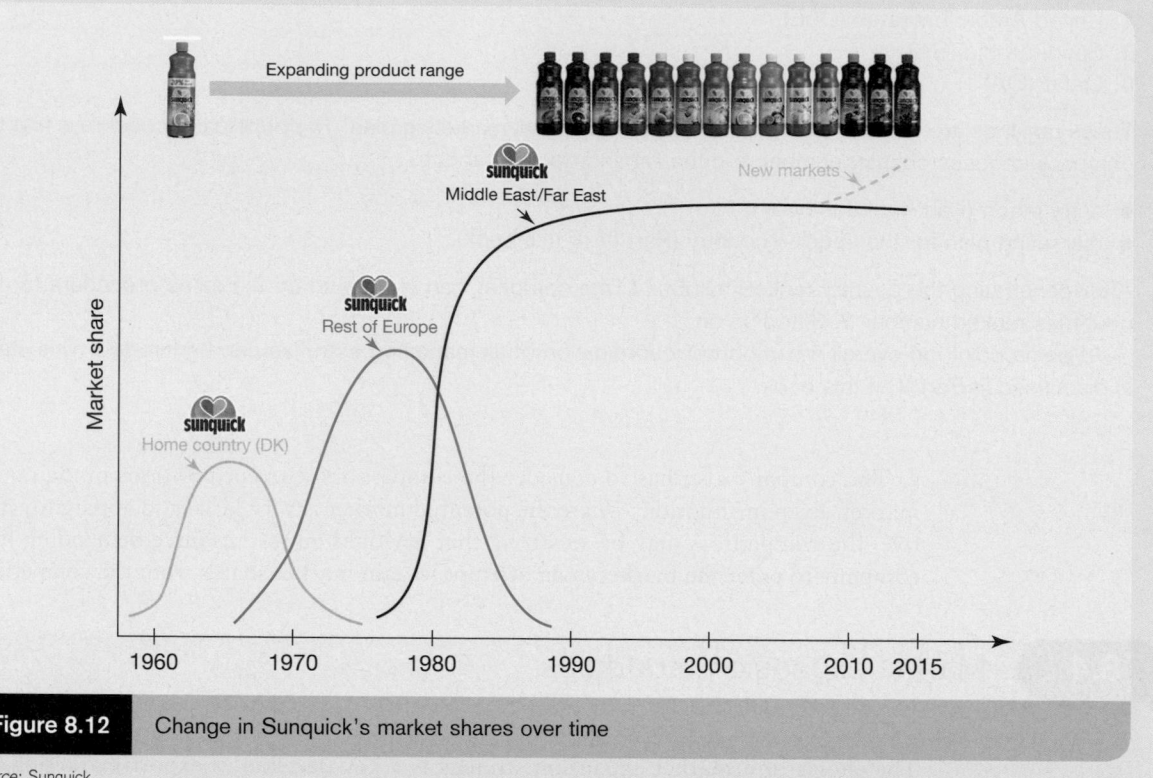

| Figure 8.12 | Change in Sunquick's market shares over time |

Source: Sunquick.

When Sunquick was introduced in the 1960s, the maker concentrated mainly on the domestic market and the European markets. During the 1970s and 1980s, Sunquick was sold mainly in the rest of Europe. In the 1980s, 1990s and the 2000s, Sunquick expanded mainly in emerging markets and less developed countries, as shown in Figure 8.12.

By 2010, Sunquick had become the market leader in Malaysia and China, with its market position constantly being expanded in less developed countries. (compare Figure 8.12 with a similar product life cycle (PLC) concept in Chapter 14 (Figure 14.9), which shows different PLCs in different countries).

Sources: based on www.sunquick.com; www.co-ro.com.

In designing their strategy firms have to answer two underlying questions:

1. Will they enter markets incrementally (the waterfall approach = trickle-down) or simultaneously (the shower approach)? (See Figure 8.13.)
2. Will entry be concentrated or diversified across international markets?

Incremental versus simultaneous entry

The waterfall approach is based on the assumption that, initially, a product or a technology may be so new or expensive that only the advanced (wealthy) countries can use it or afford it. Over time, however, the price will fall until it is inexpensive enough for developing and less developed countries to buy it. Consequently, following this approach, a firm may decide to enter international markets on an incremental or experimental basis, entering first a single key market in order to build up experience in international operations, and then subsequently entering other markets one after the other. Alternatively, a firm may decide to enter a number of markets simultaneously in order to leverage its core competence and resources rapidly across a broader market base.

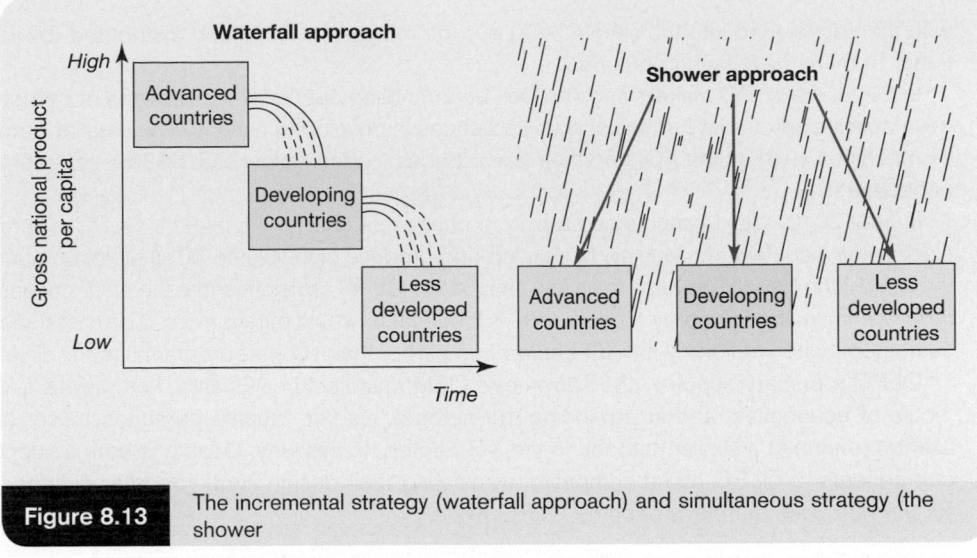

| Figure 8.13 | The incremental strategy (waterfall approach) and simultaneous strategy (the shower |

Source: Keegan, Warren J.; Green, Mark, *Global Marketing Management*, 2nd ed. p. 410; © 2000. Electronically reproduced by permission of Pearson Education, Inc., Upper Saddle River, New Jersey.

For the big global company the two strategies can be translated into the concept of the *international product life cycle* (Vernon, 1966), as illustrated in Figure 14.8.

Entry on an incremental basis, especially into small markets, may be preferred where a firm lacks experience in foreign markets and wishes to edge gradually into international operations. Information about, and familiarity with, operating in foreign markets is thus acquired step by step. This strategy may be preferable if a company is entering international markets late and faces entrenched local competition. Equally, if a firm is small and has limited resources, or is highly risk-averse, it may prefer to enter a single or a limited number of markets and gradually expand in a series of incremental moves rather than making a major commitment to international expansion immediately.

EXHIBIT 8.3 An example of the 'trickle-up' strategy

According to the waterfall approach (trickle-down), multinational corporations have stripped away features of new products or technologies, originally for advanced countries, to offer them at lower prices to people in developing countries, often adding details based on local research about user habits and needs. Now the opposite process, called 'trickle-up strategy', is happening. This is where multinationals take low-cost products initially developed for emerging markets and adapt them for bargain-hungry audiences in North America, Europe, Japan and Australia. Let us look at trickle-up in action.

One Laptop per Child.
Source: Joerg Boethling/Alamy Images.

XO laptop computer

Nicholas Negroponte founded 'One Laptop per Child' (OLPC) in 2005, with the purpose of distributing small and simple laptops (with internet access) to children who have no access to formal education. This concept was then developed into the simple 'XO Laptop', released in 2007 and distributed (by international organizations) to many developing countries.

In 2008, major PC makers such as Dell began rolling out their own versions of netbooks, intended not for developing markets but for mainstream audiences in developed nations. The smaller form factor was inspired by machines such as the XO, and their lower prices – often as low as US$300 – appeal to budget-conscious consumers.

In May 2010, OLPC announced a plan to change its offer to the market. OLPC entered a partnership with electronics manufacturer Marvell, to develop and produce high-volume XO-3 tablet computers and thus reduce the cost of the device, perhaps to as low as US$75. OLPC envisioned that the price cut and the greater product flexibility, including the ability to work with Adobe Flash, would attract more customers, including governmental customers, who would buy the XO Laptop has part of their support programmes for developing countries.

OLPC's primary supplier, the Taiwanese OEM-manufacturer Quanta, has played a key role in building a 'scale of economies' and in expanding the netbook market. Quanta persuaded Acer (another of Quanta's clients) to market a similar netbook to the XO Laptop. In this way, Quanta is both a supplier of manufactured components to OLPC and a competitor translating their design ideas for other customers' efforts, specially for the netbooks that have become OLPC rivals.

Sources: adapted from Yujuico and Gelb (2011); http://images.businessweek.com/ss/09/04/0401_pg_trickleup/11.htm.

Some companies prefer a rapid entry into world markets in order to seize an emerging opportunity or forestall competition. Rapid entry facilitates early market penetration across a number of markets and enables the firm to build up experience quickly. It also enables a firm to achieve economies of scale in production and marketing by integrating and consolidating operations across these markets. This may be especially desirable if the product or service involved is innovative or represents a significant technological advance, in order to forestall pre-emption or limitation by other competitors. While increasingly feasible due to developments in global information technology, simultaneous entry into multiple markets typically requires substantial financial and management resources and entails higher operating risk.

The appropriate expansion strategy for the SME

The SME often exploits domestic market opportunities to build up company resources which later may be used in international markets (Figure 8.14). The company strategy for market expansion should be concentrated on the product-market segment where the core competences of the company give it a competitive advantage (here product A, B, C and market 1, 2).

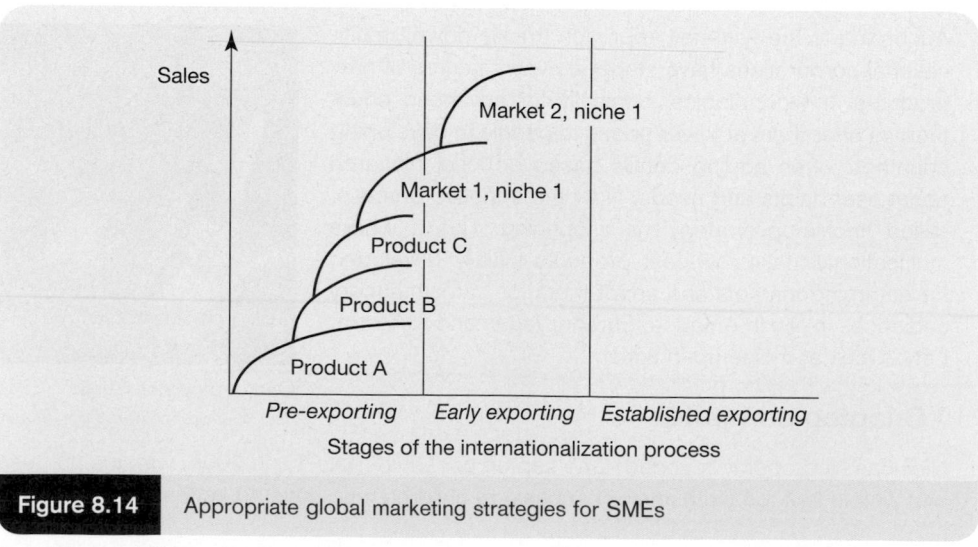

| Figure 8.14 | Appropriate global marketing strategies for SMEs |

Source: International Marketing Strategy, 2nd ed., Prentice Hall (Bradley, F. 1995) Copyright © Pearson Education Ltd.

The process might evolve step by step, taking one market at a time, market 1, niche 1, learning from it, and then using it as a bridgehead to transfer that competence to the same niche in the next market (market 2, niche 1). The company may develop its international operations by continuing to develop new markets in a step-by-step process, ensuring consolidation and profitability before moving on.

Concentration versus diversification

The firm must also decide whether to concentrate resources on a limited number of similar markets, or alternatively to diversify across a number of different markets. A company may concentrate its efforts by entering countries that are highly similar in terms of market characteristics and infrastructure to the domestic market. Management could also focus on a group of proximate countries. Alternatively, a company may prefer to diversify risk by entering countries that differ in terms of environmental or market characteristics. An economic recession in one country could be counterbalanced by growth in another market. The strength of competition also often varies from one market to another, and profits in a relatively protected or less competitive market may be funnelled into more fiercely competitive markets. Spreading out operations over a broader geographic base, and investing in different regions throughout the world, may also diversify risk, since, in some industries, markets in different regions are not interdependent (i.e. trends in one region will not spill over into another).

The question of concentrating or diversifying on the country level can be combined with concentration or diversification on the customer (segment) level. The resulting matrix (Figure 8.15) illustrates the four possible strategies.

From Figure 8.15, four expansion alternatives can be identified:

1. few customer groups/segments in few countries;
2. many customer groups/segments in few countries;
3. few customer groups/segments in many countries;
4. many customer groups/segments in many countries.

		Market/customer target group	
		Concentration	Diversification
Country	Concentration	1	2
	Diversification	3	4

Figure 8.15   The market expansion matrix

Source: Ayal and Zif (1979, p. 84).

A company can calculate its degree of export concentration and compare it over time or with other firms, using the Herfindahl index. This index is defined as the sum of the squares of the percentage of sales in each foreign country.

$$C = \sum S_i^2 \quad i = 1, 2, 3, 4, \ldots, \textbf{\textit{n}} \text{ countries}$$

where C = the export concentration index of the firm
Si = exports to country i as a percentage (measured in decimal numbers from 0 to 1) of the firm's total exports

$$\sum S_i = 1$$

There is maximum concentration ($C = 1$) when all the exports are made to one country only, and minimum concentration ($C = 1/n$) when exports are equally distributed over a large number of countries.

The factors favouring country diversification versus concentration are shown in Table 8.5.

Table 8.5	International market diversification versus market concentration
Factors favouring country diversification	**Factors favouring country concentration**
Company factors	
High management risk consciousness (accept risk)	Low management risk consciousness (risk-averse)
Objective of growth through market development	Objective of growth through market penetration
Little market knowledge	Ability to pick 'best' markets
Product factors	
Limited specialist uses	General uses
Low volume	High volume
Non-repeat	Repeat-purchase product
Early or late in product life cycle	Middle of product life cycle
Standard product saleable in many markets	Product requires adaptation to different markets
Radical innovation can trigger new global customer solutions	Incremental innovation – narrow market scope
Market factors	
Small markets – specialized segments	Large markets – high-volume segments
Unstable markets	Stable markets
Many similar markets	Limited number of markets
New or declining markets	Mature markets
Low growth rate in each market	High growth rate in each market
Large markets are very competitive	Large markets are not excessively competitive
Established competitors have large share of key markets	Key markets are divided among many competitors
Low customer loyalty	High customer loyalty
High synergy effects between countries	Low synergy effect between countries
Learning can be transferred across markets	Lack of awareness of global opportunities and threats
Short competitive lead time	Long competitive lead time
Marketing factors	
Low communication costs for additional markets	High communication costs for additional markets
Low order-handling costs for additional markets	High order-handling costs for additional markets
Low physical distribution costs for additional markets	High physical distribution costs for additional markets
Standardized communication in many markets	Communication requires adaptation to different markets

Sources: adapted from Ayal and Zif (1979); Piercy (1981); Katsikea *et al.* (2005).

EXHIBIT 8.4 Bajaj is selecting new international markets ignored by global leaders

International market success can be achieved by concentrating on markets ignored by global leaders. Indian motorcycle maker Bajaj Auto expanded into 50 countries by focusing on small motorcycles (with engines of 200cc or less) that offer exceptional value for money; Bajaj's huge line-up of simple motor bikes targets different preferences at a wide range of price points.

In 2008–09, Bajaj sold approximately 1.9 million motorcycles, of which one-third were exported. While the world's three largest motorcycle companies

Source: Bajaj Auto.

(Honda, Yamaha and Suzuki) focus on developed markets like the US and western Europe, the world's fourth-largest motorcycle manufacturer, Bajaj, has chosen to focus on developing countries (Figure 8.16).

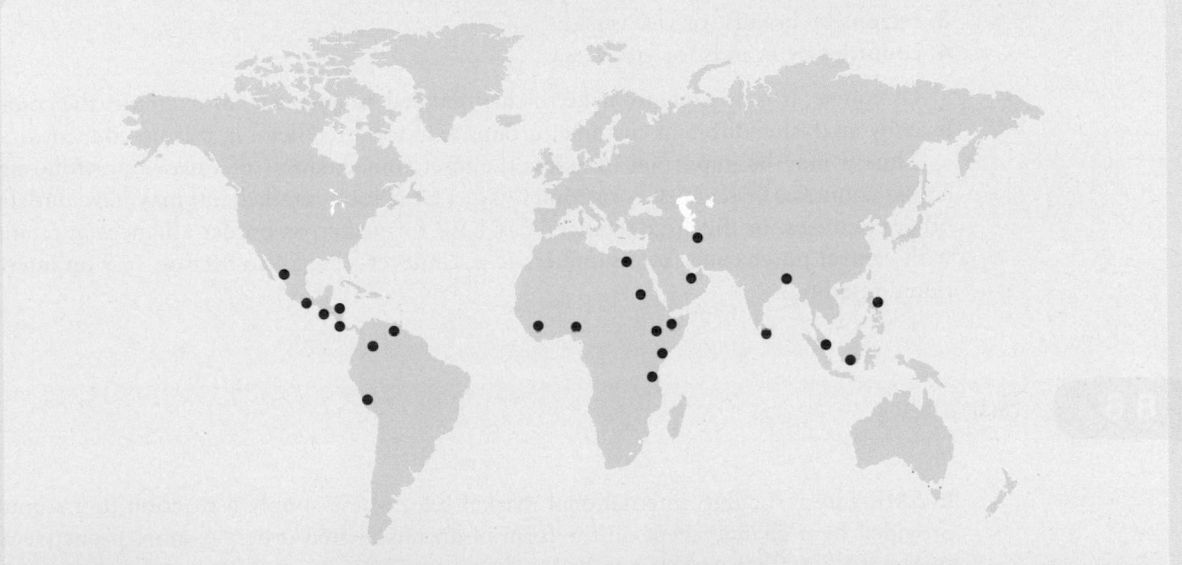

| Figure 8.16 | Location of Bajaj's international dealers |

Source: www.bajajauto.com.

Bajaj has a distribution network that covers 50 countries. It has a dominant presence in Sri Lanka, Colombia, Bangladesh, Central America, Peru and Egypt and is also gaining an increasing foothold in Africa. As a consequence, the company has commissioned an assembly unit in Nigeria with the help of its distributor to cater to the growing demand in the African markets.

As a part of the company's policy to be closer to the markets in which it operates, Bajaj Auto has its own sales offices in Monterrey (Mexico), Dubai and Colombo (Sri Lanka) in addition to its subsidiary, PT BAI, in Indonesia.

Sources: adapted from Sirkin *et al.* (2008); www.bajajauto.com.

8.5   The global product/market portfolio

The corporate portfolio analysis provides an important tool to assess how to allocate resources, not only across geographic areas but also across different product business (Douglas and Craig, 1995). The global corporate portfolio represents the most aggregate level of analysis and it might consist of operations by product businesses or by geographic areas.

As illustrated in Figure 8.17 (based on the market attractiveness/competitive strength matrix of Figure 8.4), Unilever's most aggregate level of analysis is its different product businesses. With this global corporate portfolio as a starting point, the further analysis of single corporate product business can be carried out in a product or geographic dimension, or a combination of the two.

It appears from the global corporate portfolio in Figure 8.17 that Unilever's foods business is characterized by high market attractiveness and high competitive strengths. However, a more distinct picture of the situation is obtained by analysing underlying levels. This more detailed analysis is often required to give an operational input to specific market-planning decisions.

By combining the product and geographic dimensions it is possible to analyse the global corporate portfolio at the following levels (indicated by the arrows in the example of Figure 8.17):

1. product categories by regions (or vice versa);
2. product categories by countries (or vice versa);
3. regions by brands (or vice versa);
4. countries by brands (or vice versa).

Of course, it is possible to make further detailed analysis of, for example, the country level by analysing different customer groups (e.g. food retailers) in certain countries.

Thus it may be important to assess the interconnectedness of various portfolio units across countries or regions. A customer (e.g. a large food retail chain) may have outlets in other countries, or the large retailers may have formed cross-border alliances in retailing with central purchasing from suppliers (e.g. Unilever) – see also Section 16.9 on international retailing.

8.6   Summary

In SMEs, in particular, international market selection is simply a reaction to a stimulus provided by a change agent, in the form of an unsolicited order. A more proactive and systematic approach to IMS entails:

1. selection of relevant segmentation criteria;
2. development of appropriate segments;
3. screening of segments to narrow down the list of appropriate countries (choice of target);
4. microsegmentation: development of subsegments in each qualified country or across countries.

However, the *pragmatic approach* to IMS is often used successfully by firms. Coincidences and the personal network of top managers play an important role in the 'selection' of the firm's first export market. In carrying out IMS, the firm must seek the synergy between the possible new target market and its own strengths, objectives and strategy. The firm's choice of new international markets is very much influenced by the existence of complementary markets and marketing skills gained in these markets.

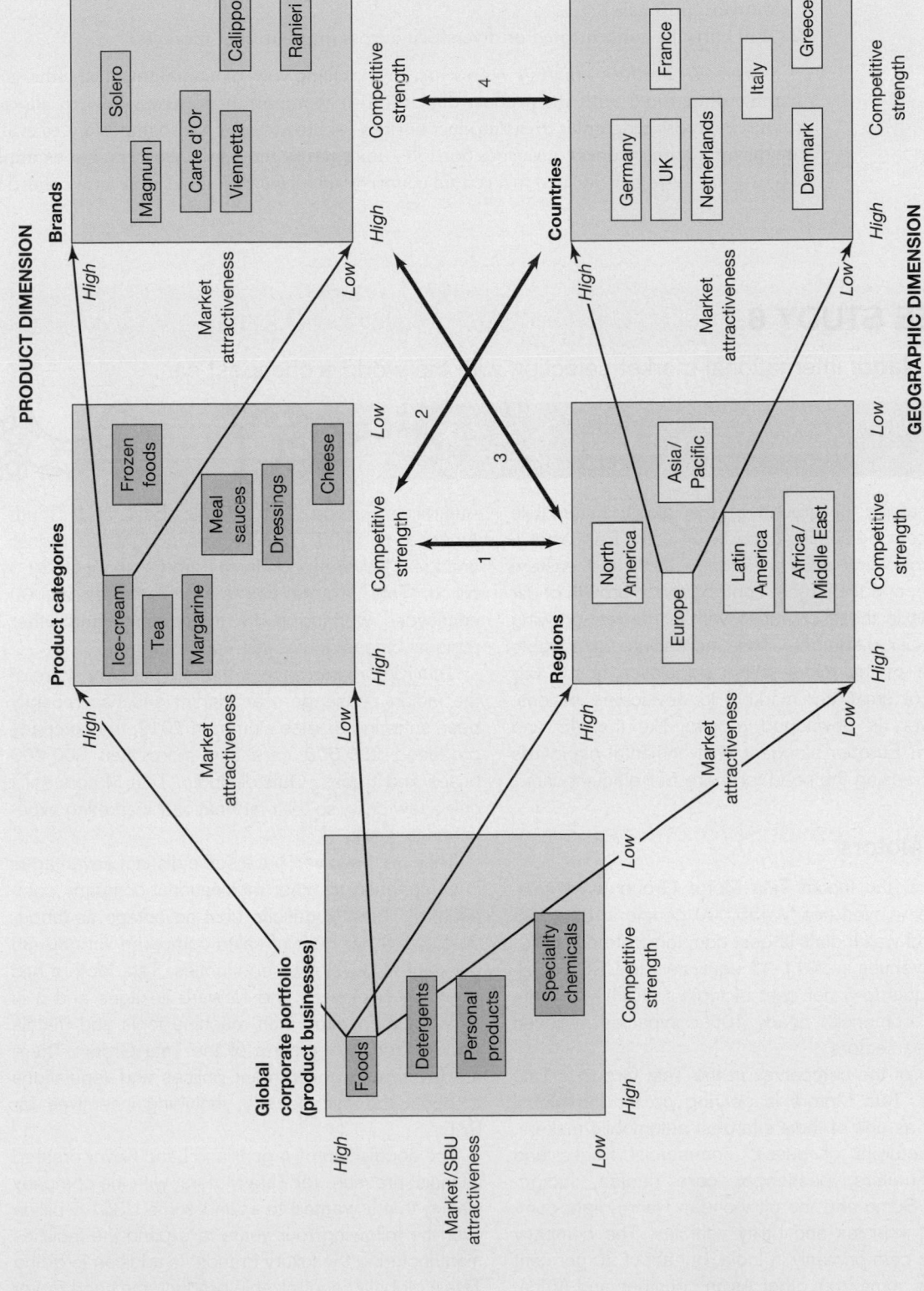

Figure 8.17 Unilever's global portfolio

After going through the four steps described above, the market expansion strategy of the chosen market is a key decision. In designing this strategy, the firm has to answer two underlying questions:

1. Will it enter markets incrementally (the waterfall approach) or simultaneously (the shower approach)?
2. Will entry be concentrated or diversified across international markets?

Corporate portfolio analysis represents an excellent way of combining IMS (the geographic dimension) with the product dimension. It is important to assess how to allocate resources across geographic areas/product businesses. However, it is also important to evaluate the interconnectedness of various portfolio units across geographic borders. For example, a particular customer (located in a certain country) may have businesses in several countries.

CASE STUDY 8.1

Tata Nano: international market selection with the world's cheapest car

The majority of growth in the global automobile industry in the coming decade will come from emerging economies such as India, China and eastern Europe, and the largest contribution to growth of car markets in these countries will be the fast-growing small car segment. The increasing disposable income of the middle-class population is the key driver of small car markets in developing nations. However, in developed regions like the US and western Europe, stringent environmental standards are increasing the need for more fuel-efficient cars.

Tata Motors

In 2012, the Indian Tata Motor Group (www.tata.com) employed nearly 455,000 people in 85 countries and was India's largest conglomerate company, with revenues in 2011–12 equivalent to US$100 billion (equal to 5 per cent of India's GDP). The Tata Group comprises nearly 100 companies in seven business sectors.

One of the companies in the Tata Group is Tata Motors. Tata Motors is gearing up for the global market as one of India's largest automobile makers, manufacturers of buses, commercial trucks and tractor-trailers, passenger cars (Indica, Indigo, Safari, Sumo and the ultra-cheap Nano), light commercial vehicles and utility vehicles. The company sells its cars primarily in India, but about 20 per cent of sales come from other Asian countries and Africa,

Australia, Europe, the Middle East and South America. In 2008, Tata Motors bought the Jaguar and Land Rover brands from Ford for about US$2.3 billion. Tata Motors has a workforce of 22,000 employees working in its three plants and other regional offices across the country.

Tata Motors has a lower than 20 per cent share of the Indian passenger car market and has recently been suffering a sales slump. In 2012, the company produced 250,000 cars and more than 300,000 buses and trucks. Outside India, Tata Motors sells only a few cars, so their international marketing experience is weak.

They do, however, have some distinct advantages in comparison to other multinational company competitors. There is definite cost advantage as labour cost is 8–9 per cent of sales compared with 30–35 per cent in developed economies. Tata Motors has extensive backward and forward linkages and it is strongly interwoven with machine tools and metals sectors from other parts of the Tata Group. There are favourable government polices and regulations to boost the car industry, including incentives for R&D.

The acquisition of Jaguar and Land Rover created financial pressure for Tata Motors, with the company stating that it wanted to spend some US$1.5 billion over the following four years to expand the facilities manufacturing the luxury brands. In addition to giving Tata a globally recognizable product, the Land Rover

The alternative to the Tata Nano
Source: David Pearson/Alamy.

and Jaguar deal also gave them an entry into the US. Through a deal with Fiat, Tata is already distributing the Italian cars in India and may expand the offering into South America, a Fiat stronghold.

Development of Tata Nano

In 2008, Tata unveiled the Nano, the cheapest car in the world, at the Auto Expo in New Delhi. The car seats up to five people, gets up to 55 miles to the gallon, and sells for about US$2,230. At first the Nano was sold only in India, but Tata hoped to export them after a few initial years of production; the Nano might also be exported to Europe in the future. First shipments to Indian customers took place at the start of 2010.

Tata Nano started with the vision of Ratan Tata, the chairman of Tata Motors' parent, the Tata Group, to create an ultra-low-cost car for a new category of Indian consumer: someone who couldn't afford the US$5,000 sticker price of what was then the cheapest car on the market and instead drove his family around on a US$1,000 motorcycle. Many drivers in India can only afford motorcycles and it is fairly common to see an Indian family of four using a motorcycle to get around.

In India alone there are 50–100 million people caught in that automotive chasm. Until now none of the Indian car makers has focused on this segment, and in this respect the Nano is a great example of the blue ocean strategy.

The customer was ever-present in the development of the Nano. Tata didn't set the price by calculating the cost of production and then adding a margin; rather it set US$2,500 as the price that it thought customers could pay and then worked back, with the help of partners willing to take on a challenge, to build a US$2,500 car that would reward all involved with a small profit.

The Nano engineers and partners didn't simply strip features out of an existing car – the tack Renault took with its Dacia Logan, which sells in India for roughly US$10,000. Instead, they looked at their target customers' lives for cost-cutting ideas. So, for instance, the Nano has a smaller engine than other cars because more horsepower would be wasted in India's jam-packed cities, where the average speed is 10–20 miles per hour.

The Nano aims to bring the joys of motoring to millions of Indians, doing for the subcontinent what the Volkswagen Beetle did for Germany and the Mini for Britain. But the plan horrified environmentalists who fear that the demand from India's aspirational and increasingly middle-class population – now numbering 50 million in a country with a total 1.1 billion people – for more cars would add to pollution and global warming.

The global automotive industry

In 2012, the worldwide production of passenger cars was 81 million cars. The distribution by country was as shown in Table 1.

Tata Nano
Source: P Cox/Alamy.

Table 1	Global distribution of passenger cars, 2012

Country	2012 (millions of cars produced)
US and Canada	17
Western Europe	13
Eastern Europe	5
Japan	5
China	19
Korea	2
India	3
Brazil/Argentina	4
Other	13
World total	**81**

Segmentation of the global low-cost car (LCC) market

There is no doubt that the competitive landscape for the global car market has been altered dramatically and permanently. Oxyer *et al.* (2008) forecasted that the global low-cost market (defined as ultra-low-cost + regular low-cost car market in Figure 1) is expected to grow from 2 million cars in 2008 to 17.5 million cars in 2020.

Moreover, the huge potential of this market is attracting the attention of manufacturers and vendors worldwide, with a number of global players recently entering the LCC sector. There is no doubt that first movers will have the opportunity to capture market share and build consumer loyalty. The dynamic and powerful ultra-low-cost car (ULCC) market is forcing car manufacturers to rethink their strategies. It is indisputable that using traditional design, manufacturing and distribution approaches to achieve ULCC entry prices below US$3,500 will be a difficult task. A low price point and low profit margins – estimated at around 3 per cent at the base model levels – will provide tough competition in the ULCC market.

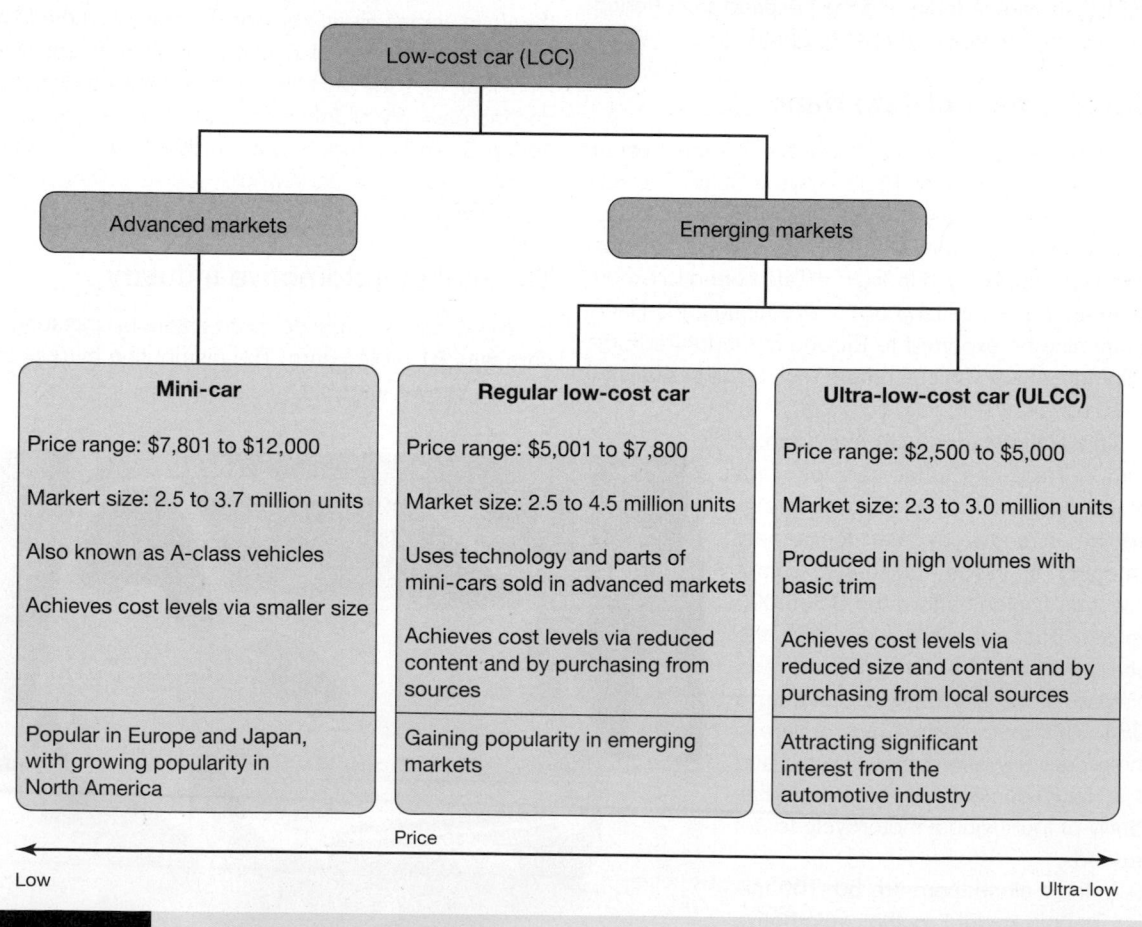

Figure 1 Segmentation of the low-cost car market

Low-cost car (LCC)

Advanced markets

Emerging markets

Mini-car

Price range: $7,801 to $12,000

Markert size: 2.5 to 3.7 million units

Also known as A-class vehicles

Achieves cost levels via smaller size

Popular in Europe and Japan, with growing popularity in North America

Regular low-cost car

Price range: $5,001 to $7,800

Market size: 2.5 to 4.5 million units

Uses technology and parts of mini-cars sold in advanced markets

Achieves cost levels via reduced content and by purchasing from sources

Gaining popularity in emerging markets

Ultra-low-cost car (ULCC)

Price range: $2,500 to $5,000

Market size: 2.3 to 3.0 million units

Produced in high volumes with basic trim

Achieves cost levels via reduced size and content and by purchasing from local sources

Attracting significant interest from the automotive industry

Price

Low

Ultra-low

Source: Oxyer *et al.* (2008).

Two of the most promising markets for Tata Nano are characterized in India and in China and Japan, which are expected to account for about 60–70 per cent of the future ULCC production and demand.

India

India is likely to evolve into a global hub for small car manufacturing. Currently it is one of the largest producers of small cars, with the small car segment accounting for about three-quarters of the Indian car market. The fast-growing small car market has encouraged several global car companies (Renault Nissan, Toyota, Hyundai) to announce plans for the launch of small cars in India. With the launch of Tata Nano, the stage is set for around a dozen new small and compact cars to be launched in India in the next two years.

In 2012, Maruti Suzuki India, the largest passenger car manufacturer in India, had more than a 60 per cent share of the domestic small car segment.

The implication of the impending advent of an inexpensive passenger car such as the Nano on urban transport in India has to be seen in the context of overall trends in motorization in the country. By the end of 2012, India was home to nearly 50 million passenger cars. In 2012, around 3 million new passenger cars were sold on the Indian market. This figure was expected to increase to 4 million cars in 2015. Compare this with the fact that in 2012 alone nearly 10 million two-wheeler motorcycles were sold in India.

China and Japan

Small car demand in China is expected to increase in the long term. However, the narrow price gap between the small car and medium car segments has made medium-segment cars a more attractive choice for consumers.

Mini-cars account for more than one-third of the total volume sales in the Japanese auto market. Suzuki and Daihatsu are the market leaders in the small car market in Japan. A large number of Japanese consumers are moving from luxury cars to mini-cars due to environmental standards and increasing gas prices.

The Tata Nano business model

Tata began the development process with 600 closely integrated suppliers, only 100 of which remain. Independent suppliers provide 80 per cent of the Nano's components, and 97 per cent of the vehicle is sourced in India. Suppliers such as Bosch worked with Tata and employed Indian engineers with motorcycle, rather than automobile, design experience to craft innovative low-cost components.

Reduce the number and complexity of parts

By focusing on the essentials and encouraging creativity in making components smaller, lighter and cheaper, Tata avoided engineering non-functional, non-essential parts. Bosch, for example, adapted a smaller and lighter motorcycle starter for use in the Nano.

European suppliers with production capacity in India had a big advantage over rivals when Tata Motors started to look for partners for its Nano. One reason the Nano is the cheapest car in the world is because 97 per cent of its parts are locally sourced. It is impossible to deliver a low-cost component out of western Europe to a different place in the world.

Half of the 100 vendors for the project are located with Tata in a 142-hectare vendor park in Singur next to the new plant that will produce the Nano. Singur is a suburb of Calcutta in eastern India. Here are some European suppliers with key parts on the Nano:

Seat belts	Autoliv
HVAC	Behr
Starter motor, engine-control module, injectors, sensors	Bosch
Transmission speed sensors, fuel-level sensor, fuel pump	Continental
Fuel filter, air cleaner	Mahle
Glazings	Saint-Gobain
Speed sensors	TT Electronics
Clutches	Valeo

Most of these suppliers can only be profitable on Nano parts because they produce high-volume parts in a low-wage country like India, where they also conduct some research and development.

Standardize at every stage of the value chain

Similar to Henry Ford's 'any colour so long as it's black' approach, the Nano offers consumers few options, and only a few have any impact on the manufacturing process.

The Nano's distribution model for India is also new. The company mobilizes large numbers of third parties to reach remote rural consumers, tailor the products and services to serve their needs, and add value to the core product or service through ancillary services. For example, one plant produces vehicle modules that are then sent to a number of strategically positioned satellite mini-factories, where the Nano is assembled and delivered to the buyer. A central warehouse stocks spare parts and accessories.

Export of Tata Nano to Europe and/or North America

There are two clear barriers for Tata Nano when considering these two regions:

- *Emission standards.* Western Europe, Japan and North America established emissions standards more than a decade ago. Emerging markets such as China and India are adopting European standards, but with a five- to seven-year lag. Cars in the lightweight low-cost car segment, with their small engines and modest fuel consumption, will meet current emissions standards.
- *Safety regulations.* North America and Europe have similar government-developed safety regulations with respect to seat belts, rollover and rear-, side- and frontal-protection standards. In developing countries, the standards are lower, and ultra-low-cost cars will encounter few, if any, difficulties in meeting those standards. As European and

North American governments continue to establish higher standards, there will be compliance issues.

As a consequence of these and other barriers (tariffs), the US$2,500 target base price of Nano for the Indian market can jump to nearly double the price in a European country:

Tata Nano	US$
Base price	2,500
+ Conversion (cost for fitting to emission standard and safety regulations)	500
+ Logistics costs	375
+ Marketing	125
+ Manufacturer profit	105
+ Dealership profit	108
+ Import tariffs	93
Expected MSRP (manufacturer's suggested retail price)	3,806
+ Sales tax	400
Total costs	4,206

The actual price that the private car buyer pays could be substantially higher in heavily taxed countries such as Denmark.

Competition

The five cheapest cars in the world at the beginning of 2012 were:

No.	Model	Producer	Price US$/€
1	Nano	Tata Motors in India	2,500/1,688
2	QQ3	Chery Automobiles in China	5,000/1,726
3	M800	Suzuki-Maruti in India	5,200/3,451
4	Merrie Star	Geely Automobiles in China	5,500/3,796
5	S-RV mini SUV	Geely Automobiles in China	5,780/3,989

Source: based on www.timesonline.co.uk.

There are now several competitors on their way into the ULLC market:

Renault-Dacia Logan

Between 2004 and 2012, Renault sold 450,000 of the bare bones US$7,200 (€4,969) Logan sedan. The price tag of this stripped-down family car is almost half the cost of competing sedans.

Hyundai

Hyundai Motors is also working on development of an ultra-cheap car that will compete against the Nano. Hyundai is the second-largest car manufacturer in India. Currently, Hyundai is the biggest rival of Indian car market leader, Maruti Suzuki India.

VW

VW also plans to launch a low-cost car called Up! in both India and Russia. The low-cost car, which will share some of the components of VW's compact Polo, is designed to be an affordable car for developing countries.

Toyota

Toyota also has plans for entering the Indian LCC market. Their new 35-billion-yen (US$343 million) production facility, located on the outskirts of the southern city of Bangalore, started production in 2010 with an initial capacity of 100,000 units a year. The unit price was around US$6,000. That will not immediately compete with Tata Motor's US$2,500 People's cars, although in the future Toyota may jump into the LCC market using Daihatsu's know-how.

Toyota holds a 16 per cent share of the US car market, but its sales in emerging markets remain small (e.g. its market share in India is 3 per cent).

QUESTIONS

In the first full year (2010–11), Tata Nano sold around 70,000 cars. This figure increased slightly to around 80,000 cars in 2011–12 but since 2012 the sales of Tata Nano have decreased. In 2012–13 sales fell to 54,000 cars, in 2013–14 they fell to 21,000 cars, and in 2014–15 they fell to 17,000 cars. The production capacity in the Indian factories is around 300,000 Nano cars per year. So far, the Nano has been sold largely to the Indian market. Only a small percentage of the production has gone for export. But now the Global Marketing Manager of Tata Nano has contacted you, as an international marketing expert, in order to expand the international sales of Tata Nano.

1. What could be the main reasons for Tata Motors entering the global ultra-low-cost car market?

2. What are the competitive advantages that Tato Motors would enjoy with the Nano in emerging markets?

3. Which screening criteria would you suggest for Tata Nano's IMS process?

4. Which world regions and specific countries would you suggest Tata Nano should enter after India and China?

Sources: based on different public sources, including www.tatanano.com, www.tatamotors.com and Oxyer, D., Deans, G., Shivaraman, S., Ghosh, S. and Pleines, R. (2008) 'A Nano car in every driveway? How to succeed in the ultra-low-cost car market', *A.T. Kearney Business Journal – Executive Agenda*, XI(2), pp. 55–62.

CASE STUDY 8.2

Philips Lighting: screening markets in the Middle East

Royal Philips Electronics of the Netherlands is one of the world's biggest electronics companies, as well as the largest in Europe, with 122,000 employees in 100 countries and sales in 2011 of €22.6 billion.

In 1891, the Dutch mechanical engineer Gerard Philips started the production of carbon-filament lamps in a former buckskin factory in Eindhoven. Among his first major clients were early electricity companies who included the provision of lamps in their power supply contracts.

Today, Philips is number one in the world market for lighting. Their lighting products (light bulbs and lamps) are found all around the world: not only everywhere in the home, but also in a multitude of professional applications, for example, in 30 per cent of offices, 65 per cent of the world's top airports, 30 per cent of hospitals, 35 per cent of cars and 55 per cent of major football stadiums.

Competition

Philips Lighting is the world leader in lighting products manufacturing. Its market shares are 50 per cent in Europe, 36 per cent in North America and 14 per cent in the rest of the world. Since the 1980s, Philips has participated intensively in the concentration of this industrial sector by purchasing smaller national companies such as Companie des Lampes (France), AEG (Germany) and Polam Pila (Poland). It has also developed joint ventures with Westinghouse Lamps, Kono Sylvania and EBT China.

GEL

General Electric Lighting (GEL) holds a 50 per cent share of the US market but had only a 2 per cent market share in Europe in 1988. In order to reach a 30 per cent market share in 2010, GEL acquired several European national companies, such as Tungsram (Czechoslovakia), Thorn Emi (UK), Sivi (Italy) and Linder Licht (Germany). In 1994 GEL built a logistics unit in France to supply France, Germany, Benelux, Switzerland, Italy and Austria. It now intends to reduce prices in connection with supermarket chains.

Osram

A 100 per cent subsidiary of the giant German holding Siemens, Osram achieves an 86 per cent share of its turnover by exporting (46 per cent in North America, 41 per cent in the EU, 6 per cent in South America and 6 per cent in Asia). The strategy for the coming years is to increase Asian market shares by doubling its turnover in Asia.

Other significant manufacturers are Sylvania Lighting International and Panasonic.

Philips Lighting market screening in the Middle East

At the beginning of the twenty-first century, Philips needed a coherent marketing strategy for the whole Middle East region. The first task was to select the most attractive markets in the region. Over the years Philips has developed a model which shows a correlation between a country's demand for lighting and its GDP per capita. During discussions with agents/distributors in many countries, Philips was completely dependent on its information about market size. If Philips underestimated market size, it missed market opportunities. That was the main reason why this model was developed, so that the company

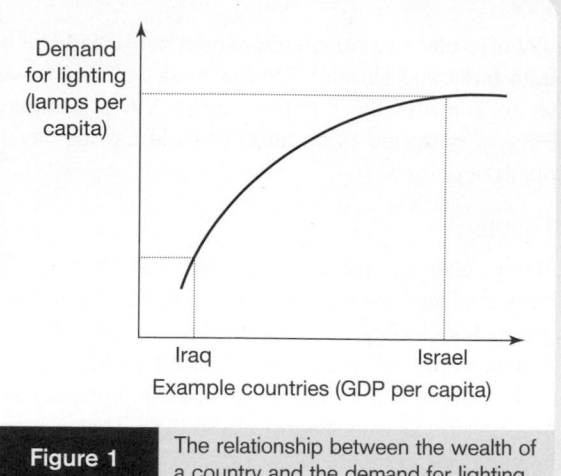

Figure 1   The relationship between the wealth of a country and the demand for lighting

could cross-check market estimations of its agents/distributors.

Figure 1 shows that lighting (demand for lamps and bulbs) is a basic need for a country and, as soon as a country starts developing, this basic need increases. However, as the country's wealth increases, the growth in the demand slows down, because at later stages of economic development basic lighting needs are covered, as can be seen in the case of Israel.

Basically, in order to find the most attractive markets Philips Lighting used the model (shown in Figure 1b and Table 1a) in combination. The demand for lighting per capita has to be multiplied by the number of inhabitants in a country. Israel and Kuwait have the highest GDP/capita, but their population size is small. On the other hand, Iraq and Iran were (and still are) large markets for lighting, but they are very tough to enter because of their politically chaotic situations.

However, the Philips Lighting Middle East managers did not use market size as the only market selection criterion for priority; instead the models were used as a starting point for discussions with agents and distributors in the countries. If the Philips sales in large lighting markets were very low, this would indicate a low Philips market share (unless the market size was also low). This would lead to a discussion with the local agents and

Table 1	Basic demographic data in the Middle East (2007)		
Markets	Population (million)	GNP 2007 (% growth)	GNP per capita (US$)
Bahrain	0.6	3.0	8,620
Egypt	61.9	5.0	1,232
Iran	66.0	3.0	1,670
Iraq	19.7	−5.0	758
Israel	5.5	7.1	15,700
Jordan	4.6	5.0	2,359
Kuwait	2.2	3.5	15,970
Lebanon	3.2	4.0	4,250
Libya	5.5	3.5	4,982
Oman	2.4	4.3	6,268
Palestine	2.1	−5.0	630
Qatar	0.6	2.0	13,520
Saudi Arabia	20.6	3.5	5,943
Syria	17.0	6.0	982
UAE	2.5	0.5	17,840
Yemen	15.0	3.0	793
Middle East	229.4	−	−

Source: Wim Wils, Eindhoven, Fontys Export Day, 13 October 2004, update via www.worldbank.org.

distributors about how to increase the local Philips market shares in cooperation with the local distributor.

QUESTIONS

1. Discuss the appropriateness of the screening model used in this case.

2. Suggest another screening model that could be relevant for Philips Lighting to use in the Middle East.

Sources: based on PowerPoint presentation from Wim Wils, Eindhoven, Fontys Export Day, 13 October 2004; www.philips.com; www.worldbank.org.

VIDEO CASE STUDY 8.3 Oreo (Mondelēz)
download from **www.pearsoned.co.uk/hollensen**

Oreo is a sandwich cookie consisting of two chocolate wafers with a sweet creme filling in between, and (as of 1974) are marketed as 'Chocolate Sandwich Cookies' on the package they are held in. The version currently sold in the US is made by the Nabisco division of Mondelēz International. Oreo has been the best-selling cookie in the US since its introduction in 1912.

Much of current Oreo production is done at the Kraft/Nabisco factory in Richmond, Virginia. Oreo cookies for the Asian markets are manufactured in Indonesia, India and China. Oreo cookies for Europe are made in Spain and in Ukraine for consumers in several CIS countries. Oreo cookies sold in Australia are manufactured in Indonesia (previously China) or Spain, depending on flavour. The Canadian produced version includes coconut oil and is sold only in that region. Manufacturing of Oreo biscuits in Pakistan began in early 2014.

Oreo is sold in more than 100 countries around the world. More than 450 billion Oreo cookies have been sold worldwide since their debut in 1912.

Source: Nenov Brothers Images/Shutterstock.com.

Questions

1. What are the foundations of Oreo's global success?

2. What demographic changes and cultural issues might influence the future global market for Oreo?

3. What are the most important screening criteria for Oreo (Mondelēz) in the IMS?

For further resources, see this book's website at **www.pearsoned.co.uk/hollensen**

Questions for discussion

1. Why is screening of foreign markets important? Outline the reasons why many firms do not systematically screen countries/markets.

2. Explore the factors that influence the IMS process.

3. Discuss the advantages and disadvantages of using only secondary data as screening criteria in the IMS process.

4. What are the advantages and disadvantages of an opportunistic selection of international markets?

5. What are the differences between a global market segment and a national market segment? What are the marketing implications of these differences for a firm serving segments on a worldwide basis?

6. Discuss the possible implications that the firm's choice of geographic expansion strategy may have on the ability of a local marketing manager of a foreign subsidiary to develop and implement marketing programmes.

References

Andersen, O. and Buvik, A. (2002) 'Firms' internationalization and alternative approaches to the international customer/market selection', *International Business Review*, 11, pp. 347–363.

Andersen, P.H. and Strandskov, J. (1998) 'International market selection', *Journal of Global Marketing*, 11(3), pp. 65–84.

Ayal, I. and Zif, J. (1979) 'Market expansion strategies in multinational marketing', *Journal of Marketing*, 43, pp. 84–94.

Brewer, P. (2001) 'International market selection: developing a model from Australian case studies', *International Business Review*, 10, pp. 155–174.

Brouthers, L.E. and Nakos, G. (2005) 'The role of systematic international market selection on small firms' export performance', *Journal of Small Business Management*, 43(4), pp. 363–381.

Douglas, S. and Craig, C.A. (1995) *Global Marketing Strategy*. McGraw-Hill, New York.

Gaston-Breton, C. and Martin, O.M. (2011) 'International market selection and segmentation: a two-stage model', *International Marketing Review*, 28(3), pp. 267–290.

Green, R.T. and Allaway, A.W. (1985) 'Identification of export opportunities: a shift-share approach', *Journal of Marketing*, 49, pp. 83–88.

Johanson, J. and Vahlne, J.E. (1977) 'The internationalization process of the firm: a model of knowledge development and increasing foreign market commitment', *Journal of International Business Studies*, 8(1), pp. 23–32.

Katsikea, E.S., Theodosiou, M., Morgan, R.E. and Papavassiliou, N. (2005) 'Export market expansion strategies of direct-selling small and medium-sized firms: implications for export activities', *Journal of International Marketing*, 13(2), pp. 57–92.

Meyer, K.E. (2009) 'Global focusing: corporate strategies under pressure', *Strategic Change*, 18, pp. 195–207.

Oxyer, D., Deans, G., Shivaraman, S., Ghosh, S. and Pleines, R. (2008) 'A Nano car in every driveway? How to succeed in the ultra-low-cost car market', *Executive Agenda*, XI(2), pp. 55–62.

Ozturk, A., Joiner, E. and Cavusgil, S. T. (2015) 'Delineating foreign market potential: a tool for international market selection', *Thunderbird International Business Review*, 57, 119–141.

Papadopoulos, N., Chen, H. and Thomas, D.R. (2002) 'Toward a tradeoff model for international market selection', *International Business Review*, 11, pp. 165–192.

Piercy, N. (1981) 'Company internationalization: active and reactive exporting', *European Journal of Marketing*, 15(3), pp. 26–40.

Rahman, S.H. (2003) 'Modelling of international market selection process: a qualitative study of successful Australian international businesses', *Qualitative Market Research: An International Journal*, 6(2), pp. 119–132.

Sinha, P., Wang, M., Scott-Kennel, J. and Gibb, J. (2015) 'Paradoxes of psychic distance and market entry by software INVs', *European Business Review*, 27(1), pp. 34–59.

Sirkin, H.L., Hemerling, J.W. and Bhattacharya, A.K. (2008) 'Globality: challenger companies are drastically redefining the competitive landscape', *Strategy and Leadership*, 36(6), pp. 36–41.

Sylvest, J. and Lindholm, C. (1997) 'Små globale virksomheder', *Ledelse & Erhvervsøkonomi*, 61 (April), pp. 131–143.

Vernon, R. (1966) 'International investment and international trade in product cycle', *Quarterly Journal of Economics*, 80, pp. 190–208.

Westhead, P., Wright, M. and Ucbasaran, D. (2002) 'International market selection strategies selected by "micro" and small firms', *Omega*, 30, pp. 51–68.

Yip, G.S., Biscarri, J.G. and Monti, J.A. (2000) 'The role of the internationalization process in the performance of newly internationalizing firms', *Journal of International Marketing*, 8(3), pp. 10–35.

Yujuico, E. and Gelb, B.D. (2011) 'Marketing technological innovation to LDCs – lessons from One Laptop per Child', *California Management Review*, 53(2), pp. 50–68.

CASE STUDY II.1

SodaStream: Managing profitable growth in an increasingly competitive global environment

SodaStream (www.sodastream.com) is the world's leading manufacturer and distributor of sparkling water makers, which enable consumers to easily transform ordinary tap water into sparkling water and flavoured sparkling water in seconds. By making ordinary water more exciting and fun to drink, SodaStream helps consumers drink more water. Sparkling water makers offer a highly differentiated and innovative solution to consumers of bottled and canned carbonated soft drinks. The products promote health and wellness, and they are environmentally friendly and cost-effective.

History

SodaStream machines became popular during the 1970s and 1980s, starting out in the UK, and later spreading to other countries, including Australia, New Zealand and Germany. SodaStream machines are associated with nostalgia for that period. Their slogan, 'Get busy with the fizzy', started as an advertising jingle in 1979 and proved so popular that they added it to their logo. The slogan was initially dropped in 1996 after 17 years but was reinstated in 2010 along with a new marketing campaign in the UK.

Originally the company operated as a subsidiary of W & A Gilbey Ltd. In 1985, after various changes of ownership, SodaStream became a wholly owned subsidiary of Cadbury Schweppes, although it operated as an autonomous business within the group. In 1998, SodaStream was bought by Soda-Club, an Israeli company founded in 1991 by Peter Wiseburgh, who from 1978 to 1991 had been Israel's exclusive distributor for SodaStream, creating the world's largest home carbonation systems supplier. In 2003, Soda-Club closed the SodaStream factory in the UK, moving the company's gas cylinder refilling and refurbishment department to Germany. Under the ownership of Soda-Club, the brand has been relaunched in many markets, with new machines and new flavours available in 41 countries. In 2012, SodaStream teamed with Yves Béhar to introduce SodaStream Source, a line of soda machines designed with a special emphasis on sustainability.

SodaStream went public on the NASDAQ stock exchange (New York) in November 2010.

SodaStream is currently headquartered in Lod, Israel and has 13 production plants; its principal manufacturing facility is located on the West Bank, creating controversy and a boycott campaign – see later.

Today, the CEO of SodaStream is Daniel Birnbaum.

The product

The SodaStream machine offers significant benefits to consumers when compared to traditional soda cans; customizability, cost savings and health benefits. SodaStream empowers consumers to make soda the way they want it: from customizing the level of carbonation in the beverage to choosing the amount of syrup flavouring. By purchasing a starter kit, the consumer gets the SodaStream soda maker, a full CO_2 cylinder and three flavourings, all for a price of less than US$100. Ongoing operating costs include refilling CO_2 canisters (US$15 per 60 litres CO_2 refill) and purchasing new flavourings. Customers usually pay between US$6 and US$10 for a 500 ml bottle which would normally produce 12 litres of flavoured sparkling water. Partnerships from large brands such as Ocean Spray, Kool-Aid and Welch's offer consumers a large selection of different flavours (concentrates) to choose from. SodaStream can only carbonate water, one litre at a time, in the supplied bottle – the concentrates are added after carbonated water is removed from the machine. This poses a limitation if one wishes to carbonate wine or fresh fruit juices.

SodaStream is almost 30 per cent cheaper on a per litre basis than traditional soda. For carbonated water, purchasing a SodaStream machine will save a user almost 70 per cent per litre.

Despite these cost-savings, SodaStream's main advantage over traditional canned soda is clear: SodaStream cola has a third of the sugar, carbs and calories of traditional Coca-Cola and Pepsi. Soda consumption is arguably one of the main causes of high obesity rates in many first-world countries, and consumers have responded by drinking less soda.

SodaStream soda is made only with cane sugar, and contains none of the highly stigmatized high-fructose corn syrup associated with intense weight gain. The relative healthiness of SodaStream products serves as a clear point of differentiation for the company moving forward, and should be even more compelling in the future as consumers continue to seek healthier alternatives to canned soda.

SodaStream's business model

When a cylinder is empty, it must be returned to a SodaStream retailer for replacement. These retailers generally maintain a stock of filled cylinders in their inventory. Customers typically exchange their empty cylinders at retail stores. In this way, they only pay for the CO_2 itself. SodaStream does not sell the CO_2 cylinders to consumers, but instead 'licenses' them to the customers. SodaStream expressly limits how the cylinders can be used in their User License Certificate. Local CO_2 vendors are generally not permitted to refill SodaStream cylinders ('canisters'), which include a proprietary valve designed to prevent refilling.

SodaStream has created a 'buy-in/follow-on' (razor + blades) business model (see Chapter 15). The razor is obviously the soda maker and SodaStream has three blades:

1. the CO_2 refill cylinders (sold through the authorized SodaStream retailers);

2. the flavour syrups (100 flavours are available);

3. the carbonation bottles (customers often purchase additional carbonation bottles – consumers typically pay US$15 for two additional plastic half-litre carbonation bottles).

These three blades are the basis for future revenue stream. SodaStream acquire users and build their installed base, and try cultivate those users for life.

Source: Bloomberg/Getty Images.

SodaStream's financial results

Table 1 shows SodaStream's latest financial results.

Table 1	SodaStream's financial development from 2010 to 2014				
US$ million	2010	2011	2012	2013	2014
Revenues	208.4	288.9	436.3	562.7	511.8
Profits (before tax)	14.9	30.9	44.6	46.7	16.2

Source: based on Sodastream Financial Report 2014.

By the end of 2014, the number of employees in SodaStream was around 1,450.

Market

The SodaStream machines are available at more than 70,000 retail stores across 45 countries, including 15,000 retail stores in the US. Worldwide, SodaStream's machines are now installed in approximately 7 million homes. A 2014 Research Report from leading market research provider Canadean, which tracks global packaged sparkling water consumption using company data, found that in 2014 SodaStream was the world leader in total volume consumption of sparkling water.

In 2014, SodaStream users worldwide consumed over 700 million litres of unflavoured sparkling water, well ahead of the next largest brands: singha (558 million litres), San Pellegrino (480 million litres) and Perrier (412 million litres), according to Canadean.

The Canadean survey also found that in the US and UK those with a SodaStream in the home consume 43 per cent more water and water-based drinks than those without one.

Table 2 shows the penetration of SodaStream machines in homes in different countries. It can be seen that Sweden is the country with highest penetration of SodaStream machines (25 per cent). In the US, UK and South Africa, only 1 per cent of households have a SodaStream machine.

SodaStream has an average of 2 per cent household penetration (HHP) in the countries where they are present. The company's overall long-term marketing objective is to achieve a minimum 10 per cent HHP per market. At present, only Sweden, Finland, the Czech Republic and Israel fulfil this long-term objective.

Table 2	Penetration in % of SodaStream machines in different countries' homes (end 2014)	
Country	Number of households (1,000 units)	Penetration of sodaStream machines in households (%)
Sweden	4,555	25%
Finland	2,500	13%
Czech Republic	4,313	11%
Israel	2,087	10%
Switzerland	3,362	8%
New Zealand	1,332	4%
Belgium	4,576	4%
Australia	7,760	4%
France	25,253	4%
Germany	40,076	3%
Austria	3,566	3%
Denmark	2,547	3%
Italy	23,848	1%
US	117,538	1%
UK	26,473	1%
South Africa	11,206	1%

Source: based on different SodaStream sources and World Bank statistics.

Marketing strategy

A key element of SodaStream's marketing strategy is to build consumer awareness and to educate consumers of the benefits of their products. Consumer demand activities are designed primarily to increase the installed base of sparkling water makers as measured in terms of percentage of household penetration in each market. As a secondary objective, SodaStream promote the concept 'users for life' so as to generate ongoing demand for their consumables (CO_2 refills, flavours and carbonation bottles). SodaStream believe that widespread availability and easy access to consumables are important in order to generate customer retention and loyalty.

SodaStream's marketing activities include brand and product marketing and management as well as sales support programmes. They use a variety of vehicles, including advertising, direct marketing and public relations campaigns, using both traditional and digital media, in-store demonstrations, infomercials and their websites to build brand awareness, educate consumers about the benefits of their home beverage carbonation systems, communicate the advantages of their products and establish brand positioning, all of which are designed to increase the installed base of sparkling water makers and active consumers in their markets. They also use marketing programmes to support the sale of their products through new channels and to enter new markets. SodaStream conduct surveys and use third-party

tracking programs in order to track household penetration, usage behaviours and consumer opinions across markets, and to measure the success of their marketing activities over time. SodaStream's internal marketing team supports sales at the point-of-sale through trade marketing, developing and executing product and brand initiatives, and consumer education.

Acquiring a new customer is only the beginning of a relationship with the customer. To this end, SodaStream continuously test and apply various marketing tools to improve customer retention. They enhance their flavour offerings in order to improve the user experience. The company works closely with leading international flavour and essence suppliers who provide research and product development services, including sensory testing, in order to enhance flavour, cater for consumers' tastes and address market trends.

SodaStream employs subscription programmes, newsletters, warranties, trade-in promotions and various other programs to keep the customer engaged. They offer easy access to CO_2 refills through mass distribution of the cylinder exchange programme and direct-to-home delivery from online orders. They also encourage consumers to purchase additional CO_2 cylinders, which also contributes to keeping customers actively using their products over time. In certain markets, they have implemented customer loyalty programs that reward customers for repeat purchases.

The marketing activities are all managed from SodaStream's headquarters in Israel. Each market has a representative (either through one of their subsidiaries or through the distribution partner) who works closely with the marketing team to localize the marketing activities in accordance with the individual tastes and preferences in a particular country.

Entry modes and distribution

In most markets the products sell through retail channels. SodaStream distribute their products in 45 countries, 24 directly (through own subsidiaries) and the remainder through intermediaries like agents (distribution partnerships). In the subsidiary markets, SodaStream typically utilize their own internal sales force and, in certain countries, subdistributors as well.

SodaStream generally employs a multi-channel distribution strategy in each geographical market that is designed to raise awareness and establish positioning of the product offerings, first in specialty retail and direct marketing channels (selective distribution) and then in larger food, drug and mass retailers (intensive distribution). The products are sold at more than 70,000 stores worldwide, including stores of many of the largest retailers operating in their markets.

In 2014, the independent intermediaries/distributors accounted for 18 per cent of their total revenues. The gross margin on sales is generally higher in markets where SodaStream distributes directly (through subsidiaries) than markets in which they use third-party intermediaries.

Intermediaries sell to retailers in their relevant markets either through their own sales force or through wholesalers, or a combination of these. Sales activities follow typical retail sales processes, including initial pitches and offers, periodic product range and price reviews, offers for seasonal or limited edition activities and promotions. Merchandising and demonstrations of the products are managed by the distributor in cooperation with the retailers. Delivery to retailer chains can be to central warehouses or to individual stores depending upon the specific agreements with the retailer.

To ensure the promotion of the brand in markets covered by intermediaries (distributors), they are provided with various forms of marketing materials. In all cases, materials that use the SodaStream brands (including the trademarks) and all promotional and sales and marketing materials must be prepared or approved by the HQ in Israel. SodaStream agrees with their intermediaries on an annual advertising and promotional budget, of which SodaStream contributes a proportion.

When SodaStream evaluate potential intermediaries/distributors, several factors are taken into consideration, including their experience with selling and marketing consumer products to retail channels; existing sales, logistics and distribution capabilities; current product portfolio; financial strength; and suitability to SodaStream brands. SodaStream work closely with their independent intermediaries/distributors to assist them in preparing and executing a multi-year strategy. Most distributors also operate e-commerce sites in their countries as well as the SodaStream website in their local language.

SodaStream continue to penetrate certain new markets. Factors that are considered in prioritizing which markets to enter include: the size of the carbonated beverage and sparkling water market; per capita consumption of carbonated beverages; the perceived quality of the tap water; household demographics; and health and wellness and environmental consciousness.

SodaStream's distribution agreements with intermediaries/distributors are generally exclusive agreements for a given country with a five-year term with an option to renew. Intermediaries/distributors are generally required to meet annual purchase targets, defined as monetary amounts, for the first year or two of the agreement, as well as to meet certain defined growth targets for each of the subsequent years until the end of the term of the agreement. In addition, annual and semi-annual discussions with intermediaries/distributors often include more specific volume targets per product type. If the distributors do not meet their defined purchase targets, they may lose their exclusivity rights and SodaStream also generally have the right to terminate the agreement after a notice period.

In addition to carrying a full selection of SodaStream products, the distributor also agrees to have the responsibility of the reverse logistics needed for the end-customers to return empty CO_2 cylinders and exchange them for filled CO_2 cylinders at the involved retailers.

Source: Mike Coppola/Getty Images.

Competition

Indirectly, Sodastream face competition from all the major CSD (carbonated soft drink) manufacturers.

Directly, SodaStream currently face limited competition from manufacturers of other home sparkling water makers. However, new competitors may enter the home carbonated beverage and sparkling water market. Current or future competitors may, for example, introduce products with features which may cause consumers to stop using SodaStream's systems or to use them less frequently, such as sparkling water makers that do not require the exchange of CO_2 cylinders or that may use other methods of carbonation. SodaStream also compete with the large global beverage companies for the money spent by consumers on non-alcoholic beverages. These include primarily manufacturers of carbonated soft drinks and sparkling water.

In February 2014, Coca-Cola announced that it was buying a 10 per cent stake in Green Mountain Coffee Roasters for US$1.25 billion. It was not a move to get into the coffee business but rather an aggressive push to compete directly with SodaStream, which sells do-it-yourself carbonation machines as well as the flavour syrups that go with them. Coca-Cola will be the first company to feature its brands in Green Mountain's new Keurig Cold machines, launched in September 2015.

Keurig Cold makes soda and non-carbonated drinks like juices and teas using pods similar to those in Green Mountain's Keurig coffee brewers. This enables consumers to make their own home-bubbled Diet Coke or Sprite. Compatibility with familiar and valued soft drink brands is clearly the selling point, just as it is with the big coffee brands such as Starbucks and Dunkin' Donuts available pods.

The strength of the Keurig Cold system is that they will have the best cold brands on it, and those are the Coca-Cola brands. Green Mountain will also look for deals with other companies.

The alliance may be bad news for SodaStream which currently dominates the DIY cold-brew market.

SodaStream's controversial TV ads

In 2013, Sodastream planned an ad to go out on Superbowl night 2013. Unfortunately for SodaStream, the ad was rejected by CBS, not because it was too risque, but because it 'disparages' other major advertisers and sponsors for Superbowl–Coca-Cola and Pepsi. SodaStream was forced to make another version of its ad, replacing Coca-Cola and Pepsi with fictional soda companies.

Fortunately, there was an upside for SodaStream. All the controversy that these ads stirred generated a buzz around them. The SodaStream 'banned Super Bowl ad' generated more than 2 million hits on YouTube in two days and created a media buzz around the company itself. And that is without having to use US$3.8 million worth of cash for a Super Bowl commercial.

For Superbowl 2014, SodaStream tried once more, this time with Scarlett Johansson. But this time offence came in the form of four words spoken at the tail end of the Israeli soda kit company's 30-second ad: 'Sorry, Coke and Pepsi.'

As was the case in 2013, SodaStream's second attempt at a Super Bowl commercial was rejected (this time by FOX) for taking aim at two of the game's biggest, most consistent advertisers.

Political controversy

SodaStream is incorporated under the laws of the State of Israel, and the HQ and a significant portion of the manufacturing facilities are located in Israel. Accordingly, political, economic and military conditions in Israel and the surrounding region directly affect the business. Since the establishment of the State of Israel in 1948, a number of armed conflicts have occurred between Israel and its Arab neighbours. States of hostility, varying in degree and intensity, have caused security and economic problems in Israel. Although Israel has entered into peace treaties with Egypt and Jordan, and various agreements with the Palestinian National Authority, there has been a marked increase in violence, civil unrest and hostility, including armed clashes, between the State of Israel and the Palestinians since September 2000. The establishment in 2006 of a government in the Gaza Strip by representatives of the Hamas militant group created heightened unrest and uncertainty in the region. In mid-2006, Israel engaged in an armed conflict with Hezbollah, a Shiite Islamist militia group based in Lebanon, and in June 2007, there was an escalation in violence in the Gaza Strip. In recent years, including in July and August 2014, Israel engaged in an armed conflict with Hamas, which involved missile strikes and violence on both sides. This negatively affected business conditions in Israel.

Furthermore, several countries, principally in the Middle East, restrict doing business with Israel, and additional countries may impose restrictions on doing business with Israel and Israeli companies whether as a result of hostilities in the region or otherwise. The State of Israel and Israeli companies have been and are today subjected to threats of economic boycotts.

In recent years, there have been increased efforts by activists to cause companies and consumers to boycott Israeli goods based on Israeli government policies.

SodaStream has been criticized for operating its primary manufacturing plant in the Mishor Adumim industrial zone, which is part of the Israeli occupied land on the 'West Bank' (Israel has occupied the 'West Bank' since the war in 1967). A number of political groups have called for consumer boycotts of products originating in this disputed territory, including Soda-Stream products.

Source: Guy Corbishley/Demotix/Corbis.

By the standards of the Geneva convention, the Rome Statute and the international court of justice, the 'West Bank' has been developed illegally by Israel. Israel has continued to build its settlements, including industrial parks such as the one that houses SodaStream.

Another controversy arose surrounding the Hollywood star, Scarlett Johansson. In 2007, Oxfam (founded in Oxford in 1942 – now working in approximately 94 countries worldwide to find solutions to poverty) turned to Scarlett Johansson to become its global ambassador. She visited a number of Oxfam projects, thereby helping Oxfam to publicize its work.

In January 2014, Johansson was appointed the Global Brand Ambassador for SodaStream. Johansson's new job posed a serious problem for Oxfam. The charity has over the years taken a strong position against Israel's settlement construction at the same time as it has worked to deliver much-needed goods and services to the population in the occupied Palestinian territories. Pro-Palestinian activists began to put pressure on Oxfam and Scarlett Johansson to make a simple choice – either she had to break her contract with SodaStream or Oxfam would have to cut itself off

from her.

Finally, around 1st February 2014, Johansson cut her ties to Oxfam. In her statement she described SodaStream as not only committed to the environment but to building a bridge to peace between Israel and Palestine, supporting neighbours working alongside each other, receiving equal pay, equal benefits and equal rights.

In July 2014, Sodastream fired 60 Palestinian workers after they complained about not receiving sufficient food to break Ramadan fasts during night shifts (the company does not permit employees to bring their own food because the plant follows Jewish dietary restrictions) and called a wildcat strike. The workers were fired after receiving due process hearings, and were given severance pay.

Around 1st November 2014, SodaStream announced that its factory in Mishor Adumim (on the 'West Bank') would be closed by the end of 2016 in order to save $9 million in production costs. The plant's operations will be transferred to a new factory in Lehavim, where it will reportedly employ a significant number of Bedouin Arabs. Lehavim is located within the pre-1967 borders of Israel.

As a consultant in International Marketing for Soda-Stream you are tasked with delivering a report answerous the following questions:

QUESTIONS

1. Please discuss and evaluate SodaStream's key competitive advantages in the home carbonated beverage market.

2. Was it a good idea for SodaStream (Daniel Birnbaum) to choose Scarlett Johansson as the Global Brand Ambassador?

3. Please evaluate the importance of political factors in SodaStream's selection of new markets.

4. Do you think that Scarlett Johansson made the right decision in leaving Oxfam?

5. Please discuss and evaluate the screening criteria that you would use for SodaStream's IMS (international market selection). Please end up with a ranking list of the three most attractive countries. You are allowed to suggest countries where SodaStream is already active, but where you think they can achieve higher sales.

Sources: Birnbaum, D. (2014) 'SodaStream's CEO on turning a banned Super Bowl Ad into Marketing Gold', *Harvard Business Review,* January–February, pp. 39–42; different public reports, available online.

CASE STUDY II.2

The Female Health Company (FHC): the female condom is seeking a foothold in the world market for contraceptive products

It's time to take control. Give your vagina a choice.

Toronto Public Health Department female condom campaign slogan (FHC 2001 Annual Report)

On one of her few days off in autumn 2013, Senior Strategic Advisor Mary Ann Leeper is thinking about the great opportunities for the female condom. The potential market for her company's product, the female condom, is huge, but over the last few years, FCH still has not been making positive net profits. Leeper is thinking about how to reach FHC's long-term goal: 3 per cent of the 12-billion-unit male condom market (US$3–4 billion in total value). She accepts that the product is still relatively young in the world market for contraceptives, but she thinks it must be possible to produce better positive financial results with such a high-quality product. The big question is how . . .

The background to the AIDS epidemic

The history of HIV and AIDS is a relatively short one. As recently as the 1970s, no one was aware of this deadly illness. Since then, the global HIV/AIDS epidemic has become one of the greatest threats to human health and development. Since the peak of the HIV/AIDS epidemic in the 1990s, much has been learned about the science of HIV and AIDS, as well as how to prevent and treat the disease. Alhough there is still no cure for the disease, HIV-positive people who take a combination of three antiretroviral drugs can expect to recover their health and live for many years without developing AIDS, as long as they keep taking the drugs every day.

Statistics for the end of 2010 indicated that around 34 million people worldwide were living with HIV, the virus that causes AIDS. Each year around 2.7 million more people become infected with HIV and 1.8 million die of AIDS. Although HIV and AIDS are found in all parts of the world, some areas are more afflicted than others. The worst affected region is sub-Saharan Africa, where in a few countries more than one in five adults is infected with HIV. The epidemic is spreading most rapidly in eastern Europe and Central Asia, where the number of people living with HIV increased by 250 per cent between 2001 and 2010.

Given the rapid spread of HIV/AIDS in these regions, the Joint United Nations Programme on HIV/AIDS (UNAIDS) estimates that the annual public health sector demand for condoms, both male and female, will reach 19 billion units by 2015.

Background to the contraceptive market

The market for contraceptives has long been heavily influenced by social and political considerations. From the early days of the pill, the growing numbers of abortions and the decision to make the pill freely available in

Source: The Female Health Company.

the early 1970s to the emergence of the AIDS threat in the 1980s, this sector has always been more than a mere product category.

The increase in the pandemic has been linked to such cultural practices as polygamy, female genital mutilation, widow inheritance and sexual practices and behaviour that are culturally imposed in some societies. In Swaziland, for example, the local culture celebrates virility or the *ingwanwa* – a man who engages in multiple sexual encounters – while the female equivalent, *igwandla*, is shunned. The AIDS disease is also fuelled by a popular myth that sex with a virgin cures AIDS.

The total market consists of a very broad range of products, with oral contraceptives (the pill) and male condoms the most popular. Other, 'natural' forms of contraception are also practised, such as withdrawal and the safe period. Men and women may also be surgically sterilized.

Contraceptive products are available in pharmacies or general retail outlets, over the counter (OTC) or via prescription. Contraceptive products are also widely distributed in public clinics. In terms of the two leading forms of contraception, the contraceptive pill is available only on prescription, while condoms are widely available in chemists, supermarkets and vending machines, etc. Growth in distribution channels has been a feature of the condom market since the second half of the 1980s in response to the AIDS crisis.

Condom usage has risen substantially over the past six years, while use of the pill has remained broadly stable. The pill remains a popular contraceptive (based upon surveys of women – surveys of men and women show use of condom and pill as about equal).

The product

The female condom was invented by a Danish physician who obtained a US patent for the product in 1988, and subsequently sold certain rights to the product to a US company. The first female condom (FC1) became available in 1992. It was marketed under the name FC female condom in the US, Femidom in the UK and Myfemy in other markets, such as Japan.

The Female Health Company manufactures, markets and sells the female condom, which is a product under a woman's control, unlike the male condom. FHC has its headquarters in Chicago.

In 2005, FHC introduced a second-generation female condom, FC2, which had been developed to expand access to female-initiated prevention by offering a more affordable product, at a lower cost. FC2 can be produced at a unit cost that is nearly 50 per cent of that of FC1. FC2 was first marketed internationally in March 2007 and has been marketed in the US since August 2009. In October 2009, FHC completed the transition from FC1 to FC2, and production of FC1 in London was ceased.

Between FC2's introduction in March 2007 and the end of 2012, approximately 170 million FC2 female condoms were distributed in 138 countries. It is sold directly to consumers in 16 countries. Between the first FDA approval in 1993 and 2012, FHC sold over 345 million FC female condoms (FC1 and FC2).

In 2012, the end-user price per unit (FC2) at retail was around €0.30.

Global market potential and FHC sales

It is estimated that the global annual market for male condoms is 12 billion units. The major segments are in the global public sector, the US, Japan, India and the People's Republic of China. However, the majority of all acts of sexual intercourse, excluding those intended to result in pregnancy, are completed without protection. As a result, it is estimated that the potential market for barrier contraceptives is much larger than the identified male condom market.

Currently it is estimated that more than eight billion male condoms are distributed worldwide by the public sector each year. The rest, four billion male condoms, is estimated to go through the traditional retailing systems. The female condom is seen as an important addition to prevention strategies by the public sector because studies show that its availability decreases the amount of unprotected sex by as much as one-third over offering only a male condom.

FHC expects to derive the vast majority, if not all, of its future revenue from the female condom, its sole current product. While management believes the global potential for the female condom is significant, the product is in the early stages of commercialization.

The competitive situation

FHC's female condom participates in the same market as male condoms but is not seen as directly competing with male condoms. Rather, FHC believes that providing female condoms is additional in terms of prevention and choice. Latex male condoms cost less and have brand names that are more widely recognized than the female condom. In addition, male condoms are generally manufactured and marketed by companies with significantly greater financial resources than FHC.

A new direct competitor has arrived on the scene: Medtech Products Ltd (MP), a male latex condom company with a manufacturing facility in Chennai,

India, has developed a natural latex female condom. MP's female condom has been marketed under various names including V-Amour, VA Feminine Condom and L'Amour.

The United States Agency for International Development (USAID) and Family Health International (FHI), have evaluated and accepted the MP female condom for consideration along with the FC2 to qualify for an in-depth phase 3 clinical study evaluation. The MP product's manufacturing process has a CE mark for distribution in Europe and is available in German stores. MP received Indian Drug Controller approval in January 2003.

Another competitor, PATH, an international, non-profit organization based in the US, also has a female condom product in the early stages of development.

Neither the MP female condom nor the PATH woman's condom have received FDA approval or been listed as essential products for procurement by WHO.

FHC customers and their purchasing behaviour

FHC has a relatively small customer base, with a limited number of (governmental) customers who generally purchase in large quantities. Over the past few years, major customers have included large global agencies, such as the United Nations Population Fund (UNFPA) and USAID, through its facilitator, John Snow, Inc. In 2011, the three biggest customers accounted for more than 80 per cent of FHC's turnover. Other customers include ministries of health or other governmental agencies, which purchase either directly or via in-country distributors, and non-governmental organizations.

Besides big governmental customers, FHC also has distribution agreements and other arrangements with commercial partners which market directly to private consumers in 16 countries, including the US, Brazil, Spain, France and India. These agreements are generally exclusive for a single country. Under these agreements, FHC sells the FC2 female condom to the distributor partners, who market and distribute the product to consumers in the established territory.

Purchasing patterns vary significantly from one customer to another. Typically, governmental agencies purchase through a formal procurement process in which a tender (request for bid) is issued for either a specific or a maximum unit quantity. Tenders also define the other elements required for a qualified bid submission (such as product specifications, regulatory approvals, unit pricing, delivery time, etc.). Bidders have a limited period of time in which to submit bids.

The entire tender process, from publication to award, may take many months to complete. Administrative issues, politics, bureaucracy and other pressures may delay the process and affect the purchasing patterns of public-sector customers.

FHC today

On 8 July 2009, FHC went to the stock exchange (NASDAQ-CM) in order to seek capital for their expansion.

Most of FHC's revenues have been derived from sales of the FC2 female condom. Since the 2008 fiscal year, revenue has also been derived from licensing of its intellectual property to its exclusive distributor in India, Hindustan Lifecare Limited. Hindustan Lifecare Ltd is authorized to manufacture FC2 at its facility in Kochi, India, for sale in India. FHC receives a royalty based on the number of units sold by Hindustan Lifecare Ltd.

Table 1 shows FHC's financial results for the years 2008–2012.

Table 1	FHC's financial development, 2008–2012				
	US$, millions				
	2012	2011	2010	2009	2008
Net revenues	35.0	18.5	22.2	27.4	25.5
Operating income	10.9	3.3	4.3	4.7	3.2

Source: based on www.femalehealth.com.

At the end of 2012, FHC had 144 full-time employees including 10 in the US, 13 in the UK, 116 in Malaysia and five in other countries to implement training programmes.

QUESTIONS

1. How would you explain FHC's internationalization process up to now?

2. What are the main cultural barriers for expanding global sales of the female condom?

3. What screening criteria would you use if FHC had plans to expand into new developing markets?

4. Besides having distribution to the public sector, particularly in Africa, Latin America and recently India, FHC is also trying to commercialize the female condom in consumer markets around the world. Where and how should FHC attack consumer markets?

CASE STUDY II.3

Zalando: how can the online apparel retailer turn financial losses into positive profits?

Zalando is an internet retailer of branded clothing and footwear for men, women and children. The company operates in the standard and premium segments, offering a wide range of products. It is expanding the number of exclusive brands offered by the www.zalando.com Internet shop.

Zalando GmbH was established in Germany by Robert Gentz and David Schneider in 2008. The company is headquartered in Berlin and has operated so far only in e-commerce. A customer service hotline and free delivery and free return of goods are offered.

Eighty per cent of Zalando's customers are women. Zalando's target customer group is women aged 20–40.

Swedish investment company Kinnevik is the biggest shareholder, with about 32 per cent ownership of Zalando.

History

2008: Zalando is founded in Germany
2009: The company starts delivering to Austria
2010: Launch of French and Dutch retail websites in France and the Netherlands
2011: Launch in the UK, Italy and Switzerland
2012–13: Launch in: Sweden, Belgium, Spain, Denmark, Finland, Poland, Norway and Luxembourg

As of January 2016, Zalando is represented with sales in the following 15 European countries: Germany, Poland, Denmark, Norway, Sweden, Finland, Holland, UK, Belgium, France, Switzerland, Austria, Italy, Spain and Luxembourg.

These countries together offer a population of 400 million people.

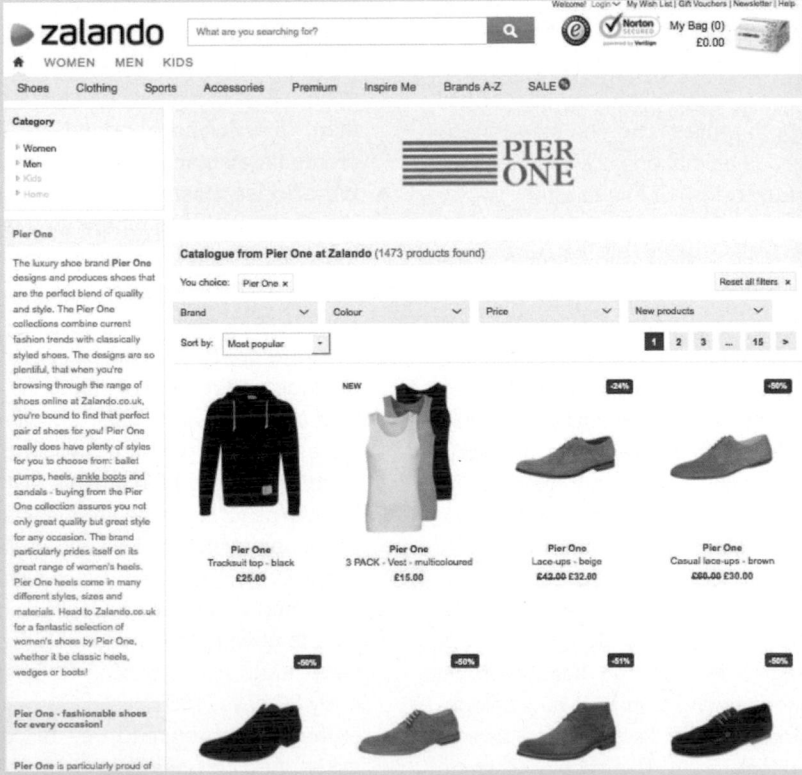

The Zalando UK website

Source: www.zalando.co.uk.

Zalando is the largest online footwear shop in Europe, offering a high number of international brands. Besides footwear, Zalando distributes women's and men's outerwear, wear, underwear, hosiery and clothing accessories, as well as bags and a number of other product types. In March 2010 Zalando expanded its product range by adding children's wear. In January 2011, the internet retailer started to sell exclusive perfume brands.

Zalando is a rapidly growing company. Its first acquisition took place in May 2010 with the buyout of MyBrands, an online designer outlet. With the acquisition of MyBrands, Zalando has broadened its target consumer group and its range of premium products.

Zalando has increased its brand awareness with the help of humorous TV spots. Its TV advertising campaign 'Scream for joy' promotes Zalando as simple to shop at. There are no minimum orders, no mailing costs and payment is made either upon receipt of invoice, by pre-payment or by credit card.

Meanwhile, Zalando has rapidly expanded into new markets and categories. The internet 'shoe-ting' star is now active in 14 European countries. The stunning revenue growth has been fired by massive investment in colourful TV spots and catchy online banners. It is estimated that Zalando has spent around €90 million in advertising and promotion per year.

Zalando has indulged its customer base with fancy store magazines, which are hardly distinguishable from conventional fashion journals yet are distributed on a complimentary basis. The lead publication, *Zalando Magazine,* has since reached a circulation of 1.5 million copies and is distributed in Germany, Austria, Switzerland, France and Holland. Needless to say, its content is also published as both e-magazine and smartphone app, along with numerous animations. Zalando exploits the potential a cross-media format has to offer.

With its new *Zalando Men* publication, Zalando seeks to approach its male audience in Germany. The 68-page magazine, produced in-house, made its debut in August 2012 with an initial circulation of 250,000 copies in Germany. Planned to appear bi-annually, distribution takes place as an insert in mail-delivered packages. In addition, the 36-page lifestyle magazine, *Zalando Wohnen* (*Zalando At Home*) aims at a predominately female and online-savvy readership in the 25 to 45 age range earning above-average net incomes. With a nicely balanced mix of journalism and subtle merchandise touting, the magazine presents offers, rating lists, seasonal themes, practical tips and recipes.

Another growth engine for Zalando has been the extension of its core shoe offering to include new categories such as clothing and household accessories, as well as own-label and designer brands. This enables Zalando to cross-sell and up-trade, which increases sales per customer. The company states that non-footwear in 2013 accounted for more than half of annual revenues.

In December 2010, Zalando opened a Christmas Sales Lounge in the centre of Berlin. The lounge attracted high consumer traffic as people sought bargains on branded clothing and footwear for Christmas. This first foray into offline retailing generated good revenues for the company.

Up until December 2013, Zalando has invested approximately €150 million in developing its logistics and technological infrastructure. More than €100 million of this went to equipping the distribution fulfilment centres in Erfurt and Mönchengladbach, Germany. A new technology hub is also being established in Dortmund to support the growth.

In July 2012, German TV channel ZDF broadcast a report on the packing and distribution centre operated for Zalando by a provider near Berlin. The report stated that some employees, who often commute more than 200 km from nearby Poland, were not allowed to sit in certain departments, and they were only paid €7 per working hour.

Considering the remarkable growth and huge expenditure of the company, some would question how sustainable a business model Zalando really has. Zalando's biggest cost-drivers, to help answer this question, are:

- **Pre-financing:** just like other trading companies, Zalando needs to pre-finance all its products. The Berlin company mass orders stock from a variety of brands to pack its warehouses. If the items prove to be unpopular among the customers, the shelves are soon full of unwanted products. It is not surprising, then, that Zalando opened the Zalando Lounge to create its own shopping club and to boost sales.
- **Warehouse costs:** When buying products there is always the issue of where they will be housed. With four huge logistical centres in Germany (see Figure 1), it is easy to imagine the complexity of Zalando's undertakings.
- **Postage costs:** As Zalando covers the costs of both postage and returns of items, the shopping giant has high costs that are most likely reflected in the product prices. The workforce required to dispatch vast quantities of products means that Zalando requires a workforce for three different shifts to ensure the work continues overnight. This is a costly procedure.
- **Returns:** An unfortunate fact within the fashion business, and particularly for online shops, is that people tend to change their minds. This returns policy is convenient and a free service for customers. Within normally 30 days (100 days in Germany), anything can be exchanged or returned free of charge, no questions asked. And here lies Zalando's Achilles heel. Rumours indicate that customers will order the same shoe model

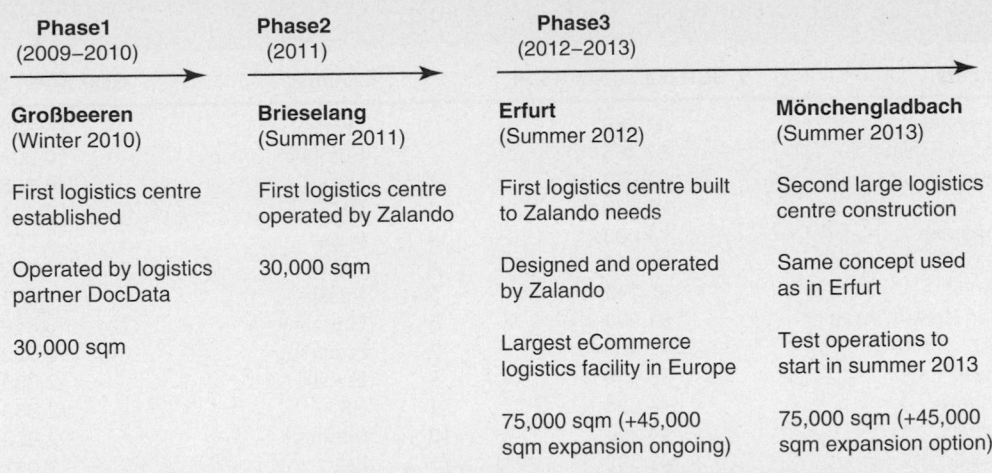

Phase1 (2009–2010)	Phase2 (2011)	Phase3 (2012–2013)	
Großbeeren (Winter 2010)	**Brieselang** (Summer 2011)	**Erfurt** (Summer 2012)	**Mönchengladbach** (Summer 2013)
First logistics centre established	First logistics centre operated by Zalando	First logistics centre built to Zalando needs	Second large logistics centre construction
Operated by logistics partner DocData	30,000 sqm	Designed and operated by Zalando	Same concept used as in Erfurt
30,000 sqm		Largest eCommerce logistics facility in Europe	Test operations to start in summer 2013
		75,000 sqm (+45,000 sqm expansion ongoing)	75,000 sqm (+45,000 sqm expansion option)

- Logistics centres are located in central locations in Germany, servicing all European countries
- Zalando is leasing land and buildings to limit capital investment
- Combined capacity of >250,000 sqm operational/in construction (~300,000 sqm including option)

Figure 1   Zalando's four warehouses (as of end 2013)

Source: Hollensen, S. (2008) *Essentials of Global Marketing*, FT/Prentice Hall, p. 61. Copyright © Pearson Education Limited.

Zalando shoes
Source: Ulrich Baumgarten/Getty Images.

in three sizes, only to return two of them, or they will return the item after a single evening's wear (though that is not sanctioned by the company of course). Industry speculation is that Zalando has figures of as high as 70 per cent in returned merchandise. Zalando refuses to comment on this figure.

- *Marketing:* From traditional advertising TV spots to spots on Germany's *Next Top Model*, expensive search engine campaigns and online marketing, Zalando is sparing no cost in marketing its products. On the plus side this advertising saturation has resulted in 60 per cent of Germany's population recognizing the brand. The brand awareness in the target group (women of 20–40 years) is as high as 90–95 per cent. On the other hand the expenses are enormous.

General market trends in footwear and apparel

Table 1 shows World Bank figures regarding the total GDP, and GDP per cap.

Apparel online (internet) B2C retailing

The internet has become an important tool for browsing or researching clothing products, whether the purchase is eventually made online or in a store (see Tables 2–4).

While the US saw the highest value growth in apparel internet retailing over the 2006–11 period, the e-commerce channel held the highest share in Taiwan, due to the number of consumers purchasing clothes from overseas sites and the prevalence of online discounts. Unlike other trends, the global online sales boom has not been driven by BRIC economies. BRICs still lag behind in online apparel. The e-commerce channel's share was less than 3 per cent in all four BRIC countries in 2011. It is particularly weak in India, where only 10 per cent of the population are internet users.

Reason for increasing internet retailing (supply side)

There are numerous underlying reasons for the rise of internet retailing on the supply side. However, the

Table 1	Word Bank statistical figures – top 20 ranking (2012)			
	Country	**$ GDP per capita (PPP)**		**Country**	**GDP (PPP) $Billion**

	Country	$ GDP per capita (PPP)		Country	GDP (PPP) $Billion
1	Luxembourg	91,388		World	85,538
	Macau (China)	87,765	–	European Union	16,805
2	Qatar	83,460	1	US	15,685
3	Norway	65,640	2	China	12,471
4	Singapore	61,803	3	India	4,793
5	Switzerland	53,367	4	Japan	4,487
6	Brunei	53,348	5	Russia	3,373
	Hong Kong (China)	51,946	6	Germany	3,349
7	US	49,965	7	France	2,372
8	Kuwait	45,455	8	Brazil	2,385
9	Australia	44,598	9	UK	2,333
10	Austria	44,208	10	Mexico	2,022
11	Ireland	43,592	11	Italy	2,017
12	Netherlands	43,198	12	South Korea	1,540
13	Sweden	43,180	13	Spain	1,510
14	Canada	42,086	14	Canada	1,484
15	Denmark	42,086	15	Turkey	1,358
16	United Arab Emirates	42,080	16	Indonesia	1,223
17	Germany	40,901	17	Australia	1,012
18	Belgium	39,788	18	Poland	854
19	Finland	38,655	19	Iran	838
20	Iceland	37,852	20	Netherlands	724

Source: based on Worldbank.com.

Table 2	Regions' development of online apparel retailing sales 2006–11 in percentage of total apparel sales (offline + online)					
Region	2006	2007	2008	2009	2010	2011
Asia Pacific	2.2	2.4	2.6	2.9	3.2	3.7
Eastern Europe	0.9	1.2	1.3	1.8	2.0	2.2
Middle East and Africa	0.5	0.5	0.4	0.6	0.5	0.6
Western Europe	2.6	3.2	4.2	5.3	6.3	7.3
Australasia	1.3	1.4	1.8	3.0	4.0	4.8
Latin America	0.3	0.3	0.4	0.48	0.5	0.5
North America	3.9	4.3	5.1	5.8	6.3	7.3

Source: based on Euromonitor.com.

fundamental reason why so many retailers set up online store fronts is that it gives them access to new consumers without having to invest in costly stores.

But there are other incentives:

1. In some markets, tax is also a huge motivator. Pure-play internet retailers in the US avoid paying sales tax in the majority of states, giving them a significant advantage over store-based retailers. The UK and Australia also have similar tax loopholes available to foreign internet retailers.

2. The information from analytics tools available to retailers also gives a major incentive for internet retail. These low-cost (or free) tools can give retailers detailed estimates on who is visiting their site, for how long and where they go next. This is invaluable information that is unavailable to store-based retailers.

Table 3	Countries' online apparel value sales in percentage of total apparel sales (offline + online)
Country	**% of apparel sales through internet retailing**
Taiwan	13.5
UK	13.0
Germany	12.4
South Korea	12.1
Denmark	10.0
France	8.3
Japan	8.1
Developed markets average	7.6
USA	7.5
Sweden	6.1
Netherlands	5.2
Australia	5.0
Austria	4.8
Norway	4.0
Singapore	3.7
Czech Republic	3.3
Canada	2.2
Portugal	1.6
Italy	1.5
Hong Kong, China	1.3
Greece	1.1
Spain	0.3
Israel	0.2

Source: based on Euromonitor.com.

Table 4	Percentage of online users (compared to total population) vs percentage of online apparel value sales compared to total apparel sales (offline + online)	
	% population using the internet 2011	**% apparel internet retailing 2011**
Germany	82	12.3
Denmark	89	9.9
UK	81	12.8
France	80	8.5
Russia	50	2.4
USA	78	7.0
Brazil	47	0.7
India	10	0.2
China	39	2.7
Japan	80	8.0
Taiwan	72	13.0
South Korea	85	12.4

Source: based on Euromonitor.com.

Reason for increasing internet retailing (demand side)

The demand for choice and convenience has fuelled the growing number of online shoppers:

1. With longer working hours, the opportunity to shop at leisure (24 hours) has drastically diminished. Historically, this has driven the growth of the hypermarket and convenience store channels. However, this same basic desire has attracted consumers to the internet, as all of their favourite brands are available around the clock.

2. In addition to the sheer variety of products available at the click of a button, consumers also benefit from the use of comparative tools. This can be either in the form of product reviews or price comparison sites.

3. Product reviews reassure the consumer that they are buying the right product for their needs. Price comparison tools have led to the perception that the best price is always found on the internet. Both these facilities further encourage consumers to browse online, which gives retailers the opportunity to sell products to them.

General development of the B2C apparel in different regions in 2012–13

Europe

Across Europe, apparel e-commerce is booming. In the EU, the share of individuals purchasing clothes and sports goods online increased in 2012, reaching over 20 per cent of individuals. In Germany, apparel is the largest e-commerce category, having grown by just under a third in terms of sales and reaching several EUR billions of sales. Among the leading players on the market, the Otto Group launched a new e-commerce fashion project named Collins in 2014, while Zalando more than doubled its apparel online sales in 2012. Asos and Debenhams were among the most prominent online shops for online fashion products in the UK in 2013. In France, nearly a half of internet users shopped for clothing online in 2012, with La Redoute, 3 Suisses and Zalando being the most popular destinations for shopping.

Eastern Europe

In Russia, apparel online sales (clothing and shoes) grew by over 40 per cent in 2012, and accounted for almost one fifth of total online value sales. Clothing, shoes and accessories became the most popular online product category in 2012, with nearly half of online shoppers making purchases. Online apparel retailers in Russia have seen significant increase in revenues, some growing by up to six times, with Wildberries, Lamoda, Quelle and KupiVip as leading online merchants.

Several players, such as KupiVip and Lamoda, attracted large investments from local venture capitalists and from abroad. Clothing and shoes is the leading online category in Poland, with a high double-digit percentage of online shoppers making purchases. The number of online shops selling clothes in Poland grows rapidly every year. In Estonia, Croatia, Macedonia and Turkey, and some other European countries, apparel was bought by a high percentage of online shoppers, and was one of the most popular online product categories in these countries.

North America

In the US, apparel and accessories was second only to consumer electronics in terms of total online value sales. This category is expected to grow by a double-digit percentage figure in 2013, with the growth continuing but slowing down throughout 2016. Nevertheless, apparel is expected to remain the fastest-growing product category in total online value sales. Players such as Abercrombie & Fitch compete to increase their share of the booming US online market for apparel.

South America

In South America, apparel ranks high in popularity for online shoppers in such countries as Peru, Uruguay and Venezuela, but is outperformed by electronics. In Brazil, apparel is the fourth most popular online product category, purchased by around a third of online shoppers in 2012. In Mexico this share is less than in Brazil, as apparel falls behind computers, electronics, books and some other products and services.

Asian-Pacific

Apparel is the most-purchased product category in online retailing in Japan. The globally active apparel retailer Gap Inc. opened an online shop in Japan in autumn 2012, joining other national and international players. In South Korea, apparel was among the highest-selling categories in 2012, growing at a one-digit percentage rate, which is slightly slower than the total online retailing market, signalling high maturity.

In China, fashion and accessories had the highest reach of online shoppers, amounting to three-quarters of females and a high, double-digit share of male online shoppers. Online apparel sales increased by over 50 per cent to several tens of EUR billions in 2012. Although C2C remains the largest segment of the online market for clothing in China, the market share of independent B2C platforms grows, with large international players, such as Levi Strauss, Inditex, Macy's and Asos, launching or planning to launch local online shops. In Australia, apparel was the second most-purchased product category in online retailing after electronics in 2012 and is expected to remain the fastest-growing product category in online retailing through the next five years.

Middle East and Africa

In the Middle East and Africa, local online fashion stores attract large investments from established capitalists, indicating a positive view of the market potential. The Middle Eastern online vendor of clothing, Namshi – a Rocket Internet's (subsidiary of Kinnevik) project – raised several USD millions of investment in May 2013, while a South African online apparel store, Zando, received an even larger sum from investors such as JP Morgan. Moreover, in South Africa, the discount sector started to emerge within the online market for clothing, with apparel discount online shopping clubs, such as Runway (launched in 2012), growing rapidly.

Zalando's financial performance to 2012

In the online business big sales often mean high costs. Thus far, Zalando is a victim of its own success. Marketing and expansion, free delivery and free returns, as well as inventory, IT and logistics costs have all weighed heavily on Zalando's bottom line – see Table 5.

The sales of shoes accounts for 50 per cent of Zalando's total turnover; the remaining sales are mostly within clothing. Fifty per cent of the Zalando sales are taking place outside Germany.

In 2012 Zalando reached break-even in its three-core DACH markets (Germany, Austria and Switzerland).

Table 5	Zalando's financial performance			
	2009 EUR	**2010 EUR**	**2011 EUR**	**2012 EUR**
Turnover	6 million	150 million	510 million	1,150 million
Net profits (before taxes)	Minus 1.6 million	Minus 20.4 million	Minus 60.0 million	Minus 90.0 million

Source: based on a variety of public sources.

Competition

Despite growing popularity, the company has to compete with other well-known internet retailers, such as Asos, Sarenza and BuyVIP in the premium segment. Initially, Zalando could convince its growing number of customers with good service and additional bonus campaigns. The increasingly strong competition will force the company to devise new strategies, such as the opening of its first retail-based outlet.

The e-commerce giant Amazon did not remain inactive and fights for its slice of the cake. It launched a new online shop, Javari.de, which operates separately from Amazon and focuses on shoes, handbags and accessories. It strives to attract customers through a free delivery service, a guarantee of low prices and a long deadline to return goods. Zalando hopes to overtake Amazon's position in the clothing and footwear category in Europe.

In addition to that, more and more manufacturers/retailers (such as Zara and H&M) are opening their own online stores due to the good growth prospects of e-commerce. This leads to an increase in competition and makes it more difficult for Zalando to maintain its high growth pace.

Zalando has been extending its lead over British primary rival Asos Plc as Europe's largest online fashion site, expanding from shoes to clothes and now selling over 1,000 brands. It doubled its 2012 net sales to €1.15 billion (£1 billion) – see Table 6.

The business model of Asos – full name, 'As seen on screen' – is to sell cheap clothes in the style of celebrities such as Lady Gaga, Kate Moss and Alexa Chung. This has given it a young and loyal customer base, which is turning from the high street to the internet for shopping.

But the growth-orientated Zalando fashion site, founded in 2008, is still loss-making as it spends to boost brand awareness to get its name out on television shows such as Germany's *Next Top Model.*

External brands sold on Zalando result in a guesstimated profit of 30–60 per cent. The profit margin could be significantly higher with an in-house brand – possibly between 60 and 80 per cent.

The role of Anders Holch Povlsen (Bestseller) as investor

In August 2013, Anders Holch Povlsen, the owner of Danish fashion company Bestseller A/S, bought a 10 per cent stake in Zalando GmbH, adding the German online clothing retailer to an investment portfolio that includes its main UK competitor, Asos Plc.

Table 6	Zalando in comparison with its primary competitor	
	Zalando Annual report 2012–13	Asos Annual report 2013
Turnover	€1,150 million	€920 million
Growth in turnover from one year earlier	+125%	+39%
Net profits (before taxes)	Minus €90 million	€66 million
Growth in net profits from one year earlier	Minus 50%	+19%
Number of employees in company group	2,000	1,360
Total number of products in the product range/number of brand	150,000 products/1,500 brands	65,000 products/800 brands
Number of countries with local country sites	14 (Germany, Austria, Switzerland, Poland, France, UK, Sweden, Denmark, Finland, Norway, Netherlands, Belgium, Spain, Italy)	9 (UK, France, Germany, Italy, Spain, Australia, US, Russia, China)
Return rate (number of customer returns compared with total number ordered)	60% (estimated)	50% (estimated)
Anders Holch Povlsen (Bestseller) ownership	10.0%	27.5%

Source: based on different public media.

Anders Holch Povlsen already holds a stake of 27.5 per cent in Asos – the UK's largest online-only fashion retailer. The Danish company first disclosed it held Asos shares in May 2010, and since then the stock has surged more than tenfold.

Alone, these two investments make Anders Holch Povlsen the biggest shareholder in Asos and the third-biggest in Zalando, after Kinnevik (37 per cent) and European Founders Fund (EFF) (18 per cent).

Founded in Denmark in 1975 by Anders Holch Povlsen's parents, Bestseller sells clothing brands including Jack & Jones and Vera Moda and has more than 3,000 stores in 38 markets. The company is the eighth-biggest retailer in the Asia-Pacific region (it is especially strong in China) and only the 29th biggest in Western Europe.

QUESTIONS

1. Compare and evaluate Zalando's and Asos' key competitive advantages and strategies in the world online apparel market.

2. Discuss and evaluate the criteria that you would use for Zalando's selection of new markets outside its current 14 countries. End up with a ranking list of the three most attractive countries.

3. Discuss and evaluate the pros and cons for Anders Holch Povlsen and Bestseller, regarding the investments in Zalando and Asos.

Source: based on a variety of public sources.

CASE STUDY II.4

Ferrari: international market selection (IMS) for the exclusive sports car brand

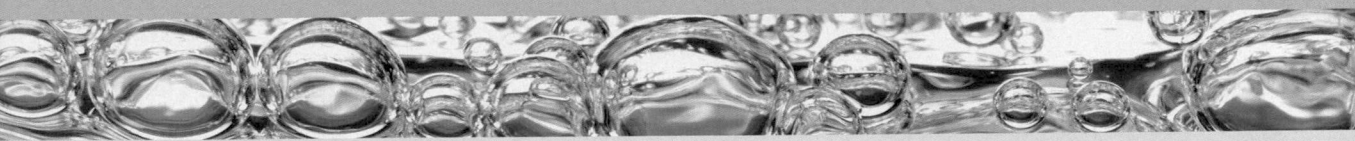

Ferrari is among the world's leading luxury brands focused on the design, engineering, production and sale of the world's most admired cars. The brand is one of the most iconic and recognizable in the world. Ferrari believe that the Ferrari brand and the prancing horse logo symbolize luxury, exclusivity, innovation, state-of-the-art sporting performance and Italian design and engineering heritage and has regularly been ranked as one of the world's most powerful brands by independent surveyors.

The Ferrari name, history and the image is closely associated with their Formula 1 racing team, Scuderia Ferrari, the most successful team in Formula 1 history, having won 222 Grand Prix races, 16 Constructor World titles and 15 Drivers' World titles. The history of excellence, technological innovation and defining style transcends the automotive industry, and is the foundation of the Ferrari brand and image. Ferrari designs, engineers and produces their cars in Maranello, Italy, and sells them in over 60 markets worldwide through a network of 182 authorized dealers.

At the end of July 2015, Fiat Chrysler (former owner of Ferrari) announced a plan to spin off Ferrari as a separate business to fund future investment in Fiat. The initial public offering was expected to take place on the New York stock exchange by the end of 2015, so that Ferrari started off as a separate company at the beginning of 2016. The company expects to start with listing 10 per cent of the shares, and later distribute a further 80 per cent to its own shareholders, completing the

Source: Dutourdumonde Photography/Shutterstock.com.

separation. The Ferrari family will retain a 10 per cent interest, held by Piero Ferrari, the son of the firm's founder, Enzo Ferrari.

Sergio Marchionne, the CEO of Fiat Chrysler, expected to reduce Fiat Chrysler's debt and fund a €48 billion investment programme to boost some of the company's other major brands worldwide: Jeep, Alfa Romeo and Maserati. He also indicated that he expected the listing to value Ferrari at more than €10 billion.

Tables 1 and 2 show the total Ferrari sales (including shipments) and the geographical split of the 2013 and 2014 shipments, respectively.

Ferrari's results on key metrics

Table 1 also shows Ferrari's latest financial results.

Table 1	Ferrari's development from 2010 to 2014 on key measures				
	2010	2011	2012	2013	2014
Shipment (number)	6,573	7,195	7,405	7,000	7,255
Revenues (€ million)	1,831	2,067	2,225	2,335	2,762
EBIT (€ million)	295	298	335	364	389
Number of employees	2,779	2,709	2,708	2,774	2,843

EBIT, earnings before interest and taxes.
Source: based on Ferrari financial reports.

Table 2	Ferrari's development of shipments from 2012 to 2014 on key geographic markets (number of cars and % of total cars)					
	2014	%	2013	%	2012	%
EMEA						
UK	705	9.7%	686	9.8%	686	9.3%
Germany	616	8.5%	659	9.4%	755	10.2%
Switzerland	332	4.6%	350	5.0%	366	4.9%
France	253	3.5%	273	3.9%	330	4.5%
Italy	243	3.3%	206	2.9%	318	4.3%
Middle East[a]	521	7.2%	472	6.7%	423	5.7%
Rest of EMEA[b]	604	8.3%	663	9.5%	825	11.1%
Total	**3,274**	**45.1%**	**3,309**	**47.3%**	**3,703**	**50.0%**
Americas[c]	2,462	33.9%	2,382	34.0%	2,208	29.8%
Greater China[d]	675	9.3%	572	8.2%	789	10.7%
Rest of APAC[e]	844	11.7%	737	10.5%	705	9.5%
Total	**7,255**	**100.0%**	**7,000**	**100.0%**	**7,405**	**100.0%**

[a] Middle East includes the United Arab Emirates, Saudi Arabia, Bahrain, Lebanon, Qatar, Oman and Kuwait.
[b] Rest of EMEA includes Africa and the other European markets not separately identified.
[c] Americas includes the US, Canada, Mexico, the Caribbean and Central and South America.
[d] Greater China includes China, Hong Kong and Taiwan.
[e] Rest of APAC mainly includes Japan, Australia, Singapore, Indonesia and South Korea.
EMEA, Europe, Middle East and Africa; APAC, Asia-Pacific.
Source: based on different Ferrari information.

Part of the revenue is also licensing of the brand. Ferrari currently has multi-year agreements with licensing partners for various Ferrari-branded products in the sports, lifestyle and luxury retail segments. They also have multi-year agreements with franchising partners for Ferrari stores and a theme park. In 2014, €416 million of the revenues (15 per cent) came from these licence agreements.

Even through the sharp macroeconomic recession in 2008–09 when a lot of luxury goods manufacturers had problems, Ferrari showed that their car sales were very stable and resilient to macroeconomic downturns.

The profile of the typical Ferrari customer looks like this:

- male (90%);
- between 35 and 55; average is 46 years old;
- higher education (college graduates);
- good jobs;
- income over US$400,000 annually.

The worldwide light car market

Ferrari's car sales are a part of sales of cars worldwide. Table 3 shows the worldwide sales of cars divided by geographic region. In 2014, 70.9 million personal cars were sold worldwide, which is 3.8 per cent more cars than in 2013.

Table 3	Global car sales 2014	
Geographic regions	Millions cars sold – 2014	% change 2013–14
Europe (EU + EFTA)	13.0	5.4
Russia	2.5	−10.3
USA	16.4	5.8
Japan	4.7	3.0
Brazil	3.3	−6.9
India	2.6	0.7
China	18.4	12.7
Other markets	10.0	–
Total	**70.9**	**3.8**

Source: based on different statistics.

Distribution

Ferrari does not own Ferrari dealers and virtually all of the sales are made through the network of Ferrari dealerships located throughout the world. Ferrari sell their cars exclusively through a network of authorized dealers (with the exception of one-offs where they sell directly to end-customers). In larger markets, they have a wholly owned subsidiary or, in China, business is done through a joint venture with a local importer, and cars are sent to dealers for resale to end-customers. In smaller markets, Ferrari generally sells the cars to a single importer. At March 31, 2015, the network comprised 182 dealers operating 204 points of sale.

Ferrari makes a careful and strict selection of the dealers. The selection criteria are based on the candidates' reputation, financial solidity and track record. They select dealers who are able to provide an in-store experience and to market and promote the cars in a manner intended to preserve the Ferrari brand integrity and to ensure the highest level of customer satisfaction.

Marketing

Ferrari promotes passion for the brand by fostering a community of enthusiasts and by rewarding loyal clients through various initiatives, such as driving events and client activities in Maranello and at motor shows and, more particularly, through providing the most loyal and active clients with preferential access to the newest and highest value cars. As a result, in 2014 approximately 60 per cent of the new Ferrari cars were sold to existing Ferrari owners and 34 per cent of Ferrari customers own more than one Ferrari car. As a testament to the enduring power of the brand, vintage Ferraris are among the most sought after cars in the collector market, with nine Ferraris ranking in the top 10 most valuable cars ever sold in public auctions.

An important factor in promoting connection to the Ferrari brand is the strong relationship with the active global community of automotive collectors and enthusiasts, particularly collectors and enthusiasts of Ferrari automobiles. This is influenced by close ties to the automotive collectors' community and by Ferrari's support of related events (such as car shows and driving events), at the company headquarters in Maranello and through the dealers, the Ferrari museum and affiliations with regional Ferrari clubs. The support of this community also depends upon the perception of the cars as collectibles, which is also supported through the Ferrari Classic services, and the active resale market for the automobiles which encourages interest over the long term.

Ferrari organizes a number of client events at Maranello and elsewhere. The factory in Maranello is the core of their customer engagement strategy and a symbolic hub attracting customers and prospects worldwide. Upon invitation, clients and prospects can visit the factory, witness some of its workings and experience several Ferrari core values such as heritage, exclusivity and customization. At the factory, customers have the opportunity to configure their cars through their personalization.

Customers are also invited to celebrations and other events that Ferrari organizes in various markets. Some recent examples include the celebration of Ferrari North America's 60th Anniversary in Beverly Hills, Los Angeles, where over 1,000 Ferraris paraded on the streets, and Ferrari's participation in the celebrations of the Year of the Horse in China.

Participation in the Formula 1 world championship with Scuderia Ferrari is the core element of Ferrari's marketing effort. The Formula 1 world championship is the highest class for single-seat auto races, attracting the best drivers, engineers and designers. Importantly, with over 425 million television viewers in 2014, it is the most watched annual sport series in the world. In return for their participation in Formula 1, the teams receive a share of the annual profits earned from Formula 1, related commercial activities. Approximately 60 per cent of earnings before interest, tax, depreciation and amortization from commercial activities and broadcasting rights are distributed to the Formula 1 teams, largely based on the relative ranking of each team in the championship.

More generally, Formula 1 racing allows Ferrari to promote and market their brand and technology to a global audience without resorting to traditional advertising activities, thereby preserving the aura of exclusivity around the brand and limiting the marketing costs that Ferrari, as a company operating in the luxury space, would otherwise incur.

As mentioned before, Ferrari enters into licence agreements with a number of licensees for the design, development and production of Ferrari branded products. Here are some examples from the licensing mix:

- accessories: Oakley sunglasses, Tod's shoes;
- sportswear: Puma;
- theme parks: Ferrari World (Abu Dhabi);
- toys: LEGO toys;
- video games: Electronic Arts, Microsoft, Ubisoft;
- watches: Hublot (co-branded high-luxury watches).

A significant portion of revenues from licensing (12 per cent of the total amount) activities consists of royalties Ferrari receive in connection with the Ferrari World theme park in Abu Dhabi. In 2014, Ferrari reached an agreement with PortAventura Entertainment S.A.U. to open Ferrari's first European theme park at the PortAventura resort near Barcelona in Spain. PortAventura Entertainment S.A.U. has announced a planned investment of €100 million and the park is expected to open in 2016. In the long term, Ferrari aims to open one theme park in each of the main geographic areas where they operate, including North America and Asia.

Marketing and selling costs (including sales personnel costs) in 2014, 2013 and 2012 amounted to €132 million, €123 million and €114 million, respectively. These costs mainly comprise marketing and events expenses, consisting primarily of costs in connection with trade and auto shows, media and client events for the launch of new models and sponsorship and indirect marketing costs incurred through the Formula 1 racing team, Scuderia Ferrari.

Service

All dealers must conform to rigorous store design, layout and corporate identity guidelines ensuring uniformity of the image and client interface. Through the Ferrari Academy, they provide training to dealers for sales, after-sales and technical activities to ensure that their dealer network delivers a consistent level of market leading standards across diverse cultural environments. They train and monitor dealers intensively and they collect and observe data relating to their profitability and financial health in order to prevent financial difficulties among dealers. Ferrari representatives visit dealerships regularly to measure compliance with the company's operating standards. They have the right to terminate dealer relationships in a variety of circumstances including failure to meet performance or financial standards, or failure to comply with the Ferrari guidelines.

Ferrari HQ provide a suggested retail price or a maximum retail price for all of the cars, but each dealer is free to negotiate different prices with clients and to provide financing. Although most Ferrari clients in certain markets purchase cars from dealers without financing, Ferrari provide direct or indirect finance and leasing services to retail customers and to dealers.

Ferrari's low volume strategy may limit potential profits

A key to the appeal of the Ferrari brand and the company's marketing strategy is the aura of exclusivity and the sense of luxury which the brand conveys. A central determinant to this exclusivity is the limited number of models and cars Ferrari produces and the strategy of maintaining the car waiting lists to reach the optimal combination of exclusivity and client service. The low volume strategy is also an important factor in the prices that customers are willing to pay for the cars. While important to the current marketing strategy, the focus on maintaining low volumes and exclusivity limits Ferrari's potential sales growth and profitability.

Conversely, if Ferrari was to increase car production they might not be able to maintain the exclusivity of the Ferrari brand. If they are unable to balance brand exclusivity with increased production, they may erode the desirability and ultimately the consumer demand for the Ferrari brand.

Ferrari's competitive position

The worldwide automotive market is highly competitive. Competition in the luxury performance car market is concentrated in a fairly small number of producers, including both large automotive companies as well as small producers exclusively focused on luxury cars.

Ferrari faces strong competition from automotive manufacturers in its various markets. The competition among various auto players is likely to intensify in light of continuing globalization and consolidation in the worldwide automotive industry.

The company's main competitors include main car manufacturers like VW/Audi, Toyota, General Motors, Daimler, Ford, among others. Ferrari's position in the car market is shown in Figure 1.

Among the pure sports car brands, Ferrari is no. 2 in revenue and profits after Porsche (see also Table 4).

Competition in the luxury performance car market is driven by the strength of the brand, and the appeal of the products in terms of performance, styling, novelty and innovation as well as on the manufacturer's ability to renew its product offerings regularly in order to continue to stimulate customer demand. Increased competition may lead to lower vehicle unit sales and

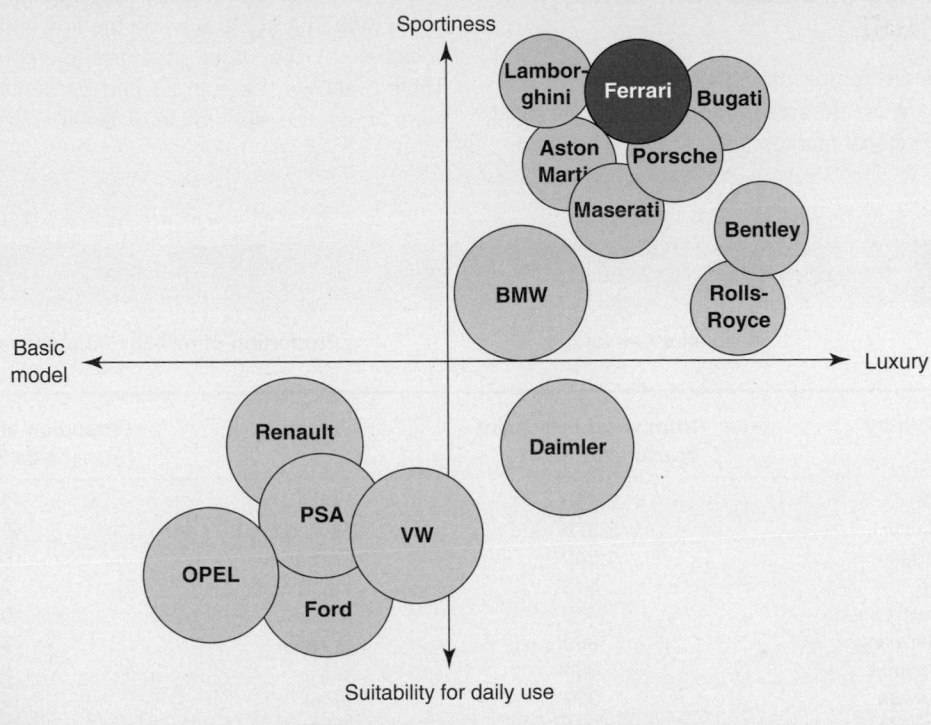

| Figure 1 | Ferrari's global positioning against other sports car brands and car brands in general |

Source: author's own figure based on different public sources.

Table 4	Comparison of sports car manufacturers		
Competitor	Revenue (€ million) 2014	Profit (€ million) 2014	Units sold 2014
Porsche	17,205	3,060	189,849
Ferrari	2,762	389	7,255
Maserati	2,760	275	36,500
Lamborghini	629	94	2,430
Aston Martin	555	−30	3,700
Bugatti	100	15	30

Source: based on different public sources.

increased inventory, which may result in a further downward price. Larger car manufacturers (like the above-mentioned) with a product offering in the luxury performance car market typically have larger financial resources compared to the small luxury car producers and therefore may have more flexibility in planning for product launches and capital spending over time.

Competition among similarly positioned luxury performance cars is also driven by price and total cost of ownership. The customers' appreciation of the value of Ferrari cars after a period of ownership is an important competitive factor because it decreases the total cost of ownership for clients and promotes repeat purchases.

Ferrari's future international market selection (IMS)

In order to secure future international growth for Ferrari, the company is interested in focusing on the most attractive international markets.

Ferrari's market research department has provided some data that could provide the first indication for the selection of the most attractive markets for Ferrari. Table 5 shows the number and percentage of millionaires among households in different countries.

Table 5	Number of millionaire households in top 15 countries				
		Millionaire households[a]		**Proportion of milli98.638 ptonaire households (%)**	
No.	Country	Number of millionaire households – 2013	Country	Proportion of millionaire households (%) – 2013	
1.	US	7,135	Qatar	17.5	
2.	China	2,378	Switzerland	12.7	
3.	Japan	1,240	Singapore	10.0	
4.	UK	513	Hong Kong	9.6	
5.	Switzerland	435	Kuwait	9.0	
6.	Germany	386	Bahrain	5.9	
7.	Canada	384	US	5.9	
8.	Taiwan	329	Israel	4.6	
9.	Italy	281	Taiwan	4.2	
10.	France	274	Oman	3.7	
11.	Hong Kong	238	Belgium	3.4	
12.	Netherlands	221	UAE	3.3	
13.	Russia	213	Saudi Arabia	3.1	
14.	Australia	195	Netherlands	3.0	
15.	India	175	Canada	2.9	

[a] Millionaire households is defined as households with more than US$1 million in net assets.
Source: based on different sources, among others BCG Global Wealth Market-sizing Database, 2014.

QUESTIONS

1. Discuss the current global position of the Ferrari brand with the starting point in Figure 1. Should Ferrari change their positioning?

2. Which screening criteria should Ferrari use in their international market selection (IMS)?

3. Which of the countries in Table 5 would you recommend as future Ferrari focus markets? Please rank 1, 2, 3.

4. Ian Fletcher, principal analyst at HIS Automotive (provides analysis to the automotive industry), said to *The Guardian*, that Ferrari may consider developing a slightly cheaper model, although still costing €100,000 plus.

If you sold 10,000 units a year that would still be exclusive – how many handbags do Louis Vuitton and Chanel sell? As Ferrari's bosses have said, if you sell one less than the market wants, you're still exclusive.*

What do you think of this statement? Do you agree? Should Ferrari launch a cheaper Ferrari model? How should this model be positioned against the other Ferrari models?

*Topham, G. (2015) 'Ferrari kickstarts split from Fiat Chrysler by filing for NYSE share listing', *The Guardian*, 23 July, http://www.theguardian.com/business/2015/jul/23/ferrari-separation-fiat-chrysler-new-york-stock-exchange-public-offering.

PART I
The decision whether to internationalize
Chs 1–4

PART II
Deciding which markets to enter
Chs 5–8

PART III
Market entry strategies
Chs 9–13

PART IV
Designing the global marketing programme
Chs 14–17

PART V
Implementing and coordinating the global marketing programme
Chs 18–19

Part III Contents

Part III Case studies

PART III
Market entry strategies

Introduction to Part III

Once the firm has chosen target markets abroad (see Part II), the question arises as to the best way to enter those markets. In Part III, we will consider the major market entry modes and criteria for selecting them. An international market entry mode is an institutional arrangement necessary for the entry of a company's products, technology and human capital into a foreign country/market.

To separate Part III from later chapters, let us take a look at Figure III.1. The figure shows the classical distribution systems in a national consumer market.

In this context, the chosen market entry mode (here, own sales subsidiary) can be regarded as the first decision level in the vertical chain that will provide marketing and distribution to the next actors in the vertical chain. In Chapter 12, we will take a closer look at the choice between alternative distribution systems at the single national level.

Some firms have discovered that an ill-judged market entry selection in the initial stages of its internationalization can threaten its future market entry and expansion activities. Since it is common for firms to have their initial mode choice institutionalized over time, as new products are sold through the same established channels and new markets are entered using the same entry method, a problematic initial entry mode choice can survive through the institutionalization of this mode. The inertia in the shift process of entry modes delays the transition to a new entry mode. The reluctance of firms to change entry modes once they are in place, and the difficulty involved in so doing, makes the mode of entry decision a key strategic issue for firms operating in today's rapidly internationalizing marketplace (Hollensen, 1991).

For most small and medium-sized enterprises (SMEs), the market entry represents a critical first step, but for established companies the problem is not how to enter new emerging markets, but rather how to exploit opportunities more effectively within the context of their existing network of international operations.

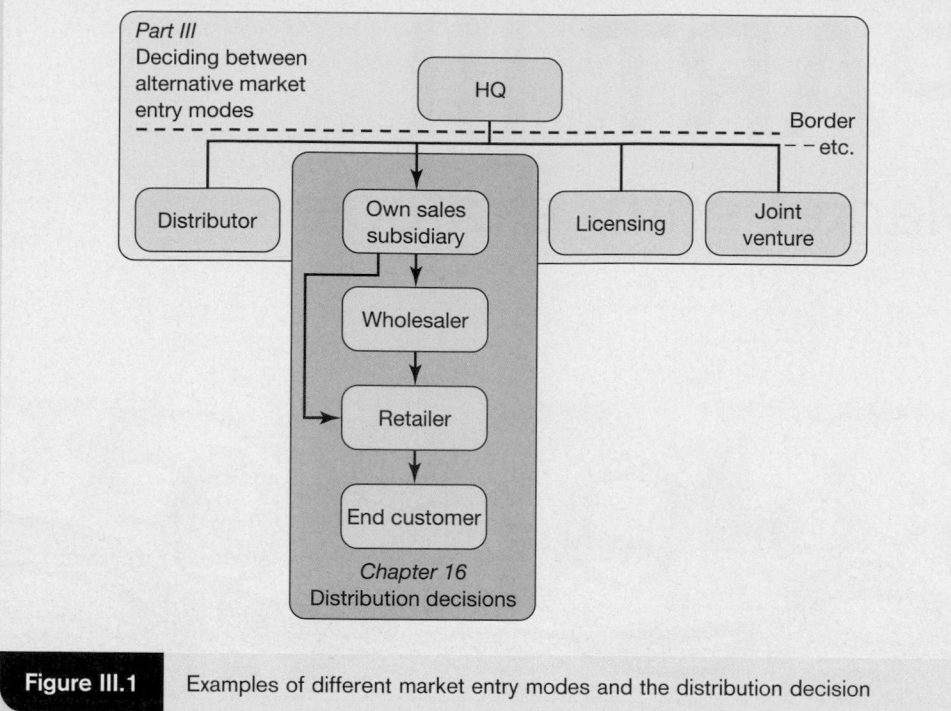

Figure III.1   Examples of different market entry modes and the distribution decision

There is, however, no ideal market entry strategy, and different market entry methods might be adopted by different firms entering the same market and/or by the same firm in different markets. Firms often combine modes to enter or develop a specific foreign market (Petersen and Welch, 2002). Such 'mode packages' may take the form of concerted use of several operation modes in an integrated, complementary way (Freeman *et al.,* 2006). In some cases, a firm uses a combination of modes that compete with each other. Sometimes this occurs when a firm attempts a hostile takeover of an export market.

According to the entry mode categorization proposed by Wrona and Trapczyński (2012, p. 301), three broad groupings emerge when one looks at the assortment of entry modes available to the firm when entering international markets (see Figure III.2). There are different degrees of control, risk and flexibility associated with each of these different market entry modes. As indicated in Figure III.2, these three concepts are important criteria for selecting on entry mode group. For example, the use of hierarchical modes (investment modes) gives the firm ownership and thereby high control, but committing heavy resources to foreign markets also represents a higher potential risk. At the same time, heavy resource commitment creates exit barriers, which diminish the firm's ability to change the chosen entry mode in a quick and easy way. So the entry mode decision involves trade-offs, as the firm cannot have both high control and high flexibility.

Figure III.3 shows three examples representing the main types of market entry mode. By using hierarchical modes, transactions between independent actors are substituted by intra-firm transactions, and market prices are substituted by internal transfer prices.

Many factors should be considered in deciding on the appropriate market entry mode. These factors (criteria) vary with the market situation and the firm in question.

Chapter 9 examines the different decision criteria and how they influence the choice

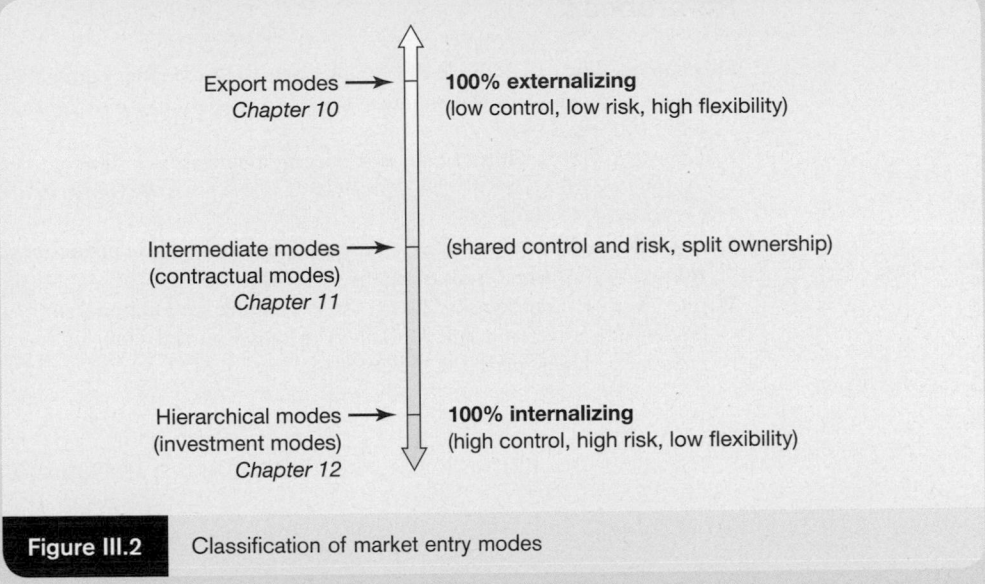

| **Figure III.2** | Classification of market entry modes |

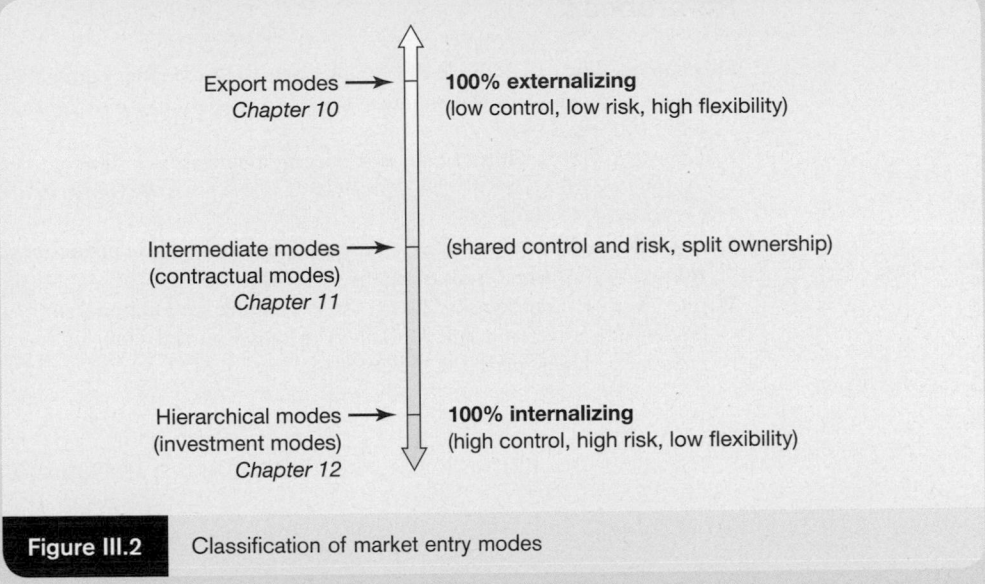

Export modes — Firm A

Intermediate modes — Firm A, Firm B

Hierarchical modes — Firm A

| **Figure III.3** | Examples of the different market entry modes in the consumer market |

among the three main groupings of market entry modes. Chapters 10–12 discuss in more detail the three main types of entry mode. A special issue for SMES is how their internationalization process is related to their much bigger customers and their sourcing and entry mode decisions. This is discussed further in Chapter 13.

The simple version of the value chain (see Figure 1.11) will be used to structure the different entry modes in Chapters 10–12.

References

Freeman, S., Edwards, R. and Schroder, B. (2006) 'How smaller born-globals firms use networks and alliances to overcome constraints to rapid internationalization', *Journal of International Marketing*, 14(3), pp. 33–63.

Hollensen, S. (1991) 'Shift of market servicing organization in international markets: a Danish case study', in Vestergaard, H. (ed.), *An Enlarged Europe in the Global Economy*, EIBA's 17th Annual Conference, Copenhagen.

Petersen, B. and Welch, L.S. (2002), 'Foreign operation mode combinations and internationalization', *Journal of Business Research*, 55, pp. 157–162.

Wrona, T. and Trapczyński (2012), 'Re-explaining international entry modes – interaction and moderating effects on entry modes of pharmaceutical companies into transition economies', *European Management*, 30, pp. 295–315.

PART III VIDEO CASE STUDY Müller Yogurts – entering the US market
download from **www.pearsoned.co.uk/hollensen**

Molkerei Alois Müller GmbH & Co. KG or Müller is a multinational producer of dairy products, with head-quarters in the German state of Bavaria. Founded as

Source: urbanbuzz/Shutterstock.com.

a family dairy farm in 1896 by Ludwig Müller, today his grandson Theo owns the successful business. The Müller group made a net turnover of €4.7 billion in 2012 and has nearly 21,000 employees worldwide. Müller is mostly well-known for its yogurts, and in this product area it is market leader in Germany and the UK, where its most well-known product is the 'Müller Corner yogurt'. The name 'corner' is in reference to the design of the product. In 2012, Müller yogurts entered the US market through a joint venture between PepsiCo and Müller. The name of the joint venture is 'Muller Quaker Dairy'. The Müller Group has subsidiaries in the nearby European markets, like the UK, Italy and Spain. However, in most export markets outside Europe, Müller mostly uses distributors for selling their yogurts to the grocery retailers in the different countries.

Questions

1. What could be the reason why Müller is using distributors (export mode) in markets outside Germany?

2. What would be the main reasons why Müller is using a joint venture solution (intermediate mode) with PepsiCo (Quaker) for the US market?

Please look at the video clips at **www.pearsoned.co.uk/hollensen**

CHAPTER 9

Some approaches to the choice of entry mode

Contents

Case studies

Learning objectives

After studying this chapter you should be able to:

- Identify and classify different market entry modes

- Explore different approaches to the choice of entry mode

- Explain how opportunistic behaviour affects the manufacturer/intermediary relationship

- Identify the factors to consider when choosing a market entry strategy.

9.1   Introduction

Entry mode
An institutional arrangement for the entry of a company's products and services into a new foreign market. The main types are export, intermediate and hierarchical modes.

We have seen the main groupings of **entry modes** available to companies that wish to take advantage of foreign market opportunities. At this point we are concerned with the question: what kind of strategy should be used for the entry mode selection?

According to Root (1994) there are three different rules:

1. *Naive rule.* The decision-maker uses the same entry mode for all foreign markets. This rule ignores the heterogeneity of the individual foreign markets.
2. *Pragmatic rule.* The decision-maker uses a workable entry mode for each foreign market. In the early stages of exporting, the firm typically starts doing business with a low-risk entry mode. Only if the particular initial mode is not feasible or profitable will the firm look for another workable entry mode. In this case, not all potential alternatives are investigated, and the workable entry may not be the 'best' entry mode.
3. *Strategy rules.* This approach requires that all alternative entry modes are systematically compared and evaluated before any choice is made. An application of this decision rule would be to choose the entry mode that maximizes the profit contribution over the strategic planning period subject to (a) the availability of company resources, (b) risk and (c) non-profit objectives.

Although many small and medium-sized enterprises (SMEs) probably use the pragmatic or even the naive rule, this chapter is inspired mainly by an analytical approach, which is the main principle behind the strategy rule.

9.2   The transaction cost approach

The principles of transaction cost analysis have already been presented in Section 3.3. This chapter will go into further details about 'friction' and opportunism.

The unit of analysis is the transaction rather than the firm. The basic idea behind this approach is that in the real world there is always some friction between the buyer and seller in connection with market transactions. This friction is mainly caused by opportunistic behaviour in the relationship between a producer and an export intermediary.

In the case of an agent, the producer specifies sales-promoting tasks that the export intermediary is to solve in order to receive a reward in the shape of commission.

In the case of an importer, the export intermediary has a higher degree of freedom, as the intermediary itself, to a certain extent, can fix sales prices and thus base its earnings on the profit between the producer's sales price (the importer's buying price) and the importer's sales price.

No matter who the export intermediary may be, there will be some recurrent elements that may result in conflicts and opportunistic actions:

- stock size of the export intermediary;
- extent of technical and commercial service to be carried out by the export intermediary for its customers;
- division of marketing costs (advertising, exhibition activities, etc.) between producer and export intermediary;
- fixing of prices: from producer to export intermediary, and from the export intermediary to its customers;
- fixing of commission to agents.

Opportunistic behaviour from the export intermediary

In this connection the export intermediary's opportunistic behaviour may be reflected in two activities:

1. In most producer–export intermediary relations, a split of the sales-promoting costs has been fixed. Thus statements by the export intermediary of too high sales promotion activities (e.g. by manipulating invoices) may form the basis of a higher payment from producer to export intermediary.
2. The export intermediary may manipulate information on market size and competitor prices in order to obtain lower ex-works prices from the producer. Of course, this kind of opportunism can be avoided if the export intermediary is paid a commission of realized turnover (the agency case).

As a consequence, high control modes (e.g. own foreign company in form of a subsidiary) may be preferred by companies, in order to protect their brand equity from possible damage done by local partners' inappropriate operations (Lu *et al.*, 2011).

Opportunistic behaviour from the producer

In this chapter we have so far presumed that the export intermediary is the one who has behaved opportunistically. The producer may, however, also behave in an opportunistic way, as the export intermediary must also use resources (time and money) on building up the market for the producer's product programme. This is especially the case if the producer wants to sell expensive and technically complicated products.

Thus the export intermediary carries a great part of the economic risk, and will always have the threat of the producer's change of entry mode hanging over its head. If the export intermediary does not live up to the producer's expectations, it risks being replaced by another export intermediary, or the producer may change to its own export organization (sales subsidiary), as the increased transaction frequency (market size) can obviously bear the increased costs.

The last case may also be part of a deliberate strategy from the producer: namely, to tap the export intermediary for market knowledge and customer contacts in order to establish a sales organization itself.

What can the export intermediary do to meet this situation?

Heide and John (1988) suggest that the agent should make a number of further 'offsetting' investments in order to counterbalance the relationship between the two parties. These investments create bonds that make it costly for the producer to leave the relationship, i.e. the agent creates 'exit barriers' for the producer (the principal). Examples of such investments are as follows:

- establish personal relations with the producer's key employees;
- create an independent identity (image) in connection with selling the producer's products;
- add further value to the product, such as a before–during–after (BDA) service, which creates bonds in the agent's customer relations.

If it is impossible to make such offsetting investments, Heide and John (1988) suggest that the agent reduces its risk by representing more producers.

These are the conditions that the producer is up against, and when several of these factors appear at the same time, the theory recommends that the company (the producer) internalizes rather than externalizes.

9.3 Factors influencing the choice of entry mode

A firm's choice of its entry mode for a given product/target country is the net result of several, often conflicting, forces. The need to anticipate the strength and direction of these forces makes the entry mode decision a complex process with numerous trade-offs among alternative entry modes.

Generally speaking, the choice of entry mode should be based on the expected contribution to profit. This may be easier said than done, particularly for those foreign markets where relevant data are lacking. Most of the selection criteria are qualitative in nature, and quantification is very difficult.

The choice of 'entry mode' in Figure 9.1 is built on a 'matchmaking' of internal capabilities (internal factors) and the external environment (external factors), moderated by the 'desired mode characteristics' and 'transaction-specific factors'. One of the other important preconditions of the model is that the 'entry mode' decision in a specific country is independent of other 'entry mode' decisions undertaken earlier on in the firm's internationalization process. This is of course not a complete realistic assumption (Shaver, 2013), and this calls for 'entry mode' researchers to study longitudinal 'entry mode' interdependences more extensively (Hennart and Slangen, 2015).

As shown in Figure 9.1, four groups of factors are believed to influence the entry mode decision:

1. internal factors
2. external factors
3. desired mode characteristics
4. transaction-specific behaviour.

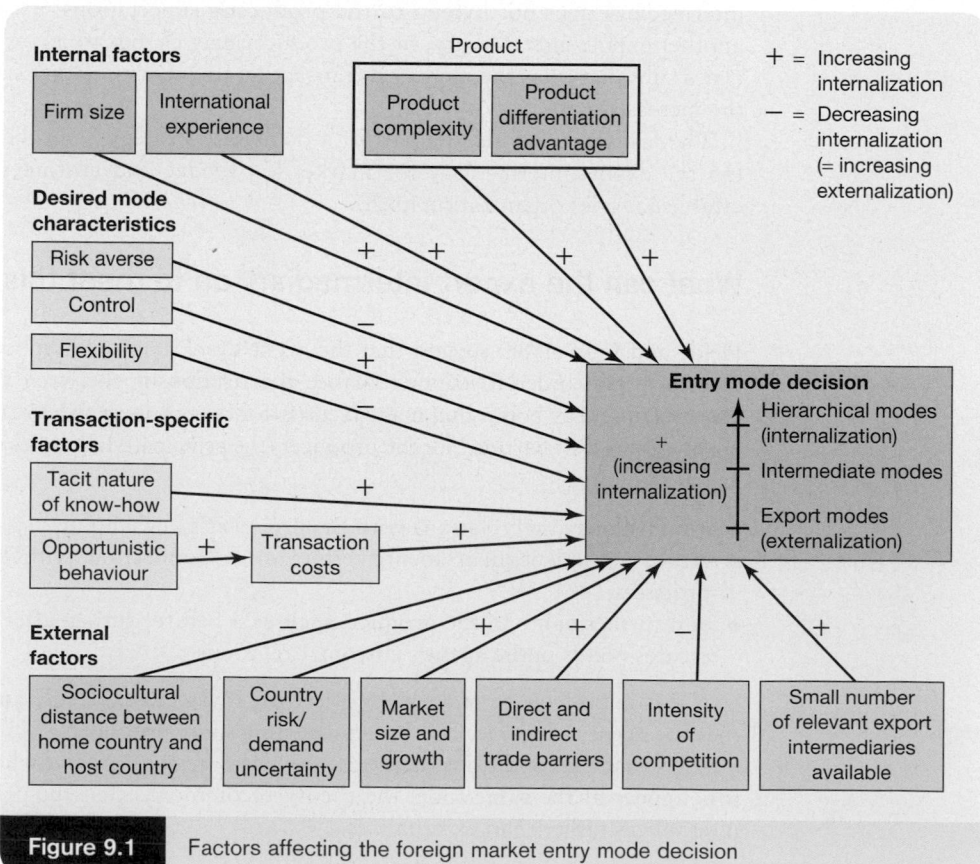

| **Figure 9.1** | Factors affecting the foreign market entry mode decision |

In what follows, a proposition is formulated for each factor: how is each factor supposed to affect the choice of foreign entry mode? The direction of influence is also indicated both in the text and in Figure 9.1. Because of the complexity of the entry mode decision, the propositions are made under the condition of other factors being equal.

Internal factors

Firm size

Size is an indicator of the firm's resource availability; increasing resource availability provides the basis for increased international involvement over time. Although SMEs may desire a high level of control over international operations and wish to make heavy resource commitments to foreign markets, they are more likely to enter foreign markets using export modes because they do not have the resources necessary to achieve a high degree of control or to make these resource commitments. Export entry modes (market modes), with their lower resource commitment, may therefore be more suitable for SMEs. As the firm grows, it will increasingly use the hierarchical model.

International experience

Another firm-specific factor influencing mode choice is the international experience of managers and thus of the firm. Experience, which refers to the extent to which a firm has been involved in operating internationally, can be gained from operating either in a particular country or in the general international environment. International experience reduces the cost and uncertainty of serving a market, and in turn increases the probability of firms committing resources to foreign markets, which favours direct investment in the form of wholly owned subsidiaries (hierarchical modes).

A high degree of international experience reinforces the use of an already preferred entry mode in subsequent entry decisions (Swoboda *et al.*, 2015). Once a firm has had success with a particular entry mode, it will to use the same entry mode in new markets, but there may also be a tendency to be less risk-averse with greater international experience, which could result in using higher-control modes in subsequent entry decisions.

Dow and Larimo (2009) conclude from their survey that practitioners should be aware that not all forms of experience are equal. International experience from similar countries (with low perceived psychic distance) is positively associated with the choice of a high control entry mode (i.e. entry by wholly owned subsidiary). This indicates that exploiting each geographic region in succession may be advisable, instead of 'jumping' from region to region. This would maximize the benefits of within-cluster experience.

In developing their theory of internationalization, Johanson and Vahlne (1977) assert that uncertainty in international markets is reduced through actual operations in foreign markets (experiential knowledge) rather than through the acquisition of objective knowledge. They suggest that it is direct experience with international markets that increases the likelihood of committing extra resources to foreign markets.

Product/service

The physical characteristics of the product or service, such as its value/weight ratio, perishability and composition, are important in determining where production is located. Products with high value/weight ratios, such as expensive watches, are typically used for direct exporting, especially where there are significant production economies of scale, or if management wishes to retain control over production. Conversely, in the soft drinks and beer industry, companies typically establish licensing agreements, or invest in local bottling or production facilities, because shipment costs, particularly to distant markets, are prohibitive.

The nature of the product affects entry mode selection because products vary so widely in their characteristics and use, and because the selling job may also vary markedly. For instance, the technical nature of a product (high complexity) may require service both before and after sale. In many foreign market areas, marketing intermediaries may not be able to handle such work. Instead firms will use one of the hierarchical modes.

Blomstermo *et al.* (2006) distinguish between *hard* and *soft services*. Hard services are those where production and consumption can be decoupled. For example, software services can be transferred to a CD, or some other tangible medium, which can be mass-produced, making standardization possible. With soft services, where production and consumption occur simultaneously, the customer acts as a co-producer and decoupling is not viable. The soft-service provider must be present abroad from their first day of foreign operations. Blomstermo *et al.* (2006) conclude that there are significant differences between hard- and soft-service suppliers regarding choice of foreign market entry mode. Managers in soft services are much more likely to choose a high control entry mode (hierarchical mode) than those in hard services. It is important for soft-service suppliers to interact with their foreign customers, and thus they should opt for a high degree of control, enabling them to monitor the co-production of the services.

Products distinguished by physical variations, brand name, advertising and after-sales service (e.g. warranties, repair and replacement policies) that promote preference for one product over another may allow a firm to absorb the higher costs of being in a foreign market. Product differentiation advantages give firms a certain amount of impulse in raising prices to exceed costs by more than normal profits (quasi-rent). They also allow firms to limit competition through the development of entry barriers, which are fundamental in the competitive strategy of the firm, as well as serving customer needs better and thereby strengthening the competitive position of the firm compared to other firms. Because these product differentiation advantages represent a 'natural monopoly', firms seek to protect their competitive advantages from dissemination through the use of hierarchical modes of entry. For example, Lu *et al.* (2011) emphasize the importance for a fashion retailer to select a higher control entry mode to ensure a successful transfer of its special assets and brand equity across borders, which are important considerations in a fashion brand's international expansion decision.

External factors

Sociocultural distance between home country and host country

Socioculturally similar countries are those that have similar business and industrial practices, a common or similar language, and comparable educational levels and cultural characteristics. Sociocultural differences between a firm's home country and its host country can create internal uncertainty for the firm, which influences the mode of entry desired by that firm.

The greater the perceived distance between the home and host country in terms of culture, economic systems and business practices, the more likely it is that the firm will shy away from direct investment in favour of joint venture agreements or even low-risk entry modes like agents or an importer. This is because the latter institutional modes enhance firms' flexibility to withdraw from the host market, should they be unable to acclimatize themselves to the unfamiliar setting. To summarize, other things being equal, when the perceived distance between the home and host country is great, firms will favour entry modes that involve relatively low resource commitments and high flexibility. Dow and Larimo (2009) found that the perceived cultural distance (psychic distance) is much more than Hofstede's cultural dimensions. Psychic distance is relevant not only on the country but also at the managerial levels. In particular, language difference seems to be one of the least important factors. Other issues, such as differences in religion, degree of democracy, industrial development and so on, have a much greater impact on the management's entry mode choice.

Country risk/demand uncertainty

Foreign markets are usually perceived as riskier than the domestic market. The amount of risk the firm faces is a function not only of the market itself but also of its method of involvement there. In addition to its investment, the firm risks inventories and receivables. When planning its method of entry, the firm must do a risk analysis of both the market and its method of entry. Exchange rate risk is another variable. Moreover, risks are not only economic; there are also political risks.

When country risk is high, a firm would do well to limit its exposure to such risk by restricting its resource commitments in that particular national domain. That is, other things being equal, when country risk is high, firms will favour entry modes that involve relatively low resource commitments (export modes).

Unpredictability in the political and economic environment of the host market increases the perceived risk and demand uncertainty experienced by the firm. This, in turn, makes firms less inclined to enter the market with entry modes requiring heavy resource commitments; on the other hand, flexibility is highly desired (Lu *et al.*, 2011).

Market size and growth

Country size and rate of market growth are key parameters in determining the mode of entry. The larger the country and the size of its market, and the higher the growth rate, the more likely management will be to commit resources to its development, and to consider establishing a wholly owned sales subsidiary or to participate in a majority-owned joint venture. Retaining control over operations provides management with direct contact and allows it to plan and direct market development more effectively.

Small markets, on the other hand, especially if they are geographically isolated and cannot be serviced efficiently from a neighbouring country, may not warrant significant attention or resources. Consequently, they may be best supplied via exporting or a licensing agreement. While unlikely to stimulate market development or maximize market penetration, this approach enables the firm to enter the market with minimal resource commitment, and frees resources for potentially more lucrative markets.

Direct and indirect trade barriers

Tariffs or quotas on the import of foreign goods and components favour the establishment of local production or assembly operations (hierarchical modes).

Product or trade regulations and standards, as well as preferences for local suppliers, also have an impact on mode of entry and operation decisions. Preferences for local suppliers, or tendencies to 'buy national', often encourage a company to consider a joint venture or other contractual arrangements with a local company (intermediate modes). The local partner helps in developing local contacts, negotiating sales and establishing distribution channels, as well as in diffusing the foreign image.

Similarly, product and trade regulations and customs formalities encourage modes involving local companies, which can provide information about and contacts in local markets and can ease access. In some instances, where product regulations and standards necessitate significant adaptation and modification, the firm may establish local production, assembly or finishing facilities (hierarchical modes).

The net impact of both direct and indirect trade barriers is thus likely to be a shift towards performing various functions, such as sourcing, production and developing marketing tactics in the local market.

Intensity of competition

When the intensity of competition is high in a host market, firms will do well to avoid internalization, as such markets tend to be less profitable and therefore do not justify heavy resource commitments. Hence, other things being equal, the greater the intensity of competition in the host market, the more the firm will favour entry modes (export modes) that involve low resource commitments.

Small number of relevant intermediaries available

Highly concentrated markets lead to 'small number bargaining', which may be executed by the few export intermediaries if they realize that they are in a kind of 'monopolistic situation'. In such a case, the market field is subject to the opportunistic behaviour of the few export intermediaries, and this will favour the use of hierarchical modes in order to reduce the scope for opportunistic behaviour.

Desired mode characteristics

Risk-averse

If decision-makers are risk-averse they will prefer export modes (e.g. indirect and direct exporting) or licensing (an intermediate mode), because these typically entail low levels of financial and management resource commitment. A joint venture provides a way of sharing risk, financial exposure and the cost of establishing local distribution networks and hiring local personnel, although negotiating and managing joint ventures often absorbs considerable management time and effort. However, modes of entry that entail minimal levels of resource commitment, and hence minimal risks, are unlikely to foster the development of international operations and may result in significant loss of opportunity.

EXHIBIT 9.1 Zara is modifying its preferred choice of entry mode, depending on the psychic distance to new markets

Zara (www.inditex.com) is a fashion retail chain that is part of the Inditex Group owned by Spanish tycoon Amancio Ortega. Zara's preferred entry mode is the hierarchical mode (direct investment), which is used in most European countries, resulting in full ownership of the stores. In 2014, 85 per cent of the Zara stores were own managed. Those markets where the hierarchical model is used are characterized by high growth potential and relatively low sociocultural distance (low country risk) between Spain and target market.

The intermediate modes (usually joint venture and franchising) are mainly used in countries where the sociocultural distance is relatively high.

A Zara shop in Shanghai, China
Source: Bloomberg/Getty Images.

Joint ventures

This is a cooperative strategy in which facilities and know-how of the local company are combined with the international fashion expertise of Zara. This particular mode is used in large, competitive markets where it is difficult to acquire property to set up retail outlets or where there are other kinds of obstacles that require cooperation with a local company. For example, in 1999 Zara entered into a 50–50 joint venture with the German firm Otto Versand, which had experience in the distribution sector and market knowledge in one of Europe's largest markets, Germany.

Franchising

Zara employs this mode for high-risk countries that are socioculturally distant or have small markets with a low sales forecast, such as Kuwait, Andorra, Puerto Rico, Panama and the Philippines.

Whatever entry mode Zara uses, the main characteristic of their franchise model is the total integration of franchised stores with own-managed stores in terms of product, human resources, training, window-dressing, interior design, logistical optimization and so on. This ensures uniformity in store management criteria and a global image in the eyes of customers around the world.

Source: adapted from the Zara case study and different public media.

Control

Mode of entry decisions also need to consider the degree of control that management requires over operations in international markets. Control is often closely linked to the level of resource commitment. Modes of entry with minimal resource commitment, such as indirect exporting, provide little or no control over the conditions under which the product or service is marketed abroad. In the case of licensing and contract manufacturing, management needs to ensure that production meets its quality standards. Joint ventures also limit the degree of management control over international operations and can be a source of considerable conflict where the goals and objectives of partners diverge. Wholly owned subsidiaries (hierarchical mode) provide the most control, but also require a substantial commitment of resources.

Flexibility

Equity
Some investment of a defined financial value.

Management must also weigh up the flexibility associated with a given mode of entry. The hierarchical modes (involving substantial **equity** investment) are typically the most costly, but they are the least flexible and most difficult to change in the short run. On the other hand, export modes provide the company with higher flexibility, because the company can terminate an agent contract on a relatively short time horizon, though the company may have to compensate the foreign agent for the lost commission for 1-2 years (depending on the agent contract).

Transaction-specific factors

The transaction cost analysis approach was discussed in Section 3.3 and earlier in this chapter. We will therefore refer to only one of the factors here.

Tacit
Difficult to articulate and express in words – tacit knowledge has often to do with complex products and services, where functionality is very hard to express.

Tacit nature of know-how

When the nature of the firm-specific know-how transferred is **tacit**, it is by definition difficult to articulate. This makes the drafting of a contract (to transfer such complex know-how) very problematic. The difficulties and costs involved in transferring tacit know-how provide an incentive for firms to use hierarchical modes. Investment modes are better able to facilitate the intra-organizational transfer of tacit know-how. By using a hierarchical mode, the firm can utilize human capital, drawing upon its organizational routines to structure the transfer problem. Hence, the greater the tacit component of firm-specific know-how, the more a firm will favour hierarchical modes.

9.4 Summary

Seen from the perspective of the manufacturer (international marketer), market entry modes can be classified into three groups:

Intermediate modes
Somewhere between using export modes (external partners) and hierarchical modes (internal modes).

1. export modes: low control, low risk, high flexibility;
2. **intermediate modes** (contractual modes): shared control and risk, split ownership;
3. hierarchical modes (investment modes): high control, high risk, low flexibility.

It cannot be stated categorically which alternative is the best. There are many internal and external conditions that affect this choice and it should be emphasized that a manufacturer wanting to engage in global marketing may use more than one of these methods at the same time. There may be different product lines, each requiring a different entry mode.

CASE STUDY 9.1

Jarlsberg: the king of Norwegian cheeses is deciding on entry modes into new markets

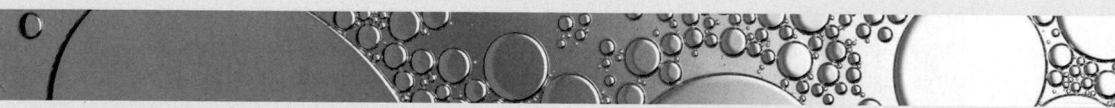

Jarlsberg cheese (www.jarlsberg.com) has been well received in the US. Nearly 50 years after entering the US it is now the imported cheese with the biggest market share of its category ('Swiss-like' cheese) in the competitive US supermarkets.

However, because of the quota introduced by the World Trade Organization (WTO) between Norway and the US, Jarlsberg can only export a limited amount of cheese from Norway to the US. The quota on Norwegian cheese to the US is approximately 8,000 tons.

To increase sales, a licensed production was set up in Ohio in 2000, with an annual production of approximately 5,000 tons. Quality control is maintained by using a cheese culture produced in Norway (based on a secret recipe from 1956), premium quality milk only, tailor-made production lines and key people with skills and know-how in dairy technology/science.

In 2008, the total export of Jarlsberg cheese (to all countries) was 16,000 tons. In that same year, the total export of Norwegian cheese to the US was approximately 8,000 tons, of which the majority

(c. 70 per cent) was Jarlsberg. This meant that the WTO quota between Norway and the US had been fulfilled, and if Norway exceeded it, they would have to pay extra import taxes on the cheese. Therefore, Jarlsberg had to find other ways of expanding sales of cheese in the US.

The story

Professor Ole M. Ystgaard and his employees at the Norwegian Agricultural School developed Jarlsberg in the 1950s. The cheese is based on traditions from Swiss cheese makers, who developed cheese with holes in the 1830s.

Jarlsberg cheese arrived in the US in 1963. In the beginning, the Jarlsberg management team travelled around the country to demonstrate how the cheese could be used for everyday meals and at parties. After just two years Jarlsberg had a sales volume of 450,000-kg in the market, and the managers understood they had a 'hot' product.

Jarlsberg has become a high-status product, served by celebrities at high-society parties.

Source: Tine SA.

Norseland Inc.

Norseland Inc. was founded in 1978. The purpose of the company was to market and distribute Jarlsberg and other Norwegian cheese in the US. The company is a wholly owned subsidiary of Tine Norwegian Dairies, which has the main responsibility for the production and marketing of Jarlsberg cheese. In 2008, Norseland had net sales of US$140 million, about half of this derived from imported Norwegian Jarlsberg, 25 per cent from Jarlsberg produced in Ohio and the remainder from sales of products from other companies, among them French Unilever Boursin. Norseland's strategy is to sell exclusive cheeses only, and the company commands respect in the US retail trade, where a 90 per cent distribution coverage has been achieved. Norseland has a regional office in Montreal, Canada, where an additional 1,350 tons of Jarlsberg were sold in 2008.

The US cheese market

In 2008, the total US market for hard cheese was approximately 400,000 tons, but the market also consumed a lot of soft cheese. Although Jarlsberg only had a small market share in the total hard cheese market (in 2008 the company sold 12,600 tons in the US, including local production), this represented the largest market share in the Swiss-like cheese category.

The largest producer of cheese for the US market is Kraft, which makes and sells the popular soft cheese, Philadelphia. The second-largest cheese producer for the US market is ConAgra Foods, which had total sales of US$13 billion in 2008.

In general, the tendency to consume cheese is higher in the eastern part of the US, whereas 'healthy' food products are focused on more in the western part of the country. There is a tendency to eat more imported cheese as personal income increases.

Jarlsberg's customers and marketing

Jarlsberg cheese has some snob appeal. Customers want to show they have good taste and they accept the higher price of Jarlsberg compared with other competitive products without complaining. The mild and creamy taste appeals to Americans, and many think that the taste of the traditional Swiss cheese, Emmenthal, is too sharp.

Characteristics of the typical Jarlsberg buyer are:

- female
- earning more than US$90,000 per year
- over 40 years old.

It is important to buyers that it is an imported cheese. The fact that it is a Norwegian cheese plays a minor role and Norseland does not use this in its marketing.

Norseland's objective is to attract new and younger consumers for its Jarlsberg cheese. To achieve this objective it wants to make contracts and deals with retail chains like 7-Eleven, which also sells sandwiches, among other things.

Besides its own sales force of about 25 people, Norseland uses nearly 500 'cheese brokers' (distributors), who sell all over the US. These are external sales representatives who visit shops, retail chains and restaurants in order to sell and market products, among them Jarlsberg.

Jarlsberg aims to be present in at least five new countries, either sourced through the existing production units (e.g. in the US or Ireland) or supplied from Norway.

QUESTIONS

1. Which kind of market entry mode would you generally suggest for Jarlsberg:

  (a) in Scandinavia?

  (b) in Asia?

2. What are the general motives for choosing a hierarchical mode (own subsidiary) in the US?

Source: based on different public sources.

CASE STUDY 9.2

Ansell condoms: is acquisition the right way to gain market shares in the European condom market?

Ansell Limited is the new name of the company formerly known as Pacific Dunlop Limited.

The company's name was changed in April 2002 as a result of its strategic repositioning to concentrate on its core business, protective products and services in a broad health care context, and following the disposition of a series of other business units that did not fit within the strategy. Ansell Limited is an Australian publicly listed company with its corporate head office located in Richmond, Australia.

In 1905, Eric Ansell, a former Dunlop employee, took the machinery and set up his own company, The Ansell Rubber Company, in Melbourne, Australia, manufacturing toy balloons and condoms. The rest is history: Ansell made strategic acquisitions and expansions and invested in the research and development necessary to bring a number of products to the world market.

Source: Ansell.

Today Ansell Limited is a global leader in barrier protective products. With operations in the Americas, Europe and Asia, Ansell employs more than 11,000 people worldwide and holds leading positions in the natural latex and synthetic polymer glove and condom markets.

Ansell Condom brands are marketed globally through the Personal Healthcare division of Ansell Healthcare, and their main office in Red Bank, NJ, US.

This 100-year-old company has fostered some innovations in latex condoms and gloves. It manufactures and markets a variety of condoms with flavours, colours, spermicide, studded and ribbed features. Ansell markets branded condoms worldwide, each with its own unique marketing strategy that has been tailored to the particular country or region. Their brands around the globe include LifeStyles (for the US market), Mates (for the UK market), KamaSutra (for the Indian market), Contempo, Manix, Primex, Pleasure and Chekmate.

Additionally, the company participates in the public sector market where condoms are supplied through health and social welfare programmes and agencies, mainly in developing countries around the world. Ansell also participates in a broad range of studies and educational activities and continues to expand its market presence with the introduction of new products. Lifestyle Ultra Sensitive condoms with spermicide, for instance, were developed to meet demand for a thinner condom that includes a spermicide to maximize protection from sexually transmitted diseases (STDs).

Global manufacturing

Estimated worldwide condom production is around 16 billion pieces annually (2014). Currently there are about 100 manufacturing plants operating globally. The majority of these plants manufacture only condoms made from natural rubber latex, and some also produce other latex products, such as gloves, finger cots and catheters. The majority of the plants are therefore in locations that have natural rubber latex plantations and where labour costs are competitive.

The production of condoms is much more labour-intensive than that of glove manufacturing, because of more stringent testing needs, more complicated packaging and significant product differentiation.

An estimate of condom production per country in 2014 is shown in Table 1.

Table 1	Estimated 2014 condom production by country

Country	Annual production in billions of pieces
India	3.3
Thailand	2.8
China	2.7
Japan	2.0
Malaysia	1.5
US	1.2
Europe	1.0
South Korea	0.5
Indonesia	0.3
South America	0.4
Vietnam	0.2
Other	0.1
Total	16.0

Source: based on different public sources.

Table 2	World market for male condoms (2014)

	Per year (billions)
Global public health sector (UN, WHO and local governments)	10
Commercial channels (mainly in the US, Japan and European nations)	6
World market	16

Source: adapted from different public sources.

World market for male condoms

Condoms offer protection against both unwanted pregnancies (contraception) and STDs (prophylaxis). The latter property is unique to condoms. Although there is considerable superficial variation in the types of condoms available (e.g. ribbed, thin and thick), there has been little fundamental change in the latex condom over the years.

Organizations that are part of the global public health sector currently distribute approximately 10 billion male condoms, generally free of charge or at a nominal cost, to sexually active people throughout the world, mostly in developing nations. It is estimated that another five billion male condoms are distributed through commercial channels, mostly in developed countries such as the US, Japan and European nations. The size of the world market for male condoms and how it is made up is shown in Table 2.

In 2014, 35 per cent of condoms were purchased by the United Nations Population Fund. The World Health Organization (WHO) is also a buyer.

Besides the direct competitors, described in Table 3, it is essential to emphasize the role of the indirect competitors, i.e. those with a product of substitution. According to the Durex Sex Survey, the male condom is globally the most popular form of contraception (41 per cent of people use it). Among the 59 per cent non-condom users, most of the population use the pill or no contraceptive at all.

With 14 per cent of the global market share for condoms, Ansell is the second largest manufacturer of condoms. The company has 50 per cent of the Polish market, 8 per cent in Germany, 20 per cent in Brazil (third largest), is number one in Australia, and is the fastest-growing brand in Canada.

In the distribution of male condoms in the commercial sector, there has been a movement from the pharmacies toward the retail chains (supermarkets). For example, in the early 1990s, supermarkets accounted for around 25 per cent of the UK retail sales of condoms while pharmacies accounted for over half. Today, the supermarkets account for around 40 per cent of retail sales, a share mostly drawn from the pharmacies, which have seen their share fall to 30 per cent. Therefore, national retailing chains (supermarkets, Boots and Superdrug) now account for at least 65 per cent of condom sales in the UK.

| Table 3 | Company shares on the world market for male condoms (2014) |

Company	Nationality	Major brands	Key strategies	Market share (%)
Seton Scholl London (SSL)	UK	Durex, Durex Avanti, Durex Pleasure, Durex Fetherlite, Durex Extra Sensitive, etc.	A true global brand with strong positions in all main markets, except the US (15 per cent MS) and Japan (5 per cent MS). In the UK the Durex MS is 85 per cent	24
Ansell Limited	Australia/ US	LifeStyles, Mates, Contempo, Manix, Primex, KamaSutra, Pleasure and Chekmate	Semi-global company with relatively strong market positions in the US, UK and the Asian and Australia/ New Zealand markets. Local/ regional brands, e.g. LifeStyles for US and Mates for UK	13
Church & Dwight Co	US	Trojan, Trojan Magnum, Trojan Pleasure, Trojan Enz	Market leader in the US market, minor position in the UK	8
Okamoto Industries	Japan	Beyond Seven, Skinless Skin	Home market-oriented: 60 per cent MS of the Japanese market, but with little exports, mainly to US	10
Others: Sagami Rubber Industries (JP), Fuji Latex Co (JP), DKT Indonesia (Indonesia), Mayer Laboratories (JP) and about 70 other manufacturers around the world			Domestic- and regional-oriented companies with strong positions in local markets	45
Total				100

MS, market share.
Source: estimations based on different public sources.

Key competitors (manufacturers) in the world male condom market

SSL International

In 1929, the London Rubber Company (LRC) registered the Durex condom trademark, whose name was derived from **du**rability, **r**eliability and **ex**cellence. The next important steps as a global condom provider came, first, in 1951 with the introduction of the first fully automated production process, and two years later with the development of the first electronic testing machines.

In the UK home market during the 1980s, Durex condoms began to be sold in public areas (e.g. supermarkets, pubs), due to the AIDS fear. That decade showed a sharp development in marketing with the first Durex poster campaign in 1982, as well as the first condom advertising on television (1987).

In the 1990s, Durex followed a marketing policy aimed at increasing the awareness of the brand with the installation of free-standing outdoor Durex vending machines (1992); the sponsorship of MTV events (1995); the first Durex Sex Survey (1995); the launch of the first selection of coloured, flavoured and ribbed condoms in the same pack (1996); and the launch (1997) of the first non-latex protection, called Avanti.

At the beginning of the twenty-first century, Durex launched www.Durex.com over 30 countries. These websites, featuring localized pages, in particular the use of local language, provide sexual information, allow people to question specialists, give details of Durex condoms and any sponsored events.

Durex is nowadays part of SSL International plc, which was formed in 1999 from the merger of the Seton-Scholl Group and London International, the former owner of the LRC. It is a worldwide company producing a range of branded products such as Scholl and Marigold gloves, sold to medical and consumer health care markets.

With a market share of approximately 24 per cent, Durex's position can be defined as the world market leader of the sector. Obviously, at different national levels, rankings can be slightly different, with, for example, 80 per cent of market share in the UK, 55 per cent in Italy, 10–15 per cent in the US and around 5 per cent in Japan.

Durex condoms are manufactured in 15 factories worldwide.

Church & Dwight Company Inc

Armkel, LLC, Church & Dwight's 50/50 joint venture with the private equity group, Kelso & Company, acquired the remainder of the Carter-Wallace consumer products businesses in 2001, including Trojan Condoms.

The Trojan brand accounts for the largest proportion of condom supplies in the US, with around 60–70 per cent market share.

The company markets condoms under the Trojan brand name in Canada, Mexico and recently, in limited distribution, in the UK. In Canada, the Trojan brand has a leading market share. It entered the UK condom market in 2003, but at present has only a small share. The company markets its condoms through distribution channels similar to those of its domestic condom business.

Okamoto

Okamoto has been in existence since 1934. It holds a remarkable 60 per cent market share in Japan, where condoms are the preferred method of birth control.

In late 1988, Okamoto introduced its condoms into the US market, but without great success until recently.

Recent developments – possible acquisition of a European key condom player

Following financial problems in 2014 at some European condom manufacturers with relatively strong local brands, Ansell is now considering acquiring one of these manufacturers.

QUESTIONS

1. What are the differences between the global strategies of Ansell and the other three competitors?

2. Which entry mode would you recommend for Ansell's sourcing (purchasing or production) of condoms?

3. What are the pros and cons for Ansell acquiring a European competitor? In your opinion, is it a good idea?

Source: based on general public media, e.g. www.ansell.com; www.durex.com.

VIDEO CASE STUDY 9.3 Understanding entry modes into the Chinese market
download from **www.pearson.co.uk/hollensen**

China became a member of the WTO on 11 December 2001 and, overall, the Chinese economy has shown exceptional economic growth over the last decade, closely associated with China's increased integration with the global economy. With a population exceeding 1.3 billion, continued economic growth and a large supply of inexpensive and productive labour, China lures businesses from around the world. Most global firms agree that companies cannot be globally successful if they ignore this huge emerging market.

Questions

1. What factors should companies consider when determining the best form of operation to use when entering the Chinese market?

2. What can be the challenges and opportunities for foreign companies in establishing collaborative arrangements, like joint ventures, in China?

3. What are the advantages for Swedish SolTech Energy to go into a joint venture with Chinese Advanced Solar Power, when starting sales in China, as featured in the video?

For further resources, see this book's website at **www.pearsoned.co.uk/hollensen**

Questions for discussion

1. Why is choosing the most appropriate market entry and development strategy one of the most difficult decisions for the international marketer?

2. Do you agree with the view that LSEs use a rational analytical approach (strategy rule) to the entry mode decision, while SMEs use a more pragmatic/opportunistic approach?

3. Use Figure 9.1 to identify the most important factors affecting the choice of foreign entry mode. Prioritize the factors.

References

Blomstermo, A., Sharma, D.D. and Sallis, J. (2006) 'Choice of foreign market entry mode in service firms', *International Marketing Review*, 23(2), pp. 211–229.

Dow, D. and Larimo, J. (2009) 'Challenging the conceptualization and measurement of distance and international experience in entry mode choice research', *Journal of International Marketing*, 17(2), pp. 74–98.

Heide, J.B. and John, G. (1988) 'The role of dependence balancing in safeguarding transaction-specific assets in conventional channels', *Journal of Marketing*, 52(January), pp. 20–35.

Hennart, J-F and Slangen, A.H.L. (2015) 'Yes, we really do need more entry mode studies! A commentary on Shaver', *Journal of International Business Studies*, 46(1), pp. 114–122.

Johanson, J. and Vahlne, J.E. (1977) 'The internationalization process of the firm – a model of knowledge', *Journal of International Business Studies*, 8(1), pp. 23–32.

Lu, Y., Karpova, E.E. and Fiore, A.M. (2011) 'Factors influencing international fashion retailer's entry mode choice', *Journal of Fashion Marketing and Management*, 15(1), pp. 58–75.

Root, F.R. (1994) *Entry Strategies for International Markets*, revised and expanded edition. The New Lexington Press, Lexington, MA.

Shaver, J. M. (2013) 'Do we really need more entry mode studies?', *Journal of International Business Studies*, 44(1), pp. 23–27.

Swoboda, B., Elsner, S. and Olejnik, E. (2015) 'How do past mode choices influence subsequent entry? A study on the boundary conditions of preferred entry modes of retail firms', *International Business Review*, 24(3), pp. 506–517.

CHAPTER 10
Export modes

Contents

Case studies

Learning objectives

After studying this chapter you should be able to:

- Distinguish between indirect, direct and cooperative export modes
- Describe and understand the five main entry modes of indirect exporting:
  - export buying agent
  - broker
  - export management company/export house
  - trading company
  - piggyback
- Describe the two main entry modes of direct exporting:
  - distributor
  - agent
- Discuss the advantages and disadvantages of the main export modes
- Discuss how manufacturers can influence intermediaries to be effective marketing partners.

10.1   Introduction

With export entry modes a firm's products are manufactured in the domestic market or a third country and then transferred either directly or indirectly to the host market. Export is the most common mode for initial entry into international markets. Sometimes an unsolicited order is received from a buyer in a foreign country, or a domestic customer expands internationally and places an order for its international operations. This prompts the firm to consider international markets and to investigate their growth potential.

Exporting is thus typically used in initial entry and gradually evolves towards foreign-based operations. In some cases where there are substantial scale economies or a limited number of buyers in the market worldwide (e.g. for aerospace), production may be concentrated in a single or a limited number of locations, and the goods then exported to other markets.

Exporting can be organized in a variety of ways, depending on the number and type of intermediaries. As in the case of wholesaling, export and import agents vary considerably in the range of functions performed. Some, such as export management companies, are the equivalent of full-service wholesalers and perform all functions relating to export. Others are highly specialized and handle only freight forwarding, billing or clearing goods through customs.

In establishing export channels, a firm has to decide which functions will be the responsibility of external agents and which will be handled by the firm itself. While export channels may take many different forms, for the purposes of simplicity, three major types may be identified:

1. *Indirect export.* This is when the manufacturing firm does not take direct care of exporting activities. Instead, another domestic company, such as an export house or trading company, performs these activities, often without the manufacturing firm's involvement in the foreign sales of its products.
2. *Direct export.* This usually occurs when the producing firm takes care of exporting activities and is in direct contact with the first intermediary in the foreign target market. The firm is typically involved in handling documentation, physical delivery and pricing policies, with the product being sold to agents and distributors.
3. *Cooperative export.* This involves collaborative agreements with other firms (export marketing groups) concerning the performance of exporting functions.

In Figure 10.1 the different export modes are illustrated in a value chain perspective.

Partner mindshare

Partner mindshare
The level of mindshare that the manufacturer's product occupies in the mind of the export partner (e.g. agent or distributor).

No matter which of the three export modes the manufacturer uses in a market, it is important to think about what level of 'mindshare' the manufacturer occupies in the mind of the export partner. **Partner mindshare** is a measurement of the strength of a relationship in terms of trust, commitment and cooperation. There is a strong and proven correlation between mindshare levels and how willing an export intermediary is to place one company brand in front of another, or how likely the intermediary is to defect. Mindshare also expresses itself very clearly in sales performance. Intermediaries who have high mindshare will typically sell more than those with low mindshare.

Mindshare can be broken down into three drivers (Gibbs, 2005):

● commitment and trust
● collaboration
● mutuality of interest and common purpose.

Good mindshare is going to depend upon scoring well across the board. For example, there are manufacturers who are good communicators but are not trusted.

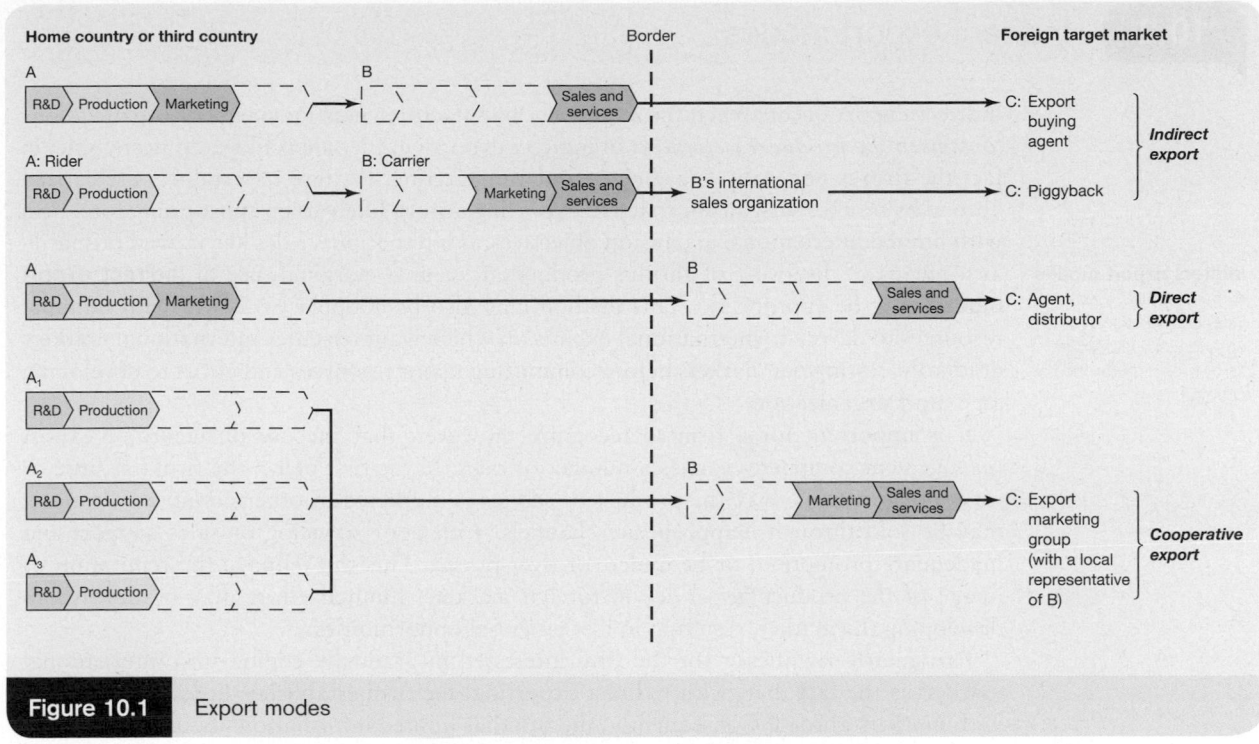

Figure 10.1   Export modes

Note: A, A₁, A₂ and A₃ are manufacturers of products/services; B is an independent intermediary (agent); C is the customer.

As well as these three mindshare drivers, there is a fourth group we need to measure – product, brand and profit. This group measures the perceived attractiveness of the supplier's product offering to the intermediary. The manufacturer can think of this as a hygiene driver. Broadly speaking, the performance of the manufacturer needs to be as good as the competition in order to garner the full benefit from strong mindshare.

Many manufacturers with excellent products and strong brands that offer good profits struggle precisely because they are seen by the export partner as arrogant, untrustworthy and unhelpful. In other words, they have low mindshare with the export partner.

Each of the three drivers can be broken down further. For instance, collaboration is based partly on a measure of how good the manufacturer is at cooperating on sales. Another constituent of collaboration measures its ability to cooperate on marketing. Other constituents measure whether it is perceived as communicating relevant information in a timely way, how much real joint planning takes place and how valuable the export intermediary finds this process.

Mindshare is severely damaged when suppliers refuse to share resources with partners. Partners may feel excluded – not part of the family. If the intermediary has no long-term stake in the manufacturer, and has more mindshare with a competitor, they could choose to simply wind down activities with that intermediary. Alternatively, the manufacturer can fight back by integrating its products and campaigns into the intermediary's business plan and going out of its way to show commitment to the intermediaries. At the multinational US computer technology corporation Oracle, they are doing this by saying: 'Our approach is to give marketing materials to our partners. Give them the things they would get if they were internal employees' (Hotopf, 2005).

Manufacturers need to understand the partners' business models, goals, their value to the manufacturer and what it would cost to replace them. However, the manufacturer also needs to look at the long-term value of the relationship (lifetime value = year-on-year value × the number of years that the manufacturer typically does business with export intermediaries). This can be used to justify investments in the relationship.

10.2   Indirect export modes

Indirect export modes
A manufacturer uses independent export organizations located in its own country (or third country).

Indirect export occurs when the exporting manufacturer uses independent organizations *located in the producer's country*. In indirect exporting, the sale is like a domestic sale; in fact the firm is not really engaging in global marketing, because its products are carried abroad by others. Such an approach to exporting is most likely to be appropriate for a firm with limited international expansion objectives. If international sales are viewed primarily as a means of disposing of surplus production, or as a marginal, use of **indirect export modes** may be appropriate. This method may also be adopted by a firm with minimal resources to devote to international expansion which wants to enter international markets gradually, testing out markets before committing major resources and effort to developing an export organization.

It is important for a firm to recognize, however, that the use of agents or export management companies carries a number of risks. In the first place, the firm has little or no control over the way the product or service is marketed in other countries. Products may be sold through inappropriate channels, with poor servicing or sales support and inadequate promotion, or be under- or over-priced. This can damage the reputation or image of the product or service in foreign markets. Limited effort may be devoted to developing the market, resulting in lost potential opportunities.

Particularly significant for the firm interested in gradually edging into international markets is the fact that, with indirect exporting, the firm establishes little or no contact with markets abroad. Consequently, the firm has limited information about foreign market potential, and obtains little input to develop a plan for international expansion. The firm will have no means to identify potential sales agents or distributors for its products.

While exporting has the advantage of the least cost and risk of any entry method, it allows the firm little control over how, when, where and by whom the products are sold. In some cases the domestic company may even be unaware that its products are being exported.

Moreover, a small and medium-sized enterprise (SME) that is already experienced in traditional exporting may have resources that are too limited to open up a great number of export markets by itself. Thus, through indirect export modes the SME is able to utilize the resources of other experienced exporters and to expand its business to many countries.

There are five main entry modes of indirect exporting:

1. export buying agent
2. broker
3. export management company/export house
4. trading company
5. piggyback (shown as a special case of indirect exporting in Figure 10.1).

Export buying agent (export commission house)

Some firms or individuals do not realize that their products or services have potential export value until they are approached by a buyer from a foreign organization, who might make the initial approach, purchase the product at the factory gate and take on the task of exporting, marketing and distributing the product in one or more overseas markets.

Export buying agent
A representative of foreign buyers who is located in the exporter's home country. The agent offers services to the foreign buyers, such as identifying potential sellers and negotiating prices.

The **export buying agent** is a representative of foreign buyers who resides in the exporter's home country. As such, this type of agent is essentially the overseas customer's hired purchasing agent in the exporter's domestic market, operating on the basis of orders received from these buyers. Since the export buying agent acts in the interests of the buyer, it is the buyer who pays a commission. The exporting manufacturer is not directly involved in determining the terms of purchase; these are worked out between the export buying agent and the overseas buyer.

The export commission house essentially becomes a domestic buyer. It scans the market for the particular merchandise it has been requested to buy and sends out specifications to manufacturers inviting bids. Other conditions being equal, the lowest bidder gets the order and there is no sentimentality, friendship or sales talk involved.

From the exporter's point of view, selling to export commission houses represents an easy way to export. Prompt payment is usually guaranteed in the exporter's home country, and the problems of physical movement of the goods are generally taken completely out of its hands. There is very little credit risk and the exporter has only to fulfil the order according to specifications. A major problem is that the exporter has little direct control over the global marketing of products.

Small firms find that this is the easiest method of obtaining foreign sales but, being totally dependent on the purchaser, they are unlikely to be aware of a change in consumer behaviour and competitor activity, or of the purchasing firm's intention to terminate the arrangement. If a company is intent upon seeking longer-term viability for its export business, it must adopt a more proactive approach, which will inevitably involve obtaining a greater understanding of the markets in which its products are sold.

Broker

Another type of agent based in the home country is the export/import broker. The chief function of a broker is to bring a buyer and a seller together. Thus the broker is a specialist in performing the contractual function, and does not actually handle the products sold or bought. For its services the broker is paid a commission (about 5 per cent) by the principal. The broker commonly specializes in particular products or classes of product. Being a commodity specialist there is a tendency for the broker to concentrate on just one or two products. Because the broker deals primarily in basic commodities, for many potential export marketers this type of agent does not represent a practical alternative channel of distribution. The distinguishing characteristic of export brokers is that they may act as the agent for either the seller or the buyer.

Export management company/export house

Export houses or export management companies (EMCs) are specialist companies set up to act as the 'export department' for a range of non-competing companies (Rosenbloom and Andras, 2008). As such, the EMC conducts business in the name of each manufacturer it represents. All correspondence with buyers and contracts are negotiated in the name of the manufacturer, and all quotations and orders are subject to confirmation by the manufacturer.

By carrying a large range, EMCs can spread their selling and administration costs over more products and companies, as well as reducing transport costs because of the economies involved in making large shipments of goods from a number of companies.

EMCs deal with the necessary documentation, and their knowledge of local purchasing practices and government regulations is particularly useful in markets that might prove difficult to penetrate. The use of EMCs, therefore, allows individual companies to gain far wider exposure of their products in foreign markets at much lower overall costs than they could achieve on their own, but there are a number of disadvantages, too:

● The export house may specialize by geographical area, product or customer type (retail, industrial or institutional), and this may not coincide with the supplier's objectives. So the selection of markets may be made on the basis of what is best for the EMC rather than for the manufacturer.

● As EMCs are paid by commission, they might be tempted to concentrate upon products with immediate sales potential, rather than those that might require greater customer education and sustained marketing effort to achieve success in the longer term.

- EMCs may be tempted to carry too many product ranges and, as a result, the manufacturer's products may not be given the necessary attention from salespeople.
- EMCs may carry competitive products that they may promote to the disadvantage of a particular firm.

Manufacturers should therefore take care in selecting a suitable EMC and be prepared to devote resources to managing the relationship and monitoring its performance.

As sales increase, the manufacturer may feel that it could benefit from increased involvement in international markets by exporting itself. However, the transition may not be very easy. First, the firm is likely to have become very dependent on the export house and, unless steps have been taken to build contacts with foreign customers and to build up the firm's knowledge of its markets, moving away from using an EMC could prove difficult. Second, the firm could find it difficult to withdraw from its contractual commitments to the export house. Third, the EMC may be able to substitute products from an alternative manufacturer and so use its existing customer contacts as a basis for competing against the original manufacturer.

Trading company

Trading companies are part of the historical legacy of colonial days and, although different in nature now, they are still important trading forces in Africa and the Far East. Although international trading companies have been active throughout the world, it is in Japan that the trading company concept has been applied most effectively. There are thousands of trading companies in Japan involved in exporting and importing, and the largest firms (varying in number from nine to 17 depending upon the source of the estimate) are referred to as general trading companies or *soge shosha*. This group of companies, which includes C. Itoh, Mitsui and Company and Mitsubishi Shoji Kaisha, handles 50 per cent of Japan's exports and 67 per cent of its imports. While the smaller trading companies usually limit their activities to foreign trade, the larger general trading companies are also heavily involved in domestic distribution and other activities.

Trading companies play a central role in such diverse areas as shipping, warehousing, finance, technology transfer, planning resource development, construction and regional development (e.g. turnkey projects), insurance, consulting, real estate and deal-making in general (including facilitating investment and joint ventures). In fact, it is the range of financial services offered that is a major factor distinguishing general trading companies from others. These services include the guaranteeing of loans, the financing of both accounts receivable and payable, the issuing of promissory notes, major foreign exchange transactions, equity investment and even direct loans.

Another aspect of their operations is to manage counter-trade activities (barter), in which sales into one market are paid for by taking other products from that market in exchange. The essential role of the trading company is to find a buyer quickly for the products that have been taken in exchange. Sometimes this can be a very resource-demanding process.

Counter-trade is still a very widespread trading form in eastern Europe and developing countries because of their lack of 'hard' currency. One of the motivations for western firms to go into counter-trade is the low-cost sources of production and raw materials for use in the firm's own production (Okoroafo, 1994).

Piggyback

In piggybacking the export-inexperienced SME, the 'rider', deals with a larger company (the carrier) which already operates in certain foreign markets and is willing to act on behalf of the rider that wishes to export to those markets. This enables the carrier to fully utilize its established export facilities (sales subsidiaries) and foreign distribution. The carrier is either paid by commission and so acts as an agent or, alternatively, buys the product outright and so acts as an independent distributor. **Piggyback** marketing is typically used for products from unrelated companies that are non-competitive (but related) and complementary (allied).

Sometimes the carrier will insist that the rider's products are somewhat similar to its own, in view of the need to deal with technical queries and after-sales service 'in the field'. Branding and promotional policies are variable in piggybacking. In some instances, the carrier may buy the products, put its own brand on them and market them as its own products (private labels). More commonly the carrier retains the brand name of the producer and the two work out promotional arrangements between them. The choice of branding and promotional strategy is a function of the importance of brand to the product and of the degree to which the brand is well established.

Piggybacking has the following advantages/disadvantages for the carrier and the rider.

Piggyback
An abbreviation of 'pick-a-back', i.e. choosing a back to ride on. It is about the rider's use of the carrier's international distribution organization.

Carrier

Advantages

A firm that has a gap in its product line or excess capacity in its export operation has two options. One is to develop internally the products necessary to round out its line and fill up its exporting capacity. The other is to acquire the necessary products outside by piggybacking (or acquisition). Piggybacking may be attractive because the firm can get the product quickly (someone already has it). It is also a low-cost way to get the product because the carrier firm does not have to invest in R&D, production facilities or market testing for the new product. It can just pick up the product from another firm. In this way the firm can broaden its product range without having to develop and manufacture extra products.

Disadvantages

Piggybacking can be extremely attractive for the carrier, but some concerns exist about quality control and warranty. Will the rider maintain the quality of the products sold by another firm? This depends in part on whose brand name is on the product. If the rider's name is on the product, the quality incentive might be stronger. A second concern is continuity of supply. If the carrier develops a substantial market abroad, will the rider firm develop its production capacity, if necessary? Each of these items should be a subject in the agreement between the two parties. If the piggybacking arrangement works out well, there is another potential advantage for the carrier. It might find that the rider is a good acquisition candidate or joint-venture partner for a stronger relationship.

Rider

Advantages

Riders can export conveniently without having to establish their own distribution systems. They can observe carefully how the carrier handles the goods and hence learn from the carrier's experience – perhaps to the point of eventually being able to take over its own export transactions.

Disadvantages

For the smaller company, this type of agreement means giving up control over the marketing of its products – something that many firms dislike doing, at least in the long run. Lack of commitment on the part of the carrier and the loss of lucrative sales opportunities in regions not covered by the carrier are further disadvantages.

In summary, piggyback marketing provides an easy, low-risk way for a company to begin export marketing operations. It is especially well suited to manufacturers that are either too small to go directly into exports or that do not want to invest heavily in foreign marketing.

10.3 Direct export modes

Direct exporting occurs when a manufacturer or exporter sells directly to an importer or buyer located in a foreign market area. In our discussion of indirect exporting we examined ways of reaching foreign markets without working very hard. Indeed, in the indirect approaches, foreign sales are handled in the same way as domestic sales: the producer does the global marketing only by proxy (i.e. through the firm that carries its products overseas). However, both the global marketing know-how and the sales achieved by these indirect approaches are limited.

Direct export modes

The manufacturer sells directly to an importer, agent or distributor located in the foreign target market.

As exporters grow more confident, they may decide to undertake their own exporting task. This will involve building up overseas contacts, undertaking marketing research, handling documentation and transportation, and designing marketing mix strategies. **Direct export modes** include export through foreign-based agents and distributors (independent intermediaries).

The terms 'distributor' and 'agent' are often used synonymously. This is unfortunate because there are distinct differences: distributors, unlike agents, take title to the goods, finance the inventories and bear the risk of their operations, whereas agents do not. Distributors are paid according to the difference between the buying and selling prices rather than by commission (agents). Distributors are often appointed when after-sales service is required, as they are more likely than agents to possess the necessary resources.

Distributors

Distributors (importers)

Independent companies that stock the manufacturer's product. They will have substantial freedom to choose their own customers and price. They profit from the difference between their selling price and the buying price from the manufacturer.

Exporting firms may work through **distributors (importers)**, which are the exclusive representatives of the company and are generally the sole importers of the company's product in their markets. As independent merchants, distributors buy on their own accounts and have substantial freedom to choose their own customers and set the conditions of sale. For each country, exporters deal with one distributor, take one credit risk and ship to one destination. In many cases, distributors own and operate wholesale and retail establishments, warehouses and repair and service facilities. Once distributors have negotiated with their exporters on price, service, distribution and so on, their efforts focus on working their own sub-operations and dealers.

The distributor category is broad and includes more variations, but distributors usually seek exclusive rights for a specific sales territory and generally represent the manufacturer in all aspects of sales and servicing in that area. The exclusivity is in return for the substantial capital investment that may be required on the part of the distributor in handling and selling products.

Agents

Agent

An independent company that sells on to customers on behalf of the manufacturer (exporter). Usually it will not see or stock the product. It profits from a commission (typically 5–10 per cent) paid by the manufacturer on a pre-agreed basis.

Agents may be exclusive, where the agent has exclusive rights to specified sales territories; semi-exclusive, where the agent handles the exporter's goods along with other non-competing goods from other companies; or non-exclusive, where the agent handles a variety of goods, including some that may compete with the exporter's products.

An agent represents an exporting company and sells to wholesalers and retailers in the importing country. The exporter ships the merchandise directly to the customers, and all arrangements on financing, credit, promotion, etc. are made between the exporter and the buyers. Exclusive agents are widely used for entering international markets. They cover rare geographic areas and have sub-agents assisting them. Agents and sub-agents share commissions (paid by the exporter) on a pre-agreed basis. Some agents furnish financial and market information, and a few also guarantee the payment of customers' accounts. The commissions that agents receive vary substantially, depending upon services performed, the market's size and importance and competition among exporters and agents.

The advantages of both agents and distributors are that they are familiar with the local market, customs and conventions, have existing business contacts and employ foreign nationals. They have a direct incentive to sell through either commission or profit margin but, since their remuneration is tied to sales, they may be reluctant to devote much time and effort to developing a market for a new product. Also, the amount of market feedback may be limited as the agent or distributor may see itself as a purchasing agent for its customers rather than as a selling agent for the exporter. If the agent or distributor is performing well and develops the market, it risks being replaced by a subsidiary of the principal. Therefore a long-term strategy is needed whereby it might be useful to include the agent in any new entry-mode decision (e.g. advent of a subsidiary) to avoid the disincentive of being replaced.

Choice of an intermediary

The selection of a suitable intermediary can be a problematic process, but the following sources may help a firm to find such an intermediary:

- asking potential customers to suggest a suitable agent;
- obtaining recommendations from institutions such as trade associations, chambers of commerce and government trade departments;
- using commercial agencies;
- poaching a competitor's agent;
- advertising in suitable trade papers.

In selecting a particular intermediary, the exporter needs to examine each candidate firm's knowledge of the product and local markets, experience and expertise, required margins, credit ratings, customer care facilities and ability to promote the exporter's products in an effective and attractive manner.

Figure 10.2 shows the matchmaking of a manufacturer and its 'wish'-profile, and two potential intermediaries and their performance profiles in a particular market.

As seen in the figure, one of the important evaluation criteria is that the intermediary's product programme should not includely competitive products. If this is not the case the exporter will experience a situation of internal competition with the intermediary's other products (Obadia and Stöttinger, 2015).

If partners 1 and 2 were the only potential candidates for the manufacturer, partner 2 would probably be chosen because of the better match of profiles between what the manufacturer wants on the market (wish profile) and the performance profile of partner 2.

The criteria listed in Figure 10.2 would probably not be the only criteria in a selection process. Some other specific desirable characteristics of an intermediary (to be included in the decision-making process) are as follows (Root, 1998):

- size of firm
- physical facilities
- willingness to carry inventories
- knowledge/use of promotion
- reputation with suppliers, customers and banks
- record of sales performance
- cost of operations
- overall experience
- knowledge of English or other relevant languages
- knowledge of business methods in manufacturer's country.

	Manufacturer's seeking criteria ('wish' profile)			Manufacturer's evaluation of the competences of the two partners			

Manufacturer's seeking criteria ('wish' profile)

- partner's activity/industry
- partner's type of customer

Manufacturer would expect similarities in activities and types of customers

Manufacturer's evaluation of the competences of the two partners

	Very strong	Very weak		Partner 1		Partner 2	
			Very strong	Very weak	Very strong	Very weak	

The partner is financially well consolidated

The partner covers the whole geographic area, e.g. the country

The partner's organization has a high level of marketing/selling expertise in the particular industry

The partner's staff have a high level of technical know-how

The partner's staff offer a high level of service support to the manufacturer's product

The partner's staff have excellent relations with industry

The partner should not have direct competitive products in the product programme

Figure 10.2 An example of matchmaking between a manufacturer and two potential distribution partners

EXHIBIT 10.1 Lofthouse of Fleetwood's (Fisherman's Friend) decision criteria when selecting new distributors

Lofthouse of Fleetwood Ltd (www.fishermansfriend.com), a family-owned company, first created Fisherman's Friend Original Extra Strong Lozenges in 1865 in Fleetwood, Lancashire. Fleetwood was one of the UK's great fishing ports and Fisherman's Friend was originally produced to help the fishermen combat the coughs, colds and bronchial problems that plagued them on their long voyages into the inhospitable waters and freezing conditions of the North Atlantic fishing grounds. Fisherman's Friend produces 13 flavours of lozenges for the global market, seven of which are available in the UK (sugar-free blackcurrant,

Source: Fisherman's Friend is a registered trademark of Lofthouse of Fleetwood Ltd.

original extra strong, aniseed, cherry, sugar-free mint, sugar-free original and sugar-free lemon). The core proposition of Fisherman's Friend as a unique, strong-tasting medicinal sweet that comes wrapped in a paper bag remains constant globally. Fisherman's Friend Original Extra Strong Lozenges are still manufactured to exactly the same formulation as in 1865, but other elements of the marketing mix vary from country to country.

It was not until 1974 that Fisherman's Friend was first exported to Norway, which remains the highest per-capita consuming market in the world today. By 2009, the lozenges were available in 120 countries worldwide and Fisherman's Friend had grown to become a major international brand. The European market accounted for 80 per cent of sales with the UK accounting for 4 per cent of total production. Germany was the largest market, followed by Asia with around 15 per cent, then North America and other regions taking up the rest. Fisherman's Friend has seen the most growth in Russia, China and India because their brand has a global taste. Generally the taste of Fisherman's Friend has been accepted worldwide, except in Japan – the Japanese find it too strong, preferring very sweet things such as Turkish delight.

Lofthouse of Fleetwood contracts (outsources) its marketing activities to an independent company, Impex Management, so that it can focus on R&D and manufacturing (Figure 10.3). In new international markets, Impex Management selects and interviews up to six candidate distributors, undertaking detailed SWOT (strengths, weaknesses, opportunities, threats) analysis on their potential. After the interviews, Impex and Lofthouse meet to choose the ideal partner for a particular market.

Among the criteria for selecting a distributor, Lofthouse and Impex have agreed on using the following:

- *Size.* Lofthouse wants a distributor to be small enough for Fisherman's Friend to have an important role and an adequate share of the distributor's total turnover and attention. Lofthouse prefers to be a big fish

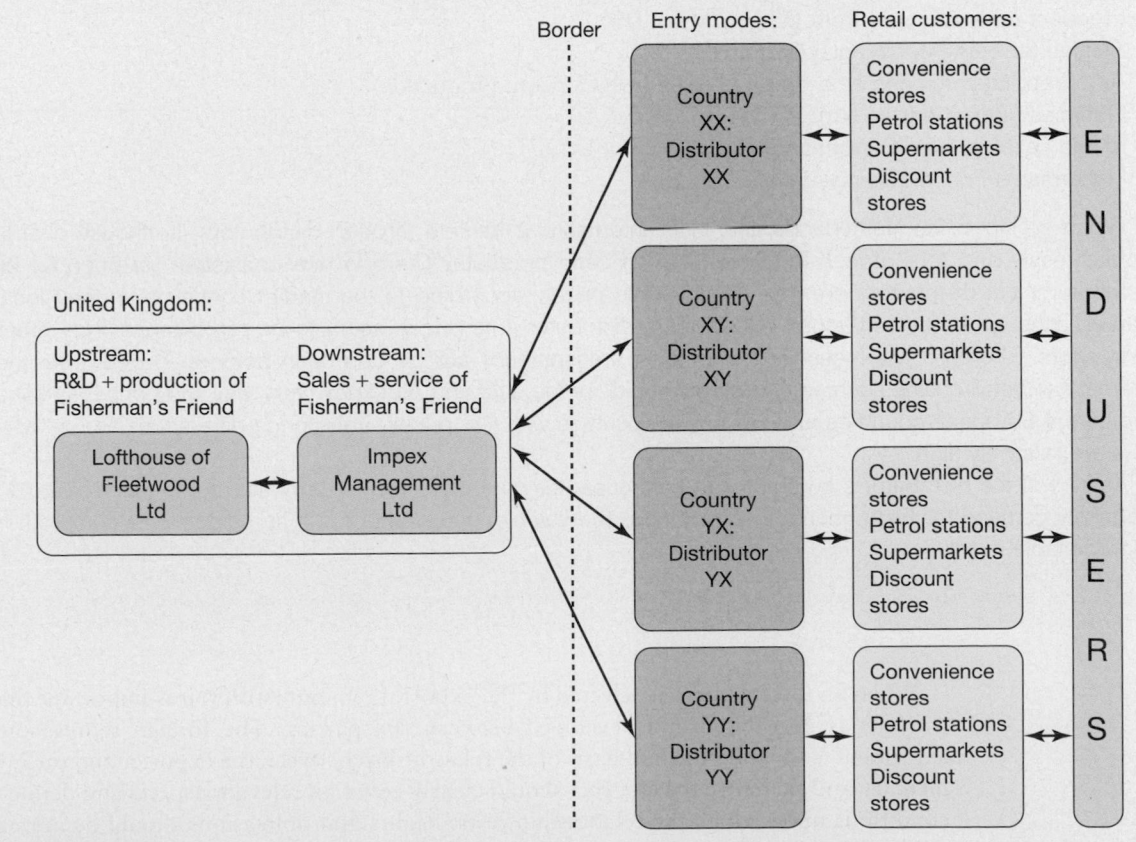

Figure 10.3   International distribution system of Fisherman's Friend

in a smaller pond. This needs to be balanced against the need to have a distributor big enough to have the right contacts to the retailers.

● *Products.* A distributor should be selling complementary product lines and have experience and suitable contacts in relevant product markets. But they should not be handling direct competitors' products – Lofthouse wants exclusivity.
● *Organizational structure for sales.* The number of sales representatives and their coverage of the market (Which geographical regions and types of retail channels are covered? How often?).
● *Financial status.* Lofthouse wants the distributor to be financially stable and secure.
● *Culture and values.* Lofthouse is looking for long-term relationships. Therefore it is important that the distributor has a similar culture and values to those of Lofthouse.
● *Family business.* As Lofthouse is a family-owned business, they are looking primarily for distributors that are also family businesses.

One distributor that has had a long-term and successful relationship with Lofthouse and Fisherman's Friend is its Dutch distributor, Concorp Brands (earlier Nedean Zoetwaren BV). Its profile fits most of the criteria above. The company distributes confectionery in the Dutch market. Fisherman's Friend was taken into the portfolio in 1974. The company employs approximately 40 people, of whom half are involved on a day-to-day basis in sales for the Dutch market. The sales force is divided in two:

1. *impulse outlets*: convenience stores, petrol stations and tobacconists;
2. *grocery channels*: supermarkets, discount stores, etc.

Around 40 per cent of Fisherman's Friends are sold through impulse outlets, the rest (60 per cent) through grocery channels.

Currently (November 2009) Concorp Brands acts as a distributor in the Netherlands representing the following brands:

● Freedent (chewing gum from Wrigley/Mars, US)
● Skittles (sweets from Wrigley/Mars, US)
● Autodrop (liquorice and acid drops from its own Concorp production)
● Oldtimes (liquorice from NL)
● Ricola (lozenge from Switzerland)
● Fisherman's Friend (lozenge from England).

When selling in the Netherlands and other international markets through distributors, Lofthouse cannot dictate resale and retail prices for Fisherman's Friend products. There is one consistent list price for all distributors, but distributors are free to set resale prices, according to the market conditions in their local market, although Lofthouse/Impex will advise a distributor if its prices seem to be too different from other distributors. The euro has meant a greater price transparency across European borders. Buyers from the international retail chains such as Carrefour, Ahold, Tesco, Lidl and Aldi know very well what prices are like in different European countries and will buy in countries with low prices, if the price differences across borders are relatively high.

As part of the distributor's contract with Lofthouse, they are expected to carry about one month's stock. Generally demand for Fisherman's Friend is fairly predictable, unless there is a flu epidemic or some other unpredictable event.

Sources: www.fishermansfriend.com; Brassington and Pettitt (2006); http://www.lz-blog.de/spotlight/2009/08/27/talk-with-fishermans-friend/.

When an intermediary is selected by the exporting manufacturer, it is important that a contract is negotiated and developed between the parties. The foreign representative agreement is the fundamental basis of the relationship between the exporter and the intermediary and therefore the contract should clearly cover all relevant aspects and define the conditions upon which the relationship rests. Rights and obligations should be mutually defined and the spirit of the agreement must be one of mutual interest. The agreement should cover the provisions listed in Table 10.1.

Table 10.1	Contracts with intermediaries

1. General provisions

Identification of parties to the contract	Definition of territory or territories
Duration of the contract	Sole and exclusive rightsa
Definition of covered goods	Arbitration of disputes

2. Rights and obligations of manufacturer

Conditions of termination	Inspection of distributor's books
Protection of sole and exclusive rights	Trademarks/patents
Sales and technical support	Information to be supplied to the distributor
Tax liabilities	Advertising/promotion
Conditions of sale	Responsibility for claims/warranties
Delivery of goods	Inventory requirements
Prices	Termination and cancellation[a]
Order refusal	

3. Rights and obligations of distributor

Safeguarding manufacturer's interests	Customs clearance
Payment arrangements	Observance of conditions of sale
Contract assignment	After-sales service
Competitive linesa	Information to be supplied to the manufacturer

[a] Most important and contentious issues.

Source: Root, F.R. (1998) *Entry Strategies for International Markets: Second Revised and Expanded Edition*, pp. 68–9. Copyright © Jossey-Bass 1998. Reprinted with permission of John Wiley & Sons, Inc.

For most exporters, the three most important aspects of their agreement with foreign representatives are sole or exclusive rights, competitive lines and termination of the agreement. The issue of agreeing territories is becoming increasingly important, as in many markets distributors are becoming fewer in number, larger in size and sometimes more specialized in their activity. The trend to regionalization is leading distributors increasingly to extend their territories through organic growth, mergers and acquisitions, making it more difficult for firms to appoint different distributors in individual neighbouring markets.

In general, there are some principles that apply to the law of agency in all nations:

- An agent cannot take delivery of the principal's goods at an agreed price and resell them for a higher amount without the principal's knowledge and permission.
- Agents must maintain strict confidentiality regarding their principal's affairs and must pass on all relevant information.
- The principal is liable for damages to third parties for wrongs committed by an agent 'in the course of his or her authority' (e.g. if the agent fraudulently misrepresents the principal's firm).

During the contract period the support and motivation of intermediaries are very important. Usually this means financial rewards for volume sold (offering superior margins to the intermediary stands out as the most effective incentive, according to Obadia and Stöttinger, 2015), but there can also be other means for increasing the sales incentives to the intermediary:

- significant local advertising and brand awareness development by the supplying firm (the exporter);
- participation (by the exporter) in local exhibitions and trade fairs, perhaps in cooperation with the local intermediary;
- regular field visits and telephone calls to the intermediary (agent or distributor);
- regular meetings of agents and distributors arranged and paid for by the supplying company (the exporter) in the latter's country;

- competitions with cash prizes, free holidays and the like for intermediaries with the highest sales;
- provision of technical training to intermediaries;
- suggestion schemes to gather feedback from agents and distributors;
- circulation of briefings (by accessing the exporter's intranet) regarding the supplying firm's current activities, changes in personnel, new product developments (NPS) and marketing plans, etc.

Measures such as these may encourage the intermediary to feel like part of the exporter's 'family'.

Evaluating international distribution partners

Even if the firm has been very careful in selecting intermediaries, a need can arise to extricate oneself quickly from a relationship that appears to be going nowhere.

In the process of evaluating international distribution partners, the matrix in Figure 10.4 can be used. According to the figure the two most important criteria for evaluating international distributor partners are:

1. the performance of the distributor partner;
2. the general attractiveness of the market where the partner operates.

Performance can be evaluated by using criteria such as achieved turnover and market share, profits generated for the manufacturer, and established network to potential customers. The country (market) attractiveness can be evaluated by using criteria such as those discussed in Chapter 8 (Table 8.2 and Figure 8.5), e.g. market size and market growth.

If the partner performance is low combined with a low attractiveness of the country (cell 1 in Figure 10.4), then the company should consider an exit from that country, especially if the low attractiveness seems to be a long-term phenomenon.

If the partner performance is high, but the country attractiveness is low (cell 3), then the company could consider a shift to another entry mode (e.g. a joint venture). In this way, the company can prevent dissatisfaction on the partner's side by rewarding it with a bigger part of the created profit pool in such a difficult market (low attractiveness).

If the partner is doing badly on a very attractive market (cell 7), the partner should be switched with another (and better) one.

If the market is very attractive and the partner is doing a good job (cell 9), the company could consider forward integration, by turning the existing entry mode (distributor) into

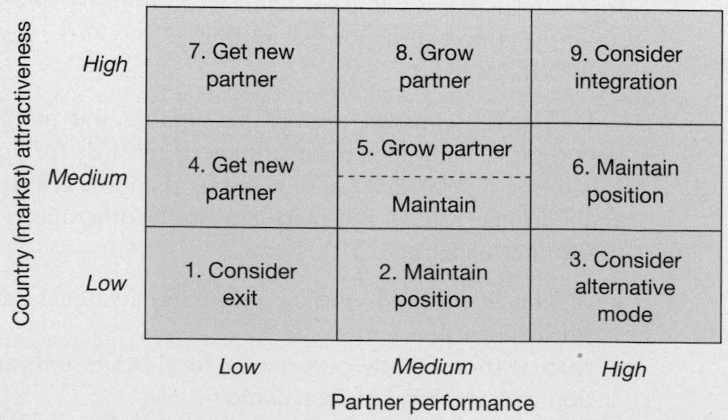

Figure 10.4 International partner matrix

a subsidiary and promoting the distributor to be the new CEO of the subsidiary, provided they have the necessary competences for such a position and have sufficient management talent.

The other cells in Figure 10.4 are mainly concerned with maintaining the current position or 'growing' the existing partner. This can be done by offering training in the company's product/service solutions at the HQ, or visiting the partner in the local market in order to show that you are committed to its selling efforts in that local market.

The intermediary may be a valuable future partner for the producer, and it may be in the interest of the principal to acquire an intermediary with whom it can have a good long-term working relationship.

Figure 10.4 is definitely seen from the producer's perspective. If we take the intermediary's perspective and if a replacement or buyout is contrary to the interest of the independent intermediary, the intermediary may actively work to prevent this by building switching costs, for example, keeping control of customer relations, building own brand, limiting the producer's access to market knowledge and letting the producer's products be a small part of the intermediary's total business (Heide and John, 1988 – see also Section 9.2). Therefore, control of the local resources (e.g. customer relations, brand and local technical competence) is always beneficial for the intermediary when the producer decides to replace the intermediary with a higher-control mode, like a sales subsidiary. This will give the intermediary a stronger bargaining position vis-à-vis the producer (Nes, 2014).

Termination of contracts with distribution partners

Cancellation clauses in distribution partner agreements usually involve rights under local legislation and it is best that a contract is scrutinized by a local lawyer before signature, rather than after a relationship has ended and a compensation case is being fought in the courts.

Termination laws differ from country to country, but the European Union situation has been largely reconciled by a directive regarding agents that has been effective in all EU member states since 1994. Under the directive, an agent whose agreement is terminated is entitled to:

● full payment for any deal resulting from its work (even if concluded after the end of the agreement);
● a lump sum of up to one year's past average commission;
● compensation (where appropriate) for damages to the agent's commercial reputation caused by unwarranted termination.

Outside western Europe some countries regard agents as basically employees of client organizations, while others see agents as self-contained and independent businesses. It is essential to ascertain the legal position of agency agreements in each country in which a firm is considering doing business. For example, laws in Saudi Arabia are extremely strong in terms of protecting agents.

10.4   Cooperative export modes/export marketing groups

Export marketing groups are frequently found among SMEs attempting to enter export markets for the first time. Many such firms do not achieve sufficient scale economies in manufacturing and marketing because of the size of the local market or the inadequacy of the management and marketing resources available. These characteristics are typical of traditional, mature, highly fragmented industries such as furniture and clothing. Frequently the same characteristics are to be found among small, recently established high-technology firms.

Figure 10.1 shows an export marketing group with manufacturers A_1, A_2 and A_3, each having separate upstream functions but cooperating on the downstream functions through a common, foreign-based agent.

One of the most important motives for SMEs to join with others is the opportunity of effectively marketing a complementary product programme to larger buyers. The following example is from the furniture industry.

Manufacturers A_1, A_2 and A_3 have their core competences in the upstream functions of the following complementary product lines:

A_1 Living room furniture
A_2 Dining room furniture
A_3 Bedroom furniture.

Together they form a broader product concept that could be more attractive to a buyer in a furniture retail chain, especially if the total product concept targets end customers with a certain lifestyle.

The cooperation between the manufacturers can be tight or loose. In a loose cooperation, the separate firms in a group sell their own brands through the same agent, whereas a tight cooperation often results in the creation of a new export association. Such an association can act as the exporting arm of all member companies, presenting a united front to world markets and gaining significant economies of scale. Its major functions are:

- exporting in the name of the association;
- consolidating freight, negotiating rates and chartering ships;
- performing market research;
- appointing selling agents abroad;
- obtaining credit information and collecting debts;
- setting prices for export;
- allowing uniform contracts and terms of sale;
- allowing cooperative bids and sales negotiation.

Firms in an association can research foreign markets more effectively together, and obtain better representation in them. By establishing one organization to replace several sellers they may realize more stable prices, and selling costs can be reduced. Through consolidating shipments and avoiding duplicated effort, firms realize transportation savings, and a group can achieve standardization of product grading and create a stronger brand name, just as the California fruit growers did with Sunkist products.

Considering all the advantages for an SME of joining an export marketing group, it is surprising that so few groups are actually running. One of the reasons for this could be that the firms have conflicting views as to what the group should do. In many SMEs there are strong feelings of independence inspired by their founders and entrepreneurs, which may be contrary, for example, to the common goal-setting of export marketing groups. One of the major tasks of the export group is to balance the interests of the different stakeholders in the group.

10.5   Summary

The advantages and disadvantages of the three main types of export mode are summarized in Table 10.2.

Table 10.2	Advantages and disadvantages of the different export modes for the manufacturer	
Export mode	**Advantages**	**Disadvantages**
Indirect exporting (e.g. export buying agent, broker or export management company)	Limited commitment and investment required. High degree of market diversification is possible as the firm utilizes the internationalization of an experienced exporter. Minimal risk (market and political). No export experience required	No control over marketing mix elements other than the product. An additional domestic member in the distribution chain may add costs, leaving smaller profit to the producer. Lack of contact with the market (no market knowledge acquired). Limited product experience (based on commercial selling)
Direct exporting (e.g. distributor or agent)	Access to local market experience and contacts with potential customers. Shorter distribution chain (compared with indirect exporting). Market knowledge acquired. More control over marketing mix (especially with agents). Local selling support and services available	Little control over market price because of tariffs and lack of distribution control (especially with distributors). Some investment in sales organization required (contact from home base with distributors or agents). Cultural differences, providing communication problems and information filtering (transaction costs occur). Possible trade restrictions
Export marketing groups	Shared costs and risks of internationalization. Provide a complete product line or system sales to the customer	Risk of unbalanced relationships (different objectives). Participating firms are reluctant to give up their complete independence

CASE STUDY 10.1

Lysholm Linie Aquavit: international marketing of the Norwegian Aquavit brand

Lysholm Linie Aquavit is marketed by the Norwegian spirits manufacturer Arcus Group (www.arcus.no). In 2010, it had approximately 1.6 billion Norwegian kroner (NOK) (€212 million) in sales, NOK 132 million in net profit and 450 employees. Around half of the Arcus sales are generated outside Norway.

Aquavit (which means 'water of life'), a slightly yellow or colourless alcoholic liquor, is produced in the Scandinavian countries by redistilling neutral spirits such as those made from grain or potatoes and flavouring them with caraway seeds. It is often consumed as an aperitif.

The alcohol content in the various aquavits varies somewhat, but starts at 37.5 per cent. Most brands contain about 40 per cent alcohol but Lysholm Linie Aquavit has an alcohol content of 41.5 per cent. (Lysholm is the name of the distillery in Trondheim

where the aquavit is made; hereafter we refer to the spirit as Linie Aquavit.)

The history of Aquavit

Aquavit was originally used for medicinal purposes, but from the 1700s stills became commonplace in Scandinavian homes.

The definition of aquavit becomes complicated when you try to distinguish it and other spirits popular in the northern climate. The term 'schnapps', for instance, is widely used in Germany, Switzerland and Scandinavia (the Danish say 'snaps') to mean any sort of neutral spirits, flavoured or otherwise. Then there's 'brannvin', a term used similarly in Sweden. (Like the Dutch word 'brandewijn' from which we derive the word 'brandy', it means burnt wine.) The famous Swedish vodka Absolut began life in 1879 as a product called 'Absolut Renat Brannvin', which might be translated as 'absolutely pure schnapps', said to have been distilled 10 times. However, the Swedish government's alcohol monopoly launched Absolut as an international brand in 1979, and labelled it vodka.

Making Linie Aquavit

Caraway is the most important herb in aquavit, but the mixture of herbs varies from brand to brand. Linie Aquavit is derived from Norwegian potato alcohol blended with spices and herbal infusions, and caraway and aniseed predominate. After the alcohol and the herbs have been mixed, the aquavit is poured into 500-litre oak barrels. Norwegian specialists travel to Spain for the express purpose of selecting the best barrels from those used in the production of Oloroso sherry. Sherry casks are used because they remove the raw, more volatile aspects of the liquor; the aquavit takes on a golden hue, and the residual sherry imparts a gentle sweetness.

Many theories have been put forward to explain how the man behind Linie Aquavit, Jørgen B. Lysholm, came up with the idea of sending aquavit around the world on sailboats in sherry casks in order to produce the special flavour. In the early 1800s, the family tried to export aquavit to the West Indies, but the ship, *Trondheim's Prøve,* returned with its cargo unsold. This is when they discovered the beneficial effects the long ocean voyage and the special storage had on the aquavit: the length of the journey, the constant gentle rocking of the boat and the variation in temperature on deck all helped give Linie Aquavit its characteristic taste. Lysholm subsequently commercialized his maturation method and this is still how things are done today.

Linie Aquavit has one of Norway's long-established shipping companies as its steady travel partner. The first Wilhelmsen liner carrying Linie Aquavit set sail in 1927. Since that time, Wilhelmsen has been the sole carrier of this distinguished product. The barrels are tightly secured in specially designed cribs before being loaded onto containers, which remain on deck during the entire journey. The journey from Norway to Australia and back again takes four-and-a-half months and crosses the equator (or the line, as sailors prefer to call it) twice. In fact, this is where Linie Aquavit gets its name. On the back of each bottle is the name of the ship and the date that it first crossed the equator.

International sales of Linie Aquavit and Vikingfjord vodka

Arcus AS is Norway's sole manufacturer of hard liquor and it is this company which produces Linie

Source: Arcus Gruppen AS (www.arcus.no).

Aquavit. The company also taps (i.e. bottles) wine from wine producers all over the world and imports a select range of bottled wines. With a market share of about 30 per cent, Arcus AS is the leading player in the Norwegian wine and spirits market.

The international aquavit markets (primarily Sweden, Norway, Denmark, Germany and the US) are dominated (except the last) by local aquavit brands. At present, Linie Aquavit is the market leader in Norway with a 20 per cent market share. In Denmark and Sweden the market share is 5 per cent. Germany is the most important export market and Linie Aqavit holds 10 per cent of the aquavit market in competition with brands like Malteserkreutz and Bommerlunde.

Arcus has established a subsidiary in Sweden, but elsewhere it only uses export modes (foreign-based intermediaries).

Until 2009, Linie Aquavit was distributed by the Berentzen Group in Germany. In April 2009, it transferred its German distribution to Racke Eggers & Franke (located in Bremen/Germany), which is a subsidiary of Racke GmbH Co. KG, Mainz. Racke offers a broad assortment of spirit brands, especially for retailers and the restaurant, hotel and catering industry, not only for Germany, but also for the rest of Europe. The current sales volume for Linie Aquavit in Germany is around 750,000 bottles a year. Their ambition is to push this figure up to one million bottles. With Racke as its distribution partner, Arcus hopes that Linie Aquavit can strengthen its market position in the southern part of Germany, and in the general on-trade segment (bars, restaurants and hotels), where Linie Aquavit has, until now, been relatively weak.

Linie Aquavit has long been the national spirit of Norway and one of the flagships in Arcus's portfolio. However, with more than 80 years' experience as a supplier and producer of spirits and wine, Arcus has a very diverse portfolio, including international premium brands such Vikingfjord Vodka. Despite the fact that the US market is usually described as the toughest vodka market in the world, Vikingfjord Vodka has become one of the eight largest imported vodka brands in the space of a few years, with a volume growth of approximately 30 per cent per year in the period 2008–2011.

QUESTIONS

1. What are the main advantages and disadvantages for Arcus of using export modes, compared with other entry modes, for its Linie Aquavit?
2. What should be Arcus's main criteria for selecting new distributors or cooperation partners for Linie Aquavit in new markets?
3. Would it be possible to pursue an international branding strategy for Linie Aquavit?
4. Which brand should be the major brand for the US market: Linie Aquavit or Vikingfjord Vodka?

Sources: www.arcus.no; Arcus Financial Report 2010.

CASE STUDY 10.2

Parle Products: an Indian biscuit manufacturer is seeking agents and cooperation partners in new export markets

A long time ago, when the British ruled India, a small factory was set up in the suburbs of Mumbai city to manufacture sweets and toffees. The year was 1929 and the market was dominated by famous international brands that were freely imported. Despite the odds and unequal competition, the company, called Parle Products (www.parleproducts.com), survived and succeeded by adhering to high quality and improvising from time to time.

Today, Parle enjoys a 40 per cent share of the total Indian biscuit market and a 15 per cent share of the total confectionery market in India. The Parle Biscuit brands, Parle G, Monaco and Krackjack, and confectionery brands, such as Melody, Poppins, Mangobite and Kismi, enjoy a strong image and appeal among consumers.

If you thought that a typical family-run Indian company could not top the worldwide charts, think again. The home-grown biscuit brand, Parle G, has proved doubters wrong by becoming the largest selling biscuit brand in the world. However, in most European markets Parle Products has to fight against one particular competitor, United Biscuits (producer of McVitie's). In all European markets the market share of Parle Products is very small.

United Biscuits (UB)

United Biscuits was founded in 1948 following the merger of two Scottish family businesses – McVitie & Price and McFarlane Lang. In 1960 UB added to its portfolio with the acquisition of Crawford's Biscuits and MacDonald's Biscuits.

In 2000 UB was bought by Finalrealm, a consortium of investors, and reverted to private limited company status.

Brand muscle

United Biscuits' brands rank number one or two in seven countries, they have five of the top 10 biscuit brands in the UK, France and Spain, and four out of the top 10 leading snack brands in the UK. More than 89 per cent of UK households bought McVitie's products in 2001. Anyone would agree that it has brand muscle.

Source: Parle Products Pvt. Ltd.

Consumer insight

United Biscuits' unique position as the largest UK snack food player, with a balanced portfolio of both sweet and savoury brands, gives it a unique understanding of how to respond effectively to changing consumer needs and wants.

Parle Products

Parle Products is the leader in the glucose and salty biscuit category but does not have a strong presence in the premium segment, with Hide-n-Seek being its only brand.

An extensive distribution network, built over years, is a major strength of Parle Products. Its biscuits and sweets are available to consumers even in the most remote places and in the smallest of villages in India, some with a population of just 500.

Parle has nearly 1,500 wholesalers, catering to 425,000 retail outlets directly or indirectly. A 200-strong dedicated field force services these wholesalers and retailers. Additionally, there are 31 depots and customs and freight agents supplying goods to the wide distribution network.

The Parle marketing philosophy emphasizes catering to the masses. The company constantly endeavours to design products that provide nutrition and fun for everyone, and most Parle offerings are in the low- and mid-range price segments based on understanding the Indian consumer psyche. This value-for-money positioning helps generate large sales volumes for the products.

The other global biscuit brands include Oreo from Nabisco and McVitie's from UB. According to market reports, Parle Products commands (with Parle G as the market leader) a 40 per cent market share in the RS 3,500 core biscuit market in India. In the confectionery segment, the company enjoys a mere 15 per cent market share and faces competition from Britannia's Tiger brand of biscuits, amongst others.

The company's flagship brand, Parle G, contributes more than 50 per cent to the company's total turnover. The other biscuits in the Parle Products' basket include Marie, Cheeslings, Jeffs, Sixer and Fun Centre.

QUESTIONS

1. Which region of the world would you recommend Parle Products to penetrate as its first choice?

2. What kind of export mode would be most relevant for Parle Products?

3. How could Parle Products conduct a systematic screening of potential distributors or agents in foreign markets?

4. What would be the most important issues for Parle Products to discuss with a potential distributor/agent before final preparation of a contract?

Sources: adapted from Jain and Zachariah (2002); http://www.bsstrategist.com/archives/2002/mar/.

VIDEO CASE STUDY 10.3 Honest Tea

download from **www.pearsoned.co.uk/hollensen**

Honest Tea (www.honesttea.com) is a beverage company based in Maryland, US, and was founded in 1998 to sell 'bottled iced tea that tastes like tea'. They are best known for their line of ready-to-drink bottled organic iced tea products and kid's juice drinks, as well as other organic beverages. Honest Tea has a strong focus on social responsibility and has become a role model of mission-driven business practices. The CEO believes a social mission is not only socially responsible but also financially sustainable because it enhances customer loyalty. The hope is that Honest Tea will become a well-known global brand and will have an impact around the world.

In March 2011, The Coca-Cola Company purchased Honest Tea after an initial 40 per cent investment in 2008, which helped expand the distribution of Honest beverages. Today, Honest Tea is run as an independent business unit under Coca-Cola.

Source: Honest Tea, Inc.

Questions

1. Discuss how its policies regarding social responsibility help Honest Tea in its exporting efforts.
2. What research method would you recommend for selecting the most suitable agent in a new export market?

For further resources, see this book's website at **www.pearsoned.co.uk/hollensen**

Questions for discussion

1. Why is exporting frequently considered the simplest way of entering foreign markets and thus favoured by SMEs?
2. What procedures should a firm follow in selecting a distributor?
3. Why is it difficult – financially and legally – to terminate a relationship with overseas intermediaries? What should be done to prevent or minimize such difficulties?
4. Identify the ways to reach foreign markets by making a domestic sale.
5. What is the difference between direct and indirect exporting?
6. Discuss the financial and pricing techniques for motivating foreign distributors.
7. Which marketing tasks should be handled by the exporter and which ones by its intermediaries in foreign markets?

8. How can the carrier and the rider both benefit from a piggyback arrangement?

9. When a firm begins direct exporting, what tasks must it perform?

10. Discuss the various ways of communicating with foreign distributors.

11. 'When exporting to a market, you're only as good as your intermediary there.' Discuss.

12. The international marketer and the intermediary will have different expectations concerning the relationship. Why should these expectations be spelled out and clarified in the contract?

References

Brassington, F. and Pettitt, S. (2006) *Principles of Marketing*. Pearson, Harlow.

Gibbs, R. (2005) 'How to measure and master mindshare', *The Routes to Market – Journal* (www.viaint.com), June, pp. 2–5.

Heide, J. B. and John, G. (1988) 'The role of dependence balancing in safeguarding transaction-specific assets in conventional channels', *Journal of Marketing,* 52(January), pp. 20–35.

Hotopf, M. (2005) 'Winning partner mindshare', *The Routes to Market – Journal* (www.viaint .com), February, pp. 13–16.

Jain, S. and Zachariah, R. (2002) 'Parle G largest-selling biscuit brand in world', *Business Standard* (Mumbai), 14 March.

Nes, E.B. (2014) 'Antecedents and consequences of replacing international independent intermediaries', *European Business Review,* 26(3), pp. 218–237.

Obadia, C. and Stöttinger, B. (2015) 'Pricing to manage export channel relationships', *International Business Review,* 24, pp. 311–318.

Okoroafo, S.C. (1994) 'Implementing international countertrade: a dyadic approach', *Industrial Marketing Management,* 23, pp. 229–234.

Root, F.R. (1998) *Entry Strategies for International Markets,* second revised and expanded edition. Jossey-Bass, San Francisco, CA.

Rosenbloom, B. and Andras, T.L. (2008) 'Wholesalers as global marketers', *Journal of Marketing Channels,* 15(4), pp. 235–252.

CHAPTER 11

Intermediate entry modes

Learning objectives

After studying this chapter you should be able to:

- Describe and understand the main intermediate entry modes:
  - contract manufacturing
  - licensing
  - franchising
  - joint venture/strategic alliances
- Discuss the advantages and disadvantages of the main intermediate entry modes

- Explain the different stages in joint-venture formation
- Explore the reasons for the 'divorce' of the two parents in a joint-venture constellation
- Explore different ways of managing a joint venture/strategic alliance.

11.1 Introduction

So far we have assumed that the firm entering foreign markets is supplying them from domestic or third country plants. This is implicit in any form of exporting. However, sometimes the firm may find it either impossible or undesirable to supply all foreign markets from domestic or third country production. Intermediate entry modes are distinguished from export modes because they are primarily vehicles for the transfer of knowledge and skills between partners, in order to create foreign sales. They are distinguished from the hierarchical entry modes in that there is no full ownership (by the parent firm) involved, but ownership and control can be shared between the parent firm and a local partner. This is the case with the (equity) joint venture.

Intermediate entry modes include a variety of arrangements, such as licensing, franchising, management contracts, turnkey contracts, joint ventures and technical know-how or co-production arrangements. In Figure 11.1 the most relevant intermediate modes are shown in the usual value chain perspective.

Generally speaking, contractual arrangements take place when firms possessing some sort of competitive advantage are unable to exploit this advantage because of resource constraints, for instance, but are able to transfer the advantage to another party. The arrangements often entail long-term relationships between partner firms and are typically designed to transfer intermediate goods, such as knowledge and/or skills, between firms in different countries.

11.2 Contract manufacturing

Several factors may encourage the firm to produce in foreign markets:

- Desirability of being close to foreign customers. Local production allows better interaction with local customer needs concerning product design, delivery and service.
- Foreign production costs (e.g. labour) are low.
- Transportation costs may render heavy or bulky products non-competitive.
- Tariffs or quotas can prevent entry of an exporter's products.
- In some countries there is government preference for national suppliers.

Contract manufacturing
Manufacturing is outsourced to an external partner, specialized in production and production technology.

Contract manufacturing enables the firm to have foreign sourcing (production) without making a final commitment. Management may lack resources or be unwilling to invest equity to establish and complete manufacturing and selling operations, but contract manufacturing keeps the way open for implementing a long-term foreign development policy when the time is right. These considerations are perhaps most important to the company with limited resources. Contract manufacturing enables the firm to develop and control R&D, marketing, distribution, sales and servicing of its products in international markets, while handing over responsibility for production to a local firm (see Figure 11.1).

Payment by the contractor to the contracted party is generally on a per-unit basis, and quality and specification requirements are extremely important. The product can be sold by the contractor in the country of manufacture, its home country or some other foreign market.

This form of business organization is quite common in particular industries. For example, Benetton and IKEA rely heavily on a contractual network of small overseas manufacturers.

Contract manufacturing also offers substantial flexibility. Depending on the duration of the contract, if the firm is dissatisfied with product quality or reliability of delivery, it

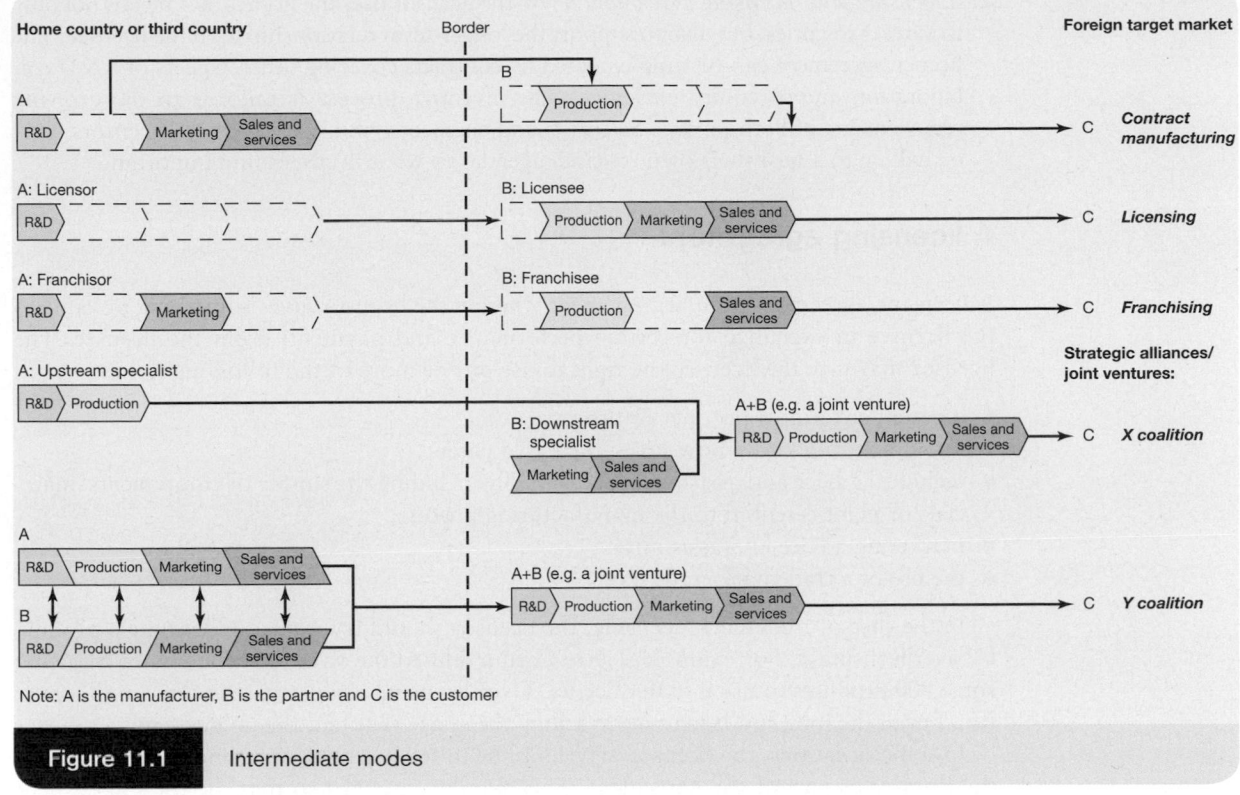

Figure 11.1   Intermediate modes

can shift to another manufacturer. In addition, if management decides to exit the market it does not have to sustain possible losses from divesting production facilities. On the other hand, it is necessary to control product quality to meet company standards. The firm may encounter problems with delivery, product warranties or fulfilling additional orders. The manufacturer may also not be as cost-efficient as the contracting firm, may reach production capacity or may attempt to exploit the agreement.

Thus, while contract manufacturing offers a number of advantages, especially to a firm whose strength lies in marketing and distribution, care needs to be exercised in negotiating the contract. Where the firm loses direct control over the manufacturing function, mechanisms need to be developed to ensure that the contract manufacturer meets the firm's quality and delivery standards.

11.3   Licensing

Licensing

The licensor gives a right to the licensee against payment, e.g. a right to manufacture a certain product based on a patent against some agreed royalty.

Licensing is another way in which the firm can establish local production in foreign markets without capital investment. It differs from contract manufacturing in that it is usually for a longer term and involves much greater responsibilities for the national firm, because more value chain functions have been transferred to the licensee by the licensor (see Figure 11.1).

The licensor can employ two main approaches to licensing (Davis, 2008):

1. *'Stand-alone' licensing agreement.* Here the licence agreement serves primarily to specify the legal basis for the transfer of rights and enable the licensor to earn royalties (or other forms of compensation such as lump sum payments). The licence fees can then finance the licensor's ongoing inventive activities.

2. *'Licensing plus' licensing agreement.* Here the licensor uses the licence as a means not only to extract royalties, but also to support the longer-term relationship with the licensee. The licence agreement can be supplemented by contracts covering other aspects of R&D collaboration and/or equity exchange. The inventive process is tailored to the evolving requirements of both parties. Scientists and engineers who work for such licensors must be willing to adjust their own research agendas to what licensees find important.

A licensing agreement

A licensing agreement is an arrangement wherein the licensor gives something of value to the licensee in exchange for certain performance and payments from the licensee. The licensor may give the licensee the right to use one or more of the following things:

● a patent covering a product or process;
● manufacturing know-how not subject to a patent;
● technical advice and assistance, occasionally including the supply of components, materials or plant essential to the manufacturing process;
● marketing advice and assistance;
● the use of a trademark/trade name.

In the case of trademark licensing, the licensor should try not to undermine a product by overlicensing it. For example, Pierre Cardin diluted the value of his name by allowing some 800 products to use it under licence. Over-licensing can increase income in the short run, but in the long run it may mean killing the goose that laid the golden egg.

In some situations, the licensor may continue to sell essential components or services to the licensee as part of the agreement. This may be extended so that the total agreement may also be one of cross-licensing, wherein there is a mutual exchange of knowledge and/or patents. In cross-licensing there might not be a cash payment involved.

Licensing can be considered a two-way street because a licence also allows the original licensor to gain access to the licensee's technology and product. This is important because the licensee may be able to build on the information supplied by the licensor. Some licensors are very interested in grantbacks and will even lower the royalty rate in return for product improvements and potentially profitable new products. Where a product or service is involved, the licensee is responsible for production and marketing in a defined market area. This responsibility is followed by all the profits and risks associated with the venture. In exchange, the licensee pays the licensor royalties or fees, which are the licensor's main source of income from its licensing operations and which usually involve some combination of:

● *a lump sum not related to output*: this can include a sum paid at the beginning of an agreement for the initial transfer of special machinery, parts, blueprints, knowledge and so on;
● *a minimum royalty*: a guarantee that at least some annual income will be received by the licensor;
● *a running royalty*: normally expressed as a percentage of normal selling price or as a fixed sum of money for units of output.

Other methods of payment include conversions of royalties into equity, management and technical fees and complex systems of counter-purchase, typically found in licensing arrangements with eastern European countries.

If the foreign market carries high political risk then it would be wise for the licensor to seek high initial payments and perhaps compress the timescale of the agreement. Alternatively, if the market is relatively free of risk and the licensee is well placed to develop a strong market share, then payment terms will be somewhat relaxed and probably influenced by other licensors competing for the agreement.

The licensing agreement or contract should always be formalized in a written document. The details of the contract will probably be the subject of detailed negotiation and hard bargaining between the parties, and there can be no such thing as a standard contract.

In the following we see licensing from the viewpoint of a *licensor* (licensing out) and a *licensee* (licensing in). This section is written primarily from the licensor's viewpoint, but licensing in may be an important element in smaller firms' growth strategies, and some consideration is therefore given to this issue too.

Licensing out

Generally there is a wide range of strategic reasons for using licensing. The most important motives for licensing out are as follows:

- The licensor firm will remain technologically superior in its product development. It wants to concentrate on its core competences (product development activities) and then outsource production and downstream activities to other firms.
- The licensor is too small to have financial, managerial or marketing expertise for overseas investment (own subsidiaries).
- The product is at the end of its product life cycle in the advanced countries because of obsolescent technology or model change. A stretching of the total product life cycle is possible through licensing agreements in less developed countries.
- Even if direct royalty income is not high, margins on key components to the licensee (produced by the licensor) can be quite handsome.
- If government regulations restrict foreign direct investment or if political risks are high, licensing may be the only realistic entry mode.
- There may be constraints on imports into the licensee country (tariff or non-tariff barriers).

When setting the price for the agreement the costs of licensing should not be underestimated. Table 11.1 presents a breakdown of costs of licensing out by Australian firms.

Table 11.1	Relative costs of licensing overseas (%)	
		%
Breakdown of total costs of licensing overseas		
Protection of industrial property		24.4
Establishment of licensing agreement		46.6
Maintenance of licensing agreement		29.0
		100.0
Breakdown of establishment costs		
Search for suitable licensee		22.8
Communication between involved parties		44.7
Adoption and testing of equipment for licensee		9.9
Training personnel for licensee		19.9
Other (additional marketing activity and legal expenses)		2.7
		100.0
Breakdown of maintenance costs		
Audit of licensee		9.7
Ongoing market research in market of licensee		7.2
Back-up services for licensee		65.0
Defence of industrial property rights in licensee's territory		11.0
Other		7.1
		100.0

Sources: based on Carstairs and Welch (1981); Young *et al.* (1989, p. 132).

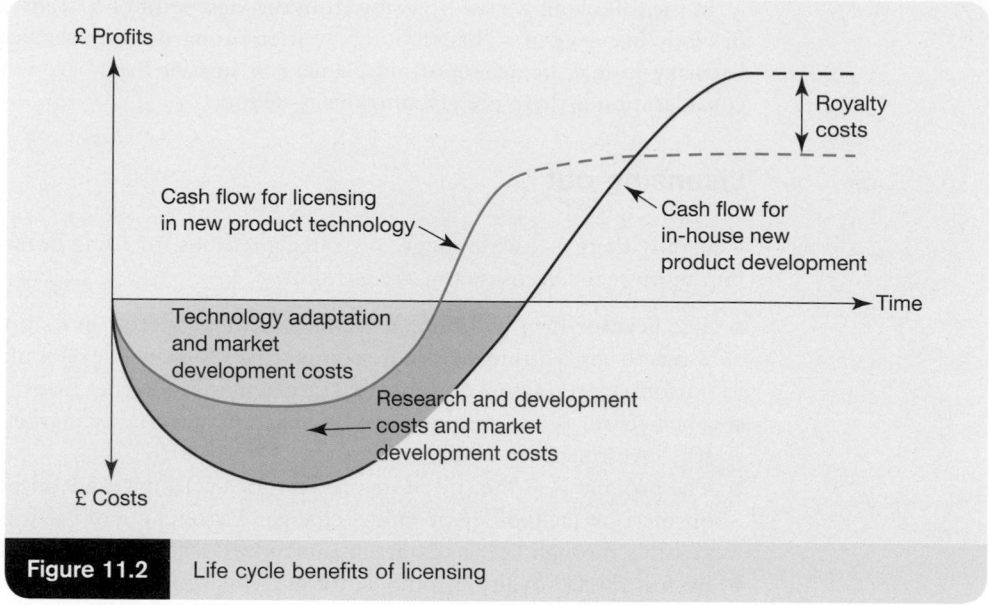

Figure 11.2 Life cycle benefits of licensing

Source: *International Marketing Strategy,* 2nd ed., Prentice Hall (Bradley, F. 1995) p. 388, Copyright © Pearson Education Ltd. Adapted from Lowe, J. and Crawford, N. (1984) *Technology Licensing and the Small Firm,* England: Gower.

Licensing in

Empirical evidence shows (Young *et al.*, 1989, p. 143) that many licensing agreements actually stem from approaches by licensees. This would suggest that the licensee is at an immediate disadvantage in negotiations and general relations with the licensor. In other cases, licensing in is the easy option, with the licence being renewed regularly and the licensee becoming heavily dependent on the technology supplier (the licensor).

As Figure 11.2 shows, licensing in can improve the net cash flow position of the licensee, but can mean lower profits in the longer term. Because technology licensing allows the firms to have products on the market sooner than otherwise, the firm benefits from an earlier positive cash flow. In addition, licensing means lower development costs. The immediate benefits of quick access to new technology, lower development costs and a relatively early cash flow are attractive benefits of licensing.

Table 11.5 summarizes the advantages and disadvantages of licensing for the licensor (see Section 11.6).

11.4 Franchising

Franchising
The franchisor gives a right to the franchisee against payment, e.g. a right to use a total business concept/system, including use of trademarks (brands), against some agreed royalty.

The term **franchising** is derived from the French, meaning 'to be free from servitude'. Franchise activity was almost unknown in Europe until the beginning of the 1970s. The concept was popularized in the US, where over one-third of retail sales are derived from franchising, in comparison with about 11 per cent in Europe (Young *et al.*, 1989, p. 111).

A number of factors have contributed to the rapid growth rate of franchising. First, the general worldwide decline of traditional manufacturing industry and its replacement by service-sector activities has encouraged franchising. It is especially well suited to service and people-intensive economic activities, particularly where these require a large number of geographically dispersed outlets serving local markets. Second, the growth in popularity of self-employment is a contributory factor to the growth of franchising. Government policies in many countries have improved the whole climate for small businesses as a means of stimulating employment.

A good example of the value of franchising is the Swedish furniture manufacturer IKEA, which franchises its ideas throughout the western world, especially in Europe and North America. In terms of retail surface area and the number of visitors to retail stores, this company has experienced very significant growth through franchising in recent years.

Franchising is a marketing-oriented method of selling a business service, often to small independent investors who have working capital but little or no prior business experience. However, it is something of an umbrella term that is used to mean anything from the right to use a name to the total business concept. Thus there are two major types of franchising:

1. *Product and trade name franchising.* This is very similar to trademark licensing. Typically it is a distribution system in which suppliers make contracts with dealers to buy or sell products or product lines. Dealers use the trade name, trademark and product line. Examples of this type of franchising are soft drink bottlers such as Coca-Cola and Pepsi.
2. *Business format* 'package' franchising.

In this section, we will focus on the latter type of franchising.

International business format franchising is a market entry mode that involves a relationship between the entrant (the franchisor) and a host country entity, in which the former transfers, under contract, a business package (or format) that it has developed and owns, to the latter. This host country entity can be either a franchisee or a master franchisee (sub-franchisor). The franchise system can be set up as a direct or indirect system – see Figure 11.3.

In the direct system, the franchisor is controlling and coordinating the activities of the franchisees directly. In the indirect system, a master franchisee (sub-franchisor) is appointed to establish and service its own subsystem of franchisees within its territory.

The advantages of the direct system include access to local resources and knowledge, more adaptation and the possibility of developing a successful master franchisee (subfranchisor) as a tool for selling the concept to other prospective franchisees within the country. The indirect system also has disadvantages, including monitoring issues because of loss of control. There have been examples of a master franchisee holding the subfranchisees hostage to compete against the franchisor. Ultimately, the success of the indirect system will be determined by the capabilities and commitment of the master franchisee (Welsh *et al.*, 2006).

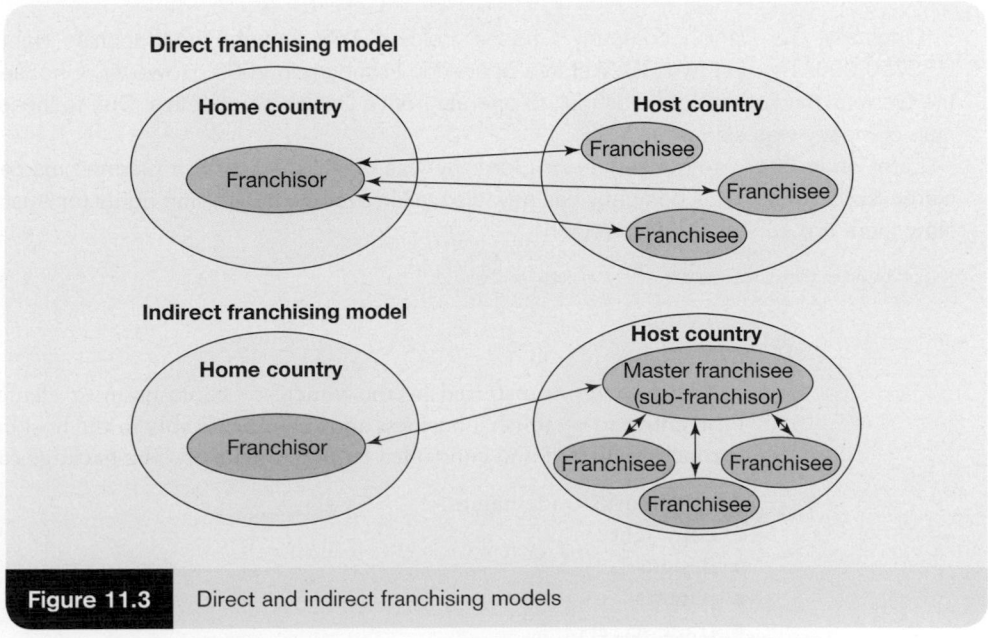

Figure 11.3   Direct and indirect franchising models

Sources: based on Welsh *et al.* (2006) in Hollensen, S. (2008) *Essentials of Global Marketing*, FT/Prentice Hall, p. 233.

EXHIBIT 11.1 Build-a-Bear workshop's use of the indirect franchising model in Germany – Austria - Switzerland

Build-A-Bear Workshop, Inc. (BBW, www.buildabear.com) is the leading and only global company that offers a create-your-own animal service in the retailing experience sector.

Founded in 1997 in the US, the company operates approximately 400 Build-A-Bear Workshop stores worldwide, mainly based on a franchising concept. Build-A-Bear Workshop posted total revenue of US$392 million in the fiscal year 2014 with a positive net income of US$14.3 million.

The indirect franchising model in BBW's case looks like that in Figure 11.4.

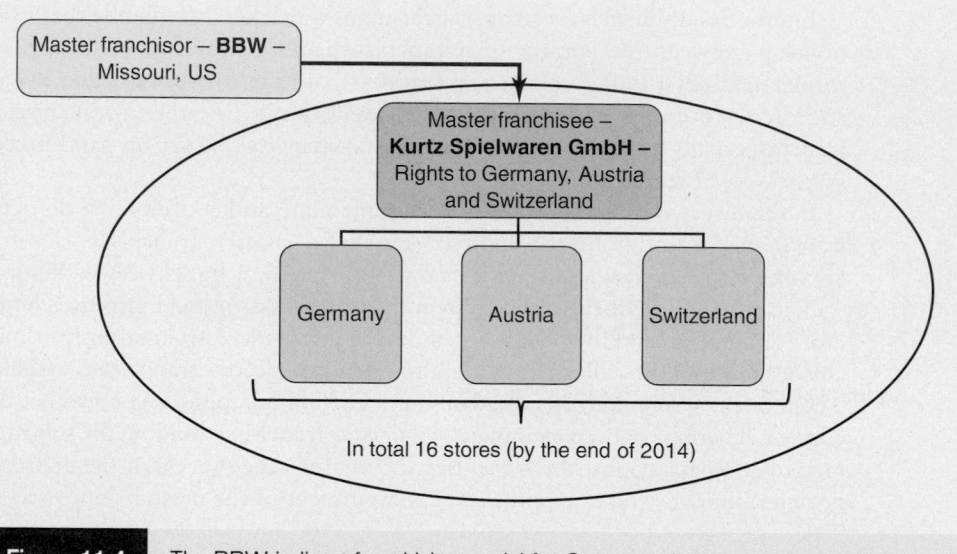

| **Figure 11.4** | The BBW indirect franchising model for Germany, Austria and Switzerland |

Originally, the Danish company Choose Holding ApS, bought the franchise rights for Germany for US$750,000. The first two BBW stores opened in Hamburg in 2006. However, Choose Holding found that the German market was quite difficult to operate from a Danish perspective. Due to these problems the German company was sold off.

Later on in 2014, a new set-up for Germany was established, with a German master franchisee, Spielwaren Kurtz GmbH. This company has now also taken over the franchising rights for Austria and Switzerland. Now there are 16 stores in this region.

Source: based on www.buildabear.com and other public services.

The package transferred by the franchisor contains most elements necessary for the local entity to establish a business and run it profitably in the host country in a prescribed manner, regulated and controlled by the franchisor. The package can contain:

- trademarks/trade names
- copyright
- designs
- patents
- trade secrets

- business know-how
- geographic exclusivity
- design of the store
- market research for the area
- location selection.

In addition to this package, the franchisor also typically provides local entities with managerial assistance in setting up and running local operations. All locally owned franchisees can also receive subsupplies from the franchisor or the master franchisees (subfranchisor) and benefit from centrally coordinated advertising. In return for this business package, the franchisor receives from the franchisee (or subfranchisor) an initial fee up front and/or continuing franchise fees, based typically on a percentage of annual turnover as a mark-up on goods supplied directly by the franchisor.

There is still a lively debate about the differences between licensing and franchising, but if we define franchising in the broader 'business format' (as here), we see the differences presented in Table 11.2.

Table 11.2	How licensing and franchising differ
Licensing	**Franchising**
The term 'royalties' is normally used.	'Management fees' is regarded as the appropriate term.
Products, or even a single product, are the common element.	Covers the total business, including know-how, intellectual rights, goodwill, trademarks and business contacts. (Franchising is all-encompassing, whereas licensing concerns just one part of the business.)
Licences are usually taken by well-established businesses.	Tends to be a start-up situation, certainly as regards the franchisee.
Terms of 16–20 years are common, particularly where they relate to technical know-how, copyright and trade marks. The terms are similar for patents.	The franchise agreement is normally for five years, sometimes extending to 11 years. Franchises are frequently renewable.
Licensees tend to be self-selecting. They are often established businesses and can demonstrate that they are in a strong position to operate the licence in question. A licensee can often pass its licence on to an associate or sometimes unconnected company with little or no reference back to the original licensor.	The franchisee is very definitely selected by the franchisor, and its eventual replacement is controlled by the franchisor.
Usually concerns specific existing products with very little benefit from ongoing research being passed on by the licensor to its licensee.	The franchisor is expected to pass on to its franchisees the benefits of its ongoing research programme as part of the agreement.
There is no goodwill attached to the licence as it is totally retained by the licensor.	Although the franchisor does retain the main goodwill, the franchisee picks up an element of localized goodwill.
Licensees enjoy a substantial measure of free negotiation. As bargaining tools they can use their trade muscle and their established position in the marketplace.	There is a standard fee structure and any variation within an individual franchise system would cause confusion and mayhem.

Sources: based on Perkins (1987, pp. 22, 157); Young *et al*. (1989, p. 148).

Types of business format franchise include business and personal services, convenience stores, car repairs and fast food. US fast-food franchises are some of the best-known global franchise businesses and include McDonald's, Burger King and Pizza Hut.

The fast-food business is taken as an example of franchising in the value chain approach of Figure 11.1. The production (e.g. assembly of burgers) and sales and service functions are transferred to the local outlets (e.g. McDonald's restaurants), whereas the central R&D and marketing functions are still controlled by the franchisor (e.g. McDonald's head office in the US). The franchisor will develop the general marketing plan (with the general advertising messages), which will be adapted to local conditions and cultures.

As indicated earlier, business format franchising is an ongoing relationship that includes not only a product or a service but also a business concept. The business concept usually includes a strategic plan for growth and marketing, instruction on the operation of the business, elaboration of standards and quality control, continuing guidance for the franchisee, and some means of control of the franchisee by the franchisor. Franchisors provide a wide variety of assistance for franchisees, but not all franchisors provide the same level of support. Some examples of assistance and support provided by franchisors are in the areas of finance, site selection, lease negotiation, cooperative advertising, training and assistance with store opening. The extent of ongoing support to franchisees also varies among franchisors. Support areas include central data processing, central purchasing, field training, field operation evaluation, newsletters, regional and national meetings, a hotline for advice and franchisor–franchisee advisory councils. The availability of these services is often a critical factor in the decision to purchase a franchise, and may be crucial to the long-term success of marginal locations or marginally prepared owners.

International expansion of franchising

Franchisors, as other businesses, must consider the relevant success factors in making the decision to expand their franchising system globally. The objective is to search for an environment that promotes cooperation and reduces conflict. Given the long-term nature of a franchise agreement, country stability is an important factor.

Where should the international expansion start? The franchising development often begins as a response to a perceived local opportunity, perhaps as an adaptation of a franchising concept already operating in another foreign market. In this case, the market focus is clearly local to begin with. In addition, the local market provides a better environment for testing and developing the franchising format. Feedback from the marketplace and franchisees can be obtained more readily because of the ease of communication. Adjustments can be made more quickly because of the close local contact.

In the strategic franchising partner (franchisee) selection process that follows, finance, business know-how, local knowledge, a shared understanding of the business and brand and, ultimately, chemistry between the partners are the key factors influencing the franchising partner selection (Doherty, 2009).

A whole variety of minor changes in the format may be necessary as a result of early experience in areas such as training, franchisee choice, site selection, organization of suppliers, promotion and outlet decoration. The early stages of franchise development represent a critical learning process for the franchisor, not just about how to adapt the total package to the market requirements but also regarding the nature of the franchising method itself. Ultimately, with a proven package and a better understanding of its operation, the franchisor is in a better position to attack foreign markets, and is more confident about doing so with a background of domestic success.

Developing and managing franchisor–franchisee relationships

Franchising provides a unique organizational relationship in which the franchisor and franchisee each bring important qualities to the business. The franchise system combines the advantages of economy of scale offered by the franchisor with the local knowledge and entrepreneurial talents of the franchisee. Their joint contribution may result in success. The franchisor depends on franchisees for fast growth, an infusion of capital from the franchise purchase fee and an income stream from the royalty fee paid by franchisees each year. Franchisors also benefit from franchisee goodwill in the community and, increasingly, from franchisee suggestions for innovation. The most important factor, however, is the franchisee's motivation to operate a successful independent business. The franchisee depends on the franchisor for the strength of the trademark, technical advice, support services, marketing resources and national advertising that provides instant customer recognition.

There are two additional key success factors (KSF), which rest on the interdependence of the franchisee and the franchisor:

1. integrity of the whole business system;
2. capacity for renewal of the business system.

Integrity of the business system

The business will be a success in a viable market to the extent that the franchisor provides a well-developed, proven business concept to the franchisee and the franchisee is motivated to follow the system as it is designed, thereby preserving the integrity of the system. Standardization is the cornerstone of franchising: customers expect the same product or service at every location. Deviations from the franchising business concept by individual franchisees adversely affect the franchisor's reputation. The need for the integrity of the system requires that the franchisor exerts control over key operations at the franchise sites (Doherty and Alexander, 2006).

Capacity for renewal of the business system

Although most franchisors conduct research and development within the parent company, the highest proportion of innovation originates from franchisees in the field. Franchisees are most familiar with customers' preferences. They sense new trends and the opportunity to introduce a new product and service. The issue is getting the franchisee to share new ideas with the parent company. Not all franchisees are willing to share ideas with the franchisor, for a number of reasons. The most common is failure of the franchisor to keep in close contact with the franchisees; the most troubling is a lack of trust in the franchisor. The franchisor needs to promote a climate of trust and cooperation for mutual benefit.

Handling possible conflicts

Conflict is inherent in the franchisor–franchisee relationship, as all aspects that are good for the franchisor may not be good for the franchisee. One of the most basic conflicts is failure of either the franchisor or the franchisee to live up to the terms of the legal agreement.

Disagreement over objectives may be the result of poor communication on the part of the franchisor, or failure on the part of the franchisee to understand the franchisor's objectives. Both franchisor and franchisee agree on the need for profits in the business, not only to provide a living but to stay competitive. However, the two parties may disagree on the means of achieving profits. The number of conflicts between franchisors and franchisees may be reduced by establishing extensive monitoring of the franchisee (e.g. computer-based accounting, purchasing and inventory systems). Another way of reducing the number of conflicts is to view franchisors and franchisees as partners in running a business; both objectives and operating procedures have to be in harmony. This view requires a strong common culture with shared values established by the use of intensive communication between franchisor and franchisees in different countries (e.g. cross-national/regional meetings, cross-national/regional advisory councils).

11.5 Joint ventures/strategic alliances

Joint venture
An equity partnership typically between two partners. It involves two 'parents' creating the 'child' (the joint venture acting in the market).

A **joint venture** or a strategic alliance is a partnership between two or more parties. In international joint ventures these parties will be based in different countries, and this obviously complicates the management of such an arrangement.

A number of reasons are given for setting up joint ventures:

- Complementary technology or management skills provided by the partners can lead to new opportunities in existing sectors (e.g. multimedia, in which information processing, communications and the media are merging).
- Many firms find that partners in the host country can increase the speed of market entry. Past research (Kuo *et al.*, 2012) has found evidence that a joint-venture arrangement can compensate for the lack of international experience. Joint ventures allow the partners to share the responsibility of management and, consequently, lower overall operation and administrative costs.
- Many less developed countries, such as China and South Korea, try to restrict foreign ownership.
- Global operations in R&D and production are prohibitively expensive, but are necessary to achieve competitive advantage.

The formal difference between a joint venture and a strategic alliance is that a strategic alliance is typically a non-equity cooperation, meaning that the partners do not commit equity into or invest in the alliance. The joint venture can be either a contractual non-equity joint venture or an equity joint venture.

In a contractual joint venture, no joint enterprise with a separate personality is formed. Two or more companies form a partnership to share the cost of investment, the risks and the long-term profits. An equity joint venture involves the creation of a new company in which foreign and local investors share ownership and control. Thus, according to these definitions, strategic alliances and non-equity joint ventures are more or less the same (Figure 11.5).

The question of whether to use an equity or a non-equity joint venture is a matter of how to formalize the cooperation. Much more interesting is to consider the roles that partners are supposed to play in the collaboration.

In Figure 11.6, two different types of coalition are shown in the value chain perspective. These are based on the possible collaboration pattern along the value chain. In the figure we see two partners, A and B, each having its own value chain. Three different types of value chain partnership appear:

1. *Upstream-based collaboration.* A and B collaborate on R&D and/or production.
2. *Downstream-based collaboration.* A and B collaborate on marketing, distribution, sales and/or service.
3. *Upstream/downstream-based collaboration.* A and B have different but complementary competences at each end of the value chain.

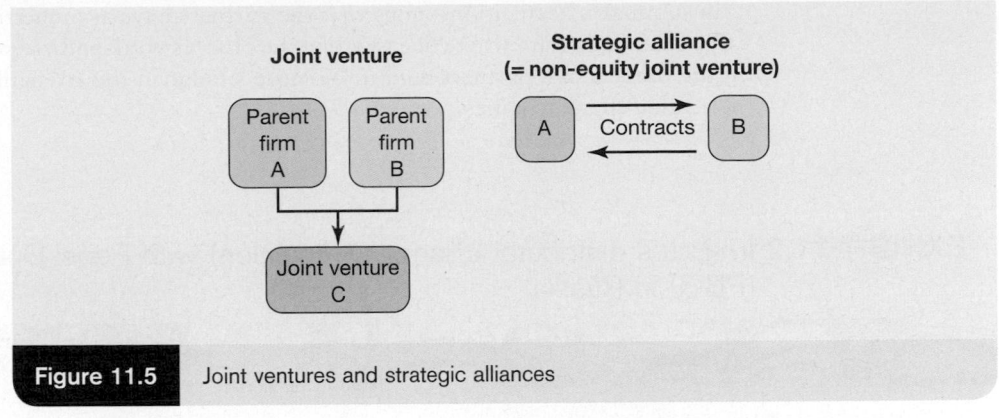

Figure 11.5 Joint ventures and strategic alliances

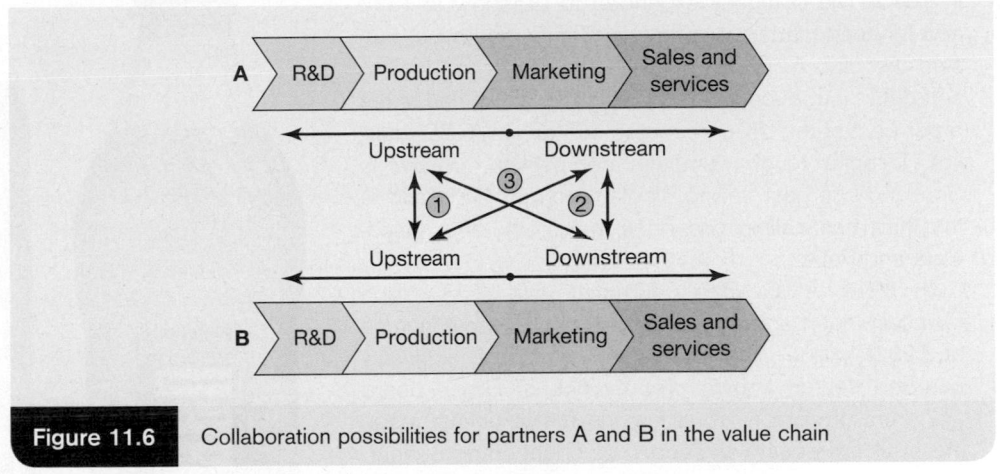

Figure 11.6 Collaboration possibilities for partners A and B in the value chain

Source: adapted from Lorange and Roos (1995, p. 16).

Y coalition

Each partner in the alliance/joint venture contributes with complementary product lines or services. Each partner takes care of all value chain activities within its product line.

X coalition

The partners in the value chain divide the value chain activities between them, e.g. the manufacturer (exporter) specializes in upstream activities, whereas the local partner takes care of the downstream activities.

Types 1 and 2 represent the so-called **Y coalition** and type 3 represents the so-called **X coalition** (Porter and Fuller, 1986, pp. 336–7):

- *Y coalitions*. Partners share the actual performance of one or more value chain activities: for example, joint production of models or components enables the attainment of scale economies that can provide lower production costs per unit. Another example is a joint marketing agreement where complementary product lines of two firms are sold together through existing or new distribution channels, and thus broaden the market coverage of both firms.

- *X coalitions*. Partners divide the value chain activities between themselves: for example, one partner develops and manufactures a product while letting the other partner market it. Forming X coalitions involves identifying the value chain activities where the firm is well positioned and has its core competences. Take the case where A has its core competences in upstream functions but is weak in downstream functions. A wants to enter a foreign market but lacks local market knowledge and does not know how to get access to foreign distribution channels for its products. Therefore A seeks and finds a partner, B, which has its core competences in the downstream functions but is weak in the upstream functions. In this way A and B can form a coalition where B can help A with distribution and selling in a foreign market, and A can help B with R&D or production.

In summary, X coalitions imply that the partners have asymmetric competences in the value chain activities: where one is strong the other is weak and vice versa. In Y coalitions, on the other hand, partners tend to be more similar in the strengths and weaknesses of their value chain activities.

EXHIBIT 11.2 Irn-Bru's distributor alliance (Y coalition) with Pepsi Bottling Group (PBG) in Russia

A. G. Barr, the UK's leading independent branded soft drinks manufacturer, was founded in Falkirk, Scotland, in 1875. The company expanded to Glasgow in 1887 and its headquarters are now in Cumbernauld just outside the city. A. G. Barr makes the renowned Irn-Bru soft drink, introduced in 1901 which, in 2014, had about 5 per cent of the UK carbonated soft drinks (CSD) market. Despite tough domestic competition, Irn-Bru is Scotland's largest selling single-flavoured CSD and is the third best-selling soft drink in the UK, after Coca-Cola and Pepsi.

In 2014, A. G. Barr's turnover was £254 million (Annual Report and Accounts, 2014) with a net income of £28.2 million. The formula for Irn-Bru is a closely guarded secret, known only by two of Barr's board members. Irn-Bru is most famous for its unique taste, maverick advertising and eccentric bright orange colour, making it easily recognisable even when not in its packaging.

In the late 1980s, Barr actively began to look at expansion through international markets. It considered France, Germany and Benelux countries, among others, but found that Coca-Cola and Pepsi dominated these mature markets. Competition was fierce and margins tight. Consequently, it examined other emerging markets and was attracted to Russia. In the years following the break-up of the Soviet Union, Russia showed much potential with a large population, growing prosperity and standard of living, and a rising demand for consumer goods. Moreover, the Russians, like the Scots, have a 'sweet tooth', leading to high soft drinks consumption. As part of the international expansion strategy, in 1994, Barr began direct exports of its trademark Irn-Bru to Russia.

Source: A. G. Barr plc.

Barr eventually parted company with its initial franchisee, but the Irn-Bru brand by that time was so well-established that, in 2002, Barr arranged a new manufacturing franchise contract with the Pepsi Bottling Group (PBG) of Russia to manufacture, distribute and sell Irn-Bru. PBG (Russia) has over 4,000 employees and distributes the PepsiCo brands throughout Russia. Since February 2002, the distribution network has been greatly enlarged, especially by using the PBG retail space and coolers in the retail outlets, improving brand availability to the trade, retailers, wholesalers and clubs. The brand is produced in 250 ml glass, 330 ml cans, 600 ml, 1.25 l and 2 l plastic bottles.

Value of the distribution alliance for both partners:

Irn-Bru:

- Irn-Bru in Russia has been a part of A. G. Barr's international expansion plan.
- Irn-Bru has provided extra turnover and profit for A.G. Barr.

PBG:

- In many Russian retail stores (with a broader PBG product range) Irn-Bru has blocked the available shelf space for Pepsi's main competitor, Coca-Cola.
- Irn-Bru has provided extra turnover and profit for PBG.
- Irn-Bru is now established as one of the leading soft drink brands in the country.

Sources: A. G. Barr plc (www.agbarr.co.uk); Irn-Bru website (www.irn-bru.co.uk).

Stages in joint-venture formation

The various stages in the formation of a joint venture are shown in Table 11.3.

Step 1: joint-venture objectives

Joint ventures are formed for a variety of reasons: entering new markets, reducing manufacturing costs and developing and diffusing new technologies rapidly. Joint ventures are

Table 11.3	Stages in joint-venture formation

1. **Joint-venture objectives**
   Establish strategic objectives of the joint venture and specify time period for achieving objectives.

2. **Cost–benefit analysis**
   Evaluate advantages and disadvantages of joint venture compared with alternative strategies for achieving objectives (e.g. licensing) in terms of:
   (a) financial commitment
   (b) synergy
   (c) management commitment
   (d) risk reduction
   (e) control
   (f) long-run market penetration
   (g) other advantages/disadvantages.

3. **Selecting partner(s)**
   (a) Profile of desired features of candidates
   (b) Identifying joint-venture candidates and drawing up a shortlist
   (c) Screening and evaluating possible joint-venture partners
   (d) Initial contact/discussions
   (e) Choice of partner.

4. **Develop business plan**
   Achieve broad agreement on different issues.

5. **Negotiation of joint-venture agreement**
   Final agreement on business plan.

6. **Contract writing**
   Incorporation of agreement in legally binding contract, allowing for subsequent modifications to the agreement.

7. **Performance evaluation**
   Establish control systems for measuring venture performance.

Source: adapted from *International Market Entry and Development*, Harvester Wheatsheaf/Prentice Hall (Young, S., Hamill, J., Wheeler, S. and Davies, J.R. 1989) p. 233, Pearson Education Ltd.

also used to accelerate product introduction and overcome legal and trade barriers expeditiously. In this period of advanced technology and global markets, implementing strategies quickly is essential. Forming alliances is often the fastest, most effective method of achieving objectives. Companies must be sure that the goal of the alliance is compatible with their existing businesses, so their expertise is transferable to the alliance. Firms often enter into alliances based on opportunity rather than linkage with their overall goals. This risk is greatest when a company has a surplus of cash.

There are three principal objectives in forming a joint venture:

1. *Entering new markets*. Many companies recognize that they lack the necessary marketing expertise when they enter new markets. Rather than trying to develop this expertise internally, the company may identify another organization that possesses those desired marketing skills. By capitalizing on the product development skills of one company and the marketing skills of the other, the resulting alliance can serve the market quickly and effectively. Alliances may be particularly helpful when entering a foreign market for the first time because of the extensive cultural differences that may abound. They may also be effective domestically when entering regional or ethnic markets.
2. *Reducing manufacturing costs*. Joint ventures may allow companies to pool capital or existing facilities to gain economies of scale or increase the use of facilities, thereby reducing manufacturing costs.
3. *Developing and diffusing technology*. Joint ventures may also be used to build jointly on the technical expertise of two or more companies in developing products that are technologically beyond the capability of the companies acting independently.

Step 2: cost–benefit analysis

A joint-venture/strategic alliance may not be the best way of achieving objectives. Therefore this entry mode should be evaluated against other entry modes. Such an analysis could be based on the factors influencing the choice of entry mode (see Section 9.3).

Step 3: selecting partner(s)

If it is accepted that a joint venture is the best entry mode for achieving the firm's objectives, the next stage is the selection of the joint-venture partner. This normally involves five stages.

Establishing a desired partner profile

Companies frequently search for one or more of the following resources in a partner:

- development know-how
- sales and service expertise
- low-cost production facilities
- strategically critical manufacturing capabilities
- reputation and brand equity
- market access and knowledge
- cash.

Identifying joint-venture candidates

Often this part of partner selection is not performed thoroughly. The first candidate, generally discovered through contacts established by mail, arranged by a banker or a business colleague already established in the country, is often the one with whom the company undertakes discussions. Little or no screening is done, nor is there an in-depth investigation of the motives and capabilities of the candidate. At other times, the personal network that executives maintain with senior managers from other firms shapes the set of prospective joint-venture partners that companies will generally consider. All too often, however, alliances are agreed upon informally by these top managers without careful attention to how appropriate the partner match may be. Instead of taking this reactive approach, the firm should proactively search for joint-venture candidates. Possible candidates can be found among competitors, suppliers, customers, related industries and trade association members.

Screening and evaluating possible joint-venture partners

Relationships get off to a good start if partners know each other. Table 11.4 gives some criteria that may be used to judge a prospective partner's effectiveness. These suggestions are merely an outline sketch of the type of information that can be used to grade partners. They cover areas where there is a reasonable chance of forming a view by the appraisal of published information and by sensible observation and questioning.

Table 11.4	Analysis of prospective partners: examples of criteria that may be used to judge a prospective partner's effectiveness by assessing existing business ventures and commercial attitudes

1. **Finance**
   Financial history and overall financial standing (all the usual ratios)
   Possible reasons for successful business areas
   Possible reasons for unsuccessful business areas

2. **Organization**
   Structure of organization
   Quality and turnover of senior managers
   Workforce conditions/labour relations
   Information and reporting systems; evidence of planning
   Effective owner's working relationship with business

3. **Market**
   Reputation in marketplace and with competitors
   Evidence of research/interest in service and quality
   Sales methods; quality of sales force
   Evidence of handling weakening market conditions
   Results of new business started

4. **Production**
   Condition of existing premises/works
   Production efficiencies/layouts
   Capital investments and improvements
   Quality control procedures
   Evidence of research (internal/external); introduction of new technology
   Relationship with main suppliers

5. **Institutional**
   Government and business contacts (influence)
   Successful negotiations with banks, licensing authorities, etc.
   Main contacts with non-national organizations and companies
   Geographical influence

6. **Possible negotiating attitudes**
   Flexible or hard line
   Reasonably open or closed and secretive
   Short-term or long-term orientation
   Wheeler-dealer or objective negotiator
   Positive, quick decision-making or tentative
   Negotiating experience and strength of team support

Sources: Walmsley (1982); Paliwoda (1993).

Initial contacts/discussions

Since relationships between companies are relationships between people, it is important that the top managers of the firm meet personally with top managers from the remaining two or three possible partners. It is important to highlight the personal side of a business relationship. This includes discussion of personal and social interests to see if there is a good chemistry between the prospective partners.

Choice of partner

The chosen partner should bring the desired complementary strength to the partnership. Ideally the strengths contributed by the partners will be unique, for only these strengths can be sustained and defended over the long term. The goal is to develop synergies between the contributions of the partners, resulting in a win–win situation for both. Moreover, the partners must be compatible and willing to trust one another.

It is important that neither partner has the desire to acquire the other partner's strength, or the necessary mutual trust will be destroyed. Dow Chemical Company, a frequent and successful alliance practitioner, uses the negotiation process to judge other corporate cultures and, consequently, their compatibility and trustworthiness.

Commitment to the joint venture is essential. This commitment must be both financial and psychological. Unless there is senior management endorsement and enthusiasm at the operating level, an alliance will struggle, particularly when tough issues arise.

Step 4: develop a business plan

Issues that have to be negotiated and determined prior to the establishment of the joint venture include:

- ownership split (majority, minority, 50–50);
- management (composition of board of directors, organization, etc.);
- production (installation of machinery, training, etc.);
- marketing (the 4-Ps, organization).

Step 5: negotiation of joint-venture agreement

As Figure 11.7 shows, the final agreement is determined by the relative bargaining power of both prospective partners.

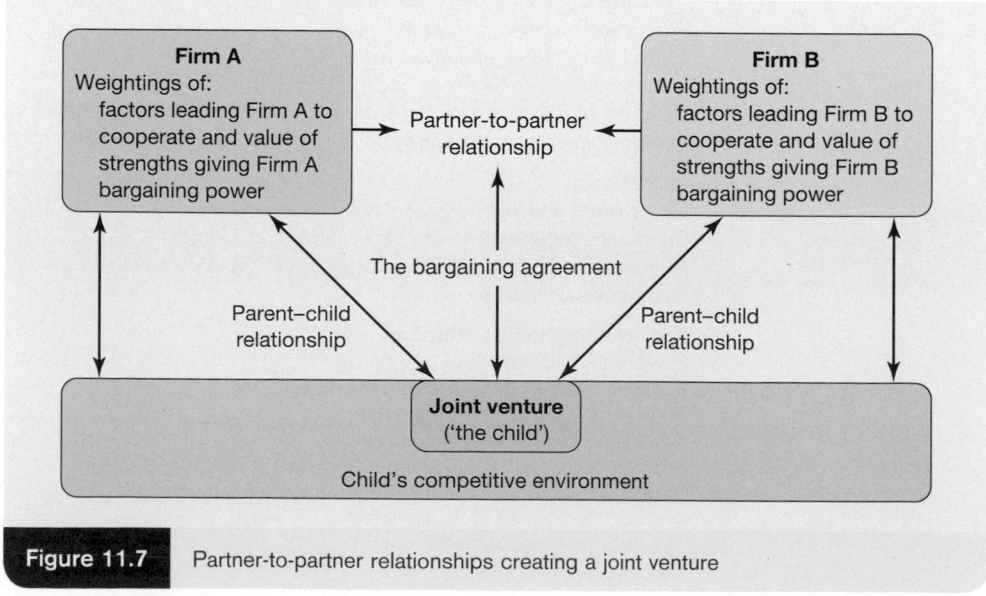

| **Figure 11.7** | Partner-to-partner relationships creating a joint venture |

Source: Harrigan (1985, p. 50).

Step 6: contract writing

Once the joint-venture agreement has been negotiated it needs to be written into a legally binding contract. Of course, the contract should cover the 'marriage' conditions of the partners, but it should also cover the 'divorce' situation, such as what happens with 'the child' (the joint venture).

Step 7: performance evaluation

Evaluating joint-venture performance is a difficult issue. Managers often fall into the trap of assessing partnerships as if they were internal corporate divisions with unambiguous goals operating in low-risk, stable environments. Bottom-line profits, cash flow, market share and other traditional financially oriented output measures become standard indicators of performance. These measures may be inappropriate for two reasons. First, they reflect a short-term orientation, and maximization of initial output too soon can jeopardize the prospects for alliances positioned for the long term. Second, the goals of many alliances may not be readily quantifiable. For instance, a partnership's objectives may involve obtaining access to a market or blocking a competitor.

Many alliances need considerable time before they are ready to be judged on conventional output measures. Only after partnerships mature (i.e. when the operations of the alliance are well established and well understood) can managers gradually shift to measure output, such as profits and cash flows.

Expecting too much too soon in terms of profit and cash flows from an alliance working under risky conditions can endanger its future success.

Managing the joint venture

In recent years, we have seen an increasing number of cross-border joint ventures. However, it is dangerous to ignore the fact that the average life span of alliances is only about seven years, and nearly 80 per cent of joint ventures ultimately end in a sale by one of the partners.

Harrigan's model (Figure 11.8) can be used as a framework for explaining this high 'divorce rate'.

Changes in bargaining power

According to Bleeke and Ernst (1994), the key to understanding the 'divorce' of the two parents is changes in their respective bargaining power. Let us assume that we have established a joint venture with the task of penetrating markets with a new product. In the initial stages of the relationship, the product and technology provider generally has the most power but, unless those products and technologies are proprietary and unique, power usually shifts to the party that controls distribution channels and thus customers.

The bargaining power is also strongly affected by the balance of learning and teaching. A company that is good at learning can access and internalize its partner's capabilities more easily, and is likely to become less dependent on its partner as the alliance evolves. Before entering a joint venture, some companies see it as an intermediate stage before acquiring the other partner. By entering a joint venture, the prospective buyer of the partner is in a better position to assess the true value of such intangible assets as brands, distribution networks, people and systems. This experience reduces the risk that the buyer will make an uninformed decision and buy an expensive 'lemon' (Nanda and Williamson, 1995).

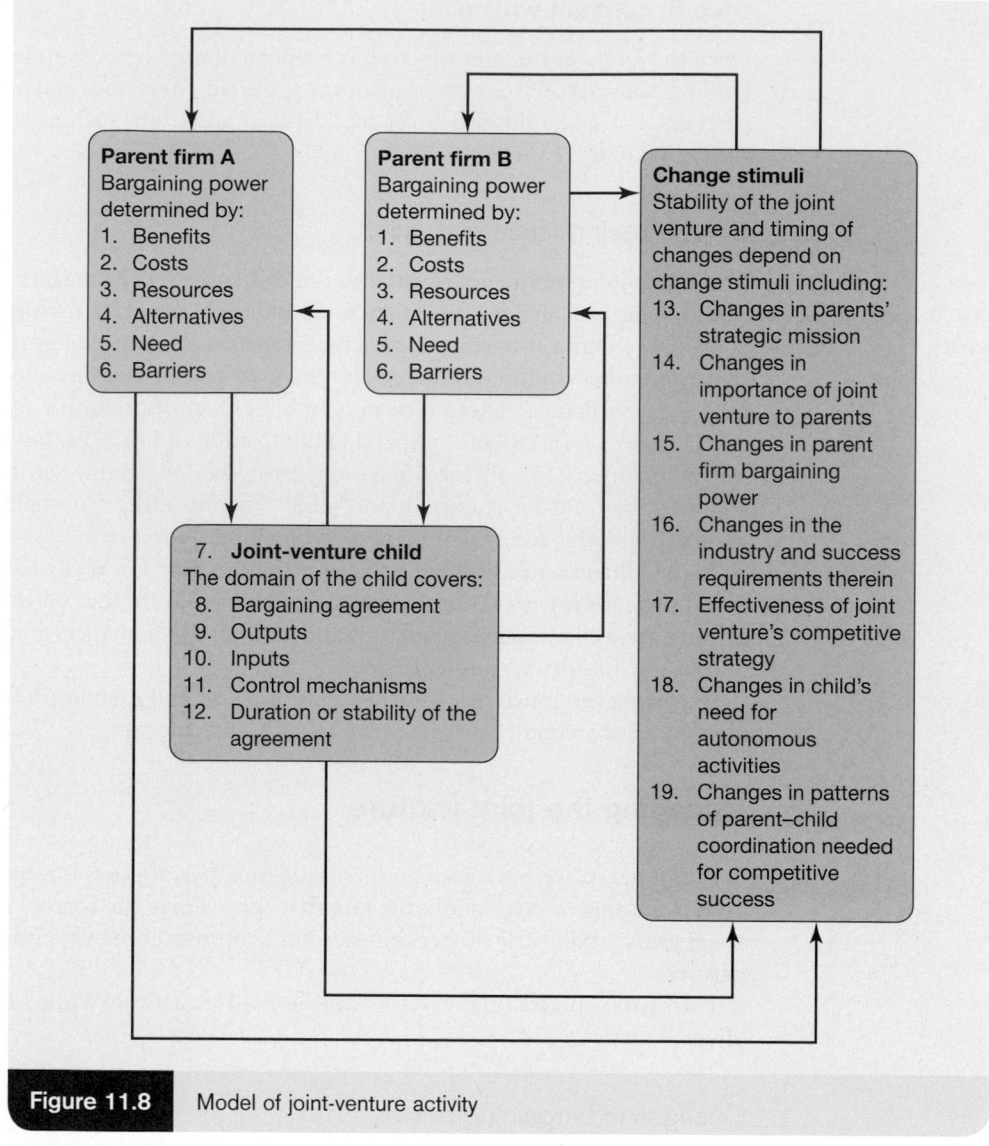

Figure 11.8   Model of joint-venture activity

Source: Harrigan (1985, p. 52).

Other change stimuli and potential conflicts

Diverging goals

As the joint venture progresses, the goals of the two partners may diverge. For example, unacceptable positions can develop in the local market when the self-interest of one partner conflicts with the interest of the joint venture as a whole, as in the pricing of a single-source input or raw material.

Diverging goals typically arise in the local market entry joint ventures. These joint ventures are created when multinational enterprises (MNEs) take local partners to enter foreign markets. The MNE is usually interested in maximizing its global income, that is, the net income of all of its affiliates, and this means that it is quite willing to run losses on some affiliates if this leads to higher net income for the whole network. The local partner, however, wants to maximize the profits of the specific affiliate of which it is part owner. Conflicts then flare up whenever the two goals are incompatible, as global income maximization is not necessarily compatible with the maximization of the separate profits of each affiliate. For example, conflicts may arise concerning the role given to the joint venture within the MNE network (and particularly on its allocation of export markets). This was the case when General Motors (GM) set up with Daewoo to manufacture subcompact cars for the Korean market and for export to the US under GM's Pontiac badge. Since GM's Opel subsidiary was selling similar subcompacts in Europe, GM limited the joint venture's export to its US Pontiac subsidiary. Dissatisfied with Pontiac's performance, Daewoo decided to export to eastern Europe in competition with Opel, a move that contributed to the dissolution of the joint venture (Hennert and Zeng, 2005).

Double management

A potential problem is the matter of control. By definition, a joint venture must deal with double management. If a partner has less than 50 per cent ownership, that partner must, in effect, let the majority partner make decisions. If the board of directors has a 50–50 split, it is difficult for the board to make a decision quickly, if at all.

Repatriation of profits

Conflicts can also arise with regard to issues such as repatriation of profits, where the local partner wants to reinvest them in the joint venture while the other partner wishes to repatriate them or invest them in other operations.

Mixing different cultures

An organization's culture is the set of values, beliefs and conventions that influence the behaviour and goals of its employees. This is often quite different from the culture of the host country and the partner organization. Thus, developing a shared culture is central to the success of the alliance.

Partnering is inherently very people-oriented. To the extent that the cultures of the partners are different, making the alliance work may prove difficult (Buck *et al.*, 2010). Cultural differences often result in an 'us versus them' situation. Cultural norms should be consistent with management's vision of the alliance's ideal culture. This may entail creating norms as well as nurturing those that already exist. The key to developing a culture is to acknowledge its existence and to manage it carefully. Bringing two organizations together and letting nature take its course is a recipe for failure. Language differences are also an obvious hurdle for an international alliance.

Ignoring the local culture will almost certainly destroy the chances of it accepting the alliance's product or service. Careful study of the culture prior to embarking on the venture is vital. Again, extensive use of local managers is usually preferred.

Shared equity

Shared equity may also involve an unequal sharing of the burden. Occasionally, international companies with 50–50 joint ventures believe that they are giving more than 50 percent of the technology, management skill and other factors that contribute to the success of the operation, but are receiving only half the profits. Of course, the national partner contributes local knowledge and other intangibles that may be underestimated. Nevertheless, some international companies believe that the local partner gets too much of a 'free ride'.

Developing trust in joint ventures

Developing trust takes time. The first times that companies work together, their chances of succeeding are very slight but, once they find ways to work together, all sorts of opportunities appear. Working together on relatively small projects initially helps develop trust and determine compatibility while minimizing economic risk. Each partner has a chance to gauge the skills and contributions of the other, and further investment can then be considered. Of course, winning together in the marketplace on a project of any scale is a great way to build trust and overcome differences. It usually serves as a precursor to more ambitious joint efforts.

Providing an exit strategy

As indicated earlier, there is a significant probability that a newly formed joint venture will fail, even if the previously mentioned key principles are followed. The anticipated market may not develop, one of the partner's capabilities may have been overestimated, the corporate strategy of one of the partners may have changed, or the partners may simply be incompatible. Whatever the reason for the failure, the parties should prepare for such an outcome by addressing the issue in the partnership contract. The contract should provide for the liquidation or distribution of partnership assets, including any technology developed by the alliance. Mata and Portugal (2015) distinguish between three modes of terminating an international joint venture: closure, acquisition by the foreign partner and acquisition by the domestic partner. When the international joint venture terminates by acquisition by one of the partners, Mata and Portugal (2015) find that it is much more likely to occur via acquisition by the foreign partner than by the domestic one.

Control mechanisms

Control mechanisms may be positive, and parents employ these in order to promote certain behaviours, or negative, used by a parent to stop or prevent the joint venture from implementing certain activities or decisions. Positive controls tend to be exercised through informal mechanisms, including staffing, reporting relationships and participation in the planning process. On the other hand, the more bureaucratic negative control includes reliance on such mechanisms as formal agreements, approval or veto by parents and the use of the venture's board of directors.

Control-related failures are likely to occur if control practices are not re-evaluated and modified in response to changing circumstances. This is the job of both partners in the joint venture. Responding to problems on an ad hoc basis will result in control-related failures (Vaidya, 2009).

Split control (50–50) or dominant control structure

Finally, a question that often causes discussion between the joint-venture parents is whether the joint venture should be based on a split (50–50) or on a dominant control structure (e.g. 60–40). Some researchers (Anderson and Gatignon, 1986) believe that dominant control structures often make joint ventures easier to manage and may be more successfully executed than when the decision-making control is shared by the parents. Other researchers (e.g. Geringer and Hebert, 1991) disagree and state that a split control structure, where each parent or the joint venture managers exert dominant control (and have responsibility) over different value chain activities of the joint venture, is also as beneficial to both the parties.

EXHIBIT 11.3 Safedom: a Chinese condom manufacturer needs a partner with which to enter the European market

Founded in 2006, the Chinese condom manufacturer Safedom has grown rapidly at home. It expected to sell one billion condoms in China, in 2012, giving it about 8 per cent of the domestic market. In China, most men used to get free condoms from the government, but more and more now buy their condoms from other branded condom manufacturers. In 2011, Safedom turned its back on the low-margin, guaranteed-business sales to the Chinese government family planning programme, and decided to shift to where the money is: the higher end of the general public market.

In China, Safedom has had good market success by targeting women. Eighty per cent of customers for Safedom's condoms in China are women, whereas in most big western markets only an estimated 40–50 per cent of condom-buyers are female. Safedom emphasizes female values with its choice of brand names. Western brands like Durex, Trojan and Australia's Ansell offer chiefly condom brands that appeal to men, with names such as Performa, Magnum and Jissbon (which means 'James Bond' in Chinese). Safedom, by contrast, sells condoms under brands such as Elegant Winter, Beautiful Girl and Green Lemon in oval-shaped, paisley-patterned tins.

The company claims to produce the first entirely virus-proof condom. However, when approaching markets outside China, such as the European market, this claim needs to be verified by international bodies. In this process, Safedom has realized that it needs a European partner for success outside China.

With regard to expansion outside China, Safedom has realized that the big problem is lack of trust in the brand. Chinese brands as a whole do not have the best reputation for quality in international markets, and birth control products require a huge leap of faith for consumers.

Elegant Winter

Calmness like water
But passion inside
Hands clenched
Enjoy intimacy
Heavy breathing, murmuring
Make you delighted

Source: www.safedom.cn.

The global sale of condoms is set to hit 27 billion by 2016, with a total worth of US$6 billion. Durex condoms account for 35–40 per cent of the global market.

Sources: based on 'Domestic condom maker targets Europe', www.beijingtoday.com.cn/tag/safedom; 'Chinese condoms: Reds in the bed', *The Economist*, 27 January 2012.

11.6   Other intermediate entry modes

Management contracting emphasizes the growing importance of services and management know-how. The typical case of management contracting is where one firm (contractor) supplies management know-how to another company that provides the capital and takes care of the operating value chain functions in the foreign country. Normally, the contracts undertaken are concerned with management operating/control systems and training local staff to take over when the contracts are completed. It is usually not the intention of the contractor to continue operating after the contract expires. Normally, it is the philosophy to operate, transfer know-how to the local staff and then depart. This will usually create a strong competitive position from which to pick up other management contracts in the area.

Management contracts typically arise in situations where one company seeks the management know-how of another company with established experience in the field. The lack of management capability is most evident for developing countries. Normally the financial compensation to the contractor for the management services provided is a management fee, which may be fixed irrespective of the financial performance, or may be a percentage of the profit (Luostarinen and Welch, 1990). The advantages and disadvantages of management contracting and different intermediate entry modes are listed in Table 11.5.

Table 11.5	Advantages and disadvantages of the different intermediate modes	
Intermediate entry mode	**Advantages**	**Disadvantages**
Contract manufacturing (seen from the contractor's viewpoint)	Permits low-risk market entry. No local investment (cash, time and executive talent) with no risk of nationalization or expropriation. Retention of control over R&D, marketing and sales/after-sales service. Avoids currency risks and financing problems. A locally made image, which may assist in sales, especially to government or official bodies. Entry into markets otherwise protected by tariffs or other barriers. Possible cost advantage if local costs (primarily labour costs) are lower. Avoids intra-corporate transfer-pricing problems that can arise with a subsidiary.	Transfer of production know-how is difficult. Contract manufacture is only possible when a satisfactory and reliable manufacturer can be found – not always an easy task. Extensive technical training will often have to be given to the local manufacturer's staff. As a result, at the end of the contract, the subcontractor could become a formidable competitor. Control over manufacturing quality is difficult to achieve despite the ultimate sanction of refusal to accept substandard goods. Possible supply limitation if the production is taking place in developing countries. The licensor is ceding certain sales territories to the licensee for the duration of the contract; should it fail to live up to expectations, renegotiation may be expensive. When the licensing agreement finally expires, the licensor may find it has established a competitor in the former licensee.
Licensing (seen from licensor's viewpoint)	Increases the income on products already developed as a result of expensive research. Permits entry into markets that are otherwise closed on account of high rates of duty, import quotas and so on. A viable option where manufacture is near the customer's base. Requires little capital investment and should provide a higher rate of return on capital employed. There may be valuable spin-off if the licensor can sell other products or components to the licensee. If these parts are for products being manufactured locally or machinery, there may also be some tariff concessions on their import. The licensor is not exposed to the danger of nationalization or expropriation of assets. Because of the limited capital requirements, new products can be exploited rapidly, on a worldwide basis, before competition develops. The licensor can take immediate advantage of the licensee's local marketing and distribution organization and of existing customer contacts. Protects patents, especially in countries that give weak protection for products not produced locally. Local manufacture may also be an advantage in securing government contracts.	The licensee may prove less competent than expected at marketing or other management activities. Costs may even grow faster than income. The licensee, even if it reaches an agreed minimum turnover, may not fully exploit the market, leaving it open to the entry of competitors, so that the licensor loses control of the marketing operation. Danger of the licensee running short of funds, especially if considerable plant expansion is involved or an injection of capital is required to sustain the project. This danger can be turned to advantage if the licensor has funds available by a general expansion of the business through a partnership. Licence fees are normally a small percentage of turnover, about 5 per cent, and will often compare unfavourably with what might be obtained from a company's own manufacturing operation. Lack of control over licensee operations. Quality control of the product is difficult – and the product will often be sold under the licensor's brand name. Negotiations with the licensee, and sometimes with local government, are costly. Governments often impose conditions on transferral of royalties or on component supply.

Table 11.5	Continued	
Intermediate entry mode	**Advantages**	**Disadvantages**
Franchising (seen from franchisor's viewpoint)	Greater degree of control compared with licensing. Low-risk, low-cost entry mode (the franchisees are the ones investing in the necessary equipment and know-how). Using highly motivated business contacts with money, local market knowledge and experience. Ability to develop new and distant international markets relatively quickly and on a larger scale than otherwise possible. Generating economies of scale in marketing to international customers. Precursor to possible future direct investment in foreign market.	The search for competent franchisees can be expensive and time-consuming. Lack of full control over franchisee's operations, resulting in problems with cooperation, communications, quality control, etc. Costs of creating and marketing a unique package of products and services recognized internationally. Costs of protecting goodwill and brand name. Problems with local legislation, including transfers of money, payments of franchise fees and government-imposed restrictions on franchise agreements. Opening up internal business knowledge may create potential future competitor. Risk to the company's international profile and reputation if some franchisees underperform ('free riding' on valuable brand names).
Joint venture (seen from parent's viewpoint)	Access to expertise and contacts in local markets. Each partner agrees to a joint venture to gain access to the other partner's skills and resources. Typically, the international partner contributes financial resources, technology or products. The local partner provides the skills and knowledge required for managing a business in its country. Each partner can concentrate on that part of the value chain where the firm has its core competence. Reduced market and political risk. Shared knowledge and resources: compared with wholly owned subsidiary, less capital and fewer management resources are required. Economies of scale by pooling skills and resources (resulting in e.g. lower marketing costs). Overcomes host government restrictions. May avoid local tariffs and non-tariff barriers. Shared risk of failure. Less costly than acquisitions. Possibly better relations with national governments through having a local partner (meets host country pressure for local participation).	Objectives of the respective partners may be incompatible, resulting in conflicts. Contributions to joint venture can become disproportionate. Loss of control over foreign operations. Large investments of financial, technical or managerial resources favour greater control than is possible in a joint venture. Completion might overburden a company's staff. Partners may become locked into long-term investments from which it is difficult to withdraw. Transfer pricing problems as goods pass between partners. The importance of the venture to each partner might change over time. Cultural differences may result in possible differences in management culture among participating firms. Loss of flexibility and confidentiality. Problems of management structures and dual parent staffing of joint ventures. Nepotism is perhaps the established norm.

Table 11.5	Continued	
Intermediate entry mode	**Advantages**	**Disadvantages**
Management contracting (seen from contractor's viewpoint)	If direct investment or export is considered too risky – for commercial or political reasons – this alternative might be relevant.	Training future competitors: the management transfer package may, in the end, create a competitor for the contractor.
	As with other intermediate entry modes, management contracts may be linked together with other forms of operation in foreign markets.	Creates a great demand for key personnel. Such staff are not always available, especially in small and medium-sized enterprises (SMEs).
	Allows a company to maintain market involvement, and so puts it in a better position to exploit any opportunity that may arise.	Considerable effort needs to be put into building lines of communication at the local level as well as back to the contractor.
	Organizational learning: if a company is in its early development stages of internationalization, a management contract may offer an efficient way of learning about foreign markets and international business.	Potential conflict between the contractor and the local government as regards the policy of the contract venture.
		Little control, which also limits the ability of a contractor to develop the capacity of the venture.

Other management contracts may be part of a deal to sell a processing plant as a project or a turnkey operation. This issue will be dealt with more intensively in Section 13.8.

11.7 Summary

Intermediate entry modes are distinguished from export modes because they are primarily vehicles for the transfer of knowledge and skills between partners, in order to create foreign sales. They are distinguished from hierarchical entry modes in that there is no full ownership (by parent firm) involved. Ownership and control can be shared between the parent firm and the local partner. This is the case, for example, with the (equity) joint venture.

CASE STUDY 11.1

Hello Kitty: can the cartoon cat survive the buzz across the world?

When, in 1974, employees at the Japanese design company Sanrio created Hello Kitty (www.sanrio.com/characters/HelloKitty/), the small, rounded cartoon cat with a red bow between her ears and no mouth, they had no idea she would become the global megastar she is today. The face of Hello Kitty adorns 50,000 products, sold in more than 130 countries. Saniro conducts its business operations through 26 subsidiaries. It has operations in Japan, the US, the UK, Brazil, Germany, Taiwan, South Korea, Hong Kong and China.

History

Hello Kitty was created with the focus of being a small gift, whatever the product is. The unique selling proposition (USP) has always been 'small gift, big smile'.

Hello Kitty's creator, Sanrio, was founded by Shintaro Tsuji in 1960; Tsuji, a qualified chemist, lost his mother when he was 13 and spent an unhappy childhood with reluctant relatives. He attended a kindergarten run by a Canadian missionary and saw for the first time the custom of birthdays, which were not traditionally celebrated in Japan. He decided he would use his company to foster the culture of gift-giving.

Source: Andrew Twort/Alamy Images.

The little half-Japanese, half-English cat has become so globally recognizable that it is, perhaps, inevitable that the Japanese board of tourism has appointed her as their official tourism ambassador to China and Hong Kong. This is not the first time the world has looked to Hello Kitty to perform an ambassadorial role; she was US children's ambassador for UNICEF in 1983.

Hello Kitty was first drawn in 1974. She was drawn without a mouth, which later made her the perfect cross-cultural representative. She wasn't given a mouth, because she speaks from the heart. She's Sanrio's ambassador to the world and isn't bound to any particular language.

Hello Kitty was made partly English because, when she was first drawn, foreign (especially English) associations were particularly popular. The Hello Kitty stationery (pencils, pencil cases, ballpoints pens, paper) and diaries were a hit among schoolgirls during the 1980s and the company soon branched out into other fancy goods.

In the 1990s, Hello Kitty had a renaissance. Shops, run by the outlet label Vivitix, marketed Hello Kitty to teens and adults, appealing to their sense of nostalgia.

As eight-year-olds they would have used Hello Kitty pencils and pencil cases in the classroom; in their late teens and early 20s, they reached for Hello Kitty satchels and make-up mirrors. Hello Kitty stands for the innocence and sincerity of childhood and the simplicity of the world. Women and girls all over the world are happy to buy in to the image of the trusting, loving childhood in a safe neighbourhood that Hello Kitty represents. They don't want to let go of that image, so as they grow up, they hang on to Hello Kitty out of nostalgia – as if by keeping a symbolic object, they can somehow keep hold of a fragment of their childhood self.

Now, although originally conceived as a character that would appeal to pre-teen girls, Hello Kitty is no longer regarded as being for children only. Along with the likes of Coca-Cola and Nike, she has become a brand phenomenon.

Hello Kitty is technically just one character who inhabits an entire, fictional world dreamt up by Sanrio. She lives in cyberspace (on the fondant-coloured Sanriotown website, www.sanrio.com/characters/HelloKitty/). Hello Kitty has her own birthday, 1 November (which makes her a Scorpio) and, as her English heritage befits, she lives in London with her parents and twin sister, Mimmy. Her many hobbies include travelling, music, reading and 'eating yummy cookies her mother Mary bakes'.

Other characters who share Hello Kitty's world include Dear Daniel, Kathy, Tippy and Thomas.

Sanrio's theme park, Puroland, opened in 1990; it features Sanrio's most popular characters, with Hello Kitty as its star draw, and with annual figures of 1.5 million visitors from around the world, it is one of Japan's most popular visitor attractions.

Hello Kitty even became an animated character. She first appeared on the American-animated Hello Kitty's Furry Tale Theater, which was shown on US television throughout 1987. She also appeared in a puppet animation 'Kitty and Mummy's New Umbrella' in 1981.

When Hello Kitty was first marketed to the US, the cultural differences meant that changes to the Japanese version had to be made. Sanrio's market research showed that American consumers responded best to pink and purple kitties and worst to anything blue, yellow or red. The American audience also took against one of Hello Kitty's friends, a little snail, which had to be eliminated from the merchandise.

However, Sanrio got it right in the end and now there are no differences in the American and Japanese lines of merchandise. Indeed, when Sanrio tried to customise Hello Kitty for its Taiwanese and Hong Kong markets, putting her in local dress and in local surroundings, the products did not sell. Her mixed English-Japanese heritage was part of her charm.

Hello Kitty business today

Its primary business is making and marketing what it calls social communication gifts. The company also operates restaurants and two theme parks in Japan, produces movies and publishes books and magazines – all based on its multitude of cute characters. Sanrio licenses or sells thousands of items – including Hello Kitty stationery, school and desk accessories, clothing, cosmetics and room decor – that turn up for sale around the world. Over 4,000 stores sell the products in the Americas alone, including some 50 Sanrio boutiques.

There are more than 50,000 Hello Kitty products available in 130 countries worldwide. The idea is to change the product range in order to match different and emerging marketing, business and cultural trends across the world. In China, Sanrio's Agents and the Franchisees operate about 160 shops.

Mobile phones are attractive products for the Hello Kitty brand with regard to licensing: children are now using mobiles as much as teenagers and adults. Mobiles or smartphones are objects that everyone carries with them and they are always visible.

Sanrio already operates a pair of Hello Kitty theme parks in Japan and the licensees operate theme parks in Malaysia, Korea and China.

Marketing and advertising

While the licensing partners may advertise Hello Kitty's products, Sanrio relies purely on its partners' marketing and word of mouth. Hello Kitty doesn't rely on animations, films or film shows to be promoted and is probably one of the only brands in the world that relies solely on its partners' advertising and word of mouth.

Licensing

Normally licensing is done as a very technical and commercial deal. However, Sanrio is very involved with the creative side and its decisions to work with certain licensee partners are more about their ability to create Hello Kitty products that appeal to the loyal consumer and protect what the brand stands for.

Competition

Sanrio does not tend to worry much about competition, as Hello Kitty has been out there as a brand for more than 30 years. However, Sanrio respects newcomers such as Don Ed Hardy, an American tattoo artist born and raised in southern California. Hardy is recognized for incorporating Japanese tattoo aesthetic and technique into his work. For example, in 2004, French fashion designer Christian Audigier licensed the rights to produce the high-end Ed Hardy clothing line, which is based on Hardy's imagery (Varley, 2009).

Sales development

The company's sales in Europe and the US have been declining, while the products have continued to grow in popularity in Japan, Asia and Brazil. The declining trend in some parts of the world may be due to the softening economy and financial crises.

Source: Markus Mainka/Alamy Images.

Despite the current problems, Sanrio is confident that the Hello Kitty phenomenon is not over yet. Overall, the Hello Kitty appeal is impossible to ignore. Her list of celebrity friends in the highly photographed entertainment industry includes Lady Gaga, who posed in a ball gown made of Hello Kitty plush and showed off a bouquet of miniature Hello Kitty roses. Heidi Klum has been seen publicly doing her make-up in front of a compact Hello Kitty mirror. Hello Kitty is also adored by others who are still young at heart, such as Nicki Minaj, Victoria Beckham and Mariah Carey.

Despite the current problems, Sanrio is confident that the Hello Kitty phenomenon is not over yet. Only the future will tell whether the iconic character will be heard in the coming decades, but currently its brand equity serves as a solid business platform for Sanrio.

QUESTIONS

1. Do you think that Hello Kitty will continue to rule the world? What are the pros and cons?

2. What are the reasons that Hello Kitty is licensed to so many different product manufacturers?

3. Suggest a future licensing strategy for Hello Kitty.

Sources: based on www.sanrio, www.sanrioeurope.com and other public sources; adapted from Walker, E. (2008) Top Cat: how 'Hello Kitty' conquered the world – Japan's new tourism ambassador, *The Independent,* 21 May, Copyright © The Independent, www.independent.co.uk.

CASE STUDY 11.2

Kabooki: licensing in the LEGO brand

The Danish toy manufacturer LEGO is known worldwide for its LEGO bricks. LEGO is a strong and well-known brand. In the 1990s, LEGO management received (among others) the results of three consumer surveys:

1. 'Image power' is a measure of brands' impact, where consumers' awareness of the world's leading brands is combined with their judgment of the brands' quality. In the US and Japan, LEGO was not placed among the top 10, but the results from Europe were impressive. Here LEGO was placed at number five, after four car brands: Mercedes-Benz, Rolls-Royce, Porsche and BMW. LEGO was ahead of brands such as Nestlé, Rolex, Jaguar and Ferrari.

2. A US survey, conducted in Europe, the US and Japan, showed that LEGO was number 13 in the list of most appreciated brands.

3. A survey by a German market analysis institute showed that LEGO was one of the most well-known toy brands in the new German Federal Republic, with an awareness share of 67 per cent. Matchbox was number two with 41 per cent.

The LEGO management decided to exploit this strong brand image and a managing director for the new business area LEGO Licensing A/S was appointed. The company's objective was to generate income from licensing suitable partners, which would use the LEGO brand in marketing their own products.

The LEGO management noticed that Coca-Cola had an income of Danish Kr 3 billion from licensing alone. Coca-Cola's strategy can be characterized as 'brand milking', where a brand is sold to the highest bidder in each product area.

Ideas become viable

In 1993, the idea of licensing the LEGO brand became viable for the Danish textile firm Kabooki, as it was given the rights to use the LEGO brand in connection with the production and sale of children's clothes. Kabooki's managing director, Torben Klausen, was previously employed in LEGO's international marketing department, where he was in charge of coordinating the European marketing of LEGO bricks. From this position, he was able to follow the development of the licensing concept. From 1993 things developed very quickly. By mid-1997, Kabooki, which had invested a considerable amount of money in the R&D of LEGO children's clothes, was selling to approximately 900 shops, primarily in Scandinavia and England.

Torben Klausen said:

We received a strong international brand from the first day. But with selling LEGO children's comes an obligation to live up to the LEGO company's unique quality demands. LEGO must approve all new models that are put on the market, and that is between 350 and 400 a year.

LEGO children's clothes distinguish themselves from other brands by being functional and having strong colours and an uncompromising quality. This means a relatively high price for the clothes, and that the products are not sold in discount shops. The clothes are sold on the basis of a shop-in-shop concept, where merchandising and display facilities are very important.

Children in Kabooki clothes (LEGO licence)
Source: © The Lego Group

QUESTIONS

You have just been employed by LEGO Licensing A/S in connection with the development of the licensing data. You are given the following assignments.

1. What are the most important factors determining future market demand for LEGO children's clothes from Kabooki?

2. Which other products could be considered for licensing out the LEGO brand?

3. List some criteria for choosing suitable licensees and future products for the LEGO brand (licensing out).

4. What values/benefits can LEGO transfer to the licensee (e.g. Kabooki) apart from the use of the LEGO brand?

5. What values/benefits can the licensee transfer to the licensor?

Source: based on different public sources.

VIDEO CASE STUDY 11.3 Marriott

download from **www.pearson.co.uk/hollensen**

Marriott (www.marriott.com) is a worldwide operator and franchisor of 4,100 hotels and related facilities in 80 countries with over 697,000 rooms. Quality and consistent service are Marriott's main focuses and these keep the company at the top of its industry. The company is responsible for pioneering segmentation in the hospitality industry. With a wide array of hotels, Marriott meets the needs of various customer segments. Before developing any additional hotel chains and their respective brands, the company always tests properties first. Marriott is active in soliciting feedback from its customer base and focuses on really understanding its customer targets.

Questions

1. What could be the main motives for Marriott in using franchising, compared to other entry modes and operation forms?

2. Identify several major categories of segmentation used by Marriott. For each, relate specific examples of hotel services tailored to various target markets; www.marriott.com offers a brief description of 13 brands of various Marriott hotels catering to different types of customers.

3. How should Marriott react to 'shared economy' internet-based services like Airbnb?

Source: Frankfurt Marriott Hotel, Marriott Hotels International Ltd.

For further resources, see this book's website at **www.pearsoned.co.uk/hollensen**

Questions for discussion

1. Why are joint ventures preferred by host countries as an entry strategy for foreign firms?

2. Why are strategic alliances used in new product development?

3. Under what circumstances should franchising be considered? How do these circumstances vary from those leading to licensing?

4. Do you believe that licensing in represents a feasible long-term product development strategy for a company? Discuss in relation to in-house product development.

5. Why would a firm consider forming partnerships with competitors?

6. Apart from the management fees involved, what benefits might a firm derive from entering into management contracts overseas?

References

Anderson, E. and Gatignon, H. (1986) 'Modes of foreign entry: a transaction cost and analysis and propositions', *Journal of International Business Studies,* Fall, pp. 1–26.

Bleeke, J. and Ernst, D. (1994) *Collaborating to Compete: Using Strategic Alliances and Acquisitions in the Global Marketplace.* John Wiley, New York.

Buck, T., Liu, X. and Ott, U. (2010) 'Long-term orientation and international joint venture strategies in modern China', *International Business Review,* 19, pp. 223–234.

Carstairs, R.T. and Welch, L.S. (1981) *A Study of Outward Foreign Licensing of Technology by Australian Companies.* Licensing Executives Society of Australia, Canberra.

Davis, L. (2008) 'Licensing strategies of the new intellectual property vendors', *California Management Review,* 50(2), pp. 6–30.

Doherty, A.M. (2009) 'Market and partner selection processes in international retail franchising', *Journal of Business Research,* 62, pp. 528–534.

Doherty, A.M. and Alexander, N. (2006) 'Power and control in international retail franchising', *European Journal of Management,* 40(11/12), pp. 1292–1316.

Geringer, J.M. and Hebert, L. (1991) 'Measuring performance of international joint ventures', *Journal of International Business Studies,* 22, pp. 249–263.

Harrigan, K.R. (1985) *Strategies for Joint Ventures.* Lexington Books and D.C. Heath, Lexington, MA.

Hennert, J.-F., Zeng, M. (2005) 'Structural determinants of joint venture performance', *European Management Review,* 2, pp. 105–115.

Kuo, A., Kao, M.S., Chang, Y.C. and Chiu, C.F. (2012) 'The influence of international experience on entry mode choice: difference between family and non-family firms', *European Management Journal,* 30, pp. 248–263.

Lorange, P. and Roos, J. (1995) *Strategiske allianser i globale strategier.* Norges Eksportråd, Oslo.

Luostarinen, R. and Welch, L. (1990) *International Business Operations.* Helsinki School of Economics, Helsinki.

Mata, J. and Portugal, P. (2015) 'The termination of international joint ventures: Closure and acquisition by domestic and foreign partners', *International Business Review,* 24, 677–689.

Nanda, A. and Williamson, P.J. (1995) 'Use joint ventures to ease the pain of restructuring', *Harvard Business Review,* November–December, pp. 119–128.

Paliwoda, S. (1993) *International Marketing*. Heinemann, Oxford.

Perkins, J.S. (1987) 'How licensing and franchising differ', *Les Nouvelles*, 22(4), pp. 155–158.

Porter, M.E. and Fuller, M.B. (1986) 'Coalition and global strategy', in Porter, M.E. (ed.), *Competition in Global Strategies*, Harvard Business School Press, Boston, MA, pp. 315–344.

Vaidya, S. (2009) 'International joint ventures: an integrated framework', *Competitiveness Review: An International Business Journal*, 19(1), pp. 8–16.

Varley, M. (2009) 'Can Hello Kitty continue to rule the world', *Brand Strategy*, 32, February, pp. 32–36.

Walmsley, J. (1982) *Handbook of International Joint Ventures*. Graham & Trotman Ltd, London.

Welsh, D.H.B., Alon, I. and Falbe, C.M. (2006) 'An examination of international retail franchising in emerging markets', *Journal of Small Business Management*, 44(1), pp. 130–149.

Young, S., Hamill, J., Wheeler, S. and Davies, J.R. (1989) *International Market Entry and Development*. Harvester Wheatsheaf/Prentice Hall, Hemel Hempstead.

CHAPTER 12
Hierarchical modes

Contents

Case studies

Learning objectives

After studying this chapter you should be able to:

- Describe the main hierarchical modes:
  - domestic-based representatives
  - resident sales representatives
  - foreign sales subsidiary
  - sales and production subsidiary
  - region centres

- Compare and contrast the two investment alternatives: acquisition versus greenfield
- Explain the different determinants that influence the decision to withdraw investments from a foreign market.

12.1   Introduction

Hierarchical mode
The firm owns and controls the foreign entry mode/organization.

The final group of entry modes is the **hierarchical mode**, where the firm completely owns and controls the foreign entry mode. Here it is a question of where the control in the firm lies. The degree of control that head office can exert on the subsidiary will depend on how many and which value chain functions can be transferred to the market. This again depends on the allocation of responsibility and competence between head office and the subsidiary, and how the firm wants to develop this on an international level. An organization that is not wholly owned (i.e. 100 per cent) will here be viewed as an export mode or an intermediate mode. The following example, though, may suggest some of the problems involved in this sharp division: a majority-owned (e.g. 75 per cent) joint venture is, according to definition, an intermediate mode, but in practice a firm with 75 per cent will generally have nearly full control, similar to a hierarchical mode.

If a producer wants greater influence and control over local marketing than export modes can give, it is natural to consider creating its own companies in the foreign markets. However, this shift involves an investment, except in the case of the firm having its own sales force, which is considered an operating cost (see Figure 12.1).

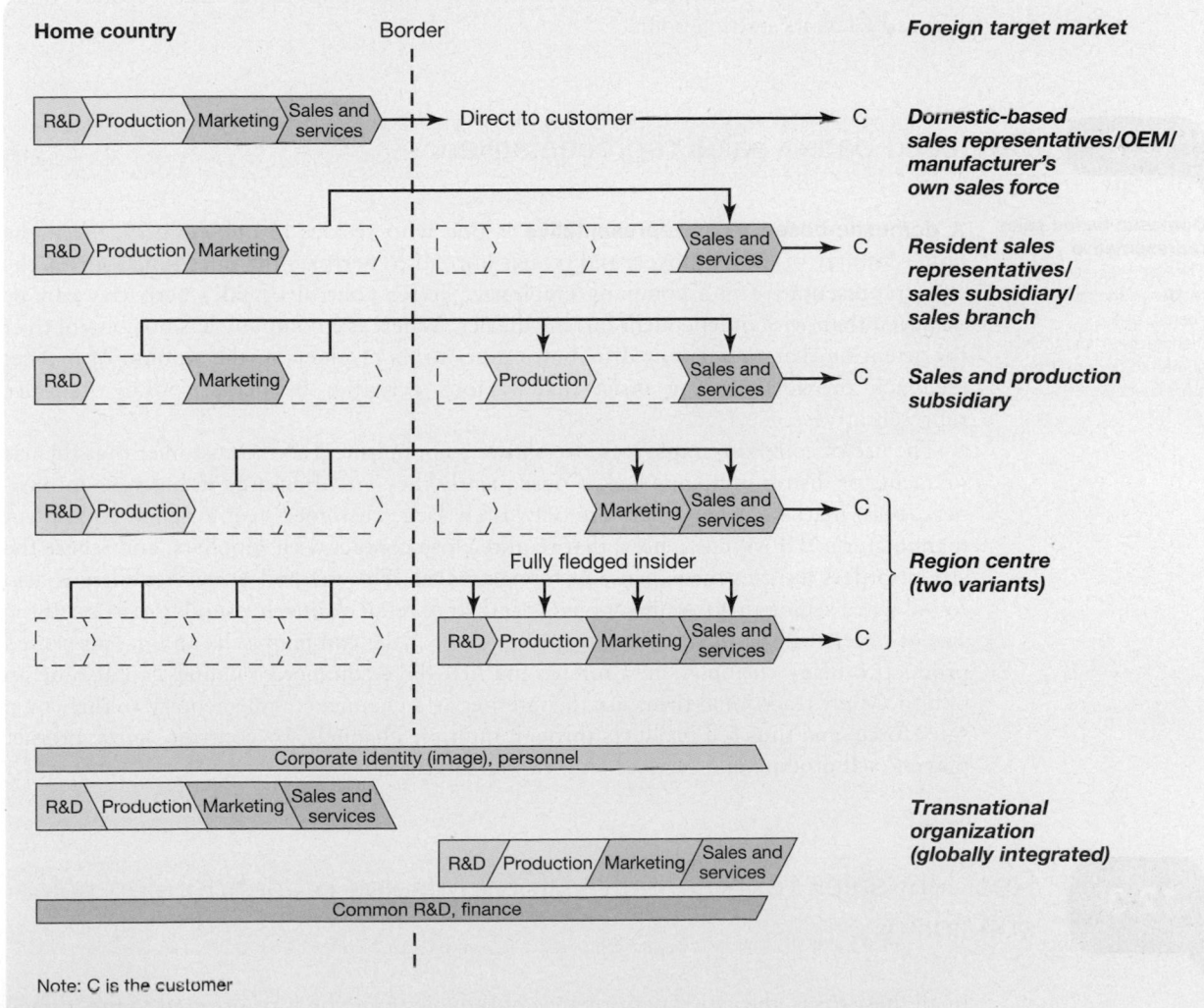

Note: C is the customer

Figure 12.1   Hierarchical modes in a value chain perspective

As a firm goes through Figure 12.1, it chooses to decentralize more and more of its activities to the main foreign markets. In other words, it transfers the responsibility of performing the value chain functions to the local management in the different countries. While moving through Figure 12.1 the firm also goes from one internationalization stage to another (Perlmutter, 1969):

- *Ethnocentric orientation*, represented by the domestic-based sales representatives. This orientation represents an extension of the marketing methods used in the home country to foreign markets.
- *Polycentric orientation*, represented by country subsidiaries. This orientation is based on the assumption that markets/countries around the world are so different that the only way to succeed internationally is to manage each country as a separate market with its own subsidiary and adapted marketing mix.
- *Regiocentric orientation*, represented by a region of the world (Section 12.6).
- *Geocentric orientation*, represented by the transnational organization. This orientation is based on the assumption that the markets around the world consist of similarities and differences and that it is possible to create a transnational strategy which takes advantage of the similarities between the markets by using synergy effects to leverage learning on a worldwide basis.

The following description and discussion concerning hierarchical modes takes Figure 12.1 as its starting point.

12.2 Domestic-based sales representatives

Domestic-based sales representative
The sales representative resides in the home country of the manufacturer and travels abroad to perform the sales function.

A **domestic-based sales representative** is one who resides in one country, often the home country of the employer, and travels abroad to perform the sales function. As the sales representative is a company employee, better control of sales activities can be achieved than with independent intermediaries. Whereas a company has no control over the attention that an agent or distributor gives to its products or the amount of market feedback provided, it can insist that various activities be performed by its sales representatives.

The use of company employees also shows a commitment to the customer that the use of agents or distributors may lack. Consequently they are often used in business-to-business (B2B) markets, where there are only a few large customers [e.g. original equipment manufacturer (OEM) customers] that require close contact with suppliers, and where the size of orders justifies the expense of foreign travel. This method of market entry is also found when selling to government buyers and large retail chains, for similar reasons. If the size of orders cannot justify the foreign travel, or if the company sells an uncomplicated product to many customers in a foreign market, the e-commerce channel can also be an option. Many traditional firms use the internet as a channel complementary to their own sales force, and thus sell products through multiple channels. By contrast, 'pure internet players' sell product and services only via the internet.

12.3 Resident sales representatives/foreign sales branch/foreign sales subsidiary

In all these cases, the actual performance of the sales function is transferred to the foreign market. These three options all display a greater customer commitment than using domestic-based sales representatives. In making the decision whether to use travelling domestic-based representatives or resident sales representatives in any particular foreign market, a firm should consider the following:

- *Order-making or order-taking.* If the firm finds that the type of sales job it needs done in a foreign market tends towards order-taking it will probably choose a travelling domestic-based sales representative, and vice versa.
- *The nature of the product.* If the product is technical and complex in nature and a lot of servicing/supply of parts is required, the travelling salesperson is not an efficient entry method. A more permanent foreign base is needed.

Foreign branch
An extension of and a legal part of the manufacturer (often called a sales office). Taxation of profits takes place in the manufacturer's country.

Subsidiary
A local company owned and operated by a foreign company under the laws and taxation of the host country.

Sometimes firms find it relevant to establish a formal branch office, to which a resident salesperson is assigned. A **foreign branch** is an extension and a legal part of the firm. A foreign branch also often employs nationals of the country in which it is located as salespeople. If foreign market sales develop in a positive direction, the firm (at a certain point) may consider establishing a wholly owned sales subsidiary. A foreign **subsidiary** is a local company owned and operated by a foreign company under the laws of the host country.

The sales subsidiary provides complete control of the sales function. The firm will often keep a central marketing function at its home base, but sometimes a local marketing function can be included in the sales subsidiary. When the sales function is organized as a sales subsidiary (or when sales activities are performed), all foreign orders are channelled through the subsidiary, which then sells to foreign buyers at normal wholesale or retail prices. The foreign sales subsidiary purchases the products to be sold from the parent company at a price. This, of course, creates the problem of intra-company transfer pricing. This problem will be discussed in further detail in Section 15.4.

One of the major reasons for choosing sales subsidiaries is the possibility of transferring greater autonomy and responsibility to these subunits, being close to the customer. However, another reason for establishing sales subsidiaries may be the tax advantage. This is particularly important for companies headquartered in high-tax countries. With proper planning, companies can establish subsidiaries in countries with low business income taxes and gain an advantage by not paying taxes in their home country on the foreign-generated income until such income is actually repatriated to them. Of course, the precise tax advantages that are possible with such subsidiaries depend upon the tax laws in the home country compared with the host country.

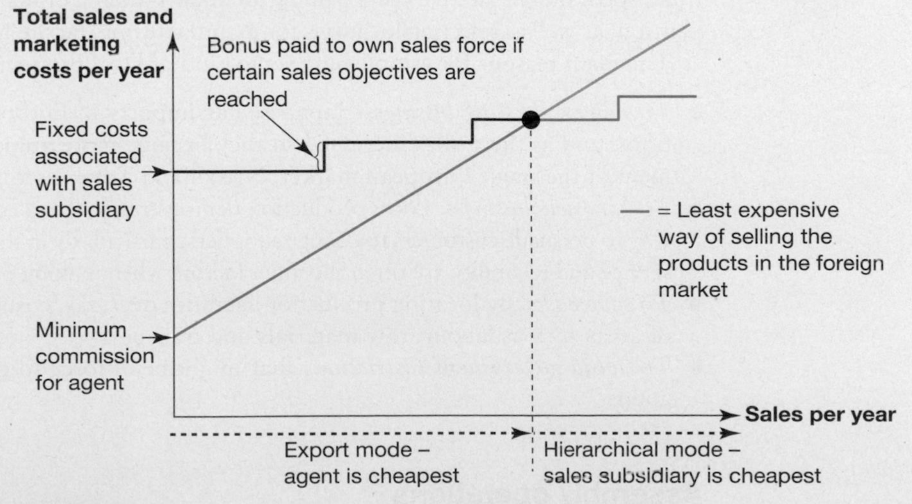

Figure 12.2   Break-even shifting from agent to sales subsidiary

Source: Hollensen, S. (2008) *Essentials of Global Marketing*, FT/Prentice Hall, p. 245. Copyright © Pearson Education Limited.

One of the most interesting things to determine for a firm doing business in a foreign market is when to switch from an agent to having its own sales subsidiary and own sales force (Ross *et al.*, 2005). Figure 12.2 shows the total sales and marketing costs associated with using two different entry modes:

1. *Agent.* This curve is based on a contract where the agents get a minimum annual commission independent of annual sales. The agents will get the same percentage in commission no matter how much they generate in annual sales.
2. *Sales subsidiary.* This curve is based on the assumption that the sales force in the sales subsidiary will have a fixed salary per annum (independent of the annual sales), but will be paid an extra bonus if they fulfil certain sales objectives.

Under these circumstances there will be a certain break-even point where it is more advantageous (from a financial standpoint) to switch from an agent to own sales subsidiary. Of course, other issues, such as control, flexibility and level of investment, must be considered before making such a switch.

12.4   ### Sales and production subsidiary

Sales subsidiaries may be perceived as taking money out of the country and contributing nothing of value to the host country in which they are based, especially in developing countries. In those countries, a sales subsidiary will generally not be in existence long before there are local demands for a manufacturing or production base.

Generally, if the company believes that its products have long-term market potential in a country that is relatively stable politically, then only full ownership of sales and production will provide the level of control necessary to meet the firm's strategic objectives fully. However, this entry mode requires great investment in terms of management time, commitment and money. There are considerable risks, too, as subsequent withdrawal from the market can be extremely costly – not simply in terms of financial outlay but also in terms of reputation in the international and domestic market, particularly with customers and staff.

Japanese companies have used this strategy to build a powerful presence in international markets over a long period of time. Their patience has been rewarded with high market shares and substantial profits, but this has not been achieved overnight. They have sometimes spent more than five years gaining an understanding of markets, customers and competition, as well as selecting locations for manufacturing, before making a significant move.

The main reasons for establishing some kind of local production are:

- *To defend existing business.* Japanese car imports to Europe were subject to restrictions, and as their sales increased so they became more vulnerable. With the development of the single European market, Nissan and Toyota set up operations in the UK.
- *To gain new business.* Local production demonstrates strong commitment and is the best way to persuade customers to change suppliers, particularly in the industrial markets where service and reliability are often the main factors when making purchasing decisions.
- *To save costs.* By locating production facilities overseas, costs can be saved in a variety of areas such as labour, raw materials and transport.
- *To avoid government restrictions* that might be in force to restrict imports of certain goods.

Assembly operations

An assembly operation is a variation of the production subsidiary. Here a foreign production plant might be set up simply to assemble components manufactured in the domestic market or elsewhere. The firm may try to retain key component manufacture in the domestic plant, allowing development, production skills and investment to be concentrated, and maintaining the benefit from economies of scale. Some parts or components may be produced in various countries (multi-sourcing) in order to gain each country's comparative advantage. Capital-intensive parts may be produced in advanced nations, and labour-intensive assemblies may be produced in a less developed country (LDC), where labour is abundant and labour costs are low. This strategy is common among manufacturers of consumer electronics. When a product becomes mature and faces intense price competition, it may be necessary to shift all of the labour-intensive operations to LDCs. This is the principle behind the international product life cycle (IPLC) – see also Chapter 14 (Figure 14.8).

12.5   Subsidiary growth and integration strategies

As multinational corporations (MNCs) face ever greater competition, their subsidiaries located in developed countries are increasingly vulnerable to being closed and having their operations relocated to low-cost eastern bloc and Asian nations. To cope with this cost differential, subsidiary managers are constantly urged to contribute beyond their core mandate, to move their subsidiary's activities up the value chain and to be innovative and entrepreneurial.

Due to continuing globalization of systems and processes, there are increasing restrictions (from the HQ) on the ability of subsidiaries to develop a unique position to ensure their survival and growth. In this process the subsidiary must clearly define its boundaries, as there are activities that may not be cost-effective or strategically beneficial to pursue. However, the subsidiary CEO must identify the value-added business that will generate strong returns and then bring the problem and its solution to HQ rather than waiting for it to take the initiative. As suggested in the following, there are several ways that a subsidiary can act against its parent company (HQ).

Transfer of company HQ culture to the subsidiary

According to the literature, an organizational culture that is valuable, rare and difficult to imitate may form the basis for international competitive advantage (Barney, 1997). Figure 12.3 illustrates the relationship between the HQ of the MNCs, their subsidiaries and the host country. A strong home culture is likely to help subsidiaries to develop their own strong culture and identity. On the other hand, a relatively strong country culture, meaning there are unique cultural values and behaviour in the local community, is likely to make barriers to the development of the MNC's unique company culture in the subsidiary.

As Figure 12.3 indicates, the MNC subsidiary operates in a host country and thus forges relationships with local actors, such as suppliers and customers, who embody country and local cultural values that differ from the home country and the HQ values. Figure 12.3 presents a framework for analysing the cultural interaction between organizations in different countries, with different cultural values. According to the framework (matrix), there are four combinations:

1. *Integration*. Here the MNC's company (HQ) values are maintained in the subsidiary. At the same time, the subsidiary develops a high level of external contact and embeddedness to the host country's national and local culture. So the subsidiary has close relationships to the local actors, such as local suppliers. At first glance, this strategy seems attractive. However, integrating two cultures is not an easy task.

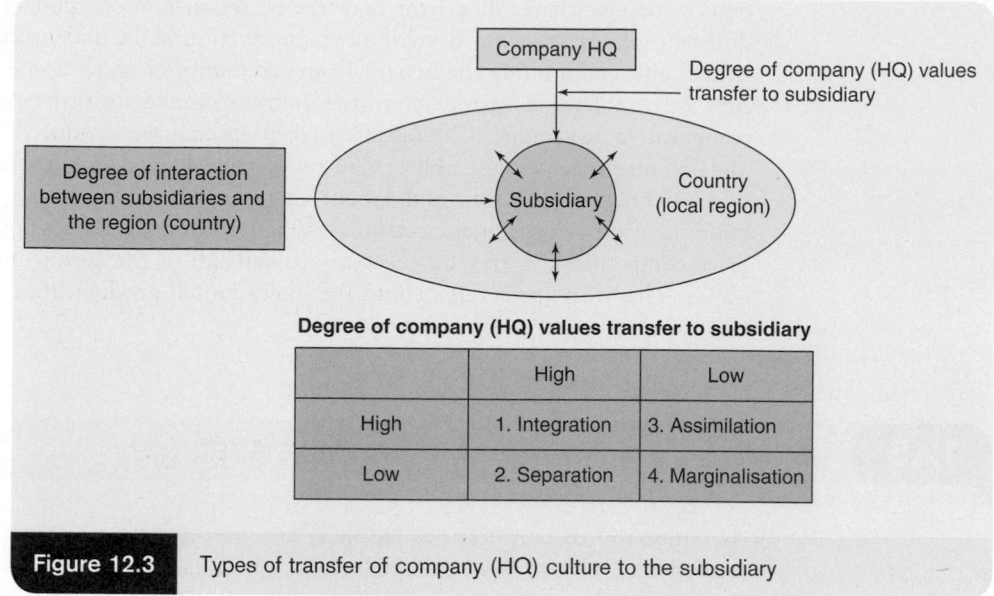

Figure 12.3   Types of transfer of company (HQ) culture to the subsidiary

Source: based on Sasaki and Yoshikawa (2014, p. 460).

2. *Separation*. Here the MNC's company (HQ) culture is also maintained, but the subsidiary limits its external embeddedness to the local actors, especially suppliers. For example, when the Japanese auto manufacturers such as Toyota, Honda and Nissan established their North American manufacturing sites they brought their own suppliers with them from Japan. In fact, many of them internalized the production of key parts in these plants. This limited the need to interact with local actors (e.g. local suppliers) who were embedded in national and local values and practices.

3. *Assimilation*. This option implies a high level of external embeddedness and lack of maintenance of the MNC HQ's own identity and culture. The subsidiary acts more on its own, and assimilates into the local region with its own cultures and values. This strategy was used by Japanese MNCs like Sony and NEC when they established subsidiaries in Silicon Valley. The subsidiary employees (even those coming from Japan) quickly adopted the risk-taking and fast-moving culture of Silicon Valley, which conflicted with the consensual risk-controlling culture from the home country HQs in Japan.

4. *Marginalization*. Here the MNC HQ culture is not established in the subsidiary and the subsidiary also limits its external embeddedness. Not the best strategy for achieving success in the country.

Before the MNC makes a choice of location for its subsidiary in a country, it could benefit from assessing the nature of the local culture and its strength in the target market. This kind of assessment would be especially important for MNCs pursuing both active interaction with local actors and close collaboration between home HQ and the subsidiary in that such a strategy requires the integration of two cultures. In addition, a lack of globalization experience would make such an assessment even more necessary (Sasaki and Yoshikawa, 2014).

12.6

Region centres (regional HQ)

Until now choice of foreign entry mode has mainly been discussed in relation to one particular country. If we suspend this condition, we consider the world as being increasingly regionalized through the formation of such groupings as the European Union, the North American Free Trade Area (NAFTA) and the Association of South East Asian Nations (ASEAN).

Region centres
The regional HQ ('lead country') will usually play the role of coordinating and stimulating sales in the whole region.

In Figure 12.1 two examples of **region centres** are shown. The first variant shows that the downstream functions have been transferred to the region. In the second variant, even greater commitment is shown to the region, because here all the value chain activities are moved to the region, whereby the firm has become a fully fledged insider in the region. At this stage the firm has all the necessary functions in the region to compete effectively against local and regional competitors. At the same time, the firm can respond to regional customer needs. This situation is also illustrated in the lower part of Figure 12.4, where many activities are coordinated across countries.

Formation of region centres implies creation of a regional HQ or appointment of a 'lead country', which will usually play the role of coordinator and stimulator with reference to a single homogeneous product group (see Figure 12.5).

The coordination role consists of ensuring three things:

1. Country and business strategies are mutually coherent.
2. One subsidiary does not harm another.
3. Adequate synergies are fully identified and exploited across business and countries.

The stimulator role consists of two functions:

1. facilitating the translation of 'global' products into local country strategies;
2. supporting local subsidiaries in their development (Lasserre, 1996).

		Number of countries involved	
		Few	*Many*
Coordination of value chain activities	*Few activities coordinated across countries (primarily logistics)*	New international market makers	
		Export/import start-up ①	Multinational trader ②
	Many activities coordinated across countries	③ Geographically focused start-up	④ Global start-up

Figure 12.4 Types of international new venture

Source: reproduced with permission of Palgrave Macmillan: *Journal of International Business Studies*, Vol. 25, No. 1, pp. 45–64, *Toward a theory of international new ventures*, by Oviatt, B.M. and McDougall, P.P., copyright 1994, published by Palgrave Macmillan.

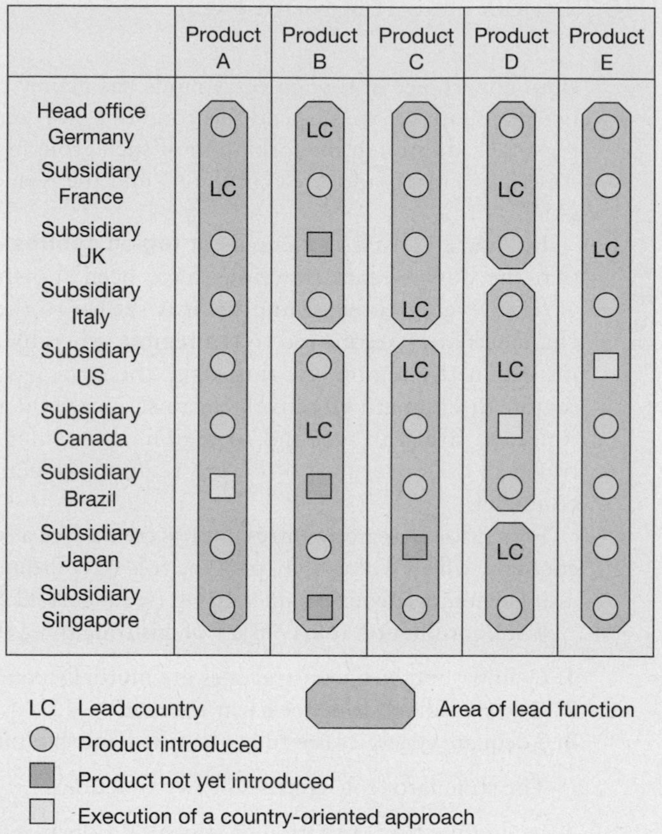

	Product A	Product B	Product C	Product D	Product E
Head office Germany	○	LC	○	○	○
Subsidiary France	LC	○	○	LC	○
Subsidiary UK	○	□	○	○	LC
Subsidiary Italy	○	○	LC	○	○
Subsidiary US	○	○	LC	LC	□
Subsidiary Canada	○	LC	○	□	○
Subsidiary Brazil	□	□	○	○	○
Subsidiary Japan	○	○	□	LC	○
Subsidiary Singapore	○	□	○	○	○

LC	Lead country	Area of lead function
○	Product introduced	
■	Product not yet introduced	
□	Execution of a country-oriented approach	

Figure 12.5 The lead country concept

Source: Raffée and Kreutzer (1989). Published with permission of Emerald Publishing Ltd; *www.emeraldinsight.com*.

Figure 12.5 (an example of a multinational company having its head office in Germany) shows that different countries/subsidiaries can have a leading function for different product groups. In the figure there is a world market such that for products A and E only one country/subsidiary has the coordination function on a global basis (France and the UK, respectively). For product D there are three regions with a lead country in each region.

The choice of a lead country is influenced by several factors:

● the marketing competences of the foreign subsidiaries;
● the quality of human resources in the countries represented;
● the strategic importance of the countries represented;
● location of production;
● legal restrictions of host countries.

The country with the best 'leading' competences should be chosen for the job as lead country.

12.7 Transnational organization

In this final stage of internationalization, companies attempt to coordinate and integrate operations across national boundaries so as to achieve potential synergies on a global scale. Management views the world as a series of interrelated markets. At this stage, the employees tend to identify more strongly with their company than with the country in which they operate.

Common R&D and frequent geographical exchange of human resources across borders are among the characteristics of a **transnational organization**. Its overall goal will be to achieve global competitiveness through recognizing cross-border market similarities and differences, and linking the capabilities of the organization across national boundaries. One of the relatively few international companies that have reached this stage is Unilever – see also Section 8.5.

In summary, managing a transnational organization requires the sensitivity to understand:

Transnational organization
Integration and coordination of operations (R&D, production, marketing and sales and services) across national boundaries in order to achieve synergies on a global scale.

- when a global brand makes sense or when local requirements should take precedence;
- when to transfer innovation and expertise from one market to another;
- when a local idea has global potential;
- when to bring international teams together fast to focus on key opportunities.

12.8 Establishing wholly owned subsidiaries – acquisition or greenfield

All the hierarchical modes presented in this chapter (except domestic-based sales representatives) involve investment in foreign-based facilities. In deciding to establish wholly owned operations in a country, a firm can either acquire an existing company or build its own operations from scratch (greenfield investment).

Acquisition

Acquisition enables rapid entry and often provides access to distribution channels, an existing customer base and, in some cases, established brand names or corporate reputations. In some cases, too, existing management remains, providing a bridge to entry into the market and allowing the firm to acquire experience in dealing with the local market environment. This may be particularly advantageous for a firm with limited international management expertise, or little familiarity with the local market.

In saturated markets, the industry is highly competitive or there are substantial entry barriers, and therefore there is little room for a new entrant. In these circumstances, acquisitions may be the only feasible way of establishing a base in the host country.

Acquisitions take many forms. According to Root (1987), acquisition may be horizontal (the product lines and markets of the acquired and acquiring firms are similar), vertical (the acquired firm becomes supplier or customer of the acquiring firm), concentric (the acquired firm has the same market but different technology, or the same technology but different markets) or conglomerate (the acquired firm is in a different industry from that of the acquiring firm). No matter what form the acquisition takes, coordination and styles of management between the foreign investor and the local management team may cause problems.

Greenfield investment

The difficulties encountered with acquisitions may lead firms to prefer to establish operations from the ground up, especially where production logistics is a key industry success factor, and where no appropriate acquisition targets are available or they are too costly.

The ability to integrate operations across countries, and to determine the direction of future international expansion, is often a key motivation to establish wholly owned operations, even though it takes longer to build plants than to acquire them. Further motives for greenfield investment can also include incentives offered by the host country.

Furthermore, if the firm builds a new plant, it can not only incorporate the latest technology and equipment, but also avoid the problems of trying to change the traditional practices of an established concern. A new facility means a fresh start and an opportunity for the international company to shape the local firm to its own image and requirements.

12.9   Location/relocation of HQ

The starting point is to consider the traditional checklist of HQ site selection criteria (Baaij *et al.*, 2005):

- corporate tax advantages
- investment incentives
- investment climate
- company law (internal restriction – the owners' wishes have to be followed)
- operational costs
- quality, availability and costs of the workforce
- quality of living (major hotels and restaurants, proximity of quality housing, cultural life and recreation, quality of schools, cultural diversity, safety, crime and health factors, personal taxes, cost of living, etc.)
- level of infrastructure (in particular, transportation, communication and IT)
- extent of high-level business services (e.g. accounting, legal and management consulting)
- sufficient representative office space
- the presence of other major corporations.

The main benefit of using this checklist is not to find suitable sites, but to eliminate unsuitable ones. Once these factors have been assessed, more strategic criteria for the right HQ location can be considered.

There are three strategic motives that can affect the HQ location decision:

1. mergers and acquisitions
2. internationalization of leadership and ownership
3. strategic renewal.

Mergers and acquisitions

When companies of equal size merge, they need to find a neutral location for the HQ of the merged corporation. In 1987, Asea from Västerås in Sweden and BBC Brown Boveri of Baden, Switzerland, merged to create ABB Asea Brown Boveri. The new HQ was not situated in either original location, but in Zurich.

Internationalization of leadership and ownership

In the case of acquisitions, the obvious solution is the most effective – the new HQ is that of the acquirer, and the acquired corporation relocates (e.g. DaimlerChrysler). The second motive – internationalization of leadership and ownership – makes corporations less sensitive to national sentiments or ties to a specific country. Foreign board executives and shareholders will be less attached to the traditional home country, and less likely to resist a cross-border relocation of the HQ.

Strategic renewal

The final reason for relocating HQ is strategic renewal. This was a key reason for Philips Electronics' relocation to Amsterdam after 106 years of emotional ties to Eindhoven, the town where Philips was founded. Relocation can be a mechanism of change because it symbolizes a fresh start and a break with the past.

12.10 Foreign divestment: withdrawing from a foreign market

While a vast theoretical and empirical literature has examined the determinants of entering into foreign direct investments, considerably less attention has been given to the decision to exit from a foreign market.

Most of the studies undertaken show a considerable 'loss' of foreign subsidiaries over time:

- Between 1967 and 1975, the 180 largest US-based multinationals added some 4,700 subsidiaries to their networks, but more than 2,400 affiliates were divested during the same period (Boddewyn, 1979).
- Out of 225 foreign direct investments (FDIs) undertaken by large Dutch multinationals in the period 1966–88, only just over half were still in existence in 1988 (Barkema *et al.*, 1996).

EXHIBIT 12.1 Tesco's withdrawal from Japan in 2012 after nine years

Tesco entered Japan in 2003 through acquisition of the local partner C Two-Network. Tesco management initially talked about plans to open a store a week, taking the total up to 500 stores by 2010. However, in June 2012, the British retailer decided to leave the Japanese market after nine years.

This was despite Tesco launching its private-label products (2006) and its Express format (2007) into the market – two initiatives that have been successful in other Asian markets. All in all Tesco invested more than US$150 million since entering Japan, but it did not succeed in making the operations profitable. The number of

Source: Imagine China/Corbis.

Tesco stores in Japan peaked at around 140 – at the time of the decision to leave Japan Tesco had 129 stores.

Tesco encountered a difficult market in Japan, one in which other international retailers had previously had serious problems as well. Carrefour of France left Japan after just five years, while giants like US-based Walmart and Germany's Metro have struggled to settle down successfully.

Why did Tesco fail in Japan?

Wrong local partner

Tesco has typically tied up with a relatively strong local player in local Asian markets – e.g. in South Korea it is tied up with Samsung. In Japan, Tesco's Japanese partner, C Two-Network, at the time of acquisition had 78 stores and annual revenues of less than US$0.5 billion. So it was obviously not a major player in the Japanese retail sector.

Tough competition

Japan is a unique retail market, as other global retailers have also discovered. Rapidly changing consumer tastes is a challenge. Launching Tesco Express seemed a logical move given the existing store portfolio and the format's success elsewhere. However, it faced stiff competition from local c-store giants such as 7-Eleven, Lawson, FamilyMart and Ministop.

Too few 'economies of scale'

For food retailers, Japan's high costs, particularly high rents and personnel costs, pose an additional challenge. One factor behind the high costs is consumers' strong preference for locally sourced fresh foods. Scale is crucial to keep costs low and this is what ultimately led to failure for Tesco. With 129 stores left, compared with Aeon's 1,900 stores, Tesco was just too small to compete with the large Japanese supermarket groups.

Immediately after the decision to leave, Tesco sold 50 per cent of its Japanese subsidiary, Tesco Japan, to Aeon Co., the dominant retail group in Japan. Later in 2012, it sold the remaining 50 per cent to Aeon.

Now Tesco will pay more attention to the UK and US markets.

Tesco has 1,400 stores in Asia, with larger businesses in China, Korea, Malaysia and Thailand, which is one of Tesco's fastest-growing markets.

Source: based on different public media.

Closing down a foreign subsidiary or selling it off to another firm is a strategic decision, and the consequence may be a change of foreign entry mode (e.g. from a local sales and production subsidiary to an export mode or a joint venture), or a complete withdrawal from a host country.

The most obvious incentive to exit is profits that are too low, which in turn may be due to high costs, permanent decreases in local market demand or the entry into the industry of more efficient competitors. Besides being voluntary, the divestment may also be a result of expropriation or nationalization in the foreign country.

In order to investigate further the question of why foreign divestments take place, it is necessary to look at the specific factors that may influence incentives and barriers to exit, and thereby the probability of exiting from a foreign subsidiary. Benito (1996) classifies the specific factors into four main groups (Figure 12.6).

Environmental stability

This is a question of the predictability of the environment – competitively and politically – in which the foreign subsidiary operates:

- *R&D intensity*. Perceived barriers to exit are likely to increase due to large market-specific investments made in R&D and the marketing of the products.
- *Country risks*. These risks are typically outside the firm's scope of control. Political risks may often lead to forced divestment, with the result that expropriation takes place.

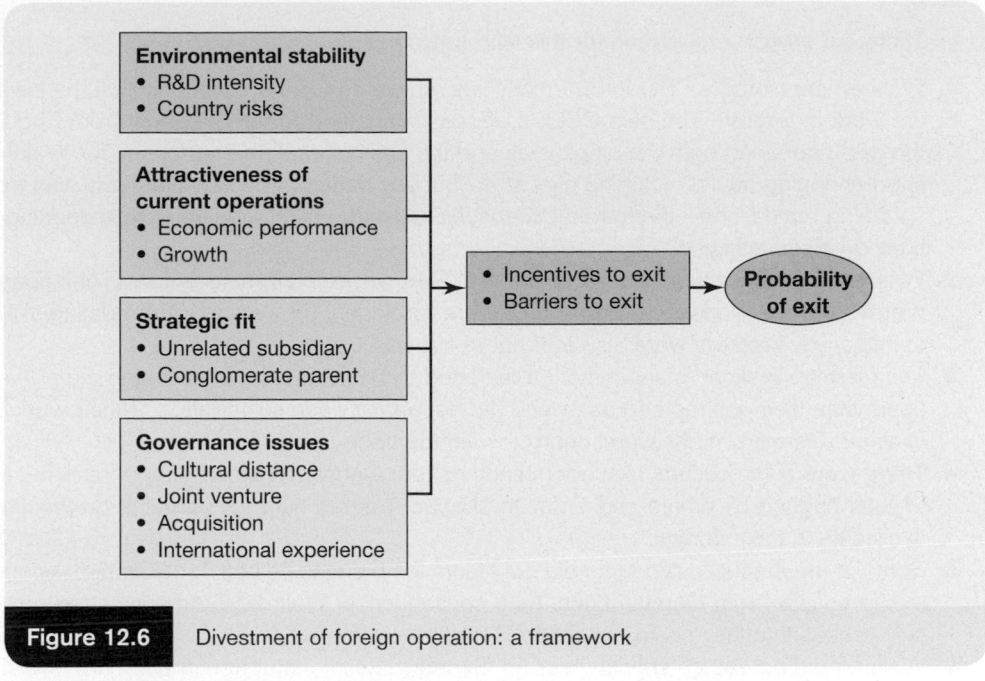

Figure 12.6   Divestment of foreign operation: a framework

Source: Benito (1996, Figure 2).

Attractiveness of current operations

- *Economic performance*. Unsatisfactory economic performance (i.e. inability to produce a net contribution to overall profits) is the most obvious reason why particular subsidiaries are sold off or shut down. On the other hand, if the subsidiary is a good economic performer, the owners may see an opportunity to obtain a good price for the unit while it is performing well.
- *Growth*. Economic growth in the host country would normally make FDI even more attractive, thereby increasing the barriers to exit from such a country. However, the attractiveness of the location would make such operations more likely targets for takeovers by other investors.

EXHIBIT 12.2 Walmart's withdrawal from the German market

Walmart (www.walmartstores.com) was founded by Sam Walton in 1962, with the opening of the first Walmart discount store. Today, there are more than 8,100 retail stores under 55 different store brands in 16 countries (Argentina, Brazil, Canada, Chile, China, Costa Rica, El Salvador, Guatemala, Honduras, India, Japan, Mexico, Nicaragua, Puerto Rico, UK and the US). With fiscal year 2009 sales of US$401 billion (only 20 per cent outside the US), Walmart employs more than 2.1 million associates worldwide. Walmart had high hopes for Germany (the world's third-largest retail market after the US and Japan) when it entered the market in 1997 by acquiring Wertkauf GmbH with its 21 hypermarkets. One year later Walmart aquired a further 74 Interspar stores of Spar AG.

However, nine years later Wal-Mart had to withdraw from the German market. What happened?

There are several explanation for this withdrawal:

1. Walmart appointed a CEO for Germany who spoke no German. Not only that, he insisted that his managers work in English. The next CEO, an Englishman, tried to run the show from England. The men at the top misunderstood both the employees and the customers. Other surprises for Walmart were Germany's short shopping hours, including almost no Sunday trading. Walmart Germany was frustrated by German shopping regulations – the feared *Ladenschlussgesetz* which regulates store opening times – and restrictions on discounting.

2. Walmart's American managers pressured German executives to enforce American-style management practices in the workplace. Employees were forbidden, for instance, from dating colleagues in positions of influence. Workers were also told not to flirt with one another.

3. The German Walmart management threatened to close certain stores if staff did not agree to work longer hours than their contracts foresaw and did not permit video surveillance of their work. As a consequence, Walmart Germany had several conflicts with the trade union.

4. There were some cultural misunderstandings too: German Walmart shoppers didn't like having their purchases bagged by others and German shoppers like to hunt for bargains on their own, without smiling assistants at their elbows.

5. Some of the American products did not fit into the German homes: for example, American pillowcases are a different size from German ones. As a consequence, Walmart Germany ended up with a huge stock of pillowcases that they could not sell to German customers.

6. Walmart did not reach 'critical mass' in Germany. Its infrastructure in Germany, which involved two HQs (for a while) and three logistics centres, piled up costs without achieving economies of scale. With its relatively low number of stores, it only reached 2 per cent of the German food market. It was up against fierce competition from Aldi and Lidl, two German discount chains. For example, Aldi had a network of 4,000 stores, compared with Walmart's approximately 100 stores.

After nine years of trying to make a go of it, in July 2006 Walmart sold its 85 stores to German rival Metro.

Walmart's attempt to apply the company's proven US success formula in an unmodified manner to the German market turned out to be a fiasco. This case shows how important it is to address cultural differences when setting up international operations.

Sources: *The Economist*, 'After struggling for years, Walmart withdraws from Germany', US Edition, 5 August, 2006; *The Independent*, 'Mighty Walmart admits defeat in Germany', 29 July 2006, London; www.walmartstores.com.

Strategic fit

Unrelated expansion (i.e. diversification) increases the governance cost of the business, and economies of scale and scope are also rarely achieved by unrelated subsidiaries. Hence these factors increase the incentives to exit.

The same arguments apply to a conglomerate parent.

Governance issues

- *Cultural distance*. Closeness between home country and host countries results in easier monitoring and coordination of production and marketing activities in the various locations. Thus culturally close countries increase the barriers to exit and vice versa.
- *Joint venture and acquisition*. A joint venture with a local partner can certainly reduce barriers to the penetration of a foreign market by giving rapid access to knowledge about the local market. On the other hand, whenever a joint venture is set up with a foreign partner, both different national and corporate cultures may have an impact on its success. Joint ventures and acquisitions are put in a difficult situation in the often critical initial phases of the integration process. Thus a lack of commitment in the parent company or companies may increase the incentive to exit.

● *Experience*. Firms learn from experience how to operate in the foreign environment and how to search for solutions to problems that emerge. As experience is accumulated, it becomes easier to avoid many of the problems involved in running foreign subsidiaries and to find workable solutions if problems should arise. This also includes the unpleasant decision to close down a subsidiary.

12.11 Summary

The advantages and disadvantages of the different hierarchical entry modes are summarized in Table 12.1.

Furthermore, this chapter discussed under what circumstances foreign divestment is likely to take place. The most obvious reason to exit from a market seems to be low profits earned in the market.

Table 12.1	Advantages and disadvantages of different hierarchical entry modes	
Hierarchical entry mode	**Advantages**	**Disadvantages**
Domestic-based sales representatives	Better control of sales activities compared with independent intermediaries Close contact with large customers in foreign markets close to home country	High travel expenses Too expensive in foreign markets, far away from home country
Foreign sales, branch/sales and production subsidiary	Full control of operation Eliminates the possibility that a national partner gets a 'free ride' Market access (sales subsidiary) Acquire market knowledge directly (sales subsidiary) Reduce transport costs (production subsidiary) Elimination of duties (production subsidiary) Access to raw materials and labour (production subsidiary)	High initial capital investment required (subsidiary) Loss of flexibility High-risk (market, political and economic) Taxation problems
Region centres/ transnational organization	Achieves potential synergies on a regional/global scale Regional/global scale efficiency Leverage learning on a cross-national basis. Resources and people are flexible and can be put into operating units around the world	Possible threats: ● increasing bureaucracy ● limited national-level responsiveness and flexibility A national manager can feel they have no influence Missing communication between head office and region centres
Acquisition	Rapid entry to new markets Gaining quick access to: ● distribution channels ● a qualified labour force ● existing management experience ● local knowledge ● contacts with local market and government ● established brand names/reputation	Usually an expensive option High-risk (taking over companies that are regarded as part of a country's heritage can raise considerable national resentment if it seems that they are being taken over by foreign interests) Possible threats: ● lack of integration with existing operation ● communication and coordination problems between acquired firm and acquirer
Greenfield investment	Possible to build in an 'optimum' format, i.e. in a way that fits the interests of the firm (e.g. integrating production with home base production) Possible to integrate state-of-the-art technology (resulting in increased operational efficiency)	High investment cost Slow entry of new markets (time-consuming process)

CASE STUDY 12.1

Polo Ralph Lauren: Polo moves distribution for South-east Asia in-house

Polo Ralph Lauren Corporation, founded in 1967 by Ralph Lauren, is a leader in the design, marketing and distribution of premium lifestyle products, including men's, women's and children's apparel, accessories, fragrances and home furnishings.

Total net revenue in 2009 was US$5 billion and net profits were US$595 million.

From 2007 to 2009 the net revenues developed as shown in Table 1.

Polo Ralph Lauren operates in three distinct but integrated segments:

1. **Wholesale.** The wholesale business (representing approximately 57 per cent of 2009 net revenues) consists of wholesale-channel sales made principally to major department stores, speciality stores and golf and pro shops located throughout the US, Europe and Asia. The number of shops where Polo Ralph Lauren is represented by wholesalers is approximately 6,097.

2. **Retail.** The retail business (representing approximately 39 per cent of 2009 net revenues) consists of retail-channel sales directly to consumers through full-price and factory retail stores located throughout the US, Canada, Europe, South America and Asia, and through the retail internet sites located at www.RalphLauren.com and www.Rugby.com. Polo Ralph Lauren has 163 own full-price retail stores and 163 own factory stores worldwide, totalling approximately 2.5 million square feet.

3. **Licensing.** Licensing business (representing approximately 4 per cent of 2009 net revenues) consists of royalty-based arrangements under which they license the right to third parties to use the various trademarks in connection with the manufacture and sale of designated products, such as apparel, eyewear and fragrances, in specified geographical areas for specified periods.

RalphLauren.com offers the customers access to the full breadth of Ralph Lauren apparel, accessories and home products, allows them to reach retail customers on a multi-channel basis and reinforces the

Table 1	Polo Ralph Lauren's net revenues in different regions 2007–9		
Net revenues	2009 (millions US$)	2008 (millions US$)	2007 (millions US$)
US and Canada	3,589	3,653	3,452
Europe	1,028	945	768
Japan	393	272	65
Other regions (including South-east Asia)	9	10	11
Total	5,019	4,880	4,296

luxury image of the brands. RalphLauren.com averaged 2.9 million unique visitors a month and acquired approximately 350,000 new customers, resulting in 1.7 million total customers in 2009.

In August 2008, the company launched Rugby.com, its second e-commerce website. Rugby.com offers clothing and accessories for purchase – previously only available at Rugby stores – along with style tips, unique videos and blog-based content. Rugby.com offers an extensive array of Rugby products for young men and women.

The business is typically affected by seasonal trends, with higher levels of sales resulting primarily from key vacation travel, back-to-school and holiday shopping periods (e.g. Christmas) in the retail segment.

By the end of March 2009, Polo Ralph Lauren had approximately 17,000 employees, both full- and part-time, consisting of approximately 12,000 in the US and approximately 5,000 in foreign countries.

Since 1967, the distinctive brand image has been consistently developed across an expanding number of products, price tiers and markets. Reflecting a distinctive American lifestyle under the direction of internationally renowned designer Ralph Lauren, they have a considerable influence on the way people dress and the way that fashion is advertised throughout the world.

Source: Ralph Lauren Fragrances.

The Company's product portfolio consists of four product lines:

1. *Apparel*: products include extensive collections of men's, women's and children's clothing.
2. *Accessories*: products encompass a broad range, including footwear, eyewear, watches, jewellery, hats, belts and leather goods, including handbags and luggage.
3. *Home*: coordinated products for the home include bedding and bath products, furniture, fabric and wallpaper, paint, tabletop and giftware.
4. *Fragrance*: fragrance products are sold under Romance, Polo, Lauren, Safari, Ralph and Black Label brands, among others.

Use of licensing in far distance markets

Polo Ralph Lauren grants a licence for the right to sell at wholesale specified categories of products in far distance markets. These geographic area licensees source products from product licensing partners and independent sources.

Each licensing partner pays Polo Ralph Lauren royalties based upon its sales of their products, generally subject to a minimum royalty requirement for the right to use the company's trademarks and design services. In addition, licensing partners may be required to allocate a portion of their revenues to advertise the products and share in the creative costs associated with these products. Larger allocations are required in connection with launches of new products or in new territories. The licences generally have three-to five-year terms and may grant the licensee conditional renewal options.

Polo Ralph Lauren works closely with their licensing partners to ensure that their products are developed, marketed and distributed so as to reach the intended market opportunity and to present consistently to consumers worldwide the distinctive perspective and lifestyle associated with their brands. Many aspects of the packaging, merchandising, distribution, advertising and promotion of the products are subject to continuing oversight by Polo Ralph Lauren. The result is hopefully a consistent identity for Ralph Lauren products across product categories and international markets.

At the beginning of 2009 Polo Ralph Lauren had four licensing partners, covering the following geographical areas:

1. Oroton Group/PRL Australia: Australia and New Zealand
2. Doosan Corporation: Korea
3. P.R.L. Enterprises, S.A.: Panama, Aruba, Curacao, The Cayman Islands, Costa Rica, Nicaragua, Honduras, El Salvador, Guatemala, Belize, Colombia, Ecuador, Bolivia, Peru, Antigua, Barbados, Bonaire, Dominican Republic, St Lucia, St Martin, Trinidad and Tobago
4. Dickson Concepts: Hong Kong, China, the Philippines, Malaysia, Singapore, Taiwan, Thailand and Indonesia

Typically, the international licensing partners acquire the right to sell, promote, market and/or distribute various categories of the Polo Ralph Lauren products in a given geographic area.

Shift from licensing to hierarchical mode in South-east Asia

In February 2009, Polo Ralph Lauren entered into an agreement with Dickson Concepts (based in Hong Kong) to assume direct control of its Polo-branded licensed apparel businesses in South-east Asia effective 1 January 2010 in exchange for a payment of US$20 million and certain other consideration. Until 1 January 2010, Dickson was the company's licensee for Polo-branded apparel in the South-east Asia region, which comprises China, Hong Kong, Indonesia, Malaysia, the Philippines, Singapore, Taiwan and Thailand. In South-east Asia, Dickson Concepts sold Polo merchandise through approximately 40 freestanding stores and nearly 100 shop-in-shops.

QUESTIONS

1. What are the likely main motives for Polo Ralph Lauren to shift the entry mode from licensing to the hierarchical mode in South-east Asia?
2. Would you recommend they take all geographical licences back in-house and turn them into hierarchical modes? If not, why?

Sources: Karmizadeh, M. (2009) 'Polo will move distribution for South-east Asia in-house', *Women's Wear Daily*, 17 February 2009, 197(35), p. 10; www.ralphlauren.com, especially Annual Report 2009.

CASE STUDY 12.2

Durex condoms: SSL will sell Durex condoms in the Japanese market through its own organization

Durex condoms will go on sale in Japan for the first time after SSL International, the manufacturer and distributor of health care products, announced it is to expand its operation in the country. SSL International was formed in June 1999 by the merger of Seton Scholl Health Care and the London International Group (LIG). Durex is the highest-selling condom brand in the world, available in more than 140 countries, and with approximately 22 per cent of the global branded condom market. The Durex brand name was registered in 1929, with the name Durex derived from durability, reliability and excellence.

Generally, the SSL managers run a brand-oriented strategy: 'We want Durex to be the Coca-Cola of the condom world.' The move into Japan was made possible by the 1999 merger. Seton Scholl has its own presence in Japan, with marketing and distribution networks set up, whereas LIG did not. Through Seton Scholl Japan, it already distributes Scholl products such as shoes and other footwear products throughout the country as well as surgical gloves, which are manufactured by the old LIG company.

SSL terminated a long-term contract with Okamoto, the largest supplier of condoms in Japan, freeing it to vie for a share of the country's 200 million condom market. The chief executive said, 'It now makes sense for us to take control of our own destiny in Japan.' SSL aimed to have won 5 per cent of the market within five years, generating £10 million worth of new revenue. SSL has bought out its partner in Seton Scholl Japan, giving it full control. The CEO added: 'We saw more prospect of generating value for shareholders by going it alone in Japan.' He said that Durex was already well known as an international brand in the country.

The Japanese market for condoms is said to be the world's largest, with annual turnover worth about £200 million. It is dominated by Okamoto (42 per cent market share) and other locally produced products. The Japanese market is as large as it is because until June 1999 the contraceptive pill was banned and most people had to rely on condoms for birth control. Experts say that it will still take one or two generations before the pill is widely used in Japan.

One reason it took 40 years for the contraceptive pill to be legalized in Japan was lobbying by condom-makers against its introduction. Japanese health officials said they were concerned that use of the pill, instead of condoms, would spread sexually transmitted diseases. It was even claimed, by other opponents, that the urine of women on the pill would pollute rivers and deform fish.

QUESTIONS

1. What were the main motives for SSL establishing its own distribution channels for condoms in Japan?

2. What are the major barriers to SSL reaching a higher market share for condoms in Japan?

Sources: adapted from: *Financial Times* (2000) 'SSL goes it alone in Japan with Durex', 3 February; *New Media Age* (1997) 'Condom brand goes global on web', 1 May.

VIDEO CASE STUDY 12.3 Starbucks

download from **www.pearsoned.co.uk/hollensen**

Starbucks Corporation (www.starbucks.com) is named after the first mate in Herman Melville's *Moby Dick.* It was founded in 1971 in Seattle. The original name of the company was Starbucks Coffee, Tea and Spices, later changed to Starbucks Coffe Company. Starbucks sells more than coffee; it sells the Starbucks experience. Leveraging a strong brand, the company is expanding into new markets at home and abroad. The challenge is to grow while maintaining a consistent, high-quality customer experience.

Questions

1. What could be the main motives for Starbucks in owning most of its coffee houses compared with other entry modes and operation forms?

2. How does Starbucks' entry into the grocery market affect the company's relationships with its retail customers?

3. How did Starbucks make the successful transition from a niche to a mainstream marketer? What can the company do to maintain its 'small company feel' as it expands globally?

Source: Pickture/Alamy Images.

For further resources, see this book's website at **www.pearsoned.co.uk/hollensen**

Questions for discussion

1. By what criteria would you judge a particular foreign direct investment activity to have succeeded or failed?

2. What are a firm's major motives in deciding to establish manufacturing facilities in a foreign country?

3. Is the establishment of wholly owned subsidiaries abroad an appropriate international market development mode for SMEs?

4. What is the idea behind appointing a 'lead country' in a region?

5. Why is acquisition often the preferred way to establish wholly owned operations abroad? What are the limitations of acquisition as an entry method?

6. What are the key problems associated with profit repatriation from subsidiaries?

References

Baaij, J.M., Berghe, D.V.D., Den Bosch, F.A.J. and Volberda, B.W. (2005) 'Rotterdam or anywhere: relocating corporate HQ', *Business Strategy Review*, summer, pp. 45–48.

Barkema, H.G., Bell, J. and Pennings, J.M. (1996) 'Foreign entry, cultural barriers and learning', *Strategic Management Journal*, 17, pp. 151–166.

Barney, J. (1997) *Gaining and Sustaining Competitive Advantage*, Addison Wesley Longman, Reading, MA.

Benito, G. (1996) *Why are Subsidiaries Divested? A Conceptual Framework*. Working Paper No. 3–93, Institute of International Economics and Management, Copenhagen Business School.

Boddewyn, J.J. (1979) 'Foreign divestment: magnitude and factors', *Journal of International Business Studies*, 10, pp. 21–27.

Lasserre, P. (1996) 'Regional headquarters: the spearhead for Asian Pacific markets', *Long Range Planning*, 29(1), pp. 30–37.

Perlmutter, H. (1969) 'The torturous evolution of multinational corporations', *Columbia Journal of World Business*, January–February, pp. 9–18.

Raffée, H. and Kreutzer, R. (1989) 'Organizational dimensions of global marketing', *European Journal of Marketing*, 23(5), pp. 43–57.

Ross, W.T., Dalsace, F. and Anderson, E. (2005) 'Should you set up your own sales force or should you outsource it? Pitfalls in the standard analysis, *Business Horizons*, 48, pp. 23–36.

Root, F.R. (1987) *Entry Strategies for International Markets*. Lexington Books, Lexington, MA.

Sasaki, I. and Yoshikawa, K. (2014) 'Going beyond national cultures – dynamic interaction between intra-national, regional, and organizational realities', *Journal of World Business*, 49(3), pp. 455–464.

CHAPTER 13

International sourcing decisions and the role of the subsupplier

Contents

Learning objectives

After studying this chapter you should be able to:

- Describe the role of subcontractors in the vertical chain
- Explore the reasons for international outsourcing
- Explain the development of a buyer–seller relationship
- Discuss alternative routes of subcontractor internationalization
- Explain how turnkey contracts differ from conventional subcontracting.

13.1 Introduction

Recent studies of subcontracting and competitiveness have emphasized the importance of outsourcing: moving functions or activities out of an organization. Outsourcing is often more efficient, except in the case of the firm's core competences, which are considered central to its success. Thus the issue is whether an organization should perform certain functions itself ('make') or source ('buy') these activities from outside. If large-scale enterprises (LSEs) outsource an increasing number of value chain functions, this provides business opportunities for small and medium-sized enterprises (SMEs) as subcontractors to LSEs (main contractors).

A subcontractor can be defined as a person or a firm that agrees to provide semi-finished products or services needed by another party (main contractor) to perform another contract to which the subcontractor is not a party. According to this definition, the characteristics of subcontractors that distinguish them from other SMEs are:

- Subcontractors' products are usually part of the end product, not the complete end product itself.
- Subcontractors do not have direct contact with the end customers, because the main contractor is usually responsible to the customer.

The position of subcontractors in the vertical production chain is shown in Figure 13.1.

OEM
Original equipment manufacturer – the customer of a subsupplier (e.g. Autoliv in Case III.3 is a subsupplier of airbags for their OEMs, the car manufacturers such as VW or BMW).

In the original equipment manufacturer contract (**OEM**), the contractor is called the OEM or 'sourcer', whereas the parts suppliers are regarded as 'manufacturers' of OEM products (= subcontractors = subsuppliers). Typically the OEM contracts are different from other buyer–seller relationships because the OEMs (contractors) often have much stronger bargaining power than the subcontractors. However, in a partner-based buyer–seller relationship, the power balance will be more equal. There are cases where a subcontractor improved its bargaining position and went on to become a major force in the market (Cho and Chu, 1994).

The structure of the remainder of this chapter is shown in Figure 13.2.

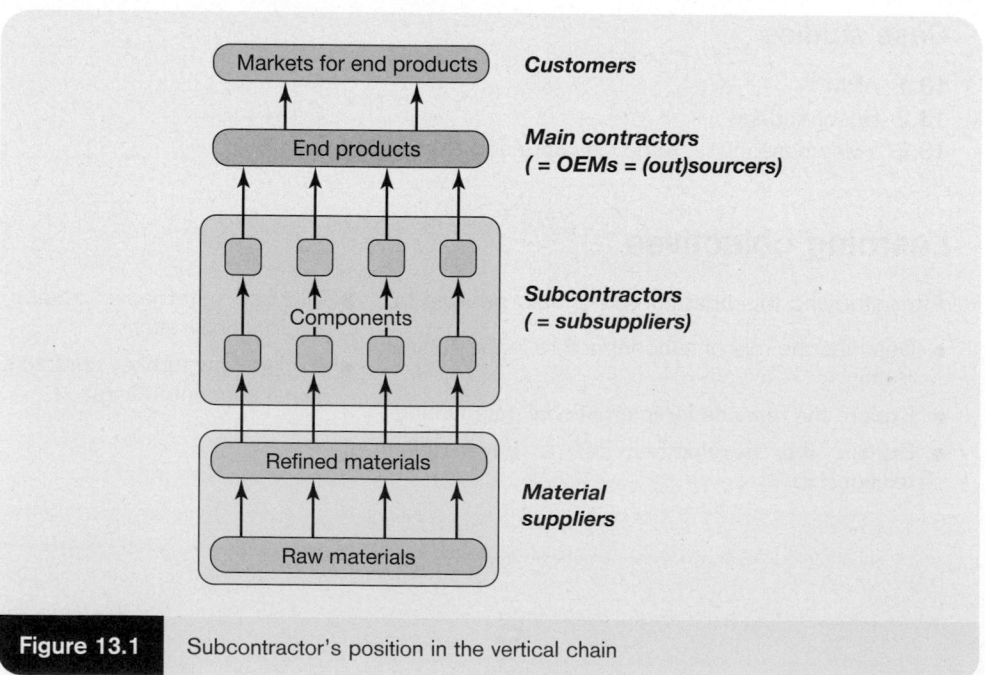

| **Figure 13.1** | Subcontractor's position in the vertical chain |

Source: adapted from Lehtinen (1991, p. 22).

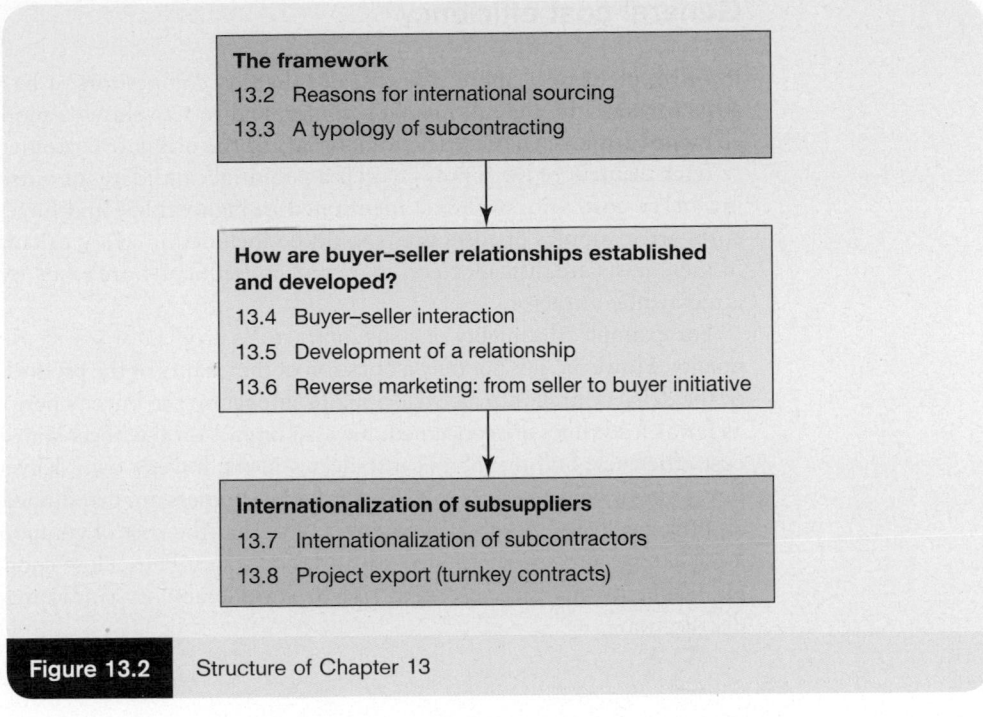

The framework

13.2 Reasons for international sourcing

13.3 A typology of subcontracting

How are buyer–seller relationships established and developed?

13.4 Buyer–seller interaction

13.5 Development of a relationship

13.6 Reverse marketing: from seller to buyer initiative

Internationalization of subsuppliers

13.7 Internationalization of subcontractors

13.8 Project export (turnkey contracts)

Figure 13.2   Structure of Chapter 13

13.2   Reasons for international sourcing

More and more international firms are buying their parts, semi-finished components and other supplies from international subcontractors. Creating competitiveness through the subcontractor is based on the understanding that the supplier can be essential to the buyer (contractor) for a number of reasons.

Concentration on in-house core competences

A contractor wishes to concentrate management time and effort on those core business activities that make the best use of in-house skills and resources. There may also be special difficulties in obtaining suitably skilled labour in-house.

Lower product/production costs

In this respect there are two underlying reasons for outsourcing:

1. *Economies of scale*. In many cases the subcontractor produces similar components for other customers, and by use of the experience curve the subcontractor can obtain lower production costs per unit.
2. *Lower wage costs*. The labour costs involved in the domestic country can make the in-house operation uneconomic and motivate international sourcing. For example, 80 per cent of the labour cost of clothing manufacture is in the sewing stage. Short production runs of different sizes of clothes permit only a low degree of mechanization. Moreover, adjusting the tooling for each run is relatively labour-intensive (Hibbert, 1993). For this reason, a large part of labour-intensive clothing production is moved to low-wage countries in eastern Europe and the Far East.

General cost efficiency

If a firm plans to be more cost-efficient than its competitors, it has to minimize the total costs towards the end (ultimate) customer. Figure 13.3 shows a model of the different cost elements, from the basic price of materials to the ultimate customer cost.

Each element of the supply chain is a potential candidate for outsourcing. Quality costs, inventory costs (not explicitly mentioned in Figure 13.3) and buyer–supplier transaction costs are examples of costs that should be included in every calculation. However, some of these costs are difficult to estimate and consequently are easily overlooked when evaluating a subcontractor.

For example, the quality of a subcontractor's product or service is essential to the buyer's quality. However, it is not only a question of the quality of the product or service. The quality of the delivery processes also has a major impact on the buyer's performance. Uncertainties, as far as lead times are concerned, have an impact on the buyer's inventory investments and cost efficiency, and they may cause delays in the buyer's own delivery processes. Thus the buyer's own delivery times towards the end customers are determined by the subcontractors and their delivery. Another important fact is that the cost of components and parts is, to a large extent, already determined at the design stage. Thus, close cooperation between buyer and seller at this stage can give rise to considerable cost advantages in production and distribution.

Ultimate customer cost/value	*Strategic business factors*
Marketability	*Intermediate customer factors*
Downstream channel costs	
Product improvement	
Supplier cost commitment	*Tactical input factors*
Supplier R&D	
Transaction overhead costs	
Payment terms	*Indirect financial costs*
Logistics chain costs	
Production costs	
Lot-size costs	*Operational/logistics costs*
Receive/make-ready costs	
Quality costs	
Warranty terms	*Quality costs/factors*
Transportation terms	*Landed costs*
Transportation costs	
Initiating/maintaining a supply relationship	*Supply relational costs*
FOB terms	*Direct transaction costs*
Cost of transaction method	
Basic price of materials	*Traditional basic input costs*

Figure 13.3   The total cost/value hierarchy model. FOB, free on board

Source: Cavinato (1992).

Increased potential for innovation

Ideas for innovation can be generated by the subcontractor due to its more in-depth understanding of the component. New ideas can also be transferred from other customers of the subcontractor.

Fluctuating demand

If the main contractor is confronted with fluctuating demand levels, external uncertainty and short product life cycles, it may transfer some risk and stock management to the subcontractor, leading to better cost and budget control.

Finally, it should be mentioned that when buying from international sources, fluctuations in exchange rates become particularly important, especially when there is a time lag between when the contract is signed and when payment is made. When the currency in the country of the main contractor is very strong in comparison to a particular country, this can be an incentive for the main contractor to buy from that country.

In summary, price is a very important reason for (international) outsourcing, but the main contractors increasingly regard cooperation with critical subcontractors as advantageous to the buying firm's competitiveness and profitability.

13.3 A typology of subcontracting

Traditionally, a subcontractor has been defined as a firm carrying out day-to-day production based on the specifications of another firm (the main contractor). The variety of subcontracting relationships that are appearing indicates a need for a more differentiated typology.

Figure 13.4 displays a typology of subcontractors based on differences in the contractor–subcontractor relationship. The typology displays the interplay between the degree of coordination needed and the complexity of the tasks to be solved:

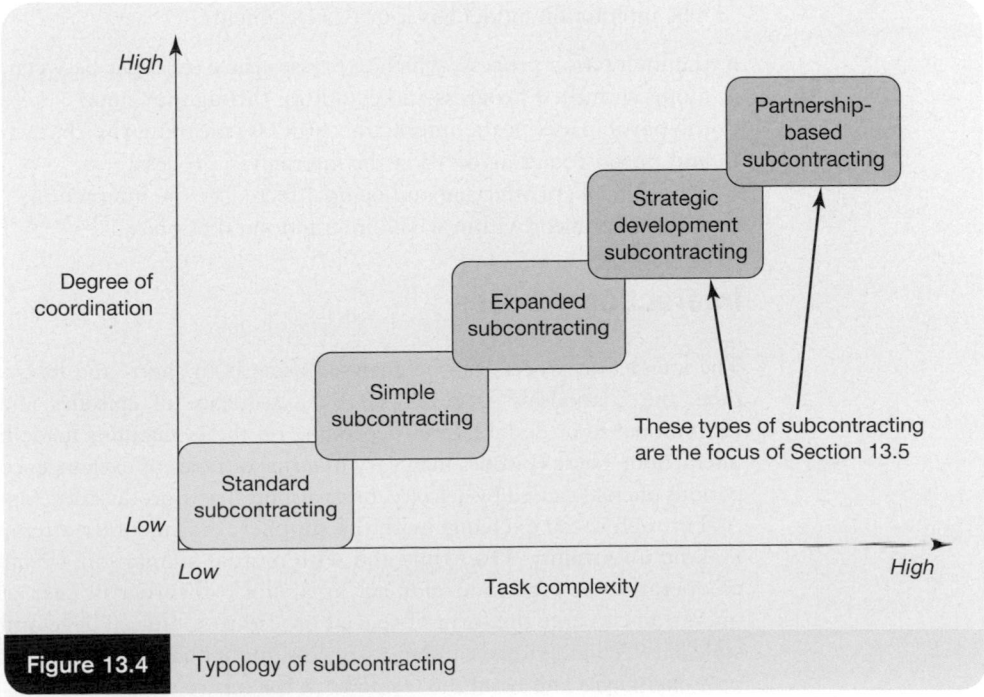

| Figure 13.4 | Typology of subcontracting |

Source: adapted from Blenker and Christensen (1994).

- *Standard subcontracting.* Economies of scale often operate in the global market with standardized products, in which case no adaptation to specific customers is needed.
- *Simple subcontracting.* Information exchange is simple because the contractor specifies criteria for contribution. The contractor's in-house capacity is often a major competitor.
- *Expanded subcontracting.* There is some mutual specialization between the two parties, and exit costs are higher for both parties. Therefore single sourcing (one supplier for a product/component) may replace multi-sourcing (more suppliers for a product/component).
- *Strategic development subcontracting.* This is very important to the contractor. Subcontractors possess a critical competence of value to the contractor. They are involved in the contractor's long-term planning, and activities are coordinated by dialogue.
- *Partnership-based subcontracting.* This is a relationship based on a strong mutual strategic value and dependency. The subcontractor is highly involved in the R&D activities of the contractor.

There is a certain overlap between the different types of subcontractor, and in a specific relationship it can be very difficult to place a subcontractor in a certain typology. Depending primarily on the task complexity, a main contractor may have both standard subcontractors and partnership-based subcontractors. Also, a subcontractor may play more than one of the roles in Figure 13.4, but only one at a time.

13.4 Buyer–seller interaction

Traditionally, subcontracting has been defined as the production activities that one firm carries out on the day-to-day specification of another firm. Outsourced activities increasingly include R&D, design and other functions in the value chain. Thus what starts with simple transactions (so-called episodes) may, if repeated over time, evolve into a relationship between buyer and seller.

Interaction theory was developed by the Swedes but spread into France, the UK, Italy and Germany when a group of like-minded researchers formed what became known as the IMP Group, basing their research on the interaction model (Figure 13.5).

The interaction model has four basic elements:

- the interaction process, which expresses the exchanges between the two organizations along with their progress and evolution throughout time;
- the participants in the interaction process, meaning the characteristics of the supplier and the customer involved in the interaction process;
- the atmosphere affecting and being affected by the interaction;
- the environment within which interaction takes place.

Interaction process

The interaction process can be analysed using both short- and long-term perspectives. Over time, the relationship is developed by a sequence of episodes and events that tends to institutionalize or destabilize it, depending on the evaluations made by the two firms in the interaction. These episodes may vary in terms of types of exchange: commercial transactions, periods of crisis caused by delivery, price disputes, new product development (NPO) stages, etc.

Through social exchange with the supplier, the customer attempts to reduce decision-making uncertainty. Over time and with mutual adaptation a relationship-specific mode of operation emerges and may act as a shock absorber in case of crisis. This mode of operation can take the form of special procedures, mutual developments, communication style between individuals and more or less implicit rules. These rules are modified through past exchanges and form the framework for future exchanges.

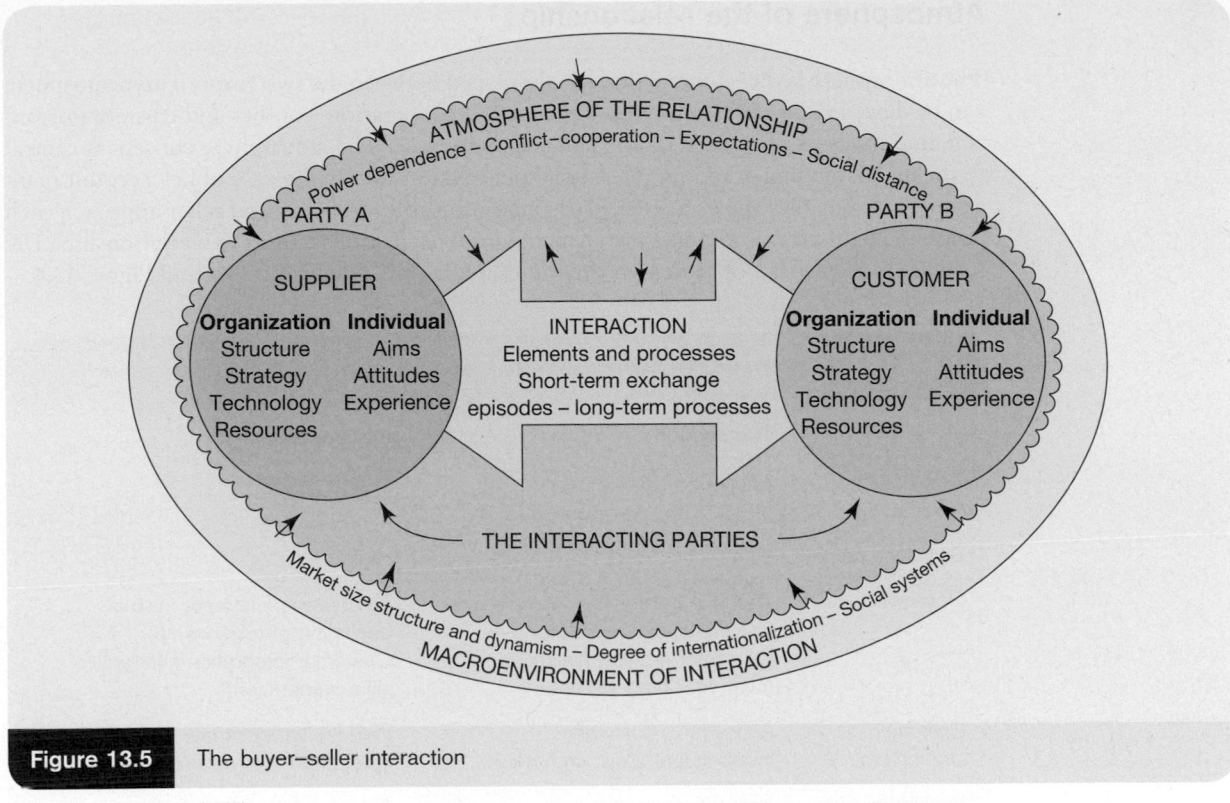

| Figure 13.5 | The buyer–seller interaction |

Source: Turnbull and Valla (1986).

Interacting parties

The participants' characteristics strongly influence the way they interact. Three analytical perspectives of buyer and seller, at different levels, may be taken into account.

The social system perspective

Dimensions such as culture – languages, values and practices – and the operating modes of the firm influence the distance between actors that will limit or encourage collaboration.

The organizational perspective

The relationship between buyer and seller is influenced by three organizational dimensions:

1. The characteristics of each firm's technology (i.e. products and production technology) strongly influence the nature of the interaction between the two organizations.
2. The complexity of products sold, for example, conditions the very nature and the density of the interaction between supplier and customer.
3. Relationship characteristics: a supplier can choose to develop a stable relationship with a customer, or the supplier can regard the relationship as a pure transaction-based exchange where the supplier typically makes 'one-shot' business with a customer purely to increase sales volume and with no further involvement.

The individual perspective

The individuals' characteristics, their objectives and their experience will influence the way social exchanges and social contacts take place, and subsequently the development of supplier–customer interaction.

Atmosphere of the relationship

The atmosphere is the 'climate' that has developed between the two firms. This atmosphere can be described in terms of power–dependence, cooperation–conflict and trust–opportunism, and in terms of understanding and social distance. The atmosphere concept is central to the understanding of the supplier–customer relationship. In the case of key account management, atmosphere plays a particularly important role. As buyer and seller approach each other, the marketing exchanges are changing from single transactions to a relationship. The further characteristics of these two situations are described in Table 13.1 and Figure 13.6.

Table 13.1	Marketing exchange understanding	
	Transaction	**Relationship**
Time Horizon	Short	Long
Switching costs	Low	Higher
Objective	To make a sale (sale is end result and measure of success) Customer needs satisfaction (customer buys values)	To create a customer (sale is beginning of relationship) Customer integration (interactive value generation).
Customer understanding	Anonymous customer Independent buyer and seller	Well-known customer Independent buyer and seller
Marketers' task and performance criteria	Assessment on the basis of products and prices. Focus on gaining new customers	Assessment on the basis of problem-solving competence. Focus on value enhancing of existing customers
Core aspects of exchange	Focus on products. Sale as a conquest. Discrete event. Monologue to aggregated broad customer segments	Focus on service. Sale as an agreement. Continuing process. Individualized dialogue

Source: based on Jüttner and Wehrli (1994). Published with permission of Emerald Publishing Ltd; www.emeraldinsight.com.

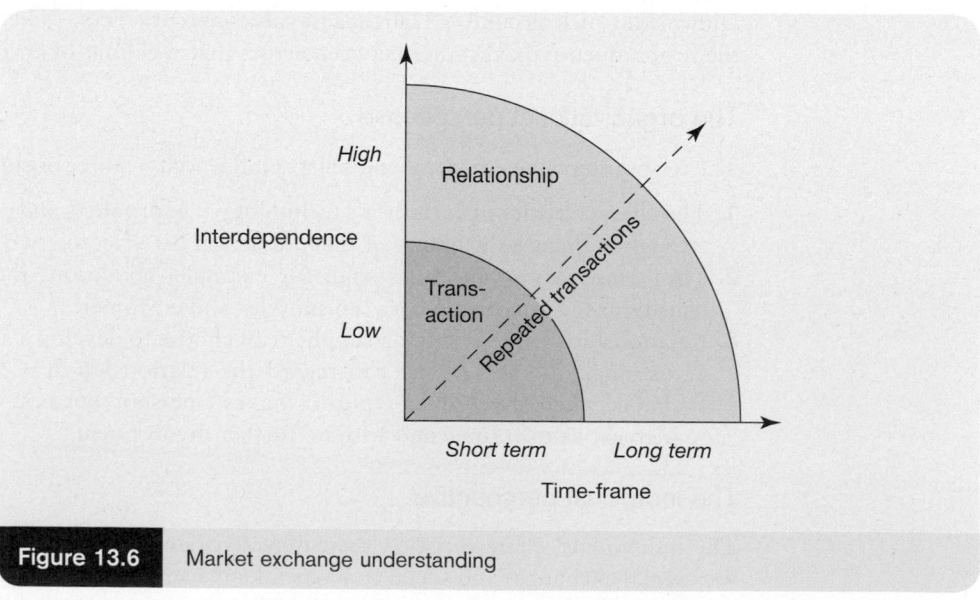

Figure 13.6	Market exchange understanding

Source: Jüttner and Wehrli (1994). Published with permission of Emerald Publishing Ltd; www.emeraldinsight.com.

At one end of the spectrum are transaction buyers in what is essentially a 'spot market'; at the other end are relationship buyers. Transaction exchanges have short time horizons when purchasing products or services in a specific category. In such markets, the lack of switching costs means that adjustments are easy to make. Because transaction buyers invest little in specialized procedures or assets when product or services are bought in the category, they are less interested in more long-term system benefits (or total life cycle costs) that may be offered. These buyers purchase a product for its product performance and at price at a point in time. This does not mean that these buyers are uninterested in quality or value. Rather, they define value as meeting specifications and do not want to pay for a product or service whose quality, applications or scope exceed what they want at that point.

In contrast, relationship buyers have a longer time horizon. There is something about the product or the service that motivates them to make larger investments in specialized procedures or assets. Once made, the investments are not easily interchangeable. Enterprise software offers a good example. Historically, the choice of an enterprise software vendor has been a multiyear choice of support, upgrade and other processes – a choice not easily altered after the choice of software supplier. Because of these investments and switching costs, buyers are interested in the wider system benefits and in choosing a longer-term business partner.

Hence, buyers are legitimately interested in knowing more about the seller's organization, commitment to the category, future plans, etc. Many sales directors prefer relationship buyers in the belief that these customers will pay higher prices and be more loyal. But the selling cycle in a relationship is also likely to be longer and more complicated, so sellers should continuously make efforts to make buyers aware of all the extra value that they can deliver, although often at a higher price, compared to the transaction situation (Cespedes *et al.*, 2013).

Interaction environment

Supplier–customer relationships evolve in a general macro environment that can influence their very nature. The following analytical dimensions are traditionally considered: political and economic context, cultural and social context, market structure, market internationalization and market dynamism (growth, innovation rate).

13.5 Development of a relationship

A relationship between two firms begins, grows and develops – or fails – in similar ways to relationships between people. The development of a relationship has been mapped out in a five-phase model: awareness, exploration, expansion, commitment and dissolution, and these are shown in Figure 13.7.

Figure 13.7 shows the initial *psychic distance* 1 between a buyer and a seller (from different countries and cultures), which is influenced by the psychological characteristics of the buyer and the seller, the firm's organizational culture and the national and industry culture to which the firm belongs. For example, a firm entering a psychically distant market is likely to perceive large differences between the two countries, resulting in high uncertainty (Magnusson and Boyle, 2009; Sousa and Lages, 2011). The apparent lack of understanding serves as a motivation to spend more resources on research and planning, leading to a reduction of the psychic distance. Figure 13.7 also shows that the initial psychic distance 1 at the beginning of the relationship is reduced to *psychic distance 2* through the interaction process of the two partners. However, relationships do not always last forever. The partners may 'move from each other' and the position may increase to *distance 3*. If the problems in the relationship are not solved, it may result in a 'divorce'.

Within such a framework, one might easily characterize a marketing relationship as a marriage between a seller and a buyer (the dissolution phase being a 'divorce'). The use of

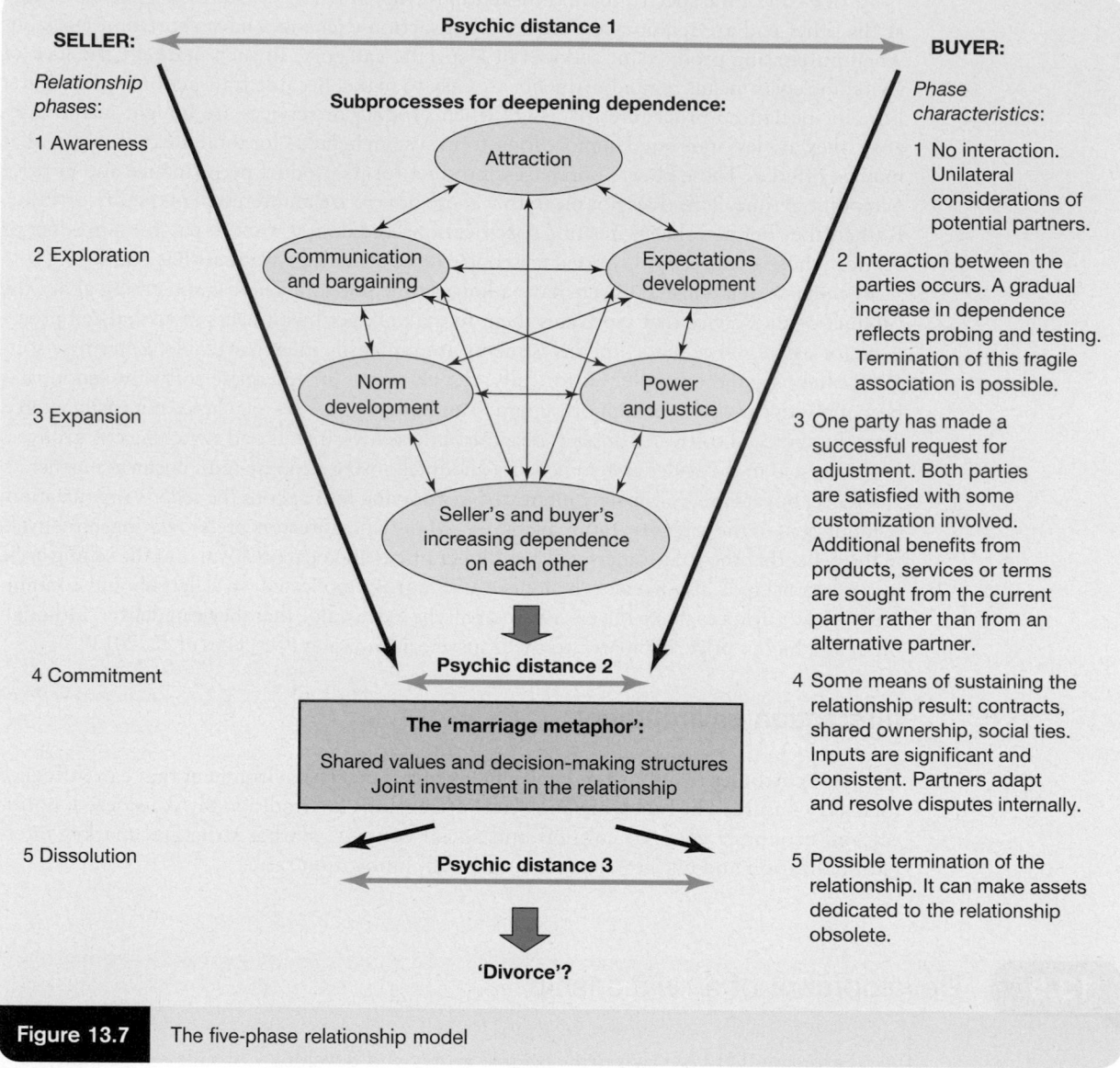

Figure 13.7   The five-phase relationship model

The marriage metaphor
The process of reducing the psychic distance + increasing dependence between buyer and seller = shared values and joint investments in the relationship.

the marriage metaphor indicates that business relationships involve inter-organizational relationships, but certainly also interpersonal relationships (Mouzas *et al.*, 2007). Dwyer *et al.* (1987) call the first phase in a relationship *awareness*, which means that the partners recognize each other as potential partners. In other words, in their model the decisions made about cooperating and choosing the partner are combined. Both types of decision-making can exist at the beginning of cooperation, but it is difficult to state any definite chronological order between them.

In SMEs it is likely that the decision-making process is reactive, in the way that the SME probably first realizes the existence of a potential partner (maybe 'love at first sight') and then decides to cooperate. The selection process may, however, be better if companies look for three key criteria (Kanter, 1994):

1. *Self-analysis*. Relationships get off to a good start when partners know themselves and their industry, when they have assessed changing industry conditions and have decided to seek an alliance. It also helps if executives have experience in evaluating potential partners. They will not be easily attracted by the first good-looking prospect that comes along.

2. *Chemistry.* To highlight the personal side of business relationships is not to deny the importance of sound financial and strategic analysis. But successful relations often depend on the creation and maintenance of a comfortable personal relationship between senior executives. This will include personal and social interests. Signs of managers' interests, commitment and respect are especially important in high-context countries. In China, as well as in Chinese-dominated businesses throughout Asia, the top manager of the western company should show they respect the potential partner's decision by investing his or her personal time.

3. *Compatibility.* The courtship period tests compatibility on broad historical, philosophical and strategic grounds: common experiences, values and principles, and hopes for the future. While analysts examine financial viability, managers can assess the less tangible aspects of compatibility. What starts out as personal rapport, philosophical and strategic compatibility and shared vision between two companies' top executives must eventually be institutionalized and made public ('getting engaged'). Other stakeholders get involved, and the relationship begins to become depersonalized. But success in the engagement phase of a new alliance still depends on maintaining a careful balance between the personal and the institutional.

In Figure 13.7's *exploration phase,* trial purchases may take place and the exchange outcomes provide a test of the other's ability and willingness to deliver satisfaction. In addition, electronic data interchange can be used to reduce the costly paperwork associated with purchase orders, production schedule releases, invoices and so on.

At the end of the exploration phase, it is time to 'meet the family'. The relations between a handful of leaders from the two firms must be supplemented with approval, formal or informal, by other people in the firms and by stakeholders. Each partner has other outside relationships that may need to approve the new relationship.

When a party (as is the case in the *expansion phase*) fulfils perceived exchange obligations in an exemplary fashion, the party's attractiveness to the other increases. Hence motivation to maintain the relationship increases, in particular as high-level outcomes reduce the number of alternatives that an exchange partner might use as a replacement.

The romance of courtship quickly gives way to day-to-day reality as the partners begin to live together ('setting up house'). In the *commitment phase,* the two partners can achieve a level of satisfaction from the exchange process that actually precludes other primary exchange partners (suppliers) who could provide similar benefits. The buyer has not ceased attending other alternative suppliers, but maintains awareness of alternatives without constant and frequent testing.

During the description of the relationship development, the possibility of a withdrawal has been implicit. The **dissolution phase** may be caused by the following problems:

Dissolution phase
'Divorce': termination of the relationship. It can make the assets dedicated to the relationship obsolete.

- Operational and cultural differences emerge after collaboration is under way. They often come as a surprise to those who created the alliance. Differences in authority, reporting and decision-making styles become noticeable at this stage.

- People in other positions may not experience the same attraction as the chief executives. The executives spend a lot of time together, both informally and formally. Other employees have not been in touch with one another, however, and in some cases have to be pushed to work with their overseas counterparts.

- Employees at other levels in the organization may be less visionary and cosmopolitan than top managers and less experienced in working with people from different cultures. They may lack knowledge of the strategic context in which the relationship makes sense and see only the operational ways in which it does not.

- People just one or two tiers from the top might oppose the relationship and fight to undermine it. This is especially true in organizations that have strong independent business units.

- Termination of personal relationships, as a result of managers leaving their positions in the companies, is a potential danger to the partnership.

Firms have to be aware of these potential problems before they enter into a relationship, because only in this way can they take action to prevent the dissolution phase. By jointly analysing the extent and importance of the attenuating factors, the partners will become more aware of the reasons for continuing the relationship, in spite of the trouble they are already in. Moreover, this awareness increases the parties' willingness to engage in restorative actions, thus trying to save the relationship from dissolution (Tähtinen and Vaaland, 2006). Consequently, many organizations allow their alliances to continue in their initial form for too long, while the original conditions change in unforeseen ways, sometimes favouring a new structure. For instance, a 2004 McKinsey study found that more than 70 per cent of companies were part of major alliances in need of restructuring. McKinsey's results further indicate that alliances that change their scope have a 79 per cent success rate compared with 33 per cent for the ventures that remain essentially unchanged (Gulati *et al.*, 2008).

13.6 Reverse marketing: from seller to buyer initiative

Reverse marketing
The buyer (and not the seller as in traditional marketing) takes the initiative in searching for a supplier that is able to fulfil their needs.

Reverse marketing describes how purchasing actively identifies potential subcontractors and offers suitable partners a proposal for long-term cooperation. Similar terms are proactive procurement and buyer initiative (Ottesen, 1995). In recent years, the buyer–seller relationship has changed considerably. The traditional relationship, in which a seller takes the initiative by offering a product, is increasingly being replaced by one in which the buyer actively searches for a supplier that is able to fulfil its needs.

Today, many changes are taking place in the utilization of the purchasing function:

- reduction in the number of subcontractors;
- shorter product life cycles, which increase the pressure to reduce the time to market ('just in time');
- upgraded demands on subcontractors (zero defects) – in addition, firms are demanding that their suppliers become certified; those that do not comply may be removed from the approved supplier list;
- purchasing that is no longer simply about getting lower prices – the traditional arm's-length relationships are increasingly being replaced by long-term partnerships with mutual trust, interdependence and mutual benefits.

Implementing a reverse marketing strategy starts with fundamental market research and with an evaluation of reverse marketing options (i.e. possible suppliers). Before choosing suppliers, the firm may include both present and potential suppliers in the analysis as well as current and desired activities (Figure 13.8).

	Current activities	**New activities**
Existing suppliers	Intensify current activities	Develop and add new activities
New potential suppliers	Replace existing suppliers Add suppliers: secure deliveries	Develop new activities not covered by existing suppliers

Figure 13.8 Supplier development strategies

Based on this analysis the firm may select a number of suitable partners as suppliers and rank them in order of preference.

13.7   Internationalization of subcontractors

In Chapter 3, the internationalization process was described as a learning process (the Uppsala school). Generally speaking, it is something that can be described as a gradual internationalization. According to this view, the international development of the firm is accompanied by an accumulation of knowledge in the hands of management and by growing capabilities and propensities to manage international affairs. The main consequence of this way of thinking is that firms tend to increase their commitment towards foreign markets as their experience grows. The number of adherents to this theory has grown, but there has also been much criticism of it.

The main problem with the model is that it seems to suggest the presence of a deterministic and mechanistic path that must be followed by firms implementing their internationalization strategy. Sometimes it happens that firms leapfrog one or more stages in the establishment chain; at other times firms stop their internationalization altogether (Welch and Luostarinen, 1988).

Concerning internationalization among contractors and subcontractors, there is a central difference. The internationalization of subcontractors is closely related to their customers. The concept of subcontractor indicates that the strategies of such a firm, including its internationalization strategy, cannot be seen in isolation from the strategies of its partner, the contractor. Therefore the internationalization of subcontractors may show irregular paths, such as leapfrogging.

Andersen *et al.* (1995) introduced four basic routes of internationalization (note that sometimes there is an overlap between the different routes, e.g. between routes 2 and 3).

Route 1: following domestic customers

If a contractor is internationalizing and establishing a production unit in a foreign market, some subcontractors (standard or simple in Figure 13.4) may be replaced with local suppliers, because they might be able to offer the standard components at cheaper prices. However, subcontractors in the upper part of Figure 13.4 and with a strategic value to the contractor will be maintained if they commit themselves to foreign direct investment: claims for direct delivery to the foreign production unit or claims for after-sales service on delivered components may result in the establishment of a local sales and/or production subsidiary by the subcontractor. In most cases, such a direct foreign investment related directly to a specific contractor is based on a guarantee of procurement over some years (until the payback period has passed).

When the furniture chain IKEA established itself in the North American market, it took along some strategically important Scandinavian subcontractors, some of which also established subsidiaries in North America. Other examples are the Japanese car manufacturers that established production units in the US and pulled along a lot of Japanese subcontractors to establish subsidiaries there. This route is similar to the 'late starters' in the model of Johanson and Mattson (1988).

Route 2: internationalization through the supply chain of a multinational corporation

Deliveries to one division of a multinational corporation may lead to deliveries to other divisions, or to parts of its network. One case is when mergers and acquisitions take place between firms and create new business opportunities for dynamic subcontractors.

The strategic alliance between the French car manufacturer Renault and the Swedish Volvo is one example, where Swedish subcontractors have become involved in the subcontracting system of Renault, and French subcontractors have opportunities to get into the subcontracting system of Volvo (Christensen and Lindmark, 1993).

Route 3: internationalization in cooperation with domestic or foreign system suppliers

In collaboration with other specialized subcontractors, system suppliers may be involved in international system supplies by taking over the management of whole supplies of subsystems (see Figure 13.9).

Systems supplies result in the development of a new layer of subcontractors (second-tier subcontractors). Through the interaction between a system supplier and a domestic main contractor, the system supplier can get access to the network of a global contractor (the dotted line in Figure 13.9) because of the network/contract between the contractor and the global contractor. For example, a Japanese car seat supplier supplies the Japanese Toyota factory (domestic main contractor). This can eventually give the supplier access to other Toyota factories around the world (global contractors) and their global networks.

In many cases, the collaboration between the subcontractors will be characterized by the exchange of tacit, not easily transferable, knowledge. The reason for this is that the complete subsystem is frequently based on several fields of competence, which have to be coordinated by use of tacit knowledge and communication. In the case of the Japanese car seat supplier, the system supplier should have a tight relationship with the subcontractors (suppliers of leather head rests, etc.) in order to adapt the car seat to the individual car models (see also Exhibit 13.1).

Route 4: independent internationalization

The need to gain economies of scale in production forces the standard contractor, in particular, to use the route of independent internationalization. In other cases, it cannot be recommended that small subcontractors follow the independent route. The barriers of independent internationalization are too high for small firms with limited resources. For these firms, route 3 (collaboration with other subcontractors) seems to be a more realistic way to internationalize.

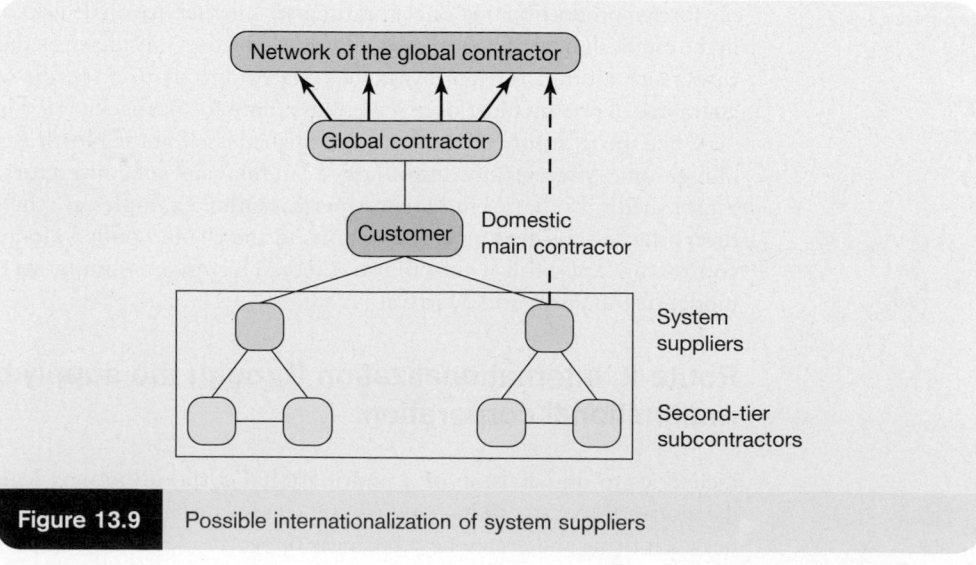

Figure 13.9   Possible internationalization of system suppliers

EXHIBIT 13.1 An example of Japanese network sourcing: the Mazda seat-sourcing case

Mazda adopts a policy of splitting its seat purchases between two suppliers, Delta Kogyo and the Toyo Seat Company. The present division is approximately 60 per cent to Delta and 40 per cent to Toyo. Each of these companies is responsible for different models of seats. Note that each individual item, such as a seat for the Mazda 626, is single-sourced for the product life cycle of typically three to five years, but seat production in general is, in effect, dual-sourced.

Both Delta Kogyo and the Toyo Seat Company are informally assured of a certain percentage of the Mazda seat business at any one time. This percentage is approximately one-third of the total Mazda seat purchases. Thus each firm has an assured long-term share of Mazda's seat business. When asked about the length of relationship that Mazda has with its suppliers, Mr Nakamichi of Mazda's marketing division said that relationships with all suppliers, whether they are affiliates, subcontractors or common part suppliers, were established for an 'indefinite' period of time. In addition, the last third of the seat business was available to whichever of the suppliers had performed the best over the life cycle of previous car models.

The two seat makers rely on Mazda for a very high percentage of their business. In the case of Delta Kogyo, Mazda business represents around two-thirds of its total sales. In addition, both suppliers are members of Mazda's *keiretsu* (network) and hence come into direct contact with each other on a regular basis. Additionally, since they are direct competitors for only a third of Mazda's seat business, there is a significant degree of openness between the two firms. This openness in some instances takes the form of cooperation in solving mutual or individual problems, because the other seat supplier is often in a better position to give advice than Mazda itself.

However, competition for the remaining third of the Mazda seat business is very intense, since both firms know that they have only one chance to gain the orders for a new car model every three to five years. The most interesting aspect of this competition is that it is based primarily on performance since the last contract was awarded. The areas of competition include design abilities, management strength, cost-reduction progress, quality record and, perhaps surprisingly, the amount of assistance that the supplier has given to its direct competitor either within the auspices of the *keiretsu* or on separate occasions. Thus either firm can obtain new business as long as the other does not fall below 33 per cent of Mazda's total seat purchases. A situation has been created in which there is creative tension between cooperation and competition.

Indeed, when one of the suppliers approaches the lower limit of its 33 per cent supply, Mazda typically uses its own engineers, and possibly those of the supply competitor, to help the weaker supplier in terms of a joint value analysis/value engineering programme. Because neither supplier wants to be forced into this situation, both will work diligently to avoid this fate – and at the same time enhance their own competitiveness.

Mazda is careful to ensure that neither supplier is forced into a situation of unprofitability, since this would obviously mean that Mazda would suffer in the long term. This is not to say that either supplier is allowed to make excessive profits. Indeed, profit as a percentage of sales is roughly equalized throughout the supply network, including the Mazda organization itself. During recessionary periods Mazda and its network of suppliers would make no more than about 2 per cent profit on sales. Thus members of the supply network stand or fall together, increasing the shared bonds and the willingness to help any member of the network.

Source: reproduced with permission from the publisher, John Wiley & Sons, Inc., 'Network sourcing: a hybrid approach', *Journal of Supply Chain Management* (formerly *The International Journal of Purchasing and Materials Management*), by Peter Hines, 5 April 2006, pp. 17–24.

This chapter has dealt mainly with sourcing (subcontracting) in the industrial market. Although marketing of subsupplies to international projects has a number of similarities with subsupplies in the industrial market in general, it also has the characteristics of the special marketing situation in the project market, e.g. the long and often very bureaucratic selection of subsuppliers for ad hoc supplies.

The subsupplier market in project export, however, is also very internationalized, and the main part of marketing should be conducted in those centres or countries where the main contractor is domiciled. For example, London is the domicile of a number of building contracting businesses, which work in those countries that used to be in the British Empire.

Project export is a very complex international activity, involving many market players. The preconditions for project export are a technology gap between the exporting and importing countries and that the exporter possesses the specific product and technology know-how that are being demanded in the importing country.

Project export involves supplies or deliveries that contain a combination of hardware and software. When the delivery is concluded, it will constitute an integrated system that is able to produce the products and/or the services, which the buyer requires. An example of this type of project is the construction of a dairy in a developing country.

Hardware is the blanket term for the tangible, material or physical contribution of the project supply. Hardware is composed of buildings, machines, inventory, transport equipment, etc., and is specified in the quotation and contract between buyer and seller in the form of drawings, unit lists, descriptions and so on.

Software is the blanket term for the intangible contributions in a project supply. Software includes know-how and service. There are three types of know-how:

1. *technology know-how,* comprising product, process and hardware know-how;
2. *project know-how,* comprising project management, assembly and environmental know-how;
3. *management know-how,* which in general terms involves tactical and operational management, and specifically includes marketing and administrative systems.

Service includes advisory services and assistance in connection with various applications and approvals (environmental approval, financing of the project, planning permission, etc.).

The marketing of projects is different from the marketing of products in the following respects:

- Decision of purchase, apart from local business interests, often involves decision processes in national and international development organizations. This implies the participation of a large number of people and a heavily bureaucratic system.
- The product is designed and created during the negotiation process, where the requirements are put forward.
- It often takes years from the disclosure of needs to the purchase decision being taken. Therefore total marketing costs are very large.
- When the project is taken over by the project buyer, the buyer–seller relations cease. However, by cultivating these relations before, during and after the project, a 'sleeping' relationship can be woken up again in connection with a new project (Hadjikhani, 1996).

Financing a project is a key problem for the seller as well as the buyer. The project's size and the time used for planning and implementation result in financial demands that make it necessary to use external sources of finance. In this connection, the following main segments can be distinguished. The segments arise from differences in the source of financing for the projects:

- Projects where *multilateral organizations,* such as the World Bank or regional development banks, are a primary source of finance.
- Projects where *bilateral organizations* are a primary or essential source of finance.

Project export
Combination of hardware (e.g. buildings and infrastructure) and software (technology and project know-how), e.g. in the form of a factory for ice-cream production.

● Projects where a *government institution* acts as buyer. This was normal in the command economies, where government companies acted as buyers. However, it can also be found in liberal economies, e.g. in connection with the development of social infrastructure or the building of a bridge.

● Projects where a *private person or firm* acts as buyer, such as when Unilever builds a factory in Vietnam for the production of ice-cream.

For large-scale projects, such as a new airport, there may be many partners forming a consortium, involving the concept of a 'leader firm', but with each partner undertaking financing, organization, supervision and/or construction, etc. of a part of the project on the basis of their specific expertise.

Organizing export projects involves establishing an interaction between different firms from the west, on the one side, and firms and authorities typically from developing countries, on the other. Creating or adapting an organization that is able to function under these conditions is a precondition of project marketing.

13.9   Summary

This chapter has analysed the buyer–seller relationship from different angles in the internationalized environment. The advantages and disadvantages for the contractor and subcontractor of entering into a relationship are summarized in Table 13.2.

Table 13.2	Advantages and disadvantages of buyer–seller relationships for contractor and subcontractor	
	Advantages	**Disadvantages**
Contractor (buyer)	The contractor is flexible by not investing in manufacturing facilities. The subcontractor can source the products more cheaply (because of e.g. cheaper labour costs) than by own production The contractor can concentrate on in-house core competences Complement of the contractor's product range New ideas for product innovation can be carried over from the subcontractor	The availability of suitable manufacturers (subcontractors) cannot be assumed. Outsourcing tends to be relatively less stable than in-house operations The contractor has less control over the activities of the subcontractor Subcontractors can develop into competitors Quality problems of outsourced products can harm the business of the contractor Assistance to the subcontractor may increase the costs of the whole operation
Subcontractor (seller)	Access to new export markets because of the internationalization of the contractor (especially relevant for the so-called late starters) Exploits scale economies (lower cost per unit) through better capacity utilization Learns product technology of the contractor Learns marketing practices of the contractor	Risk of becoming dependent on the contractor because of expanding production capacity and concurrent overseas expansion of sales and marketing activities in order to meet the demands of the contractor

The project export situation differs from the 'normal' buyer–seller relationship in the following ways:

- The buying decision process often involves national and international development organizations. This often results in very bureaucratic selection of subcontractors.
- Financing of the project is a key problem.

CASE STUDY 13.1

ARM: challenging Intel in the world market of computer chips

ARM Limited (www.arm.com) is the leading provider of embedded microprocessor architecture with commanding market share in everything from mobile devices to sensors. ARM provides leading microprocessor intellectual property (IP) and supporting technology including physical IP, system IP, graphic processors, design tools and software to a massive ecosystem of partners that in turn develop and support a broad range of industrial and consumer products. ARM licenses and sells its technology and products to international electronics companies, which in turn manufacture, market and sell microprocessors, application-specific integrated circuits (ASICs) and application-specific standard processors (ASSPs) based on ARM's technology to systems companies for incorporation into a wide variety of end products. The company primarily operates in the UK, the US, Europe, South-east Asia and India. It is headquartered in Cambridge, in the UK.

ARM was established in 1990 as a result of collaboration between Acorn and Apple Computer, to develop a commercial reduced instruction set computing (RISC) processor. VLSI Technology soon became an investor in ARM. In 1991, the company introduced its first embeddable RISC core, the ARM6 solution.

Cirrus Logic and Texas Instruments licensed ARM technology and Nippon Investment and Finance became ARM's fourth investor and introduced the ARM7 core in 1993.

In 1994, the company experienced international expansion, when Samsung and AKM (Asahi Kasei Microsystems) licensed its technology. In the same year, it opened offices in the US (Los Gatos, California) and Japan (Tokyo), also introducing the ARM7500 'system chip' for multimedia applications

In 2014, ARM had 30 offices around the world, including design centres in China, Taiwan, France, India, Sweden and the US.

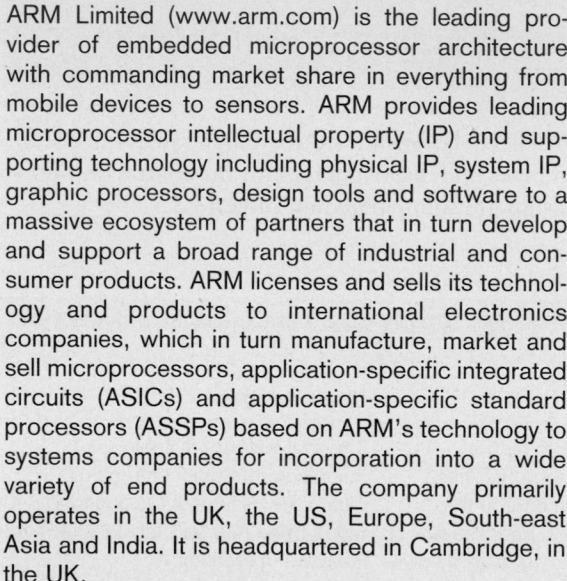

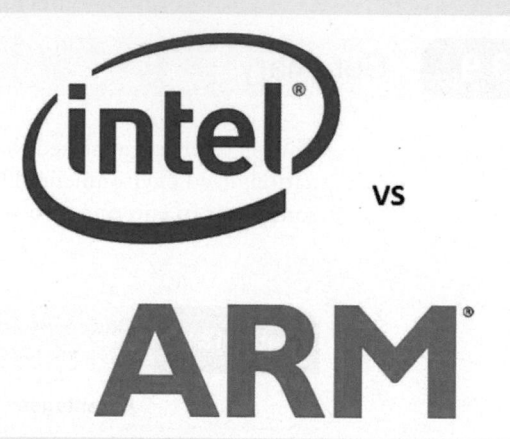

What is a microprocessor ('chip')?

Microprocessors are found at the heart of many electronic systems. They are semiconductor devices capable of interacting with other components of the system, such as memory, disk drives, keyboards, and so on, either directly or via intermediate devices ('chip sets'). The processor coordinates the functioning of these devices and manipulates digital data.

Typically, the processor performs various procedures on data stored in the memory or received from peripheral devices, and transfers the results to the appropriate locations. For example, a processor can compress a file by copying data from RAM, carrying out a compression algorithm and then copying the resulting data to a disk drive.

In order to provide this level of 'intelligence', a processor executes programs ultimately written by a human programmer. A processor of a given design has a specific instruction set. This is a set of the very logical, arithmetical and other operations that the device can perform in a single step.

In order to execute the program, the processor steps through the sequence of instructions at a rate determined by its clock. This is a device that provides a steady stream of timing pulses at a rate of anywhere between one million and several billion per second.

The power consumption of a processor depends on its clock speed, its power supply voltage and the number of transistors it contains. Because RISC architectures (which ARM uses) can be implemented in silicon with far fewer transistors than CISC architectures (which Intel uses), they tend to consume far less power in operation.

Low-power processors are ideal for small, battery-operated products

For products such as desktop computers, which are physically large and mains-operated, the power consumption of processors is not a very important design consideration. Thus CISC processors remain dominant in the desktop PC market, even though their very fast clock speeds and very high transistor counts lead to high power consumption and the need for large heat sinks to ensure that excess heat is safely dissipated.

For products which must be physically small and battery-operated, processor power consumption is a critically important design factor. A key factor in ARM's success was the recognition by the company and its customers that its RISC processor designs offered significant computational capabilities with low electrical power consumption.

The key to ARM's business model is that it offers its manufacturing customers access to its designs, rather than making silicon chips itself, which is Intel's business model. When producing a processor chip, the design phase can be separated from the physical fabrication phase. Design can be completed largely with software, and therefore needs little capital expenditure compared with establishing a fabrication facility. A company like Intel would invest approximately US$1 billion in setting up a new production facility.

The high up-front outlay and running costs associated with advanced semiconductor manufacturing translate into high entry barriers to this industry. This means that it is difficult to challenge Intel, which is vertically integrated from initial concept, through design, to production (see Figure 1).

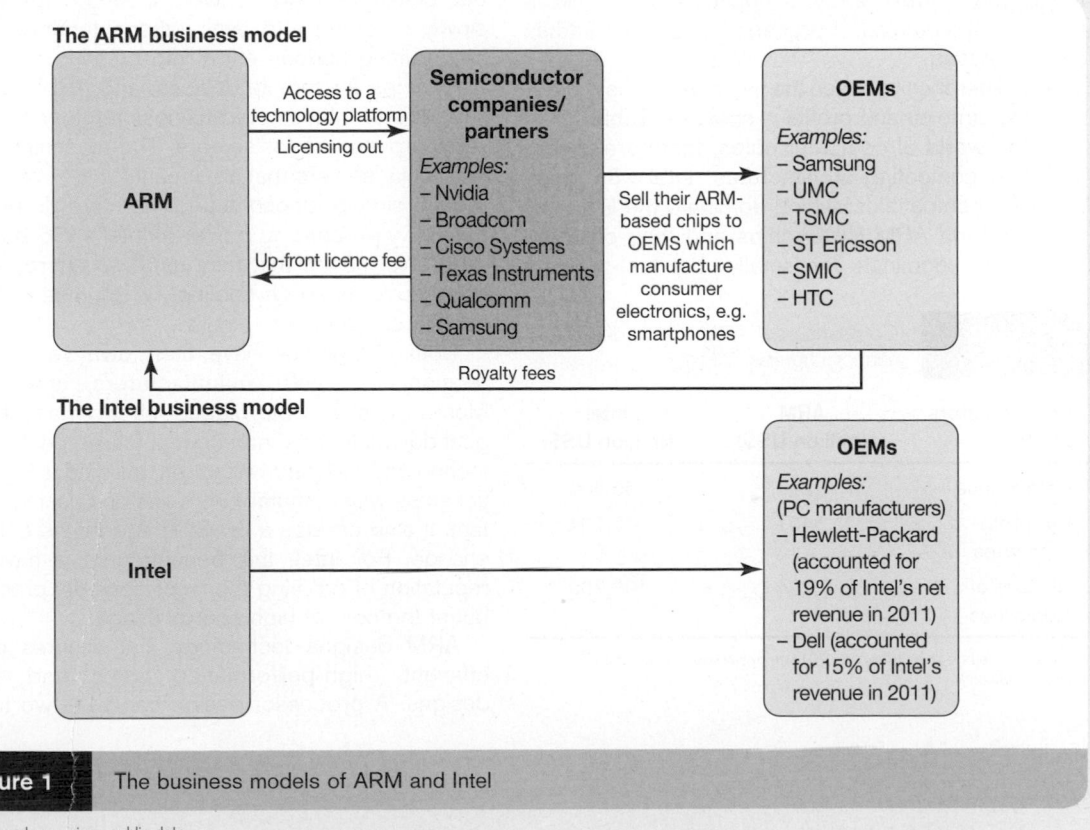

Figure 1   The business models of ARM and Intel

Source: based on various public data.

Therefore, ARM uses a different model. It confines itself to designing RISC processor cores. It then offers this intellectual property to its chip manufacturer customers. Revenues are generated from (see Figure 1):

- *Licence fees.* The fee is charged in exchange for giving the customer access to ARM's design. Licence fees are set at a level designed to recover ARM's development costs. Having paid the fee, each customer then integrates ARM's IP into its own chip design, a process that typically takes three to four years.
- *Royalties.* For each chip incorporating ARM's IP that is shipped, the manufacturer pays a small royalty. The size of the royalty is scaled to the price of the physical processor chip. It is typically less than $1 per chip, but the high volume at which chips are manufactured and the possibility that a design can be in production for 20 years mean that this is a significant revenue stream.

For the last 30 years or so, the processor industry has been dominated by the race to create even more powerful chips for servers and PCs. Intel is the undisputed leader in this market, having innovated aggressively over the years while simultaneously bringing down the prices. Processors can now be found in a massive array of applications and products, and the number of processors per product has also increased.

The difference between the two companies regarding size, turnover and profits is shown in Table 1.

In the world of computer chips, there are essentially two competing architectures: Intel ×86 chips and their compatibles, which dominate the PC marketplace; and ARM RISC chips and their compatibles, which dominate the smaller but fast-growing

Table 1	Comparison of ARM and Intel's key financial figures, 2014	
Key indicators (2014)	**ARM (million US$)**	**Intel (million US$)**
Net revenue	1,248	55,900
Net profit after taxes	401	11,704
Number of employees	3,294	106,700

Source: based on financial reports 2014 from (www.arm.com) and Intel (www.intel.com).

mobile devices sector. What makes this interesting is that Intel and ARM do not simply compete on price and technical specifications, they also compete on business model, application models and perception and relationships with the industry.

In addition to both companies serving different types of products and needs, they also operate vastly different business models. Intel designs, manufactures and sells chips directly to the marketer of the product, one step before the final consumer. The benefit of this is that, should there be a problem with a processor, the company can quickly respond and fix its supply chain, from design to production. Intel is famously known to be incredibly good at doing this, with a quick turnaround of its designed chips to the end user. However, the problem with this structure is that the original equipment manufacturers (OEMs) cannot customize the chips for their own purposes, unlike ARM chips.

ARM simply designs its chips and then sells the design to the manufacturer for licence and royalty fees. This means that ARM can generate large revenues without having to make huge capital investments, and enables manufacturers to customize their chips to certain specifications.

ARM processor-based chips are extremely power-efficient. Intel chips, on the other hand, are powerful but consume more power. Both companies are slowly creeping into each other's territory. Intel is now putting serious effort into creating energy-efficient chips for mobile devices, and ARM is making inroads into Intel's core business territory by making ARM processors for servers. The reasoning behind this is that servers that are meant for the internet only require simple functions and therefore do not need the heavy processing power of Intel's x86 infrastructure. This means that they use less energy and do not require as much cooling, which means that the servers can be made smaller.

Both companies have their own very complex relationships with manufacturers and OEMs. Moreover, this is the biggest strength and the biggest downfall of the non-commoditized portion of the technology industry. Although building strong relationships with manufacturers and end users is important, it also creates a brand image that is difficult to change. For Intel, this benefit/curse is having the reputation of creating the most powerful processors but at the cost of high energy usage.

ARM designs technology that ensures energy-efficient, high-performance chips and system designs. A processor design can take two to three years to develop. In most years, ARM introduces two to three new processors per year with a range of capabilities making them suitable for different end-markets.

The companies that choose ARM's technology pay an up-front licence fee to gain access to a design. They incorporate the ARM technology into their chip – a process that often takes three to four years. When the chip starts to ship, ARM receives a royalty on every chip that uses the design. Typically the royalty is based on the price of the chip. ARM expects to recoup a chip's development costs from the sale of the first 10 licences.

Each ARM processor and physical IP design is suitable for a wide range of end applications and so can be reused in different chip families addressing multiple markets. Each new chip family generates a new stream of royalties. An ARM design may be used in many different chips and may ship for over 20 years.

The majority of ARM's revenues are earned from semiconductor companies based all over the world. These companies sell their ARM-based chips to OEMs building consumer electronics, which are also based in all major economies. The OEMs sell their products to consumers and enterprises in every country. ARM's royalty revenues are derived from the chips in these OEM products, and ARM therefore benefits from the growth in all economies and countries around the world.

Demand for consumer products has been growing rapidly, especially in emerging markets such as India and China.

Why do semiconductor companies buy ARM technology instead of developing it themselves?

It is simply too expensive for the semiconductor companies' R&D teams to develop the technology themselves. Each company would need to spend over US$100 million every year to reproduce what ARM does. This represents more than US$20 billion of annual costs for the industry. By designing once and licensing many times, ARM spreads the R&D costs over the whole industry, making digital electronics cheaper.

Every licence represents the opportunity for a future royalty stream. In recent years ARM has added over 100 processor licences per year to its existing base of licences. In 2014, ARM signed a record 163 processor licences, taking the licence base to nearly 1,198 licences with 389 semiconductor companies.

ARM's development in the smartphone industry

ARM's first mobile phone design win was in a Nokia handset in the mid-1990s. This was one of the world's first 2G mobile phones. The software running on the ARM processor in this phone managed both the protocol-stack and the user interface. This user interface gradually became more sophisticated and engaging for the phone's users, changing the configuration of the phone, running games and managing contact lists.

In low-cost mobile phones there is one chip per phone. In the new smartphones there are often many more. The average number of ARM-based chips in a phone went up from 2.6 in 2011 to nearly 4 in 2015. A smartphone can, in the best case, bring the company eight times more royalties as a basic phone, a tablet computer 11 times more.

The price of the chip varies a great deal, but if we take an average price of US$5, the typical royalty per chip will be 2 per cent = 10 cents.

ARM's market position in 2014

In 2014, the production of chips based on ARM's technology was 12 billion, which results in a 'market share' for ARM's technology platform of about 37 per cent, up from 35 per cent in 2013. ARM has a specially strong position (80–90 per cent market share) in the small electronic devices market, such as smartphones, smartwatches, tablets and laptops. In other industries, such as home (e.g. PCs and digital TVs) and enterprise systems (desktop PCs and network systems), ARM has a much weaker position. In these industries Intel is more dominating.

QUESTIONS

1. Explain the role of ARM as a supplier in the 'chip' value chain.

2. What are the strengths and the weaknesses of ARM's business model compared with Intel?

3. In which end-user application market should ARM strengthen its relationships to potential partners, and how?

Sources: based on: www.arm.com; www.intel.com; other publicly available data. ARM is a registered trademark of ARM Limited (or its subsidiaries) in the EU and/or elsewhere. All rights reserved.

CASE STUDY 13.2

Bosch Indego: how to build B2B and B2C relationships in a new global product market – robotic lawnmowers

Before the traditional lawnmower, people used scythes to out the grass. In 1827, the English engineer Edwin Beard Budding invented the first lawnmower. Colonel Edwin George manufactured the first gasoline-powered mower in 1919. The Australian company Victa started production of the first rotary mowers in 1952. After that several models were made. The latest, the robotic lawnmower, entered the market in the year 1995 (by Husqvarna).

Types of lawnmowers

There are hundreds of lawnmower models on the market. To get an overview they can be categorized into five general groups (see Figure 1):

1. *Reel (cylinder)*: normally pushed by hand or drawn by a small tractor on large lawns.
2. *Electrical*: normally based on the rotary principle.
3. *Motor*: will normally be based on the rotor principle, but the motor can also be found on cylinder lawnmowers.

4. *Riding*: riding lawnmowers or ride-on mowers (UK) are mostly popular in the US and Canada for large lawns. The operator is provided with a seat and literally rides on the machine. Most use the rotary principle with horizontal multiple rotating blades. A common form of riding mowers is the lawn tractor which is designed to resemble a small agricultural tractor (e.g. John Deere).
5. *Robotic*: normally robotic lawnmowers are based on battery charging. A border wire around the lawn defines the area to be mowed. The robot uses the wire to locate the boundary of the area to be trimmed and, in some cases, to locate a recharging dock. Robotic lawnmowers are becoming increasingly sophisticated – they are usually self-docking and contain rain sensors, thereby eliminating human interaction from the grass-mowing process. Multiple mowers can be used to mow an even larger area.

Small electrical rotary and reel mowers are the most common in the small lawnmower category, but

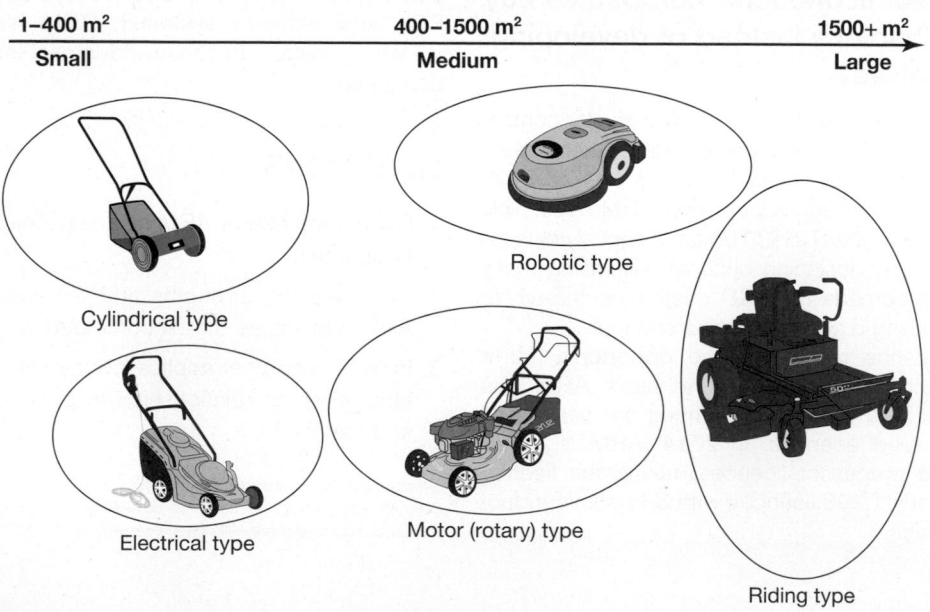

Figure 1 — Five categories of lawnmowers

The Bosch Indego robotic lawnmower at work
Source: Robert Bosch GmbH.

accessories. In 2011, its workforce generated sales of some €3.8 billion, 90 per cent of which came from outside Germany. With brands such as Bosch, Skil and Dremel, the division stands for customer focus and great engineering progress. The core success factors are innovative strength and pace of innovation. Each year, Bosch Power Tools launches more than 100 new products onto the market. The division generated about 40 per cent of its sales in 2011 with products that have been on the market for less than two years. The business segments electric power tools, accessories, measuring tools and electric garden tools of Bosch Power Tools outperformed the market.

manual reel mowers and classical motor-driven mowers are also represented in this group. In the medium lawn size category, the most common mower is the classical motor-driven lawnmower. The robot mower could also be considered part of this group. The reason for the low number is because of the high price compared with the cutting area.

The ride-on mower is the one that dominates the large lawn category, but you will also find the robot mower in small numbers. If you want a robot mower fitted to cut a large lawn, this is a very expensive option.

The Bosch Group

The Bosch Group (**www.bosch.com**) is a leading global supplier of technology and services. In the areas of automotive and industrial technology, consumer goods and building technology, more than 300,000 associates generated €51.5 billion of sales in the fiscal year 2011. The Bosch Group comprises Robert Bosch GmbH and its roughly 350 subsidiaries and regional companies in some 60 countries. If its sales and service partners are included, then Bosch is represented in roughly 150 countries. This worldwide development, manufacturing and sales network is the foundation for further growth. Bosch spent some €4.2 billion on R&D in 2011, and applied for over 4,100 patents worldwide. With all its products and services, Bosch enhances the quality of life by providing solutions which are both innovative and beneficial.

The new robotic lawnmower from Bosch – Indego – is part of the Bosch Power Tools Division.

The Bosch Power Tools Division

The Power Tools Division of the Bosch Group is the world market leader for power tools and power tool

Gardening and lawnmowing

There are around 110 million homes with gardens in the western world, generating sales of 10–15 million lawnmowers (all types) every year.

	Number of homes with gardens (2011)
US	55 million
Europe	45 million
Australia and South Africa	10 million
Total	110 million

Source: based on different public sources.

The most important competitors in the robotic lawnmower industry

The Swedish firm Husqvarna pioneered the engineering of the robotic mower in 1995, a device that mows lawns by itself. Since then, the Husqvarna Group has (at the end of 2012) manufactured more than 200,000 robotic mowers.

With more than 20,000 units sold, Husqvarna is the world leader in robotic lawnmowers, with the widest range of the market. The Automower model can handle up to 6,000 square metres of lawn and can send text messages to its owner's mobile phone.

Husqvarna's most successful markets in terms of volume are Sweden, Germany and Switzerland. During 2011, the offering was being expanded with the Automower 305, a model for small gardens with lawns up to 500 square metres. The recommended retail price for the Husqvarna Automower 305 is €1,490 (US $1,999).

By the end of 2012, about 500,000 robotic lawn-mowers had been sold, mainly by companies such as the market leader Husqvarna, Zucchetti Robotica (Italian), Friendly Robotics (Israeli), Stihl (German) and a few others. New competitors from Asia are now entering the market with low-price design copies to win a share of the growing garden care market. New marketing concepts have also been developed to defend the market positions in growing markets.

In 2011, new models were introduced by Husqvarna/Gardena, focusing on the growing number of elderly people as well as small garden owners. In 2012, John Deere, the well-known US manufacturer of gardening equipment, also entered the robotic lawnmower market with the introduction of the John Deere Tango E5. Hong Kong-based Positec Industrial introduced the Landroid robotic lawnmower in 2010 and is now selling in several European countries.

United States

In the biggest robotic lawnmower market of the world, the Israeli-made Friendly Robotics Robo-mower robotic lawnmower has a huge market share, leading the Italian-made, Zucchetti Lawnbott Evolution automatic lawnmower. Since the beginning of the 2000s the Robomower has enjoyed dominance of the US market.

Honda, launched its own robotic lawnmower for cutting household grass – the Miimo–in 2013, only in Europe, with a target of 4,000 sales per year.

Overall, worldwide sales of robotic lawnmowers reached approximately 150,000 units, in 2013 with Husqvarna as the world market leader (–30 per cent market share).

Bosch enters the robotic lawnmower market

In January 2013, Bosch Indego (www.bosch-pt. co.uk/gardentools/) entered the rapidly growing robotic lawnmower market.

The Indego is recommended for a lawn area of up to 1,000 square metres. It is powered by a lithium-ion battery and has a cutting width of 26 centimetres. The height of cut can be adjusted to 10 different settings from 20 mm to a maximum of 60 mm. If the Indego encounters an obstacle in its path while mowing, it is recognized with the aid of sensitive touch sensors, allowing the mower to manoeuvre safely around it.

The robotic lawnmower spreads the finely cut grass clippings across the lawn, where they fertilize the grass roots. It can operate for up to 20 minutes per full charge, during which it can mow 200 square metres. It then needs to juice itself for 90 minutes before resuming operation.

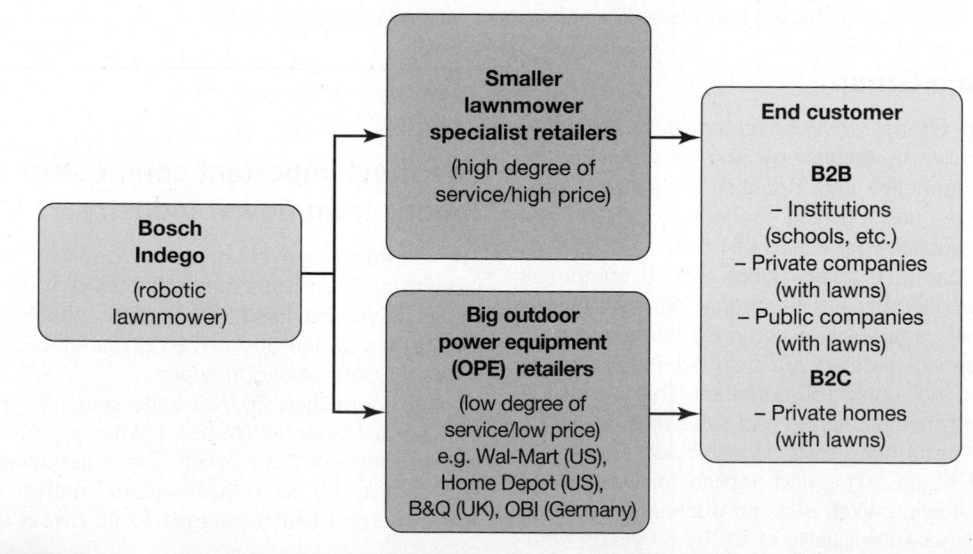

Figure 2 Two different distribution systems for the Bosch Indego

Source: based on different public sources.

Bosch claims the Indego is three to four times quicker than other robotic mowers. One reason for this is that it mows in orderly sequential rows, like a farmer harvesting crops. By contrast, some robotic mowers move more or less randomly, the idea being that they will eventually get the whole lawn done.

The Indego has been available in retail outlets since January 2013 at the recommended price of **€1,499**, including VAT. It is supplied in a carton with a docking station and a 150-metre wire including 300 fixing nails.

The global distribution of the Bosch Indego

The distribution of the Bosch Indego is of course to be handled by the Bosch sales force in the local subsidiaries together with the rest of the products in the Bosch Power Tools Division.

In principle there are two different distribution alternatives for Indego Bosch, according to Figure 2.

QUESTIONS

1. As a supplier of the Indego, how should Bosch's approaches differ in the two types of distribution in Figure 2.

2. Which of the two distribution set-ups should Bosch focus on most?

3. Would you also recommend that Bosch build relationships with the end customer? If yes, which target group should they focus on?

Sources: based on www.bosch-pt.co.uk/gardentools/; www.husqvarna.com; other public sources.

VIDEO CASE STUDY 13.3 Kone elevators and escalators

download from www.pearsoned.co.uk/hollensen

The Finnish company is one of the largest manufacturers of elevators and escalators worldwide, and also provides maintenance services and modernization solutions. In addition, Kone builds and services automatic doors and gates. The company provides local service for builders, developers, building owners, designers and architects in 1,000 offices in over 50 countries. Since 1924, Kone has been owned by

Source: copyright © KONE Corporation.

one of Finland's wealthiest families, the Herlin family.

There are four global large elevator and escalator companies. These are, in addition to KONE: Otis (part of the United Technologies group), Schindler and ThyssenKrupp Elevator (part of the Thyssen-Krupp group). Otis is regarded as the world market leader for new equipment. Kone has around 18.5 per cent market share in the world market for new equipment. There are also many more local competitors. The new equipment business has a much higher degree of consolidation than the service business, which is more local.

Questions

1. Try to describe the complex decision-making process regarding choice of supplier for installation of new elevators and escalators in a building.

2. What are Kone's key challenges in establishing long-term relationships with its new global customers?

For further resources, see this book's website at **www.pearsoned.co.uk/hollensen**

Questions for discussion

1. What are the reasons for the increasing level of outsourcing to international subcontractors?

2. Describe the typology of subcontractors based on the differences in the contractor/subcontractor relationship.

3. Explain the shift from seller to buyer initiative in subcontracting.

4. Explain the main differences between the US and the Japanese subsupplier systems.

5. How are project exports/turnkey projects different from general subcontracting in the industrial market?

6. Project export is often characterized by a complex and time-consuming decision-making process. What are the marketing implications of this for the potential subcontractor?

References

Andersen, P.H., Blenker, P. and Christensen, P.R. (1995) *Internationalization of Subcontractors: In Search of a Theoretical Framework.* The Southern Denmark Business School, Kolding.

Blenker, P. and Christensen, P.R. (1994) 'Interactive strategies in supply chains: a double-edged portfolio approach to SME', Subcontractors Positioning Paper presented at the 8th Nordic Conference on Small Business Research.

Cavinato, J.L. (1992) 'A total cost/value model for supply chain competitiveness', *Journal of Business Logistics,* 13(2), pp. 285–301.

Cespedes, F.V., Dougherty, J.P. and Skinner III, B.S. (2013) 'How to identify the best customers for your business', *MIT Sloan Management Review,* 54(2), pp. 53–59.

Cho, Dong-Sung and Chu, Wujin (1994) 'Determinants of bargaining power in OEM negotiations', *Industrial Marketing Management,* 23, pp. 342–355.

Christensen, P.R. and Lindmark, L. (1993) 'Location and internationalization of small firms', in Lindquist, L. and Persson, L.O. (eds), *Visions and Strategies in European Integration,* Springer Verlag, Berlin/Heidelberg.

Dwyer, R.F., Schurr, P.H. and Oh, S. (1987) 'Developing buyer–seller relationships', *Journal of Marketing,* 51 (April), pp. 11–27.

Gulati, R., Sytch, M. and Mehrotra, P. (2008) 'Breaking up is never easy: planning for exit in a strategic alliance', *California Management Review*, 50(4), pp. 147–163.

Hadjikhani, A. (1996) 'Project marketing and the management of discontinuity', *International Business Review*, 5(3), pp. 319–336.

Hibbert, E.P. (1993) 'Global make or buy decisions', *Industrial Marketing Management*, 22, pp. 67–77.

Johanson, J. and Mattson, L.G. (1988) 'Internationalization in industrial systems', in Hood, N. and Vahlne, J.E. (eds), *Strategies in Global Competition*, Croom Helm, Beckenham, pp. 287–314.

Jüttner, U. and Wehrli, H.P. (1994) 'Relationship marketing from a value system perspective', *International Journal of Service Industry Management*, 5, pp. 54–73.

Kanter, R.M. (1994) 'Collaborative advantage', *Harvard Business Review*, July–August, pp. 96–107.

Lehtinen, U. (1991) 'Alihankintajarjestelma 1990-luvulla [Subcontracting system in the 1990s]', *Publications of SITRA*, 114, Helsinki.

Magnusson, P. and Boyle, B.A. (2009) 'A contingency perspective on psychic distance in international channel relationships', *Journal of Marketing Channels*, 16(1), pp. 77–99.

Mouzas, S., Henneberg, S. and Naudé, P. (2007) 'Trust and reliance in business relationships', *European Journal of Marketing*, 41(9/10), pp. 1016–1032.

Ottesen, O. (1995) *Buyer Initiative: Ignored, but Imperative for Marketing Theory*. Working Paper, Department of Business Administration, Stavanger College, Norway.

Sousa, C.M.P. and Lages, L.F. (2011) 'The PD scale: a measure of psychic distance and its impact on international marketing strategy', *International Marketing Review*, 28(2), pp. 201–222.

Tähtinen, J. and Vaaland, T. (2006) 'Business relationships facing the end: why restore them?', *Journal of Business & Industrial Marketing*, 21(1), pp. 14–23.

Turnbull, P.W. and Valla, J.P. (1986) *Strategies for International Industrial Marketing*. Croom Helm, London.

Welch, L.S. and Luostarinen, R. (1988) 'Internationalization: evolution of a concept', *Journal of General Management*, 14(2), pp. 36–64.

CASE STUDY III.1

Raleigh Bicycles: does the iconic bicycle brand still have a chance on the world market?

The name Raleigh (www.raleigh.co.uk) has been synonymous with bicycles since the company was founded in a small workshop on Raleigh Street, Nottingham, by three men in 1886. Frank Bowden, a successful lawyer and convert to cycling, bought the firm in 1887, and in December 1888 founded The Raleigh Cycle Company as a limited liability private company. During its 130 years in existence, Raleigh has sold more than 250 million bicycles.

From the start, Raleigh was very successful. In the 1960s, it was the largest bicycle manufacturer in the world. At that time, Raleigh was like an empire. Wherever the Commonwealth was, Raleigh was there too. In the late 1960s, Raleigh was manufacturing four million bicycles a year, 75 per cent of which were exported. By 1970, Raleigh owned over 160 different brand names, each country having its own brand. From that point Raleigh decreased in size, sales and importance in the global bicycle industry. Its whole product portfolio was also rationalized and standardized. However, Raleigh still experienced hard financial times, and the company changed ownership several times during the following decades.

Source: Raleigh International Ltd.

The bicycle world market

Currently only 18 per cent of the world population sometimes uses a bicycle. This means that there is still a huge potential number of customers out there: 82 per cent of the world population.

According to Table 1 the global bicycle market, including bicycles, parts and accessories, is estimated to have total retail sales of about €36 billion. In 2014, worldwide demand for bicycles was approximately 90 million units, of which approximately 60 per cent are produced (but not bought) in China (with Taiwan as the core bicycle production centre). In comparison, roughly 40 million cars were produced worldwide.

During the 1980s' Taiwan took over Japan's role as the world's leading supply nation. The world bicycle market is highly fragmented. The world's biggest bicycle producer, Giant in Taiwan, produces almost two million bicycles, securing them a market share of 2.2 per cent. Taiwanese firms have opened their own overseas production centres. Meanwhile, Japan retains its prime role in the supply of cycle components, again drawing on cheap labour in other parts of the Far East. Japan's Shimano is one example of a huge component supplier.

The world electric bicycle (e-bike) market

The modern electric bicycle (e-bike) is true to the concept of a pedal bicycle with assisting propulsion, being rideable without power. Batteries have finite capacity, which means that the hybrid human/electric power mix is much more likely to be emphasized than is the case with a combustion engine. Electric bicycles are gaining acceptance, especially in Europe and Asia, in response to increasing traffic congestion, an ageing population and concern about the environment.

Electric motorized bicycles can be *power-on-demand,* where the motor is activated by a handlebar-mounted throttle, and/or a *pedelec* (from **ped**al **elec**tric), also known as *electric assist,* where the electric motor is regulated by pedalling. These have a sensor to detect the pedalling speed or the pedalling force, or both. An electronic controller provides assistance as a function of the sensor inputs, the vehicle speed and the required force. Most controllers also provide for manual adjustment.

Table 1   Total European and world bicycle market e-bikes (2014)

Market volume (1,000 units of bicycles – consumption)	Germany	France	UK	Italy	NL	Rest of EU	Total EU	Japan	China (incl. Taiwan)	US	Total world (incl. rest of world)
Total market (1,000)	4,500	3,500	3,400	2,000	1,400	13,200	28,000	10,000	28,000	18,000	90,000
Most important manufacturers/brands	MIFA Derby Cycle Werke	Eddy Merckx Peugeot	Raleigh Universal	Bianchi Alan Cinelli	Gazelle	??	Raleigh Derby	??	Giant Co Tianjin Xinri Shandong	Connoncale Merlin	Giant man Ltd (Taiwan) Trek
Raleigh brand market shares %	??	??	20%	??	??	??	??	??	??	??	??
% volume – e-bikes	2.6	1.5	2.1	1.5	7.0	1.0	1.8	3.0	54.0	1.7	20.0
Total e-bikes market (1,000)	117	52	71	30	98	132	500	300	15,000	300	18,000
Market value (mill. €)											
Total value (mill. €) – all bicycles including parts and accessories (average price €400 per unit – unless for China)	1,800	1,400	1,360	800	560	5,280	11,200	4,000	5,600 (average price €200 per unit)	7,200	36,000
Total value – e-bikes (mill. €) (average price €1,500 per unit – unless for China)	175	78	96	45	147	198	739	450	4,500 (average price €300 per unit)	450	9,000
% value – e-bikes	9.7	5.5	7.1	5.6	26.0	3.8	6.6	11.36	80.4	6.3	25.0

Sources: www.bike-eu.com (market reports); China Sourcing Reports (bicycles).

Raleigh website

Source: Raleigh International Ltd (www.raleigh.com).

Range is a key consideration with electric bikes, and is affected by factors such as motor efficiency, battery capacity, efficiency of the driving electronics, aerodynamics, hills and weight of the bike and rider. The range of an electric bike is usually stated as somewhere between 7 km (uphill on electric power only) and 70 km (minimum assistance) and is highly dependent on whether or not the bike is tested on flat roads or hills.

There have been some interesting advances in materials science and battery technology that now make electric bicycles more practical than in previous years. Much of this has come from the computer industry. For example, battery technology has advanced a great deal. The battery systems to choose from include lead-acid, nickel–cadmium (NiCd) nickel–metal hydride (NiMH) and lithium-ion batteries.

Three factors are important when choosing the right battery: weight, how long the battery lasts and how long it takes to recharge.

Lithium-ion batteries are very common in consumer electronic devices, especially the portable type. The qualities that make them ideal in consumer electronics also make them ideal for bicycles. For example, they have one of the best energy-to-weight ratios of any battery type and recharging them is straightforward. Additionally, they do not suffer from 'memory effect' – which is when a battery that is only partially discharged is subsequently recharged but never regains its full capacity again. Furthermore, the charge lost over time when not in use is negligible.

However, lithium-ion batteries do have certain drawbacks. For one, the shelf life is limited in comparison to NiCd batteries. From time of manufacturing, regardless of the number of charge and discharge cycles, the battery's capacity will decline. This means that the battery has to be exchanged every second or third year.

Worldwide, the total e-bike market (which in Table 1a is regarded as a part of the total world bicycle market) is estimated to be 18 million units, which represents a value of approximately €9 billion. Most of the worldwide demand for e-bikes is found in China, where consumers are buying 54 per cent of all e-bikes sold worldwide.

The share of e-bikes (of the total bicycle market) varies a lot from market to market. In Europe (apart from the Netherlands), the percentage is still relatively low, whereas in Asia the percentage is as high as 50 per cent (e.g. in China).

In April 2009, the EN 15194 standard for 'Electronically Power-assisted Cycles' (EPAC) was officially announced by the National Standards Boards (NSBs) of 30 countries (27 EU member states and Iceland, Norway and Switzerland of the European Free Trade Association).

Current Raleigh international marketing strategy

By the 1930s, Raleigh was already exporting from Nottingham all over the world. This was done not merely by sending a single model of bicycle to all these countries, but by gathering information about each market and adapting the design of bicycles to the local market. The policy of adaptation was continued until the 1960s when Raleigh had 60,000 different models of bicycle in its range, each of which had a demand to fill. After the 1960s takeover of Raleigh by TI, the Raleigh product range was gradually rationalized and standardized. However, the consequence was that Raleigh lost market share in many countries, mainly to local competition, as customers would not accept the 'standardized' changes being made.

In international markets, Raleigh has cancelled their bicycle manufacturing units (the bicycles are now sourced from the Far East). Instead they mainly rely on a licensing concept: revenue is generated by finding partners around the world who are willing to pay a royalty fee for having the exclusive right to sell under the Raleigh brand, or one of the other Raleigh companies' brands in their chosen market. By taking this approach, Raleigh can choose the international partners they want to work with, and can refuse to work with partners wishing to sell inferior quality bicycles with the Raleigh name. Raleigh can keep control of its brand by having the contractual right to veto any bicycle that it feels is not appropriate.

When the partners have been chosen, Raleigh is quite flexible in how the licensing contracts are drawn up, by allowing licensees a relatively free reign on how they market the Raleigh name locally. Through this strategy Raleigh is becoming a stronger brand in a lot of countries, for example in Finland where Raleigh bicycles had not been sold before. The licensee spent a lot of time and effort promoting Raleigh and the licensee reports it is now the third biggest brand in the country.

The licensing strategy has also resulted in the Raleigh brand being perceived differently in different countries. Here are some examples:

R09 Power Elegance (e-bike)
Source: Raleigh International Ltd.

- Holland – the Raleigh bicycle is the managing directors' bicycle; it is seen as exclusive and has a very high price to match the image.
- Ireland – a Raleigh bicycle is seen as a family bicycle which cannot command a higher price than other internationally branded competitors' bicycles.
- Germany – the Raleigh bicycle is used mainly for leisure and exercise.
- Kuwait – the rise in income has meant the bicycle is perceived as a poor man's transport so the majority of bicycles sold are for the immigrant workforce to get to work cheaply.
- Africa – Raleigh has sponsored a successful national cycling team and based all of their marketing around this team, thus suggesting Raleigh is 'setting the pace' in South Africa.

Team Raleigh
Source: Raleigh International Ltd.

In 2004, Raleigh UK started its Cyclelife initiative. Cyclelife is based on a franchising concept and was created to compete effectively with chain stores in the UK by giving all Cyclelife participants a national identity. Raleigh is the main supplier for these Cyclelife stores. In September 2009, the first Cyclelife dealership started in Ireland. By 2012, Cyclelife was one of the biggest retailing networks in the UK, with around 150 stores. The result is that in 2014 Raleigh's share of the UK bicycle market was around 25 per cent – in its heyday it was 60 per cent.

Today (2014), Raleigh operates through production and distribution companies in the UK, US and Canada, along with worldwide licensing activities and a sourcing arm in Taiwan. Raleigh's best-known brands are Raleigh, Avenir and Diamondback. Raleigh has approximately 430 employees. In 2011, they realized sales of over US$260 million (€195 million) and sold approximately 850,000 bicycles at a small profit of €2 million. Geographically, the Raleigh revenues are roughly split between Europe (43 per cent), North America (48 per cent) and the rest of the world (9 per cent).

The strategy to license the Raleigh name to partners has minimized the fixed costs and the financial situation today is much better than it used to be: the Raleigh Group's latest financials (2011) show the company with a profit of €2 million on turnover. In 2002 the business lost nearly €6 million.

In April 2012, the Dutch Accell Group acquired Raleigh and its international operations for US$80 million. This acquisition further strengthened Accell Group's position in North America and the UK.

QUESTIONS

1. Characterize the internationalization 'balance' between standardization and adaptation over the history of Raleigh.

2. Does the iconic bicycle brand still have a chance in the world market?

3. Please compare and evaluate Raleigh's current entry modes (business models), franchising and licensing, with other alternatives.

4. E-bike sales are increasing across Europe. Electric bicycles are being seen as a commuting alternative to the car, allowing customers to travel to work by bicycle without having to shower and change. This is an area where Raleigh already has a product. Should Raleigh sell a standardized e-bike concept, or should it adapt its marketing mix to each local market depending on the culture and potential future e-bike sales?

Sources: www.bike-eu.com market reports; Global bicycle stats http://quickrelease.tv/?p=279; http://www.bikebiz.com/news/29247/Guardian-profiles-Gouldthorp; http://www.guardian.co.uk/business/2007/nov/23/cycling; http://tectrends.com/tectrends/article/00169044.html; special thanks to Gerry Appleton and John MacNaughtan from Raleigh.

CASE STUDY III.2

Netflix Inc.: the US internet subscription service company is dominating the television and movies streaming world

Netflix, Inc. began operations on April 14, 1998. The Company is now the world's leading internet television network with 69 million members in nearly 50 countries (most countries are in South America) enjoying more than 2 billion hours of TV shows and movies per month, including original series, documentaries and feature films. Members can watch as much as they want, anytime, anywhere, on nearly any internet-connected screen. Members can play, pause and resume watching, all without commercials or commitments. Additionally, in the US, members can receive DVDs.

The company has three reportable segments:

1. Domestic streaming
2. International streaming
3. Domestic DVD

A majority of Netflix's revenues are generated in the US, and substantially all of the company's long-lived tangible assets are held in the US. The company's revenues are derived from monthly membership fees (for the streaming part, the flat monthly payment is US$9).

Netflix history

How did it all start? Of course, there is always an interesting story associated with any business. Reed Hastings and *Marc Randolph* founded Netflix in 1997 in Scotts Valley, California. The idea of Netflix came to Hastings when he was charged US$40 late fees after returning *Apollo 12*. The fact that consumers need to pay high overdue fees frustrated Hastings; at the same time, Hastings was trying to come up with a better way to provide customers with better video rental service.

With this objective in mind, Hastings started Netflix, which at that time offered home movie delivery service. Netflix used the US Postal Service to deliver all the DVDs to its subscribers. Different from the industry giant Blockbuster Inc., which offered the traditional pay per movie rental delivery/pick-up service, Netflix's subscription plan was unlimited monthly rentals with a flat rate of US$17.99. Netflix allowed its customers to hold up to three movies at any one time in a month. Another

significant difference between Netflix and Blockbuster Inc. at that time was that Blockbuster Inc. attracted customers to their various retail locations whereas Netflix offered home delivery through the mail. In 2000, Netflix introduced an extensive personalized video recommendation system where the system recommends movies to customers based on their preferences, movie ratings and reviews by other customers. This innovation has given Netflix a competitive edge compared to its rivals.

It was not until 2007 that Netflix finally introduced the new video-on-demand and streaming services, which allow consumers to play, pause and play again anytime and anywhere without limit.

According to the recent statistics on the Netflix website, the company has reached 70 million users globally (as per 1st September 2015), which is a tremendous increase compared with that of 2014. Table 1 shows the key figures for Netflix from 2012 to 2014.

Table 1	Netflix financial and membership development 2012–14		
	2012 (US$ million)	2013 (US$ million)	2014 (US$ million)
Revenues	3,609	4,375	5,505
• marketing costs	439	470	607
• other costs	3,140	3,737	4,549
Net profits (before taxes)	30	171	349
Global streaming members	2012 (millions of members)	2013 (millions of members)	2014 (millions of members)
Total (end of the year)	33	44	57
US members	27	33	39
International members	6	11	18
Domestic (US) DVD customers	8.0	6.7	5.7

Source: based on the Netflix Financial Report 2014.

At 1st September 2015, there were 69 million streaming members (42 million US members and 27 million international members).

By the end of 2014, there were 2,189 full-time employees in Netflix.

Revenues

Revenues come mainly from membership fees in the streaming business. Netflix offers three types of streaming membership plans.

In the US, the basic plan is priced at US$7.99 per month and includes access to standard definition quality streaming on a single screen at a time.

The most popular streaming plan, which includes access to high-definition quality streaming on two screens concurrently, is priced at US$8.99 per month. Existing members were grandfathered in at US$7.99 for two years, as long as they remain a member.

The premium plan, introduced in the second quarter of 2013, is priced at US$11.99 per month and includes access to high-definition and ultra-high-definition quality content on four screens concurrently.

Internationally, pricing for the three types of membership plans is structured similar to the US and ranges from the US dollar equivalent of approximately US$6.00 per month to US$19.00.

Costs

Payment for content

For the domestic and international streaming segments, content expenses, which include the amortization of the streaming content library and other expenses associated with the licensing and acquisition of streaming content, represent the vast majority of cost of revenues. Streaming content rights are generally specific to a geographic region and accordingly international expansion will require the company to obtain additional streaming content to support new international markets. Other costs of revenues such as streaming delivery expenses, customer service and payment processing fees tend to be lower as a percentage of total cost of revenues as compared to content expenses.

Netflix utilizes both their own and third-party content delivery networks to help them efficiently stream a high volume of content to the members over the internet. Streaming delivery expenses, therefore, also include equipment costs related to the content delivery network and all third-party costs associated with delivering streaming content over the internet.

Cost of revenues in the domestic DVD segment consist primarily of delivery expenses, content expenses, including amortization of DVD content library and revenue sharing expenses, and other expenses associated with their DVD processing and customer service centres. Delivery expenses for the domestic DVD segment consist of the postage costs to mail DVDs to and from the members and the packaging and label costs for the mailers.

Marketing

For the domestic and international streaming segments, marketing expenses consist primarily of advertising expenses and payments made to affiliates and device partners. Advertising expenses include promotional activities such as television and online advertising. Payments to the affiliates and device partners include fixed fee and/or revenue sharing payments. Marketing expenses are primarily incurred by the domestic and international streaming segments given the focus on building consumer awareness of the streaming offerings. Marketing expenses incurred by the international streaming segment have been significant and will fluctuate dependent upon the number of international territories where Netflix is marketed.

Source: IanDagnall Computing/Alamy Images.

International expansion

The company first began offering an instant streaming service to the international market in 2010. It was in that year, on September 22, that the service became available in Canada. At the time, Canadians could subscribe to Netflix for US$7.99 a month. However, despite the proclaimed low price, content selection in Canada was extremely limited. In 2012, data showed that in the US there were 10,625 unique titles in Netflix's library, whereas in Canada there were only 2,647. This could be blamed on differences in distribution deals in the US and Canada. At 1st September 2015, there are about 6 million Netflix members in Canada.

On July 5 2011, Netflix announced its plans to launch a streaming service in Latin America, its largest expansion to date. At the time, Netflix had 23 million subscribers in the US and Canada. Entering the Latin American market meant Netflix had access to approximately 600 million people, or twice the number of people living in the US. Although high-speed internet in Latin America is not as accessible as it is in the US and Canada, upon the announcement of its expansion to Latin America, Netflix stock immediately surged 8 per cent.

Beginning in September 2011, the company began its expansion to 43 countries and territories in Central and South America, as well as the Caribbean, offering content in English, Spanish and Portuguese. Brazil became the first country in Latin America to launch the service on September 5. There the service was offered at $BR14.99 or approximately US$9.10 per month, making it more expensive than in the US and Canada. Rounding out the first five countries to launch streaming service in Latin America were Argentina, which followed on the 7th September, Chile on the 8th, Colombia on the 9th and Mexico on the 12th. Service spread to the other 38 countries in the following weeks. Among the content distributed to Latin America was programming from CBS, Showtime, and Miramax.

The launch in Latin America was not as successful as the company had hoped. While in Latin America Netflix had no streaming competitors as it did in Canada, the digital divide (a lack of high broadband internet penetration) hindered rapid growth. In Brazil, for example, only 20 per cent of the population had an internet speed greater than 500-kbs a second; 800-kbs a second are needed to stream Netflix's content.

Further, the lack of competitors in some ways slowed growth as well. Whereas in Canada new subscribers had been exposed to streaming content by other companies, the concept was newer to a wide Latin American audience, making some sceptical of the prospect. A banking system unused to recurrent monthly transactions exacerbated the problem. Still, while Latin American expansion happened more slowly than expected, their Canadian expansion happened at a faster rate than expected, making their first two forays into the international market fairly successful.

The initial launches in Canada and in Latin America happened before Netflix's 2011 controversy in the US. In September of that year, the company decided to switch to two separate plans (one for streaming and one for DVD), hiked its prices accordingly, and attempted a move to two websites (one for streaming and one for DVD rentals). The change to its business model was accompanied by a loss of approximately 1 million American users and a plunging stock price.

Prior to announcing the change to service, stock was valued at just around US$300; after the announcement the price plunged to less than US$53 a share. Prior to this debacle, Netflix had been having its most successful quarter, mainly due to the decision to expand to Latin America. The company quickly lost all the money it made in the quarter it announced growth to Latin America, and was forced to apologize and rethink its changing model.

Bringing people back to Netflix after the 2011 controversy came in two forms. First, it began work on producing its own original content – announcing its adaptation of *House of Cards* in 2011 for a 2013 air date and its revival of *Arrested Development* in 2012 for a 2013 air date. Second, it continued international expansion.

Netflix started its expansion to Europe in 2012, launching in the UK and Ireland on January 4. By September 18, it had expanded to Denmark, Finland, Norway and Sweden.

At that time, Netflix had developed a strategy for its international expansion. They start with a limited offer which does not cost them very much money and minimizes the risk. Then they collect very detailed data about what people like, and structure programming and investment around consumer behaviour. This takes into account cultural taste differences and allows distribution deals to develop accordingly. For example, by September 2013, Netflix had added content from Channel 4, ITV and the BBC.

Netflix UK and Ireland reached its millionth subscriber faster than Netflix Canada, nabbing its millionth member by July 2012. In the UK, BARB (Broadcasters Audience Research Board) reported Netflix as being extremely successful in the UK market. More than one in ten households in the country subscribed to the service by 2014. More than twice as many people subscribed to Netflix than to Amazon Prime. As of autumn 2014, Netflix had 3 million UK subscribers which was more than twice as many as it had in 2013.

Following the UK and Scandinavia, the next country in Europe to receive Netflix service was The Netherlands, on September 11, 2013. The Netherlands was the only country that Netflix expanded to in 2013, although, as the company decided to slow expansion in order to control subscription costs. The company spent US$3 billion on subscription content that year. Netflix said that shows that performed well on BitTorrent networks and other pirate sites were more likely to be offered as part of the expansion. Netflix thinks that illegal downloading helps to create demand, as users may switch to legal services for an improved user experience.

In the final quarter of 2013, Netflix gained more new subscribers from its pool of international countries than it did from the US for the first time since it began its European expansion, making international expansion increasingly important. At the end of 2013, the company had reached approximately 32 million users in the US and additionally had approximately 10 million users internationally.

By September 19, 2014, the service was also available in Austria, Belgium, France, Germany, Luxembourg and Switzerland. While reception throughout the rest of Europe was relatively warm, it was fairly hostile in France because of fears that the launch of Netflix would begin to ruin the country's cultural exception – its focus on culturally specific media. This led to Netflix's decision to create a series called *Marseille,* essentially a remake of its hit series *House of Cards* within a French context and one of the company's first non-English language shows.

Prior to its international expansion in 2010, Netflix's subscriber base grew on average by 2.4 million people a year. Following its arrival in Canada, Latin America and eventually Europe, its subscriber base has grown on average by 7 million people a year, making international expansion key to Netflix's continued growth in the global marketplace. Notably, the company has over 20 original shows planned for release in 2015 and 2016. In that bunch are Netflix's first non-English language series.

Expansion to Australia and New Zealand occurred on March 24, 2015. On February 4, 2015, expansion to Japan was announced to begin during the fall of 2015. In May 2015, Netflix revealed it was in talks with Jack Ma's Wasu Media Holding (part of Alibaba) and other partners to enter China's online video market. Also Spain and Portugal is in reach for further expansion.

Competition

Table 2 compares the major suppliers in the streaming video business:

HBO

Netflix has long considered HBO (owned by Time Warner Inc.) to be its biggest rival in terms of content, but HBO has a long way to go to catch up with Netflix's subscriber numbers. HBO has over 114 million subscribers globally through their cable and satellite television network.

In Spring 2015, HBO offered a new service – HBO Now – which is available as a standalone service and does not require a television subscription to use. The new service targets customers who prefer 'pure' streaming services like Netflix and Hulu. HBO Now contains access to shows like *Girls* and *Game of Thrones* and other premium TV series and films, whereas Netflix now focuses on its original content shows such as *House of Cards, Unbreakable Kimmy Schmidt* and more. HBO Now charges US$15 per month – nearly double the price of Netflix, but they claim it contains more original content. Of course, HBO has had 25 years to position its brand as one delivering quality content that's worth a premium. The network piled up a record 126 Emmy nominations in 2015, while Netflix is just beginning to make its presence felt in that sphere. But Netflix has had a strong start and received 34 Emmy nominations of its own in 2015 for *House of Cards, Orange Is the New Black* and *Unbreakable Kimmy Schmidt.*

However, in September 2015, *HBO Now* was already considering lowering its price of US$15 per month, in order to meet the competition from Amazon Prime and Netflix.

Table 2	Comparison of major suppliers of video streaming services – number of subscribers at September 2015 (million)		
	US Millions of subscribers	**International Millions of subscribers**	**Total Millions of subscribers**
Netflix (app. US$10 per month)	42.0	27.0	69.0
Amazon Prime / Instant Video (US$99 membership per year)	45.0	10.0	55.0
HBO Television service/cable owned by Time Warner (US$15–20 per month)	36.0	78.0	114.0 (mainly cable subscribers)
HBO NOW (app. US$15 per month)	NA	NA	NA
Hulu Co-owned by Fox, Disney and Comcast (US$8 per month)	7.0	?	-
Google Play (US$ per movie – 2 day watch	?	?	?

Source: based on different public sources.

Source: epa european pressphoto agency b.v./Alamy Images.

Amazon

As the largest e-commerce company in the US, Amazon's entry into 'video on demand' is no surprise. The company rebranded its video services as Amazon Instant Video in 2011, and Amazon Prime members now have unlimited access to a large library of movies and TV shows. The price of a Prime membership is US$99 per year, which then also provides access to the following services:

- free two-day shipping
- free access to Prime Instant Video (access to 40,000 videos)
- prime Music Library (access to 1 million music tracks, compared to Spotify's 30 million)
- instant access to over 500,000 Kindle book titles to borrow for free.

Amazon's own research has shown that Prime members spend more than double, compared to what non-members spend on Amazon.

Amazon Prime had between 3 and 5 million subscribers around October 2011, but this had increased to around 45 million by September 2015 in the US alone. Amazon has expanded the Prime membership to other countries such as the UK, Spain, Japan, Italy, Germany, France, Austria and soon also India.

Amazon has aggressively added content to its service, so that in some countries for exmple Germany, they are actually market leader.

A Prime membership will not give the customer access to every streaming video on Amazon. The company offers only certain TV shows and movies for unlimited streaming. When it comes to brand-new movies and recently broadcast episodes of TV shows, for example, the customer will have to pay US$2–3 per episode/movie. Amazon marks its unlimited streaming shows and movies with a Prime graphic across the top of the box art; everything else is pay-as-you-go. In total,

the Prime service offers about 150,000 videos, of which about 40,000 are available for unlimited streaming with a Prime subscription (compared to Netflix's estimated 75,000).

Amazon Prime now hosts two (own) original series: *Alpha House* (starring John Goodman) and *Betas*, with more shows planned to debut in 2016.

Hulu

While Netflix initially began as a DVD rental service, Hulu's business model was established as a video streaming service founded by NBC Universal, Fox and ABC to satisfy consumer demand for web-based content. Hulu currently offers basic services free of charge or a premium service, Hulu Plus, for US$7.99 per month. Unlike Netflix, Hulu is structured to source revenue from monthly subscribers and on-screen advertisements. In an attempt to replicate the cable industry, Hulu distributes videos from major networks aside from NBC, ABC and Fox. Through its 200 content partners, it is reported that Hulu retains between 50 and 70 per cent of advertising revenue generated from its videos. With 7 million Hulu Plus subscribers and US$1 billion in revenue, Hulu's business model, in contrast to that of Netflix, supplements cable television rather than replaces it.

Amazon is both supplier and competitor for Netflix

Netflix relies upon Amazon Web Services (AWS) to operate certain aspects of their service and any disruption of or interference with use of the AWS operation would impact their operations and their business would be negatively impacted.

Figure 1 shows the supplier-competitor relationship.

Amazon Prime / Instant Video is Amazon's own solution targeted at end users. AWS provides a distributed computing infrastructure platform for Netflix's web platform. This is also commonly referred to as a cloud computing service. Netflix has architected their software and computer systems so as to utilize data processing, storage capabilities and other services

Source: Carlo Allegri/Reuters/Corbis.

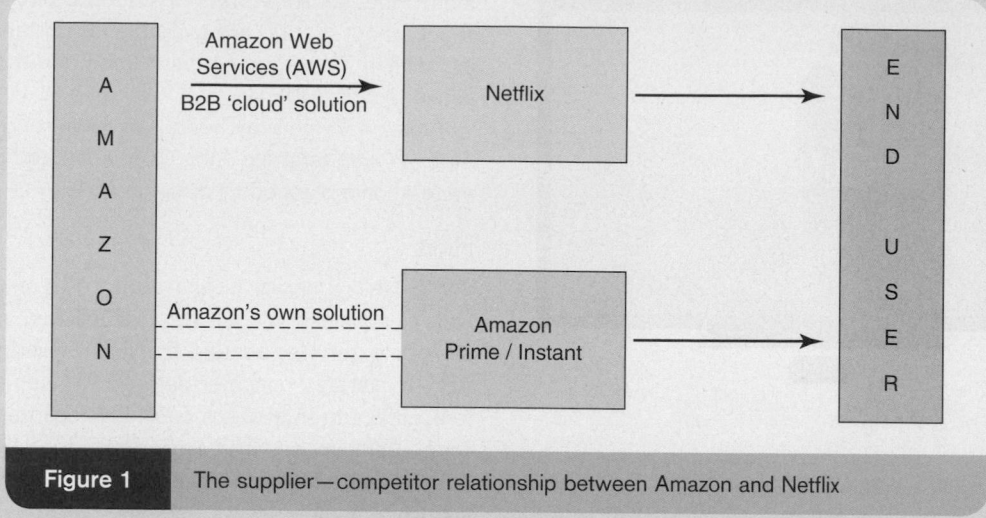

Figure 1 The supplier—competitor relationship between Amazon and Netflix

provided by AWS. Currently, Netflix run the vast majority of their computing on AWS. This, along with the fact that Netflix cannot easily switch their AWS operations to another cloud provider, makes Netflix dependent on Amazon as a supplier of cloud computing services. Consequently, any further Netflix international expansion would also benefit AWS, which now comprises more than 10 per cent of Amazon's total revenue, but much more if we measure the importance of AWS for Amazon's total profits. On the other hand, the retail side of Amazon (Amazon Prime – Instant Video) also competes with Netflix towards the end-customers.

QUESTIONS

You are hired by Reed Hastings (CEO of Netflix) as a specialist in International Marketing and given the following tasks to carry out.

1. Which of the following strategic options would you recommend Netflix for future implementation in order to increase revenues:

   (a) create more own original content, like *Wet Hot American Summer*;
   (b) increase the price of monthly subscription;
   (c) allow advertising to be integrated in the service?

2. Which countries (mentioned in Appendix 1) would you recommend as future Netflix markets? Please argue for your ranking 1, 2 and 3.

3. Does the supplier relationship to Amazon (through AWS) harm the international competitiveness of Netflix? If yes, how?

Source: based on www.netflix.com and other public sources.

APPENDIX 1	Ranking of country statistics regarding Netflix relevant data

Country	2014 Population (million)	2014 Persons using the internet during 2014 from any device (access % internet)	2014 CIA World FactBook Billion US$ – GDP total (PPP)	2014 GDP per capita (PPP) – US$	Netflix already there Y= Yes N = No
1. China	1,370	45%	17,630	12,869	N
2. India	1.271	20%	7,277	5,725	N
3. USA	321	86%	17,460	54,393	Y
4. Indonesia	255	15%	2,554	10,016	N
5. Brazil	204	54%	3,473	17,025	Y
6. Pakistan	190	15%	884	4,653	N
7. Nigeria	184	33%	1,058	5,750	N
8. Bangladesh	158	6%	536	3,392	N
9. Russia	146	59%	3,568	24,438	N
10. Japan	126	86%	4,807	38,151	Y
11. Mexico	121	38%	2,143	17,711	Y
12. Philippines	101	36%	695	6,881	N
13. Vietnam	92	40%	510	5,543	N
14. Ethiopia	90	2%	139	1,544	N
15. Egypt	89	44%	945	10,618	N
16. Germany	81	84%	3,621	44,704	Y
17. Iran	78	26%	1,284	16,462	N
18. Turkey	78	45%	1,512	19385	N
19. Congo	71	6%	56	789	N
20. France	66	83%	2,587	39,197	Y
21. Thailand	65	27%	990	15,231	N
22. United Kingdom	65	87%	2,435	37,462	Y
23. Italy	61	58%	2,066	33,869	N
24. South Africa	54	41%	683	12,648	N
25. South Korea	51	92%	1,786	35,020	N

Source: based on CIA World Factbook.

CASE STUDY III.3

Autoliv Airbags: transforming Autoliv into a global company

Chief executive officer of Autoliv Inc., Jan Carlson, is in the middle of a board of directors' meeting in Stockholm in December 2014, discussing how to further globalize Autoliv. He takes out a situation report for the business area of airbags. As there are a couple of new members on the board, Carlson takes the opportunity to give a broader introduction to the business area than he usually does. The following is his status report.

Situation report for the business area of airbags

Business concept

Autoliv Inc., which is a Fortune 500 company, is the world's largest automotive safety supplier with sales to all the leading car manufacturers in the world. Autoliv's shares are listed on the New York Stock Exchange and on the Stockholm Stock Exchange. The company develops, markets and manufactures airbags, seat belts, safety electronics, steering wheels, anti-whiplash systems, seat components and child seats. Autoliv has 80 subsidiaries (production plants) and joint ventures in 30 vehicle-producing countries, with around 34,000 employees. In addition, Autoliv has technical centres in nine countries with 20 crash test tracks – more than any other automotive safety supplier.

Autoliv aims to develop, manufacture and market systems and components worldwide for personal safety in automobiles. This includes the mitigation of injuries to autombile occupants and pedestrians and the avoidance of accidents. Autoliv wants to be the systems supplier and the development partner to car producers that satisfies all the needs in the area of personal safety. To fulfil its business concept, Autoliv has strong product lines:

- frontal and side-impact airbags (including all key components such as inflators with initiators, textile cushions, electronics with sensors and software, steel and plastic parts);
- seat belts (including all key components such as webbing, retractors and buckles);
- seat belt features (including pre-tensioners, load limiters, height adjusters and belt grabbers);
- seat subsystems (including anti-whiplash systems);

- steering wheels (including integrated driver airbags);
- roll-over protection (including sensors, pre-tensioners and airbag curtains).
- night-vision system with pedestrian detection and warning (this product was introduced in BMW cars in 2008).

Autoliv's short- and medium-range radar system provides all-weather object detection and tracking to improve safety and to provide assistance to the driver. The radar can be used for blind spot detection, lane change assist, adaptive cruise control, collision mitigation by braking and for back-up and park assist functions. The radar could also provide front and side pre-crash sensing that scans up to 30 metres around the vehicle to provide an advanced warning of an imminent collision. This additional time could be used to prime airbags and active seat belts. (An active seat belt has an electrically driven pre-tensioner that tightens the belt as a precaution in hazardous situations.) Autoliv already delivers active seat belts to four premium-brand vehicle models for three different customers.

In 2014, the penetration rate of frontal and side airbags in Europe was nearly 100 per cent. For curtain airbags in new cars, the penetration rate was 80 per cent in Europe, 60 per cent in North America, 45 per cent in Japan and 35 per cent in the rest of the world.

The following concentrates on the business area of airbags.

Production strategy

Autoliv has final assembly of restraint systems, located close to major customers' plants for just-in-time supply (see Figure 1). Most of the component production (textiles and stamped metal components, etc.) has been outsourced since 2009.

Since major automobile manufacturers are continually expanding production into more countries, it is also Autoliv's strategy to have manufacturing capacity where the major vehicle manufacturers have or are likely to set up production facilities. As a consequence, Autoliv has more plants for automotive safety products in more countries than any other supplier.

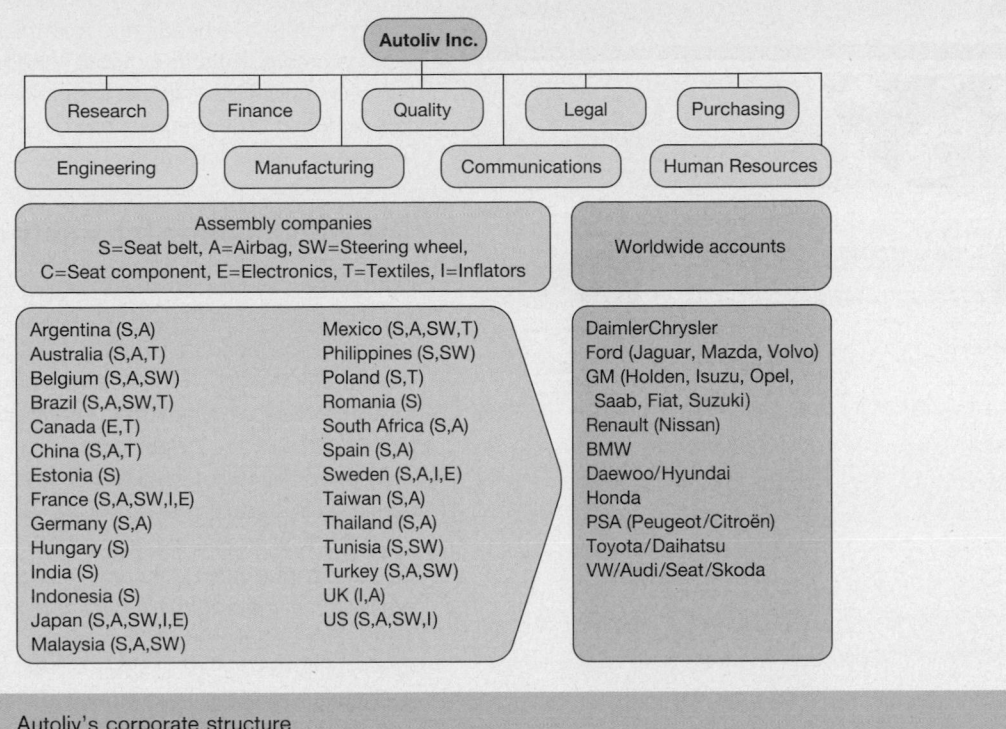

Autoliv Inc.

Research — Finance — Quality — Legal — Purchasing

Engineering — Manufacturing — Communications — Human Resources

Assembly companies
S=Seat belt, A=Airbag, SW=Steering wheel,
C=Seat component, E=Electronics, T=Textiles, I=Inflators

Worldwide accounts

Argentina (S,A)
Australia (S,A,T)
Belgium (S,A,SW)
Brazil (S,A,SW,T)
Canada (E,T)
China (S,A,T)
Estonia (S)
France (S,A,SW,I,E)
Germany (S,A)
Hungary (S)
India (S)
Indonesia (S)
Japan (S,A,SW,I,E)
Malaysia (S,A,SW)

Mexico (S,A,SW,T)
Philippines (S,SW)
Poland (S,T)
Romania (S)
South Africa (S,A)
Spain (S,A)
Sweden (S,A,I,E)
Taiwan (S,A)
Thailand (S,A)
Tunisia (S,SW)
Turkey (S,A,SW)
UK (I,A)
US (S,A,SW,I)

DaimlerChrysler
Ford (Jaguar, Mazda, Volvo)
GM (Holden, Isuzu, Opel,
   Saab, Fiat, Suzuki)
Renault (Nissan)
BMW
Daewoo/Hyundai
Honda
PSA (Peugeot/Citroën)
Toyota/Daihatsu
VW/Audi/Seat/Skoda

Figure 1   Autoliv's corporate structure

The product: the airbag

Even the best belt designs cannot prevent all head and chest injuries in serious head-on crashes. This is where airbags help, by creating an energy-absorbing cushion between an occupant's upper body and the steering wheel, instrument panel or windshield. Independent research has shown that driver deaths in head-on crashes are about 20 per cent lower in cars with frontal airbags than in similar cars with belts only. In all kinds of crashes, deaths are down by about 15 per cent over and above lives already being saved by belts.

Although airbags may seem complicated, they are in fact relatively simple. In moderate and severe head-on crashes, sensors signal inflators to fill the bags with harmless gas. The bags fill in a fraction of a second and begin deflating the instant they cushion people. Peak inflation occurs in less than one-twentieth of a second, faster than the blink of an eye. The speed and force of airbag inflation may occasionally cause injuries, mostly minor abrasions or bruises, but in the US some occupants have died from broken necks caused by airbags that inflated with great force. Those at the greatest risk of injury caused by an airbag are those who drive or ride unbelted, small children, short or obese adults, and certain disabled people.

Injury risk from the bag itself can be reduced by choosing a driving or passenger position that does not put your face or chest close to the steering wheel or instrument panel. The combination of seat belt and airbag provides maximum protection in all kinds of crash.

Together with Volvo, Autoliv has also developed the first side airbags to protect drivers and front-seat passengers in side-impact crashes. These bags are typically smaller than frontal airbags and they inflate more quickly. Volvo was the first manufacturer to offer side airbags in its 850 model in 1994. Volvo's bag is mounted on the outside of the driver and front-seat passenger's seat backs. Since 1996, side bags have been standard in all Volvo models.

The history of airbags goes back to the early 1950s. The product idea was patented in 1951 by Walter Linderer from Munich. It was in the US, however, that the concept came into existence, driven by the North Americans' reluctance to use seat belts and hindered by the car manufacturers, who initially ridiculed the idea. In 1981, only 2,636 airbag systems were produced.

However, in late 1989 automatic restraint systems became compulsory in all passenger cars in the US on the driver's side and, while this included automatically fastening seat belts, it seemed that the airbag had at last arrived. By 1992, 10 million airbag-equipped cars had been delivered to the US. In 1993 came the requirement that all new light vehicles of model year 1999 produced in the US had to be fitted with frontal airbags for the driver and the front-seat occupant. The

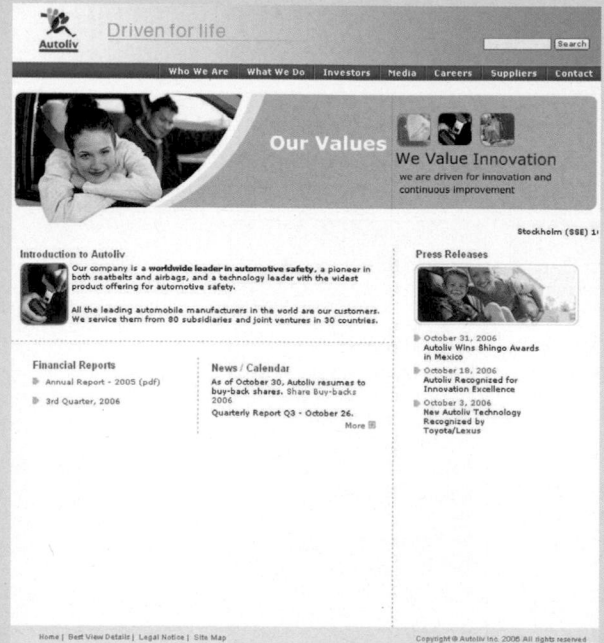

Source: www.autoliv.com.

next stage will be the compulsory fitting of airbags to both the driver and front passenger sides.

Autoliv introduced its first airbag system in 1990. It was designed to meet US requirements, where not all states have laws on wearing seat belts. The airbag therefore had to be relatively large. Autoliv has developed a special system (the Eurobag system) for markets where wearing a seat belt is compulsory. In this system, the airbags are of smaller volume (but they are still effective) and therefore the price can be kept at a lower level than some of the competitors. In the Eurobag system, the airbags are 30–45 litres on the driver's side and 60–100 litres on the passenger's side. Furthermore, the Eurobag system is lighter and less bulky.

An airbag system consists of an electronic control unit and an airbag module. The electronic control unit contains (among other things) a sensor, while the module essentially consists of a gas generator, a nylon bag and a cover for the steering wheel centre or the instrument panel, depending on where the airbag module is placed. Autoliv typically supplies entire systems adapted to individual car models.

Organization

In France, Germany, Spain, Sweden, the UK and the US, local management is regionally responsible for Autoliv's operations in countries around them. As a result, the main customers have the advantage of dealing with Autoliv both in their home market and when they have established or are going to establish production in other markets. Together with two regional

coordination offices, this organization contributes to low corporate overheads and short response times for the customers. (Autoliv's global headquarters in Stockholm has only 40 employees.) Autoliv's business directors and their organizations coordinate all activities with major customers on a global basis.

The world market for safety content

With its successful growth strategy, Autoliv has become the global leader in the US$21 billion automobile occupant restraint market (including airbags, seat belts and related electronics). Frontal and side airbags account for 55 per cent of that market, seat belts for 25 per cent and electronics for 20 per cent.

The world market for airbags was an area of spectacular growth during the 1990s.

In the US, frontal airbags – both on the driver and the passenger side – became compulsory under federal law in all new light vehicles sold after 1 September 1998. The US market for frontal airbags therefore fluctuates with the car production cycle, but sales of side airbags are now about to take off. Their penetration rate was less than 20 per cent among new US light vehicles in 2001. Both Ford and General Motors have announced aggressive plans for curtain side airbags such as Autoliv's Inflatable Curtain. In addition, new regulations in the US required vehicle manufacturers to phase in more valuable 'advanced airbags'.

In Europe, Autoliv estimates that, more or less, all new vehicles have dual airbags. Installations of side impact airbags began in 1994, but by 2001 two-thirds of all new vehicles in Europe had such systems for chest protection. In addition, 25 per cent had a separate side-impact airbag for head protection (such as the inflatable curtain). By 2014, the European penetration rate for both frontal and side airbags was nearly 100 per cent for new cars.

In Japan and China, where development started later than in Europe, penetration rates for frontal airbags are nearly as high as in Europe, while the penetration rate for side airbags is below the level in Europe.

In the rest of the world, penetration rates vary greatly from country to country, but the average is still less than 50 per cent for both driver and passenger airbags.

In Table 1 the total new car production (light vehicles) is split into the different regions, and the total safety value per vehicle is mentioned.

Although the safety content in mature markets is expected to increase, it is estimated that the global average safety content per vehicle will remain almost unchanged at approximately US$300 (see Table 1) during the next three-year period 2014–17, because of the downward price pressure in the industry. China, for

Table 1	The world market for passenger passenger car safety (airbags, seat belts and electronics) and Autoliv market share per major region (2014)			
	Production of passenger cars	Safety value per vehicle (US$ per vehicle)	Total market for passenger car safety (billion US$)	Autoliv market shares by region
Europe	19 million (27%)	380	7.2	43%
North America	11 million (16%)	430	4.7	39%
Japan	10 million (15%)	300	3.0	18%
Rest of the world	29 million (42%)	210	6.1	34%
Total	69 million (100%)	300	21.0	37%

Sources: Autoliv Financial Report 2004; Autoliv PowerPoint presentations.
Note: In 2014: Total light vehicle production = passenger car production + commercial car production = 69 million + 20 million = 89 million. In Table 1 only passenger cars are included. Autoliv also deliver car safety to commercial cars, but that is not included in Table 1

instance, introduced a crash-test rating programme in 2006, similar to the European programme and Brazil has plans to make frontal airbags mandatory. However, the safety market is only expected to grow by a small percentage in the next years due to the effect of an increasing number of low-end vehicles with low safety content, primarily for emerging markets in Eastern Europe and Asia. For instance, the safety content in India is, presently, less than one-fifth of the average safety value per vehicle in North America or western Europe.

In North America, Autoliv estimates that in 2014 it accounted for a little more than one-third of the airbag products market and the same for the seat belt market compared with just over 10 per cent in 1999. (Autoliv did not sell seat belts in the US until 1993.) Autoliv made its big entry into the North American market in 1996 when it acquired Morton Automotive Safety Products, which at that time was North America's largest airbag producer. The airbag business has given Autoliv an opportunity to expand its seat belt business as a result of complete systems sourcing. In 2000, Autoliv acquired the North American seat belt business of NSK. Autoliv's market share for seat belts also increased as a result of new contracts and the increasing number of new US vehicles with seat belt pre-tensioners.

In Europe, Autoliv estimates its market share to be about 43 per cent with a somewhat higher market share for seat belts than for airbags. In Japan, Autoliv has a strong position in the airbag inflator market, but its market share is still behind the European market share. Local assembly of airbag modules began in 1998. In 2000, Autoliv acquired the second largest Japanese steering wheel company, with a market share exceeding 20 per cent, and 40 per cent of NSK's Asian seat belt operations, with the option to acquire the remaining shares in two steps in 2002 and 2003. Including NSK's sales, Autoliv accounts for approximately a fifth of the Japanese seat belt market.

In other countries, such as Argentina, Australia, China, India, Malaysia, New Zealand, South Africa and Turkey, where Autoliv established production early, the company has achieved strong market positions in several places.

Competitors

In the late 1990s, the number of major suppliers of occupant restraint systems was reduced from nine to four. As a result of the consolidation among producers of light vehicles, the new entities that have been formed require suppliers to be cost-efficient and to have the capability to deliver the same products to all the companies' plants worldwide.

The four leading car occupant restraint suppliers now account for approximately 80 per cent of the world market as opposed to 50 per cent 10 years ago. During this period Autoliv has increased its share to slightly more than 35 per cent and has replaced TRW (a US publicly traded company) as the market leader. Another important car safety supplier is Takata (a privately owned Japanese company). Both TRW and Takata have about 25 per cent market share. Delphi (the world's largest automotive components supplier) and KSS (Key Safety Systems) have less than 5 per cent each.

In Japan, Korea and China, there are a number of local manufacturers that often have close ties with the domestic vehicle manufacturers in these countries. Toyota, for instance, has in-house suppliers for seat belts, airbags and steering wheels that receive the majority of the Toyota business in Japan for these products. Consequently, these safety product suppliers are often the toughest competitors in these markets.

Customers

Several of the world's largest car producers are among Autoliv's customers (see Table 2). Autoliv typically accounts for between 25 and 75 per cent of customers' purchases of seat belts and airbags and supplies all major car makers in the world and most car brands.

Table 2	Autoliv's customer mix, 2014	
Car manufacturer	Share of total global passenger car production (69 million vehicles) (%)	Share of Autoliv's total sales (%)
General Motors	11	13
Renault/Nissan	9	10
Ford	7	10
Daimler	2	7
Fiat/Chrysler	5	7
PSA (Citroën and Peugeot)	4	4
VW	12	8
Toyota	12	5
BMW	2	5
Hyundai/Kia	9	9
Honda	5	5
Others (primarily Chinese OEMS – Volvo also included here)	22	17
Total	100	100

Source: based an different public sources.

In the development of a new car model, a process that takes several years, Autoliv in many cases functions as a development partner for the car manufacturer. This typically means that Autoliv gives advice on new safety-enhancing products and assists in adaptation and conduct testing (including full-scale crash tests with the vehicle) of the safety systems.

In Table 2, the category 'Others' represents Autoliv's growing order intake from Chinese manufacturers like Chery, Great Wall and other local Chinese vehicle manufacturers, including Volvo, which is now Chinese owned. The same trend goes for other Asian OEMs.

The fact that premium vehicles are especially important for Autoliv is evidenced by e.g. BMW and Daimler.

No customer accounts for more than 13 per cent of Autoliv's sales (Table 2). Most of these car makers can be characterized as Autoliv's global accounts – see also Chapter 19. Traditional customers are also increasingly turning to global contracts rather than regional contracts as before. Consequently, Autoliv believes these trends in the vehicle industry tend to strengthen Autoliv's competitive position in the long term.

The contracts are generally divided among a car maker's different car models, with each contract usually running for the life of the car model, normally between 5 and 7 years. No contract accounts for more than 5 per cent of consolidated sales.

Table 3	Five years of economic development at Autoliv Inc.		
Key figures	2014	2013	2012
Sales (US$ million)	9,240	8,803	8,267
Pre-tax profit (US$ million)	723	761	705

Sources: based on www.autoliv.com; financial reports from 2012 to 2014.

Of the 2014 total sales in Table 3, Europe accounts for 33 per cent, Americas 33 per cent, Japan 8 per cent and the rest of the world 26 per cent. Now China alone accounts for 16 per cent of Autoliv's total sales.

The total number of employees (whole Autoliv Group, including subsidiaries) in December 2014 was about 50,800.

QUESTIONS

1. Describe Autoliv's role as a subsupplier for large car manufacturers in a market that is characterized by consolidation.

2. Which car manufacturer should Autoliv target to strengthen its global competitive position?

3. What strategic alternative does Autoliv have to strengthen its competitive position outside Europe?

CASE STUDY III.4
IMAX Corporation: globalization of the film business

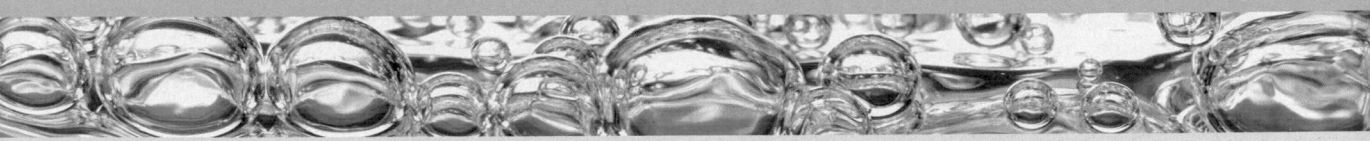

Back in 1997 the CEO of IMAX, Richard L. Gelfond, was sceptical about building a story with Hollywood movie stars into the big-screen format. At that time his answer to the criticism of IMAX® films' missing story was: 'It is too expensive and risky for us to put all our eggs in one basket and hire a major movie star.'

However, by 2003, new technological achievements had made it possible to show, for example, *Matrix Reloaded* on the giant-screen format. This did not just involve the projection of the standard theatrical print on to an IMAX screen – the film underwent the patented IMAX DMR® (digital remastering) process, which enhances the quality of the image and soundtrack to the huge 15/70 film format, the same thing that was done to *Apollo 13,* featuring Oscar-winning actor Tom Hanks.

So though IMAX have been through financial tough times the company now seems to be looking towards a brighter future.

IMAX Corporation

IMAX Corporation is involved in a wide variety of out-of-home entertainment business activities. It designs and manufactures projection and sound systems for giant-screen theatres based on a patented technology. IMAX Corporation is the world's largest producer and distributor of films for giant-screen cinemas.

IMAX Corporation, together with its wholly owned subsidiaries, is one of the world's leading entertainment technology companies whose principal activities are:

- the design, manufacture, marketing and leasing of proprietary projection and sound systems for IMAX theatres principally owned and operated by institutional and commercial customers in more than 50 countries (end of 2011);
- the development, production, digital remastering, post-production and distribution of certain films shown in the IMAX cinema network;
- the operation of certain IMAX cinemas located primarily in the US and Canada;

- the provision of other services to the IMAX cinema network, including designing and manufacturing IMAX camera equipment for rental to film-makers and providing ongoing maintenance services for the IMAX projection and sound systems.

While IMAX's roots are in the institutional market, it believes that the commercial market is potentially larger. To increase the demand for IMAX cinema systems, it is currently working to position the network as a new window for Hollywood event films. To this end, IMAX has both developed a technology that allows standard 35-mm movies to be converted to its format and is also working to build strong relationships with Hollywood studios and commercial exhibition companies.

IMAX theatre systems combine advanced, high-resolution projection systems, sound systems and screens as much as eight storeys high (approximately 80 feet) that extend to the edge of a viewer's peripheral vision to create the audiovisual experience. As a result, audiences feel as if they are a part of the on-screen action in a way that is more intense and exciting than in traditional cinemas. In addition, IMAX's 3D cinema systems combine the same projection and sound systems and up to eight-storey screens with 3D images that further increase the audience's feeling of immersion in the film. IMAX believes that its network of 3D cinemas is the largest out-of-home, 3D distribution network in the world.

History

The IMAX system has its roots in EXPO '67 in Montreal, Canada, where multi-screen films were the hit at the fair. A small group of Canadian film-makers/entrepreneurs (Graeme Ferguson, Roman Kroitor and Robert Kerr), who had made some of those popular films, decided to design a new system using a single powerful projector rather than the cumbersome multiple projectors used at that time. The result was the IMAX motion picture projection system, which would revolutionize giant-screen cinema. As the IMAX screen is about 10 times the size of a conventional movie screen, picture quality has to be very good. The camera required is also much bigger than a conventional movie camera, but for anyone with film experience it is not hard to learn to use it.

The much acclaimed *Fires of Kuwait* was nominated for an Oscar in the feature documentary category in 1993. Since the premiere in 1970 more than 700 million people have enjoyed The IMAX Experience®.

In 1977, IMAX was awarded the sole Oscar® for scientific and technical achievement by the Academy of Motion Picture Arts and Sciences. The award recognized IMAX's innovation in creating the world's best film capture and projection system as well as IMAX's acceptance as part of the entertainment mainstream.

IMAX Ridefilm: entry and departure

Historically, another part of the corporation was the IMAX® Simulation Ride System, which combined giant-screen technology with aspects of an amusement park ride.

One of Ridefilm Corporation's new state-of-the-art projects became a reality in 1993. *Back to the Future – The Ride,* directed by Douglas Trumbull, premiered in June at Universal Studios, Hollywood. This high-tech attraction was considered by entertainment industry experts to be the paradigm for the film experience of the future. The Ridefilm concept consisted of 18-person projection rooms in which the seats were equipped with seat belts and moved with the action on the screen. The film is projected on a 180-degree screen, with digital surround sound.

IMAX never succeeded in becoming profitable in the Ridefilm business. One reason for this might be that it never reached the critical mass of about 100 cinemas needed to support the three or four Ridefilms per year required for profitability. In the fiscal year 1999, IMAX was forced to write off Ridefilm's assets, resulting in a charge of US$13.6 million.

Development of IMAX's businesses and products

Generally speaking, IMAX does not own its cinemas, but leases its projection and sound systems and licenses the use of its trademarks. IMAX derives revenue principally from cinema system lease agreements, maintenance agreements, film production agreements and distribution of films.

In 2002, IMAX introduced a technology allowing the conversion of live-action 35-mm films to its 15/70-format at a modest incremental cost, while meeting IMAX's high standards of image and sound quality.

IMAX believes that this proprietary system, known as IMAX DMR (Digital Re-Mastering), has positioned IMAX cinemas as a new release window or distribution platform for Hollywood's biggest event films. As of 31 December 2005, IMAX, along with its studio partners, had released 11 IMAX DMR films. In 2005, IMAX released four films converted through the IMAX DMR process contemporaneously with the releases of the films to conventional 35 mm theatres, re-released one IMAX DMR film that had previously been released in 2004, and released one film made specifically for IMAX cinemas. In March 2003, IMAX introduced IMAX MPX, a new cinema projection system designed specifically for use by commercial multiplex operators. The IMAX MPX system, which is highly automated, was designed to reduce the capital and operating costs required to run an IMAX cinema while still offering consumers the image and sound quality of the trademarked 'The IMAX Experience'.

Cinema system leases

IMAX's system leases generally have 10–20 year initial terms and are typically renewable by the customer for one or more additional 10-year terms. As part of the lease agreement, IMAX advises the customer on design and custom assemblies and supervises the installation of the system; provides training in using the equipment to cinema personnel; and for a separate fee provides ongoing maintenance of the system. Prospective cinema owners are responsible for providing the location, the design and construction of the building, the installation of the system and any other necessary improvements. Under the terms of the typical lease agreement, the title to all cinema system equipment (including the projection screen, the projector and the sound system) remains IMAX's. IMAX has the right to remove the equipment for non-payment or other defaults by the customer. The contracts are generally not cancellable by the customer unless IMAX fails to perform its obligations. The contracts are generally denominated in US dollars, except in Canada and Japan, where contracts are generally denominated in Canadian dollars and Japanese yen, respectively.

The typical lease agreement provides for three major sources of revenue: initial rental fees; ongoing additional rental payments; and ongoing maintenance fees. Rental payments and maintenance fees are generally received over the life of the contract and are usually adjusted annually based on changes in the local consumer price index. The terms of each lease agreement vary according to the system technology provided and the geographic location of the customer.

IMAX films

IMAX produces films that are financed internally and through third parties. With respect to the latter, IMAX generally receives a film production fee in exchange for producing the films and is appointed the exclusive distributor of the film. When IMAX produces films, it typically hires production talent and specialists on a project-by-project basis, allowing IMAX to retain creative and quality control without the burden of significant ongoing overhead expenses. Typically the ownership rights to films produced for third parties are held by the film sponsors, the film investors and IMAX.

IMAX is a significant distributor of 15/70 format films, with distribution rights to more of these films than any competing distributor, and generally distributes films that it produces, and it has acquired distribution rights to films produced by independent producers. As a distributor, IMAX generally receives a percentage of box office receipts.

International marketing

IMAX markets its cinema systems through a direct sales force and marketing staff located in offices in Canada, the US, Europe, China and Japan. In addition, IMAX has agreements with consultants, business brokers and real estate professionals to find potential customers and cinema sites for IMAX on a commission basis.

IMAX has experienced an increase in the number of commercial cinema and international signings since 1995. The commercial cinema segment of IMAX's network is now its largest. As of 31 December 2014, 54 per cent of all theatres were outside North America. IMAX's institutional customers include science and natural history museums, zoos, aquaria and other educational and cultural centres. IMAX also leases its systems to theme parks, tourist destination sites, fairs and expositions. See Table 1 for an outline of IMAX's operations by area.

With regard to revenues, IMAX had a clearly negative financial development from 2006 to 2009. During that period, IMAX lost US$77.3 million. However, since 2009 IMAX has been in financially positive territory, mainly carried by the film *Avatar,* which had an enormously positive effect on the 2010 result.

Since then (up to 2015) IMAX has been in a state of positive and stable development (see Table 2b).

No one customer represents more than 5 per cent of IMAX's installed base of cinemas. IMAX has no dependence upon a single customer, or a few customers, the loss of any one or more of which would have a materially adverse effect on IMAX.

Table 1	IMAX breakdown of installations by geographic segment as at 31 December 2014 and 31 December 2010	
	2014 installed base	2010 installed base
Canada	46	26
US	385	291
Mexico	15	19
Europe	101	76
Asia (excluding China)	68	18
China	215	40
Rest of World	104	48
Total	**934**	**518**

Source: based on www.imax.com.

Table 2	IMAX revenues and net income (US$ million)		
	2014	2013	2012
Total revenues	290.5	287.9	282.8
Net income (million US$)	42.2	44.4	41.8

Source: based on www.imax.com.

As of 31 December 2014, IMAX had 600 employees, excluding hourly employees at company-owned and operated cinemas.

IMAX enters the Chinese market

The first IMAX projection system in a cinema in China was installed in December 2001, and there are currently 215 IMAX cinemas operating there (see Table 1). China is now IMAX's second-largest market (after the US) and the fastest-growing. In order to enable further growth in China, in 2011, IMAX formed IMAX China, a wholly owned subsidiary. Also in 2011, IMAX entered into key joint revenue sharing relationships in China, including a 75-cinema arrangement with Wanda Cinema Line, which is the Company's largest single international partnership to date, and reflects an even greater financial investment in China. As IMAX furthers its commitment to China, it is increasingly exposed to risks in that region. These risks include changes in laws and regulations and currency fluctuations. Some of these risks and uncertainties of doing business in China are solely within the control of the Chinese government, and Chinese law regulates both the scope of IMAX's investment in China and the business conducted by IMAX within China.

Competition in the industry

The out-of-home entertainment industry is very competitive, and IMAX faces a number of challenges. IMAX competes with other large-format film projection system manufacturers, as well as, indirectly, conventional motion picture exhibitors.

Most of the manufacturers of large-format film projection systems that IMAX competes with utilize smaller film formats, including eight-perforation film frame, 70-mm and 10-perforation film frame and 70-mm formats, which IMAX believes deliver an image that is inferior to The IMAX Experience. As already mentioned, the IMAX cinema network and the number of 15/70 format films to which IMAX has distribution rights are substantially larger than those of its competitors, and IMAX DMR films are available exclusively to the IMAX network. IMAX's customers generally consider a number of criteria when selecting a large-format theatre, including quality, reputation, brand name recognition, type of system, features, price and service. IMAX believes that its competitive strengths include the value of the IMAX brand name, the quality and historic uptime of IMAX cinema systems, the number and quality of 15/70 format films that it distributes, the quality of the sound system in the IMAX cinema, the potential availability of Hollywood event films to IMAX cinemas through IMAX DMR technology and the level of IMAX's service and maintenance efforts. Nearly all of the best-performing large-format cinemas in the world are IMAX cinemas.

In addition to existing competitors, IMAX may also face competition in the future from companies in the entertainment industry with new technologies and/or substantially greater capital resources. IMAX also faces in-home competition from a number of alternative motion picture distribution channels such as home video, pay-per-view, video-on-demand, DVD, internet and syndicated and broadcast television. IMAX further competes for the public's leisure time and disposable income with other forms of entertainment, including gaming, sporting events, concerts, live theatre, social media and restaurants.

Furthermore, the out-of-home entertainment industry in general is undergoing significant changes. Primarily due to technological developments and changing consumer tastes, numerous companies are developing, and are expected to continue to develop, new entertainment products for the out-of-home entertainment industry, which may compete directly with IMAX's products.

The motion picture exhibition industry is in the early stages of conversion from film-based to electronic-based media. IMAX is similarly in the early stages of

Audience watching a film in an IMAX cinema
Source: LOOK Die Bildagentur der Fotografen GmbH/Alamy Images.

developing a digital projection system that can be utilized in IMAX cinemas.

In recent years, a number of companies have introduced digital 3D projection technology. According to the National Association of Theater Owners, there are approximately 1,700 conventional-sized screens in US multiplexes equipped with digital 3D systems. However, IMAX believes that its IMAX brand name and its IMAX DMR technology, including its patented cinema geometry, differentiate it significantly from other 3D presentations. Until now the IMAX cinemas have outperformed the conventional cinemas on a per-screen revenue basis.

However, the competitive risks could include the need for IMAX to raise additional capital to finance remanufacturing of cinema systems and associated conversion costs, capital that may not be available to IMAX on attractive terms.

The commercial success of IMAX's products is ultimately dependent on consumer preferences. The out-of-home entertainment industry in general continues to go through significant changes, primarily due to technological developments and changing consumer tastes. Numerous companies are developing new entertainment products for the out-of-home entertainment industry and there are no guarantees that some of these new products will not be competitive with, superior to or more cost-effective than IMAX's products.

Latest film releases

At the end of September 2009, IMAX Corporation and Sony Pictures announced that the highly anticipated motion picture, Michael Jackson's *This is it,* would be released for a special run in selected digital IMAX cinemas worldwide during the film's limited two-week engagement in thousands of cinemas globally starting on 28 October 2009. *This is it* was to be digitally remastered by the use of IMAX DMR technology. When screened, the crystal-clear images coupled with IMAX's customized cinema geometry and powerful digital audio created a unique environment that made audiences feel as if they were in the film. Chronicling the months from March through to June 2009, the film was produced with the full support of the estate of Michael Jackson and drew from more than 100 hours of behind-the-scenes footage, featuring Jackson rehearsing a number of his songs for the show that never took place because of his death on 25 June 2009.

In March 2010, *Avatar: An IMAX 3D Experience* completed its initial run as the all-time highest grossing IMAX release; the worldwide IMAX box office total for the film climbed to more than US$220 million since the film's launch in December 2009. This success was the main reason for the fantastic financial result in 2010, which saw a net income of US$100.8 million.

In 2014, the biggest successes were with *Robocop* and *Captain America.*

In 2015, IMAX reported results with key franchise title including *Games of Thrones, Jurassic World, Mission Impossible 5, The Hunger Games* and not least *Star Wars,* which was released in December 2015 in a cooperation with Walt Disney Studios.

QUESTIONS

1. Discuss the statement back in 1997: 'It is too expensive and risky for us to put all our eggs in one basket and hire a major movie star.'

2. What were the main reasons for the failure of IMAX Ridefilm?

3. Can IMAX's core competences be transferred to the marketing of high-volume commercial products? Which types of product could these be?

4. What are the possibilities of growing the IMAX business with the new IMAX MPX system combined with their new IMAX DMR technology, which enables Hollywood studios to digitally remaster their films into IMAX's 15/70?

5. In 2011, a wholly owned subsidiary, IMAX China, was formed. What are the advantages and disadvantages for IMAX of this entry mode initiative?

Sources: based on IMAX press releases; www.imax.com; other publicly available information. IMAX®, IMAX DMR®, The IMAX Experience® and An IMAX 3D Experience® are registered trademarks of IMAX Corporation. OSCAR® is the registered trademark and service mark of the Academy of Motion Picture Arts and Sciences.

PART I
The decision whether to internationalize
Chs 1–4

PART II
Deciding which markets to enter
Chs 5–8

PART III
Market entry strategies
Chs 9–13

PART IV
Designing the global marketing programme
Chs 14–17

PART V
Implementing and coordinating the global marketing programme
Chs 18–19

Part IV Contents

14 Product decisions
15 Pricing decisions and the terms of doing business
16 Distribution decisions
17 Communication decisions (promotion strategies)

Part IV Case studies

IV.1 **Absolut Vodka:** defending and attacking for a better position in the global vodka market

IV.2 **Guinness:** how can the iconic Irish beer brand compensate for declining sales in the home market?

IV.3 **Dyson Vacuum Cleaner:** the iconic vacuum cleaner manufacturer launches the robotic version

IV.4 **Triumph Motorcycles Ltd:** rising from the ashes in the international motorcycle business

PART IV
Designing the global marketing programme

Introduction to Part IV

Once the firm has decided how it will enter the international market(s) (see Part III), the next issue is how to design the global marketing mix.

Part IV is based mainly on the traditional '4P' marketing mix:

- Chapter 14–15: Product and pricing decisions
- Chapter 16–17: Distribution and communication decisions

The original 4P marketing mix was primarily derived from research on manufacturing business to consumer (B2C) companies, where the essence of the marketing mix concept is the idea of a set of controllable variables or a 'toolkit' (the 4Ps) at the disposal of marketing management which can be used to influence customers. However, especially in business to business (B2B) marketing, the marketing mix is also influenced by the interaction process itself between buyer and seller, so that the influence process is negotiation and not persuasion as implied by the traditional 4P mix. Furthermore, there has been concern that the classic 4Ps do not incorporate the characteristics of services – namely inherent intangibility, perishability, heterogeneity (variability), inseparability and ownership.

The most influential of the alternative frameworks is, however, Booms and Bitner's (1981) *7Ps mix* where they suggest that the traditional 4Ps need to be extended to include an additional three Ps: *participants (people), physical evidence* and *process*. Their framework is discussed in the following.

Participants (people)

Any person coming into contact with customers can have an impact on overall satisfaction. This is especially true when the person is interacting with customers from different cultures (Czinkota and Samli, 2010). Participants are all human actors who play a part in service delivery, namely the firm's personnel and other customers. Because of the simultaneity of production and consumption, the firm's personnel occupy a key position in influencing customer perceptions of product quality. This is especially the case in 'high-contact' services, such as restaurants, airlines and professional consulting services. In fact, the firm's employees are part of the product and hence product quality is inseparable from the quality of the service provider. It is important, therefore, to pay particular attention to the quality of employees and to monitor their performance. This is especially important in services because employees tend to be variable in their performance, which can lead to variable quality.

The participants' concept also includes the customer who buys the service and other customers in the service environment. Marketing managers therefore need to manage not only the service provider–customer interface but also the actions of other customers. For example, the number, type and behaviour of people will partly determine the enjoyment of a meal at a restaurant.

Process

This is the process involved in providing a service to the customers. It is the procedures, mechanisms and flow of activities by which the service is acquired and delivered. The process of obtaining a meal at a self-service, fast-food outlet such as McDonald's is clearly different from that at a full-service restaurant. Furthermore, in a service situation customers are likely to have to queue before they can be served and the service delivery itself is likely to take a certain length of time. Marketers have to ensure that customers understand the process of acquiring a service and that the queuing and delivery times are acceptable to customers.

Physical evidence

Unlike a product, a service cannot be experienced before it is delivered, which makes it intangible. This means that potential customers perceive greater risk when deciding whether or not to use a service. To reduce the feeling of risk, thus improving success, it is often vital to offer customers some tangible clues to assess the quality of the service provided. This is done by providing physical evidence, such as case studies or testimonials. The physical environment itself (i.e. the buildings, furnishings, layout, etc.) is instrumental in customers' assessment of the quality and level of service they can expect, for example in restaurants, hotels, retailing and many other services. In fact, the physical environment is part of the product itself.

It can be argued that there is no need to amend or extend the 4Ps, as the extensions suggested by Booms and Bitner can be incorporated into the existing framework. The argument is that consumers experience a bundle of satisfactions and dissatisfactions that derive from all dimensions of the product whether tangible or intangible. The process can be incorporated in the distribution. Buttle (1989), for example, argues that the product and/or promotion elements may incorporate participants (in the Booms and Bitner framework) and that physical evidence and processes may be thought of as being part of the product. In fact, Booms and Bitner (1981) themselves argue that product decisions should involve the three extended elements in their proposed mix.

Therefore Part IV of this text still uses the structure of the 4Ps, but at the same time the three extended Ps will be incorporated in Chapters 14–17.

Globalization

Since the beginning of the 1980s the term 'globalization' has increasingly become a matter of debate. In his article 'The globalization of markets', Levitt (1983) provoked much controversy concerning the most appropriate way for companies to become international. Levitt's support of the globalization strategy received both support and criticism. Essentially the two sides of this debate represented local marketing versus global marketing and focused on the central question of whether a standardized, global marketing approach or a country-specific, differentiated marketing approach has the most merits. In Part IV we learn that there are different forces in the international environment that may favour either increasing globalization or increasing adaptation of a firm. The starting point is illustrated by the existing balance point on the scale illustrated in Figure IV.1. Which force will win depends not only on the environmental forces but also on the specific international marketing strategy that the firm might favour. Figure IV.2 shows the extremes of these two strategies.

Hence, a fundamental decision that managers have to make regarding their global marketing strategy is the degree to which they should standardize or adapt their global marketing mix. The following three factors provide vast opportunities for marketing standardization (Meffert and Bolz, 1993):

1. *Globalization of markets.* Customers are increasingly operating on a worldwide basis and are characterized by an intensively coordinated and centralized purchasing process. As a countermeasure, manufacturers establish a global key account management in order to avoid individual country subsidiaries being played off against each other in separate negotiations with, for example, global retailers.
2. *Globalization of industries.* Many firms can no longer depend on home markets for sufficient scale economies and experience curve effects. Many industries, such as computers, pharmaceuticals and automobiles, are characterized by high R&D costs that can be recouped only via worldwide, high-volume sales.

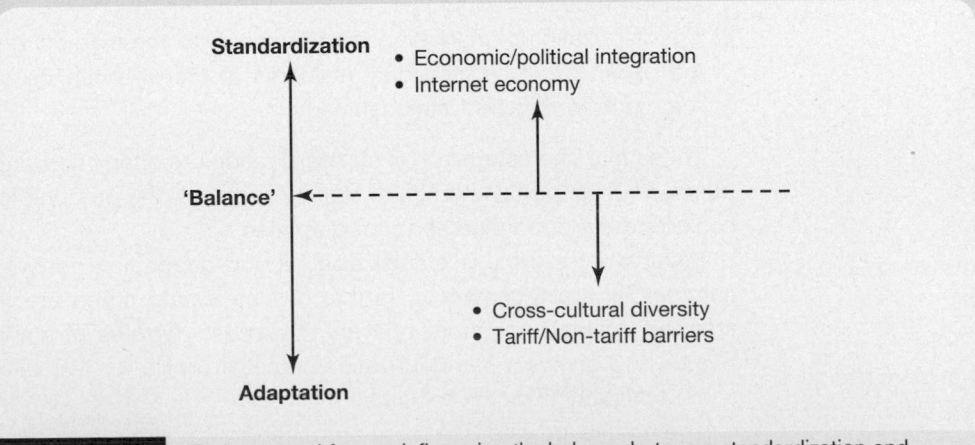

| Figure IV.1 | Environmental factors influencing the balance between standardization and adaptation |

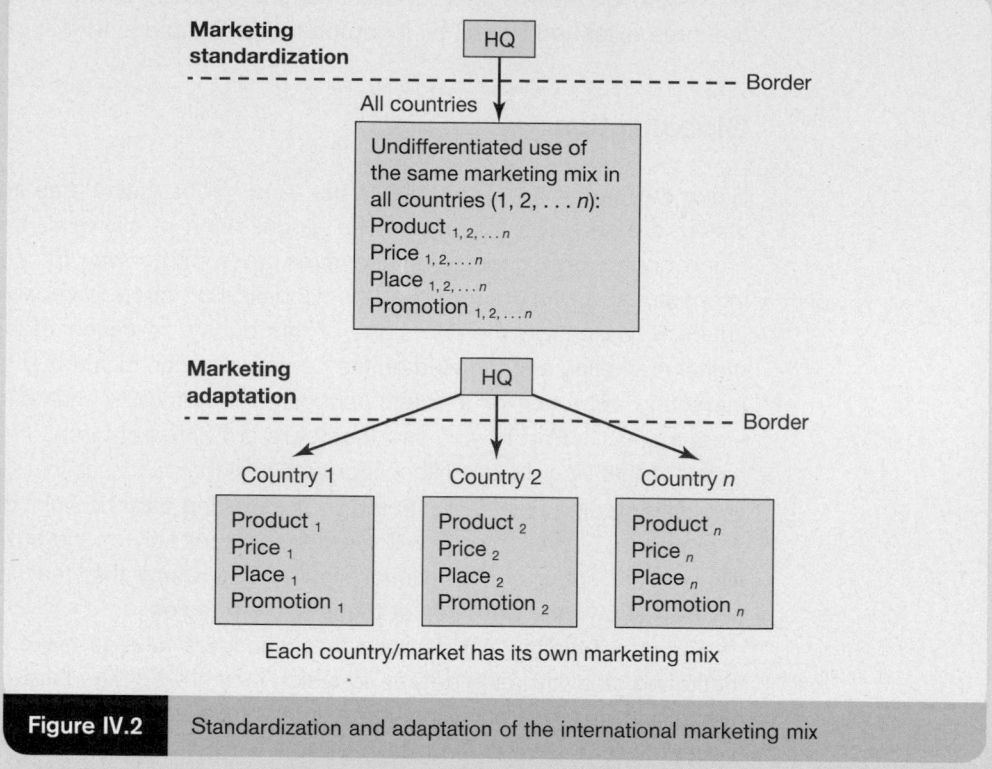

Figure IV.2 Standardization and adaptation of the international marketing mix

3. *Globalization of competition.* As a consequence of the worldwide homogenization of demand, the different markets are interrelated. Therefore firms can plan their activities on a worldwide scale and attempt to establish a superior profile vis-à-vis other global competitors. Hence, country subsidiaries no longer operate as profit centres, but are viewed as parts of a global portfolio.

The standardized marketing concept can be characterized by two features:

1. Standardization of marketing processes is mainly concerned with a standardized decision-making process for cross-country marketing planning. By standardizing the launch of new products, controlling activities, etc., rationalization of the general marketing process is sought.
2. Standardization of marketing programmes and the marketing mix is concerned with the extent to which individual elements of the 4Ps can be unified into a common approach for different national markets.

These two characteristics of standardization are often interrelated: for many strategic business units, process-oriented standardization is the precondition for the implementation of standardized marketing programmes.

Many writers discuss standardization and adaptation as two distinct options. The commercial reality, however, is that few marketing mixes are totally standardized or adapted. Instead it is more relevant to discuss *degrees* of standardization. Therefore Figure IV.3 shows a standardization-potential profile for two different products by the same company (Procter & Gamble).

The results indicate that there are different ways of realizing a standardized concept within the marketing mix. In the case of both products, it is possible to standardize the package at least on an average level. Difficulties arise as far as the price policy is concerned. Here it is possible to reach a standardized price positioning only for disposable nappies. So Procter & Gamble selects only those markets that possess the necessary purchasing power to pay a price within the target price range. In the case of alcoholic drinks, it is nearly impossible to gain a standardized price positioning due to legal constraints. In Denmark, for example, consumers have to pay twice as much for the same Johnnie Walker whisky as they do in Germany because of tax regulations. In many cases, it is possible to use one brand name on a worldwide basis. There are negative effects connected with particular names in only a few cases; you have to change brand names to avoid these unintentional images.

Table IV.1 lists the main factors favouring standardization versus adaptation of the global marketing programme.

Supporters of *standardization* view markets as increasingly homogeneous and global in scope and scale and believe that the key for survival and growth is the ability to standardize goods, services and processes. The overall conceptual argument is that the world is becoming increasingly similar in terms of environmental factors and customer requirements and that, irrespective of geographical locations, consumers have the same demands.

Supporters of *adaptation* indicate difficulties in using a standardized approach and therefore support adaptation to fit the unique dimensions of different international markets. Proponents of adaptation claim that there are substantial differences between countries and even between regions in the same country.

• Standardization profile of a special disposable nappy (e.g. Pampers)
■ Standardization profile of a special drink (e.g. Johnnie Walker)

| **Figure IV.3** | Analysis of a company's standardization potential |

Source: adapted from Kreutzer (1988). Reproduced with kind permission from Emerald Group Publishing Ltd; www.emeraldinsight.com.

Since competitive advantages play a critical role in the global marketing strategy, similarity in the nature of competitive advantages across international markets would favour the use of similar strategies across markets, facilitating a standardization of the strategy. Competitive advantages arise from core competences (see also Chapter 4), so firms possessing core competences would be in a better position to standardize their marketing strategies than firms that do not possess core competences (Viswanathan and Dickson, 2007).

Companies operating internationally should not make a one-time choice between the poles of absolute standardization or adaptation. Multinational companies operating in several countries using diverse entry modes must integrate different international marketing approaches. They should focus attention on aspects of the business (value chain activities) that require global standardization and aspects that demand local adaptation (Vrontis *et al.*, 2009).

Fuchs and Köstner (2015) analyse which factors are most important for choosing either standardization or adaptation (Figure IV.1). Their survey demonstrates that competitive pressure in an export market is positively related to promotion adaptation, price adaptation and distribution adaptation in European countries. Their findings also reveal that product adaptation will only be financially profitable for European small and medium-sized enterprises (SMEs) in familiar European countries. Outside Europe, it seems to be difficult for managers of SMEs to correctly interpret the reality in unfamiliar countries in order to successfully customize the product strategy regarding product design, brand name, variety of product lines and so on.

In these markets outside Europe, SMEs benefit from standardizing their marketing strategies, because an inappropriate adaptation in non-European markets with high psychic distance often results in poor performance (Fuchs and Köstner, 2015).

Table IV.1	Main factors favouring standardization versus adaptation
Factors favouring standardization	**Factors favouring adaptation**
• Economies of scale in R&D, production and marketing (experience curve effects)	• Local environment-induced adaption: sociocultural, economic and political differences (no experience curve effects)
• Global competition	• Local competition
• Convergence of tastes and consumer needs (consumer preferences are homogeneous)	• Variation in consumer needs (consumer needs are heterogeneous because of cultural differences)
• Centralized management of international operations (possible to transfer experience across borders)	• Fragmented and decentralized management with independent country subsidiaries
• A standardized concept is used by competitors	• An adapted concept is used by competitors
• High degree of transferability of competitive advantages from market to market	• *Low* degree of transferability by competitive advantages from market to market
Further issues:	*Further issues:*
• Easier communication, planning and control (through internet and mobile technology)	• Legal issues – differences in technical standards
• Stock cost reduction	

Source: Essentials of Global Marketing, FT/Prentice Hall (Hollensen, S. 2008) p. 299, Table 1, Copyright © Pearson Education Limited.

References

Booms, B.H. and Bitner, M.J. (1981) 'Marketing strategies and organization structures for service firms', in Donnelly, J.H. and George, W.R. (eds), *Marketing of Services*, American Marketing Association, Chicago, IL, pp. 47–51.

Buttle, F. (1989) 'Marketing services', in Jones, P. (ed.), *Management in Service Industries*, Pitman, London, pp. 235–259.

Czinkota, M. and Samli, A.C. (2010) 'The people dimension in modern international marketing: neglected but crucial', *Thunderbird International Business Review*, 52(5), pp. 391–401.

Kreutzer, R. (1988) 'Standardization: an integrated approach in global marketing', *European Journal of Marketing*, 22(10), pp. 19–30.

Levitt, T. (1983) 'The globalization of markets', *Harvard Business Review*, May–June, pp. 92–102.

Meffert, H. and Bolz, J. (1993) 'Standardization of marketing in Europe', in Halliburton, C. and Hünerberg, R. (eds), *European Marketing: Readings and cases*, Addison–Wesley, Wokingham, England, pp. 45–62.

Viswanathan, N.K. and Dickson, P.R. (2007) 'The fundamentals of standardizing global marketing strategy', *International Marketing Review*, 24(1), pp. 46–63.

Vrontis, D., Thrassou, A. and Lamprianou, I. (2009) 'International marketing adaptation versus standardization of multinational companies', *International Marketing Review*, 26(4/5), pp. 477–500.

Further reading

Berman, B. (2002) 'Should your firm adopt a mass customization strategy?', *Business Horizons*, July–August, pp. 51 60.

Biemans, W. (2001) 'Designing a dual marketing program', *European Management Journal*, 19(6), December, pp. 670–677.

Birnik, A. and Bowman, C. (2007) 'Marketing mix standardization in multinational corporations: A review of the evidence', *International Journal of Management Reviews*, 9(4), pp. 303–324.

Fuchs, M. and Köstner, M. (2015) 'Standardisation and adaptation of firms' export marketing strategies in familiar European and non-familiar non-European markets', *European Journal of International Management*, 9(3), pp. 306–325.

Solberg, C.A. (2000) 'Educator insights: standardization or adaptation of the international marketing mix: the role of the local subsidiary/representative', *Journal of International Marketing*, 8(1), pp. 78–98.

PART IV VIDEO CASE STUDY Tequila Avión

download from **www.pearsoned.co.uk/hollensen**

Tequila Avión is a company created in 2009 by Ken Austin and Kenny Dichter aiming at producing, promoting and distributing Avión, a premium tequila that is produced by fifth generation agave growers in Mexico. Avión's distinct flavours are achieved through a combination of slow-roasting at lower temperatures to protect the natural flavours of the agave and an ultra-slow filtration process that creates an unusually smooth taste profile. Tequila Avión defines their target customer group as females aged 25–34 and males aged 35–45.

The Tequila Avión brand became famous in the US market by a product placement in 2010. The spirit played a major role in the seventh (2010) season of the HBO series *Entourage,* which saw the character Turtle trying to convince his actor friend Vince to promote the brand. Since Tequila Avión was still so new in 2010, it was sold only in two states at the time, so most viewers assumed it was just an invention of the show's writers. The challenge for the management was to make it available in stores and bars — and fast in order to capitalize on its new-found fame.

In 2012, the company Tequila Avión announced the signing of a joint venture agreement with Pernod Ricard for the purpose of producing and promoting

Source: Brian Ach/Getty Images.

Source: Brian Ach/Getty Images.

tequila brand Avión. Pernod Ricard will hold a minority interest in this joint venture and will be the exclusive worldwide distributor of the brand.

Also in 2012 the first TV commercial was created for Tequila Avión.

Questions

1. Why is a product placement often more effective than a television commercial?

2. What is the target group and the main 'message' in the Tequila Avión commercial?

3. Why is it a good idea to hand over the worldwide distribution of Tequila Avión to Pernod Ricard?

Please look at the video clips at **www.pearsoned.co.uk/hollensen**

CHAPTER 14
Product decisions

Contents

Case studies

Learning objectives

After studying this chapter you should be able to:

- Discuss the influences that lead a firm to stand-ardize or adapt its products
- Explore how international service strategies are developed
- Distinguish between the product life cycle and the international product life cycle
- Discuss the challenge of developing new prod-ucts for foreign markets

- Explain and illustrate the alternatives in the product communication mix
- Define and explain the different branding alternatives
- Discuss brand piracy and the possible anti-counterfeiting strategies
- Discuss alternative environmental management strategies.

14.1 Introduction

The product decision is among the first decisions that a marketing manager makes in order to develop a global marketing mix. This chapter examines product-related issues and suggests conceptual approaches for handling them. Also discussed are international brand (labelling) strategies and service policies.

14.2 The dimensions of the international product offer

In creating an acceptable product offer for international markets, it is necessary first to examine what contributes to the 'total' product offer. Kotler (1997) suggests five levels of the product offer that should be considered by marketers in order to make the product attractive to international markets. In the product dimensions of Figure 14.1, we include not just the core physical properties, but also additional elements such as packaging, branding and after-sales service that make up the total package for the purchaser.

We can also see from Figure 14.1 that it is much easier to standardize the core product benefits (functional features, performance, etc.) than it is to standardize the support services, which often have to be tailored to the business culture and sometimes to individual customers.

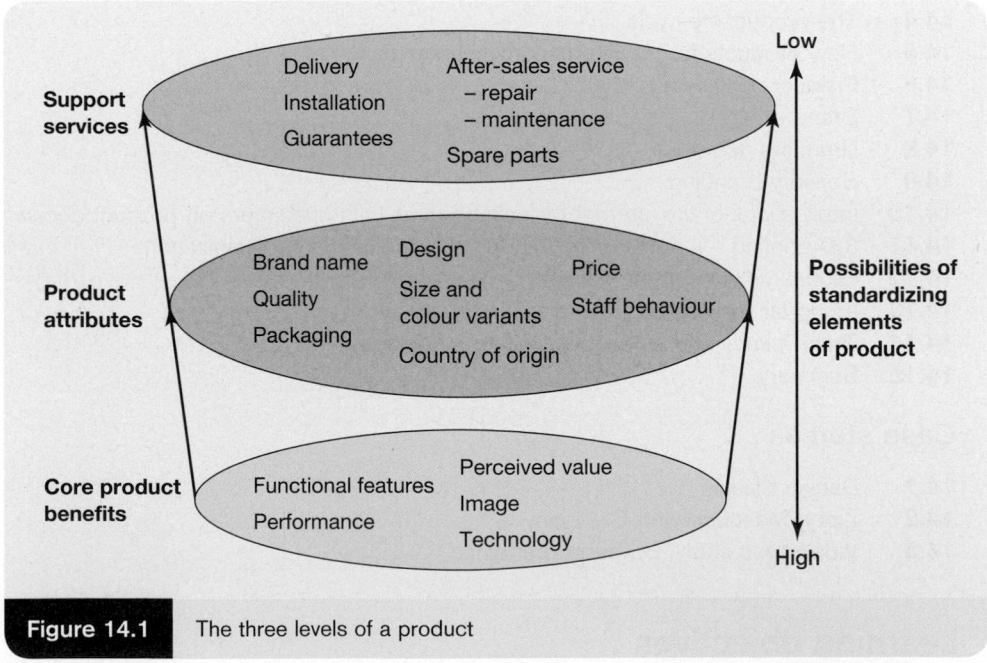

Figure 14.1   The three levels of a product

14.3 Developing international service strategies

We have seen from the definition of a product that services often accompany products, but products are also an increasingly important part of our international economy in their own right. As Figure 14.2 shows, the mix of product and service elements may vary substantially. The figure assumes that the customer is more or less passive in the buying and consuming process. That is, of course, not always realistic. More and more, offerings cannot be represented accurately by points on either end of a tangibility continuum. Rather, offerings are complex mixes of concrete objects, rendered services and customer participation. Customers do not seek products; they seek satisfaction. Products thus represent vehicles for service, because they enable customers to pursue their individualized satisfaction. For instance, when customers purchase new software for their computer, they may get a tangible product (CDs) to take home and install on their computer. However, what they are truly buying is the ability to perform a new task or an existing task in a new way. The installation CDs are filled up with knowledge, encrypted with the capabilities of various service providers, which then require that the customer demonstrate the competence and willingness to liberate this stored knowledge (Michel *et al.*, 2008).

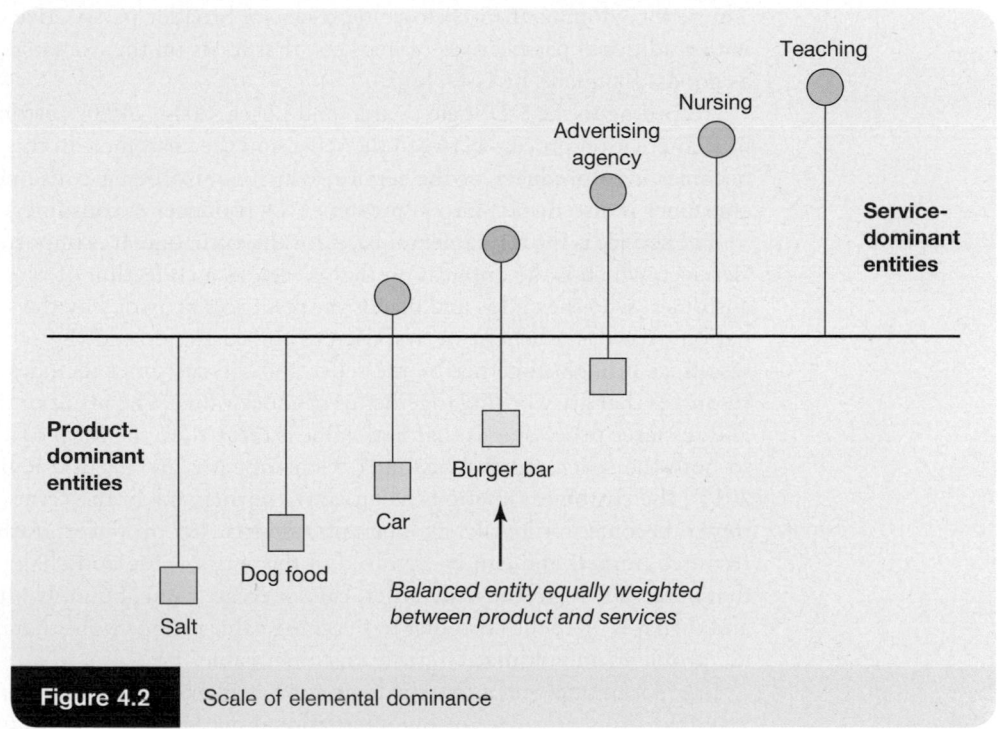

| **Figure 4.2** | Scale of elemental dominance |

Source: *International Marketing*, 4th ed. (Czinkota, M.R. and Ronkainen, I.A. 1995) p. 526, © 1995 South-Western, a part of Cengage Learning, Inc., reproduced by permission, www.cengage.com/permissions.

Characteristics of services

Before considering possible international service strategies, it is important to consider the special nature of global service marketing. Services are characterized by the following features:

- *Intangibility*. As services such as air transport or education cannot be touched or tested, the buyers of services cannot claim ownership of anything tangible in the traditional sense. Payment is for use or performance. Tangible elements of the service, such as food or drink on airlines, are used as part of the service in order to confirm the benefit provided and to enhance its perceived value.
- *Perishability*. Services cannot be stored for future use – for example, unfilled airline seats are lost once the aircraft takes off. This characteristic causes considerable problems in planning and promotion in order to match supply and demand. To maintain service capacity constantly at levels necessary to satisfy peak demand is very expensive.

The marketer must therefore attempt to estimate demand levels in order to optimize the use of capacity.

- *Heterogeneity*. Services are rarely the same because they involve interactions between people. Furthermore, there is high customer involvement in the production of services. This can cause problems of maintaining quality, particularly in international markets where there are quite different attitudes towards customer service.
- *Inseparability*. The time of production is very close to or even simultaneous with the time of consumption. The service is provided at the point of sale. This means that economies of scale and experience curve benefits are difficult to achieve, and supplying the service to scattered markets can be expensive, particularly in the initial setting-up phase.

The service-dominant logic (S-D logic)

The service-dominant (S-D) logic represents a broader perspective of markets compared with traditional perspectives of markets, that focus on the exchange of goods (referred to as goods-dominant, or G-D, logic).

According to the S-D logic (Vargo and Lusch, 2004, 2008), customer value is produced in a co-creation process between the seller and the customer. In this process the customer becomes a co-producer of the service, which is also being consumed. Consequently the consumer is also turned into a 'prosumer' (= producer + consumer).

The service is the fundamental basis for the exchange. It is important to clarify the term 'service', which is the application that is seen as a collection of resources available to the customer, who then adds and blends the resources provided by the seller, which in combination provides a benefit or a service to the customer and the seller. This collection of resources brought together by the seller and the customer includes an entire network of resources that are working together to produce value. The result of this resource 'meeting' and resource processing is that new value is created, in the form of a service (value added) to both the seller and the customer. Consequently, in this S-D logic view (Vargo, 2009, 2011), the customer functions as an active participant in the creation of value. The customer becomes primarily an operant resource (co-producer) rather than an operand resource (target) and can be involved in the entire value and chain. Vargo (2009) argues that in the S-D logic, the firm (seller) cannot create value, but only offer value propositions and then it is up to the customer to select the value propositions that are necessary to 'solve the problem' and ultimately create customer value.

In order to implement the S-D logic approach where the customer is a co-producer, the way that firms organize for the international marketing activities must also support this approach. For example, in global supplier–manufacturer collaboration in product development, the supplier sets up global account management (GAM) teams that are organized around a 'global' customer to work with the customer to produce joint solutions to problems and joint value for both organizations (see also Section 19.3). Some of these teams are even located near the customer's worldwide premises. These can include members from manufacturing, sales, logistics, finance, accounting and human resources. Suppliers need to match their sales reps with buyers, their finance and accounting with the customer's accountants and payers, and their customer service with the customer's users. The supplier's GAM teams interface with multiple and cross-border entities of the customer's global organization (Gruen and Hofstetter, 2010). This is also the principle behind the transition from the so-called 'bow-tie' organization to the 'diamond' type of organization (see also Figure 19.8).

Global marketing of services

There are some specific problems in marketing services internationally. There are particular difficulties in achieving uniformity of the different marketing parameters in remote locations where exerting control can be especially problematic. Pricing, too, can be extremely difficult, because fixed costs can be a very significant part of the total service costs. Consumers' ability to buy and their perceptions of the service they receive may vary considerably between markets, resulting in significantly different prices being set and profits generated. Moreover, preserving customer loyalty in order to obtain repeat business may prove difficult because of the need to provide personalized services.

Categories of service

All products, both goods and services, consist of a core element that is surrounded by a variety of optional supplementary elements. If we look first at the core service products, we can assign them to one of three broad categories depending on their tangibility and the extent to which customers need to be physically present during service production. These categories are presented in Table 14.1.

In summary, the information-based services offer the best opportunities of global standardization. The two other types of service (people-processing and possession-processing) both suffer from their inability to transfer competitive advantages across borders. For example, when Euro Disneyland in Paris opened, Disney suffered from not being able to transfer the highly motivated staff of its US parks to Europe.

The accelerating development within information technology (the internet) has resulted in the appearance of new types of information service (e.g. information on international flight schedules), which offer great opportunities for standardization.

Table 14.1	Three categories of service		
Categories of service	Characteristics	Examples (service provider)	Possibilities of worldwide standardization (hence utilizing economies of scale, experience effects, lower costs)
People processing	Customers become part of the production process. The service firm needs to maintain local geographic presence	Education (schools, universities) Passenger transport (airlines, car rental) Health care (hospitals) Food service (fast-food, restaurants) Lodging service (hotel)	No good possibilities: because of 'customer involvement in production' many local sites will be needed, making this type of service very difficult to operate globally
Possession processing	Involves tangible actions to physical objects to improve their value to customers. The object needs to be involved in the production process, but the owner of the object (the customer) does not. A local geographic presence is required	Car repair (garages) Freight transport (forwarding agent) Equipment installation (e.g. electrician) Laundry service (launderette)	Better possibilities: compared with people-processing services, this involves a lower degree of contact between the customer and the service personnel. This type of service is not so culture-sensitive
Information-based services	Collecting, manipulating, interpreting and transmitting data to create value. Minimal tangibility. Minimal customer involvement in the production process	Telecommunication services (telephone companies) Banking News Market analysis Internet services (producers of homepages on the web, database providers)	Very good possibilities: of worldwide standardization from one central location (single sourcing) because of the 'virtual' nature of these services

Service in the business-to-business (B2B) market

Business-to-business markets differ from customer markets in many ways:

- fewer and larger buyers, often geographically concentrated
- a derived, fluctuating and relatively inelastic demand
- many participants in the buying process
- professional buyers
- a closer relationship
- absence of intermediaries
- technological links.

For services in consumer markets, an alternative for dissatisfied consumers is always to exit from the supplier–consumer relationship, as the number of firms offering the same kind of products is usually high, making it easy to switch between products and firms.

In the B2B market, however, bonds between the buyer and seller make the firms more unwilling to break the relationship. Of course, the exit opportunity also exists to some extent in the B2B market, but the loss of investment in bonds and commitment tends to create exit barriers, because the costs of changing supplier are high. Furthermore, it can be difficult to find a new supplier.

Professional service firms, such as consulting engineering firms, have similarities with typical B2B service firms, but they involve a high degree of customization and have a strong component of face-to-face interaction. The service frequently takes the form of a hundred-million-dollar project and is characterized by the development of long-term relationships between firms, but also the management of day-to-day relationships during the project. When a professional service firm (whether it be an accountant, architect, engineer or management consultant) sells to its clients, it is less the services of the firm than the services of specific individuals that it is selling. As a consequence, professional service firms require highly skilled individuals.

The inherent characteristics of services imply that local presence and customer–supplier interactions become much more vital than is the case for traditional product offerings (Kowalkowski *et al.*, 2011).

Filiatrault and Lapierre (1997) made a study of the cultural differences in consulting engineering projects between Europe (France) and North America (Canada). In North America the consulting engineering firms are generally smaller and they work in an economic environment closer (than in Europe) to pure competition. The contracts in Europe are very large and often awarded by governments. The French consultants recognized that there is more flexibility in managing in North America than in Europe. Subcontracting also appears to be more popular in North America.

e-Services

Due to the continuing expansion of the internet, consumer behaviour has changed and new needs have emerged. As an interactive medium, the internet combines the best of mass production (based on the manufacture of products) and customization (typically found in services). The ultimate tool for mass customizing can treat each customer as being unique.

Enterprises devoted to combining new technologies with traditional service concepts have created a new type of services called **e-services**. E-services deliver particular intangible information-based products and services through interaction with online users. Basically an e-service can be defined as a business activity of value exchange that is accessible through electronic networks, which include the internet and mobile networks. It involves distributing and personalizing resources in realtime over the internet.

e-services
A business activity of value exchanges that is accessible through electronic networks, which include the internet and mobile networks. It involves distributing and personalizing resources in real-time over the internet.

The e-services include services that use only the internet as the user interface and also situations where the actual service fulfillment might include non-electronic channels (e.g. shopping), as well as services that are entirely delivered electronically (e.g. music streaming and download).

Currently, services delivered over the internet offer entirely new opportunities in the era of the digital economy. E-service has become increasingly significant, not only for determining the success or failure of e-commerce ventures but by delivering a superior overall experience for customers. The emergence of the internet regarding services has enhanced cost benefits for enterprises, as well as the speed, efficiency and flexibility of online transactions. Furthermore, this unique approach to delivering services provides a novel experience and alters customer expectations.

Development of new e-service offerings takes place in many industries, such as financial services, health care, telecommunications services, leisure and hospitality services, information services, legal and educational services, and many more. Development of new e-services stresses core differences between products and services: intangibility, heterogeneity and simultaneity.

e-Services through 'cloud computing'

Cloud computing
Cloud computing is a general term for anything that involves delivering hosted services over the internet. In cloud computing, the word cloud is used as a metaphor for 'the internet'.

In the simplest terms, **cloud computing** means storing and accessing data and programs over the internet instead of your computer's hard drive. The cloud is just a metaphor for the internet.

The innovations in cloud computing result from its ability to share information resources in a self-service fashion with little interaction from the internet service provider. Information can be accessed from any location or device, which provides better utilization of a consumer's digital information. For consumers, the ability to access information at any time or geographic location has resulted in better access to marketing information that was previously expensive and difficult to obtain (Ratten, 2015). This aspect of 'cloud computing' is of course important from a global marketing perspective.

For international marketers, cloud computing provides global access to computing resources that can be reconfigured based on international location. As more companies and consumers are working in the international business world, cloud computing provides a cheaper and better alternative to traditional information technology data storage and access services.

Cloud computing has changed the way business apps are developed and deployed. Companies no longer need to buy and maintain their own infrastructure of servers, storage and development tools in order to create and run business apps. Instead, companies can gain access to a variety of business apps via an internet browser or mobile device on an as-needed basis, without the cost and complexity of managing the hardware or software in-house.

The broad shift to social networking has transformed the way people collaborate and is accelerating the adoption of technologies that connect people and products through 'feeds' and status updates. There is a significant transition underway from desktops to smartphones and tablets, making it possible for people to get business done right from their mobile devices. And increasingly, customers want to be connected to the products they use.

The worldwide demand for cloud computing services is expected to record strong growth in coming years. Cloud computing is a computing infrastructure model, which enables delivery of software-as-a-service (SaaS). Appeal to cloud computing has been increasing as it enables companies to reduce expenses like upfront royalty or licensing payments, investment in hardware infrastructure and other operating expenses.

One company that is in the forefront on 'cloud' customer relations management (CRM) solutions is Salesforce.com – see Exhibit 14.1.

EXHIBIT 14.1 Salesforce.com as provider of CRM 'cloud' services

Salesforce.com was founded on the concept of delivering CRM applications via the internet, or 'cloud'. They introduced their first CRM solution in February 2000 and they have expanded their offerings with new editions, solutions and enhanced features, through internal development and acquisitions.

Their mission is to help customers transform themselves into 'customer companies' by empowering them to connect with their customers in entirely new ways.

Salesforce.com derive their revenues primarily from subscription fees (one year at a time) for their services. In the financial year 2015, Salesforce.com achieved US$5.4 in revenue, with US$263 in net loss. Approximately 30 per cent of their revenue comes from customers outside of the Americas (North and South America). On the 1st February 2015, Salesforce.com had 13,000 employees.

Growing demand for cloud CRM software services will facilitate the company's revenue and market share growth in coming years. However, Salesforce.com operates in the CRM solutions market, which is highly competitive, rapidly evolving and fragmented. The company primarily competes with vendors of packaged business software and companies offering CRM apps. Salesforce.com also faces competition from internally developed applications. The major direct competitors of the company include Microsoft, NetSuite, Oracle and SAP.

Source: based on Salesforce.com and other public sources.

14.4 The product life cycle

PLC
Product life cycle concerns the life of a product in the market with respect to business/ commercial costs and sales measures. Simply explained, it is a theory in which products or brands follow a sequence of stages, including introduction, growth, maturity and sales decline.

Time to market
The time it takes from the conception of an idea until it is available for sale. TTM is important in those industries where products become quickly outmoded:

The concept of the product life cycle (**PLC**) provides useful inputs into making product decisions and formulating product strategies.

Products, like individuals, pass through a series of stages. Each stage is identified by its sales performance and characterized by different levels of profitability, various degrees of competition and distinctive marketing programmes. The four stages of the PLC are introduction, growth, maturity and decline. The basic model of the PLC is shown in Figure 14.3, where also the stages prior to the actual sales are included. In total these stages represent the so-called time to market (TTM).

Time to market is the length of time it takes from a product being conceived until it becomes available for sale. TTM is important in industries where products become outdated quickly, for example in the IT industry.

Rapid TTM is important for the competitive success of many companies for the following reasons:

- competitive advantage of getting to market sooner;
- premium prices early in life cycle;
- faster break-even on development investment and lower financial risk;
- greater overall profits and higher return on investment.

The key process requirements for rapid TTM are:

- clear understanding of customer needs at the start of the project and stability in product requirements or specifications;
- a characterized, optimized product development process;
- a realistic project plan based on this process;

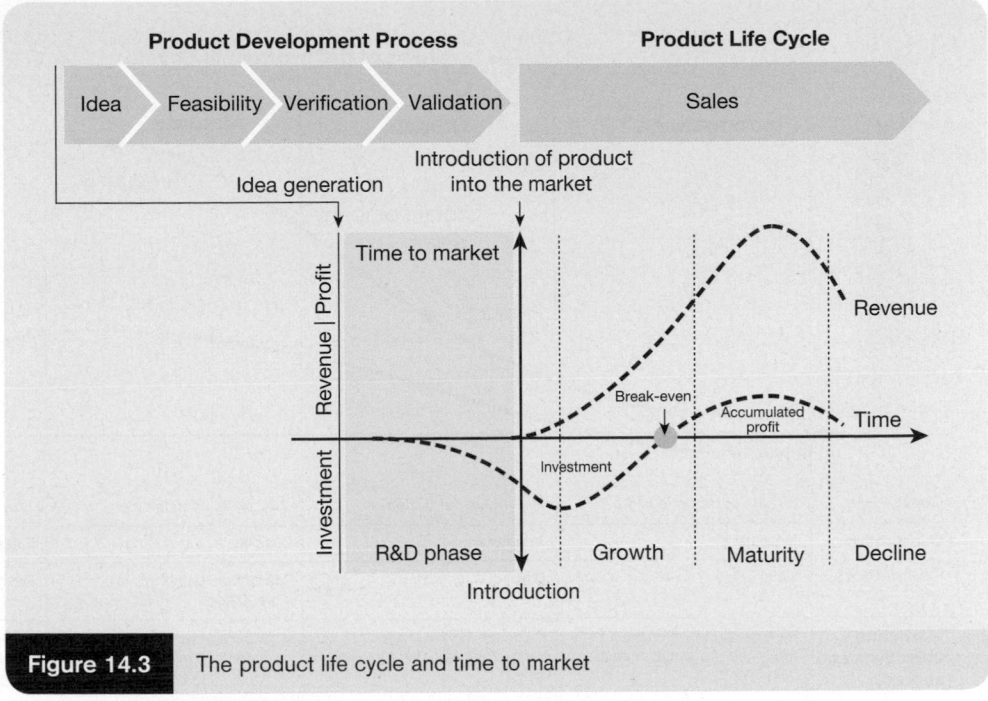

Figure 14.3   The product life cycle and time to market

Source: Marketing Management: A relationship approach, 2nd ed., Financial Times/Prentice Hall (Hollensen, S. 2010) Figure 11.7, Copyright © Pearson Education Limited.

- availability of needed resources to support the project and use of full-time, dedicated personnel;
- early involvement and rapid staffing build-up to support the parallel design of product and process;
- virtual product development including digital assembly modelling and early analysis and simulation to minimize time-consuming physical mock-ups and testing;
- design re-use and standardization to minimize the design content of a project.

Pure speed, i.e. bringing the product to market as quickly as possible, is valuable in fast-moving industries but is not always the best objective. Many managers calculate that the shorter the product development project, the less it will cost, so they attempt to use TTM as a means of cutting expenses. Unfortunately, a primary means of reducing TTM is to staff the project more heavily, so a faster project may actually be more expensive.

The PLC emphasizes the need to review marketing objectives and strategies as products pass through various stages. It is helpful to think of marketing decisions during the lifetime of a product. However, sometimes it is hard to know when a product is leaving one stage and entering the next. The life cycle concept helps managers to think about their product line as a portfolio of investments.

Most organizations offer more than one product or service, and many operate in several markets. The advantage here is that the various products – the product portfolio – can be managed so that they are not all in the same phase in their life cycles. Having products evenly spread out across life cycles allows for the most efficient use of both cash and human resources. Figure 14.4 shows an example of such life cycle management and some of the corresponding strategies that follow the different stages of the product life cycle.

The current investment in C, which is in the growth phase, is covered by the profits being generated by the earlier product B, which is at maturity. This product had earlier been funded by A, the decline of which is now being balanced by the newer products. An organization looking for growth can introduce new goods or services that it hopes will be

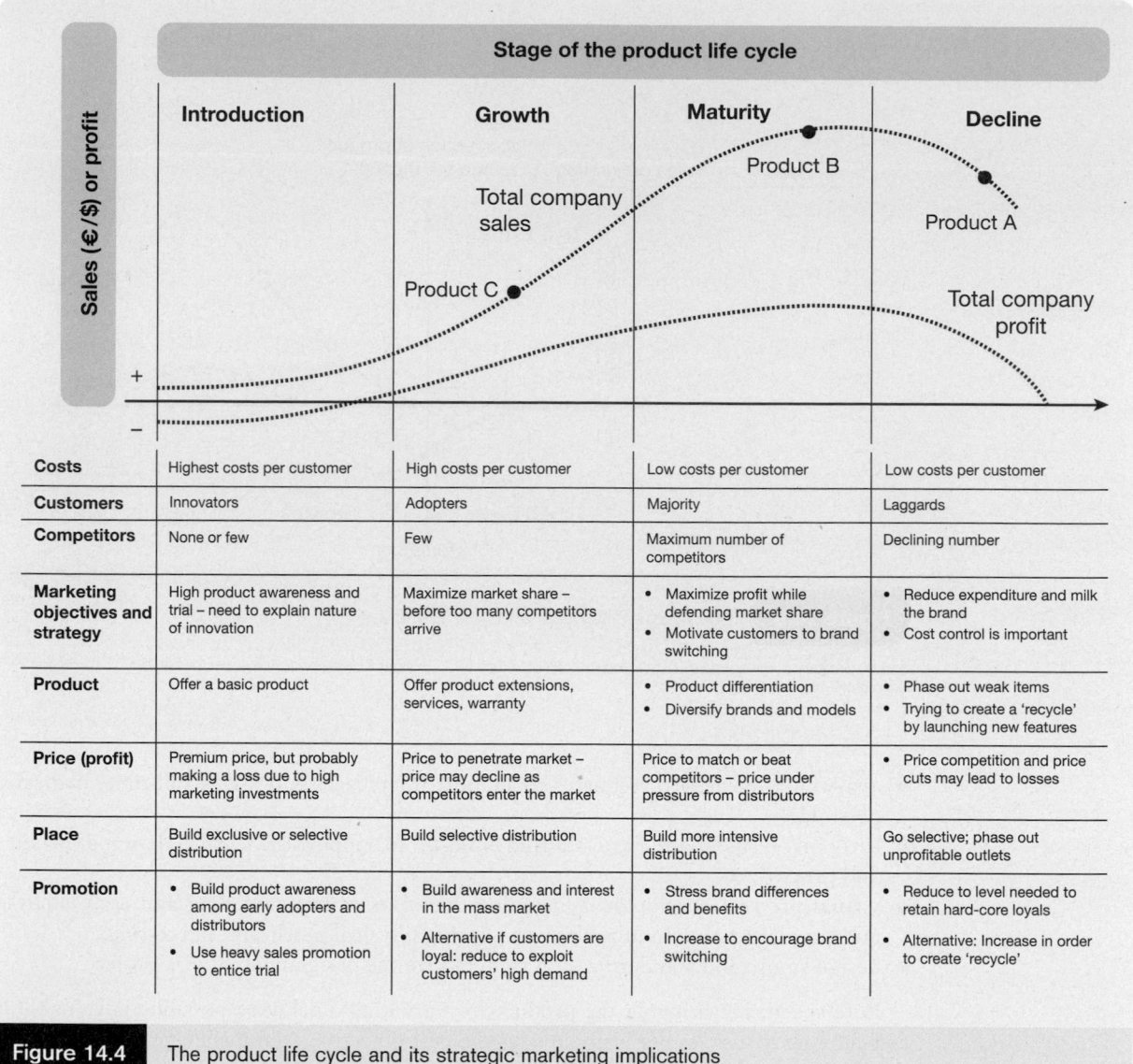

Stage of the product life cycle			
Introduction	**Growth**	**Maturity**	**Decline**

	Introduction	**Growth**	**Maturity**	**Decline**
Costs	Highest costs per customer	High costs per customer	Low costs per customer	Low costs per customer
Customers	Innovators	Adopters	Majority	Laggards
Competitors	None or few	Few	Maximum number of competitors	Declining number
Marketing objectives and strategy	High product awareness and trial – need to explain nature of innovation	Maximize market share – before too many competitors arrive	• Maximize profit while defending market share • Motivate customers to brand switching	• Reduce expenditure and milk the brand • Cost control is important
Product	Offer a basic product	Offer product extensions, services, warranty	• Product differentiation • Diversify brands and models	• Phase out weak items • Trying to create a 'recycle' by launching new features
Price (profit)	Premium price, but probably making a loss due to high marketing investments	Price to penetrate market – price may decline as competitors enter the market	Price to match or beat competitors – price under pressure from distributors	• Price competition and price cuts may lead to losses
Place	Build exclusive or selective distribution	Build selective distribution	Build more intensive distribution	Go selective; phase out unprofitable outlets
Promotion	• Build product awareness among early adopters and distributors • Use heavy sales promotion to entice trial	• Build awareness and interest in the mass market • Alternative if customers are loyal: reduce to exploit customers' high demand	• Stress brand differences and benefits • Increase to encourage brand switching	• Reduce to level needed to retain hard-core loyals • Alternative: Increase in order to create 'recycle'

Figure 14.4 The product life cycle and its strategic marketing implications

Source: Marketing Management: A relationship approach, 2nd ed., Financial Times/Prentice Hall (Hollensen, S. 2010) Figure 11.7, Copyright © Pearson Education Limited.

bigger sellers than those they succeed. However, if this expansion is undertaken too rapidly, many of these brands will demand investment at the beginning of their life cycles, and even the earliest of them will be unlikely to generate profits fast enough to support the numbers of later launches. Therefore, the producer will have to find another source of funds until the investments payoff.

However, managers also need to be aware of the limitations of the PLC so they are not misled by its prescriptions.

Limitations of the product life cycle

Misleading strategy prescriptions

The PLC is a dependent variable that is determined by the marketing mix; it is not an independent variable to which firms should adapt their marketing programmes (Dhalla and Yuspeh, 1976). If a product's sale is declining, management should not conclude that

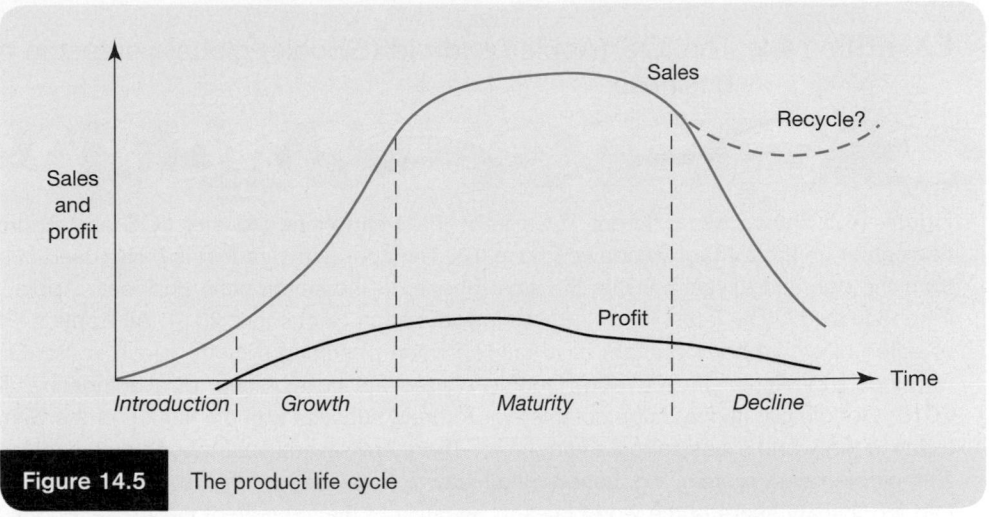

Figure 14.5 | The product life cycle

the brand is in the decline stage. If management withdraws marketing resources from the brand, it will create a self-fulfilling prophecy and the brand's sales will continue to decline. Instead management might increase marketing support in order to create a recycle (see Figure 14.5). This could be realized by the use of one or more of the following measures:

● product improvements (e.g. new product packaging);
● reposition perception of the product;
● reach new users of the product (via new distribution outlets);
● promote more frequent use of the product (fulfilling same need);
● promote new uses of the product (fulfilling new needs).

Fads

Not all products follow the classic PLC curve. Fads are fashions that are adopted very quickly by the public, peak early and decline very quickly. It is difficult to predict whether something will be only a fad, or how long it will last. The amount of mass-media attention together with other factors will influence the fad's duration.

Unpredictability

The duration of the PLC stages is unpredictable. Critics charge that markets can seldom tell what stage the product is in. A product may appear to be mature when, in fact, it has merely reached a temporary plateau prior to another upsurge.

Levels of product life cycle

The PLC concept can be examined at various levels, from the life cycle of a whole industry or product form (the technological life cycle, or TLC) (Popper and Buskirk, 1992) to the life cycle of a single model of a specific product. It is probably most useful to think in terms of the life cycle of a product form such as photocopiers or operating systems for smartphones (see Exhibit 14.2). Life cycles for product forms (TLCs) include definable groups of direct and close competitors and a core technology. These characteristics make life cycles for product forms easier to identify and analyse, and would seem to have more stable and general implications. An example of different PLC levels is shown in Figure 14.6.

EXHIBIT 14.2 The iOS (Apple)/Android (Google) global contest in the smartphone business

Figure 14.6 shows two different TLCs from the smartphone industry (iOS and Android), and a possible newcomer, in the form of Windows Phone 10. The core software that is being used in smartphones derives from the operating system inside the smartphone. In the smartphone business, Apple introduced their first iPhone in 2007. The latest iPhone 6 was introduced in September 2014. All Apple's iPhone models (PLCs of different smartphone brands) have one common operating system, which is the iOS (= TLC), which is developed by Apple. In 2007–08, Google started the development of a competing TLC, the Android. In 2010, Google got its first huge commercial Android success with the launch of the Samsung Galaxy, which today is the world's bestselling smartphone. There are several smartphone manufacturers who use Android as their operating system, e.g. Lenova and Huawei. In the beginning of the smartphone industry, Apple's iOS had a dominant share of the world market, because of the strength of the Apple iPhone. This continued until the beginning of 2012 when the Android took over the world leadership. Today (2015), Android has a world market share of around 70 per cent, whereas iOS has around 20 per cent. The rest is divided among other operating systems (TLCs) like BlackBerry 10. Now new TLCs are being supported to get a foothold in the world market, e.g. the Windows Phone 10, which is being used by e.g. Microsoft's Lumia.

In principle, the aggregation of the different smartphone models and brands in Figure 14.6 forms the total TLC.

Besides smartphones, the same operating systems (iOS and Android) can also be used for tablets.

In conclusion, the fierce competition among the different formats (TLCs) has resulted in better software for the smartphones, to the benefit of the smartphone end-buyers.

Another example of a TLC shift happened when the compact disc (CD) format was introduced as a result of a joint development between Philips and Sony. A key factor in the success of the CD format displacing the old LP vinyl record format was the ownership by Sony of CBS in the US, and by Philips of Polygram in Europe, two of the biggest music

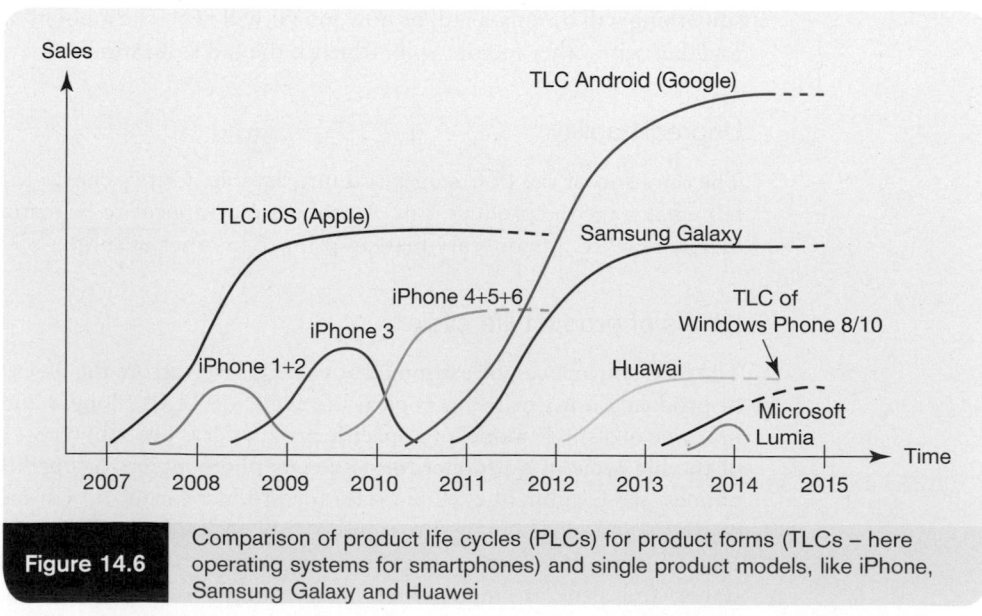

Figure 14.6   Comparison of product life cycles (PLCs) for product forms (TLCs – here operating systems for smartphones) and single product models, like iPhone, Samsung Galaxy and Huawei

software companies in the world. This contributed to the new CD format establishing itself as the industry standard. However, there were also a number of barriers to the adoption of the new format. The potential users had already invested in LP record collections and the prices of discs and players were relatively high at the beginning of the TLC.

Product life cycles for different products of the firm

So far in this chapter we have treated products as separate, distinct entities. However, many firms are multi-product, serving multiple markets. Some of these products are 'young' and some are 'older'. Young products will require investment to finance their growth, while others will generate more cash than they need. Somehow firms have to decide how to spread their limited resources among the competing needs of products so as to achieve the best performance of the firm as a whole. Figure 14.7 shows an example of a company (British Leyland) that did not succeed in achieving a balanced product portfolio (note that the PLC curves are represented by profit and not sales).

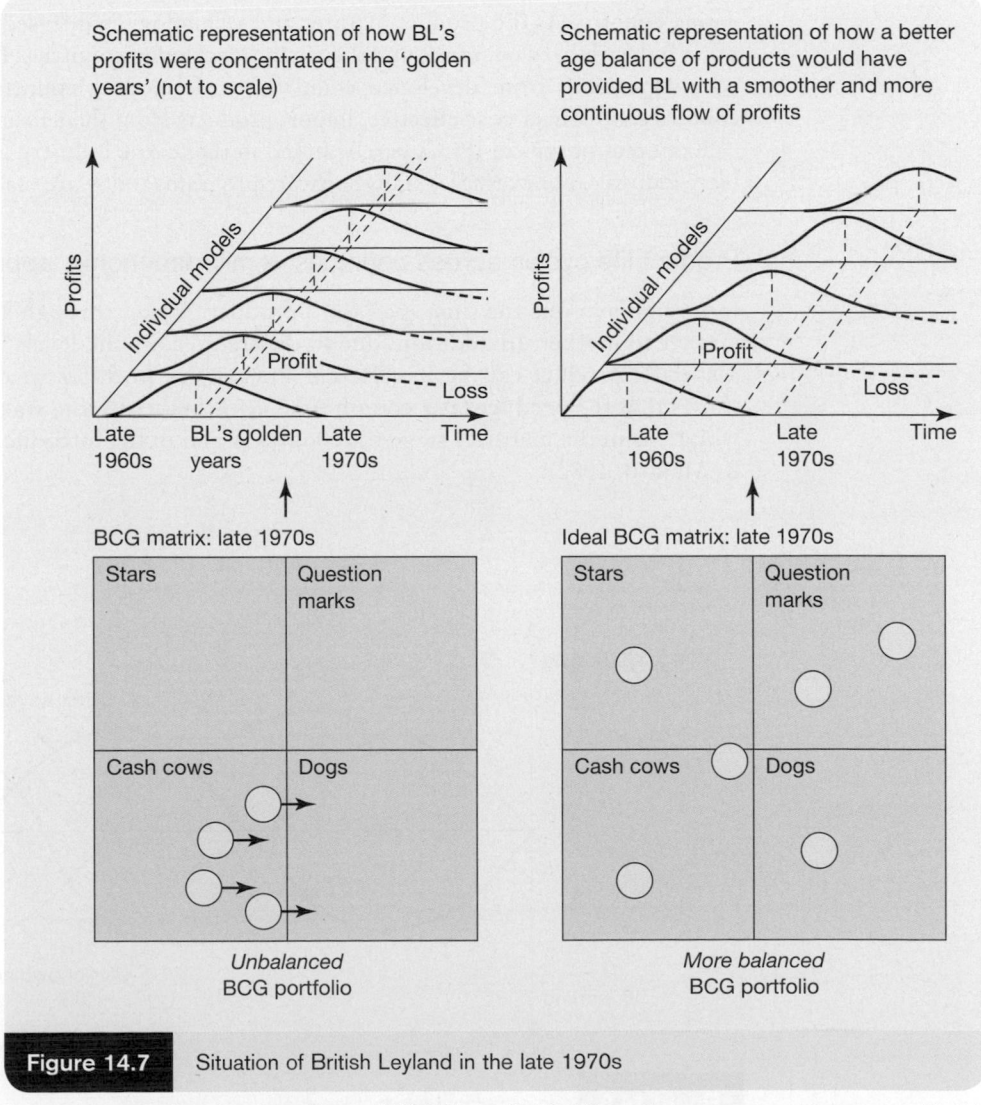

| Figure 14.7 | Situation of British Leyland in the late 1970s |

Source: partly reprinted from *Long Range Planning*, 17(3), McNamee, P. (1984) 'Competitive analysis using matrix displays', pp. 98–114, copyright 1984, with permission from Elsevier.

Product life cycles for different countries

When expanding the concept of the PLC to international markets, two different approaches appear:

1. international product life cycle (IPLC) – a macroeconomic approach;
2. PLCs across countries – a microeconomic approach.

The IPLC

The IPLC theory (originally Vernon, 1966) describes the diffusion process of an innovation across national boundaries (Figure 14.8). For each curve, net export results when the curve is above the horizontal line; if the curve is below the horizontal line, net import results for a particular country.

Typically, demand first grows in the innovating country (here the US). In the beginning excess production in the innovating country (greater than domestic demand) will be exported to other advanced countries where demand also grows. Only later does demand begin in less developed countries. Production, consequently, takes place first in the innovating country. As the product matures and technology is diffused, production occurs in other industrialized countries and then in less developed countries. Efficiency/comparative advantages shift from developed countries to developing countries. Finally, advanced countries, no longer cost-effective, import products from their former customers.

Examples of typical IPLCs can be found in the textile industry and the computer/software industry. For example, many software programs today are made in Bangalore, India.

Product life cycles across countries: a microeconomic approach

In foreign markets the time span for a product to pass through a stage may vary from market to market. In addition, due to different economic levels in different countries, a specific product can be in different PLC stages in different countries. Figure 14.9 shows that the product (at a certain time, t_1) is in the decline stage in the home market while it is in the maturity stage for country A and in the introduction stage for country B (Majaro, 1982).

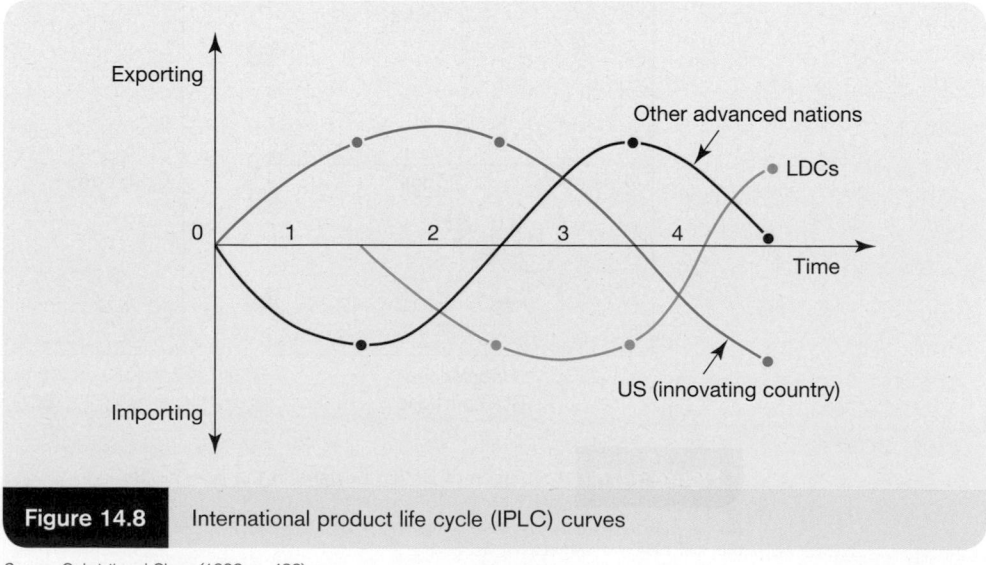

| **Figure 14.8** | International product life cycle (IPLC) curves |

Source: Onkvisit and Shaw (1993, p. 483).

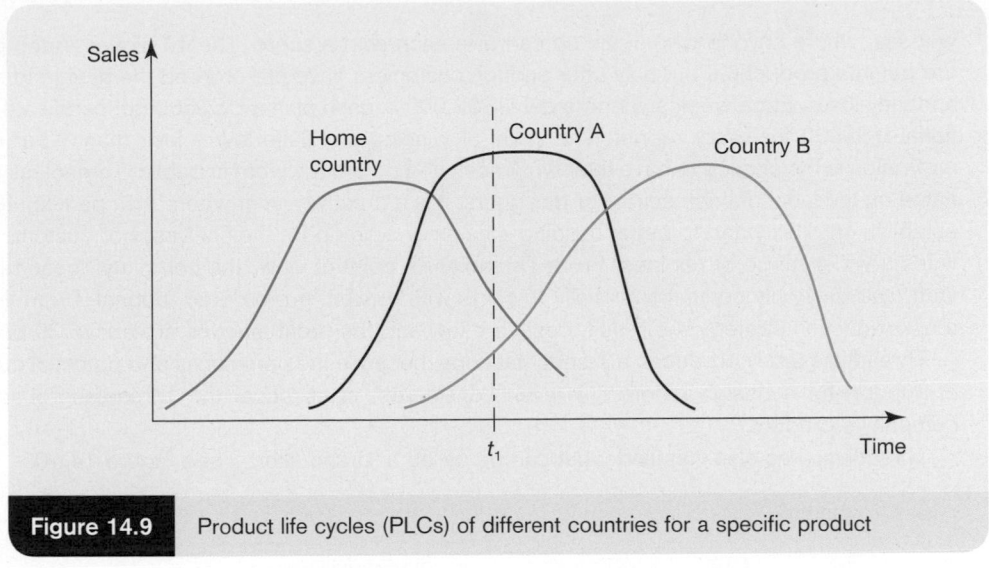

Figure 14.9   Product life cycles (PLCs) of different countries for a specific product

Crowd-sourcing

Some companies try to involve their (potential) customers and their online community directly in the product development process.

Crowd-sourcing
A company or institution that takes a function once performed by employees and outsources it to an undefined and large community of people in the form of an open call.

Jeff Howe, who coined the term **crowd-sourcing** back in 2006, defines crowd-sourcing as the act of a company taking a function once performed by employees and outsourcing it to a large community of people in the form of an open call (Howe, 2006).

Procter & Gamble, Nike, Best Buy, Threadless (see Exhibit 14.3) and Starbucks have all created digital platforms that allow customers to respond to 'open calls' with a view to involving them in creating new products and messages.

EXHIBIT 14.3 Threadless T-shirt crowdsourcing business

Threadless is a Chicago-based T-shirt maker whose design process consists entirely of an online contest. Today (2015) Threadless sells millions of custom, community-designed T-shirts in over 150 countries. Designs for the T-shirts come from all over the world and the community carefully selects the best and brightest.

Each week the company receives around 1,500 design submissions from amateur and professional artists. Threadless posts these to its

Source: www.threadless.com

website, where anyone who signs up can give each shirt a score. The 10 highest-rated designs each week are put into production, but only after enough customers have pre-ordered the design to ensure it will not be a money-loser. Each week's winners get US$2,000 in cash plus a US$500 gift certificate as well as an additional US$500 for every reprint. The odds of winning are quite low – less than 1 per cent – but the real motivation is the chance to have their work seen and potentially worn in public. Threadless puts the designer's name on the label of each shirt. For designers, it is a creative outlet where they participate mainly to learn, to establish credibility and to begin building a name or a brand for themselves. For customers, Threadless provides a wider range of choices. From Threadless's point of view, the company doesn't have to hire design staff, and they only commit financially to shirts with proven, pre-ordered, appeal. From that perspective it is a risk-reduction strategy. As result, costs are low and the profit margins are above 30 per cent.

Threadless rarely produces a T-shirt that flops, because the community and potential customers cast votes of support for a design before it is even considered. In essence, the Threadless customers develop the company's product.

Threadless has also installed what can be called a 'brand filter' – see Figure 14.10.

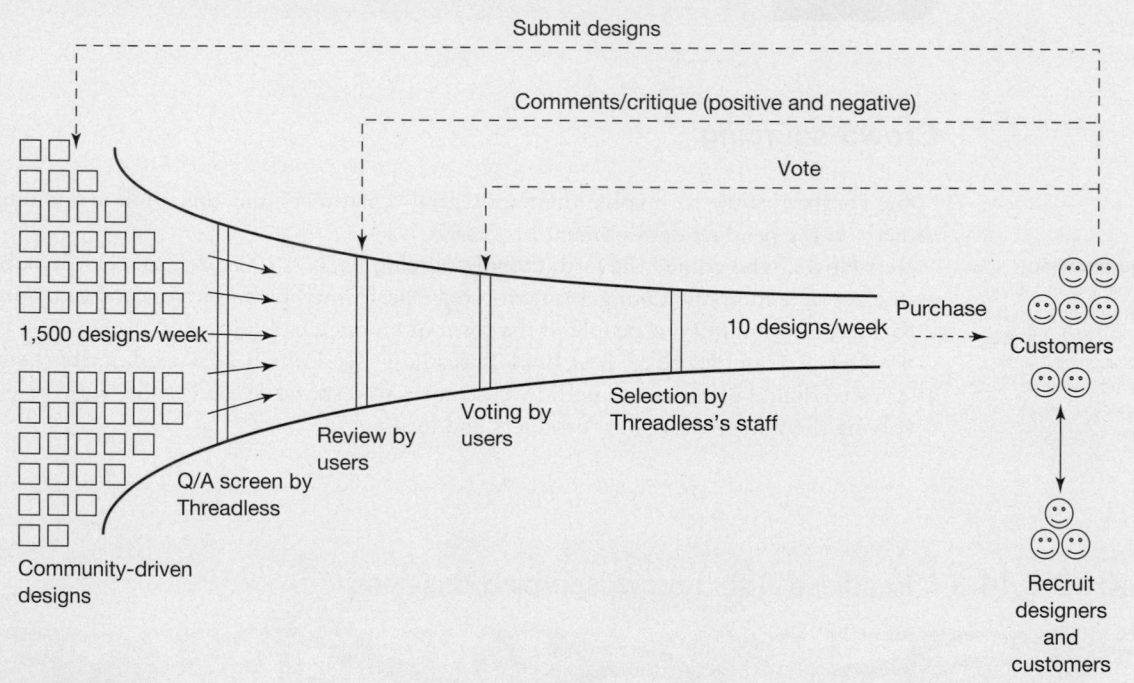

| **Figure 14.10** | Threadless's crowd-sourced brand-filter process |

After all the designs have been uploaded to the Threadless website (with a built-in Q&A screen) the community members can post comments and critique the different designs. After the designs have been discussed, and people have supported and recommended specific designs by forwarding links to other members of the community, the final voting is done – all within a week.

It is true that the 'crowd', meaning anyone, submits designs and the community votes to filter these designs from the clutter of weekly submissions, but the Threadless staff still make the final selection in a democratic process that helps to ensure both quality and purpose.

In 2008, Threadless Kids opened its own store in Chicago (see the photo). In addition to featuring the new adult T-shirts for the week, it has a constant rotation of other interesting designs, also for children.

Sources: adapted from Parent *et al.* (2011) and various orther public sources, e.g. Threadless.com.

Thanks to the recent internet technologies, companies can now tap into collectives on a greater scale than ever before. Crowds can bring together more data, leading to more accurate and intimate understanding of the market. So crowd-sourcing requires the collaboration of a larger number of people. Until recently, this was difficult to achieve. However, Web 2.0 offers new opportunities for collaboration and for the involvement of large crowds. Across hierarchies and functions, individuals can easily share knowledge and collaborate at almost no cost (Stieger *et al.*, 2012; Boudreau and Lakhani, 2013).

14.5   New products for the international market

Customer needs are the starting point for product development, whether for domestic or global markets. In addition to customer needs, conditions of use and ability to buy the product form a framework for decisions on new product development (NPD) for international markets.

Developing new products/cutting the time to market

As a consequence of increasing international competition, time is becoming a key success factor (KSF) for an increasing number of companies that manufacture technologically sophisticated products. This time competition and the level of technological development mean that product life cycles are getting shorter and shorter.

In parallel to shorter PLCs, the product development times for new products are being greatly reduced. This applies not only to technical products in the field of office communication equipment, but also to cars and consumer electronics. In some cases there have been reductions in development times of more than half.

Similarly, the time for marketing/selling, and hence also for R&D cost to pay off, has gone down from about four years to only two years. This new situation is illustrated in Figure 14.11.

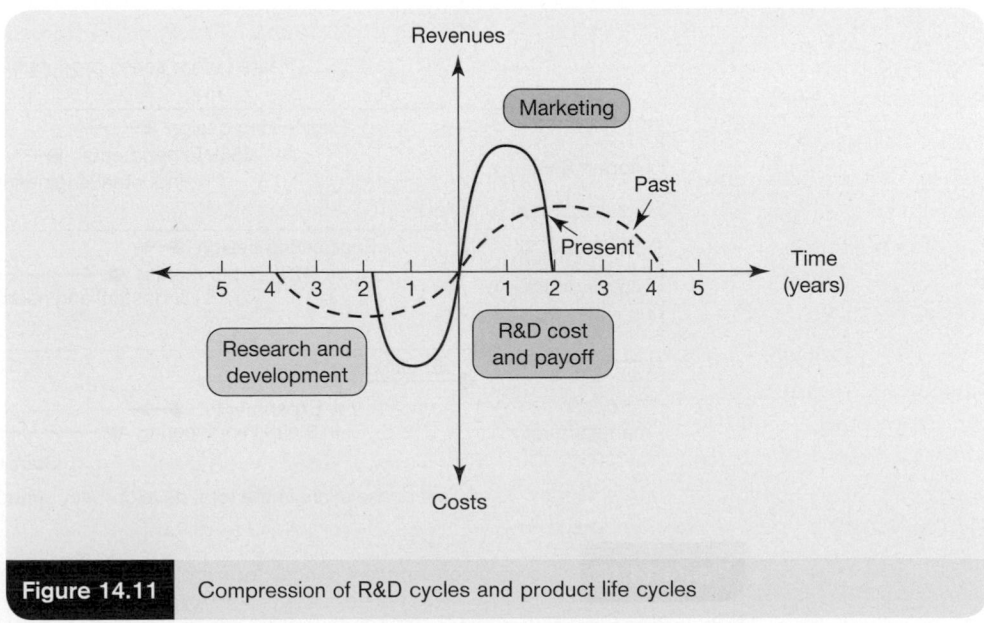

| **Figure 14.11** | Compression of R&D cycles and product life cycles |

Source: reprinted from *Long Range Planning*, 28(2), Töpfer, A. (1995) 'New products: cutting the time to market', p. 64, Copyright 1995, with permission from Elsevier.

For all types of technological product it holds true that the manufactured product must have as good a quality as required by the customer (i.e. as good as necessary), but not as good as technically feasible. Too frequently technological products are over-optimized and therefore too expensive from the customer's point of view (a good analysis of 'quality' is to be found in Guiltinan *et al.*, 1997).

As we have indicated in earlier chapters, Japanese and European suppliers to the car industry have different approaches to the product development process. Figure 14.12 shows an example with suppliers of dashboard instruments for cars. The two Japanese manufacturers start the engineering design phase two years later than the European manufacturer. This enables the Japanese to develop a product fully in a shorter time using the newest technology and to launch it almost simultaneously with their competitors.

The reason for the better time competition of the Japanese manufacturers is the intensive use of the following measures:

- early integration of customers and suppliers;
- multiskilled project teams;
- interlinking of R&D, production and marketing activities;
- total quality management (TQM);
- parallel planning of new products and the required production facilities (simultaneous engineering);
- high degree of outsourcing (reduction of internal manufacturing content).

Today, product quality is not enough to reach and to satisfy the customer. Quality of design and appearance play an increasingly important role. A highly qualified product support and customer service is also required.

Quality deployment function

Quality deployment function (QDF) is considered a main tool for 'listening to the voice of the customer' in the NPD process. It may be used to identify opportunities for product improvement or differentiation. QDF is a useful technique for translating customer needs

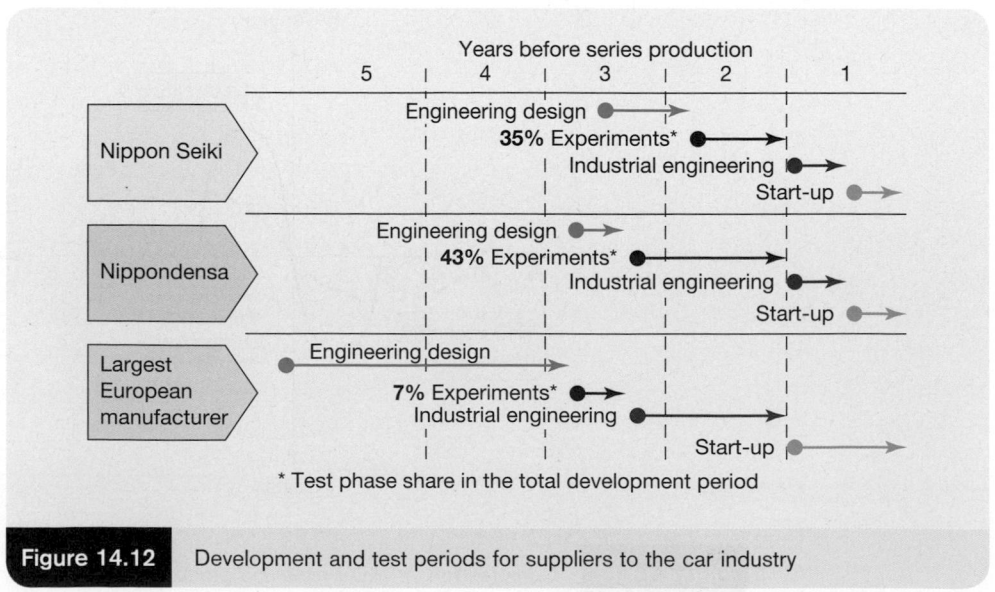

| **Figure 14.12** | Development and test periods for suppliers to the car industry |

Source: reprinted from *Long Range Planning*, 28(2), Töpfer, A. (1995) 'New products: cutting the time to market', p. 72, Copyright 1995, with permission from Elsevier.

into new product attributes and for responding to requirements of the successful development process. It encourages communication among engineering, production and marketing. Besides the involvement of customer requirements in the NPD process, QDF permits the reduction of design time and design cost while maintaining or enhancing the quality of the design. QDF originated in 1972 at Mitsubishi's Kobe shipyard and is used widely both in Japan and in the US. It has reduced design time and cost at Toyota by 40 per cent. The time- and cost-reducing effect arises because more effort is allocated in the early stages of the product innovation process.

Degrees of product newness

A new product can have several degrees of newness. It may be an entirely new invention (new to the world) or it may be a slight modification of an existing product. In Figure 14.13, newness has two dimensions: newness to the market (consumers, channels and public policy) and newness to the company. The risk of market failure also increases with the newness of the product. Hence the greater the newness of the product, the greater the need for a thorough internal company and external environment analysis, in order to reduce the risk involved.

The product communication mix

Having decided upon the optimum standardization/adaptation route and the newness of the product, the next most important (and culturally sensitive) factor to be considered is that of international promotion.

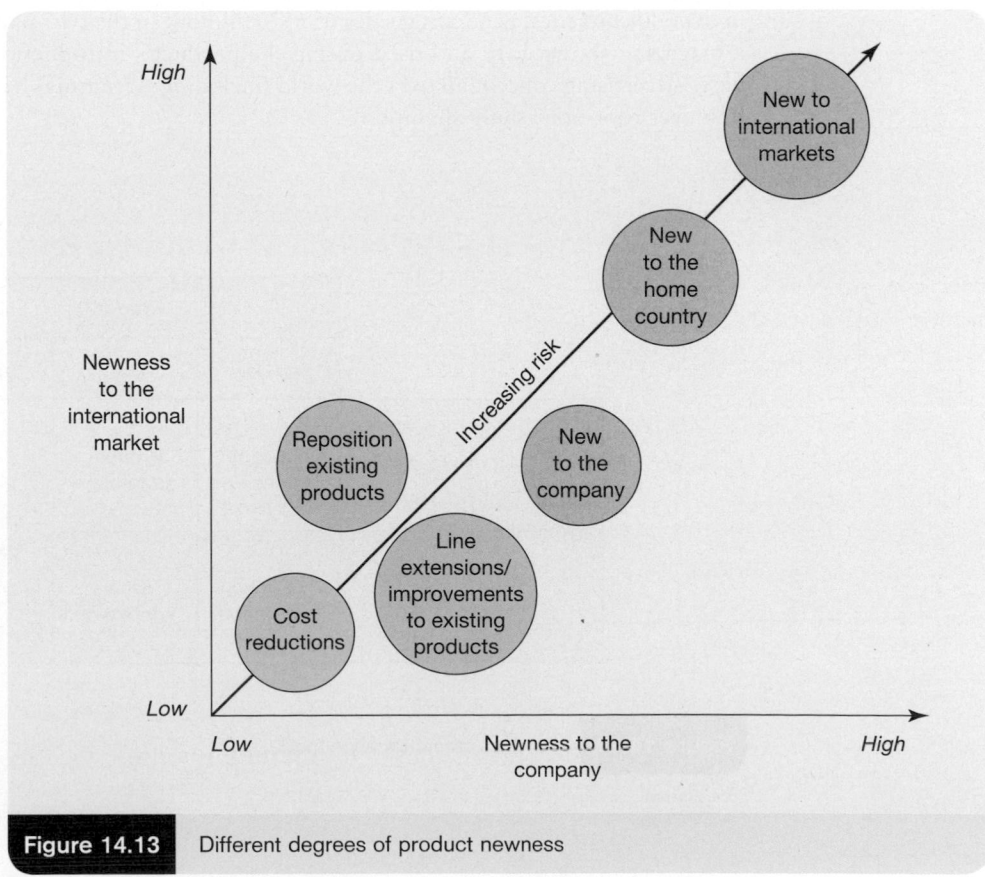

| **Figure 14.13** | Different degrees of product newness |

Product and promotion go hand in hand in foreign markets and together are able to create or destroy markets in very short order. We have considered the factors that may drive an organization to standardize or adapt its product range for foreign markets. Equally important are the promotion or the performance promises that the organization makes for its product or service in the target market. As with product decisions, promotion can be either standardized or adapted for foreign markets.

Keegan (1995) has highlighted the key aspects of marketing strategy as a combination of standardization or adaptation of the product and promotion of elements of the mix, and offers five alternative and more specific approaches to product policy. These approaches are shown in Figure 14.14.

Straight extension

This involves introducing a standardized product with the same promotion strategy throughout the world market (one product, one message worldwide). By applying this strategy successfully, major savings can be made on market research and product development. Since the 1920s, Coca-Cola has adopted a global approach, which has allowed the company to make enormous cost savings and benefits from continual reinforcement of the same message. While a number of writers have argued that this will be the strategy adopted for many products in the future, in practice only a handful of products might claim to have achieved this already. A number of firms have tried and failed. Campbell's soups, for example, found that consumers' taste in soup was by no means international.

An example of successful extension is Unilever's worldwide introduction of Organics Shampoo, which was first launched in Thailand in late 1993 after joint development work by Unilever's Hair Innovation Centres in Bangkok and Paris. By 1995, the brand was sold in over 40 countries, generating sales of £170 million. In the two-page advertisement from a magazine shown here and used during the product's introduction into Argentina, the basic advertising concept all over the world (including Argentina) has been 'Organics – the first ever root-nourishing shampoo'.

		Product		
		Standard	*Adapt*	*New*
Promotion	*Standard*	Straight extension	Product adaptation	Product invention
	Adapt	Promotion adaptation	Dual adaptation	

Figure 14.14   Product/communication mode

Source: based on Keegan (1995), pp. 489–94, p. 498, Table 13–1.

'Straight extension' of Organics shampoo to Argentina

Promotion adaptation

Use of this strategy involves leaving a product unchanged but fine-tuning promotional activity to take into account cultural differences between markets. It is a relatively cost-effective strategy, as changing promotion messages is not as expensive as adapting products. An example of this strategy is illustrated by Lux.

LUX soap (Unilever): the UK versus India

The UK version of the LUX advertisement is based on the classic transborder advertising campaign, 'the beauty soap of film stars', which has been standardized to a high degree. In India, the LUX campaign has been given a special local touch.

The Indian version is one of three advertisements that trace LUX's association with film stars from the past era to the current stars of today and the potential film stars of tomorrow. The advertisement focuses on three legendary beauties of Indian cinema who have endorsed the brand in the past. The creative statement is in the style of a cinema poster, keeping the brand image in mind, and in a sepia tone to give it a nostalgic feel.

Product adaptation

By modifying only the product, a manufacturer intends to maintain the core product function in the different markets. For example, electrical appliances have to be modified to cope with different electrical voltages in different countries. A product can also be adapted to function under different physical environmental conditions. Exxon changed the chemical composition of petrol to cope with the extremes of climate, but still used the 'Put a tiger in your tank' campaign unchanged around the world.

Advertisements for Lux in the UK and India

Dual adaptation

By adapting both product and promotion for each market, the firm is adopting a totally differentiated approach. This strategy is often adopted by firms when one of the previous three strategies has failed, but particularly if the firm is not in a leadership position and is therefore reacting to the market or following competitors. It applies to the majority of products in the world market. The modification of both product and promotion is an expensive but often necessary strategy.

Kellogg's dual adaptation for the Indian market

An example of dual adaptation is shown here, with the launch of Kellogg's Basmati Flakes in the nascent breakfast cereal market in India. This product was specially created to suit Indian tastes, India being a large rice-eating country, and the advertising campaign was a locally adapted concept based on international positioning.

Product invention

Product invention is adopted by firms, usually from advanced nations, that are supplying products to less developed countries. Products are specifically developed to meet the needs of the individual markets. Existing products may be too technologically sophisticated to operate in less developed countries, where power supplies may be intermittent and local skills limited. Keegan (1995) uses a hand-powered washing machine as a product example.

EXHIBIT 14.4 Product invention – solar-powered portable charging systems for India

By developing a solar-powered portable charging system for its digital cameras and photo printers, Hewlett-Packard (HP) has been able to make successful inroads into the vast Indian rural market. This incremental innovation has enabled HP to successfully sell digital cameras and printers to consumers living in villages in India that have not yet benefited from the national rural electrification programme. The business model employed by HP to tap into the potential of the rural market is innovative. Unlike in urban markets where the camera and printer are sold outright to customers, the village entrepreneurs lease the equipment and purchase consumables from HP. Another major contributing factor to HP's success in penetrating the rural market in India was the knowledge gained about rural communities by a team of HP employees who stayed in the homes of local families for a couple of days, and from attending community meetings.

Source: adapted from Varadarajan (2009).

14.6   Product positioning

Product positioning is a key element in the successful marketing of any organization in any market. The product or company that does not have a clear position in the customer's mind consequently stands for nothing and is rarely able to command more than a simple commodity or utility price. Premium pricing and competitive advantage are largely dependent upon the customer's perception that the product or service on offer is markedly different in some way from competitive offers (Devaney and Brown, 2008). How can we achieve a credible market position in international markets?

Since it is the buyer/user perception of benefit-generating attributes that is important, product positioning is the activity by which a desirable 'position' in the mind of the customer is created for the product. Positioning a product for international markets begins with describing specific products as comprising different attributes that are capable of generating a flow of benefits to buyers and users.

The global marketing planner puts these attributes into bundles so that the benefits generated match the special requirements of specific market segments. This product design problem involves not only the basic product components (physical, package, service and country of origin) but also the brand name, styling and similar features.

Viewed in a multidimensional space (commonly denoted as 'perceptual mapping'), a product can be graphically represented at a point specified by its attributes. The location of a product's point in perceptual space is its 'position'. Competitors' products are similarly located (see also Johansson and Thorelli, 1985). If points representing other products are close to the point of the prototype then these other products are close competitors of the prototype. If the prototype is positioned away from its closest competitors in some international markets and its positioning implies important features for customers, then it is likely to have a significant competitive advantage.

Country-of-origin effects

The country of origin (COO) of a product, typically communicated by the phrase 'made in [country]', has a considerable influence on the quality perception of that product. Some countries have a good reputation and others a poor reputation for certain products. For example, Japan and Germany have good reputations for producing cars. The COO effects are especially critical among eastern European consumers. A study by Ettensén (1993) examined the brand decision for televisions among Russian, Polish and Hungarian consumers. These consumers evaluated domestically produced television products much lower than western-made products, regardless of brand name. There was a general preference for televisions manufactured in Japan, Germany and the US.

The country of origin is more important than the brand name, and this can be good news for western firms that are attempting to penetrate the eastern European region with imports whose brand name is not yet familiar. Another study (Johansson *et al.*, 1994) showed that some products from eastern Europe have done well in the west, despite negative COO perceptions. For example, Belarus tractors have sold well in Europe and the US not only because of their reasonable price but also because of their ruggedness. Only the

---

EXHIBIT 14.5 Chinese piano manufacturers are experiencing the 'country of origin' (COO) effect

The Chinese piano industry is a useful example to show the opportunities and challenges facing Chinese brands. China has overtaken Japan and South Korea to become the world's largest piano-producing nation. One of the brand manufacturers, Pearl River, has become the world's largest piano manufacturer with annual sales of about 100,000 units. As piano-making is still a labour-intensive industry, Chinese manufacturers enjoy a big cost and price advantage. This also motivates international dealers to stock Chinese pianos, because of a larger profit margin. However, the biggest branding dilemma facing Chinese piano manufacturers is negative perceptions of 'made in China' as a label. It is difficult for individual firms to change this perception and requires the country to change its image in general, which may take a generation. It has taken Japan's Yamaha more than 30 years to change its image from a cheap 'me too' product to a leading global brand. An important buying influence also comes from music teachers, and many of them advise their students not to buy Chinese-made instruments.

To overcome this difficulty, Chinese manufacturers could try to link their brands to western-oriented values and names. For example, Longfeng Piano could emphasize that its Kingsburg model is designed by the world-renowned German designer Klaus Fenner.

Source: adapted from Fan (2007). From Hollensen, S. (2008) *Essentials of Global Marketing*, FT/Prentice Hall, p. 311, Exhibit 11.1.

lack of an effective distribution network has hindered the firm's ability to penetrate western markets to a greater degree.

When considering the implications of product positioning, it is important to realize that positioning can vary from market to market, because the target customers for the product differ from country to country. In confirming the positioning of a product or service in a specific market or region, it is therefore necessary to establish in the consumer's perception exactly what the product stands for and how it differs from existing and potential competition. In developing a market-specific product, positioning the firm can focus upon one or more elements of the total product offer, so the differentiation might be based upon price and quality, one or more attributes, a specific application, a target consumer or direct comparison with one competitor.

EXHIBIT 14.6 Madame Tussauds – a brand that brings people closer to celebrities on a global basis

The attraction's history is a rich and fascinating one with roots dating back to the Paris of 1770. It was here that Madame Tussaud learnt to model wax likenesses under the tutelage of her mentor, Dr Philippe Curtius. Her skills were put to the test during the French Revolution when she was forced to prove her allegiance by making the death masks of executed aristocrats. It was in the early nineteenth century that she came to Britain, bringing with her a travelling exhibition of revolutionary relics and effigies of public heroes and rogues.

In March 2007, the Tussauds Group was sold to the Blackstone Group in a £1 billion deal. The company has been merged with the Merlin Entertainments Group. In 2009, Merlin attracted around 30 million visitors to all its attractions, making them the world's second-largest visitor attraction operator after Disney. The Merlin Entertainments Group operates in 12 countries and has more than 13,000 employees.

Brand experience

The future for brands is about building memorable consumer experiences. Experience-oriented companies like Madame Tussauds need to have something that goes beyond the product. Madame Tussauds' selling point is not about waxworks, it is about bringing people closer to celebrities and what they do in life.

Choice of new location

The choice of a new location is based on many different criteria. Madame Tussauds has a product development team that investigates how many tourists visit a city, whether they fit the profile of the attraction's visitors and whether there's enough space. Detailed research is vital to take a concept into a new market. After opening in Hong Kong, Madame Tussauds opened its second Asian branch in Shanghai in 2006. As China's largest and wealthiest city with over 13 million residents and nearly 40 million tourists a year, Shanghai represents a good opportunity for the company.

Interactivity with the waxwork figures

The Shanghai branch has the most interactivity of all the attractions, with fewer waxwork figures and more to do around them. The Tiger Woods exhibit allows visitors to putt on the green and see their scores come up. The latest guest to have a hole-in-one is recorded on the leaderboard. Visitors can also go into a karaoke booth with models of some famous Chinese popstars, called Twins, sing with them and view themselves on video. People can also dress up like Charlie Chaplin and see themselves on a movie screen in black and white.

Kim Kardashian

The Queen

Source: Madame Tussauds.

Balancing local and global branding

Research on Madame Tussauds shows a 98 per cent brand recognition in the UK market. However, in Asia, the term 'madame' sometimes implies a bar or club to many consumers, and saying that the brand is a 'wax attraction' does not mean anything in the Asian market as there is no tradition of that type of museum there.

For Madame Tussauds it is important to make sure the brand maintains a good mix of local and global content. This is a delicate balance: too much local content does not fit with the idea of a global brand, while too little emphasis on global figures can disappoint international customers. The Chinese venue overwhelmingly features local faces, such as actor Ge You, kung fu king Jackie Chan, the pop-group Twins and basketball superstar Yao Ming; it also has global figures such as David Beckham, Michael Jackson and Brad Pitt. The London attraction has a wide range of global figures such as Angelina Jolie, Beyonce Knowles and Barack Obama, but international tourists also love Margaret Thatcher, Princess Diana, Winston Churchill and the Queen.

Expanding the Madame Tussauds brand on a global scale is a challenge, but when it comes down to the essentials, Madame Tussauds is not about waxworks – it is about consumer experiences and bringing people into interaction with the celebrities.

Sources: with kind permission from Madame Tussauds Group, especially Global Marketing Director Nicky Marsh from London (www.madame-tussauds.com) and Cathy Wong, External Affairs Consultant from Shanghai (www.madame-tussauds.com.cn); Marsh, N. (2006) 'Translating experiences across the world', *Brand Strategy*, June, p. 11; Macalister, T. (2005) 'Madame Tussauds to open in Shanghai', *The Guardian* (London), 19 September, p. 20.

14.7　Brand equity

Brands have become omnipresent in all parts of the global culture (Cayla and Arnould, 2008). A study by Citibank and Interbrand in 1997 found that companies basing their business on brands had outperformed the stock market for 15 years. The same study, however, noted the risky tendency of some brand owners to reduce investments in brands in the mid-1990s, with negative impacts on their performance (Hooley *et al.*, 1998, p. 120).

The following two examples show that brands add value for customers:

- The classic example is that in a blind test 51 per cent of consumers prefer Pepsi to Coca-Cola, but in open tests 65 per cent prefer Coca-Cola to Pepsi: soft drink preferences are based on brand image, not taste (Hooley *et al.*, 1998, p. 119).
- Skoda cars were once best known in the UK as the butt of bad jokes, reflecting a widespread belief that the cars were of very low quality. In 1995, when Skoda was preparing to launch a new model in the UK, and did 'blind and seen' tests of consumers' judgment of the vehicle. The vehicle was rated as better designed and worth more by those who did not know the make. With the Skoda name revealed, perceptions of the design were less favourable and estimated value was substantially lower. This leads us from the reputation of the company to branding (Hooley *et al.*, 1998, p. 117). However, since being taken over by German car giant Volkswagen in 1991, the reputation of the much-criticized Czech manufacturer has rapidly improved. Since then, although lots of parts have been shared between VW and Skoda, not to mention SEAT, the Skoda identity has regained strength and is now the gold standard for the Czech economy.

Definitions of brand equity

Brand equity
A set of brand assets and liabilities that can be clustered into five categories: brand loyalty, brand awareness, perceived quality, brand associations and other proprietary brand assets. Brand equity is the premium a customer/consumer would pay for the branded product or service compared with an identical unbranded version of the same product/service.

Although the definition of **brand equity** is often debated, the term deals with the brand value, beyond the physical assets associated with its manufacture.

David Aaker of the University of California at Berkeley, one of the leading authorities on brand equity, has defined the term as 'a set of *brand assets and liabilities* linked to the brand, its name and symbol, that add to or subtract from the value provided by a product or service to a firm or to the firm's customers' (Aaker, 1991, p. 15).

Aaker has clustered those assets and liabilities into five categories:

1. *Brand loyalty*: encourages customers to buy a particular brand time after time and remain insensitive to competitors' offerings.
2. *Brand awareness*: brand names attract attention and convey images of familiarity; may be translated as what percentage of customers know the brand name.
3. *Perceived quality*: 'perceived' means that the customers decide upon the level of quality, not the company.
4. *Brand associations*: the values and the personality linked to the brand.
5. *Other proprietary brand assets*: include trademarks, patents and marketing channel relationships.

Brand equity can be thought of as the additional cash flow achieved by associating a brand with the underlying values of the product or service. In this connection it is useful (although incomplete) to think of a brand's equity as *the premium a customer/consumer would pay for the branded product or service compared with an identical unbranded version of the same product/service.*

Hence brand equity refers to the strength, depth and character of the consumer–brand relationship. A strong equity implies a positive force that keeps the consumer and the brand together, in the face of resistance and tension. The strength, depth and character of the customer–brand relationship is referred to as the *brand relationship quality* (Marketing Science Institute, 1995).

14.8   Branding decisions

Closely linked to product positioning is the question of branding. The basic purposes of branding are the same everywhere in the world. In general, the functions of branding are:

- to distinguish a company's offering and differentiate one particular product from its competitors;

- to create identification and brand awareness;
- to guarantee a certain level of quality and satisfaction;
- to help with promotion of the product.

All of these purposes have the same ultimate goals: to create new sales (market shares taken from competitors) or induce repeat sales (keep customers loyal).

Figure 14.15 demonstrates the four levels of branding decisions. Each alternative at the four levels has a number of advantages and disadvantages, which are presented in Table 14.2. We will discuss these options in more detail in the following.

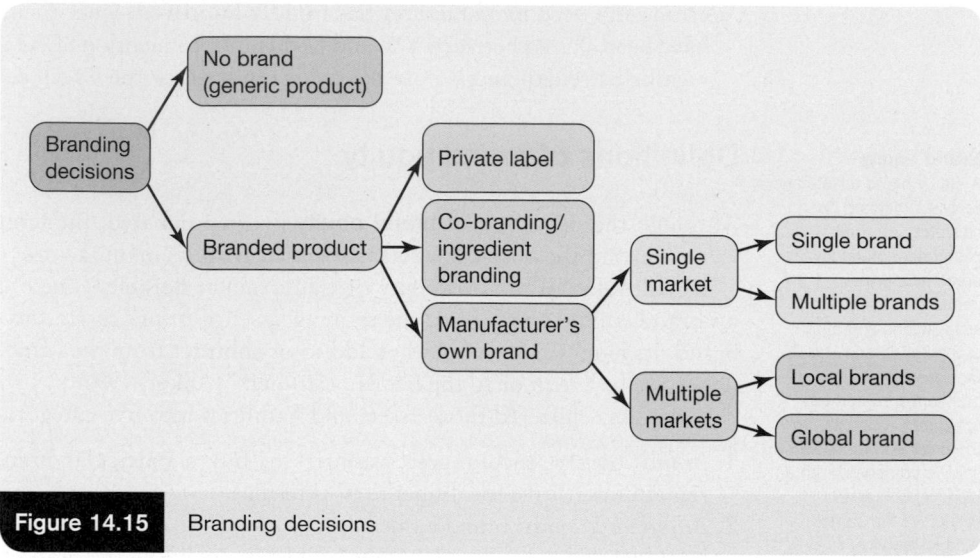

| **Figure 14.15** | Branding decisions |

Source: adapted from Onkvisit and Shaw (1993, p. 534).

EXHIBIT 14.7 Unilever's Snuggle fabric softener – an example of local brands in multiple markets

An effective example of promotion adaptation is illustrated by Unilever's Snuggle fabric softener. The product was initially launched in Germany as an economy brand in a category dominated by Procter & Gamble. In order to counteract the negative quality inferences associated with low price, Unilever emphasized softness as the product's key point of difference. The softness association was communicated through the name, 'Kuschelweich', which means 'enfolded in softness', and this was illustrated through a picture of a teddy bear on the package. When the product was launched in France, Unilever kept the brand positioning of economy and softness but changed the name to 'Cajoline', meaning softness in French. In addition, the teddy bear that had been inactive in Germany now took centre-stage in the French advertising as the brand symbol for softness and quality. Success in France led to global expansion and in each case the brand name was changed to connote softness in the local language while the advertising featuring the teddy bear remained virtually identical across global markets. By the 1990s, Unilever was marketing the fabric softener around the globe with over a dozen brand names, all with the same product positioning and advertising support. More importantly, the fabric softener was generally the number one or two brand in each market.

Source: adapted from Keller and Sood (2001).

Brand versus no brand

Branding is associated with added costs in the form of marketing, labelling, packaging and promotion. Commodities are 'unbranded' or undifferentiated products. Examples of products with no brand are cement, metals, salt, beef and other agricultural products.

Private label versus co-branding versus manufacturer's own brand

These three options can be graded as shown in Figure 14.16.

Table 14.2	Advantages and disadvantages of branding alternatives	
	Advantages	**Disadvantages**
No brand	Lower production cost Lower marketing cost Lower legal cost Flexible quality control	Severe price competition Lack of market identity
Branding	Better identification and awareness Better chance for production differentiation Possible brand loyalty Possible premium pricing	Higher production cost Higher marketing cost Higher legal cost
Private label	Possibility of larger market share No promotional problems	Severe price competition Lack of market identity
Co-branding/ ingredient branding	Adds more value to the brand Sharing of production and promotion costs Increases manufacturer's power in gaining access to retailers' shelves Can develop into long-lasting relationships based on mutual commitment	Consumers may become confused Ingredient supplier is very dependent on the success of the final product Promotion cost for ingredient supplier
Manufacturer's own brand	Better price due to higher price inelasticity Retention of brand loyalty Better bargaining power Better control of distribution	Difficult for small manufacturer with unknown brand Requires brand promotion
Single market, single brand	Marketing efficiency Permits more focused marketing Eliminates brand confusion Good for product with good reputation (halo effect)	Assumes market homogeneity Existing brand's image harmed when trading up/down Limited shelf space
Single market, multiple brands	Market segmented for varying needs Creates competitive spirit Avoids negative connotation of existing brand Gains more retail shelf space Does not harm existing brand's image	Higher marketing cost Higher inventory cost Loss of economies of scale
Multiple markets, local brands (see also Exhibit 14.5)	Meaningful names Local identification Avoidance of taxation on international brand Allows variations of quantity and quality across markets	Higher marketing cost Higher inventory cost Loss of economies of scale Diffused image

Table 14.2	Contd.		
	Advantages		**Disadvantages**
Multiple markets, global brand	Maximum marketing efficiency Reduction of advertising costs Elimination of brand confusion Good for culture-free product Good for prestigious product Easy identification/recognition for international travellers Uniform worldwide image		Assumes market homogeneity Problems with black and grey markets Possibility of negative connotation Requires quality and quantity consistency LDCs' opposition and resentment Legal complications

LDC, less developed country.
Source: adapted from Onkvisit and Shaw (1989). Published with permission from Emerald Publishing Ltd. www.emeraldinsight.com.

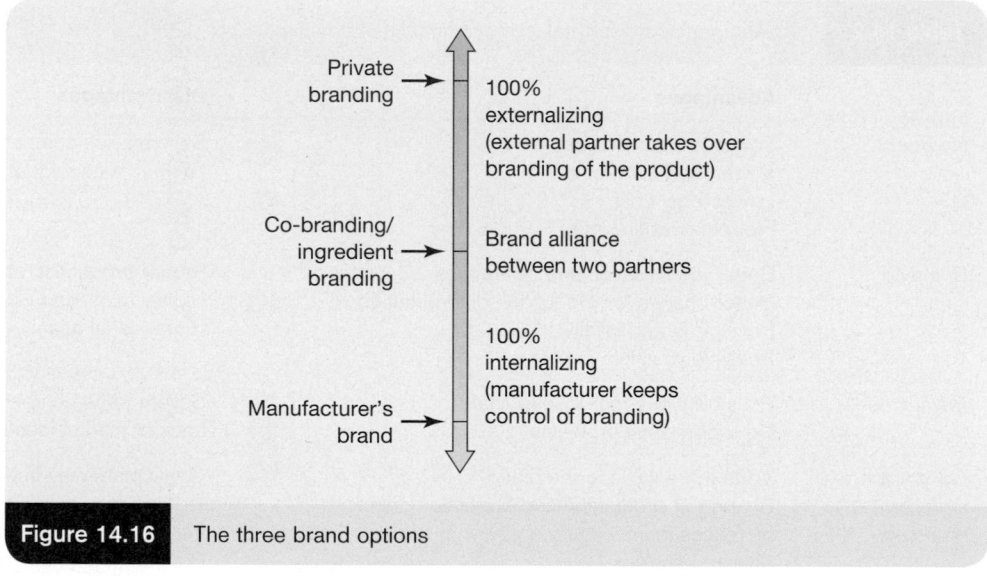

Figure 14.16	The three brand options

The question of consumers having brand loyalty or shop loyalty is a crucial one. The competitive struggle between the manufacturer and the retailer actualizes the need for a better understanding of shopping behaviour. Both actors need to be aware of determinants of shop choice, shopping frequency and in-store behaviour. Where manufacturers pay little attention to the shopping behaviour of their consumers, this helps to anticipate the increasing power of certain retail chains.

Private label

Private label
Retailer's own brand, e.g. Sainsbury's 'Taste the difference'.

Private labelling is most developed in the UK, where Marks & Spencer, for instance, mostly sells own-label (**private label**) products. At Sainsbury's, own labels account for 60 per cent of the sales. The average market share of private labels across Europe have reached 23 per cent.

Compared with the high share of private labelling in northern Europe, the share in southern Europe (e.g. Spain and Portugal) is less. In Europe, the highest shares of private labels are found in the UK (46 per cent) and Switzerland (45 per cent). Moreover, the growth of private labels significantly exceeds that experienced by manufacturer brands.

The situation in the US is similar to western Europe, where penetration rates across categories have reached 24 per cent. In other regions of the world, private label shares are relatively low. In South America and Asia, the shares are typically around 5 per cent but there is widespread diversity across markets in terms of the level of private label penetration (Europanel, 2009).

The retailer's perspective

For the retailer there are two main advantages connected with own-label business:

1. *Own labels provide better profit margins.* The cost of goods typically makes up 70–85 per cent of a retailer's total cost. So if the retailer can buy a quality product from the manufacturer at a lower price, this will provide a better profit margin for the retailer. In fact, private labels have helped UK food retailers to achieve profit margins averaging 8 per cent of sales, which is high by international standards. The typical figure in France and the US is 1–2 per cent (Steenkamp and Kumar, 2009).

2. *Own labels strengthen the retailer's image with its customers.* Many retail chains try to establish loyalty to their particular chain of shops by offering their own quality products. In fact, premium private-label products (e.g. Sainsbury's 'Taste the Difference') that compete in quality with manufacturers' top brands have seen a growth in market share, whereas the share of cheap generics is declining.

The manufacturer's perspective

Although private brands are normally regarded as threats for manufacturers, there may be situations where private branding is a preferable option:

- Because there are no promotional expenses associated with private branding for the producer, the strategy is especially suitable for small and medium-sized enterprises (SMEs) with limited financial resources and limited competences in the downstream functions.
- The private brand manufacturer gains access to the shelves of the retail chains. With increasing internationalization of the big retail chains, this may also result in export business for the SME that has never been in international markets.

There are also a number of reasons why private branding is bad for the manufacturer:

- By not having its own identity, the manufacturer must compete mainly on price, because the retail chain can always switch supplier.
- The manufacturer loses control over how its products should be promoted. This may become critical if the retailer does not do a good job in pushing the product to the consumer.
- If the manufacturer is producing both its own brands and private brands, there is a danger that the private brands will cannibalize the manufacturer's brand-name products.

Furthermore, in many countries, private labels have undergone a deep transformation, evolving from a low-price/low-quality image to competing in some categories with the strongest brands in the market. Clearly, manufacturer brands in many countries such as the US and those in western Europe are facing a competitive threat from the expansion of private labels.

It is assumed that retailers' market power (measured by retail concentration = aggregated percentage of market shares of the top three retailers) is the key determinant for the private label share in a specific country. Studies have confirmed that retail concentration rates are positively associated with private label shares in different countries, because they signal both the market power of retailers in the marketplace and their negotiating power versus the brand manufacturers' (Rubio and Yagüe, 2009).

Cuneo et al. (2015) confirm that a well-developed modern trade structure (i.e. supermarkets, hypermarkets and/or discounters) in a country is a prerequisite for the growth of private labels because only large retailers are able to build sufficient market power to realize the high volumes required to attain scale advantages. Thus, as retail distribution systems in a market transform from more traditional channels to more modern trade, it is likely that the private label share will grow and pose a greater threat to manufacturer brands in those markets.

Even local manufacturer brands in markets with low private-label brand (PLB) share are likely to experience enormous competitive pressure that will threaten their very existence as:

- global discounters expand their market reach;
- local retailers develop PLBs that mimic global retailers;
- international manufacturer brands competing in markets where PLBs have a stronghold may plan to enter new markets where PLB market share is low.

Exhibit 14.8 shows an example with Kellogg, which supplemented its manufacturer brand strategy with a private label strategy in Germany.

EXHIBIT 14.8 Kellogg under pressure to produce under Aldi's own label

In February 2000, Kellogg (the cereal giant) made an own-label deal with German supermarket chain Aldi. It was the first time that Kellogg had supplied own-label products.

A slogan on Kellogg's cereal packets claimed: 'If you don't see Kellogg's on the box . . . it isn't Kellogg's in the box.' But then Kellogg negotiated a deal with Aldi to supply products in Germany bearing a different brand name. Reports in Germany suggested the deal was made after Aldi announced it would no longer pay brand suppliers' prices and threatened to cut top brands from its shelves.

Source: adapted from various public media.

Manufacturer's own brand

From World War II until the 1960s, brand manufacturers managed to build a bridge over the heads of the retailers to the consumers. They created consumer loyalty for their particular brand by using sophisticated advertising (culminating in TV advertising) and other promotional techniques.

Since the 1960s, various sociological changes (notably the car) have encouraged the rise of large, efficient retailers. Nowadays the distribution system is being turned upside down. The traditional supply chain, powered by manufacturer 'push', is becoming a demand chain, driven by consumer 'pull'. Retailers have won control over distribution not just because they decide the price at which goods are sold, but also because both individual shops and retail companies have become much bigger and more efficient. They are able to buy in bulk and to reap economies of scale, mainly due to advances in transport and, more recently, in information technology. Most retail chains have not only set up computer links between each store and distribution warehouses, but they are also hooked up with the computers of the firm's main suppliers, through an electronic data interchange system.

After some decades of absence, private labels reappeared in the 1970s as generic products pioneered by Carrefour in France, but were soon adopted by UK and US retailers. Ten years ago there was a distinct gap in the level of quality between private-label and brand-name products. Today the gap has narrowed: private-label quality levels are higher than ever before and they are more consistent, especially in categories historically characterized by little product innovation.

Co-branding/ingredient branding

Despite the similarities between co-branding and ingredient branding there is also an important difference, as we shall see below.

Co-branding

Co-branding
Form of cooperation between two or more brands, which can create synergies that create value for both participants, above the value they would expect to generate on their own.

Co-branding is a form of cooperation between two or more brands with significant customer recognition, in which all the participants' brand names are retained. It is of medium- to long-term duration and its net value creation potential is too small to justify setting up a new brand and/or legal joint venture. The motive for co-branding is the expectation of synergies that create value for both participants, above the value they would expect to generate on their own (Bengtsson and Servais, 2005).

In the case of co-branding, the products are often complementary, in the way that one product can be used or consumed independently of the other (e.g. Bacardi Rum and Coca-Cola). Hence co-branding may be an efficient alternative to traditional brand extension strategies (Figure 14.17).

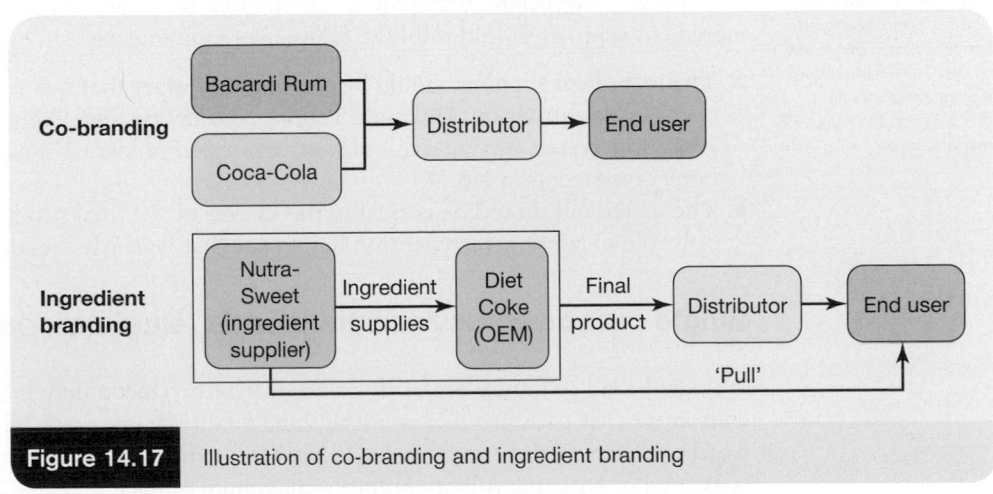

Figure 14.17   Illustration of co-branding and ingredient branding

EXHIBIT 14.9 Shell's co-branding with Ferrari and LEGO

In 1999–2000 Shell ran a £50 million co-branding campaign with Ferrari and LEGO. Some people might have thought that this was an attempt to persuade people, mainly in the west, that Shell's controversial attempt to dump the Brent Spar oil platform in the North Sea was not a true reflection of the company.

However, it may be more accurate to say that Shell was seeking a 'brand image transfer'. In the petrol retailer market traditionally driven by price and more price promotions, Shell wanted both Ferrari's sexy, sporty image and the family values of LEGO. Furthermore, Shell was, and is, no longer only in the petroleum and oils business, where price promotions are the main focus of marketing activity. The company is also involved in food retailing, where loyalty programmes are important.

What were the benefits for Ferrari and LEGO? Ferrari gained sponsorship and royalty income from model car sales, while LEGO got improved global distribution. The co-branding strategy involved the use of 10 exclusive small boxed toys and a big Ferrari LEGO car carrying a Shell logo. Shell wanted to sell between 20 and 40 million units of LEGO globally, and the deal made Shell one of the world's largest toy distributors.

Source: adapted from various public media.

Ingredient branding

Normally the marketer of the final product (OEM) creates all of the value in the consumer's eyes. In the case of Intel and NutraSweet, the ingredient supplier is seeking to build value in its products by branding and promoting the key component of an end product. When promotion of the key component brand is initiated by the ingredient supplier, the goal is to build awareness and preference among consumers for that ingredient brand ('pull' strategy: see Figure 14.17). Simultaneously, it may be the manufacturer (OEM) that seeks to benefit from a recognized ingredient brand; for example, some computer manufacturers are benefiting from the quality image of using an Intel chip.

Ingredient branding
The supplier delivers an important key component to the final OEM product, e.g. Intel delivers its processor to the major PC manufacturers.

However, **ingredient branding** is not suitable for every supplier of components. An ingredient supplier should fulfil the following requirements:

● The ingredient supplier should be offering a product that has a substantial advantage over existing products. DuPont's Teflon, NutraSweet, Intel chips and the Dolby noise reduction system are all examples of major technological innovations, the result of large investments in R&D.
● The ingredient should be critical to the success of the final product. NutraSweet is not only a low-calorie sweetener, but has a taste that is nearly identical to that of sugar.

Single brand versus multiple brands (single market)

A single brand or family brand (for a number of products) may be helpful in convincing consumers that each product is of the same quality or meets certain standards. In other words, when a single brand in a single market is marketed by the manufacturer, the brand is assured of receiving full attention for maximum impact.

The company may also choose to market several (multiple) brands in a single market. This is based on the assumption that the market is heterogeneous and consists of several segments.

EXHIBIT 14.10 Roundup – a global brand for multiple markets

Roundup is the brand name of a broad-spectrum herbicide produced by the US company Monsanto. Containing the active ingredient glyphosate, Roundup is referred to as a non-selective herbicide, meaning it removes most weeds. Monsanto developed and patented glyphosate herbicide in the 1970s. The original Roundup was introduced in 1974 in the US. The brand is registered in more than 130 countries. Glyphosate is the most used herbicide in the world, and Roundup is the number one-selling herbicide worldwide since at least 1980.

In the late 1990s, Roundup became the best-selling agricultural chemical of all times and a profitable product for Monsanto. This success was the result of several factors. One was a conscious strategy to reduce price in the US, where patent protection gave it a strong market position until September 2000. Prices were lower outside the US, where patents expired earlier, and between 1995 and 2000, Monsanto reduced the price by an average of 9 per cent a year.

The Roundup line of products represented just over one quarter of Monsanto's revenue in 2012 of US$13.5 billion.

It retained exclusive rights in the US until its US patent expired in 2000, and maintained a predominant market share in countries where the patent expired earlier. Monsanto also produces seeds which grow into plants genetically engineered to be tolerant to glyphosate, which are known as Roundup Ready crops. The glyphosate tolerance-imparting gene contained in these seeds is patented. Such crops allow farmers to use glyphosate as a post-emergence herbicide against most broadleaf and narrowleaf weeds.

Today (2015) more than companies worldwide make glyphosate, and many of them are in China. In 2009–2011, the growing number of producers resulted in an oversupply of generic glyphosate to the world market, and a downward pressure on the world market price. In 2012, this development was reversed as a result of very strong demand caused by sky-high crop commodity prices. As a result the world market price increased by around 70 per cent.

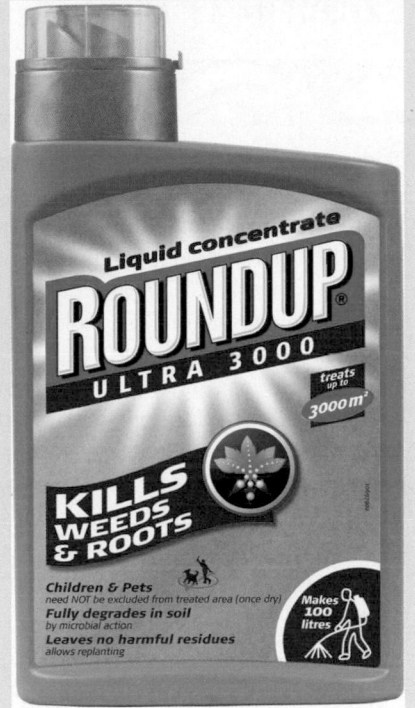

Source: Monsanto Europe S.A.

Overall, in the post-patent world markets, Roundup has maintained its market leadership and a premium position. In consumers' minds, Roundup has become identical with a whole product category.

Source: based on www.monsanto.com and additional public sources. With permission from Monsanto Europe S.A.

Local brands versus a global brand (multiple markets)

A company has the option of using the same brand in most or all of its foreign markets or of using individual, local brands.

A single, global brand is also known as an international or universal brand (see also Exhibit 14.10 regarding Monsanto's Roundup brand). A Eurobrand is a slight modification of this approach, as it is one product for market of 15 or more European countries, with an emphasis on the search for intermarket similarities rather than differences.

A global brand is an appropriate approach when a product has a good reputation or is known for quality. In such a case, a company would be wise to extend the brand name to other products in the product line. Examples of global brands are Coca-Cola, Shell and the Visa credit card. Although it is possible to find examples of global brands, local brands are probably more common among big multinational companies than people realize

The big MNCs prefer to acquire some local brands instead of using a global brand. This result was confirmed by a 2008 survey, sponsored by Millward Brown. Here the conclusion was that there are relatively few truly global brands and fewer still that manage to create a really strong connection with consumers in many countries (Hollis, 2009).

EXHIBIT 14.11 Maggi – local brands for multiple markets through acquisitions

Today Maggi is a Nestlé brand of instant soups and other instant food products. The original company came into existence in 1872 in Switzerland, when Julius Maggi took over his father's mill. It quickly became a pioneer of industrial food production, aiming to improve the nutrition of workers' families. It was the first to bring a protein-rich legume meal to the market, which was followed by ready-made soup based on a legume meal in 1886. In 1897, Julius Maggi founded the company Maggi GmbH in the German town of Singen where it is still established today. Maggi cubes are used as part of the local cuisine. Throughout many countries, Maggi products, especially bouillon cubes, are widely sold with some repackaging to reflect local terminology. Many multinational companies, such as Nestlé, follow a 'multi-local' strategy like this, preferring to follow specific trends. Thus Nestlé's ready-made soups were launched in different markets in the following ways:

Source: Société des Produits Nestlé SA.

- *Germany*: under the name 'Maggi, 5 Minuten Terrine' and positioned as a practical nutritious food for men and women between 30 and 40;
- *France*: under its own name 'Bolino' (with Maggi in small print) and positioned as an instant snack for the young, single person;
- *UK and Switzerland*: under the name 'Quick Lunch', and positioned as a quick meal approved by mothers;
- *Poland*: under the name 'Flaki – Danie to 5 minut'. Here Nestlé had to adjust the taste of the soup to Polish recipes. At the time of the launch of the Maggi brand there was already a strong Polish brand in existence. However, Nestlé acquired this competitor and the Maggi products were launched under the umbrella brand 'Wineary' (under which Flaki was also introduced).

Generally, Nestlé's international brand strategy within ready-to-made soups is that it wants to behave as a local, and if they cannot do this with Maggi, they acquire a local brand.

Source: adapted from various public sources.

14.9   Sensory branding

Sensory branding
Normally brand communication involves just two senses – sight and hearing. Sensory branding involves all five senses: sight, hearing (sound), smell, touch and taste.

Branding is essentially about building emotional ties between consumer and product. Nearly all the brand communication we experience encompasses just two senses – sight and hearing (e.g. print advertising, TV commercials). Yet the way in which we engage with the world around us uses all five senses: sight, sound, smell, touch and taste. Almost our entire understanding of the world is experienced through our senses. Our senses are our link to memory and can tap right into emotion. Sensory perception is an untapped strategic resource that can have a direct impact on purchasing decisions (Derval, 2012).

It is important to build a 'sensory footprint' for your product to optimize this communication. For example, in Figure 14.18, Product 1 may be a food. It smells nice, tastes good and has a decent texture in the mouth. But it doesn't have a unique sound (like crunching/chewing of the food or the opening of the wrapper) or very engaging package branding. In contrast, another product, Product 2, may be a generic soda and has a recognizable fizzy

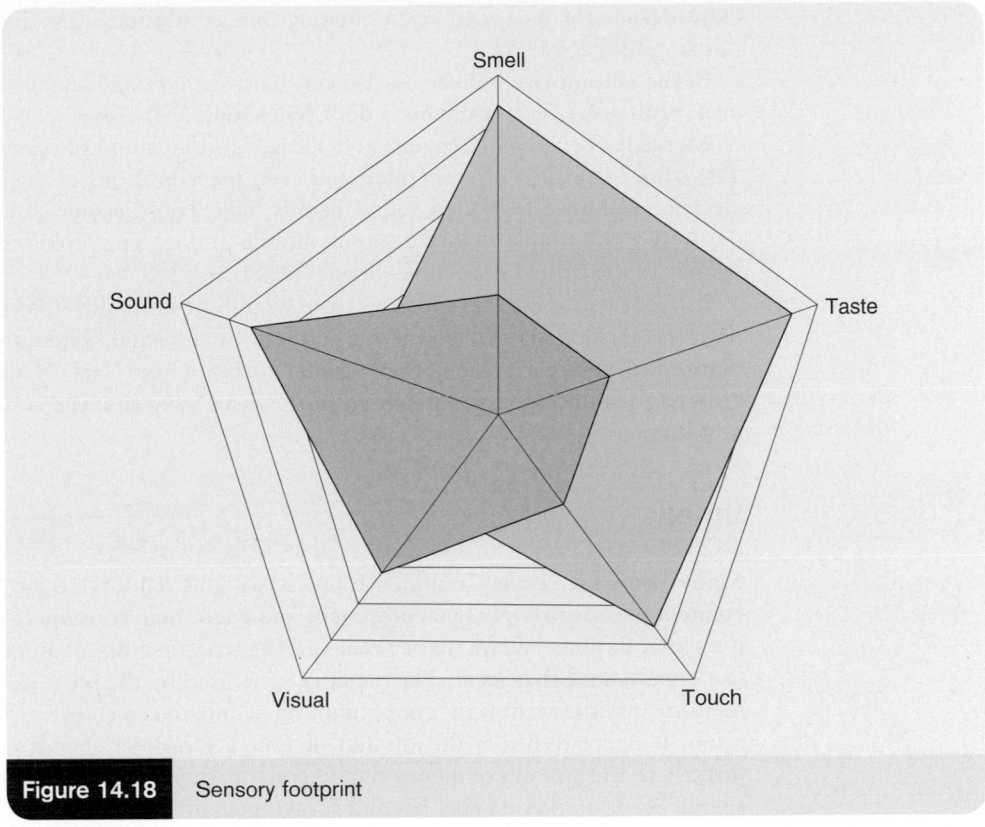

| Figure 14.18 | Sensory footprint |

sound when it's opened and a distinctive logo, but the smell, taste and texture surface (touch) may not be recognizable.

Sight

In some sectors the revolution in sight is already underway. Drinks companies have become expert at using colour to revitalize ageing brands and catch the interest of younger consumers. Gordon's Gin is a classic example. In 2004, the company took its Sloe Gin out of its trademark emerald green bottle (still used for the Original Gin) and repackaged it in clear glass to reveal the rich sloe purple of its ingredients. The move was followed by high-profile advertising, focusing on the 'colourful flavours' and aromas imparted by the herbs in Gordon's three different formulations (Original, Distiller's Cut and Sloe), and positioning the brand as the 'Colorful Gin'.

Drinks companies (perhaps with an eye to the day when alcohol advertising might eventually be banned) are also adept at building sensory cues into brand communications. For an example look no further than Smirnoff Ice, which builds TV, web-based and experiential marketing campaigns (featuring public snowball fights) around Uri – a fictitious Smirnoff Ice drinker who lives in the frozen wastes of eastern Europe – aimed, one might guess, at forging a mental link between Smirnoff's fantasy world of ice and the generic pleasure of drinking ice-cold spirits.

Sound

'Sonic branding' represents the process of using music and sound in the branding process. For example, a 'music' has for many years been used as a part of the retail experience as a means of strengthening and communicating the retail brand identity (Gustafsson, 2015).

In the automotive industry, advances in acoustic design enable manufacturers to engineer, with great precision, how a door will sound as it closes.

Mercedes-Benz has 12 engineers dedicated to the sound of opening and closing doors. The sound is artificially generated and even the vibrations in the door are generated by electric impulses. Neglected sound details have even become powerful tools. In earlier days, take the simple ring of a Nokia mobile phone. The Nokia tune created awareness similar to the 'Intel Inside' tune (Steiner, 2014).

It is not enough for brands to create a sound that is different from that of the competitors; it must also be distinctive enough for the legal system to allow it to be trademarked. Kellogg's trademarked crunchy sound and feel of eating cornflakes was created in sound labs and patented in the same way that the company owns its recipe and logo.

Smell

Many firms use scents to influence purchases and reinforce their brands. Smells aim to create a pleasant shopping environment and encourage consumers to spend more time in the store. Experts believe that a scent can trigger a memory of an occasion when a person last experienced that scent. The memory generated by the scent is known as a contextual memory and the scent is the cue prompting people to remember a specific or familiar situation. It is believed that the amount of time a customer spends in a retail store relates directly to the amount of money they spend, i.e. the longer they stay the more money they spend. Scent marketing goes beyond spraying an air freshener to make a room smell nice; the choice of smell is based on specific research analysing what smells encourage customers to visit a store and purchase the products (on offer) once they have entered the store. The choice of smell will depend on the retailer and its products (see Exhibit 14.11 regarding Starbucks' use of scent marketing).

When Rolls-Royce started getting complaints about its new models not quite living up to the predecessors, it found out that the only difference was the smell. The interiors of older Rolls-Royce cars smelt of natural substances like wood, leather, hessian and wool. Modern safety regulations mean that most of these materials are no longer used, and have been replaced by foams and plastics. Using a 1965 Silver Cloud as a reference, the Rolls-Royce team spent a considerable amount of time recreating the 'original' smell of Rolls-Royce. Today, before each new Rolls-Royce leaves the factory, the unique smell of Rolls-Royce is added to the underside of the car's seats to recreate the 'classic' Rolls-Royce.

Early in 2000, Crayola needed to protect its brand from the many unauthorized competitors in Asia. It is difficult to protect a colour pen which draws generic colours, and even harder to differentiate the product when the logo is barely recognizable. Crayola decided to leverage the smell. By analysing the scent of the original pen, Crayola artificially manufactured the smell and patented it, making it impossible to imitate. Today the smell of Crayola colour pens takes adults back to their childhood. The very characteristic smell is an essential component of the Crayola product with the aim of stimulating the memory of generations of kids in years to come.

Print magazine ads have also been finding creative new ways to engage readers. One method that some print magazine advertisers have been using is so called 'call-to-sniff' ads, or scented paper ads. It is a way to grab readers 'by the nose' and engage them for a longer period of time, hence enhancing the overall reader experience. Surveys show that the awareness and recall of these scented paper ads are significantly higher compared to control groups, who were not exposed to the scented ads (GfK, 2011; Kinzinger et al., 2014).

EXHIBIT 14.12 Starbucks' expanding product line strategy is causing problems for its 'scent marketing strategy'

In the early 2000s, Starbucks increasingly included food products, other than coffee in their product range. This was done in order to increase the average turnover per restaurant. However, the smell of warm breakfast sandwiches was causing a major brand crisis for the coffee giant around 2008 as the earnings per Starbucks shop fell. The warming breakfast aroma was its biggest problem, overwhelming the coffee aroma that Starbucks views as critical to its experience.

In light of the underperforming stores, Starbucks Chairman and newly-reinstated CEO Howard Shultz pushed a return to his original vision with the emphasis on premium coffee and customer focus. Shultz also announced that the company would be doing away with its heated breakfast sandwiches by 2008 in an effort to make the Starbucks ambiance more about coffee. Starbucks even created an aroma task force to fix the smell 'problem'.

Today, Starbucks enhances the smell of coffee in its stores by injecting coffee smells directly into each store. The idea behind the extra coffee smell is to create the alluring smell that customers expect in a particular environment.

Starbucks wants to create an attractive and comfortable space that is the perfect place to be between work and home. Indeed, the doors of the coffee shop chain are opened not only to offer coffees, but also to create a powerful sensorial experience. In other words, as well as coffee, the Starbucks' marketing strategy can be experienced with the five senses.

Source: based on Nassauer (2014) and other public sources.

Touch

One brand that epitomizes sensory stimulation is Lush, the hand-made cosmetics company. Pass the entrance of a Lush store and you are hit by a rush of fragrance. Lush co-founder Mark Constantine says: 'Packaging is so boring. Smelling and touching is just more fun for the senses.' What is more, he adds, 'If you don't use packaging you can use higher-quality ingredients' (Lindstrom, 2004).

Taste

Taste is an obvious sense for companies that deal with food and beverages, for example Hennessy Cognac, KFC Fried Chicken and Coca-Cola. Every brand in these industries wants to create a unique and specific taste to associate with their brand.

Of all the senses, taste most relies on the others. In fact, nearly 80 per cent of taste is derived from your sense of smell. In order to get a full sensory experience with taste, all other senses must be appealed to:

- sight – appearance, attractiveness, colour, shape
- smell – aroma
- touch – texture, temperature
- sound – consistency, texture.

By its nature, the use of taste is limited primarily to food and beverage products. Kellogg's has spent years experimenting with taste and synergy between sound (crunch) and the taste. When Kellogg's introduced their unique crunch to the market, the brand moved up the ladder.

There are some non-food or beverage products that have been able to incorporate this sense, such as dental products. It is important to remember that everyone is different in relation to which sense(s) they rely on to validate their experience.

In summary, the general rule of thumb is that the more senses a brand appeals to, the stronger the message will be perceived. Interestingly, stronger bonding directly translates to higher prices that consumers will be prepared to pay.

14.10   Implications of the internet for collaboration with customers on product decisions

Firms are realizing the importance of collaboration for creating and sustaining competitive advantage. Collaboration with partners and even competitors has become a strategic imperative for firms in the networked world of business. More recently, scholars in strategy and marketing have focused on collaboration with customers to co-create value (Prahalad and Ramaswamy, 2004).

The internet is an open, cost-effective and ubiquitous network. These attributes make it a global medium with unprecedented reach, contributing to reduced constraints of geography and distance. The internet enhances the ability of firms to engage customers in collaborative innovation in several ways. It allows firms to transform episodic and one-way customer interactions into a persistent dialogue with customers. Internet-based virtual environments allow the firm to engage in interaction with a much larger number of customers without significant compromises on the richness of the interaction (Evans and Wuster, 2000).

Customization and closer relationships

The new business platform recognizes the increased importance of customization of products and services. Increased commoditization of standard features can only be countered through customization, which is most powerful when backed up by sophisticated analysis of customer data.

Mass-marketing experts such as Nike are experimenting with ways of using digital technology to enable customization. Websites that can display three-dimensional images, for example, will certainly boost the attractiveness of custom tailoring.

The challenge is clear: to use IT to get closer to customers. There are already many examples of this. Dell is building a closer relationship with its end-customers by letting them design their own PCs on the internet. These customers can then follow their computers along the various stages of the production process in real time on a personalized website. Such experimentation is advisable because the success of 'build-to-order' models such as Dell's represents a challenge to current 'build-to-stock' business platforms, which Compaq generally uses. Dell's basic business principle is the close relationship between the PC manufacturer and the end-customer, without further intermediaries in the distribution channel. This allows Dell to individualize the computers more to customers' specific needs.

These days computers can also be remotely diagnosed and fixed over the internet, something that may soon be true of many other appliances. Airlines now communicate special fares to preferred customers through e-mails and special websites. Cars will soon have internet protocol addresses, which will make possible a range of personal, in-vehicle information services.

Customers can also be involved in the early stages of product development so that their inputs can shape product features and functionality. Pharmaceutical companies are experimenting with the possibility of analysing patients' genes to determine precisely what drugs should be administered in what dosages.

The transformation in the business platform can be seen in university textbook publishing. This industry – which has seen little innovation since the advent of the printing press – is now in the midst of major changes. Publishers are creating supplementary website links to provide additional ways for students and lecturers to be connected during courses (e.g. www.pearsoned.co.uk and www.wiley.com). The publisher's role, which traditionally was selling textbooks at the beginning of term, is becoming that of an educational consultant or value-adding partner throughout the term.

Dynamic customization of product and services

The second stage of the customer interaction vector focuses on the opportunities and challenges in dynamically customizing products and services. Competitive markets are rapidly eroding margins due to price-based competition, and companies are seeking to enhance margins through customized offerings. Dynamic customization is based on three principles:

1. *Modularity*: an approach for organizing complex products and processes efficiently. Product or service modularity requires the partitioning of a task into independent modules that function as a whole within overall architecture.
2. *Intelligence*: continuous information exchange with consumers allows companies to create products and processes using the best possible modules. Website operators can match buyer and seller profiles and make recommendations based on their shared interests. The result is intelligent sites that learn their visitors' (potential buyers') tastes and deliver dynamic, personalized information about products and services.
3. *Organization*: dynamic customization of products and services requires a customer-oriented and flexible approach that is fundamentally committed to operating in this new way.

How can the internet be integrated in future product innovation?

Figure 14.19 shows some of the implications of the internet on future product innovation. The internet is seen as the medium through which each 'box' communicates with the R&D function in the company, as follows:

- *Design*. Data is gathered directly from the product and is part of designing and developing the product. New product features (such as new versions of software programs) may be built into the product directly from the internet.
- *Service and support*. The service department can perform troubleshooting and correction directly through the internet set-up; for example, a Mercedes car driving on the highway may be directly connected to the Mercedes service department. It will monitor the main functions of the car and, if necessary, make online repairs of, for example, the software of the car.
- *Customer relations*. Data gathered from the product may form part of statistics, comparisons between customers, etc. In this way customers can compare the performance of their product (e.g. a car) with other customers' product, a kind of benchmarking. This may also strengthen an existing customer relationship.
- *Logistics*. Concurrently with increasing demands for just-in-time deliveries, the internet will automatically find the distribution and transport that will take the goods from the subsupplier to the producer and then to the customer in the cheapest and most efficient way (and on time).

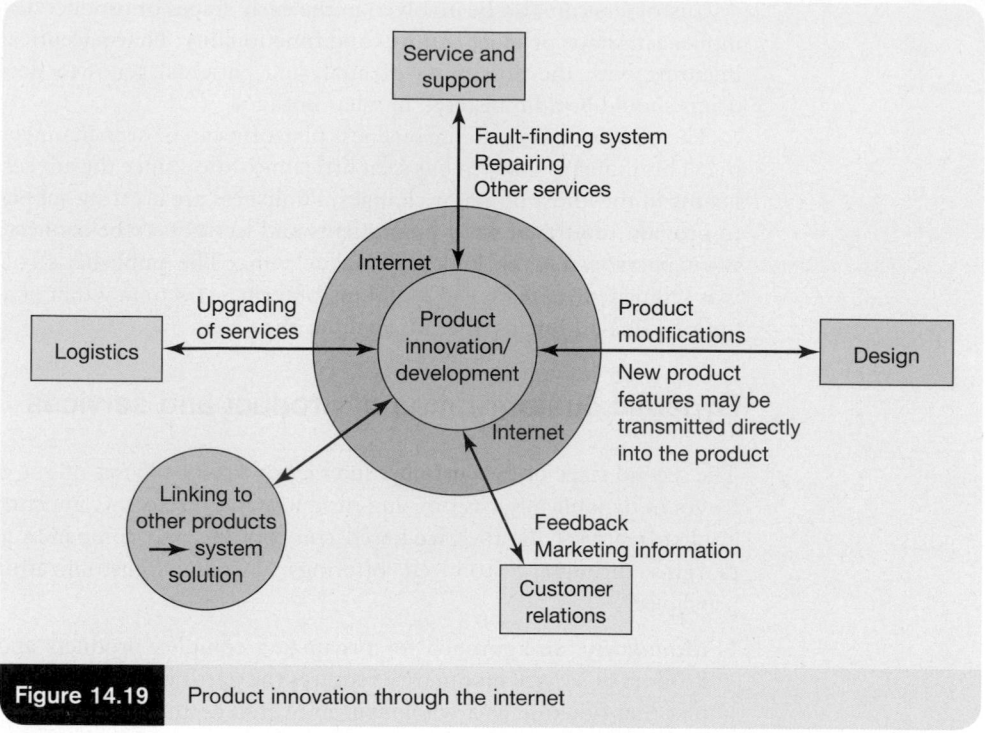

Figure 14.19   Product innovation through the internet

A fundamental shift in thinking is to replace the term 'supply chain' with 'demand chain'. The critical difference is that demand-chain thinking starts with the customers and works backwards. This breaks away from parochial approaches that focus solely on reducing transport costs. It supports a 'mass customization' viewpoint, in which bundles of goods and services are offered in ways that support customers' individual objectives.

This does not necessarily imply product differentiation. In fact, the service aspects often require differentiation. For example, a company such as Unilever will provide the same margarine to both Tesco and Sainsbury's. However, the ways in which the product is delivered, transactions are processed and other parts of the relationship are managed can and should be different, since these two competing supermarket chains each have their own ways of evaluating performance. The information systems required to coordinate companies along the demand chain require a new and different approach to that required within individual companies. Some managers believe that if they and their suppliers choose the same standard software package, such as SAP, they will be able to integrate their information systems.

- *Link to other products*. Sometimes a product is used as a subcomponent in other products. Through links in the internet, such subcomponents may be essential inputs for more complex product solutions. The car industry is an example of an industry that already makes a targeted effort in this direction. New cars may be linked together by the internet in order to communicate, e.g. about technical problems while driving. In the wake of this development, a new industry is created, the purpose of which is to provide integrated transport. In this new industry, developing and producing cars are only two of several important services. In addition, there will be systems that can diagnose cars (and correct the error) while the car is running, systems for regulation of traffic, interactive systems that enable drivers to have the desired transport at their disposal when and where they want it without tiresome rental agreements, and so on.

The music industry is also undergoing a change. Today you can buy portable players that can download music from the internet using the MP3 format, and subsequently play the music that is stored in the player. The CD is becoming obsolete – as is the whole distribution facility. The music industry will become completely altered through these different economic conditions. The struggle will be about creating the best portal to the internet, where the consumer can find the best information on music and the largest selection of music. The problems regarding rights are, however, still being discussed, and the lawyers and politicians have to find a final solution before the market can increase significantly.

Thus innovative product development of the future demands that a company possesses the following characteristics:

- *Innovative product development and strategic thinking.* Product development will contain much technology and demand an interdisciplinary, strategic overview and knowledge in order to find out what new services are worth aiming at.
- *Management of alliances.* Few companies have all the necessary qualifications themselves – innovative product development and the resulting services demand that companies enter into alliances dynamically and in a structured way.
- *New customer relations.* The car industry example above clearly shows that the customers are not car buyers any longer, but *buyers of transport services,* and that is quite another matter. This means that companies have to focus on understanding the customers' needs in a quite different way.

14.11   3-D printing – a possible new industrial revolution in customization

3-D printing

An additive manufacturing process that turns a computer-aided design (CAD) file created on a computer or with a 3-D scanner into a physical object. 3-D printing enables firms to economically build custom products in small quantities, which also allow firms to profitably serve small market segments.

3-D printing, also known as additive manufacturing, turns a computer-aided design (CAD) file created on a computer or with a 3-D scanner into a physical object, allowing users to make almost anything. Unlike traditional manufacturing, which uses subtractive processes, such as grinding, forging, drilling, and cutting, 3-D printing is an additive process, whereby products are built on a layer-by-layer basis, through a series of cross-sectional slices (Berman, 2012).

The largest commercial application for 3-D printing today is rapid prototyping, which accounts for the majority of the 3-D printing market. Rapid prototyping shortens the development life cycle, enables easy experimentation and innovation and saves costs by allowing for easy tweaks and changes to the design.

Increasingly, 3-D printers are being used for direct digital manufacturing. 3-D printing has been applied to making prototypes, mockups, replacement parts, dental crowns and artificial limbs (for the human body). However, the fashion industry is now adopting 3-D printing with designers now 3-D printing jewellery and clothing. 3-D printing will eventually change the way lifestyle products are made and sold. Tailors could customise clothing on a computer and print the products in the local stores. With low-cost 3-D printing, anyone with a digital design can bypass traditional supply chains and self-manufacture a product. Not surprisingly, 3-D printing has created a new generation of at-home and do-it-yourself manufacturers. Microsoft has adapted its popular Kinect device (for its Xbox games console) to make 3-D scanning easy and inexpensive. This can, for example, be used for scanning the human body in order to get the right sizes and styles in clothing.

On the macro level, 3-D printing has the potential to disrupt or destroy traditional models of manufacturing, distribution, warehousing, shipping and retailing. This means that products can be made where they are needed. Future sales will be of designs, not products and, warehouses may be replaced with digital inventories. Lower entry barriers will allow more local and small businesses to prosper. Instead of relying on traditional manufacturing chains, people will design and print their own products or have a local service bureau print it for them. 3-D printing enables firms to economically build custom products in small quantities, which also allow them to profitably serve small market segments.

A shorter travelling distance for products or parts does not only save money; it saves time. Owners of vehicles will appreciate that in future the waiting time at a repair shop while the mechanic waits for a part will be reduced. BMW and Honda, among other automakers, are moving toward the additive manufacturing of many industrial tools and end-use car parts in their factories and dealerships – especially as new metal, composite plastic and carbon-fibre materials become available for use in 3-D printers. Distributors in many industries are taking note, eager to help their business customers capitalize on the new efficiencies. UPS, for example, is building on its existing third-party logistics business to turn its airport hub warehouses into mini-factories. By reducing the need to ship physical products and efficiently using raw materials, 3-D printing saves energy.

3-D printing will eliminate some manufacturing jobs, but it should create others. New jobs, coupled with diminishing cost savings from off-shoring and outsourcing, give 3-D printing the potential to foster a manufacturing come-back in countries with strong intellectual capital but high manufacturing and labour costs.

However, when 3-D printing of complex structures, such as electronic devices, becomes commonplace in the home, 3-D printing may threaten the utility patent system in the same manner that the digital revolution, the internet and file sharing threatened the music industry and the copyright system. Products that are copyrightable, such as dolls, action figures and figurines, and toys, are especially vulnerable to 3-D printing at home. Toys can be scanned and 3-D printed at home, and the designs can be shared peer-to-peer, thereby threatening copyright and design patent protection for such products. Trademark owners may also be affected when branded products are copied at home (Kietzmann *et al.*, 2015).

Managers will need to determine whether it is wise to wait for this fast-evolving technology to mature before making certain investments or whether the risk of waiting is too great. Their answers will differ, but for all of them it seems safe to say that the time for long-term strategic decisions is now.

14.12   Global mobile app marketing

In recent times, perhaps no other consumer electronic device has impacted consumers as much as mobile phones. Mobile devices are everywhere. The total number of unique individual mobile subscribers worldwide is estimated to be around 4.5 billion.

Smartphones make up an increasing share of mobile devices. Mobile penetration is expected to rise from 61 per cent to 70 per cent of the global population between 2013 and 2017.

Due to the roll out of 3G and 4G mobile services across the globe, along with the increasing penetration of smartphones and tablets, the app industry is gaining traction and social media offer new opportunities for the vendors. However, privacy concerns are some of the challenges being faced by the marketers in the app ecosystem.

Mobile app
An application or computer program designed to run on smartphones, tablet computers and other mobile devices.

According to a market research report (MarketsandMarkets, 2015), the global **mobile app** market is expected to grow with an average yearly growth of 15 per cent.

By July 2014, there were 1.3 million Android apps and 1.2 million Apple apps available. On average, smartphone users have about 40 apps on their phones and regularly use about 15. For companies, apps provide ample revenue opportunities. Worldwide revenue from apps was approximately US$12 billion in 2012 and is estimated to increase to over US$60 billion in 2017.

As free apps become increasingly prevalent, paid app downloads are expected to decline, and advertising and in-app purchases are likely to become the main revenue streams in the coming years. With the rise in smartphones and tablets across the globe, the mobile app industry has been rapidly growing. Mobile advertising has seen triple-digit percentage growth each year since 2010.

Mobile apps can be classified into **mobile commerce** and **mobile value-added services** (**MVAS**) (see also the mobile app spectrum in Figure 14.20):

Mobile value-added services (MVAS)

Service for users in a co-production process that works in an integrative and interactive manner via mobile services and offers additional value to the core service or product that it supports.

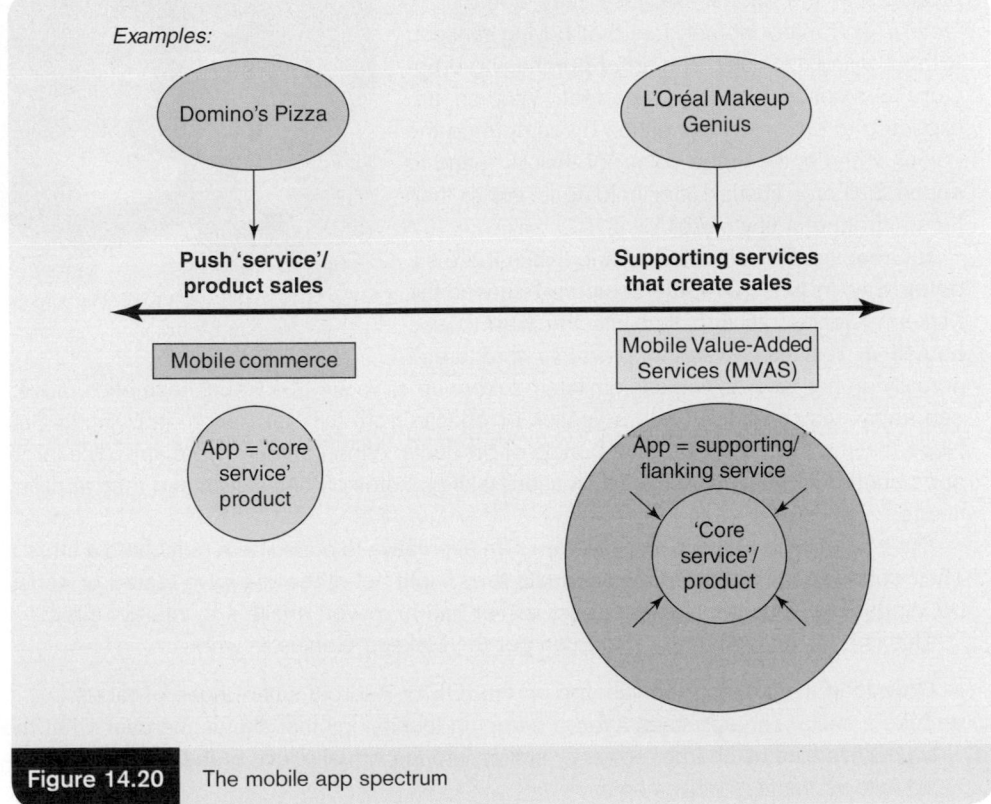

| Figure 14.20 | The mobile app spectrum |

- *Mobile commerce.* Here the app mostly has the purpose of selling a product or a service. For example, the Domino's Pizza app is designed to generate sales and promote special deals to customers.
- *Mobile value-added services (MVAS).* Here the app offers services that are not directly tied to sales but are designed to help customers solve problems or make decisions. Such an app enriches the total customer experience of a product/service offering.

An example of an MVAS is an airline app that can be used to generate a mobile boarding pass (QR code) in a co-production process between the airline and the customer. Conceptually, the core service (the flight) and the MVAS (mobile boarding pass) need to be seen as interrelated constructs building the final customer experience – flight from A to B (Asche and Kreis, 2014).

Similarly, the Makeup Genius app from L'Oreal can be seen as assisting the user in selecting the best makeup in order to build the final service ('looking good and attractive') – see Exhibit 14.13.

EXHIBIT 14.13 L'Oréal is extending the customers' buying experience with the mobile app Makeup Genius

Digitalization is reinventing the rules of the game in the beauty industry.

Many beauty stores found that people unwrap products in the shops, because they don't carry testers, and many women feel that buying makeup without trying it is risky. The art of purchasing drug-store cosmetics is wildly imperfect. Women are expected to choose a foundation by comparing the colour of the bottle to the colour of their arm and to spend $10 on a lipstick after holding it next to their face in front of a tiny mirror.

L'Oréal, the French beauty giant, thinks there's a better way. In June 2014, the company released the Makeup Genius, an app that lets the woman see herself in real time wearing products that aren't

Source: Motoo Naka/AFLO/Nippon News/Corbis.

actually on her face. When she smiles, puckers up or winks, the virtual cosmetics move along with her. She can apply, say, a lip liner with a lipstick or choose from full looks such as Evening Smokey and Jennifer's Nude (as in J. Lo), created with a bundle of products. Although there were already a large number of makeup apps out there, these were based on users taking photos of themselves and then applying makeup to the still image.

For L'Oréal, the Makeup Genius app is an alternative to consumers going into a store to try out cosmetics. Their consumers can try out the products they might not otherwise have tested or considered. This used to be impossible since the manufacturers earlier had to rely on retailers to interact directly with consumers.

This is how the woman (or man) can get the Makeup Genius to work:

● Download the Makeup Genius app on the IOS or Android smartphone or tablet.
● Take a selfie. The app uses a facial mapping technology that shows the user what the makeup looks like on her/his face as she/he moves or smiles into the virtual mirror of the phone's camera. The virtual make-up follows the face movements.

Make-up products (limited to L'Oréal's product range) can be tried out virtually at the touch of a button. The app allows the user to save the results of these virtual makeovers and share them with friends on social media or via e-mail. The app also features different looks from makeup artists – some of them modelled by L'Oréal brand ambassadors such as Freida Pinto.

Once decided, the user can buy the cosmetic products online directly from L'Oréal. A barcode scanner means that the shopper can also try the products virtually in stores too.

Guive Balooch has a PhD in biomaterials and came up with the idea for Makeup Genius together with a fellow biologist during a brainstorming session in 2012. At the time, several cosmetics companies, including L'Oréal, were offering virtual makeup counters on their websites and at drugstores, but most required users to upload a picture and Photoshop lipstick and eye shadow onto the static image – a time-consuming process. Guive Balooch and his Balooch's tech lab (now with 15 engineers and scientists) developed the app for L'Oréal.

Balooch's team tested eye, lip and cheeked products on hundreds of models with varying complexions, capturing how each shade and texture transforms under 400 different lighting conditions. The company also collected more than 100,000 images to compare how the makeup looks on the models in real life vs on-screen.

During development, L'Oréal worked together with Image Metrics, a creator of facial recognition software for video games and movies, including 2008's *The Curious Case of Benjamin Button,* in which the title character, played by Brad Pitt, ages in reverse.

Of course, L'Oréal hopes that the Makeup Genius will lead to more purchases, either through its built-in e-commerce platform or at a local store. Today (2015), around 16 per cent of L'Oréal's media budget goes to digital media, but this is proving very effective. In 2014 alone, L'Oréal's e-commerce beauty sales increased by 20 per cent, up to €800 million. By the end of 2015, the app had been downloaded approximately 15 million times.

Sources: based on Korporaal (2015), Daneshkhu (2014).

Another MVAS app is Kraft Foods, iFood Assistant app, which allows users to browse recipes by occasion or category and then add the necessary ingredients to a shopping list. It includes a recipe box option that lets users access favourite recipes (Urban and Sultan, 2015).

On the spectrum from mobile commerce to mobile services (MVAS), many apps offer on-the-go services paired with location-based technology. Companies employ technology for both geo-coding (based on location latitude and longitude) and reverse geo-coding (translating coordinates into a street address) to deliver accurate locations. One example of a location-based app is the Tinder dating app, which is a social discovery application that facilitates communication between mutually interested users. The Tinder 'matchmaking' app is based on criteria like geographical location and number of mutual friends and common interests. Based on these criteria, the app then makes a list of geographically nearby potential candidates. The app then allows the user to anonymously like another user by swiping right or pass by swiping left on them. If two users like each other it then results in a 'match' and they are then able to chat within the app.

14.13   'Long tail' strategies

Long tail
Long tail refers to a graph showing fewer products selling in large quantities versus many more products selling in low quantities. The low-quantity items (the very broad product range) stretch out on the x-axis of the graph, creating a very long tail that generates more revenue overall. Even though a smaller quantity of each item is sold, there is a much greater variety of these items to sell, and these 'rare' items are very easy to find via today's online search tools.

Anderson's (2006) **'long tail'** is basically a theory of selling that suggests that in the internet era, selling fewer copies to more people is a new strategy that can be successfully pursued. In the past, all the interesting business was around a few hits, and many businesses focused entirely on producing the next hit. The group of people who buy the hard-to-find or 'non-hit' items is the customer demographic called the long tail. Given a large enough availability of choice, a large population of customers, efficient search engines and negligible stocking and distribution costs, it becomes possible, in Chris Anderson's view, to profitably target the long tail.

Anderson (2006) advances two distinct but related ideas:

1. Merchandise assortments are growing because when goods don't have to be displayed on store shelves, physical and cost constraints on selection disappear. Search and recommendation tools can keep a selection's vastness from overwhelming customers. In Figure 14.21 all possible offerings in an imagined product sector are ranked by their sales volume, with the 'blue' part representing products that are unprofitable through brick-and-mortar channels. The long tail, in other words, reveals a previously untapped demand.

2. Online channels actually change the shape of the demand curve, because consumers value niche products geared to their particular interests more than they value products designed for mass appeal. As internet retailing enables them to find more of the former, their purchasing will change accordingly. In other words, the tail will steadily grow not only longer, as more obscure products are made available, but also *fatter* (including the red part in Figure 14.21), as consumers discover products better suited to their tastes.

In Figure 14.21 the power of the long tail is illustrated by an example: the online Rhapsody.com download music company, which has an inventory of some 11 million tracks, receives 40 per cent of its revenue from songs that are simply not available in retail stores. By contrast, a typical Walmart store has a maximum of approximately 40,000 songs on CDs on the shelves, and their top 200 CD albums account for 90 per cent of Walmart's sales because they do not have the space to inventory songs that might sell only once a month. For online stores that use technology to cut their cost of inventory, the amount of total business for objects in the tail increases.

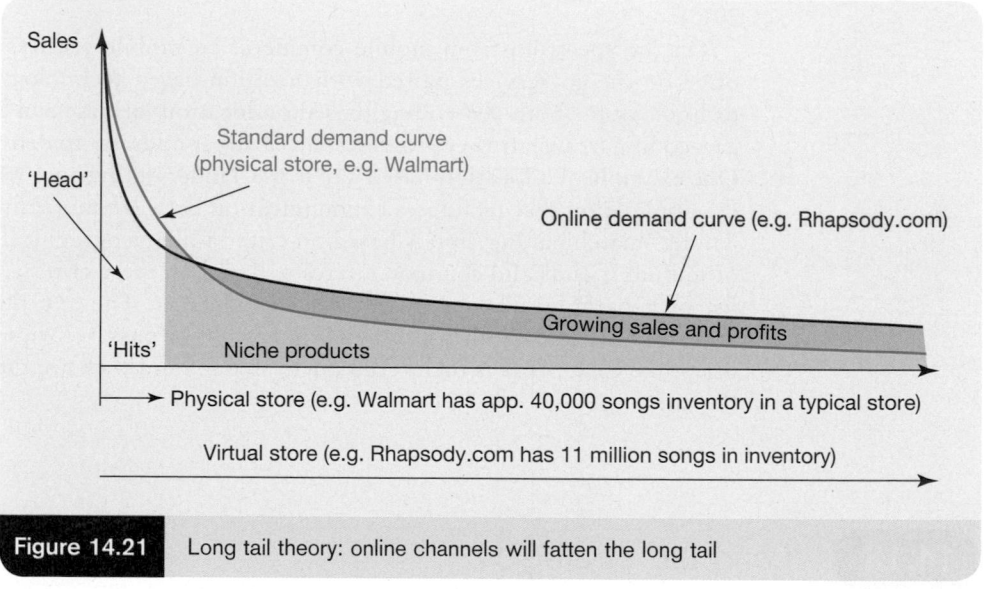

| Figure 14.21 | Long tail theory: online channels will fatten the long tail |

Elberse (2008) tries to prove that Anderson's 'long tail' concept is problematic, and says that consumers are not finding 'hidden gems' out in the long tail: in fact, they are not even venturing into the tail that much. She gives evidence that the activity in the head is even more unusual. What happened? Elberse's (2008) research implies that anything good out on the long tail will quickly be elevated to the head if it has any broad appeal at all because of the way the internet works. It will only be those products of an extremely limited appeal that do not make that jump. Suddenly, a perfectly legitimate long tail buying process has resulted in the 'discovery' of a blockbuster and in the process has ignored the fact that it started out in the long tail.

14.14 Brand piracy and anti-counterfeiting strategies

Until the 1980s, counterfeiting was a relatively small-scale business, restricted mainly to copying luxury fashion items, such as watches and leather goods, in limited quantities. Since the 1990s, it has been transformed into a much bigger, broader industry, with large-scale production and distribution of false versions of different brands (see Exhibit 14.14).

A firm that finds itself exposed to brand piracy has a number of strategic options. These range from identifying and punishing retail outlets to destroying the production facilities of the pirates. The brand manufacturer can also try to convert the pirates into legitimate businesses.

However, piracy is not all negative for the brand manufacturer, if the fake brand and the original brand can be distinguished from each other. In fact, decisions to purchase counterfeits usually reaffirm the brand's values because the recipient buys the product to project the very image that the company is trying to portray through its advertising and promotions. Brand piracy can be seen as a positive indicator of a brand's value as it highlights a brand's strengths. If the company's product is copied, it means it is doing the right thing. Some brands embrace the counterfeit market rather than seeing it as a threat. When Giorgio Armani was on a trip to Shanghai in 2004, he purchased a fake Armani watch for US$22 instead of the US$710 price tag on his authentic watches. He said: 'It was an identical copy of an Emporio Armani watch . . . it is flattering to be copied. If you are copied, you are doing the thing right' (Whitwell, 2006). Although this was a publicity stunt, it does highlight the fact that consumers of fake brands are the opposite of consumers of the authentic product and so pose no significant threat to the brand owner.

EXHIBIT 14.14 The next stage in pirating, faking an entire company – NEC

After two years' investigation, in 2006 the Japanese company NEC discovered a piracy network in China where the pirates were faking their entire company. The counterfeiters had set up a parallel NEC brand with links to a network of more than 50 electronics factories in China, Hong Hong and Taiwan. Using the name NEC, the pirates copied NEC products and went as far as developing their own range of consumer electronic products – everything from home entertainment centres to MP3 players. They even coordinated manufacturing in the way that they required factories to pay royalties for 'licensed' products and issued official-looking warranty and service documents. The products were shipped and packaged in authentic-looking boxes and display cases.

The investigation records showed that the counterfeiters even carried NEC business cards, commissioned product research and development in the company's name and signed production and supply orders.

Many multinational companies (like NEC) are now facing similar challenges as piracy expands and becomes better organized.

Source: adapted from 'Next step in pirating: faking a company – for NEC an identity crisis in China', *Herald Tribune*, 28 April 2006.

Another element of counterfeiting is that it closes off the competition, as the competitors are 'stuck-in-the-middle'. High-priced branded goods encourage the competition to enter the market at a slightly lower price point. Counterfeiters produce branded goods and sell significantly below the cost of competition. This means the competition is squeezed out as it has nowhere to go: it is priced out of the top market by the original brand and cannot compete with the counterfeit whose prices are too low.

14.15 Summary

In deciding the product policy abroad, it is important to decide what parts (product levels) should be standardized and what parts should be adapted to the local environment. This chapter has discussed the variety of factors that are relevant to this decision.

One very important issue is the question of branding. Different branding alternatives have been discussed. For example, because large (often transnational) retail chains have won control over distribution, they try to develop their own labels. For the retailer, private labels provide better profit margins and strengthen its image with its customers. Because of the power shift to the retailers, the percentage of retail grocery sales derived from private brands has increased in recent years.

The basic purposes of branding are the same everywhere in the world. In general, the functions of branding are:

- to distinguish a company's offering and differentiate one particular product from its competitors;
- to create identification and brand awareness;
- to guarantee a certain level of quality and satisfaction;
- to help with promotion of the product.

The products sold over electronic markets and the internet can be grouped into two categories: physical products and purely digital goods and services.

Traditional marketing often views the customer as a passive participant. However, customization sees the customer as a more active partner in the product development and consumption process. An extreme version of customization is the 3-D printing concept. By manufacturing locally on 3-D printers, 3-D printing enables firms to economically build totally customized products in small quantities, which also allow firms to profitably serve small market segments.

Mobile application (or Mobile Apps) is the user-friendly software designed for operation on mobile devices such as smartphones, tablet computers and other hand-held devices. With the rising demand for smartphones and tablet PCs globally, the mobile applications market is expected to grow exponentially during the forecast period. In addition, the demand for mobile application is also driven by the rising penetration of internet-based services across the globe.

The 'long tail' is a theory of selling that suggests that, in the internet era, selling fewer copies to more people is a strategy that can be pursued successfully.

CASE STUDY 14.1

Danish Klassic: launch of a cream cheese in Saudi Arabia

In the spring of 1987, the product manager of Danish Cheese Overseas, KA, was pleased to note that after some decline (e.g. in Iran) feta sales were improving in the Middle East. However, the company was a little concerned that the feta, according to several expert opinions, could lose ground to a cream cheese that was apparently becoming more and more popular among Arabs in both the cities and provincial areas.

Saudi Arabia in general

Because of its immense income from oil, Saudi Arabia had developed fantastically over the previous 30

Table 1	Development in population in the three biggest cities in Saudi Arabia	
	Population (million)	
	1974	**2000**
Riyadh	0.7	2.4
Jeddah	0.6	2.1
Dammam	0.2	0.8

Table 2	Total import of cheese in 1986 (tons)
	Total import
Processed cheese (including cream cheese)	29,500
Feta	18,400
Other types of cheese	2,400
Total	50,300

Source: Saudi Arabian import statistics.

years. With Islamic tradition as its basis, the country had become more modern. In 1987, the population was 11.5 million, more than 50 per cent of whom were under 15 years of age, making Saudi Arabia a 'young' nation. The Saudi Arabian Ministry of Agriculture had forecast that the population would rise to 19 million by 2000. The expected development in population in the three biggest cities at that time is shown in Table 1.

The cheese market in Saudi Arabia

Traditionally Danish Cheese Overseas had had a strong position in Saudi Arabia, having been the market leader for several years, especially as regards feta and some other types of cheese. However, Danish Cheese Overseas had encountered some difficulties in the cream cheese market. The market had risen, but up to that point two large global exporters of cheese had dominated it – France and Australia.

The total import of cheese into Saudi Arabia in 1986 (there was very little local production) is shown in Table 2. The share of cheese from Denmark at that time was about 25 per cent (£10 million). On the basis of this, Danish Cheese decided to develop a new cream cheese in order to compete with the big exporters of cheese within the cream/processed segment. The product was to be targeted at the Middle East, where Saudi Arabia was the main market, but was also to form the basis of an international brand: Danish Klassic.

In order to plan the specific details of the product parameter, Danish Cheese contacted an international market research bureau that specialized in the Middle East. The objective was to analyse the cream cheese consumption among typical Middle East families living in

cities. The final result showed that between 85 and 100 per cent of all family members ate cream cheese on a regular basis (mostly in the middle of the day), and that consumption was especially high among children. Different product concepts were tested among typical families, and the outcome was a 200g cream cheese in brick cartons. This was a new type of packaging – until then cream cheese had mostly been sold in glass packaging.

Marketing plan for Danish Klassic

The following describes the launch actually made by Danish Cheese Overseas in 1987.

An introduction was held in October of that year, in the form of three trade seminars in the largest cities – Riyadh, Jeddah and Dammam. Here the product concept and the advertising campaign were presented to a large number of distributors and wholesalers (see photos a–e).

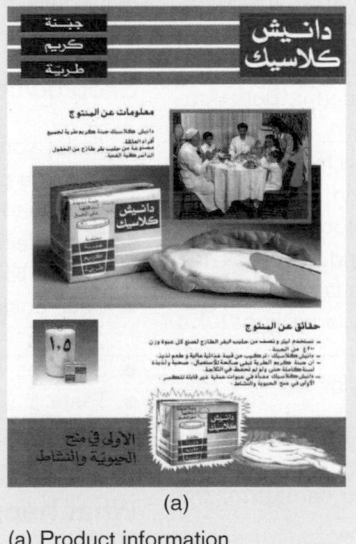

(a)

(a) Product information
Source: Arla Foods.

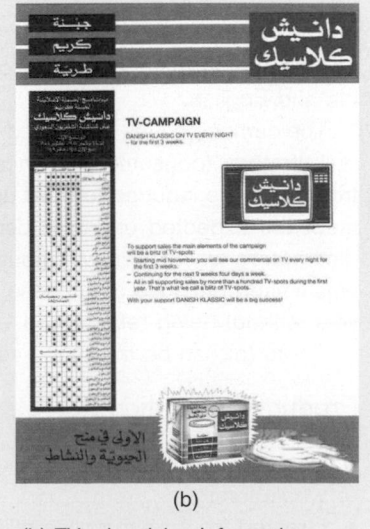

(b)

(b) TV advertising information

(c)

(d)

(e)

(c) Print advertising information   (d) Point-of-sale equipment   (e) Packaging system

Source: Arla Foods.

TV commercials

In Saudi Arabia, television is considered the most effective medium for mass communication. It therefore became the foundation of the company's marketing. In total, 128 commercial spots were planned for the first year (photo b).

Print advertisements

- *Consumer-oriented*: the most popular newspapers and family magazines in the big cities, especially directed at women as the decisive buyer unit (photo c).
- *Distributor-oriented*: trade magazines.
- *In-store promotion*: displays, taste sample demonstrations, etc. (photo d).

The campaign material was introduced in both Arabic and English.

The campaign was influenced by a high degree of pull strategy (consumer influence). In this way, distributors were induced to build up stocks in order to meet the expected end-user demand. The risk the distributors would face when buying large quantities was limited because the cheese could be kept for a year without being refrigerated.

Photo (a) can be translated as follows:

Product information

- Danish Klassic – a cream cheese spread for the whole family.
- Created from fresh cow's milk from the vigorous fields of Denmark.

Product facts

- It takes 1.5 litres of fresh cow's milk to produce a single box of 200-g cheese.
- Danish Klassic is packed in a practical, unbreakable box.
- This cream cheese spread will remain healthy and delicious for a whole year after production – even if not kept under refrigeration.
- Danish Klassic, a combination of high nutritional value and a delicious taste.

This enclosure was also used as an advertisement for many consumer-oriented newspapers and magazines.

Photo (d) can be translated as follows:

Shop demonstrations

- To let your customers know Danish Klassic is in town we plan shop demonstrations in a number of supermarkets all over the country.
- The selected shops will be decorated with giant Danish Klassic boxes.
- Your customers are bound to notice this cream cheese.
- Samples will be distributed.
- Taste it. It's delicious. It's healthy and full of energy.

What happened to Danish Klassic?

About six months after the introduction in Saudi Arabia, a Danish newspaper, the *Jyllands-Posten* (the

Jutland Post), published an article on the new product (24 October 1988):

So far MD Foods has shipped 700–800 tons of the new, long-life cheese from the harbour of Esbjerg, but sales are expected to rise to 5,000 tons per year during the next few years . . . According to the plan, 'Danish Klassic' is to be marketed in Denmark and in other parts of the world such as South America, where it has scored top marks in recent taste tests.

The new long-life cheese that comes in completely sealed 200 g packages is marketed massively through TV spots, the company's own sales representatives, shop promotions and print advertisements. About half of the total investment of DKr30–35 million is allocated to marketing. In this way MD Foods is challenging the multinational food concern, Kraft Foods which, through its various types of cheese in glass packaging, controls the majority of the markets in the Middle East.

Source: Hassan Ammar/Getty Images.

However, at the beginning of 1993 MD Foods realised that Danish Klassic could not meet its international sales budgets: later that year MD Foods withdrew the product from the market.

In 2015 Arla Foods (previously MD Foods) sells cheese to the Middle East through its sales company. The cream cheese and other types of cheese are now sold under the brand 'Puck' (photo e) in glass packaging (the 140 g and 240 g round containers). Its market share of cream cheese is increasing again and today the total sales are very close to those of the market leader Kraft Food.

QUESTIONS

1. What might have been the reasons that Danish Klassic was not able to meet expectations? Comment on the following:
   (a) the change of packaging – from glass to plastic brick carton;
   (b) the consumer-oriented advertisement (photo a) – is it targeted at the Saudi Arabian market?
2. What do you think of the brand name Danish Klassic?

Postscript

On 30 September 2005, the *Jyllands-Posten* published an article entitled '*Muhammeds ansigt*' ('The face of Muhammad'). The article consisted of 12 cartoons, some of which depicted Muhammad.

In late 2005, the Muhammad cartoon controversy received only minor media attention outside of Denmark. Six of the cartoons were reprinted in the Egyptian newspaper *El Fagr* in October 2005, along with a highly critical article, but publication was not considered noteworthy. January 2006, saw some of the pictures reprinted in Scandinavia, then in major newspapers of Denmark's southern neighbours Germany, Belgium and France. Soon after this, as protests grew, the cartoons were reprinted around the globe, but mostly in continental Europe. Several editors in the Middle East were fired for their decision, or even their intention, to republish the cartoons. Critics of the cartoons argued that they were blasphemous to people of the Muslim faith.

Organized boycotts of Danish goods began in several Islamic countries. In Saudi Arabia, people called for a boycott on Danish products on 20 January 2006 and carried it out from 26 January. The boycott primarily targeted dairy products produced by Arla Foods, but also hit other products such as Bang & Olufsen and LEGO. The Foreign Minister of Denmark, Per Stig Møller, stated that the boycott had not been initiated by the Saudi Arabian government. The dairy company Arla Foods launched a massive ad campaign in Saudi Arabia, aiming to improve its reputation and stop the boycott. This happened after sales in Saudi Arabia came to an almost complete stop. Arla's exports to Saudi Arabia were almost €380 million a year. Arla halted production in the Saudi capital Riyadh and sent home 170 employees. Denmark was concerned about the potential loss of 11,000 jobs resulting from boycotts against Danish products in the Islamic world.

However, during 2008 and 2009 the situation eased and by the end of 2009 and forward the sales of Arla products were again above the level for the Middle East region (compared to before the Muhammad cartoons).

Sources: adapted from *The Copenhagen Post Online* (2009): 'Arla back on shelves in Mid-East', Tuesday 20 October, http://www.cph-post.dk/news/international/89-international/47250-arla-back-on-shelves-in-the-mid-east.html; Simmons, J. (2006), 'A war of ideas', 10 February, www.BaghdadMuseum.org; www.arla.com.

CASE STUDY 14.2

Zippo Manufacturing Company: has product diversification beyond the lighter gone too far?

History

Zippo (www.zippo.com) was founded in Bradford, Pennsylvania, in 1932 when George G. Blaisdell decided to create a lighter that would look good and be easy to use. Blaisdell obtained the rights for an Austrian windproof lighter with a removable top, and redesigned it to his own requirements. He made the case rectangular, attached the lid to the bottom with a welded hinge and surrounded the wick with a windhood. Fascinated by the sound of the name of another recent invention, the zipper, Blaisdell called his new lighter 'Zippo', and backed it with a lifetime guarantee. The 80-year-old brand's fame took off during World War II, when Zippo's entire production was distributed through commercial outlets run by the US military.

Zippo's current business model

By June 2012, Zippo had produced over 500 million windproof lighters since its founding in 1932. Except for improvements in the flint wheel and modifications in case finishes, Blaisdell's original design remains virtually unchanged. The lifetime guarantee that accompanies every Zippo lighter still guarantees that 'It works or we fix it free™'.

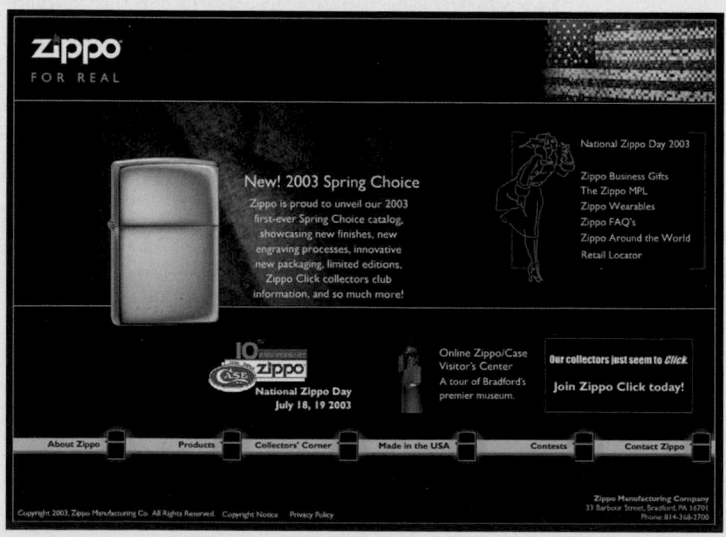

Source: reprinted by permission of Zippo Manufacturing Company.

Source: reprinted by permission of Zippo Manufacturing Company.

Although the windproof lighter is the most popular Zippo product, Zippo has been hurt by anti-smoking campaigns. Its business is fundamentally tied to smokers and it has suffered from US tobacco regulations. Cigarette makers order thousands of Zippos to promote their brands, distributing them to smokers in exchange for coupons.

Due to significant decrease in sales from 18 million lighters a year in the mid-1990s to about 12 million lighters in 2011, combined with increasing pressure on people not to smoke, Zippo decided to try offering a wider variety of products using Zippo brands, such as watches, leisure clothing and eau de cologne.

At the same time, Zippo has expanded its sales operations nationally and internationally through a wide network of sales representatives. In more than 120 countries throughout the world, Zippo is synonymous with US-made quality and craftsmanship.

Zippo windproof lighters enjoy a widespread and enviable reputation as valuable collectibles. The company produces the *Zippo Lighter Collectors' Guide,* containing illustrations of the lighters and descriptions of the series, as well as an explanation of the date code found on the bottom of every Zippo lighter. Clubs for lighter collectors have been organized in the UK, Italy, Switzerland, Germany, Japan and the US. Zippo also sponsors it own collectors' club, Zippo Click.

QUESTIONS

1. What are the pros and cons of the product diversification strategy that Zippo has been following recently?

2. In a US marketing campaign in the late 1990s, Zippo was repositioned as an essential tool for avid outdoorsmen. Individual tin and sleeve packaging was developed that reflected the 'tool' position of the lighter. For continuity, similar packaging and graphics were developed for the cans of Zippo lighter fluid, and the lighters and fluid were delivered to retailers in handy self-shipping counter-top displays. To support the national roll-out, the advertising company (Swanson Russell) developed a communications programme that included direct mail to major outdoor product distributors, as well as advertising at both the trade and consumer levels (pictured on page 552).

   However, the outdoor market was entirely new to the Zippo sales force, who were accustomed to calling on tobacconists and convenience stores. How would you use the product life cycle (PLC) concept for this case study?

3. What obstacles would Zippo Manufacturing Company face if it repeated the outdoor campaign in other countries?

Source: based on different public sources.

VIDEO CASE STUDY 14.3 Burberry branding
download from **www.pearsoned.co.uk/hollensen**

Burberry Group plc (www.burberry.com) is a British luxury fashion house, distributing outerwear, fashion accessories, sunglasses, fragrances and cosmetics. Its distinctive tartan pattern has become one of its most widely copied trademarks. Burberry is most famous for its trench coat, which was designed by founder Thomas Burberry. The company has branded stores and franchises around the world and also sells through concessions in third-party stores. Burberry has more than 500 stores in over 50 countries.

Angela Ahrendts joined Burberry in January 2006, and took up the position of CEO on July 1, 2006 replacing Rose Marie Bravo. The company

Source: David Paul Morris/Bloomberg/Getty Images.

value rose during her stay in Burberry from £2 billion to over £7 billion.

Burberry is nearly 160 years old; its coats were worn in the trenches of World War I by British soldiers, and for decades thereafter they were so much a part of British culture that the company earned a royal warrant, making it an official supplier to the royal family. Sir Ernest Shackleton wore a Burberry during his Antarctic expedition. Movie legends wore them on the silver screen. For more than a century, the Burberry trench coat was cool.

But then in the 1990s and beginning of the 2000s, the Burberry trench coat became uncool. Angela Ahrendts and the rest of the team decided to reinforce their heritage, their Britishness, by emphasizing and growing them into core luxury products, innovating them and keeping them at the heart of everything that they would do. Trench coats are now among the most expensive items burberry sell (many of them are priced at over $1,000), but the staff is least equipped to sell them.

The company transformation paid off. Today, 60 per cent of their business is apparel, and outerwear makes up more than half of that. At the end of the fiscal year 2012/13, Burberry's revenues and profit (before taxes) had doubled over the previous five years, to £2.0 billion and £350 million, respectively.

On October 15, 2013, it was announced that Ahrendts would leave Burberry in Spring 2014 to join Apple Inc. as a member of its executive team as Senior Vice President of Retail and Online Stores. She was followed in spring 2014 by Christopher Bailey. In 2014/15, the revenues were £2.5 billion and the profits (before taxes) were £445 million.

QUESTIONS

1. What are the main motives behind the product line extension from the original Burberry trench coat into other product areas?

2. Please describe the brand transformation process of Burberry. What were the main reasons why Angela Ahrendts were so successful with this brand transformation?

For further resources, see this book's website at **www.pearsoned.co.uk/hollensen**

Questions for discussion

1. How would you distinguish between services and products? What are the main implications of this difference for the global marketing of services?

2. What implications does the product life cycle (PLC) theory have for international product development strategy?

3. To what degree should international markets be offered standardized service and warranty policies that do not differ significantly from market to market?

4. Why is the international product policy likely to be given higher priority in most firms than other elements of the global marketing mix?

5. Describe briefly the international PLC (IPLC) theory and its marketing implications.

6. What are the requirements that must be met so that a commodity can effectively be transformed into a branded product?

7. Discuss the factors that need to be taken into account when making packaging decisions for international product lines.

8. When is it appropriate to use multiple brands in: (a) a single market; (b) several markets/countries?

9. What is the importance of 'country of origin' in international product marketing?

10. What are the distinguishing characteristics of services? Explain why these characteristics make it difficult to sell services in foreign markets.

11. Identify the major barriers to developing international brands.

12. Discuss the decision to add or drop products to or from the product line in international markets.

13. Why should customer-service levels differ internationally? Is it, for example, ethical to offer a lower customer-service level in developing countries than in industrialized countries?

14. What are the characteristics of a good international brand name?

References

Aaker, D. (1991) *Managing the Brand Equity: Capitalizing on the Value of the Brand Name*. The Free Press, New York.

Anderson, C. (2006) *The Long Tail: Why the Future of Business is Selling Less of More*. Hyperion, New York.

Asche, M. and Kreis H. (2014) 'Apps as Crucial Value Components and their Impact on the Customer Experience', *Marketing Review St. Gallen*, 5, pp. 42–50.

Berman, B. (2012) '3-D printing: The new industrial revolution', *Business Horizons*, 55, pp. 155–162.

Bengtsson, A. and Servais, P. (2005) 'Co-branding on industrial markets', *Industrial Marketing Management*, 34, pp. 706–713.

Boudreau, K.J. and Lakhan, K.R. (2013) Using the Crowd as an Innovation Partner, *Harvard Business Review*, April, 61–69.

Cayla, J. and Arnould, E.J. (2008) 'A cultural approach to branding in the global marketplace', *Journal of International Marketing*, 16(4), pp. 86–112.

Cuneo, A., Milberg, S.J., Benavente, J.M. and Palacios-Fenech, J. (2015) 'The Growth of Private Label Brands: A Worldwide Phenomenon?, *Journal of International Marketing*, 23(1), pp. 72–90.

Daneshkhu, S. (2014) 'Make-up enters age of selfie', *Financial Times Europe*, 29 July, p. 8

Derval, D. (2012), 'Tapping the untapped – marketers can learn from product preferences that are simply linked to consumers' physiology', *Marketing Management*, Spring, pp. 24–27.

Devaney, T. and Brown, J. (2008) 'The new brand landscape', *Marketing Health Services*, 28(1), pp. 14–17.

Dhalla, N.K. and Yuspeh, S. (1976) 'Forget the product life concept', *Harvard Business Review*, January–February, pp. 102–112.

Elberse, A. (2008) 'Should you invest in the long tail', *Harvard Business Review*, July, pp. 88–96.

Europanel (2009) *Key Facts for Decision Makers*, Special Edition Report, Europanel, London, June, pp. 2–30.

Ettensén, R. (1993) 'Brand name and country of origin: effects in the emerging market economies of Russia, Poland and Hungary', *International Marketing Review*, 5, pp. 14–36.

Evans, P.B. and Wuster, T.S. (2000) *Blown to Bits: How the New Economics of Information Transforms Strategy*. Harvard Business School Press, Boston, MA.

Fan, Y. (2007) 'Marque in the making', *Brand Strategy*, June, pp. 52–54.

Filiatrault, P. and Lapierre, J. (1997) 'Managing business-to-business marketing relationships in consulting engineering firms', *Industrial Marketing Management*, 26, pp. 213–222.

Fuchs, M. and Köstner, M. (2015) 'Standardisation and adaptation of firms' export marketing strategies in familiar European and non-familiar non-European markets', *European Journal of International Management*, 9(3), pp. 306–325.

GfK (2011) 'Call-to-Sniff: Scented Paper Ads that Appeal to the Senses', *Cover-to-Cover: Insights from Starch Advertising Research into Print Ad Effectiveness*, 8, pp. 1–4

Gruen, T.W. and Hofstetter, J.S. (2010) 'The relationship marketing view of the customer and the Service Dominant Logic perspective', *Journal of Business Marketing Management*, 4, pp. 231–245.

Guiltinan, J.P., Paul, G.W. and Madden, T.J. (1997) *Marketing Management: Strategies and Programs*, 6th edn. McGraw-Hill Companies, Inc., New York.

Gustafsson, C. (2015) 'Sonic branding: A consumer oriented literature review', *Journal of Brand Management*, 22(1) pp. 20–37.

Hollis, N. (2009) 'Rethinking globalization', *Marketing Research*, Spring, pp. 12–18.

Hooley, G.J., Saunders, J.A. and Piercy, N. (1998) *Marketing Strategy and Competitive Positioning*, 2nd edn. Prentice Hall, Hemel Hempstead.

Howe, J. (2006) 'The rise of crowdsourcing', *Wired,* 14 June 2006, pp. 1–4.

Johansson, J.K. and Thorelli, H.B. (1985) 'International product positioning', *Journal of International Business Studies*, 16(Fall), pp. 57–75.

Johansson, J.K., Ronkainen, I.A. and Czinkota, M.R. (1994) 'Negative country-of-origin effects: the case of the new Russia', *Journal of International Business Studies*, 25(first quarter), pp. 1–21.

Keegan, W.J. (1995) *Global Marketing Management*, 5th edn. Prentice-Hall, Englewood Cliffs, NJ.

Keller, K.L. and Sood, S. (2001) 'The ten commandments of global branding', *Asian Journal of Marketing*, 8(2), pp. 97–108.

Kinzinger, A., Stumpf, M., Stiller, B. (2014) 'Duftmarketing: Wirkung von dedufteter Printwerbung, *PRAXIS,* 3, pp. 27–32.

Kietzmann, J., Pitt, L. and Berthon, P. (2015) 'Disruptions, decisions, and destinations: Enter the age of 3-D printing and additive manufacturing', *Business Horizons*, 58, pp. 209–215.

Kotler, P. (1997) *Marketing Management: Analysis, Planning, Implementation and Control*, 9th edn. Prentice-Hall, Englewood Cliffs, NJ.

Korporaal, G. (2015) 'The Changing Face of Cosmetics', *The Deal*, 20th March, pp. 28–21.

Kowalkowski, C, Kindstrom, D. and Brehmer, P.O. (2011) 'Managing industrial service offerings in global business markets', *Journal of Business & Industrial Marketing* 26(3), pp. 181–192.

Lindstrom, M. (2004) *Brand Sense: Build Powerful Brands through Touch, Taste, Smell, Sight, and Sound*. Free Press, New York.

Majaro, S. (1982) *International Marketing: A Strategic Approach to World Markets*, revised edn. George Allen & Unwin, London.

Marketing Science Institute (1995) *Brand Equity and Marketing Mix: Creating Customer Value*, Conference Summary, Report no. 95–111, September, p. 14. Cambridge, MA: MSI.

MarketsandMarkets (2015) *Mobile Value Added Services (MVAS) Market by Solution (SMS, MMS, Mobile Money, Mobile Infotainment, and Others), by End User (SMBs and Enterprises), & by Vertical (BFSI, Government, and Others)–Global Forecast and Analysis to 2020*, Dallas, USA

Michel, S., Brown, S.W. and Gallan, A.S. (2008) 'Service-logic innovations: how to innovate customers, not products', *California Management Review*, 50(3), pp. 49–65.

Nassauer, S. (2014) 'Using Scent as a marketing tool, stores hope it – and shoppers – will linger', *Wall Street Journal*, 20th May, p. 8

Onkvisit, S. and Shaw, J.J. (1989) 'The international dimension of branding: strategic considerations and decisions', *International Marketing Review*, 6(3), pp. 22–34.

Onkvisit, S. and Shaw, J.J. (1993) *International Marketing: Analysis and Strategy*, 2nd edn. Macmillan, London.

Parent, M., Plangger, K. and Bal, A. (2011) 'The new WTP: willingness to participate', *Business Horizons*, 54, 219–229.

Popper, E.T. and Buskirk, B.D. (1992) 'Technology life cycles in industrial markets', *Industrial Marketing Management*, 21, pp. 23–31.

Prahalad, C.K. and Ramaswamy, V. (2004) *The Future of Competition: Co-creating Unique Value with Customers*. Harvard Business School Press, Boston, MA.

Quelch, J.A. and Harding, D. (1996) 'Brands versus private labels: fighting to win', *Harvard Business Review*, January–February, pp. 99–109.

Ratten, V. (2015) 'International Consumer Attitudes Toward Cloud Computing: A Social Cognitive Theory and Technology Acceptance Model Perspective', *Thunderbird International Business Review*, 57(3), May/June, pp. 217–228.

Rubio, N. and Yagiie M.J. (2009), 'The Determinants of Store Brand Market Share: A Temporal and Cross-National Analysis', *International Journal of Market Research*, 51(4), pp. 501–519.

Sawhney, M., Verona, G. and Prandelli, E. (2005) 'Collaborating to create: the Internet as a platform for customer engagement in product innovation', *Journal of Interactive Marketing*, 19(4), pp. 4–17.

Steenkamp, J.-B. and Kumar, N. (2009) 'Don't be undersold', *Harvard Business Review*, 87(12), pp. 90–95.

Steiner, P. (2014) 'Sound Branding: Beispiele aus der Markenführungspraxis', *Praxis*, 60(3), pp. 52–58.

Stieger, D., Matzler, K., Chatterjee, S. and Ladstaetter-Fussenegger, F. (2012) 'Democratizing Strategy: How Crowdsourcing Can Be Used For Strategy Dialogues', *California Management Review*, 54(4), Summer, pp. 44–68.

Urban, G.L. and Sultan, F. (2015) 'The Case for 'Benevolent' Mobile Apps', *MIT Sloan Management*, 56(2), pp. 31–37.

Varadarajan, R. (2009) 'Fortune at the bottom of the innovation pyramid: the strategic logic of incremental innovations', *Business Horizons*, 52, pp. 21–29.

Vargo, S.L. (2009) 'Toward a transcending conceptualization of relationship: a Service-dominant Logic perspective', *Journal of Business and Industrial Marketing*, 24(5), pp. 373– 378.

Vargo, S.L. (2011) 'On marketing theory and service-dominant logic: connecting some dots', *Marketing Theory*, 11(1), pp. 3–8.

Vargo, S.L. and Lusch, R.L. (2004) 'Evolving to a new dominant logic for marketing', *Journal of Marketing*, 68(1), pp. 1–17.

Vargo, S.L. and Lusch, R.L. (2008) 'Service-dominant logic: continuing the evolution', *Journal of the Academy of Marketing Science*, 36(1), pp. 1–12.

Vernon, R. (1966) 'International investment and international trade in the product life cycle', *Quarterly Journal of Economics*, May, pp. 190–207.

Whitwell, S. (2006) 'Faking it can be good', *Brand Strategy*, May, pp. 30–31.

CHAPTER 15

Pricing decisions and terms
of doing business

Contents

Case studies

Learning objectives

After studying this chapter you should be able to:

- Explain how internal and external variables influence international pricing decisions

- Explain why and how prices escalate in export selling

- Discuss the strategic options in determining the price level for a new product

- Explain the necessary sales volume increase as a consequence of a price decrease

- Explain what is meant by experience curve pricing

- Explore the special roles and problems of transfer pricing in global marketing

- Discuss how varying currency conditions challenge the international marketer

- Identify and explain the different terms of sale (price quotations)

- Discuss the conditions that affect terms of payment

- Discuss the role of export credit and financing for successful export marketing.

15.1   Introduction

Pricing is part of the marketing mix, and therefore pricing decisions must be integrated with the other three Ps of the marketing mix. Price is the only area of the global marketing mix where policy can be changed rapidly without large direct cost implications. This characteristic, plus the fact that overseas consumers are often sensitive to price changes, results in the danger that pricing action may be resorted to as a quick fix instead of changes being made in other areas of the firm's marketing programme. It is important that management realizes that constant fine-tuning of prices in overseas markets should be avoided and that many problems are not best addressed by pricing action.

Generally, pricing policy is one of the most important yet often least recognized of all the elements of the marketing mix. The other elements of the marketing mix all lead to costs. The only source of profit to the firm comes from revenue, which in turn is dictated by pricing policy. In this chapter we focus on a number of pricing issues of special interest to international marketers.

15.2   International pricing strategies compared with domestic pricing strategies

For many small and medium-sized enterprises (SMEs) operating in domestic markets, pricing decisions are based on the relatively straightforward process of allocating the total estimated cost of producing, managing and marketing a product or service and adding an appropriate profit margin. Problems for these firms arise when costs increase and sales do not materialize, or when competitors undercut them. In international markets, however, pricing decisions are much more complex, because they are affected by a number of additional external factors, such as fluctuations in exchange rates, accelerating inflation in certain countries and the use of alternative payment methods such as leasing, barter and counter-trade.

Of special concern to the global marketing manager are pricing decisions on products made or marketed locally, but with some centralized influence from outside the country in which the products are made or marketed. Broadly speaking, pricing decisions include setting the initial price as well as changing the established price of products from time to time.

15.3   Factors influencing international pricing decisions

An SME exporting for the first time, with little knowledge of the market environment that it is entering, is likely to set a price that will ensure that the sales revenue generated at least covers the costs incurred. It is important that firms recognize that the cost structures of products are very significant, but they should not be regarded as the sole determinants when setting prices.

Pricing policy is an important strategic and tactical competitive weapon that, in contrast to the other elements of the global marketing mix, is highly controllable and inexpensive to change and implement. Therefore pricing strategies and action should be integrated with the other elements of the global marketing mix.

Figure 15.1 presents a general framework for international pricing decisions. According to this model, factors affecting international pricing can be broken down into two main groups (internal and external factors) and four subgroups, which we will now consider in more detail (see also Kohli and Suri, 2011, for a more comprehensive literature review on these different factors).

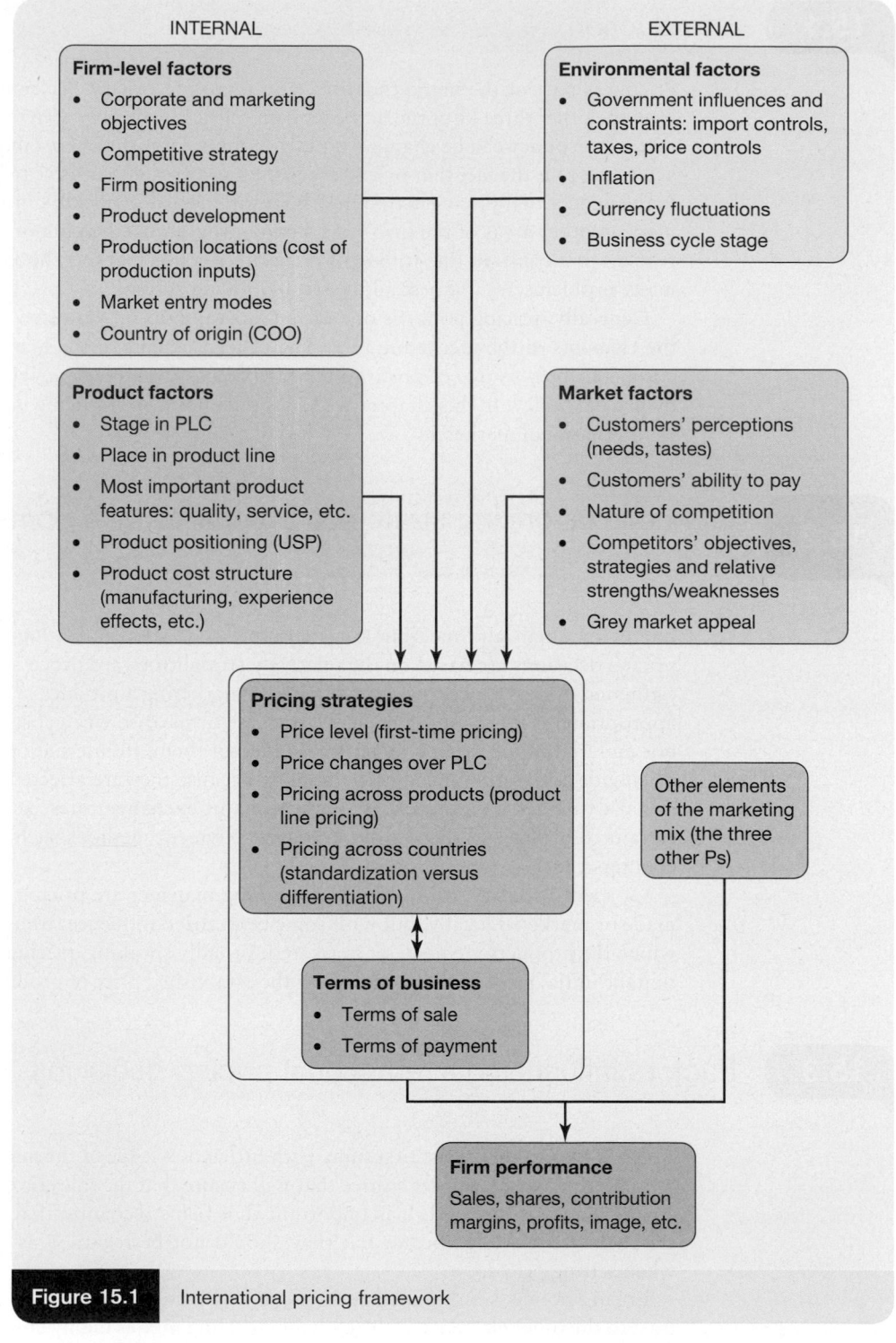

Figure 15.1 International pricing framework

Firm-level factors

International pricing is influenced by past and current corporate philosophy, organization and managerial policies. The short-term tactical use of pricing in the form of discounts, product offers and reductions is often emphasized by managers at the expense of its strategic role, yet in recent years pricing has played a very significant part in the restructuring of many industries, resulting in the growth of some businesses and the decline of others. In particular, Japanese firms have approached new markets with the intention of building market share over a period of years by reducing price levels, establishing the brand name and setting up effective distribution and servicing networks. The market share objectives of these Japanese firms have usually been accomplished at the expense of short-term profits, as international Japanese firms have consistently taken a long-term perspective on profit. They are usually prepared to wait much longer for returns on investments than some of their western counterparts.

Country of origin (COO) is also a major factor that consumers take into account when they make a decision about the maximum price they are willing to pay for a branded product. Managers can use this information in their pricing decisions. If their brand originates and is produced in a country with a good reputation and image, the implementation of a premium pricing strategy will be easier, because consumers' willingness to pay is also likely to be higher. For example, for many years Volkswagen's (VW) slogan has been 'Das Auto' ('The Car'), indicating that the car is developed and manufactured in Germany, although today's car production also takes place in China and other parts of the world. However, this provides the opportunity for VW to charge a higher price to its consumers, compared with, for example, French-produced cars (Koschate-Fischer *et al.*, 2012).

The choice of foreign market entry mode also affects the pricing policy. A manufacturer with a subsidiary in a foreign country has a high level of control over the pricing policy in that country.

Product factors

Key product factors include the unique and innovative features of the product and the availability of substitutes. These factors will have a major impact on the stage of the product life cycle, which will also depend on the market environment in target markets. Whether the product is a service or a manufactured or commodity good sold into consumer or industrial markets is also significant.

The extent to which the organization has had to adapt or modify the product or service, and the level to which the market requires service around the core product, will also affect cost and thereby have some influence on pricing.

Costs are also helpful in estimating how rivals will react to the setting of a specific price, assuming that knowledge of one's own costs helps in the assessment of competitors' reactions. Added to the above is the intermediary cost, which depends on channel length, intermediary factors and logistical costs. All these factors add up and lead to **price escalation**.

Price escalation
All cost factors (e.g. firms' net ex-works price, shipping costs, tariffs, distributor mark-up) in the distribution channel add up and lead to price escalation. The longer the distribution channel, the higher the final price in the foreign market.

The example in Table 15.1 shows that due to additional shipping, insurance and distribution charges, the exported product costs some 21 per cent more in the export market than at home. If an additional distribution link (an importer) is used, the product costs 39 per cent more abroad than at home.

Many exporters are not aware of rapid price escalation; they are preoccupied with the price they charge to the importer. However, the final consumer price should be of vital concern because it is on this level that the consumer can compare prices of different competitive products and it is this price that plays a major role in determining the foreign demand.

Price escalation is not a problem for exporters alone. It affects all firms involved in cross-border transactions. Companies that undertake substantial intra-company shipment of goods and materials across national borders are exposed to many of the additional charges that cause price escalation.

The following management options are available to counter price escalation:

● *Rationalizing the distribution process.* One option is to reduce the number of links in the distribution process, either by doing more in-house or by circumventing some channel members.
● *Lowering the export price from the factory* (firm's net price), thus reducing the multiplier effect of all the mark-ups.

Table 15.1	Examples of price escalation

	Domestic channel	Foreign marketing channel	
	(a)	(b)	(c)
	Firm	Firm	Firm
	↓	↓	↓
		Border	Border
	↓	↓	↓
	Wholesaler	Wholesaler	Importer
	↓	↓	↓
	Retailer	Retailer	Wholesaler
	↓	↓	↓
	Consumer	Consumer	Retailer
			↓
			Consumer
	£	£	£
Firm's net price	100	100	100
Insurance and shipping costs	–	10	10
Landed cost	–	110	110
Tariff (10% of landed cost)	–	11	11
Importer pays (cost)	–	–	121
Importer's margin/mark-up (15% of cost)	–	–	18
Wholesaler pays (cost)	100	121	139
Wholesaler's margin/mark-up (20% of cost)	20	24	28
Retailer pays (cost)	120	145	167
Retail margin/mark-up (40% of cost)	48	58	67
Consumer pays (price) (exclusive of VAT)	168	203	234
per cent price escalation over domestic channel	–	21	39

- *Establishing local production of the product* within the export market to eliminate some of the cost.
- *Pressurizing channel members to accept lower profit margins.* This may be appropriate if these intermediaries are dependent on the manufacturer for much of their turnover.

It may be dangerous to overlook traditional channel members. In Japan, for example, the complex nature of the distribution system, which often involves many different channel members, makes it tempting to consider radical change. However, existing intermediaries do not like to be overlooked, and their possible network with other channel members and the government may make it dangerous for a foreign firm to attempt to cut them out.

Environmental factors

The environmental factors are external to the firm and thus uncontrollable variables in the foreign market. The national government control of exports and imports is usually based on political and strategic considerations.

Generally speaking, import controls are designed to limit imports in order to protect domestic producers or reduce the outflow of foreign exchange. Direct restrictions commonly take the form of tariffs, quotas and various non-tariff barriers. Tariffs directly increase the price of imports unless the exporter or importer is willing to absorb the tax and accept lower profit margins. Quotas have an indirect impact on prices. They restrict supply, thus causing the price of the import to increase.

Since tariff levels vary from country to country, there is an incentive for exporters to vary the price somewhat from country to country. In some countries with high customs duties and high price elasticity, the base price may have to be lower than in other countries if the product is to achieve satisfactory volume in these markets. If demand is quite inelastic, the price may be set at a high level, with little loss of volume, unless competitors are selling at lower prices.

Government regulations on pricing can also affect the firm's pricing strategy. Many governments tend to have price controls on specific products related to health, education, food and other essential items. Another major environmental factor is fluctuation in the exchange rate. An increase (revaluation) or decrease (devaluation) in the relative value of a currency can affect the firm's pricing structure and profitability.

Market factors

Oligopoly
A market structure characterized by a small number of sellers who control the market.

Monopoly
Exists if there is one seller in the market, such as a state-owned company, e.g. a local electricity supplier, postal service company or a gas company. The seller has the control over the market and can solely determine the price of its product.

One of the critical factors in the foreign market is the purchasing power of the customer – the customer's ability to pay. The pressure of competitors may also affect international pricing. The firm has to offer a more competitive price if there are other sellers in the market. Thus the nature of competition (e.g. **oligopoly** or **monopoly**) can influence the firm's pricing strategy.

Under conditions approximating pure competition, price is set in the marketplace. Price tends to be just enough above costs to keep marginal producers in business. Thus, from the point of view of the price-setter, the most important factor is cost. The closer the substitutability of products, the more nearly identical the prices must be, and the greater the influence of costs in determining prices (assuming a large enough number of buyers and sellers).

Under conditions of monopolistic or imperfect competition, the seller has some discretion to vary the product quality, promotional efforts and channel policies in order to adapt the price of the total product to serve preselected market segments. Nevertheless, the freedom to set prices is still limited by what competitors charge, and any price differentials from competitors must be justified in the minds of customers on the basis of differential utility, i.e. perceived value.

When considering how customers will respond to a given price strategy, Nagle (1987) has suggested nine factors that influence the sensitivity of customers to prices:

1. more distinctive product;
2. greater perceived quality of products;
3. consumers are less aware of substitutes in the market;
4. difficulty in making comparisons (e.g. in the quality of services such as consultancy or accountancy);
5. the price of a product represents a small proportion of total expenditure of the customer;
6. the perceived benefit for the customer increases;
7. the product is used in association with a product bought previously, so that, for example, components and replacements are usually extremely highly priced;
8. costs are shared with other parties;
9. the product or service cannot be stored.

Price sensitivity is reduced in all these nine cases.

In the following sections we discuss the different available pricing strategies.

15.4 International pricing strategies

In determining the price level for a new product, the general alternatives are as shown in Figure 15.2.

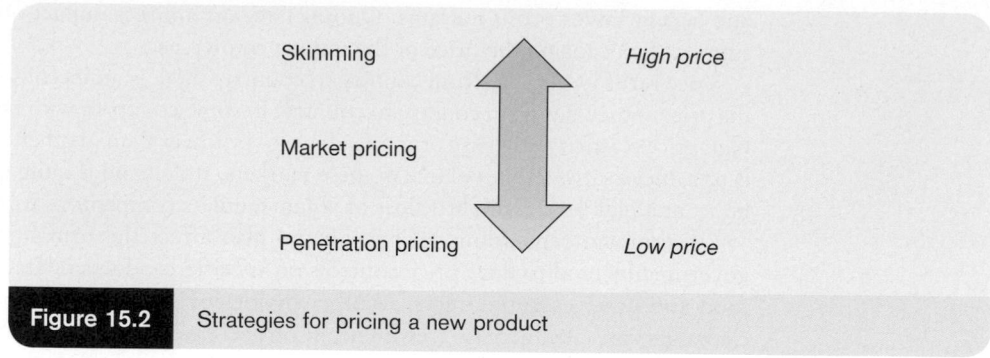

| **Figure 15.2** | Strategies for pricing a new product |

Skimming

In this strategy a high price is charged to 'skim the cream' from the top end of the market, with the objective of achieving the highest possible contribution in a short time. For a marketer to use this approach, the product has to be unique, and some segments of the market must be willing to pay the high price. As more segments are targeted and more of the product is made available, the price is gradually lowered. The success of skimming depends on the ability and speed of competitive reaction.

Products should be designed to appeal to affluent and demanding consumers, offering extra features, greater comfort, variability or ease of operation. With skimming, the firm trades off a low market share against a high margin. One way of calculating the final price is to use the concept of 'customer value-based pricing' by asking: 'How can we create additional customer value and increase the customer willingness to pay'.

Problems associated with skimming are as follows:

- Having a high price but a small market share makes the firm vulnerable to aggressive local competition.
- Maintenance of a high-quality product requires a lot of resources (promotion, after-sales service) and a visible local presence, which may be difficult in distant markets.
- If the product is sold more cheaply at home or in another country, grey marketing (parallel importing) is likely.

EXHIBIT 15.1 German car manufacturers are using 'skimming' price strategy in China

Chinese people just love German cars, especially the premium brands.

From 2009 to 2013, German automobile sales in China more than doubled, from 1.6 to 3.7 million units. German car makers now enjoy a record 23 per cent market share in China – and an increasing proportion of German cars sold in China are being made there. A price analysis of the most popular German brands (Table 1) shows that the premium car brands also get a price premium in China compared to the EU and US, although several factors may contribute to unequal pricing in different markets, including location of manufacturing, volume manufactured, sales volume and different taxation of cars in different countries.

Overall it is estimated that the annual contribution of China to German car makers' total net profits is nearly 50 per cent. However, the flip side of German car makers' growing success in China is their growing

Table 1	Prices of German premium car brands in China compared to EU and US		
All prices are converted to EUR	Audi A6	BMW 5 series	Mercedes E-class
China	€54,000	€60,900	€61,400
EU	€48,600	€51,800	€51,000
US	€37,100	€41,100	€40,700

Note: EU prices are an average of prices in France, Germany, Italy, Spain and UK

dependence on regulatory changes in the Chinese market. In 2014, Chinese regulators took a run at foreign car makers – including Daimler (Mercedes), BMW and VW (Audi), among others – accusing them of monopolistic pricing of spare parts. The car makers have responded by reducing some of the spare part prices.

Source: based on Mitchell, T. (2014) Chinese car probe takes an unexpected turn, *Financial Times Europe*, 22nd August, p. 15; other public sources.

Market pricing

If similar products already exist in the target market, market pricing may be used. The final customer price is based on competitive prices. This approach requires the exporter to have a thorough knowledge of product costs, as well as confidence that the product life cycle is long enough to warrant entry into the market. It is a reactive approach and may lead to problems if sales volumes never rise to sufficient levels to produce a satisfactory return. Although firms typically use pricing as a differentiation tool, the global marketing manager may have no choice but to accept the prevailing world market price.

From the price that competitors are charging in average, it is possible to make a so-called **retrograde calculation** where the firm uses a 'reversed' price escalation to calculate backwards (from market price) to the necessary (ex factory) net price, which should then be compared with the variable costs. If this net price can create a satisfactory contribution margin then the firm can go ahead.

The main advantage of this approach is that the competitive situation is taken into account. The main disadvantage is that aspects related to the demand function are ignored. In addition, a strong competitive focus can increase the risk of a price war (Hinterhuber and Liozu, 2012).

Retrograde calculation
When the firm uses a 'reversed' price escalation to calculate backwards (from market price) to the necessary (ex factory) net price.

Penetration pricing

A penetration pricing policy is used to stimulate market growth and capture market shares by deliberately offering products at low prices. This approach requires mass markets, price-sensitive customers and reduction in unit costs through economies of scale and experience curve effects. The basic assumption that lower prices will increase sales will fail if the main competitors reduce their prices to a correspondingly low level. Another danger is that prices might be set so low that they are not credible to consumers. There are confidence levels for prices below which consumers lose faith in the product's quality.

Motives for pricing at low levels in certain foreign markets might include:

● intensive local competition from rival companies;
● lower income levels of local consumers;

● the belief in some firms that, since their R&D and other overhead costs are covered by home sales, exporting represents a marginal activity intended merely to bring in as much additional revenue as possible by offering a low selling price.

Japanese companies have used penetration pricing intensively to gain market share leadership in a number of markets, such as cars, home entertainment products and electronic components.

EXHIBIT 15.2   A 'market pricing' ('mass point') strategy in use: the Converse brand is making a comeback under Nike ownership

In February 1908, Marquis Mills Converse opened the Converse Rubber Shoe Company in Malden, Massachusetts. The company was a rubber shoe manufacturer, providing winterized rubber-soled footwear for men, women and children. By 1910, Converse was producing 4,000 shoes daily.

The company's main turning point came in 1917 when the Converse All-Star basketball shoe was introduced. Then in 1921, a basketball player named Charles H. 'Chuck' Taylor walked into Converse complaining of sore feet. Converse gave him a job. He worked as a salesman and ambassador, promoting the shoes around the US, and in 1923 his signature was added to the All Star patch. He continued this work until shortly before his death in 1969.

Source: Emka74/Shutterstock.com.

Converse is a less clearly athletic brand, although its roots are in sports and much of its brand equity depends on the vintage Chuck Taylor basketball brand. So today Converse is a much more fashion-aligned brand. Nike has made the brand even edgier and more 'rock and roll'.

Despite its comparatively small size, Converse was an influential player in the sports footwear category for much of the 20th century. A subculture built up around the brand, originally among wannabe basketball players, and it became linked to a perception of non-mainstream 'cool' or trendiness. There was also elitism about the brand. Indeed, despite its mass price point, Converse All Stars were not for everyone, only those with a 'certain knowledge'.

However, Converse shoes started to look dated as the Nike generation came of age and by the early 1990s, Converse was on the brink of bankruptcy. Converse navigated troubled financial waters for the next 10 years before Nike threw the company a buyout lifeline in 2003, in the form of a US$305 million acquisition. It seems unlikely that Converse would have survived much longer on its own, yet that did little to appease diehard fans. To their minds, the independence of the company was integral to its free-spirited identity. There was a feeling that by selling to Nike, the maker of Chuck Taylor All Stars had sold its soul to the enemy.

Despite its 'mass price' point (compared with Nike's premium price point), Converse has paradoxically managed to achieve a bigger 'cool factor'.

At the time of its purchase in 2003, Converse's annual turnover was about US$205 million, compared with US$11 billion at Nike. Eight years later (2011) Converse reported a turnover of US$ 1,150 million. It seems, therefore, that the Converse brand has become 'cooler' and more 'rock and roll' than it was before the Nike acquisition.

Sources: based on Elek, M. (2012), 'How brands close to the edge can keep their cool,' *Marketing Week*, 17/05/2012; Nike annual report, 2011; www.converse.com.

Price changes

Price changes on existing products are called for when a new product has been launched or when changes occur in overall market conditions (such as fluctuating foreign exchange rates).

Table 15.2 shows the percentage sales volume increase or decrease required to maintain the level of profit. An example (the figure in bold type in Table 15.2) shows how the table functions. A firm has a product with a contribution margin of 20 per cent. The firm would like to know how much the sales volume should be increased as a consequence of a price reduction of 5 per cent, if it wishes to keep the same total profit contribution. The calculation is as follows:

Before price reduction

Per product	Sales price	£100
	Variable cost per unit	£80
	Contribution margin	£20

Total contribution margin: 100 units @ £20 =   £2,000

After price reduction (5 per cent)

Per product	Sales price	£95
	Variable cost per unit	£80
	Contribution margin	£15

Total contribution margin: 133 units @ £15 =   £1,995

As a consequence of a price reduction of 5 per cent, a 33 per cent increase in sales is required.

If a decision is made to change prices, related changes must also be considered. For example, if an increase in price is required, it may be accompanied, at least initially, by increased promotional efforts.

When reducing prices, the degree of flexibility enjoyed by decision-makers will tend to be lower for existing products than for new products. This follows from the high probability that the existing product is now less unique, faces stronger competition and is aimed at a broader segment of the market. In this situation, the decision-maker will be forced to pay more attention to competitive and cost factors in the pricing process.

The timing of price changes can be nearly as important as the changes themselves. For example, a simple tactic of time-lagging competitors in announcing price increases can produce the perception among customers that you are the most customer-responsive supplier. The extent of the time lag can also be important.

In one company, an independent survey of customers (Garda, 1995) showed that the perception of being the most customer-responsive supplier was generated just as effectively by a six-week lag in following a competitor's price increase as by a six-month lag. A considerable amount of money would have been lost during the unnecessary four-and-a-half-month delay in announcing a price increase.

Table 15.2	Sales volume increase or decrease (%) required to maintain total profit contribution								
	Profit contribution margin (price – variable cost per unit as % of the price)								
Price reduction (%)	5	10	15	20	25	30	35	40	50
	Sales volume increase (%) required to maintain total profit contribution								
2.0	67	25	15	11	9	7	7	5	4
3.0	150	43	25	18	14	11	9	8	6

Table 15.2	Continued

	Profit contribution margin (price – variable cost per unit as % of the price)								
Price reduction (%)	5	10	15	20	25	30	35	40	50
	Sales volume increase (%) required to maintain total profit contribution								
4.0	400	67	36	25	19	15	13	11	9
5.0		100	50	33	25	20	17	14	11
7.5		300	100	60	43	33	27	23	18
10.0			200	100	67	50	40	33	25
15.0				300	150	100	75	60	43
	Profit contribution margin (price – variable cost per unit as % of the price)								
Price increase (%)	5	10	15	20	25	30	35	40	50
	Maximum sales volume reduction (%) required to maintain total profit contribution								
2.0	29	17	12	9	7	6	5	5	4
3.0	37	23	17	13	11	9	8	7	6
4.0	44	29	21	17	14	12	10	9	7
5.0	50	33	25	20	17	14	12	11	9
7.5	60	43	33	27	23	20	18	16	13
10.0	67	50	40	33	29	25	22	20	17
15.0	75	60	50	43	37	33	30	27	23

Experience curve pricing

Combination of the experience curve (lowering costs per unit with accumulated production of the product) with typical market price development within an industry.

Experience curve pricing

Price changes usually follow changes in the product's stage in the life cycle. As the product matures, more pressure will be put on the price to keep the product competitive because of increased competition and less possibility of differentiation.

Let us also integrate the cost aspect into the discussion. The experience curve has its roots in a commonly observed phenomenon called the learning curve, which states that as people repeat a task they learn to do it better and faster. The learning curve applies to the labour portion of the manufacturing cost. The Boston Consulting Group extended the learning effect to cover all the value-added costs related to a product – manufacturing plus marketing, sales, administration and so on.

The resulting experience curves, covering all value chain activities (see Figure 15.3), indicate that the total unit costs of a product in real terms can be reduced by a certain percentage with each doubling of cumulative production. The typical decline in cost is 30 per cent (termed a 70 per cent curve), although greater and lesser declines are observed (Czepiel, 1992, p. 149).

If we combine the experience curve (average unit cost) with the typical market price development within an industry, we will have a relationship similar to that shown in Figure 15.4.

Figure 15.4 shows that after the introduction stage (during part of which the price is below the total unit cost), profits begin to flow. Because supply is less than demand, prices do not fall as quickly as costs. Consequently the gap between costs and prices widens, in effect creating a price umbrella, attracting new competitors. However, the competitive situation is not a stable one. At some point the umbrella will be folded by one or more competitors reducing the prices in an attempt to gain or retain market share. The result is that a shake-out phase will begin: inefficient producers will be shaken out by rapidly falling market prices, and only those with a competitive price/cost relationship will remain.

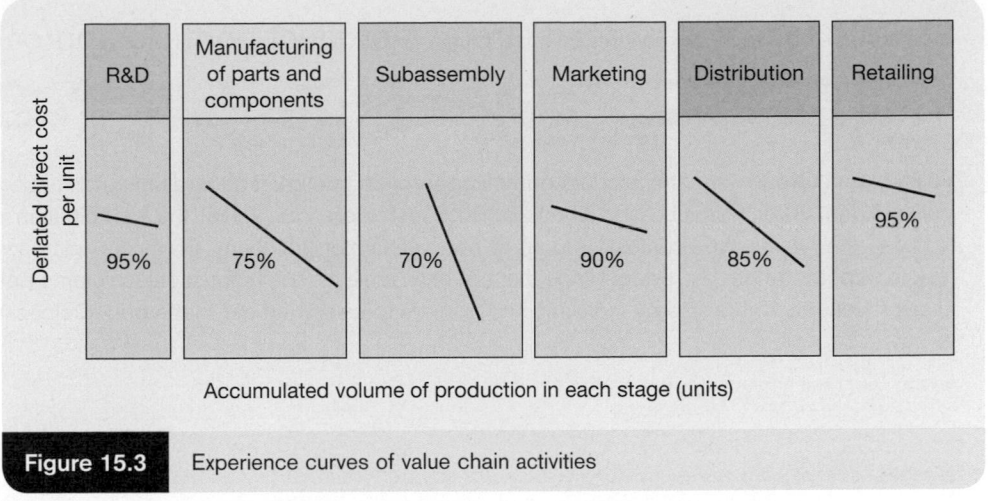

Figure 15.3   Experience curves of value chain activities

Source: Hax, Arnoldo C., Majluf, Nicholas S., *Strategic Management: An Integrative Perspective, 1st*, p. 121 © 1984. Electronically reproduced by permission of Pearson Education, Inc., Upper Saddle River, New Jersey.

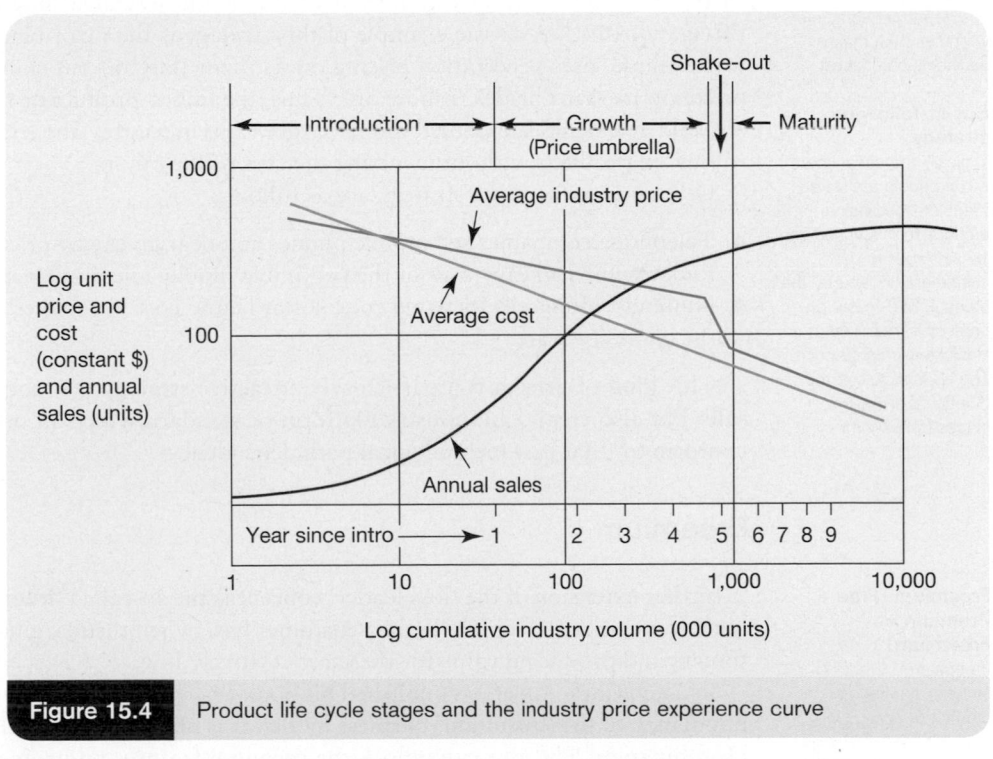

Figure 15.4   Product life cycle stages and the industry price experience curve

Source: Kotler, Philip, *Marketing Management: Analysis, Planning, Implementation and Control, 7th edn.*, p. 350, Prentice Hall © 1991. Electronically reproduced by permission of Pearson Education, Inc., Upper Saddle River, New Jersey.

Pricing across products (product line pricing)

With across-product pricing, the various items in the line may be differentiated by pricing them appropriately to indicate, for example, an economy version, a standard version and a top-of-the-range version. One of the products in the line may be priced to protect against competitors or to gain market share from existing competitors.

EXHIBIT 15.3 Volkswagen Group's product portfolio approach to pricing

Volkswagen Group uses the product portfolio approach to market an array of autos under brands that include Volkswagen, Audi, Porsche and Lamborghini. Customers can select the combination of brand, price and features that yields the greatest amount of net satisfaction for them. From the company's perspective, the task is to put together a product range that not only achieves the highest sales volume possible but also maximizes revenues and profits by motivating customers to select the car that's priced closest to their willingness to pay.

Source: based on Bertini and Koenigsberg (2014).

Loss leader
A product priced below cost to attract consumers, who may then make additional purchases.

Buy-in/follow-on strategy
Typically the case where two products are linked together: the original product item is priced very low, in order to get customers 'in' and try the product. The follow-on product is then sold at a significantly higher price. The classic case is the Gillette razor (buy-in) + blades (follow-on).

Products with less competition may be priced higher to subsidise other parts of the product line, so as to make up for the lost contribution of such fighting brands. Some items in the product line may be priced very low to serve as **loss leaders** and induce customers to try the product. A special variant of this is the so-called '**buy in/follow-on**' strategy (Weigand, 1991). A classic example of this strategy is the razor blade link where Gillette, for example, uses penetration pricing on its razor (buy in) but skimming (relatively high price) on its razor blades (follow on). Thus, the linked product or service – the follow on – is sold at a significant contribution margin. This inevitably attracts others who try to sell follow on products without incurring the cost of the buy-in.

Other examples of the strategy are as follows:

- Telephone companies sell mobile phones at a near giveaway price, hoping that the customer will be a heavy user of the profitable mobile telephone network.
- Nintendo often sells its game consoles at below cost but makes a handsome profit on the game software.

This kind of pricing is a particularly attractive strategy if it not only generates future sales but also creates an industry platform or standard which all other rivals must use or conform to (that is, a technological path dependency).

Freemium

Freemium (Free + Premium = Freemium)
Freemium is a pricing strategy by which a product or service is provided free of charge (free), but money is then charged afterwards for more advanced features or functionality (premium).

A further extension of the 'loss leader' concept is the so-called '**freemium**' model, which a marketer can use to rapidly build a customer base when the marginal costs of adding customers and producing value for these are relatively low.

In 2009, Chris Anderson published his book *Free* (Anderson, 2009), which examines the popularity of the 'freemium' business model. It is often used by Web 2.0 and open source IT companies. The user can unlock the premium features on payment of a licence fee, as per the freemium model. Other software manufacturers make all the premium features available for a trial period after which the software stops working. This is not to be confused with the freemium model, where the user has access to a limited free version without time restraint.

For example, in March 2013 Spotify (online music provider, www.spotify.com) had 6 million paying subscribers and 24 million active free users. For revenue, Spotify's free users can stream unlimited music on their desktop, but need to listen to ads every once in a while, providing a revenue stream of 15 per cent of their total revenue. Users can also pay $4.99/month to eliminate the ads and then $9.99/month to eliminate the ads and stream music on any or all devices.

EXHIBIT 15.4 The Gillette price premium strategy

An incrementally innovative new product can enable a firm to command a higher price as well as realize higher margins than the product it replaces in the marketplace. For example, in 1971 the Gillette Safety Razor Company (acquired by Procter & Gamble in 2005) introduced the Gillette Trac II brand, a razor with two blades fitted in a shaving cartridge. In 2006, it introduced the Gillette Fusion brand, fitted with five blades in a cartridge for shaving, plus a sixth blade for trimming. The history of the price per replacement cartridge for Gillette brand razors, spanning the 35-year period from 1971 to 2006, summarized in Table 1, is instructive in this regard.

Table 1	Gillette's price per replacement cartridge (2006 prices, adjusted for inflation)
Gillette product version	**Price per replacement cartridge (2006 prices)**
Gillette II (1971, two-bladed cartridge) – 'Two blades are better than one'	$1.00
Gillette Sensor (1990, spring-mounted blades) – 'Can sense and adjust to the contours of your face'	$1.22
Gillette Mach3 (1998, three blades) – 'You take one stroke, it takes three'	$2.02
Gillette Fusion (2006, five blades plus a trimmer) – 'The comfort of five blades, the precision of one'	$3.00

The price per replacement cartridge adjusted for inflation has increased by 200 per cent.

Source: based on Varadarajan (2009).

Product–service bundle pricing

Bundling product and services together in a system-solution product. If the customer thinks that entry price is a key barrier, service contracts can be priced higher, which allows for lower entry product pricing – the practice in many software businesses.

Product–service bundle pricing

Bundling is selling two or more products or services as a package. For instance, a Colgate toothbrush with Colgate toothpaste. This is a very useful practice: customers get a good price and companies increase their profitability if the probability of the customers buying the second item from them is rather low. It is also helpful in inducing trial for the second item (Kohli and Suri, 2011; Hinterhuber and Liozu, 2014).

The structure and level of pricing are perhaps the most crucial design choice in embedded services. To get pricing right, a company needs a clear grasp of its strategic intent and its sources of competitive advantage and must often make trade-offs between product penetration and the growth and margins of its *service* business.

A company's strategic intent largely determines the appropriate extent of product–service bundling and the *value* attributed to services in such bundles. Companies that focus on enhancing or protecting core products should price their services to improve their product penetration. The pricing strategy to achieve such product pull-through varies according to customer purchasing decisions. Companies can raise the *value* of the product in use and increase its pull-through by bundling products and services into a higher-value solution. If the entry price is a key factor, service contracts can be priced higher, which allows for lower product pricing – the practice in many software businesses. In some cases, companies can raise the price of maintenance service contracts to accelerate the rate of product upgrades. The strategic goal of product pull-through also means that sales and field agents should have some flexibility and authority in the pricing of services. However, companies must still actively manage pricing discipline by ensuring that these salespeople are accountable for the total profitability of the bundles they sell.

By contrast, companies aiming to create an independent, growth-oriented service business should price their offerings to achieve profitable growth and set pricing targets as close to the service's value to customers as competitive alternatives permit. These companies should set pricing guidelines and delegate authority centrally, with relatively limited freedom for sales and field personnel and clear rules for discounting. Bundling prices for services and products is usually a bad idea for a growth platform in services, because within any given customer's organization, the person who buys the service might not be the one who buys the product. It is also difficult to bundle prices while holding both product and service business units accountable for their independent sales and margin targets.

EXHIBIT 15.5 Kodak is following the reverse 'buy-in/follow-on' strategy for its printer and cartridge division

Kodak is a multinational US corporation which focuses on two major markets: digital photography and digital printing. Its revenues in 2011 were US$6 billion, but with a negative operating income of $600 million. In attempting to build a new position in the printer market, Kodak has challenged industry convention with low prices for the ink cartridges for its newest printers. This strategy presents a price opportunity for buyers. The conventional approach by printer manufacturers is the 'buy-in/follow-on' price strategy (cheap printers but expensive cartridges), while Kodak was charging slightly more for the printer and substantially less for replacement ink cartridges.

While the traditional approach means high-volume users effectively subsidize low-volume users, Kodak was targeting high-volume printer users with a better deal based on a different pricing architecture. The role of price is a critical element of the Kodak business model in this sector.

Source: adapted from Piercy *et al.* (2010).

Source: MacFormat Magazine/Getty Images.

The source of competitive advantage – scale or skill – mainly affects pricing structures. If economies of scale drive a business, its pricing should be based on standard units (such as terabytes of storage managed) and it should offer volume discounts to encourage growth in usage. Such companies ought to make the price of any customized variation from their standard service offerings extremely high, since these exceptions push up costs throughout the business.

By contrast, if a service business relies mostly on special skills, it should base its prices on the costs its customers avoid by using its services or on the cost of the next-best alternative. Such value-based pricing requires a sophisticated analysis of a customer segment's total cost of ownership and a deep understanding of the cost structure of the service business. Competitive benchmarks and the cost of deploying the skills should determine the respective upper and lower bounds for these price levels. In the best case, companies can package this intelligence into pricing tools that allow sales and field agents to estimate customer value more accurately and thus improve field-level pricing decisions (Auguste *et al.*, 2006).

Pricing across countries (standardization versus differentiation)

A major problem for companies is how to coordinate prices between countries. There are two essential opposing forces: first, to achieve similar positioning in different markets by adopting largely standardized pricing; and, second, to maximize profitability by adapting pricing to different market conditions. In determining to what extent prices should be standardized across borders, two basic approaches appear:

1. *Price standardization.* This is based on setting a price for the product as it leaves the factory. At its simplest it involves setting a fixed world price at the headquarters of the firm. This fixed world price is then applied in all markets after taking account of factors such as foreign exchange rates and variance in the regulatory context. For the firm, this is a low-risk strategy, but no attempt is made to respond to local conditions and so no effort is made to maximize profits. However, this pricing strategy might be appropriate if the firm sells to very large customers, who have companies in several countries. In such a situation, the firm might be under pressure from the customer only to deliver at the same price to every country subsidiary, throughout the customer's multinational organization. In Figure 15.5 this is exemplified, for example, by the international activities of large retail organizations. Another advantage of price standardization is the potential for rapid introduction of new products in international markets and the presentation of a consistent (price) image across markets.

2. *Price differentiation.* This allows each local subsidiary or partner (agent, distributor, etc.) to set a price that is considered to be the most appropriate for local conditions, and no attempt is made to coordinate prices from country to country. Cross-cultural empirical research has found significant differences in customer characteristics, preference and purchasing behaviour in different countries (Theodosiou and Katsikeas, 2001). The weakness with 'price differentiation' is the lack of control that the headquarters has over the prices set by the subsidiary operations or external partner. Significantly different prices may be set in adjacent markets, and this can reflect badly on the image of multinational firms. It also encourages the creation of parallel importing/grey markets

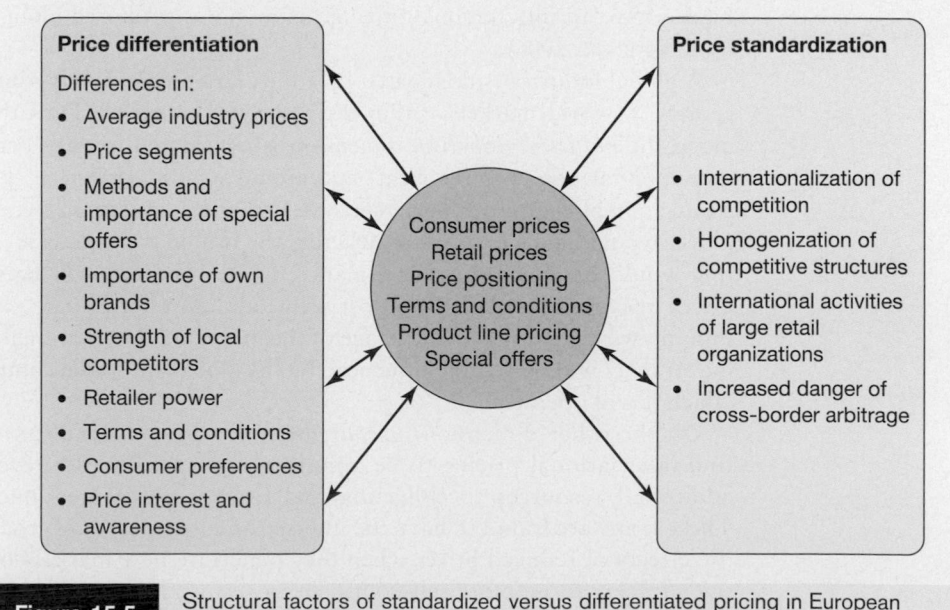

| Figure 15.5 | Structural factors of standardized versus differentiated pricing in European consumer goods markets |

Source: reprinted from *European Management Journal,* vol. 12, no. 2, Diller, H. and Bukhari, I. (1994) 'Pricing conditions in the European Common Market', p. 168, Copyright 1994, with permission from Elsevier.

(which are dealt with in greater detail in Chapter 16), whereby products can be purchased in one market and sold in another, undercutting the established market prices in the process.

A special case arises when the company is selling through intermediaries (agent or importers). Here the cross-border price to the intermediary is set by the manufacturer (the exporter), as this part of the pricing process is under the exporter's control. However, in this case the intermediaries usually carry products from more than one supplier, giving them the freedom to decide which products to promote and not to promote. This puts the exporter in a situation of internal competition with the intermediary's other product lines. To gain the intermediary's attention, the exporter needs to provide a package of attractive benefits to the intermediary, such as value support (in terms of letting the intermediary get access to newest product/service information), high margins, product support payments or cooperative advertising. From an agency theory perspective, such incentives are supplemental revenues provided by the principal to the agent (Obadia and Stöttinger, 2015).

The underlying forces favouring standardization or differentiation are shown in Figure 15.5.

An international pricing taxonomy

As we discussed previously, pricing decisions in the international environment tend to be a function of the interplay between the external, market-related complexities that shape a firm's operations and the capabilities of the firm to respond effectively to these contingencies. Solberg's (1997) framework captures this interface in a meaningful way and leads to sufficiently important consequences for the export pricing behaviour of firms in foreign markets. Solberg suggests that firms' international strategic behaviour is shaped primarily by two dimensions: (a) the degree of globalism of the firm's industry (a measure of the market-related factors); and (b) its degree of preparedness for internationalization (a measure of the firm's abilities to respond to these factors). These two dimensions are discussed in Chapter 1 (Figure 1.1) with the purpose of suggesting under which circumstances the firm should stay at home, strengthen the global position or something in between. In Figure 15.6, an international pricing taxonomy is proposed along these two dimensions (Solberg *et al.*, 2006).

A global industry is dominated by a few, large major competitors that 'rule' their categories in world markets within their product category. Thus the degree of globalism along the *industry globalism* dimension is considered to vary between two extremes: a monopoly at one end (the right) and atomistic competition at the other (the left). The strategic implication of this perspective is that the monopolistic and oligopolistic global player would be the price setter, whereas the firm in the atomistic (multilocal) market setting would be exposed to local market forces, finding itself needing to follow market prices in every case. Although most firms fall into intermediate positions along this continuum, we believe that the leverage of the individual international firm in setting its pricing strategy will be greatly influenced by the globalism of the competitive environment in which it will operate.

On the other dimension, *preparedness for internationalization*, experienced firms find international pricing to be a more complicated matter, even though they devote additional resources to collecting and processing greater amounts of information. These firms are found to have the international preparedness that is necessary to offset the effects of reduced prices when they penetrate new markets or respond to competitive attacks, to be more self-confident in setting pricing strategies and, in general, to enjoy higher market shares in the export market. By contrast, smaller and more inexperienced firms seem to be too weak, both in relation to their local counterparts and in terms of generating local market insight, to be able to determine effective price levels

3 Multi-local price setter • Local market leaders in selected markets • Market-oriented, adapted prices • Local competition	**4 Global price leader** • Global market leaders • Market and cost-oriented 'global' prices • Global competition but local differences
1 Local price follower • Limited resources and leverage • Dependent on local export intermediary • Cost-oriented, standard prices • Unexposed to global forces	**2 Global price follower** • Newcomers to global markets • Market-oriented, standard prices • Global competition but local differences

High / Low — Preparedness for internationalization

Multi-local markets — Global markets

Industry globalism

Figure 15.6 A taxonomy of international pricing practices

Source: adapted from Solberg *et al.* (2006, p. 31). In the original article Solberg has used the concept 'globality' rather than 'globalism'.

for their products in foreign markets. Therefore, they tend to possess smaller shares in their markets and to follow the pricing practices of their competitors or segment leaders.

Looking through the lens of this framework we assume that large, internationally experienced exporters will be likely to centralize their pricing decisions and will prefer higher degrees of control over those decisions, whereas smaller, often new to export and internationally inexperienced firms will be likely to experiment with decentralized and often opportunistic modes of price-setting behaviour in their market.

The following discusses the characteristics of each of the four strategic prototypes in Figure 15.6.

Prototype 1: the local price follower firm

In this cell the firm (manufacturer) will only have limited international experience, and consequently the firm's local export intermediate (agent or distributor) will serve as the key informant for the firm. This information asymmetry bears the danger that the export intermediate might mislead the exporter by exercising opportunism or by pursuing goals that are in conflict with those of the exporter. That may cause further transaction costs, and lead to internalization (see Section 3.3 on transaction cost analysis). Because of limited market knowledge, the exporter is prone to calculate its prices crudely and most likely on the basis of cost and the (sometimes insufficient or biased) information from its local export intermediary. In the extreme case, such an exporter would respond only to unsolicited offers from abroad, and will tend to follow a pricing procedure based on internal cost information, thus missing potential international business opportunities.

Prototype 2: the global price follower firm

Firms that fall into the global price follower cell have limited preparedness for internationalization. By contrast, however, global price follower firms are often more motivated in expanding their international market involvement, as they are 'pushed' by the global market. Firms in this cell are expected to charge a standardized price in all countries because the interconnected international markets have more or less the same price level.

Given their marginal position in global markets, such firms have limited bargaining leverage and may be compelled to adopt the price level set by global market leaders, often very large global customers (see also the discussion about global account management [GAM] in Chapter 19). The prototype 2 firms are typically under constant pressure from their more efficient distribution and globally branded counterparts to adjust their prices.

Prototype 3: the multi-local price setter firm

Firms in this cell are well-prepared international marketers with well-entrenched positions in local markets. Typically they are capable of assessing local market conditions through in-depth analyses and evaluation of market information, established market intelligence systems and/or deeply rooted market knowledge. They tend to have a tight control of their local market distribution networks through information and feedback systems. Prototype 3 firms adapt their prices from one market to the next in light of the differentiated requirements of each local market and manage the different market and pricing structures they cope with in their many (multidomestic) markets with relatively high sophistication.

In contrast to their local price follower counterparts (prototype 1), however, these firms are often the pricing leaders in their local markets and base their pricing strategy primarily on local market conditions in each market. Given their multidomestic orientation, these firms tend to shift pricing decision-making authority to local subsidiary managers, even though their headquarters personnel closely monitor sales trends in each local market. Firms in this cell face challenges from grey market imports in their local markets that are motivated by the opportunity for cheaper producers to exploit price differences across markets (see also Section 16.10 on grey marketing).

Prototype 4: the global price leader firm

Firms in this cell hold strong positions in key world markets. They manage smoothly functioning marketing networks, operating mainly through hierarchical entry modes or in combination with intermediate modes such as joint ventures or alliances in major world markets. Prototype 4 firms compete against a limited number of competitors in each major market, similar to a global (or a regional) oligopoly. Typical of oligopoly players, they tend to be challenged by the cross-border transparency of the price mechanism; manage global (or regional) constraints, such as demand patterns and market regulation mechanisms; and set prices pan-regionally (e.g. across the EU). Global price leaders tend to maintain relatively high price levels in their markets, although possibly not as effectively as their multi-local counterparts. Compared with the global price leader firm, the multi-local price setter more effectively erects local entry barriers, such as brand leadership, and has closer relationships with its local distributors and a deeper understanding of local conditions in each local market, thus protecting itself from the downside of international price competition (Solberg *et al.*, 2006).

Establishing global-pricing contracts

Global-pricing contract
A customer requiring one global price (per product) from the supplier for all its foreign strategic business units (SBUs) and subsidiaries.

As globalization increases, the following is heard frequently among global suppliers and global customers: 'Give me a **global-pricing contract** (GPC) and I'll consolidate my worldwide purchase with you.' Increasingly, global customers are demanding such contracts from suppliers. For example, in 1998 General Motors' Powertrain Group told suppliers of components used in GM's engines, transmissions and subassemblies to charge GM the same for parts from one region as they did for parts from another region.

Suppliers do not need to lose out when customers globalize. The most attractive global-pricing opportunities are those that involve suppliers and customers working together to identify and eliminate inefficiencies that harm both. Sometimes, however, suppliers do not have a choice – they cannot afford to shut themselves out of business with their largest and fastest-growing customers.

Suppliers and customers have different advantages and disadvantages with GPCs, and Table 15.3 illustrates some of these.

One chemicals manufacturer concentrated on relationships with a few select customers. It had decided that its strength lay in value-added services but that potential customers in emerging markets were fixated on price. The select customers, however, were interested in money-saving supply and inventory management initiatives developed jointly with the supplier.

Global customers' demands for detailed cost information can also put suppliers at risk. Toyota, Honda, Xerox and others force suppliers to open their books for inspection. Their stated objectives are to help suppliers identify ways to improve processes and quality while reducing costs – and to build trust. However, in an economic downturn, the global customer might seek price reductions and supplementary services.

Table 15.3	Global pricing contracts: advantages and disadvantages	
	Customers	**Suppliers**
Advantages	Lower prices worldwide coupled with higher levels of service	Easily gain access to new markets and grow the business
	Standardization of products and services offered across markets	Consolidate operations and achieve economies of scale
	Efficiencies in all processes, including new product development, manufacturing, inventory, logistics and customer service	Work with industry leaders and influence market development by using them as showcase accounts
	Faster diffusion of innovations globally	Collaborate with customers and develop strong relationships that are difficult for potential competitors to break into
		Rectify price and service anomalies in a customer relationship across country markets
Disadvantages	Customer might be less adaptable to local market variance and changes over time	Local managers sometimes resist change, and supplier may get caught in the crossfire between customer's HQ and country managers
	Supplier might not have capabilities to provide consistent quality and performance across markets	Supplier might lose the ability to serve other attractive customers
	Supplier might use customer's over-dependence to extract higher prices	Customer might not be able to deliver on promises
	Local managers might resist global contracts and prefer dealing with local suppliers	Customer might take advantage of cost information shared in the relationship
	Costs of monitoring global contracts might outstrip the benefits	Supplier might become over-dependent on one customer, even when there are other, more attractive customers to serve
		Supplier might have a conflict with existing channels of distribution in the new markets

Source: based on Narayandas *et al.* (2000, pp. 61–70).

European pricing strategy

In 1991, price differentials for identical consumer goods across Europe were around 20 per cent on average, but much greater differences were apparent in certain products (Simon and Kucher, 1993). In another study by Diller and Bukhari (1994), there were also considerable price differences for identical take-home ice-cream products.

The causes of price differentials are differences in regulations, competition, distribution structures and consumer behaviour, such as willingness to pay. Currency fluctuations can also influence short-term price differences. The pressures of regionalization are accelerating the move to uniform pricing, but Simon and Kucher (1993) warn that this is a potential time bomb, as the pressure is for uniform pricing to be at the lowest pricing levels.

Europe was a price differentiation paradise as long as markets were separated, but it is becoming increasingly difficult to retain the old price differentials. There are primarily two developments that may force companies to standardize prices across European countries:

1. International buying power of cross-European retail groups.
2. Parallel imports/grey markets. Because of differentiated prices across countries, buyers in one country are able to purchase at a lower price than in another country. As a result there will be an incentive for customers in lower-price markets to sell goods to higher-price markets in order to make a profit. Grey marketing will be examined further in Section 16.10.

Simon and Kucher (1993) suggest a price 'corridor' (Figure 15.7). The prices in the individual countries may only vary within that range. Figure 15.7 is also interesting in light of the euro, which was implemented fully by January 2002. However, price differences that can be justified by transportation costs and short-term competitive conditions, etc. may still be maintained.

The main detailed implications of the euro are that it will:

- lower prices for consumers by making prices transparent across Europe;
- create a real single market by reducing 'friction' to trade caused by high transaction costs and fluctuating currencies;
- enhance competition by forcing companies to concentrate on price, quality and production instead of hiding behind weak currencies;
- benefit SMEs and consumers by making it easier for the former to enter foreign markets and allowing the latter, increasingly via the internet, to shop in the lowest-priced markets;
- establish inflation and interest rate stability via the new European Central Bank;
- lower the costs of doing business through lower prices, lower interest rates, no transaction costs or loss through exchanging currencies and the absence of exchange rate fluctuations.

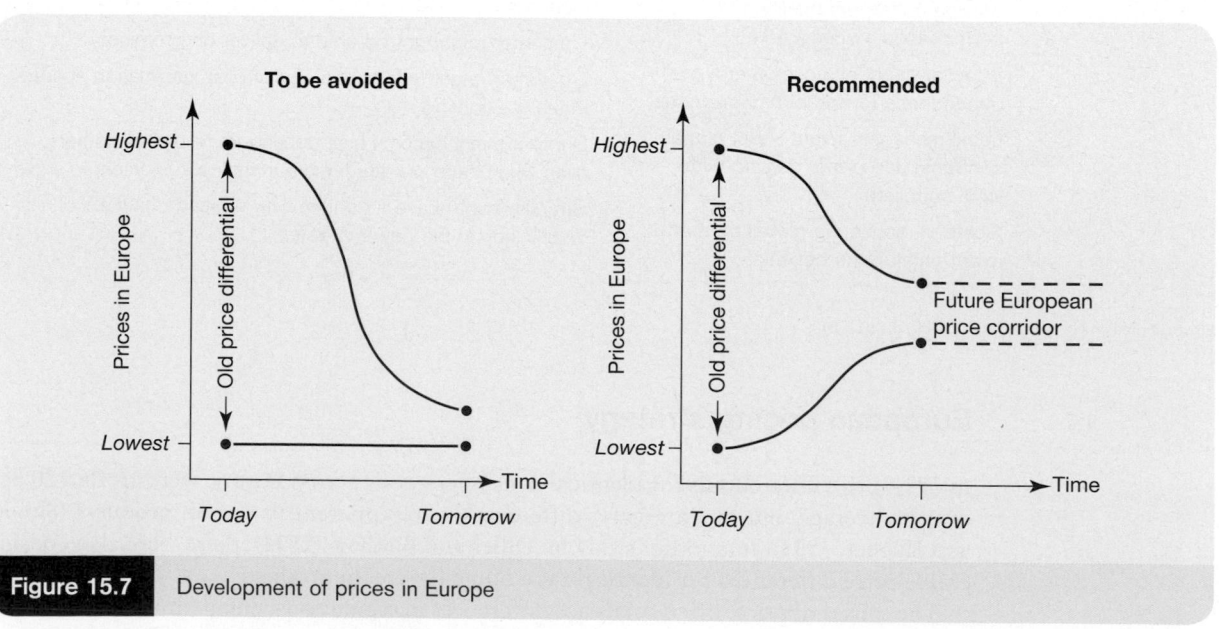

Figure 15.7   Development of prices in Europe

Source: Simon and Kucher (1993, p. 26). Copyright ESOMAR.

In short, the single currency will significantly increase competition, lower transaction costs and bring about greater certainty. These new forces will bring about structural reforms in Europe.

Transfer pricing

Transfer pricing
Prices charged for intra-company movement of goods and services. While transfer prices are internal to the company, they are important externally for cross-border taxation purposes.

Transfer prices are those charged for intra-company movement of goods and services. Many purely domestic firms need to make transfer-pricing decisions when goods are *transferred* from one domestic unit to another. While these transfer prices are internal to the company, they are important externally because goods being transferred from country to country must have a value for cross-border taxation purposes.

The objective of the corporation in this situation is to ensure that the transfer price paid optimizes corporate rather than divisional objectives. This can prove difficult when a company is organized internationally into profit centres. For profit centres to work effectively, a price must be set for everything that is transferred, be it working materials, components, finished goods or services. A high transfer price – for example, from the manufacturing division to a foreign subsidiary – is reflected in an apparently poor performance by the foreign subsidiary (see the high mark-up policy in Table 15.4), whereas a low price would not be acceptable to the domestic division providing the goods (see the low mark-up policy in Table 15.4). This issue alone can be the cause of much mistrust between subsidiaries.

The 'best' of Table 15.4's two mark-up policies seen from the consolidated point of view is to use a high mark-up policy, since it generates a net income of US$550, as compared with US$475 from using a low mark-up policy. The 'best' solution depends on the tax rates in the countries of the manufacturing and distribution affiliates (subsidiaries).

For obvious reasons multinational companies would like to place as much profit in countries with the lowest tax rates. In order to place as much profit in a certain country, the company should set a relatively low transfer price to the subsidiary in the 'low tax rate' country.

Table 15.4	Tax effect of low versus high transfer price on net income (US$)		
	Manufacturing affiliate (division)	**Distribution/selling affiliate (subsidiary)**	**Consolidated company total**
Low mark-up policy			
Sales	1,400	2,000	2,000
Less cost of goods sold	1,000	1,400	1,000
Gross profit	400	600	1,000
Less operating expenses	100	100	200
Taxable income	300	500	800
Less income taxes (25%/50%)	75	250	325
Net income	225	250	475
High mark-up policy			
Sales	1,700	2,000	2,000
Less cost of goods sold	1,000	1,700	1,000
Gross profit	700	300	1,000
Less operating expenses	100	100	200
Taxable income	600	200	800
Less income taxes (25%/50%)	150	100	250
Net income	450	100	550

Note: Manufacturing affiliate pays income taxes at 25%. Distribution affiliate pays income taxes at 50%.
Source: based on Eiteman and Stonehill (1986).

The OECD Transfer Pricing Guidelines were first released in 1995. The latest revision took place in 2010 (OECD, 2010). The OECD Transfer Pricing Guidelines 2010 are more detailed and contain practical suggestions for the comparison of the transaction conditions between associated enterprises and transaction conditions between third parties.

There are three basic approaches to transfer pricing:

1. *Transfer at cost.* The transfer price is set at the level of the production cost and the international division is credited with the entire profit that the firm makes. This means that the production centre is evaluated on efficiency parameters rather than profitability. The production division normally dislikes selling at production cost because it believes it is subsidizing the selling subsidiary. When the production division is unhappy, the selling subsidiary may get sluggish service, because the production division is serving more attractive opportunities first.

2. *Transfer at arm's length.* An 'arm's length price' is a price the subsidiary has to pay for the delivery of goods, services or intangibles under the conditions of perfect competition. In other words, an arm's-length price would be the result of supply and demand in a particular market. That's why it is also called 'market-based pricing'. Here the international division is charged the same as any buyer outside the firm. Problems occur if the overseas division is allowed to buy elsewhere, when the price is uncompetitive or the product quality is inferior, and further problems arise if there are no external buyers, making it difficult to establish a relevant price. Nevertheless the arm's-length principle has now been accepted worldwide as the preferred (not required) standard by which transfer prices should be set (Fraedrich and Bateman, 1996). The 'arm's length principle' is defined in Article 9 of the OECD Model Tax Convention (Buter, 2011).

3. *Transfer at cost plus.* This is the usual compromise, where profits are split between the production and international divisions. The actual formula used for assessing the transfer price can vary, but usually it is this method that has the greatest chance of minimizing executive time spent on transfer-price disagreements, optimizing corporate profits and motivating the home and international divisions. A senior executive is often appointed to rule on disputes.

A good transfer-pricing method should consider total corporate profile and encourage divisional cooperation. It should also minimize executive time spent on transfer-price disagreements and keep the accounting burden to a minimum.

The tax jurisdictions of EU member states have adopted transfer pricing rules which are similar to the OECD guidelines. The predominant preferred transfer pricing rule by countries' tax authorities is the arm's-length principle.

Generally the possibility of manipulation of cross-border transfer prices increases with the complexity of the market conditions. Taking into account the intangibles characteristics of international product markets and the comprehensive price setting of intragroup services being traded between associated enterprises, the arm's-length principle is a fairly theoretical approach, which may be hard to implement in practice.

Currency issues

A difficult aspect of export pricing is the decision about what currency the price should be quoted in. The exporter has the following options:

- the foreign currency of the buyer's country (local currency);
- the currency of the exporter's country (domestic currency);
- the currency of a third country (usually US dollars);
- a currency unit such as the euro.

If the exporter quotes in the domestic currency, this makes it administratively much easier, and also means the risks associated with changes in the exchange rate are borne by the customer. By quoting prices in the foreign currency, on the other hand, the exporter bears the exchange rate risk. However, there are benefits to the exporter in quoting in foreign currency:

- Quoting in foreign currency could be a condition of the contract.
- It could provide access to finance abroad at lower interest rates.
- Good currency management may be a means of gaining additional profits.
- Customers normally prefer to be quoted in their own currency, in order to be able to make competitive comparisons and know exactly what the eventual price will be.

Another difficult problem that exporters face is caused by fluctuating exchange rates. A company in a country with a devalued currency can (all other things being equal) strengthen its international competitive position. It can choose to reduce prices in foreign currencies or it can leave prices unchanged and instead increase profit margins.

When the Italian lira dropped by 15–20 per cent in value against the German mark, it gave the Italian car producer Fiat a competitive advantage in pricing. The German car exporters, such as Volkswagen, were adversely affected and had to lower their list prices. In this respect, the geographic pattern of a firm's manufacturing and sales subsidiaries compared with those of its main competitors becomes very important, because a local subsidiary can absorb most of the negative effects of a devaluation.

15.5   Implications of the internet for pricing across borders

In 2013, nearly 35 per cent of the world's population had access to the internet. By 2015, global online retail sales were expected to reach US$940 billion.

The variation of prices for pure internet sellers is considerably lower than the prices for duo-channel retailers (having both traditional stores and online sales). Buyers perceive less risk in buying online products, which they believe vary little in perceived quality across online sellers. Then buyers are also more likely to minimize the price paid for such items.

Searching for the lowest possible price from alternative sellers can be quite time-consuming in traditional shopping. By contrast, searching online for the lowest price for 'standard' products such as books, airline tickets and pet supplies is normally very convenient, quick and relatively cheap.

Reduction of asymmetric information between sellers and buyers ('lock-in' effects)

The internet search engines help to reduce the asymmetric information between buyers and sellers. Furthermore, demand aggregation sites can connect individual buyers for the same product into buying groups with increased buying power and higher-volume discounts.

As a result, customers may come to think of the price as something they can influence and control, rather than as being given to them.

Although this suggests that prices are lower on the internet, this is not always the case. The online customers are not always as price-sensitive as had previously been thought. Customers become less price-sensitive and more loyal as the level of quality information on the site increases. Also attributes other than price can influence buyers' purchasing decisions, e.g. customer support, online delivery, shipping and handling, product content, ease of ordering and product information.

For example, most customers of Amazon.com are loyal, even though Amazon.com often charges higher prices than other online book retailers. It seems that customers are prepared to pay more to use a reputable seller and will pay more if they have previously visited the seller's website.

Dual-channel pricing

The winning business model in the internet economy seems to be that of the hybrid company using both the traditional retail (physical) stores and the online channels at the same time (the dual-channel strategy). These firms are the so-called 'click and mortar' or 'click and brick' companies. By this strategy, the company can benefit from both online and offline shopping. The internet channel provides the advantages that are mentioned in this section. Compared with the internet channel, the traditional retailing has the advantage that it can provide better personal service, such as sales explanation, immediate response and personal interaction to customers.

When pricing is taken into account, this dual-channel strategy poses a challenge, with possible channel conflicts and 'cannibalism' across channels. However, firms have different options when solving these potential channel conflicts, by taking advantage of different customers' value perceptions. They can choose to offer different products in the two channels (physical stores and online), thus avoiding any possible confusion and conflict. Other companies might choose to offer their products in both channels at the same price, which will also minimize channel conflicts. This is the case, for example, when Vodafone offers its services of a prepaid telephone credit card at the physical points of sale (shop) and then also on its website at the same price conditions.

Other firms may choose to use a mix of the two strategies by offering their products in both channels, but at different prices for different products. In this case, discrimination of prices is again the critical point. Many banking and financial institutions are implementing dual-channel pricing policies by offering their customers different conditions for trading and financial operations in the traditional branch or online. However, most banks offer their customers better price conditions if they do their banking online, resulting in the closure of many physical bank branches.

Dynamic and time-based pricing

The internet provides marketers with the ability to offer special deals tailored specifically for individual customers on all types of products and services. Furthermore, the internet also offers companies the opportunity to test prices, discover new segments and continuously change prices over time, based on customer preferences. For example, airlines may charge different prices online for the same product, resulting in price changes several times per day for the same seat in the aircraft.

Implementing pricing strategies

In implementing pricing strategies on the internet, there are different options:

- *Fixed price mechanism.* Here the seller sets a fixed price for products and services offered to the customer and the latter has to decide whether to buy or not – negotiation is not allowed.
- *Auction mechanism.* Here we can distinguish between classic auctions, where buyers compete to obtain the product on auction by offering the highest price, and reverse auctions, where sellers compete in deciding whether to accept (or not) the price set by the buyer, in a reverse pricing mechanism. For example, Ticketmaster.com (owed by Live Nations Entertainment, Inc.), the ticket sales company based in West Hollywood, California, uses classic auctions to allocate tickets for in-demand concerts to people who value the events the most. The Priceline.com case (with the 'Name your price' slogan) is the best known case of reverse auction.
- *Negotiated price mechanism.* Here sellers and buyers begin a negotiation process in digital networks, starting from a fixed price. Generally speaking, negotiations are more

private and less structured than auctions, and the context of interpersonal relationships often shapes the outcome (Bertini and Koenigsberg, 2014). This version also covers the co-buying process, where some infomediaries can aggregate customers to increase the bargaining power and obtain lower prices.

Since these three 'pure' pricing mechanisms can be mixed, it is possible to have combinations of fixed and negotiated pricing, fixed pricing and auctions, and so on. Thus, when pricing in the digital economy, companies can take advantage of the flexibility and possible combination of these different price mechanisms.

15.6 Terms of sale and delivery

The price quotation describes a specific product, states the price for the product and a specified delivery location, sets the time of shipment and specifies payment terms. The responsibilities of the buyer and the seller should be spelled out as they relate to what is and what is not included in the price quotation and when ownership of goods passes from seller to buyer.

Incoterms (**international commercial terms**) are the internationally accepted standard definitions for terms of sale set by the International Chamber of Commerce (ICC). Thus by agreeing on an Incoterms rule and incorporating it into the sales contract, the buyer and seller can achieve a precise understanding of what each party is obliged to do, and where responsibility lies in event of loss or damage.

The Incoterms rules are revised from time to time in order to reflect developments in commercial practice. The most recent revision is *Incoterms 2010*, which came into force on 1 January 2011 (Ramberg, 2011). *Incoterms 2010* defines 11 rules, reducing the 13 used in *Incoterms 2000* by introducing two new rules (DAT = 'Delivered at terminal' and DAP = 'Delivered at place') that replace four rules of the prior version (DAF = 'Delivered at frontier', DES = 'Delivered ex ship', DEQ = 'Delivered ex quay' and DDU = 'Delivered duty unpaid').

The 11 terms contained in *Incoterms 2010* are:

EXW Ex-works   (. . . named place)
FCA Free carrier   (. . . named place)
FAS Free alongside ship   (. . . named port of shipment)
FOB Free on board   (. . . named port of shipment)
CFR Cost and freight   (. . . named port of destination)
CIF Cost, insurance and freight   (. . . named port of destination)
CPT Carriage paid to   (. . . named place of destination)
CIP Carriage and insurance paid to   (. . . named place of destination)
DAT Delivered at terminal   (. . . named terminal)
DAP Delivered at place   (. . . named place)
DDP Delivered duty paid   (. . . named place of destination)

Table 15.5 describes the point of delivery and risk shift for some terms of sale.
The following is a description of some of the most popular terms of sale:

- *Ex-works (EXW)*. The term 'ex' means that the price quoted by the seller applies at a specified point of origin, usually the factory, warehouse, mine or plantation, and the buyer is responsible for all charges from this point. This term represents the minimum obligation for the exporter.
- *Free alongside ship (FAS)*. Under this term the seller must provide for delivery of the goods free alongside, but not on board, the transportation carrier (usually an ocean vessel) at the point of shipment and export. This term differs from that of FOB, since

Table 15.5	Point of delivery and where risk shifts from seller to buyer						
	EXW	**FAS**	**FOB**	**CFR**	**CIF**	**DAT**	**DDP**
Supplier's factory/warehouse	×						
Dock at port of shipment (export dock)		×					
Port of shipment (on board vessel)			×	×	×		
Port of destination (import dock/terminal)					×[a]	×	
Buyer's warehouse (destination)							×
Main transit risk on	Buyer	Buyer	Buyer	Buyer	Seller	Seller	Seller

[a]The seller transfers the risk to its insurance company.
Sources: based on Ramberg (2011); Onkvisit and Shaw (1993, p. 799).

the time and cost of loading are not included in the FAS term. The buyer has to pay for loading the goods onto the ship.

- *Free on board (FOB)*. The exporter's price quote includes coverage of all charges up to the point when goods have been loaded on to the designated transport vehicle. The designated loading point may be a named inland shipping point, but is usually the port of export. The buyer assumes responsibility for the goods the moment they pass over the ship's rail.
- *Cost and freight (CFR)*. The seller's liability ends when the goods are loaded on board a carrier or are in the custody of the carrier at the export dock. The seller pays all the transport charges (excluding insurance, which is the customer's obligation) required to deliver goods by sea to a named destination.
- *Cost, insurance and freight (CIF)*. This trade term is identical to CFR except that the seller must also provide the necessary insurance. The seller's obligations still end at the same stage (i.e. when goods are loaded or aboard), but the seller's insurance company assumes responsibility once the goods are loaded.
- *Delivered at terminal (DAT)*. This can be used for any transport mode, or where there is more than one transport mode. The seller is responsible for arranging carriage and for delivering the goods, unloaded from the arriving conveyance, at the named place. Risk transfers from seller to buyer when the goods have been unloaded. 'Terminal' can be any place – a quay, container yard, warehouse or transport hub. The buyer is responsible for import clearance and any applicable local taxes or import duties. The place for delivery should be specified as precisely as possible, as many ports and transport hubs are very large.
- *Delivered duty paid (DDP)*. The export price quote includes the costs of delivery to the importer's premises. The exporter is thus responsible for paying any import duties and costs of unloading and inland transport in the importing country, as well as all costs involved in insuring and shipping the goods to that country. These terms imply maximum exporter obligations. The seller also assumes all the risks involved in delivering to the buyer. DDP used to be known as 'Franco domicile' pricing.

Export price quotations are important because they spell out the legal and cost responsibilities of the buyer and seller. Sellers favour a quote that gives them the least liability and responsibility, such as ex-works, which means the exporter's liability finishes when the goods are loaded on to the buyer's carrier at the seller's factory. Buyers, on the other hand, would prefer either DDP, where responsibility is borne by the supplier all the way to the customer's warehouse, or CIF port of discharge, which means that the buyer's responsibility begins only when the goods are in its own country.

Generally, the more market-oriented pricing policies are based on CIF, which indicates a strong commitment to the market. By pricing ex-works an exporter is not taking any steps to build a relationship with the market and so may be indicating only short-term commitment.

15.7   Terms of payment

The exporter will consider the following factors in negotiating terms of payment for goods to be shipped:

● practices in the industry
● terms offered by competitors
● relative strength of the buyer and the seller.

If the exporter is well established in the market with a unique product and accompanying service, price and terms of trade can be set to fit the exporter's desires. If, on the other hand, the exporter is breaking into a new market or if competitive pressures call for action, pricing and selling terms should be used as major competitive tools.

The basic methods of payment for exports vary in terms of their attractiveness to the buyer and the seller, from cash in advance to open account or consignment selling. Neither of the extremes will be feasible for longer-term relationships, but they do have their uses in certain situations. The most common payment methods are presented in Figure 15.8.

The most favourable term to the exporter is cash in advance because it relieves the exporter of all risk and allows for immediate use of the money. On the other hand, the most advantageous option seen from the buyer's perspective would be consignment or open account.

The most common arrangements, in decreasing order of attractiveness to the exporter, are described in the following sections.

Cash in advance

The exporter receives payment before shipment of the goods. This minimizes the exporter's risk and financial costs, since there is no collection risk and no interest cost on receivables. However, importers will rarely agree to these terms, as it ties up their capital and the goods may not be received. Consequently, such terms are not widely used. They are most likely either when the exporter lacks confidence in the importer's ability to pay (often the case in initial export transactions) or where economic and political instability in the importing country could result in foreign exchange not being made available for importers.

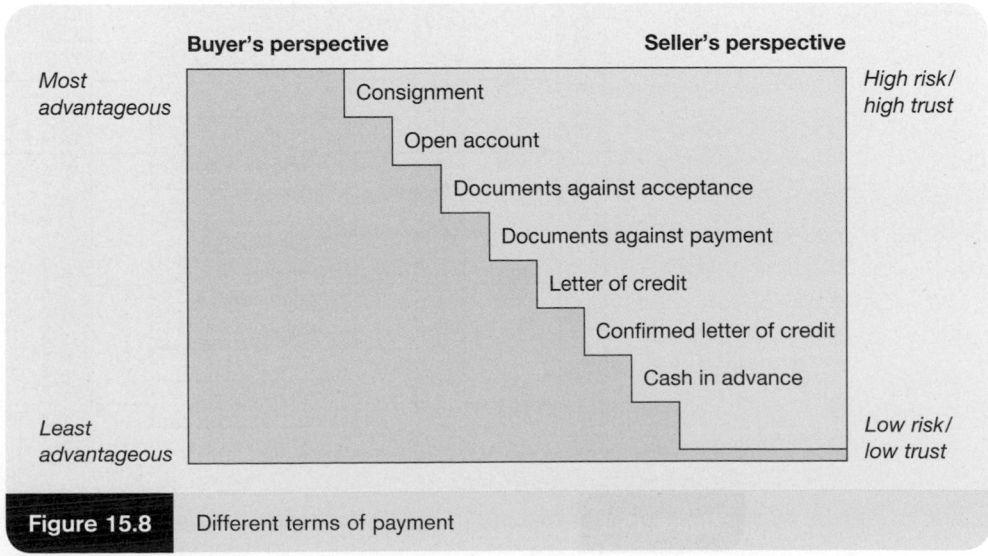

Figure 15.8   Different terms of payment

Source: Chase Manhattan Bank (1984, p. 5).

Letter of credit

Worldwide letters of credit are very important and very common. A letter of credit is an instrument whereby a bank agrees to pay a specified amount of money on presentation of documents stipulated in the letter of credit, usually the bill of lading, an invoice and a description of the goods. In general, letters of credit have the following characteristics:

- They are an arrangement by banks for settling international commercial transactions.
- They provide a form of security for the parties involved.
- They ensure payment, provided that the terms and conditions of the credit have been fulfilled.
- Payment by such means is based on documents only and not on the merchandise or services involved.

The process for handling letters of credit is illustrated in Figure 15.9.

In the process the customer agrees to payment by a confirmed letter of credit. The customer begins the process by sending an enquiry for the goods (1). The price and terms are confirmed by a pro forma invoice (2) by the supplier, so that the customer knows for what amount (3) to instruct its bank (the issuing bank) to open a letter of credit (4). The letter of credit is confirmed by a bank (5) in the supplier's country.

When the goods are shipped (6), the shipping documents are submitted by the supplier to its bank (7), so that shipment is confirmed by their presentation (8) together with the letter of credit and all other stipulated documents and certificates for payment (9). The

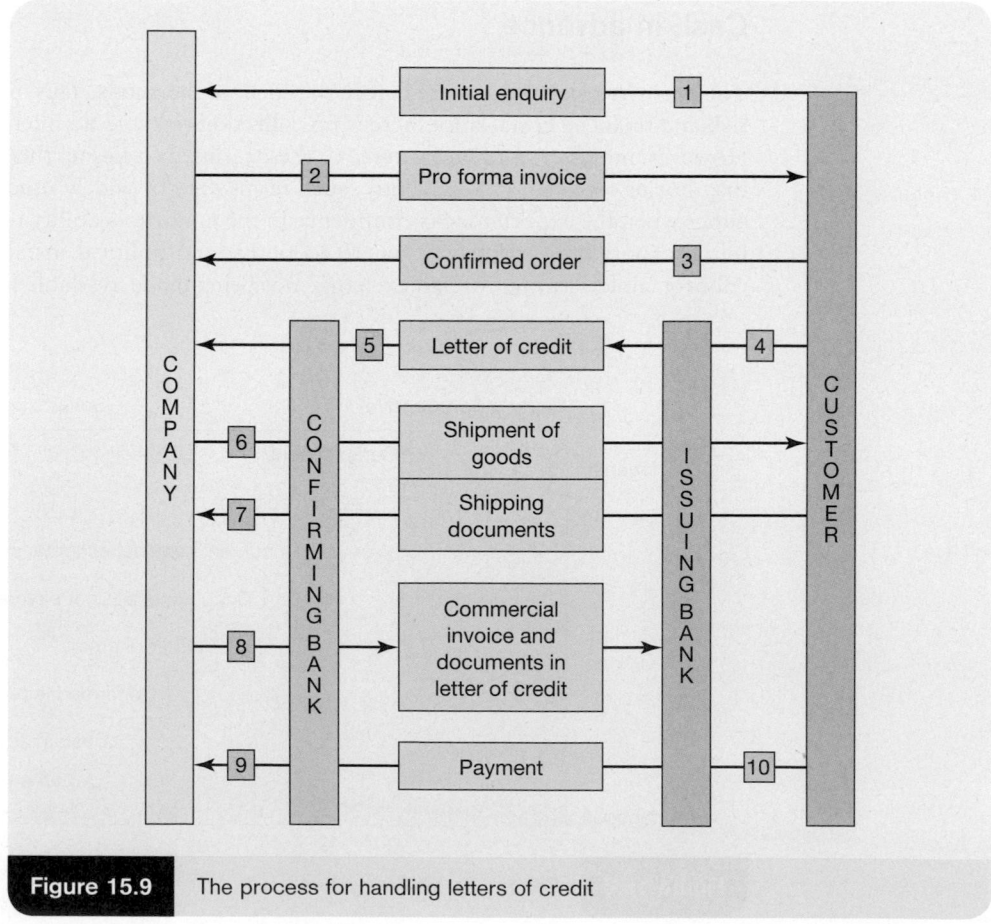

| **Figure 15.9** | The process for handling letters of credit |

Source: Phillips *et al.* (1994, p. 454). With permission from Cengage Learning.

money is automatically transmitted from the customer's account via the issuing bank. The customer may collect the goods (10) only when all the documents have been delivered to it by its bank – the issuing bank (adapted from Phillips *et al.*, 1994, p. 453).

The letter of credit (L/C) has three forms:

1. *Revocable L/C.* Now a rare form, this gives the buyer maximum flexibility as it can be cancelled without notice to the seller up to the moment of payment by the bank.
2. *Irrevocable but unconfirmed L/C.* This is as good as the credit status of the establishing bank and the willingness of the buyer's country to allow the required use of foreign exchange. An unconfirmed L/C should not necessarily be viewed with suspicion. The reason for the lack of confirmation may be that the customer has been unwilling to pay the additional fee for confirmation.
3. *Confirmed irrevocable L/C.* This means that a bank in the seller's country has added its own undertaking to that of the issuing bank, confirming that the necessary sum of money is available for payment, awaiting only the presentation of shipping documents. While it guarantees the seller its money, it is much more costly to the buyer. Generally the buyer pays a fixed fee plus a percentage of the value, but where the letter of credit is confirmed, the confirming bank will also charge a fee. On the other hand, the confirmation of an irrevocable letter of credit by a bank gives the shipper the most satisfactory assurance that payment will be made for the shipment. It also means that the exporter does not have to seek payment under any conditions from the issuing bank – invariably located in some foreign country – but has a direct claim on the confirming bank in the exporter's home country. Thus the exporter need not be concerned about the ability or willingness of the foreign bank to pay.

Documents against payment and acceptance

In the following two 'documents against' situations, the seller ships the goods and the shipping documents, and the draft (bill of exchange) demanding payment is presented to the importer through banks acting as the seller's agent. There are two principal types of bill of exchange: sight draft (documents against payment) and time draft (documents against acceptance).

1. *Documents against payment.* Here the buyer must make payment for the face value of the draft before receiving the documents conveying title to the merchandise. This occurs when the buyer first sees the draft (*sight draft*).
2. *Documents against acceptance.* When a draft is drawn, 'documents against acceptance' credit is extended to the buyer on the basis of the buyer's acceptance of the draft calling for payment within a specified time and usually at a specified place. Acceptance means that the buyer formally agrees to pay the amount specified by the draft on the due date. The specified time may be expressed as a certain number of days after sight (*time draft*). A time draft offers less security for the seller than a sight draft, because the sight draft demands payment prior to the release of shipping documents. The time draft, on the other hand, allows the buyer a delay of 30, 60 or 90 days in payment.

Open account

The exporter ships the goods without documents calling for payment, other than the invoice. The buyer can pick up the goods without having to make payment first. The advantage of the open account is its simplicity and the assistance it gives to the buyer, which does not have to pay credit charges to banks. The seller in return expects that the invoice will be paid at the agreed time. A major weakness of the method is that there are no safeguards for payment. Exporters should sell on open account only to importers they know very well or that have excellent credit ratings, and to markets with no foreign exchange problems. Open account sales are less complex and expensive than drafts, as there are no documentation requirements or bank charges.

Consignment

Here the exporter retains title of the goods until the importer sells them. Exporters own the goods longer in this method than any other, and so the financial burden and risks are at their greatest. The method should be offered only to very trustworthy importers with an excellent credit rating in countries where political and economic risks are very low. Consignments tend to be mainly used by companies trading with their own subsidiaries.

The credit terms given are also important in determining the final price to the buyer. When the products of international competitors are perceived to be similar, the purchaser may choose the supplier that offers the best credit terms, in order to achieve a greater discount. In effect, the supplier is offering a source of finance to the buyer.

15.8 Export financing

Exporters need financing support in order to obtain working capital and because importers will often demand terms that allow them to defer payment. Principal sources of export finance include commercial banks, government export financing programmes, export credit insurance, factoring houses and counter-trade.

Commercial banks

The simplest way of financing export sales is through an overdraft facility with the exporter's own bank. This is a convenient way to finance all the elements of the contract, such as purchasing, manufacturing, shipping and credit. The bank is generally more favourably disposed towards granting an overdraft if the exporter has obtained an export credit insurance policy.

Export credit insurance

Export credit insurance is available to most exporters through governmental export credit agencies or through private insurers (Griffith and Czinkota, 2012). Such insurances usually cover the following:

- *political risks* and non-convertibility of currency;
- *commercial risks* associated with non-payment by buyers.

Exporters may be able to use credit insurance to enable them to grant more liberal credit terms or to encourage their banks to grant them financing against their export receivables. The costs of such insurance are often quite low in many markets, ranging from 1–2 per cent of the value of the transaction. Specialized insurance brokers handle such insurance.

Factoring

Factoring means selling export debts for immediate cash. In this way, the exporter shifts the problems of collecting payment for completed orders over to organizations or factors that specialize in export credit management and finance.

Ideally the exporter should go to the factor before any contract is signed or shipment made, and secure its willingness to buy the receivable. The factor will check out the credit rating and so forth of the prospective buyer(s), typically by having a correspondent in the importer's country do the necessary checking. Thus the factor acts as a credit approval agency as well as a facilitator and guarantor of payment.

The factor does not usually purchase export debts on terms exceeding 120 days. Factors normally charge a service fee of between 0.75 and 2.5 per cent of the sales value, depending on the workload and the risk carried by the factor.

Forfeiting

This is a finance method developed in Switzerland in the 1950s. It is an arrangement whereby exporters of capital goods can obtain medium-term finance (between one and seven years). The system can briefly be explained as follows.

An exporter of capital goods has a buyer that wishes to have medium-term credit to finance the purchase. The buyer pays some of the cost at once and pays the balance in regular instalments for, say, the next five years. The principal benefit is that there is immediate cash for the exporter and, along with the first cash payment by the buyer, forfeiting can finance up to 100 per cent of the contract value.

Bonding

In some countries (e.g. in the Middle East) contracts are cash or short term. Whereas this is an ideal situation for suppliers, it means that the buyer loses some of its leverage over the supplier as it cannot withhold payment. In this situation, a bond or guarantee is a written instrument issued to an overseas buyer by an acceptable third party, either a bank or an insurance company. It guarantees compliance of its obligations by an exporter or contractor, or the overseas buyer will be indemnified for a stated amount against the failure of the exporter/contractor to fulfil its obligations under the contract.

Leasing

Exporters of capital equipment may use leasing in one of two ways:

1. to arrange cross-border leases directly from a bank or leasing company to the foreign buyer;
2. to obtain local leasing facilities either through overseas branches or subdivisions of international banks or through international leasing associations.

With leasing the exporter receives prompt payment for goods directly from the leasing company. A leasing facility is best set up at the earliest opportunity, preferably when the exporter receives the order.

Counter-trade

Counter-trade is a generic term used to describe a variety of trade agreements in which a seller provides a buyer with products (commodities, goods, services, technology) and agrees to a reciprocal purchasing obligation with the buyer in terms of an agreed percentage (full or partial) of the original sales value.

Barter

This is a straightforward exchange of goods for goods without any money transfer. Bilateral barter, where only two parties are involved, is relatively uncommon. The bartering process can, however, be facilitated when a third (trilateral barter) or even more countries (multi-lateral barter) become involved in a trading chain.

Compensation deal

This involves the export of goods in one direction. The 'payment' of the goods is split into two parts:

1. Part payment in cash by the importer.
2. For the rest of the 'payment' the original exporter makes an obligation to purchase some of the buyer's goods. These products can be used in the exporter's internal production or they may be sold on in the wider market.

Buy-back agreement

The sale of machinery, equipment or a turnkey plant to the buyer's production is financed at least in part by the exporter's purchase of some of the resultant output. Whereas barter and compensation deals are short-term arrangements, buy-back agreements are long-term agreements. The contract may last for a considerable period of time, such as five to 10 years. The two-way transactions are clearly linked, but are kept financially separate.

Counter-trade has arisen because of shortages of both foreign exchange and international lines of credit. Some estimates of the extent of counter-trade put it as high as 10–15 per cent of world trade.

15.9   Summary

The major issues covered in this chapter include the determinants of price, pricing strategy, how foreign prices are related to domestic prices, price escalation, the elements of price quotation and transfer pricing.

Several factors must be taken into consideration in setting price, including cost, competitors' prices, product image, market share/volume, stage in product life cycle and number of products involved. The optimum mix of these ingredients varies by product, market and corporate objectives. Price-setting in the international context is further complicated by such factors as foreign exchange rates, different competitive situations in each export market, different labour costs and different inflation rates in various countries. Local and regional regulations and laws in setting prices also have to be considered.

The international marketer must quote a meaningful price by using proper international trade terms. When there is doubt about how to prepare a quotation, freight forwarders may be consulted. These specialists can provide valuable information with regard to documentation (e.g. invoice, bill of lading) and the costs relevant to the movement of goods. Financial documents, such as letters of credit, require a bank's assistance. International banks have international departments that can facilitate payment and advise clients regarding pitfalls in preparing and accepting documents.

CASE STUDY 15.1

Harley-Davidson: does the image justify the price level?

Source: TonyV3112/Shutterstock.com.

The Harley-Davidson (HD) Corporation has dominated the motorcycle industry for many decades and continues to have a strong presence in the world market for heavy-weight cruisers. In the financial year 2011, the net revenues of HD were US$5.3 billion. In 2011, HD had 1,450 dealers selling 300,000 HD motorcycles worldwide and employed about 6,000 people worldwide. In the heavyweight section (651+ cc), HD was a clear market leader in North America with a 55 per cent market share, and their market share in Europe was 12 per cent. The mission statement of the company is to fulfil dreams through the experience of motorcycling, by providing to the motorcyclists and the general public an expanding line of motorcycles, and branded products and services, in selected market segments. HD offers a complete range of motorcycles, parts, accessories, apparel and general merchandise. Strategic licensing of the HD brand helps create future generations of Harley-Davidson enthusiasts.

HD celebrated its 100-year anniversary in 2003. Over the previous century, the company managed to create a strong brand image and a loyal customer base within the marketplace. Much of the value of a Harley resides in its tradition – the look, sound and heritage that have made it an all-American symbol.

The bikes represent something very basic – a desire for freedom, adventure and individualism.

HD maintains a close relationship with its customers through a variety of programmes (Harley Owners' Group), product offerings and events such as the Daytona bike week, motor shows and rallies. However, the company is facing rigorous competition from Japanese manufacturers, specifically Honda and Yamaha. HD's strength is its brand image within the marketplace, but its weakness is related to production capacity and unfulfilled demand for its products. HD tries to continue to strengthen its positioning strategy by building on the 'Own an American Icon' slogan.

As its average customer's age rises, and sales go down, HD faces the task of attracting younger customers. Part of retooling its image included releasing a new motorcycle, the Buell, designed for young professionals.

According to the Motorcycle Industry Council (www.mic.org), an industry trade group based in Irvine, California, the women's market accounts for about 11 per cent of the total motorcycling population.

Pricing

The international price competition is getting tougher. Compared with similar models from Honda, HD still has a 30 per cent price premium; even though Harley bikers still wear T-shirts saying 'I'd rather push a Harley than drive a Honda'.

In 2011, HD's sales of motorcycles outside the US comprised around 25 per cent of its annual total. Europeans like cruiser bikes, but they are not so keen on Harley prices. In 2011, the European market share of HD in the heavyweight segment (over 650 cc) was around 12 per cent. The 2011 market leaders in Europe were Honda, Yamaha, Suzuki and BMW, each with around 15 per cent market share.

On 15 October 2009, Harley-Davidson Inc. announced the end of production of Buell Motorcycles to focus more on the HD brand.

QUESTIONS

1. Describe HD's general pricing strategy. What does the company's positioning have to do with its pricing strategy?

2. Should HD alter its prices, given strong price pressures from rivals?

3. What should HD do to improve its market share in Europe?

Sources: www.harley-davidson.com/; www.mic.org/; www.motorcy-clenewswire.com/; www.neobike.net/industry.

CASE STUDY 15.2

Gillette Co.: is price standardization possible for razor blades?

In the battle to out-blade the competition, Gillette's 2005 creation, a five-bladed razor called Fusion, leapfrogged the Schick Quattro by one blade and aimed to provide an even closer shave to the millions of men who were apparently having trouble with only three or four blades.

Fusion (launched in September 2005) was the first entirely new men's razor system from Gillette since Mach 3, which was launched in 1998. Gillette's previous flagship razor, the Mach 3, had three blades, while the Schick Quattro had four, but Gillette president James Kilts insisted this latest 'innovation' had nothing to do with the competition: 'The Schick launch has nothing to do with this, it's like comparing a Ferrari to a Volkswagen as far as we're concerned. . . There was never a plan to go to four.'

Fusion had one more blade than the Quattro sold by rival Schick, a unit of Energizer Holdings Inc., plus a trimming blade on the back of the pivoting cartridge for shaping facial hair, trimming sideburns and shaving under the nose.

QUESTIONS

1. Evaluate the price level of Gillette's Fusion.

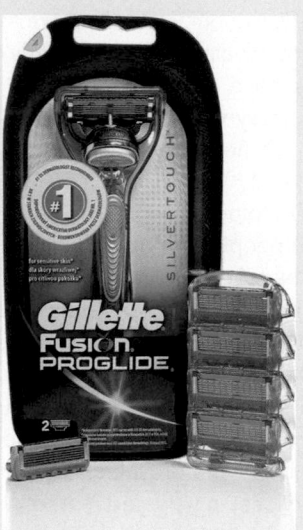

Source: Melica/Shutterstock.com.

2. Discuss whether it is possible for Gillette to standardize pricing across borders for its new five-blade Fusion. Which factors would favour price standardization and which factors would favour price differentiation?

Source: based on different public sources.

VIDEO CASE STUDY 15.3 Vaseline pricing strategy

download from **www.pearsoned.co.uk/hollensen**

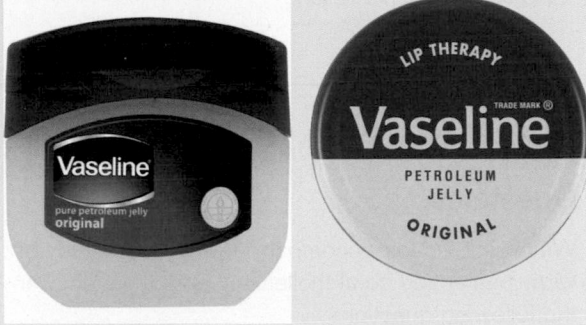

The Vaseline® journey started in 1859, when a 22-year-old chemist from Brooklyn, New York, named Robert A. Chesebrough, went to Pennsylvania to investigate an oil well. The oil industry was in its infancy, and Chesebrough, like many, was hoping to profit from it.

While Chesebrough was there, he discovered a gooey substance known as 'rod wax' that was causing the oil rig workers problems, as it stuck to the drilling rigs, causing them to seize up.

Chesebrough noticed that oil workers would smear their skin with the residue from their drills, as it appeared to aid the healing of cuts and burns. His curiosity led him to take some rod wax home with him and start experimenting with it. After months of testing, he managed to successfully extract usable petroleum jelly.

By 1870, Chesebrough was marketing his petroleum jelly product by the name of Vaseline, and within 10 years, the product's increased exposure and popularity meant that almost every household in America had a jar of Vaseline.

Chesebrough expanded his business to Canada, the UK and British colonies all over the world. New mothers used it as an absorbent shield for nappy rash. Professionals working in extreme cold weather used it to relieve their dry chapped skin. Even Commander Robert Peary took Vaseline with him when he became (as is generally accepted) the first man to reach the North Pole, because it wouldn't freeze.

By the late 1880s, Chesebrough was selling Vaseline petroleum jelly nationwide at the rate of one jar per minute and most medical professionals recognized it as the standard remedy for skin complaints.

By 1911, the company began opening operation plants and factories in Europe, Canada and Africa in order to facilitate the manufacture and distribution of the product. In 1955, Chesebrough Manufacturing Co. merged with Pond's Extract Company to form Chesebrough, Ponds, Inc. Like Chesebrough, Pond's had a passionate interest in and curiosity about skin.

During the 1960s, the company continued to expand, moving to places such as Argentina, Australia, Brazil and India.

Vaseline's 100th anniversary was in 1970, and to mark the occasion a major new product, Vaseline

Source: Reproduced with kind permission of Unilever PLC and group companies.

Intensive Care Lotion, was launched in the USA (1968) and in the UK (1971), with huge success. The brand was later extended to include hand and nail moisturizers and deodorants for men and women.

In 1987, Unilever purchased Chesebrough-Pond's, acquiring successful, internationally known brands such as Pond's and Vaseline. Today, Vaseline products are available in over 60 countries around the world. Its rich heritage, healing qualities and efficacy have been passed on from generation to generation for over 130 years.

One way of expanding revenues is through established product categories in which a firm currently does not have a market presence. In 1980, Chesebrough-Pond's entered the market for lip care, a product category in which it did not have a market presence, with Vaseline Constant Care lip balm, and in 1985 they launched Vaseline brand petroleum jelly packaged in a 0.35-ounce plastic tube, directly applicable to the lip, under the brand name Vaseline Lip Therapy. Applying Vaseline petroleum jelly to dry or cracked lips, particularly during the winter season, is one of the many uses for which the product has long been promoted.

Besides facilitating entry into a new product market, it is conceivable that the Vaseline profit margins associated with the incremental innovation are considerably higher (see Table 1). While Vaseline brand petroleum jelly in a 13-ounce plastic jar retailed for about US$2.99 (US$0.23 per ounce of jelly), the same product packaged in a 0.35-ounce tube retailed for US$1.99 (US$5.69 per ounce of jelly).

Table 1	Vaseline pricing: pure petroleum jelly versus Lip Therapy	
Vaseline product	**List price in US (US$)**	**Price per ounce of jelly (US$)**
Vaseline Pure Petroleum Jelly (13 ounces in a plastic jar)	2.99	0.23 per ounce of jelly
Vaseline Lip Therapy (0.35 ounces in a tube)	1.99	5.69 per ounce of jelly

Source: based on various sources.

Questions

Watch the videos accompanying this case study at www.pearsoned.co.uk/hollensen and then answer the following questions:

1. If you were a representative of the Vaseline (Unilever) management, how would you justify the price difference? What extra customer value do you create by selling the jelly as lip therapy in small tubes?

2. How would you price the Vaseline Intensive Care lotion in the Philippines compared with the UK?

Sources: adapted from Varadarajan (2009); History of Vaseline, www.vaseline.co.uk, with the kind permission of Unilever.

For further resources, see this book's website at **www.pearsoned.co.uk/hollensen**

Questions for discussion

1. What are the major causes of international price escalation? Suggest possible courses of action to deal with this problem.

2. Explain how exchange rates and inflation affect the way you price your product.

3. In order to protect themselves, how should marketers price their product in a country with high inflation?

4. International buyers and sellers of technology frequently disagree on the appropriate price for knowledge. Why?

5. What methods can be used to compute a transfer price (for transactions between affiliated companies)?

6. What relevance has the international product life cycle theory for pricing strategy in international firms?

7. Why is it often difficult to compute fair arm's length transfer prices?

8. Explain these terms of sale: EXW, FAS, FOB, CFR, CIF, DEQ and DDP. Which factors will determine the terms of sale?

9. Explain these types of letter of credit: revocable/irrevocable, confirmed/unconfirmed. Under what sets of circumstances would exporters use the following methods of payment:

   (a) revocable letter of credit
   (b) confirmed letter of credit
   (c) confirmed irrevocable letter of credit
   (d) time draft (i.e. bill of exchange)?

10. Name some of the financing sources for exporters.

11. How does inflation affect a country's currency value? Is it a good idea to borrow or obtain finance in a country with high inflation?

12. How and why are export credit financing terms and conditions relevant to international pricing?

13. What is counter-trade? Why should firms be willing to consider counter-trade arrangements in their global marketing efforts?

References

Anderson, C. (2009) *Free: The Future of a Radical Price*, Hyperion, New York

Auguste, B.G., Harmon, E.P. and Pandit, V. (2006) 'The right service strategies for product companies', *McKinsey Quarterly*, 1, March, pp. 10–15.

Bertini, M. and Koenigsberg, O. (2014) 'When customers help set prices', *MIT Sloan Management Review*, Summer, pp. 56–64.

Buter, C. (2011) 'International transfer pricing and the EU Code of Conduct', *European Integration Studies*, 5, pp. 110–115.

Chase Manhattan Bank (1984) *Dynamics of Trade Finance*. New York.

Czepiel, J.A. (1992) *Competitive Marketing Strategy*. Prentice-Hall, Englewood Cliffs, NJ.

Diller, H. and Bukhari, I. (1994) 'Pricing conditions in the European Common Market', *European Management Journal*, 12(2), pp. 163–170.

Eiteman, D.K. and Stonehill, A.I. (1986) *Multinational Business Finance*, 4th edn. Addison-Wesley, Reading, MA.

Fraedrich, J.P. and Bateman, C.R. (1996) 'Transfer pricing by multinational marketers: risky business', *Business Horizons*, 39(1), pp. 17–22.

Garda, R.A. (1995) 'Tactical pricing', in Paliwoda, S.J. and Ryans, J.K. (eds), *International Marketing Reader*. Routledge, London, pp. 257–265.

Griffith, D.A. and Czinkota, M.R. (2012) 'Release the constraints: Solving the problems of export financing in troublesome times', *Business Horizons*, 55, pp. 251–260.

Hinterhuber, A. and Liozu, S.M. (2012) 'Is it time to rethink your pricing strategy?', *MIT Sloan Management Review*, 53(4), pp. 68–77

Hinterhuber, A. and Liozu, S.M. (2014) 'Is innovation in pricing your next source of competitive advantage?', *Business Horizons*, 57, pp. 413–423.

Kohli, C. and Suri, R. (2011) 'The price is right? Guidelines for pricing to enhance profitability', *Business Horizons*, 54, pp. 563–573.

Koschate-Fischer, N., Diamantopoulos, A. and Oldenkotte, K. (2012) 'Are consumers really willing to pay more for a favorable country image? A study of country-of-origin effects on willingness to pay', *Journal of International Marketing*, 20(1), pp. 19–41.

Nagle, T.T. (1987) *The Strategies and Tactics of Pricing*. Prentice-Hall, Englewood Cliffs, NJ.

Narayandas, D., Quelch, J. and Swartz, G. (2000) 'Prepare your company for global pricing', *Sloan Management Review*, Fall, pp. 61–70.

Obadia, C. and Stöttinger, B. (2015) 'Pricing to manage export channel relationships', *International Business Review*, 24, pp. 311–318.

OECD (2010) *OECD Transfer Pricing for Multinational Enterprises and Tax Administrations 2010*. OECD Publishing, Paris.

Onkvisit, S. and Shaw, J.J. (1993) *International Marketing Analysis and Strategy*, 2nd edn. Macmillan, London.

Piercy, N.F., Cravens, D.W. and Lane, N. (2010) 'Thinking strategically about pricing decisions', *Journal of Business Strategy*, 31(5), pp. 38–48.

Phillips, C., Doole, I. and Lowe, R. (1994) *International Marketing Strategy: Analysis, Development and Implementation*. Routledge, London.

Ramberg, J. (2011) 'ICC Guide to Incoterms 2010', *ICC Publications*, No. 720, Paris.

Simon, H. and Kucher, E. (1993) 'The European pricing bomb – and how to cope with it', *Marketing and Research Today*, February, pp. 25–36.

Solberg, C.A. (1997) 'A framework for analysis of strategy development in globalizing markets', *Journal of International Marketing*, 5(1), pp. 9–30.

Solberg, C.A., Stöttinger, B. and Yaprak, A. (2006) 'A taxonomy of the pricing practices of exporting firms: evidence from Austria, Norway and the United States', *Journal of International Marketing*, 14(1), pp. 23–48.

Theodosiou, M. and Katsikeas, C.S. (2001) 'Factors influencing the degree of international pricing strategy standardization of multinational corporations', *Journal of International Marketing*, 9(3), pp. 1–18.

Varadarajan, R. (2009) 'Fortune at the bottom of the innovation pyramid: the strategic logic of incremental innovations', *Business Horizons*, 52, pp. 21–29.

Weigand, R.E. (1991) 'Buy in–follow on strategies for profit', *Sloan Management Review*, Spring, pp. 29–38.

CHAPTER 16
Distribution decisions

Contents

Case studies

Learning objectives

After studying this chapter you should be able to:

- Explore the determinants of channel decisions
- Discuss the key points in putting together and managing global marketing channels
- Discuss the factors influencing channel width (intensive, selective or exclusive coverage)
- Explain what is meant by integration of the marketing channel
- Describe the most common export documents
- Define and explain the main modes of transportation
- Discuss the consequences of online distribution
- Explain how the internationalization of retailing affects the manufacturer
- Define grey markets and explain how to deal with them.

16.1 Introduction

Access to international markets is a key decision area facing firms into the 2000s. In Part III we considered the firm's choice of an appropriate market entry mode that could assure the entry of a firm's products and services into a foreign market. After the firm has chosen a strategy to get its products into foreign markets, the next challenge (and the topic of this chapter: see Figure 16.1) is the distribution of the products within those foreign markets. The first part of this chapter concerns the structure and management of foreign distribution. The second part is concerned with the management of international logistics.

Distribution channels typically account for 15–40 per cent of the retail price of goods and services in an industry.

Over the next few years, the challenges and opportunities for channel management will multiply, as technological developments accelerate channel evolution. Data networks are increasingly enabling end-users to bypass traditional channels and deal directly with manufacturers and service providers.

The following presents a systematic approach to the major decisions in international distribution. The main channel decisions and their determinants are illustrated in Figure 16.1. Distribution channels are the links between producers and final customers. In general terms, an international marketer distributes either directly or indirectly. As we saw in Chapter 10, direct distribution amounts to dealing with a foreign firm, while the indirect method means dealing with another home country firm that serves as an intermediary. Figure 16.1 shows that the choice of a particular channel link will be strongly influenced by various characteristics of the host markets. We will now consider these in more detail.

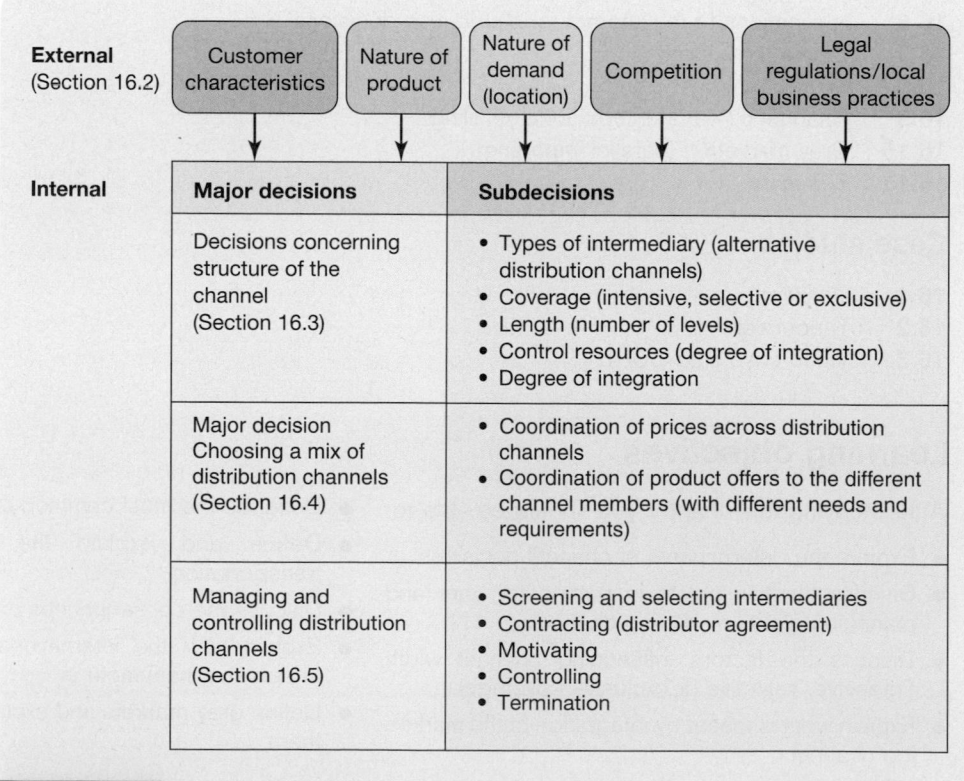

Figure 16.1 Channel decisions

Communication is the fourth and final decision to be made about the global marketing programme. The role of communication in global marketing is similar to that in domestic operations: to communicate with customers so as to provide information that buyers need to make purchasing decisions. Although the communication mix carries information of interest to the customer, in the end it is designed to persuade the customer to buy a product – at the present or in the future.

To communicate with and influence customers, several tools are available. Advertising is usually the most visible component of the promotion mix, but personal selling, exhibitions, sales promotions, publicity (public relations) and direct marketing (including the internet) are also part of a viable international promotion mix.

One important strategic consideration is whether to standardize worldwide or to adapt the promotion mix to the environment of each country. Another consideration is the availability of media, which varies around the world.

16.2   External determinants of channel decisions

Customer characteristics

The customer, or final consumer, is the keystone in any channel design. Thus the size, geographic distribution, shopping habits, outlet preferences and usage patterns of customer groups must be taken into account when making distribution decisions.

Consumer product channels tend to be longer than industrial product channels because the number of customers is greater, the customers are more geographically dispersed and they buy in smaller quantities. Shopping habits, outlet preferences and usage patterns vary considerably from country to country and are strongly influenced by sociocultural factors.

Nature of product

Product characteristics play a key role in determining distribution strategy. For low-priced, high-turnover convenience products, the requirement is an intensive distribution network. On the other hand, it is not necessary or even desirable for a prestigious product to have wide distribution. In this situation a manufacturer can shorten and narrow its distribution channel. Consumers are likely to do some comparison shopping and will actively seek information about all brands under consideration. In such cases, limited product exposure is not an impediment to market success.

Transportation and warehousing costs of the product are also critical issues in the distribution and sale of industrial goods such as bulk chemicals, metals and cement. Direct selling, servicing and repair and spare parts warehousing dominate the distribution of such industrial products as computers, machinery and aircraft. The product's durability, ease of adulteration, amount and type of customer service required, unit costs and special handling requirements (such as cold storage) are also significant factors.

Nature of demand/location

The perceptions that the target customers hold about particular products can force modification of distribution channels. Product perceptions are influenced by the customer's income and product experience, the product's end use, its life cycle position and the country's stage of economic development. The geography of a country and the development of its transportation infrastructure can also affect the channel decision.

Competition

The channels used by competing products and close substitutes are important because channel arrangements that seek to serve the same market often compete with one another. Consumers generally expect to find particular products in particular outlets (e.g. speciality stores), or they become accustomed to buying particular products from particular sources. In addition, local and global competitors may have agreements with the major wholesalers in a foreign country that effectively create barriers and exclude the company from key channels.

Sometimes the alternative is to use a distribution approach totally different from that of the competition and hope to develop a competitive advantage.

Legal regulations/local business practices (Japan)

A country may have specific laws that rule out the use of particular channels or intermediaries. For example, until recently, all alcoholic beverages in Sweden and Finland had to be distributed through state-owned outlets. Other countries prohibit door-to-door selling. Channel coverage can also be affected by law. In general, exclusive representation may be viewed as a restraint of trade, especially if the product has a dominant market position. EU anti-trust authorities have increased their scrutiny of exclusive sales agreements. The Treaty of Rome prohibits distribution agreements (e.g. grants of exclusivity) that affect trade or restrict competition.

Furthermore, local business practices can interfere with efficiency and productivity and may force a manufacturer to employ a channel of distribution that is longer and wider than desired. Because of Japan's multi-tiered distribution system, which relies on numerous layers of intermediaries, foreign companies have long considered the complex Japanese distribution system as the most effective non-tariff barrier to the Japanese market.

Figure 16.2 shows how the complex Japanese distribution system escalates prices by a factor of 5 through both vertical transactions and horizontal transactions (e.g. from one wholesaler to another wholesaler).

While western firms understand integration as ownership of other suppliers and/or buyers, Japanese firms forge tight collaborations, known as **keiretsu**, instead of buying

Keiretsu

A network of businesses that own stakes in one another as a means of mutual security, especially in Japan, and usually including large manufacturers and their suppliers of raw materials and components. The original *keiretsu* were each centred around one bank, which lent money to the *keiretsu*'s member companies and held equity positions in the companies.

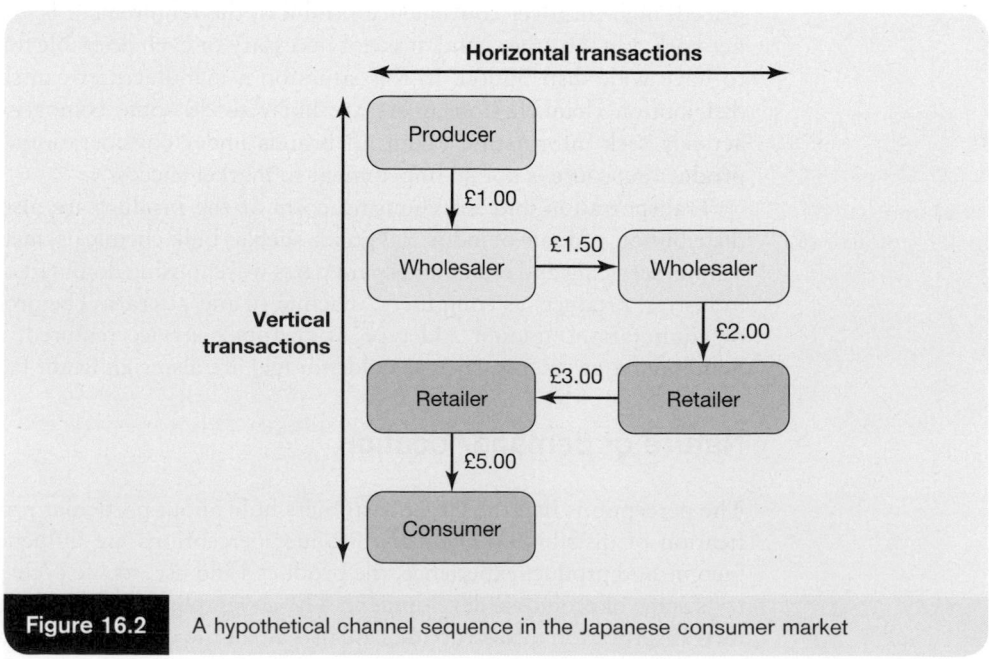

Figure 16.2   A hypothetical channel sequence in the Japanese consumer market

Source: Lewison (1996, p. 271).

channel members. These alliances are not contractual, but consist of strong links among channel members that originate from personal exchanges and trust to giving long-term supply agreements and technology, sharing vital information and managing resources into developing new products and processes. Accordingly, wholesalers and retailers push the products of one manufacturer, and share information extensively.

These collaborative companies behave as if they were one company in which it becomes very difficult for channel firms to refuse to buy from *keiretsu* members, even when the price is far from being competitive.

The tight-knit *keiretsu* and intimate grouping among affiliated Japanese producers, wholesalers and retailers attempt to form one company by buying high-priced goods and services of group members, rather than acquiring them competitively from non-group members. For example, Matsushita, a leading manufacturer in Japan, formed a *keiretsu* with hundreds of wholesalers and thousands of retailers nationwide. By buying goods and services only from group members, the Matsushita *keiretsu* tries to avoid competition among its member firms, which helps to keep prices high, as they are able to securely control the price and distribution of goods and services from the supplier to the consumer (Rawwas *et al.*, 2008).

Let us now return to the major decisions concerning the structure of the distribution channel (Figure 16.1).

16.3 The structure of the channel

Market coverage

Market coverage
Coverage can relate to geographical areas or number of retail outlets. Three approaches are available: intensive, selective or exclusive coverage.

The amount of **market coverage** that a channel member provides is important. Coverage is a flexible term. It can refer to geographical areas of a country (such as cities and major towns) or the number of retail outlets (as a percentage of all retail outlets). Regardless of the market coverage measure(s) used, the company has to create a distribution network (dealers, distributors and retailers) to meet its coverage goals.

As shown in Figure 16.3, three different approaches are available:

1. *Intensive coverage.* This calls for distributing the product through the largest number of different types of intermediary and the largest number of individual intermediaries of each type.
2. *Selective coverage.* This entails choosing a number of intermediaries for each area to be penetrated.
3. *Exclusive coverage.* This involves choosing only one intermediary in a market.

Channel coverage (width) can be identified along a continuum ranging from wide channels (intensive distribution) to narrow channels (exclusive distribution). Figure 16.4 illustrates some factors favouring intensive, selective and exclusive distribution.

Channel length

Channel length
Number of levels (middlemen) in the distribution channel.

Channel length is determined by the number of levels or different types of intermediary. A country's economic development provides the need for more efficient channels, first lengthening as more intermediaries enter the distribution system, but later shortening as the number of channel layers decreases, as a result of efficiencies such as vertical integration (Jaffe and Yi, 2007). Longer channels, those with several intermediaries, tend to be associated with convenience goods and mass distribution. Japan and China have longer channels for convenience goods because of the historical development of their systems. One implication is that prices increase considerably for the final consumer (price escalation: see Section 15.3).

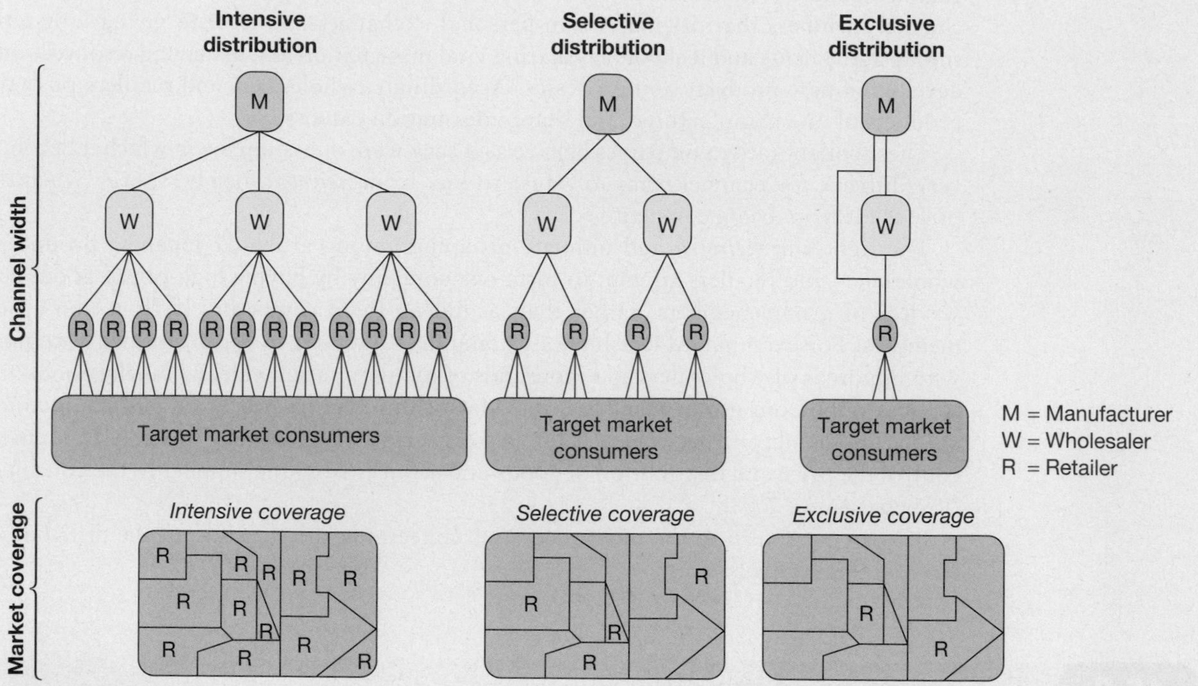

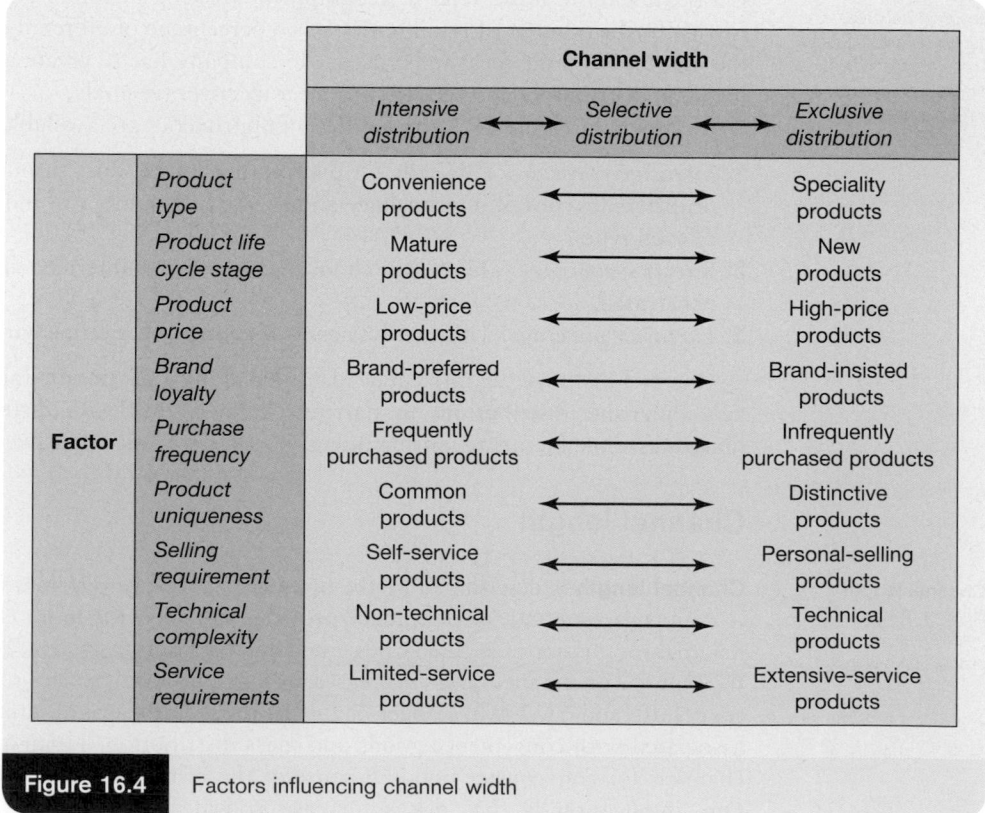

Figure 16.3   Three strategies for market coverage

Source: Lewison (1996, p. 271).

		Channel width	
		Intensive distribution ⟷ Selective distribution ⟷ Exclusive distribution		
Factor	Product type	Convenience products ⟷	Speciality products
	Product life cycle stage	Mature products ⟷	New products
	Product price	Low-price products ⟷	High-price products
	Brand loyalty	Brand-preferred products ⟷	Brand-insisted products
	Purchase frequency	Frequently purchased products ⟷	Infrequently purchased products
	Product uniqueness	Common products ⟷	Distinctive products
	Selling requirement	Self-service products ⟷	Personal-selling products
	Technical complexity	Non-technical products ⟷	Technical products
	Service requirements	Limited-service products ⟷	Extensive-service products

Figure 16.4   Factors influencing channel width

Source: adapted from Lewison (1996, p. 279).

Control/cost

The 'control' of one member in the vertical distribution channel means its ability to influence the decisions and actions of other channel members. Channel control is of critical concern to international marketers wanting to establish international brands and a consistent image of quality and service worldwide.

The company must decide how much control it wants to have over how each of its products is marketed. The answer is partly determined by the strategic role assigned to each market. It is also a function of the types of channel member available, the regulations and rules governing distribution activity in each foreign market and, to some extent, the roles traditionally assigned to channel members.

Normally a high degree of control is provided by the use of the firm's own sales force in international markets. The use of intermediaries will automatically lead to loss of some control over the marketing of the firm's products.

An intermediary typically performs certain functions:

- carrying of inventory
- demand generation, or selling
- physical distribution
- after-sales service
- extending credit to customers.

In getting its products to end-user markets, a manufacturer must either assume all of these functions or shift some or all of them to intermediaries. As the old saying goes, 'You can eliminate the intermediary, but not the functions of the intermediary.'

In most marketing situations, there is a trade-off between a producer's ability to control important channel functions and the financial resources required to exercise that control. The greater the number of intermediaries involved in getting a supplier's product to user customers, the less control the supplier can generally exercise over the flow of its product through the channel and the way it is presented to customers. On the other hand, reducing the length and breadth of the distribution channel usually requires that the supplier perform more functions itself. In turn, this requires the supplier to allocate more financial resources to activities such as warehousing, shipping, credit, field selling or field service.

In summary, the decision to use an intermediary or to distribute via a company-owned sales force requires a major trade-off between the desire to control global marketing efforts and the desire to minimize resource commitment costs.

Degree of integration

Control can also be exercised through integration. Channel integration is the process of incorporating all channel members into one channel system and uniting them under one leadership and one set of goals. There are two different types of integration:

Vertical integration
Seeking control of channel members at different levels of the channel, e.g. the manufacturer's acquisition of the distributor.

1. **vertical integration**: seeking control of channel members at different levels of the channel;
2. **horizontal integration**: seeking control of channel members at the same level of the channel (i.e. competitors).

Horizontal integration
Seeking control of channel members at the same level of the channel, e.g. the manufacturer's acquisition of the competitor.

Integration is achieved either through acquisitions (ownership) or through tight cooperative relationships. Getting channel members to work together for their own mutual benefit can be a difficult task. However, today cooperative relationships are essential for efficient and effective channel operation.

Figure 16.5 shows an example of vertical integration. The starting point in the figure is the conventional marketing channels, where the channel composition consists of isolated and autonomous participating channel members. Channel coordination is here achieved through arm's-length bargaining. At this point, the vertical integration can take two forms – forward and backward:

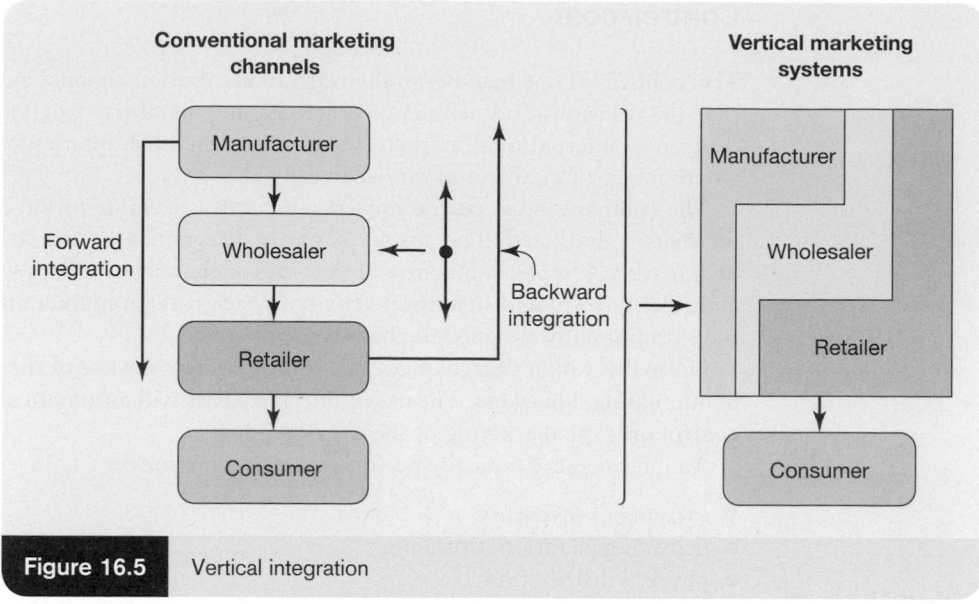

| **Figure 16.5** | Vertical integration |

- The manufacturer can make forward integration when it seeks control of businesses of the wholesale and retail levels of the channel. De Beers (see Case Study 16.1 at the end of this chapter) is a good example of a company which has followed this strategy.
- The retailer can make backward integration, seeking control of businesses at wholesale and manufacturer levels of the channel. The internet retailer Amazon.com, for example, is aggressively moving into the publishing domain. It contracts directly with authors and has released hundreds of books in both print and e-book format. This trend is likely to become more widespread in other product categories, such as music, electronics and clothing.
- The wholesaler has two possibilities: both forward and backward integration.

The result of these manoeuvres is the vertical marketing system (Figure 16.5). Here the channel composition consists of integrated participating members, where channel stability is high due to assured member loyalty and long-term commitments.

EXHIBIT 16.1 Burberry: the iconic British luxury brand targets 25 of the world's wealthier cities

Burberry is a global luxury brand with a distinctive British heritage, core outerwear and large leather goods base and some of the most recognized icons in the world. Burberry designs and sources apparel and accessories, selling through a diversified network of retail (including digital), wholesale and licensing channels worldwide.

Burberry, which is today headquartered in London, was founded in 1856 by Thomas Burberry, who opened a store in Basingstoke, England, where he sold men's outerwear.

In 2011/12, Burberry's revenues were £1.9 billion with operating profits of £377 million.

Source: Thinglass/Shutterstock.com.

At 30 September 2012, Burberry had a global portfolio of 198 retail stores, 215 concessions, 49 outlets and 62 franchise stores. The number of employees was approximately 8,000.

Targeting 25 of the world's wealthier cities

Burburry has transformed itself in the last few years in an attempt to attract a new, younger customer base while hanging on to its current customers. The brand has shifted away from the conservativism of the British upper class as it has been adopted by teenagers and young adults from the working classes. Today, the company is targeting young, digitally aware customers in the world's wealthier markets.

Source: Jo Yong Hak/Reuters/Corbis.

As part of this strategy, Burberry now targets 25 of the wealthier cities around the world. Key markets include London, New York and Beijing and, according to Burberry, these account for more than half of the global luxury fashion trade. These markets also benefit from high levels of tourism and high-net-worth residents. While the US remains by far the world's largest consumer of luxury products, the middle classes in developing countries are creating new opportunities for luxury goods providers.

Social media is capturing a new generation of Burberry fans

Unlike many luxury brands, Burberry is not afraid to become more accessible to the masses and has been engaging with social media such as Facebook, Twitter and YouTube. In late 2010/11, the brand was launched on Chinese social media sites Sina Weibo, Kaixin001, Douban and Youku. Country-specific Twitter accounts were launched in Brazil, Mexico, Japan, Turkey and South Korea. Additionally, the company has its own social media site, **artofthetrench.com**, which allows customers to post pictures of themselves in Burberry trenches and to comment and like pictures posted by others.

Sources: based on www.burberryplc.com; Barrett, C. and Massoudi, A. (2012) 'Burberry reports strong sales growth', *Financial Times*, 17 January 2012, http://www.ft.com/intl/cms/s/0/93395426-40ef-11e1-b521-00144feab49a.html#axzz28yGrSiHB; Barrett, C. (2012) 'Burberry plans for slump despite results', *Financial Times*, 12 October 2012, www.ft.com/intl/cms/s/0/82a54208-f4a7-11e0-a286-00144feab49a.html#axzz28yGrSiHB.

16.4   Multiple channel strategy

Multiple channel strategy
A product/service is available to the market through two (dual distribution) or more channels of distribution. Multiple channels may include the internet, sales force, distributors, call centres, retail stores and direct mail.

A **multiple channel strategy** is employed when a firm makes a product available to the market through two or more channels of distribution. Multiple channels include internet (online sales), own sales force, external intermediaries/distributors, retail stores (own and external) and call centres (selling services).

This strategy has been a very popular channel design during the 2000s (Valos, 2008). Its increasing popularity results from the potential advantages provided: extended market coverage and increased sales volume; lower absolute or relative costs; better accommodation of customers' evolving needs; and more and better information. However, the strategy can also produce potentially disruptive problems: consumer confusion; conflicts with intermediaries and/or internal distribution units; increased costs; loss of distinctiveness; and, eventually, an increased organizational complexity.

A case that is often seen in online (internet) channel distribution is that the prices offered to the customers through that channel are frequently lower than through other channels. The same price problem can also arise more or less where the same product is sold through other multiple channels at the same time. There are several ways for the supplier (manufacturer) to get around that and other across-channel problems (Brynjolfsson et al., 2013):

1. *Avoiding direct price comparisons*. While customers benefit from easy search, such capabilities can be damaging to sellers. Taking steps to make direct comparisons

difficult can protect suppliers from poaching by competitors and mitigate the effects of price competition. Consider the following options:

- *Distinctive features*. Suppliers offering a distinctive version of a product will see less price competition. The basic strategy for manufacturers is to make minor modifications for each distribution channel and thus have different target segments. However, unless the changes add value, the risk is that the manufacturer will annoy distributors and customers. With continually falling search costs and rich information resources, achieving differentiation can be difficult.
- *Exclusivity*. Suppliers may want to focus on product development partnerships/innovations to create exclusive products. This would mean offering products (values) that are not available to competitors). Such exclusive offerings might include distinctive versions of products, as opposed to cost-focused brands.
- *Bundles*. Bundling products can make it difficult for channel members and distributors to do a direct comparison of the value of the supplier's offering with those of competitors as long as the same bundle is not available through other distribution channels. A bundling strategy can be quite powerful in generating additional sales and profits if it is created by using historical purchase data and finding the meaningful relationships between products from past transactions.

For non-exclusive products (in other words, products that are also offered by competitors), especially popular ones, cost and efficiency are critical in determining the winner, because mobile apps enable customers to make instant price comparisons across channels. This will intensify the level of competition.

2. *Learning to sell niche products*. If a supplier sells through the online channel they will have advantages over the physical distribution channel in that they can focus on 'long tail' (see Section 14.13) products that are not economical for physical stores to carry. In between the long tail products and popular products are 'middle of tail' products, which are often available through physical distribution channels but do not enjoy a huge demand. Finding these products in local stores has traditionally been unpredictable and time-consuming. But with inventory information available online, finding the products in nearby stores has become much easier.

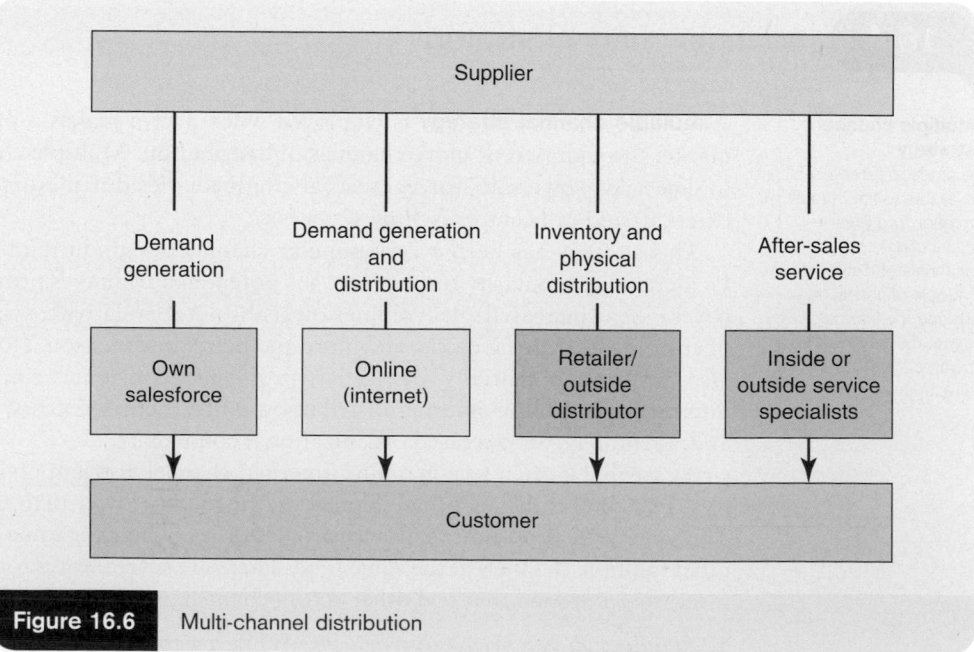

Figure 16.6 Multi-channel distribution

3. *Establishing switching costs.* Suppliers can reduce the amount of competition among the channel members they face by creating switching costs. Loyalty programmes similar to airline frequent-flyer programmes can be important vehicles for retaining customers and maintaining margins.

Besides the threat to the supplier (manufacturer) that different channels will offer customers different prices, there is also the problem that many manufacturers will no longer be able to offer the same product to all the channel members. The distributors and retailers will be looking for customized and exclusive merchandise, which will add complexity for manufacturers.

As a result, manufacturers will need to become agile at producing smaller and more customized batches of products. Further, as channel members pursue a strategy of seeking unique products, the boundaries between manufacturing and retailing will also blur (see the discussion about forward and backward integration earlier in this chapter).

Despite the difficulties involved in operating a multiple distribution platform (see Figure 16.6), doing so will expand the pie for the supplier by extending their market reach and by introducing customers to products they have not hitherto been aware of.

EXHIBIT 16.2 Dell's use of the multi-channel distribution strategy

At the beginning of the 21st century, Dell realized that the highly responsive configure-to-order strategy that had made its online store the world's largest channel for PCs no longer met the needs of some of its fastest-growing businesses. As a consequence, in 2008 for example, Dell entered the retail channel with its highly standardized PCs, at lower prices. Clearly, Dell needed to transform its distribution channel strategy to serve new customers in new channels with new products. Around 2010, the company started offering laptops and in 2012 Dell even entered the highly competitive tablet market with its Venue brand (using the Android platform). The current multidistribution channel strategy is illustrated in Figure 16.7.

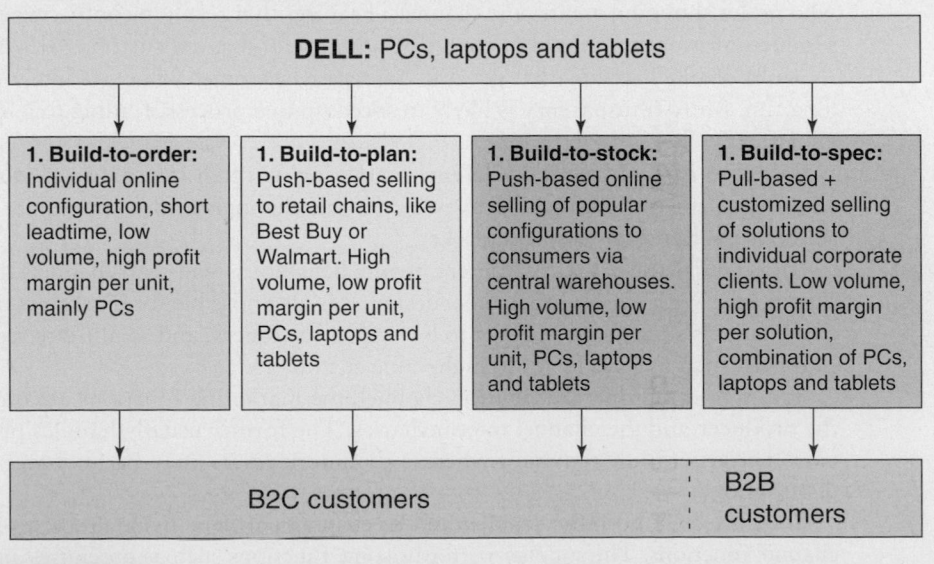

| **Figure 16.7** | Dell's four major worldwide distribution channels |

The four channel strategies are as follows:

1. *Build-to-order.* This represents the traditional Dell business model: satisfying consumers' individual needs, online with millions of possible configurations.
2. *Build-to-plan.* Here the production of popular products is planned in cooperation with the big retail chains, like Best Buy and Walmart. The final products are then sent to the central warehouses of the retailers.
3. *Build-to-stock.* Here Dell identified another customer segment with low demand uncertainty and loose customer relationships: popular products/configurations sold online directly from Dell warehouses to private consumers.
4. *Build-to-spec.* Here product solutions (combination of different products) are designed and delivered directly to individual corporate clients (B2B).

Source: courtesy of Dell, Inc.

An important challenge for implementing this multi-channel distribution strategy has been to utilize the synergies across the different channels and supply chains, in order to reduce complexity and exploit 'economies of scale' in production. In general, there are five possible areas that can yield synergies: procurement, product design, manufacturing, planning and order fulfilment.

Source: based on Simchi-Levi *et al.* (2013).

The shift toward multiple distribution channels also allows customers to accumulate product knowledge (for example, the name, product size, colour, shape, material content, etc.) in one channel and then purchase from another channel. Therefore, manufacturers (suppliers) need to do a better job of sharing product knowledge across their entire platform. Doing so will facilitate channel integration and will overall attract more customers who prefer shopping in multiple channels. Features that result in conflicting and confusing product information should of course be minimized to avoid customer frustration.

Multi-channel set-ups that generate increased customer value are likely to win in the long run. More transparency is likely to speed up this process, leading to a 'winner-takes-all' effect.

Dual marketing
Marketing the same product to two different customer groups, typically both consumers (B2C) and business customers (B2B), through two different distribution channels.

A special case of 'multiple channel marketing' is often referred to as **dual marketing** where the same product is sold to two different channels at the same time, for example, the consumer and the business market.

Different customers with different buying behaviours will seek channels that best serve their needs. With a multiple channel design, it is also possible for marketers to match low-cost channels such as the internet to low-value customers, and to allocate more expensive channels, such as sales force, to high-value customers.

In a hybrid multiple distribution channel, the marketing functions are often shared by the producer and the channel intermediaries. The former usually handles promotion and customer-generation activities, whereas the intermediary may be in charge of sales and distribution.

In Figure 16.5, both the supplier and its channel partners divide up the execution of the channel functions. The supplier performs some functions such as brochures and advertising material, while its channel partners deliver local sales negotiation, physical distribution and order fulfilment. Other channel members might specialise in functions such as after-sales service. The members work together with certain members specialising in certain functions.

16.5 | Managing and controlling distribution channels

At the beginning of a market entry, partnerships with local distributors make good sense: distributors know the distinctive characteristics of their market, and most customers prefer to do business with local partners. Arnold (2000) proposes the following guidelines to the international marketer (manufacturer) in order to anticipate and correct potential problems with international distributors:

- *Select distributors – do not let them select you.* Typically, manufacturers are approached by potential distributors at international fairs and exhibitions, but the most eager potential distributors are often the wrong people to partner with.
- *Look for distributors capable of developing markets, rather than those with a few obvious contacts.* This means sometimes bypassing the most obvious choice – the distributor who has the right customers and can generate quick sales – in favour of a partner with a greater willingness to make long-term investments and an acceptance of an open relationship.
- *Treat the local distributors as long-term partners, not temporary market-entry vehicles.* Many companies actively signal to distributors that their intentions are only for the short term, drawing up contracts that allow them to buy back distribution rights after a few years. Under such a short-term agreement, the problem is that the local distributor does not have much incentive to invest in the necessary long-term marketing development.
- *Support market entry by committing money, managers and proven marketing ideas.* Many manufacturers are reluctant to commit resources at the early stages of a market entry. However, to retain strategic control, the international marketer must commit adequate corporate resources. This is especially true during market entry, when companies are least certain about their prospect in new countries.
- *From the start, maintain control over marketing strategy.* An independent distributor should be allowed to adapt the manufacturer's strategy to local conditions. However, only companies providing solid leadership for marketing will be in a position to exploit the full potential of a global marketing network.
- *Make sure distributors provide you with detailed market and financial performance data.* Most distributors regard data like customer identification and local price levels as key sources of power in the relationship with the manufacturer. However, the manufacturer's ability to exploit its competitive advantages in the international market depends heavily on the quality of information it obtains from the market. Therefore a contract with the distributor must include the exchange of such information, e.g. detailed market and financial performance data.
- *Build links among national distributors at the earliest opportunity.* The links may take the form of creating an independent national distributor council or a regional corporate office. The transfer of ideas within local markets can improve performance and result in greater consistency in the execution of international marketing strategies, because links to other national distributor networks could be established. This could lead to a cross-national transfer of efficient marketing tools.

Once the basic design of the channel has been determined, the international marketer must begin to fill it with the best available candidates, and must secure their cooperation.

Screening and selecting intermediaries

Figure 16.8 shows the most important criteria (qualifications) for selecting foreign distributors, grouped into five categories.

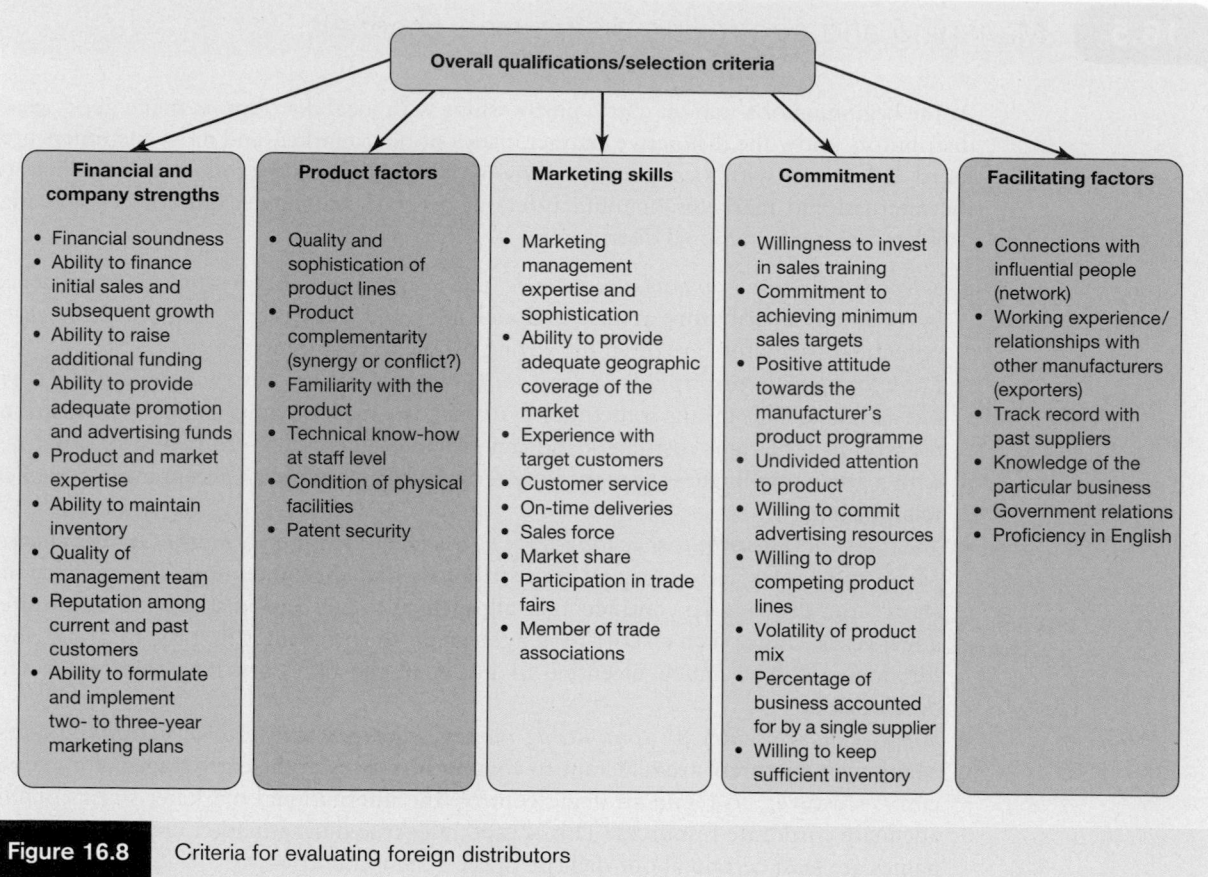

| **Financial and company strengths** | **Product factors** | **Marketing skills** | **Commitment** | **Facilitating factors** |

Overall qualifications/selection criteria

Financial and company strengths
- Financial soundness
- Ability to finance initial sales and subsequent growth
- Ability to raise additional funding
- Ability to provide adequate promotion and advertising funds
- Product and market expertise
- Ability to maintain inventory
- Quality of management team
- Reputation among current and past customers
- Ability to formulate and implement two- to three-year marketing plans

Product factors
- Quality and sophistication of product lines
- Product complementarity (synergy or conflict?)
- Familiarity with the product
- Technical know-how at staff level
- Condition of physical facilities
- Patent security

Marketing skills
- Marketing management expertise and sophistication
- Ability to provide adequate geographic coverage of the market
- Experience with target customers
- Customer service
- On-time deliveries
- Sales force
- Market share
- Participation in trade fairs
- Member of trade associations

Commitment
- Willingness to invest in sales training
- Commitment to achieving minimum sales targets
- Positive attitude towards the manufacturer's product programme
- Undivided attention to product
- Willing to commit advertising resources
- Willing to drop competing product lines
- Volatility of product mix
- Percentage of business accounted for by a single supplier
- Willing to keep sufficient inventory

Facilitating factors
- Connections with influential people (network)
- Working experience/ relationships with other manufacturers (exporters)
- Track record with past suppliers
- Knowledge of the particular business
- Government relations
- Proficiency in English

Figure 16.8   Criteria for evaluating foreign distributors

Source: adapted from Cavusgil *et al.* (1995).

After listing all important criteria (as in Figure 16.8), some of these must then be chosen for a more specific evaluation, where the potential candidates are compared and contrasted against determining criteria.

The example in Table 16.1 uses the first two criteria in each of Figure 16.8's five categories for screening potential channel members, in total ten criteria. The specific criteria to be used depend on the nature of a firm's business and its distribution objectives in given markets. The list of criteria should correspond closely to the marketer's own determinants of success – all the things that are important to beating the competition.

The hypothetical manufacturer (a consumer packaged goods company) used in Table 16.1 considered the distributor's marketing management expertise and financial soundness to be of greatest importance. These indicators will show whether the distributor is making money and is able to perform some of the necessary marketing functions such as extension of credit to customers and risk absorption. Financial reports are not always complete or reliable, or may lend themselves to differences of interpretation, pointing to the need for a third-party opinion. In order to make the weighting and grading in Table 16.1, the manufacturer must have had some personal interviews with the management of each potential distributor. In the example in the table, Distributor 1 would be selected by the manufacturer.

Alternatively, an industrial goods company may consider the distributor's product compatibility, technical know-how and technical facilities and service support of high importance, and the distributor's infrastructure, client performance and attitude towards its products of low importance. Quite often global marketers find that the most desirable distributors in a given market are already handling competitive products and are therefore unavailable.

Table 16.1	An example of distributor evaluation by the use of selection criteria from Figure 16.8						
Criteria (no ranking implied)	Weight	Distributor 1		Distributor 2		Distributor 3	
		Rating	Score	Rating	Score	Rating	Score
Financial and company strengths							
Financial soundness	4	5	20	4	16	3	12
Ability to finance initial sales and subsequent growth	3	4	12	4	12	3	9
Product factors							
Quality and sophistication of product lines	3	5	15	4	12	3	9
Product complementarity (synergy or conflict?)	3	3	9	4	12	2	6
Marketing skills							
Marketing management expertise and sophistication	5	4	20	3	15	2	10
Ability to provide adequate geographic coverage of the market	4	5	20	4	16	3	12
Commitment							
Willingness to invest in sales training	4	3	12	3	12	3	12
Commitment to achieving minimum sales targets	3	4	12	3	9	3	9
Facilitating factors							
Connections with influential people (network)	3	5	15	4	12	4	12
Working experience/relationships with other manufacturers (exporters)	2	4	8	3	6	3	6
Score			**143**		**122**		**97**

Scales:

Rating
5 Outstanding
4 Above average
3 Average
2 Below average
1 Unsatisfactory

Weighting
5 Critical success factor
4 Prerequisite success factor
3 Important success factor
2 Of some importance
1 Standard

A high-tech consumer goods company, on the other hand, may favour financial soundness, marketing management expertise, reputation, technical know-how, technical facilities, service support and government relations. In some countries, religious or ethnic differences might make an agent suitable for one part of the market coverage but unsuitable for another. This can result in more channel members being required in order to give adequate market coverage.

Contracting (distributor agreements)

When the international marketer has found a suitable intermediary, a foreign sales agreement is drawn up. Before final contractual arrangements are made, it is wise to make personal visits to the prospective channel member. The agreement itself can be relatively simple but, given the numerous differences in the market environments, certain elements are essential, as follows:

- names and addresses of both parties;
- date when the agreement goes into effect;
- duration of the agreement;
- provisions for extending or terminating the agreement;

- description of sales territory;
- establishment of discount and/or commission schedules and determination of when and how paid;
- provisions for revising the commission or discount schedules;
- establishment of a policy governing resale prices;
- maintenance of appropriate service facilities;
- restrictions to prohibit the manufacture and sale of similar and competitive products;
- designation of responsibility for patent and trademark negotiations and/or pricing;
- the assignability or non-assignability of the agreement and any limiting factors;
- designation of the country and state (if applicable) of contract jurisdiction in the case of dispute.

Source: from *International Marketing Management 5th Edition* by Jain, 1996. Reprinted with permission of Professor Subhash C. Jain.

The long-term commitments involved in distribution channels can become particularly difficult if the contract between the company and the channel member is not carefully drafted. It is normal to prescribe a time limit and a minimum sales level to be achieved, in addition to the particular responsibilities of each party. If this is not carried out satisfactorily, the company may be stuck with a weak performer that either cannot be removed or is very costly to buy out from the contract.

Contract duration is important, especially when an agreement is signed with a new distributor. In general, distribution agreements should be for a specified, relatively short period (one or two years). The initial contract with a new distributor should stipulate a trial period of either three or six months, possibly with minimum purchase requirements. Duration is also dependent on the local laws and their stipulations on distributor agreements.

Geographic boundaries for the distributor should be determined with care, especially by smaller firms. Future expansion of the product market might be complicated if a distributor claims rights to certain territories. The marketer should retain the right to distribute products independently, reserving the right to certain customers.

The *payment section* of the contract should stipulate the methods of payment as well as how the distributor or agent is to draw compensation. Distributors derive compensation from various discounts, such as the functional discount, whereas agents earn a specific commission, a percentage of net sales (typically 10–20 per cent). Given the volatility of currency markets, the agreement should also state the currency to be used.

Product and conditions of sale need to be agreed on. The products or product lines included should be stipulated, as well as the functions and responsibilities of the intermediary in terms of carrying the goods in inventory, providing service in conjunction with them, and promoting them. Conditions of sale determine which party is to be responsible for some of the expenses (e.g. marketing expenses) involved, which will in turn have an effect on the price to the distributor. These conditions include credit and shipment terms.

Means of communication between the parties must be stipulated in the agreement if a marketer–distributor relationship is to succeed. The marketer should have access to all information concerning the marketing of its products in the distributor's territory, including past records, present situation assessments and marketing research.

Motivating

Geographic distance and cultural distance make the process of motivating channel members difficult. Motivating is also difficult because intermediaries are not owned by the company. Since intermediaries are independent firms, they will seek to achieve their own objectives, which will not always match the objective of the manufacturer. The international marketer may offer both monetary and psychological rewards, and intermediaries will be strongly influenced by the earnings potential of the product. If the trade margin is poor and sales are difficult to achieve, intermediaries will lose interest in the product and concentrate on products with a more rewarding response to selling efforts, because they make their sales and profits from their own assortment of products and services from different companies.

It is important to keep in regular contact with agents and distributors. A consistent flow of all relevant types of communication will stimulate interest and sales performance. The international marketer may place one person in charge of distributor-related communications and put into effect an exchange of personnel so that both organizations gain further insight into the workings of the other.

Controlling

Control problems are reduced substantially if intermediaries are selected carefully. However, control should be sought through the common development of written performance objectives. These performance objectives might include some of the following: sales turnover per year, market share growth rate, introduction of new products, price charged and marketing communications support. Control should be exercised through periodic personal meetings.

Evaluation of performance has to be done against the changing environment. In some situations, economic recession or fierce competition activity prevents the possibility of objectives being met. However, if poor performance is established, the contract between the company and the channel member will have to be reconsidered and perhaps terminated.

Termination

Typical reasons for the termination of a channel relationship are:

- The international marketer has established a sales subsidiary in the country.
- The international marketer is unsatisfied with the performance of the intermediary.

Open communication is always needed to make the transition smooth. For example, the intermediary can be compensated for investments made, and major customers can be visited jointly to assure them that service will be uninterrupted.

Termination conditions are among the most important considerations in the distribution agreement. The causes of termination vary and the penalties for the international marketer may be substantial. It is especially important to find out what local laws say about termination and to check what type of experience other firms have had in the particular country.

In some countries, terminating an ineffective intermediary can be time-consuming and expensive. In the EU, one year's average commissions are typical for termination without justification. A notice of termination has to be given three to six months in advance. If the cause for termination is the manufacturer's establishment of a local sales subsidiary, then the international marketer may consider engaging good employees from the intermediary as, for example, managers in the new sales subsidiary. This can prevent a loss of product know-how that has been created at the intermediary's firm. The international marketer could also consider an acquisition of this firm if the intermediary is willing to sell.

16.6 Implications of the internet for distribution decisions

The internet has the power to change drastically the balance of power among consumers, retailers, distributors, manufacturers and service providers. Some participants in the distribution chain may experience an increase in their power and profitability. Others will experience the reverse; some may even find that they have been bypassed and have lost their market share.

Disintermediation
The elimination of a layer of intermediaries from a marketing channel or the displacement of traditional resellers by radically new types of intermediaries.

Channel conflict
Disagreement among marketing channel members on goals and roles – who should do what and for what rewards. A significant threat arising from the introduction of an internet channel is that, while disintermediation gives the opportunity for a company to sell direct and increase the profitability of products, it also threatens distribution arrangements with existing partners.

Physical distributors, and dealers in goods and services that are more conveniently ordered and/or delivered online are indeed subject to increasing pressure from e-commerce. This **disintermediation** process, with increasing direct sales through the internet, leads manufacturers to compete with their resellers, which may also result in **channel conflict**.

The reality is that the internet may eliminate the traditional 'physical' distributors, but in the transformation process of the value chain new types of intermediaries may appear. So the disintermediation process has come to be balanced by a reintermediation force – the evolution of new intermediaries tailor-made for the online world (Figure 16.9).

Many scholars believe that the direct internet-based exchange (direct distribution from manufacturer to buyer in Figure 16.9) is much more likely to reduce transaction costs, which are the expenditures associated with the transaction process regarding the distributor contract that a manufacturer sets up with a distributor: searching costs, bargaining costs and monitoring costs. If this were true, then traditional market distributors would have disappeared in e-commerce. However, they continue to play important roles (Cho and Tansuhaj, 2013).

What typically happens is: the transformation of any industry structure in the internet economy is likely to go through the intermediation–disintermediation–reintermediation (IDR) cycle. The IDR cycle will occur because new technologies are forcing change in the relationships among buyers, suppliers and middlemen. Intermediation occurs when a firm begins as a middleman between two industry players (e.g. buyer–supplier, buyer–established intermediary or established intermediary–supplier). Disintermediation occurs when an established middleman is pushed out of the value chain. Reintermediation occurs when a once disintermediated player is able to re-establish itself as an intermediary.

What can the intermediaries (typically wholesalers and distributors) do in order to limit the dis-intermediation? The answer is anti-disintermediation. By this, measures are carried out through business incentives (or disincentives) and legal actions to ensure that intermediary positions are not eliminated. Since a good deal of profit is made by individuals or businesses serving as intermediaries between the primary source of a good or service and the consumer, intermediaries are using anti-disintermediation measures to re-establish their niche in the changing economy. In one example of anti-disintermediation, Home Depot sent a letter to 1,000 of its suppliers (including Black & Decker and General

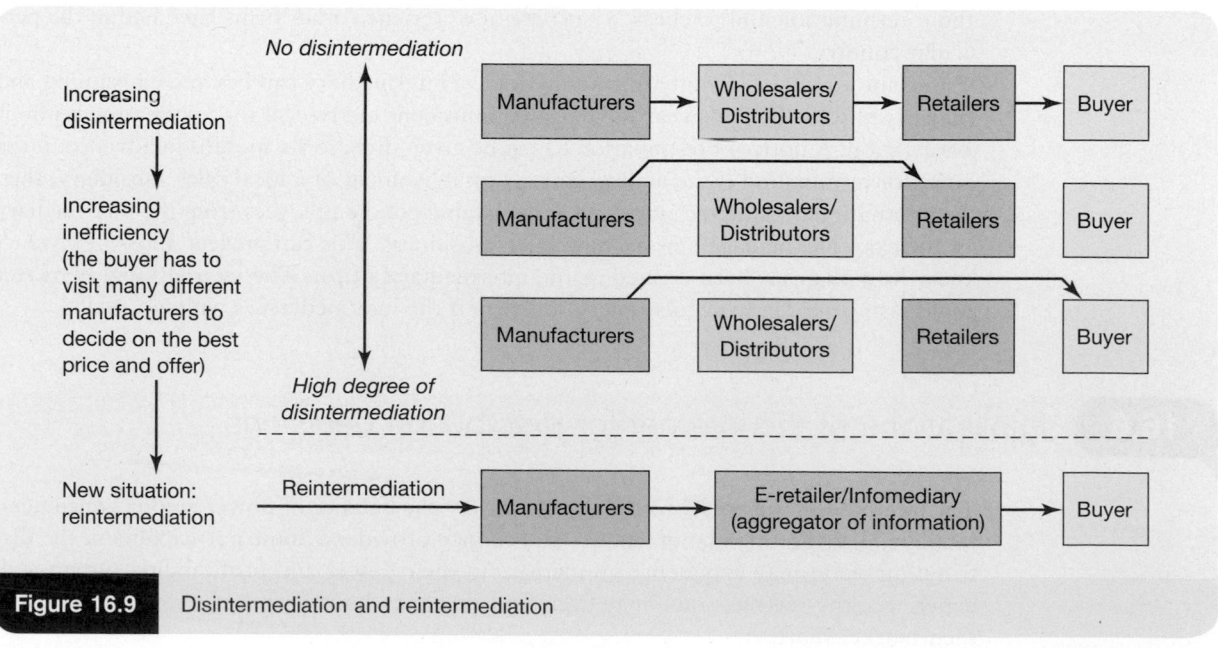

Figure 16.9   Disintermediation and reintermediation

Electric, for example) warning them that the company would be less likely to do business with those among them who also marketed their goods online.

Anti-disintermediation through high level of personalized services is also a way to address the increasing trend toward disintermediation. Instead of focusing on lower value-added transactions that can be replaced easily by internet technology, wholesalers and distributors can choose to focus on personalized service that technology cannot duplicate.

16.7   Online retail sales

Online retailing is one of the fastest-growing market sectors in Europe, the US and Asia (China). Worldwide, online retail sales will grow around 10–15 per cent per year over the next five years as shoppers continue to shift their spending from physical stores ('bricks') to online ones ('clicks'). Key drivers of this growth include increased use of smartphones and tablet computers, greater merchandise selection online and new business models. Consumers feel more confident with purchasing various categories online, and with broader web shopping capabilities with their mobile and tablet devices. It seems that consumers are now more willing to consider purchasing a greater number of categories of products online than before. Many consumers are expanding from an early emphasis on items such as books and CDs (which can be described precisely online in terms such as title, product number and shipping time) to other types of merchandise such as fashion apparel and gourmet food. These products also contain 'non-digital' attributes such as the fit and feel (Bell *et al.*, 2012).

In the past, brick-and-mortar retail stores were unique in allowing consumers to touch and feel merchandise and provide instant gratification. As the retailing industry evolves towards seamless '**omnichannel retailing**' experience, the distinctions between physical and online will vanish, turning the world into a showroom without walls (Brynjolfsson *et al.*, 2013).

The two-dimensional framework (resulting in the 2 × 2 matrix) in Figure 16.10 is based on basic questions:

1. *Information delivery*. How will the customers get the information they need to facilitate their purchase decisions? Two options: will they visit the stores to obtain (offline) information or will they seek information online, through websites or online catalogues?

Omnichannel retailing (or multi-channel retailing)
The use of a variety of channels in a customer's shopping experience, including research before a purchase. Such channels include: retail stores, online stores, mobile stores, mobile app stores, telephone sales and any other method of transacting with a customer. Transacting includes browsing, buying, returning as well as pre-sale and after-sale service.

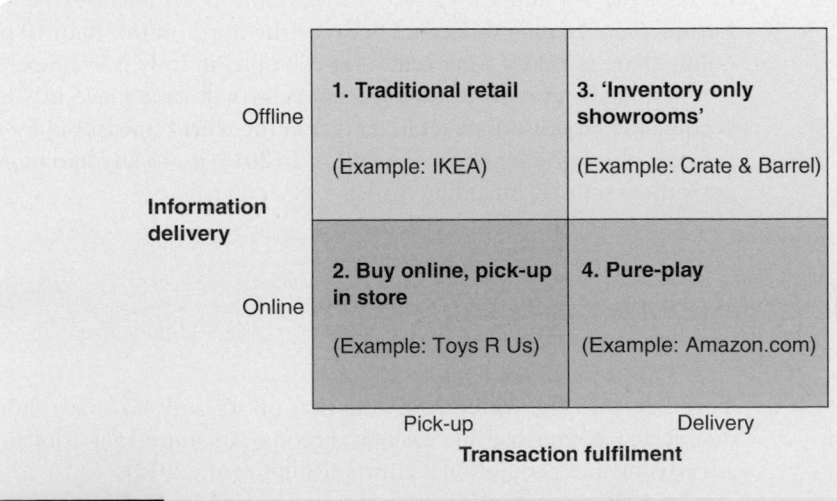

| Figure 16.10 | The information and fulfilment matrix |

Source: based on Bell *et al.* (2014), © 2014 from MIT Sloan Management Review/Massachusetts Institute of Technology.

Table 16.2	Online share of all retail business (2015)
	2015 online share of total retail sales
UK	15.2%
Germany	11.6%
Sweden	7.8%
Netherlands	7.4%
Spain	3.5%
Poland	3.3%
Italy	2.5%
Average Europe	8.4%
US	12.7%
China	8.5%

Source: based on figures from Centre for Retail Research (www.retailresearch.org).

2. *Transaction fulfilment.* How will the transactions be fulfilled? Two options: will the customers either visit the store to pick up the items or will the store come to them, when the products are being delivered?

Most of the company examples mentioned in Figure 16.10 should be well known. Of course several of the companies pursue a retail strategy where they combine two or more of the four strategies in Figure 16.10. For example, Crate & Barrel is an American chain of up-market retail stores, functioning as showrooms, specializing in housewares, furniture and home accessories. Their customers typically come to their showrooms after which the furniture will be delivered to their homes via central warehouses ('inventory only showrooms' – option 3).

Option 4 ('Pure play') is growing at a rapid pace all over the world. For example, Amazon.com uses multiple third-party carriers such as UPS, FedEx or DHL, to ship products to customers. Amazom.com is even testing the use of drones to ship products directly to customers' homes.

The average share that online retail sales have of the total retail sales is quite similar in Europe, the US and China (see Table 16.2), at around 8–9 per cent. However, within Europe there is a big difference between the north (more than 10 per cent) and where the online share is below 5 per cent – for example, in Italy it is 2.5 per cent.

The biggest growth in online retail sales will take place in China, which is likely to become the largest online retail market in the world (measured by value), with close to 10 per cent of retail sales occurring online. In 2015, it already had more online shoppers than any other country, including the US.

16.8   Smartphone marketing

Together with the widespread adoption of 3G and 4G smartphones among consumers, mobile marketing has increasingly become an important tool in brands' international advertising and promotional efforts (Rohm *et al.*, 2012).

The next generation of the internet standard in mobile marketing (m-marketing) will allow programs to run through a web browser rather than a specific operating system. That means consumers will be able to access the same programs and cloud-based content from any device – personal computer, laptop, smartphone or tablet – because the browser is the common platform. This ability to work seamlessly anytime, anywhere, on any device could change consumer behaviour and shift the balance of power in the distribution systems towards the end of the distribution system – the end-buyer, who has cheaper and cheaper access to the new mobile devices. It will create opportunities for marketers to distribute goods and services more directly to the end-buyers and it will present increasing challenges for the intermediaries between the manufacturers and the end-buyers (Korkmaz *et al.*, 2011).

Rapidly emerging innovations have also delivered the possibility of smartphones able to use product bar codes to access product-related information and phones able to act as e-wallets, as either a prepaid card for small purchases or a fully functioning credit/debit card unit.

However, the mobile industry will also see a lot more enforcement in the are of mobile security and privacy in the coming years, as many questions have been raised regarding mobile payments, coupons and applications. Mobile commerce is on the rise, which means people are more comfortable with the idea of paying with their phones. However, there is still a critical view throughout the mobilized world regarding the safety of this kind of payment system.

Benefits of m-marketing

The introduction of m-marketing should bring a series of benefits to consumers, merchants and telecommunication companies. As with all technologies, many benefits will arise in the future that have not yet even been imagined. Some benefits that are apparent now, however, include the following:

For consumers

- *Comparison shopping*. Consumers can access on demand, at the point of purchase, the best prices in the marketplace. This can be done now without mobility, with services such as pricescan.com.
- *Bridge the gap between bricks and clicks*. Services permitting users to examine merchandise in a store and still shop electronically for the best price.
- *Opt-in searches*. Customers may receive alerts from merchants when products they are looking for become available.
- *Travel*. Ability to change and monitor scheduled travel any time, any place.

For merchants

- *Impulse buying*. Consumers may buy discounted products from a web page promotion or a mobile alert, increasing their willingness to buy when they are near or even inside the store, thus increasing merchants' sales.
- *Drive traffic*. Companies will guide their customers to where it is easier to carry out the transaction, to either online or offline stores, due to the time-sensitive, location-based and personalized characteristics of the mobile device.
- *Education of consumers*. Companies will send information to customers about product benefits or new products.
- *Perishable products*. This is especially important for products that do not retain their value when unused, such as service-based products, an example being the use of an aeroplane seat, which, when unused, generates no revenue and is lost value. This will enable companies to manage inventory more effectively.
- *Drive efficiency*. Companies will save time with their clients. Because information is readily available on the mobile device, they will not have to talk about the benefits of the different products or about prices.
- *Target market*. Companies will be better able to target their products and promotions to those in a given geographic area at a specific time.

For telecommunication companies, the advantages are primarily more airtime used by the consumers and higher fees charged to content providers for each m-commerce transaction.

M-marketing requires direct marketers to rethink their strategies to tap into already existing communities – such as sports fans, surfers and music fans; time-context communities such as spectators at sports events and festivals; and location-sensitive communities such as gallery visitors and small shoppers – and develop ways to get them to opt in to m-marketing. Applications must be responsive to location, customer needs and device capabilities. For example, time- and location-sensitive applications, such as travel reservations, cinema tickets and banking, will be excellent vehicles for young, busy, urban people.

Finally, as highlighted, m-marketing enables distribution of information to the consumer at the most effective time, place and in the right context. This suggests that m-marketing, via mobile devices, will cement further the interactive marketing relationship. Greater adoption of mobile technology can help the marketer deliver messages to consumers when in a relevant environment. Smartphones are a vital piece of technology, as their owners take them wherever they go and they can be used to deliver a message based on consumers' shopping preferences just before the point of purchase.

16.9   Channel power in international retailing

For too long, manufacturers have viewed vertical marketing channels as closed systems, operating as separate, static entities. The most important factors creating long-term, integrated strategic plans and fostering productive channel relationships were largely ignored. Fortunately, a new philosophy about channel management has emerged, but to understand its potential we must first understand how power has developed at the retailer level.

Channel power
The ability of a channel member to control marketing variables of any other member in a channel at a different level of distribution.

Power in channel relationships can be defined as the ability of a channel member to control marketing decision variables of any other member in a channel at a different level of distribution. A classic example of this **channel power** is the amount of power wielded by retailers against the food and grocery manufacturers. One result of this may be found in Exhibit 16.3, where the 'banana split' shows that increasing retailing power has resulted in a retail share of the total value chain in the banana business of 40 per cent. As the balance of power has shifted, more merchandise is controlled by fewer and fewer retailers.

EXHIBIT 16.3 The 'banana split' model

At the level of production, bananas tend to be produced either on very small land holdings or on very large plantations. It is estimated that 80 per cent of global exports originate from large-scale plantations and the rest from smaller farms. There is considerable diversity of production systems both within and between banana-exporting countries. There is considerably less diversity in the chain after the farm gate. The process of transporting, ripening and distributing bananas is highly concentrated, with five very large corporations controlling as much as 80 per cent of banana exports. The remaining 20 per cent of exports is nonetheless very fragmented: a large number of smaller exporting companies are involved in sourcing and marketing of bananas.

The five large transnational banana exporters – Dole, Del Monte, Chiquita, Fyffes and Noboa – are vertically integrated to varying degrees into production, transportation, ripening and distribution. Of the five large transnationals, only Fyffes is not directly involved in producing bananas on company-owned farms. The other large companies own plantations in Latin America, Africa and Asia. The large banana exporters own, or have owned, the infrastructure for shipping and transport.

Once the bananas are offloaded at ports in Europe, the US and Asia, they are transported to ripening facilities so that the fruit can be prepared for distribution. All of the transnational banana exporters own their own ripening and distribution facilities in the markets they supply. In Europe, investment by these companies in ripening and distribution infrastructure increased in the period after 1993 with the shift to a single European market for bananas.

The five transnationals are as follows:

- **Chiquita** controls 25 per cent of the global banana market. Bananas generate 67 per cent of Chiquita's revenues; other interests are in fresh fruit, juices and canned vegetables.
- **Dole** claims to be the world's largest producer of bananas, with approximately 30 per cent of the global banana market. Dole has been 100 per cent owned by CEO David Murdock and family since late 2002.
- **Del Monte Fresh Produce** (completely separate from Del Monte Foods since the break-up of RJR Nabisco in 1989) has around 15 per cent of the banana market, and also sells pineapples, melons and other tropical fruit and speciality vegetables.
- **Fyffes** is the largest fresh produce distributor in Europe. It has about 20 per cent of the global banana market and is headquartered in Ireland.
- **Noboa (Exportadora Bananera Noboa)** is part of a conglomerate of 110 companies (Grupo Noboa) privately owned by Alvaro Noboa, Ecuador's richest man and twice presidential candidate. It has 10 per cent of the global banana market.

Only around 12 per cent (10 per cent + 2 per cent) of revenues from banana retail sales (see Figure 16.11) remain in producing countries, despite the very limited amount of product transformation outside of the farm or plantation. Forty per cent of retail value may stay with the supermarket even though this is the least demanding part of the chain. The dominance of retailers has had an increasing influence over the structure and distribution of value along the banana chain. The shift of profits towards the downstream end of the chain has been dramatic over the last decade, and the transnationals' margins on bananas are decreasing, whereas the retailers' share of the value chain is increasing. The banana value chain has shifted from being producer-driven to one that is increasingly buyer-driven. A structural oversupply of bananas has also led to lower prices and intense competition. Since the mid-1990s, the supermarket chains have consolidated (fewer but more powerful retail chains) and exercised their growing market power over banana transnationals by demanding higher product quality and service, and by passing value functions 'up the chain'. In response, the transnationals are increasingly integrating vertically into ripening, shipping, packing and distribution, but also moving away from direct ownership of production. The transnationals are also trying to provide a wider range of fruit and more value-added products in order to increase profits and improve their chances of becoming a preferred supplier of a supermarket chain.

Sources: adapted from Vorley (2003); Marther (2008).

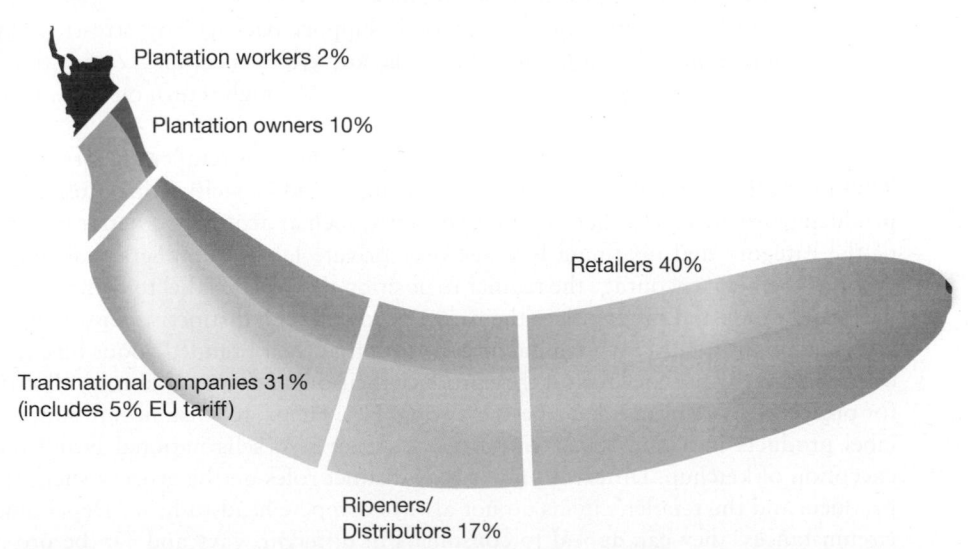

Plantation workers 2%

Plantation owners 10%

Retailers 40%

Transnational companies 31%
(includes 5% EU tariff)

Ripeners/
Distributors 17%

There is a high degree of overlap between the transnational companies and the ripeners/distributors.
Four of the five transnationals are also involved with ripening: Chiquita, Dole, Del Monte and Fyffes.

Figure 16.11   The 'banana split' model. How much (in percentages of the retail value in the UK) stays with each chain actor to cover costs and margin

Source: adapted from Vorley, B. (2003, Fig. 7.2, p. 52).

There is a worldwide tendency towards **concentration in retailing** (fewer and fewer retail chains dominate more and more of the retail trade), resulting huge buying power among huge retail chains, like Walmart. The concentration in the European food sector is most evident in the northern part of Europe. Since the mid-1990s, new players have arrived on the European grocery market, for example, the German discount-chain, Lidl, which is now second in the German discount sector after Aldi. Lidl is also expanding to the remaining European area (e.g. to Scandinavia, the UK and France). In the UK in 2014, Tesco was number one and Sainsbury's number two.

A consequence of this development is that there has been a worldwide shift from manufacturer to retailer dominance. Power has become concentrated in the hands of fewer and fewer retailers, and the manufacturers have been left with little choice but to accede to their demands. This often results in manufacturing of the retailers' own brands (private labels). This phenomenon was introduced in Section 14.8.

Therefore we can see that traditional channel management, with its characteristics of power struggles, conflict and loose relationships, is no longer beneficial. New ideas are emerging to help channel relationships become more cooperative. This is what is known as 'trade marketing'. Trade marketing is when the manufacturer (supplier) markets directly to the trade (retailers) to create a better fit between product and outlet. The objective is to create joint marketing and strategic plans for mutual profitability.

For the manufacturer (supplier), it means creating twin marketing strategies: one to the consumer and another to the trade (retailers). However, as Figure 16.12 shows, potential channel conflicts exist because of differences in the objectives of the channel members.

Despite potential channel conflicts, what both parties share, but often forget, is their common goal of consumer satisfaction. If the desired end result is to create joint marketing plans, a prerequisite must be an improved understanding of the other's perspective and objectives.

Retailers are looking for potential sales, profitability, exclusivity in promotions and volume. They are currently in the enviable position of being able to choose brands that fulfil those aims.

A private-label manufacturer has to create different packages for different retailers. By carefully designing individual packages, the manufacturer gains a better chance of striking up a relationship with the best-matched retailer.

Manufacturers can offer retailers a total 'support package' by stressing their own strengths. These include marketing knowledge and experience, market position, proven new product success, media support and exposure and a high return on investment (ROI) in shelf space.

Manufacturers should also think about partnering with retailers to produce **private-label products**. In addition to the obvious volume and capacity utilization gained from producing private labels, there are more benefits, such as acquiring a better understanding of the category and obtaining leverage over private labels. Suppliers that manufacture private labels can encourage the retailer to position the private label to compete with other national brands and differentiate their own products with distinctive packaging, product sizes and quantities. Many manufacturers worry that their branded goods business will be overwhelmed by private labels if they produce their own private-label entry. But strategies for protecting core brands have been evolving. H.J. Heinz, for instance, produces private-label products in a number of categories where it also sells national brands, with the exception of ketchup. Different brands play distinct roles on the grocery shelf; the Heinz products and the retailer's items do not always compete head-to-head. Depending on the circumstances, they can appeal to consumers in different ways and can be promoted at different times (Dawar and Stornelli, 2013).

If such a joint strategy is going to be successful, manufacturers and retailers must work together at every level, perhaps by matching counterparts in each organization. As a consequence of the increasing importance of the individual customer (the retail chain as one buying unit), the concept of the key account (key customer) has been introduced.

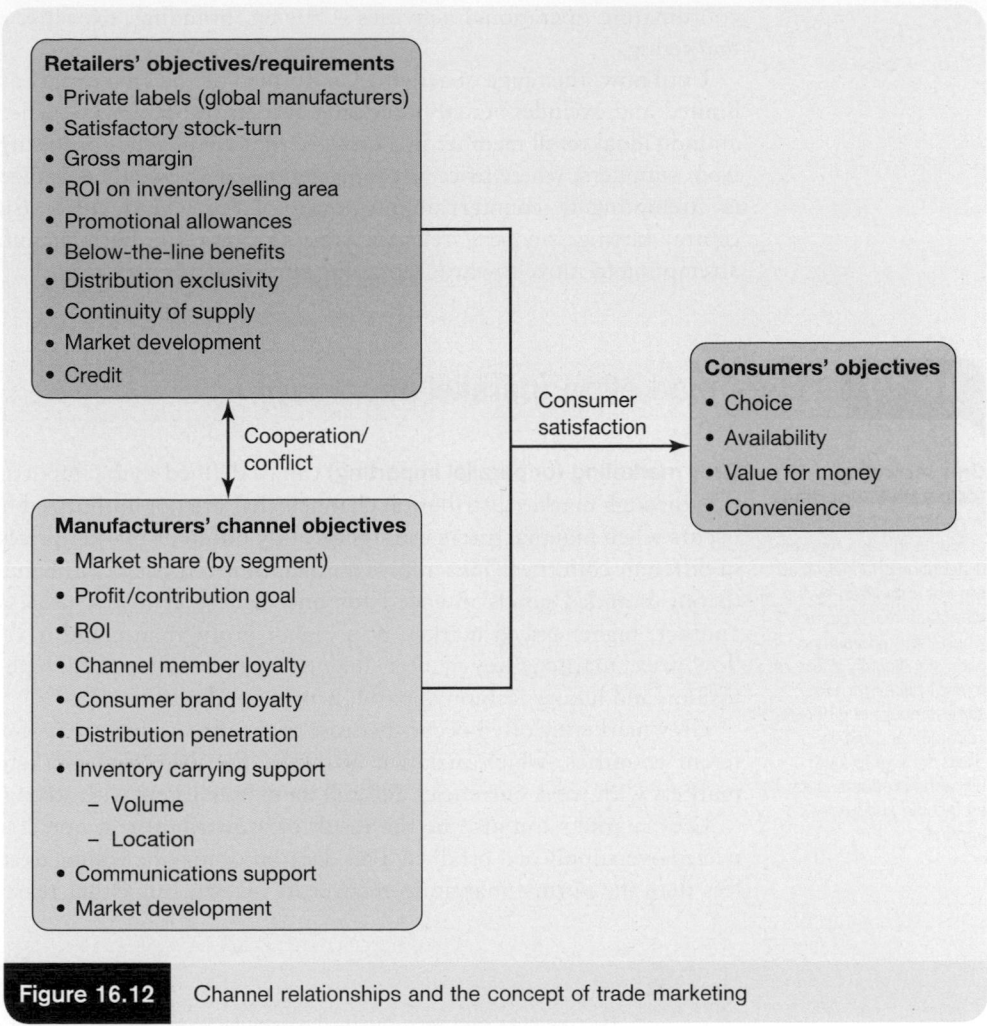

Figure 16.12   Channel relationships and the concept of trade marketing

Key accounts
The most important
customers for the
manufacturer, as they
contribute to a large
portion of the company's
sales. Creating and
maintaining long-term
relationships to key
accounts is the most
important role of key
account managers.

Key accounts are often large retail chains with a large turnover (in total as well as of the
supplier's products), which are able to decide quantity and price on behalf of different
outlets.

Segmentation of customers is therefore no longer based only on size and geographic
position but also on customers' (retailers) structure of decision-making. This results in a
gradual restructuring of sales from a geographic division to a customer division. This
reorganization is made viable by creating key account managers (managers responsible for
customers).

Cross-border alliances in retailing

The focus of this section is alliances between retailers that are both horizontal (i.e. retailer
to retailer) and also international, in that they cross the boundaries of nation states. Cross-
border retailer alliances are emerging predominantly between western European retailers
and can, in many cases, be interpreted as explicit responses to the perceived threats and
opportunities of the EU internal market.

None of the cross-border alliances in Europe can be described as 'equity participating
alliances', which include a cross-shareholding between members. None of the alliances
involves the sharing of equity, but they all have a central secretariat with the function of

coordinating operational activities – buying, branding, expertise exchange and product marketing.

Until now, the range of activities performed by the secretariats of the alliances has been limited and excludes actual processing and central payments. The present advantage for an individual retail member in a cross-border alliance lies primarily in central purchasing from suppliers, where price advantages flow to all members, suggesting that the alliance is attempting to countervail the power of the manufacturer (supplier). Cross-border central buying can be a relevant starting point for both manufacturers and retailers attempting to move towards a pan-European supply network.

16.10   Grey marketing (parallel importing)

Grey marketing (or parallel importing)
Importing and selling of products through market distribution channels that are not authorized by the manufacturer. It occurs when the manufacturer uses significantly different market prices for the same product in different countries and mainly exists for high-priced, high-end products, such as fashion and luxury apparel.

Grey marketing (or parallel importing) can be defined as the importing and selling of products through market distribution channels that are not authorized by the manufacturer. It occurs when manufacturers use significantly different market prices for the same product in different countries. This allows an unauthorized dealer (in Figure 16.13, a wholesaler) to buy branded goods intended for one market at a low price and then sell them in another, higher-priced market, at a higher profit than could have been achieved in the 'low-price' market. Grey markets mainly exist for high-priced, high-end products, such as fashion and luxury fashion apparel, watches and perfume.

Grey marketing often occurs because of the fluctuating value of currencies between different countries, which makes it attractive for the 'grey' marketer to buy products in markets with weak currencies and sell them in markets with strong currencies.

Grey markets can also be the result of a distributor in one country having an unexpected oversupply of a product. This distributor may be willing to sell its excess supply for less than the normal margin to recover its investment. Other reasons for lower prices in

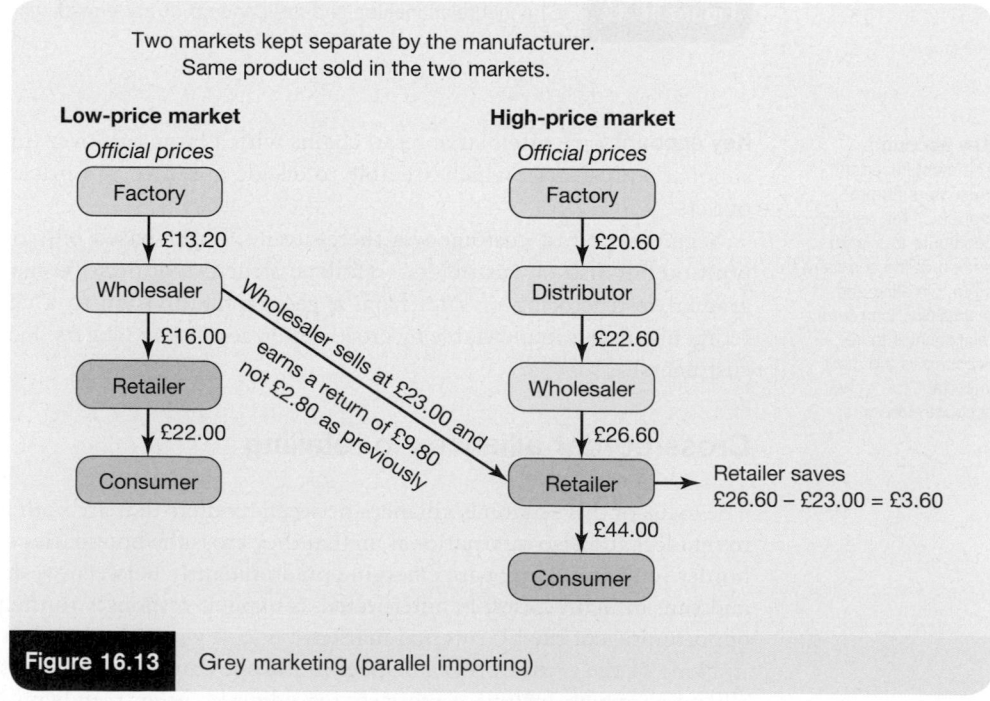

| **Figure 16.13** | Grey marketing (parallel importing) |

Source: Paliwoda (1993, p. 300). Reprinted with permission from Butterworth-Heinemann Publishers, a division of Reed Educational & Professional Publishing Ltd.

some countries (which can result in grey marketing) might be lower transport costs, fiercer competition and higher product taxes (high product taxes put pressure on the ex-works price to keep the end-consumer price at an acceptable level).

The particular problem with grey marketing for the manufacturer is that it results in authorized intermediaries losing motivation. The grey marketer usually competes only on price and pays little attention to providing marketing support and after-sales service.

Grey markets are fed by many sources in the e-business. Perhaps the most common are authorized dealers who can make a profit, or at least minimize a loss, by selling to unauthorized dealers. The internet makes it easier for firms operating in grey territory to reach a wide range of customers. Companies can buy in bulk and resell to unauthorized distributors, a situation that has characterized the market for computer parts for some time. Sometimes a manufacturer itself will sell into the grey market as salespeople struggle to meet quotas or managers attempt to cover costs or make year-end sales goals (Antia *et al.*, 2004).

Possible strategies to reduce grey marketing

Sometimes companies hope that grey marketing is a short-term problem and that it will disappear – and it might well do if the price difference is the result of the fluctuating value of currencies. At other times, a more proactive approach to the problem is needed:

- *Seek legal redress*. Although the legal option can be time-consuming and expensive, some companies (e.g. Seiko) have chosen to prosecute grey marketers.
- *Change the marketing mix*. This involves three elements:
  - *Product strategy*. This strategy is about moving away from the standardization concept (same product for all markets), and introducing a differentiated concept with a different product for each main market.
  - *Pricing strategy*. The manufacturer can change the ex-works prices to the channel members to minimize price differentials between markets. The manufacturer can also narrow the discount schedules it offers for large orders. This will reduce the incentive for intermediaries to over-order to get lower prices and later sell unsold stock on the grey market, still at a profit.
  - *Warranty strategy*. The manufacturer may reduce or cancel the warranty period for grey market products. This will require that the products can be identified through the channel system.

16.11 Summary

In this chapter we have examined the management of international distribution channels and logistics. The main structure of this chapter was given in Figure 16.1, and from the discussion it is evident that the international marketer has a broad range of alternatives for selecting and developing an economical, efficient and high-volume international distribution channel.

In many instances, the channel structure is affected by external factors and it may vary from nation to nation. Physical distribution (external logistics) concerns the flow of goods from the manufacturer to the customer. This is one area where cost savings through efficiency are feasible, provided the decision is made systematically. The changing nature of international retailing influences distribution planning. During the last decade, the balance of power (between manufacturers and retailers) has shifted in favour of the retailers. The manufacturer often has no other choice than to cooperate with large and increasingly concentrated retailers in terms of the 'trade marketing' concept.

Online distribution has dramatically changed the balance of power among the members in the distribution chain. The reality is that the online distribution may eliminate the traditional 'physical' distributors through the disintermediation process.

An increasingly popular distribution strategy is the multiple channel strategy, which is employed when a firm makes a product available to the market through two or more channels of distribution. Multiple channels include the internet, sales force, call centres, retail stores and direct mail.

A phenomenon of growing importance in international markets is the grey market, which consists of unauthorized traders buying and selling a company's product in different countries. Companies confronted with a grey market situation can react in many ways. They may decide to ignore the problem, take legal action or modify elements of their marketing mix. The option chosen is strongly influenced by the nature of the situation and its expected duration.

CASE STUDY 16.1

De Beers: forward integration into the diamond industry value chain

De Beers is a private holding company engaged in the exploration, mining and marketing of diamonds. The company primarily operates in Africa and markets its products across the globe. It is headquartered in Johannesburg, South Africa, and employs nearly 13,500 people. In the 2010 financial year, the company recorded revenues of US$5,877 million and operating profits of US$478 million.

Since the late 1800s, the South African multinational De Beers (www.debeersgroup.com) has regulated both the industrial and gemstone-diamond markets and effectively maintained an illusion of diamond scarcity. It has developed and nurtured the belief that diamonds are precious, invaluable symbols of romance. Every attitude consumers hold today about diamonds exists – at least in part – because of the persistent efforts of De Beers.

Moreover, by monitoring the supply and distribution of diamonds throughout the world, De Beers has introduced and maintained an unprecedented degree of price stability for a surprisingly common mineral: compressed carbon. Such unique price stability lies within the cartel's tight control over the distribution of diamonds. De Beers' operating strategy has been pure and simple: to restrict the number of diamonds released into the market in any given year and to perpetuate the myth that they are scarce and, therefore, should command high prices.

Source: Imagine China/Corbis.

De Beers spends about US$200 million a year to promote diamonds and diamond jewellery. 'A diamond is for ever', and the firm controls nearly 70 per cent of the rough diamond market.

De Beers controls a producer's cartel that operates as a quantity-fixing entity by setting production quotas for each member (as does OPEC). De Beers has successfully convinced the producers that the diamond supply must be regulated in order to maintain favourably high prices and profits.

During the early part of the last century much of the diamond cartel's strength rested with De Beers' control of the South African mines. Today, the source of power no longer comes from rough diamond production alone, but from a sophisticated network of production, marketing sales and promotion arrangements, all administered by De Beers.

It is interesting to note that diamond prices have little or no relation to the cost of extraction (production). Table 1 shows average or 'normal' price mark-ups on gemstones along the channel of distribution.

A diamond that may cost US$100 to mine can end up costing a consumer $920 at a local jewellery store. Business cycles and individual commercial practices may positively or negatively influence these figures, together with the gemstone quality. Diamond

Table 1	Mark-ups on diamonds	
Stage of distribution	Mark-up (%)	Average value of 0.5 carat gem ($/carat)
Cost of mining	–	100
Mine sales	67	167
Dealers of rough gems	20	200
Cutting units	100	400
Wholesaler dealers	15	460
Retail	100	920

Sources: based on Ariovich (1985); Bergenstock and Maskulka (2001).

sales, known in the trade as 'sights', are held 10 times a year in London, Lucerne, Switzerland and Kimberley, South Africa. The sales are limited to approximately 160 privileged 'sight-holders', primarily owners of diamond-cutting factories in New York, Tel Aviv, Mumbai and Antwerp, who then sell to the rest of the diamond trade.

Diamond output from De Beers' self-owned and self-operated mines constitutes only 43 per cent of the total world value of rough diamonds. Because it is not the sole producer of rough stones in the world,

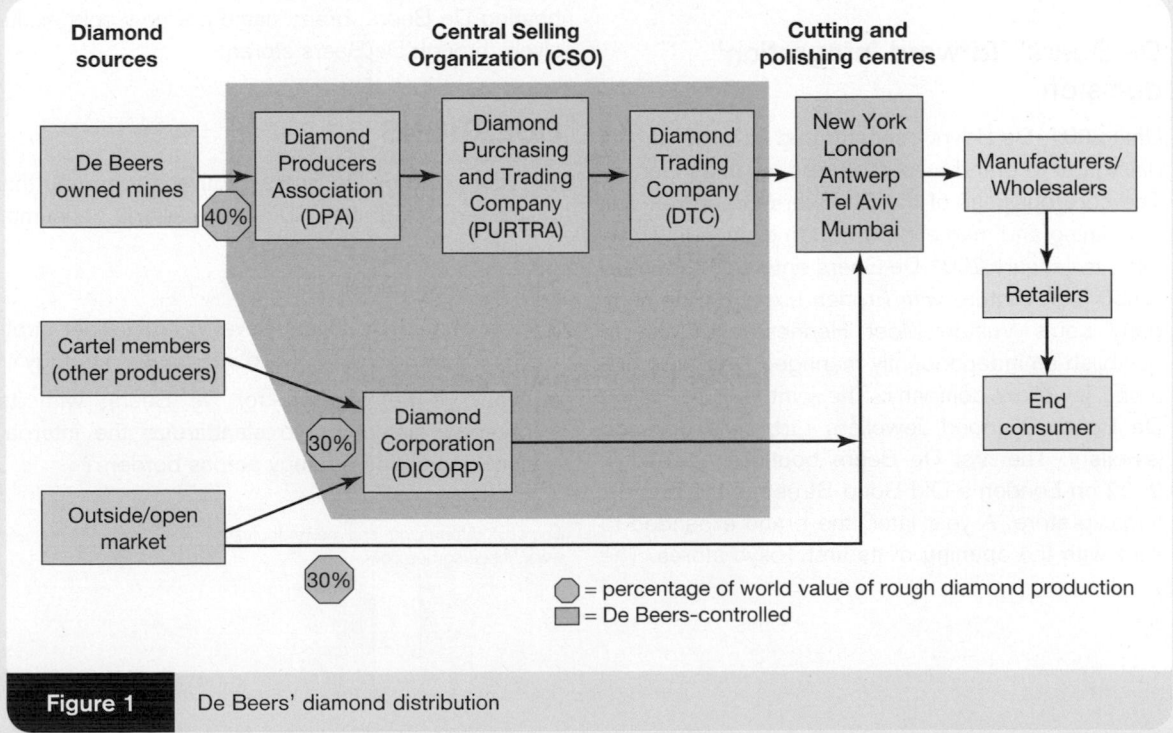

Figure 1 De Beers' diamond distribution

Sources: adapted from De Beers Annual Report and Bergenstock and Maskukla (2001).

De Beers has had to join forces with other major diamond-producing organizations, forming the international diamond cartel that controls nearly three-quarters of the world market.

De Beers has constructed a controlled supply and distribution chain whereby all cartel producers are contracted to sell the majority of their entire output to a single marketing entity: the De Beers-controlled Central Selling Organization (CSO) (see Figure 1).

The total rough diamond supply controlled by the CSO comes from three sources: De Beers/ Centenary-owned mines, outside suppliers contracted to the CSO (cartel members) and open market purchases via buying offices in Africa, Antwerp and Tel Aviv (rough output purchased from countries that have not signed an agreement with De Beers). De Beers functions as the sole diamond distributor. In any given year, approximately 75 per cent of the world's diamonds pass through the CSO to cutters and brokers.

The economic success of the cartel depends highly on strict adherence to their rules, written or unwritten. Clients who follow the rules are rewarded with consistent upgrades in the quality and quantity of rough stones in their boxes, while those who circumvent them find progressively worse allocations and risk not being invited back to future sights.

De Beers' 'forward integration' decision

Until 2001, De Beers concentrated on supplying its diamonds to brand manufacturers, such as Cartier. The core business of the De Beers Group remains the mining and marketing of rough diamonds. However, in January 2001 De Beers entered into a retail 50:50 joint venture with French luxury goods company Louis Vuitton Moet Hennessy (LVMH) to establish an independently managed De Beers diamond jewellery company. The joint venture, called De Beers Diamond Jewellers Ltd, sells diamond jewellery. The first De Beers boutique opened in 2002 on London's Old Bond Street as the brand's flagship store. A year later, the brand expanded to Asia with the opening of its first Tokyo stores. The brand expanded into the US with stores on Fifth Avenue in New York and Rodeo Drive in Beverly Hills in 2005. De Beers further expanded in the US in 2007 with stores in Las Vegas, Houston and McLean, VA, coinciding with the launch of a website with e-commerce capability. By 2010, there were De Beers retail stores in England, France, the US, Ukraine, Russia, Japan, Taipei, Hong Kong, Dubai and Macau. The joint venture's worldwide store network of 40 shops extended across the US (11), Europe (8), Middle East (4), East Asia (7) and Japan (10).

LVMH is the home of premier brands in the categories of fashion and leather goods, watches and jewellery, wine and spirits, cosmetics and perfumes. LVMH will contribute with its extensive experience in both developing luxury brands and rolling out premium retail concepts.

The 'mother' company, De Beers SA, contributes to the joint venture with its over 100 years of experience in the form of technology and individual experts to allow for the selection of the most beautiful diamonds.

As part of the joint venture agreement, De Beers SA transferred to De Beers LV the worldwide rights to use the De Beers brand name for luxury goods in consumer markets. From that point, De Beers would design, manufacture and sell premium diamond jewellery under its own brand name. The diamonds bearing De Beers' brand name are now sold exclusively through De Beers stores.

QUESTIONS

1. What could be De Beers' motives for making this 'forward integration' into the retail and consumer market?

2. Is it a wise decision?

3. How should De Beers develop its internet strategy following this 'forward integration' strategy?

4. Would it be possible for De Beers, with its branded diamonds, to standardize the international marketing strategy across borders?

Sources: information and news found on www.diamonds.net and www.debeersgroup.com.

CASE STUDY 16.2

Tupperware: the global direct distribution model is still working

Company founder Earl Tupper was an early plastics pioneer. The young inventor found work at DuPont in the 1930s without the benefit of a college education. By 1938, Tupper was ready to strike out on his own and devote himself to research in plastics. That year he started his own company, leaving DuPont with only his experience and a discarded piece of poly-ethylene. In 1946, he founded a new company, Tupperware, and began manufacturing food storage and serving containers with Poly-T.

Tupperware Corporation (www.tupperware.com), whose well-known Tupperware parties have spread to more than 100 countries, is one of the largest direct sellers in the world. Relying on independent consultants rather than employees for sales, the company generated more than US$1 billion in revenues, already in 1998. Although Tupperware's mainstay for 50 years had been plastic food storage containers, in the 1990s the company expanded into kitchen tools, small appliances and baby and toddler products. Although US sales declined steadily in the 1980s and 1990s, international sales expanded, with the result that more than 85 per cent of company revenues came from international business in the mid-1990s. The economic declines in the Far East and Latin America in the late 1990s left Tupperware with overall falling sales and an unsure outlook for the coming years.

Tupperware's direct selling model

The most successful early direct seller of Tupperware was Brownie Wise, a Detroit secretary and single mother. Tupper hired her in 1951 to create a direct selling system for his company. Within a few months, Tupper had established the subsidiary Tupperware Home Parties, Inc. and had abandoned selling his products through retail stores. Wise's home party system used a sales force of independent consultants who earned a flat percentage of the goods they sold and won incentives in the form of bonuses and products.

By the late 1950s, Tupperware had become a household name. With almost no advertising,

Tupperware had created phenomenal brand awareness. The company's rapid success can be attributed to its recruitment of almost 9,000 independent consultants by 1954, most of them women, and their enthusiastic spread of Tupperware parties, because Tupperware home parties provided an easy entry into the workforce for women. Tupperware understood what women at that time were going through. The company wanted to give them a sense of self-esteem and so came up with the idea of 'Tupperware parties'. Here women came together in their homes to talk about kitchen goods and other issues. In this way the women had the opportunity to own a business and make some money. This was the fore runner to what many marketing systems now call 'direct marketing'.

During the 1960s and 1970s, Tupperware created a range of toys targeted at various stages of a child's development.

In the 1980s, Tupperware launched products designed to minimize cooking time and products specially designed for microwave and conventional ovens.

Despite encountering some financial problems at the beginning of the 1990s, overall sales continued to improve in the mid-1990s, in part fuelled by massive product introductions. Tupperware brought out approximately 100 new products between 1994 and 1996, including entire new product lines and speciality items catering to particular needs internationally, such as Kimono Keepers in Japan. As had been the case during the last decade, international sales growth outstripped that in the US. Sales in the Far East and Latin America boomed, while sales in the US improved slowly. As a result, by 1996, Tupperware relied on international business for 85 per cent of its revenues and 95 per cent of its profits.

In 2005, Tupperware acquired all the assets in International Beauty from Sara Lee. Following the acquisition, the company changed its corporate name from the Tupperware Corporation to the Tupperware Brands Corporation.

Tupperware in 2014

The company's product brands and categories include preparation, storage and serving solutions for the kitchen and home through the Tupperware brand, and beauty and personal care products. Its products are sold under eight brand names: Tupperware, Armand Dupree, Avroy Shlain, BeautiControl, Fuller, Natur-Care, Nutrimetics and Nuvo.

The company recorded revenues of US$2,606 million during the financial year ended December 2014 (FY2014), an decrease of 12.5 per cent compared to FY2013. The operating profit of the company was US$403.5 million in FY2014, an decrease of 22 per cent compared to FY2013.

By the end of 2014, the number of employees was 13,000 (not including the worldwide sales force) (see also Table 1).

Competition

Tupperware competes with both established players and local manufacturers in the kitchen storage segment. The company competes on the basis of marketing, price, quality and innovation of products. However, the company has to compete mainly with local manufacturers on the price factor. The low-quality raw material employed by local manufacturers

Source: www.tupperware.com.

gives them significant leverage over the price factor. As a result, the company has to maintain its competitive position through the use of strong incentives and promotional programmes, as well as innovative launches. The company's beauty and personal care brands have also been witnessing strong competition from companies such as Avon, Oriflame Cosmetics, Revlon, L'Oréal, Procter & Gamble, Unilever and Estée Lauder. These companies have increased their focus to gain market share in beauty and personal care products in the US as well as emerging markets.

In recent years, brand recognition has emerged as a key differentiator and companies across the globe have invested heavily in advertising, promotional campaigns and innovative marketing strategies to increase market share. Tupperware has also increased its advertising outlay considerably. The rise in advertising expenses will have put pressure on operating margins, and the competitive pressure on prices will also have led to revenue decline.

The Tupperware distribution system

The direct selling business model and a large sales force have been among the strengths of Tupperware over the years. Since direct selling is inherently a low-cost business model with relatively low start-up costs, it helps the company in expanding to new markets and in its sales growth.

The company mainly follows the direct selling distribution model. Tupperware-branded products are primarily sold directly to distributors, directors,

Table 1	Tupperware's 2014 revenues and geographical split

Tupperware total revenues	2014 US$2,606 million
Sales regions	
Europe	28%
Asia-Pacific	33%
North America (Beauty North America and Tupperware North America)	25%
South America	14%
Total	100%

Source: based on www.tupperware.com.

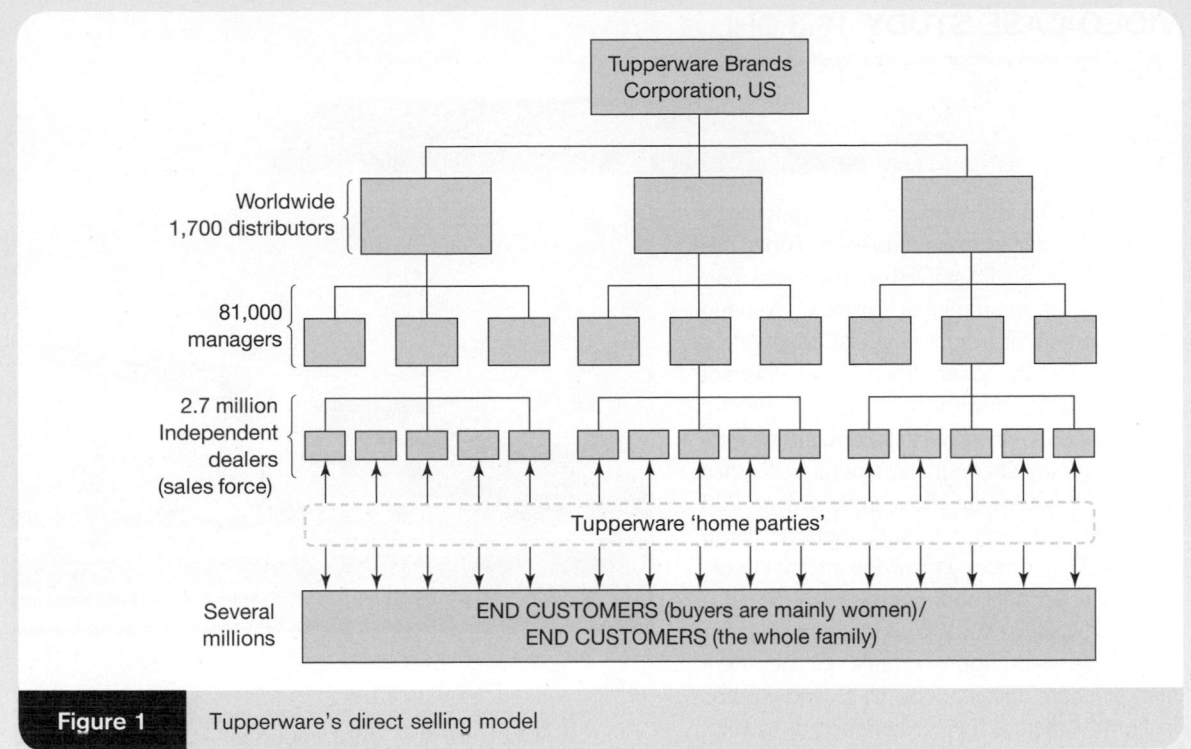

| Figure 1 | Tupperware's direct selling model |

Source: based on www.tupperware.com and other public data.

managers and dealers (sales force) throughout the world. The company also awards distributorships, who gain the right to market Tupperware products.

The vast majority of the sales force or dealers are independent contractors and not employees of Tupperware. Tupperware-branded products are primarily sold directly to these distributors, directors, managers and dealers (sales force) throughout the world. At the end of 2014, the Tupperware distribution system had approximately 1,700 distributors, 81,000 managers and 2.7 million dealers worldwide. Figure 1 illustrates the Tupperware distribution system.

Besides the 'party' method of selling, which includes demonstrations of the features and benefits of Tupperware products in homes, offices, social clubs and the like, the company also sells via the internet. It has also entered into a limited number of business-to-business transactions, in which it sells products to a partner company for sale to consumers.

Tupperware products are also promoted through brochures. In addition, Tupperware utilizes catalogues, and television and magazine advertising.

QUESTIONS

1. How will you characterize Tupperware's distribution strategy in relation to the theoretical models?

2. What are the advantages and disadvantages of Tupperware's distribution model?

3. How do you evaluate the future for this distribution model?

4. In the last few years, Tupperware has witnessed sales decline across some of its markets, namely, Russia, Australia and Japan. Which criteria would you use in order to find out which of the three countries should have Tupperware's focus in the next three years?

Sources: based on www.tupperware.com; other public media.

VIDEO CASE STUDY 16.3 DHL

download from **www.pearson.co.uk/hollensen**

DHL International (www.dhl.com) specializes in cross-border express deliveries. Today it is part of Deutsche Post. DHL is the global market leader in international express, overland transport and air freight. It is also the world's number one in ocean freight and contract logistics. DHL offers a full range of customized solutions – from express document shipping to supply chain management. DHL links about 120,000 destinations in more than 220 countries and territories and operates cargo airlines. The company provides internet tracking and order fulfilment services.

Source: InsectWorld/Shutterstock.com.

In 2014, DHL was a logistics market leader in Europe with approximately 19 per cent market share followed by UPS and FedEx. In North America, DHL was second to UPS and FedEx with around 10 per cent market share.

Questions

1. What are the macroeconomic drivers for the growth of the logistics business?

2. What are the most important issues in keeping DHL's international competitiveness?

3. How can DHL be perceived as a local company in most countries of the world?

For further resources, see this book's website at **www.pearsoned.co.uk/hollensen**

Questions for discussion

1. Discuss current distribution trends in world markets.

2. What are the factors that affect the length, width and number of marketing channels?

3. In attempting to optimize global marketing channel performance, which of the following should an international marketer emphasize: training, motivation or compensation? Why?

4. When would it be feasible and advisable for a global company to centralize the coordination of its foreign market distribution systems? When would decentralization be more appropriate?

5. Do grey marketers serve useful marketing functions for consumers and manufacturers?

6. Why is physical distribution important to the success of global marketing?

7. What are the main advantages and disadvantages of following a Multiple Distribution Channel Strategy?

8. Discuss the implications for the international marketer of the trend towards cross-border retailing.

9. Many markets have relatively large numbers of small retailers. How does this constrain the international marketer?

10. How is retailing know-how transferred internationally?

11. What services would the manufacturer like to receive from the retailer?

12. What are the advantages and disadvantages of global online distribution compared to the physical distribution?

References

Antia, K.D., Bergen, M. and Dutta, S. (2004) 'Competing with gray markets', *MIT Sloan Management Review,* Fall, pp. 63–69.

Ariovich, G. (1985) 'The economics of diamond price movements', *Managerial Decision Economics,* 6(4), pp. 234–240.

Arnold, D. (2000) 'Seven rules of international distribution', *Harvard Business Review,* November–December, pp. 131–137.

Bell, D., Choi, J.H. and Lodish, L. (2012) 'What matters most in internet retailing', *MIT Sloan Management Review,* 54(1), pp. 27–33.

Bell, D.R., Gallino, S. and Moreno, A. (2014), 'How to win in an omnichannel world', *MIT Sloan Management Review ,*56(1), pp. 44–53.

Bergenstock, D.J. and Maskulka, J.M. (2001) 'The De Beers story: are diamonds forever?', *Business Horizons,* 44(3), pp. 37–44.

Brynjolfsson, E., Hu, Y.J. and Rahman, M.S. (2013) 'Competing in the age of omnichannel retailing', *MIT Sloan Management Review,* 54(4), pp. 23–29.

Cavusgil, S.T., Yeoh, P.-L. and Mitri, M. (1995) 'Selecting foreign distributors – an expert systems approach', *Industrial Marketing Management,* 24, pp. 297–304.

Cho, H. and Tansuhaj, P.S. (2013) 'Becoming a global SME: determinants of SMEs decision to use e-intermediaries in export marketing', *Thunderbird International Business Review,* 55(5), pp. 513–530.

Dawar, N and Stornelli, J. (2013) 'Rebuilding the relationship between manufacturers and retailers', *MIT Sloan Management Review,* 54(2), pp. 83–90.

Jaffe, E.D. and Yi, L. (2007) 'What are the drivers of channel length? Distribution reform in The People's Republic of China', *International Business Review,* 16, pp. 474–493.

Jain, S. (1996) *International Marketing Management,* 5th edn. South-Western College Publishing, Cincinnati, OH.

Korkmaz, B., Lee, R. and Park, I. (2011) 'How new Internet standards will finally deliver a mobile revolution', *McKinsey Quarterly,* I 3, pp. 46–53.

Lewison, D.M. (1996) *Marketing Management: An Overview.* Fort Worth, TX, The Dryden Press/Harcourt Brace College Publishers.

Marther, C. (2008) 'Value chains and tropical products in a changing global regime', *ICTSD,* Issue Paper No. 13, Switzerland (www.ictsd.org).

Paliwoda, S. (1993) *International Marketing.* Heinemann, Oxford.

Rawwas, M.Y.A., Konishi, K., Kamise, S. and Al-Khatib, J. (2008) 'Japanese distribution system: the impact of newly designed collaborations on wholesalers' performance', *Industrial Marketing Management,* 37, 104–115.

Rohm, A.J., Gao, T.T., Sultan, F. and Pagani, M. (2012) 'Brand in the hand: a cross-market investigation of consumer acceptance of mobile marketing', *Business Horizons,* 55, pp. 485–493.

Simchi-Levi, D., Clayton, A. and Raven, B. (2013) 'When one size does not fit all', *MIT Sloan Management Review,* 54(2), pp. 14–17.

Valos, M. J. (2008) A qualitative study of multi-channel marketing performance measurement issues, *Journal of Database Marketing & Customer Strategy Management,* 15(4), pp. 239–248.

Vorley, B. (2003) *Food, Inc. – Corporate Concentration from Farm to Consumer.* UK Food Group, London.

CHAPTER 17
Communication decisions (promotion strategies)

Contents

Case studies

Learning objectives

After studying this chapter you should be able to:

- Define and classify the different types of communication tool

- Describe and explain the major steps in advertising decisions

- Describe the techniques available and appropriate for setting the advertising budget in foreign markets

- Discuss the possibilities of marketing via the internet

- Explain how important personal selling and sales force management are in the international marketplace

- Define and explain the concept of viral marketing and social media marketing

- Discuss how standardized international advertising has both benefits and drawbacks.

17.1   Introduction

Communication is the fourth and final decision to be made about the global marketing programme. The role of communication in global marketing is similar to that in domestic operations: to communicate with customers so as to provide information that buyers need to make purchasing decisions. Although the communication mix carries information of interest to the customer, in the end it is designed to persuade the customer to buy a product – at present or in the future.

To communicate with and influence customers, several tools are available. Advertising is usually the most visible component of the promotion mix, but personal selling, exhibitions, sales promotions, publicity (public relations) and direct marketing (including the internet) are also part of a viable international promotion mix.

One important strategic consideration is whether to standardize worldwide or to adapt the promotion mix to the environment of each country. Another consideration is the availability of media, which varies around the world.

17.2   The communication process

In considering the communication process, we normally think about a manufacturer (sender) transmitting a message through any form of media to an identifiable target segment audience. Here the seller is the initiator of the communication process. However, if the seller and the buyer have already established a relationship, it is likely that the initiative in the communication process will come from the buyer. If the buyer has positive post-purchase experience with a given offering on one occasion, this may dispose the buyer to purchase again on future occasions, i.e. take the initiative in the form of making enquiries or placing orders (so-called reverse marketing).

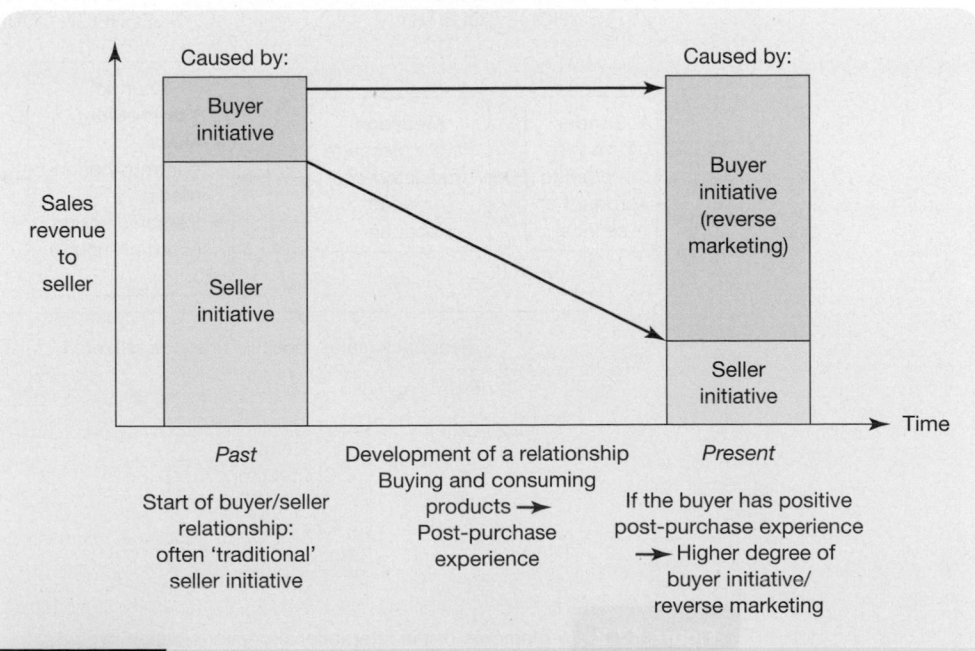

Figure 17.1   The shift from seller initiative to buyer initiative in buyer–seller relationships

The likely development of the split between total sales volume attributable to buyer and seller initiatives is shown in Figure 17.1. The relative share of sales volume attributable to buyer initiative will tend to increase over time. Present and future buyer initiatives are a function of all aspects of a firm's past market performance – that is, the extent, nature and timing of seller initiative, the competitiveness of offerings, post-purchase experience, the relationships developed with buyers as well as the way in which buyer initiative has been dealt with (Ottesen, 1995).

Key attributes of effective communication

The rest of the chapter will be devoted to the communication process and communicative tools based on seller initiatives. All effective marketing communication has four elements: a sender, a message, a communication channel and a receiver (audience). The communication process in Figure 17.2 highlights the key attributes of effective communication.

To communicate in an effective way, the sender needs to have a clear understanding of the purpose of the message, the audience to be reached and how this audience will interpret and respond to the message. However, sometimes the audience cannot hear clearly what the sender is trying to say about its product because of the 'noise' of rival manufacturers making similar and often contradictory claims about their products.

Another important point to consider in the model of Figure 17.2 is the degree of 'fit' between medium and message. For example, a complex and wordy message would be better for the press than for a visual medium such as television or cinema.

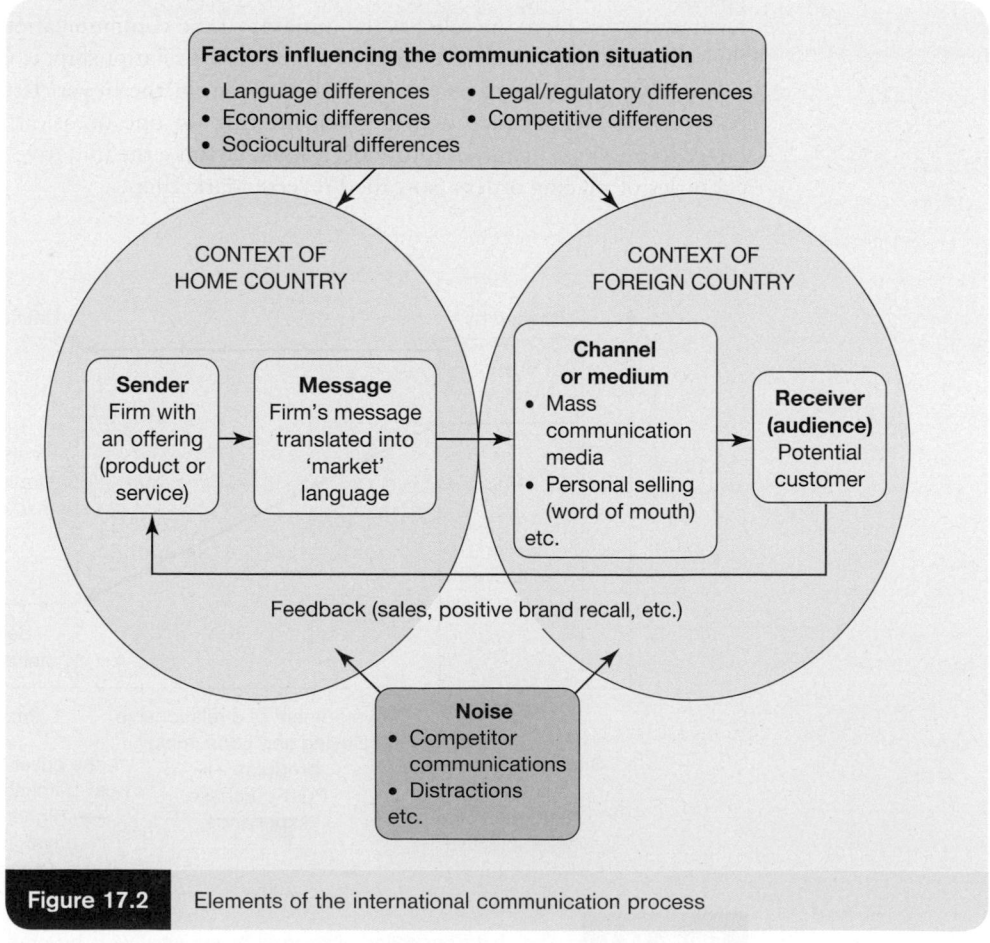

Figure 17.2   Elements of the international communication process

Other factors affecting the communication situation

Language differences

A slogan or advertising copy that is effective in one language may mean something different in another language. Thus the trade names, sales presentation materials and advertisements used by firms in their domestic markets may have to be adapted and translated when used in other markets.

There are many examples of unfortunate translations of brand names and slogans. General Motors has a brand name for one of its models called the Vauxhall Nova – this does not work well in Spanish-speaking markets because there it means 'no go'. In Latin America, 'Avoid embarrassment – Use Parker Pens' was translated as 'Avoid pregnancy – Use Parker Pens'. Scandinavian vacuum manufacturer Electrolux used the following in a US ad campaign: 'Nothing sucks like an Electrolux.'

A Danish company made up the following slogan for its cat litter in the UK market: 'Sand for Cat Piss'. Unsurprisingly, sales of the firm's cat litter did not increase! Another Danish company translated 'Teats for baby's bottles' as 'Loose tits'. In Copenhagen Airport the following poster could be seen until recently: 'We take your baggage and send it in all directions.' Thus a slogan used to express the desire to give good service might instead cause concern about where the baggage might end up (Joensen, 1997).

Economic differences

In contrast to industrialized countries, people in developing countries may be more likely to have radios than television sets. In countries with low levels of literacy, written communication may not be as effective as visual or oral communication.

Sociocultural differences

Dimensions of culture (religion, attitudes, social conditions and education) affect how individuals perceive their environment and interpret signals and symbols. For example, the use of colour in advertising must be sensitive to cultural norms. In many Asian countries, white is associated with grief; hence an advertisement for a detergent where whiteness is emphasized would have to be altered for promotional activities in, say, India.

Legal and regulatory conditions

Local advertising regulations and industry codes directly influence the selection of media and content of promotion materials. Many governments maintain tight regulations on content, language and sexism in advertising. The type of product that can be advertised is also regulated. Tobacco products and alcoholic beverages are the most heavily regulated in terms of promotion. However, the manufacturers of these products have not abandoned their promotional efforts. Camel engages in corporate-image advertising using its Joe Camel. Regulations are found more in industrialized economies than in developing economies, where the advertising industry is not yet as highly developed.

Competitive differences

As competitors vary from country to country in terms of number, size, type and promotional strategies used, a firm may have to adapt its promotional strategy and the timing of its efforts to the local environment.

EXHIBIT 17.1 Husqvarna's consumer wheel

Husqvarna is the world's largest producer of outdoor power products, including chainsaws, trimmers, lawn-mowers and garden tractors. The product range includes items for both consumers and professional users. Husqvarna's products are sold in more than 100 countries. Sales in 2011 generated €3.5 billion, with €0.18 billion in operating income. At the end of 2011, Husqvarna had 16,000 employees.

The global market for Husqvarna's products is estimated at approximately €17 billion annually. North America accounts for approximately 60 per cent of this market, Europe for more than 30 per cent, and the rest of the world for less than 10 per cent.

Husqvarna's global garden products (GGP)

Within the garden segment, Husqvarna (as a group) sells its products to both specialized dealers and mass retailers, which then sell to end users.

Specialized dealers in outdoor power equipment sell to professional users and private consumers who demand high levels of performance and service. This channel normally offers products in the high-price segments. It is the only channel in which the Husqvarna brand is sold.

Mass retailers sell products in the low- and medium-price segments to consumers. These retailers also include do-it-yourself (DIY) stores and supermarkets. Prices and margins are lower than for the specialized dealers. Examples of these dealers are Wal-Mart (US), Home Depot (US), B&Q (UK) and OBI (Germany).

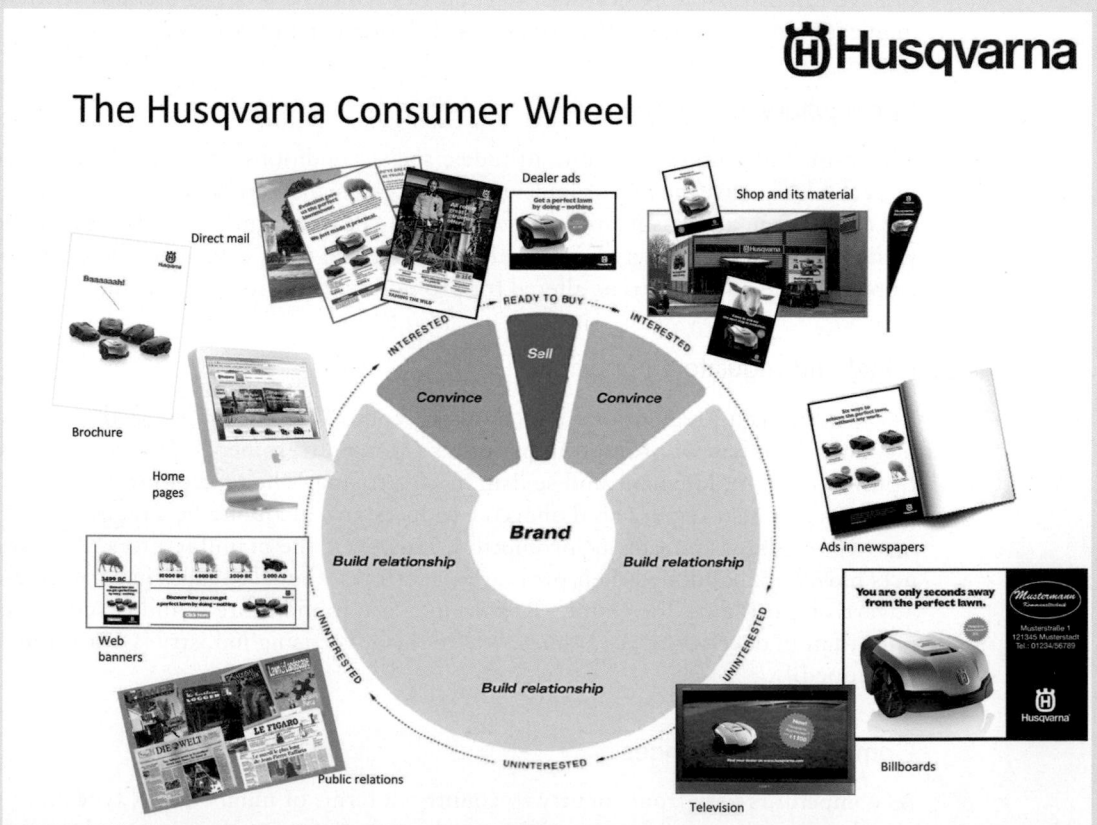

The Husqvarna consumer wheel
Source: based on material from Husqvarna.

The Husqvarna brand is not sold through this channel. Instead, other Husqvarna group brands are used, such as Gardena, McCulloch, Weedeater or Poulan.

The 'Husqvarna consumer wheel' shows how the company tries to build up relationships to potential end-customers in the robotic lawnmower segment (the Husqvarna brand in this case is called 'Automower').

As shown in the consumer wheel, most of the time, potential customers are not in the actual process of buying a lawnmower (private home owners only buy such products every five or 10 years), so consequently in the time between the actual buying processes, the relationship-building is mainly based on market communication activities in order to keep the brand at the 'top awareness' level among competitive brands. These market communication activities include ads in newspapers, billboards, television and public relations. As the potential customer reaches the 'interest' stage (before the actual buying), Husqvarna makes more use of web banners, the home page and brochures. In the process of actually buying the product, Husqvarna makes use of direct mail, dealer ads and shopping materials at the Husqvarna special dealer, in order to convince the customer to actually buy the Automower robotic lawnmower. After the sale of the product, customers may still be in the 'interest' stage, as the dealer may be involved in some aftersales service activities with them.

Source: based on material from Husqvarna and www.husqvarna.com.

17.3   Communication tools

Earlier in this chapter we mentioned the major forms of promotion. As shown in Table 17.1 the communication tools can be classified from mass communication tools (one-way) from a transactional marketing approach to very personal and close (two-way) communication tools (Centeno and Hart, 2012). In this section the different communication tools, listed in Table 17.1, will be further examined.

Table 17.1   Typical communication tools (media)

One-way communication			Two-way communication	
Advertising	**Public relations**	**Sales promotion**	**Direct marketing**	**Personal selling**
• Newspapers	• Annual reports	• Rebates and price discounts	• Direct mail/database marketing	• Sales presentations
• Magazines	• Corporate image	• Catalogues and brochures	• Internet marketing (WWW)	• Salesforce management
• Journals	• House magazines	• Samples, coupons and gifts	• Telemarketing	• Trade fairs and exhibitions
• Directories	• Press relations	• Competitions	• Mobile marketing	
• Radio	• Public relations		• SMS	
• Television	• Events		• Viral marketing	
• Cinema	• Lobbying		• Social media (Facebook, Twitter, LinkedIn, etc.)	
• Outdoor	• Sponsorship			
	• Celebrity endorsement			
	• Product placement			
	• Ambush Marketing			

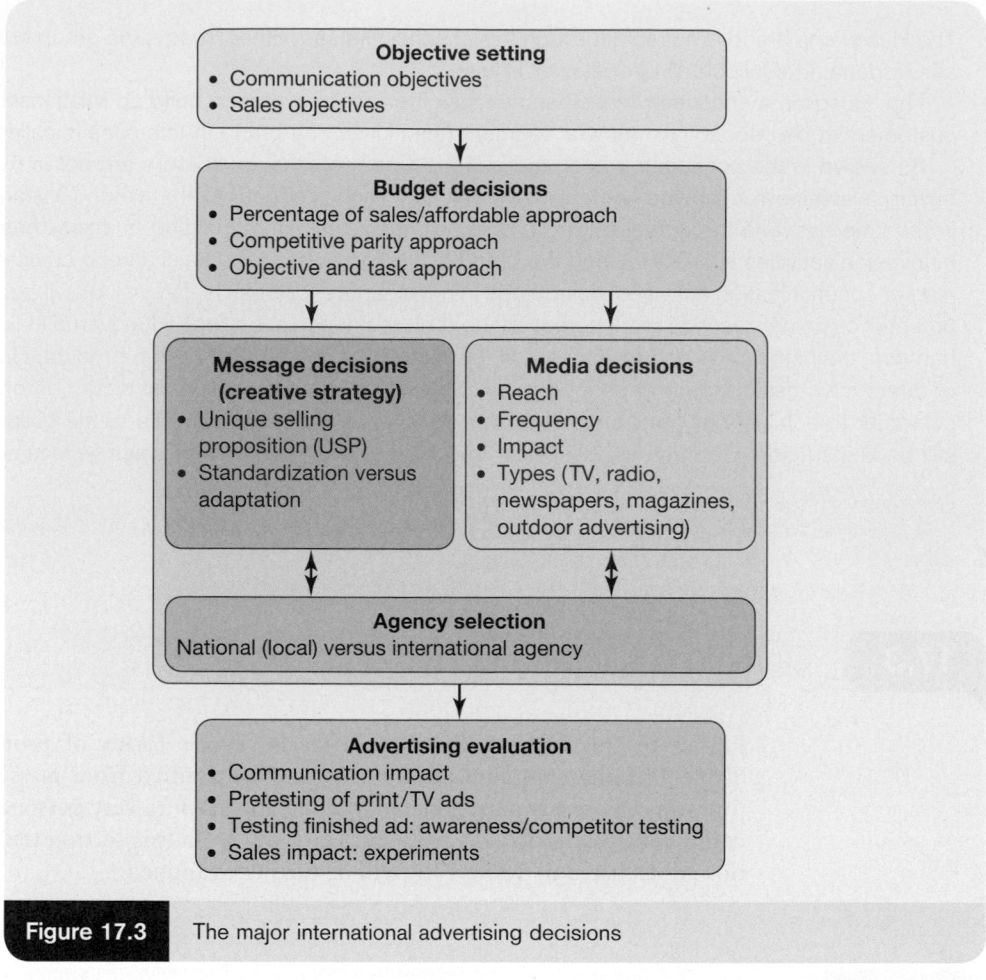

Figure 17.3   The major international advertising decisions

Advertising

Advertising is one of the most visible forms of communication. Because of its wide use and its limitations as a one-way method of communication, advertising in international markets is subject to a number of difficulties. Advertising is often the most important part of the communications mix for consumer goods, where there are a large number of small-volume customers who can be reached through mass media. For most business-to-business markets, advertising is less important than the personal selling function.

The major decisions in advertising are shown in Figure 17.3. We will now discuss these different phases.

Objective setting

Advertising objective
A specific communication task to be accomplished with a specific target audience during a specific period of time.

Although advertising methods may vary from country to country, the major **advertising objectives** remain the same. Major advertising objectives (and means) might include:

- increasing sales from existing customers by encouraging them to increase the frequency of their purchases; maintaining brand loyalty via a strategy that reminds customers of the key advantages of the product; stimulating impulse purchases;
- obtaining new customers by increasing consumer awareness of the firm's products and improving the firm's corporate image among a new target customer group.

Budget decisions

Controversial aspects of advertising include determining a proper method for deciding the size of the promotional budget, and its allocation across markets and over time.

In theory, the firm (in each of its markets) should continue to put more money into advertising, as money spent on advertising returns more money than money spent on anything else. In practice, it is not possible to set an optimum advertising budget. Therefore, firms have developed more practical guidelines. The manager must also remember that the advertising budget cannot be regarded in isolation, but has to be seen as one element of the overall marketing mix.

Affordable approach/percentage of sales

Affordable approach
Setting the promotion budget at the level management thinks the company can afford.

Affordable approach budgeting techniques link advertising expenditure directly to some measure of profits or, more commonly, to sales. The most popular of these methods is the percentage of sales method, whereby the firm automatically allocates a fixed percentage of sales to the advertising budget.

Advantages of this method:

● For firms selling in many countries, this simple method appears to guarantee equality among the markets. Each market seems to get the advertising it deserves.
● It is easy to justify in budget meetings.
● It guarantees that the firm only spends on advertising as much as it can afford. The method prevents wastage.

Disadvantages of this method:

● It uses historical performance rather than future performance.
● It ignores the possibility that extra spending on advertising may be necessary when sales are declining, in order to reverse the sales trend by establishing a 'recycle' on the product life cycle curve (see Section 14.4).
● It does not take into account variations in the firm's marketing goals across countries.
● The percentage of sales method encourages local management to maximise sales by using the easiest and most flexible marketing tool: price (that is, lowering the price).
● The method's convenience and simplicity encourage management not to bother investigating the relationships between advertising and sales or analysing critically the overall effectiveness of advertising campaigns.
● The method cannot be used to launch new products or enter new markets (zero sales = zero advertising).

Competitive parity approach

Competitive parity approach
Setting the promotion budget to match competitors' outlays.

The **competitive parity approach** involves estimating and duplicating the amounts spent on advertising by major rivals. Unfortunately, determining the marketing expenditures of foreign-based competitors is far more difficult than monitoring home country businesses, whose financial accounts (if they are limited companies) are open to public inspection and whose promotional activities are obvious the moment they occur. Another danger in following the practice of competitors is that they are not necessarily right.

Furthermore, the method does not recognize that the firm is in different situations in different markets. If the firm is new to a market, its relationships with customers are different from those of existing companies. This should also be reflected in its promotion budget.

Objective and task approach

Objective and task approach
Developing the promotion budget by defining specific objectives, determining the tasks that must be performed to achieve these objectives, and estimating the costs of performing these tasks. The sum of these costs is the proposed promotion budget.

The weaknesses of the above approaches have led some firms to follow the **objective and task approach**, which begins by determining the advertising objectives and then ascertaining the tasks needed to attain these objectives. This approach also includes a cost–benefit analysis, relating objectives to the cost of achieving them. To use this method, the firm must have good knowledge of the local market.

Hung and West (1991) showed that only 20 per cent of companies in the US, Canada and the UK used the objective and task approach. Although it is the theoretically correct way of determining the promotion budget, it is sometimes more important to be operational and to use a percentage of sales approach. This is not necessarily a bad method if company experience shows it to be reasonably successful. If the percentage is flexible, it allows different percentages to be used in different markets.

Message decisions (creative strategy)

Unique selling proposition (USP)
A unique characteristic of a product or brand identified by the marketer as the one on which to base a promotional campaign. It is often used in a product-differentiation approach to promotion.

This concerns decisions about what **unique selling proposition (USP)** needs to be communicated, and what the communication is intended to achieve in terms of consumer behaviour in the country concerned. These decisions have important implications for the choice of advertising medium, since certain media can better accommodate specific creative requirements (use of colour, written description, high definition, demonstration of the product, etc.) than others.

An important decision for international marketers is whether an advertising campaign developed in the domestic market can be transferred to foreign markets with only minor modifications, such as translation into appropriate languages. Complete standardization of all aspects of a campaign over several foreign markets is rarely attainable. Standardization implies a common message, creative idea, media and strategy, but it also requires that the firm's product has a USP that is clearly understood by customers in a cross-cultural environment.

Standardizing international advertising can lead to a number of advantages for the firm. For example, advertising costs will be reduced by centralizing the advertising campaign in the head office and transferring the same campaign from market to market, as opposed to running campaigns from different local offices.

However, running an advertising campaign in multiple markets requires a balance between conveying the message and allowing for local nuances. The adaptation of global ideas can be achieved by various tactics, such as adopting a modular approach, adapting international symbols and using international advertising agencies.

Media decisions

The selection of the media to be used for advertising campaigns needs to be done simultaneously with the development of the message. A key question in media selection is whether to use mass media or a targeted approach. The mass media (television, radio and newsprint) are effective when a significant percentage of the general public are potential customers. This percentage varies considerably by country for most products, depending on, for example, the distribution of incomes in different countries.

Reach
The number of people exposed to an advertisement carried by a given medium.

The selection of the media to be used in a particular campaign typically starts with some idea of the target market's demographic and psychological characteristics, regional strengths of the product, seasonality of sales, and so on. The media selected should be the result of a careful fit of local advertising objectives, media attributes and target market characteristics.

Frequency
Average number of times within a given timeframe that each potential customer is exposed to the same ad.

Furthermore, media selection can be based on the following criteria:

- **reach**: total number of people in a target market exposed to at least one advertisement in a given time period ('opportunity to see', or OTS);
- **frequency**: average number of times within a given time period that each potential customer is exposed to the same advertisement;

Impact
Depends on the compatibility between the medium used and the message (the 'impact' on the consumer's brain).

- **impact**: depends on compatibility between the medium used and the message. *Penthouse* magazine continues to attract advertisers for high-value-added consumer durables, such as cars, hi-fi equipment and clothes, which are geared primarily to a high-income male segment.

High reach is necessary when the firm enters a new market or introduces a new product so that information about, for example, the new product's availability is spread to the widest possible audience. A high level of frequency is appropriate when brand awareness already exists and the message is about informing the consumer that a campaign is under way. Sometimes a campaign should have both a high frequency and extensive reach, but limits on the advertising budget often create the need to trade off frequency against reach.

A media's **gross rating points (GRPs)** are the result of multiplying its reach by the frequency with which an advertisement appears within the media over a certain period. Hence it contains duplicated exposure, but indicates the 'critical mass' of a media effort. GRPs may be estimated for individual vehicles, for entire classes of media or for a total campaign.

Hence it contains duplicated exposure, but indicates the critical mass of a media effort. GRPs may be estimated for individual vehicles, for entire classes of media or for a total campaign.

The cost of running a media campaign also has to be taken into consideration. Traditionally, media planning is based on a single measure, such as **cost per thousand (CPM)** GRPs. When dealing with two or more national markets, the selection of media also has to take into account differences in:

- the firm's market objectives across countries;
- media effectiveness across countries.

Since media availability and relative importance will not be the same in all countries, plans may require adjustment in cross-border campaigns.

As a way of distributing advertising messages through new communication channels, co-promotion now has a strong foothold.

Let us now take a closer look at the main media types.

Television

Television is an expensive but commonly used medium in attempting to reach broad national markets. In most developed countries, coverage is no problem. However, television is one of the most regulated communications media. Many countries have prohibited the advertising of cigarettes and alcohol other than beer. In other countries (e.g. Scandinavia, the UK), there are limits on the number of minutes that TV advertising is permitted to be shown. Some countries also prohibit commercial breaks in TV programmes.

Radio

Radio is a lower-cost broadcasting activity than television. Commercial radio started several decades before commercial television in many countries. Radio is often transmitted locally and therefore national campaigns have to be built up area by area.

Newspapers

In virtually all urban areas of the world, the population has access to daily newspapers. In fact, the problem for the advertiser is not having too few newspapers, but rather having too many of them. Most countries have one or more newspapers that can be said to have a truly national circulation. However, in many countries newspapers tend to be predominantly local or regional and, as such, serve as the primary medium for local advertisers. Attempting to use a series of local papers to reach a national market is considerably more complex and costly.

Many countries have English-language newspapers in addition to local-language newspapers. For example, the aim of the *Asian Wall Street Journal* is to supply economic information in English to influential Asian business people, politicians, senior government officials and intellectuals.

Magazines

In general, magazines have a narrower readership than newspapers. In most countries, magazines serve to reach specific segments of the population. For technical and industrial

Gross rating points (GRPs)
Reach multiplied by frequency. GRPs may be estimated for individual media vehicles. Media planning is often based on 'cost per 1000 GRPs'.

Cost per thousand (CPM)
Calculated by dividing the cost of an ad placed in a particular advertising vehicle (e.g. certain magazine) by the number of people (expressed in thousands) who are exposed to that vehicle.

products, magazines can be quite effective. Technical business publications tend to be international in their coverage. These publications range from individual businesses (e.g. beverages, construction, textiles) to worldwide industrial magazines covering many industries.

Marketers of international products have the option of using international magazines that have regional editions (e.g. *Newsweek, Time* and *Business Week*). In the case of *Reader's Digest,* local-language editions are distributed.

Cinema

In countries where it is common to subsidize the cost of showing films by running commercials prior to the feature film, cinema advertising has become an important medium. India, for example, has a relatively high level of cinema attendance per capita (few have television at home). Therefore cinema advertisements play a much greater role in India than in, for example, the US.

Cinema advertising has other advantages, one of the most important being that it has a truly captive audience (no channel hopping!).

Outdoor advertising

Outdoor advertising includes posters/billboards, shop signs and transit advertising. This medium shows the creative way in which space can be sold to customers. In the case of transit advertising, for example, a bus can be sold as an advertising medium. The use of transit media is expanding rapidly in China, her example. Outdoor posters/billboards can be used to develop the visual impact of advertising. France is a country associated with the effective use of poster and billboard advertising. In some countries, legal restrictions limit the amount of poster space available.

EXHIBIT 17.2 LEGO Ninjago's 360 degree marketing communication

LEGO's main activity is the development, production, marketing and sale of play materials. The market for traditional toys, in which LEGO operates, has been slightly decreasing in recent years. So far the weakening toy market has not had an effect on LEGO which has enjoyed double-digit growth rates in consumer sales in virtually all LEGO markets. LEGO gained significant market shares from competitors and is today the world's leading brand on construction toys.

Apart from its classic product lines like City and licensed product line like Star Wars LEGO has introduced a 'big bang' product every year since 2009. A big bang is a product line with a short scheduled life cycle (between two and three years) accompanied by substantial above-the-line marketing spends.

The Ninjago concept arose when a team of LEGO designers made an inspirational trip to Japan searching for ideas for a theme for the next major product launch. The designers were inspired by the whole ninja mythology with the different elements, i.e. fire, earth, ice and lightning, and they have developed a product line which is somewhere between the traditional and the new.

When the Ninjago series was introduced in January 2011 it became one of the 'best selling' new series ever in LEGO history. In 2012, Ninjago was the third biggest series by consumer sales after Star Wars and City.

Ninjago was continued in 2014, despite an initial suggestion that it would be replaced by Legends of Chima in 2013. However, the two themes in fact co-exist.

360-degree marketing communication

Children spend more and more time playing online. They see it as a natural extension of the physical world and boundaries between the two are blurring. LEGO needs to make its products available for children in their digital playroom and be present in social media. Social play is an important aspect for Ninjago.

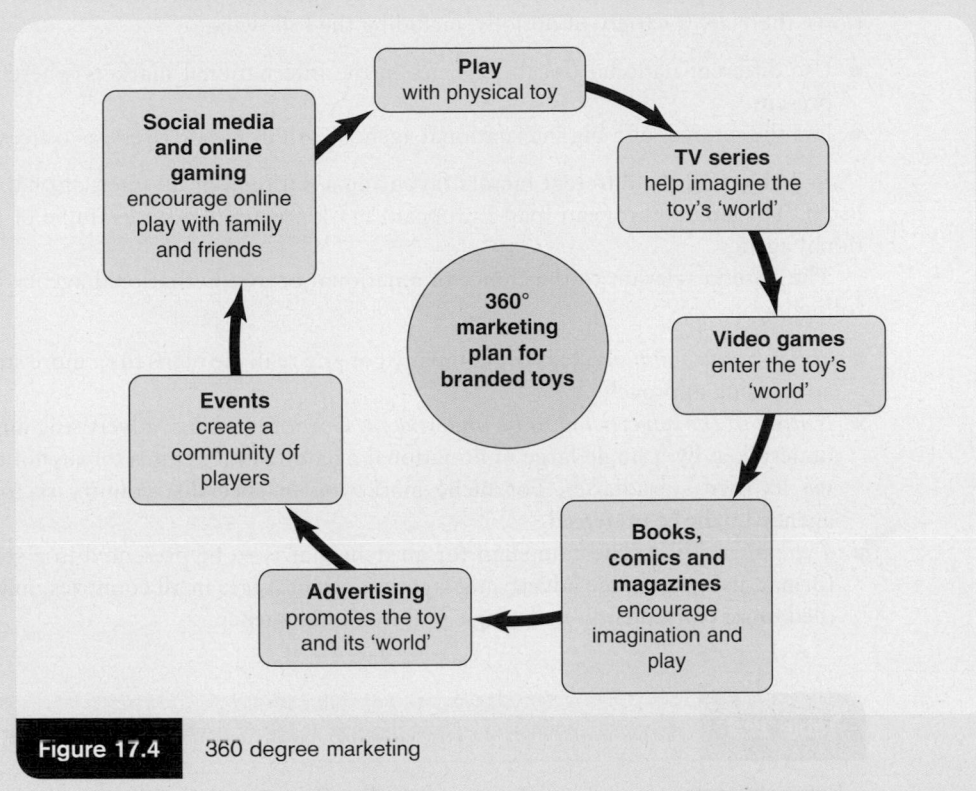

Figure 17.4 360 degree marketing

LEGO chose to use a 360 degree strategy campaign to promote Ninjago. Integrated 360 degree marketing communications are the practice of blending different elements of the communication mix in mutually reinforcing ways to inform, persuade and induce consumer action, as shown in Figure 17.4. For Lego, the goal of communication was not just to induce initial purchases; it was also an attempt to achieve post-purchase satisfaction, thus increasing the probability of repeat sales. In the case of Ninjago, all points of consumer contacts, e.g. TV series, video game, LEGO.com, advertising, were used.

LEGO reinforces its core business of building sets and complements it with expanded offerings to reach new children and the 360 degree brand experience that bridges physical and virtual play worlds to engage children's imagination and compel them to keep building.

The Ninjago Story provides a context for drama in children's play. Therefore, even although the investment is high, TV series play an important role in communicating the story of Ninjago, characters and missions.

Traditional marketing to children will continue to play a crucial role, but LEGO has increasingly made social media, viral media and networks an integral part of the mix in order to enhance the experience of physical play and build brand loyalty.

The marketing approach and strategy contains elements that will support the objective of reaching new consumers (by TV shows, in-store) while also including elements that stimulate engagement and involvement. Traffic to Ninjago's online content among LEGO users aged between 6 and 11 years is thereby increased.

Source: different LEGO Ninjago materials. Special thanks to Pat Madsen and Marketing Manager, Michael Stenderup, LEGO for their contribution.

Agency selection

Confronted with the many complex problems that international advertising involves, many businesses instinctively turn to an advertising agency for advice and practical assistance. Agencies employ or have instant access to expert copywriters, translators, photographers, film-makers, package designers and media planners who are skilled and experienced in the international field. Only the largest of big businesses can afford to carry such people in-house.

If the international marketer decides to outsource the international advertising functions, there are a variety of options, including the following:

- Use different national (local) agencies in the international markets where the firm is present.
- Use the services of a big international agency with domestic overseas offices.

In Table 17.2 the different factors favouring a national or an international agency are listed. The single European (pan-European) market is used as an example of an international agency.

The criteria relevant to the choice of a national or an international agency include the following:

- *Policy of the company.* Has the company got any realistic plans for a more standardized advertising approach?
- *Nature of the advertising to be undertaken.* Corporate image advertising might be best undertaken by a single large multinational agency that operates throughout the world via its own subsidiaries. For niche marketing in specialist country sectors, a local agency might be preferred.
- *Type of product.* The campaign for an item that is to be presented in a standardized format, using the same advertising layouts and messages in all countries, might be handled more conveniently by a single multinational agency.

Table 17.2	European agency selection: national (local) or pan-European (international)	
National (local)	**Pan-European (international)**
Supports national subsidiary	Reflects new European reality and trends
Investment in existing brand best handled nationally	Economies of scale in new product development and branding
Closer to marketplace	Uniformity of treatment across Europe
Smaller size is more conducive to personalized service and greater creativity	Resources and skills of major European or global agency
Diversity of ideas	Easier to manage one agency group

Source: adapted from Lynch, (1994), *European Marketing,* Table 11–4 pub. Irwin Professional Publishing, Homewood, IL.

Advertising evaluation

Advertising evaluation and testing is the final stage in the advertising decision process shown in Figure 17.3. Testing advertising effectiveness is normally more difficult in international markets than in domestic markets. An important reason for this is the distance and communication gap between domestic and foreign markets. Thus it can be very difficult to transfer testing methods used in domestic markets to foreign ones. For example, the conditions for interviewing people can vary from country to country. Consequently, many firms try to use sales results as a measure of advertising effectiveness, but awareness testing is also relevant in many cases, e.g. brand awareness is of crucial importance during the early stages of a new product launch.

Testing the impact of advertising on sales is very difficult because it is difficult to isolate the advertising effect. One way to solve this problem is to use a kind of *experiment,* where the markets of the firm are grouped according to similar characteristics. In each group of countries, one or two are used as test markets. Independent variables to be tested against the sales (dependent variable) might include the amount of advertising, the media mix, the unique selling proposition and the frequency of placement.

Public relations

Word-of-mouth advertising is not only cheap, but it is also very effective. Public relations (PR) seeks to enhance corporate image building and influence favourable media treatment. PR (or publicity) is the marketing communications function that carries out programmes which are designed to earn public understanding and acceptance. It should be viewed as an integral part of the global marketing effort.

PR activities involve both internal and external communication. Internal communication is important to create an appropriate corporate culture. The target groups for public relations are shown in Table 17.3.

The range of target groups is far wider in public relations than it is for the other communications tools. Target groups are likely to include the main stakeholder groups of employees, customers, distribution channel members and shareholders. For companies operating in international markets, this gives a very wide range of communication tasks. Internal communications in different country subsidiaries, employing people from a number of different countries, with different cultural values, will be particularly challenging.

Table 17.3	Target groups for public relations
Public or target groups: domestic markets	**Extra factors: international markets**
Directly connected with the organisation	
● Employees	● Wider range of cultural issues
● Shareholders	● The degree of remoteness of the corporate headquarters
Suppliers of raw materials and components	
● Providers of financial services	● Is this to be handled on a country-by-
● Providers of marketing services (e.g. marketing research, advertising, media)	country basis, or is some overall standardization desirable?
Customers of the organisation	
● Existing customers	● May have less knowledge of the company
● Past customers	● The country-of-origin effect will influence
● Those capable of becoming customers	communications
Environment	
● The general public	● Wide range of general publics
● Government: local, regional, national	● Host governments
● Financial markets generally	● Regional grouping (e.g. EU), world groupings

Source: adapted from Phillips, C., Poole, I. and Lowe, R. (1994) *International Marketing Strategy: Analysis, Development and Implementation,* Routledge, Andover. Reproduced with permission from Cengage Learning.

In a more market-oriented sense, the PR activity is directed towards an influential, though relatively small, target audience of editors and journalists who work for newspapers/ magazines, or towards broadcasting aimed at the firm's customers and stakeholders.

Since the target audience is small, it is relatively inexpensive to reach. Several methods can be used to gain PR. Such methods can include contributing prizes at various events, press releases of news about the firm's products, plant and personnel, announcements of the firm's promotional campaign and lobbying of governments. Other strategies worth pursuing are:

● sponsorship
● celebrity endorsement
● product placement.

Sponsorship

Sponsorship
A business relationship between a provider of funds, resources or services and an individual, event or organization which offers in return some rights and association that may be used for commercial advantage.

According to Meenaghan (1996), one of the fastest growing aspects of marketing and marketing communications is the practice of corporate **sponsorship**. Sponsorship takes two forms: event sponsorship (such as athletic and entertainment events) and cause-oriented sponsorship. Event marketing is growing rapidly because it provides companies with alternatives to the cluttered mass media, an ability to segment on a local or regional basis, and opportunities for reaching narrow lifestyle groups whose consumption behaviour can be linked with the local event (Milliman *et al.*, 2007). Cause-related marketing, a form of corporate philanthropy with benefits accruing to the sponsoring company, is based on the idea that a company will contribute to a cause every time the customer undertakes some action. In addition to helping worthy causes, corporations satisfy their own tactical and strategic objectives when undertaking cause-related efforts. By supporting a deserving cause, a company can enhance its corporate or brand image, generate incremental sales, increase brand awareness, broaden its customer base and reach new market segments;

Celebrity endorsement

Celebrity endorsement
The use of famous spokespersons or celebrities in marketing communications.

Research indicates that **celebrity endorsement** can result in more favourable advertisement ratings and product evaluations and can have a substantial positive impact on financial returns for the companies that use them (Silvera and Austad, 2004). One possible explanation for the effectiveness of celebrity endorsers is that consumers tend to believe that major stars are motivated by genuine affection for the product rather than by endorsement fees. Celebrities are particularly effective endorsers because they are viewed as highly trustworthy, believable, persuasive and likeable. Although these results unequivocally support the use of celebrity endorsers, other research suggests that celebrity endorsements might vary in effectiveness depending on other factors such as the 'fit' between the celebrity and the advertised product (Hosea, 2007; Seno and Lukas, 2007). The selection process behind finding the right celebrity endorser for the company's product or service, can be either very complex (involving many possible celebrity endorser candidates) or very simple (only one candidate is involved from the beginning). In both types of selection processes, the celebrity's agent will often (on behalf of the celebrity) play an important role in the negotiation process with the company or its creative advertising company (Hollensen and Schimmelpfennig, 2013). See also Exhibit 17.3 regarding Ricola's Celebrity endorsement.

EXHIBIT 17.3 Ricola is using celebrity endorsement in the international marketing of its herbal drops

Ricola AG (www.ricola.com) is a modern and innovative producer of herb drops. Ricola's herb specialities are exported to more than 50 different countries and are famous for their fine Swiss quality.

Founded in 1930, Ricola products now include about 30 different herb speciality flavours. All the herbs used in Ricola products are organically cultivated in the Swiss mountains and the herbal drops are all produced in Switzerland. In order to obtain enough herbs for the production of its herbal drops, Ricola contracts with over 100 self-managed farms in the area surrounding the factory. Ricola exports to over 50 countries in Asia, North America and Europe, through its subsidiary and distributors. Ricola entered the Asian market in 2006 via a representative office in Hong Kong and the Australian market in 2007, where it has been well received.

In 1967, the founder family Richterich renamed the company **Ricola,** an abbreviation of **Ri**chterich & **Co**mpagnie **La**ufen. Export began in the 1970s, introducing Ricola's products to foreign markets. At the end of the decade, Ricola moved to a new factory in Laufen, where its headquarters are still located.

Today, the company is now managed by Felix Richterich, son of Hans Peter and grandson of the founder.

Ricola generated 300 million Swiss francs in sales in 2011 and employs 400 workers.

Endorsement by celebrity singers

Ricola is a world brand and the company is carefully expanding its brand image internationally. For example, the company now has a page on its website dedicated to celebrity endorsement of its product.

Many famous singers always keep a pack of Ricola herb drops to hand. Why? Because sucking Ricola herb throat drops 'oils' into the vocal cords. This is important for musicians and actors whose voices must be at their peak throughout concerts, operas and thea-

Source: Helen Sessions/Alamy Images

tre performances. In Switzerland and the US, Ricola supports all those involved in musicals and classical concerts by providing Swiss herb specialities. These stars appreciate Ricola products. Among the stars who endorse Ricola herb drops are Robbie Williams, Mariah Carey, Justin Timberlake, Madonna and Placido Domingo.

Source: based on www.ricola.com.

Product placement

Product placement
Product placement is the inclusion of a branded product in media, usually without explicit reference to the product. Most commonly, branded products are featured in movies, television shows and video games.

Product placement is a form of advertisement, where branded products or services are placed in a context usually without ads, such as films, the storyline of television shows or news programmes. Product placement is common practice on reality television, e.g. *American Idol*. As the costs of making such shows accelerate, the television networks are looking for partners who want to finance programmes in return for some screen time for their products.

For the brand manufacturer the practice is considered a type of pull marketing, designed to increase consumer awareness of the brand and product and strengthen demand. Product placement can be much more cost-effective than other types of marketing. Apple, for example, claims that they never pay for product placement – they just provide devices.

Another example of a company that has decided to focus more on product placement is Harley-Davidson. Only 3 per cent of US consumers own a motorcycle (mainly males aged 35+), but there are another 15–20 million individuals in the US (outside the core target group) who have a desire to buy one. The motorcycle brand announced in November 2009 that it had teamed up with an entertainment consulting agency for a major product placement push in film, TV, music and video games.

Surveys show that product placements in films are an effective tool to market brands on a global basis with a standardized strategy. Product placement in a film has been seen to drive purchase intention (Srivastava, 2015). Nielsen Media Research has shown that product placement in television shows can raise brand awareness by 20 per cent (Cebrzynski, 2006).

The degree of control of the PR message is quite different. Journalists can use PR material to craft an article of so many words, or an interview of so many seconds.

How material is used will depend on the journalist and the desired storyline. On occasions a thoroughly negative story can result from a press release that was designed to enhance the company image.

Hence, PR activity includes anticipating criticism. Criticisms may range from general ones against all multinational corporations to more specific ones. They may also be based on a market; for example, doing business with prison factories in China.

Source: FOX/Getty Images.

EXHIBIT 17.4 Ambush marketing strategy – Dutch Bavaria vs Anheuser Busch's Budweiser during the Fifa World Cup 2010

Ambush marketing occurs when one brand pays to become an official sponsor of an event and another competing brand connects itself to the event without paying the sponsorship fee and without breaking any laws.

There was good example of ambush marketing during the FIFA football World Cup in June 2010 in South Africa. The Dutch brewery, Bavaria, gave some orange mini-dresses to female spectators at the Netherlands vs Denmark match as part of a gift pack. (Orange is the historic national colour of the Netherlands, originating from the coat of arms of the Dutch founding father, Prince William of Orange, who led the campaign for independence against Spanish rule in 1568.)

The mini-dresses only had a tiny outer label carrying the brand's name but, prior to the stunt, the firm made sure they were instantly recognizable in the Netherlands by arranging for one to be worn by top-ranking Dutch Wag Sylvie van der Vaart, the wife of Real Madrid's Rafael van der Vaart.

When 36 young women wearing orange mini-dresses associated with the Dutch brewers Bavaria entered the stands at South Africa's Soccer City Stadium for the Netherlands vs Denmark match, it was no surprise that all the cameras turned towards them, capturing shots that would attract picture editors worldwide.

The women were subsequently ejected from the stadium under the Contravention of Merchandise Marks Act, which prevents companies benefiting from an event without paying for advertising. The 36 women were accused of being part of a campaign to promote a Dutch brewery. South African police arrested two of the women at their hotel in the Johannesburg district of Roodepoort, two days after they were questioned at the game. They appeared at Johannesburg Magistrate's Court and were released on bail of 10,000 rand (£900) each.

Anheuser Busch's Budweiser was the official beer of the tournament and world football's governing body fiercely protects its sponsors from brands that are not FIFA partners.

The Netherlands' foreign minister, Maxime Verhagen, was quoted by *De Telegraaf* newspaper as saying the arrest was disproportionate and senseless.

Source: Kevork Djansezian/Getty Images.

Source: WENN Ltd/Alamy Images.

What did the Bavaria Brewery get out of it?

The resulting publicity from the stunt heightened the popularity and awareness of the brand. At the time, a quick Google news search for Bavaria beer returned many pages of articles reporting the incident. Furthermore, several TV channels also reported on the marketing stunt. Most of the TV channels didn't mention the name 'Bavaria' – but that only triggered people's curiosity further regarding which brewery it could be.

Source: based on: Laing, A. (2010) 'World Cup 2010: Police arrest women in Dutch orange dresses'. *Telegraph*, 16.06.2010, http://www.telegraph.co.uk/sport/football/competitions/world-cup-2010/7830319/World-Cup-2010-Police-arrest-women-in-Dutch-orange-dresses.html.

Sales promotion

Sales promotion is defined as those selling activities that do not fall directly into the advertising or personal selling category. Sales promotion also relates to so-called below-the-line activities such as point-of-sale displays and demonstrations, leaflets, free trials,

Advertising agency
A marketing services firm
that assists companies in
planning, preparing,
implementing and
evaluating all or portions
of their advertising
programmes.

Point-of-sale displays
Includes all signage –
posters, signs, shelf cards
and a variety of other
visual materials – that are
designed to influence
buying decisions at the
point of sale.

Cross-selling
Selling an additional
product or service to an
existing customer.

competitions and premiums such as 'two for the price of one'. Unlike media advertising which is above the line and earns a commission, below-the-line sales promotion does not. To an **advertising agency**, above the line means traditional media for which they are recognized by the media owners, entitling them to commission.

Sales promotion is a short-term effort directed primarily to the consumer and/or retailer, in order to achieve specific objectives such as:

● consumer product trial and/or immediate purchase;
● consumer introduction to the shop;
● encouraging retailers to use **point-of-sale displays** for the product;
● encouraging shops to stock the product.

When a manufacturer owns two or more brands, current loyal customers are excellent candidates for **cross-selling**, promoting another of the brands or using one product to boost sales of another, often an unrelated product. Different companies also may work together to cross-sell.

In the US, the sales promotion budgets for fast-moving consumer goods (FMCG) manufacturers are larger than the advertising budgets. In Europe, the European Commission estimates that the rate of spending growth on sales promotions was double that for conventional advertising throughout the period 1991–94 (Bennett, 1995, p. 321). Factors contributing to the expansion of sales promotion activities include:

● greater competition among retailers, combined with increasingly sophisticated retailing methods;
● higher levels of brand awareness among consumers, leading to the need for manufacturers to defend brand market shares;
● improved retail technology (e.g. electronic scanning devices that enable coupon redemptions, etc., to be monitored instantly);
● greater integration of sales promotion, public relations and conventional media campaigns.

In markets where the consumer is hard to reach because of media limitations, the percentage of the total communication budget allocated to sales promotions is also relatively high. Some of the different types of sales promotion are as follows:

● *Price discounts*. There are very widely used. A variety of different price reduction techniques is available, such as cash-back deals.
● *Catalogues/brochures*. The buyer in a foreign market may be located at quite a distance from the closest sales office. In this situation, a foreign catalogue can be very effective. It must be able to close the gap between buyer and seller such that the potential buyer is supplied with all the necessary information, from prices, sizes, colours and quantities to packing, shipping time and acceptable forms of payment. In addition to catalogues, brochures of various types are useful for salespeople, distributors and agents. Translations should be done in cooperation with overseas agents and/or distributors.
● *Coupons*. Coupons are a classic tool for FMCG brands, especially in the US. A variety of coupon distribution methods exists: door-to-door, on packs, in newspapers. Some European countries do not allow coupons.
● *Samples*. A sample gives the potential foreign buyer an idea of the quality that cannot be attained by even the best picture. Samples may prevent misunderstandings over style, sizes, models and so on.
● *Gifts*. Most European countries have a limit on the value of the premium or gift given. Furthermore, in some countries it is illegal to offer premiums that are conditional on the purchase of another product. The US does not allow beer to be offered as a free sample.
● *Competitions*. This type of sales promotion needs to be communicated to the potential customers. This can be done on the pack, in stores via leaflets or through media advertising (Friel, 2008).

The success of sales promotion depends on local adaptation. Major constraints are imposed by local laws which may not permit premiums or free gifts to be given. Some countries' laws control the amount of discount given at the retail level; others require permits for all sales promotions. Since it is impossible to know the specific laws of each and every country, international marketers should consult local lawyers and authorities before launching a promotional campaign.

Direct marketing

According to Onkvisit and Shaw (1993, p. 717), direct marketing is the sum total of activities by which products and services are offered to market segments in one or more media for informational purposes or to solicit a direct response from a present or prospective customer or contributor by mail, telephone or personal visit.

Direct marketing covers direct mail (marketing database), telephone selling and marketing via the internet – in the light of the developments in internet technologies it is highly relevant to consider the web as a direct marketing tool.

Personal selling

The differences between advertising and personal selling are indicated in Table 17.1. Advertising is a one-way communication process that has relatively more 'noise', whereas personal selling is a two-way communication process with immediate feedback and relatively less 'noise'. Personal selling is an effective way to sell products, but it is expensive. It is used mainly to sell to distribution channel members and in business-to-business (B2B) markets. However, personal selling is also used in some consumer markets, e.g. for cars and consumer durable products. In some countries, labour costs are very low and here personal selling will be used to a greater extent than in high-cost countries.

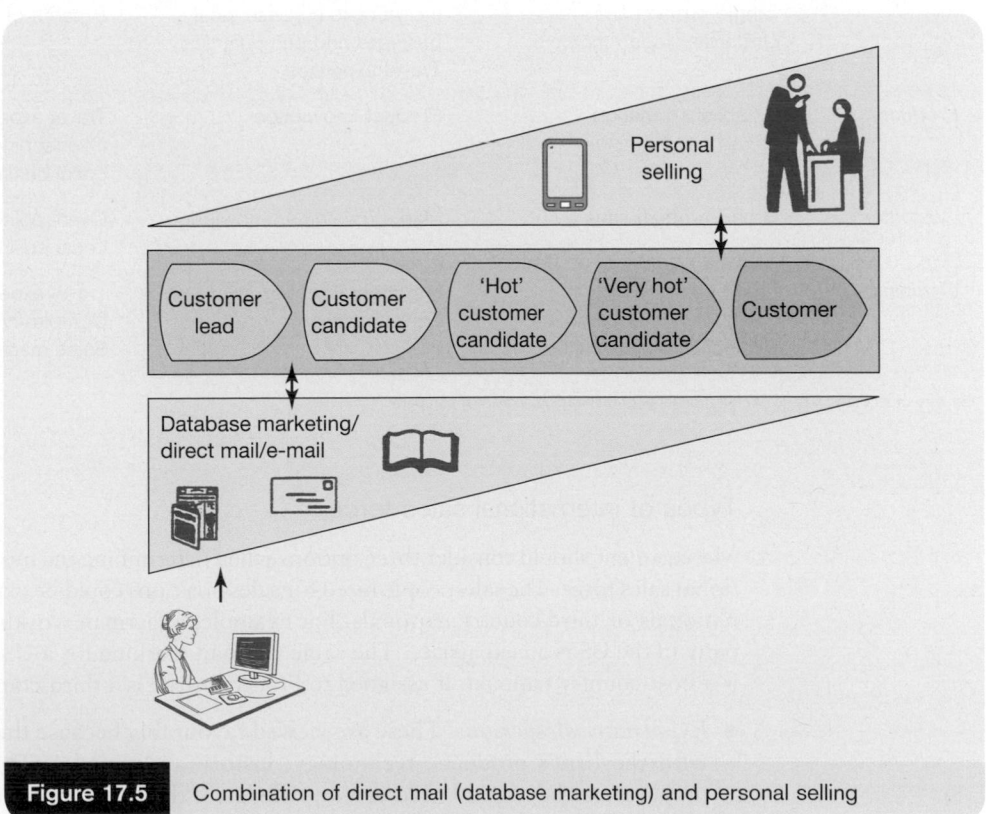

| **Figure 17.5** | Combination of direct mail (database marketing) and personal selling |

If personal selling costs in B2B markets are relatively high, it is relevant to economize with personal selling resources, and to use personal selling only at the end of the potential customer's buying process (Figure 17.5). Computerized database marketing (e.g. direct mail) is used in a customer-screening process to identify possible customers, who will then be 'taken over' by salespersons. Their job is to turn 'hot' and 'very hot' customer candidates into real customers.

The international sales force organization

In international markets, firms often organize their sales forces similarly to their domestic structures, regardless of differences between one country and another. This means that the sales force is organized by geography, product, customer or some combination of these (Table 17.4).

A number of firms organize their international sales force along simple geographical territories within a given country or region. Firms that have broad product lines and large sales volume, and/or operate in large, developed markets may prefer more specialized organizations, such as product or customer assignment. The firm may also organize the sales force based upon other factors such as culture or languages spoken in the targeted foreign markets. For example, firms often divide Switzerland into different regions, reflecting French, Italian and German language usage.

Table 17.4	Sales force organizational structure		
Structure	**Factors favouring choice of organizational structure**	**Advantages**	**Disadvantages**
Geographic	Distinct languages/cultures Single product line Underdeveloped markets	Clear, simple Incentive to cultivate local business and personal ties Travel expenses	Breadth of customers Breadth of products
Product	Established market Broad product lines	Product knowledge	Travel expenses Overlapping territories/customers Local business and personal ties
Customer[a]	Broad product lines	Market/customer knowledge	Overlapping territories/products Local business and personal ties
Combination	Large sales volume Large/developed markets Distinct language/cultures	Maximum flexibility Travel expenses	Travel expenses Complexity Sales management

[a] By type of industry, size of account, channel of distribution, individual company.

Types of international sales force

Management should consider three options when determining the most appropriate international sales force. The salespeople hired for sales positions could be expatriates, host-country nationals or third-country nationals. For example, a German working for a German company in the US is an expatriate. The same German working for a US company in Germany is a host-country national. If assigned to France, he/she is a third-country national.

- *Expatriate salespersons*. These are viewed favourably because they are already familiar with the firm's products, technology, history and policies. Thus the 'only' kind of preparation they would need is a knowledge of the foreign market. Yet this could be a big problem for the expatriate salesperson. Whereas some may enjoy the challenge and adjustment, other expatriate personnel find it difficult to come to terms with a new and unfamiliar business environment. The failure to understand a foreign culture and its customers will hinder the effectiveness of an expatriate sales force. The family of the expatriate may also face adaptation problems. However, very expensive items often require selling directly from the head office, which usually involves expatriates.

● *Host-country nationals.* These are personnel who are based in their home country. As native personnel they have extensive market and cultural knowledge, language skills and familiarity with local business traditions. Since the government and local community undoubtedly prefer that their own nationals be hired instead of outsiders, the firm can avoid charges of exploitation while gaining goodwill at the same time. Using local sales representatives also permits the firm to become active more quickly in a new market because the adjustment period is minimized.

● *Third-country nationals.* These are employees transferred from one country to another. They tend to be born in one country, employed by a firm based in another country and working in a third country.

Table 17.5	Advantages and disadvantages of sales force types	
Category	**Advantages**	**Disadvantages**
Expatriates	Product knowledge High service levels Train for promotion Greater home control	Highest costs High turnover High training cost
Host country	Economical High market knowledge Language skills Best cultural knowledge Implement actions sooner	Needs product training May be held in low esteem Importance of language skills declining Difficult to ensure loyalty

Third country	Cultural sensitivity
	Language skills
	Economical
	Allows regional sales coverage
	May allow sales to country in conflict
	  with the home country
		Face identity problems
		Blocked promotions
		Income gaps
		Needs product/company
		  training
		Loyalty assurance

Source: reprinted from *Industrial Marketing Management,* Vol. 24, Honeycutt, E.D. and Ford, J.B. (1995) 'Guidelines for managing an international sales force', p. 138, Copyright 1995, with permission from Elsevier.

The advantages and disadvantages of the three types of international sales force are summarized in Table 17.5.

Expatriates and third-country nationals are seldom used in sales capacities for long periods of time. They are used for three main reasons: to upgrade a subsidiary's selling performance, to fill management positions and to transfer sales policies, procedures and techniques. However, most companies use local nationals as their sales personnel. They are familiar with local business practices and can be managed accordingly.

Trade fairs and exhibitions

A trade fair (TF) or exhibition is a concentrated event at which manufacturers, distributors and other vendors display their products and/or describe their services to current and prospective customers, suppliers, other business associates and the press.

Trade fairs can enable a company to reach, in a few days, a concentrated group of interested prospects that it might otherwise take several months to contact. Potential buyers can examine and compare the outputs of competing firms in a short period at the same place. They can see the latest developments and establish immediate contact with potential suppliers. TFs also offer international firms the opportunity to gather vital information quickly, easily and cheaply. For example, within a short period, a firm can learn a considerable amount about its competitive environment, which would take much longer and cost much more to get through other sources (e.g. secondary information).

Whether a marketer should participate in a TF depends largely on the type of business relationship it wants to develop with a particular country. A company looking only for one-off or short-term sales might find the TF expense prohibitive, but a firm looking for long-term involvement may find the investment worthwhile.

17.4 International advertising strategies in practice

In the introduction to Part IV, the question of standardization or adaptation of the whole marketing mix was discussed. Standardization allows the realization of economies of scale in the production of advertising materials, reducing advertising costs and increasing profitability. On the other hand, since advertising is based largely on language and images, it is mostly influenced by the sociocultural behavior of consumers in different countries.

In reality, it is not a question of either/or. For the internationally oriented firm it is more a question of the degree of standardization/localization. Many of the global companies using standardized advertising are well known (e.g. Coca-Cola, Intel, Philip Morris/Marlboro).

It is important to separate the global/local marketing challenge into two parts — the creative challenge and the implementation challenge. The creative concept is arguably the most crucial and powerful force in any campaign. However, implementation is too often not given the priority it needs. Successful campaigns recognize that making the big idea *work* (the implementation) is as important as the big idea itself (Freedman, 2015):

1. *The creative challenge*: creating a global campaign concept that meets the global brand aims and is adaptable for local market needs. Many obstacles await brand directors who fail to take local market needs fully into account, for example:
   - *Images*. Landscape, typical background and, of course, images of people will vary from market to market.
   - *Humour*. This is so easy to get wrong. Something that is hilarious in Europe may not go down well at all in Asia. Worse still, it could be offensive.
   - *Animals*. Be aware of the varying connotations animals carry in different cultures. A picture of children playing with a dog in the back garden is an image of household happiness in Europe and the Americas, but would cause offence in the Middle East.
   - *Metaphors*. Metaphors related to local superstitions (religion) or proverbs may not apply to other markets, or resonate less strongly, weakening the campaign.
   - *Colours*. Colours are very important in some markets; they will have positive and negative associations and values that could support or have negative impact on the campaign's values.
   - *Traditions*. Local traditions can work really well, but be cautious when using 'international' traditions like Valentine's Day for all markets, as they do differ.

This list could go on, but it is a useful bottom line to be aware of when working on any global creative project.

If using humour, metaphors or festivities, make sure that they are universal or it may result in considerable time working with local markets on major adaptation. Try to make key campaign elements transferable.

2. *The implementation challenge:* planning and managing the project from inception, through the key localization stages all the way to launch. A focus on implementation right from the start is key to global marketing success. This requires a specialist skillset and smart technology and systems. It also needs a certain kind of focus, determination and attitude, and forward-thinking, agile project managers to oversee and drive projects to success. There are four main elements to consider when implementing a global campaign:

- *Roles and accountabilities.* Ensure that the right people are on the team, and that everyone knows what they are doing.
- *Defined budgets.* The global marketing manager should ensure that the marketing teams are aware of the budgets.
- *A global creative brief.* Good briefing will ensure that global and local marketing assets are generated according to the company's vision and mission. For example, the global marketing manager could have the responsibility to create a toolkit of assets for local markets to adapt locally.
- *Clear project management and communication.* In under to improve project management and communication for the campaign, assign an implementation captain. The role of the implementation captain is to govern the implementation plan, act as a central point of contact and appoint experienced local campaign managers who understand the whole picture.

Solving the global/local creative challenge

What may resonate compellingly in one market, however, may have little to no impact in a number of others. Major brands want to implement a single message globally, and empower it to perform locally with a single high-impact creative concept. The benefits are obvious: although information moves faster than ever, local culture, language, history, values, climate and other aspects still differentiate one market from another and, as a consequence, impact on the effectiveness of the message. In this connection, relying on central assumptions from the HQ can be a recipe for disaster. Working closely with local markets and the local organizations (subsidiaries or local agents) is the only way to get the most out of global campaigns.

Brand directors may well think they have developed the very best creative as far as the global team is concerned, but the real test of whether or not it will fly is when the time comes for the idea to be implemented in the local markets. Many global brand owners describe keeping all the markets in the picture as a nightmare. However, inviting local brand managers into the conversation around the creative concept is essential to the success of a global campaign. Ultimately, collaboration is the name of the game when getting local markets involved.

Example of standardization strategies

The Cathay Pacific advertisements show that the company uses a standardized strategy in the South-east Asian area. The only element of adaptation is the translation of the English text into Japanese.

Examples of adaptation (localization) strategies

Cognac: Hong Kong/China versus Europe

The Chinese love affair with western alcohol goes back a long way. The first imported brandy arrived in Shanghai in 1859 when Hennessy unloaded its first cargo. Then in 1949

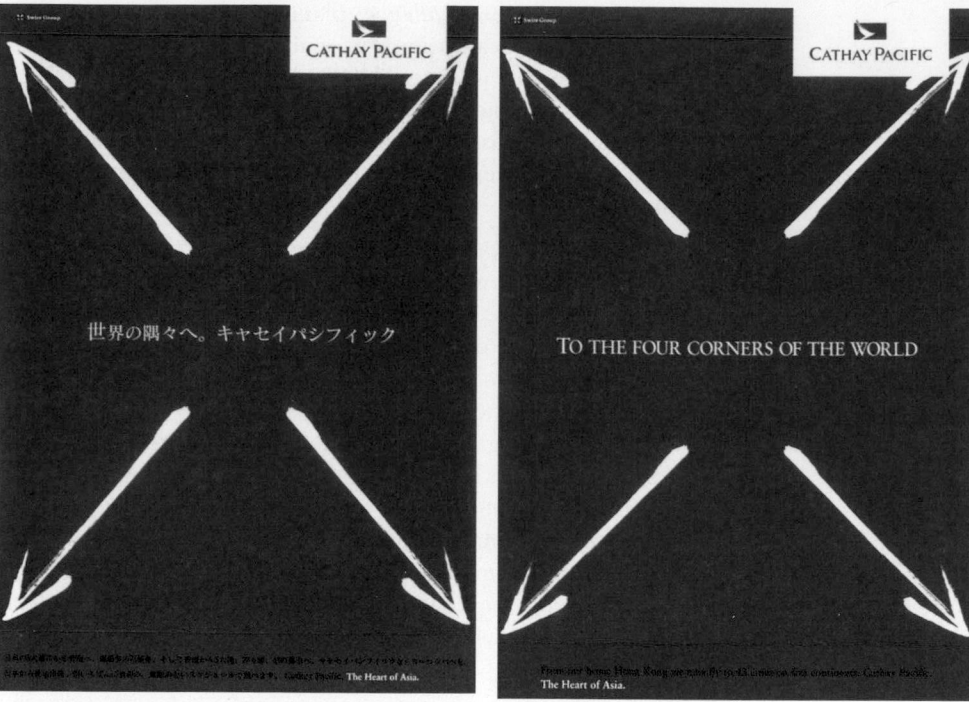

Standardized advertisements from Cathay Pacific
Source: Cathay Pacific Airways Ltd.

the favourite drink of 'the Paris of the East' suddenly became a symbol of western capitalist decadence; alcohol shipments came to an abrupt halt and did not resume for the next 30 years. However, when foreign liquor once again became available in the late 1970s, cognac quickly resumed its place as a guest at the Chinese banquet table.

Today cognac and brandy still account for about 80 per cent of all imported spirits in China. Most of the imported brandy goes through Hong Kong via grey markets (see also Section 16.10). Chinese awareness of brand and category of cognac is particularly high in the south of the country, where the drinking habits of visiting Hong Kong businessmen set a strong example. This impact is reinforced by alcohol advertising on Hong Kong television, available to millions of viewers in Guangdong province.

The key to Chinese consumption patterns lies in the importance of 'face'. Whatever the occasion, be it the father of the bride toasting his son-in-law's family in Beijing or a Shenzhen entrepreneur's night out on the town, brandy is of paramount importance. Unlike their western counterparts, who like to curl up on the couch with a snifter of brandy, the Chinese consider cognac drinking an extremely social – and conspicuous – pastime.

For this reason, companies will carefully tailor their advertisements to their market so that an advert intended for the western European market might show couples drinking cognac with their coffee, whereas an advert intended for the Asian market might show people drinking cognac from beer glasses during the meal.

Folklore as much as marketing has propelled the growth of cognac sales. Cognac has long had the inestimable commercial benefit of being widely regarded by the Chinese as enhancing a man's sexual prowess. And much to the delight of the liquor companies, the Chinese believe that the older (and pricier) the cognac, the more potent its effect.

Prince cigarettes: UK versus Germany

The Danish cigarette company House of Prince has high market share (50–90 per cent) in Scandinavian countries, but outside this area its market share is very low, typically 1–2 per cent.

Western alcohol is highly popular in South-east Asia, with cognac and brandy accounting for about 80 per cent of all imported spirits.

Source: Bloomberg/Getty Images.

Advertisements for Prince cigarettes in the UK and Germany

Source: House of Prince A/S.

The House of Prince cigarette images show advertisements used in the UK and Germany. The UK version is based on an invitation to try the product ('I go for Prince'). The target group is also above average in education and income. The German advertisement is somewhat different. Prince is promoted as an 'original import from Denmark'. Apparently there is no 'buy German' mentality working against the use of this slogan. In the German consumer's mind, Danish cigarettes are strongly positioned compared with light German cigarettes. Therefore the product's position is emphasized as 'men's business', with Viking associations and ideas of freedom. Incidentally, the two products, Prince and Prince Denmark, are not identical. The German Prince Denmark has a milder taste than does Prince.

Gammel Dansk (Danish Distillers/Danisco): Denmark versus Germany

The Danish bitter Gammel Dansk has a 75 per cent share of the bitter market in Denmark. Thus the product has a high degree of recognition there (nearly all Danish adults know the label). The objective of the Danish advertisement has therefore primarily been to maintain Gammel Dansk's high degree of recognition.

Although the market share in Denmark is very high, Gammel Dansk does not have any position worth mentioning outside Denmark. In Germany, the situation is totally different. Here the knowledge (and trial share) is at a minimum. The Germans have their own Jägermeister and competition is tough. The strategy behind the German campaign has therefore been to make people try Gammel Dansk by letting them fill out a coupon. By sending it in they receive a little bottle of Gammel Dansk and two original Gammel Dansk glasses.

Advertisements for Gammel Dansk in Denmark and Germany
Source: Det Danske Spirituskompagni A/S.

LEGO FreeStyle: Europe versus the Far East

The LEGO images show European and Far Eastern versions of an advertisement for LEGO FreeStyle. The Asian version, 'Build your child's mind', appeals to Asian parents' desire for their children to do well in school.

The Asian educational system is very competitive and only those with the highest grades are admitted to university. In many places in Asia it is a defeat for parents if their child does not do well in school. The Asian version has been run in Hong Kong, Taiwan and Korea (preferably in the local languages because the majority of consumers do not understand English). In Hong Kong, the advertisements are run in English or Chinese (depending on the language of the magazine).

The European version implies creativity when playing with the different FreeStyle bricks: 'What will your child make of it?'

Advertisements for LEGO® Freestyle in the Far East (left) and Europe (right)

Source: © 2010 the Lego Group. Used with permission.

EXHIBIT 17.5   Jarlsberg cheese – cross-border communication

Jarlsberg, the Norwegian cheese brand, is a mild, Swiss-Emmentaler type of cow's milk cheese that has large, irregular holes. The history of this cheese can be traced back to the middle 1850s. Its creator, Anders

Russia

Source: Tine.

UK

Source: Tine.

US

Source: Tine.

Australia

Source: Tine.

Larsen Bakke, was a local farmer/entrepreneur and a pioneer in Norway's dairy industry. He produced the cheese in the village of Våle in the county of Vestfold, some 80 km south of Oslo. The cheese came to be named 'Jarlsberg' because 'Jarlsberg & Larviks Amt' was the name of the county until 1918.

Today, the producer of Jarlsberg, TINE SA, is Norway's largest producer, distributor and exporter of dairy products. Since the start of 1961, the exports of Jarlsberg have grown substantially. Annually, more than 23,000 tonnes of Jarlsberg are consumed worldwide. Jarlsberg is currently the most sold foreign cheese on the US and Australian markets. In the US market alone, Jarlsberg cheese is sold in 30,000 supermarkets.

Until now, Jarlsberg's assorted agents and partners in various export countries have been responsible for the local ads. The four photographs included here illustrate this approach of localized advertising.

QUESTIONS

1. Explain the different cultural characteristics behind the different ads.
2. Would it be a good idea for Jarlsberg to standardize the international advertising?

Source: based on different public sources.

<table>
<tr><td>**17.5**</td><td>Implications of the internet for communication decisions</td></tr>
</table>

In the physical marketplace, different communication tools are used in the customers' buying process (see Figure 17.6). Traditional mass communication tools (print advertising, TV and radio) can create awareness and this can result in consumers' identification of new needs. From then on, other elements of the communication mix take over, such as direct marketing (direct marketing, personal selling) and in-store promotion. Unlike marketing in the physical marketplace, the internet/e-commerce encompasses the entire 'buying' process. Of course, the online markets also make use of traditional mass advertising in order to get potential customers into the online buying process (from the left in Figure 17.6).

Market communication strategies change dramatically in the online world. On the internet, it is easier than ever to actually *communicate* a message to large numbers of people. However, in many cases, it is much harder for your message to be heard above the noise by your target audience. Various strategies for conducting online marketing have been developed in the past several years – from the most common (website linking) to the most expensive (banner advertising) to the most offensive (e-mail spamming), and everything in between. It is almost certain that a continual stream of new market communication strategies will emerge as the internet medium evolves.

How, then, can a web audience be created? One of the new possibilities in this field is social media marketing.

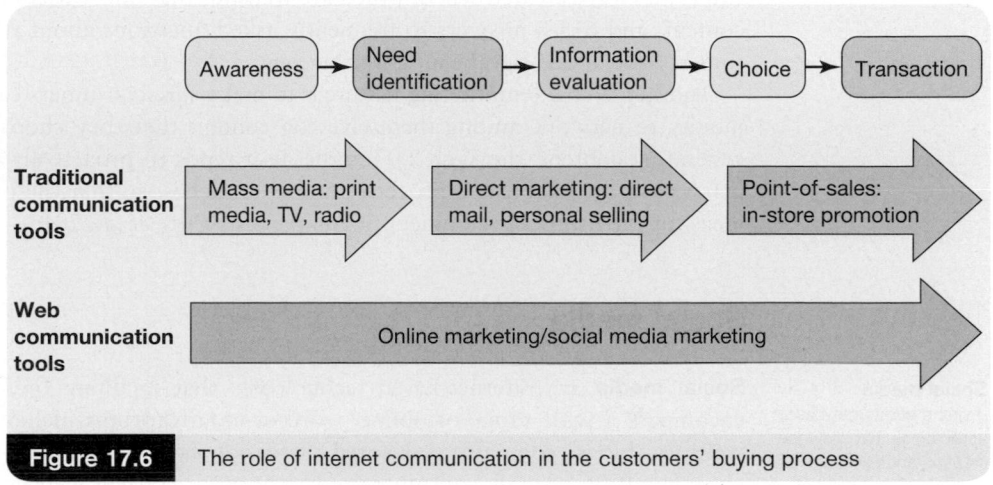

| **Figure 17.6** | The role of internet communication in the customers' buying process |

17.6   Social media marketing

Word-of-mouth (WoM)
The sharing of information about a product, promotion, etc., between a consumer and a friend, colleague or other acquaintance.

When you sell and buy you will experience that it is part of a social process. It involves not only a one-to-one interaction between the company and the customer but also many exchanges of information and influence among the people who surround the customer. Consumers are much more trusting in friends and colleagues than they are in TV advertising or corporate communication. **Word-of-Mouth (WoM)** has shown many more times more effective than traditional print advertising in impacting brand switching decisions.

Word-of-mouth and conversations can take place off-line and online. Like any conversation, in a café, the content varies. Some conversations are serious and some fun, some are short and some long, some happy and some angry and intense. In online conversations, consumers' experiences with brands and services are often openly discussed, whether companies are involved or not. In this way, consumers are becoming more powerful. Clearly monitoring the online conversations and intervening, when appropriate, has advantages to brand managers in any B2B or business-to-consumer (B2C) company. Such monitoring can lead to a better understanding of consumer behaviour and feelings of the market mood. It can lead to changes in the different parts of the marketing mix (Woodcock *et al.*, 2011).

Web 2.0

Web 2.0 websites allow you to do more than just retrieve information, as this was mainly the case with Web 1.0. Web 2.0 transforms broadcast media monologues (one-to-many =

Web 1.0) into social media dialogues (many-to-many). The term Web 2.0 was first used in 2004 to describe a new way software developers and end users started to utilize the internet to create content and applications that were no longer created and published by individuals, but instead continuously modified by all users in a participatory and collaborative fashion. The popularity of the term Web 2.0, along with the increasing use of blogs, wikis and social networking technologies, has led many in academia and business to work with these 'new' phenomena.

For marketers, Web 2.0 offers an opportunity to engage consumers. A growing number of marketers are using Web 2.0 tools to collaborate with consumers on product development, service enhancement and promotion. Companies can use Web 2.0 tools to improve collaboration with both business partners and consumers. Among other things, company employees have created wikis, which are websites that allow users to add, delete and edit content, and to list answers to frequently asked questions about each product, and consumers have added significant contributions.

Another Web 2.0 marketing feature is to make sure consumers can use the online community to network among themselves on content that they choose themselves. Besides generating content, the Web 2.0 internet user tends to proactively bring in a whole new perspective on established processes and approaches, so that the users create innovative ideas for the future development of companies (Wirtz *et al.*, 2010).

Social media

Social media
A group of internet-based applications that allow the creation and exchange of user-generated content. Examples are blogs, YouTube, networking sites (e.g. Facebook, MySpace, LinkedIn, Twitter), photo-sharing (e.g. Flickr) and aggregating channels (e.g. comparison sites).

Social media are internet-based technologies that facilitate online conversations and encompass a wide range of online, word-of-mouth forums including social networking websites, blogs, company sponsored discussion boards and chat rooms, consumer-to-consumer (C2C) e-mail, consumer product or service ratings websites and forums, internet discussion boards and forums, and sites containing digital audio, images, movies or photographs, to name a few. Since 2009, the official company and brand websites have typically been losing audience. This decline is believed to be due to the emergence of social media marketing by the brands themselves, an increasingly pervasive marketing practice (Hutton and Fosdick, 2011).

According to ebizmba.com the world's largest social networking site is Facebook, which was initially founded by Mark Zuckerberg in order to stay in touch with his fellow students from Harvard University. In May 2015, according to www.ebizmba.com, the five most popular social websites (excluding YouTube and Google) were (number of unique visitors worldwide per month):

1. Facebook   900 million
2. Twitter   310 million
3. LinkedIn   255 million
4. Pinterest   250 million
5. Google+   120 million

For social media usage and development, the diversity of languages is creating communication challenges on a global basis. Facebook has 900 million weekly users, with more than 70 per cent outside the US. To effectively communicate with non-English users, Facebook has 70 translations available on its site made possible by a vast network of 300,000 volunteers and translators (Singh *et al.*, 2012). Facebook and Twitter are mostly interactive social media on an intimate level. As such, these platforms offer direct selling companies means of communicating with key stakeholders (customers and distributors) in the industry. On the other hand, YouTube, with its more traditional one-way audience communication, appears to be used more effectively for recruiting consumers to become distributors of information or products (Ferrell and Ferrell, 2012).

One of the 'shooting stars' since 2010 is LinkedIn, which is a social networking website for people in professional occupations. Launched in 2003, it is mainly used for professional networking. While Facebook, YouTube and Twitter continue to dominate social media in the US and Europe, the global scene tells a different story. In Germany, Russia, China and Japan, the most visited social networking site is not Facebook but home-grown rivals.

Integrated marketing communications (IMC) have traditionally been considered to be largely one-way in nature ('bowling' – see Figure 17.7 below). In the old paradigm, the organization and its agents developed the message and transmitted it to potential consumers, who may or may not have been willing participants in the communication process. The control over the dissemination of information was in the hands of the firm's marketing organization. The traditional elements of the promotion mix (advertising, personal selling, public relations and publicity, direct marketing and sales promotion) were the tools through which control was asserted.

The twenty-first century is witnessing an explosion of internet-based messages transmitted through these media. They have become a major factor in influencing various aspects of consumer behaviour including awareness, information acquisition, opinions, attitudes, purchase behaviour and post-purchase communication and evaluation. Unfortunately, the popular business press and academic literature offers marketing managers very little guidance for incorporating social media into their IMC strategies.

Social networking as a communication tool has two interrelated promotional roles (Mangold and Faulds, 2009):

1. Social networking should be consistent with the use of traditional IMC tools. That is, companies should use social media to talk to their customers through such platforms as blogs, as well as Facebook and Twitter groups. These media may either be company-sponsored or sponsored by other individuals or organizations.
2. Social networking is enabling customers to talk to one another. This is an extension of traditional word-of-mouth communication. While companies cannot directly control such C2C messages, they do have the ability to influence the conversations that consumers have with one another. However, consumers' ability to communicate with one another limits the amount of control companies have over the content and dissemination of information. Consumers are in control; they have greater access to information and greater command over media consumption than ever before.

Marketing managers are seeking ways to incorporate social media into their IMC strategies. The traditional communications paradigm, which relied on the classic promotional mix to craft IMC strategies, must give way to a new paradigm that includes all forms of social media as potential tools in designing and implementing IMC strategies. Contemporary marketers cannot ignore the phenomenon of social media, where available market information is based on the experiences of individual consumers and is channeled through the traditional promotion mix. However, various social media platforms, many of which are completely independent of the producing/sponsoring organization or its agents, enhance consumers' ability to communicate with one another.

From 'bowling' to 'pinball'

Although a little oversimplified, marketing in the pre-social media era was comparable to 'bowling' (see Figure 17.7).

A game of bowling shows how you may have traditionally communicated with your consumers, with the firm and the brand (the bowler) rolling a ball (the brand communication message) towards the pins (our target customers). Clearly this is a very direct one-way communication approach. This is the old traditional push model. Marketers targeted certain customer groups and sent out their advertising messages like precisely bowled bowling balls. They used traditional media to hit as many bowling pins as possible. One key characteristic of this bowling marketing game was the large amount of control the company retained over marketing communication because consumers were given only limited freedom of action.

For many bigger companies a large TV-budget has been the ball that marketers rolled down the lane, trying to hit as many pins as possible. Marketers were in control, happily counting how many 'pins' they had hit, and how often. Success in this game was clear-cut, and the metrics clear.

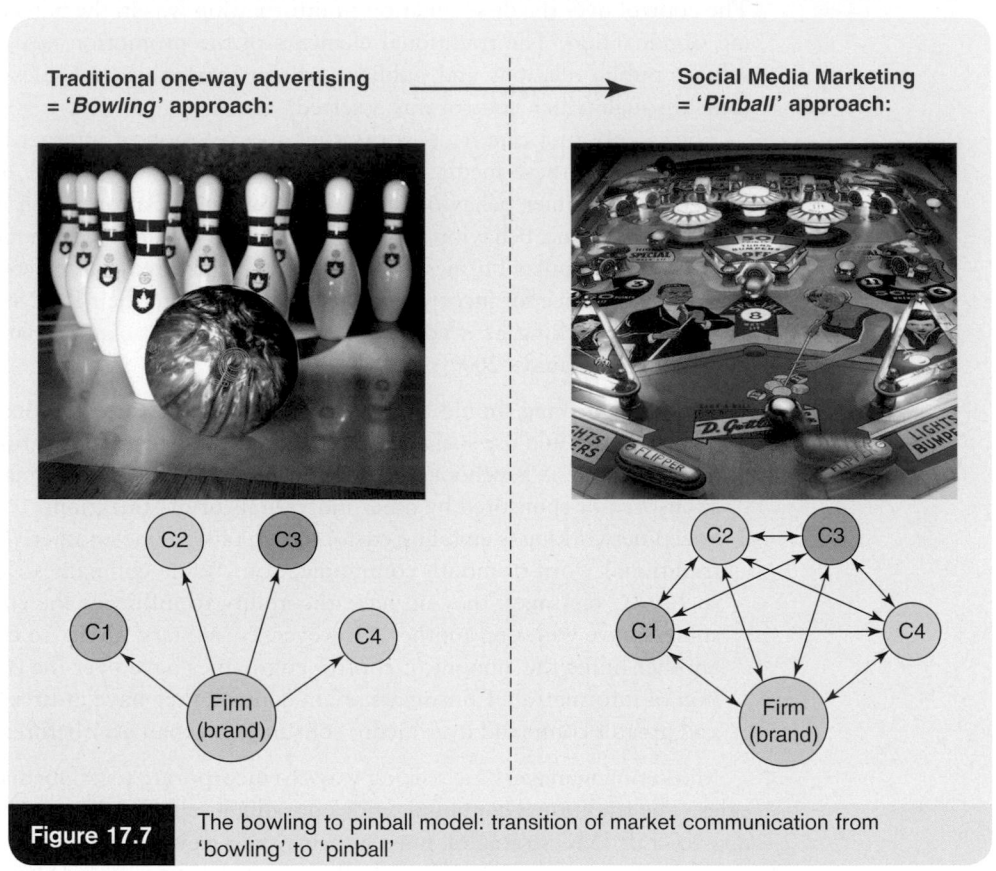

| Figure 17.7 | The bowling to pinball model: transition of market communication from 'bowling' to 'pinball' |

Note: C = consumer.

Source: images from Imagemore Co., Ltd (left) and 5AM Images/Alamy Images (right).

Times are changing

In a social media marketing world, the bowling metaphor does not fit anymore. On this arena marketing can be better described as playing 'pinball'. Companies serve up a 'marketing ball' (brands and brand-building messages) into a dynamic and chaotic market environment. The 'marketing ball' is then diverted and often accelerated by social media 'bumpers', which change the ball's course in chaotic ways. After the marketing ball is in play, marketing managers may continue to guide it with agile use of the 'flippers', but the ball does not always go where it is intended to.

Consequently, in the 'pinball' world, you cannot know outcomes in advance. Instead, marketers have to be prepared to respond in real time to the spin put on the ball by consumers. When mastered well, the pinball game can deliver big point multipliers and, if the company is very good, even more balls can be shot into the game. A reason for this may be that today consumers have a large audience to bring up new topics on the communication agenda. In the ideal situation, you are reaching networked influencers, advocates and other high-value consumers, who may sustain and spread positive conversations about the brand across multiple channels.

Occasionally, the marketing ball will come back to the company. At this point, the firm (brand) has to use the flippers to interact and throw it back into the social media sphere. If the company or the brand do not feed the social marketing media sphere by flipping communications back, the ball will finally drop through the flippers and in the longer term, the two-way relationship between consumers and the firm (brand) will die.

The extended model of interactive market communication

In Figure 17.8 (below) the 'bowling to pinball' model is further elaborated into an extended model of interactive market communication.

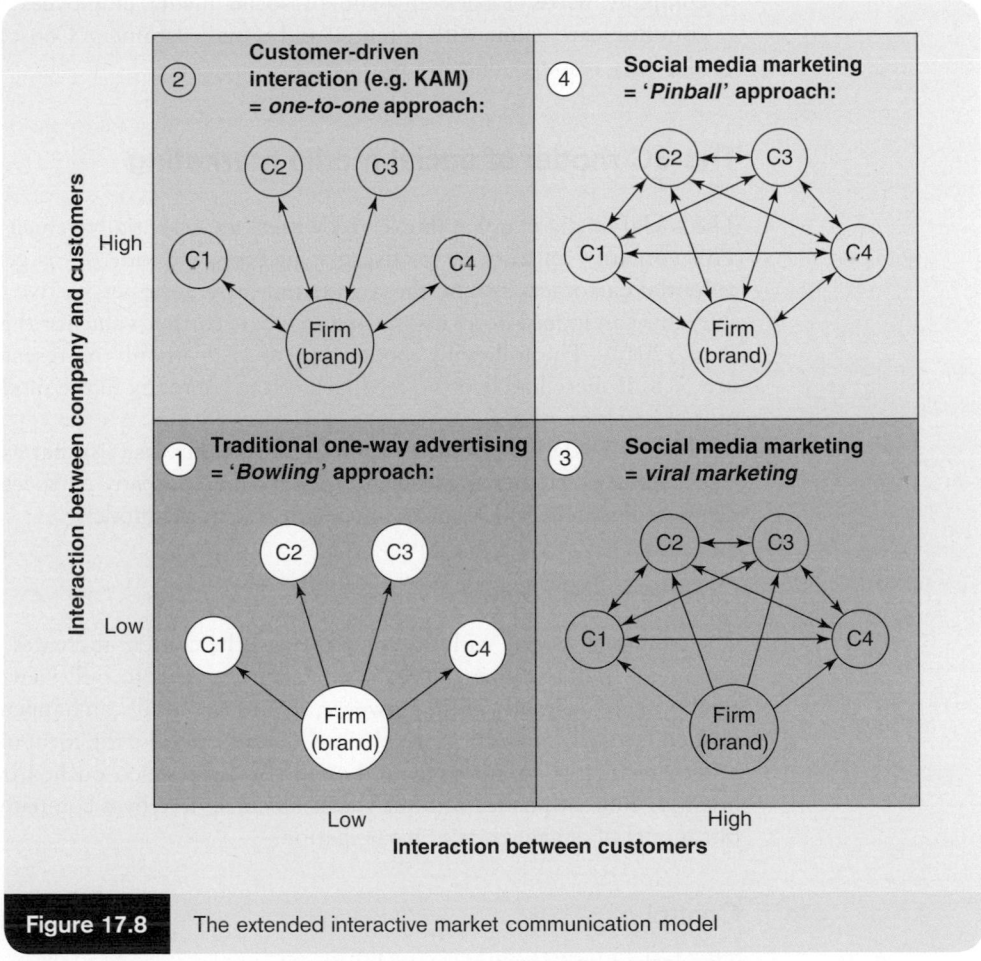

| **Figure 17.8** | The extended interactive market communication model |

Note: C = consumer.

The four different communication styles, represented in Figure 17.8, are:

1. The traditional one-way advertising (mass media advertising like television advertising, newspaper/magazine advertising etc.) represents the 'bowling' approach where the firm attempts to 'hit' as many customers with 'shotgun' mass media methods. Normally this approach is a one-way communication type.

2. Customer-driven interaction represents a higher degree of interaction between the company and its different key customers. Often the company finds some key account managers, who have the responsibility of taking care of the one-to-one interaction between the firm and its key accounts (customers).

3. Viral marketing represents version 1.0 of social media marketing, where the company uses an non-traditional medium, such as a YouTube video for example, to attract attention and build brand awareness. The interaction between the potential 'customers' is quite high (blogging sites, etc.), but the feedback to the company is relatively low (no double arrows back to the company).

4. Social media marketing represents version 2.0 of social media marketing, where there is also an extensive feedback to the company itself (double arrows back to the company). Here the company has proactively chosen to be a co-player in the discussion and blogging on the different relevant social media sites (Facebook, Twitter, etc.). This also means that the company here tries to strengthen interaction with the customers in a positive direction, in order to influence customer behaviour. In order to do so, the company needs a back-up team of social media employees who can interact and communicate online with potential and actual customers. Consequently, this strategy is also very resource demanding.

The 6C model of social media marketing

The social media (e.g. Facebook or Twitter) are essentially vehicles for carrying content. This content – in form of words, text, pictures and videos – is generated by millions of potential customers around the world, and from your perspective (= company's perspective) this can indeed be an inspiration to create further value for these customers (Berthon *et al.*, 2012). The following model (Figure 17.9) mainly represents alternative 4 in Figure 17.8. If there had been no feedback to the company in the model, it would have been more like alternative 3.

Figure 17.9 defines six distinct, interrelated elements (Cs) that explain the creation and retention of consumer engagement, seen from a company perspective; however the user-generated content still plays an important role in the model.

Company and content

The 6C model begins with the company and the content it creates. Basically, the internet remains a 'pull' medium, in the way that firms seek to pull viewers to its content, and finally to the company itself. However, before any 'pull' can happen, the content has to be pushed (seeded) forward in the chain. Content can take the form of, for example, a Facebook product or brand page, and/or a YouTube video pushed out to viewers. Consequently, content pushed into the social media sphere by a company acts as a catalyst for our model of engagement or participation.

Control

The dashed line denoting control in the 6C model (Figure 17.9) is intended to represent a wall beyond which the company passes over control of its brand to the online community and the customers. In order to accelerate the viral uptake of its brand messaging, the company sometimes gives up the digital rights and blocks in order to encourage online community members to copy, modify, re-post and forward the content. The content is intended to be copied and/or embedded into people's websites, blogs and on Facebook walls. The key point to this stage in the process is that the company (the content creator) must accept, and even embrace, the fact that they no longer have full control over the content: it is free to be taken, modified, commented on and otherwise appropriated by the community of interest. This may challenge the conventional 'brand management' wisdom stating that managers must keep control of brand image and messaging.

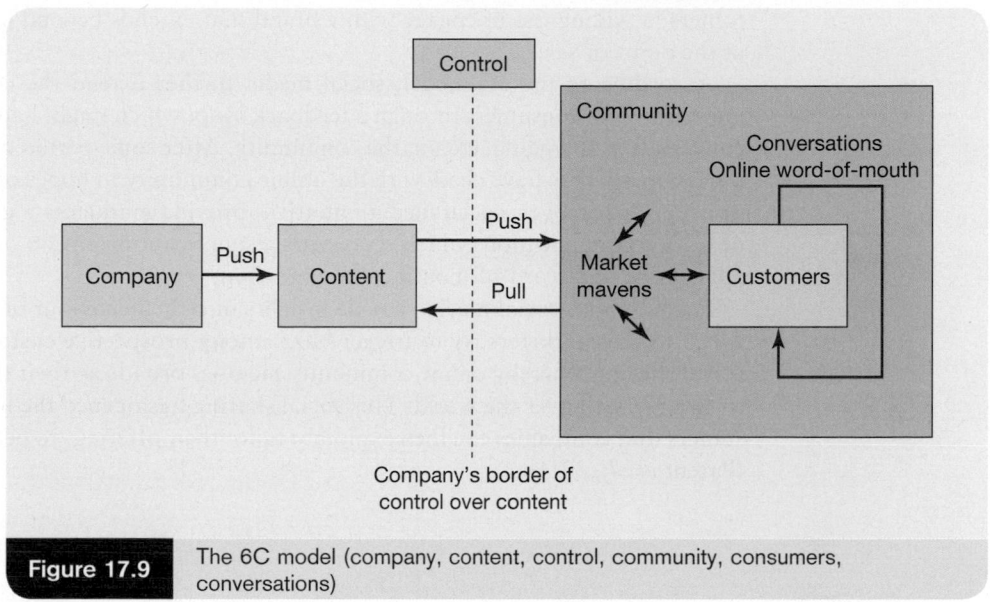

| Figure 17.9 | The 6C model (company, content, control, community, consumers, conversations) |

Source: based on Parent *et al.* (2011).

Community

The company creates content and pushes it over the symbolic border of control to the other side, where a community of interested consumers now takes it up. At this point, communication becomes bidirectional. The use of arrows in Figure 17.9 for push and pull attempts to reflect the 'give-and-take' that goes on between a community and the company, represented by the content creators. In its simplest form, it is reflected in the art of commenting: posting reactions, on Facebook or YouTube, to the content. In some cases, the company can even learn about 'customer behaviour' in the market by following these online community discussions. In an ideal world, a series of reflexive conversations take place in the community, independent of any action by the company, which will often have a passive role as an observer (Kaplan and Haenlein, 2011).

When transferring the 'content' into the online community, the company and the content providers often try to target the 'market mavens', which are defined as individuals who have access to a large amount of marketplace information, and proactively engage in discussions with other online community members and customers to diffuse and spread this content.

Market mavens are typically the first to receive the message and transmit it to their immediate social networks. They function as connectors or bridges between different subcultures' and their network of social hubs can facilitate immediate transmission of the content to thousands of online community members.

Customers and online conversation

The ultimate expression of engagement occurs when a multitude of online conversations circle around the phenomenon and content, as illustrated above and in Figure 17.9. The 6C model distinguishes between the online community and potential customers, as the latter are usually a subset of the former. The online community may also include people who have heard of the web-based initiative but not directly participated in it.

In general, there seems to be a growing escalation in participation on the part of customers; a willingness to engage with a brand that extends beyond just purchase decisions at the point of sale.

According to the 6C model, social media further extend the conversations between marketers and consumers through a feedback loop, which might happen after some online conversation (blogging, etc.) in the community. After some period of online conversation, the company may have chats with the online community in hopes of influencing purchase decisions. Moreover, social media initiatives provide marketers a glimpse into the world of C2C communication, which represents a significant extension of the more traditional advertising and word-of-mouth communication.

Furthermore, social media provide insights into the behaviour of non-customers. Most social media marketers try to trigger buzz among prospective customers. This has led to social sharing whereby online community member broadcast their thoughts and activities to strangers all over the world. This social sharing has opened the lives of individual consumers that companies can then exploit to tailor their offerings to better match preferences (Parent *et al.*, 2011).

EXHIBIT 17.6 Generating buzz in the pre-communication stage for BMW 1 Series M Coupé

A good example of how to leverage social media marketing in communication campaigns can be found in the 2011 worldwide introduction of BMW 1 Series M Coupé. This case shows how social media can generate buzz even in the pre-communication phase. BMW's systematic use of such a buzz strategy (using Facebook and video clips, involving car journalists and TV shows like *Top Gear*) was highly effective in sparking interest in the target group and generating leads with a relatively small budget. With a rich information base and the prospect of an exclusive test drive, prospective buyers were motivated to register on M-power.com. The contact details and insights of users enabled targeted follow-up communication and gave BMW more control over this campaign.

Source: Mark Scheuern/Alamy Images.

For you as a marketer, what you can learn from this case is that generating leads should be the main driver in the pre-communication stage. All marketing stimuli such as communication and events have to encourage registration. Therefore, a consistent landing platform should be an essential part of each social media campaign. All social media marketing activities have to encourage registration of the potential customers, in order to follow up with more personalized communication, which could lead to a specific purchase of the product.

Source: based on Mrkwicka *et al.* (2012).

17.7 Developing a viral marketing campaign

Viral marketing
Online word-of-mouth is a marketing technique that seeks to exploit existing social networks to produce exponential increases in brand awareness.

The internet has radically changed the concept of word-of-mouth, so much so that the term **viral marketing** was coined by venture capitalist Steve Jurvetson in 1997. The term was used to describe Hotmail's e-mail practice of appending advertising for itself to outgoing mail from its users. In the Hotmail case each e-mail sent arrived with the appended message '*Get your private, free e-mail from Hotmail at* http://www.hotmail.com'.

Viral marketing is by no means a substitute for a comprehensive and diversified marketing strategy. In employing viral marketing to generate peer-to-peer endorsement, the technique should not be considered as a standalone miracle worker.

While the messaging and strategy ranges radically from campaign to campaign, most successful campaigns contain some commonly used approaches. These approaches are often used in combination to maximize the viral effect of a campaign.

Successful viral campaigns are easily spread. The key is to get your customers to do the hard work for you by recommending your company or its promotional offers to friends and colleagues, who in turn will recommend it to their friends and so on. An effective viral marketing campaign can get your marketing message out to thousands of potential customers at phenomenal speeds.

When creating a campaign, marketers should evaluate how people will communicate the message or campaign to others.

Creating compelling content

Creating quality content can often be more expensive than simply offering a free product, but the results are often better. Fun is often a vital part of any viral marketing campaign. The general rule of thumb is that the content must be compelling, it must evoke a response on an emotional level from the person viewing it. This fact alone has allowed many smaller brands to capitalize on content-based viral campaigns. Traditionally, larger brands are more reserved and risk adverse to the possibility of negative reaction. Central to the success of these campaigns is one or more of the following: their entry timing (early), their visibility or the simplicity of the idea.

Targeting the right audience

If a campaign is skewed towards a certain audience or certain regions (countries), marketers should make sure they seed towards that audience. Failure to due so may kill a campaign before it ever gets off the ground.

The influence and, in some cases, the power of reference groups or opinion leaders in individual decision-making is significant.

Campaign seeding

'Seeding' the original message is a key component of a viral campaign. Seeding is the act of planting the campaign with the initial group who will then go on to spread the campaign to others. The internet provides a wide array of options for seeding, including:

- e-mail/SMS
- online forums (Google groups)
- social networks (Facebook.com, MySpace.com)
- chatroom environment (MSN Messenger)
- blogs
- podcasts.

When determining where to seed it is important that marketers consider the audience they are aiming for. Is the target audience using the above-mentioned media (technologies) and to what degree?

Companies often use a combination of technologies to 'spread the virus'. Many use SMS. An example of an SMS campaign is that of Heineken, which linked an SMS promotion with the British pub tradition of playing quiz games. Heineken combined both online and off-line promotions through point-of-sale signs in pubs, inviting customers to call from their mobile phones, type in the wordplay and receive a series of multiple-choice questions to answer. Food and beverage prizes were awarded for correct answers. From a promotional perspective, the idea was successful as customers told others what they were doing, prompting them to call in too.

Control/measuring results

The goal of a viral campaign is explosive reach and participation. To measure the success of a viral marketing campaign, establish specific and obtainable goals within a timeframe. For example, you would like to see a 20 per cent increase in traffic to a website within three months or to double your subscriber rate to an e-mail newsletter in one year.

Marketers should also be adequately prepared to meet the needs of participants in the event that the campaign is successful. Server space, bandwidth, support staff, fulfilment and stocking should be taken into consideration well in advance of campaign launch. The marketer should have the ability to capitalize on the full success of the campaign.

17.8 Summary

Six main ingredients of international communication have been presented in this chapter:

1. advertising
2. public relations
3. sales promotion
4. direct marketing
5. personal selling
6. social media marketing.

As international marketers manage the various elements of the promotions mix in differing environmental conditions, decisions must be made about what channels are to be used in the communication, the message, who is to execute or help execute the programme, and how the results of the communication plan are to be measured. The trend is towards greater harmonization of strategy, at the same time allowing for flexibility at the local level and early incorporation of local needs into the communication plans.

Hence an important decision for international marketers is whether the different elements of the communication should be standardized worldwide or localized. The main reasons for seeking standardization are as follows:

- Customers do not conform to national boundaries.
- The company is seeking to build an international brand image.
- Economies of scale can be achieved.
- The few high-quality creative ideas can be exploited as widely as possible.
- Special expertise can be developed and exploited.

However, some communication tools, especially personal selling, have to be localized to fit conditions of individual markets. Another reason for the localization of the personal selling tool is that distribution channel members are normally located firmly within a country. Consequently, decisions concerning recruitment, training, motivation and evaluation of salespeople have to be made at the local level.

The process of selecting agencies has also been considered. The requisite blend of local knowledge, cultural understanding and management expertise across international markets is elusive. Too much centralization and standardization results in inappropriate marketing communications.

A very important communication tool for the future is the internet. Any company eager to take advantage of the internet on a global scale must select a business model for its internet ventures and estimate how information and transactions delivered through this new direct marketing medium will influence its existing distribution and communication system.

Social media marketing can be understood as a group of internet-based applications that build on the foundations of Web 2.0, allowing the creation and exchange of user-generated content. Social media are particularly suited to viral marketing, as the community element in them makes it convenient to transmit the marketing message to a large group of people.

Viral marketing is by no means a substitute for a comprehensive and diversified marketing strategy. Viral marketing is a credible marketing tactic that can deliver positive return on investment when properly executed as a component of an overarching strategic plan. Marketers should utilize viral marketing when the messaging can coincide and support a measurable business goal.

CASE STUDY 17.1

Helly Hansen: sponsoring fashion clothes in the US market

On a warm autumn day in 1997, Johnny Austad, President of the Norwegian clothing manufacturer Helly Hansen Co. (HH), arrives at the company's US subsidiary. Johnny still cannot quite understand the incredible development that HH has seen in the US market. During the last couple of years, he notes, Helly Hansen USA has had an increase in turnover of 10 per cent per year, but in 1996 turnover doubled, amounting to one-third of HH's worldwide sales.

How it all started

Helly Hansen Co. was founded in 1877 by the Norwegian captain Helly Juell Hansen. During the era of the sailing ship, he felt the forces of nature when he had to stand at the helm in all kinds of weather. Many hours were spent oiling clothes so they would become waterproof before rough weather set in. However, the clothes became stiff and sticky, so when Hansen finally went ashore he decided to develop better rainwear for Norwegian sailors. Today HH sells its products in more than 20 countries. Production takes place in the company's own factories in Norway and Portugal, as well as in the Far East and via contract manufacturing. Design of the new collections takes place at the company's headquarters in Norway.

American rap group Bad Boys in Helly Hansen clothes
A/S Helly Hansen.

From a producer of functional clothing to a supplier of fashion clothes to the US 'underground'

The honourable 100-year-old Norwegian producer of functional clothing for sailors has by chance become the supplier of fashion clothes to black hip-hoppers in New York's underground scene. The label, which for generations has been associated with wind and waterproof leisurewear, and work clothes for the quality-conscious consumer who likes to dress 'sensibly', has now become a symbol of the avant-garde and the exotic. Young people think the clothes are 'cool' and they don't care if they have taped seams or that it might be difficult to breathe through four layers of waterproof coating.

In the past, the first and last thing that HH designers thought about when making jackets was functionalism. The result was a very large collection of jackets with small specialized differences that only real enthusiasts could appreciate. HH's prices, on the other hand, became unreasonably high. By gathering several of the functions in the same jacket, HH is able to make allowances for its more discerning customers, as well as producing at a price that a larger part of the market is able to afford. Where HH used to direct its collections at alpine skiers, fishermen, those involved in water sports and snowboarders, it now also considers the current fashion trends. HH aims to link its look to street fashion and hopes that in this way its core customers will feel smarter, while new customers will be encouraged to buy because of the look of the clothes.

Before Johnny Austad gets on the plane back to Norway, the US subsidiary receives an enquiry about sponsorship from one of the most well-known rap groups in the US. The manager of the rap group in question, Bad Boys, is seeking US$200,000 from HH for the group to perform in HH clothes at all their concerts over the next six months as well as in their forthcoming music video.

QUESTIONS

As a newly employed marketing assistant in the US HH subsidiary, you are asked to take care of this enquiry. You are specifically asked the following questions.

1. Would you recommend that HH sponsors Bad Boys? Give reasons for your answer.

2. How can an eventual sponsorship be integrated into the total marketing plan for HH clothes in the US market?

Source: based on different public sources.

CASE STUDY 17.2

Morgan Motor Company: can the British retro sports car brand still be successful after 100 years?

The once-proud British car industry has all but vanished. However, there is one famous producer left in the UK: the Morgan Motor Company. It is the oldest privately held car company in the world and today the company is still 100 per cent family-owned.

The company was founded in 1909 by H.F.S. Morgan and was run by him until 1959. Peter Morgan, the son of H.F.S., ran the company until a few years before his death in 2003. The company was then run until 2013 by his son, Charles Morgan.

Morgan is based in Malvern Link, in Worcestershire, and in 2013 employed 180 people. All the cars are assembled by hand and the waiting list is one to two years, although it has been as high as 10 years in the past.

Business is strong, despite the economic slowdown. In 1997, Morgan made 480 cars; 14 years later, in 2011, the figure was 700. Morgan hopes that one day it will make as many as 900–1,000 cars a year, but only if that can be done the Morgan way – and what a totally unique and utterly inimitable way to make sports cars that is!

In 2011, the estimated revenue was around £25 million. The operating profits were £320,000 in 2011, compared with £665,000 in 2009. The company employs 160 people, of whom 130 are production floor employees.

Source: Morgan Motor Company.

Morgan history

The first Morgan design was, of course, the famous Threewheeler. H.F.S. Morgan designed a fun car, the Morgan Runabout, for people with little money but with a sense of adventure. The car was a great success and in the 1920s the Morgan factory in Malvern was making 2,500–3,000 cars a year, with a smaller number being built under licensee in France under the Darmont Morgan brand. Nevertheless, each year production always sold out in advance, as customers were desperate for small cars at this time.

Morgan Threewheeler sales declined and by 1935 there were only 300 new orders. The reason for this was the arrival of mass-produced popular cars from Ford, Morris and Austin at a similar price but offering more features for the money.

H.F.S. Morgan had to come up with a new design. He did this in 1936 and announced the Morgan Four Four, a light sports car with four wheels and a four-cylinder Coventry Climax engine. From the start, the Morgan Four Four made its name in competition and finished well at Le Mans in 1938 and 1939.

In 1962, Morgan won the two-litre class at Le Mans. A production Morgan beat the specially modified Porsche and Lotus racing cars and then drove home: the car averaged 98 mph for the 24-hour race. Following the race, the Morgan Plus Four Supersports was launched as a factory model so that customers could buy a Le Mans class winner.

Morgan's cars became regular winners in production sports car races across the US.

At this time the Morgan Motor Company was one of the first companies to benefit from celebrity endorsement – Ralph Lauren, Brigitte Bardot and David Bailey all drove Morgans in the 1960s.

In 1989, a visit was made by businessman Sir John Harvey Jones and makers of the BBC programme *Troubleshooter*. Sir John criticized the company's strategy of having a long waiting list and making everything by hand in such a labour-intensive way. Morgan is probably the only car company that still makes cars the way they were made in the early 1900s – building them on a wooden frame and crafting them mainly by hand.

Sir John did not really understand Morgan's market. Coachbuilding (by wood) and a waiting list are strengths, not weaknesses, of the business. Coachbuilding the cockpit area produces a light, strong cabin that is durable and the waiting list maintains second-hand prices. There was much humour over the 'Sir John Hardly Knows' T-shirts that subsequently appeared at Morgan Sports Car Club meetings.

There were, however, some very beneficial commercial effects of Sir John's visit. Morgan experienced a big increase in orders and the long waiting list encouraged a price increase, which led to the company making significant profits that could be reinvested.

In April 2009, Princess Anne officially opened the brand new Morgan Visitor Centre, a modern museum bedecked with memorabilia, photos, films and the inevitable gift shop, housing a remarkable range of merchandise for 'Moggie' enthusiasts, young and old.

The Morgan philosophy and product range

The company's whole business model is based on longevity and brand reinforcement. This is not a get-rich-quick business. Among the many other distinctions Morgan enjoys is that of being one of just a few family dynasties left in the car industry. The traditional family influence has engendered a long-time dedication to craft, as well as a determination not to grow the company too large for fear of increasing costs and jeopardizing quality. The sense of family ties isn't lost on customers, either. Eager buyers often visit their unborn vehicles in the company's factory as the cars are being built. It is a kind of Build-a-Bear transferred to the car industry. All Morgan cars have a customer's name on them before they begin production. Customers can choose from myriad variants of body, engine size, paint colour, dashboard and leather trim. However, component supply and storage have been complicated by the Morgan customization model, but this has been simplified where possible to make it easier for the business to deliver product.

Morgan's speedy roadsters are entirely hand-crafted, which is perhaps fitting for the oldest privately held sports car manufacturer in the world. As a result, each car takes 130 hours to build and the waiting list is at least 12 months. By comparison, the average US-made Nissan takes just over 28 hours to build and can be had pretty much when you want it. Unlike commonplace vehicles, Morgans feature ash wood frames, hand-moulded body panels and hand-stitched leather.

Such craftsmanship doesn't come cheap. For the US market, a basic two-seat roadster starts at nearly US$50,000 and the top-of-the-line Aero 8 two-seat road rocket starts at around US$140,000 – before adding custom cosmetic, luxury or performance upgrades. Aero 8 (launched in 2000) was the first completely new Morgan for 30 years and customers wanting to buy one must wait nine months. The two-door Morgan roadsters may look old-fashioned, but they perform as well as the best of today's technologically advanced sports cars.

The Aero 8 is Europe's first AIV (aluminium-intensive vehicle) and is 20 per cent lighter than comparable vehicles. It is equipped with a BMW-sourced 4.4-litre V8 engine that gets the car from 0 to 60 in just 4.5 seconds.

As part of the centenary celebrations (100 years in 2009), Morgan announced a truly special model. The brand new Aero SuperSports was launched at the Geneva Motor Show in 2009 and the first customer models were finished at the factory in January 2010. The two Aero models, intended for a production run of 100 units, were launched from rendered drawings, with up-front deposits of £25,000 per car required 12 months before build. They quickly sold 100 on plan.

Designed and engineered in-house, the Morgan Aero SuperSports is a lightweight aluminium sports car with a luxurious specification. The interior features a comfortable combination of polished hardwoods, hand-stitched leather and electronic technology to create a driving environment that is efficient and ergonomic. In spite of all this opulence, the overall weight of the car is still relatively low, so the car is responsive to driver inputs and economical to run. Morgan can achieve this because of their unique use of aircraft-style super-formed aluminium outer panels and the skills of their craftsmen in hand-finishing the assembly of each car.

The technology debuted in the 100 AeroMax coupes built by the factory in 2008 and 2009. Such was the demand for the Aero SuperSports model that Morgan took the decision to produce the new model in greater numbers.

Morgan Aero Supersport (2010 model) including interior
Source: Morgan Motor Company.

Customer target groups

Morgan is not a company that deliberately targets the recession-proof super-rich, but the cars' name and caché have made the marque resilient. Morgan's business model has been robust. First, the cars have great residual value – an AeroMax that sells for £110,000 new can go on sale in Germany for €160,000 within a year. Today, 98 per cent of all the Morgans ever made are still in existence.

Of growing importance is the number of women who are wealthy in their own right who are potential customers. In North America where the number of Morgan distributors has doubled in recent years, women represent nearly 40 per cent of the top wealth holders, with gross assets of more than US$625,000, and in the UK there are now as many woman millionaires as men in the age group 18–44. However, Morgan buyers are not necessarily terribly wealthy, especially not owners of the 1.6 base model, costing around £30,000 in the UK. The BMW-engined Aero 8 costs nearly eight times this amount.

Over the years a lot of celebrities have joined the Morgan spirit: Mick Jagger has joined Catherine Deneuve and Jean-Paul Belmondo. Even Miss Piggy has been among the elite alumni of Morgan owners. Morgan cars have appeared in a host of films and TV programmes, including *Moonraker, Monty Python's Flying Circus, My Girl* and *The Trip*. Several books have been published about Morgan cars.

The Morgan community

A Morgan community is in place for the firm's huge network of enthusiasts:

- Cars can be ordered online or through the global dealer network (26 in the UK, 28 in Europe, eight in the US and six in the rest of the world).

- The Morgan Sports Car Club: this owners' club, which represents owners in many countries, provides a sense of identity and community for many of the buyers. It has strong links and influences with the factory, and the Morgan community is often consulted on product and brand development. The club is a powerful, though informal, symbol and promoter of the Morgan core brand proposition. There is an active agenda of meetings and social gatherings. For example, during the 100th anniversary celebrations in 2009, many Morgan owners met with the Morgan family at the factory in Malvern Link.

- The Worcester-based Morgan Works racing team. The racing events also create a strong relational bond between owners and the factory.

All these activities represent classic examples of customer relationship marketing.

International marketing

Morgan builds about 700 cars per year, around 30 per cent of which are sold in the UK. Besides the UK and the US, Morgan cars are sold throughout most of western Europe, as well as in Australia, Japan, New Zealand and South Africa.

For part of the 1950s and 1960s, the US provided the company with its largest market worldwide, taking up to 85 per cent of all production. This ended with the first wave of US safety and emission regulations in 1971. For many years (1974 to 1992), all Morgans imported into the US were converted to run on propane, in order to meet the requirements of the US emissions regulations. However, this conversion, along with bringing the cars into compliance with US vehicle safety leglislation, was carried out by the dealership and not by the factory, making the cars grey market vehicles.

Comeback in the US

In 2003, Morgan sold 100 cars in the US, and by 2012 it had already pre-sold the same number of the Aero 8 which replaces its Plus 8 model. Sales were then expected to rise to 200–250 per year. The Aero 8 was the first Morgan model sold in the US since the 1950s and 1960s.

QUESTIONS

1. How is Morgan's international communication strategy different from mainstream mass-produced cars?

2. How can Morgan use celebrities in the communication strategy?

3. How can Morgan make use of social media?

4. Prepare a global communication plan for the new Aero SuperSports.

Sources: http://www.morgan-motor.co.uk; *The Manufacturer* (2009) 'Morgan Motor Company, 100 not out', August, http://www.the-manufacturer.com/uk/profile/9493/Morgan_Motor_Company?PHPSESSID=8a965626552f15dc0f04fdf53a4d9836.

VIDEO CASE STUDY 17.3 BMW Motorcycles

download from **www.pearson.co.uk/hollensen**

Bayerische Motoren Werke (BMW) (www.bmw.com) is one of the leading manufacturers of premium passenger cars and motorcycles in Europe. Although car buyers are extremely familiar with the BMW brand, the brand has a much lower profile among motorcycle buyers. This is a major challenge for BMW Motorcycles, which has been producing high-end motorcycles for more than 80 years. The company's main promotional goal is to attract serious riders who are looking for an exceptional riding experience. To do this, its marketers carefully coordinate every promotional detail to convey a unified brand message positioning the BMW motorcycle as 'the ultimate riding machine', as its advertising slogan states.

Source: Car Culture/Corbis.

Questions

1. What are the advantages of using more personal advertising copy and encouraging customers to become missionaries for BMW motorcycles?

2. Should BMW use standardization or adaptation in promoting the motorcycles outside the US and Germany?

3. Why is BMW using its website as a virtual showroom rather than also selling online directly to consumers?

4. Should BMW develop and promote a new motorcycle brand to differentiate its motorcycles from competing motorcycle brands (i.e. selling to new target groups), as well as differentiating them from BMW cars?

For further resources, see this book's website at **www.pearsoned.co.uk/hollensen**

Questions for discussion

1. Identify and discuss problems associated with assessing advertising effectiveness in foreign markets.
2. Compare domestic communication with international communication. Explain why 'noise' is more likely to occur in the case of international communication processes.
3. Why don't more companies standardize advertising messages worldwide? Identify the environmental constraints that act as barriers to the development and implementation of standardized global advertising campaigns.
4. Explain how personal selling may differ between the overseas and home markets.
5. What is meant by saying that advertising regulations vary around the world?
6. Evaluate the 'percentage of sales' approach to setting advertising budgets in foreign markets.
7. Explain how multinational firms may have an advantage over local firms in training the sales force and evaluating its performance.
8. Identify and discuss problems associated with allocating the company's promotion budget across several foreign markets.
9. How can a company increase its communication effectiveness through the use of social media?

References

Bennett, R. (1995) *International Marketing: Strategy, Planning, Market Entry and Implementation*, Kogan Page, London.

Berthon, P.R., Pitt, L.F., Plangger, K. and Shapiro, D. (2012) 'Marketing meets Web 2.0, social media, and creative consumers: implications for international marketing strategy', *Business Horizons*, 55, pp. 261–271.

Centeno, E. and Hart, S. (2012) 'The use of communication activities in the development of small to medium-sized enterprise brands', *Marketing Intelligence & Planning*, 30(2), pp. 250–265.

Cebrzynski, G. (2006). Lights! Camera! Product placement! Nation's Restaurant News, New York, December 4, 40 (49), pp. 1–5

Ferrell, L. and Ferrell, O.C. (2012) 'Redirecting direct selling: High-touch embraces high-tech', *Business Horizons*, Vol. 55, pp. 273–281.

Freedman, K. (2015) 'Practice papers: How to run a global marketing campaign that meets local needs without damaging the brand', *Journal of Brand Strategy*, 4(1), pp. 15–26.

Friel, A. L. (2008) 'No purchase necessary', *Marketing Management*, March/April, pp. 48–51.

Hosea, M. (2007) 'Bigger bucks', *Brand Strategy*, February, pp. 12–13.

Hung, C.L. and West, D.C. (1991) 'Advertising budgeting methods in Canada, the UK and the USA', *International Journal of Advertising*, 10, pp. 239–250.

Hutton, G. and Fosdick, M. (2011) 'The globalization of social media – consumer relationships with brands evolve in the digital space', *Journal of Advertising Research*, December, pp. 564–570.

Joensen, S. (1997) 'What hedder it now on engelsk?', *Politikken* (Danish newspaper), 24 April.

Kaplan, A.M. and Haenlein, M. (2011) 'Two hearts in three-quarter time: how to waltz the social media/viral marketing dance', *Business Horizons*, 54, pp. 253–263.

Mangold, W.G. and Faulds, D.J. (2009) 'Social media: the new hybrid element of the promotion mix', *Business Horizons*, 52, pp. 357–365.

Meenaghan, T. (1996) 'Ambush marketing: a threat to corporate sponsorship', *Sloan Management Review*, Fall, pp. 103–113.

Milliman, J. F., Olson, E. M. and Slater, S. F. (2007) 'Courting excellence', *Marketing Management*, March–April, pp. 14–17.

Mrkwicka, K., Resinger, F. and Schögel (2012), 'Leveraging the buzz – From fan to lead generation in BMW's pre-communication, *Marketing Review St. Gallen*, 4, pp. 28–34.

Onkvisit, S. and Shaw, J.J. (1993) *International Marketing: Analysis and Strategy*, 2nd edn. Macmillan, London.

Ottesen, O. (1995) 'Buyer initiative: ignored, but imperative for marketing management – towards a new view of market communication', *Tidsvise Skrifter*, 15, avdeling for Økonomi, Kultur og Samfunnsfag ved Høgskolen i Stavanger.

Parent, M., Plangger, K. and Bal, A. (2011) 'The new WTP: willingness to participate', *Business Horizons*, 54, 219–229.

Schimmelpfennig, C. and Hollensen, S. (2014) 'Celebrity Endorsements – Exploring the process for finding the right celebrity endorser for your brand', *Journal of Brand Strategy*, 2(4), pp. 366–378.

Seno, D. and Lukas, B. A. (2007) 'The equity effect of product endorsement by celebrities', *European Journal of Marketing*, 41(1/2), pp. 121–134.

Silvera, D. H. and Austad, B. (2004) 'Factors predicting the effectiveness of celebrity endorsement advertisements', *European Journal of Marketing*, 38(11/12), pp. 1509–1527.

Singh, N., Lehnert, K. and Bostick, K. (2012) 'Global social media usage: insights into reaching consumers worldwide', *Thunderbird International Business Review*, 54(5), September/October, pp. 683–700.

Srivastava, R. K. (2015) 'Product placement by global brands as an alternative strategy: is it worth in emerging market?', *Journal of Strategic Marketing*, 23(2), 141–156.

Wirtz, B.W., Schilke, O. and Ullrich, S. (2010) 'Strategic development of business models – implications of the Web 2.0 for creating value on the internet, *Long Range Planning*, 43, pp. 272–290.

Woodcock, N., Green, A. and Starkey, M. (2011) 'Social CRM as a business strategy', *Database Marketing & Customer Strategy Management*, 18(1), pp. 50–64.

CASE STUDY IV.1

Absolut Vodka: defending and attacking for a better position in the global vodka market

On a lovely day in August 2015 the new CEO of Absolut Company AB in Stockholm, Paul Duffy, packs his suitcase for the third time this month for a business trip to the subsidiary in New York. After many years with only increasing market shares, it seems that Absolut Vodka, at least in the US market, is under fierce attack from some of the other imported vodka brands, e.g. the super-premium brand, Grey Goose from France (owned by Bacardi).

In March 2008, France's Pernod Ricard won the battle to buy the maker of Absolut vodka in a costly €5.63 billion (US$8.9 billion) deal that brought it nearly level in sales with global spirits leader Diageo. As of July 2008, The Absolut Company became a company within the Pernod Ricard group.

The head office is located in Stockholm, Sweden. Pernod Ricard's main gain with the acquisition of V&S Absolut Spirits was Absolut Vodka. It is the world's second-largest vodka brand, and the world's leading premium vodka. Before the acquisition, Pernod Ricard had a limited vodka portfolio and was only among the world's leading 20 vodka manufacturers. Since the acquisition, Pernod Ricard has increased its total revenues to €8.2 billion (2014) and it has become the second-largest vodka producer, behind Diageo (known for its Smirnoff brand). Pernod now has a total annual volume of 47 million 9-litre cases of spirits (in 2014), of which Absolut Vodka, with 11 million cases (⊠100 million litres), comprises the largest share.

While packing, Duffy thinks about how hard the company must fight to keep and increase its market share for Absolut Vodka in the US and other markets. In the last five years Absolut Vodka has increased its world market share, but can it continue?

Absolut accounts for more than half of all imported vodka sales in the US: it is the fourth-largest international premium spirit and is available in 130 markets. Among premium vodkas, Absolut Vodka is number two worldwide, after Smirnoff, which sells around 200 million litres (double the sales of Absolut Vodka).

When Duffy gets on the plane at Stockholm's airport bound for New York, there are two things that worry him:

- Apparently the market share of Absolut Vodka in the US has reached saturation point. Has Absolut Vodka reached its maximum market share in that country, or is it time for a frontal attack on the number one brand, Smirnoff?
- Until now, the market share for Absolut Vodka in Europe (especially in eastern Europe) has been somewhat smaller. This could be a problem, as 80 per cent of the world's vodka is consumed in Russia and the other countries of eastern Europe (see Table 1, p. 682).

Marketing of Pernod's Absolut Vodka is primarily dealt with by The Absolut Company's head office in Stockholm and via the subsidiary company, The Absolut Spirits Company, Inc., in the US. Worldwide marketing control of the Absolut Vodka brand is centralized to guarantee consistency and focus, as well as responsibility for the content. In agreements with co-owned and independent distribution organizations, The Absolut Company has ensured that responsibility for marketing lies with the company itself.

On his way over the Atlantic, Paul thinks back on the story and adventure of Absolut Vodka.

The history of Absolut Vodka

The Swedish state-owned Vin & Sprit AB could justly call the launch of its Absolut Vodka an absolute success. Absolut Vodka is probably the biggest success story in the world of spirits. It has become an icon.

The shape of the bottle

The shape of the bottle dates back to the mid-eighteenth century, but is based on a traditional design: in the sixteenth century, Swedish pharmacies sold a clear, distilled liquid as a cure for ailments such as colic and even the plague. The custom was to ingest it by the spoonful, not by the shot glass.

Rediscovered in an antique store in Stockholm by Gunnar Broman, of the now defunct advertising agency Carlsson & Broman, the clear medicine bottle has since been fine-tuned by Absolut's team of shrewd marketers. The neck was lengthened, curves were adjusted and labels were replaced with printed type-face. To top it off, a medallion bearing the portrait of Lars Olsson Smith, known as 'The King of Vodka', was stamped on each bottle. In 1879, Smith successfully broke Stockholm's spirit monopoly by distilling and marketing Absolut Rent Bränvin (i.e. Absolute Pure Vodka). His tipple was the beginning of a dynasty.

In 2013, the Absolut family comprised of the following variants/flavours:

- *Absolut Vodka* has a rich taste, and is smooth and mellow with a distinct character of grain. Introduced in 1979.
- *Absolut Peppar* is aromatic, complex and spicy. The peppery flavour is a combination of the spicy components in the capsicum pepper family and the fresh green jalapeño pepper. Introduced in 1986.
- *Absolut Citron* is flavoured with citrus fruits. Lemon is dominant, but other citrus flavours are added to give a fuller body. Absolut Citron has a distinctive character made up of lemon and lime with a hint of sweetness. Introduced in 1988.
- *Absolut Kurant* is flavoured with blackcurrant, a distant cousin to the grape. This is a fragrant dark berry that grows on shrubs up to six feet in height. Absolut Kurant has a distinct character, with a hint of tartness and sweetness. Introduced in 1992.
- *Absolut Mandrin* is flavoured with citrus fruits. Mandarin and orange are dominant, but other citrus flavours are added to give a fuller body. Absolut Mandrin has a distinctive character with a hint of sweetness. Introduced in 1999.
- *Absolut Vanilia* has a rich, robust and complex taste of vanilla with notes of butterscotch and hints of dark chocolate. Introduced in 2003.
- *Absolut Raspberri* is rich and intense, revealing the fresh and fruity character of ripened raspberries. Introduced in 2004.
- *Absolut Apeach* is smooth and mellow, with a sophisticated and fruity character of peach. Introduced in 2005.
- *Absolut Ruby Red* is smooth and fruity with a crisp and refreshing character of zesty grapefruit. Introduced in 2006.
- *Absolut Pears* has the fresh and clear aroma of mellow pears with a slight touch of sweet almonds. It is fruity, smooth and full-bodied with a long and slightly dry aftertaste. Introduced in 2007.
- *Absolut Disco,* launched in December 2007.
- *Absolut New Orleans* (mango and black pepper flavour launched in August 2007).

This was a special edition in an annual city-themed series: 100 per cent of the profits went towards various Gulf Coast charities after the flood damage from Hurricane Katrina.

- *Absolut 100* 100 proof, black bottle, flavour launched in 2007.
- *Absolut Los Angeles* (blueberry flavour mix launched in July 2008). This was the second in the city-themed series. Other cities followed in the series.
- *Absolut Wild Tea* (black tea and elderflower flavour with a clear bottle and a green label). Launched in August 2009.
- *Absolut Orient Apple* (red apple and ginger flavoured vodka). Launched in 2011.
- *Absolut Hibiskus* (mixology with inspiration from the garden). A slightly acidic, berry-flavoured hibiscus underlined by the sweet notes of pomegranate. Launched in 2013.
- *Absolut Unique* (launched in October 2012). The idea was to make four million unique bottles, so that each and every bottle became a limited edition in itself. To realize this idea, the Absolut Company had to rebuild the production line and use every possible aspect of glass decoration in a new and randomized, but controlled, way. The Absolut team defined colours, coatings, patterns and paint methods and then waited to see what the machines would create. Using a mix of 38 different colours and 51 pattern types, applied through splash guns and colour-generating machines, it was ensured that each bottle produced was one-of-a-kind. Every bottle was numbered (1–4,000,000) and the numbers were mixed before the cases were sent out to the world, primarily to the travel retail markets at the international airports. In most markets, bottles were sold at the regular price for a bottle of Absolut. The campaign was a big success and it created impressive media awareness.

Source: © The Absolut Company AB. Used under permission from The Absolut Company AB.

Source: © The Absolut Company AB. Used under permission from The Absolut Company AB.

Introduction to the US market

Independent market research in the US concluded, in 1979, that no one would buy Swedish vodka. Nevertheless, the first shipment of Absolut Vodka was sent off to that country in April 1979; its destination was Boston. Some 90,000 litres were sold worldwide in 1979; and in 2014 worldwide Absolut Vodka sales were 100 million litres (11 million 9-litre cases), of which about 50 per cent was exported to the US. Apart from the US, the most important markets are (in decreasing order of importance): Canada, Germany, Brazil, Spain, the UK, Mexico and France.

The marketing of the bottle

For more than 25 years, advertisements for Absolut Vodka have been based on the same fundamental concept, with the focus being on the product. The very first advertisement, 'Absolut Perfection', was created in 1980 and today it is the one that is used most often.

Ever since Andy Warhol, patron saint of pop art, created his first Absolut painting in 1985 ('Absolut Warhol'), artists around the world have been asked to render their interpretation of the bottle. Distinctive advertising campaigns such as 'Absolut London', in which the door of 10 Downing Street was made to look like an Absolut bottle, have made the vodka brand nearly as famous as Coca-Cola or Nike. In the advertisement 'Absolut Essence', magazine readers were able to fold back the cover and smell the scent of Absolut Kurant. Most countries maintain strict rules concerning alcohol advertisements to consumers, but Absolut's PR machine has milked the free publicity that its advertising generates.

The Absolut Vodka CEO's thoughts have become dream-like on the plane to New York, but Paul Duffy wakes with a start when passengers are asked to buckle their seatbelts. To use his time sensibly before landing, he takes a report out of his suitcase describing conditions in the US and world markets. The following is the essence of the report, which also describes recent Absolut Vodka initiatives in this market.

The world market for vodka

Table 1 shows that eastern European countries account for 80 per cent of the world's total vodka sales, and the area's average consumption per capita per year is also high (5 litres). In Poland, the average vodka consumption per capita per year is about 10 litres, while the average in Russia is 5 litres. By comparison, average consumption in the US is 1.3 litres and in the UK 0.6 litres. It should be noted that all these figures are based on registered sales and don't include the home-made products that are distilled in quite a large part of eastern Europe as well as in Sweden and Finland.

The markets of eastern Europe are distinguished not only by their high vodka consumption but also by how

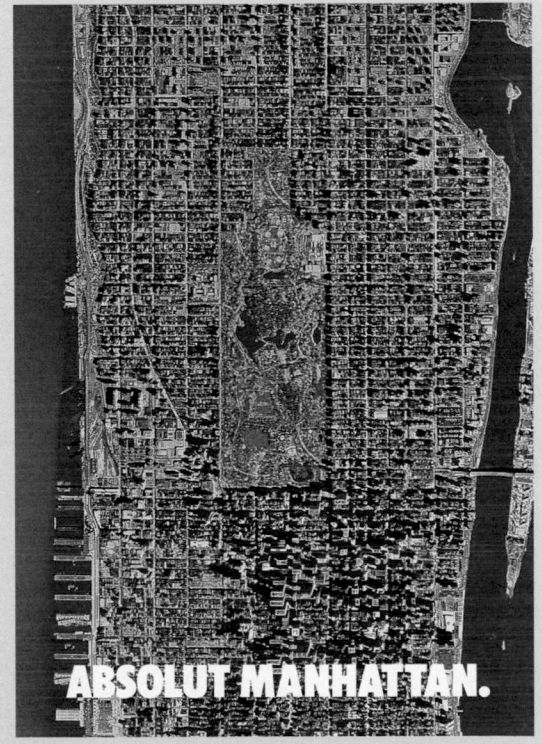

Source: © The Absolut Company AB. Used under permission from The Absolut Company AB.

much consumers know about alcoholic beverages and their appreciation of quality. However, political uncertainty and the lack of a well-functioning infrastructure in several eastern European countries make short-term developments difficult to predict. The biggest vodka market (in volume) in eastern Europe is Russia, followed by the Ukraine.

Absolut Vodka has long been exported to most eastern European countries – it was introduced into Poland in 1995. Fifteen years later (in 2010), Poland was the seventh-largest Absolut Vodka market. Thus Absolut Vodka is now represented in all the major vodka markets of the world.

The US market for vodka

In the last 20 years the consumption of alcohol in the US has decreased by 20 per cent. There are several reasons for this. One of the main reasons is the 'health trend' in the country, which has led to a greater awareness of the harmful effects of alcohol. At the same time, a tendency has developed for drinking 'less but better'; thus many people now drink cleaner and purer alcohol. This has meant that the sale of 'super-premium' (high-quality) brands has not fallen but has been stable since 2010. Nearly all imported brands are in the super-premium segment and this is the main reason that vodka imports have not fallen. Although the vodka importers' share of the total market is only 12–15 per cent, the gross margin on imported vodka represents about 40 per cent of the total gross margin of all vodka sales in the US.

Historically vodka has not been a differentiated product, but more and more flavoured brands have gradually been introduced to the market, including Absolut Citron, Absolut Peppar and Absolut Kurant. However,

it is risky introducing new brands into the American market, as consumers' tastes there are so volatile. A producer can introduce a flavour that is popular one year and unpopular the next.

Product segments

The different product segments are as follows:

- *Platinum.* The most expensive category, with prices around US$25 per bottle or more. Brands in this category include Stolichnaya Cristall. This segment accounts for less than 1 per cent of total US vodka consumption.
- *Super-premium.* Nearly all brands are imported, the leaders being Swedish Absolut, Russian Stolichnaya, Finnish Finlandia and French Grey Goose. The price level is US$15–20 per bottle. This category's share of the total vodka consumption in the US is about 10 per cent.
- *Premium.* Here we find the world's most popular vodka, American Smirnoff, sold for US$10–14 a bottle. This group's share of the US's total vodka consumption is 22 per cent.
- *Standard priced.* These include the two English labels Gilbey's and Gordon's, which are sold for US$8–9 a bottle. This category's share is 14 per cent.
- *Popular priced.* This is the largest group. Its share of total US vodka consumption is about 54 per cent, and the group consists of a number of local labels at about US$6 a bottle.

Worldwide, the three largest *imported* brands are Absolut (number two), Stolichnaya (number six) and Finlandia (number 15). Absolut's main competitors are Smirnoff, Finlandia and Stolichnaya, which may be characterized as follows:

Table 1	Distribution of world vodka sales by volume and value. V&S Absolut Spirits' market share, 2014			
World	Volume (% of total)	Value (% of total)	The Absolut Company (% of total)	Absolut marketshare (%)
Eastern Europe	80.9	63.0	6.0	1.3
North America	9.7	20.7	50.0	10.3
Western Europe	4.3	11.7	18.0	6.3
Latin America	1.3	1.5	9.0	7.0
Africa and the Middle East	1.8	1.2	5.0	2.4
Asia-Pacific	1.4	0.9	6.0	10.9
Australasia	0.6	1.0	6.0	3.8
Total world	100.0 (= 4,000 million litres)	100.0 (= US$20 billion)	100.0 (= 11 million 9-litre cases ~ 100 million litres)	2.5 (= 100/4,000)

Source: adapted from Impact International and *Euromonitor*.

- *Stolichnaya* (brand owner: Sojuzplodimport or SPI Group). The pioneer among imported vodka brands, this was the first vodka into be introduced into the US, in 1972. Stolichnaya was at the time a good alternative to the US-produced vodka brands as it tasted milder due to a more refined distilling process, but its popularity has been dependent on the political climate between the US and the former USSR. Today (2014), Stolichnaya is distributed by their own import organization. In Eminem's 2010 music video for *Love the Way You Lie,* Stolichnaya vodka was included in several scenes. The world-wide sales of the brand is around three million 9-litre cases.
- *Finlandia* (brand owner: Brown-Forman). Thanks to its name, Finlandia is widely associated with Finland on the international market. Finlandia was launched in Scandinavia in 1970 and in the US in 1971 – much earlier than Absolut Vodka. Despite many marketing campaigns, Finlandia has never been able to get a grip on the vodka market. In the trade it is estimated that Finlandia has the most exposed position, as all new importers go for the esteemed third place (which seems to be a realistic goal for a new brand). In 2002, Findlandia celebrated its 30th anniversary in style by forming a partnership with MGM Pictures for their James Bond film, *Die Another Day.* Bond still likes his martinis shaken, not stirred, but his vodka in that particular film was Finlandia, not Smirnoff. Finlandia sells around two million 9-litre cases worldwide.
- *Smirnoff* (brand owner: Diageo plc). Diageo was created in December 1997, following the merger of Guinness plc and Grand Metropolitan plc. Among the wine and spirits companies included in the merger were Carillon Importers Ltd, The Paddington Corporation, UDV, Glenmore, Schieffelin & Somerset, Heublein Inc. and International Distillers & Vintners North America. Guinness/UDV's primary US division is United Distillers & Vintners North America (UDVNA). In 2011–12, UDVNA was the second-largest spirits company in the US market, with a 14 per cent volume share. Three of the top 10 US spirits brands in 2008 were UDVNA brands: Smirnoff vodka, José Cuervo tequila and Gordon's gin and vodka. After a four-year interruption, Smirnoff was re-confirmed as the 'vodka of choice' for James Bond in *Casino Royale.* The renewed strategic alliance between Smirnoff and Bond involved a fully integrated multi-million-dollar global media campaign. In several countries, the campaign included on-pack promotions offering two-for-the-price-of-one cinema tickets to *Casino Royale* and a fully interactive *Casino Royale* microsite.

One of the newcomers to the super-premium segment is Grey Goose. It is distilled in Cognac, France, from French wheat, then imported by the Sidney Frank Importing Company based in New York. In 1997, it quickly gained a reputation for quality and has won several prestigious awards in distilled spirit competitions. In 2004, Sidney Frank sold the manufacturing rights to Bacardi for US$2.2 billion.

The distribution system for vodka in the US

Generally, the sale of spirits goes through the distribution system shown in Figure 1. For US producers, the roles of producer/supplier and importer/agent coincide. The retail ('off-premise') sale of wine, spirits and beer takes place through two different distribution systems. In 'open states' (licensed states) the market is free, and spirits are distributed via liquor stores, supermarkets or other grocery stores where the owner has a licence to sell spirits. In 'controlled states' spirits can only be sold in liquor stores owned by the state, similar to the Nordic monopoly system.

The importer/agent usually has only a small sales force, which concentrates on selling to and servicing a distributor. An importer/agent usually cooperates with one distributor in each state (although one distributor can handle several states), and in large states a distributor can have up to 500 salespeople geographically divided. Generally these salespeople pay for their own cars and receive a low basic wage, plus commission. The salesperson in the area concerned visits both the wholesale and the retail markets, often once a week, taking orders and in exceptional cases delivering goods and collecting payment.

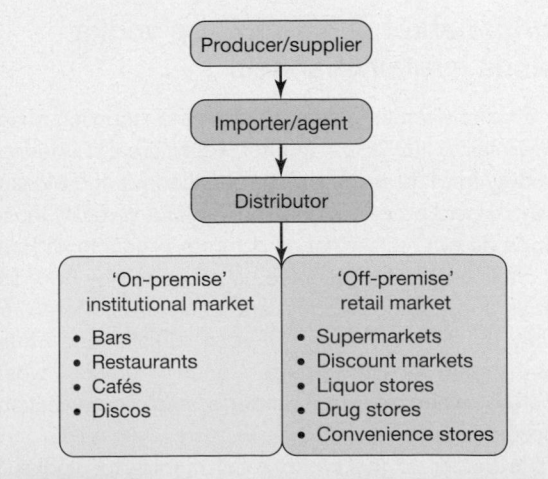

| Figure 1 | The general distribution system for spirits in the US |

Absolut Vodka – advertising campaigns

As part of a fightback against a new range of super-premium brands such as Grey Goose, nibbling into Absolut's image of 'coolness in a bottle', the Absolut Company rolled out a new marketing campaign in January 2006 to raise the brand's profile with a new generation of vodka drinkers. The multi-million-dollar push in the US was Absolut's first all-new campaign in 25 years – and it also marked the first time the brand was advertised on TV. The ads from Absolut's global agency, TBWA/Chiat/Day in New York, positioned the liquor as 'The Absolute Vodka', while highlighting other classics that are 'absolutes' in pop culture. One spot featured footage from the Apollo moon landing under the banner 'Absolute Road Trip'. Another showed Marilyn Monroe entertaining troops with the tag line 'Absolute Morale Booster'. The 30-second spots were shown on cable channels such as Comedy Central, Fox Sports Net and E! Absolut also continued its iconic print ads starring the Absolut bottle dressed up by fashion designers, famous photographers and artists, with a two-word tagline.

In March 2012, there was world premiere of the multidimensional cocktail experiences Absolut Greyhound, featuring new music by Swedish House Mafia. The music video ad (which can be seen on YouTube: https://www.youtube.com/watch?v=PDboaDrHGbA) shows a futuristic fantasy world where three groups of people in bizarre costumes meet in the middle of the desert. As they drink Absolut cocktails served by a masked waiter, the guests are entertained by the members of Swedish House Mafia, who have been transformed into robotic greyhounds and chase after a floating orb as the guests watch through binoculars. *Greyhound* reached No. 5 on the UK dance chart.

World market shares for top vodka brands – retail channels

If we include vodka sales through all distribution channels [retail + HORECA (HOtel, REstaurant, CAtering) and duty free], brands such as Stolichnaya and Moskovskaya would be very highly ranked. But in reality these brands do not really exist as discrete products: in Russia, Stolichnaya, for instance, is produced by 800 distilleries and in various bottle and case sizes. Moreover, products differ widely between distilleries. Thus, brands such as Stolichnaya are only 'brands' when exported, when control is under a single organisation, Sojuzplodimport.

The leader of the world retail market for vodka is Kristal, with around a 7 per cent share of the world market. Kristal is a local Russian brand, but it is mainly being sold in the world's biggest vodka market – Russia. Diageo's Smirnoff is the leading international brand of vodka. These are the only two brands of vodka worldwide commanding more than 5 per cent of the global vodka market.

Western Europe

Smirnoff, with a regional market share of 15 per cent, was the brand leader in western Europe in 2014. Its nearest rival brand, Gorbatschow, comprised just over 7 per cent of regional sales. Only three brands in western Europe – Smirnoff, Gorbatschow and Absolut – accounted for more than 5 per cent of regional vodka sales in 2014.

Eastern Europe

The vodka market in eastern Europe is large and diverse, with hundreds of brands on the market. Consequently regional leader Kristal controlled 'only' 6 per cent of regional sales in 2014, with its nearest rival brand, Smirnov, holding 4 per cent of the regional market. Diageo's Smirnoff was the largest international brand on the market.

North and Latin America

Diageo's Smirnoff brand was the leader of the North American vodka market in 2014, accounting for 19 per cent of regional sales. Its main rival was the premium Absolut brand. Smirnoff was also the largest vodka brand in Latin America, where it controlled 25 per cent of the regional market. Smirnoff has few serious rivals in Latin America. Its closest competitor, Oso Negro from José Cuervo, held only 8 per cent of regional sales in 2014.

Rest of the world

In the rest of the world, Smirnoff is the dominant brand of vodka. In 2014, it led the market in Asia-Pacific, Australasia, Africa and the Middle East.

Absolut Vodka and the FAB market

The market for RTD (ready to drink) pre-mixed alcoholic beverages or FAB (flavoured alcoholic beverages) has developed at a rapid pace in the last decade. It is also a market that Absolut Vodka entered in 2004.

The international FAB market

Demand for FAB has grown sharply in the UK, with spirit-based beverages Bacardi Breezer and Smirnoff Ice being the key brands driving the market.

A significant proportion of FABs are consumed on licensed premises, with modern town bars and nightclubs being the most popular venues for consuming these products. They are perceived as trendy, desirable products and are particularly popular among image-conscious consumers within the 18–30 age group, who drink directly from the bottle. To a large extent, it is through strong branding that the industry has managed the transition from alcopops, with their connotation of under-age drinking, to the positive, premium image FABs currently enjoy. The use of energy drinks in combination with alcohol has become a popular trend in nightclubs and bars.

Consumption of FABs generally declines steadily with age (particularly after the age of 35), although this category is beginning to attract a wider audience: consumer research, for instance, shows that brands such as Smirnoff Ice are popular with consumers right up to the age of 65! It is clear that there is scope to push the category further among consumers of all ages and backgrounds. Although women continue to consume more than men, the difference in consumption levels according to gender is narrowing.

'Opinion leaders' form the segment of the consumer base that is socially influential in terms of fashions, and the product is taken to places where opinion leaders congregate in an attempt to secure acceptance by these trend-setters. Consequently, this expands the appeal of the product to consumers who are driven by peer-led drinking. In the designer alcoholic drinks market, opinion leaders tend to be young professional adults who frequent city-centre bars. In the international FAB market, the club scene (on-premise) is also very important – allying a product with the nightclubbing market increases brand exposure and means that the product acquires acceptance by the socially influential nightclub audience. Both of these are integral to the development of designer alcoholic drinks. The trend for going to stylish bars and drinking expensive cocktails mixed at the bar is another affirmation of wealth and style and it has experienced a resurgence due to rising disposable incomes. 'Cocktail culture' has influenced flavour trends, especially in the premixed spirits market.

The 'cult of the individual' is also a major aspect of culture and is a growing trend across all markets. This term refers to the trend for individuality in consumption. For instance, rather than drinking the same brand as one's peers, consumers drink something that is particular to their own consumption habits in order to assert their own character and individuality. This trend is manifesting itself in both an assertion of individuality and a rejection of blanket marketing. This is a strong driver for sales of designer alcoholic drinks, even though brands have targeted opinion leaders in an attempt to capture more peer-led consumption. Ultimately, the brands' contribution to consumers'

perception of their own individuality is key to the success of designer alcoholic drinks, despite the inherent contradictions.

Consumers are becoming more adept at discerning which products are qualitatively better than others; they are also becoming quicker to abandon those that do not appeal to them. This is increasing the pressure on producers to create products that are obviously better than others. Despite the importance of image, poor quality in the premium market is less tolerated among consumers now.

Absolut Vodka's entrance into – and disappearance from – the international FAB market

As consumer preferences evolved, Absolut Vodka saw an opportunity to launch a more sophisticated product into the international FAB market.

In 2004, Absolut Vodka started selling vodka in Canada. Here the 7 per cent abv (alcohol by volume) vodka drink was aimed at the more mature drinker – rather than the younger generation traditionally targeted by RTDs – offering the ease of a pre-mix but with a less sugary taste.

Absolut intended to take a more mature approach in its advertising, moving away from the image-based campaigns of other brands that were so frequently criticized for glamourizing alcohol consumption and tempting under-age drinkers. The 'product' was to be the centrepiece of any advertising rather than the 'image'.

Source: © The Absolut Company AB. Used under permission from The Absolut Company AB.

By the end of 2006, the Absolut Cut had been launched in three flavours:

- *Absolut Cut,* containing a fresh citrus flavour;
- *Absolut Clear Cut,* containing a mandarin flavour enhanced by kiwi;
- *Absolut Crisp Cut,* containing a crisp apple flavour and a fresh finish of lime.

Absolut Cut had the same distinctive bottle shape as its parent brand and was rolled out to both the on- and off-trade FAB markets in Canada, Australia and the UK. However, in July 2007 management concluded that Absolut Cut had failed to deliver sufficient volume in these countries, prompting it to be taken off the production line in all three markets.

Having read the above report, Absolut's CEO, Paul Duffy, acknowledges that it is necessary to get external input on some essential strategic questions. When he lands in New York he has written down the following questions, which he asks you to answer.

QUESTIONS

1. What was the main motive for Pernod Ricard's acquisition of V&S (including Absolut Vodka) in 2008?

2. Which alternative marketing strategies should The Absolut Company have to increase its market share for:

   (a) Absolut Vodka in the US?
   (b) Absolut Vodka in Europe (including eastern Europe)?
   (c) Absolut Vodka in other parts of the world?

3. In which region (country) of the world would you recommend Absolut Vodka to allocate more marketing resources?

4. Did Absolut Vodka have the right competences for achieving international success for its Absolut Cut?

5. Should Absolut Vodka relaunch a mixer product in the global FAB market?

The photographs in this case study represent trademarks owned by The Absolut Company AB. Absolut® Vodka, Absolut Country of Sweden Vodka & Logo, Absolut, Absolut Bottle Design and Absolut Calligraphy are trademarks owned by The Absolut Company AB.

Sources: based on different sources from *Euromonitor* and public sources.

CASE STUDY IV.2

Guinness: how can the iconic Irish beer brand compensate for declining sales in the home market?

Beer is an alcoholic beverage made by brewing and fermenting cereals, especially malted barley, usually with the addition of hops as a flavouring agent and stabilizer. One of the oldest of alcoholic beverages (there is archaeological evidence dating to *c.* 3000 bc), beer was well known in ancient Egypt, where it may have been made from bread. At first brewed chiefly in households and monasteries, it became a commercial product in late medieval times and is now made by large-scale manufacture in almost every industrialized country. Although British, European and American beers can differ markedly in flavour and content, the brewing processes are similar. A mash, prepared from crushed malt (usually barley), water and, often, cereal adjuncts such as rice and corn, is heated and rotated in the mash tun to dissolve the solids and permit the malt enzymes to convert the starch into sugar. The solution, called wort, is drained into a copper vessel, where it is boiled with the hops (which provide beer with its bitter flavour), then run off for cooling and settling. After cooling, it is transferred to fermenting vessels where yeast is added, converting the sugar into alcohol. Modern beers contain about 3–6 per cent alcohol. After brewing, the beer is usually a finished product. At this point the beer is kegged, casked, bottled or canned. Beers fall into two broad categories:

- *Lighter beer (lagers).* Lagers use yeast that ferments more slowly at cooler temperatures and tends to settle, and they are aged at cold temperatures for weeks or months, hence the name (German, lager = storage place). Lagers are the most commonly consumed beer in the world, with brands like Budweiser, Heineken, Fosters, Carlsberg, Beck's, Carling, Kronenbourg and Stella Artois.
- *Darker beer.* Included in this broad category are ales, stouts and porters. Stouts (and porters) are dark beers made using roasted malts or roast barley. Porter is a strong and dark beer brewed with the addition of roasted malt to give flavour and colour. Stout (today more or less identical to Guinness) is normally darker and maltier than porter and has a more pronounced hop aroma. Porter was first

recorded as being made and sold in London in the 1730s. It became very popular in the British Isles, and was responsible for the trend towards large regional breweries with tied pubs. Originally, the adjective 'stout' meant 'proud' or 'brave', but later, after the fourteenth century, 'stout' came to mean 'strong'. The first known use of the word *stout* about beer was in 1677, the sense being that a stout beer was a strong beer. The expression *stout-porter* was applied during the 1700s for strong versions of porter, and was used by Guinness of Ireland in 1820, although Guinness had been brewing porters since 1759. 'Stout' still meant only 'strong' and it could be related to any kind of beer, as long as it was strong: in the UK, it was possible to find 'stout pale ale', for example. Later 'stout' was eventually associated only with porter, becoming a synonym for dark beer. At the end of the nineteenth century, stout porter beer (especially the so-called 'milk stout' – a sweeter version) got the reputation of being a healthy strengthening drink, so it was used by athletes and nursing women, while doctors often recommended it to help recovery. Stouts can be classed into two main categories, sweet and bitter, and there are several kinds of each. Irish stout or dry stout is the original product, equivalent to the Guinness beer. It is very dark in colour and it often has a 'toast' or coffee-like taste. Major brands in this broad category include Murphy's (Heineken), Castle Milk Stout (SAB Miller) and, of course, Guinness (Diageo).

Diageo

UK-based Diageo was formed in 1997 through the merger of Guinness and Grand Metropolitan. Both companies were themselves products of earlier mergers and acquisitions – Guinness had acquired Distillers in 1986 while Grand Metropolitan had diversified from its origins as a hotel chain into spirits (IDV), food (Pillsbury), restaurants (Burger King) and pubs. Diageo sold off Pillsbury and Burger King and the Guinness

Table 1	Key financial figures of Diageo (2008–10)		
	2008 (£m)	2009 (£m)	2010 (£m)
Total net sales	10,643	12,283	12,958
Profit before taxation	2,015	2,093	2,239

Source: based on www.diageo.com.

business was integrated into the global spirits organization.

Today, Diageo is a Fortune 500 company listed on both the New York and London stock exchanges. The firm is the world's leading premium drinks enterprise, with a broad selection of brands. It currently occupies a 30 per cent share of the global market, and owns nine of the world's top 20 spirit brands, including Smirnoff vodka, Bushmills Irish whiskey, Johnnie Walker Scotch whisky, Captain Morgan rum, Gordon's dry gin, J&B Scotch whisky, Crown Royal whiskey and Baileys cream liqueur. The portfolio also includes Guinness stout. In 2019 the company had over 20,000 employees, and traded in over 180 markets around the world. Its annual turnover in the fiscal year 2010 reached nearly £13 billion, with a total market capitalization of over £20 billion. The financial development of Diageo during 2008–10 is illustrated in Table 1.

Diageo plc has one major beer brand, Guinness, which is the world's leading stout brand. However, in the world beer market the stout only accounts for 1.0 per cent of world beer sales (see Table 2). As a result of Guinness' status, Diageo plc's beer performance is heavily reliant on the fortunes of the Guinness brand. However, cracks have started to appear in the brand as an aggressive price-increase policy was employed to mask volume declines in key markets. Diageo plc fails to disclose operating profit figures for its beer sector or for the flagship Guinness stout brand. However, it is estimated that beer accounts for 20 per cent of company sales, while its contribution to profits is thought to be smaller, at around 15 per cent.

Diageo's top management has growing concern over the company's principal beer brand, Guinness. The company reported a volume sales decline of 2 per cent for the brand in 2010, with value sales growth of 5 per cent only being achieved as a result of aggressive price increases in its main markets. The adoption of such a strategy has raised doubts over the sustainability of brand profitability. The Guinness brand has suffered on a number of levels, being hit by deteriorating demographics, with younger drinkers turning away from stout in general, a growing preference for wine and spirits, and a shift towards off-trade consumption

(buying beers in the shops to drink them at home), which puts the on-trade (pubs and bars) Guinness at a distinct disadvantage.

One of the reasons for this shift away from traditional pub consumption towards home drinking is the banning of smoking in public places, both in the UK and in Ireland. Nowhere have these trends been more evident than in these key markets. In general, Diageo plc in 2010 reported a 2 per cent decline in Guinness worldwide volume sales, while in the UK and Ireland the fall was steeper, at 3 per cent. Nevertheless, on the back of notable price rises, value growth of 4 per cent was achieved in both markets.

Guinness – an iconic Irish brand

As an adopted Irish national icon (although it is not Irish-owned), the Guinness brand is readily recognizable throughout the world, even by non-consumers. Indeed, it is one of only a few truly global beer brands, possessing a geographic coverage that spans all international regions. Brewed in over 50 countries, the Guinness recipe is modified to suit different market tastes in type and strength, with around 20 different variants sold worldwide. Its prime line is Guinness Draught, launched in 1959 and marketed in over 70 countries. This sub-brand accounts for around 55 per cent of all Guinness sold worldwide.

Widget technology saw Guinness Draught move into cans in 1989, and into bottles in 1999. To entice younger lager drinkers to stout, Guinness Draught Extra Cold was added to its range in its core markets of the UK and Ireland in 1998. The sub-brand actually comes from the same barrel as Guinness draught but goes through a super cooler on the way to the glass, and is served at a temperature around one-third lower than regular Guinness. This product is generally served

Source: Guinness® brand images, Diageo plc.

| Table 2 | World market for beer and stout (2010) |

Beer/stout 2008	Western Europe	Eastern Europe	North America	Latin America	Asia Pacific	Australia and Asia	Africa and Middle East	World total
Beer volume sales (million litres)	30,000	20,000	26,000	24,000	48,000	2,000	10,000	160,000
Stout volume sales (million litres)	637	121	122	21	88	25	720	1,600 (1.0% of total beer sales)
Brand (company) market shares	%	%	%	%	%	%	%	%
Guinness (Diageo)	80	12	86	5	64	66	45	60
Murphy's/Legend (Heineken)	8	6	3				15	8
Zywiec Porter (Heineken)		14						2
Kelt (Heineken)		8						1
Beamish (Heineken)	4	1						3
Carlsberg (Carlsberg)	1	1						1
Okocim Porter (Carlsberg)		4						1
Danish Royal Stout (Carlsberg)					5			
Lvivske (BBH)		12				1		11
Baltica 6 Porter (BBH)		5						
Tyskie Porter (SAB Miller)		10				1		1
Castle Milk Stout (SAB Miller)							35	12
Morenita (CCU)				94				1
Speight's (Lion Nathan)						12		
Monteith's (Asia Pacific Breweries)						12		
Hite Stout (Hite Brewery)					10			1
Others	7	27	11	1	21	8	5	8
Total	100	100	100	100	100	100	100	100
Beer distribution	%	%	%	%	%	%	%	%
On-trade (bars, pubs etc.)	48	22	25	39	33	26	34	34
Off-trade (retail)	52	78	75	61	67	74	66	66
Total	100	100	100	100	100	100	100	100

Source: based on Euromonitor.

in more modern outlets, where people prefer their beer cooler than standard.

Other line extensions include: Guinness Bitter, a dark beer primarily sold in the UK; Guinness Extra Stout, which is mainly distributed in Europe in bottles and cans; and Guinness Foreign Extra Stout. The last is a higher-strength, carbonated stout with a strong oaky flavour and no head, which is distributed throughout Africa, Asia and the Caribbean. Malta Guinness, an alcohol-free beer sold in Africa, and Guinness Extra Smooth, a smoother and creamy variation on traditional Guinness Draught, complete the Guinness portfolio.

The world market for beer and stout

Although Guinness holds 60 per cent of the world stout market, the brand accounts for only 0.6 per cent (60 per cent of 1 per cent) of the total world beer market (see Table 2).

Guinness's world market share is pretty stable at around 55–60 per cent. Today, the largest market growth for stout is in Africa: Nigeria, Cameroon and Kenya.

Competitors

Despite recent regional declines, the global strength of Diageo pic's Guinness brand has left little room for other major brands to become established in stout. Its main international rivals are SAB Miller's Castle Milk Stout, Heineken with its Murphy's brand, and Beamish (a former Scottish & Newcastle brand).

Castle Milk Stout (SAB Miller)

Castle Milk Stout is only present in South Africa, but it is very strongly placed there. This country has a considerable base, equivalent in size to the US stout environment, and combined with relatively low consumption of stout on a global level, this means that Castle Milk Stout had a heavy influence on the global market, with a volume share of 12 per cent in 2010. The product's performance of late has been dramatic. Under the guidance of SAB Miller, the brand is by far the leading stout product in South Africa, with a share of 70 per cent, a notable leap from the 60 per cent posted in 2005. It appears that Diageo plc's decision to cut back marketing spend and implement aggressive price increases has backfired in South Africa.

Murphy's/Legend (Heineken)

Murphy's features in most markets across western and eastern Europe and North America, but most significantly it holds a 7 per cent volume share of the largest stout market: the UK. Here, Murphy's has exerted

The Guinness Surger
Source: Guinness® brand images, Diageo plc.

limited pressure on Guinness in recent years, although its own share is partially under threat, facing similar problems in appealing to younger demographics. Conversely, notable brand growth in 2010 was evident in Slovakia, while forward momentum was maintained in Italy, France, the Netherlands, Norway and Russia.

Legend Extra Stout is Heineken's main brand in Africa's biggest stout market: Nigeria. There it is number two after Guinness.

Beamish (Heineken)

Beamish remains the most popular stout after Guinness in Ireland, posting a notable increase in volume share in 2004, up from 7 per cent to 8 per cent. Beamish is less of a threat in the UK, and is also present in the smaller stout markets of Canada, Portugal, France, Spain and the Ukraine. In 2003, Beamish was also introduced to the Finnish off-trade environment. Carlsberg is another international player in stout, but its competitive position is diluted by the fragmentation of its brand portfolio, which includes Carlsberg, Danish Royal Stout and Okocim Porter.

Local brand competition

Other local brands that generate reasonable volumes include Zywiec Porter in Poland and Kelt in Slovakia. Both of these brands are owned by Heineken and contributed to the company retaining its position as the number three player in stout, with a volume share of 8 per cent in 2008. That said, it remains some way behind the two leaders. Asahi Stout and Kirin Stout in Japan are also strong localized brands. Across eastern Europe, Asia-Pacific, Australasia and Africa and the Middle East, Guinness has to contend with strong local brands. Aside from Castle Milk Stout, SAB Miller's other key brand is Tyskie Porter, which is hugely popular in Poland. Overall, SAB Miller sits in second place in global sales of stout, reflecting the strong performance of Castle Milk Stout in its domestic market.

Guinness market shares across regions

As seen in Table 2, Guinness is the market leader in five of the seven regions: western Europe, North America, Africa and Middle East, Asia, Pacific and Australia and Asia. In the remaining two regions, Guinness is number two or three.

Western Europe

Focusing on stout, in western Europe Diageo plc led every national market with the exception of Denmark and Greece. Despite this strength, the company experienced its second successive year of volume sales decline in the region. At the heart of this downward trend in 2008 was a notable volume sales decline in Ireland, at 5 per cent, and stagnation in the UK. The other markets in the region are also declining. Key to this decline is the ageing profile of stout drinkers, with younger consumers failing to connect with the product. In addition, wine and spirits have grown in popularity, taking share from beer, and momentum behind the off-trade sector has grown, placing the on-trade-focused Guinness brand at a disadvantage. The main driver of the lower growth of stout is the shift from on-trade to off-trade. In the UK and Ireland around 80 per cent of Guinness sales take place in the on-trade.

Eastern Europe

The strength of local brands also poses a problem to Guinness in eastern Europe, with limited market shares in markets such as Poland (10 per cent in 2008), the Ukraine (3 per cent) and Slovakia (4 per cent). Guinness's volume share of stout is at 12 per cent in the region, its second lowest showing, with only its presence in Latin America smaller. Notably, Diageo posted a steady increase in its volume share of stout between 2004 and 2008 as consumers enjoyed rising disposable income levels and looked to trade up from low to middle-end local brands. By contrast, Heineken, in pole position with its standard brand (Zywiec Porter), steadily lost share over the same period.

North America

Guinness also suffered a decline in North America, with sales volume falling in 2005. Poor US beer market conditions, with a price war taking place among leading players, were the main reason for the downbeat performance, as performance in Canada was stronger.

Nevertheless, the company remained the dominant force in stout in the region, with a volume share of 86 per cent in 2005.

Latin America

In Latin America a relatively new arrival in stout is Cía de Cervecerías Unidas SA (CCU) in Chile, although its global presence is negligible. CCU is dominating the Latin American market, and its entry with its Morenita brand has knocked Guinness off the top spot.

Asia-Pacific

Demand for stout is underdeveloped in Asia-Pacific, where an almost total lack of demand in the populous markets of China and India is a notable barrier to growth. The Guinness sales volume declined in Hong Kong and experienced a marked dip in Indonesia and Thailand. A key force behind Diageo plc's decline was the success of local player, Hite Brewery Company Ltd, whose Hite Stout products quickly and confidently gained volume share of stout following its entry in 2000. Given its performance to date, this product constitutes a considerable threat to Diageo plc in the region. In addition, other local players performed well in recent years, negatively affecting Diageo plc's regional position. Despite the dip in volume share, Diageo plc remained the number one player in stout, even maintaining the top spot in Hong Kong, where decline was at its steepest. Another source of positive momentum in 2004 was Japan, where the company took its volume share to over 40 per cent.

This growth was a notable achievement, given the extent of local competition from Asahi and Kirin, which both have rival products to Guinness (Asahi Stout and Kirin Stout) and both enjoy significant price advantages. In Asia-Pacific, the introduction of ginseng-flavoured stout brands signaled repositioning of stout. Examples of ginseng stout brands are Danish Royal Stout Ginseng (Carlsberg), Partner Stout Ginseng (Bali Hai Brewery) and ABC Extra Stout Ginseng (Asia Pacific Breweries). These new ginseng stout brands were developed for fans who seek a full-bodied stout with additional benefits. The key end target market for this product segment is the middle-income male consumer.

Australia and Asia

This region is one of the strongest markets for Guinness, which enjoys a market share of 66 per cent in the region as a whole.

Africa and the Middle East

Africans have been drinking Guinness since the slave-trading days of the 1820s, company documents say.

European merchant sailors preferred to load up with Guinness rather than other beers because a higher concentration of alcohol, at 7.5 per cent, gave the stout a longer shelf life. By 1827, Guinness was exporting its stout, from its brewery on the banks of Dublin's Liffey River to Sierra Leone.

In 2013, Guinness employed 5,000 people in Africa in breweries. African countries – Nigeria, Kenya, Cameroon, Ivory Coast and South Africa – accounted for five of the 10 largest markets by volume in the world for Guinness and about 50 percent of worldwide profit.

This region is one of the most important for the company in terms of growth potential, as the level of stout consumption is among the highest in the world, and much growth is expected in the short term. The majority of Diageo's worldwide brewing facilities are in Africa, where its majority-owned brewing operations, such as in Kenya, Nigeria, Cameroon, Ghana and the Seychelles, brew both Guinness and local brands. Guinness is also produced by third-party brewers in other African countries where volumes are not so strong.

Overall, Guinness is a stout market leader in Africa and Middle East. Guinness's strongest markets are the markets in East Africa (Kenya, Uganda and Tanzania), although the majority of volumes are sold in Nigeria, which is the brand's second-largest market globally. For example, Guinness has a market share of 80 per cent in Kenya, while SAB Miller's strength is based on its dominance (70 per cent market share) in South Africa with its Castle Milk Stout. Heineken is especially strong in Nigeria and Cameroon. Consequently, company performances are very reliant on local geographic conditions. Diageo has started to develop its presence outside the core markets in Africa, such as Nigeria and Kenya. The company started to do that in 2010, by acquiring a majority stake in Tanzania'a second-ranked brewer, Serengeti Brewery.

The international marketing strategy

In the ensuing paragraphs, Guinness's initiatives within the international marketing mix will be explained.

New product innovation/packaging

Diageo plc moved its Guinness Draught into bottles in late 1999 following the development of a new 'rocket widget', which enabled Guinness to retain its distinctive foamy white head when consumed from its packaging. Presented in long-neck bottles, this line positioned Guinness alongside premium lagers and flavoured alcoholic beverages (FABs), such as Diageo plc's popular Smirnoff Ice.

The beer market in the UK is seeing a dynamic shift away from traditional pub consumption towards home drinking experiences, partially due to the banning of smoking in public places. The impact of banning smoking in pubs in Ireland and the UK has been a switch from on-trade (pubs, bars) into off-trade as more people opted to smoke and drink at home.

In February 2006, the 'Guinness Surger' was launched. It is a plug-in unit promising to deliver the perfect pint at home by sending ultrasonic sound waves through the special Guinness Draught Surger beer. By releasing this new product, Diageo aimed to recreate the 'pub experience' in consumers' own homes. Consumers purchasing drinks for at-home occasions want to mimic the on-trade experience as much as possible, particularly in terms of presentation and quality. The new Surger gadget delivered exactly this, as well as having a 'shareability' factor to enhance consumers' at-home drinking experience through the novelty of using the ultrasound device. The price in the UK was £17 for the starter kit, which included one Surger, a pint glass and two cans of Surger beer.

Diageo thought the Guinness Draught Surger would help to capitalize on the growing movement towards the off-trade. The product had already been released with success in Japan and Singapore, and was the focus of a £2.5 million marketing campaign in the UK. However, the Guinness Surger Unit was withdrawn from the UK market in April 2008 and sales of the cans were withdrawn from Tesco stores.

In 2009, the Surger Unit was again available in the UK and worldwide, including countries such as the US, Italy, France, Spain, Austria, Australia and Japan. Guinness Surger cans are available to licensed premises in different sizes – UK and Spain 520 ml, US 14.9 fluid ounces, Europe 330 ml, Japan 350 ml and Australia 375 ml.

Distribution

Diageo plc handles its own distribution as a rule. However, in many countries stout occupies a very small niche in the beer environment, making it uneconomical for Guinness to set up its own production and distribution network. It therefore operates in partnership with a number of local and international brewers. Sometimes the company appoints third-party distributors or agrees a joint venture for the purpose.

Distribution agreements most often include licensing and distribution agreements for beer. These include both Guinness and rival brands. For example, with Carlsberg it is allowing them the production of their beer in Ireland. In return, Carlsberg helps Guinness with distribution in some countries. Japanese Sapporo beer is also produced in the Guinness breweries. As compensation, Guinness gets access to Japanese distribution.

Diageo has also entered into a three-way joint venture with Heineken and Namibia Breweries Limited in southern Africa, called Brandhouse, to take advantage of the consumer shift towards premium brands. The company has also merged its business in Ghana (Guinness Ghana Limited) with Heineken's Ghana Breweries Limited in order to achieve operational synergy benefits.

Diageo terminated its rights agreement for the distribution of Bass Ale in the US with effect from 30 June 2003. According to the original agreement Diageo had the rights to distribute Bass Ale in the US until 2016. After negotiation, the distribution rights reverted to the global brand owner, Interbrew, for £69 million.

Advertising of Guinness

Guinness advertising spend has been reduced in recent years. Whether this caution is a wise move in times of increased competition remains to be seen. As a largely unique product that leads its category, Guinness has historically been supported by a high degree of creative and ground-breaking marketing and advertising, beginning with the 'Guinness for Strength' girder-man in 1934, and its long-surviving Toucan character, which ran from 1935 to 1982. Guinness has increasingly developed below-the-line campaigns to target existing and potential consumers with the development of customer relationship marketing (CRM). However, above-the-line spend in 2002 was notable, with Guinness's first ever global campaign entitled 'believe'. This focused on the concept of 'self belief' and 'belief in Guinness', and was created by BBDO. The campaign featured a logo with the V in 'believe' replaced with the Guinness harp, and was designed to reinforce brand loyalty among existing consumers and, of course, attract new ones.

Advertising in the UK and Ireland

Particularly in the UK and Ireland, the Guinness marketing campaigns have been very high-profile, turning the brand into one of the most successful and fast-moving consumer goods in the UK, with very strong top-of-mind recall awareness. In Ireland, however, repeated attempts to reinvigorate the Guinness brand have met with limited success. In February 2004, Diageo plc launched a new advertising campaign for Guinness in the UK called 'Out of Darkness Comes Light'. The first advert in the series – Moth – represented the start of a campaign marking a new chapter in the heritage of Guinness advertising. This advert was followed up by the Mustang execution, which has all the epic drama and scale characteristic of Guinness advertising. It was supported by a total media spend of £15 million, and first appeared on national TV in September 2004.

In 2005, Diageo plc launched a new advertising campaign for the core Guinness brand in the UK and Ireland late in the year. The 'Evolution' campaign featured an advert depicting three men in a bar taking a sip of Guinness and then being transported back in time, going back through the main stages of evolution. The new advert had a more contemporary and youthful feel than previous showings, suggesting that Diageo plc has responded to the problem of deteriorating demographics affecting the brand.

In 2007, Diageo launched the 'Hands' campaign, a £2.5 million campaign for Guinness, which included an online presence as well as traditional TV and print executions.

Advertising in Africa

As the biggest growth markets for Guinness are African countries, the greatest marketing innovation generated by Diageo plc is being implemented here. Guinness spent more than £25 million on advertising in Africa, where the brand commands premium pricing through its reputation. Following on from Saatchi & Saatchi's 1999 creation of the character Michael Power, in a series of five-minute, action-thriller advertisements, the concept has culminated in a full-length promotional film production shown across Africa. Guinness Nigeria shot a new Michael Power film, which was screened in 2004. In a further display of commitment to this growth region, Guinness Nigeria has worked with local communities to provide them with clean, safe water. Royalties from the Guinness-sponsored feature film *Critical Assignment,* which highlights the need for clean drinking water, have helped fund a Water of Life project.

How to attract the young consumer

Despite its previous marketing successes, Guinness is suffering from a lack of take-up among younger consumers in preference for more fashionable lagers and FABs. An interesting trend in Diageo plc's marketing strategy was a further change in the way the company marketed its flagship Guinness brand. For a time, on its Guinness.com website, the company actively encouraged consumers to mix Guinness with other products to produce various 'cocktails'. This was clearly a further effort to appeal to the youth segment, given that many consumers in this age group find the taste of Guinness too bitter. Examples of mixers suggested by the company included champagne, blackcurrant juice, lime juice or curacao, cacao and Dubonnet.

Sponsorships

The positioning of Guinness has been centred on the brand's traditional associations with sports. In 2005, Guinness made a notable investment in sports sponsorship, putting its name to the 2005 tour of the British and Irish Lions rugby union team to New Zealand and paying £20 million to sponsor the 2005–06 season of top domestic rugby union league in the UK. In addition, the brand was the sponsor of the G-8 Summit in Gleneagles, Scotland.

In 2008, Diageo announced that Guinness would be the title sponsor for Singapore Rugby. The three-year deal saw Guinness sponsoring the Guinness Premiership in the UK and Ireland, the Irish national rugby team and the club Hong Kong Sevens. In Singapore, Guinness sponsored three divisions, as well as the elite knock-out competition, the Singapore Cup.

Investments in a new Irish-theme pub concept

Guinness consumption rose partly because of the development of the Irish-theme pub. In the UK, Diageo plc invested £13 million in 2001 in developing a new bar concept that it encouraged independent owners of Irish-theme pubs to adopt.

The idea was to make traditional pubs less cluttered and more contemporary, lighter and cleaner and thereby more appealing to women. This new concept also put a stronger focus on spirits rather than draught beer, thereby signalling that Diageo plc saw its spirits brands driving future revenue growth rather than Guinness beer.

The top management in Diageo is in doubt as to what to do about Guinness in the future. Should they continue the 'milking strategy' by withdrawing marketing resources (lowering costs) and increasing revenues (by increasing the end-consumer prices)? At least that would maximize profits over a shorter term, and Diageo could use the financial resources in acquiring other beer brands. Or should Diageo instead make a long-term investment in developing the brand, by implementing new global marketing initiatives?

Latest Guinness initiatives

According to the Diageo's 2014 annual report, sales of Guinness fell by 5 per cent globally in 2014. In order to reverse the negative sales development (especially happening, on the UK market), Guinness has come up with new marketing ideas.

In March 2014, Guinness launched the '1759' limited edition with a run of 90,000 bottles, but at a price of £22 per bottle-about five times what you would normally pay for a traditional Guinness at the local pub. However, '1759' is not an Irish dry stout. It is an amber ale with peated malt, the same smoky stuff that goes into certain types of Scotch whisky. The reason it is called '1759' is that it is the year when Arthur Guinness set up his shop in Dublin.

Guinness '1759' is meant to be a gift product. Also the packaging is a bit special – It is topped off with a cork. Guinness suggest serving it in a Champagne-like glass (preferably stemless – see picture).

Source: Guinness® brand images, Diageo plc.

QUESTIONS

As an international marketing consultant, you are asked to give an independent assessment of Guinness's opportunities in the world beer market. You are specifically asked the following questions:

1. How would you explain the Guinness pricing strategy and the underlying assumptions about consumer behaviour when Diageo reports for 2005 that in the UK and Ireland Guinness sales volume fell by 3 per cent, but a value growth of 4 per cent was achieved in both markets, mainly due to price increases?

2. Motivated by the success of this pricing strategy, should Diageo continue to increase the price of Guinness?

3. In Choueke (2006), an anonymous beer retail buyer comments on Guinness's decreasing sales volume:

   Guinness has an older profile of drinker and with an ever-increasing availability of continental lagers and a fast-growing range of alcopops, the younger generation of drinkers simply haven't bought into it. Innovation – widgets and gadgets – will keep the brand alive for a while but where else can Diageo go? Flavoured Guinness? No thanks. It is in decline and Diageo's best minds can't do much about it. The brand may have only a couple of decades' worth of life in it and I would milk it for everything before getting rid of it and concentrating on spirits.

   Do you agree with this statement? Explain your reasons.

4. What elements of the Guinness international marketing strategy would you focus on in order to increase both global sales volume, value and profits?

5. What do you think about the '1759' marketing idea? Should Guinness introduce more special edition beer brands with a limited lifetime for special occasions or as a gift product?

Sources: based on different materials from www.diageo.com and www.euromonitor.com; Choueke, M. (2006) 'Dark times for the black stuff?', *Marketing* Week, 15 June.

CASE STUDY IV.3

Dyson Vacuum Cleaner: the iconic vacuum cleaner manufacturer launches the robotic version

The Dyson history

It is impossible to separate the very British Dyson vacuum cleaner from its very British inventor. Together they are synonymous with innovation and legal battles against established rivals.

James Dyson was born in Norfolk in 1947. He studied furniture design and interior design at the Royal College of Art from 1966 to 1970 and his first product, the Sea Truck, was launched while he was still studying.

Dyson's foray into developing vacuum cleaner technology happened by chance. In 1978, while renovating his 300-year-old country house, Dyson became frustrated with the poor performance of his conventional vacuum cleaner. Whenever he went to use it, there was poor suction. One day he thought he would find out what was wrong with the design. He noted that the appliance worked by drawing air through the bag to create suction, but when even a fine layer of dust got inside, it clogged its pores, stopping the airflow and suction.

In his usual style of seeking solutions from unexpected sources, Dyson noticed how a nearby sawmill used a cyclone – a 30-foot-high cone that spun dust out of the air by centrifugal force – to expel waste. He reasoned that a vacuum cleaner that could separate dust by cyclonic action and spin it out of the airstream which would eliminate the need for both bag and filter. James Dyson set out to replicate the cyclonic system.

Over the next eight years, Dyson tried to license his dual cyclone concept to established vacuum manufacturers, only to be turned down. At least two of these initial contacts forced him to file patent infringement lawsuits, which he won in out-of-court and in-court settlements. Finally in 1985, a small company in Japan contacted him out of the blue after seeing a picture of his vacuum cleaner in a magazine. Mortgaged to the hilt and on the brink of bankruptcy, Dyson took the cheapest flight to Tokyo to negotiate a deal. The result was the G Force vacuum cleaner, priced at US$2,000, which became the ultimate domestic appliance status symbol in Japan.

In June 1993, using money from the Japanese license, Dyson opened a research center and factory in Malmesbury, Wiltshire. Here he developed the Dyson dual cyclone and within two years it was the fastest-selling vacuum cleaner in the UK.

Dyson was nearly bankrupted by the legal costs of establishing and protecting his patent. It took him more than 14 years to get his first product into a shop and it is on display in the Science Museum. Other products can be seen in the Victoria & Albert Museum, the San Francisco Museum of Modern Art and the Georges Pompidou Centre in Paris.

Dyson went on to develop the Root 8 Cyclone, which removes more dust by using eight cyclones instead of two. In 2000, he launched the Contra-rotator washing machine, which uses two drums spinning in opposite directions and is said to wash faster and with better results than traditional washing machines. It was soon withdrawn from the market because of disappointing sales.

The company has developed a portfolio of innovative product designs including its expansion of hand-held vacuum cleaners and products focused on pet owners and allergy sufferers. But other different products have also been developed by Dyson's innovative R&D department.

The Dyson Airblade (hand dryer) was introduced in 2006 (UK) and 2007 (US). It has been a reasonable success for Dyson, and it is still on the market.

The company launched its Air Multiplier Fan range in 2009. In line with the launch of the Dyson Air Multiplier desk fan in 2009, the company extended this technology to standing fans (AM03) and tower fans (AM02) range. Both new fans retailed at £299.99 and both products are still on the market.

In 2010, the company launched its compact cylinder vacuum cleaner called Dyson City (model DC26). The company claimed that 90 per cent of the UK's population is city dwellers and this new model, fitting on a sheet of A4 paper, offered the best storage solution for consumers. The company took five years to re-engineer all the 275 parts of the DC26 so that it was presented in a compact size while not compromising on suction power or performance. The model has since been replaced by the Dyson Cordless.

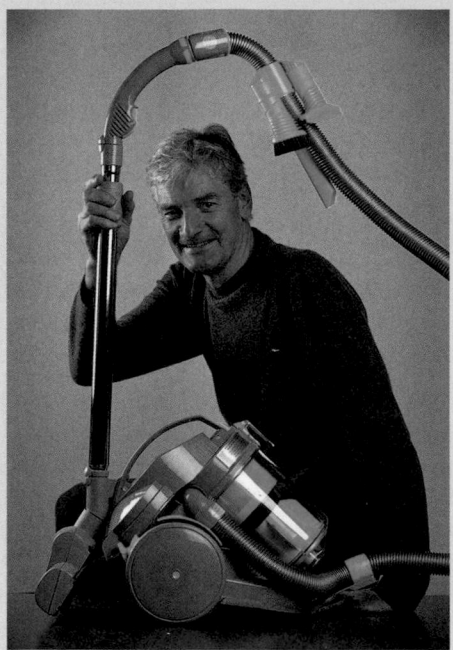

Source: Adrian Sherratt/Alamy Images.

In 2013, Dyson's global sales reached £1.3 billion, roughly two-thirds of which came from outside the UK, while pre-tax profit for the year was £382 million, up 50 per cent compared to 2010. Most of the sales come from vacuum cleaners – a product in which Dyson has built large sales in the US, Japan and Australia. Nearly 1,500 of Dyson's 3,600 global employees are in the UK.

In Spring 2015, Dyson took a step closer to floor cleaning systems with the launch of Dyson Cordless V6 in the US and UK (see the picture). Dyson is riding on the economic recovery and is looking to entice consumers who are more likely to prioritize convenience when income allows. As one of the first of its kind, Dyson

Source: Roger Parkes/Alamy Images.

combines advanced vacuum technology with mopping function. Procter & Gamble can be credited with kick-starting floor cleaning systems in 2001 with the launch of the Swiffer WetJet. Dyson V6's launch is further capitalizing on consumer demand for multisurface convenience by combining the essential need for two-step floor cleaning – sweeping/vacuuming and mopping – with interchangeable carpet and hard floor heads, along with attachments to convert it to a handheld cleaner. Although coming with a hefty price tag, £300 in the UK for example, the cost may well be affordable (£5/month) when considered against a typical five-year life cycle for such an appliance.

Marketing the Dyson vacuum cleaner

Dyson believes the most effective marketing tool is word-of-mouth, and today the company claims 70 per cent of its vacuum cleaners are sold on personal recommendation. As an enthusiastic self-publicist, James Dyson believes that if you make something, you should sell it yourself, so he often appears in his own advertisements.

When a Belgian court banned Dyson from denigrating old-style vacuum cleaner bags, he was pictured wearing his trademark blue shirt and holding a Dyson vacuum cleaner in a press advertisement that had the word 'bag' blacked out several times. A note at the bottom said: 'Sorry, but the Belgian courts won't let you know what everyone has a right to know'.

Dyson has sometimes shunned advertising altogether, sometimes preferring to use sponsorship instead. For example, in 1996–97 the company produced a limited edition model to sponsor Sir Ranulph Fiennes' solo expedition to Antarctica, in order to raise money for the charity Breakthrough Breast Cancer.

As rivals started to manufacture their own bagless cleaners, Dyson knew he would have to advertise more aggressively and in 2000 he appointed an advertising agency to promote the £2 million business. The marketing strategy, however, remains true to Dyson's original principles, with an emphasis on information and education rather than brand-building. Moreover, it seems to be working; in 2014, one in every five vacuum cleaners bought in the UK was a Dyson. See also Table 1 on p. 700.

The world market for vacuum cleaners

The use of vacuum cleaners is largely related to national preferences for carpets rather than floor tiles. In many warm countries floor tiles are more usual than carpets, and these can be swept rather than vacuumed. In countries where houses are predominantly carpeted, such as in Northern Europe, Eastern Europe and North America, the number of households owning vacuum cleaners is high. In 2014, approximately 95 per cent of households owned vacuum cleaners in Belgium, Germany, Japan, the Netherlands, Sweden, the US and the UK. Many Belgian households possess more than one vacuum cleaner, as traditional vacuum cleaners are often complemented with hand-held cleaners (cleanettes). In parts of Eastern Europe, it is also common to carpet walls, which provides additional demand for vacuum cleaners.

Relatively few vacuum cleaners are sold in China and India. Vacuum cleaners have only been available in China for 15 years, but ownership has not become widespread. In India, many of the rural population do not have the means for such appliances and power supply is erratic. The Asia-Pacific total market for vacuum cleaners is 14 million units per year.

The world market for vacuum cleaners is fairly mature and stable. As average prices fell throughout 2009–14, value growth amounted to only approximately 3 per cent overall. In 2014, the number of vacuum cleaners sold throughout the world was 85 million units. Demand is driven mainly by replacement purchases at the end of a product's life cycle (the commercial lifetime of a vacuum cleaner is about eight years), although new product developments such as bagless models and robotic vacuum cleaners spurred growth in some markets.

The most sold vacuum cleaner types are the upright and the cylinder. The distinction between upright and cylinder vacuum cleaners became less clear in recent years, with the addition of hoses and tools to the upright version and cylinders mimicking uprights by adding turbo brushes to eradicate dust from carpets.

Cylinder, or canister, vacuum cleaners make up the majority of the global market, but do not take a strong lead, accounting for 70 per cent of European volume sales in 2014, compared with 30 per cent for upright models. As upright vacuum cleaners are more expensive, their share is higher by value, amounting to 35 per cent of the market by value.

Generally, the sales of upright vacuum cleaners grew faster than cylinders over the five-year period from 2009 to 2014. This largely reflected trends in the US, which was the world's leading market for vacuum cleaners (especially upright vacuum cleaners). Here, the addition of new features fuelled the upright subsector, including bagless operation, HEPA (high-efficiency particulate air) filtration and self-propulsion, which are available in various combinations on models selling for less than US$200.

In other markets, such as in Eastern Europe, cylinder vacuum cleaners are the most popular type as they are more practical for use on wall carpets, which are common, for example, in Russia.

Among the top markets for vacuum cleaners, preferences also vary between bag and bagless. In the US and South Korea, the bagless format accounts for 80–90 per cent of volume sales. In other countries, such as Germany, bagless still holds the smallest share, (30 per cent) and its penetration is growing very slowly. In most of the emerging markets, the bagless format is still largely non-existent and consumers are still opting for more conservative models with lower unit prices.

Hand-held vacuum cleaners do not play an important role in the market, and are ignored in the rest of this case study.

The market for vacuum cleaners tends to be dominated by leading white goods manufacturers. Electrolux was world market leader in this sector in 2014 with a world volume share of approximatley 12% through its brands Electrolux, Eureka and AEG. In Table 1, the robotic vacuum cleaner manufacturers (like iRobot) are hidden in the 'others' category for the total market (under 'Manufacturer'). At the bottom of Table 1, the Robotic vacuum cleaner market is then specified more, including the CAGR growth forecast.

Since the 1990s, one of the most significant developments in the market is bagless technology. Dyson UK pioneered its dual cyclone technology back in 1993 and it is protected by patent, but other manufacturers were quick to develop bagless versions. In the US, bagless vacuum cleaners increased their unit share from just 2.6 per cent in 1998 to over 65 per cent in 2014.

The western European market is rather fragmented. In 2014, Dyson was some way behind Electrolux with a share of 10 per cent. Although Dyson's overall market share is not high, it used to be one of the dominating brands in the high-priced segment.

The Asia-Pacific market for vacuum cleaners is highly concentrated, with the top five players accounting for 80 per cent of sales in 2014. These were all Japanese companies, led by Matsushita. The latter also led the Australasian market, slightly ahead of Dyson. Interestingly, Samsung did not rank among the top five Asian manufacturers in 2014, although it led the Eastern European market.

In the US, Dyson sells more than 1 million units, equal to a total market share of 6 per cent in 2014. However, in the high-priced segment (US$400 – plus) Dyson is taking market shares in the high end, which Hoover used to dominate and, at the same time, Hoover lost the low-cost market to non-brand Asian competitors. While not as expensive as ultra-premium lines, such as Miele and Kirby, upright models of Dyson vacuum cleaners are resolutely high-end, with models retailing for US$350–550. The company does not engage in discounting, maintaining the brand's high prices as part of an overall image of quality. Even its hand-held model retails for US$150, which is significantly higher than its competitors. In US, vacuum cleaners can be found in a growing number of retail outlets, such as Best Buy, Sears Bed, Bath & Beyond, Target and WalMart.

Robotic vacuum cleaners

After the bagless technology, one of the most significant developments in the market is the robotic vacuum cleaner. Dyson will play a significant role in this area in the future. The remainder of the case will concentrate on this growth market in vacuum cleaners.

It has been more than ten years since robotic vacuum cleaners debuted, although as early as 2001, Dyson built and demonstrated a robot vacuum cleaner known as the DC06. However, due to its high price, the product was never released to the market.

In 2002, the American advanced technology company iRobot launched the 'Roomba' robotic vacuum robot cleaner, which is the world market leader today (2015).

Nevertheless, sales of robotic vacuum cleaners remain small, accounting for less than 2 per cent of total volume sales of vacuum cleaners globally in 2014. Despite having already posted explosive growth, robotic vacuum cleaners' volume sales are expected to continue to increase by nearly 60 per cent between 2013 and 2018.

Robotic vacuum cleaners are, however, considered extravagant, due to their high price; for example, in the US, the average unit price for a robotic vacuum cleaner is US$184 compared to US$104 for a standard vacuum cleaner.

The volume share of robotic vacuum cleaners mostly comes from developed countries such as the US, South Korea, France and Japan, which together accounted for nearly 70 per cent of total robotic vacuum cleaners' volume sales in 2014. The common factor in these developed countries is transition of household format and lifestyle. As the number of one- or two-person households grows in developed countries, the demand for appliances that provide convenience is increasing. Thanks to technological advance, robotic vacuum cleaners have changed the conventional concept of cleaning which still needed human touch and effort. These days, people have the option to enjoy their free time through relying on smart appliances like robotic vacuum cleaners that can be programmed to clean their homes in their absence.

In contrast, robotic vacuum cleaners' penetration in much of the Middle East and Africa and some Asia-Pacific countries is very low. For example, the total vacuum cleaner penetration in Middle Eastern and African countries was just 33 per cent in 2014. Consumers in these areas largely still prefer cleaning in the traditional way. This is mainly due to the availability of cheap labour and differences in floor type. In the United Arab Emirates, for instance, affluent consumers who can afford robotic vacuum cleaners tend to hire maids instead. They do not see the need to purchase either robotic vacuum cleaners or standard vacuum cleaners while they can still rely on manual labour to keep their homes clean. Furthermore, according to Euromonitor International's Home and Garden research, 63 per cent of volume sales of floor coverings in the United Arab Emirates are carpets. Consumers' cleaning style tends towards sweeping and scrubbing carpets manually with cleaners. Manufacturers are therefore faced with the challenge of positioning robotic vacuum cleaners to suit existing cleaning styles.

Competition between robotic vacuum cleaner manufacturers

iRobot dominates robotic vacuum cleaners sales globally, with approximately 50 per cent volume share in 2014. One reason for iRobot's exceptional global performance stems from its leading position in the US, the world's biggest market for robotic vacuum cleaners. Its first-mover advantage also means that iRobot's geographic footprint is more comprehensive compared to its competitors. That said, it is worth noting that iRobot's share has dropped by 20 percentage points since 2006, when it had a near-monopoly status.

In September 2015, iRobot entered the smart home with the launch of its connected Roomba 980 (see picture below).

Furthermore in early 2016 iRobot launched its Braava jet floor mopping robot for private homes.

Source: iRobot Corporation.

i-Robot's current closest competitors in robotic vacuum cleaners are Samsung and LG, although they trail behind iRobot and have only managed to gain volume shares of 8 per cent and 2 per cent, respectively, in 2014. Other players, including Ecovacs, Electrolux, Miele, Sharp and Toshiba, have less than 1 per cent volume share each in 2014.

Competition between Korean manufacturers (mainly Samsung and LG) in particular is becoming very intense, and characterized by dynamic growth. While iRobot focuses on its strong brand image, with its Roomba and Braava brands, Samsung and LG are focused on launching innovative technologies. Samsung, the leading robotic vacuum cleaner in South Korea, launched Smart Tango in 2011, with a camera to detect obstacles in its cleaning path, the ability to pre-set cleaning routes, and remote operation via smart devices such as a Samsung smartphone. Comparably, LG launched the Robot King Triple Eye in 2011. This comes with three built-in cameras for detecting objects in its way, measuring the distance to these objects and monitoring cleaning status; it also features voice control and a smart diagnosis function which informs users of potential issues with the machine.

Smaller-sized robotic vacuum cleaner companies in China, Taiwan and South Korea also continue to chip at the market, increasing total global sales volume of robotic vacuum cleaners. Some of these companies specialize in robotic vacuum cleaners exclusively. Unlike multinational brands which have the resources to compete through investing heavily in aggressive marketing and advertisement activities, these smaller companies need to come up with alternative strategies. These have tended to be through competitive prices, patent technologies and strategic alliances with multinational brands.

Over the next five years, sales volume of robotic vacuum cleaners globally are predicted to grow from approximately 4 million units in 2014 to 6 million units in 2016. Relatively new in consumer appliances, robotic vacuum cleaners still have strong potential for growth. Technological developments along the lines of those launched by Samsung and LG will need to continue in order to convince consumers to upgrade from standard to robotic vacuum cleaners.

Further development can be expected in the longer term. There are still many manufacturers such as Haier and Midea who have yet to launch robotic vacuum cleaners, but can be expected to, in order to offer a complete consumer appliances portfolio to customers. Major multinational brands coming into the market can be expected to quickly intensify competition, bringing price competition and stimulating interest via new technology.

Extending geographical coverage is another opportunity for expansion. Despite challenges faced in changing consumers' traditional cleaning habits, manufacturers stand to benefit from increasing awareness in developing regions like Latin America and the Middle East and Africa. Pioneers in developing markets will have firm ground to grow shares globally.

World region sales of robotic vacuum cleaners

Almost negligible five years ago, the robotic vacuum cleaner market in western Europe is now the world's largest in volume terms, having overtaken north America in 2012. More significantly, western Europe is also far and away the most valuable market.

In North America, robotic vacuum cleaners are not experiencing the same momentum, with sales in the US, which account for well over 90 per cent of the regional market, not expected to grow more than 0.4 per cent annually in value between 2013 and 2017 – growth that other categories can only dream of, but still significantly lower than in western Europe. When the recession first hit in 2008, the US market entered a three-year decline and it was not expected to return to 2007 levels before 2015. The bullish growth that robotic vacuum cleaners enjoyed following their first launch seems to be proving short-lived. Table 1 illustrates the total market share of various vacuum cleaner manufacturers together with the market share specific to the robotic type.

Characteristics of key national markets

UK

Volume sales of vacuum cleaners in the UK registered flat growth in 2014 while value sales were boosted by a premium trend. Even though volume growth stagnated in 2014, vacuum cleaners generally show some resilience as sales are chiefly driven by replacement. Consumers shift towards high added-value products for better quality and long-lasting use.

Robotic vacuum cleaners, albeit niche, achieved a good performance in both retail volume and current value terms in 2014. Such vacuum cleaners are considered as complementary to standard vacuum cleaners and do not cannibalize other types such as cylinder vacuum cleaners. However, robotic vacuum cleaners offer benefits such as time-saving in daily cleaning. Technology and advanced features allow robotic vacuum cleaners to be positioned high-end in terms of pricing.

The fastest growth within vacuum cleaners in 2013 was in robotic vacuum cleaners, led by iRobot UK in 2014 with a retail volume share of 46 per cent. However, the company has seen slow but growing

Table 1 Market share of vacuum cleaner (traditional + robotic) manufacturers in most important countries – 2014

	UK	Germany	France	USA	Japan	China	Australia
Total market (traditional + robotic):							
Total volume (1,000 units)	5,960	5,349	4,723	43,162	5,669	5,176	2,324
Total value (€ millions)	902	854	602	3,884	788	555	336
CAGR value growth forecast 2013–18	3.7%	0.0%	-1.2%	3.1%	-0.4%	6.2%	5.9%
Manufacturer:	% (volume)	% (volume)	% (volume)	% (volume)	% (volume)	% (volume)	% (volume)
Electrolux (incl. Eureka, AEG)	4	13	14	14	2	–	29
TTI Floor Care NA (incl. Hoover, Dirt Devil, Royal)	8	18	4	32	–	–	–
Bissell Inc.	3	–	–	21	–	–	1
Dyson	20	8	15	6	5	–	18
Philips	–	3	5	–	–	25	–
Miele	2	9	4	–	–	–	6
BSH (Bosch Siemens Home)	4	15	–	–	–	–	–
Panasonic	–	–	–	1	33	15	–
SEB	–	–	17	–	–	1	–
Samsung	5	–	–	–	–	–	–
LG	2	–	1	–	–	–	4
Private label	15	5	9	5	5	5	10
Others	37	29	26	22	55	54	32
Total	100	100	100	100	100	100	100
Total robotic vacuum cleaner market:							
Total volume (1,000 units)	51	255	234	729	357	38	65
Total value (€ millions)	27	90	75	156	89	9	26
% of total vacuum cleaner market (volume)	0.9%	4.8%	4.9%	1.7%	6.3%	0.7%	2.8%
% of total vacuum cleaner market (value)	3.0%	10.5%	12.5%	4.0%	11.3%	1.6%	7.7%
Market leaders in the robotic market – 2014	iRobot, Samsung	iRobot (Klein Robotics GmbH is the distributor)	iRobot (Robopolis SA), Zicom, LG, Samsung	iRobot, Neato Robotics	iRobot (Sales On Demand Corporation), Sharp, Toshiba	Ecovacs, Fmart	iRobot (Salton Pty), Samsung, LG
CAGR growth forecast 2013-18 (value)	19.7%	7.3%	2.5%	0.4%	8.8%	16.3%	24.7%

CAGR, compound annual growth rate.
Notes: In Europe and the US, Hoover and Dirt Devil are manufactured by TTI Floor Care North America (Hoover) and its subsidiary Royal Appliance Manufacturing (Dirt Devil). The SEB group took over the Rowenta brand in 1988. In 2001, the SEB Group took over Moulinex SA and the SEB Group now markets the Moulinex vacuum cleaner.
Source: Euromonitor and other public sources.

competition from Samsung Electronics (UK) Ltd in robotic vacuum cleaners. The latter increased its retail volume share, albeit still marginal, in 2014, thereby enabling Samsung Electronics to maintain its overall retail volume share of vacuum cleaners in the UK at 5 per cent in 2013.

Germany

Upright vacuum cleaners have continued to suffer from a lack of interest among German consumers and, as a result, the majority of German consumers continue to ignore this relatively small category. According to the key players in vacuum cleaners in Germany, the focus has instead been placed on the development of other vacuum cleaner categories. For example, Miele introduced hybrid technology into its range of compact vacuum cleaners and in 2014 they also introduced a robotic vacuum cleaner. The innovative new Miele vacuum cleaner line features ground-breaking technology which is pending patent approval.

Robotic vacuum cleaners remained the vacuum cleaner category with the highest growth during 2014, increasing in volume by 30 per cent to 255,000 units. Since the introduction of robotic vacuum cleaners into Germany, the category has enjoyed consistently high volume growth rates. The leading brand of robotic vacuum cleaners in Germany in 2013 remained Klein Robotics GmbH (an iRobot distributor), which accounted for approximately 60 per cent of total robotic vacuum cleaner retail volume sales in 2013. Klein Robotics GmbH is a distributor for Germany and a subsidiary of French Robopolis SAS, which distributes iRobot's products all over Europe. In Germany, Klein Robotics GmbH is mainly selling iRobot's products.

The emerging presence of multinational players in robotic vacuum cleaners and the increase in the range of products offered in the category at affordable prices led to a decline in the average unit price in the category.

Philips GmbH entered the robotic vacuum cleaner market in 2012 with its Philips Robot Vacuum Cleaner FC9910/01. This product is positioned at the same price point as the robotic vacuum cleaners of existing leading players such as Samsung Electronics Deutschland GmbH. Further competition from key players in consumer appliances is expected to boost the future sales of robotic vacuum cleaners in Germany.

An increasing share of robotic vacuum cleaners (20 per cent in 2014) is now sold and distributed through internet retailing. The main distribution channel for vacuum cleaners, however, remains specialist electronics and appliance retailers and chain stores, Media-Saturn-Holding GmbH being the most popular outlet for vacuum cleaner purchase among the German population.

France

The phenomenal success of robotic vacuum cleaners and other technologically advanced vacuum cleaners reflects the outlook of French households when it comes to cleaning homes. This attitude involves a high propensity to spend money on convenient types of vacuum cleaners which save consumers time on cleaning their homes.

Many French consumers are now happy to have two vacuum cleaners in the home, a standard vacuum cleaner and a robotic vacuum cleaner.

Internet retailing accounts for approximately 15 per cent of the total retail distribution of vacuum cleaners in France.

Purchasing robotic vacuum cleaners and stick vacuum cleaners through home shopping is especially popular among elderly French people, many of whom have readily adopted the new technological advances in vacuum cleaners as these help them to clean their homes effortlessly. Hypermarkets remain the main channel of distribution vacuum cleaners in France with 45 per cent of total volume sales in 2014.

US

The rise of allergies and asthma over the last decade has had a profound influence on the kinds of vacuum cleaners in which consumers were interested. As such, there has been an increasing trend for upright vacuum cleaners to adapt HEPA filtration technology. Many companies, such as Electrolux Home Products North America, Bissell, and TTI Floor Care North America (Hoover), offer HEPA filtration systems, which effectively trap nearly 100 per cent of airborne particles. Another trend born from this rise in hygiene considerations has been the growth of steam mop cleaners. Whilst these steam mop models have inferior suction power, they offer an alternative method for providing the best sterilization and sanitation, which is a factor for homes with children and pets.

The most popular type of vacuum cleaner is the upright, which accounted for a 55 per cent share of volume sales of vacuum cleaners in 2014. Hand-held was the second most popular type of vacuum cleaner, holding a 13 per cent share of volume sales. The third and fourth largest types of vacuum cleaners were other vacuum cleaners, which includes steam cleaners and stick vacuum cleaners. Cylinder vacuum cleaners, whilst popular in Europe, receive little promotion and attention in the US market.

Vacuum cleaners enjoy wide distribution in the US, being sold in traditional large appliance outlets, such as Sears, Best Buy and Home Depot, as well as in small appliance channels, such as Wal-Mart, Target and Bed, Bath & Beyond. The leading distribution channels are similar to those of other small electrical appliances: hypermarkets, mass merchandisers and furniture and furnishings stores. Online retailing has not had a major impact as an alternative channel. However, 11 per cent of vacuum purchases are made online, and the online trend is increasing.

At the end of 2012, iRobot, the leading manufacturer of robotic vacuum cleaners in the US, acquired Evolution Robotics Inc. for an estimated US$74 million. Evolution Robotics is known for its wet robotic floor cleaners, and has expanded the robotic floor care offerings that iRobot offers. iRobot's launch of its Braava floor mopping robot is a result of this acquisition.

Japan

Japanese standard vacuum cleaners are divided into two dust-collection formats – dust bag and cyclone. Over the review period, the rise of the cyclone format was fuelled by Dyson. However, the dust bag remained the predominant format.

The robotic vacuum cleaners' growth rate outperformed standard vacuum cleaners in 2014. The category developed over the review period to account for 6 per cent of the total vacuum cleaners' volume sales in 2014. Robot's Roomba has been a household name for robotic vacuum cleaners in recent years and revolutionized the way Japanese householders clean, as it offers greater time-saving benefits and sets the household free from such demanding housework. These benefits were in line with changing socioeconomic trends in Japan, such as the increasing number of double-income households and the ageing population. The high price points of robotic vacuum cleaners were accepted by these households as they are more affluent and less price sensitive.

Thus iRobot is a pioneer in the robotic vacuum cleaner category and its key brand Roomba has almost become a generic term for robotic vacuum cleaners among Japanese consumers. This reputation was driven by its strong marketing campaigns in consumer electronics stores. These efforts were successful in educating Japanese consumers, enabling iRobot to benefit from a boom in robotic vacuum cleaners after 2010. Its rivals, including Toshiba, Sharp, CCP and LG Electronics, also followed the leader entering the market between 2011 and 2014. These companies differentiated their offerings: Toshiba highlighted its robotic vacuum's superior cleaning abilities as a key

differentiator; low-cost manufacturer CCP appealed to consumers' wallets with its low priced product offerings that lacked the key features of other larger players; while LG Electronics featured robotic vacuum cleaners that offered greater noise reduction.

Cocorobo, Sharp's robotic vacuum cleaner, achieved substantial press coverage for its voice recognition technology, enabling it to respond to commands in many languages, such as Japanese, Chinese and English. With a camera attached to the product, consumers are able to monitor their pets or babies at home when they are away as the product automatically sends pictures to consumers' smartphones. Although the major consumer segments of robotic vacuum cleaners were busy households and the elderly, due to their limited time and physical disabilities, respectively, the added value of these offerings opened them up to wider segments including gadget lovers looking for advanced technology in their household electronics.

Electrolux, the Swedish headquartered manufacturer, is expected to perform well in the cylinder vacuum cleaner category over the coming years. In 2012, the company offered a new vacuum cleaner, Ergothree, with value-added functions, such as filtered expelling air and lower noise-levels. These product features were in response to the growing awareness of cleanliness and hygiene among Japanese consumers. Given that there was a rise in pollen allergy and other allergies among the population, such features will benefit from strong demand and will provide the company with a competitive edge in the Japanese vacuum cleaner market.

China

Vacuum cleaner sales in China are still at a low level compared to other countries, but the rapid growth of high-end vacuum cleaners, including upright vacuum cleaners and robotic vacuum cleaners, is driven by consumers' improving living standards. With ongoing urbanization in China, more households are choosing to use machines instead of labour to do housework; thus vacuum cleaners are becoming popular amongst local consumers. Due to smaller households in China and limited living space, smaller-sized cylinder vacuum cleaners are preferred by many consumers. In the meantime, upright vacuum cleaners are also considered space-saving and hence are popular amongst Chinese households.

The unit price of vacuum cleaners continues to rise in constant terms, thanks to increasing sales of high-end products.

Philips China leads the Chinese vacuum cleaner market benefiting from the company's established brand reputation. Philips's success lies in its wide product portfolio, including all types of vacuum cleaners, from, low- to high-end products in addition to intelligent robotic vacuum cleaners, catering to consumers' various needs. Philips's strong nationwide distribution network is another important factor in its success.

Albeit starting from a low base, robotic vacuum cleaners enjoyed faster volume growth than other vacuum cleaner types in 2014, due to Chinese consumers' developing interest in high-end products. Robotic vacuum cleaners boast intelligent functions and convenience of operation and are presented as fun to use, and this appeals to Chinese consumers' changing priorities – from saving money to enjoying life. There are two major brands which hold the lead in robotic vacuum cleaners, Ecovacs from Ecovacs Electrical and Fmart from Beijing Lierpu Appliances. Meanwhile, the dynamic growth of robotic vacuum cleaners attracted many players in standard vacuum cleaners to enter this niche. Philips and Puppy, for example, both launched robotic vacuum cleaners to gain more share. To defend themselves against the newcomers, Ecovacs and Fmart expanded their product ranges from the low-to high-end of the market in order to meet the needs of a wider range of consumers.

Australia

The category, cylinder vacuum cleaners, is the product area with the highest level of household penetration, reaching almost 72 per cent in 2014. More households have acquired vacuum cleaners, as they seek to make house cleaning easier, while many households acquired additional vacuum cleaners for smaller jobs, with this trend particularly benefiting stick vacuum cleaners (with battery chargers).

Robotic vacuum cleaners have seen a strong growth over the latest years, as these products moved further into the mainstream. Sales benefited strongly from the entry of major players Samsung in 2010 and LG in 2011, with these mainstream brands benefiting from wide distribution and strong consumer awareness. The high price of robotic vacuum cleaners, however, resulted in these products remaining a tiny niche in overall vacuum cleaners.

Electrolux continued to be the clear leader in vacuum cleaners in 2014 with close to 29 per cent retail volume share. The company offers the upper-mid-priced Electrolux brand and the entry-level Volta brand.

Private label continued to gain share in vacuum cleaners in 2014, with many consumers seeking basic products at the best available price. Private label is particularly strong in standard vacuum cleaners, where many are less interested in value-added features. In this product area, leading private label players are Woolworths and Wesfarmers.

The 2015 introduction of the Dyson 360 Eye

iRobot is now facing a threat as Dyson marks its foray into the robot vacuum cleaner market with its 360 Eye automated robot cleaner that claims to be more powerful, effective and intelligent than Roomba and other smart floor cleaners.

The Dyson 360 Eye, that took 16 years and an investment of around US$47 million, is equipped with a 360-degree panoramic camera that can 'see' an entire room and navigate accordingly. The camera captures up to 30 frames per second. These images are then processed by the internal software to assess the room's geometry and potential obstacles. The 360-degree panoramic camera is a breakthrough in the field of robotic vacuum cleaners, given that most of the other robotic vacuum cleaners are only equipped with some sensor system to look or feel around a room.

The 360 Eye also employs a set of flexible tank treads that will help it to climb over smaller obstacles enabling it to easily transition between rooms with subtle lips, ledges or steps.

Dyson's robotic vacuum is equipped with the cyclone technology and a full-width brush bar to suck up dirt and dust. According to the company, its powerful digital motor provides it with a suction capacity higher than that of any robotic vacuum cleaner. Dyson's 360 Eye can also be controlled by an app available on the iOS and Android platforms, which will enable users to schedule their cleaning (see picture below). It also enables the user to view maps of cleaning progress.

iRobot's Roomba has so far ruled the world of intuitive, higher-end robotic vacuum cleaners. Since the launch of Roomba in 2002, iRobot has sold more than 15 million robotic vacuum cleaners globally. Eight generations of Roomba have been introduced so far. Although more and more robotic vacuum cleaner

Source: Hannibal Hanschke/Reuters/Corbis.

brands have been introduced in the market by players like LG Electronics and Samsung, they have not been able to seriously cut Roomba's market share, and Roomba continues to be a household name.

Robotic floor cleaners have proved to be one of the fastest-growing consumer products in the past few years, and iRobot has capitalized on the demand. In such an evolving robot vacuum cleaner market, Dyson's 360 Eye camera is surely a breakthrough, providing it with a competitive edge. However, it is a bit early to determine the extent of the competitive threat to Roomba, given that Dyson's product is yet to be used in a real-world environment.

Dyson's new robot is also taller than Roomba, which might make it a bit difficult for it to clean under low furniture but it is better for cleaning between chair legs, for example. Moreover, pricing is an important factor. The Dyson 360 Eye will retail at the high-end of the market, for about £850, compared to the Roomba 980 that sells for £630.

Following the footsteps of Roomba, local electronics companies have also been developing robot cleaners with unique functions For instance, Sharp Corp.'s Cocorobo has voice communications, while Toshiba Corp.'s Torneo Robo automatically dumps dust into a box built into the charging dock. Robotic vacuum cleaners have been the key growth driver for iRobot. In this highly competitive market, it is expected that iRobot will not be far behind in bringing some innovation to Roomba to topple Dyson.

Meanwhile, it remains to be seen how Dyson's new cleaner is received in Japan, one of the biggest markets in the world for robotic vacuums. Roomba is already a market leader in Japan commanding around 80 per cent share of the Japanese market for robot cleaners.

QUESTIONS

1. Please discuss and evaluate Dyson's key competitive advantages in the home cleaning market, including the vacuum cleaner market.

2. Please discuss and evaluate Dyson's key competitive advantages in the robotic vacuum cleaner market.

3. Please discuss and evaluate the screening criteria that you would use for Dyson's IMS (International Market Selection) regarding the new Dyson 360 Eye. Please end up with a ranking list of the three most attractive countries of the seven countries in Table 1 (in answering this question you do not have to agree with Dyson's selection of Japan as the first market to enter).

4. Please select 'Distribution' (Place) and one other of the four 'Ps' from the marketing mix and argue how they should be designed for the Dyson 360 Eye introduction in the countries which were ranked 1, 2 and 3 in Question 3.

Source: different public reports, available online.

CASE STUDY IV.4

Triumph Motorcycles Ltd: rising from the ashes in the international motorcycle business

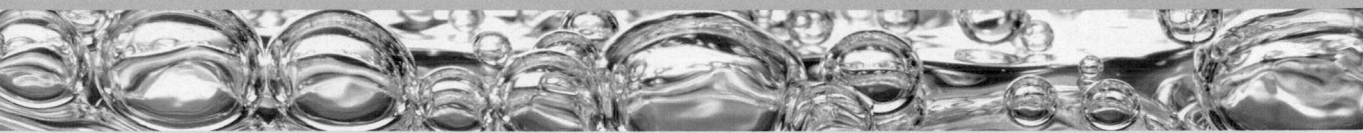

When Marlon Brando led a group of outlaw bikers in the 1950s film *The Wild One,* he rode a Triumph. It was the obvious choice back then. Britain was the biggest motorbike maker in the world and led the motorcycling world in performance and engineering innovation with such bygone makers as BSA, Matchless and Vincent, to name just a few. And Triumph was winning every race in sight. But after bad management and botched rescue attempts by successive governments, Triumph went bankrupt in 1983. However, the marque is back, starring in films such as *Mission Impossible 2.* When Tom Cruise roared on to the screen on a sleek motorcycle, it wasn't a Harley or a Honda but a Triumph, which also featured in Arnold Schwarzenegger's *Terminator 3.* The Triumph bike has captured approximately 75 per cent of the 'Hollywood' market, one of few US markets where Triumph is the market leader.

Product segments in the motorcycle market

Motorcycles are often classified by engine capacity in three categories:

- lightweight (50–250cc)
- middleweight (251–650cc)
- heavyweight (651cc and up).

Triumph's motorcycles are in the middleweight and heavyweight category only, competing mainly with companies such as Harley-Davidson, Ducati, BMW and, of course, the main Japanese motorcycle manufacturers.

Motorcycles are also classified by types of use, generally separated into four groups: standard, which emphasizes simplicity and cost; performance, which focuses on racing and speed; touring, which emphasizes comfort and amenities for long-distance travel; and custom, which features styling and individual owner customization. The standard models tend to have the smaller engines, while the performance motorcycles often have an engine capacity of more than 251cc. The touring models typically have a comfortable seating position and their engines range from middleweight to super heavyweight types.

Source: Adriano Castelli/Shutterstock.com.

History

The credit for Triumph's rebirth goes to John Bloor, a builder who bought the company's remains (the Triumph brand name and the company's designs and tooling) for about US$200,000. He has invested £80 million on, among other things, a new plant in Leicestershire. The product has been completely revamped. New engines were crucial. Most have a distinctive three-cylinder layout, which makes them more powerful than the two-cylinder bikes made in Europe and the US, and more relaxing than the high-revving four-cylinder bikes made in Japan.

Bloor was betting on the nostalgic power of the Triumph brand. Back in the 1950s and 1960s, Triumph and Harley-Davidson were fierce rivals. The original Triumphs offered lighter weight and better handling than Harley's machines, and sales of the British bikes were stronger in the US than they were in their home market. The bikes are also part of US folklore. Despite what flag-waving Harley fans in bars may mistakenly claim, Steve McQueen in *The Great Escape* and Marlon Brando in *The Wild One* rode Triumphs. James Dean had one too. Legend and myth and the power of branding do not come any better.

Bloor's first act as a prospective motorcycle manufacturer was to hire three employees of the original Triumph company who had been involved in developing new models. Bloor realized that the engine is everything in a motorcycle, and there is no way to make a bike with a dull motor feel red-hot to the customer. So while he outsourced other parts of the bike, he put his team of engineers and metalworkers to work designing new liquid-cooled, three- and four-cylinder engines that would save costs by sharing internal parts.

Bloor's decision to keep a three-cylinder engine from the original line-up turned out to be a great marketing move, and it has helped the company stand out from the crowd. Most other bikes use two- or four-cylinder engines. Triumph's soulful three-cylinder has won a place in the hearts of many bikers, who tend to be a discriminating bunch when it comes to how an engine feels and delivers power on the road. Three-cylinder engines are also perfect for middle-aged men who are getting back into bikes.

Today

Big-bike sales doubled in Britain between 2005 and 2010, and the buyers are no longer youngsters needing cheap wheels but older people with the money to spend on expensive toys. Many of these born-again bikers have not touched a motorbike since their teens, and find Japanese offerings just a bit too fast and flash for their taste.

Triumph's sales have risen from 2,000 in 1991 to approximately 50,000 in 2014 – similar to the old Triumph's peak of 50,000 in the late 1960s. Most buyers now are aged between 35 and 55. US sales (which make up 27 per cent of the total) have increased since 2001 when Triumph introduced a retro-styled bike, called the Bonneville, and are now rising at an annual rate of 40 per cent. The Bonneville (a twin-cylinder, 800cc machine, priced at US$7,000–8,000) is about 85 per cent faithful to the 650cc Bonneville of yore, which was the machine to ride in the 1960s if you were not a Harley fan. Further, introduction of a Harley-style cruiser bike is being considered by the Triumph management team. Taking marketing cues from Harley-Davidson, Triumph also offers a line of clothing and accessories.

Growth should be consistent. Sales are rising by 15 per cent a year, putting Triumph within sight of European rivals such as BMW and Ducati. Triumph's marketing manager believes there is plenty of scope for growth in the US, where 550,000 big bikes are sold each year. Triumph currently accounts for around 3 per cent of that market, compared with 14 per cent of the British market. To grab more, it needs to exploit not just its classic name but also its old race-winning reputation.

Total sales in 2014 were approximately £345 million, the number of employees was about 550 and the net profit was approximately £22 million.

The company currently sells its 50,000 units per year through a global network of around 700 dealers in more than 25 major national markets. In these markets, Triumph also offers a clothing and accessories line designed according to bike and rider style.

Of the motorcycles Triumph produces, 56 per cent are sold in Europe, 27 per cent in the US and Canada, 3 per cent in Japan and 14 per cent in the rest of the world. The company is actively reviewing niche markets for other specialized forms of motorcycles to add to its line-up, and is keeping to the trend of dealers who stock a full range of branded motorcycles, and only motorcycles.

The downturn of the Japanese manufacturers' market shares

In 1981, Japan's motorbike industry was in a state of blissful ignorance. Its manufacturers had managed to dominate the world in not much over a decade and annual production had hit 7.4 million units. Although they did not know it, this was to be their best year.

Three decades later and Japanese manufacturers are nowhere near as dominant. While they still loom large on the global motorbike market, 1981's record domestic production has declined to just 2.4 million. This serves as a stark reminder of a painful trend for all types of Japanese manufacturers as their domestic costs have risen, their markets have matured and their rivals have sharpened their game.

In 2001, two Japanese manufacturers – Suzuki and Kawasaki – joined forces to jointly produce and develop new bikes, marking the end of the 'big four' in Japan, where they ruled alongside much bigger rivals Honda and Yamaha.

The hollowing out shift to overseas production through joint ventures and wholly owned plants has also cut into domestic production in Japan.

The Suzuki–Kawasaki tie-up also serves as a symbol for what has happened to Japan's motorbike industry in the last two decades. Once lazy and inefficient rivals such as Ducati, BMW and Harley-Davidson have found a way of replying to the competitive threat from Japan and are clawing back market share. In Europe, for example, Japan's market share fell from 80 to 50 per cent in 2005–2010, although numbers have risen. In the vital US market its share fell by 10 per cent between 2000 and 2010.

The rise and rise of the Japanese motorbike manufacturers owed as much to luck as to design. Manufacturers were servicing a huge domestic market for many years, which generated the profits that financed the export drive. It also gave the Japanese a finely honed design and production machine that churned out faster, more reliable and better-looking bikes – and did so every year. The weak yen also made Japanese exports intensely competitive.

In addition, they were up against severely weakened domestic manufacturers in the west. Triumph, BSA and Norton in the UK, for example, were spent forces, and the country was in the middle of labour disputes that generated a lazy attitude towards design and technology, producing machines that looked old-fashioned in comparison to their Japanese rivals.

The Japanese manufacturers, perhaps complacent in their success, failed to spot a key change in the motorbike-buying world. They were too obsessed with technology and assembly quality and did not recognize that motorbikes had become consumer goods that had a brand value. Harley-Davidson led the way, with branded goods ranging from desk clocks to women's thongs adding hugely to profits.

Japanese manufacturers based their bikes on racing models. Undoubtedly Japanese bikes are lighter and faster, but it takes a lot of skill to ride them. Western manufacturers have been designing for people who like to ride normal bikes in a normal environment. As Japan's rivals have caught up with the technology, they have also managed to inject something extra.

Ducati conveys on two wheels the kind of image its Italian counterpart, Ferrari, has on four. Triumph has capitalized on its Britishness and the appeal of the marque's previous incarnation with such models as the Bonneville. Harley-Davidson has built up an appeal for weekend rebels with US$70,000-plus salaries. BMW has combined engineering excellence with design flair.

However, to talk of the demise of the Japanese motorbike industry would be unwise. Honda remains the largest manufacturer of motorbikes in the world, but the Japanese are removing themselves from the big bike category. Honda, Yamaha and Suzuki are concentrating on 100–500cc bikes for mass production in the developing countries of Asia. The bulk of Japanese-made bikes are small and service the growing economies of Asia, where having a 50cc or 100cc bike is the first step on a transportation ladder that eventually leads to a Toyota Corolla. India and China are huge and growing markets for the Japanese, and Suzuki says it hopes its new link with its smaller rival will help its efforts in China.

The alliance between Suzuki and Kawasaki has more to do with these markets than the competition in the superbike league. It allows them to pare costs considerably by jointly procuring parts and joining forces on product design, development and production. It also matches similar moves by Honda, which has reduced the number of its Japanese motorcycle production lines

from five to two in recent years. While Japanese manufacturers may be facing competition at the top end of the market, motorbikes are a high-volume game – and in this game the Japanese are still the winners.

The global competitive situation today

The competitive market situation in the three main regions of the world is shown in Table 1.

Market trends

In industrialized wealthy economies such as Japan, the US and Europe, motorcycles are often purchased for recreation in addition to basic transport. In developing economies and others with low income per capita, motorcycles or smaller two-wheelers were purchased primarily for basic transport, and the market was distinctly different. Historically, large touring bikes, cruisers and racers sold almost exclusively in the wealthy economies while motorcycles with small engine displacement and mopeds made up the vast majority of sales in the developing nations. Decreasing trends in the overall market in some nations were due, in large part, to the replacement of two-wheeled vehicles by automobiles as the countries became more affluent.

The challenge

A big problem for Triumph is still the relative low unit volume of motorcycles. Triumph sells about 15 per cent of the Harley-Davidson sales volume. Being so small makes it hard to develop new bikes or to buy good components at a decent price. To maintain quality, Triumph makes about a third of its components

Table 1	The three main market areas for heavyweight motorcycles (651cc) number of registrations 2014		
	North America	Europe	Asia/ Pacific
Total industry (000s)	480	397	80
Market share	%	%	%
Harley-Davidson/Buell	47.0	9.6	24.5
Honda	14.3	12.3	17.8
Yamaha	9.2	13.6	12.0
Kawasaki	7.5	11.3	13.8
Suzuki	12.7	15.5	10.7
BMW	2.0	15.1	4.4
Ducati	–	5.9	3.2
Triumph	3.0	7.5	1.5
Others	4.3	9.2	12.1
Total	**100.0**	**100.0**	**100.0**

Source: adapted from Harley-Davidson Financial Report (2014), and other public sources.

in-house, and imports many from China and Japan. That clobbers profits. In 2003, Triumph also lost money. Bloor's building business, which is quite profitable, could cover those losses, but that is not a long-term solution.

As a consequence, the strategy was set for increasing sale and market share in the area of large motorcycles. In 2003, Bloor hired a McKinsey consultant, first as an advisor and, later, as a commercial director (Tue Mantoni). Among other projects, Mantoni worked on the introduction of the world's biggest motorcycle; the Rocket III, which has a 2,294cc engine. As Bloor thinks that Triumph's market share in North America is not satisfactory, and he considers the potential for Triumph in the US is huge, he has collected the following information about US motorcycle consumers.

The motorcycle market in the US

The Hollywood myth of the young and wild motorcycle rider became less and less a reality in the 1990s and beginning of 2000s, according to Motorcycle Industry Council statistics regarding heavyweight motorcycle owners (see also Table 2).

The 1990s rider was more mainstream and less likely to be a part of some counterculture motorcycle gang. 'The end of the road for today's motorcyclist is just as likely to be a boardroom as a burger joint,' said Beverly St Clair Baird, Managing Director of Discover Today's Motorcycling, a public awareness campaign of the Motorcycle Industry Council. The average motorcyclist is male, 33 years old, married, a university graduate and his annual household income or US$95,100 – significantly more than the average US household.

The average income of the motorcyclist of the 2000s has more than doubled since 1980. In 1980, fewer than 10 per cent of riders made over US$50,000 per year: by 2010, more than 90 per cent of riders had attained that income level. Riders from the 1990s onwards were also much older. They used their bikes more for leisure and recreation than had the riders of the early 1980s. The typical rider was interested in the outdoors. In surveys about their other interests, fishing and hunting topped the list. The demographic profile showed that motorcyclists came from all walks of life and a variety of occupational, educational and economic backgrounds.

Motorcycle accidents and fatalities dropped by more than half between 1985 and 2010. In addition to state helmet laws, this was attributed in part to an increasing

Table 2	Motorcycle owner profile in the US		
	% of total owners		
	2000	**2005**	**2010**
Age (years)			
<17	24.6	14.9	8.3
18–24	24.3	20.7	15.5
25–29	14.2	18.7	17.1
30–34	10.2	13.8	16.4
35–39	8.8	8.7	14.3
40–49	9.4	13.2	16.3
>50	5.7	8.1	10.1
Not stated	2.8	1.9	2.0
Median age	24.0	27.1	32.0
Mean age	26.9	28.5	33.1
Marital status			
Single	51.7	47.6	41.4
Married	44.3	50.3	56.6
Not stated	4.0	2.1	2.3
Highest level of education			
Grade school	13.5	7.5	5.9
Some high school	18.9	15.3	9.5
High school graduate	34.6	36.5	39.4
Some college	17.6	21.6	25.2
College graduate	9.2	12.2	12.4
Postgraduate	3.1	5.2	5.2
Not stated	3.1	1.7	2.4
Occupation of owner			
Labourer/semi-skilled	20.7	23.2	24.1
Professional/technical	18.8	19.0	20.3
Mechanic/craftsman	23.3	15.1	13.1
Manager/proprietor	8.6	8.9	9.3
Clerical/sales	9.3	7.8	6.8
Service worker	7.1	6.4	6.6
Farmer/farm labourer	4.6	5.1	2.1
Military	1.9	1.6	1.5
Other	0.0	4.6	13.1
Not stated	5.7	8.3	3.1
Household income for prior year			
<$24,999	9.1	6.9	3.4
$25,000–$49,999	10.0	9.3	4.4
$50,000–$69,999	16.9	11.6	7.8
$70,000–$89,999	17.9	15.4	15.8
$90,000–$109,999	12.5	18.3	26.4
$110,000–$149,999	5.9	11.4	19.6
>$150,000	2.4	6.1	9.9
Don't know	25.3	21.0	12.7
Median	$80,500	$92,600	$95,100

Source: based on Motorcycle Industry Council.

trend for rider education and training programmes. Enrolment in these programmes, sponsored by individual manufacturers and industry groups such as the Motorcycle Industry Council, rose dramatically in the 1990s and 2000s. Motorcyclists today are likely to be more skilled and responsible than the riders of the 1970s and 1980s.

Women and motorcycling

Women, though not more than 10 per cent of the US riding population, are a growing segment of the industry. The AMA (American Motorcycle Association) has had women members since 1907. In 2010, nearly a million women in the US rode their own motorcycles. The average female rider was almost 48 years old compared with her 32-year-old male counterpart. Of the women riders, 74 per cent were married, and 44 per cent attended college. The largest segment of women riders had professional/technical careers. They belonged to a riders club and were passengers for a few years before they purchased their first bike. Most women used their motorcycles for either long-distance touring (36 per cent of riding time) or for local street use (31 per cent). Only 10 per cent of their riding time was spent commuting or running errands. More women's families positively supported their riding than the families of male riders (64 vs 55 per cent); however, more men's friends than women's friends supported their riding.

Profile of the typical Harley-Davidson rider

As with the average, Harley-Davidson (H-D) has about 85 per cent male and 15 per cent female riders. However, the household average income is higher than for the average rider, about US$100,000. The manufacturer has researched the 2010 purchases of H-D motorcycles. It shows that 41 per cent previously owned a H-D; 31 per cent were competitor motorcycles and the rest (28 per cent) were new to motorcycling.

Fashion trends

Motorcycling was a major fashion trend in the 1990s.

The sales of motorcycles increased 50 per cent from 1995 to 2010, and motorcycle accessories, fashions and parts followed this upward trend. Owners were making personal statements by customizing their bikes with accessories, and more than 60 per cent of all owners purchased accessories in 2010 (compared with only 30 per cent in 1985). Many non-motorcycle riders or owners invested in motorcycle fashions. Men spent more on average on motorcycle fashions than women (US$227 per year for men vs US$180 for women). Overseas motorcyclists followed the trend as well. Motorcycle fashions and accessory sales rose in both Europe and Japan in the 1990s and 2000s.

The motorcycle market in general

Motorcycle registration requires compliance with state and federal Motor Vehicle Safety Standards. Over one-third of the nation's motorcycles were concentrated in just five states: California, Texas, New York, Florida and Ohio. Over 15 per cent of the motorcycles in the US were in California alone. Overall, there were an average of 1.5 motorcycles per 100 people in the US in 2010. Most motorcycles in the country were registered for on-highway use: over half of these had engine displacements over 749cc, and more than 80 per cent over 450cc.

QUESTIONS

1. Design a global marketing programme for Triumph, including a suggestion for the priority of the 4Ps: product, price, place and promotion.

2. How should the marketing programme for the US market differ from your suggested marketing programme in Question 1?

3. A member of Triumph's management team has proposed designing a special motorcycle for women. Do you think this is a good idea?

Sources: Stuart F. Brown (2002) 'A sweet Triumph', *Fortune Small Business,* 12(3/4), pp. 48–51; Kampert, P. (2003) 'British motor-cycles "Triumphant" return – Triumph motorcycles are roaring back into the American market', http://money.cnn.com/2003/08/04/pf/autos/triumph/index.htm; http://www.mic.org/.

PART I
The decision whether
to internationalize
Chs 1–4

PART II
Deciding which
markets to enter
Chs 5–8

PART III
Market entry
strategies
Chs 9–13

PART IV
Designing the
global marketing
programme
Chs 14–17

PART V
Implementing and
coordinating the
global marketing
programme
Chs 18–19

Part V Contents

Part V Case studies

PART V
Implementing and coordinating the global marketing programme

Introduction to Part V

While the first four parts of this book have considered the set-up necessary to carry out global marketing activities, Part V will discuss the implementation and coordination phase.

An essential criterion for success in selling and negotiating internationally is to be able to adapt to each business partner, company and situation. Chapter 18 therefore discusses how the international negotiator should cope with the different cultural background of its counterparts. A part of this chapter will also deal with how knowledge and learning can be transferred across borders within the company and between cooperation partners.

As companies evolve from purely domestic firms to multinationals, their organizational structure, coordination and control systems must change to reflect new global marketing strategies. Chapter 19 is concerned with how organizational structures and marketing budgets (including other control systems) have to be adjusted as the firm itself and market conditions change.

PART V VIDEO CASE STUDY Stella & Dot

download from **www.pearson.co.uk/hollensen**

Despite co-founding the successful WeddingChannel.com, Jessica Herrin found herself re-evaluating her personal and entrepreneurial priorities. In 2004, she decided to align the two with the founding of Stella & Dot, for which she also serves as CEO. San Francisco-based Stella & Dot is a direct-sales jewellery business, which allows women all over the country to sell bracelets, necklaces, rings and other accessories to friends and acquaintances, similarly to how Tupperware or beauty supplies were peddled in the past.

At the heart of the business model is 'social selling'. Stella and Dot representatives, or 'stylists' (of which there are more than 30,000), organize 'trunk parties' at the homes of friends, contacts or family members where the jewellery is showcased. In return, the stylist gets paid a percentage of the sales in cash. And the person who hosted the party gets a percentage of the sales in jewellery. Stella & Dot's stylists get started by paying US$199 for catalogues, order forms and other training materials, and receive US$350 worth of jewellery to show off at 'trunk shows'.

In 2011, Sequoia Capital acquired 10 per cent of the shares for US$37 million, setting the total value of Stella & Dot at $370 million.

In 2014, Stella & Dot had a turnover of approximately US$250 million, with around US$25 million in profit. Since its start, Stella & Dot has paid in total US$200 million in sales commission to the approximately 30,000 stylists around the world (right now Stella & Dot is working in six countries). That provides approximately US$6,700 on average for each stylist.

Source: Ari Perilstein/Getty Images.

Questions

1. Describe the business and distribution model that Stella & Dot build on.

2. What are the opportunities and challenges in globalizing the Stella & Dot's business model?

3. When Stella & Dot globalize their business, how should they incorporate all the 'stylists'' operations into a consolidated international marketing budget?

Please look at the video clips at **www.pearsoned.co.uk/hollensen**

CHAPTER 18
Cross-cultural sales negotiations

Contents

Case studies

Learning objectives

After studying this chapter you should be able to:

- Discuss why intercultural selling through negotiation is one of the greatest challenges in global marketing
- Explain the major phases in a cross-cultural negotiation process
- Discuss how BATNA can be used in international negotiation
- Discuss how learning and knowledge transfer across borders can increase international competitiveness
- Discuss the implications of Hofstede's research for the firm's cross-cultural negotiation
- Explain some important aspects of intercultural preparation
- Discuss opportunities and pitfalls with global multicultural project groups
- Explain the complexity and dangers of transnational bribery.

18.1 Introduction

Culture is a dimension that intervenes at each stage of the negotiation. It plays a role in the way people conceive of the situation even before any discussion starts because it contributes to structuring the problem. It influences the strategic approach developed in terms of competition or cooperation.

To remain competitive and to flourish in the complex and fast-changing world of international business, companies must look worldwide not only for potential markets but also for sources of high-quality but less expensive materials and labour. Even small business managers who never leave their home countries will deal with markets and a workforce whose cultural background is increasingly diverse. Those managers with the skills to understand and adapt to different cultures are better positioned to succeed in these endeavours and to compete successfully in the world market.

Culture contributes to orchestrating behaviours, drawing a line between what is desirable and what is not acceptable. It conditions perception in providing meaning to what is observed, organizing and codifying communication. It influences the choice of norms for fairness that will seal the final agreement. By the importance and significance that it gives to the context, culture directly influences the negotiation process. Fundamentally, negotiation as a process which is intended to reach a goal is a process of a strategic nature, taking place in a cultural context and conducted by people who are themselves cultural vectors. It would be unrealistic not to take this into account. Culture is the variable that distinguishes international negotiation from any other type. Before engaging in such a lengthy and complex negotiation process as establishing a joint venture, it is essential for an international negotiator, whether a buyer or a seller, to assimilate basic elements of the counterpart's culture. Such a task will enable a better understanding of what really goes on around the negotiation table and in the immediate environment, to avoid misunderstandings, to communicate more effectively, to be better equipped to solve deadlocks that may surface and to be able to diagnose the real problems.

Consequently, conducting business with people from other cultures will never be as easy as doing business at home.

In the early stages of internationalization, small and medium-sized enterprises (SMEs) may treat cross-cultural markets as purely short-term economic opportunities to be pursued in order to maximize short-term profit. However, learning more about the nature of culture and how it affects business practices can increase the chances of success, even in the early cross-cultural business negotiations. When people from two different cultures are conducting business, making assumptions about another culture is often detrimental and can result in miscommunication. Managers in SMEs should develop realistic assumptions based on a truthful appreciation of the culture and should refrain from any thoughts of cultural stereotyping. Exhibit 18.1 shows that cultural influences can be difficult to predict.

EXHIBIT 18.1 Google gives a clock as gift in China

As Google was growing and consolidating their purchase in Asia, one Christmas they decided to give away clocks to their worldwide clients. When they sent the clock to their Chinese partners they didn't realize that it was actually considered a very offensive gift, because in the Chinese (and Asian) culture it means that 'your time is up'.

Source: based on Kim (2011).

All successful international marketers have personal representation abroad: face-to-face negotiations with the customer are the heart of the sales job. Negotiations are necessary to reach an agreement on the total exchange transaction, comprising such issues as the product to be delivered, the price to be paid, the payment schedule and the service agreement.

International sales negotiations have many characteristics that distinguish them from negotiations in the domestic setting. First and foremost, the cultural background of the negotiating parties is different. Successful negotiations therefore require some understanding of each party's culture and may also require the adoption of a negotiating strategy that is consistent with the other party's cultural system. It is interesting to note that Japanese negotiators, among other things, routinely request background information on US companies and key negotiators. Japanese negotiators therefore often know in advance the likely negotiating strategies and tactics of the other side.

Two different negotiation cultures: rule-based and relationship cultures

Basically, we meet two distinctly different negotiation cultures:

1. *Rule-based negotiation cultures* are found primarily in the western world. Westerners tend to trust this system, while people elsewhere trust their friends and family. Westerners organize their business around discrete deals that are drawn up as contracts or agreements and enforced by a legal system. Rule-based cultures are universalist precisely because they are rule-based. While relationship-based cultures invest authority in human beings, rule-based cultures respect the rules for their own sake. Western rulers derive their authority from the rules they enforce and by which they are chosen, not from who they are. Rules can command this kind of respect only if they are seen as inherently logical and reasonable; but logic is universal, and rules worthy of observance are therefore viewed as universally valid.
2. *Relationship negotiation cultures* (e.g. Asian cultures), by contrast, are based primarily on loyalty and obligation to friends, family or superiors rather than on a system of rules. There is a traditional preference for building relationships rather than making deals, and the relationship-based approach remains the more effective one today in many contexts. Bargaining across the table tends to be regarded as confrontation rather than negotiation, even when it is strictly regulated by protocol, as in Japan. Confrontational bargaining is prevalent in street markets precisely because the parties typically do not have a working relationship. This kind of bargaining is acceptable when long-term collaboration is not required. However, when undertaking the major projects on which civilization rests, it is best to develop harmony and trust among the parties rather than rely on western-style negotiation.

Bribery tends to be more prevalent in relationship-based cultures because building a relationship requires time and effort. There is always a temptation to take a short cut. Rule-based systems, on the other hand, are particularly vulnerable to cheating. This stems from the fact that behaviour is regulated as much by respect for rules as respect for people (Hooker, 2009).

18.2 Cross-cultural negotiations

A firm entering a psychically distant market is likely to perceive large differences between the two countries, resulting in high uncertainty (Magnusson and Boyle, 2009).

Faced with such different customs, perceptions and language, the most common human tendency is to stereotype the other party in a negative way. A crucial perception is knowing what to look for and thoroughly researching the characteristics of a culture before conducting negotiations.

One thing to look for concerns *time*, the perception of which is often culturally patterned. Thus, there are great differences in people's views of time all over the world. Western cultures in general, and industrialized societies in particular, view time as unilinear, so activities need be scheduled. They view time as valuable, as a commodity, a thing that can be saved, spent or wasted. They budget their time as they budget their money. Hence the saying 'Time is money'. They value promptness and deplore the waste and passing of time. They don't like to be kept waiting.

Westerners often rush into a business and their impatience is often exploited, especially by the Chinese and Japanese negotiators. As Oriental nations, deeply influenced by Confucian ideas, the Chinese and Japanese businesspeople place a high value on rituals and the establishment of personal rapport before really getting down to business. They usually do not consider the time it might take them to do so. In business negotiations they will keep on saying 'yes, yes' instead of a straightforward 'no' to the proposals or terms they don't want to accept. Their view of time is much more flexible than that of westerners (Mayfield, 1997; Huang, 2010).

In the Middle East and Africa, people typically lack a strict sense of time. The punctual westerner who insists on the meeting of deadlines will surely be kept waiting. However, once a businessperson is finally invited into the manager's office, the interview will last as long as is necessary to transact the business, even though the next visitor may be kept waiting for a long time.

Understanding other cultures is often based on tolerance. Trust and respect are essential conditions in several cultures, e.g. the Japanese, Chinese, Mexican and most Latin American cultures. The Japanese may require several meetings before actual negotiation issues are discussed, while North Americans and northern Europeans are inclined to do business as soon as possible. Culture affects a range of strategies, including the many ways they are implemented. Israelis prefer direct forms of negotiation, whereas Egyptians prefer an indirect form. Egyptians interpret Israeli directness as aggressive, and are insulted, while the Israelis view Egyptian indirectness with impatience, and consider it insincere. This cultural difference endangers any negotiation between business people in the two countries.

Even the language of negotiation can be deceptive. Compromise for North Americans and western Europeans is equal to morality, good faith and fair play. To the Mexicans and other Latin Americans, compromise means losing dignity and integrity; in Russia and the Middle East it is a sign of weakness. Furthermore, members of other cultures may regard the common western ideal of a persuasive communicator as aggressive, superficial and insincere.

The cross-cultural negotiation process

Negotiation process
A process in which two or more entities come together to discuss common and conflicting interests in order to reach an agreement of mutual benefit.

A **negotiation process** can be defined as 'a process in which two or more entities come together to discuss common and conflicting interests in order to reach an agreement of mutual benefit' (Harris and Moran, 1987, p. 55). The negotiation process is significantly influenced by the cultures within which the negotiators (typically a buyer and a seller) have been socialized and educated. Cultural differences prevalent in the international sales negotiation process can have a tremendous impact upon the process itself as well as its outcome.

The cross-cultural negotiation process can be divided into two different parts: the non-task-related interaction and the task-related interaction (see Figure 18.1) – each will be discussed in the following sections (Simintiras and Thomas, 1998; Simintiras and Reynolds, 2001; Salacuse, 2010).

Figure 18.1 shows that the cross-cultural negotiation process is very much influenced by the cultural 'distance' between seller and buyer. This perspective is further developed in Figure 18.2.

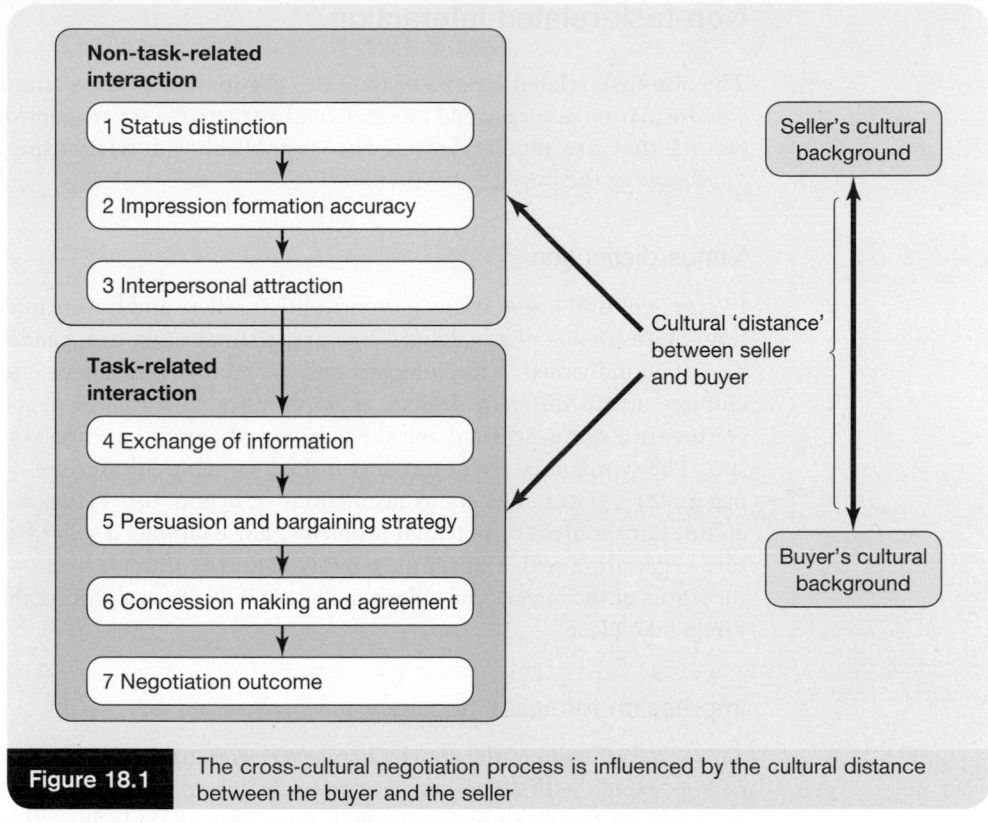

Figure 18.1   The cross-cultural negotiation process is influenced by the cultural distance between the buyer and the seller

Sources: adapted from Simintiras, A.C. and Thomas, A.H. (1998) and Simintiras, A.C. and Reynolds, N. (2001).

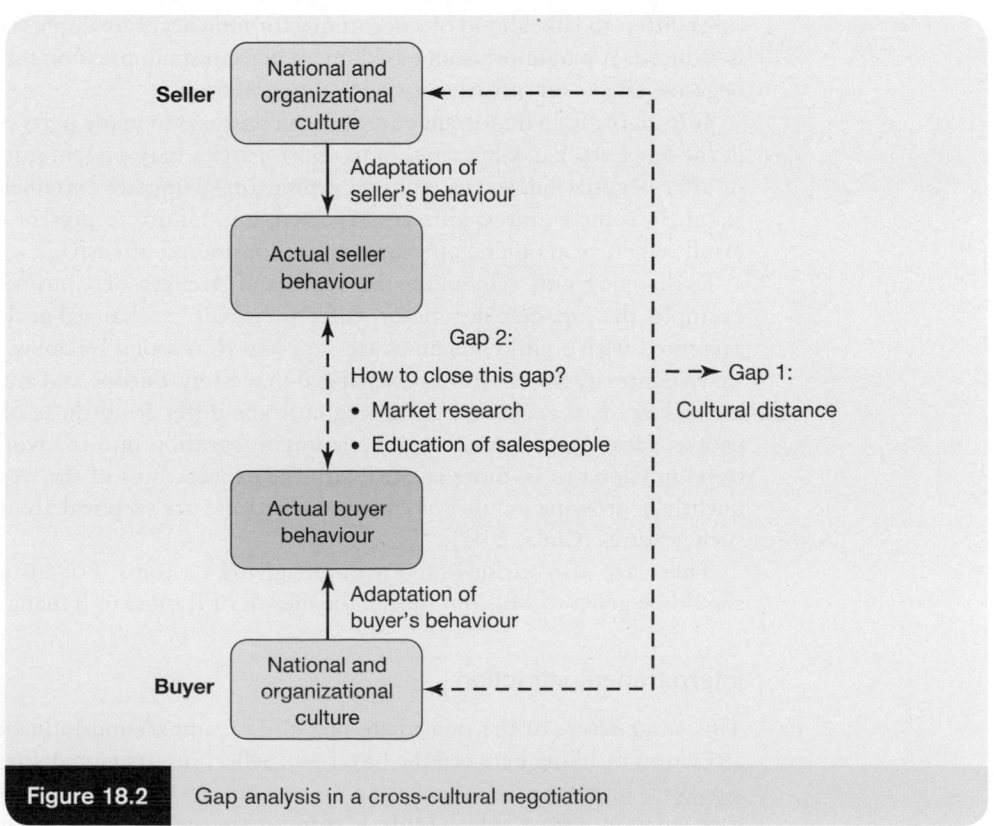

Figure 18.2   Gap analysis in a cross-cultural negotiation

Non-task-related interaction

The non-task-related aspects of the sales negotiation process (status distinction, impression formation accuracy and interpersonal attractiveness) are considered first, as it is these factors that are more relevant when establishing a relationship with the buyer, i.e. *approaching* the buyer.

Status distinction

In cross-cultural negotiations it is critical that sellers and buyers understand status distinction. Status distinction is defined by interpersonal rank, age, gender, education, the position of an individual in the company and the relative position of one's company. Different cultures attach different degrees of importance to status in negotiations. High-context cultures are status-oriented and the meaning of communication is internalized in the person. The words used by negotiators in high-context cultures are not as important as the negotiator's status. The status distinctions of negotiators between high- and low-context cultures are sources of potential problems. For example, a seller from a high-context culture negotiating with a buyer from a low-context culture is likely to attach importance to the status of the buyer. The seller expects the buyer to reciprocate this respect, but this will rarely take place.

Impression formation accuracy

This stage refers to initial contact between negotiators. The first two minutes that a salesperson spends with a prospect are the most important (the 'moment of truth'). Meeting someone for the first time, individuals have immediate feelings that precede rationalized thought processes; these feelings lead to the formation of instant opinions that are often based on minimal information. As the perceptions of the individuals from dissimilar cultures differ, the likelihood of a negotiator forming accurate impressions of the counterpart is reduced. A bad impression based on an inaccurate impression formation may also have negative effects on subsequent stages of negotiation.

Gift-giving is an important part of doing business in many parts of the world, especially in the Far East, e.g. China and India. Both parties may present gifts to each other before or after negotiation, so customs concerning gift-giving are extremely important to understand. In some cultures, gifts are expected, and failure to present them is considered an insult, whereas in others, offering a gift is considered offensive.

Exchanging gifts symbolizes the depth and strength of a business relationship to, for example, the Japanese negotiator. Gifts are usually exchanged at the first meeting. When presented with a gift, companies are expected to respond by doing the same in return. In sharp contrast, gifts are rarely exchanged in western Europe and are usually not appropriate. Likewise, the Chinese gift-giving customs differ from those of the English-speaking people. However, with China's increasing integration into the world economy there is a trend in China to be more aligned with the expectations of the western partners. Consequently, a growing number of Chinese companies are sceptical about gift giving and other such gestures (Chua, 2012).

There are also various taboos in gift-giving customs. For instance, no gifts of food should be given to Muslims during the month of Ramadan (Huang, 2010).

Interpersonal attraction

This stage refers to the immediate face-to-face impression influenced by the feelings of attraction or liking between the buyer and seller. Interpersonal attraction can have either a positive or a negative influence on the negotiation outcome. Similarity between negotiators can induce trust, which leads, in turn, to interpersonal attraction. Individuals who are attracted to each other are likely to make concessions in the bargaining process. Thus an individual negotiator may give up economic rewards for the rewards of the satisfaction derived from the relationship with an attractive partner.

Zhang and Dodgson (2007) offered an interesting character sketch of the founder of a Korean start-up IT company, Mr Lee:

> *We found Mr Lee was influenced by his partners, and sometimes followed their advice – even though he knew they were not necessarily right, because he could not face losing business relations from his personal networks. (p. 345)*

Korean negotiation culture is based on Confucianism and its values permeate every aspect of society. Like other Asian countries, Korea is a society where group harmony within social networks, and company loyalty and commitment, are greatly appreciated collectivistic attributes.

Task-related interaction

Once a relationship has successfully been established between buyer and seller, the task-related aspects of the cross-cultural negotiation process become more important. However, it should be remembered that even though the non-task-related factors are not of prime importance at this stage, they could still have an impact on the negotiation process and the final outcome.

Exchange of information

At this point in the process, a clear understanding of the negotiator's needs and expectations is essential as a point of departure for an effective communication flow between the partners. More specifically, there is an emphasis on the participants' expected utilities of the various alternatives open to them. The amount of information that has to be exchanged explicitly will vary from culture to culture, and with the extra complexity of several thousand languages and local dialects in the world, communication in cross-cultural negotiations through verbal means is complex and difficult. Even in cases when participants understand each other and are mutually fluent, the meaning of the information exchanged can be lost as a result of different meanings of words and across cultures. In addition to difficulties with verbal communication, cross-cultural sales negotiations are subject to non-verbal problems, such as body language, which can reduce the possibility that the negotiators will understand their differences and their similarities accurately.

Persuasion and bargaining strategy

This phase of the negotiation process refers to a negotiator's attempts to modify the performance expectations of the other party through the use of various persuasive tactics. There are various styles of persuasion and each culture has its own style of persuasion. According to Anglemar and Stern (1978), there are two basic approaches to the negotiation process: representational and instrumental strategies.

When *representational strategies* are used, communication is based on identification of problems, a search for solutions and the selection of the most appropriate course of action; for example, the salesperson may cooperate with the buyer and seek information on the buyer's views of the situation.

When *instrumental strategies* are used, communication involves affecting the other party's behaviour and attitudes; for example, a salesperson may influence the buyer with persuasive promises, commitments, rewards and punishments. The existence of a friendly and cooperative negotiation climate favours the use of the representational bargaining strategy.

Concession-making and agreement

This stage refers to the manoeuvring of negotiators from their initial position to a point of agreement on what is being negotiated. Negotiators from different cultures have different approaches to concession-making. For example, while in low-context cultures negotiators are likely to use logic, individuals in high-context cultures are more likely to use personalized arguments.

BATNA

Best alternative to a negotiated agreement. Negotiators cannot make a wise decision about whether to accept a negotiated agreement unless they know what the alternatives are. If the proposed agreement is better than the negotiators' BATNA, then they should accept it. Having a good BATNA increases negotiation power.

BATNA (best alternative to a negotiated agreement) is a term coined by Roger Fisher and William Ury in their 1981 bestseller, *Getting to Yes: Negotiating Without Giving In*. BATNAs are critical to negotiation because negotiators cannot make a wise decision about whether to accept a negotiated agreement unless they know what the alternatives are. The BATNA is the only standard that can protect both from accepting terms that are too unfavourable and from rejecting terms that it would be in their best interest to accept. In the simplest terms, if the proposed agreement is better than the negotiators' BATNA, then it should be accepted. If the agreement is not better than their BATNA, then they should reopen negotiations. If the negotiators cannot improve the agreement, they should at least consider withdrawing from the negotiations and pursuing their alternative, although the costs of doing that must be considered as well. Furthermore, the more negotiators can learn about the BATNA of their counterpart, the better prepared they will be for negotiation. Then they will be able to develop a more realistic view of what the outcomes may be and what offers are reasonable.

Having a good BATNA increases negotiating power. Therefore, it is important to improve the BATNA whenever possible. Good negotiators know when their opponent is desperate for an agreement. When that occurs, they will demand much more, knowing their opponent will have to give in. If the opponent apparently has many options outside of negotiation, however, they are likely to get many more concessions in an effort to keep them at the negotiating table. Making the BATNA as strong as possible before negotiating and making that BATNA known to one's opponent will strengthen the negotiating position.

BATNA also affects the so-called 'ripeness', the time at which a dispute is ready or 'ripe' for settlement. When parties have similar ideas or 'congruent images' about what BATNAs exist, then the negotiation is ripe for reaching agreement. Having congruent BATNA images means that both parties have similar views of how a dispute will turn out if they do not agree, but rather pursue other options. In such a situation, it is often smarter for them to negotiate an agreement without continuing the disputing process, thus saving the transaction costs.

Put in other terms, a conflict becomes ripe for resolution when the parties realize that the status quo – no negotiation – is a negative sum (or 'lose–lose') situation, not a zero-sum ('win–lose') situation. To avoid the mutual loss, the negotiators must consider negotiation in an attempt to reach a positive sum (or 'win–win') outcome.

Ripeness is a matter of perception. Finding a ripe moment requires research and intelligence studies to identify the objective and subjective elements.

On the other hand, disputants may hold 'dissimilar images' about what BATNAs exist. For example, both sides may think they can win a dispute if they decide to pursue it in court or through force. If both sides' BATNAs tell them they can pursue the conflict and win, the likely result is a power contest. If one side's BATNA is indeed much better than the other's, the side with the better BATNA is likely to prevail. If the BATNAs are about equal, however, the parties may reach a stalemate. If the conflict is costly enough, eventually the parties may come to realize that their BATNAs were not as good as they thought they were. Then the dispute will again be 'ripe' for negotiation.

Negotiation outcome

Agreement is the last stage of the negotiation process. The agreement should be the starting point for the development of a deeper relationship between buyer and seller. The final agreement of a negotiation process may take the form of a gentleman's agreement, which is common in high-context cultures, or more formal contracts, which are more prevalent in low-context countries.

Implications of Hofstede's work

From Hofstede's (1983) work we see that there are differences (gaps) between national cultures. Each of five dimensions is reflected in the corporate culture patterns exhibited across countries. In the following, implications of Hofstede's five dimensions on the firm's international negotiation strategies will be discussed (Rowden, 2001; McGinnis, 2005; Volkema and Fleck, 2012).

Masculinity/femininity

Masculine cultures value assertiveness, independence, task orientation and self-achievement. Masculine cultures' strategy for negotiation is usually competitive, resulting in a win–lose situation. Conflict is usually resolved by fighting rather than compromising, reflecting an ego-boosting approach. In this situation, the person with the most competitive behaviour is likely to gain the most. On the other hand, feminine cultures value cooperation, nurturing, modesty, empathy and social relations, and prefer a collaborative or a compromising style or strategy to assure the best possible mutually accepting solution to obtain a win–win situation.

When negotiating, individuals from masculine countries are more likely to focus on the specifics of the agreement and not show much concern for its overall impact on the other party. Negotiators from feminine cultures are more likely to be concerned with the agreement's aesthetics and longer-range effects; they feel that the details can be worked out later.

Uncertainty avoidance

This dimension refers to the comfort level of a person in an unclear or risky situation. High-uncertainty avoidance cultures have formal bureaucratic negotiation rules, rely on rituals and standards and trust only family and friends. They require a clearly defined structure and guidelines. Low-uncertainty avoidance cultures prefer to work informally with flexibility. They do not like hierarchy, and are likely to seek resolving solutions and compromises rather than the status quo.

Negotiators from high-risk avoidance cultures are likely to seek specific commitments in terms of volume, timing and requirements. Their counterparts from low-uncertainty avoidance cultures are likely to be comfortable with rough estimates of volume and timing and with constantly changing requirements. During the negotiating process, discussions around delays in new product availability, for example, might cause great concern to those high on uncertainty avoidance. On the other hand, it would be regarded as an opportunity to improvise creatively by those who are low on uncertainty avoidance.

Power distance

This dimension refers to the acceptance of authority differences between those who have power and those affected by power. High power distance is authoritarian, and protocol, formality and hierarchy are considered important. In high-power distance cultures the CEO of the company is often directly involved in the negotiations and is the final decision-maker.

The idea of business negotiations between equals (low power distance) is basically a western concept and is not found in status-oriented societies such as Japan, Korea or Russia. Western Europeans and North Americans are normally informal and downplay status by using first names, dressing in casual attire, etc.

The Japanese dress conservatively – they always prefer dark business suits; to be dressed casually during negotiations with the Japanese would, therefore, be inappropriate. The Japanese do not believe in using first names unless in the very best of personal relationships. In Asia, honours, titles and status are extremely important: counterparts should be addressed by their proper titles. Frankness and directness are important in the western world, but are not desirable in Asia.

The valued European handshake is often out of place in Japan, where bowing is customary. When meeting a devout Muslim, never shake with the left hand or utilize the left hand for any purpose – it is considered rude and a personal affront.

When a person from a high masculine culture negotiates with a high-power distance culture, conflict will most likely result if neither party makes an effort to understand the cultural balance. Competence is valued over seniority, which yields a consultative management style. Dealings between cultures with low masculinity and low power distance usually result in more cooperative and creative behaviour.

Negotiators from low-power distance cultures may be frustrated by the need of negotiators from high-power distance cultures to seek approval from their supervisors. On the other hand, negotiators from high-power distance cultures may feel pressured by the pace imposed by those from low-power distance cultures. The key here is to understand the power distance mindset of the people one is negotiating with. That understanding is the first step towards closing the deal and setting realistic expectations for the relationship that follows.

Individualism/collectivism

Individualistic cultures tend to put tasks before relationships and value independence highly. These cultures tolerate open conflict and place the needs of the individual over the needs of a group, community or society. In negotiations, the individualistic society expects the other party to have the authority to make decisions unilaterally. In a highly individualist country such as the US, it is considered socially acceptable to pursue one's own ends without understanding the benefits for others. By contrast, managers from a collectivistic culture, such as China, will seek a stable relationship with a long-term orientation, stressing above all the establishment of a personal relationship. A collectivistic society values solidarity, loyalty and strong interdependence among individuals, and the members define themselves in terms of their membership within groups. Collectivist managers assume that details in the negotiation process can be worked out and show more concern for the needs of the other party by focusing on group goals. Members of collectivist societies are often irritated when members from individualistic societies promote their own positions and ideas during negotiations.

On the other hand, negotiators from individualistic societies are more likely to focus on the short term, make extreme offers and view negotiations from a competitive perspective. A critical factor in such negotiations is for each party to understand the other's main interests rather than focusing solely on its own.

Long-term/short-term orientation

Following his seminal study of national cultures, Hofstede added a fifth dimension that differentiates cultures of east and west (Hofstede and Bond, 1998, see also Chapter 7).

Given these differences, it is expected that negotiators from cultures with a short-term orientation feel more comfortable with making a request. By contrast, someone from a culture with a long-term orientation (typical Asian cultures) would be more inclined to respond to the personal need by deferring action to another time (i.e. thinking of the longer-term, more holistic picture). This includes waiting for the other party to 'drive' the subject once engaged, if not deferring personal engagement. Business negotiation may also take a longer time to develop in a long-term-oriented culture. Long-term traditions and commitments would be more likely to support the status quo and impede change.

Different organizational models

The British model of organization seems to be that of a village market with no decisive hierarchy, flexible rules and a resolution of problems by negotiating. The German model is more like a well-oiled machine. The exercise of personal command is largely unnecessary because the rules settle everything. The French model is more of a pyramidal hierarchy held together by a united command issuing strong rules. If we look at international buyer–seller relations, the national culture is only one level in the cultural hierarchy that will influence the behaviour of the individual buyer or seller. When members of different cultures come together to communicate, whether within the sales organization or in buyer–seller encounters, they typically do not bring the same shared values, thought patterns and actions to the situation. Common ground is typically limited. This increases the degree of uncertainty about the outcome of the interaction and can limit the efficiency and effectiveness of communication. To reduce uncertainty, communicators must predict accurately how others will behave and be able to explain those behaviours (Bush and Ingram, 2001).

The gap model in international negotiation

In negotiation situations the most fundamental gap influencing the interaction between buyer and seller is the difference between their respective cultural backgrounds (gap 1 in Figure 18.2). This cultural distance can be expressed in terms of differences in communication and negotiation behaviour, the concepts of time, space or work patterns and the nature of social rituals and norms (Madsen, 1994). The cultural distance between two partners tends to increase the transaction costs, which may be quite high in cross-cultural negotiations.

Cultural influence on people, and therefore international negotiations, can be analysed at various levels of society. Furthermore, there is a learning 'effect' in the way that a person's cultural identity formed in one specific cultural setting will affect how that person views other situations in other cultural settings. Both seller and buyer are influenced by (at least) the national and organizational culture they belong to. As seen in Chapter 7 (Figure 7.2), there are probably more levels in the understanding of individual negotiation behaviour.

The level of adaptation that is necessary is dependent on how culturally similar the seller and buyer are in the first place. However, the cultural differences between buyer and seller are likely to be less than the cultural differences between their two nations, as, to a certain extent, they will share a 'business' culture.

The influence of national culture

The national culture is the macro/societal culture that represents a distinct way of life of a group of citizens in a certain country. This national culture is composed of the norms and values that members hold as well as their level of, for example, economic development, education system, national laws and other parts of the regulatory environment (Harvey and Griffith, 2002). All these factors play an important role in socializing individuals into a specific pattern of belief (Andersen, 2003). Therefore it is typical that when individuals encounter cultural differences in their international interactions/relationships, they tend to view people from different national cultures as strangers, i.e. unknown people who belong to different groups. This feeling of distance can have a direct impact on trust and personal bonding, which increases the probability of conflict between seller and buyer in the negotiation process. The earlier discussion of the five dimensions of Hofstede's research gives several examples of differences in national culture and how they may affect intercultural negotiations between two partners.

The influence of organizational culture

Organizational culture is the pattern of shared behaviour, values and beliefs that provides a foundation for understanding the organizational functioning processes (Schein, 1985). When two or more organizations are negotiating with each other, the relative level of consistency of core elements between organizational cultures can directly influence the effectiveness of communication and negotiation.

The overall complexity of a firm's communication environment will vary tremendously when elements of national culture and organizational culture are examined. In instances where the national cultural distance between buyer and seller is great and the organizational cultures are inconsistent (i.e. high interorganizational distance), the negotiation environment will be highly complex, necessitating careful planning and monitoring of the firm's intercultural negotiation strategies. Alternatively, when the national cultural distance is low and the cultures of the buyer's and seller's organizations are consistent, both partners will find it easier to employ effective negotiation strategies without too much adaptation (Griffith, 2002).

In the case of a national and organizational cultural 'distance' between buyer and seller, both the buyer and (especially) the seller will try to adapt their own behaviour to suit the other party. In this way, the initial gap 1 may be reduced to gap 2, through adaptation of behaviour (Figure 18.2). The extent to which sellers can adjust their behaviour to another culture's communication style is a function of their skills and experience. The necessary skills include the ability to handle stress, initiate conversation and establish a meaningful relationship.

However, neither the seller nor the buyer will have a full understanding of the other party's culture, so the final result will often still be a difference between the cultural behaviour of the seller and the buyer (gap 2). This gap can create friction in the negotiation and exchange process and hence give rise to transaction costs.

Gap 2 can be reduced through market research and the education of salespeople (see Section 18.3). However, salespeople bring different 'baggage' with them in the form of attitudes and skills that result in different stages of intercultural awareness. The different stages of intercultural preparedness are highlighted in the next section. For example, if a trainer chooses to give a basic cultural awareness exercise to salespeople who are already at the acceptance stage and willing to learn about behaviour strategies, they are likely to be bored and not see the value of some types of diversity training.

Furthermore, face-to-face communication skills remain an important topic in international sales training. This is especially true in consultative selling, where questioning and listening skills are essential in the global marketing context. However, learning about cultural diversity through training programmes should help salespeople and marketing executives be better prepared to predict the behaviours they encounter with diverse customers or co-workers. Yet many salespeople are sceptical of training and question its value. In fact, employees may view diversity training as simply a current fad or the 'politically correct thing to do'. However, if not prepared, salespeople often do not realize the impact of cultural diversity until they encounter an unfamiliar cultural situation.

EXHIBIT 18.2 Euro Disney becomes Disneyland Resort Paris – Disney learns to adapt to European cultures

The Walt Disney Company began scouting locations for a European theme park in the mid-1980s, with France and Spain emerging as the strongest possibilities. The city of Marne-la-Vallée (about 20 miles east of Paris) eventually won the battle for the new mouse house, and in 1987 Disney created the subsidiary Euro Disney. It broke ground on the US$4.4 billion project the following year, and in 1989 Euro Disney went public (Walt Disney retained a 49 per cent stake).

In preparing the opening of Euro Disney in 1992, the company's first chairman proudly announced that his company would 'help change Europe's chemistry'.

However, there were some cross-cultural issues:

● Prior to opening the park, Disney insisted employees comply with a detailed written code regarding clothing, jewellery and other aspects of personal appearance. Women were expected to wear 'appropriate undergarments' and keep their fingernails short. Disney defended its move, noting that similar codes were used in its other parks. The goal was to ensure that guests received the kind of experience associated with the Disney name. Despite these statements, the French considered the code to be an insult to French culture, individualism and privacy.

● The extension of Disney's standard 'no alcohol' policy from the US meant that wine was not available at Euro Disney. This, too, was deemed inappropriate in a country renowned for its production and consumption of wine.

It took a series of adaptations, such as renaming the park Disneyland Resort Paris and the addition of some special attractions, to make the park profitable as of 1996.

At the time of the renaming Disney's CEO, Michael Eisner, commented (Snyder, 2002):

As Americans, the word 'Euro' is believed to mean glamorous or exciting. For Europeans it turned out to be a term they associated with business, currency and commerce. Renaming the park 'Disneyland Paris' was a way of identifying it with one of the most romantic and exciting cities in the world.

The Disneyland Resort Paris theme park is now Europe's top tourist attraction. Attendance has surpassed the Eiffel Tower as Europe's number one tourist destination, with more than 14 million visits per year (2014).

Over the years, the company has learned to cater more to European tastes, e.g. by serving food and beverages, such as sausage and wine. Disney Studios' virtual tour guides also use European actors.

Sources: Tagliabue (2000); Della Cava (1999); www.eurodisney.com; Hoovers Company Records: Euro Disney S.C.A, December 2006.

One of the main problems frequently encountered in providing salespeople with meaningful educational experience that includes cultural diversity (distance) is the inability to provide on-location experiential learning opportunities routinely. This is due to lack of time and resources. Although desirable, in many instances one cannot expose salespeople to the culture beforehand to analyse and learn from their reactions. A viable alternative to this dilemma is to expose trainees to a simulated culturally diverse experience. The advantages of this approach are that it is more efficient and requires the active involvement of individuals, resulting in experiential learning. Simulations based on role-plays and result-oriented learning have been very successful in teaching salespeople and managers (Bush and Ingram, 2001).

Negotiating strategies

An essential part of negotiating is, of course, knowing your own strengths and weaknesses, but also knowing as much as possible about the other side, understanding their way of thinking and recognizing their perspective. Even starting from a position of weakness, there are strategies that salespeople can pursue to turn the negotiation to their advantage.

18.3   Intercultural preparation

Many salespeople may be aware that cultural diversity is an important issue in their work environment. However, as evidenced by many stories of cultural blunders (see the example in Exhibit 18.2), salespeople may not realize the impact of diversity on their ability to predict behaviour in a selling situation. Thus individuals may progress through a kind of self-revelation about their own perceived skills and how these skills impact on their interactions with co-workers or buyers from culturally diverse backgrounds. Participating in such an experimental exercise can help sales and marketing personnel begin to understand the impact of cultural diversity in different ways.

General intercultural preparation

The following five-step approach is proposed to help firms with preparing their salespeople for coping with cultural diversities when entering different international markets (Bush and Ingram, 2001):

1. Build awareness about how cultural differences impact upon them in the sales organization.
2. Motivate salespeople and managers to rethink their behaviour and attitude towards customers.
3. Allow salespeople to examine their own biases in a psychologically safe environment.
4. Examine how stereotypes are developed, and how they can create misunderstandings between buyers and sellers.
5. Identify diversity issues that need to be addressed in the international sales organization.

This simulation may be perceived as a valuable starting point for learning about communication styles and cultural differences. Most firms realize that cultural diversity training requires much more time than expected. One of the difficulties in educating individuals about communicating between cultures or subcultures is that a two-hour session will not suffice. Respecting and successfully interacting with members of diverse cultures are part of a long-term process. By participating in a long-term exercise, salespeople may begin to realize that the concept of diversity goes beyond 'the right thing to do' or satisfying affirmative action requirements. Valuing diversity can also have an impact on the bottom line of an organization.

Specific evaluation of a partner's intercultural communication and negotiation competences

To address the issues involved with the fit and reduction of 'gaps' in negotiation processes, a firm must be proactive and develop specific strategies to enhance communication effectiveness. Most organizations have not formalized their management of cross-cultural communication, but at least three steps are necessary in order to improve the selling firm's cross-cultural communication and negotiation competences:

1. *Assessing communication competences of salespersons.*Given the importance of salespeople's communication competences for relationship success, it is critical that selling firms assess their competences. Once the technical level (e.g. technical and standard language competences) is assessed, the firm could use the above-mentioned simulation and experiential methods to gauge behavioural competences.
2. *Assessing communication competences of negotiators in the buying firm.*If possible, the same procedure as in (1) should be carried out for the buyers in the foreign culture. However, it might be difficult to get this information about the negotiators in the buying firm.
3. *Matching communication and negotiation competences of buying and selling firm.* Only if there is a match (and not too large a gap) between the communication competences of the two firms can they realistically expect success in the international negotiation and in the possible future relationship. Of course, it should be noted that the selling firm is only able to control its internal competences, and not those of the buying firm.

This issue of communication assessment can also be integrated into the firm's partner selection and retention criteria. As the selling firm begins to integrate these communication competences into its partner selection and retention criteria, it is also important that it shows flexibility and willingness to improve the existing competences in relation to its partner (the buying firm).

18.4 Coping with expatriates

The following discussion can be applied not only to expatriate salespeople but also to other jobs in the firm based in a foreign country (e.g. an administrative position in a foreign subsidiary). Expatriate salespeople negotiating in foreign cultures often experience a culture shock when confronted with a buyer. Culture shock is experienced more intensely by **expatriates** whose cultures are most different from the ones in which they are now working. What can the management of the international firm do to minimize the risk of culture shock? The following areas should be considered (Guy and Patton, 1996).

Expatriates
Employees sent out from the HQ to work for the company in the foreign markets, often in its subsidiaries.

The decision to employ an expatriate salesperson

The first major decision to make is whether the use of home-country expatriates is the best choice for entering and serving foreign markets. The firm should first examine its own past experience with culture shock and adjustment of its sales representatives in other cultures. Inexperienced firms would probably be best advised to evaluate possible agents and distributors rather than using home-country expatriates. Other options for firms with their own sales force are host-country or third-country nationals (see also Section 17.3).

The firm should try to identify the elements in the expatriate sales job that suggest potential problems with culture shock. If the job is highly technical, is located in an area with other home-country nationals and involves similar tastes and lifestyles as in the home country, then the expatriate sales force may be appropriate.

If, however, the job places the expatriate salesperson in an unfamiliar post with conflicting expectations, the firm should consider other options. The likelihood of greater culture shock and adjustment problems increases with greater cultural distance. The greater the high-context/low-context contrast, the greater is the chance of difficulty. When entering a different culture, many familiar symbols and cues are missing. The removal of these everyday reassurances can lead to feelings of frustration, stress and anxiety.

Selection of expatriates

Being an expatriate salesperson is a critical task and the selection process should be given considerable thought, not be decided too quickly. The selection should not be based primarily on the technical competence of the salesperson. Substantial emphasis must also be placed on the following attributes:

- foreign-language skills
- general relational abilities
- emotional stability
- educational background
- past experience with the designated culture
- ability to deal with stress.

Previous research (Guy and Patton, 1996) suggests that the following characteristics are associated with a lower level of cultural shock for the expatriate:

- open-mindedness
- empathy
- cultural sensitivity
- resilience
- low ego identity.

An assessment of the potential expatriate alone is not sufficient if the person has family members who will be making the move as well. Family issues that must be considered include marital stability, the overall emotional stability of family members and family cohesiveness. In-depth interviews with at least the rep's spouse, but preferably other family members as well, can be very useful in determining the status of these variables.

Training

Selecting the most appropriate training programme for each expatriate requires methods for classifying people into various levels of intercultural skills. Each level needs a different training programme. The initial requirement is to train the expatriate, and any accompanying family member, to understand the main sociocultural, economic, political, legal and technological factors in the assigned country.

The training activities may include:

- area/country description
- cultural assimilation training
- role-playing
- handling critical incidents
- case studies
- stress reduction training
- field experience
- extensive language training.

Obviously many firms will not be able to provide all the training needed in-house or through a single source, but they may need to coordinate a variety of methods and external programmes for their expatriates, to take place before and during the foreign assignment.

Support

It is very important to provide a solid support network from the head office so that the expatriate is not simply left alone to sink or swim. Support during expatriate assignment may include a number of elements:

- adequate monetary compensation or other benefits;
- constant communication from the home base regarding ongoing operations at head office and in the assigned country/area;
- providing opportunities for periodic travel to the home country to maintain contacts and relationships within the firm; the home base could also send copies of forthcoming job postings in which the expatriate may be interested.

Expatriates should identify and contact individuals in the host country who can become a part of their social network. It is also important that their spouse and family are included in a social support network.

Repatriation

Companies employing expatriates should develop an integrated career plan, identifying likely subsequent job positions and career progression. If the expatriates are exposed to a series of international assignments during their careers, each assignment should be selected to develop their awareness of different cultures. For example, for a UK company, the first non-UK assignment could be a culturally similar or proximate country, say Germany or the US, the next assignment might be South Africa or Australia, the next Hong Kong, then Japan and so on. In this way, cultural shock is minimized, because the process encourages the ability to manage situations in more and more distant cultures.

The return of the expatriate to the home country is sometimes difficult. Lack of job guarantees is one of the most critical challenges faced by expatriates. Some months prior to return an internal position search should be started with a home visit arranged for the expatriate to meet with appropriate managers. An internal sponsor in the head office should be appointed to maintain ongoing contact and to help the expatriate secure a desirable position upon return.

Sometimes, expatriate families also experience a culture shock upon returning to the home country; therefore some support is needed during repatriation. This includes spouse job-finding assistance and time to readjust before going back to work.

18.5 Knowledge management and learning across borders

Managing global knowledge that crosses the lines between business units, subsidiaries and departments that are dispersed geographically across continents is highly complex and requires consideration of different issues and factors. The global strategy exploits the knowledge of the parent organization (headquarters) through worldwide diffusion and adaptation. It strives to achieve the slogan 'think globally but act locally', through dynamic interdependence between the headquarters and the subsidiaries. Organizations following such a strategy coordinate efforts, ensuring local flexibility while exploiting the benefits of global integration and efficiencies, as well as ensuring worldwide diffusion of innovation (Desouza and Evaristo, 2003).

A key element in knowledge management is continuous learning from experience (Stewart, 2001). In practical terms, the aim of knowledge management, as a learning-focused activity across borders, is to keep track of valuable capabilities used in one market that could be used elsewhere (in other geographic markets), so that firms can continually update their knowledge without 'reinventing the wheel'. See the example in Figure 18.3 for a systematic approach to global learning from transferring best practices in the firm's different international markets.

The steps in transferring the firm's best practices to other international markets are:

1. By benchmarking (comparing) the different procedures in the firm's international markets, the firm should be able to pick up best practices – in Figure 18.3 the best practices are found in the UK and Sweden. Subsequently, the possible implications of the best practices are discussed in the 'top management' group.
2. After the procedures for diffusion of the best practices have been established in the top management group, the next step is to see if these best practices can be used elsewhere in the firm's international markets. In order to disseminate global knowledge and best practices, meetings (with representatives from all international markets) and global project groups should be established. If done successfully, the benchmarking could result in a global learning process, where the different international marketing managers would select the most useable elements from the presented best practices and adapt these in the local markets.

However, as noted earlier in this chapter, knowledge developed and used in one cultural context is not easily transferred to another. The lack of personal relationships, the absence of trust and cultural distance all conspire to create resistance, frictions and misunderstandings in cross-cultural knowledge management (Bell *et al.*, 2002).

As globalization becomes a centrepiece in the business strategy of many firms – be it firms engaged in product development or providing services – the ability to manage the 'global knowledge engine' to achieve a competitive edge in today's knowledge-intensive economy is one of the keys to sustainable competitiveness. In the context of global marketing, the management of knowledge is, *de facto*, a cross-cultural activity, whose key task is to foster and continually make more sophisticated collaborative cross-cultural learning (Berrell *et al.*, 2002). Of course, the kind and/or the type of knowledge that is strategic for an organization and which needs to be managed for competitiveness varies depending on the business context and the value of different types of knowledge associated with it.

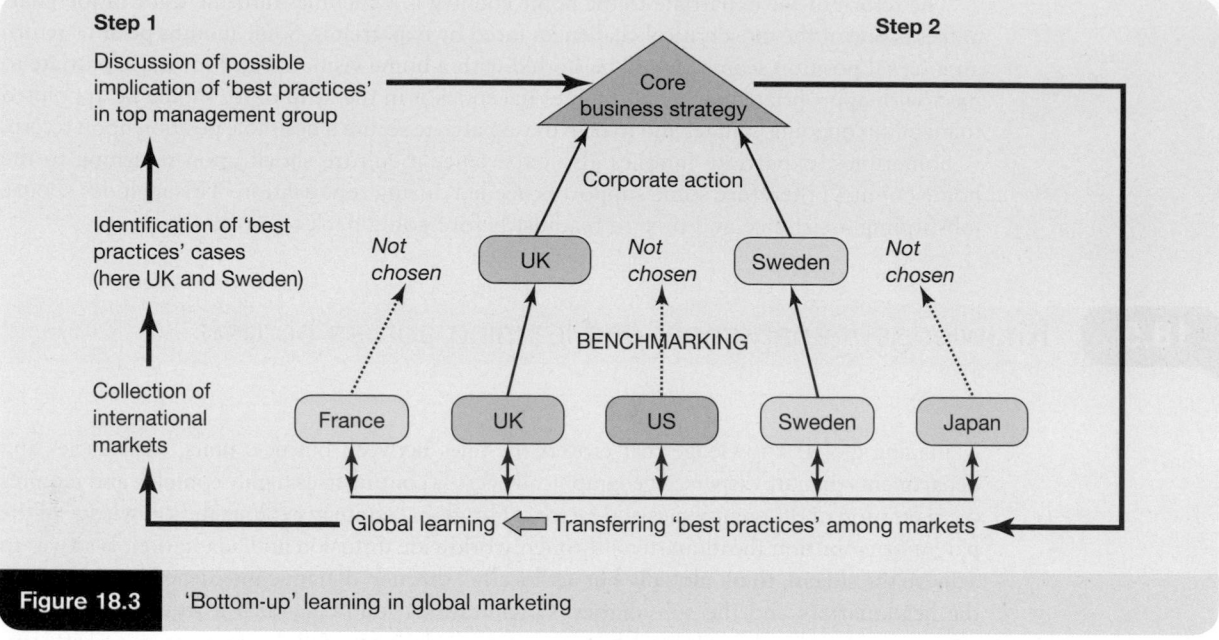

Figure 18.3 'Bottom-up' learning in global marketing

Explicit and tacit knowledge

New knowledge is created through the synergistic relationship and interplay between *tacit* and *explicit* knowledge.

Explicit knowledge is defined as knowledge that can be expressed formally using a system of symbols, and can therefore be easily communicated or diffused. It is either object- or rule-based. It is object-based when the knowledge is codified in symbols (e.g. words, numbers, formulas) or in physical objects (e.g. equipment, documents, models). Object-based knowledge may be found in examples such as product specifications, patents, software codes, computer databases and technical drawings. Explicit knowledge is rule-based when the knowledge is codified into rules, routines or standard operating procedures (Choo, 1998).

Tacit knowledge is the implicit knowledge used by organizational members to perform their work and to make sense of the world. It is knowledge that is uncodified and difficult to diffuse across borders and subsidiaries. It is hard to verbalize because it is expressed through action-based skills and cannot be reduced to rules and recipes. Instead, tacit knowledge is learned through extended periods of experiencing and doing a task, during which the individual develops a feel for and a capacity to make intuitive judgments about the successful execution of the activity. Tacit knowledge is vital to an organization because organizations can only learn and innovate by somehow levering on the implicit knowledge of its members. Tacit knowledge becomes substantially valuable when it is turned into new capabilities, products, services or even new markets for the firm. Organizational knowledge creation is a process that organizationally amplifies the knowledge created by individuals in different countries and subsidiaries and crystallizes it as a part of the international knowledge network of the company. There are two sets of dynamics that drive the process of international knowledge amplification (Nonaka and Takeuchi, 1995):

1. converting tacit knowledge into explicit knowledge;
2. moving knowledge from the individual level to the group, organizational and inter-organizational levels (across subsidiaries in different countries).

A central issue in internationalized firms concerns where knowledge is created and diffused: capabilities in creating knowledge centres of excellence may be formed in certain subsidiaries, for example, regarding specific functions such as product development or international marketing.

Global project groups

Today's business, with its growing emphasis on globalization, increasingly requires people to collaborate in workgroups that cross cultural and geographic boundaries. The trend to multicultural workgroups emerged as a reaction to changed economic conditions, forcing organizations to develop new structures in order to minimize costs and maximize flexibility. One consequence of these changes is that, as a result of rapid knowledge growth and increasingly complex work environments, more and more tasks can only be accomplished in international project groups by cooperation of functionally and culturally different experts. Based on the assumption of diversity creating value, and therefore competitive advantage, by bringing together different ideas and pooling knowledge, multicultural project groups have become a prevailing tendency in multinational organizations. However, the use of such groups often turns out, in practice, to be a lot more problematic than expected. It seems that the cognitive advantages that can be gained by a diverse workforce are counter-balanced by relational problems such as miscommunication and distrust, and therefore high turnover rates (Wolf, 2002). Nevertheless, with today's economy facing an ever-increasing need to cross all kinds of borders, the existence of culturally diverse project groups has become inevitable.

Given the communication problems and trust issues that plague ad hoc global project groups, structuring the project team is particularly critical to success. Three questions need to be addressed by the firm's top management (Govindarajan and Gupta, 2001), as discussed in the following.

1. Is the objective clearly defined?

One of the first concerns for any global project team must be to discuss the group's agenda explicitly and ensure that the objective/problem is defined clearly and correctly. Many project groups do not fully resolve and discuss the issues involved and they immediately run into problems. Different framing of the same problem can produce different outcomes. Because the project group typically has members from different subsidiaries that usually compete with one another for scarce corporate resources, they tend to have a high degree of internal conflict, combined with a low level of trust.

As a result, it is generally best to frame the problem of the project group in terms of the company's position vis-à-vis the external marketplace instead of emphasizing internal issues. An external focus encourages benchmarking, fosters creativity and provides a compelling rationale for making the tough decisions inherent in any manufacturing rationalization and workforce reduction. Given the possible communication problems in the global project group, it is imperative that the members understand the agenda of the project group: the scope of the project, the expected deliverables and the timeline. Cultural and language differences may complicate the task of getting group members to agree on the agenda and the problems to be solved. Clarity is essential to promoting commitment and accountability.

2. Choosing group members

Another key to creating a successful global team is choosing the right group members. Two issues are of particular importance: how do you balance diversity within the team and what should be the size of the group? Normally we will see high levels of diversity. Why? First, members come from diverse cultural and national backgrounds – this refers to so-called *behavioural diversity*. Second, members generally represent subsidiaries whose agenda may not be congruent. Third, because members often represent different functional units and departments, their priorities and perspectives may differ. The last two issues refer to so-called *cognitive diversity*.

Let us take a closer look at an example of behavioural diversity. Consider, for example, a cross-border project group in a Swedish–Chinese joint venture. The norm in most Chinese teams is that the most senior member presents the team's perspective, but in a Swedish team the most junior member typically does so. Unless the members of the team are sensitized to such differences, misunderstandings can easily emerge and block communication. So behavioural diversity is best regarded as a necessary evil: something that no global project group can avoid, but the effects of which the group must attempt to minimize through training in cultural sensitivity.

Let us also take a closer look at an example of cognitive diversity. This diversity refers to differences in the substantive content of how members perceive the group's challenges and opportunities. Differences in functional backgrounds can account for substantive cognitive differences on issues of 'market pull' (preferred by people in marketing departments) and 'technology push' (preferred by people in engineering departments). Because no single member can ever have a monopoly on wisdom, cognitive diversity is almost always a source of strength. Divergent perspectives foster creativity and a more comprehensive search for and assessment of options, but the group must be able to integrate the perspectives and come to a single solution.

3. Selection of team leadership

Structuring the leadership of a global project team involves critical decisions around three roles: the *project leader,* the *external coach* and *the internal sponsor.* The project leader plays a pivotal role in cross-border project groups. They must contribute to the development of trust between the members and perhaps have the biggest stake in the outcome of the project. They must possess conflict-resolution and integration skills and expertise in process management, including diagnosing problems, assessing situations and generating and evaluating options. An external coach serves as an ad hoc member of the project group and is an expert in process more than content. The need for such a coach is likely to be high when the process-management skills of the best available project leader are inadequate. This might happen if the appointed leader has some major stake in the project's outcome, for example if a cross-border task force has to rationalize and decrease the number of subsidiaries around the world by 30 per cent. The internal sponsor of a global project group is typically a senior executive with a strong interest in the success of the team. Among the responsibilities of the sponsor are to provide ongoing guidelines and to facilitate access to resources.

At any given time, a global company will typically have many project groups working on different cross-border coordination issues. Therefore it makes sense for the company to undertake initiatives to create interpersonal familiarity and trust among key managers of different subsidiaries. For example, Unilever uses several approaches to do this – such as bringing together managers from different subsidiaries in executive development education programmes.

When a project group consists of members with distinct knowledge and skills drawn from different subsidiaries in different countries, the potential for cognitive diversity is high, and this can also be a source of competitive strength. However, intellectual diversity will almost always bring with it some degree of interpersonal incompatibility and communication difficulty. Process mechanisms that recognize and anticipate such pitfalls – and integrate the best of individuals' ideas and contributions – are needed to help the project group reconcile diverse perspectives and arrive at better, more creative and novel solutions.

18.6   Transnational bribery in cross-cultural negotiations

On first consideration, **bribery** is both unethical and illegal, but a closer look reveals that bribery is not really a straightforward issue. The ethical and legal problems associated

Bribery
Involving a company from an industrialized country offering an illicit payment to a developing country's public official with perceived or real influence over contract awards. Bribery may range from gifts to large amounts of money.

with bribery can be quite complex. Thus the definition of bribery can range from the relatively innocuous payment of a few pounds to a minor official or business manager in order to expedite the processing of papers or the loading of a truck, to the extreme of paying millions of pounds to a head of state to guarantee a company preferential treatment. Scott *et al.* (2002) generally define bribery as 'involving a company from an industrialized country offering an illicit payment to a developing country's public official with perceived or real influence over contract awards' (p. 2).

The difference between lubrication and bribery must be established. Lubrication payments accompany requests for a person to do a job more rapidly or more efficiently. They involve a relatively small cash sum, gift or service made to a low-ranking official in a country where such offerings are not prohibited by law, the purpose being to facilitate or expedite the normal, lawful performance of a duty by that official. This practice is common in many countries. Bribery, on the other hand, generally involves large sums of money, which are frequently not properly accounted for, and is designed to entice an official to commit an illegal act on behalf of the one paying the bribe.

Another type of payment that can appear to be a bribe, but may not be, is an agent's fee. When a businessperson is uncertain of a country's rules and regulations, an agent may be hired to represent the company in that country. This person will do a more efficient and thorough job than someone unfamiliar with country-specific procedures.

There are many intermediaries (attorneys, agents, distributors and so forth) who function simply as channels for illegal payments. The process is further complicated by legal codes that vary from country to country: what is illegal in one country might be winked at in another and legal in a third. In some countries, illegal payments can become a major business expense. Hong Kong companies report that bribes account for about 5 per cent of the cost of doing business in China. In Russia, the cost is 15–20 per cent, and in Indonesia it can be as high as 30 per cent (Gesteland, 1996, p. 93).

In a survey of bribery practice in the US, Sanyal (2012) found that the principal reason (80 per cent of the cases) to give bribes to foreign officials is for the firm or individual to secure a specific contract or renew a contract. Much less common is a bribe given to change the law in the foreign country to favour the business prospects of the briber or to reduce tax liabilities. In 30 per cent of the cases, the bribes were paid directly to the recipients (no agents or intermediaries involved). However, intermediaries were used in over 50 per cent of the cases.

The answer to the question of bribery is not an unqualified one. It is easy to generalize about the ethics of political payoffs and other types of payment; it is much more difficult to make the decision to withhold payment of money, when not making the payment may affect the company's ability to do business profitably, or at all. With the variety of ethical standards and levels of morality that exist in different cultures, the dilemma of ethics and pragmatism that faces international business cannot be resolved until more countries decide to deal effectively with the issue.

18.7 Summary

When marketing internationally, negotiation skills are needed. Negotiation skills and personal selling skills are related. Personal selling typically occurs at the field sales force level and during formal negotiation processes. Cultural factors are critical to understanding the negotiation style of foreigners.

The negotiation process is significantly influenced by the cultures within which the negotiators (typically a buyer and a seller) have been socialized and educated. Cultural differences prevalent in the international sales negotiation process can have a tremendous impact upon the process itself, as well as its outcome.

The cross-cultural negotiation process can be divided into two different parts: the *non-task-related interaction* and the *task-related interaction*. The non-task-related aspects of the sales negotiation process (status distinction, impression formation accuracy and interpersonal attractiveness) are considered first, as it is these factors that are more relevant when approaching the buyer. Once a contact has successfully been established, the task-related aspects of the sales negotiation process begins (exchange of information, persuasion and bargaining strategies and concession-making and agreement).

Before the two partners begin the negotiation process, there is a cultural distance between them. This cultural distance causes some transaction costs, which may be quite high. To reduce the cultural distance, training of the negotiators is required.

The culture shock felt by expatriates indicates that sending negotiators and salespeople to foreign markets is often difficult and complex to implement successfully. Five important areas of implementation include: (1) making the initial decision to employ an expatriate sales force; (2) identifying and selecting qualified candidates; (3) providing adequate training; (4) maintaining ongoing support; and (5) achieving satisfactory repatriation.

In global knowledge management, a key element is the continuous learning from experiences in different markets. In practical terms, the aim of knowledge management as a learning-focused activity across borders is to keep track of valuable capabilities used in one market that could be used elsewhere (in other geographic markets), so that firms can continually update their knowledge without reinventing the wheel.

The ethical question of what is right or appropriate poses many dilemmas for international marketers. Bribery is an issue that is defined very differently from country to country. What is acceptable in one country may be completely unacceptable in another.

CASE STUDY 18.1

ZamZam Cola: marketing of a 'Muslim' cola from Iran to the European market

The brand ZamZam Cola is a cola-flavoured soft drink produced in Iran by ZamZam Soft Drink Manufacturing Co.

Originally a subsidiary of Pepsi, created in Iran in 1954 as the first Iranian carbonated soft drink producer, ZamZam founded its own corporation following the 1979 Islamic Revolution.

The product's name is a reference to the Well of Zamzam in Mecca, which is one of the stops on the Islamic pilgrimage of the Hajj (to Mecca).

ZamZam Cola is particularly popular in Iran and parts of the Arab world, having gained a cult status there as a Muslim alternative to 'western' products such as Coca-Cola and Pepsi, although these two manufacturers together still have nearly 80 per cent of the total cola market in Middle East and Africa.

The director of the ZamZam Soft Drink Manufacturing Co is Ahmad-Haddad Moghaddam. The firm is owned by the *Bonyad-e Mostazafen va Janbazan,* the Foundation for the Oppressed and Disabled, a powerful state charity run by clerics.

Following the 2002 boycott of Coca-Cola by Saudi Arabia, ZamZam was unofficially dubbed the soft drink of the Hajj. A Saudi firm owned by one of the kingdom's princes, Turki Abdallah al-Faisal, signed an agreement with the ZamZam Group in January 2003, giving the Saudi company some exclusive distribution rights in Saudi Arabia, Egypt and a number of other Arab countries. It is also sold on a limited basis in Europe and in some parts of Asia.

The headquarters of ZamZam are in the Iranian capital, Tehran. The bottling facility in Tehran is a popular attraction where people can see for themselves the drink being bottled. Due to the bottling facility's proximity to Mehrebad airport, tourists often stop for a visit.

The production was at first a single production line, but the firm now owns 17 beverage plants in Iran as well as several international companies, which produce and distribute ZamZam products under licence. The ZamZam company has developed the most well equipped beverage concentrate

Source: Zam Zam Refreshment.

Table 1	Cola market shares in Middle East

Middle East company	% market share (off-trade market) – 2010
Coca-Cola	51%
Pepsico Co	27%
ZamZam	5%
Others	17%
Total	100%

Source: adapted from Euromonitor.com and other public sources.

plant in the Middle East. ZamZam Iran Co has had significant presence in domestic and international markets, and produces over 100 diverse products including cola, lemon, orange, lemonade, mango, mineral water and a non-alcoholic malt beverage. ZamZam is also available in the United Arab Emirates and other surrounding nations.

Competitive situation

Cola carbonates are still the most popular soft drinks in many countries in the Middle East. Despite various boycotts against Pepsi-Cola and Coca-Cola, the cola sector remains a cash cow for the two American giants, which seem to have gained back the market shares that were lost during the boycotts around 2002. Pepsi-Cola and Coca-Cola seem to be more active than ever in terms of marketing and promotional campaigns.

In 2010, the total market for cola carbonates in Middle East was around eight billion litres, of which 18 per cent was drunk in Iran, the home country of ZamZam. For the whole Middle East region it is expected that from 2010 to 2015 the yearly cola consumption will increase by more than 10 per cent per year.

The market shares (2010) for the whole Middle East region are shown in Table 1.

In Iran, ZamZam has a market share of around 16 per cent of the cola market.

Cola drinks from across the Arab and Muslim world, such as ZamZam Cola, Arab Cola, Parsi Cola and Mecca Cola, have emerged to push an Arab and Muslim identity to the cola market. Mecca Cola encouraged consumers to 'shake your conscience' on the side of the bottle and reminds all consumers that the drink should not be mixed with any alcoholic beverages. Drinking is taboo in most Islamic countries and is explicitly forbidden in the Koran.

Subsequent developments

In 2012, ZamZam opened a US$10 million manufacturing facility in the Dubai Investment Park, with a production capacity of 80 million bottles per year. ZamZam Cola already has manufacturing plants in Palestine, Iraq, Oman and Jordan with a total capacity of 600 million bottles. The next stage of the Dubai project will be a water filling line and juices – all in glass, cans and PET.

Ahmad-Haddad Moghaddam is still considering how future growth can be secured for ZamZam Cola, and he thinks that Europe could be a future market, because of the large number of Muslims there. The total number of Muslims in Europe in 2010 was about 53 million (7 per cent of the population in Europe), excluding Turkey. The biggest Muslim populations in Europe are in Russia (25 million) and France (six million). The total number of Muslims in the European Union (EU) in 2010 was about 16 million (3 per cent of the population of the EU).

If ZamZam chose to make a more proactive entry into the UK cola market, it would face competition from other UK based 'Muslim cola' competitors, such as Evoca Cola and Mecca Cola (this brand seems to have been withdrawn from the European market).

The manufacturer of the Evoca Cola, Evoca Enterprises Limited, was established in May 2003 in the UK and officially launched this flagship brand in

January 2004. Evoca Cola is currently sold in the UK, France and Algeria.

Evoca has highlighted the ingredient black seed, as it is well known in Islamic culture (amongst others), and there are recorded hadiths from the prophet Muhammad that mention its healing properties. As Muslims are keen to follow the example of their Prophet, taking great interest in his every speech, thoughts and actions, an argument can be made to support the fact that, where available and marketed appropriately, Muslim-centric produce and services can in fact succeed (Wilson and Liu, 2010).

Despite the addition of black seed being a possible advantageous marketing angle, the product has not been positioned or sold as a 'Muslim cola' due to its growing mainstream appeal as a result of its unique composition of 100 per cent mineral water, its only being made from natural ingredients and its authentic cola taste.

QUESTIONS

1. What were the main reasons for the success of the ZamZam Cola in the Middle East?

2. How should Ahmad-Haddad Moghaddam prepare his sales force culturally for selling ZamZam Cola to European supermarket chains?

3. Do you think Ahmad-Haddad Moghaddam can repeat the international ZamZam Cola success with a new coffee shop chain and a new energy drink?

Sources: Wilson, J.A.J. and Liu, J. (2010), 'Shaping the Halal into a brand?', *Journal of Islamic Marketing*, 1(2), pp. 107–123; publicly available information about ZamZam.

CASE STUDY 18.2

TOTO: the Japanese toilet manufacturer seeks export opportunities for its high-tech brands in the US

An average person visits the toilet 2,500 times per year, about 6–8 times per day. People spend at least three years of their lives using the toilet, and women take three times as long to use the toilet as men (www.worldtoilet.org).

Founded in 1917, Japanese toilet maker TOTO (www.toto.co.jp) is the largest toilet manufacturer in the world, producing more than 12 million toilets annually. TOTO's net sales in the financial year 2012 were US$4.5 billion; with a net profit of US$90 million. Their total number of employees at the end of March 2012 was 25,000.

Over the years, TOTO has made a sales success in Japan. Japanese Government statistics show that the 'innovative toilet seat' that features an integrated bidet (represented by TOTO's Washlet-brand) are now installed in 69 per cent of Japanese homes compared to just 14 per cent in 1992. TOTO, which employs around 1,500 engineers, dominates this 'innovative toilet seat' market with a 50 per cent share. Its closest rival, Japan's Inax Corp., trails at 25

Source: TOTO.

per cent. Numbers for Japan's overall toilet market in 'water closets' are like this: TOTO's market share is 60 per cent while Inax is about 30 per cent. TOTO's market share is only very small outside Japan, with 14 per cent of TOTO's total net sales coming from overseas in 2012. The Chinese market is the number one target (54 per cent of overseas sales), and the US is the second (24 per cent of overseas sales), but still the US is a key target for TOTO.

US market for toilets

The US is one of the largest and most competitive markets in the world: in 2012, 14 million toilets were sold in the US market. TOTO's sales to the US in 2012 were approximately US$150 million. In 1989, TOTO began to make inroads into the US market with the establishment of TOKI KiKi USA, Inc., but in 2012 their overall market share of the US toilet market was still only very small – approximately 6 per cent.

Americans are said to move residences once every seven or eight years, creating a used-home market larger than that in Japan. As a consequence, remodelling is effectively the same level as (or better than) that of new homes. Compared with Japan, the US has stricter water conservation regulations for toilets and spurred by these regulations, industry specialists expect to see demand for replacement toilets in the future.

New housing starts are over 1.6 million annually, thanks in part to low interest rates in the US new housing market. Even when you consider the 1.1 million new housing starts in Japan, the US housing market is substantially larger in scale, and therefore has more potential. TOTO is targeting high value-added markets in the US through the kitchen/bath shop and waterworks channels, and bypassing the home improvement centre channel. Through the kitchen/bath shop and waterworks channels TOTO provides customers with services, including consulting and installation for its products. In this way TOTO is hoping to capture market shares in the high-end of the US toilet market.

TOTO penetrates the US market but is facing cultural barriers

TOTO made toilet history in 1980 when, improving on a US model that combined the bidet and the toilet seat, it produced the 'Washlet', bringing warm water to the user's nether regions. TOTO did what the American toilet makers were reluctant to try – they brought electronics into the water closet. Top-of-the-line Washlets now came with wall-mounted control panels as complex as those of stereo systems. Their manifold buttons allow adjustment of the nozzle position, water pressure and type of spray, plus blow-drying, air purification and seat warming for those cold winter mornings. Water and seat temperatures are adjustable. The controls can also be set so the lid rises as the user approaches the Washlet. Globally, more than 20 million Washlets have been sold (mainly in Japan) since their introduction in 1980. The US, however, is a country without a history with the bidet. Bidets – usually stand-alone fixtures used in conjunction with toilets – originated in France and have been in use throughout the southern part of Europe since the 1700s. Ironically, almost three decades ago TOTO began importing hospital-grade bidets from the US to sell to Japan's ageing population. It soon discovered there was a larger market for the fixtures and adapted the traditional bidet into a toilet seat attachment, which fits onto existing toilet bowls.

While US consumers are just waking up to Washlets, the Japanese are going even more upmarket. TOTO's new Neorest model, Washlet integrated toilet (introduced in 2003) gets rid of the inner rim of the bowl and brings in 'the tornado flush'. The Neorest (priced at US$5,200) has all the features of TOTO's Washlet, including a heated seat for cold nights, built-in back-and-front bidet with oscillating or pulsating spray massage and a warm-air dryer, all with temperature controls on a wall-mounted remote. Add to these features the smart toilet's built-in air purifier and motion sensors that detect your approach and automatically raise the lid. Males can lift the seat with the touch of a button and in doing so instruct the unit to flush with less water. Complete your business and the toilet automatically shuts the lid (while putting the seat down!) and flushes.

QUESTIONS

1. What cultural barriers would the Japanese managers from Toto meet when negotiating with American managers from building societies about new contracts for toilets in US luxury apartments?

2. Some analysts argue that tackling cultural toilet norms and barriers is not worth the effort and that Toto would be better off pulling its Washlets and Neorests out of the US and Europe altogether and concentrating on more receptive Asian markets like China, and of course Japan. Do you agree? Why? Why not?

Sources: Toto annual and financial report 2012; adapted from Helms T. (2003, 'The toilet marketplace', *Supply House Times,* September 2003, pp. 72–78; www.ceramicindustry.com; www.toto.co.jp; www.worldtoilet.org.

VIDEO CASE STUDY 18.3 Dunkin' Donuts
download from **www.pearsoned.co.uk/hollensen**

Dunkin' Donuts (www.dunkindonuts.com) is a coffee and baked goods chain, selling 5 million doughnuts and 4 million cups of coffee daily. Dunkin' Donuts sell a variety of doughnuts and bakery products such as muffins and bagels as well as beverages such as iced coffee. In the US in 2014 there were over 8,000 Dunkin' Donuts locations across 41 states. Internationally, there were over 3,200 Dunkin' Donuts locations in 48 countries. Dunkin' Donuts' most significant presence overseas is in the Philippines, Indonesia, South Korea and Thailand. Their international locations are mainly concentrated in Asia-Pacific and Latin America.

Source: Northfoto/Shutterstock.com.

In July 2011, Dunkin' Brands (also including Baskin-Robbins icecream shops) was introduced on the stock exchange. The total revenues were $749 million in 2014. Profits before taxes were $255 million.

Questions

1. Dunkin' Donuts wants to get a better market position in Europe, and set up a meeting in London with potential franchisees from different European countries in order to negotiate franchising deals that could provide a higher growth in this region. What potential dangers should the US negotiator be aware of in this kind of cross-national negotiation?

2. What is Dunkin' Donuts' value perception and positioning strategy?

3. How has Dunkin' Donuts responded to competitive changes in the global marketplace?

For further resources, see this book's website at **www.pearsoned.co.uk/hollensen**

Questions for discussion

1. Explain why the negotiation process abroad may differ from country to country.

2. You are a European preparing to negotiate with a Japanese firm for the first time. How would you prepare for the assignment if it is taking place: (a) in the Japanese headquarters; (b) in one of its European subsidiaries?

3. Should expatriate personnel be used? What are some of the difficulties they may encounter overseas? What can be done to minimize these problems?

4. Compare and contrast the negotiating styles of Europeans and Asians. What are the similarities? What are the differences?

5. What are your views on lobbying efforts by foreign firms?

6. Why is it so difficult for an international marketer to deal with bribery?

References

Andersen, P.H. (2003) 'Relationship marketing in cross-cultural contexts', in Rugimbana, R. and Nwankwo, S. (eds), *Cross-cultural Marketing.* London: Thomson, pp. 209–225.

Anglemar, R. and Stern, L.W. (1978) 'Development of a content analytical system for analysis of bargaining communication in marketing', *Journal of Marketing Research,* February, pp. 93–102.

Bell, D.B., Giordano, R. and Putz, P. (2002) 'Inter-firm sharing of process knowledge: exploring knowledge markets', *Knowledge and Process Management,* 9(1), pp. 12–22.

Berrell, M., Gloet, M. and Wright, P. (2002) 'Organizational learning in international joint ventures: implications for management development', *Journal of Management Development,* 21(2), pp. 83–100.

Bush, V.D. and Ingram, T. (2001) 'Building and assessing cultural diversity skills: implications for sales training', *Industrial Marketing Management,* 30, pp. 65–76.

Choo, C. (1998) *The Knowing Organization.* Oxford University Press, New York.

Chua, R.Y.J. (2012) 'Building Effective Business Relationships in China', *MIT Sloan Management Review,* 53(4), pp. 27–33.

Della Cava, R.R. (1999) 'Magic kingdoms, new colonies: theme parks are staking bigger claims in Europe', *USA Today,* 17 February.

Desouza, K. and Evaristo, R. (2003) 'Global knowledge management strategies', *European Management Journal,* 21(1), pp. 62–67.

Fisher, R. and Ury, W. (1981) *Getting to Yes: Negotiating Agreement Without Giving In.* Penguin Books, New York.

Gesteland, R.R. (1996) *Cross-cultural Business Behaviour.* Copenhagen Business School Press, Copenhagen.

Govindarajan, V. and Gupta, A.K. (2001) 'Building an effective global business team', *MIT Sloan Management Review,* Summer, pp. 63–71.

Griffith, D.A. (2002) 'The role of communication competencies in international business relationship development', *Journal of World Business,* 37(4), pp. 256–265.

Guy, B.S. and Patton, P.W.E. (1996) 'Managing the effects of culture shock and sojourner adjustment on the expatriate industrial sales force', *Industrial Marketing Management,* 25, pp. 385–393.

Harris, P.R. and Moran, R.T. (1987) *Managing Cultural Differences.* Houston, TX: Gulf Publishing Company.

Harvey, M.G. and Griffith, D.A. (2002) 'Developing effective intercultural relationships: the importance of communication strategies', *Thunderbird International Business Review,* 44(4), pp. 455–476.

Hofstede, G. (1983) 'The cultural relativity of organizational practices and theories', *Journal of International Business Studies,* Fall, pp. 75–89.

Hofstede, G. and Bond, M.R. (1988) 'The Confucius connection: from cultural roots to economic growth', *Organizational Dynamics,* 16(4), pp. 4–21.

Hooker, J. (2009) 'Corruption from a cross-cultural perspective', *Cross Cultural Management,* 16(3), pp. 251–267.

Huang, L. (2010) 'Cross-cultural communication in business negotiations', *International Journal of Economics and Finance,* 2(2) (May), pp. 196–199.

Kim, Y.H. (2011) 'Google boss searches for local style', *The Wall Street Journal,* March 22, p. 31.

Madsen, T.K. (1994) 'A contingency approach to export performance research', *Advances in International Marketing,* 6, pp. 25–42.

Magnusson, P. and Boyle, B.A. (2009) 'A contingency perspective on psychic distance in international channel relationships', *Journal of Marketing Channels,* 16, pp. 77–99.

Mayfield, M. (1997) 'Time perspective of the cross cultural negotiation process', *American Business Review,* January, pp. 78–85.

McGinnis, M.A. (2005) 'Lessons in cross-cultural negotiations', *Supply Chain Management Review,* April, pp. 9–10.

Nonaka, I. and Takeuchi, H. (1995) *The Knowledge-creating Company.* Oxford University Press, New York.

Rowden, R.W. (2001) 'Research note: how a small business enters the international market', *Thunderbird International Business Review,* 43(2), pp. 257–268.

Salacuse, J.W. (2010) 'Teaching international business negotiation: reflections on three decades of experience', *International Negotiation*, 15, pp. 187–228.

Sanyal, R. (2012) 'Patterns in international bribery: Violations of the foreign corrupt practices act', *Thunderbird International Business Review*, 54(3), pp. 299–309.

Schein, E.H. (1985) *Organizational Culture and Leadership*. Jossey-Bass Publishers, San Francisco, CA.

Scott, J., Gilliard, D. and Scott, R. (2002) 'Eliminating bribery as a transnational marketing strategy', *International Journal of Commerce & Management*, 12(1), pp. 1–17.

Simintiras, A.C. and Reynolds, N. (2001) 'Toward an understanding of the role of cross-cultural equivalence in international personal selling', *Journal of Marketing Management*, 16(8), pp. 829–851.

Simintiras, A.C. and Thomas, A.H. (1998) 'Cross-cultural sales negotiations: a literature review and research propositions', *International Marketing Review*, 15(1), pp. 10–28.

Snyder, D. (2002) *Euro Disney S.C.A.: Individual Term Paper International Marketing*. John Hopkins University, Baltimore, MD.

Stewart, D. (2001) 'Reinterpreting the learning organization', *The Learning Organization*, 8(4), pp. 141–152.

Tagliabue, J. (2000) 'Lights, action in France for second Disney Park', *New York Times*, 13 February.

Volkema, R.J., and Fleck, D. (2012) 'Understanding propensity to initiate negotiations: an examination of the effects of culture and personality', *International Journal of Conflict Management*, 23(3), pp. 266–289.

Wolf, J. (2002) 'Multicultural workgroups', *Management International Review*, 42(1), pp. 3–4.

Zhang, M.Y. and Dodgson, M. (2007) 'A roasted duck can still fly away: a case study of technology, nationality, culture and the rapid and early internationalization of the firm', *Journal of World Business*, 42, pp. 336–349.

CHAPTER 19
Organization and control of the global marketing programme

Contents

Learning objectives

After studying this chapter you should be able to:

- Examine how firms build their organizational structure internationally and what roles headquarters can play
- Identify the variables that affect the reorganization design
- Describe and evaluate functional, geographic, product and matrix organizations as the key international structural alternatives

- Explain the pitfalls and opportunities of global account management
- Describe the key elements of the marketing control system
- List the most important measures for marketing performance
- Explain how a global marketing budget is established
- Understand the steps in developing the global marketing plan.

19.1   Introduction

The overall objective of this chapter is to study intra-organizational relationships as part of the firm's attempt to optimize its competitive response in areas most critical to its business. As market conditions change, and companies evolve from purely domestic entities to multinationals, their organizational structure, coordination and control systems must also change.

First, this chapter will focus on the advantages and disadvantages of the main organizational structures available, as well as their appropriateness at various stages of internationalization. Then the chapter will outline the need for a control system to oversee the international operations of the company.

19.2   Organization of global marketing activities

The way in which a global marketing organization is structured is an important determinant of its ability to exploit the opportunities available to it effectively and efficiently. It also determines the capacity for responding to problems and challenges. Companies operating internationally must decide whether the organization should be structured along functions, products, geographical areas or combinations of the three (a matrix). The evolutionary nature of organizational changes is shown in Figure 19.1. The following pages discuss the different organizational structures.

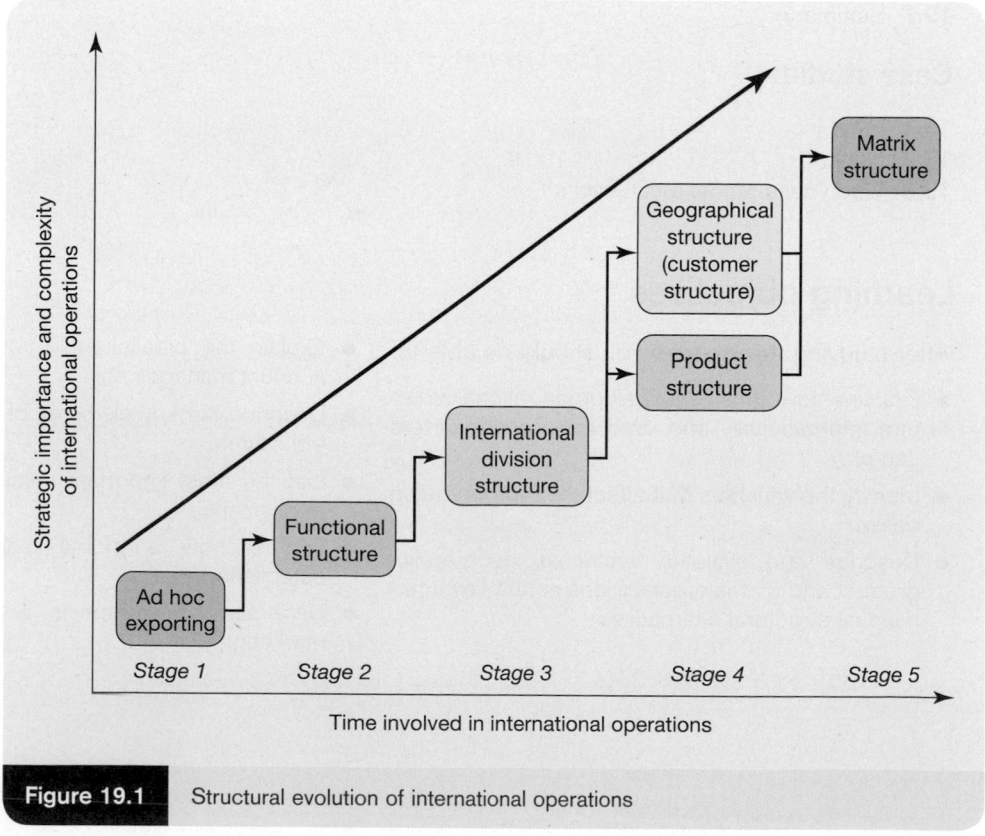

Figure 19.1   Structural evolution of international operations

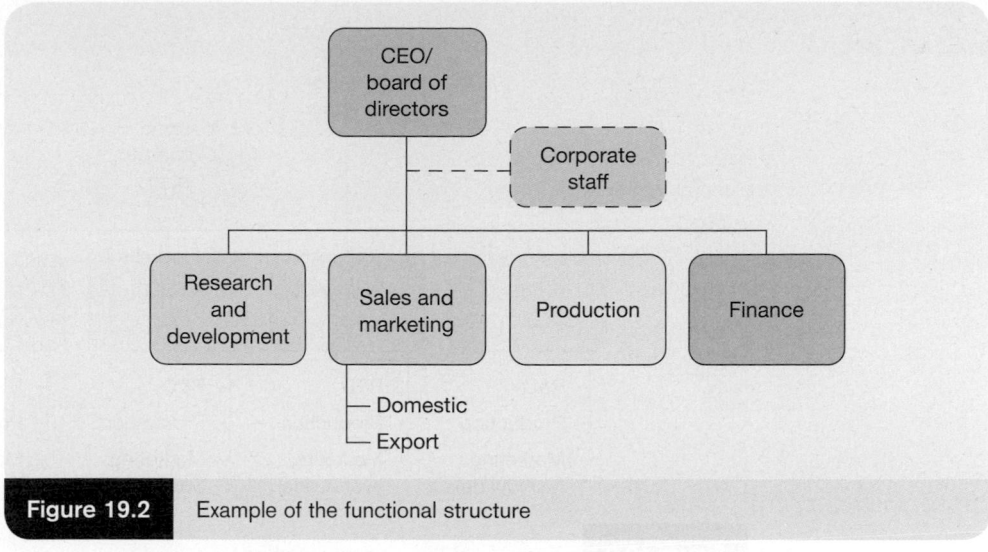

Figure 19.2   Example of the functional structure

Functional structure

Functional structure
Here, the next level after top management is divided into functional departments, e.g. R&D, sales and marketing, production and finance.

Of all the approaches, the **functional structure** (Figure 19.2) is the simplest. Here management is concerned primarily with the functional efficiency of the company.

Many companies begin their international business activities as a result of having received enquiries from abroad. The company, being new to international business, has no international specialist and typically has few products and few markets. In this early stage of international involvement, the domestic marketing department may have the responsibility for global marketing activities but, as the international involvement intensifies, an export or international department may become part of the organizational structure. The export department may be a sub-department of the sales and marketing department (as in Figure 19.2) or may have equal ranking with the other functional departments. This choice will depend on the importance assigned to the export activities of the firm. Because the export department is the first real step in internationalizing the organizational structure, it should be a fully fledged marketing organization and not merely a sales organization. The functional export department design is particularly suitable for small and medium-sized enterprises (SMEs), as well as larger companies, that are manufacturing standardized products and are in the early stages of developing international business, having low product and area diversities.

International divisional structure

International divisional structure
As international sales grow, at some point the international division may emerge at the same level as the functional departments.

As international sales grow, at some point an **international divisional structure** may emerge. This division becomes directly responsible for the development and implementation of the overall international strategy. The international division incorporates international expertise, information flows about foreign market opportunities and authority over international activities. However, manufacturing and other related functions remain with the domestic divisions in order to take advantage of economies of scale.

International divisions best serve firms with new products that do not vary significantly in terms of their environmental sensitivity, and whose international sales and profits are still quite insignificant compared with those of the domestic divisions.

Product divisional structure

Product divisional structure
The next level after top management is divided into product division, e.g. product A, B, C and D.

A typical **product divisional structure** is presented in Figure 19.3.

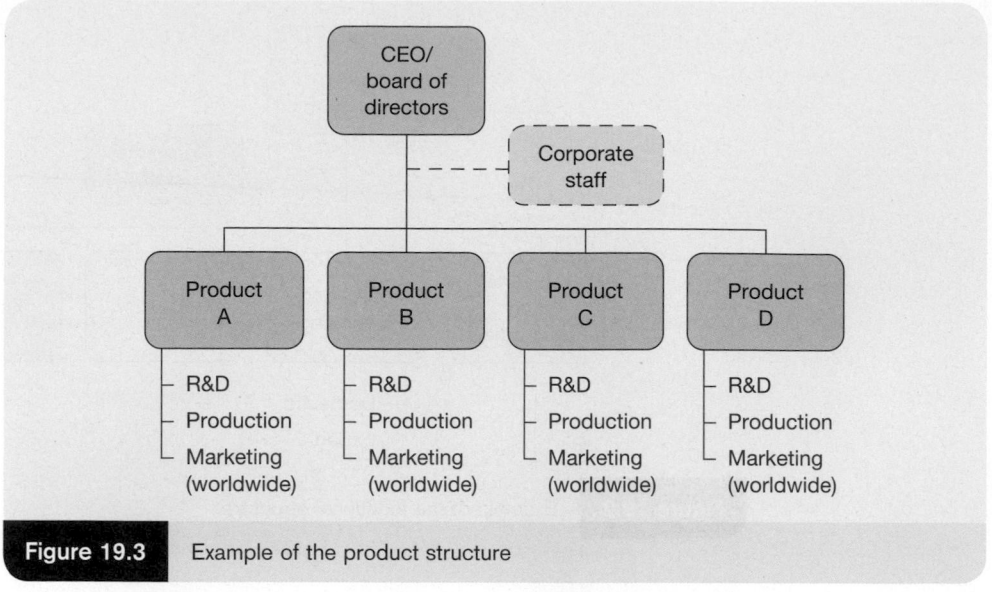

Figure 19.3   Example of the product structure

In general, the product structure is better suited to companies with more experience in international business and marketing, and with diversified product lines and extensive R&D activities. The product division structure is most appropriate under conditions where the products have the potential for worldwide standardization. One of the major benefits of the approach is improved cost efficiency through centralization of manufacturing facilities for each product line. This is crucial in industries in which competitive position is determined by world market share, which in turn is often determined by the degree to which manufacturing is rationalized (utilization of economies of scale). The main disadvantages of this type of structure are:

● It duplicates functional resources: you will find R&D, production, marketing, sales force management, etc. in each product division.
● It under-utilizes sales and distribution facilities (subsidiaries) abroad. In the 'product structure' there is a tendency that marketing of products is taken care of, centrally from the home base ('marketing [worldwide]'). Therefore there is less need for the facilities in the local sales subsidiary.
● The product divisions tend to develop a total independence from each other in world markets. For example, a global product division structure may end up with several subsidiaries in the same foreign country reporting to different product divisions, with no one at headquarters responsible for the overall corporate presence in that country.

Geographical structure

Geographical structure
The next level after top management is divided into international divisions, e.g. Europe, North America, Latin America, Asia-Pacific and Africa/ Middle East.

If market conditions with respect to product acceptance and operating conditions vary considerably across world markets, then the **geographical structure** is the one to choose. This structure is especially useful for companies that have a homogeneous range of products (similar technologies and common end-use markets), but at the same time need fast and efficient worldwide distribution. Typically, the world is divided into regions (divisions), as shown in Figure 19.4.

Many food, beverage, car and pharmaceutical companies use this type of structure. Its main advantage is its ability to respond easily and quickly to the environmental and market demands of a regional or national area through minor modifications in product design, pricing, market communication and packaging. Therefore the structure encourages adaptive global marketing programmes. Moreover, economies of scale can be achieved within regions. Another reason for the popularity of this structure is its tendency to create area autonomy.

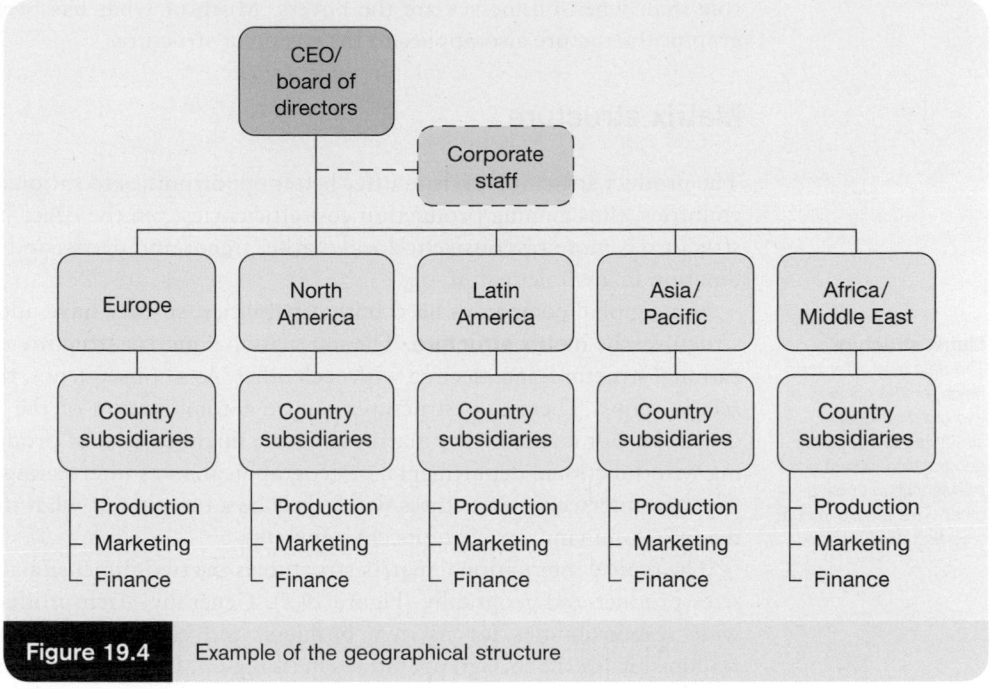

Figure 19.4   Example of the geographical structure

However, this may also complicate the tasks of coordinating product variations and transferring new product ideas and marketing techniques from one country to another.

Hence the geographical structure ensures the best use of the firm's regional expertise, but it means a less than optimal allocation of product and functional expertise. If each region needs its own staff of product and functional specialists, duplication and also inefficiency may be the result. As indicated in Figure 19.4, the geographical structure may include both regional management centres (e.g. Europe, North America) and country-based subsidiaries.

Regional management centres

There are two main reasons for the existence of regional management centres (RMCs):

1. When sales volume in a particular region becomes substantial, there need to be some specialized staff to focus on that region, to realize more fully the potential of an already growing market.
2. Homogeneity within regions and heterogeneity between them necessitate treating each important region separately. Therefore a regional management centre becomes an appropriate organizational feature.

Country-based subsidiaries

Instead of, or parallel to, a regional centre, each country has its own organizational unit. Country-based subsidiaries are characterized by a high degree of adaptation to local conditions. Since each subsidiary develops its own unique activities and its own autonomy, it is sometimes relevant to combine local subsidiaries with an RMC: for example, to utilize opportunities across European countries.

Firms may also organize their operations using a customer structure, especially if the customer groups they serve are very different, e.g. businesses and governments. Catering to these diverse groups may require the concentration of specialists in particular divisions. The product may be the same, but the buying processes of the various customer groups may differ. Governmental buying is characterized by bidding, in which price plays a larger role than when businesses are the buyers. Much of what has been said about the geographical structure also applies to the customer structure.

Matrix structure

The product structure tends to offer better opportunities to rationalize production across countries, thus gaining production cost efficiencies. On the other hand, the geographical structure is more responsive to local market trends and needs, and allows for more coordination in a whole region.

Some global companies need both capabilities, so they have adopted a more complex structure: the **matrix structure**. The international matrix structure consists of two organizational structures intersecting with each other. As a consequence, there are dual reporting relationships. These two structures can be a combination of the general forms already discussed. For example, the matrix structure might consist of product divisions intersecting with functional departments, or geographical areas intersecting with global divisions. The two intersecting structures will largely be a function of what the organization sees as the two dominant aspects of its environment.

The typical international matrix structure is the two-dimensional structure that emphasizes product and geography (Figure 19.5). Generally, each product division has worldwide responsibilities for its own business, and each geographical or area division is responsible for the foreign operations in its region. If national organizations (subsidiaries) are involved, they are responsible for operations at the country level.

Because the two dimensions of product and geography overlap at the affiliate level, both enter into local decision-making and planning processes. It is assumed that area and product managers will defend different positions, but this will lead to tensions and creative conflict. Area managers will tend to favour responsiveness to local environmental factors, and product managers will defend positions favouring cost efficiencies and global competitiveness. The matrix structure deliberately creates a dual focus to ensure that conflicts between product and geographical area concerns are identified and then analysed objectively.

Matrix structure
The next level after top management consists of two organizational structures (product and geographical areas) intersecting with each other. This results in dual reporting relationships.

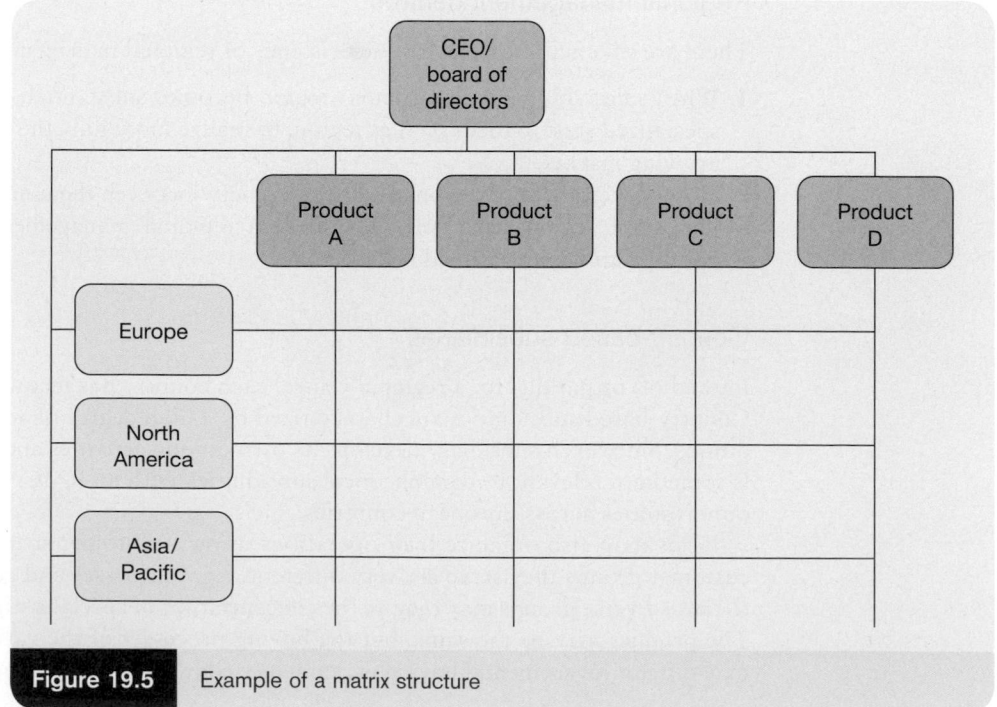

Figure 19.5   Example of a matrix structure

The structure is useful for companies that are both product-diversified and geographically spread. By combining a product management approach with a market-oriented approach, one can meet the needs of both markets and products.

The future role of the international manager

At the end of the 1980s, many internationally oriented companies adopted the transnational model (Bartlett and Ghoshal, 1989). It held that companies should leverage their capabilities across borders and transfer best practices to achieve global economies and respond to the local market. In this way, companies avoided duplicating their functions (product development, manufacturing and marketing). However, it required that senior managers could think, operate and communicate along three dimensions: function, product and geography. Surely there are few such 'supermanagers' around!

In a study by Quelch (1992), one manager says of changing managerial roles: 'I am at the fulcrum of the tension between local adaptation and global standardization. My boss tells me to think global and act local. That's easier said than done' (p. 158).

There is no universal solution to the ideal profile for an international manager, but Quelch and Bloom (1996) have predicted the 'fall of the transnational manager and the return of the country manager'. They studied the behaviour of country managers in different countries and concluded that the opportunities in expanding emerging markets (e.g. eastern Europe) have to be grasped by entrepreneurial country managers. The transnational manager is better suited to stable and saturated markets, such as western Europe.

This also underlined by the conclusion on Ghemawat and Vantrappen (2015) that despite globalization, the vast majority of the world's largest corporations (87 per cent of Fortune Global 500) are run by CEOs native to the country in which the company is headquartered (one notable exception, however, is Satya Nadella, who was born in India, but became CEO of Microsoft in 2014). As a consequence of this native CEO orientation, more executive diversity at the top is needed. National and cultural diversity at the top of the multinationals should be a topic of conversation for the board of directors.

19.3   The global account management organization

Global account management
A relationship-oriented marketing management approach focusing on dealing with the needs of an important global customer (an account) with a global organization (foreign subsidiaries all over the world).

Global account management (GAM) can be understood as a relationship-oriented marketing management approach focusing on dealing with the needs of an important global customer (i.e. an account) in the business-to-business (B2B) market.

Global account management can be defined as an organizational form (a person or a team) in a global supplier organization used to coordinate and manage worldwide activities, by servicing an important customer centrally from headquarters (Harvey *et al.*, 2002) (see also Figure 19.6).

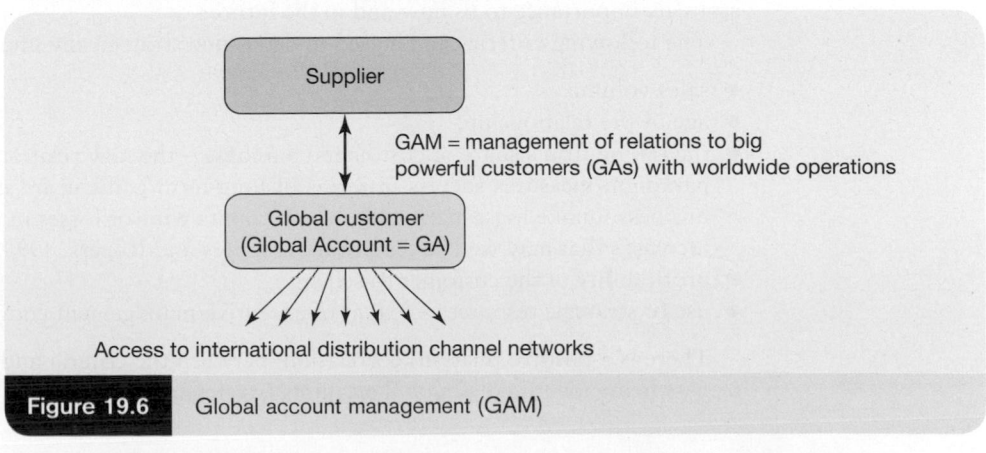

Figure 19.6   Global account management (GAM)

For the small supplier enterprises that are ambitious and growth-oriented, it is imperative that they learn to find ways of engaging with large multinational corporations (MNCs) (global customers) who have the complementary resources and capabilities that can lead to, for instance, an innovative product offering being rolled out on a global scale, through the international distribution system of the global customer (global account). In other words, these small suppliers must seriously consider, as Prashantham and Birkinshaw (2008) put it, learning how to 'dance with the gorillas'.

A global account is a customer that is of strategic importance to the achievement of the supplier's corporate objectives, pursues integrated and coordinated strategies on a worldwide basis, and demands a globally integrated product/service offering (Wilson and Millman, 2003).

A global account manager is the person in the selling company who represents that company's capabilities to the buying company, the buying company's needs to the selling company, and brings the two together (Hollensen and Wulff, 2010).

The importance of GAM strategies will grow in future (Harvey *et al.*, 2002; Shi *et al.*, 2004, 2005) because of the consolidation [mergers and acquisitions (M&As) and global strategic alliances] that takes place in most industries. This development means that big MNC customers are getting even bigger and more powerful, with increasing buying power. In the following we discuss what the supplier can do about this development.

Successful GAM often requires an understanding of the logic of both product and service management. Moreover, excellent operational level capabilities are useless if strategic level management is inferior, and vice versa – the GAM approach combines strategic and operational level marketing management.

The starting point for the following is the firm that wishes to implement GAM. Afterwards the development of GAM is regarded in a dyadic perspective.

Implementation of GAM

The firm that wants to implement successful GAM with suitable global accounts may go through the following four steps (Ojasalo, 2001):

1. identifying the selling firm's global accounts
2. analysing the global accounts
3. selecting suitable strategies for the global accounts
4. developing operational level capabilities to build, grow and maintain profitable and long-lasting relationships with global accounts.

Identifying the selling firm's global accounts

This means answering the following question: which existing or potential accounts are of strategic importance to us now and in the future?

The following criteria can be used to determine strategically important customers:

● sales volume;
● age of the relationship;
● the selling firm's share of customers' purchase – the new relationship marketing (RM) paradigm measures success in terms of long-term gains in its share of its customers' business, unlike mass marketing, which counts wins or losses in terms of market share increases that may well be temporary (Peppers and Rogers, 1995);
● profitability of the customer to seller;
● use of strategic resources – extent of executive/management commitment.

There is a positive relation (correlation) between the criteria and the likelihood of customers being identified as global accounts (strategic customers).

Analysing global accounts

This includes activities such as analysing:

- *The basic characteristics of a global account.* Includes assessing the relevant economic and activity aspects of their internal and external environments. This, for example, includes the account's internal value chain inputs, markets, suppliers, products and economic situation.
- *The relationship history.* Involves assessing the relevant economic and activity aspects of the relationship history. This includes volume of sales, profitability, global account's objectives, buying behaviour (the account's decision-making process), information exchange, special needs, buying frequency and complaints. Among the above-mentioned aspects, knowing/estimating relationship value plays a particularly important role. The revenues from each global account (customer lifetime value) should exceed the costs of establishing and maintaining the relationship within a certain time span.
- *The level and development of commitment to the relationship.* The account's present and anticipated commitment to the relationship is important, since the extent of the business with the account depends on that.
- *Goal congruence of the parties.* Goal congruence, or commonality of interests between buyer and seller, greatly affects their cooperation at both the strategic and operational levels. Common interests and relationship value together determine whether two companies can be partners, friends or rivals. The organization that aims its sights lower than the sort of partnership relationship an account is looking for risks losing long-term share of that account's business.
- *Switching costs.* It is useful to estimate both the global account's and the selling company's switching costs in the event that the relationship dissolves. Switching costs are the costs of replacing an existing partner with another. These may be very different for the two parties and thus affect the power position in the relationship. Switching costs are also called transaction costs and are affected by irretrievable investments in the relationship, the adaptations made and the bonds that have developed. High switching costs may prevent a relationship from ending, even though the global account's accumulated satisfaction with the selling company may be non-existent or negative.

Selecting suitable strategies for the global accounts

This depends greatly on the power positions of the seller and the global account. The power structure within different accounts may vary significantly. Thus the selling company may typically not freely select the strategy – there is often only one strategic alternative to be chosen if there is a desire to retain the account.

The selling firm might prefer to avoid very powerful accounts. Sometimes the selling firm realizes that accounts that are less attractive today may become attractive in future. Thus, in the case of certain accounts, the objective of the strategy may be merely to keep the relationship alive for future opportunities.

Developing operational level capabilities

This refers to customization and development of capabilities related to the following.

Product/service development and performance

Joint R&D projects are typical between a selling company and a global account in industrial and high-tech markets. In addition, information technology (IT) applied in just-in-time production and distribution channels increases the possibilities of customizing the offering in consumer markets as well.

New products developed in a partnership are not automatically more successful than those developed in-house. However, R&D projects may bring other kinds of long-term benefits, such as access to account organization and learning. Improving capabilities for providing services to global accounts is extremely important, because even when the core product is a tangible good, it is often the related services that differentiate the selling company from its competitors and provide competitive advantage.

Organizational structure

The selling company's *organizational ability* to meet the global account's needs can be developed, for example, by adjusting the organizational structure to correspond to the global account's global and local needs and by increasing the number of interfaces between the selling company and the account, and thus also the number of interacting persons. Organizational capabilities can also be developed by organizing teams, consisting of people with the necessary competences and authorities, to take care of global accounts.

Individuals (human resources)

A company's capabilities related to individuals can be developed by selecting the right people as global account managers and for global account teams, and by developing their skills. The global account manager's responsibilities are often complex and varied, and therefore require a large number of skills and qualifications, which should be taken into account in the selection and development of global account managers.

It is quite common to find that the current set of global account managers may be good at maintaining their own relationships with their contacts in the account but lack the total set of skills required to lead an account team through a transition in the account relationship. Therefore an assessment of the total desired interfaces between the seller and the customer needs to be considered. It may be that a change is required by moving the relationship from a dependency on a one-to-one relationship (between the global account manager and the chief buyer) to a network of organizational relationships spanning many different projects, functions and countries.

Information exchange

Information exchange between the selling company and a global account is particularly important in GAM. An important relationship-specific task is to search, filter, judge and store information about the organizations, strategies, goals, potentials and problems of the partners. However, this mainly depends on the mutual trust and attitudes of the parties, and on the technical arrangements. A global account's trust is something that the selling company has to earn over time by its performance, whereas the technical side can be developed, for example with IT.

Company and individual level benefits

Successful long-term GAM in a business-to-business context always requires the ability to offer both company and individual level benefits to global accounts.

Company level benefits are rational and may be either short- or long-term, direct or indirect, and typically contribute to the global account's turnover, profitability, cost savings, organizational efficiency and effectiveness and image. Individual level benefits, in turn, may be rational or emotional. From the relationship management point of view, global individuals are the ones with the power to continue or terminate the relationship. Rational individual level benefits contribute, for example, to the individual's own career, income and ease of job. Emotional individual level benefits include friendship, a sense of caring and ego enhancement.

The dyadic development of GAM

The Millman–Wilson model in Figure 19.7 describes and demonstrates the typical dyadic progression of a relationship between buyer and seller through five stages – pre-GAM, early GAM, mid-GAM, partnership GAM and synergistic-GAM (Wilson and Millman, 2003).

Pre-GAM describes preparation for GAM. A buying company is identified as having key account potential, and the selling company starts to focus resources on winning some business with that prospect. Both seller and buyer are sending out signals (factual information) and exchanging messages (interactions) prior to the decision to engage in transactions. There is a need to develop networks of contacts, to gain knowledge about the customer's operations and to begin to assess the potential for relational development.

Early GAM. At this stage, the selling company is concerned with identifying the opportunities for account penetration once the account has been won. This is probably the most typical sales relationship, the classic 'bow tie'.

Adapted solutions are needed, and key account managers will be focused on understanding more about their customers and the market in which those customers are competing. The buying company will still be market-testing other selling companies. Detailed knowledge of the global customer and its core competences, the depth of the relationship and the potential for creating relation-specific entrepreneurial value are all limited at this stage. There is an increasing need for political skills to be applied as the potential of the account is identified and the global account manager is called upon to ensure that the resources of the supplier configure to best serve the needs of the customer (Wilson and Millman, 2003). The selling company must concentrate hard on product, service and intangibles – the buying company wants recognition that the product offering is the prime reason for the relationship – and expects it to work.

Mid-GAM. This is a transition stage between the classic 'bow tie' and the 'diamond' of the partnership GAM stage (see Figure 19.8).

At this stage, the selling company has established credibility with the buying company. Contacts between the two organizations increase at all levels and assume greater importance. Nevertheless, buying companies still feel the need for alternative sources of supply. This may be driven by their own customers' desire for choice. The selling company's offering is still periodically market-tested, but is reliably perceived to be of good value. The selling company is now a 'preferred' supplier.

Partnership GAM. This is the stage where benefits should start to flow. When partnership GAM is reached, the selling company is seen by the buying company organization as a strategic external resource. The two companies will be sharing sensitive information and engaging in joint problem-solving. Pricing will be long-term and stable, but it will have been established that each side will allow the other to make a profit.

If a major disadvantage of the bow tie of early GAM was the denial of access to customers' internal processes and to their market, the main advantage of the 'diamond' relationship is in seeing and understanding the 'opening' of the 'global account'.

Global accounts will test all the supplier company's innovations so that they have first access to, and first benefit from, the latest technology. The buying company will expect to be guaranteed continuity of supply and access to the best material. Expertise will be shared. The buying company will also expect to gain from continuous improvement. There may be joint promotions, where appropriate.

Synergistic GAM. This is the ultimate stage in the relational development model. The experience gained at the partnership stage – coordinating the team-sell, coaching the team on its interface roles – will be a good starting point for moving to synergistic GAM. The closer the relationship, the greater the knowledge about the customer and the greater the potential for creating entrepreneurial value.

The selling company understands that it still has no automatic right to the customer's business. Nevertheless, exit barriers have been built up. The buying company is confident that its relationship with the selling company is delivering improved quality and reduced cost. Costing systems become transparent. Joint research and development will take place.

There will be interfaces at every level and function between the organizations. Top management commitment will be fulfilled through joint board meetings and reviews.

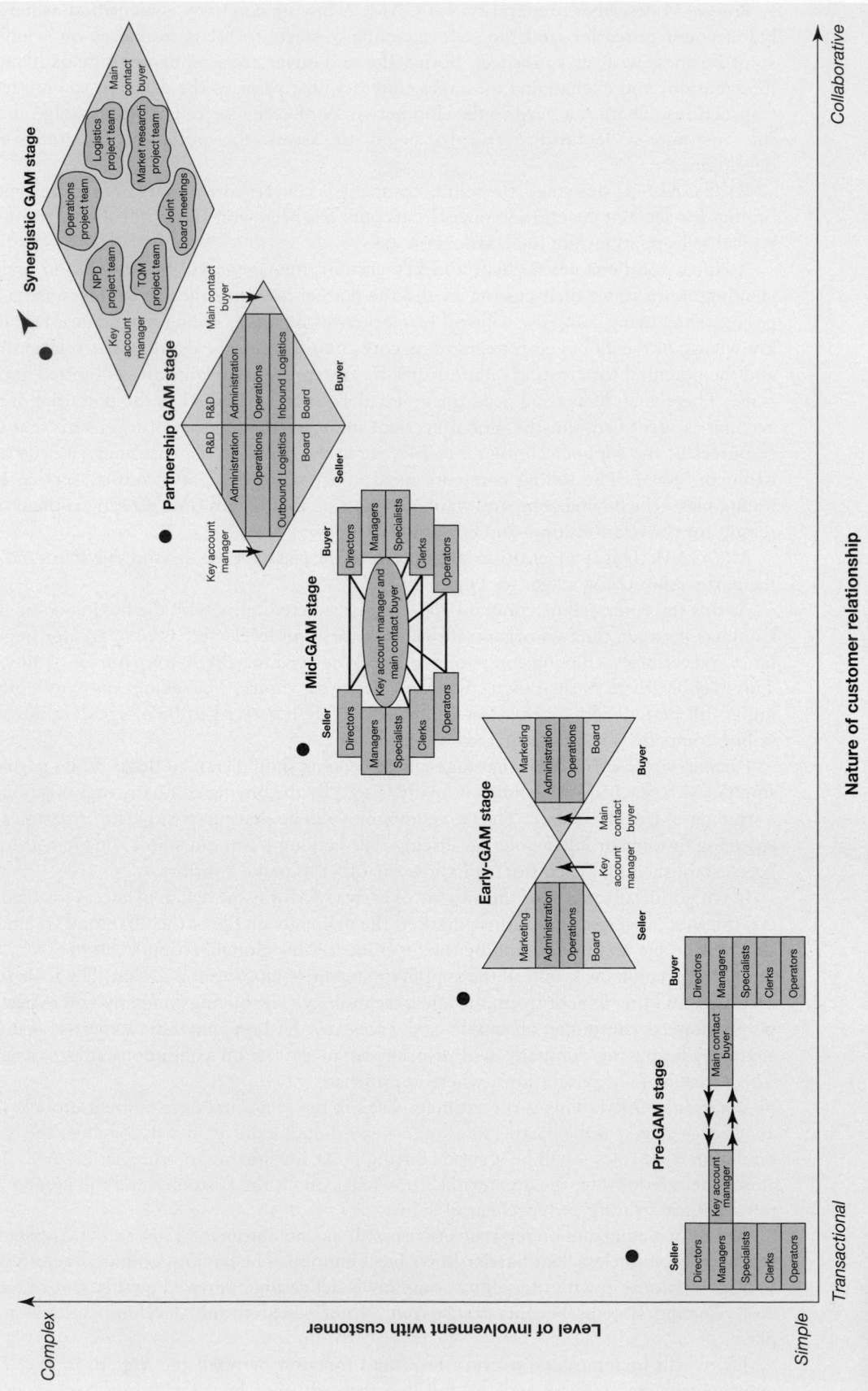

Figure 19.7   Rational development model

Sources: adapted from Millman and Wilson (1995); Wilson and Millman (2003).

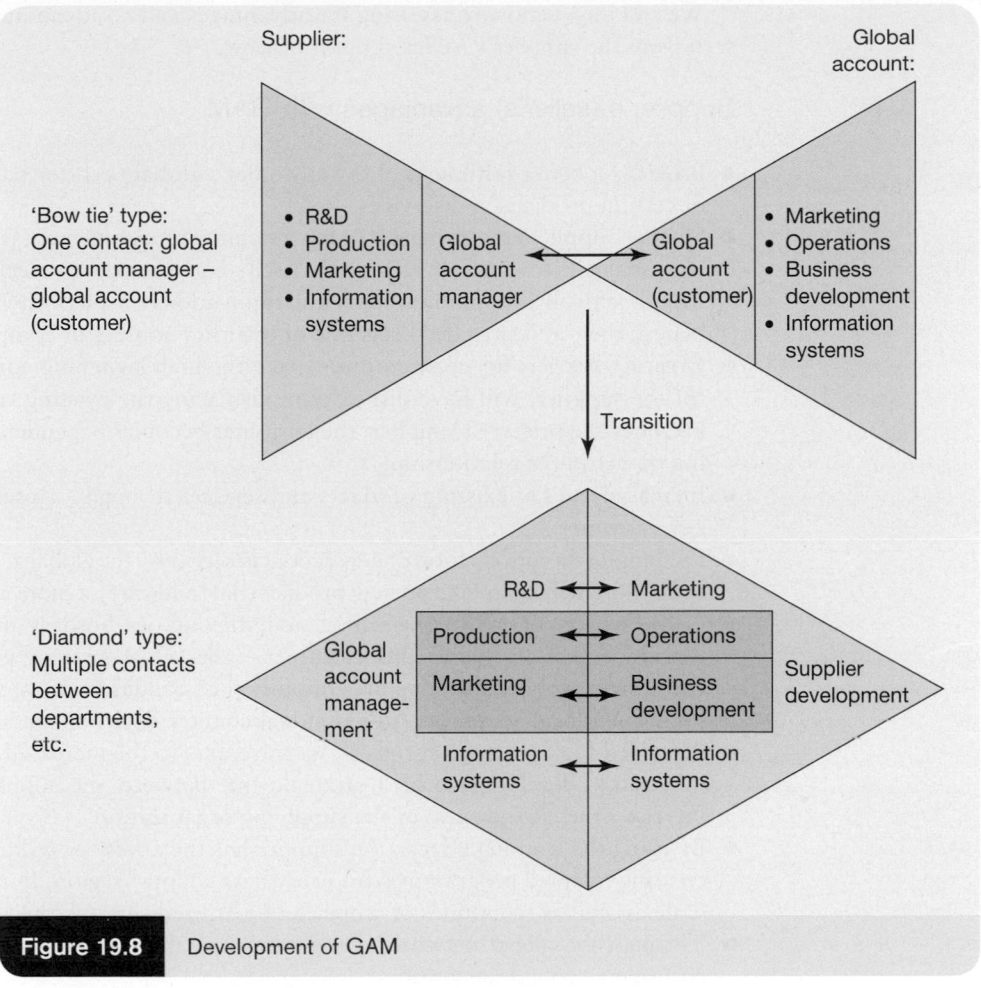

Figure 19.8   Development of GAM

There will be a joint business plan, joint strategies and joint market research. Information flow should be streamlined and information systems integration will be planned or in place as a consequence. Transaction costs will be reduced.

Although there are clear advantages for both partners in moving through the different GAM stages, there are also pitfalls. As the contacts proliferate through the stages, so does the speed of activity – and the risk of saying and doing the wrong things. Through the stages the key account manager changes from 'super salesperson' to 'super coach'. In the last two stages, the key account manager moves on to a 'super coordinator', who conducts the orchestra.

If the key account manager does not move along then the potential of losing control is great, resulting in well-meaning but misdirected individuals following their own quite separate courses.

Key account management requires process excellence and highly skilled professionals to manage relationships with strategic customers. For most companies this represents a number of revolutions. A revolution is needed in the way activity is costed and costs are attributed, from product or geographical focus to customer focus. Currently few financial or information systems in companies are sophisticated enough to support the higher levels of key account management. A transformation is needed in the way the professional with responsibility for a customer relationship is developed, from an emphasis on selling skills to management skills, including cross-cultural management skills (McDonald *et al.*, 1997).

We end this section by assessing the advantages and disadvantages of going into GAM, seen from the supplier's (seller's) point of view.

Supplier's (seller's) advantages with GAM

- Provides a better fulfilment of the customer's global need for having only one supplier of certain products and services.
- Smaller supplier enterprises often have significant complementary assets that the MNC will struggle to develop efficiently itself, e.g. proprietary technologies. Most large MNCs actively seek out new ideas and innovations on a worldwide basis; indeed, many believe their ability to do this is one of their key sources of competitive advantage.
- Creating barriers for competitors – given the high switching costs, global competitors (of the supplier) will have difficulty in displacing the existing supplier. If the supplier becomes the preferred supplier, the customer becomes dependent on the supplier shifting power in the relationship.
- Increased sales of existing products and services through a closer relationship with the key customer.
- Facilitating the introduction of new products/services – the global account (GA) is perceived to be more willing to take on new product trials and carry a more complete product line.
- Coordination of marketing/selling activities across borders may increase the total worldwide sales value to this customer – the GAM strategy enables the supplier to coordinate global marketing programmes (i.e. standardization) while at the same time permitting local adaptation to individual country environment.
- Perceived high potential for profit increase, due to the increased sales and global coordination – development of a strategic 'fit' between the supplier and the customer increases the effectiveness of the supplying organization.
- By using the learning effects, the supplier has the ability to reduce the marginal cost of creating adapted programmes for every new country/region. In this way, economies of scale as well as economies of scope can be utilized through the GAM strategy.
- Through the global network of the customer, the supplier might gain access to new customers around the world.

Supplier's (seller's) disadvantages with GAM

- The supplier will feel pressure from the global customers to improve global consistency – they may force the supplier to institute GAM to maintain their global 'preferred' supplier status.
- Small enterprises have restricted access to the attention of key decision-makers in the MNC, which is very different from the situation in an MNC–MNC relationship where the executives are equal partners. Thus, with smaller suppliers, there is a problem of *asymmetry in resources*. Smaller supplier enterprises lack the reputation, financial muscle and human resources of their potential partners, which is in direct contrast to the situation in a balanced MNC–MNC relationship. Indeed, in many respects small supplier enterprises and MNCs are entirely different organizations, which makes communication and knowledge transfer extremely difficult. MNCs typically have a clear separation between line and staff roles, many functional specialists and explicit processes for every activity. Small supplier enterprises are full of generalists, many of whom perform multiple functions, and they get things done through ad hoc and informal processes (Prashantham and Birkinshaw, 2008).
- Normally the supplier would use different prices for the customer's different subsidiaries in the different countries. However, the global customer may attempt to use GAM as a means to lower prices globally, by using the argument that there should be equity/commonality of pricing throughout the global network of the customer's subsidiaries. However, research done by Yip and Bink (2007) concludes that the suppliers' globally consistent service performance is more important than lower prices to the global

customers. So suppliers adopting the GAM can build relationships with their global customers that go beyond price discounts.

- Pressure to 'standardize' all terms of trade on a global basis, and not just price. So global accounts increasingly demand uniformity in such issues as volume discounts, transportation charges, overheads, special charges and so forth.
- The supplier's loss of a global account due to major competitors utilizing the GAM strategy – the supplier may feel compelled to form a GAM team to match or counteract the strategy of key customers.
- Most often a GAM strategy is linked to the use of some kind of matrix organization. Consequently, there may be multiple decision-makers in the supplier organization making the same decision from different perspectives (e.g. global vs local). The cost of managing may increase due to the parallel structures at global and local levels. Moreover, the parallel structures might slow down the decision-making process.

The organizational set-up of global account management

According to Figure 19.9, three different organizational models will be presented.

1. Central HQ–HQ negotiation model

This model shows a situation where the product in question is standardized. The customer HQ will collect the demands from the different subsidiaries around the world. Thereafter, the customer will meet with the supplier and the HQ-to-HQ negotiations will take place. In this situation the customer will typically exercise significant buying power, because the supplier will not have any international organization that can offset this buying power. For the supplier, a standardized (high) quality is the condition for being invited to the discussions with the customer HQ. Subsequently, the discussion will quickly come down to a question of the 'right' price. The supplier will always be under pressure to lower the price and cut costs of producing the product package (including services).

IKEA is an example of a customer that puts its furniture suppliers under constant pressure to reduce their prices and make their production more efficient, in order to reduce costs. Around 2005, IKEA planned to reduce its distribution warehouse costs by 10 per cent per year. In order to achieve this goal, they ran weekly batch global-demand forecasts for each of its three major regions: North America, Asia and EMEA (Europe, Middle East and Africa). The fulfilment solution would balance demand forecasts with inventory levels and replenish accordingly through IKEA's ordering system (Scheraga, 2005). Orders would be sent to IKEA's suppliers weekly or daily, depending on how active they were with the retailer.

IKEA suppliers were pressurized to deliver furniture to IKEA more frequently and more directly to its stores around the world. If a European subsupplier of furniture was invited by the IKEA headquarters to be a global supplier to IKEA, it should be ready to establish production and assembling factories in the other two main IKEA regions of the world (outside Europe): North America and Asia. That would require big investments from these European furniture suppliers. On the other hand, that investment would also provide them with access to new large furniture markets, by following their key international (global) customer (IKEA).

2. Balanced negotiation model

In this situation the central HQ-to-HQ negotiation is supplemented with some decentralized and local negotiations on a country basis. Typically this will take place in the form of negotiations between the local subsidiaries of the customers and the different partners (e.g. agents) or subsidiaries of the supplier. The HQ-to-HQ negotiations will set the possible range of outcomes for the following negotiations on a local basis. This will allow for some degree of price differentiation across the involved countries, dependent on the degree of necessary product adaptation to local conditions. Danfoss Power Solutions (www.powersolutions.danfoss.com) is an example of a subsupplier working to this model (see Exhibit 19.1).

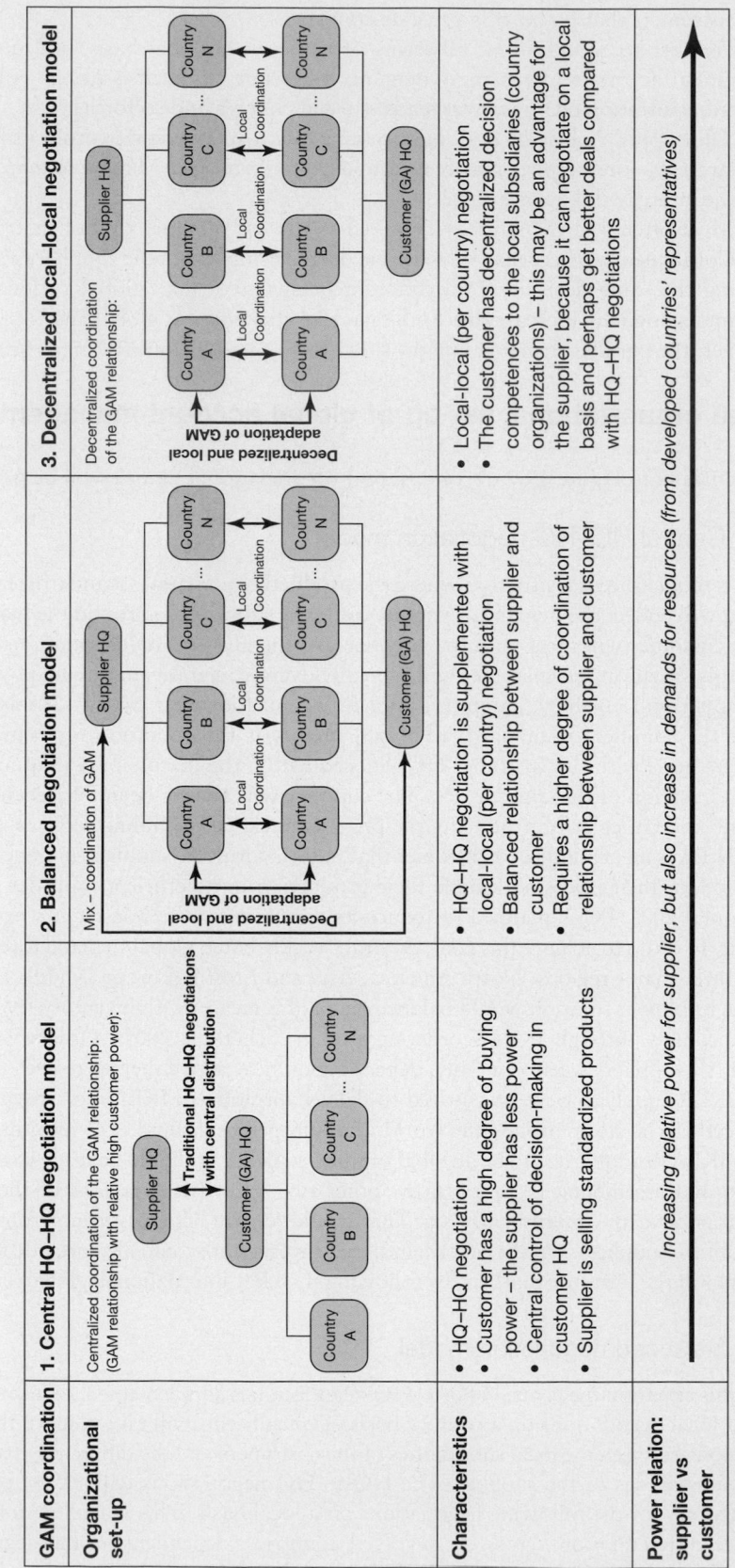

Figure 19.9   The organizational set-up in GAM

Source: based on Hollensen (2006).

EXHIBIT 19.1 Danfoss Power Solutions' GAM

Danfoss Power Solutions is one of the world's leading companies for the development, production and sale of hydraulic power transmission systems – primarily for use in mobile work vehicles. Danfoss Power Solutions has sales, manufacturing and engineering capabilities in Europe, the Americas and the Asia-Pacific region. Danfoss Power Solutions's key global customers are John Deere, Case New Holland, Ingersoll-Rand, Agco and Caterpillar (see also Case study 6.2).

One of Danfoss Power Solutions's main global accounts (OEM customers), Case New Holland (CNH), is the number one manufacturer of agricultural tractors and combines in the world and the third-largest maker of construction equipment. Revenue in 2014 totalled US$33 billion. Based in the US, CNH's network of dealers and distributors operates in over 160 countries. CNH agricultural products are sold under the Case IH, New Holland and Steyr brands. CNH construction equipment is sold under the Case, FiatAllis, Fiat Kobelco, Kobelco, New Holland and O&K brands.

As a result of a merger in 1999, CNH is an example of consolidation on the OEM customer side. The consequence of this consolidation is that fewer than the 10 largest OEM customers will represent more than half of Danfoss Power Solutions's potential sales over the medium to long term. There is no doubt that the price-down pressure will continue worldwide. The global business culture trend is leading towards a more professional buying process on the customer side. This development requires a new way of structuring the Danfoss Power Solutions organization, and the answer is GAM. As illustrated below, Danfoss Power Solutions has met the requirements of CNH's worldwide production units by forming local production locations and GAM team groups in India, China, Poland, North America, Italy, Brazil, Germany and the UK (CNH's French production unit is being sourced by Danfoss Power Solutions German production side). In partnership with CNH, the GAM teams try to find more cost-effective solutions, rather than simply reduce prices. Danfoss Power Solutions is following CNH into low-cost manufacturing countries, such as India and China. At all of CNH's worldwide production units there is pressure for a higher degree of outsourcing and a request for value-added packages. Danfoss Power Solutions tries to fulfil this requirement by supplying pre-assembled kit packages and delivering more system solutions to CNH.

Sources: different Danfoss Power Solutions material (as at 2014); Hollensen (2006).

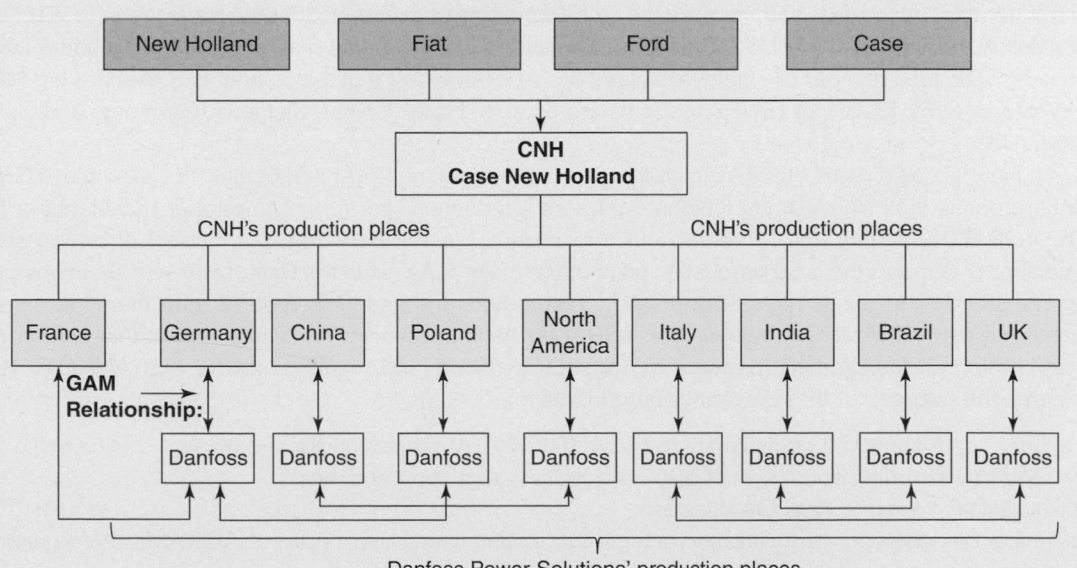

The Danfoss–CNH global account management relationship

3. Decentralized local–local negotiation model

According to this model, the negotiations will only take place on a local basis, partly because the supplier is often selling system solutions which require a high degree of adaptation to the different markets (countries). This means that the HQs are disconnected from the negotiation processes. A consolidation process in the customer's industry may cause this outcome. If the customer has been involved in several M&As, it will have difficulties in understanding the overall picture of the decision structures in the new merged multinational company. In such a situation, the customer will tend to decentralize even important decisions to the country subsidiaries, because it has lost its overview of the whole multinational company. It can be really difficult to control and coordinate decision processes in recently merged companies. For that reason, top managers will often refer the buying decisions to local decision-makers in local country subsidiaries.

This will give the supplier better opportunities for sub-optimization by negotiating only locally with a customer's country-based organizations. By using this approach, the supplier may be in a better relative negotiation position and may also achieve better (higher) prices in some markets by using this model. However, the supplier may have higher costs connected to fulfilling the different requirements of the customer's local subsidiaries. Also this model requires that the supplier has an established network of subsidiaries or partners (e.g. agents) who are familiar with the product solutions of the supplier and who can offer local adapted product solutions for the customer's subsidiaries in the different countries (see Exhibit 19.2).

EXHIBIT 19.2 AGRAMKOW – working to model 3

AGRAMKOW (www.agramkow.com) is an example of a company working to this model. AGRAMKOW (Denmark) has a goal to become one of the world's leading developers and suppliers of filling equipment for fluid refrigerants, which are used, for example, in refrigerators or in automotive air conditioners. In 2011, their total sales were approximately US$35 million, of which 95 per cent was realized outside the home country (Denmark). The total number of employees was 130. AGRAMKOW's global accounts (GAs) are big MNCS like Whirlpool (US), Electrolux (Sweden), Samsung (Korea), Haier (China), Siemens (Germany) and General Electric (US).

It is a fact that, as a result of M&As, global customers are getting fewer and bigger. For example, AGRAMKOW's process fluid fill system is fitted into the total production line of the refrigerator manufacturer Electrolux. AGRAMKOW has 'only' three or four subsidiaries around the world, but instead of having several subsidiaries to support the local production units of the major GAs (as in the Danfoss Power Solutions case), it has transferred the values of AGRAMKOW to distributors and agents in order to turn them into partners with internalized AGRAMKOW values. The AGRAMKOW management has implemented this partner strategy by inviting all the potential partners to common seminars and meetings at the AGRAMKOW HQ in Denmark. The purpose of these meetings is to increase:

- common team spirit and commitment to the AGRAMKOW shared values and goals – this has also been achieved by including some common social activities (e.g. sport activities);
- sales skills for winning local GA business;
- technical competence for installation, integration, maintenance and repair of AGRAMKOW equipment/ solutions;
- understanding of the necessity for constant feedback to AGRAMKOW on performance and other market activities (e.g. competitor activity).

Afterwards the individual partner and their organization (e.g. the Chinese partner) is in a better position to take care of customized products, local service and customer care directed towards the local GA unit (e.g. the local Electrolux refrigerator production unit in China). This also means that AGRAMKOW has increased its relative power on the local basis towards one of its important GAs, Electrolux.

Despite this positive development, there have been some difficulties in the process of turning the distributors and agents into partners. Those organizations with small turnovers of AGRAMKOW products and services have been somewhat reluctant to take part in this process (Hollensen, 2006).

Source: different AGRAMKOW material.

In summary, the importance of GAM strategies will grow in the future because of consolidation in most industries across the world. The development of relational contracting with a large, global customer – the cooperation between a customer and a supplier into a long-term global relationship – has a number of positive outcomes. However, a great deal of learning is necessary when deciding to implement a GAM strategy, because high stakes and high exit barriers accompany the implementation.

19.4 Controlling the global marketing programme

The final, but often neglected, stage of international market planning is the control process. Not only is control important to evaluate how the company has performed, but it completes the circle of planning by providing the feedback necessary for the start of the next planning cycle.

Figure 19.10 illustrates the connection between the marketing plan, the marketing budget and the control system.

After building the global marketing plan, its quantification appears in the form of budgets. The budget is the basis for the design of the marketing control system that may give the necessary feedback for a possible reformulation of the global marketing plan. The marketing budgets should represent a projection of actions and expected results, and they should be capable of accurate monitoring and controlling. Indeed, measuring performance against budget is the main (regular) management review process, which may cause the feedback in Figure 19.10.

The purpose of a marketing budget is to pull all the revenues and costs involved in marketing together into one comprehensive document. It is a managerial tool that balances what needs to be spent against what can be afforded and helps make choices about priorities. It is then used in monitoring the performance in practice. The marketing budget is usually the most powerful tool with which you think through the relationship between desired results and available means. Its starting point should be the marketing strategies and plans that have already been formulated in the marketing plan itself. In practice, the strategies and plans will run in parallel and will interact.

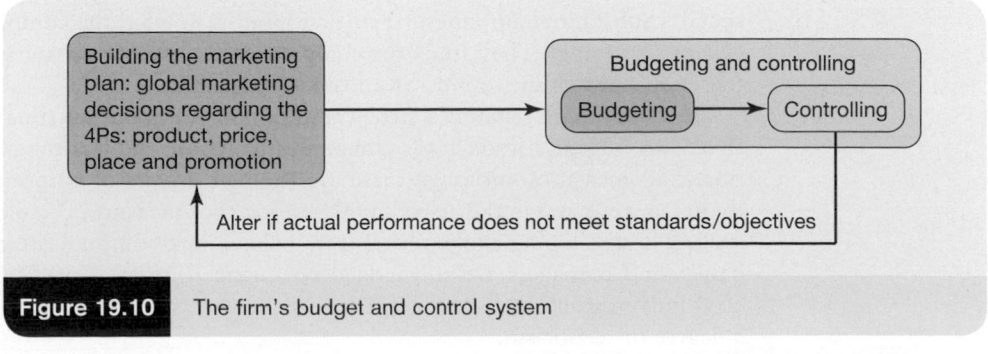

| **Figure 19.10** | The firm's budget and control system |

Unfortunately, however, 'control' is often viewed by the people of an organization as being negative. If individuals fear that the control process will be used not only to judge their performance, but also as a basis for punishing them, then it will be feared and reviled.

The evaluation and control of global marketing probably represent the weakest areas of marketing practice in many companies. Even the organizations that are otherwise strong in their strategic marketing planning have poor control and evaluation procedures for their global marketing. There are a number of possible reasons for this: primarily, there is no such thing as a 'standard' system of control for marketing.

The function of the organizational structure is to provide a framework in which objectives can be met. However, a set of instruments and processes is needed to influence the behaviour and performance of organization members to meet the goals. The critical issue is the same as with organizational structures: what is the ideal amount of control? On the one hand, headquarters needs information to ensure that international activities contribute maximum benefit to the overall organization. On the other hand, controls should not be construed as a code of law.

The global question is to determine how to establish a control mechanism capable of early interception of emerging problems. Considered here are various criteria appropriate for the evaluation process, control styles, feedback and corrective action. These concepts are important for all businesses, but in the international arena they are vital.

Design of a control system

In designing a control system, management must consider the costs of establishing and maintaining it and trade them off against the benefits to be gained. Any control system will require investment in a management structure and in systems designs.

The design of the control system can be divided into two groups, dependent on the objective of control:

1. output control (typically based on financial measures)
2. behavioural controls (typically based on non-financial measures).

Output control
Regular monitoring of output, such as profits, sales figures and expenditures (typically based on financial measures).

Behavioural controls
Regular monitoring of behaviour, such as sales people's ability to interact with customers (typically based on non-financial measures).

Output control may consist of expenditure control, which involves regular monitoring of expenditure figures, comparison of these with budget targets, and taking decisions to cut or increase expenditure where any variance is believed to be harmful. Measures of output are accumulated at regular intervals and are typically forwarded from the foreign subsidiary to headquarters, where they are evaluated and criticized based on comparison to the plan or budget.

Behavioural controls require the exercise of influence over behaviour. This influence can be achieved, for example, by providing sales manuals to subsidiary personnel or by fitting new employees into the corporate culture. Behavioural controls often require an extensive socialization process, and informal, personal interaction is central to the process. Substantial resources must be spent to train the individual to share the corporate culture, i.e., 'the way things are done at the company'.

To build common vision and values, managers at the Japanese company Matsushita spend a substantial amount of their first months in what the company calls 'cultural and spiritual training'. They study the company credo, the 'Seven Spirits of Matsushita', and the philosophy of the founder, Kanosuke Matsushita.

However, there remains a strong tradition of using output (financial) criteria. A fixation with output criteria leads companies to ignore the less tangible behavioural (non-financial) measures, although these are the real drivers of corporate success. However, there is a weakness in the behavioural performance measures. To date there has been little success in developing explicit links from behaviour to output criteria. Furthermore, companies and managers are still judged on financial criteria (profit contribution). Until a clear link is established, it is likely that behavioural criteria will continue to be treated with a degree of scepticism.

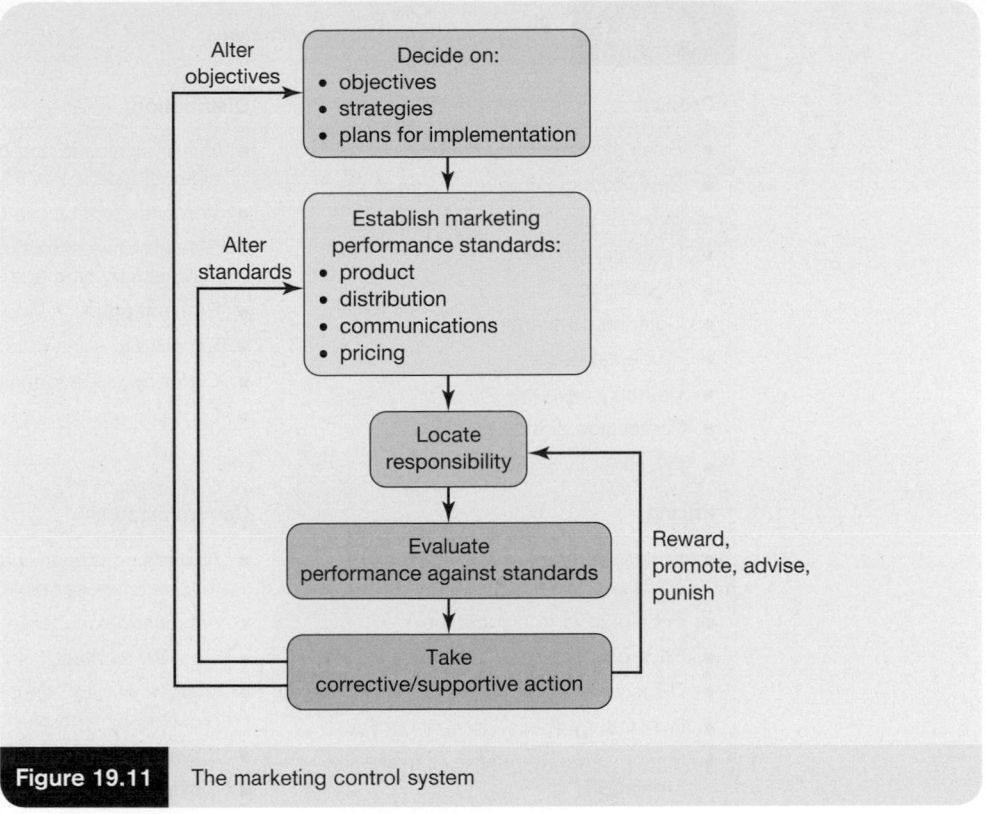

Figure 19.11   The marketing control system

We will now develop a global marketing control system based primarily on output controls. Marketing control is an essential element of the marketing planning process because it provides a review of how well marketing objectives have been achieved. A framework for controlling marketing activities is given in Figure 19.11.

The marketing control system begins with the company setting some marketing activities in motion (plans for implementation). This may be the result of certain objectives and strategies, each of which must be achieved within a given budget. Hence budgetary control is essential.

The next step in the control process is to establish specific performance standards that will need to be achieved for each area of activity if overall objectives and sub-objectives are to be achieved. For example, in order to achieve a specified sales objective, a specific target of performance for each sales area may be required. In turn, this may require a specific standard of performance from each of the salespeople in the region with respect to, for example, number of calls, conversion rates and, of course, order value. Table 19.1 provides a representative sample of the types of data required. Marketing performance measures and standards will vary by company and product according to the goals and objectives delineated in the marketing plan.

The next step is to locate responsibility. In some cases, responsibility ultimately falls on one person (e.g. the brand manager); in others it is shared (e.g. the sales manager and sales force). It is important to consider this issue, because corrective or supportive action may need to focus on those responsible for the success of marketing activity.

In order to be successful, the people involved and affected by the control process should be consulted in both the design and implementation stages of marketing control. Above all, they will need to be convinced that the purpose of control is to improve their own levels of success and that of the company. Subordinates need to be involved in setting and agreeing their own standards of performance, preferably through a system of management by objectives.

Table 19.1	Measures of marketing performance

Product	Distribution
• Sales by market segments	• Sales, expenses and contribution margin by channel type
• New product introductions each year	
• Sales relative to potential	• Percentage of stores carrying the product
• Sales growth rates	• Sales relative to market potential by channel, intermediary type and specific intermediaries
• Market share	
• Contribution margin	• Percentage of on-time delivery
• Product defects	• Expense-to-sales ratio by channel, etc.
• Warranty expense	• Order cycle performance by channel, etc.
• Percentage of total profits	• Logistics cost by logistics activity by channel
• Return on investment	

Pricing	Communication
• Response time to price changes of competitors	• Advertising effectiveness by type of media (e.g. awareness levels)
• Price relative to competitor	• Actual audience/target audience ratio
• Price changes relative to sales volume	• Cost per contact
• Discount structure relative to sales volume	• Number of calls, enquiries and information requests by type of media
• Bid strategy relative to new contacts	
• Margin structure relative to marketing expenses	• Sales per sales call
	• Sales per territory relative to potential
• Margins relative to channel member performance	• Selling expenses to sales ratio
	• New accounts per time period
	• Lost accounts per time period

Source: adapted from Jobber, D. (1995) *Principles and Practice of Marketing,* published by McGraw-Hill.

Performance is then evaluated against these standards, and this relies on an efficient information system. A judgment has to be made about the degree of success and failure achieved and what corrective or supportive action is to be taken. This can take various forms:

- Failure that is attributed to the poor performance of individuals may result in the giving of advice regarding future attitudes and actions, training and/or punishment (e.g. criticism, lower pay, demotion, termination of employment). Success, on the other hand, should be rewarded with praise, promotion and/or higher pay.
- Failure that is attributed to unrealistic marketing objectives and performance may cause management to lower objectives or lower marketing standards. Success that is thought to reflect unambitious objectives and standards may cause them to be raised in the next period.

Many firms assume that corrective action needs to be taken only when results are less than those required or when budgets and costs are being exceeded. In fact, both 'negative' (under-achievement) and 'positive' (over-achievement) deviations may require corrective action. For example, failure to spend the amount budgeted for, say, sales force expenses may indicate that the initial sum allocated was excessive and needs to be reassessed, and/or that the sales force is not as 'active' as it might be.

It is also necessary to determine such things as the frequency of measurement (e.g. daily, weekly, monthly or annually). More frequent and more detailed measurement usually means more cost. Care must be taken to ensure that the costs of measurement and the control process itself do not exceed the value of such measurements and do not overly interfere with the activities of those being measured.

The impact of the environment must also be taken into account when designing a control system:

● The control system should measure only dimensions over which the organization has control. Rewards or sanctions make little sense if they are based on dimensions that may be relevant for overall corporate performance, but over which no influence can be exerted (e.g. price controls). Neglecting the factor of individual performance capability would send the wrong signals and severely impair the motivation of personnel.

● Control systems should harmonize with local regulations and customs. In some cases, however, corporate behavioural controls have to be exercised against local customs, even though overall operations may be affected negatively. This type of situation occurs, for example, when a subsidiary operates in markets where unauthorized facilitating payments are a common business practice.

Feedforward control

Feedforward control
Monitors variables other than performance – variables that may change before performance itself. In this way, deviations can be controlled proactively before their full impact has been felt.

Much of the information provided by the firm's marketing control system is feedback on what has been accomplished in both financial (profits) and non-financial (customer satisfaction, market share) terms. As such, the control process is remedial in its outlook. It can be argued that control systems should be forward-looking and preventive, and that the control process should start at the same time as the planning process. Such a form of control is **feedforward control** (Figure 19.12).

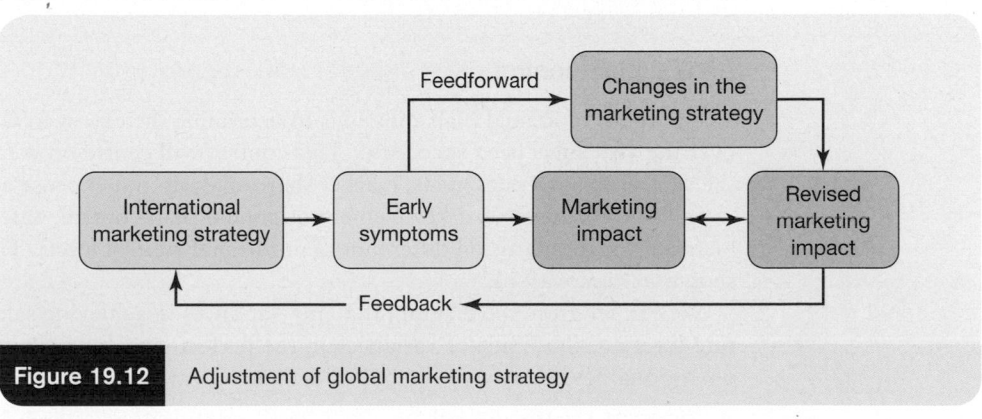

| **Figure 19.12** | Adjustment of global marketing strategy |

Source: Samli *et al.* (1993, p. 421).

Feedforward control would continuously evaluate plans, monitoring the environment to detect changes that would call for revising objectives and strategies. Feedforward control monitors variables other than performance; variables that may change before performance itself changes. The result is that deviations can be controlled before their full impact has been felt. Such a system is proactive in that it anticipates environmental change, whereas after-the-fact and steering control systems are more reactive in that they deal with changes after they occur. Examples of early symptoms (early performance indicators) are presented in Table 19.2.

Feedforward control focuses on information that is prognostic: it tries to discover problems waiting to occur. Formal processes of feedforward control can be incorporated into the business marketer's total control programme to enhance its effectiveness considerably. Utilization of a feedforward approach would help to ensure that planning and control are treated as concurrent activities.

Key areas for control in marketing

Kotler (1997) distinguishes four types of marketing control, each involving different approaches, different purposes and a different allocation of responsibilities. These are

Table 19.2	Some key early performance indicators
Early performance indicators	**Market implication**
Sudden drop in quantities demanded	Problem in marketing strategy or its implementation
Sharp decrease or increase in sales volume	Product gaining acceptance or being rejected quickly
Customer complaints	Product not debugged properly
A notable decrease in competitors' business	Product gaining acceptance quickly or market conditions deteriorating
Large volumes of returned merchandise	Problems in basic product design
Excessive requests for parts or reported repairs	Problems in basic product design, low standards
Sudden changes in fashions or styles	Product (or competitors' product) causing a deep impact on the consumers' lifestyles

Source: Samli *et al.* (1993, p. 425).

shown in Table 19.3. Here we will focus on annual plan control and profit control, as they are the most obvious areas of concern to firms with limited resources (e.g. SMEs).

Annual plan control

The purpose of annual plan control is to determine the extent to which marketing efforts over the year have been successful. This control will centre on measuring and evaluating sales in relation to sales goals, market share analysis and expense analysis.

Sales performance is a key element in annual plan control. Sales control consists of a hierarchy of standards on different organizational control levels. These are interlinked, as shown in Figure 19.13.

We can see from the diagram that any variances in achieving sales targets at the corporate level are the result of variances in the performance of individual salespeople at the operational level. At every level of sales control, variances must be studied with a view to

Table 19.3	Types of marketing control		
Type of control	**Prime responsibility**	**Purpose of control**	**Examples of techniques/approaches**
Strategic control	Top management Middle management	To examine if planned results are being achieved	Marketing effectiveness ratings Marketing audit
Efficiency control	Line and staff management Marketing controller	To examine ways of improving the efficiency of marketing	Sales force efficiency Advertising efficiency Distribution efficiency
Annual plan control	Top management Middle management	To examine if planned results are being achieved	Sales analysis Market share analysis Marketing expenses to sales ratio Customer tracking
Profit control (budget control)	Marketing controller	To examine where the company is making and losing money	Profitability by, e.g., product, customer group or trade channel

Source: adapted from Kotler, Philip, *Marketing Management: Analysis, Planning, Implementation and Control*, 9th edn., © 1997. Electronically reproduced by permission of Pearson Education, Inc., Upper Saddle River, New Jersey.

Figure 19.13   The hierarchy of sales and control

determining their causes. In general, variances may be due to a combination of factors in volume and/or price.

Profit control

In addition to the previously discussed control elements, all international marketers must be concerned to control their profit. The budgetary period is normally one year because budgets are tied to the accounting systems of the company. In the following section we will explore further how global marketing budgets are developed, the starting point being the GAM organization and the country-based structure of the company.

19.5 The global marketing budget

The classic quantification of a global marketing plan appears in the form of budgets. Because these are so rigorously quantified, they are particularly important. They should represent a projection of actions and expected results, and they should be capable of accurate monitoring. Indeed, performance against budget is the main (regular) management review process.

Budgeting is also an organization process that involves making forecasts based on the proposed marketing strategy and programmes. The forecasts are then used to construct a budgeted profit-and-loss statement (i.e. profitability). An important aspect of budgeting is deciding how to allocate the last available dollars across all of the proposed programmes within the marketing plan.

Recognizing the *customer* as the primary unit of focus, a market-based business will expand its focus to customers and countries/markets, not just products or units sold. This is an important strategic distinction because there is a finite number of potential customers, but a larger range of products and services can be sold to each customer. A business's volume is its customer share in a market with a finite number of customers at any point in time, not the number of units sold.

Global marketing strategies that affect customer volume include marketing strategies that:

- attract new customers to grow market share;
- grow the market demand by bringing more customers into a market;
- enter new markets to create new sources of customer volume.

All marketing strategies require *some* level of marketing effort to achieve a certain level of market share. Expenses associated with sales effort, market communications, customer service and market management are required to implement a marketing strategy designed to obtain a certain customer volume. The costs of this marketing effort are the *marketing expenses* and they must be deducted from the total contribution to produce a *net marketing contribution*.

Figure 19.14 illustrates the traditional marketing budget (per country or customer group) and its underlying determinants. One of the most important budget figures is the 'Total Net Marketing Contribution' which is now explained, together with the final 'Net Profit' (before tax).

Net marketing contribution

All marketing strategies require some level of marketing effort to achieve a certain level of market share. Expenses associated with sales effort, market communications, customer service and market management are required to implement a marketing strategy designed to obtain a certain customer sales volume in a specific country. The cost of this marketing effort is shown in Table 19.4 as marketing costs and must be deducted from the total contribution to produce a *net marketing contribution*. This is the net contribution produced after the marketing expenses are deducted from the total contribution produced:

net marketing contribution = total contribution − marketing expenses

In effect, this is how the marketing function contributes to the company's profits. If the marketing team develops a marketing strategy that fails and, therefore, produces a lower net marketing contribution, then that marketing strategy has, in effect, lowered the net profits of the company.

Marketing strategies are generally designed to affect total contribution, mainly by increasing market demand, market share or revenue per customer in a specific local market. The net marketing contribution equation should make it clear that such strategies are profitable only if the increase in total contribution exceeds the increase in marketing expenses required to produce that increase in total contribution. That is, for a marketing strategy to improve profits for the company, it has to improve net marketing contribution.

Net profit (before tax)

Although marketing strategies contribute to net profits through net marketing contribution, net profit (before tax) is generally beyond the control of the marketing function or the marketing management team. Marketing strategies produce a certain level of net marketing contribution from which all other business expenses must be deducted before a net profit is realized, as illustrated in Table 19.4. These operating expenses include fixed expenses, such as human resources management, R&D and administrative expenses, and other operating expenses, such as utilities, rent and fees. In most instances, corporate overheads would also be allocated, which includes company expenses such as legal fees, corporate advertising and executive salaries:

net profit (before tax) = net marketing expenses − other operating expenses

However, there are instances when a marketing strategy can affect other operating expenses. For example, a strategy to improve a product to attract more customers and build market share could involve increased R&D expenses to develop the new product.

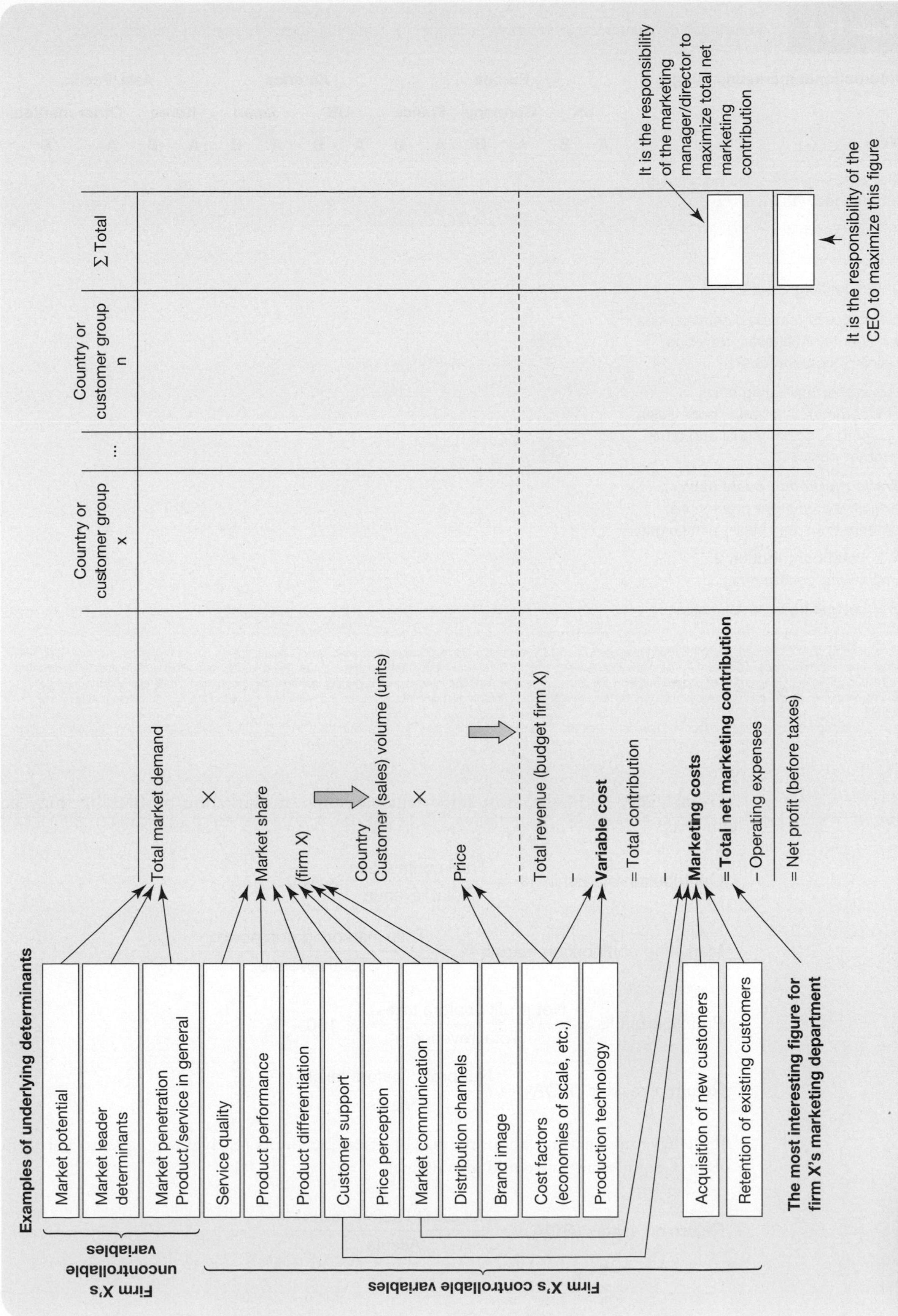

Figure 19.14 Marketing budget 200X and its underlying determinants

Table 19.4	An example of an international marketing budget for a manufacturer exporting consumer goods												
International marketing budget		Europe				America				Asia/Pacific			
		UK		Germany		France		US		Japan		Korea		Other markets
Year = _____		A	B	A	B	A	B	A	B	A	B	A	B	A	B
Net sales (gross sales lesscounts, allowances, etc.)															
+ Variable costs															
= Contrtion 1															
+ Marketing costs:															
Sales costs (salaries, commissions for agents, incentives, travelling, training, conferences)															
Consumer marketing costs (TV commercials, radio, print, sales promotion, social media and other internet costs)															
Trade marketing costs (fairs, exhibitions, in-store promotions, contributions for retailer campaigns)															
= Σ **Total contribution 2** (marketing contribution)															
B = budget figures; A = actual.															

Note: on a short-term (one-year) basis, the export managers or country managers are responsible for maximizing the actual figures for each country and minimizing their deviation from budget figures. The international marketing manager/director is responsible for maximizing the actual figure for the total world and minimizing its deviation from the budget figure. Cooperation is required between the country managers and the international marketing manager/director to coordinate and allocate the total marketing resources in an optimum way. Sometimes certain inventory costs and product development costs may also be included in the total marketing budget (see main text).

Source: *Marketing Management: A relationship approach*, 2nd ed., Financial Times/Prentice Hall (Hollensen, S. 2010) p. 583, Copyright © Pearson Education Limited.

From Figure 19.14 the most important measures of marketing profitability may be defined as:

$$\text{Contribution margin in \%} = \frac{\text{Total contribution}}{\text{Total revenue}} \times 100$$

$$\text{Marketing contribution margin \%} = \frac{\text{Total marketing contribution}}{\text{Total revenue}}$$

$$\text{Profit margin \%} = \frac{\text{Net profit (before taxes)}}{\text{Total revenue}} \times 100$$

$$\text{Return on assets (ROA)} = \frac{\text{Net profit (before taxes)}}{\text{Assets}}$$

If we have information about the size of assets (accounts receivable + inventory + cash + plant + equipment) we could also define:

$$\text{Return on assets (ROA)} = \frac{\text{Net profit (before taxes)}}{\text{Assets}}$$

ROA is similar to the well-known measure ROI, return on investment.

Besides the above-mentioned financial metrics there are a great many other relevant marketing metrics, especially within 'social media' such as (Kumar and Mirshandani, 2012; Srinivasan, 2015):

- *Awareness*: how large a share (percentage) of the potential customer group knows about the brand. Normally, awareness would affect new product trial. For example, all else equal, marketing spending aimed at awareness building will have greater potential impact if the initial awareness level is 20 per cent as opposed to 70 per cent.
- *Conversion rate*: how big a percentage of website visitors are actually being converted into paying customers.
- *Advocates*: total number of social media participants who actively write positively about a brand. Being 'engaged' is a necessary condition for reaching the final stage of brand commitment. Being an 'advocate' for the brand, by creating and uploading content that actively promotes the brand.

Table 19.4 presents an example of a global marketing budget for a manufacturer of consumer goods. Included in the budget are those marketing variables that can be controlled and changed by the sales and marketing functions (departments) in the home country and in the export market. In Table 19.4 the only variable that cannot be controlled by the international sales and marketing departments is variable costs.

The global marketing budget system (as presented in Table 19.4) is used for the following (main) purposes:

- Allocation of marketing resources among countries/markets to maximize profits. In Table 19.4 it is the responsibility of the global marketing director to maximize the total contribution 2 for the whole world.
- Evaluation of country/market performance. In Table 19.4 it is the responsibility of export managers or country managers to maximize contribution 2 for each of their countries.

Note that besides the marketing variables presented in Table 19.4, the global marketing budget normally contains inventory costs for finished goods. As the production sizes of these goods are normally based on input from the sales and marketing department, the inventory of unsold goods will also be the responsibility of the international marketing manager or director. Furthermore, the global marketing budget may also contain customer-specific or country-specific product development costs, if certain new products are preconditions for selling in certain markets.

In contrast to budgets, long-range plans extend over periods from two to 10 years, and their content is more qualitative and judgmental in nature than that of budgets. For SMEs, shorter periods (such as two years) are the norm because of the perceived uncertainty of diverse foreign environments.

19.6   The process of developing the global marketing plan

The purpose of the global marketing plan is to create sustainable competitive advantages in the global marketplace. Generally, firms go through some kind of mental process in developing global marketing plans. In SMEs this process is normally informal; in larger organizations it is often more systematized. Figure 1.2 (pp. 8–11) offers a systematized approach to developing a global marketing plan.

19.7 Summary

Implementation of a global marketing programme requires an appropriate organizational structure. As the scope of a firm's global marketing strategy changes, its organizational structure must be modified in accordance with its tasks and technology and the external environment. Five ways of structuring an international organization have been presented: functional structure, international divisional structure, product structure, geographical structure (customer structure) and matrix structure. The choice of organizational structure is affected by such factors as the degree of internationalization of the firm, the strategic importance of the firm's international operations, the complexity of its international business and the availability of qualified managers.

Control is the process of ensuring that global marketing activities are carried out as intended. It involves monitoring aspects of performance and taking corrective action where necessary. The global marketing control system consists of deciding marketing objectives, setting performance standards, locating responsibility, evaluating performance against standards and taking corrective or supportive action.

In an after-the-fact control system, managers wait until the end of the planning period to take corrective action. In a feedforward control system, corrective action is taken during the planning period by tracking early performance indicators and steering the organization back to desired objectives if it goes out of control.

The most obvious areas of control relate to the control of the annual marketing plan and the control of profitability. The purpose of the global marketing budget is mainly to allocate marketing resources across countries to maximize worldwide total marketing contribution.

CASE STUDY 19.1

Mars Inc.: merger of the European food, pet care and confectionery divisions

Mars Inc. is a diversified multifunctional company whose primary products include foods, petcare, confectionery, electronics and drinks. Owned and controlled by the Mars family, this US giant is one of the world's biggest private companies, but also one of the most secretive.

Mars' decision in January 2000 to merge its food, pet care and confectionery divisions across Europe – and eventually with headquarters in the UK – split the marketing industry.

The most well-known brands within the three divisions are:

- *foods*: Uncle Ben's rice and sauces;
- *pet care*: Whiskas, Pedigree;
- *confectionery*: M&Ms, Snickers, Milky Way, Mars Bar.

Mars UK said the decision to pool the businesses was taken to strike at the company's international

Source: Roman Samokhin/Shutterstock.com.

competitors in food and confectionery, such as Nestlé and Unilever. The move also coincided with plans to create a single European market and highlighted the company's belief that its consumers' needs are the same across the continent.

However, the combination of food and confectionery with pet care was not clear to all industry observers. One industry analyst commented:

Generally speaking, Mars is doing the right thing by merging divisions to squeeze profits out of them. Before the advent of the euro it was acceptable to run separate companies in different European countries but not any more.

Another analyst said: 'I can't imagine it marketing all three sides of the business together. They're too different.'

The only visible benefit appeared to be an improvement in distribution. Tastes across European markets are very different, whether you're selling products for animals or people.

It's all very well Mars saying it will tackle competitors such as Nestlé and Unilever, but they are only rivals in food and confectionery.

If Mars starts laying down too many controls by merging all its businesses – and therefore also its marketing and management strategies – it may streamline communications, but could lose the creativity available in different regions.

QUESTIONS

1. Discuss the two views of organizing Mars' European activities.

2. Did Mars Inc. do the right thing in your opinion?

Source: McCawley (2000).

CASE STUDY 19.2

Henkel: should Henkel shift to a more customer-centric organization?

Henkel is a multinational company headquartered in Düsseldorf, Germany. In 2012, the total turnover was €16.5 billion. It has about 47,600 employees worldwide and counts among the most internationally aligned German-based companies in the global marketplace. The company was founded in Aachen, Germany, in 1876 by the 28-year-old Fritz Henkel and two partners. Its first product was washing powder based on water-glass. In contrast to all similar products, which at that time were sold loose, this heavy-duty detergent was marketed in handy packets.

In 2012, the company's products and technologies were distributed in approximately 125 countries around the world. Henkel had three globally product-oriented operating business sectors:

Laundry and home care has always played an important role for Henkel, particularly because the company started with a product from this business sector. It consists of household cleaning products such as laundry detergent and dishwashing liquid. One of its most well-known products is the washing powder Persil.

Beauty care is the second key business sector. Henkel's cosmetic division is one of the largest of its kind in the world. It consists of beauty and oral care products, such as shampoo, toothpaste, hair colourants and shower gel.

Persil – Henkel's laundry detergent brand in Germany
Source: Henkel.

Le Chat – Henkel's laundry detergent brand in France
Source: Henkel.

The *adhesive technologies* market is where Henkel is the undisputed market leader. Here the company produces adhesives, sealants and surface treatments for consumers, craftsmen and industrial applications.

Henkel is an innovation-driven company that controls a well-balanced portfolio of international, regional and local brands. The annual research and development investment is 2.7 per cent of sales. The target groups for Henkel's products are consumers, craftsmen and industrial users. Henkel's credo is to provide superior (customized) solutions and innovative technologies for the individual business-to-consumer (B2C) and business-to-business (B2B) client.

Its main competitors in the laundry and home care division are Unilever, Procter & Gamble and Reckitt Benckiser. In its cosmetics and toiletries division, its competitors are Unilever, Procter & Gamble and L'Oréal.

In order to live up to this commitment, Henkel's employees work closely with B2C (lead users) and B2B customers (global accounts) and focus on their current needs as well as on the challenges which they will face in the future. This customer-centric philosophy is the main reason why Henkel has become a partner of choice for many leading companies.

Henkel-Walmart

In 2003, Walmart, the world's largest public corporation by revenue, according to Fortune Global 500, and one of Henkel's global customers, increasingly demanded an intensified, global relationship. Retailers are slowly becoming more powerful, than manufacturers, because they are launching their own brands. At the same time, overall trade revenues are growing due to the retailer's internationalization strategy. Prices are slowly approaching the production costs of the products. Henkel has now shifted its strategy from a product-centric to a more customer-centric approach. Consequently, the CEO, Kasper Rorsted, implemented a 'glocal' approach, coordinating multidimensional global processes and local/regional distribution. This is now embedded in a global account management programme with Walmart.

For example, in 2012 Henkel organized a sustainability week together with Walmart Mexico and Walmart Central America, in order to share experiences in sustainable development. The week was accompanied by an educational campaign where Henkel conducted in-store experiments in Walmart to demonstrate to consumers how the correct use of products can save energy.

QUESTIONS

1. Was it a good idea to shift the Henkel organization from a more product- to a more customer-centric approach?

2. What are the challenges of being a customer-driven multinational that serves both B2B and B2C customers?

3. How can Henkel further intensify the B2B relation with its key global customers?

Source: This case was developed in cooperation with former PhD researcher Vlad Stefan Wulff, University of Southern Denmark.

VIDEO CASE STUDY 19.3 McDonald's

download from www.pearsoned.co.uk/hollensen

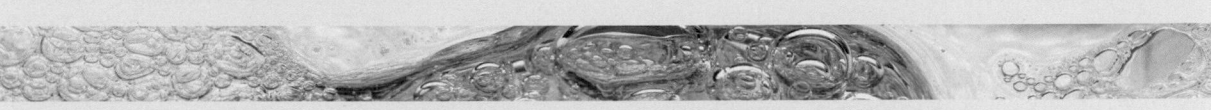

McDonald's Corporation (www.mcdonalds.com) is the world's largest food service retailing chain. The company is known for its burgers and fries, but also breakfast.

At the end of 2014, McDonald's was serving around 68 million customers daily in 119 countries across 36,000 restaurants. Approximately 30,000 are franchised and around 6,000 are operated by McDonald's Corp itself. In 37 countries there is a subsidiary.

McDonald's generated revenues of US$27.4 billion in 2014 and US$7.4 billion in net profit before taxes.

Questions

1. What could be the reason why McDonald's have both franchised and own restaurants?

2. Which financial measures should McDonald's use to control the global marketing programme in the single countries and in single restaurants?

3. What problems might arise if individual McDonald's restaurants were required to enter sales data directly onto the company's centralized accounting website at the HQ in USA, instead of following the current procedure of sending it through country (subsidiaries) and through other regional channels?

For further resources, see this book's website at **www.pearsoned.co.uk/hollensen**

Questions for discussion

1. This chapter suggests that the development of a firm's international organization can be divided into different stages. Identify these stages and discuss their relationship with the international competitiveness of the firm.

2. Identify appropriate organizational structures for managing international product development. Discuss key features of the structure(s) suggested.

3. What key internal/external factors influence the organizational structure? Can you think of additional factors? Explain.

4. Discuss the pros and cons of standardizing the marketing management process. Is a standardized process of more benefit to the company pursuing a national market strategy or a global market strategy?

5. Discuss to what degree the choice of organizational structure is essentially a choice between headquarters centralization and local autonomy.

6. Discuss how the international organization of a firm may affect its planning process.

7. Discuss why firms need global marketing controls.

8. What is meant by performance indicators? Why does a firm need them?

9. Performance reviews of subsidiary managers and personnel are required rarely, if at all, by headquarters. Why?

10. Identify the major weaknesses inherent in the international division structure.

11. Discuss the benefits gained by adopting a matrix organizational structure.

References

Bartlett, C. and Ghoshal, S. (1989) *Managing Across Borders: The Transnational Solution.* Boston, MA, Harvard University Press

Ghemawat., P. and Vantrappen, H. (2015) 'How global is your C-Suite?', *MIT Sloan Management Review,* 56(4), pp.73-82

Harvey, M., Myers, M.B. and Novicevic, M.M. (2002) 'The managerial issues associated with global account management', *Thunderbird International Business Review,* 44(5), pp. 625–647.

Hollensen, S. (2006) 'Global account management (GAM): two case studies illustrating the organizational set-up', *The Marketing Management Journal,* 16(1), pp. 244–250.

Hollensen, S. and Wulff, V. (2010) 'Global Account Management (GAM) – creating companywide and worldwide relationships to global customers', *International Journal of Customer Relationship Marketing and Management,* 1(1), pp. 28–47.

Kotler, P. (1997) *Marketing Management: Analysis, Planning, Implementation and Control,* 9th edn. Prentice-Hall, Englewood Cliffs, NJ.

Kumar, V. and Mirchandani, R. (2012) 'Increasing the ROI of Social Media Marketing', *MIT Sloan Management Review,* 54(1), pp. 55-61

McCawley, I. (2000) 'Can Mars bridge gaps in merger?' *Marketing Week,* News Analysis, 13 January.

McDonald, M., Millman, T. and Rogers, B. (1997) 'Key account management: theory, practice and challenges', *Journal of Marketing Management,* 13, pp. 737–757.

Millman, T. and Wilson, K. (1995) 'From key account selling to key account management', *Journal of Marketing Practice: Applied Marketing Science,* 1, pp. 9–21.

Ojasalo, J. (2001) 'Key account management at company and individual levels in B2B relationships', *The Journal of Business and Industrial Marketing,* 16(3), pp. 199–220.

Peppers, D. and Rogers, M. (1995) 'A new marketing paradigm: share of customer, not market share', *Harvard Business Review,* July–August, pp. 105–113.

Prashantham, S. and Birkinshaw, J. (2008) 'Dancing with gorillas: how small companies can partner effectively with MNCs', *California Management Review,* 51(1), pp. 6–23.

Quelch, J.A. (1992) 'The new country managers', *The McKinsey Quarterly,* 4, pp. 155–165.

Quelch, J.A. and Bloom, H. (1996) 'The return of the country manager', *The McKinsey Quarterly,* 2, pp. 30–43.

Samli, A.C., Still, R. and Hill, J.S. (1993) *International Marketing: Planning and Practice.* Macmillan, London.

Scheraga, P. (2005) 'Balancing act at IKEA', *Chain Store Age,* 81(6), pp. 45–46.

Shi, Linda, H., Zou, Shaoming and Cavusgil, S. Tamer (2004) 'A conceptual framework of global account management capabilities and firm performance', *International Business Review,* 13, pp. 539–553.

Shi, Linda, H., Zou, Shaoming, White, J. Cris, McNally, Regina, C. and Cavusgil, S. Tamer (2005) 'Executive insights: global account management capability: insights from leading suppliers', *Journal of International Marketing,* 13(2), pp. 93–113.

Srinivasan, S. (2015) 'Mind-Set Metrics: Consumer attitudes and the bottom line', *GfK Marketing Intelligence Review,* 7(1), pp. 28–33.

Wilson, K. and Millman, T. (2003) 'The global account manager as political entrepreneur', *Industrial Marketing Management,* 32, pp. 151–158.

Yip, G.S. and Bink, A.J.M. (2007) 'Managing global accounts', *Harvard Business Review,* September, pp. 103–111.

CASE STUDY V.1

Sony Music Entertainment: new worldwide organizational structure and the marketing, planning and budgeting of Pink's new album

On a sunny June day in 2013 the Executive Vice President Marketing for Sony Music Entertainment (SME), David Scott, gets on a plane from New York bound for London. There, among other things, he is going to meet megastar Pink about the marketing campaign for her new CD release in spring 2014. Pink is one of SME's best-selling artists, and David is looking forward to meeting the star personally.

New in his job as Executive Vice President, David uses the plane trip over the Atlantic to study the global music industry more thoroughly.

In August 2008, the international media and entertainment companies Sony Corporation and Bertelsmann AG announced that Sony had agreed to acquire Bertelsmann's 50 per cent stake in Sony BMG. The new music company, to be called Sony Music Entertainment Inc. (SME), became a wholly owned subsidiary of Sony Corporation of America. SME's HQ is in New York.

Sony Music Entertainment operates music labels such as Arista Records, Upstate Records, Columbia Records, Epic Records, J Records, Jive Records, RCA Records, LaFace Records and Zomba Records.

After landing in London, David hurries to the meeting with Pink, but on the way he thinks about the new global organizational structure of SME.

In spring 2009, SME introduced a new organizational strategy for its music labels and corporate staff that would allow the company to focus on creating global music superstars who reach across geographical boundaries. The streamlining of the organization eliminated regional corporate groups in Europe, Asia and Latin American regions, and created four new strategic groups within SME: Office of the Chairman, Label Group, Territory Management and Corporate Center. All management from the groups report directly to the CEO, Doug Morris.

Sony Music Entertainment wants to strengthen relationships with its artists. The top management of the company thinks this structure allows its creative executives to be closer to artists, while allowing managers to better support their creative executives. SME wants an organization built on record labels with global reach. The labels and the creative executives should be able to work more closely with artists while being able to rely on effective global marketing capabilities.

Reporting to the Office of the Chairman, David Scott is the company's highest-ranking marketing executive, overseeing global marketing campaigns for Sony Music Entertainment artists. Also reporting to the Office of the Chairman are Human Resources, Strategy and New Technology, and Corporate Communications.

One of David's first tasks in the summer of 2013 is to create the worldwide marketing plan for the UK-singer Pink and her new album released in spring 2014. Hence, at David's meeting with Pink in London, they agree that the launch of Pink's new album in 2014 should start up in the UK in an effort to get to the top of the charts as quickly as possible.

First some general market data from the global music industry.

The world music industry in 2012

A general trend in the world music industry is that, since 2000, sales of recorded music have dropped off substantially, while live music has increased in importance.

A small handful of music companies (operating through several hundred subsidiaries and over a thousand labels) account for most records sold in the advanced economies. Music publishing – production and licensing of intellectual property rights – is even more concentrated.

The global recorded music industry has fallen from around US$30 billion in 2000 to around US$20 billion in 2012. The approximate market shares on the world market are shown in Table 1.

Development in 2011–12

The 'Big 5' major record companies became the 'Big 4' in 2004 when Sony acquired BMG, and the 'Big 3' when EMI was acquired by Universal Music Group in

Table 1	The global recorded music industry	
Record company	Market shares (%) on the world market for recorded music (2011)	Market shares (%) on the world market for recorded music (2012)
Universal Music Group	27	35
Sony Music Entertainment	24	26
EMI Group	10	–
Warner Music	14	15
Independent labels	25	24
Total	100	100

Sources: based on www.ifpi.com, musicandcopyright.files.wordpress.com, New Music First, www.cmj.com and other public sources.

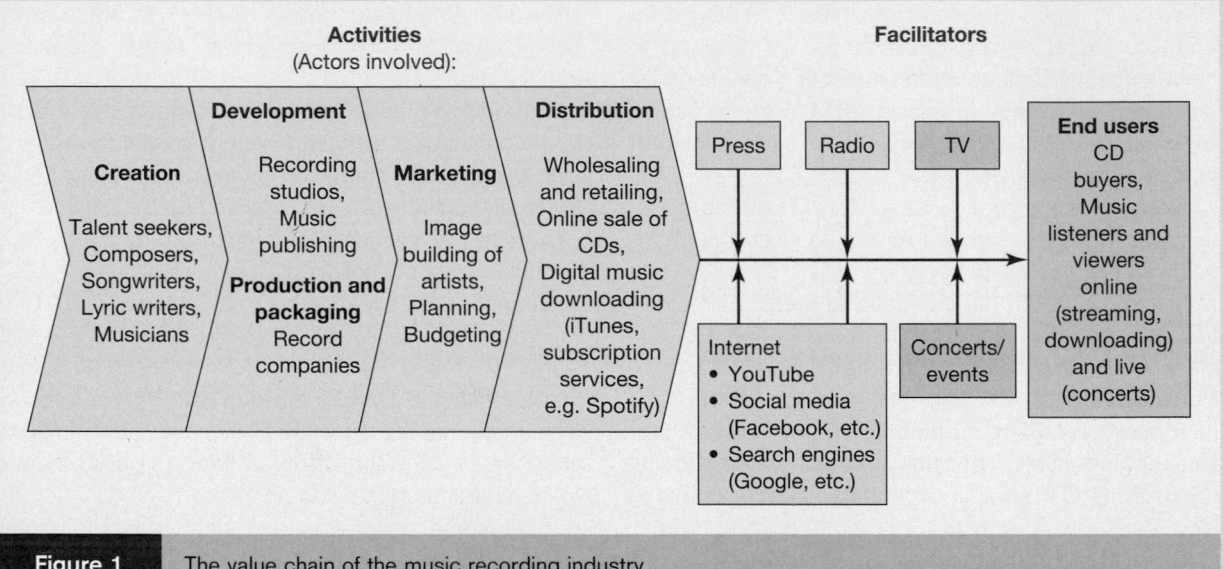

Figure 1   The value chain of the music recording industry

November 2011 (see also Table 1). EMI is the world's oldest music label and is home to legendary artists like the Beatles, David Bowie and Pink Floyd. In September 2012, the deal was finally approved in both the US and Europe.

This is a considerable shake-up in the music industry as it will make Universal even more dominant among the top music companies.

A label (like RCA under SME) typically enters into an exclusive recording contract with an artist to market the artist's recordings in return for royalties on the selling price of the recordings. Contracts may extend over short or long durations, and may or may not refer to specific recordings. Established, successful artists tend to be able to renegotiate their contracts to get terms more favourable to them.

Over the past 100 years, we have seen the music industry evolve through three basic stages, characterized by different technologies and different publishing

organizations. Prior to the gramophone, when sheet music was the primary vehicle for disseminating popular music, the industry was dominated by music publishing houses. With the rise of recording (and subsequently broadcasting, which was driven by the availability of 'canned content'), those publishers were displaced by the record companies.

Today, increasingly the industry has involved entertainment groups that bring together a broad range of content distribution and repackaging activities – broadcast, film, video, booking and performance management agencies, records, music licensing and print publishing.

See also the value chain of the music recording industry in Figure 1. In the early days of the recording industry, record labels were absolutely necessary for the success of any artist. The first goal of any new artist or band was to get signed to a contract as soon as possible. Through the advances of the internet, the role of labels is diminishing, as artists are able to distribute their own material freely through web radio, YouTube and other services, for little or no cost.

The business model of digital music

The digital music sector is pushing the limits of consumer choice, extending its business models and reaching out to consumers across the world. In 2011, digital channels accounted for an estimated 32 per cent of the record companies' revenues globally, up from 29 per cent in 2010. Some markets now see more than half of the revenues derived from digital channels, including the US (52 per cent), South Korea (53 per cent) and China (73 per cent). Around 3.6 billion downloads (combining singles and album downloads) were purchased globally in 2011, an increase of 17 per cent from 2010.

Ten years after the first online stores emerged in the US and Europe, the music download sector continues to expand internationally and improve its offer to consumers. Download stores account for a large proportion of digital revenues and account for most of the 500 legitimate services worldwide, offering libraries of up to 20 million tracks.

Digital music is now broadly segmented into two main consumption models – 'ownership' (Apple's iTunes) and 'access' (streaming, e.g. through Spotify). The growth per year of digital music has been between 5 and 10 per cent between 2007 and 2012.

Also driving growth is the global surge in consumer demand for smartphones and tablets. These, along with steadily growing broadband penetration, are a major factor in the increased uptake of both download and subscription services.

iTunes

In 2003, Apple introduced a new business model in the form of iTunes. iTunes is based on the iTunes store concept and the single song purchase. The user acquires full rights to enjoy music by paying a fee for each song. In this model, the user becomes owner of the music. The acquired songs can be moved freely to an iPod or other mobile devices. The development of iTunes put pressure on the CD as a medium for music. In response, artists often produce only four or eight tracks instead of a complete album. The iTunes end user typically pay US$1 for a downloaded song. Of this amount, Apple takes 30 per cent, the artist gets around 10 per cent and the rest goes to the record company.

Spotify

Spotify was founded as a subscription service in 2006 in Sweden. Spotify makes music available in a legal way by providing (partly free) access to songs and albums. The Spotify business model (access to music through streaming) challenges that of iTunes (owning music). Spotify provides music to anyone with internet access, via PC or mobile device, for free. The Spotify model is based on 'music anytime, anyhow, anywhere'. Users determine whether they take the free version (with advertising) or the premium version (without advertising). Spotify introduced the model of 'providing access to music' with or without advertising. The user starts using Spotify in the free version, with advertising. While getting to know the application, a complete new world opens up. You can play anything you like. And after a while, users who are bothered by the advertising shift towards the paid subscription model. This concept 'free drives paid' is fully recognized by Spotify and built into their business model.

The total number of Spotify users reached 20 million in January 2013, five million of them paying monthly either US$4.99 (ad-free, desktop version) or US$9.99 (adfree, available on all platforms: smartphone, offline, etc.). As of February 2013, the service is available in 25 countries, including the US, Australia and New Zealand.

Spotify allows registered users to integrate their account with existing Facebook and Twitter accounts. Once users integrate their Spotify account with other social media profiles, they are able to access their friends' favourite music and playlists.

There has been some criticism of the business model, especially from the artists' side. Spotify has been accused of failing to compensate artists fairly. Spotify has responded to the criticism by stating that 70 per cent of Spotify's revenue is paid out in royalties, and that the per-stream royalty rate has doubled since the service was launched. Spotify also argues that the royalties are paid to the record labels, who then pass it on to their artists. The specific royalty that the artists receive depends on the contract that they have with their record company. Typically an artist will get US$1.50 every time a song is streamed 1,000 times on Spotify.

'360 degree' business partnerships

The turmoil in the recorded music industry changed the twentieth-century balance between artists, record companies, promoters, retail music stores and the consumer. As of 2010, big retail chains such as Walmart and Best Buy sell more records than music-only stores, which have ceased to function as a player in the industry. Recording artists now rely on live performance and merchandise for the majority of their income, which in turn has made them more dependent on music promoters such as Live Nation (which dominates tour promotion and owns a large number of music venues). In order to benefit from all of an artist's income streams, record companies increasingly rely on the '360 deal', a new business relationship pioneered by Robbie Williams and EMI in 2007. The terms of these '360 degree' deals commit record companies to greater investment across a range of artist' activities in return for a proportion of the revenue stream from all of that. This form of non-traditional licensing income is becoming an increasingly important revenue channel for record companies. In the UK, income from non-traditional rights and licensing deals in 2012 reached 20 per cent of all the music industry income.

Online piracy

Widespread piracy is the biggest factor undermining the growth of the digital music business. It undermines the incentive to obtain music using legitimate paid models and depresses spending, even among those consumers willing to purchase music. The vast scale of the problem is widely recognized, as is the recent evolution of new forms and channels. Globally, it is estimated that 28 per cent of internet users access unauthorized services on a monthly basis. For some countries, the piracy rate is extremely high. China is a market with huge potential for the music industry. However, in recent years it has suffered from an estimated 99 per cent digital piracy rate. China has nearly twice as many internet users as the US, but registered digital music revenues per user are currently only 1 per cent of that of the US.

Pink – one of the best-selling pop-rock artists

Pink (Alecia Beth Moore) was born on 8 September 1979 in Pennsylvania. To date she has sold over 31 million albums worldwide. Her songs are characterized by their rebellious tone and a strict use of the first person. Her stage name, 'Pink', is a nickname she has had since she was a child. She would get embarrassed easily and her face would turn pink.

Pink's career accomplishments include three Grammy Awards, five MTV Video Music Awards and two Brit Awards. On the 2 June 2011, Pink and her husband, Carey Hart (a professional US motocross racer), had their first child, Willow Sage Hart.

Pink returned to work four months after giving birth to her daughter Willow to begin filming the dramatic comedy *Thanks for Sharing* (released in 2012), starring alongside Gwyneth Paltrow and Mark Ruffalo.

Pink's musical career

Pink released her first single, *There You Go,* and her first album, the R&B-oriented *Can't Take Me Home,* in

Pink
Source: Kevork Djansezian/Getty Images.

2000 via LaFace Records, which garnered commercial success. Her more pop rock-oriented second studio album, *Missundaztood,* which began a marked shift in the sound of her music, was released in 2001, and was a worldwide success. The CD *Can't Take Me Home* was certified double platinum in the US, sold five million copies worldwide and produced more top 10 singles.

On the second album, Pink took her sound in a new direction and sought more creative control during its recording. She recruited Linda Perry, former singer of 4 Non Blondes (one of Pink's favourites in her teenage years). The album, titled *Missundaztood* because of Pink's belief that people had got the wrong idea about her, was released in November 2001.

The first single, *Get the Party Started* (written and produced by Perry), went into the top five in the US and many other countries, and number one in Australia. Pink's third and fourth studio albums went well but sales were not excellent.

Funhouse, the fifth studio album by Pink, was released by LaFace Records worldwide in October 2008. Upon its release, the album reached number one in the charts in Australia, New Zealand and the UK, while debuting at number two in Germany, Ireland, France and the US. The album's main single, *So What,* was the biggest solo success of Pink's career up to that point, topping the charts in 11 countries so far, including her native US, the UK, Germany and Australia, and reaching the top five in many others.

By the end of 2009, *Billboard* magazine named Pink the number one pop artist of the decade, as well as naming her the 13th overall music artist of the decade.

In 2009, Pink went on a worldwide tour, and during 2009–10 she sold a total of 3,000,000 concert tickets.

In the first week of October 2010, Pink released *Raise Your Glass,* the first single from her first compilation album, *Greatest Hits. . . So Far!!!.* The song celebrates a decade since Pink's debut in 2000 and is dedicated to her fans who have supported her over the years. The song peaked at number one on the Billboard Hot 100, becoming Pink's 10th top ten hit, and her second solo number one on the chart. On 12 November 2010, Pink released the compilation album *Greatest Hits...So Far!!!,* and month a later she released her second single from the album, called *Fuckin' Perfect.* The song reached number two on the Billboard Hot 100 and peaked at number one in Germany.

Pink's sixth studio album (*The Truth About Love*) was released in autumn 2012. The single *Blow Me (One Last Kiss)* was released as the first single from that album. The song topped the German Airplay Chart, becoming Pink's 10th consecutive single to do so and increasing her record for the greatest number of consecutive number one singles in Germany. The song also appeared on the South African Airplay Chart, reaching a peak position of number two. As of October 2012, Pink was placed third behind Rihanna and Beyoncé for greatest number of top 10 hits for a female artist since 2000. On 5 February 2013, Pinks' music video for *Just Give Me a Reson* featuring Nate Reuss (from the group FUN.) was released on her official Vevo channel on YouTube.

Pink's second single from the album (*The Truth About Love*) was *Try,* which was a commercial success for Pink in Spring 2013, reaching number one in Spain and top ten in several other countries.

The typical value chain for a CD

The following shows how the 'value added' of a typical physical CD album is split among the various players in the value chain:

	£
Retail price to consumers (exclusive VAT)	11
Price to retail	8
(Price to distributor from record company)	5

Creation and development

In the music industry, record labels will actively seek to sign up bands and artists on long-term exclusive contracts. A key to success in development is to spot talent and to sign it up early. Discovering, developing and promoting talent can be extremely expensive. In recent years, a new wave of reality TV competitions has drawn huge audiences. Many talented stars have been found through such shows, from Kelly Clarkson in the US to Leona Lewis in the UK, but these are only one means of discovering talent and they complement, rather than substitute, the talent work done by the record labels.

Production and packaging

Production is relatively cheap in the music industry, and the cost of digital recording equipment and production of CDs is falling rapidly. Some consumers do not understand why the sale price of a CD is so much higher than the cost of producing the actual physical disc. However, as described below, there are many different activities and costs involved in creating songs and marketing the end result, the album.

Distributors

Major distributors have a global network of branch offices to handle the sales, marketing and distribution process. Sometimes the distributors outsource the physical distribution process.

Retail

Retailers put in orders to the wholesalers as and when albums and singles are required. In the UK, the retailing of CDs is dominated by the big department store chains, such as Marks & Spencer, and specialized music stores. However, because of the popularity of the online business model (e.g. iTunes, Spotify), these 'bricks-and-mortar' retailers are now struggling financially.

The costs of a hit

Singles are released with the purpose of getting to the top of the charts. The financial risks involved in mounting an attack on the UK charts have never been greater. Securing a top 10 hit in the UK in the current climate is likely to cost a minimum of £150,000. Ever-increasing amounts of financial resources are being thrown at marketing and promotion in the hope that a single will be picked up by television, radio and, perhaps most importantly, the major retailers, in order to secure the highest chart entry.

Biggest cost categories

Of course, the most important component of a CD is the artist's effort that goes into developing the music. Artists spend a large portion of their creative energy writing song lyrics and composing music or working with producers and creative executives to find great songs from great writers. This task can take weeks, months or even years. The creative ability of these artists to produce the music, combined with the time and energy they spend throughout that process, is in itself priceless. But while the creative process is priceless, it must be compensated. Artists receive royalties on each recording, which vary according to their contract, and the songwriter gets royalties too. In addition, the label incurs the costs of finding and signing new artists.

Once an artist or group has songs composed, they go into a studio and begin recording. The costs of recording, including studio fees, musicians, sound engineers, producers and others, must all be recovered by the price of the CD. Professional studio recording costs vary widely, but for a pop or rock album, they commonly exceed £100,000. This investment includes the livelihoods of the community of professionals working on a recording, including studio producers, sound engineers and session musicians.

Then come the marketing and promotion costs – perhaps the most expensive part of the music business today. Increasingly they include expensive video clips, public relations, tour support, marketing campaigns and promotion to get the songs played. Labels make investments in artists by paying for both the production and the promotion of the album. The internet offers new ways for artists to reach music fans, but it still requires that some entity, whether a traditional label or another kind of company, market and promote the artist so that fans are aware of new releases.

For every album released in a given year, a marketing strategy is developed to make that album stand out from the others hitting the market. Artwork must be designed for the CD box, and promotional materials (posters, store displays and music videos) have to be developed and produced. For many artists, a costly concert tour is essential to promote their recordings.

Another factor commonly overlooked in assessing album prices is the assumption that all albums are somehow profitable. In fact, the vast majority are never profitable. For example, in the US, 27,000 new releases hit the market every year. Most of these albums never sell enough to recover costs. In the end, fewer than 10 per cent are profitable and, in effect, it is these recordings that finance the rest.

Marketing and promotion costs

The singles charts – compiled each week by different organizations, radio- and TV stations – have always been the cornerstone of the UK music industry. Singles are essentially 3–4 minute adverts for the albums. Singles' sales guarantee chart places and, in turn, radio play – and that is why music label companies persist with them. They are a kind of loss-leader for albums, where the real money is made.

The biggest expense is normally the promotional videos, which for a mainstream artist starts at about £50,000 and can cost anything up to £1 million (however, this is exceptional). Videos are an essential tool for reaching music fans through services such as YouTube and social networking sites as well as specialist TV channels, e.g. MTV. A series of three professionally shot music videos to promote an album might cost around £150,000. The digital technology and social media, such as FaceBook, can be used to develop relationships between artists and fans. Record companies show online what is happening in-studio or backstage.

New artists in particular need to be heavily supported by record companies. The level of tour support required is highly dependent on the nature of the artist. Typically, rock acts require heavier support than pop acts, while artists who require a backing band or orchestra could receive up to £200,000 in tour support.

In summary, here are some of the basic costs for a 'typical' UK top 10 album:

	£
Recording	100,000
Promotion videos	150,000
Remixes (of the original single)	10,000
Merchandising	20,000
Posters	15,000
Stickers	10,000
PR (press)	10,000
Promotion copies to radio stations, etc.	10,000
Website/social media (e.g. Facebook, Twitter)	30,000
Manufacturing costs (20p per CD)	10,000
Optional:	
Press ads	15,000
Billboard campaign	50,000
TV/radio/internet advertising	300,000
Tour support	200,000

These are often the biggest budget items for a record company bringing the contents (the music) to the public. Marketing builds the brand identity from which artists can earn money from numerous sources, such as live touring to merchandise. Record companies often work with broadcasters, news media and specialist advertising and PR companies who also benefit from the investment.

QUESTIONS

1. What do you think of the change in Sony Music Entertainment's organizational structure, from a geographical structure to an artist-driven organization?

2. How would you produce a sales and marketing budget for Pink's forthcoming single and album?

3. How would you control your budgets? What key figures would you monitor?

4. Which marketing mix would you suggest to increase Sony Music Entertainment's share in the UK market, where the company has less than 20 per cent market share?

5. What are the pros and cons for Sony Music Entertainment and Pink making all Pink's music available on an online music service like Spotify.

6. What can Sony Music Entertainment do to reduce the level of digital piracy of their music?

Sources: based on International Federation of the Phonographic Industry (IFPI), www.ifpi; www.sonymusic.com; www.sonybmg.com; and other publicly available information on the internet.

CASE STUDY V.2

Red Bull: the global market leader in energy drinks is considering further market expansion

The beginning

Energy drinks may well have come from Scotland in the form of Irn-Bru, first produced in the form of 'Iron Brew' in 1901. In Japan, the energy-drink phenomenon dates at least as far back as the early 1960s, with the release of Lipovitan. Most such products in Japan bear little resemblance to soft drinks, and are sold instead in small brown glass medicine bottles or cans styled to resemble such containers. These so-called 'genki drinks', which are also produced in South Korea, help employees to work long hours, or to stay awake on the late commute home.

In the UK, Lucozade Energy was originally introduced in 1929 as a hospital drink for 'aiding the recovery'; in the early 1980s, it was promoted as an energy drink for 'replenishing lost energy'.

Red Bull dates back to 1962 when the original formula was developed by Chaleo Yoovidhya, a Thai businessman, and sold under the name Krating Daeng by a local pharmaceutical company to treat jetlag and boost energy for truck drivers.

Dietrich Mateschitz grew up in a small village in Styria, Austria. When he turned 18, he attended the University of Vienna. It took Mateschitz 10 years to finally graduate with a degree in world trade. His friends said that Mateschitz liked to play, party and pursue pretty women. After graduation he decided to get serious and become a 'really good marketing man'. His natural charm helped him land a training position at Unilever, and soon he was promoting dishwashing detergents and soap all over Europe. Colleagues described him as 'funny, full of ambition and always filled with crazy ideas'.

Mateschitz had a natural talent for selling. He was creative and had a knack for getting things done. He soon got promoted to the position of marketing director for a leading international toothpaste brand called Blendax.

After years of travelling and selling toothpaste around the globe, Mateschitz became obsessed with the idea of creating his own business. In the summer of 1982, Mateschitz read a story about the top 10 taxpayers in Japan. He was surprised that a certain Mr Taisho, who had introduced a high-energy drink to Japan, was the top of the list. On the next stop of his sales trip – in Thailand – he learned from a local toothpaste distributor that energy drinks were a popular item among tired drivers stopping at gas stations. The top brand was Krating Daeng, meaning water buffalo. The ingredients were clearly written on the can. Like the original *Yellow Pages,* there was no trademark or patent to protect the formula.

Dietrich Mateschitz met up with Chaleo Yoovidhya (owner of Krating Daeng) shortly afterwards and they decided to start an energy drink company together. Each partner would contribute about half a million dollars in start-up capital. Yoovidhya provided the beverage formula and his partner contributed the marketing flair.

Red Bull was then founded by the pair in 1984, and was headquartered in Austria.

The start-up in Austria and the further international expansion

The optimistic 40-year-old Mateschitz quit his job and applied for a licence to sell the high-energy drink in Austria. However, Austrian bureaucracy would not allow the drink to be sold without scientific tests. It took three years and many sales calls to get a licence to sell the product. While waiting for the official licence, Mateschitz asked his old school friend Johannes Kastner, who ran an advertising agency in Frankfurt, Germany, to design the can and logo. Mateschitz rejected dozens of samples before settling on a macho logo with two red bulls charging each other. Kastner worked diligently on a snappy slogan, but Mateschitz rejected one after the other, each time saying, 'Not good enough.'

Kastner told Mateschitz to find someone else to come up with a better slogan, but Mateschitz pleaded, 'Sleep on it, and give me one more tag line.' The next morning Kastner called and said, 'Red Bull – gives you wings.' The slogan turned into a prophecy for the Red Bull brand, which continues to soar around the globe.

Mateschitz still had to find a bottler to produce his drink. Every bottler he called told him that Red Bull had no chance of success. Finally, Mateschitz found a sympathetic ear in Roman Rauch, the leading soft-drink bottler in Austria, and soon the shiny silver cans were rolling off the production line. Within two years, and after many creative promotions, sales began to grow, but so did his losses. While a million-dollar loss in two years may scare some entrepreneurs into closing the business, Mateschitz was undaunted. He financed everything without outside capital, and by 1990 Red Bull was in the black. He soon realized that Austria was not a big enough market and, in 1993, he expanded to neighbouring Hungary and then focused his energies on conquering the German market.

Once the news of Red Bull's advancing sales spread in Europe, dozens of copycat competitors came on the market. Red Bull's initial move into the German market was highly successful. However, after three months of increasing demand, Mateschitz could not get enough aluminium to produce the cans anywhere in Europe, and sales of Red Bull fell quickly. A competitor named Flying Horse became the market leader. It took Red Bull four years to reclaim the top spot in the German market.

In 1995, Red Bull hit Britain; in 1997, the US, starting in California. There, in a marketing trick typical of Mateschitz's unusual style, he hired students to drive around in liveried Minis with a Red Bull can on the roof to promote the drink.

The rest is history. Red Bull has become extremely popular over recent years with almost 1 billion 250 ml cans sold in 2000 to more than 3 billion cans sold in 2006 in over 130 countries. In 2006, Red Bull generated over €2.6 billion throughout the world with the help of its 3,900 employees.

In 2010, a total of 4.2 billion cans of Red Bull were sold worldwide, representing an increase of 8 per cent against 2009. However, due to currency and price factors, company turnover increased by 16 per cent from €3.3 billion to €3.8 billion.

Sales, revenues, productivity and operating profit not only matched 2006 levels, they exceeded them to such an extent that the figures recorded were the best in the company's history so far.

The main reasons for such positive figures included outstanding sales in the Red Bull markets in Turkey (+86 per cent), Japan (+80 per cent), Brazil (+32 per cent), Germany (+13 per cent) and the US (+11 per cent), combined with efficient cost management and ongoing brand investment even in the challenging economic climate of recent years.

Growth and investment continues – as is customary at Red Bull – to be financed from the operating cash flow.

At the end of 2010, Red Bull employed 7,758 people in 161 countries (end 2009: 6,900 in 160 countries). In addition, more than 5,000 students were getting their first work experience every year within Red Bull promotion teams.

In spite of the still very difficult and uncertain financial and global economic climate, the Red Bull plans for growth and investment in 2012 and beyond remain just as ambitious, and a continued upward trend is expected.

Red Bull is produced at a single facility in Austria and distributed around the world via a network of local subsidiaries and distributors. At the end of 2010, Red Bull had subsidiaries in the following countries:

- *Europe:* Germany, Switzerland, Ireland, Italy, Netherlands, Finland, Greece, Portugal, Czech Republic and Slovakia.
- *Outside Europe:* Australia, New Zealand and United Arab Emirates.

Marketing orientation and consumers

Red Bull devised an innovative viral marketing approach to target mainly consumers seeking an energy boost: young adults (16–29), young urban professionals, post-secondary school students and club-goers.

The company also set about promoting the Red Bull brand directly to Generation Y, the so-called 'millennials', people born after 1981 who were believed to be cynical about traditional marketing strategies. Part of this idea involved recruiting 'student brand managers' who would be used to promote Red Bull on university campuses. These students would be encouraged to throw a party at which cases of Red Bull would be distributed. The brand managers would then report back to the company, giving the firm a low-cost form of market research data.

Red Bull tries to portray its products as drinks for energetic, physically active and health-conscious consumers, characterized by the sugar-free version. People in need of energy boosts include, but are not limited to, club-hoppers, truck drivers and students.

The Red Bull marketing strategy

Red Bull essentially threw the traditional marketing book out of the window. Its highly acclaimed strategy has been variously described as: grassroots, guerilla, word-of-mouth, viral marketing, underground, buzz-marketing and, without doubt, successful.

The first marketing trials of Red Bull failed miserably. The respondents didn't like the taste, colour or the 'stimulates mind and body' concept. At this point, many companies would have abandoned their plan or reformulated to make it more appealing to the consumer. However, Mateschitz rejected any suggestion that this testing of consumer taste should be the basis for their marketing strategy. Mateschitz's message was that Red Bull was not selling a beverage; rather, it was selling a 'way of life.' Red Bull will *give you wings* . . . Red Bull is an enabler for what you desire. Red Bull needed to be enjoyed in the right context – where an energy boost was needed.

One effective brand builder was not initiated by the company. Red Bull faced many obstacles in gaining regulatory approval in several countries because of its unique ingredients. During this time a rumour circulated that the taurine used came from bulls' testicles and Red Bull was 'liquid Viagra', which made the drink even more mystic. Adding to the allure was the fact that the beverage was at one time banned in several countries such as France and Denmark.

Source: Costi Iosif/Shutterstock.com.

The product

Red Bull is sold as an energy drink to combat mental and physical fatigue. Active ingredients include, but are not limited to, 27 g of sugar, B-complex vitamins and 80 mg of caffeine – which is a little less than the amount of caffeine found in an average cup of coffee and about two times as much caffeine as many leading cola drinks. Besides water, sugar and caffeine, the drink contains an ingredient named taurine, an amino acid that, according to Japanese studies, benefits the cardiovascular system.

A sugar-free version has been available since the beginning of 2003. The drink tastes of citrus and herbs, and is commonly used as a mixer in alcoholic drinks such as Red Bull Wings (Red Bull and vodka) or a base ingredient in the famous Jägerbomb (a cocktail combining one shot of Jägermeister dropped into a glass of Red Bull).

Red Bull specializes in energy drinks. Red Bull is the company's main brand, and with only two flavour varieties and one packaging size this allows the company to focus its efforts and expand its footprint quickly while leveraging marketing and promotions used in other regions. In most countries and regions, Red Bull was the first energy drinks brand and, as a result, is the leading brand in almost all regions where it is sold.

Red Bull distinguishes itself from a lot of the beverage market by only offering its product in one size, 8.3 ounce (250 ml) cans, which is smaller than a typical soft drink. The cans are small, sleek vessels with distinctive printing, which have been described as more 'European' styling. With the exception of mandated warning labels, the can design does not vary by country. Furthermore, unlike soft drinks or vodka, Red Bull is only offered in two varieties: original and sugar-free. This recognizable packaging provides Red Bull with an advantage, and the one size that is used worldwide creates production efficiencies.

On 24 March 2008, Red Bull introduced 'Simply Cola', or Red Bull Cola. The cola, which contains natural flavouring and caffeine, was introduced in several countries (as of 2008, Red Bull Cola was available in the Netherlands, Austria, Czech Republic, Egypt, Switzerland, Spain, Poland, Germany, Belgium, Italy, the UK, Ireland, Thailand, Romania, Hungary, Russia and the US). Red Bull Cola is not manufactured by Red Bull itself, but in Switzerland by Rauch Trading AG for Red Bull GmbH. It is the company's own take on a cola beverage. The product was the first major brand extension since Red Bull Sugar-Free was introduced in 2003. It was available in both the original 250 ml cans and the newer 355 ml version. Red Bull Cola also has slightly more caffeine, at 45 mg per 355 ml (12-ounce) can, than Coca-Cola (34 mg) or Pepsi-Cola (37.5 mg), but less than Diet Coke (47 mg).

In May 2009, food regulators from Germany discovered trace amounts of cocaine in Red Bull Cola. The amounts in question were very small, around 0.13 micrograms of cocaine in a can of Red Bull Cola, so about 12,000 litres of the cola would need to be consumed for the cocaine to be harmful. But in light of this, the drink was ordered off the shelves in some German shops. The product was also banned in Taiwan for the same reason. In the summer of 2009, the 'Red Bull Energy Shots' were introduced globally. It is a small version of the regular drink, with the same energy power.

The idea of energy shots started decades ago in the Far East, notably in Japan, where small 'tonics' became very popular among consumers, highly concentrated and without carbonation. With the introduction of energy drinks as of the late 1980s, the efficacy of these energy shots started to travel the world as a new product format. In 2004, the first suppliers, like 5-Hour Energy, took up the idea and launched these energy shots in the US, opening up a sub-segment in the energy drink market. In 2008, there were over 25 brands offering energy shots in the US alone. As of September 2011, there were approximately 250 energy shot brands in the US, with 5-Hour Energy owning 70 per cent of the market share. Although originally marketed in the US, energy shots are becoming more popular in other parts of the world, such as Europe, Asia and Australia.

However, in July 2011 it was announced that Red Bull North America had discontinued production of both its energy shot and cola. Red Bull would sell through existing inventories of Red Bull Cola and Red Bull Energy Shot, but not proceed with additional production. Instead it would refocus efforts on growth of its core brand within the expanding energy drink category.

Since its debut in 2008, Red Bull Cola has struggled to excite US consumers and retailers, in part due to the cola's premium price point, which has been its biggest impediment to success. A 12-ounce can of Red Bull Cola sells for around US$1.50 in comparison to US$1.00 or less for a similarly sized Coke or Pepsi product.

Despite its late entry into the energy-shots segment, Red Bull was a well-known manufacturer and thus many experts predicted that there would be carry-over success from its canned energy drinks. However, in the US the energy-shot market seemed already overcrowded. Though well-known as an energy-drink brand, the competition was more fierce for Red Bull Energy Shots as many entrants were already in the category, and the shelf space for energy shots was extremely limited – not to mention the premium price point (50 cents higher than '5-hour Energy' and other competitors), which served as a stronger deterrent, given the absolute price points range anywhere from $2.49 to $3.49.

To date (2013), sales of the Red Bull Cola and the Energy Shot have not been discontinued in Red Bull international markets, other than North America.

Price

This clear positioning has created a foothold in key markets such as the UK, Germany and the US. Sales in key markets help drive the global positioning of the company, as well as providing the opportunity to sell Red Bull at a premium price over other brands. A single can is generally around €2, which is up to five times the cost of other branded soft drinks.

Premium pricing is a feature of the energy drinks category, and especially for Red Bull. Since its inception, the category has been positioned as providing products that not only refresh you, but also give you the energy and related brain power to make the most of your time. While it could never be said that energy drinks position themselves as healthy, there is little doubt that they claim to provide a functional benefit to the consumer, which is the main reason why they can command a premium price. In 2010, the average price per litre for an energy drink across the world was around US$6.00, almost four times the average price of a litre of carbonates, like cola (US$1.50), and similarly ahead of the average price per litre in the soft drinks category as a whole.

Red Bull Original
Source: © Red Bull Media House.

Red Bull Sugarfree
Source: © Red Bull Media House.

Red Bull Simply Cola
Source: Red Bull GmbH.

Red Bull Energy Shot
Source: ©   Bull Photofiles.

Distribution

A key growth strategy at Red Bull has been increased international distribution. It has consistently worked on growing international sales, first making moves outside its domestic market in 1992, only five years after the first cans of Red Bull appeared in Austria. Now available in over 100 countries worldwide, Red Bull has a well-developed network of local subsidiaries set up in key markets to oversee distribution in any given region. These subsidiaries are responsible for importing Red Bull from Red Bull GmbH in Austria and either setting up an independent distribution network or working with a partner, such as in Australia where Red Bull Australia uses Cadbury Schweppes's distribution network. In this case, Red Bull Australia imports and sells on to Cadbury Schweppes, which then sells to vendors in its network.

The typical Red Bull national distribution strategy for new markets is, like everything else, atypical. Instead of targeting the largest distributors with the greatest reach, Red Bull targets small distributors who often become exclusively Red Bull distributors. They even went to the extreme of hiring teenagers/college students and giving them vans to distribute the product.

Small independent venues were the first targets. Red Bull would find the small bars, restaurants and stores and give them a small cooler to sell the beverage from. This was their preferred method rather than

Red Bull X Fighters Exhibition Tour, Egypt 2009
Source: © Balazsgardi.com/Red Bull Photofiles.

dealing with the demands of the larger stores, which eventually were begging to sell the product.

Promotion/advertising

Many product launches are coupled with large advertising campaigns, both in print and on TV, taste tests, give-aways and celebrity endorsements to get the brand and product out to the public. This is not a technique that is used by Red Bull.

Red Bull does not use traditional advertising to enter a market. Only after the product is in the market does advertising serve as a reminder. Furthermore, they never use print media since they are too dull and flat to express the product. Television ads are often cartoon drawings using the 'Red Bull gives you wings' slogan and are very carefully placed. Stations and programming are carefully selected to maximize exposure to the target audience such as late-night TV shows.

Red Bull does not hire celebrity endorsers, but they do enable celebrity endorsers. Some of the earliest deliveries of Red Bull in the US were to Hollywood movie sets for consumption during long days of filming, even before the beverage was readily available. This created a situation where the celebrities were doing what they could to get Red Bull and instantly became endorsers for the brand to the masses. Celebrities are not the only ones who were enabled for endorsements. Again, before the product was widely available, the company made it available to bartenders in New York's trendiest spots for their own consumption. This led to an unpaid endorsement to the club patrons by the bartenders.

Every year the company sponsors dozens of extreme sporting events, like the climbing of ice-covered silos in Iowa or kite sailing in Hawaii, as well as cultural events like breakdancing contests and rock music jam sessions. Red Bull also sponsors a DJ camp where some of the up-and-coming DJs get a chance to learn from some of the masters, courtesy of Red Bull. Red Bull also sponsors some 500 athletes around the world, the type of person who would surf in Nova Scotia in January or jump out of a plane to 'fly' across the English Channel.

It also hosts events such as the 'Red Bull Flugtag' (German for 'flight day' or 'flying day'), a competition where entrants launch themselves off a 30-foot ramp in homemade 'flying machines' into a body of water. It takes place in big cities such as London (see photo).

The local subsidiaries are also responsible for local marketing content such as buzz marketing, local sponsorships and arranging media, including TV, billboards and radio. In addition to local marketing and advertising, local subsidiaries also acquire marketing material from Red Bull GmbH and its exclusive advertiser Kastner & Partners.

Red Bull is also involved with more popular sports, such as football and racing. Red Bull has extended its presence in sports to purchasing and entirely rebranding a number of sports teams.

Red Bull owns four soccer teams – New York's Red Bulls (and their stadium), Red Bull Salzburg, Red Bull Brasil and RB Leipzig – a Nascar team and two Formula 1 racing teams. One Formula 1 team has on occasion been sufficient to cripple a billionaire's finances but, like everything at Red Bull, it finances the annual US$200 million cost of its F1 teams out of the company's healthy operating income.

Red Bull Racing is one of two Formula 1 teams owned by Red Bull (the other being Scuderia Toro Rosso). The team is based in Milton Keynes in the UK but holds an Austrian licence.

In 2010, 2011 and 2012, the Red Bull Racing team won both the constructors' and drivers' Formula 1 championships, with young German driver Sebastian Vettel.

In addition to sports sponsorships, Red Bull has developed the Mobile Energy Team programme consisting mostly of outgoing college students who drive specially designed Red Bull Mini Coopers with the blue can on the roof to promote the drink. They go to all types of events and arrange sampling of the energy drink. They are usually employed by Red Bull on a part-time basis and often have teams running on 24/7 formats.

Red Bull Flugtag in Vienna
Source: © Marcel Lammerhirt/Red Bull Photofiles/Red Bull GmbH.

Red Bull Mini

Source: Red Bull GmbH.

On 14 October 2012, Red Bull received a monumental amount of attention as a result of the 39-km free space jump by Austrian Felix Baumgartner, who was sponsored by Red Bull. He set the record for highest jump and fastest freefall velocity when he became the first person to break the sound barrier without the aid of a jet or spacecraft. Baumgartner has made a career out of risky jumps, including skydiving across the English Channel and parachuting off the Petronas Towers in Malaysia. The jump was five years in preparation for the sponsor, the Red Bull Stratos team. We saw Baumgartner in his custom-made suit splashed with the Red Bull logo and got updates from the Red Bull command centre. It was a huge PR success for Red Bull.

All in all, Red Bull spends relatively little on traditional print and TV advertising, instead relying on sponsorships of sports or giving away samples at local events. Since its introduction, Red Bull has invested heavily in building the brand, spending around 40 per cent of revenue on marketing and promotion. As a comparison, Coca-Cola spends 9 per cent.

Competition

By definition, Red Bull operates within the functional drinks market, which is mostly made up of sales from energy drinks and sports drinks – Red Bull is only active in the energy drinks market. Sports drinks are not to be confused with energy drinks. Sports drinks are intended to replenish electrolytes, sugar, water and other nutrients, and are usually isotonic (containing the same proportions as found in the human body) and

used after strenuous training or competition. Energy drinks, on the other hand, mainly provide sugar and caffeine in order to increase concentration or mental and physical capacities. The most well-known sports drink is 'Gatorade' (PepsiCo), which was introduced in 1965.

Red Bull, despite being widely known as an energy drink, has other uses such as a coffee, tea and soda substitute, a vitamin/energy supplement and a mixer for alcohol.

The majority of consumers use Red Bull as a vitamin supplement or energy stimulant in place of preferred stimulants such as ginseng. Red Bull, with its liquid B-vitamin supplement, competes in the niche market for vitamins and is competing with the larger pharmaceutical companies. Red Bull also competes indirectly with various drink mixers such as juice, sour mix and tonic. Red Bull initially marketed its energy drink mixed with alcohol to the average club-goer. However, due to various health concerns and fatal incidents associated with Red Bull when mixed with alcohol, explicit warnings have been placed on product labels discouraging improper use.

The market for energy drinks is characterized by the presence of specialized manufacturers as well as food and beverage powerhouses. Key players in the marketplace include Pepsi, Coca-Cola, Danone, Hansen Beverage Company, Monarch Beverage Co., Red Bull, Dark Dog, GlaxoSmithKline, Extreme Beverages, Taisho Pharmaceuticals and Otsuka Pharmaceuticals. In terms of market share, Gatorade and Red Bull lead the sports and energy drinks segments, respectively. Most of the soft drink multinationals (e.g. Pepsi, Coca-Cola, Danone, GlaxoSmithKline) also cover the functional drinks market. For example, Coca-Cola added the 'Von Dutch' and 'Tab Energy' brands to its energy drinks portfolio in 2006. While smaller players have proven the most innovative, the production, distribution and marketing resources of the major multinationals represent a considerable threat to Red Bull.

The total market for functional drinks (including energy drinks)

As indicated, the global soft drink market can be divided into different types of soft drinks, of which the 'functional drinks' sector is one. However, the volume share of functional drinks is only 3 per cent (see Table 1).

Table 1	Global soft-drink market (volume share, 2012)
Type of drink	**Percentage**
Bottled water	37
Carbonates (primarily cola)	35
Fruit/vegetable juice	11
Functional drinks (sports drinks and energy drinks)	3
Rest (RTD coffee, RTD tea, concentrates, etc.)	14
Total	100

Source: based on Euromonitor.com information.

Within the functional-drinks category, the volume share of 'sports drinks' is twice as high as energy drinks.

The global sports-drinks market

In global sports drinks, PepsiCo is the world market leader (world market share is 46 per cent), driven by its dominance in North America, where the PepsiCo brand, Gatorade, has a 75 per cent off-trade volume share of sports drinks in its region.

The world's number two in sports drinks is Coca-Cola Co., which has 22 per cent of the world market. Its main brand, Powerade, has a more regionally balanced sports drinks business than PepsiCo. For example, in Australia, Powerade is the leading brand with 50 per cent market share, compared with Gatorade with 36 per cent.

The global energy-drinks market

Although the global market size is bigger for sports drinks, the segment growth is faster for energy drinks than sports drinks. From 2005 to 2010, energy drinks showed a compound annual growth rate (CAGR) of 16 per cent vs just 5 per cent for sports drinks.

While North America has the highest volume share of the energy drinks market (37 per cent – see Table 2), it is not as dominant as it is in the sports drinks market.

Australasia is also quite developed. The brand competition in energy drinks is more diverse than in sports drinks. Red Bull is the only global brand, with a 25 per cent share (see Table 2) of the global off-trade volume sales. Typically, Red Bull enjoys a price premium of 20–30 per cent compared with other companies in the market. This also means that Red Bull's value share of the world market is higher than the 25 per cent volume share.

The two top energy drinks companies, Red Bull and Hansen, together have 35 per cent of the world market, although Hansen derives nearly all of its volume sales from North America (US). In 2010, the total world energy drinks market reached 4.5 billion litres, with a total value of about US$15.0 billion.

In western Europe, GSK's Lucozade is number one due to its dominance in the UK and Ireland. Outside UK and Ireland, Red Bull is the market leader. In eastern Europe, the competition is very diffuse, but overall Red Bull is the market leader. In North America, Hansen's Monster is the leading brand by off-trade volume,

Table 2	Energy drinks market shares (off-trade volume) in different regions (2010)					
	Western Europe	**Eastern Europe**	**North America**	**Australasia**	**Other areas (Latin Am., Africa)**	**World total**
Regional distributions of energy drinks – volume 2010 (%)	23%	7%	37%	25%	8%	100%
Market shares of the manufacturers (brands)	%	%	%	%	%	%
Red Bull, Austria (Red Bull)	29	24	20	27	25	26
Hansen, US (Monster)	1	–	27	–	–	11
PepsiCo, US (SoBe, AMP, Adrenaline Rush)	–	9	17	–	8	10
Coca-Cola, US (Burn, Full Throttle)	6	12	8	17	8	9
Rockstar, US (Rockstar)	1	–	12	–	–	6
Suntory, Japan (V)	–	–	–	48	–	3
GSK, UK (Lucozade)	38	–	–	–	–	9
Private labels	12	6	1	–	15	7
Others (e.g. Tiger in Poland)	13	49	15	8	44	19
Total	100	100	100	100	100	100

Source: based on Euromonitor and other public sources.

surpassing Red Bull in 2008. However, Monster does not have significant distribution and market share outside North America. Hansen has entered an agreement to distribute Monster in western Europe.

In Australasia, Suntory's 'V' is number one. Suntory is a relatively new player in the global energy-drinks scene. By acquiring a locally strong brand, 'V', from Danone, and the distribution network of 'Orangina', it has broadened its distribution outside Japan.

On-trade and off-trade challenges

Red Bull was originally targeted at the on-trade market (bars, discos, etc.), and still in Spain, for example, the popularity of Red Bull as a mixer underpins the fact that on-trade channels accounted for 55 per cent of energy drinks volume sales in 2010. The role of fashion in determining product choice in the on-trade channel presents Red Bull with the opportunity to generate sales by developing new combinations with alcoholic drinks.

Off-trade (retail) has now become the principal channel for energy drinks, with approximately two-thirds of worldwide volume being sold through these channels. This picture is pretty consistent worldwide, other than in Central and South America where the split is far more even, and North America where the emphasis is far heavier on the retail channels (85 per cent). In many markets, the UK being a good example, the volume sold through on-trade channels is heavily impacted by energy drinks being sold as mixers with spirits, primarily vodka.

Overall, the energy drinks market has seemed to shift from impulse-dependent to planned purchases with the expansion through supermarkets/hypermarkets. The development of non-impulse-oriented off-trade distribution creates opportunities to develop new packaging formats, including larger cans, multipacks and bottles. Furthermore, the shift to supermarket/hypermarket distribution may further encourage Red Bull to engage in agreements with major multinationals that have strong relationships with large and powerful retailers. The expansion of a non-impulse off-trade presence carries a risk of undermining Red Bull's fashionable image, especially given the emergence of rival brands targeting cutting-edge niches.

Red Bull is challenged in the US market by 'Monster'

When 'Monster' and other brands launched a larger 16-ounce can, Red Bull reacted too slowly. It was costly: from 2001 to 2006, Red Bull's market share in dollar terms went from 91 per cent to well under 50 per cent, and much of that loss was Monster's gain.

From 2006 to 2008, California-based Hansen Natural Corp.'s line of Monster energy drinks gained further market shares from Red Bull, and Monster is now the top US energy drink in terms of both unit volume and value (dollars) in the important convenience store channel. Monster has strong momentum in the US across all channels. However, taken together (off-trade plus on-trade), Monster is still the nation's number two selling energy drink (in value) behind Red Bull. Both companies had around 25 per cent value market share in 2008. Rockstar is a distant third with approximately 14 per cent market share in 2008.

In October 2008, Monster and Coca-Cola Enterprises (Coca-Cola's bottler) made a 20-year deal to distribute Monster energy drinks in about 20 US states, Canada and in six western European countries. This deal with Monster could give Coca-Cola a stronger position in the growing energy drink market. Conversely, it could help Monster by giving it access to Coca-Cola's distribution system in Europe. In January 2009, Coca-Cola began distributing the Monster line in France, Monaco, Belgium, Holland, Luxembourg and Canada (Much, 2009).

In February 2009, it was announced that the number three brand in US energy drinks, 'Rockstar', had signed a 10-year distribution deal with PepsiCo Inc., which in future will distribute Rockstar to most parts (approximately 80 per cent) of the US and Canada. Both companies hope the deal will give the brand more consistent coverage across the US and increase PepsiCo's presence in the energy drink category. Rockstar had in fact signed a distribution agreement with Coca-Cola Enterprises in 2005, and renegotiated the deal in 2008 as Coke was in negotiations with Monster's parent, Hansen Natural (Casey, 2009).

In contrast to Monster and Rockstar, Red Bull still has full confidence in its own distribution model in the US, by having its sales subsidiary Red Bull North America taking care of the overall distribution strategy and then relying on smaller distributors (often young, committed entrepreneurs) in order to penetrate local markets.

Strategic options

Dietrich Mateschitz is preparing for the next top management meeting: he summarizes some current strategic options for Red Bull in random order:

(a) *Expansion in emerging markets.* The top management team of Red Bull is considering focusing its further expansion on new markets such as India, Turkey, Russia, Mexico, Japan, China or the

Middle East. These markets are seeing demand for energy drinks grow strongly in urban areas thanks to rising purchasing power, accelerated lifestyles and improving distribution. Red Bull's prime consumers are in their 20s and the large youth population in the region can potentially become energy-drink consumers in the long term. India boasts the highest number of 20- to 24-year-olds (98 million), followed by China (82 million) and Indonesia (21 million). The liberalization of the Chinese and Indian economies is set to raise living standards and improve levels of disposable incomes, which will benefit sales of highly valued consumer products. Along with total increases in the consumption of soft drinks, China, India and Indonesia will continue to see high sales growth of energy drinks in years to come, implying optimistic business prospects for Red Bull.

(b) *International production.* Expanding the Red Bull production infrastructure would help the company to diminish the negative impact of exchange rate fluctuations and provide greater flexibility on price in the context of international expansion.

(c) *Healthier product variants.* Rising consumer health-consciousness is creating opportunities to develop energy drinks with healthier ingredients and more specific functional properties.

(d) *Hybrid products.* As busy consumers look for quick energy boosts, there are growing opportunities to develop hybrid products which combine energy-giving properties with other drink categories, such as tea, fruit/vegetable juice and bottled water. Another example is the emergence of malt-based alcohol brands with added energy components. In the US in 2005, Anheuser-Busch launched 'B to the E', a beer with added ginseng and guarana. In 2006, Miller Brewing purchased Sparks, a malt beverage with added caffeine, ginseng and taurine. Such drinks pose a particular threat to Red Bull's position as a mixer for alcoholic beverages in on-trade establishments.

(e) *Strategic alliances.* Red Bull may consider engaging in more agreements with major multinational partners, such as Cadbury-Schweppes in Australia, which would allow it to exploit established distribution networks and accelerate its penetration of new markets. This has also been the strategy of the main US competitor, Monster, which has allied itself with Coca-Cola Enterprises as its US and European distributor.

Dietrich Mateschitz is interested in your input for the tasks/questions below.

QUESTIONS

1. How would you characterize Red Bull's overall marketing strategy (global, glocal or local)?

2. Argue for the most relevant segmentation (screening) criteria to be used by Red Bull in the process of international market selection (IMS).

3. Was it a wise decision of Red Bull to:
   (a) launch Red Bull Cola and Red Bull Energy Shots?
   (b) launch Red Bull Cola and Red Bull Energy Shots in many markets at the same time?

4. Should Red Bull counteract the new marketing initiatives of its US competitor, Monster? If yes, what should Red Bull do in response?

5. Which of the five strategic options would you recommend for Red Bull's future strategy? Present arguments in support of your suggested priority list.

Sources: Cirillo, J. (2008) 'Energy drinks are on steady track', *Beverage World,* 127(4), 15–17; Casey, M. (2009) 'PepsiCo signs deal to distribute Rockstar via Pepsi Bottlers', Bevnet.com (www.bevnet.com/news/2009/2-19-2009-rockstar_pepsi); *Datamonitor* (2007) Red Bull GmbH, company profile, *Datamonitor,* 25 April; *Euromonitor International* (2006) Functional drinks: Japan, *Euromonitor,* October, 1–11; *Euromonitor International* (2007) Red Bull GmbH: softdrink – world, global company profile, *Euromonitor,* March, 1–15; Gschwandtner, G. (2004) 'The powerful sales strategy behind Red Bull', *Selling Power Magazine,* September; Hosea, M. (2007) 'Running with bulls', *Brand Strategy,* September, 30, 20–23; Lerner, M. (2007) 'Running with "Red Bull" and an arena of speciality drinks', *American Metal Market,* August, 20–22; *Marketing Week* (2006) 'Red Bull spreads its wings', 6 January, 33; Much, M. (2009) 'Coke distribution deal could be a Monster boost for drink maker', Investers.com (http://beta.investors.com/NewsAndAnalysis/Article.aspx?id=459831).

CASE STUDY V.3

Tetra Pak: how to create B2B relationships with the food industry on a global level

'A package should save more than it costs.'

Dr Ruben Rausing, founder of Tetra Pak (1895–1983)

In other words, what Dr Rausing is saying is that the benefits to the customer and society from packaging should outweigh the resources used and the costs of its manufacture.

Most efforts to reduce world hunger focus on increasing food production, building sustainable food chains and making food available and affordable. It is also important to do something about the fact that up to 50 per cent of the annual world food production is lost between the place where it is grown and the consumer. Food is wasted everywhere due to maturation and poor storage, products are crushed, become oxidized, suffer water damage or are attacked by vermin and microorganisms – mostly as a result of having either poor packaging or none at all.

Tetra Pak (www.tetrapak.com) helps with solving these huge global problems of food security by offering, for example, aseptic processing, and its packaging can preserve delicate products such as milk, juice and water safely for months without needing any preservatives or refrigeration.

Tetra Pak

Tetra Pak is one of three companies in the Tetra Laval Group – a private group that started in Sweden. The other two companies are DeLaval and Sidel. Tetra Laval is headquartered in Switzerland. Tetra Pak is a specialist in complete solutions for the processing, packaging and distribution of food products.

Tetra Pak develops, produces and markets complete processing, packaging and distribution systems, primarily for liquid foodstuffs. Tetra Pak has expanded its business to include much more than packaging of liquid food products. Today, ice-cream, cheese, dry foods, fruits, vegetables and pet food are examples of products that can be processed or packaged in Tetra Pak processing and packaging lines.

The first products packed in Tetra Pak cartons were milk and cream. Accounting for about two-thirds of the total volume of the foodstuffs packed in Tetra Pak packages, they remain the firm's most important products.

A wide variety of food products are process treated and aseptically packaged. Thanks to the aseptic processing and packaging systems, these products retain their taste and nutritional value, even when stored for months without refrigeration.

This packaging system has also facilitated rational and economical distribution of products in large volumes such as milk and milk-based products, juices and fruit drinks, tea drinks, soy drinks, tomato products and wine.

The Tetra Pak products are divided into several categories:

- packages
- processing equipment
- filling machines
- distribution equipment
- service products.

Source: Tetra Pak International SA.

Tetra Pak operates in more than 170 countries around the globe, employing almost 23,000 people. Their customers come from different parts of the food industry, such as the dairy, cheese, ice-cream, beverage and prepared food sectors.

In 2012, 8.2 billion packages of milk and other nutritious drinks in Tetra Pak packages were provided to 67 million children in schools in over 60 countries. School feeding programmes can have a considerable impact on the local community and economy. Not only do they improve the health and learning capabilities of children, but they often act as a catalyst for agricultural and economic development.

In 2011, Tetra Pak expanded its support for school feeding programmes in Senegal, Sudan, Zambia, Honduras and Argentina among many others. School feeding programmes play a vital part in their business strategy and commitment to dairy customers around the world to make food safe and available everywhere.

The company envisaged that these programmes would be expanded in subsequent years.

Development of Tetra Pak

Ruben Rausing, the founder of Tetra Pak, was born near Helsingborg, Sweden. He graduated from the Stockholm School of Economics in 1918 at the end of World War I. By 1920, he had earned his Master of Science from Columbia University, in New York.

During his studies in the US, Rausing came across the 'self-service grocery stores' system in America, which was unknown in Europe at the time. He realized that pre-packaging was part of the future in food retailing as a more hygienic and practical way of distributing staple groceries, all of which were at the time sold over the counter in glass bottles or impractical paper wraps in most European countries.

Rausing's team got the order to produce a viable packaging for milk that was cheap enough to compete with the current milk distribution system, based on loose milk sold in reusable glass bottles. The key to this was to use as little packaging material as possible. The research laboratory had tried and failed with a number of different solutions. One of the engineers in the team, Erik Wallenberg, got the idea of using one single sheet of paper rolled into a cylinder and folded from two different sides, creating a geometrical figure – a *tetrahedron* (this form later gave the name 'Tetra' to the company). The volume created only needed to be sealed in three places and the packages could be produced in one subsequent sequence from one roll of paper, using a minimum of material, with a minimum of waste. The package is still sold today under the name of Tetra Classic Aseptic.

In 1951, AB Tetra Pak was founded in Lund Sweden, by Ruben Rausing. It started as a subsidiary of Åkerlund & Rausing.

Tetra Pak's commercial breakthrough did not arrive until the mid-60s with the new Tetra Brik® package, introduced in 1963, and the development of the aseptic technology.

International expansion had already begun at the beginning of the 1960s, when the first production plant for packaging material outside of Sweden was established in Mexico (1960), soon to be followed by another one in the US (1962). In 1964, the first Tetra Classic Aseptic machine outside Europe was installed in Lebanon. The late 1960s and the 1970s saw a global expansion of the company, much of it due to the new Tetra Brik® Aseptic package.

Tetra Pak acquired Alfa-Laval AB in 1991, a venerable Swedish company producing industrial and agricultural equipment and milk separators, a world leader in its industry. In 1993, Group Tetra Laval was created, with joint headquarters in Lund and Lausanne.

Food waste and the role of packaging

Throwing food away is tremendously wasteful. Food that is bought, cooked and then thrown away is of no use to anyone. It has been produced, packaged, transported and stored, as well as using raw materials, energy, water and packaging, completely unnecessarily. Food that is thrown away instead of being eaten is a waste of both resources and money.

Approximately the same amount of food goes to waste in industrialized countries as in developing countries (670 and 630 million tonnes, respectively) but for different reasons. Around 30–50 per cent of the food in developing countries is unfit for human consumption, owing to inadequate packaging and distribution, compared with 2–3 per cent in western Europe and other industrial countries.

The main aim of food packaging is to protect the product from physical damage and keep out bacteria. The product waste saved due to packaging has been calculated as 10 times greater than the amount of waste created by the packaging itself. In less developed countries, over 30 per cent of all food is wasted simply because of poor packaging, lack of packaging, and inadequate transport and refrigeration facilities. In other countries, where packaging is common, this figure is significantly lower.

Technical attributes of packaging can influence how much food we waste. The following examples make a difference and are also features that consumers appreciate:

- protects the contents
- hygienic

- easy to open
- reclosability
- easy to portion
- easy to empty completely
- different volume sizes
- ambient storage.

More intense global competition

Tetra Pak's current main competitor is the Swiss manufacturer SIG Combibloc. Swedish Elopak/Pure-Pak produces similar style carton packages and has historically been Tetra Pak's principal competitor. However, Tetra Pak's main competition generally no longer comes from companies producing similar packaging but from industries and companies producing other types of packaging with a lower cost of production, such as the PET bottle. From 2012, the Chinese packaging company, GA Pack, began producing spin-offs of Tetra Pak products and challenging Tetra Pak in the important Chinese market. Tetra Pak's competitors are developing packaging machines with smaller capacities in order to secure business from customers requiring lower volumes, with the aseptic milk market proving a particularly attractive target. Tetra Pak's approach to tackling this involves broadening its product portfolio, improving its service offering and continuing to enhance quality in all respects.

With increasingly fierce competition in China, Tetra Pak has increased its resources and further adapted its products to suit the local market. As an example of the increased investment in the country, Tetra Pak opened a product development centre in Shanghai in November 2011. It provides dairy and beverage companies with processing, packaging and powder-handling

Tetra Pak filling machine – the firm's 'cash cow'
Source: Tetra Pak International SA.

equipment, as well as the expertise to enable Tetra Pak to develop high-quality products quickly and efficiently.

Table 1 shows that the efforts in China have paid off. By the end of 2011, 15 per cent of the total installed base of filling machines (in total 8,700) was located in Greater China (including Taiwan). Furthermore, 19 per cent of the new installed filling machines in 2011 were put into operation in Greater China.

Tetra Pak's green profile

Environmental efficiency has always been a part of Tetra Pak's strategy, because it is critical to both business performance and society as a whole.

Table 1	Installed base of filling machines and new installed filling machines in 2011	
Region	**Total installed base by the end of 2011**	**Installed in 2011**
	8700	(Numbers not available)
	%	%
Greater China	15	19
Southern Europe	14	5
Central and South America	13	21
Greater Middle East	12	15
Central Europe	9	6
Eastern Europe and Central Asia	8	3
North-east Asia and Oceania	8	3
South and South-east Asia	7	17
North America	6	7
North Europe	5	1
Sub-Saharan Africa	3	3
	100%	100%

Source: based on information in Tetra Pak Annual Report, 2011.

The 10-year targets are part of an ambitious environmental programme that aims to provide sustainable packaging using only renewable materials, achieve a minimal environmental footprint and create zero waste.

Tetra Pak is committed to helping double the global recycling rate of its used beverage cartons to 40 per cent by 2020. This means valuable raw materials can be provided for new products. With a compound annual growth rate of 5 per cent, this goal would lead to almost 100 billion used beverage cartons being recycled in 2020 alone. In 2011, more than 36 billion used Tetra Pak cartons were recycled.

Tetra Pak's current packaging types
Source: Tetra Pak International SA.

Tetra Pak's financial results

Table 2 shows the financial development of Tetra Pak from 2009 to 2011.

The total net sales (2011) in the whole Tetra Laval Group were €12,665 million. Of the total net sales in 2011, the market segment liquid dairy products (milk, etc.) accounts for 64 per cent. Juices and nectars accounts for 18 per cent. The remaining 18 per cent comprises still drinks, wine and spirits, and other food products.

Tetra Pak's value chain and the role of the 'actors' in it

In Figure 1 Tetra Pak's value chain is illustrated with the main stakeholders included.

Tetra Pak

Tetra Pak should develop more efficient packaging systems based on the requirements and needs of

Table 2	Tetra Pak's net sales and number of employees 2009–11		
	2011	**2010**	**2009**
Net sales (millions €)	10,360	9,980	8,955
Number of employees	22,896	22,623	21,672

Source: based on Tetra Pak's financial reports.

producers (direct B2B customers), retailers and consumers. Efforts are being made to improve packaging strength and at the same time reduce the environmental impact. Efforts are also being made to increase the shelf life of food in order to achieve longer expiry dates and thus less food waste. Demand for aseptically filled carton packaging will therefore increase over the next few years, particularly in South America and Asia. The benefits of convenience and cost also suggest a global increase of aseptic systems.

Direct B2B customers (producer of e.g. dairy products)

By investing in an extensive range of packaging solutions, Tetra Pak helps to foster a long-term B2B relationship

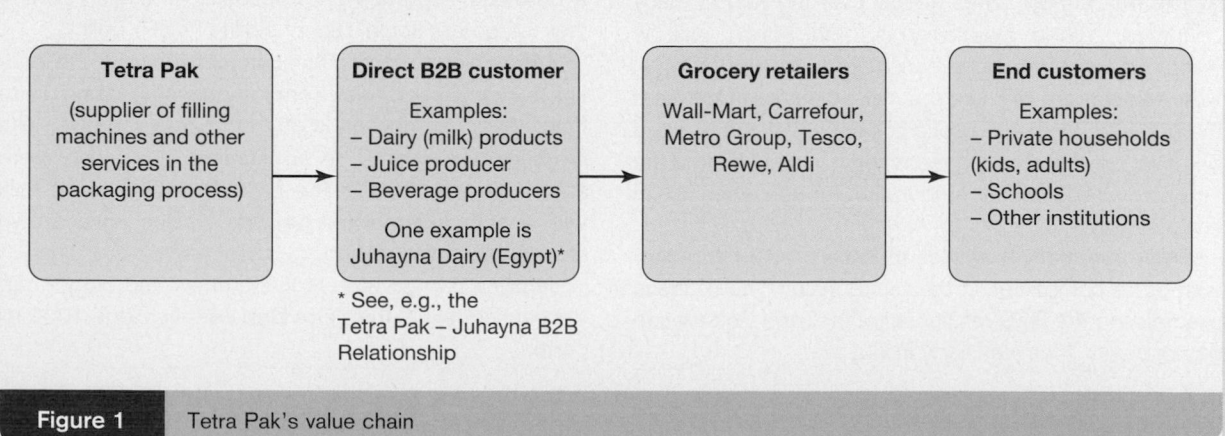

Figure 1   Tetra Pak's value chain

with their customers. Tetra Pak does its best to earn respect through a profound knowledge of the food industry in every step, from processing to consumption.

Retailers

Tetra Pak's packaging distribution solutions protect profitability for retailers. Tetra Pak makes sure that packaged products are well protected on shelves, and helps distributors brand their products, helping protect and increase retailers' image.

Retailers can do a lot to make this easier for the consumers of food products. One way is to provide several sizes of packaging to meet the needs of different consumers, especially single-person households, whose numbers are growing.

End-customers

Consumers have responsibility for the economic management of their own kitchens. Consumers can take responsibility by buying food in the right size of package when this option is available. The packaging manufacturer can assist by supplying reclosable packaging that is easy to empty, and especially by producing packaging that provides a good protective barrier against light, oxygen and moisture. Clear information and easy-to-understand date marking are also needed so that perfectly edible food is not thrown away unnecessarily.

Tetra Pak has started school feeding programmes in more than 50 countries – 49 million schoolchildren throughout the world receive milk or nutritious drinks in Tetra Pak packaging. Around 30 million of these children live in low-income countries, where improvements in health and education are vital for positive development. Experience shows that school milk can act as a catalyst for encouraging an entire milk value chain to develop in a country.

The milk supply varies greatly over the year in many countries. When availability is high, much milk is wasted if local industries cannot process the surplus. When things are difficult, the milk volume cannot meet the demand. With an aseptic solution, all the milk could be processed and packaged when it is plentiful and the surplus stored without refrigeration for use when it is in short supply.

There are many examples of value creation together with other companies in the value chain. One of these examples is the B2B relationship that Tetra Pak tries to develop with Juhayna Diary, in Egypt.

The Juhayna Dairy

Juhayna began operations in 1983 with a state-of-the-art manufacturing facility in the Sixth of October City, a suburb west of Cairo that was being developed as one of Egypt's new industrial hubs. Juhayna was the first Egyptian company to partner with Tetra Pak (called Alfa-Laval at the time) and thus became a market pioneer in producing packed milk, yoghurt and juice.

In 1988, Juhayna began exporting its products and established a wide customer base in Europe and the Middle East. By 2012, Juhayna had become the leading dairy in Egypt with the highest market shares in dairy products.

In 2009, Juhayna, Tetra Pak, the Egyptian Ministry of Health, Chamber of Food Industries, Alexandria University and other dairy companies joined forces in the 'Loose Milk Conversion Initiative'. The purpose was to create awareness of the benefits of packaged milk and the potential hazards of loose milk. The partners also wanted to raise awareness about pasteurization and UHT.

Increase of packaged milk in Egypt

At the start of the 1980s, packaged milk comprised less than 1 per cent of the total milk market. By 2009, this had increased to 10 per cent and by 2011 the ambient white (packaged) milk market had risen to 22.5 per cent.

Loose milk is unprocessed, unpackaged milk, straight from the cow or buffalo. Consumers buy it from milkmen on their doorsteps or from corner shops, usually poured into plastic bags. Studies have repeatedly shown it is not safe; it has a high bacteria count and high levels of formalin and other additives.

Converting loose milk into packaged milk is not only a business opportunity for Juhayna; it is also part of their corporate social responsibility (CSR) policy.

Tetra Pak has helped its customer Juhayna, the leading dairy in Egypt, to become successful. Using Tetra Fino® Aseptic, Juhayna is offering packaged milk, with its many advantages, to consumers in a much more affordable way than in the past, replacing loose milk with a safer alternative. Juhayna's sales have grown steadily since the launch.

Juhayna has gave on to launch new and bigger carton packages, i.e. the Tetra Brik Aseptic Edge 1000 ml carton.

Example of Tetra Fino® Aseptic
Source: Tetra Pak International SA.

Advantages of Tetra Fino® Aseptic

The advantages of Tetra Fino Aseptic are clear. It was introduced to Egypt by Juhayna in 1997 to benefit low-income individuals who would normally buy loose milk. Production costs of the package are low, so it is economical for consumers. Most importantly, it is reliable and convenient to use, keeping milk fresh and pleasant-tasting. Since the introduction of Tetra Fino Aseptic, consumers have increasingly accepted it and sales have grown.

Stakeholders in the 'Loose Milk Conversion Initiative' put much effort into marketing, including educational TV commercials, seminars, workshops and other initiatives to gain customer and consumer acceptance of the product, particularly among women. Recently, the focus was expanded to include young people, with seminars in schools delivering the message through interactive learning, prompting high levels of engagement among the students.

Juhayna's production started with one milk production line, including a Tetra Pak filling machine. The steady growth of sales put pressure on Juhayna's production line (filling machine) and further Tetra Pak filling machines were added. Efficiency was increased, and costs and resources reduced. In 2011, Juhayna increased capacity by adding two new production lines. Juhayna is also receiving fewer complaints from the market regarding leaking products.

The 'Loose Milk Conversion Initiative' aims to reach the long-term objective of 80 per cent packaged milk in the Egyptian market in 2020.

QUESTIONS

1. Which 'P' of the marketing mix should Tetra Pak concentrate on in the development of its global marketing plan?

2. Would it be relevant for Tetra Pak to work with global account management (GAM)? If yes, how should it be organized and which organizational set-up should Tetra Pak make use of?

Sources: based on different types of information on www.tetrapak.com; WHO/World Health Organization www.who.int/en/; different public sources.

CASE STUDY V.4

Polaroid Eyewear: can the iconic brand achieve a comeback in the global sunglasses industry?

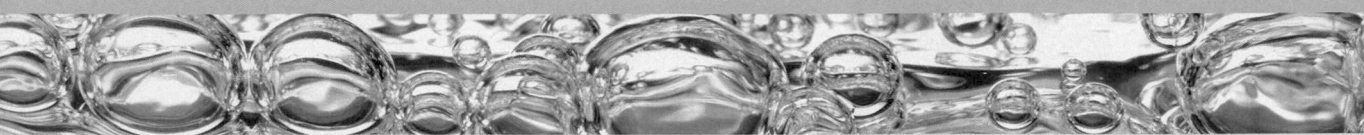

Polaroid Corporation was an international consumer-electronics and eyewear company, originally founded in 1937 by Edwin H. Land. It is most famous for its instant film cameras, which reached the market in 1948, and continued to be the company's flagship product line until the February 2008 decision to cease all production in favour of digital photography products. The company's original dominant market was in polarized sunglasses, an outgrowth of Land's self-guided research in polarization after leaving Harvard University after his freshman year – he later returned to Harvard to continue his research.

Polaroid was also one of the early manufacturers of digital cameras, with the PDC-2000 in 1996; however, they failed to capture a large share in that market.

On 11 October 2001, the Polaroid Corporation filed for bankruptcy. Almost all the company's assets (including the 'Polaroid' name itself) were sold to a subsidiary of Bank One. It went on to form a new company, which also operated under the name 'Polaroid Corporation'. It stopped making Polaroid cameras in 2007 and stopped selling Polaroid film after 2009, to the consternation of some users.

On 18 December 2008, after the reorganization, Polaroid Corp. again filed for bankruptcy. The filing for bankruptcy came shortly after the criminal investigation of its parent company, Petters Group Worldwide, and the parent company's founder, Tom Petters.

Polaroid Corp.'s bankruptcies were widely believed to be the result of a failure by its senior management to anticipate the effect of digital cameras on its film business.

Already within the Polaroid Corporation, the Eyewear division was treated as its own profit centre with its own management, sales and marketing structure and, in 1998, it became its own company (Polaroid Eyewear AG), with its headquarters based in Zürich, Switzerland.

Shortly before the second bankruptcy, Petters Group Worldwide, the owner of the Polaroid brand at the time, sold Polaroid Eyewear AG to the specialist eyewear company Stylemark Inc., in March 2007. The company name was changed from Polaroid Eyewear AG to StyleMark AG, and the headquarters remained in Zürich, Switzerland. StyleMark AG is an autonomous business owned by Stylemark Inc., which is a global distributor of fashion, sport and children's sunglasses.

In total, the StyleMark group manufactured approximately 70 million units per year, of which roughly 7.5 million sunglasses units (according to www.stylemark.net) were sold under the Polaroid brand. This makes the StyleMark group the world's biggest sunglasses manufacturer, but obviously only a part of this production was sold under the Polaroid brand.

In 2011, the Polaroid Eyewear business generated approximately US$63 million in sales and an EBITDA of about US$8.75 million. StyleMark AG owned the Polaroid Eyewear business from March 2007 until the end of 2011. On 17 November 2011, Safilo Group (see p. 802) announced that it had acquired the Polaroid Eyewear business from StyleMark AG for US$87.5 million.

This case study will focus mainly on the Polaroid-branded sunglasses business.

The Polaroid sunglasses brand's USP is the Polaroid premium polarized lenses. When sunlight reflects off a horizontal surface like a road or water, it often becomes concentrated horizontally. This phenomenon is called glare, which makes it difficult for people not wearing polarized sunglasses to see clearly. The polarized lenses block the glare, ensuring perfect vision (see Photosets 1 and 2).

The marketing strategy of Polaroid sunglasses

Today, Polaroid-branded sunglasses are sold into over 60 different markets. According to a GFK consumer survey in eight countries (Switzerland, France, Italy, Netherlands, Sweden, UK, Russia and Germany), Polaroid has the fourth highest brand awareness in the sunglasses market (see Figure 1).

Today, Polaroid sunglasses are mostly sold through the optical trade and department stores. Polaroid has achieved a solid distribution in continental Europe since the 1980s, and by the mid-1990s the brand had also become widely available in the eastern European markets.

Photoset 1 Left: using non-polarized sunglasses; right: using Polaroid polarized sunglasses
Source: Polaroid Eyewear.

Photoset 2 Polaroid sunglasses
Source: Polaroid Eyewear.

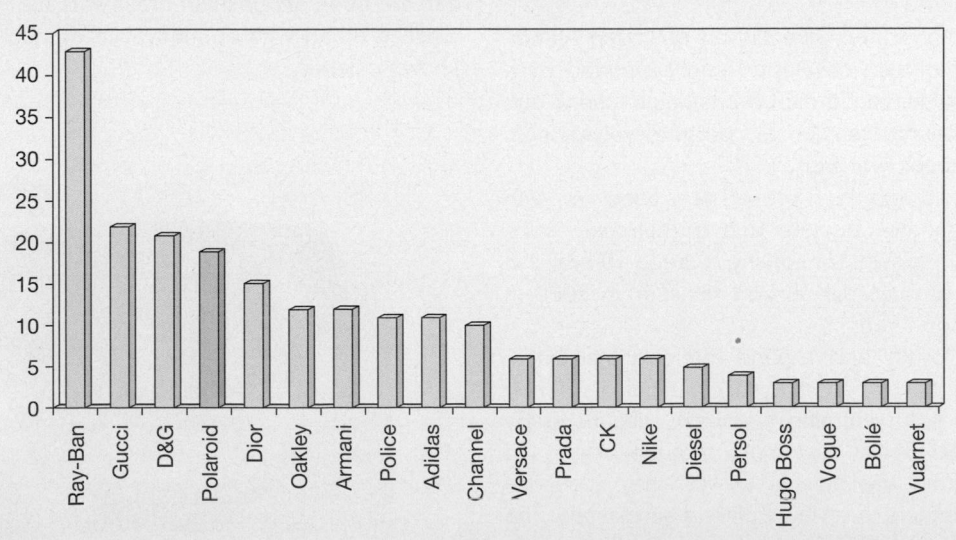

| Figure 1 | Brand awareness in Europe of different brands of sunglasses |

Source: Polaroid Eyewear. With kind permission.

The UK marketing strategy in 2007

This successful marketing strategy was based on a small budget but big aspirations. The UK market remained unconquered so, in 2007, the company decided that it was time to focus on this important market. At the same time, the company also wanted to strengthen the brand in the markets where they had remained strong, and invested in a new marketing concept to reach that goal: a new, global and fully unified communications campaign – wholly focused on the brand's USP of premium polarized sunglasses – to build the brand and rally retail sales in combination with a new channel strategy that would ensure the brand was getting the needed awareness back fast, even though budgets were limited. When people go on holiday, sunglasses are definitely on their minds, so airport sales in the UK were a natural place to start.

Polaroid developed three guiding principles for its work with airport retailers and to build all-important brand awareness:

- *Educate.* In 2007 it kicked off the communications campaign by sharing the secrets of Polaroid's polarizing technology – and some great style tips – with sales staff at airport retailers. If they passed their quiz, they were given a pair of Polaroid sunglasses.
- *Demonstrate.* As part of their training, retailers were also given lens testers to demonstrate the benefits of polarization to customers. Seeing the difference between unpolarized and polarized lenses goes a long way to explaining the benefits.
- *Incentivize.* When the sales started rolling in, teams with the best results won prizes on a monthly and seasonal basis.

To reach consumers directly, an optimized e-commerce site was also developed and supported by a search-engine marketing (SEM) campaign (check out: www.polaroidsunglasses.co.uk, polaroideyewear.com and the Facebook website).

This Polaroid approach proved very effective. With backlit point-of-sale posters and a motivated sales force, Polaroid grew from nothing to a top 10 brand in nine months at major UK airport retailers. In 2009, it reached the top three.

To retain loyalty and expand the customer base, Polaroid has developed a loyalty campaign offering discounts to both returning and new customers. By getting closer to the customers through blogs and forums, Polaroid was able to answer their questions and find influencers to review Polaroid sunglasses. The company's Facebook followers are loyal and growing.

The airport marketing campaign in the UK has also made it possible for Polaroid to broaden its distribution in the UK into the classic Polaroid sunglasses channels. Now, customers can buy Polaroid polarized sunglasses in Specsavers (optical retailers in the UK) and in a growing number of independent opticians and department stores, including John Lewis.

StyleMark AG has used its new marketing campaign concepts all over Europe, and now wants to push further into other markets, such as the US (formerly a big market for the Polaroid brand) as well as new territories like South America and Asia.

Figure 2 shows how Polaroid considers itself in comparison with key competitive brands.

The Lady Gaga endorsement

In January 2011, almost a year to the day since Polaroid signed Lady Gaga as its creative director, the popular singer unveiled the fruits of her labours at the Polaroid booth at the consumer electronics show in Las Vegas. Called 'Grey Label by Haus of Gaga', the gadgets include a pair of sunglasses with embedded camera and display, a mobile photo printer and a Polaroid camera. She unveiled the GL20 sunglasses to a packed crowd and a storm of photo flashes.

The glasses can shoot both photos and video, which are stored in memory embedded in one of the earpieces. The earpiece can be removed and connected via USB to a printer, or the images can be transferred via Bluetooth. The glasses also feature a screen in front of each eye that can play back recorded images. Lady Gaga said inspiration for the product, which never went beyond a prototype, came from a pair of glasses she once used on tour. StyleMark AG used this endorsement and the camera glasses for getting back into the trade and fashion press with the Polaroid sunglasses brand with an innovative product and a well-known celebrity.

Polaroid GL20 camera glasses, designed by Lady Gaga
Source: Ethan Miller/Getty Images.

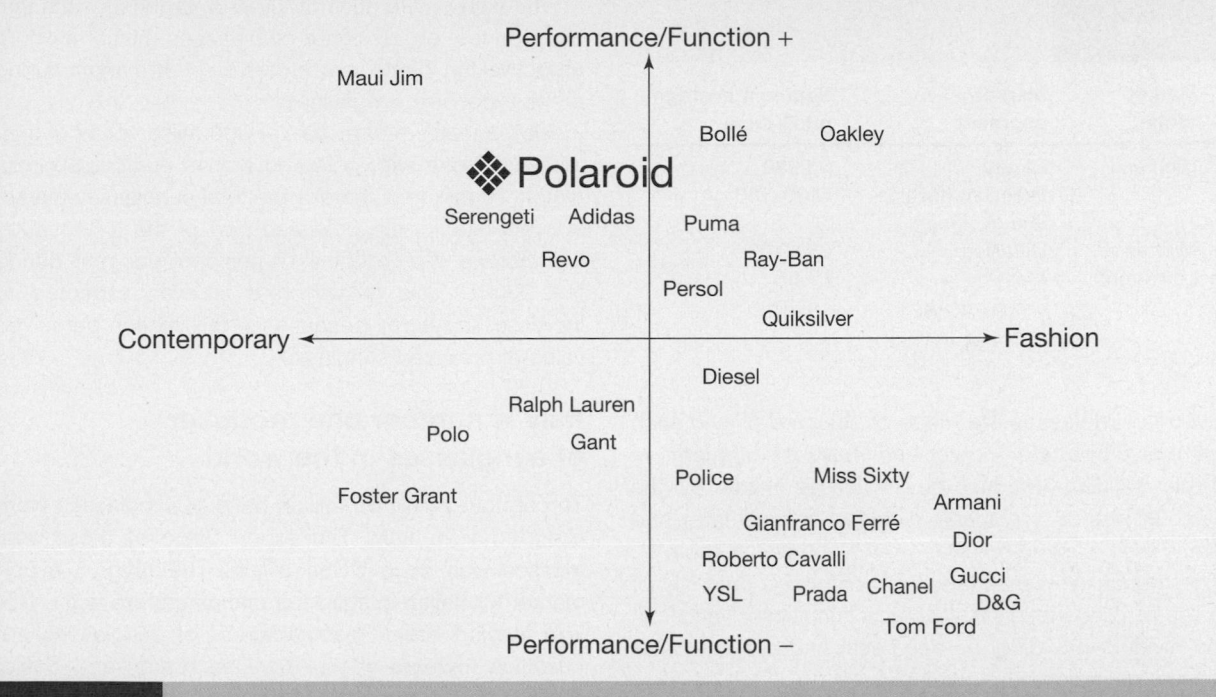

| Figure 2 | Polaroid's brand position |

Source: Polaroid Eyewear.

The 'Best under the sun' (BUTS) collection and campaign

In spring 2011, Polaroid Sunglasses launched its 'Best under the sun' collection and campaign. The collection consists of bestselling and iconic Polaroid sunglass models from their collection archives, from the 1930s to the 1980s. The goal of this special collection was to show the rich heritage of the brand and make the brand relevant again with fashionistas and opinion leaders, both in trade and with consumers. Polaroid Eyewear put together a whole marketing campaign around this collection, to strengthen the brand and to get back into the fashion press. Apart from a big push in PR, Polaroid is mostly using social media tools to communicate the 'Best under the sun' range cost-effectively and connect with its (new) consumers. Activities include tools like a special webpage (www.polaroidsunglasses1937.com), a special Facebook page (Polaroid Best under the sun), a viral, interactive You-Tube spot and an interactive online design competition.

The world market for sunglasses

Sunglasses are used to protect the eyes from the sun's harmful UV rays. They are also worn as a style statement according to the current trend. Most of the lenses

Polaroid Best under the sun – campaign visual
Source: Creative Circle GmbH/Polaroid Eyewear GmbH

Table 1	Segmentation of the sunglass market	
Market range	Market segment	Segment average retail price
High end	Luxury	> €230
	Premium (fashion and designer)	€130–230
Mid-range	Diffusion	€50–130
Lower end	Mass	< €50
	Discount	< €20

Source: based on Polaroid Eyewear and public sources.

used in sunglasses are made of coloured plastic such as polycarbonate (lower-end market segment in Table 1). But the high-quality lenses made by the famous brands are made of glass or triacetate, and some are polarized (mid-range and high end in Table 1). The global eyewear market is composed primarily of sales of prescription frames and sunglasses, and can be divided into different segments and average retail prices, as indicated in Table 1.

The major proportion of sunglasses (80–90 per cent) is sold at the lower end of the market. In the worldwide sunglasses market, North America is the largest market, but it is also growing at the slowest rate. North America is followed by Europe and Asia-Pacific, with the Asia-Pacific region experiencing the most rapid growth rate. Major eyewear players are targeting emerging markets such as India and China. Italian companies like Safilo Group and Luxottica Group (including the Ray-Ban brand), and the US-based Viva International Group are entering emerging markets in Asia.

The worldwide sunglasses market is usually segmented by price and function, and the two major price segments are premium and value. The premium segment is growing rapidly in comparison to the value segment.

With consumers treating sunglasses as their fashion statement, eyewear designers are focusing on bright, multicoloured and bejewelled designs of sunglasses. Different designs of sunglasses are being developed for the office, casual wear, party wear or beach wear.

In 2011, the total world market value was around US$6 billion with an estimated sales volume of 300 million pairs of sunglasses. This provides an average sales price of US$20, but the variation of prices is huge across the regions of the world. New producers of sunglasses in the Far East have caused increased competition, and prices have come down at the high end. Also the increasing 'piracy' of designer brands is playing a role in the downward trend in pricing of sunglasses.

The high proliferation of 'pirated' brands means that high prices on designer sunglasses make it more attractive for 'pirate' producers to start manufacturing these expensive sunglasses.

Of the total world market of 300 million pairs of sunglasses, those with polarized lenses number approximately 70 million. Whereas the total sunglasses market is pretty stable, the polarized part of the total market has increased by roughly 15 per cent per year during the 2000s. This growth rate is even expected to increase in future, because of the higher perceived value of polarized sunglasses.

Italy is number one producer of sunglasses in the world

Throughout 2010, 55 million pairs of sunglasses were exported from Italy. The export value of these sunglasses was circa US$2 billion. The biggest export market for Italian sunglasses manufacturers is the US. The leading Italian manufacturers of sunglasses are Luxottica (owners of the Ray-Ban brand) and Safilo. Table 2 describes some of the major markets for sunglasses. It shows that the global market for sunglasses is rather fragmented.

One of the key characteristics of the sunglasses industry is that the big multinational companies (like Luxottica and Safilo) have a few own 'house' brands, and they buy the licensing rights to sell famous designer brands through their company. For example, Luxottica has its own Ray-Ban brand, but it also has the right to distribute, e.g., Dolce & Gabbana and Polo Ralph Lauren sunglasses worldwide.

Distribution trends

The general worldwide trend in distribution is consolidation. Earlier, the multinational companies (like Luxottica) entered the international market for sunglasses through independent and domestic retail companies. This is changing, as these smaller optical retail chains are being taken over by bigger ones.

An example from the UK market

Consolidation is also indicative of the general trend in the UK spectacles market of global multinational companies entering the market at the expense of independent and domestic companies. Vision Express has been owned by French parent Grand Vision since 1997, and with the loss of Dollond & Aitchison to Boots there is now only one independent British, high-street optician left. However, this happens to be Specsavers, the market leader, which remains directly controlled by the husband-and-wife team Doug and Mary Perkins, who founded the company in 1984.

Unlike Specsavers, Vision Express and Boots, most of the other leading manufacturers are focused on the design of spectacles and they do not operate related optician services. As such, they lack a high-street presence but they are still key suppliers to the opticians. For the most part, this group consists of multinationals like Luxottica and Safilo.

Important manufacturers of branded sunglasses

In the following, the two Italian sunglasses companies Luxottica and Safilo are presented.

Luxottica (Italy)

Luxottica Group S.p.A. is a global leader in the design, manufacture and distribution of fashion, luxury, sport and performance eyewear, primarily in the sunglasses sector. Founded in 1961 by Leonardo Del Vecchio, the Luxottica Group (based in Milan, Italy) is now a vertically integrated organization whose manufacturing of prescription frames, sunglasses and lenses is backed by a wide-reaching wholesale and retail distribution network comprising 6,350 retail locations, as of 31 December 2010, mostly in North America, Asia-Pacific and China. Product design, development and manufacturing take place in six production facilities in Italy, two wholly owned factories in China and two sports sunglasses production facilities in the US. Luxottica also has a small plant in India serving the local market. In 2010, production reached approximately 57 million units.

House brands include Ray-Ban, one of the world's best known brands, Oakley, Vogue, Persol, Oliver Peoples, Arnette and REVO, and the licence brands include Bvlgari, Burberry, Chanel, Dolce & Gabbana, Donna Karan, Polo Ralph Lauren, Paul Smith, Prada, Stella McCartney, Tiffany, Tory Burch, Versace and Coach.

Table 2	Market share in the major markets for sunglasses (2010)							
		UK	Germany (D)	Italy (I)	US	China	Other countries	Total market
Total sales of sunglasses (million US$)		363	675	1,270	1,980	572	1,140	6,000
Sunglasses company	Company brands	% market share	% market share	% market share	% market share	% market share	% market share	% market share
Luxottica (Italy)	Ray-Ban Oakley Dolce & Gabbana Polo Ralph Lauren	18	7	28	7	16	15	12
Safilo (Italy)	Gucci Diesel Carrera	–	2	20	1	11	5	5
Other sunglasses companies	Polaroid Specsaver Adidas Fossil Esprit Diesel Dior Calvin Klein Police UV3 Bolle Nike Prosun Porpoise	34	76	42	72	68	70	73
Private-label companies	Different private labels	48	15	10	20	5	10	10
Total		100	100	100	100	100	100	100

Note. The Polaroid brand of sunglasses is under the 'other' category – Euromonitor does not publish any specific market share data about Polaroid.
Source: based on Euromonitor.com and public sources.

The group's wholesale distribution network, covering 130 countries across five continents, has 18 distribution centres and over 40 commercial subsidiaries providing direct operations in key markets. The group is currently seeking to penetrate emerging markets and is exploring new channels of distribution such as department stores, airports and railway stations. Direct wholesale operations are complemented by an extensive retail network.

In the retail sun business, the Luxottica Group operates approximately 2,480 retail locations in North America, Asia-Pacific, South Africa, Europe and the Middle East, mainly through the Hut brand of sunglasses. In North America, Luxottica operates the points of sale for its licensed brands, with over 1,140 stores under the Sears Optical and Target Optical brands.

In 2010, its total net sales reached a record €5.8 billion, net income increased to more than €400 million, with a headcount of approximately 62,000 employees, and the company enjoyed a strong global presence.

Luxottica's most famous brand, Ray-Ban
Debuting in 1937 with the Aviator model created for American Air Force pilots, Ray-Ban joined Luxottica's brand portfolio in 1999. Unaffected by the conceptual transience of fashion, Ray-Ban immediately made a name for itself thanks to the absolute quality and authenticity of its eyewear, now more 'modern' than ever and worn by countless movie celebrities and trendsetters all over the world. Over the years, Ray-Ban has grown into a fashion icon, more than just a brand of sunglasses. The brand has a touch of retro, yet it is widely demanded for its avant-garde style.

Safilo

Safilo Group S.p.A. (based in Padua, Italy) is Italy's second-largest sunglasses company. It designs, produces and distributes prescription frames, sunglasses, sports-eyewear, ski goggles, ski and cycling helmets. Its products are primarily manufactured in six self-owned plants, three in Italy and one each in Slovenia, China and the US, and through third parties. The products are marketed in around 130 countries worldwide through 30 direct commercial subsidiaries and more than 170 independent distributors. The company has 38 principal brands, of which five are directly owned (the two most important are Safilo and Carrera). The rest are licensed from other well-known designer companies, e.g. Armani, Balenciaga, Alexander McQueen, BOSS, Bottega, Veneta, Valentino, Dior, Banana Republic, Emporio Armani and others. Safilo's major competitor is the Milan-based Luxottica SpA.

Safilo Group S.p.A. was founded in 1934 after Guglielmo Tabacchi purchased Italy's first industrial complex for producing lenses and frames in Pieve di Cadore. Exports in the 1930s expanded to many European countries, North Africa, the Middle East and South Africa.

In 2010, the Safilo Group's net sales reached €1,080 million. Sales have been determined by prescription frames (38 per cent), sunglasses (54 per cent) and sport and other products (8 per cent). Safilo's products are primarily sold to wholesale and retail clients through approximately 80,000 points of sale in about 130 countries in the world. Safilo's main sales area in 2010 was America (43 per cent), followed by Europe (41 per cent) and Asia and the rest of the world (16 per cent).

Overall, Safilo's strategy is based on the following three pillars:

- *Enhance the brand portfolio.* Safilo intends to continue to improve its portfolio of both licensed and owned brands.
- *Strengthen the distribution network and expand in new markets.* Safilo wishes to continue its policy of strengthening its distribution network in the markets in which it operates and to enter new markets with high-growth potential.
- *Improve financial capabilities.* Safilo strives to improve its financial capabilities by means of higher operating profitability and increased retention of cash flows.

Safilo's marketing and communication activities comprise both activities dedicated to customers and trade marketing at their points of sale (at retailers).

- *End-customer-oriented activities* constitute about two-thirds of Safilo's advertising and promotional investments. The group mostly uses the press (weekly and monthly magazines), posters, sponsorships (in particular for Carrera and Smith sports goggles), public relations with fashion journalists and product placement with fashion, sports and showbusiness personalities.
- *Trade marketing activities* (primarily towards optical retailers), which take up about one-third of the advertising and promotional investments, are important to foster customer confidence. The group provides marketing material for points of sale, such as posters, banners, displays, specialized window displays, and training courses and brochures for the brands and products.

In its licensing relationships, Safilo (licensee) coordinates promotional material and activities with licensors. The licence agreements also provide for a mandatory payment by the licensee, who benefits from the advertising activities carried out directly by the licensors, for the advertising and promotion of the brand linked to the previous year's sales.

As mentioned above, since 2012 the Polaroid Eyewear business has been controlled by the Safilo Group. In connection with the acquisition of Polaroid Eyewear (in November 2011), Roberto Vedovotto, Chief Executive Officer of the Safilo Group, made the following comment (Safilo, 2011):

> We are extremely happy to announce that a historical yet contemporary brand like Polaroid is becoming part of the new Safilo, bringing along its reputation of leader in the manufacturing of high-quality polarizing lenses and the distribution of world-class polarized sunglasses around the world. The size of the polarizing-eyewear market is rising steadily as more and more consumers realize the benefits and the value of glare-free vision. I am confident that a brand like Polaroid will help us in giving a strong push in the use of such important technology. More importantly we are taking a further step towards what we define as a great growth opportunity for our Group, Safilo's own brands.

QUESTIONS

In some former key markets, such as the US, Polaroid has still not reached a satisfactory level for image and market share. Other geographic regions (e.g. South America and Asia) also offer further potential that has not yet been conquered.

The management of Polaroid Eyewear constantly considers how it can utilize the high brand awareness of the Polaroid brand for further international expansion.

As an international marketing consultant you are asked to provide an assessment of Polaroid Eyewear's opportunities for achieving a global comeback with its iconic Polaroid sunglasses brand. You are specifically asked the following questions:

1. Make a comparison of the competitive strategies and competitive strengths of Luxottica Group and Safilo Group on a company level – before and after the Polaroid Eyewear business became part of the Safilo Group at the beginning of 2012.

2. The new marketing strategy of Polaroid has worked well in the UK and its other markets. Should the Polaroid brand strategy just repeat in new territories what it has done in the UK, or should it do it differently in other international markets?

3. In the US, where Polaroid was 'born' and where Polaroid sunglasses used to have a big market share, the Polaroid brand needs to be repositioned and relaunched. What should be the key elements of the relaunch and repositioning strategy?

4. Prepare an international marketing plan which can secure international expansion for Polaroid sunglasses in the coming years, also including new markets in South America and Asia.

Sources: Safilo (2011), 'Safilo Group announces the acquisition of the Polaroid Eyewear business', Safilo Press Release, Padua, 17 November; StyleMark websites; Euromonitor and Datamonitor data.

INDEX